BIOGRAPHICAL DICTIONARY
OF REPUBLICAN CHINA

VOLUME IV: YANG-YÜN
BIBLIOGRAPHY

BIOGRAPHICAL DICTIONARY OF REPUBLICAN CHINA

HOWARD L. BOORMAN, *Editor*

RICHARD C. HOWARD, *Associate Editor*

VOLUME IV: YANG-YÜN

BIBLIOGRAPHY BY JOSEPH K. H. CHENG

COLUMBIA UNIVERSITY PRESS

NEW YORK

BIOGRAPHICAL DICTIONARY
OF REPUBLICAN CHINA

HOWARD L. BOORMAN, Editor
RICHARD C. HOWARD, Associate Editor
O. EDMUND CLUBB
RUSSELL MAETH

STAFF

ANNE B. CLARK

SHEN-YU DAI

LIENCHE TU FANG

PEI-JAN HSIA

YANG-CHIH HUANG

MELVILLE T. KENNEDY, JR.

DONALD W. KLEIN

ROBERT H. G. LEE

BERNADETTE LI

ALBERT LU

SUSAN H. MARSH

YONG SANG NG

LORETTA PAN

A. C. SCOTT

PEI-YI WU

CONTRIBUTORS

John S. Aird
Cyril Birch
Scott A. Boorman
Conrad Brandt
Robert A. Burton
C. M. Chang
K. N. Chang
Kwang-chih Chang
Fu-ts'ung Chiang
Tse-tsung Chow
M. W. Chu
Samuel C. Chu
Wen-djang Chu
James I. Crump, Jr.
John Dardess
James E. Dew
John Philip Emerson
Albert Feuerwerker
Yi-tsi Feuerwerker
Wolfgang Franke
Donald Gillin

Merle Goldman
Jerome B. Grieder
Marus Fang Hao
James P. Harrison
Judy Feldman
  Harrison
David Hawkes
Nicole Hirabayashi
Ping-ti Ho
C. T. Hsia
Ronald Hsia
Kung-chuan Hsiao
Francis C. P. Hsu
Kai-yu Hsu
Chün-tu Hsüeh
Paul V. Hyer
Chalmers A. Johnson
Paula S. Johnson
William R. Johnson
Olga Lang
Kan Lao

Shu-hua Li
C. T. Liang
H. H. Ling
Arthur Link
Chun-jo Liu
Ch'ung-hung Liu
James T. C. Liu
Wu-chi Liu
John T. Ma
Meng Ma
Eduardo Macagno
Robert M. Marsh
Harriet C. Mills
Donald Paragon
Robert W. Rinden
David T. Roy
Harold Schiffrin
Stuart R. Schram
William R. Schultz
T. H. Shen
Tsung-lien Shen

James E. Sheridan
Stanley Spector
E-tu Zen Sun
Rufus Suter
S. Y. Teng
Te-kong Tong
T. H. Tsien
T'ung-ho Tung
Lyman P. Van Slyke
Richard L. Walker
Farrell Phillips
  Wallerstein
Chi-kao Wang
Y. T. Wang
Holmes H. Welch
Hellmut Wilhelm
Hsiang-hsiang Wu
K. T. Wu
William C. C. Wu
William A. Wycoff
Isabella Yen

Editor for the Columbia University Press: Katharine Kyes Leab

EXPLANATORY NOTES

NAMES

The romanization systems used are the Wade-Giles (with the omission of some diacritical marks) for Chinese and the Hepburn (with the omission of some macrons) for Japanese. The major exception to this rule is Chinese place names for large cities, which are given according to the Chinese Post Office system. In the case of Kwangtung province, Cantonese spellings often have been indicated: Nanhai (Namhoi). For place names in Manchuria and in the case of Peking, we generally have followed contemporary usage. In such outlying areas as Sinkiang, Mongolia, and Tibet, any given place might have several names. For convenience, we have standardized the place names in all outlying areas according to the dictates of common sense.

Chinese personal names are given in the Chinese order, that is, with the surname first. In general, the articles are arranged alphabetically by the Wade-Giles romanization of the subject's surname and given personal name (ming). However, the biographies of Chiang Kai-shek, Eugene Ch'en, H. H. K'ung, T. V. Soong, Sun Yat-sen, and a few others appear under the name most familiar to Western readers. The courtesy, literary, Western, alternate, and common pen names of subjects of biographies are listed at the beginning of each article (*see* ABBREVIATIONS). The reader should note that the ming and the tzu (courtesy name) frequently are confused in modern Chinese sources.

THE CALENDAR

Dates are given according to the Western calendar, converted in many cases from the Chinese calendar. The word sui often is used in referring to age. In China, a person is regarded as being one year old at birth and two years old at the beginning of the next Chinese calendar year. Thus, a person's age by Western calculation will be less than his sui. We have retained the sui form in many articles because of the difficulties of conversion and, frequently, the lack of precise information about month and day of birth.

MEASURES OF MONEY AND LAND

From 1911 to 1949 the values of Chinese monetary units varied so greatly that it is impossible to assign them standard values in Western terms. Until 1933 the official unit of value was the Customs tael (Hai-kuan liang). Other monies, such as silver dollars (yuan), also were current. In 1933 the silver dollar (yuan) became the standard legal tender of China. In 1935, by law, a managed paper currency (fapi) replaced the silver. A gold dollar unit (yuan) was briefly introduced in 1948, but the Chinese monetary system remained unstable until after the establishment of the Central People's Government at Peking in October 1949.

Standard units of land measurement used in this work are li and mu.

    1 li = 1/3 mile
    1 mu (or mou) = 733 sq. yards
    6.6 mu = 1 acre

MILITARY ORGANIZATION

We have used Western military terms to describe the organization of Chinese armies. Thus:

chün = army	ying = battalion
shih = division	lien = company
lü = brigade	p'ai = platoon
t'uan = regiment	

The reader should note that the organization of Chinese armies was not so standardized as that of Western armies, and the size of units varied considerably. During the second phase of the Northern Expedition (1928) armies were combined for field operations to form larger units, although they retained their individual designations (e.g., First Army). The combined forces were known variously as army groups (chün-t'uan), direction armies (fang-mien chün), and route armies (lu-chün). Above this level was that of group army (chi-t'uan-chün). Although these were temporary designations, they achieved the permanence of organizational categories.

PROVINCIAL ADMINISTRATION

The administrative divisions, in ascending order, of each province at the end of the Ch'ing period were:

hsien = districts or counties
chou = departments
fu = prefectures
tao = circuits composed of
2 or more fu

We have used the terms military governor and civil governor in referring to provincial rulers of the 1912–28 period. At the beginning of the republican period the Chinese title for the military governor of a province was tutuh. The official designation was changed to chiang-chün in 1914 and to tuchün in 1916. Beginning about 1925, the title was changed in some areas to tupan, a designation which implied that the governor's primary responsibilities were demilitarization and social rehabilitation.

We have used the term governor in referring to the top-ranking officer of a provincial government after 1928, rather than the more literal rendering of the Chinese (sheng cheng-fu chu-hsi) as chairman.

The term tao-t'ai refers to the official in charge of a circuit. A number of the men who held this office during the Ch'ing period were important in foreign relations because often the tao-t'ai was the highest Chinese official available for negotiations with foreigners.

Mention should be made of the likin, an inland tax on the transit of goods which was introduced by the imperial government at the time of the Taiping Rebellion (1850–64). Likin stations soon proliferated throughout China.

The tax revenues were beyond Peking's control and often were used to finance regional armies. The likin tax on local trade was not suppressed officially until 1933.

THE EXAMINATION SYSTEM

In the Ch'ing period, the official class was defined by statute, and its composition was determined by the results of examinations in literary and classical subjects. Although the examination system was abolished in 1905, a brief discussion of it is necessary because many prominent people in the republican period were members of this class by achievement or purchase and because the examinations and degrees have no Western equivalents.

Preliminary examinations were conducted on three successive levels: the hsien; the fu; and the sheng, which was conducted at the prefectural capital. Successful candidates received the sheng-yuan degree, which entitled them to assume the dress of the scholar and exempted them from forced labor. However, they had no legal right to or opportunity for official appointment. They were subject to sui-k'ao, examinations given regularly in the prefectural capitals under provincial supervision. Success in the sui-k'ao meant that they received a small stipend annually to further their studies. Roughly equivalent to the sheng-yuan degree was the chien-sheng degree, which, however, could be purchased. Accordingly, holders of the chien-sheng degree were not subject to periodic examination. Holders of the chien-sheng and the sheng-yuan degrees, who were neither commoners nor officials, comprised a large and changing group.

Those who wished to qualify for official status took the provincial examinations, composed of a preliminary examination, or k'o-k'ao, and a hsiang-shih, or provincial examination. Successful candidates received the degree of chü-jen, which made the holder eligible for office. The kung-sheng degree was roughly equivalent to the chü-jen, but was acquired by appointment, by examination, or by purchase.

The examinations for the highest degree, the chin-shih, which brought appointment to the middle levels of the imperial bureaucracy, were held at Peking. They were composed of the hui-shih, or metropolitan examination; the tien-shih, or palace examination; and the ch'ao-k'ao, an examination in the presence of the emperor which led to specific appointment. Chin-shih who ranked near the top of their group usually were appointed to the Hanlin Academy, where their duties included drawing up government documents and compiling materials for official histories. Service at the Hanlin Academy frequently afforded access to the highest positions in the imperial government.

Candidates who passed the examinations in the same year were linked in the t'ung-nien (same year) relationship, a bond somewhat similar to that linking, for example, members of the Class of 1928 at Harvard College.

FINAL DATE FOR VOLUME IV

The final date for inclusion of information about the subjects of biographies in Volume IV was February 1970.

BIBLIOGRAPHY

This, the final volume of the *Biographical Dictionary of Republican China* contains a comprehensive bibliography. It lists the published writings, if any, of the subject of each article and the sources, both personal and written, used in preparing the article.

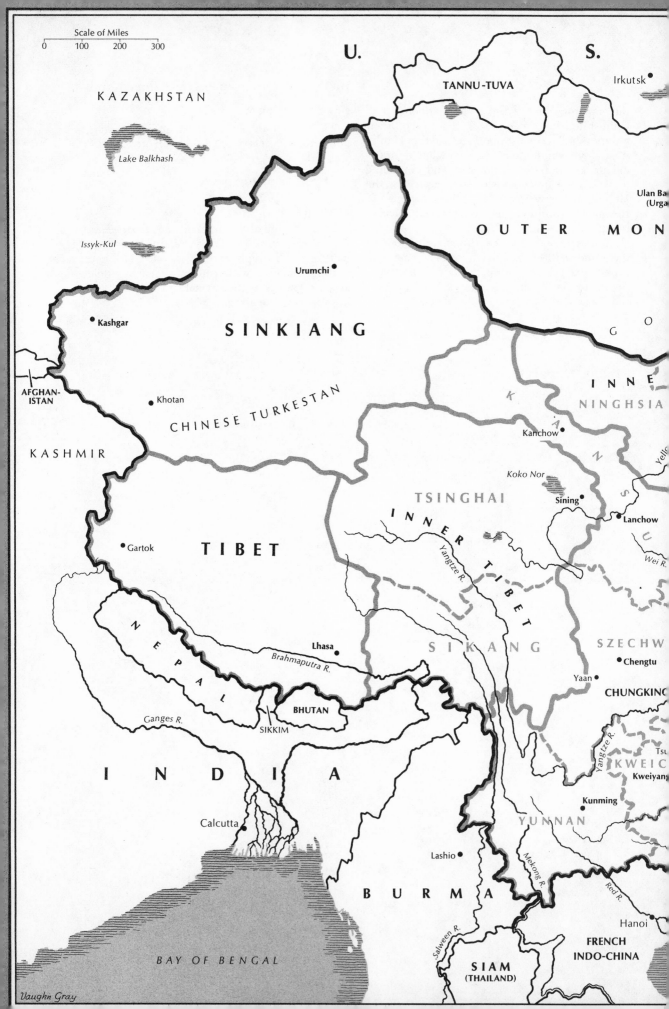

Scale of Miles

0   100   200   300

KAZAKHSTAN

Lake Balkhash

Issyk-Kul

U.   S.

TANNU-TUVA   Irkutsk

OUTER   MON

Ulan Ba
(Urga

Urumchi

SINKIANG

Kashgar

G   O

INNE

NINGHSIA

AFGHAN-
ISTAN

Khotan

CHINESE TURKESTAN

Kanchow

K
A
N
S
U

KASHMIR

Koko Nor

Sining

Lanchow

TSINGHAI

Yello

Gartok

TIBET

INNER   TIBET

Yangtze R.

Wei R.

U

NEPAL

Lhasa

Brahmaputra R.

SIKANG

SZECHW

Chengtu

Yaan

CHUNGKING

BHUTAN

SIKKIM

Ganges R.

Yangtze R.

Tsu

KWEIC

Kweiyang

INDIA

Kunming

YUNNAN

Calcutta

Lashio

Mekong R.

Red R.

BURMA

Hanoi

Salween R.

FRENCH
INDO-CHINA

SIAM
(THAILAND)

BAY OF BENGAL

Vaughn Gray

S.   R.

LAKE
BAIKAL

Shilka R.

Argun R.

Amur R.

• Khabarovsk

Kerulen R.

HEILUNGKIANG

• Tsitsihar

Nonni R.

Sungari R.

Ussuri R.

• Harbin

L. Khanka

MANCHURIA

KIRIN

• Changchun

• Kirin

• Vladivostok

MONGOLIA

CHAHAR

JEHOL

• Mukden   • Fushun

• Anshan
• Yingkow
Antung

KOREA

SEA OF
JAPAN

Kalgan •

• Chengte

T'angshan

• Shanhaikuan

KWANTUNG
(Japan)

• Dairen
Port Arthur

Tokyo

Kaotow

• Kweisui

KUIYUAN

PEKING
(Peiping)

Tatung •

TIENTSIN

Tangku •
Taku •

Chinwangtao

• Weihaiwei

Seoul •

J A P A N

Paoting •

HOPEI
(CHIHLI)

Shihchiachuang •

• Taiyuan

SHANSI

Yellow R.

• Chefoo

Tsushima Strait

SHENSI

(Hwang Ho)

Grand

• Tsinan

SHANTUNG

• Tsingtao

YELLOW
SEA

Nagasaki •

Sian

• Loyang
Chengchow •

• Kaifeng

• Hsuchow

Canal

Quelpart I.

HONAN

Han R.

Hwai R.

Hofei •

KIANGSU

Yangchow •
Pukow •

• Chinkiang   Nant'ung •

• Woosung

ANHWEI

NANKING
• Wuhu

Wusih •
Soochow •

SHANGHAI

HUPEH

Ichang •

Hankow •
Hanyang •

WUHAN

Anking •

Wuchang •

Hangchow •

EAST
CHINA
SEA

PACIFIC

*Tungting
Lake*

• Yochow

Kiukiang •

*Poyang
Lake*

Ningpo •

CHEKIANG

RYUKYU ISLANDS

OCEAN

• Changsha

Nanchang •

KIANGSI

HUNAN

Hengyang •

• Foochow

• Kweilin

Juichin •

FUKIEN

• Taipei

Formosa Strait

West R.

NGSI

• Amoy

TAIWAN
(FORMOSA)

KWANGTUNG

• CANTON

• Swatow

• HONG KONG (Br.)

Macao (Port.)

KWANGCHOWAN
(Fr.)

SOUTH
CHINA
SEA

*HAINAN
(to Kwangtung)*

PHILIPPINES

REPUBLICAN CHINA
IN 1928

BIOGRAPHICAL DICTIONARY
OF REPUBLICAN CHINA

VOLUME IV: YANG-YÜN

ABBREVIATIONS

Alt. = alternate name
H. = hao, a literary name
Orig. = original name
Pen. = pen name

Pseud. = pseudonym
Studio. = pieh-hao (alternate hao)
T. = tzu, courtesy name
West. = Western name

ECCP = *Eminent Chinese of the Ch'ing Period*, ed. by
Arthur W. Hummel. Washington, 1943–44.

Yang Ch'ang-chi   楊昌濟
T. Huai-chung   懷中

Yang Ch'ang-chi (c.1870–17 January 1920), Western-trained scholar who taught ethics at the First Provincial Normal School in Changsha (1912–17) and at Peking University (1918–19). He is best remembered as the teacher of Mao Tse-tung and the father of Mao's first wife.

Precise information about the life of Yang Ch'ang-chi is scanty. A native of Changsha, Hunan, Yang spent the period 1902–11 studying abroad in Japan, England, and Germany. After several years in Japan, he went to England with his elder brother (or nephew, according to some authorities), Yang Shou-jen. When Yang Shou-jen committed suicide by drowning himself in England in May 1911, Chang Shih-chao (q.v.), who was then studying at Edinburgh, came to assist Yang Ch'ang-chi in making burial arrangements. Chang, also a native of Changsha, had been a close associate of Yang Shou-jen in anti-Manchu activities in China. During his European sojourn, Yang Ch'ang-chi also studied in Germany and came to regard himself as a neo-Kantian idealist.

After his return to China, Yang Ch'ang-chi taught ethics at the First Provincial Normal School at Changsha from 1912 to 1918. There he gave his students some exposure to Western ethical theory as well as solid grounding in the writings of principal Chinese philosophers of the Ming and Ch'ing periods. Although vigorous in criticizing certain aspects of Confucianism and in rejecting many conventional Chinese behavior patterns, Yang did place emphasis on many traditional Chinese virtues, notably self-discipline, patriotism, and resistance to alien rule. One of Yang's favorite students in ethics at the First Normal School was Mao Tse-tung, who studied there for five years before 1918. Yang was appointed to the faculty of Peking University in 1918 and taught there until his death two years later. When Mao made his first trip to Peking in September 1918, Yang provided him with an introduction to the university librarian, Li Ta-chao (q.v.). On Mao's second trip to Peking at the beginning of 1920, he and Yang met for the last time. On that trip Mao renewed his acquaintance with Yang's daughter, Yang K'ai-hui, whom he later married. It is as Mao Tse-tung's teacher and as the father of Mao's first wife that Yang Ch'ang-chi is best remembered in the West.

Although biographical data are elusive, some information regarding Yang's thought and writings is available. One starting point is his *Exposition and Critique of Western Ethical Theories* (1923). In this book, in the course of explaining and criticizing selected Western schools of thought, Yang expounded his own views at some length and in systematic fashion. He began with a discussion of asceticism, which he criticized on the grounds that desire and reason cannot be regarded simply as opposites. Desire may be a source of evil or good. Moreover, pleasure and desire are incentives to action. Without them, men would cease to act and therefore cease to exist. Moral conduct consists in disciplining desire by reason in order to attain a goal. At the same time, one may regard desire and pleasure only as facts of experience and not as moral principles, for desire and pleasure are fluctuating and unstable. The basis of society is not self-interest but altruism, which assures the unity of the race. For all these reasons, Yang rejected both the "quantitative" hedonism of Jeremy Bentham and the "qualitative" hedonism of John Stuart Mill. The principle of the greatest good of the greatest number, he maintained, though it appears universal, is in fact merely a multiplication of egoism. In any case, the whole idea of a calculus of pleasure is meaningless, for one cannot add pleasures and pains and get zero as a result as one can add positive and negative numbers.

Yang believed that evolutionary hedonism, as exemplified by Herbert Spencer and Leslie Stephen, has the advantage of explaining the development of ethics; all other ethical systems are static. But this system also presents difficulties, for the process of evolution cannot take itself as its goal. There are actions, said Yang, which are harmful according to the laws of biological life but which have the greatest moral value. Examples are the sacrifice of one's life for right or for humanity. Moreover, the struggle for survival of the fittest is incompatible with such ethical concerns as kindness to the weak. Spencer's "moral" society also can be criticized on many counts, for the principle of happiness and the principle of the progression of life are contradictory.

A better ideal is that of self-realization. Aristotle was a partisan of it, as were Kant, Fichte, and Hegel. F. H. Bradley and especially T. H. Green developed theories based on this principle. According to them, the goal of action is to perfect oneself and society through both pleasure and pain. But this theory too has its weaknesses. Green's idealistic philosophy, though it affirms man's existence, cannot explain it by the laws of nature. This philosophy does, however, have the merit of steering a middle course between hedonism and asceticism. Yang Ch'ang-chi believed that a satisfactory moral philosophy could be achieved by combining Green's ideal of self-realization with a greater emphasis on man's responsibility to society. Man, he said, can influence the development of the world, and by developing the world he develops himself.

These aims of individual self-realization and responsibility to society were the two main themes in all of Yang Ch'ang-chi's life and thought. The first aim seems contradictory to traditional Confucian philosophy. Like many intellectuals of his generation, however, Yang sought to buttress ideas which were derived largely from Western thought with references to Chinese authorities. He compiled a small volume of extracts from the *Lun-yü* (*Analects*) which he used to teach individualism to his students. Nevertheless, Yang was vigorous in his rejection of certain patterns of behavior which characterized Chinese society. He wrote a number of articles which gave evidence of his impatience with traditional Chinese ways in three important areas: economic activity, religion, and family relationships.

The problems of the individual's livelihood and its relation to social patterns were the subject of a two-part article which appeared in the *Hsin Ch'ing-nien* [new youth] in 1916. Here Yang emphasized the contrast between the Chinese family system, which gives to everyone a certain security and hence does not encourage people to work hard, and the English system, under which each son must create a separate establishment for his family and rely on his own efforts to do so. He held that British inheritance laws, which incited younger sons to seek their fortune beyond the seas, were an important factor in the success of the British colonial effort. Self-reliance, honesty, economy, and industry are desirable not only because they will help the individual to get ahead but also because they will assure the welfare of society. Independent-spirited individuals make possible an independent country. The Chinese, said Yang, must learn not to put the welfare of their families before that of their country. Fathers should make provision for their old age rather than becoming burdens to their sons. One's role as a citizen should be considered when choosing a profession—being an opium dealer might benefit one's family, but it harms the nation. Yang averred that business rather than the army is the basis of a nation's strength.

Yang Ch'ang-chi set forth his radical views on the Chinese family system in an article which appeared in the *Chia-yin tsa-chih* [tiger magazine] of Chang Shih-chao in 1915. He praised the Western family system because of the autonomous character of the husband-wife relationship and because of the free choice of partners and the equal rights enjoyed by women. He denounced arranged marriages on both individual and social grounds. Under the Chinese system, he pointed out, marriages are arranged for mentally and physically weak persons who should not perpetuate these weaknesses. People should marry late, after the husband is able to support a family, and should take into account the mental endowments, character, appearance, and bodily condition of their potential partners. Yang also opposed concubinage as immoral and destructive of basic family relationships. Returning to the idea of the independent household, he pointed out that rural life and ancestor worship made it difficult for Chinese to marry late and live in a separate establishment. That pattern is easier for people in the West, where city life predominates. He summed up the situation by saying: "An agricultural country easily gives rise to clanism; an industrial and commercial country easily demolishes clanism."

Yang's views on religion were less radical than his opinions on marriage and the family. He believed that the disputes about whether or not Confucianism is a religion were merely linguistic quibbles. Confucianism is not a religion in the narrow sense; its founder is not regarded as a supernatural being; there are no places of worship for the population at large; and Confucius never spoke of a future life but only of the problems of this life. However, Confucianism may be considered a religion in a broad sense of the word, for Confucius has been held in reverence by Chinese for more than 2,000 years. Although Yang admired the Confucian way, he was unalterably opposed to the establishment of Confucianism as a state religion. As for Christianity, he said: "I cannot approve of those who wish to save China by Christianity, but I consider superfluous the efforts of those who attempt to fight against Christianity with Confucianism."

Such were the beliefs that Yang Ch'ang-chi imparted to his students at Changsha and Peking. His personality and example appear to have made a profound impression on all who came in contact with him. Mao Tse-tung deemed Yang his most influential teacher, saying that "he tried to imbue his students with the desire to become just, moral, virtuous men, useful in society."

Yang Chieh 楊 杰
T. Keng-kuang 耿 光

Yang Chieh (25 January 1889–19 September 1949), outstanding military strategist who headed the Chinese Army Staff College from 1931 to 1935 and served as ambassador to the Soviet Union from 1938 to 1940.

Little is known about Yang Chieh's family background or early years except that he was born in Tali hsien, Yunnan, and that in the spring of 1911 he enrolled at the Shimbu Gakkō [military preparatory academy] in Japan. He returned to China when the revolution began in October 1911 and joined the republican forces at Shanghai as a battalion commander. In 1912, with the establishment of the Chinese

republic, he became commander of the 1st Cavalry Regiment of the Kweichow Army, with the rank of colonel. At this time, his fellow provincial T'ang Chi-yao (q.v.) was governor of Kweichow. In 1913 Yang was promoted to command of the 5th Brigade. After the so-called second revolution (*see* Li Lieh-chün) began in 1913, Kweichow forces moved into Szechwan, and Yang served briefly as Chungking garrison commander, Chungking chief of police, and Szechwan commissioner for civil affairs. With the failure of the second revolution in September, Yang returned to Yunnan. In 1914, after T'ang Chi-yao became military governor of Yunnan, Yang was appointed an instructor at the Yunnan Military Academy. He participated in the anti-Yuan Shih-k'ai movement of Ts'ai O (q.v.) and T'ang Chi-yao in 1915 and early 1916, returning to Yunnan after Yuan's death in 1916 to serve as adviser to T'ang.

In 1920, on the recommendation of T'ang Chi-yao, Yang Chieh enrolled at the Shikan Gakkō [military academy] in Japan, where one of his classmates was Hsiung Shih-hui (q.v.). Yang was graduated first in his class in 1924, and his wife, the former Chao Shih-chün, was graduated at the same time from Tokyo Normal University for Women. Upon his return to China, Yang served briefly in the forces of Chang Tso-lin (q.v.) as a staff officer. In December 1924 he joined the forces of Feng Yü-hsiang (q.v.) as chief of staff of the Third Army of the Kuominchün. After Feng consolidated control of Honan province, Yang was appointed dean of the Honan Military Training Institute in September 1925.

At the invitation of Ch'eng Ch'ien (q.v.), the commander of the Sixth Army of the National Revolutionary Army, Yang Chieh went to Canton in May 1926 to become commander of the 17th Division. He participated in the first stage of the Northern Expedition, and by the late spring of 1927 he had risen to become acting commander of the Sixth Army. Yang supported Chiang Kai-shek during the Kuomintang split over the question of alliance with the Communists. In November 1927 he received membership in the Military Affairs Commission at Nanking, and in December of that year he became president of the Central Military Academy. He was named director of the Military Affairs Commission's administrative department in January 1928. That April, during the final stage of the Northern Expedition, he served as director of Chiang Kai-shek's field headquarters and chief of staff of the First Army Group. After the successful completion of the Northern Expedition, he received an additional appointment in October as president of the Peiping Gendarmerie School.

Yang Chieh was a delegate to the Third National Congress of the Kuomintang in March 1929. He then became chief of staff in the field headquarters of the commander in chief (Chiang Kai-shek) of the land, sea, and air forces. In October, he took to the field as commander of the Tenth Army in a successful campaign against Feng Yü-hsiang. After the capture of Loyang from the rebel forces on 20 November, Yang also became director of Chiang Kai-shek's Loyang field headquarters, but he was forced to flee the area when T'ang Sheng-chih (q.v.) staged a revolt in December. In April 1930 Yang was appointed commander of the Yangtze River forts at Nanking, Chinkiang, Chenghai, and Woosung, with responsibility for the reorganization and reconstruction of the river fortifications from Woosung to Nanking. He returned to the field in May to lead the 2nd Artillery Corps against the so-called northern coalition of Feng Yü-hsiang and Yen Hsi-shan (q.v.). In the course of that campaign, which ended with the collapse of the northern coalition in September, Yang also served as chief of staff of Chiang Kai-shek's field headquarters. Yang became an alternate member of the Central Executive Committee of the Kuomintang in 1931. He assumed office as president of the Chinese Army Staff College in January 1932 and retained that post until May 1938. In March 1933 he led the Eighth Army Group against the Japanese at the Great Wall, and in September 1933 he headed a military mission to Europe, returning to China in the autumn of 1934.

After carefully studying the battle doctrines of the Japanese and German armies, Yang Chieh endeavored to adapt those principles to Chinese conditions and to modernize the Staff College. Using his lectures at the college as a basis, he compiled such works as the *Pao-lin ch'eng-yuan i-chien shu* [book of thoughts on the retention of city walls], *Chan-cheng chueh-yao* [extracted essentials of warfare], *Tsung-ssu-ling hsueh* [the art of the commander in chief], and

Sun Tzu chien-shih [a simple exposition of Suntzu]. These volumes demonstrated his brilliance as a military strategist.

On 18 December 1935 Yang Chieh was appointed deputy chief of the general staff, serving under Ch'eng Ch'ien. Also in 1935 Yang became a full member of the Kuomintang Central Executive Committee. In October 1937, after the Sino-Japanese war began, he headed a mission charged with negotiating a loan from the Soviet Union for the war effort. Yang encountered difficulties, and in March 1938 Sun Fo (q.v.), who had negotiated a previous loan agreement with the Soviet Union, arrived in Moscow to assist Yang. On 12 May 1938 Yang was appointed Chinese ambassador to the Soviet Union, replacing T. F. Tsiang (Chiang T'ing-fu, q.v.). Later that month, he signed the formal agreements covering both the first and second Soviet war loans to China. Sun Fo then returned home. A Sino-Soviet commercial treaty was signed at Moscow on 16 June 1939, but this time the documents were signed by Sun Fo rather than Yang Chieh. On 16 April 1940 the Executive Yuan appointed Shao Li-tzu (q.v.) to replace Yang as ambassador.

Yang went to Paris and remained there for a time before proceeding to Chungking, the National Government's wartime capital. He received no substantive posts after his return to China. Yang lectured to the Central Training Corps and in 1942 wrote a book entitled *Kuofang hsin-lun* [new treatise on national defense]. In it he surveyed ancient and modern systems and theories of national defense and considered practical issues related to national defense in the then-current war. Early in 1944 Yang was appointed head of a five-man military observation group which went to London early in February and returned to Chungking at the end of the month. The only other appointment he received from the National Government came in 1946, when he was named to the Strategic Advisory Commission.

In 1949, after a brief trip to Yunnan, Yang Chieh went to Hong Kong, where he became a central executive committee member of the dissident Kuomintang Revolutionary Committee (*see* Li Chi-shen). He accepted an invitation that summer to attend the Chinese People's Political Consultative Conference, which was to be held at Peiping to establish the People's Republic of China. Yang was waiting for transportation by ship from Hong Kong when, on 19 September 1949, he was assassinated, allegedly by a Kuomintang agent.

Yang Ch'uan　　　　　　　楊 銓
T.　Hsing-fo　　　　　　　 杏 佛
Alt. Yang Chien

Yang Ch'uan (1893–18 June 1933), founder of the Science Society of China and secretary general of the Academia Sinica. In 1932 he also became secretary general of the China League for Civil Rights. Yang was assassinated in 1933.

Yushan, Kiangsi, was the birthplace of Yang Ch'uan. He was the fifth child born to Yang Yung-ch'ang, an official who then was serving in Huichou, Anhwei. At the age of six sui, Yang Ch'uan was enrolled at an old-style private school. When he was 13 sui, his father lost his position, and the family experienced the hardships of poverty for a time. About 1908 Yang went to Shanghai to acquire a modern education. He enrolled at the famous Chung-kuo kung-hsueh (China National Institute), where one of his teachers was Hu Shih (q.v.). Yang soon joined the T'ung-meng-hui, and he participated in the republican revolution in 1911.

With the establishment of the republican government in January 1912, Yang Ch'uan served briefly as a presidential secretary to Sun Yat-sen. In 1913 he received a government scholarship for study abroad. He went to the United States to study mechanical engineering at Cornell University. In Ithaca he joined with H. C. Zen (Jen Hung-chün, q.v.) and others in organizing the Science Society of China, later serving as its secretary from 1919 to 1922, and as editor of its journal, *Science*, from 1919 to 1921. Upon graduation from Cornell, he enrolled at Harvard, where he received a master's degree in business administration in 1918. Yang returned to China in mid-1918 to become director of the cost accounting division of the Han-yeh-p'ing Iron and Coal Company. In 1919 he left the company to become professor and chairman of the department of commerce at Nanking Normal College. He later served successively as professor of economics, engineering, and factory manage-

ment. After the college was reorganized as Southeastern (Tung-nan) University in 1921, he remained on the faculty as professor of engineering until the summer of 1924, when the engineering college was abolished at the behest of Ch'i Hsieh-yuan (q.v.), the military governor of Kiangsu. Throughout this period, Yang feuded with the university's president, Kuo Ping-wen (q.v.), and with the board of trustees. This feud was responsible for his transfer from department to department and for his dismissal after the engineering college was abolished. Disagreement over educational policies, divergence in political sympathies, and personal animosities made Yang a bitter enemy of Kuo, whose replacement he advocated publicly. Whereas Yang was a loyal follower of Sun Yat-sen who maintained an uncompromisingly antagonistic attitude toward the Peking government and the provincial warlords, Kuo had to maintain a smooth working relationship with the authorities in order to keep the university operating.

After leaving Southeastern University, Yang Ch'uan went to Canton to join Sun Yat-sen's government. He accompanied Sun to north China, serving as a secretary. After Sun's death in March 1925, Yang acted as general director of the preparatory office for the funeral of Sun Yat-sen, which was responsible for selecting and preparing a permanent burial site. Yang then went to Shanghai, where he devoted his time to a variety of Kuomintang activities. After the May Thirtieth Incident in 1925, when British police fired on Chinese, Yang founded, on 10 June, the *Min-tsu jih-pao*, which maintained an uncompromising attitude toward foreign imperialism and which strongly attacked the equivocal stand of the Peking government. By the time the Shanghai authorities suppressed the *Min-tsu jih-pao* on 25 June, Yang had won renown as a Kuomintang propagandist and organizer. In the spring of 1927, after the Nationalists won control of Shanghai, Yang Ch'uan was appointed to the Shanghai branch of the Central Political Council and to the executive committee of the Shanghai branch of the Kuomintang. He also served as chief of the Shanghai propaganda bureau and helped in the reorganization of the China Merchants' Steam Navigation Company.

In June 1927 the National Government announced the reorganization of the ministry of education as the Ta-hsueh-yuan [board of universities], with Ts'ai Yuan-p'ei (q.v.) as president. The new board was patterned after the French system. In October, Yang Ch'uan became Ts'ai Yuan-p'ei's chief executive assist-ant, with the official title of director of the office of educational administration. On 28 January 1928 he became vice president of the Ta-hsueh-yuan. In the meantime, the National Government decided to establish a scientific research organization. A preparatory commit-tee of some 30 members was set up in November 1927 with Ts'ai as its president and Yang as its secretary general. In April 1928 the Ta-hsueh-yuan was abolished, and the ministry of education was reestablished. At that time, the central research organization, known as the Academia Sinica (Chung-yang yen-chiu-yuan) became an independent organ under the direct jurisdiction of the National Government. Ts'ai became president of the Academia Sinica, with Yang as secretary general. Yang, a conscientious and able administrator, took charge of the financial and developmental operations of the Academia Sinica, which was inaugurated on 9 June 1928.

Before long, Yang Ch'uan became increas-ingly critical of the National Government, particularly of its seeming inability to counter Japanese encroachments upon China's sover-eignty. During the 1932 Sino-Japanese conflict at Shanghai, he sponsored the establishment of a technical cooperation committee to aid the embattled Chinese troops and collaborated with Sun Yat-sen's widow, Soong Ch'ing-ling (q.v.), in setting up a hospital for wounded soldiers. On 23 October 1932 Yang, Ts'ai Yuan-p'ei, Lin Yü-t'ang (q.v.), and others made an unsuccessful appeal for the release of Ch'en Tu-hsiu (q.v.), who had been arrested on charges of endangering the republic. In December, Yang, Ts'ai, Soong Ch'ing-ling, and others established the China League for Civil Rights to defend the civil rights of the increasing number of political prisoners held by the National Government. Yang served as secretary general of the new organization. On 14 May 1933 the noted Communist novelist Ting Ling (q.v.) was abducted by Kuomintang underground agents in Shanghai. Yang's unsuccessful efforts to secure her release caused him to receive anonymous letters warning him to disband the league and to stop meddling in the anti-Communist campaigns. Yang ignored all such warnings.

On 18 June 1933 Yang Ch'uan and the elder of his two sons, Yang Hsiao-fu, went for their customary Sunday morning drive. At 8:45 a.m., just as they were seating themselves in the car, which was parked in front of the Academia Sinica's office of international publications exchange in Shanghai, they were ambushed by four or five gunmen. Yang was killed instantly, and his son was wounded in the leg. Policemen near the scene of the murder gave chase and brought down one of the assassins, Kuo Te-tsung, who then committed suicide. The officers of the China League for Civil Rights held the National Government responsible for Yang's death, but they were unable to prove their contention.

Yang Hu-ch'eng   楊 虎 城

Yang Hu-ch'eng (1883–September 1949), gover-nor (1931) and pacification commissioner (1932–36) of Shensi. He joined with Chang Hsueh-liang in precipitating the Sian Incident of December 1936. Yang was arrested in 1937, imprisoned for 11 years, and murdered in 1949.

Little is known about Yang Hu-ch'eng's family background or early life except that he was born in Pucheng, Shensi, and that he became a bandit. At the time of the 1911 revolution, he led a group of some 200 men, presumably bandits, which joined the republican forces in Shensi. He took part in the so-called second revolution in 1913 (see Li Lieh-chün) and steadily rose in rank in the Shensi forces. In 1918 these forces were reorganized as the Ching-kuo-chün [national pacification army], with Yü Yu-jen (q.v.) as commander in chief, to fight the northern warlords. Yang served with this army until it was disbanded in June 1922, by which time he had become a brigade commander.

When Sun Yüeh (1878–1928; T. Yü-hsing), the commander of the Third Army of the Kuominchün (see Feng Yü-hsiang), became military governor of Shensi late in 1924, Yang Hu-ch'eng received command of the Third Army's 3rd Division. In 1926 he was sent to garrison Sian, where he was trapped in April when troops commanded by Liu Chen-hua, a supporter of Wu P'ei-fu (q.v.), encircled the city. The siege of Sian lasted for eight months, and several thousand inhabitants of the city starved to death. Yang and his remaining troops finally were rescued on 28 November by Kuominchün forces, led by Sun Liang-ch'eng, which had been stationed in Kansu. After Feng Yü-hsiang (q.v.) declared allegiance to the Kuomintang in September 1926, the Kuominchün became the Second Group Army, with Yang as commander of its Tenth Army. He served as field commander in chief of the Second Group Army's eastern route and fought against the Chihli-Shantung forces on the Lunghai front in 1927. His forces moved into Shantung but suffered a setback soon afterwards. At this point, Yang retired from the field and went to Japan.

Yang Hu-ch'eng returned to China in 1928 and received command of the 21st Division of the Second Group Army, stationed at Linyi, Shantung. When the situation in Shantung was thrown into confusion with the sudden withdrawal of Sun Liang-ch'eng from the province in April 1929, Yang shifted his allegiance to the Nationalists. He received command of the 14th Division and was assigned to garrison Nanyang, Honan. In 1930 he took part in the Nationalist campaign against the northern coalition of Yen Hsi-shan (q.v.) and Yang's former chief, Feng Yü-hsiang. With the collapse of the northern coalition in October, Yang was sent to Sian as commander of the 17th Division. In 1931 he became a member of the Kuomintang Central Supervisory Committee and governor of Shensi. He held the governorship until 1932, when he was appointed pacification commissioner of Shensi and commander of the Seventeenth Route Army.

In 1936 Chang Hsueh-liang (q.v.) and Yang Hu-ch'eng unsuccessfully argued with Chiang Kai-shek about the cessation of the civil war against the Communists and the formation of a united front against the Japanese. Finally, after Chang, Yang, and the Northeastern commanders held a conference, they arrested Chiang Kai-shek at Sian on 12 December 1936 and confronted him with eight demands (for details, see Chang Hsueh-liang). In the negotiations that ensued, Chang stated his willingness to settle for a private oral agreement on the united front, but Yang demanded a public announcement of Chiang's support of all eight points. Chang's view prevailed, and he accompanied Chiang Kai-shek back to Nanking on 25 December. Yang and the Northeastern generals, however, refused to support National Government policies and established the "Sian Military Commission of the Anti-Japanese Allied Army," with Yang as its head. On 5 January 1937 the National Government responded by removing Yang from his official posts and sending Ku Chu-t'ung (q.v.) to north China as director of Chiang Kai-shek's Sian headquarters and commander in chief of five group armies. Yang and his associates met with Ku at Loyang, but no agreement was reached. They demanded, among other things, the immediate release of Chang Hsueh-liang. Ku then moved to T'ungkuan to prepare for battle. On 29 January, the rebels resumed negotiations and agreed to troop reorganization. Ku Chu-t'ung moved to Sian and began the work of reorganization in February. At the beginning of June 1937, Yang was sent on a year's tour of Europe and America as a "special military investigator."

On his return to China in 1938, Yang Hu-ch'eng was arrested by the Nationalist authorities and sent to a detention camp at Chungking. His wife went on a hunger strike in protest, and died. Yang, his younger son, a daughter, his secretary, and his secretary's wife remained prisoners at the camp throughout the Second World War and the Nationalist-Communist civil war. In September 1949, when the National Government was preparing for the move from its Chungking refuge to Taiwan, they all were shot. Yang Hu-ch'eng was survived by his elder son, Yang Chi-min, who commanded Communist forces in southwest China.

Yang Sen   楊 森
T. Tzu-hui   子 惠

Yang Sen (c.1887–), Szechwanese military and political leader who served as commander in chief of the Twenty-seventh Group Army and deputy commander of the Ninth War Area in 1938–44. He was governor of Kweichow in 1945–47 and mayor of Chungking in 1948–49.

A native of Kuangan, Szechwan, Yang Sen was born into a scholarly family of landowners.

Although many members of the family were interested in things military, Yang's father did not wish him to pursue a military career. Accordingly, Yang was sent to a private school for the classical education that would prepare him for the imperial examinations and a civil service career. But military exercises interested Yang more than books, and he secretly took up such training with a cousin. Some time later, when members of the Yang clan assembled in the village square for an exhibition of military skills on the occasion of the Dragon Boat festival, Yang Sen, at the urging of his cousin, displayed his skills in horsemanship and archery. As a result, Yang's father relented and allowed him to enroll at the Szechwan Army Primary School.

Upon graduation in 1906, Yang Sen enrolled at the Szechwan Short-Term Military Academy, where one of his classmates was Liu Hsiang (q.v.). In 1910 he began active service as a platoon leader in the 65th Regiment of the Szechwan forces. About this time, he joined the T'ung-meng-hui, and in 1911 he was among those who actively opposed the Ch'ing government's plans for nationalization of the projected Szechwan-Hankow railroad and who supported the republican revolution. In 1912 he and Liu Hsiang were selected for service in the guards battalion of Chang Lan (q.v.). After participating in the so-called second revolution (*see* Li Lieh-chün) in 1913, Yang fled to Yunnan, where he joined the military staff of Ts'ai O (q.v.). When Ts'ai returned to Yunnan in December 1915 to organize a revolt against Yuan Shih-k'ai, Yang became a staff officer in the First Army, led by Ts'ai, of the National Protection Army. He marched into Szechwan with that force at the beginning of 1916. The Yunnan force remained in Szechwan long after the deaths of both Yuan Shih-k'ai and Ts'ai O. Finally, in May 1920, Szechwanese troops began a campaign against the "guest armies" from Yunnan and Kweichow. Yang, as a loyal Szechwanese, promptly joined the Second Army of Liu Hsiang as a regimental commander. When that campaign ended, the provincial military leaders declared Szechwan's independence and elected Liu Hsiang commander in chief of all Szechwan armies. Yang succeeded Liu as commander of the Second Army.

In 1922, after launching a campaign against Tan Mou-hsin, Liu Hsiang and Yang Sen were forced out of Szechwan by a coalition headed by Liu Ch'eng-hsun. Yang then entered the service of Wu P'ei-fu (q.v.) as commander of a mixed brigade (reorganized from the remnants of his own army) at Ichang, Hupeh. Liu became his director of reorganization. With the aid of Wu P'ei-fu's forces, they fought their way back to power in Szechwan in 1923. Yang then became Szechwan military rehabilitation commissioner, with Liu as Szechwan-Yunnan border defense commissioner. But when Wu P'ei-fu fell from power at Peking late in 1924, Liu decided to move against Yang. In March 1925 Liu's uncle Liu Wen-hui, Teng Hsi-hou (qq.v.), Yuan Tsu-ming, and Lai Hsin-hui moved against Yang and drove him from Szechwan. In the spring of 1926, however, Yang returned to power, with the aid of Wu P'ei-fu and with the support of Teng Hsi-hou and Yuan Tsu-ming. That May, Yang became civil governor of Szechwan, with Teng as military governor and Yuan as Szechwan-Kweichow border defense commissioner.

When the Northern Expedition began in mid-1926, Yang Sen decided to support the Nationalists. In June, he was appointed commander of the Fifth Route Army. Later that year, he became commander of the Twentieth Army, stationed in the Wanhsien-Ichang sector. The head of the Twentieth Army's political department was Chu Teh (q.v.), who had served with Yang in Ts'ai O's forces. When Yang discovered that his troops were being indoctrinated with Marxist-Leninist principles, he caused the arrest and execution of 23 cadres in the 14th Division. Chu Teh, readily perceiving the significance of this development, abandoned his post and went to Kiangsi. When the Kuomintang split into factions in 1927 over the question of cooperation with the Communists, Yang decided to support Chiang Kai-shek. Although he aided Chiang in campaigns against the Wuhan regime, early in 1928 he was relieved of his command because of his continuing association with Wu P'ei-fu. When it became apparent that Yang had no ambitions involving Wu, he was restored to command and was appointed to the Szechwan government council. In December 1928 he and other Szechwanese leaders issued a public telegram denouncing Liu Wen-hui, then the governor of Szechwan. Internal conflict again plagued Szechwan as the forces of Yang Sen and Liu Hsiang took to the field. Yang did well in the conflict until his supporter Kuo Ju-tung defected to the two Lius. In January 1929 Yang was forced out of Wanhsien and was dismissed from his posts by the National Government. Yang remained at the head of his army and consolidated his position in Nanchung, Kwangan, Chühsien, Yingshan, Pengan, and Yuehchih. He remained aloof from civil conflict until late 1932, when he joined with Liu Hsiang and Teng Hsi-hou in a campaign against Liu Wen-hui.

After the Communist Fourth Front Army of Hsü Hsiang-ch'ien (q.v.) inflicted a defeat on Yang Sen in the autumn of 1933, Yang accepted an appointment as commander in chief of the Fourth Route of the so-called bandit-suppression forces in Szechwan, serving under Liu Hsiang. The campaign against Liu Wen-hui also continued, and in October Liu Hsiang succeeded him as governor of Szechwan. With the help of Nationalist troops commanded by Hu Tsung-nan (q.v.), Yang Sen and Liu Hsiang countered the Communist threat to Szechwan in 1935.

When the Sino-Japanese war broke out in July 1937, Yang Sen was the first Szechwanese general to accept orders to move his troops out of the province and to the front. He fought bravely on the Shanghai front and at Anking, Anhwei, and he received command of the Sixth Army Group. In 1938 he became commander in chief of the Twenty-seventh Group Army and deputy commander of the Ninth War Area (Hunan and western Kiangsi), serving under Hsueh Yueh (q.v.). After he repulsed major attacks on Changsha in September 1939, September 1941, and December 1941, he was promoted to the rank of full general. In 1942–43 his forces held the Hsinchiang River line without much difficulty. In 1944, however, the Japanese launched the offensive known as Operation Ichi-go and virtually destroyed Yang's forces, capturing Changsha on 18 June. Yang was transferred to the Hunan-Kwangsi border in September and was relieved of his command in December. On 16 January 1945 he was appointed governor of Kweichow. He held that post until April 1948, when he became mayor of Chungking and director of its Kuomintang headquarters. When the Chinese Communists forced the National Government to retreat to Chungking

in the autumn of 1949, Yang received the concurrent post of Chungking garrison commander. He remained loyal to the Nationalists even though most of the Szechwan militarists declared allegiance to the Chinese Communists. He finally left Szechwan for Taiwan when ordered to do so by Chiang Kai-shek in December. Some of his forces continued to fight the Chinese Communists in the early 1950's. In Taipei, Yang served as an adviser on national strategy in the presidential office and as chairman of the Chinese National Athletic Foundation.

Yang Sen married several times and had many children, most of whom remained on the mainland after 1949.

Yang Shou-ching   楊 守 敬
T. Hsing-wu   惺 吾

Yang Shou-ching (27 May 1839–9 January 1915), leading bibliophile and bibliographer who was also known for his accomplishments in the fields of epigraphy, calligraphy, historical geography, and printing.

Born into a merchant family in Ich'ang, Hupeh, Yang Shou-ching was taught to read by his mother when very young and subsequently had a few years of traditional schooling with a local teacher. Because of the early death of his father, he had to interrupt his schooling from 1849 to 1852 to assist his grandfather in the family business. While working in the family store, however, he continued his studies in the evenings. He was able to resume his formal education in 1852, and he passed the sheng-yuan examinations in 1857 and the chü-jen examinations in 1862. In the years following, he unsuccessfully participated several times in the metropolitan examinations. During this long period of preparation for the examinations, Yang made his living by teaching and by managing the family business.

While in Peking in 1863 for the metropolitan examinations, Yang Shou-ching encountered two scholars who stimulated his interest in bibliography and epigraphy. He began to collect books, bronze and stone inscriptions, and antique objects.

It was during one of his trips to Peking that Yang became acquainted with Ho Ju-chang

(1838–1891), who in 1877 was appointed Chinese minister to Japan. Ho was an enthusiastic admirer of Yang's calligraphy, and in 1880 he invited Yang to join his staff in Japan. Although Ho Ju-chang left his post soon afterwards, Yang Shou-ching remained in the Chinese legation at Tokyo until 1884 as secretary to Ho's successor, Li Shu-ch'ang (ECCP, I, 483–85). Yang's stay in Japan greatly enriched his experience as a bibliophile. With his knowledge and keen interest, he searched tirelessly through book stores and sought out Japanese collectors, discovering many rare Chinese works which he had not seen before or which were not to be found in China. He bought some items and obtained others in exchange for rubbings, old coins, old seals, or other objects he had brought from China. His notes on early editions of Chinese works which he found in Japan were assembled and printed in 1901 under the title *Jih-pen fang-shu chih*. It was on the basis of these materials and under Yang's supervision that Li Shu-ch'ang prepared the well-known collectanea of rare books no longer extant in China, the *Ku-i ts'ung-shu*, which was printed in Tokyo in 1882–84. Through his experience in Japan, Yang Shou-ching broadened his knowledge of book publishing and of the technique of carving wood blocks. When he returned to China in 1884, be brought back many rare and valuable books as well as a personal reputation as a bibliophile and authority on wood-block printing.

From 1884 to 1899, Yang served as district director of studies of Huangkang hsien in his native Hupeh. There in 1888 he built his library, the Lin-su yuan. The name Lin-su, meaning "neighbor of Su," was taken from Su Tung-p'o's essay on the Red Cliff, situated north of the city of Huangkang. During this period Yang began to print his own works and to reprint old and rare books. He also trained Chinese wood-block carvers to meet the standards which he had learned in Japan.

In 1899 Chang Chih-tung, then governor general of Hupeh and Hunan, invited Yang Shou-ching to teach geography at the Liang-Hu shu-yuan, the provincial academy at Wuchang. Three years later, as part of a program to modernize the school system, the shu-yuan [old style academies] were converted into hsueh-t'ang [modern schools]. The Liang-Hu shu-yuan became the Ch'in-cheng hsueh-t'ang in 1902 and the Ts'un-ku hsueh-t'ang in 1907. Yang Shou-ching served as director of the school from 1902 until 1908.

Early in 1906 Yang made a trip to Nanking at the invitation of Tuan-fang, then governor general of Liang-Kiang, who was a lover of books and antiques. There Yang wrote descriptive and critical notes on Tuan-fang's collection of rubbings of inscriptions from bronzes and stones. From Nanking he proceeded to Shanghai, where, as a result of the admiration and publicity of a friend, he sold samples of his calligraphy for good prices. He made another trip to Nanking and Shanghai, with similar material success, in 1909.

After the outbreak of the revolution of 1911, Yang, then 72, took refuge in Shanghai. He derived his principal income from the sale of his calligraphy. In 1914, the Peking government appointed as advisers a number of elderly men of distinction, including Yang Shou-ching. Yang went to Peking, where he lived until his death on 9 January 1915. His acceptance of this position under the republic brought unfavorable criticism from conservative Chinese who believed that a man who had been an official under the former dynasty should not serve the new regime.

Of the two dozen or more works in the various fields of his special interest left by Yang Shou-ching, a number of volumes are particularly notable. In bibliography, the *Jih-pen fang-shu chih* not only re-introduced many ancient Chinese books to China but also revived interest in collecting Chinese books in Japan. The *Liu-chen p'u* and its supplement (1901–17) are two collections of examples in facsimile of rare books. They are important to bibliophiles because, unlike most catalogues, they provide pictures of the actual items rather than mere descriptions in words. In geography, the historical atlas *Li-tai yü-ti yen-ko hsien-yao t'u* (1904–11), is still a useful reference work for students of Chinese history. Of Yang's three works on the *Shui-ching chu* [water classic], the *Shui-ching chu shu* is the most comprehensive and finished product. This manuscript was completed after Yang's death by his student Hsiung Hui-chen (d.1936; T. Ku-chih) and was photographically reproduced in Peking in 1957. Yang's two collections of epigraphs, the *Wang-t'ang chin-shih wen-tzu* and *Erh-pien*, were published in 1870–77 and 1909. His collected essays, *Hui-ming hsuan-chi*, were printed in 1895. An annalistic autobiography, the *Lin-su lao-jen nien-p'u* stopped at the end of 1911 but was completed by Hsiung Hui-chen and printed in 1915 shortly after Yang's death.

Yang Tseng-hsin   楊 曾 新
T. Ting-ch'en   鼎 臣

Yang Tseng-hsin (1867–7 July 1928), governor of Sinkiang from 1912 until his death by assassination in 1928.

During the Ming dynasty, the ancestors of Yang Tseng-hsin had lived in Kiangsu, but the family later had moved to Mengtze in Yunnan province, and it was there that Yang was born. His father, Yang Chi-yuan, saw that Yang and his two brothers, Tseng-ling and Tseng-ping, received a thorough education in the Chinese classics. Yang Tseng-hsin passed the examinations for the chü-jen degree in 1889 and became a chin-shih in 1890.

Yang's first official appointment sent him to Kansu, where he served as paymaster in the provincial treasury and as a hsien magistrate. After returning to Yunnan to observe the conventional mourning period when his father died, Yang was again ordered to Kansu to serve as district magistrate at Weiyuan. On his way there, he received a temporary assignment in the Ninghsia area at the time of the Sino-Japanese war of 1894–95.

In 1896 Yang returned to Kansu. Because of the major Muslim rebellion of 1862–77 that had devastated much of northwest China, relations between Chinese and Muslims in the province were poor. As district magistrate at Linhsia (Hochow), Yang devoted himself for four years to planning and supervising reconstruction work, notably the improvement of civil-military relations and rehabilitation of the educational system. He was responsible for the restoration of a number of schools in Linhsia and surrounding districts, and he recruited scholars to teach in the area. In 1900 he was appointed private secretary to Wei Kuang-yin, the governor general of Shensi-Kansu, and in 1901 he was promoted to the rank of circuit commissioner. After a trip to Peking, Tientsin, and the lower Yangtze valley to observe

educational developments and to recruit staff, Yang established the Kansu Academy as well as normal schools and other institutions designed to provide training in military, police, and industrial subjects and to prepare specialists for government service.

When a new governor general of Shensi-Kansu was appointed in 1907, Yang's position in Kansu became difficult. The official in charge of the provincial treasury in neighboring Sinkiang at this time was Wang Shu-t'ang, an official who had served in Kansu and who thus was acquainted with Yang's capabilities. At Wang's suggestion, the governor of Sinkiang petitioned Peking to recommend Yang Tseng-hsin for appointment as circuit commissioner at Aksu. The transfer was approved, and Yang assumed office in 1908. His years of experience in Kansu, a province with a mixed Chinese-Muslim population, proved to be of great value in Sinkiang. He soon was promoted, becoming circuit intendant and commissioner for judicial affairs at Urumchi, the provincial capital.

Sinkiang, or Chinese Turkestan, the largest and western-most administrative region of China, had become a province of the Chinese empire in 1884. Because its populace was ethnically heterogeneous and largely non-Chinese, the republican revolution of 1911 caused new administrative problems there. Yuan Ta-hua, the last governor of Sinkiang under the Ch'ing dynasty, proclaimed the allegiance of the province to the Chinese republic in March 1912, but he soon found himself unable to cope with the discord that prevailed in Sinkiang. He delegated authority to Yang Tseng-hsin and fled from Urumchi. Yang thus found himself the involuntary inheritor of political authority in Sinkiang. He immediately expressed his allegiance to the Chinese republic, and in an official communication to Yuan Shih-k'ai at Peking he emphasized the importance of retaining indigenous Muslim, rather than Chinese, troops to support his regime. In May 1912 the Peking government confirmed Yang as civil and military governor of Sinkiang province, with the concurrent post of military governor of the Ili region, which comprised the districts of Ili, Ashan (Altai), and T'ach'eng (Chuguchak) in the far northwest adjacent to the Russian border.

Yang recognized that preservation of practical power in Sinkiang depended largely on his own resources. He also understood the importance of insulating Sinkiang from the internecine military and political strife then endemic within the Great Wall. The attitudes of officials at Peking were unpredictable; the loyalties of regional militarists with territorial bases of power in China's Muslim northwest were problematical. In attempting to insulate Sinkiang from the vagaries of outside authority, Yang was aided both by the geographical remoteness of Sinkiang and by the underdeveloped transportation and communications systems in northwest China.

The new regime of Yang Tseng-hsin also confronted difficult internal problems. Without military forces, Yang had to rule a heterogeneous population overwhelmingly composed of non-Chinese elements, many of which were mutually antagonistic. The Han Chinese comprised less than ten percent of the population. The remainder was a melange of Uighurs, Kazakhs, and Kirghiz, with smaller numbers of Mongols, Tajiks, Uzbeks, Tatars, and other minority groups. Yang's immediate objectives were unification of the province and consolidation of control. To attain these goals, Yang dealt sharply with a separatist revolt in the Ili region; incorporated the three districts of Ili, Altai, and Chuguchak into his realm; suppressed the potentially disruptive activities of the Ko-lao-hui [brothers and elders society] in both northern and southern Sinkiang; and countered Muslim resistance at Hami, Kuche, Khotan, and other places. In addition to political and security problems, Yang had to deal with economic problems created by currency instability and by inflation during the early years of his administration. By imposing new controls, he was able to bring reasonable stability to the provincial finances by 1918.

Throughout his rule in Sinkiang, Yang Tseng-hsin was troubled by anti-Chinese sentiment in the province. Using divide-and-rule tactics which Chinese administrators had long employed, Yang strove to sustain a balance among ethnic groups and economic regions within Sinkiang to prevent unrest and rebellion. Traditional patterns of economic-social life in Chinese Turkestan, based on oasis agriculture and nomadic animal husbandry, continued under Yang's rule. If the non-Chinese majority of the populace was to acquiesce to Chinese rule, the provincial administration and its representatives would have to avoid exploitation that would focus discontent on the ruling Chinese minority. Yang retained tight control over the administrative bureaucracy and reinforced his security system with an extensive espionage network. The administration of justice, if harsh, was reasonably effective, and Sinkiang did not lapse into the conditions of banditry and brigandage that prevailed in many provinces of China proper during these years.

Yang Tseng-hsin also attempted to preserve the political and territorial integrity of his domain by isolating Sinkiang from external influence. Provincial borders were carefully guarded, and casual travelers were discouraged from entering the area. Imports and exports were controlled, and strict censorship was maintained over communications. During the early years of his administration, Yang had to deal with problems on the Sinkiang border with Outer Mongolia and with troubles created by movement of nomadic Kazakhs across the Sinkiang border with Russia. During the late nineteenth century, Russia had developed significant economic interests in Central Asia. The growth of trade with geographically adjacent areas of Chinese Turkestan had been aided by the fact that the Muslim peoples on both sides of the Russian-Sinkiang border were related ethnically and linguistically. Before the First World War, trade relations were conducted under the provisions of the Sino-Russian Treaty of St. Petersburg concluded in 1881.

The impact of the war and the Russian Revolution led to the closing of the Russian-Sinkiang border and to suspension of trade and official intercourse in 1918. Lacking effective military or political support from Peking, which did not officially recognize the Soviet government until 1924, Yang Tseng-hsin pursued a general policy of neutrality toward the unrest in Russian Central Asia. However, he did provide asylum to anti-Bolshevik refugees and to remnants of the White Russian armies of Generals Annenkov and Dutov which fled across the border into Sinkiang in 1920–21. In May 1920 Yang negotiated a new trade agreement with the Russian authorities at Tashkent. This so-called Ili agreement provided for the resumption of Sinkiang-Russian trade and for the establishment of two Soviet consulates in Sinkiang and two Chinese (actually Sinkiang) consulates in Soviet Central Asia. The agreement also provided for the abandonment of Russian extraterritorial rights in Sinkiang. White Russian resistance in Central Asia ended in late 1921, and a measure of stability returned to Sinkiang.

In May 1924 the Peking government, to which Yang Tseng-hsin was nominally subordinate, formally recognized the Soviet Union. The specific problems of Sinkiang, however, required separate negotiations between Yang and the Soviets. These negotiations led to a new trade agreement, signed in October 1924, which provided for five Chinese consulates in neighboring Soviet territory (at Semipalitinsk, Tashkent, Alma Ata, Zaisan, and Andijan) and for five Soviet consulates in Sinkiang (at Urumchi, Ining, Chugachak, Sharasume, and Kashgar). After the conclusion of the 1924 agreement, the Soviet Union came to play an increasingly dominant role in the economic life of Sinkiang. This process of commercial and financial penetration was aided by the fact that much of the trading activity of northern Chinese Turkestan tended normally to be oriented toward Russian Turkestan across a political border which, in respect to economic geography, was largely artificial. The development was also aided by Moscow's post-1925 policy of relaxing controls over trade with technologically underdeveloped areas of the Middle East and Asia judged to be "not dominated by foreign capital." Soviet-Sinkiang political and commercial relations based on the 1924 agreement negotiated by Yang continued even after 1927, when the Kuomintang's break with the Communists led to expulsion of both Russian advisers and consular officials from China proper.

Despite his isolationist policies, Yang Tseng-hsin continued to accept Chinese political sovereignty over Sinkiang throughout his tenure as governor. After the completion of the second stage of the Northern Expedition and the Nationalist entry into Peking in June 1928, Yang ordered that the Kuomintang flag be raised in Sinkiang, thereby acknowledging the authority of the new National Government at Nanking. At a ceremony in Urumchi on 1 July 1928, Yang officially assumed the post of chairman of the Sinkiang provincial government under the National Government.

Only a week later, on 7 July 1928, Yang was assassinated while attending an official banquet in Urumchi. The planner of the murder allegedly was Fan Yao-nan, then Sinkiang provincial commissioner for foreign affairs. Within a few hours after Yang's death, Fan Yao-nan, his accomplices, and members of their immediate families were put to death on orders from another aspirant to power, Chin Shu-jen (q.v.), who then had himself named governor.

During his 16 years of control over Sinkiang after 1912, Yang Tseng-hsin accomplished the unusual feat of providing the major frontier area of Chinese Central Asia with reasonably consistent and coherent rule. He maintained a relatively high level of political order within Sinkiang despite the rapid changes that took place in the pre-1928 period not only in China but also in adjacent Russia and Outer Mongolia.

An important source for the study of Yang Tseng-hsin's public career is the *Pu-kuo-chai wen-tu*, published privately at Nanking in 1921. This work comprises a total of 12 volumes and provides an important collection of Yang's official papers documenting the first decade of his administration of Sinkiang.

Yang Tu   楊　度
T. Hsi-tzu   晳　子

Yang Tu (10 January 1875–17 September 1931), student of Wang K'ai-yün and advocate of constitutional monarchy who became an adviser to Yuan Shih-k'ai. In 1915 he organized the Ch'ou-an-hui [society to plan for stability] to implement Yuan's plans for establishing a monarchy.

Hsiangt'an, Hunan, was the birthplace of Yang Tu. He lost his father, a scholar-official, at an early age and was put under the care of a paternal uncle, Yang Jui-sheng, who had once served as military commandant at Chao-yang-chen, where Wang Shih-chen (q.v.), subsequently one of the "Big Three" in the Peiyang military clique, had been his bodyguard. Yang Tu and his younger sister Yang Chuang became students of Wang K'ai-yün (q.v.), a distinguished classical scholar and poet from Hsiangt'an. When Yang Chuang later married Wang's fourth son Wang Tzu-yü,

Yang Tu became even closer to his teacher. He followed Wang to the Tung-chou Academy at Hengshan, Hunan, and he favorably impressed him with his originality in interpretation of the classics.

After passing the provincial examinations held in Changsha in the autumn of 1897, Yang Tu continued his studies at the Tung-chou Academy. While studying Chinese classics he also became interested in Western studies and in the reform programs which the Hunan provincial government was then sponsoring. Despite Wang K'ai-yün's opposition, in March 1902 Yang left for Japan, where he enrolled at the Kōbun Intensive Teacher Training School. Like many Chinese students in Japan at that time, Yang Tu soon became convinced of the necessity of reform for China. Under his supervision, in October 1902 a monthly called *Yu-hsüeh i-pien* [overseas students' translations] was published. It was the first journal to be published by Chinese students in Japan. Yang stated in the inaugural editorial that the aim of the journal was to acquaint the Chinese people with new knowledge which would serve as a basis for transformation of their country. In addition to articles on education, military science, and foreign relations, it introduced new literature and advocated use of the pai-hua [the vernacular] in fiction for the purpose of rousing the spirit of the people. It advocated education in nationalism and self-government in Hunan as preliminary steps toward achieving revolution. Subsequently, Yang established the Hu-nan pien-i she [Hunan compilation and translation society], which published translations and textbooks for use in primary and middle schools.

In December 1902 Yang Tu returned to Hunan. In July 1903 he went to Peking for a special examination on political economy and emerged as the second-best candidate in the competition, the first being Liang Shih-i (q.v.). Immediately afterwards, however, both he and Liang were accused of being followers of K'ang Yu-wei and Liang Ch'i-ch'ao (qq.v.) and their names were removed from the list of successful candidates. Moreover, an imperial edict for their arrest was issued. Yang Tu hurriedly left Peking for Shanghai and then went to Japan. This incident aroused much criticism of the Ch'ing government, and, ironically, made Yang Tu famous among Chinese intellectuals.

After staying in Japan for about six months, Yang Tu returned to Shanghai. In the summer of 1904 he again won public applause when he acquired documents pertaining to foreign investments in the Canton-Hankow railway and sent them to Liang Ch'i-ch'ao for publication in the Shanghai *Shih-pao*. He next published a pamphlet entitled *Yüeh-Han t'ieh-lu chiao-she pi-mi tang-an* [secret archives of the negotiations over the Canton-Hankow railway]. Finally, he wrote the "Song of Hunan Youth," which contained the lines: "If China is truly to face national extinction, it will happen only after all the people of Hunan have died." In November 1904 he again had to flee to Japan.

Yang Tu declined Sun Yat-sen's invitation to join the T'ung-meng-hui in 1905 on the grounds that he was for constitutional monarchy, but he remained on friendly terms with Sun and many other Chinese revolutionaries in Japan, including Chang Chi and Huang Hsing (qq.v.). In fact, Yang was a leader of Chinese students, being the secretary general of the Chinese Students' General Association, of which Lin Ch'ang-min, Chiang Fang-chen, and Chang Chi (qq.v.) served as secretaries. In December 1905 Chinese students in Japan called a strike in protest against the control measures announced by the Japanese ministry of education. They demanded that the Chinese legation intervene for the abolition of the new rules, failing which they would all return to China. Yang Tu, however, suggested that negotiations be conducted for the revision of certain of the rules, saying that it would not help matters for all students to return to China *en bloc*. The more violent students declared that the conduct of the two Yangs (referring to Yang Tu and the Chinese minister to Japan Yang Chu) was inexcusable, and some even waited for Yang Tu with weapons in an attempt to kill him. Yang disguised himself and fled Tokyo for the countryside. The trouble only subsided in January of the following year. At this time, Hsiung Hsi-ling (q.v.) accompanied Tuan-fang (ECCP, II, 780–82), special envoy of the Ch'ing government for the study of constitutional government, on a tour of Europe and the United States. When they passed through Japan, Hsiung entrusted Yang Tu with the task of studying and translating the constitutions and laws of different countries. Yang seized the opportunity and (together with Liang

Ch'i-ch'ao) submitted a number of recommendations, some of which were accepted by Tuan-fang and his committee.

Though an advocate of constitutional monarchy, Yang Tu was not entirely in agreement with the K'ang Yu-wei and Liang Ch'i-ch'ao group. He rejected Liang's suggestion about organizing a new political party to counter Sun. When the *Hsing-min ts'ung-pao* [renovation of the people] and the *Min-pao* [people's journal] engaged in their fierce debates in 1905–6, he remained aloof from the battle. In January 1907 he founded *Chung-kuo hsin-pao* [new China journal] and the Cheng-su tiao-ch'a hui [society for investigation of political behavior]. Despite these activities, however, Yang Tu's attitude remained ambiguous and inconsistent. Although he was not anti-Manchu, he believed that the Ch'ing government should and could be replaced—not by resorting to force, but by exercise of public opinion. In the end, his vacillation and aloofness estranged him from both the Chinese revolutionaries and the constitutionalists.

In the autumn of 1907 Yang Tu returned to Hunan because of the death of his uncle Yang Jui-sheng. In December, while still observing the traditional mourning period, he wrote a memorial to the throne advocating the early convocation of a parliament. The memorial also was signed by Wang K'ai-yün and others. In the spring of 1908, Yang went to Peking to become an attaché to the Hsien-cheng pien-ch'a kuan [bureau for the drawing up of regulations for constitutional government]. In the capital he met Yuan Shih-k'ai (q.v.), who recommended him to Prince Ch'ing (ECCP, II, 964–65) and other court nobles. Encouraged by Yuan, he explained the idea of constitutional government to various high officials. When the Hsien-cheng kung-hui [association for constitutional government] was established in Peking, he became its chief executive officer. In May 1908 Yang suffered a spate of unfavorable publicity when newspapers revealed that he had spent 2,000 yüan redeeming a sing-song girl for use as a concubine. The influential *Ching-yeh hsün-pao* [the struggle], of which Hu Shih (q.v.) was then an editor, and the Kobe *Jih-hua hsin-pao* were particularly critical. Accordingly, Yang renounced the girl and presented her to a friend, an action which did little, however, to mollify his critics. Yang Tu's

influence further declined following the dismissal of Yuan Shih-k'ai in January 1909.

In August 1911 Yang Tu was appointed director of the statistical bureau of "the royal cabinet," which had been established that April. After the revolution began in October, Yang Tu served as an intermediary between Yuan Shih-k'ai and the revolutionaries. Together with Wang Ching-wei (q.v.), he organized the Kuo-shih kung-chi hui [association for assisting national affairs], which was credited with making arrangements for the abdication of P'u-yi (q.v.). As Yuan's representative, he negotiated with Huang Hsing (q.v.), the leader of the revolutionary army in the Wuhan area. On 9 December 1911 he received a reply from Huang agreeing to the election of Yuan as the president of the republic. He was thus appointed by Yuan to accompany T'ang Shao-yi (q.v.) to the south for peace talks. Yang Tu's pronouncement that Yuan was China's Napoleon and would restore monarchical government aroused wide criticism. Furthermore, in opposition to T'ang, he insisted that Yuan should remain in the north. Accordingly, when T'ang became premier in early 1912, Yang Tu was excluded from the cabinet.

In the first two years of the republican era, Yang spent most of his time in Tsingtao. When Hsiung Hsi-ling became premier in 1913, he nominated Yang for minister of communications, but because of the opposition of Liang Shih-i, chief secretary in the presidential office, Hsiung's suggestion was dropped. Yuan then asked Yang Tu to be minister of education, but he declined. In December 1913, Yang was ordered by Yuan to supervise the development of commerce in Hankow. About six months later he left that post to become a member of the Ts'an-cheng-yüan [political council]. During this period, he persuaded his teacher Wang K'ai-yün to take the post of director of the national history bureau in Peking. When Wang resigned in early 1915, Yang Tu was appointed deputy director of the bureau, in temporary charge of its affairs.

Meanwhile, Yang Tu continued to court the favor of Yuan Shih-k'ai. In April 1915 Yang published an essay entitled "Chün-hsien chiu-kuo lun" [national salvation through constitutional monarchy] in which he argued that only constitutional monarchy was suitable for China. Yuan, delighted by the essay, ordered it reprinted and circulated. In August, Yang announced the organization of the Ch'ou-an-hui [society to plan for stability], and he became its director. The original members of this organization (known as the liu chün-tzu, or six gentlemen) included Yen Fu and Liu Shih-p'ei (qq.v.), although Yen later claimed that he was "abducted" by Yang Tu. The purpose of the Ch'ou-an-hui, as its prospectus proclaimed, "is to study whether monarchism or republicanism is more suitable for China." Yang asked military and civil authorities to show their preference for either monarchism or republicanism. Despite vehement criticism and protest, he proceeded with Yuan's and his plans for a monarchy. In October, he announced the dissolution of the Ch'ou-an-hui and the organization of the Hsien-cheng hsieh-chin-hui [constitutional government promotion society]. In early 1916, as the anti-Yuan movement gained momentum, Yang Tu became an important target of criticism. In April, he asked Yuan Shih-k'ai to permit him to resign. When Yuan died in June, Yang Tu was indicted for "betraying" the republic. He escaped punishment by fleeing to Tsingtao.

In 1926 Yang Tu joined the Kuomintang and moved to Peking, where he studied painting with Ch'i Pai-shih (q.v.) and became a Buddhist convert. In 1927 he reportedly conducted some underground work on behalf of the Kuomintang. A year later, he moved to Shanghai, where he made a living by selling his calligraphy and paintings. Because the fees he charged were high, he had few patrons. Later, he managed to supplement his income by serving as private secretary to Tu Yueh-sheng (q.v.).

In 1930 Yang Tu joined the Tzu-yu ta-t'ung meng, or Freedom League, organized by Lu Hsün (Chou Shu-jen) and T'ien Han (qq.v.). In June, he became a member of the Chung-kuo she-hui k'o-hsüeh-chia lien-meng [league of Chinese social scientists], an organization of leftist intellectuals. It is said that Chou En-lai (q.v.) frequently visited him during this period. Yang Tu died of tuberculosis at Shanghai on 17 September 1931. He was survived by two sons: Yang Kung-shu, a chemist; and Yang Kung-chao, a mining engineer. Yang Tu also had a daughter named Yang Yün-hui, who married Kuo Yu-shou, a sometime senior staff member of UNESCO.

Yang Yung-ch'ing　　　　　楊永淸
West. Y. C. Yang

Yang Yung-ch'ing (26 June 1891–6 March 1956), known as Y. C. Yang, prominent Methodist lay leader and long-time president of Soochow University.

Wusih, Kiangsu, was the birthplace of Y. C. Yang. His father, a physician and a second-generation Christian, was a doctor at the Methodist mission hospital at Soochow who later joined the staff of the Soochow University Bible School at Sungkiang. His aunt, Dora Yui, was among the first widely known women evangelists in China. After being graduated from Soochow University in 1910, Y. C. Yang taught there for a year. He then went to the United States for advanced study at George Washington University in Washington, D.C. He received an LL.B. degree in 1918 and an M.A. degree in 1919. While a student in the United States, he also served in 1916 as private secretary to V. K. Wellington Koo (Ku Wei-chün, q.v.), then Chinese ambassador to the United States. Yang also was an editor of the *Chinese Students Monthly* and president of the Chinese Student Conference in 1917.

After completing his academic work, Y. C. Yang was appointed secretary in the Chinese legation at London in 1920. Because his training and talents were well suited to staff work at international conferences and because of his association with Wellington Koo, Yang was assigned as secretary and adviser to the Chinese delegations at three important meetings: the International Labor Conference at Washington in 1919, the first meeting of the League of Nations Assembly at Geneva in 1920, and the Washington Conference of 1921–22. He then returned to China, where he served under Wellington Koo in the ministry of foreign affairs at Peking. In the next five years he directed several important commissions, and in 1926 he served briefly as consul general at London.

In 1927 Y. C. Yang left government service to become the first Chinese president of Soochow University, succeeding Dr. W. B. Nance. As Yang undertook his new responsibilities, Soochow University was in the process of complying with the new registration requirements established by the National Government's ministry of education at Nanking. The colleges of science and of liberal arts were registered separately; and as distinct and somewhat competitive institutions, they were spurred to rapid expansion of their student bodies, facilities, and equipment during the first years of Yang's administration. Yang was absent from Soochow for a time after the Japanese attack on Mukden in September 1931. He served as senior secretary and director of a department of the ministry of foreign affairs at Nanking.

In addition to his administrative tasks at Soochow University, Y. C. Yang continued to devote time and energy to a variety of Christian activities in China. His prominence as a Methodist layman led to his election in 1930 to the National Christian Council of China and to its executive committee. Two years later, he became a member of the national committee of the YMCA. In 1937 he was a leader in the "Bishops' Crusade" to raise funds in the United States to liquidate the debts of the Methodist Board of Foreign Missions. Traveling 15,000 miles in two months, he spoke in every section of the United States. During this period, he also served as a Chinese delegate to three general conferences of the Methodist Episcopal Church, South. In 1938 he represented China at the meeting of the International Missionary Council at Madras, and in 1939 he participated in the special sessions of that body in the United States.

Y. C. Yang made another trip to the United States during the Sino-Japanese war. At the end of his sabbatical leave, he found himself unable to return to Soochow University because of the war. He then accepted an offer from Bowdoin College to become its Tallman Professor of Chinese Civilization. He also lectured at Emory, Duke, and Ohio Wesleyan universities and at Lake Erie College; and in 1945 he was named the first Mayling Soong Foundation resident lecturer at Wellesley College. His Emory University lectures of 1942 were published in 1943 as *China's Religious Heritage*, described by its author as the first book in English on the religions of China written by a Chinese. During this period, Yang also served as head of the speakers bureau of the Chinese News Service in the United States, in which capacity he addressed many American audiences in an attempt to increase support for the Chinese war effort.

In 1945 Y. C. Yang served as associate secretary of the Committee on the Security Council at the United Nations Conference on International Organization at San Francisco. He became a member of the Preparatory Commission and associate chief of the section on specialized agencies at the first meeting of the General Assembly at London in 1946. He also was named an adviser to the Economic and Social Council and to the Chinese delegation to the General Assembly.

Late in 1946 Y. C. Yang resigned these posts and turned his attention to the task of rehabilitating Soochow University in postwar China. The pressing problems created by the necessity of raising funds in the United States to permit rebuilding in the face of mounting inflation in China required Yang to cross the Pacific five times between the end of 1946 and mid-1948. Yang remained in China when the Chinese Communists gained power in 1949 but apparently played no active role in the new regime. He died at Shanghai on 6 March 1956, at the age of 64.

Yang Yung-t'ai   楊 永 泰
T. Ch'ang-ch'ing   暢 卿

Yang Yung-t'ai (1880–25 October 1936), revolutionary propagandist, leader of the so-called Political Science Group, and one of the most influential bureaucrats in Chiang Kai-shek's entourage in the early 1930's. From 1932 to 1936 he was secretary of Chiang's Nanchang headquarters. Soon after becoming governor of Hupeh in 1936, he was assassinated.

Maoming, Kwangtung, was the birthplace of Yang Yung-t'ai. After attending the Canton High School and the Liang-Kwang Preparatory School, he enrolled in the law school of Peking Methodist University, the forerunner of Yenching University. Upon graduation, he went to Japan for advanced study. From the outset of his career he was interested in revolutionary politics and in journalism as an entry into political life. He returned to Canton shortly before the revolution of 1911 to become editor of a revolutionary daily, the *Kwang-nan pao*. After Kwangtung declared its independence in

November 1911, Yang, as a member of the provincial assembly, helped organize the provincial republican government. He then went to Nanking as a Kwangtung delegate to the provisional National Assembly. In 1913 he was elected to the Senate as a Kuomintang member. At the time of the so-called second revolution (*see* Li Lieh-chün) in 1913, he collaborated with Ku Chung-hsiu in publishing the *Ching-i Journal* in Shanghai. The collapse of the second revolution and the dissolution of the Parliament by Yuan Shih-k'ai in January 1914 served only to strengthen Yang's anti-Yuan sentiments.

After the outbreak of the First World War in 1914, such exiled revolutionaries in Japan as Li Ken-yuan, Li Lieh-chün, Huang Hsing, Ch'eng Ch'ien, and Hsiung K'o-wu (qq.v.) founded the Ou-shih yen-chiu-hui [European affairs research society], the forerunner of the Cheng-hsueh-hsi, or Political Science Group. Yang Yung-t'ai headed a Chinese branch of this society, with headquarters at Peking. In 1915 he joined with Ku Chung-hsiu and Hsü Fu-lin in founding the *Chung-hua hsin-pao*, a violently anti-Yuan newspaper which was published in Shanghai. When a military council was established at Chaoch'ing, Kwangtung, to serve as the legitimate government of China until Yuan Shih-k'ai retired, Yang became director of the financial bureau. Ts'en Ch'un-hsuan (q.v.) served as acting head of the council, with Liang Ch'i-ch'ao as chief of the political committee and Li Ken-yuan as staff officer to the allied northern expeditionary forces and liaison officer in Shanghai. Li and Yang became close political associates at this time.

After Yuan Shih-k'ai died in June 1916, Yang Yung-t'ai returned to Peking to resume his seat in the Senate. He and Li Ken-yuan urged the election of either Ts'en Ch'un-hsuan or Lu Jung-t'ing (qq.v.) to the vice presidency so that both northern and southern interests would be represented in the government headed by Li Yuan-hung (q.v.). When Feng Kuo-chang (q.v.) became vice president, Li Ken-yuan, Yang Yung-t'ai, and their associates organized the Political Science Group, with Li, Ku Chung-hsiu, Chang Yao-tseng, and Niu Yung-chien (q.v.) as its secretaries. When the Parliament was dissolved in 1917, Yang went to Canton to take part in the rump session which established the military government at

Canton with Sun Yat-sen at its head. At this time, members of the Political Science Group were allied with Ts'en Ch'un-hsuan and the other southern militarists who caused the reorganization of the Canton regime in 1918. Supreme authority was given to a seven-man directorate which was headed by Ts'en. Sun Yat-sen withdrew from the government and went to Shanghai in May 1918, though he did not resign his directorship until August. Yang became Kwangtung commissioner of finance, and from May to October 1920 he served as civil governor of Kwangtung. He then was driven out of Canton by the forces of Ch'en Chiung-ming (q.v.). After a period of political inactivity, Yang returned to Peking in 1922 as a member of the Senate.

In 1925 Yang Yung-t'ai was appointed to membership in a new financial rehabilitation commission at Peking. That October, he was appointed a delegate to the customs tariff conference, which held sessions in 1926. One of his colleagues on the commission and the conference was Huang Fu (q.v.). It was through Huang's influence that Yang joined the National Government in 1929 as director of the general affairs department of the Hwai River Conservancy Commission. The following year, he won admittance to Chiang Kai-shek's personal entourage, becoming an adviser in the Generalissimo's headquarters. It was said that Yang had gained Chiang's favor by submitting thought-provoking memoranda on political affairs, especially on the suppression of Communists.

From 1932 to 1936 Yang Yung-t'ai exercised considerable power as chief secretary in the headquarters of the chairman of the Military Affairs Commission. These were the years of Chiang Kai-shek's campaigns against the Chinese Communists, particularly in Kiangsi. Beginning in 1933, Yang was stationed at Nanchang. The Nanchang headquarters was the administrative center for political, military, and party affairs in the provinces of Honan, Hupeh, Anhwei, and Kiangsi. Another member of the Political Science Group, Hsiung Shih-hui (q.v.), was chief of staff at the Nanchang headquarters, and he and Yang became active in promoting the New Life Movement (*see* Chiang Kai-shek). During this period, Yang and Hsiung were among the most influential bureaucrats in Chiang Kai-shek's entourage.

They became deeply involved in factional intrigues within the Kuomintang, incurring the enmity of Hu Han-min (q.v.) and of the CC clique (*see* Ch'en Kuo-fu; Ch'en Li-fu).

On 1 January 1936 Yang Yung-t'ai was appointed governor of Hupeh. He was an efficient administrator, and he immediately set to work on a project for bridging the Yangtze River at Wuhan. He was not a popular governor, however, for he was thought to favor the continuance of anti-Communist campaigns rather than the formation of a united front against the Japanese. On 25 October 1936, as he was returning home from a luncheon party at the American consulate, Yang was assassinated by a Szechwanese named Ch'en Hsi-chao. Although Ch'en said that he killed Yang because Yang supported a policy of appeasement toward Japan, the plot later was traced to Liu Lu-yin, a staunch supporter of Hu Han-min. Liu received a ten-year prison sentence. He was not confined to prison, although he was deprived of his freedom of movement in wartime Szechwan. Yang Yung-t'ai was survived by his wife, two concubines, a son, and six daughters.

Yang Yü-t'ing　　　　　　楊 宇 霆
T. Lin-ko　　　　　　　　　麟 閣

Yang Yü-t'ing (1885–10 January 1929), Manchurian military officer who served as chief of staff under Chang Tso-lin (q.v.) and who later was executed by Chang's son Chang Hsueh-liang (q.v.).

The Fak'u district of Fengtien (Liaoning) was the birthplace of Yang Yü-t'ing. Little is known of his family background or early years except that he decided on a military career and went to Japan to study at the Shikan Gakkō [military academy], from which he was graduated with an outstanding record in the artillery course. He then returned to Manchuria, where he served in the Fengtien military forces during the final years of the Ch'ing period.

After the establishment of the new republican government and the accession to power of Yuan Shih-k'ai in 1912, the Manchurian provinces came under the nominal jurisdiction of Peking. In the reorganization of Fengtien forces at that time, Yang became a weapons specialist in the 27th Division at Mukden commanded by

Chang Tso-lin (q.v.). After the death of Yuan Shih-k'ai in 1916, Chang Tso-lin moved to consolidate personal control of southern Manchuria and became military and civil governor of Fengtien. Yang continued to serve Chang, becoming chief of staff of the 27th Division. Early in 1918 the Fengtien faction lent military forces to Tuan Ch'i-jui and Hsü Shu-cheng (qq.v.) in north China, a move that led to the appointment of Chang Tso-lin as inspector general of the Three Eastern Provinces. During this interlude of cooperation between Chang Tso-lin and Tuan Ch'i-jui, Yang resided at Tientsin in north China.

In 1921 Chang Tso-lin named Yang Yü-t'ing chief counselor in the office of the inspector general of the Three Eastern Provinces. Although the Fengtien forces met defeat in the first Chihli-Fengtien war of 1922, Chang Tso-lin retained authority at Mukden and soon proclaimed himself commander in chief of the peace preservation forces of the Three Eastern Provinces. Yang Yü-t'ing was reappointed chief counselor in Chang Tso-lin's headquarters, with concurrent assignment as director of the Mukden Arsenal and supervisor of training of the Fengtien military forces.

The second Chihli-Fengtien war late in 1924 ended in defeat for the Chihli faction and left Chang Tso-lin's Manchurian army, with Yang Yü-t'ing as chief of staff, in a strong position in north China. Early in 1925 Yang and Chang Tsung-ch'ang (q.v.) pushed southward through Shantung to the Nanking-Shanghai area, where they defeated Ch'i Hsieh-yuan (q.v.) in Kiangsu. Yang was promoted to the rank of lieutenant general, and in August 1925 he became military governor of Kiangsu. That success was shortlived, however, for the armies of Sun Ch'uan-fang (q.v.) defeated the Fengtien forces in October and forced them to retreat northward.

Yang Yü-t'ing returned to Mukden, where he continued to serve as chief of staff in Chang Tso-lin's military establishment and played a role in the planning which led to the formation of a new coalition by Chang and Wu P'ei-fu (q.v.) against Feng Yü-hsiang (q.v.). Feng, whose action in 1924 had led to the defeat of Wu P'ei-fu in north China, had made a covert arrangement with Kuo Sung-ling, a leading Fengtien general; and he counted heavily on Kuo's defection to undermine the power of Chang Tso-lin. When war broke out late in

1925, however, quick action by Yang Yü-t'ing led to the defeat of Kuo Sung-ling's troops and to the capture and execution of Kuo himself in December. Chang Tso-lin then moved to Peking in mid-1926, leaving Yang Yü-t'ing in charge at Mukden. Although the Kuominchün armies of Feng Yü-hsiang were defeated in north China, a new challenge appeared as the forces of the National Revolutionary Army under the over-all command of Chiang Kai-shek drove forward from Canton in 1926 to establish a new Nationalist base of control in the lower Yangtze valley. To counter this threat, Chang Tso-lin and the northern generals, after a strategy conference at Tientsin in December, organized the Ankuochün [national pacification army], a coalition force that included Fengtien, Chihli, and Shantung units. At the beginning of 1927 Chang ordered Yang Yü-t'ing and Mo Te-hui (q.v.), civil governor of Fengtien province, from Mukden to Peking.

By the spring of 1927 the Nationalist armies had defeated Fengtien forces committed in Anhwei and Honan; while Feng Yü-hsiang in southern Honan and Yen Hsi-shan (q.v.) in Shansi had both shifted allegiance to the Nationalist side. The Chinese military situation was further complicated by Japanese interests and by conflicting views within the Fengtien high command itself. Yoshizawa Kenkichi, Japanese minister to China, held conversations with Yang Yü-t'ing in which he emphasized Japan's concern with the surging tide of radical Chinese nationalism and the continued intention of his government to view Manchuria as a special area in which Japan had recognized rights of long standing. Within the Fengtien military faction, Wu Chün-sheng recommended withdrawal of forces outside the Great Wall in order to preserve the integrity of Chang Tso-lin's power base in Manchuria. Yang Yü-t'ing, on the other hand, proposed a plan for preservation of the *status quo* through cooperation with the Nationalists at Nanking, where Chiang Kai-shek had established himself in opposition to the Nationalist-Communist group at Wuhan, and with Yen Hsi-shan in Shansi. Yang's counsel prevailed, and in June 1927 Chang Tso-lin decided to make a stand in north China and assumed the title of Ta-yuan-shuai, or generalissimo, at Peking.

In the summer of 1927, when the continued disarray of Kuomintang political factions in the Yangtze valley was accompanied by the temporary retirement to Japan of Chiang Kai-shek, it appeared that Yang Yü-t'ing's estimates would prove sound. During the year that followed, however, plans based on Yang's estimates brought military debacle to the northern forces and disaster to the leader of the Fengtien faction. In January 1928, when Chiang Kai-shek resumed command of the National Revolutionary Army, it quickly became apparent that Nationalist strategy did not envisage coexistence with continued regional military power in the north. In a planning conference at Peking in late January, Chang Tso-lin then decided to strike first at the forces of Feng Yü-hsiang. As chief of staff, Yang Yü-t'ing was assigned to direct operations from Paoting. But in April, when Nationalist armies began a coordinated offensive drive into north China, the position of the Fengtien-Chihli-Shantung warlord coalition quickly proved untenable. Its forces began a general retreat northward toward Shanhaikuan. And on 4 June 1928 the railroad coach in which Chang Tso-lin was returning to Manchuria was wrecked by a bomb explosion as it neared Mukden.

The death of Chang Tso-lin, the Old Marshal, ended a chapter in the history of modern Manchuria and introduced a six-month interregnum. In early June of 1928 Yang Yü-t'ing and the Old Marshal's eldest son, Chang Hsueh-liang (q.v.), withdrew from Peking to Tientsin. A fortnight later, Chang Hsueh-liang returned to Mukden. Yang remained behind at Luanchow to supervise evacuation of the Fengtien forces. At the beginning of July, Chang Hsueh-liang, the Young Marshal, assumed the position of commander in chief of the Northeast Peace Preservation forces, though his control of Manchuria was hardly secure.

On 13 July 1928 Yang Yü-t'ing returned to Mukden to assess the situation. Another leading candidate for power there was Chang Tso-hsiang, also a long-time associate of Chang Tso-lin and governor of Kirin province. Chang Tso-hsiang, however, removed himself from the competition by pledging personal support to Chang Hsueh-liang. The position of Yang Yü-t'ing thus became delicate. As Chang Tso-lin's chief of staff for over ten years, he regarded himself as a major contender for the position of power which the Old Marshal had long held in Manchuria. However, Yang had become the target of much personal criticism because of the 1928 Fengtien military debacle. The able, ambitious, and impatient Yang thus found himself confronting the possibility that his future career might be dependent on the good graces of Chang Hsueh-liang, a younger and much less experienced officer.

During the autumn of 1928, Yang Yü-t'ing, who regarded the Young Marshal as a political upstart and an ineffectual weakling, refused to accept appointment under him and continued to act independently without consulting Chang. Ch'ang Yin-huai, civil governor of Heilungkiang province, head of the Manchurian railroad system, and former head of military police under Chang Tso-lin, was closely associated with Yang Yü-t'ing during this period. Rumors flew. Japanese agents reportedly were hoping to use Yang as a channel for exerting indirect control over Chang Hsueh-liang. Yang reportedly was hoping to interfere with arrangements which Chang Hsueh-liang was attempting to work out with Chiang Kai-shek's new regime at Nanking. But the most persistent report was that Yang Yü-t'ing was planning to overthrow the Young Marshal and to seize power himself.

At the end of December 1928 Chang Hsueh-liang pledged the allegiance of Manchuria to the National Government at Nanking and raised the Nationalist flag at Mukden. By this time, he had recognized the danger of permitting the contest with Yang to go unresolved. On the evening of 10 January 1929 the Young Marshal invited Yang Yü-t'ing and Ch'ang Yin-huai to his headquarters for dinner and a game of mahjong. Chang greeted his guests and then excused himself to get a morphine injection. Although there are several versions of the events that followed, the generally accepted story is that, after the Young Marshal's exit, unidentified gunmen moved into the room and shot down both Yang and Ch'ang.

A statement issued by Chang Hsueh-liang's office the next day reported that detailed investigations over a period of months had revealed overwhelming evidence that the two men had been guilty of treason, disobedience to orders, and corruption. The Young Marshal, recalling the lesson of the 1925 rebellion of Kuo Sung-ling against his father, was aware that Yang Yü-t'ing stood as a major obstacle to establishment of

control over Manchuria. The elimination of Yang's rivalry was doubtless the chief motive for the double killing. What actually transpired on the chilly night of 10 January 1929 at Mukden may never be known.

Yao Yung-p'u 姚永樸
T. Chung-shih 仲實
H. T'ui-ssu lao-jen 蛻私老人

Yao Yung-p'u (1862–16 July 1939), scholar who was one of the last outstanding literary figures of the T'ung-ch'eng school.

T'ungch'eng, Anhwei, was the birthplace of Yao Yung-p'u. He came from a noted scholar-official family. His grandfather, Yao Ying (ECCP, I, 239), was a chin-shih of 1808 who later became judicial commissioner of Kwangsi province. His father, Yao Chün-ch'ang (1833–1899; T. Meng-ch'eng), served in the secretariat of Tseng Kuo-fan (ECCP, II, 751–56) and later was magistrate of various counties in Kiangsi and Hupeh. He also achieved some note as a poet. Yao Yung-p'u's elder brother, Yao Yung-k'ai (T. Hsien-po), died young, but not before showing considerable literary ability. His younger brother, Yao Yung-kai (1866–1923; T. Shu-chieh), became an accomplished poet and essayist. And Yao Yung-p'u's brothers-in-law, Ma Ch'i-ch'ang (ECCP, I, 235) and Fan Tang-shih (see ECCP, II, 871), were noted representatives of the T'ung-ch'eng school of writing. Thus, Yao Yung-p'u grew up in a predominantly T'ung-ch'eng literary atmosphere which was rich in scholarly tradition.

The T'ung-ch'eng school, named for the native district of its prominent men, played an influential role in Ch'ing and early republican literary life. The school began with Fang Pao (ECCP, I, 235–37) in the early eighteenth century, and it gained recognition as a coherent movement under the leadership of Yao Nai (ECCP, II, 800–1) in the 1760's. Tseng Kuo-fan revitalized the school in the nineteenth century, and it was brought to north China by Wu Ju-lun (ECCP, II, 870–72) and Chang Yü-chao (ECCP, I, 65), both of whom taught at the Lien-ch'ih shu-yuan at Paoting.

In 1892–93 Yao Yung-p'u served as a secretary in Tientsin and Port Arthur. While in north China, he studied under Wu Ju-lun, then the leading teacher of the T'ung-ch'eng school. Wu's advocacy of new ideas in education had an important influence on the curricula of various institutions in China. Yao Yung-p'u passed the examinations for the chü-jen degree in 1894. He then accompanied his father to various posts in Kiangsi and Anhwei. After his father died in 1899, he decided to devote himself to education.

Because many of Yao Yung-p'u's works were written primarily as textbooks, their introductory notes often provide clues to his whereabouts at various stages of his career. In 1901, while he was teaching in Kwangtung, his work on the *Shu-ching*, the *Shang-shu i-lüeh*, was published. In 1903 he left a teaching post in Shantung for another at a newly opened college in his native Anhwei. In 1903–4 he completed *Hsiao-hsüeh kuang*, a textbook on ethics, and the *Chu-tzu k'ao-lüeh*, a work on the ancient Chinese philosophers. Yao later revised the *Chu-tzu k'ao-lüeh* and published it as the *Chün-ju k'ao-lüeh*. In the 1903–8 period Yao Yung-p'u also compiled a biographical dictionary of the Yao family, the *T'ung-ch'eng Yao-shih pei-chuan lu*, which was published with financial aid from an uncle.

About 1909 Yao Yung-p'u was appointed a consulting expert at the Board of Education and a professor at Peking University. After the republic was established, he taught at Chung-hua College, established by Wang I-t'ang (q.v.). When Hsü Shu-cheng (q.v.) established the Cheng-chih Middle School at Peking in 1915, such leading literary men of the T'ung-ch'eng group as Yao Yung-p'u, Lin Shu (q.v.), and Yao Yung-kai joined its teaching staff. From 1914 to 1919 Yao Yung-p'u also served as an editor at the Ch'ing-shih kuan (*see* Chao Erh-sun), helping to compile the *Ch'ing-shih kao* [provisional history of the Ch'ing]. In his collected literary works, the *T'ui-ssu hsuan-chi*, published in 1921, there is a letter to the Ch'ing-shih kuan expressing his views on the scope and methods of compiling such a history. Yao Yung-p'u returned to Anhwei in 1919 and became a teacher at the Hung-i hsüeh-she, established by the Chou family (*see* Chou Hsueh-hsi). In 1925–35 he was a professor at Anhwei University. Japanese advances following the outbreak of the Sino-Japanese war in 1937 forced Yao to move to Kiangsi, then to Hunan, and finally to Kwangsi. He died at Kweilin on 16 July 1939. He was survived by a grandson, Yao Yung. Yao Yung-p'u's wife, *née* Ma, had died about 1915; their sons, Yao Huan and Yao Ang, had died in 1914. A daughter, who also died early, married Fang Yen-ch'en.

Yeh Ch'ang-ch'ih　　葉 昌 熾
　T. Sung-lu　　頌 魯
　Chü-shang　　鞠 裳

Yeh Ch'ang-ch'ih (30 October 1849–6 November 1917), scholar whose major work was the *Ts'ang-shu chi-shih shih*, a comprehensive history of private book collecting in China. He also made studies of bronze and stone inscriptions.

Little is known of Yeh Ch'ang-ch'ih's family background or early education. His early association with such prominent men as Feng Kuei-fen (ECCP, I, 241–43) and P'an Tsu-yin (ECCP, II, 608–9) doubtless exerted a significant influence on his developing scholarly interests. Yeh was a student of Feng Kuei-fen and in the 1870's assisted him in the compilation of the local history of Soochow, *Su-chou fu-chih*. Later, as a tutor to the younger brother of P'an Tsu-yin in 1883, Yeh had the opportunity to associate with an established bibliophile and high official, while P'an's excellent library initiated him into bibliography and the study of bronze and stone inscriptions.

Yeh Ch'ang-ch'ih became a chü-jen in 1876 and a chin-shih in 1889, with the additional honor of being selected as a member of the Hanlin Academy. From 1889 until 1901 he held various positions traditionally awarded to Hanlin scholars in Peking: proctor in the state historiographer's office, tutor in the imperial academy, and composer of the national academy. Since the duties connected with these official posts were not burdensome, he had excellent opportunities to pursue his scholarly interests in the rich cultural environment of Peking.

From 1901 to 1905 Yeh Ch'ang-ch'ih was commissioner of education in Kansu province, where he conducted studies of the historical relics found in northwest China. He found 103 stone tablets of T'ang, Sung, Chin, and Yuan times in a Buddhist temple in Pinchou, Shensi. A collection of rubbings of these tablets, with notes, was printed in 1915 under the title

Pin-chou shih-shih lu. Yeh's period of residence in northwest China also made possible the further checking of a previously completed manuscript on stone inscriptions entitled *Yü-shih*, which was published in 1909 and reissued by the Commercial Press in 1936.

When the educational system was reorganized in 1905, Yeh left his post in Kansu. In 1907–8 he was an adviser in the newly established Li-hsueh-kuan [school of ceremonies] in Peking. From 1908 to 1910 he was professor of history in the Ts'un-ku hsueh-t'ang in Soochow. After the revolution of 1911, Yeh, then 62, refused to participate in the republican government and regarded himself as an "i-lao," a man who belonged to the previous dynasty. He died in November 1917 of natural causes.

Yeh Ch'ang-ch'ih's collected prose, the *Ch'i-ku-ch'ing wen-chi*, was printed in 1921, and his collected poetry, the *Ch'i-ku-ch'ing shih-chi*, appeared in 1926. The *Han-shan-ssu-chi*, a history of the famed Buddhist monastery in Soochow, was printed in 1922. For nearly 50 years, from 1870 until shortly before his death in 1917, Yeh Ch'ang-ch'ih regularly kept a diary in which he recorded observations on current events, scholarly notes, and impressions of his contemporaries, as well as personal and family happenings. This diary, the *Yen-tu-lu jih-chi ch'ao*, was printed in 1933 in an edition by Wang Chi-lieh. Yeh's entries for the years 1900 and 1901 provide valuable materials on the Boxers in the Peking area and are included in a documentary collection, the *I-ho-t'uan*, which was part of the series of source materials on modern Chinese history published in Shanghai in 1951. His diary was also one of the four sources of the *Chin-shih jen-wu-chih*, a collection of biographical sketches on modern Chinese compiled by Chin Liang.

Yeh Ch'ang-ch'ih's most notable scholarly contribution, however, was the *Ts'ang-shu chi-shih shih*, a comprehensive history of private book collecting in China. Written in poetry with extensive notes, it includes information on 1,175 collectors from the Five Dynasties period through the 1880's. There are three different editions of this work: the 1895 edition in the *Ling-chien-ko ts'ung-shu* and later editions of 1909 and 1931. An index to this work, *Ts'ang-shu chi-shih shih yin-te*, was compiled by Ts'ai Chin-chung and published by the Harvard-Yenching Institute in 1937. A supplement covering book collectors of the republican period was prepared by Lun Ming (T. Che-ju) and was published in installments in the periodical *Cheng-feng tsa-chih*.

Yeh Chien-ying　　　葉劍英

Yeh Chien-ying (1898–), Chinese Communist general who served as chief of staff of the Communist military forces during and after the Sino-Japanese war. During the American mediation effort in 1946, he was chief Communist delegate at the Executive Headquarters in Peiping. From late 1949 until mid-1954 he was based at Canton, and he became the dominant figure in the new Communist control structure in south China.

Meihsien, the principal district of the Hakka people of Kwangtung, was the native place of Yeh Chien-ying. He was the eldest of three sons born into a Hakka merchant family. As a boy, Yeh received a solid education in the classical Chinese curriculum in a private tutoring school. He then enrolled at the Tung-shan Middle School, a well-known institution in the culturally advanced district of Meihsien. In 1913, at the age of 16 sui, Yeh was sent to Malaya to live with an uncle and to prepare for a career in business.

In December 1915, when Ts'ai O, T'ang Chi-yao, and Li Lieh-chün (qq.v.) led a revolt in Yunnan against the monarchical campaign of Yuan Shih-k'ai, they attracted national attention as potential saviors of the Chinese republic. Overseas Chinese communities in Southeast Asia zealously supported the Yunnan protest movement, and this support was often accompanied by financial contributions to the Yunnan leaders. To express appreciation and to encourage continued support, T'ang Chi-yao, then governor of Yunnan, offered to accept selected Chinese youths from Southeast Asia for admission to the provincial military academy at Kunming. Yeh Chien-ying, who had failed to develop an interest in commercial matters, was in the first group of Chinese students from Malaya who went to the Yunnan Military Academy in 1916. He was graduated as a member of the academy's twelfth class in July 1919. At that time, to avoid open conflict with the Kwangsi forces at Canton, Sun Yat-sen had ordered the newly organized Kwangtung Army, under the command of Ch'en Chiung-ming and Hsü Ch'ung-chih (qq.v.), to withdraw to southern Fukien, where it was undergoing vigorous training at Changchow. The third-ranking officer in the Kwangtung Army at that time was its chief of staff, Teng K'eng (q.v.), a native of Meihsien. Another officer from the same district was Chang Ming-ta, whose family also had business connections in Malaya, and it was through this association that Yeh Chien-ying joined the Kwangtung Army in Fukien. During his initial period of duty, Yeh was exposed to the new and radical political ideas that were spreading as a result of the Russian Revolution and the May Fourth Movement. Ch'en Chiung-ming had developed an interest in socialist ideas, and he had talked with a number of socialists, both Chinese and Russian.

Yeh Chien-ying accompanied the Kwangtung Army when it returned to Canton late in 1920. In mid-1922, when Ch'en Chiung-ming revolted against Sun Yat-sen, the Kwangtung forces divided. Yeh remained with the units under the command of Hsü Ch'ung-chih, who remained loyal to Sun Yat-sen, and he was assigned as chief of staff in the division commanded by Chang Ming-ta. During this period, Yeh also served briefly as magistrate of his native district, Meihsien, and of the native place of Sun Yat-sen, Hsiangshan.

In 1924 Sun Yat-sen organized the Whampoa Military Academy and appointed Chiang Kai-shek as commandant and Liao Chung-k'ai (q.v.) as senior Kuomintang representative. Yeh was also assigned there as deputy director of the (classroom) instruction department, then headed by Wang Po-ling and staffed by such Nationalist officers as Ch'ien Ta-chün, Ku Chu-t'ung, and Liu Chih (qq.v.). Yeh's position at Whampoa in 1924–26 thus placed him at a level equivalent to that of Chou En-lai (q.v.), deputy director of the political department headed by Tai Chi-t'ao (q.v.), and of Teng Yen-ta (q.v.), deputy director of the (field) training department headed by Li Chi-shen (q.v.). During the first stage of the Northern Expedition, launched in July 1926, Yeh Chien-ying served as chief of staff in the First Army, commanded by Chiang Kai-shek but actually led by Ho Ying-ch'in (q.v.). Later, when substantial numbers of opposing troops under

Sun Ch'uan-fang (q.v.) were captured in Kiangsi, they were reorganized as a new 2nd Division, with Yeh in command. After the Nationalist capture of Wuhan in October 1926 and the appointment of Chang Fa-k'uei (q.v.) as commander of the Fourth Army, Yeh was assigned to that army as chief of staff and commander of its training regiment.

Official Communist sources state that Yeh Chien-ying formally joined the Chinese Communist party in September 1927, though other evidence suggests that he had party connections during his period at Whampoa. In any event, after Chang Fa-k'uei's forces returned to Canton late in 1927, Yeh Chien-ying's model regiment provided principal military support for the short-lived Canton Commune of December 1927 (*see* Chang T'ai-lei). Although Yeh T'ing (q.v.) was commander of the Workers and Peasants Red Army, Yeh Chien-ying, his deputy, actually commanded the Communist troops. With the collapse of the Canton Commune, Yeh fled to Hong Kong, whence he proceeded to Shanghai to establish contact with the central apparatus of the Chinese Communist party. Soon afterwards, he went to the Soviet Union, where he studied Marxist-Leninist doctrine and military affairs and came to know Liu Po-ch'eng and Tso Ch'üan (qq.v.), who were also receiving military training in Moscow. Yeh also visited Germany to observe military affairs. He then returned to China and arrived at the central soviet base in Kiangsi in the autumn of 1931.

In Kiangsi, Yeh Chien-ying played an active and influential role in the Chinese Communist military forces. The Chinese Workers and Peasants Red Army was under the over-all command of Chu Teh (q.v.), also a graduate of the Yunnan Military Academy. At Juichin, Yeh alternated with Liu Po-ch'eng in two key posts: chief of staff of the Red Army and president of the Red Army Academy. He also saw action on several occasions, notably in 1933 when the Communists launched an eastward offensive into Fukien. When Nationalist military pressure forced the Communists to withdraw from their Kiangsi base in the autumn of 1934, Yeh was named chief of staff of the field army, which then comprised the greater part of the Communist forces. Yeh's organizational abilities were confirmed during the Long March. As chief of staff of the Third Red Army Group, he was with the advance contingent which arrived in northern Shensi in October 1935.

In December 1936 Yeh Chien-ying accompanied Chou En-lai and Ch'in Pang-hsien (qq.v.) to Sian to represent the Chinese Communists in the negotiations which led to the release of Chiang Kai-shek after his forcible detention by Chang Hsueh-liang and Yang Hu-ch'eng (qq.v.). In 1937, while discussions were underway between the Nationalists and Communists for formation of a united front against Japan, Yeh was successively assigned to direct the Chinese Communist liaison missions maintained at Sian, Nanking and Hankow. After the Sino-Japanese war began in July, he was invited by the Nationalists to supervise a guerrilla warfare training center at Hengshan, Hunan. The Chinese Communist forces in northern Shensi were reorganized in October 1937 as the Eighth Route Army, and in January 1938 Communist guerrilla forces in east and central China were reorganized as the New Fourth Army. These two armies were incorporated into the Nationalist military organization as the Eighteenth Army Group. Chu Teh served as commander in chief of the Eighth Route Army and the entire Eighteenth Army Group, with Yeh as his chief of staff. Yeh retained that post throughout the war years until 1949. When the Chinese Communists held their Seventh National Party Congress at Yenan in mid-1945, he was elected to membership in the Central Committee.

After the Japanese surrender, negotiations were begun for possible peaceful settlement of the political and military problems then separating the Nationalists and the Communists in China. Yeh Chien-ying played an important role in the talks between the two major contending parties in the hope of averting civil war. When Mao Tse-tung flew to Chungking in August 1945 for discussions with Chiang Kai-shek, Yeh was a member of the Communist group that accompanied him. In January 1946 Yeh was a member of the Chinese Communist delegation to the Political Consultative Conference in Chungking; that group was headed by Chou En-lai and also included Tung Pi-wu, Ch'in Pang-hsien, Wang Jo-fei, Wu Yü-chang, and Teng Ying-ch'ao. One result of the early postwar negotiations conducted under the prodding of General George C. Marshall, then the chief United States representative in China,

was the establishment at Peiping of a tripartite Executive Headquarters designed to monitor and enforce Nationalist-Communist ceasefire arrangements of January 1946. Yeh Chien-ying was appointed chief Chinese Communist representative to the new Executive Headquarters; his opposite numbers were Cheng Kai-min, representing the Chinese Nationalists, and Walter S. Robertson, representing the United States government. The effort proved to be fruitless, and civil war resumed later that year. Yeh Chien-ying then returned to the Chinese Communist headquarters at Yenan.

After the breakdown of United States mediation efforts in China and the outbreak of full-scale civil war, the Communists renamed their military forces the People's Liberation Army. Chu Teh continued as commander in chief, with Yeh Chien-ying as chief of staff. Yeh was the top-ranking Communist military officer present at the time of the Communist entry into Peiping in January 1949, and he became the first chairman of the Peiping Military Control Commission and mayor of that city. At this time, Yeh relinquished the post of chief of staff of the Chinese Communist military forces. Hsü Hsiang-ch'ien nominally succeeded him, though Nieh Jung-chen (q.v.) assumed responsibility as acting chief of staff. Nieh also replaced Yeh as mayor of Peiping, which became Peking again when the People's Republic of China was established on 1 October 1949. At that time, Yeh Chien-ying became a member of the Central People's Government Council, the People's Revolutionary Military Council, and the Overseas Chinese Affairs Commission.

Even as the new government was being inaugurated at Peking, Communist victory celebrations in the north were enhanced by the fall of Canton, the principal city of south China, to the People's Liberation Army on 14 October 1949. By that time, Yeh Chien-ying had moved southward to assume responsibility for organizing Communist control over his native Kwangtung province. In 1949–50 he held virtually all significant posts in the new control structure at Canton: first secretary of the south China sub-bureau of the Chinese Communist party; governor of Kwangtung; commander and political commissar of the Kwangtung military district; mayor of Canton; and secretary of the Canton municipal committee of the Chinese Communist party. Yeh gained such extensive powers in the Canton area that he was dubbed T'ien-nan-wang [king of the southern heavens], a title that had been applied by the Cantonese to Ch'en Chi-t'ang (q.v.) in the early 1930's and to Chang Fa-k'uei in 1945–46.

When a regional administrative system was established in China in 1950, Kwangtung province was included in the so-called Central-South region, which embraced six provinces and had its headquarters at Wuhan. Yeh then assumed added responsibilities as vice chairman of the Central-South Military and Administrative Committee and chairman of its financial-economic committee. During the 1952–54 period, when Lin Piao (q.v.) reportedly was ill, Yeh Chien-ying's south China responsibilities were for a time extended to the entire central-south region. He was then identified as acting secretary of the regional bureau of the Chinese Communist party and acting commander of the Central-South Military District. The system of regional administrations was abolished in 1954, and Yeh's domination of the Communist party, military, and governmental apparatus in south China came to an end. In 1954 he was assigned to Peking as director of the armed forces supervision department of the People's Liberation Army and a vice chairman of the National Defense Council. In 1955 he was one of the ten senior Chinese Communist officers awarded the rank of Marshal of the People's Republic of China. He also received the three top military orders established by Peking: the Order of August First, Order of Independence and Freedom, and Order of Liberation, all first class. In March 1958, when the Chinese Academy of Military Science was established, Yeh was named its president and political commissar.

In 1954 Yeh Chien-ying represented Kwangtung at the National People's Congress, and he was elected to its Standing Committee. He represented the armed forces at the National People's Congress in 1959 and 1964. In the Chinese Communist party structure, Yeh Chien-ying was reelected to the Central Committee at the Eighth National Congress in 1956. In July 1966 he was named to membership on the Secretariat, and in August of that year he became a member of the Political Bureau and a vice chairman of the party's Military Affairs Commission.

In December 1956 Yeh led a Chinese Communist military delegation to Burma; early in 1958 he headed a similar mission to India. He served as deputy leader, under P'eng Te-huai (q.v.), of a Chinese military delegation to the Soviet Union in 1957. In October 1958 he led a group from Peking to Poland to participate in observance of the fifteenth anniversary of the Polish Army. He attended the ceremonies marking the fifteenth anniversary of the establishment of the Democratic Republic of North Viet-Nam in August 1960; and in January 1962 he again visited Hanoi. In September 1963 he accompanied Liu Shao-ch'i to North Korea.

Yeh Chien-ying married twice. His first wife reportedly was the daughter of a prosperous overseas Chinese from Malaya. In 1936 he married Wei Kung-chih, then head of the Chinese People's Anti-Japanese Dramatic Society at Yenan. They had two sons and two daughters. In 1963 one daughter married Liu Shih-k'un, who headed the piano department of the Central Conservatory of Music at Peking and who had won second prize in a 1958 piano competition in Moscow.

Yeh Ch'ien-yü   葉 淺 予

Yeh Ch'ien-yü (1907–), cartoonist and painter. He won fame as the creator of the comic strip "Mr. Wang and Little Ch'en." He later became head of the Chinese painting department at the Peking Academy of Fine Arts.

Little is known of Yeh Ch'ien-yü's early years. He was a native of Chekiang province and was educated at Amoy University. Largely self-taught, he began his professional career in 1929 by drawing cartoons for the *Shanghai Sketch*, a weekly paper. He leapt to fame with a comic strip entitled "Mr. Wang and Little Ch'en," which appeared regularly in the *Shanghai Morning Post* and the *Nanking Post*. Mr. Wang was the typical middle-class Chinese, proud possessor of all the philistine vices; Little Ch'en was his foil. Yeh's cartoons, done with a pen, showed great technical skill and were reminiscent of the style of the English cartoonist Gilbert Wilkinson. During this period, Yeh also edited *Modern Miscellany*, a fortnightly pictorial.

The Sino-Japanese war, which erupted in

the summer of 1937, gave Chinese cartoonists a new importance and a free hand with their satire, provided that it was directed at officially approved targets. In August 1937 Yeh Ch'ien-yü, in cooperation with other artists, organized China's first cartoonist propaganda corps. After the fall of Shanghai and Nanking, the group moved to Hankow, where it became a section of the political department of the Military Affairs Commission. At Hankow, the cartoonist section produced a series of propaganda posters calling for national mobilization and resistance against the Japanese.

From Hankow, Yeh Ch'ien-yü moved westward again to Chungking, where he edited the pictorial magazine *China Today*, a government-sponsored monthly. During the war years, Yeh traveled widely as an official artist. In 1942 and 1943 he visited India, Tibet, and the Miao tribal country in Kweichow province to record his impressions of people and places. In 1944 United States government officials in China invited him to draw cartoons for the Office of War Information. Exhibitions of his work were held at Chungking, Kweiyang, Calcutta, and Bombay. During the war years, Yeh's interests turned away from pure cartooning to sketching with a Chinese brush and the development of a painting style using traditional methods. A portrait of his wife, the dancer Tai Ai-lien (q.v.), typifies his work of the late war years. Its delicate rendering shows the strong influence on Yeh of Buddhist cave paintings.

In 1946 Yeh Ch'ien-yü was invited to the United States on a year-long visit under a cultural exchange program administered by the Department of State. He was at the time a member of the Shanghai Artists Association and had just received an invitation from Hsü Pei-hung (q.v.) to become head of the Chinese painting department at the Peking Academy of Fine Arts. Deferring assumption of that post, Yeh accepted the invitation to the United States. Accompanied by his wife, he arrived at Washington on 7 September 1946. He was entertained at a luncheon at Blair House on 18 September. During the ensuing months, Yeh visited museums and art centers throughout the United States. He had brought a collection of Chinese cartoons by himself and other artists. This collection was exhibited in New York, Boston, Philadelphia, Detroit, Chicago, Minneapolis, Los Angeles, San Francisco, and

Seattle at the time of his visits to those cities. In February 1947 he was entertained at an official reception given by the Artists' League of America in New York, and he also attended the annual meeting of the American Federation of Arts. His wife, Tai Ai-lien, gave dance recitals in New York during the winter.

Yeh Ch'ien-yü arrived back in China with his wife in August 1947. He then proceeded to north China to take up his post at the Peking Academy of Fine Arts. In the summer of 1949 he was a delegate to the initial meeting of the All-China Federation of Literary and Arts Circles, the principal organization used to channel Chinese Communist party directives into the fields of literature and the fine arts. After the People's Republic of China was established, in 1951 he became a vice chairman of the Union of Chinese Artists, the national organization under the literary-arts federation responsible for coordinating activities in the field of painting. In 1960 he was elected to membership on the third national committee of the All-China Federation of Literary and Arts Circles.

Although a few new cartoons by Yeh Ch'ien-yü appeared in China during the Korean conflict in the early 1950's, he generally eschewed cartooning in favor of illustrations based on life sketches, some of which appeared in publications of the Foreign Languages Press at Peking. Various collections of Yeh's work were published in the early 1960's. These included: *Ch'ien-yü su-hsieh 1958–1959* [sketches by Yeh Ch'ien-yü, 1958–1959], *Yeh Ch'ien-yü tso-p'in hsiao-chi* [a small collection of Yeh Ch'ien-yü's works], and *Tsai Nei-meng yü Kuang-hsi* [in Inner Mongolia and Kwangsi], all of 1963; and *Jen-wu hua-chi* [pictures of people and things], of 1964.

Yeh Ch'ing: *see* JEN CHO-HSUAN.

Yeh Ch'u-ts'ang   葉 楚 滄
T. Hsiao-feng   小 鳳

Yeh Ch'u-ts'ang (1883–14 February 1946), literary figure, anti-Manchu revolutionary, and editor of the *Min-kuo jih-pao* who later served as director of the propaganda department and secretary general of the Kuomintang. During the Sino-Japanese war, he was minister of information and secretary general of the National Government.

The son of an unsuccessful vendor of condiments and soybean products, Yeh Ch'u-ts'ang was born at Wuchiang, Kiangsu. After classical training in local schools, Yeh at the age of 25 succeeded Ch'en Ch'ü-ping as the editor of the Swatow *Chung-hua hsin-pao* [new China news]. At about the same time, he was inducted into Sun Yat-sen's T'ung-meng-hui. With the coming of the 1911 revolution Yeh entered on a political career and was appointed an administrative officer in Swatow. He declined this post, however, to accept a staff position under Yao Yü-p'ing, then commander in chief of the Kwangtung Expeditionary Army, which was organized in early November 1911 to undertake a march against the Manchu forces remaining in the north. Although this army seems not to have made an active campaign, it is reported that Yeh was present at the capture of Nanking in December 1911 by combined Kiangsu and Chekiang forces, under the command of the Cantonese Hsü Shao-chen, and that Yeh participated in the pursuit of the Manchu army north of the Yangtze.

After the founding of the Chinese republic, Yeh returned to journalism. In 1912 he journeyed to Shanghai on behalf of Yao Yü-p'ing to found a newspaper to support the cause of the successful revolution. The paper, which became the *T'ai-p'ing-yang pao* [Pacific journal], boasted a staff which included such illustrious literary figures as Liu Ya-tzu, Su Man-shu (qq.v.), and Li Hsi-shuang. Owing to financial difficulties, it was obliged to suspend publication in October 1912. Yeh served as editor of the *Min-li pao* [people's livelihood] in 1912–13 and in the same capacity on the *Sheng-huo jih-pao* [life daily] in 1913–14. The next year, Yeh and Shao Li-tzu (q.v.) established the *Min-kuo jih-pao* [republican daily], which served effectively as the mouthpiece of Sun Yat-sen and the Kuomintang. The paper was particularly conspicuous for its opposition to Yuan Shih-k'ai, with whom it engaged in a running polemic battle which ended only with Yuan's death in 1916, and, after 1919, for its literary supplement, *Chiao-wu*. In time, the *Min-kuo jih-pao* became one of the publications for which the new

generation of progressive intellectuals in China had the highest respect.

During this period, Yeh also turned his hand to several other pursuits. He wrote fiction, producing first a long story of Chinese patriots and foreign spies on the Mongolian border entitled *Meng-pien ming-chu chi* [watchtower on the tartar border]. His next work was a book of anecdotes concerning such business, political, and literary leaders of Shanghai of the time as Chang Ping-lin, Su Man-shu, Liu Ya-tzu, and Chang Chien. This book was called *Lung-t'ao jen-yü* [speaking of dragons]. He then wrote two novels in the satirical tradition of the eighteenth century *Ju-lin wai-shih* [unofficial history of the literati]: *Ch'ien-pei hsien-sheng* [gentlemen of the old school] and *I-kuan ch'in-shou* [wolves in sheep's clothing]. He taught at the Shen-chou Girls School, one of the pioneer private girls schools in Shanghai, then under the direction of Chang Mo-chün (q.v.), and at Fu-tan University. In addition, he was active in the Nan-she, or Southern Society (*see* Liu Ya-tzu), the literary group founded to link traditional literary forms with the new concepts of nationalist politics. The *Min-kuo jih-pao*, which flourished under the editorial direction of Yeh Ch'u-ts'ang and Shao Li-tzu, also became the headquarters of the Hsin Nan-she, or New Southern Society, also organized by Liu Ya-tzu in 1923. The manifesto of the group, drafted by Yeh, declared the organization's aims to be the introduction of Western thought to China and the revaluation of classical Chinese literature in the light of modern values. The political nature of the group was also delineated by Yeh and expressed to be close cooperation with the Kuomintang and with the mass of the Chinese people.

In 1924, at the First National Congress of the reorganized Kuomintang, Yeh Ch'u-ts'ang was elected a member of the Central Executive Committee and director of the department of youth and women in the party's Shanghai headquarters. In November 1925, after the death of Sun Yat-sen, Yeh joined Lin Sen, Chü Cheng, Tsou Lu (qq.v.), and several others at a gathering of Kuomintang conservatives held near Sun's temporary tomb in the Western Hills, outside Peking. The group, which came to be known as the Hsi-ling-p'ai or Western

Hills clique, demanded the expulsion of Com-munists and other left-wingers from the party and the dismissal of Borodin and the other Soviet advisers from the Canton government. Despite his endorsement of this strong stand, however, Yeh was anything but dogmatic. In 1926 he went to Canton, and soon became secretary general of the central political council. In the fall of 1926 he participated in the first stage of the Northern Expedition, remaining briefly at Wuhan after its capture by the National Revolutionary Army and then moving on to Shanghai when that city fell to Nationalist control in April 1927.

Yeh Ch'u-ts'ang's connection with the central apparatus of the Kuomintang was long and uninterrupted. The key posts which he held over the years were director of the department of propaganda, in which position he functioned in 1924, 1928–29, 1935, and 1939, and secretary general of the party, an office which he assumed in 1931 and held until 1938. During his incumbency in these posts, Yeh was responsible for a steady stream of propaganda of high technical quality. In 1935 he wrote *Hsin-sheng yü ch'ing-ts'ao* [new life and character], an influential statement of the precepts of the New Life Movement (*see* Chiang Kai-shek). The following year saw the publication of *Ko-ming hsien-lieh ku-shih-hsüan* [selected stories of martyrs of the 1911 revolution], a work calculated to instill a martyr-like hardihood in the Chinese people, then facing Japanese aggression. *Tang-wu shih-shih-shang chih wen-t'i* [questions on the carrying-out of party duties], of 1939, dealt with the problems of maintaining party structure under wartime conditions. He excelled at these activities, but the extent of his power in the inner circles of the party is open to question.

For four years, during the early period of Kuomintang consolidation of power from 1927 to 1931, Yeh also played a prominent role in the politics of his native Kiangsu. He served successively as commissioner of reconstruction, secretary general of the provincial government, and governor. In 1931 Yeh resigned the gover-norship to assume greater responsibilities in Nanking. In 1931 he became a member of the State Council and participated in the drafting of the provisional constitution. He also became active in banking and business circles as director of the Central Bank, chairman of the supervisory

committee of the Kiangsu Provincial Farmers Bank, and a trustee of the Kiangnan railroad. In 1935 Yeh was elected vice president of the Legislative Yuan, a position which he held until 1945.

During the Sino-Japanese war, Yeh moved to Chungking with the National Government. There he became a member of the Supreme National Defense Council, minister of informa-tion, and secretary general of the National Government. In addition, he continued his editorial and literary activities, serving as chief editor of the *Yüeh-fu shih-hsüan* [anthology of early Chinese ballads], published in 1942, the *Yüan Ming Ch'ing ch'ü-hsüan* [lyrics of the Yüan, Ming, and Ch'ing periods], published in 1943, and the *San-kuo Chin Nan-pei-ch'ao wen-hsüan* [literary anthology for the Three King-doms, Chin, and Northern and Southern dynasties periods], published in 1944. Also in 1944, he produced a collection of his own prose entitled *Ch'u-ts'ang wen-ts'un.*

At war's end Yeh was appointed rehabilita-tion commissioner for Kiangsu, Chekiang, and Anhwei. He arrived at Shanghai in December 1945 to take up his duties, but he soon fell ill. Yeh Ch'u-ts'ang died at Shanghai on 14 February 1946.

A versatile writer who could produce poems, essays, editorials, or short stories with equal facility, Yeh was a thorough-going advocate of the pai-hua [vernacular] style. At the same time, he was a skillful poet in the classical metres. His classical poems were collected and published in 1946 under the title *Shih-hui-lou shih-kao.* That year also saw the publication of a collection of his literary and critical essays, *Yeh Ch'u-ts'ang Chung-kuo wen-hsueh p'i-p'ing.* Like his editorials, Yeh's scholarly writings were noted for their lucid style and persuasive tone.

Yeh Kung-ch'ao   葉 公 超
West. George Kung-ch'ao Yeh

Yeh Kung-ch'ao (20 October 1904–), known as George K. C. Yeh, Western-trained scholar and university professor who entered public life during the Sino-Japanese war. In 1945 he directed the ministry of information's United Kingdom office in London. He later served as vice minister (1947–48), acting minister (1949), and minister (1950–57) of foreign affairs in the

National Government and as Chinese Nationalist ambassador to the United States.

Born at Canton, George K. C. Yeh was the second son of the scholar-official Yeh Tao-sheng. He came from a family with a long tradition of scholarly activity. His great-grandfather, Yeh Yen-lan, had been a district magistrate in Kiukiang and had become known as a scholar, poet, and art collector. Soon after George Yeh's birth, his mother, *née* Tsou Ching-yü, died. Although his father later remarried, the boy was raised in the family of his uncle, Yeh Kung-cho (q.v.). At the age of four, he began to study the Chinese classics, calligraphy, art and art criticism, and English. His schooling was interrupted for one year when he went to England. Yeh received his secondary education at the Nankai Middle School in Tientsin (*see* Chang Po-ling), from which he was graduated in 1919. He then went to the United States, where he spent a year at the Urbana (Illinois) High School and a year at Bates College in Maine before enrolling at Amherst College. At Amherst, the linguistic and poetic abilities of the young Chinese student attracted the attention of Robert Frost, and Yeh became a favorite of the prominent American poet. After being graduated *magna cum laude* in 1924, Yeh went to England, where he studied at Cambridge University and received an M.A. degree in Indo-European linguistics early in 1926. He spent the next few months traveling and studying at the Sorbonne before returning to China at the end of 1926.

For the next 12 years, George Yeh devoted his time to teaching and scholarship. He first served as assistant professor of English at Peking University and then moved to Chinan University in Shanghai, where he spent two years. He returned to north China in 1929 to become professor of English literature at Tsinghua University. In the autumn of 1935 Yeh left Tsinghua and returned to Peking University to become head of the department of Western languages and literature. After the Japanese occupation he moved with his university to Kunming, where he taught at the Southwest Associated University until 1939.

The years in north China were fruitful for George Yeh. While in Peiping he married Edna Yung-hsi Yuan in June 1931. Two children were born to Yeh and his wife:

Marian T'ung (1932–) and Max Wei (1937–). In his professional life he made close friendships with such prominent scholars and intellectuals as Hu Shih, Fu Ssu-nien, and Mei Yi-ch'i (qq.v.). He joined with other young literary leaders in founding the *Hsin-yueh yueh-k'an* [the crescent moon] and became one of its editors, contributing an article to the inaugural issue in 1928 entitled "The Fate of Realistic Novels." In later issues he dealt with problems of translation and the use of fiction in promoting cultural understanding. Yeh was considered one of the leaders of a group of young scholars who lived and expounded on "the full life" in Peiping in the early 1930's, and he became a subject of controversy among his colleagues and students. Some thought that his rapid rise in academic life had brought conceit; others regarded him as "modern China's Dr. Samuel Johnson," as one of his students put it. All agreed, however, that he was an outstanding scholar and a provocative teacher. Yeh was capable of intense bursts of energy and concentration. For example, when the Chinese author Lu Hsün (Chou Shu-jen, q.v.) died in 1936, Yeh closeted himself for a week, read all of Lu Hsün's published writings, and produced a brilliant appraisal of them.

Although George Yeh began his career as a scholar and literary figure, he, like many predecessors in the Confucian tradition, was summoned to government service. Yeh had joined the Kuomintang in Chicago in 1921; and after the Sino-Japanese war began, he was called upon to serve the party. In 1939 he joined the ministry of information of the Kuomintang, and in 1940–41 he served as director of the British Malaya office of the ministry at Singapore. When the Japanese began their drive into Malaya in 1942, Yeh helped organize guerrilla resistance. Following a short stay in wartime Chungking, he was posted to London in 1942 as director of the ministry of information's United Kingdom office. In London, his remarkable command of English stood him in good stead. He was particularly effective in contacts with the leaders of the wartime British government, including Winston Churchill, Anthony Eden, Stafford Cripps, and others. His reputation as a scholar fitted him for the role of "cultural ambassador," one of the major functions of his mission. In line with the policies of the National

Government, he also lent informal assistance to members of the Indian Congress party in pressing for Indian independence. He also found time in London for research, lecturing, and writing. His lecture on "The Confucian Concept of *Jen*" was published as an occasional paper by the China Society of London in 1943, and his lecture on "Cultural Life in Ancient China" was awarded the medal of the Royal Society of Arts that same year. With the British historian C. P. FitzGerald, he wrote a book about Chinese culture entitled *Introducing China*, which was published in 1948.

At war's end, George Yeh returned to China, stopping in India on the way to visit friends whom he had helped support during his years in London. In 1946 he was named counselor and concurrently director of European affairs in the ministry of foreign affairs, and in 1947 he was promoted to administrative vice minister of foreign affairs. He was named political vice minister early in 1949, and he served later that year as acting minister of foreign affairs in the cabinet headed by Yen Hsi-shan (q.v.).

After the move of the National Government to Taiwan, George Yeh became minister of foreign affairs in March 1950 when Ch'en Ch'eng (q.v.) organized his first cabinet. Yeh played a major role in negotiating with Secretary of State John Foster Dulles the Mutual Defense Treaty between the United States and the Government of the Republic of China signed in December 1954. That agreement pledged the United States to give direct assistance to the Chinese Nationalists in the event of an attack on Taiwan or the Pescadores. In July 1958, after the longest tenure of any Chinese Nationalist foreign minister after 1928, Yeh was appointed to succeed Hollington Tong (Tung Hsien-kuang, q.v.) as ambassador to the United States. The following year, he received an honorary LL.D. degree from Amherst College at his son's commencement. In October 1961 he was recalled by his government in connection with the failure of Chinese Nationalist diplomacy to prevent the admission of the Mongolian People's Republic to the United Nations. T. F. Tsiang (Chiang T'ing-fu, q.v.) was named to succeed him as ambassador to the United States. Yeh then was named minister without portfolio in the cabinet. For the first time in more than a quarter of a

century he found time to return to the study of art and to painting and calligraphy.

Yeh Kung-cho   葉 恭 綽
T. Yü-hu   譽 虎

Yeh Kung-cho (1881–), government official who specialized in railway administration. He was a protégé of Liang Shih-i (q.v.) and a prominent member of the so-called communications clique. In 1921 he founded Chiao-t'ung University, which became one of China's leading engineering schools.

A native of Panyü, Kwangtung, Yeh Kung-cho was born into a well-to-do family with a long and brilliant scholarly tradition. He received a thorough education in the Chinese classics and showed great promise as a scholar. When Yeh was 11 sui, he and his father, Yeh Chung-luan, went to live in Kiangsi. During his five-year residence in that province, the young Yeh made the acquaintance of such young scholars as Ou-yang Ching-wu (q.v.), Wen Yung-yü, and Ts'ai Kung-chan. In 1897 he took a trip to Peking and then went to Canton, where he joined with Wu Han-ming in founding the Ts'ui-lu School. A few months later, he went to Shanghai and established the Kuang-yu Book Company with Shen Hsiao-i. In the autumn of 1898 he went to Peking, where he enrolled in the law department at Imperial University (the forerunner of Peking University). His studies were interrupted in 1900 by the Boxer Uprising, and in 1901 he went to Wuchang, where he taught history and geography at a modern languages school for four years.

In 1906 Yeh Kung-cho entered official life as an aide to Liang Shih-i (q.v.), who then was serving under T'ang Shao-yi (q.v.) as chief clerk of the railway administration. In 1907, after T'ang became vice president of the Board of Communications, that board created a directorate general of railways, with Liang as its head and Yeh as Liang's assistant. Yeh held office until 1911, when the new president of the Board of Communications, Sheng Hsuan-huai (q.v.), dismissed Liang. Yeh then resigned.

After Yuan Shih-k'ai succeeded Sun Yat-sen in 1912 as provisional president of the Chinese republic and moved the seat of government from Nanking to Peking, Yeh Kung-cho became director of the railways division of the ministry of communications. At that time his patron, Liang Shih-i, was chief secretary in the presidential office and general manager of the Bank of Communications. In the autumn of 1912 Sun Yat-sen visited Peking and accepted an appointment as national director of railway development. The National Railway Federation was organized at Peking, with Sun as honorary president. It was then that Yeh met Sun, and he made a strong impression on the revolutionary leader. Early in 1913, when Sun organized the National Railway Company in Shanghai, he invited Yeh there to give a lecture on railways.

Late in 1913 Yeh Kung-cho was appointed vice minister of communications in charge of railway affairs. Beginning in August 1914, he also represented the ministry of communications on the board of directors of the domestic loan office, headed by Liang Shih-i. During the First World War, Liang organized the Hui-min Corporation for the recruitment of Chinese laborers to serve with the Allies in Europe. Yeh and Liang Su-ch'eng managed the company, which sent more than 200,000 Chinese workers to France during the war years in accordance with an agreement it made with the French government. In July 1916, after Yuan Shih-k'ai died, Liang Shih-i was among the eight officials whose arrest was ordered because of their alleged participation in Yuan's monarchical plot. Liang fled to Hong Kong, and Yeh, because of his close relationship with Liang, resigned from office. For a time, Yeh served as secretary to the new vice president, Feng Kuo-chang (q.v.). He also continued to aid Liang in recruiting workers for the war effort in France.

In July 1917, when Chang Hsün (q.v.) attempted to restore the Ch'ing dynasty, Liang Shih-i instructed Yeh Kung-cho, then in charge of the Bank of Communications in Tientsin, to arrange for a loan to Tuan Ch'i-jui (q.v.) to finance Tuan's military campaign against Chang. With the successful completion of this campaign and the assumption of the premiership by Tuan Ch'i-jui, Yeh was appointed vice minister of communications at Peking. In 1918 Yeh resigned after quarreling with the minister of communications, Ts'ao Ju-lin (q.v.). He

then undertook a government mission to Europe to study postwar industrial and railway rehabilitation.

On his return from Europe in 1920, Yeh Kung-cho participated in the talks at Mukden which led to the formation of a coalition, composed of the Fengtien clique of Chang Tso-lin (q.v.) and the Chihli clique of Ts'ao K'un (q.v.), for a joint attack on the Anhwei clique of Tuan Ch'i-jui. After Tuan had been ousted, Yeh became minister of communications in the cabinet formed by Chin Yün-p'eng (q.v.). Early in 1921 Yeh merged four technical institutions which were under the control of the ministry to form Chiao-t'ung University, and he became its first president. Chiao-t'ung University, sometimes called Communications University, became one of China's best known engineering schools.

Dissension about the financing of the Peking government soon wracked the cabinet. Chin Yün-p'eng wanted to turn to Chinese banking circles for funds. Yeh and finance minister Chou Tzu-ch'i (q.v.), both prominent members of the so-called communications clique, believed that the government should restore public confidence by placing the old domestic loans on a proper basis before floating new loans. Chin reorganized the cabinet in May 1921 and replaced both Yeh and Chou.

In December 1921, at the behest of Chang Tso-lin, Hsü Shih-ch'ang (q.v.), who then held the presidency at Peking, called on Liang Shih-i to form a new cabinet. Yeh Kung-cho returned to office as minister of communications. Wu P'ei-fu (q.v.) opposed Liang's appointment as premier and drove him from office on 19 January 1922. Chang Tso-lin, affronted by Wu's action, responded by launching the Chihli-Fengtien war in April, but he was defeated in May. Hsü Shih-ch'ang then ordered the arrest of Liang Shih-i and Yeh Kung-cho, who fled to Japan.

While in exile, Yeh Kung-cho wrote an essay on "National Salvation Through Communications," which he completed in November 1922. This essay won him the favor of Sun Yat-sen, who appointed him minister of finance in the government at Canton in May 1923. Yeh also served as Canton's intermediary in unsuccessful negotiations with Chang Tso-lin and Lu Yung-hsiang, who then controlled the Shanghai area, concerning the formation of a triple alliance against the Chihli clique of Ts'ao K'un. In October 1923 Ts'ao assumed the presidency at Peking, and early in 1924 Yeh left the Canton government and returned to north China to take part in the movement to oust Ts'ao. After Feng Yü-hsiang (q.v.) staged a coup at Peking in October 1924 and ousted Ts'ao, Yeh became minister of communications in the government formed by Tuan Ch'i-jui. On 2 November, Sun Yat-sen announced that he had accepted an invitation to go to Peking and participate in negotiations for the formation of a new government. Because of illness, Sun interrupted his trip at Tientsin. By that time, the northern and southern governments each had announced policies and programs which were unacceptable to the other. In early December 1924 Yeh Kung-cho and Hsü Shih-ying (q.v.) arrived in Tientsin for discussions without Sun, but no agreement was reached. Yeh returned to Peking to work on plans for the development of new rail systems and for the unification of control over various types of communication. His plans received little support, and he was dropped from the cabinet in the governmental reorganization of December 1925.

Yeh Kung-cho then retired from politics and devoted his time to cultural activities. He had achieved considerable reputation as an essayist, poet, calligrapher, and archaeologist. He put these talents to work as director of Peking University's classical studies research institute. He held that post until mid-1928, when the Northern Expedition forces reached Peking. Yeh then went to live in Shanghai. From December 1931 to February 1932 he served as minister of railways in the cabinet of Sun Fo (q.v.), and later in 1932 he became a member of the National Economic Council.

After the Sino-Japanese war began in July 1937, Yeh Kung-cho moved to Hong Kong. He was detained there when the Japanese occupied Hong Kong in December 1941, and was held in custody until April 1942, when he was flown to Shanghai. He remained there for the rest of the war, devoting his time to calligraphy and research.

Yeh Kung-cho lived quietly in mainland China after the People's Republic of China was established in October 1949. In 1951 he was named to the Government Administration Council's culture-education committee, and in

1953 he was listed as a director of the China Buddhist Association and the All-China Federation of Literary and Arts Circles. He was elected to the National Committee of the Chinese People's Political Consultative Conference in 1954 and 1959. Throughout the 1950's, he also served on various committees which were concerned with the reform of the Chinese written language. In 1961 he was a member of the preparatory committee for the fiftieth anniversary celebrations of the 1911 revolution.

Yeh Sheng-t'ao   葉 聖 陶
Orig. Shao-chün   紹 鈞

Yeh Sheng-t'ao (1894–), a writer of stories and an essayist noted for his high literary standards. He was a founding member of the Wen-hsüeh yen-chiu hui (Literary Research Society), which for the period of 1921–28 dictated through its influential *Hsiao-shuo yüeh-pao* [short story magazine] the major trends of modern Chinese literature. Yeh was also notable as an advocate of educational reform, and as an editor. In the People's Republic of China he became a high cultural official, his most important post being that of vice minister of education.

Born in Soochow to a rent collector, Yeh Sheng-t'ao was originally called Yeh Shao-chün, a name which he continued to use publicly until the end of the Second World War. When Yeh was six, his father sent him to an old-fashioned primary school. Six years later, Yeh entered the Western-style Soochow Middle School, where he majored in Western languages and had for a classmate and friend Ku Chieh-kang (q.v.), later famous as a historian. Yeh was graduated from this school in 1911, the year of the republican revolution. Financial difficulties prevented further formal study, and Yeh, much against his will, turned to primary-school teaching as a profession. First in Shanghai and subsequently in Soochow, Yeh taught for ten years in various schools, and these ten years were crucial for his subsequent development as a writer. He acquired a deep sympathy for the plight of young children caught up and sometimes broken in the tyrannical and insensitive school system of the time as well as for the impoverished intellectuals like himself who staffed the schools and who slowly gave up their youthful ambitions as family cares and school routine increasingly came to constitute the substance of their daily lives. Yeh, however, had no intention of abandoning his own ambition to be a writer, and during his years as a teacher, he determined to use his talents in defense of the weak. Ku Chieh-kang gave him unflagging encouragement. As early as 1914, Yeh published a story called "Poverty," written in classical Chinese, which described a young boy's filial piety in the face of extreme hardship.

Although Yeh had discovered his theme, it was several years before he found an appropriate means of expressing it. In 1917 Ch'en Tu-hsiu and Hu Shih (qq.v.) sounded the battle cry of what was to become a literary revolution by publicly demanding emancipation from classical literary values and styles of thought through the use of pai-hua [the vernacular] for literary purposes and the realistic depiction of contemporary society. In May 1919 there began the even more momentous May Fourth Movement. Caught up in this atmosphere of reformist zeal, Yeh began writing exclusively in pai-hua. At first he wrote only essays, mostly for the progressive Peking journal Hsin-ch'ao [new tides], but he soon began to contribute stories as well. In November 1920 Yeh joined with Chou Tso-jen, Mao Tun (Shen Yen-ping), Cheng Chen-to, Hsü Ti-shan (qq.v.), Wang T'ung-ch'ao and several others to form the Wen-hsüeh yen-chiu hui (Literary Research Society) with the threefold mission of introducing European and American literature to the Chinese public, evaluating traditional Chinese literature in the light of the standards of modern literary criticism, and creating a modern pai-hua literature responsive to China's revolutionary needs. In January 1921 the society obtained control of Hsiao-shuo yüeh-pao [short story magazine], in which Yeh was to publish some of his most notable stories.

During the years from 1921 to 1937 Yeh produced six collections of short stories—Ko-mo [misunderstanding], of 1922; Huo-tsai [conflagration], of 1923; Hsien-hsia [under the line], of 1925; Ch'eng-chung [in the city], of 1926; Wei-yen chi [sans ennui], of 1928; and Ssu-san chi [at forty-three], of 1936. In addition, in 1927 he published Tao-ts'ao-jen [the scarecrow], a collection of children's stories, and in 1930 he

completed a novel, Ni Huan-chih [schoolmaster Ni Huan-chih]. Focusing on the passing scene in China of the 1930's, Yeh wrote as a critical realist, feeling compelled, in his own words, "to give 'a critical onceover' to those aspects of society which I found unsatisfactory or displeasing." Yeh often chose the schoolroom as the setting for stories and educational reform as the theme, as, for example, in the story called "I erh" [adopted son], where the cruel suppression of a young student's natural talent for painting is poignantly depicted. In other stories he satirized current thought and practice, gently attacked traditional values, or took a stand against social evils. His "Ku-tu" [solitude] ranks with the "K'ung I-chi" of Lu Hsün (Chou Shu-jen, q.v.) as a probing psychological study of the "marginal man" in traditional society. His "To shou-le san-wu-tou" [richer by three or five pecks] is one of his few stories about peasants and one of the few in the literature which captures in a few pages the helpless plight of the Chinese peasantry, to whom even a bumper crop meant no improvement of their lot. "Ch'iu" [autumn] exhibited another facet of Yeh's talent, his capacity to understand and portray female psychology. Often, however, Yeh pointed his pen at less obvious social blemishes and depicted the elements of futility and despair in the grey lives of the dwellers in provincial cities and of petty intellectuals. A typical Yeh hero is the impoverished middle school or college graduate who is dissatisfied with his own capacity for action. A full-length portrait of such a type was offered in Yeh's novel, Ni Huan-chih; and in a subsequent short story, "Ying-wen chiao-shou" [the professor of English], this essence was further distilled. The "professor of English" is a Harvard-trained student who has worked hard in the cause of the revolution and who suffers a nervous breakdown as a result of the 1927 massacre of the Communists. When the narrator in the story encounters him, he has taken a job teaching freshman English in a backwater college, and he now devotes most of his time to Buddhist ritual and to preaching pacificism. This narrator's judgment is harsh, but Yeh's gently ironic and sympathetic treatment of the professor suggests that, like him, Yeh had doubts about the possibility of meaningful action. Like the professor, too, Yeh was a devotee of Buddhism, which he had studied under the guidance of the eminent monk Hung-i (Li Shu-t'ung, q.v.), in the company of the distinguished artist Feng Tzu-k'ai (q.v.). As a technician, Yeh was capable of ingenious plot construction, but he excelled at the plotless "mood piece." These moods were generally ones of loneliness, anxiety, and fear. His writing had its optimistic side, too, and certain of his stories describe with simple charm the everyday life of ordinary families. Such scenes are probably reflections of his own family life, which was contented and peaceful. Displaying a constant devotion to the perfecting of his craft, Yeh during his years of greatest activity set high standards for the further development of the modern Chinese short story.

Throughout this period, Yeh made secondary careers of teaching and editing. Between 1921 and 1923 he lectured on Chinese literature at a number of middle schools and colleges in Woosung, Hangchow, and Peking. In 1923 he moved to Shanghai, where he remained until 1937. In addition to writing and teaching at Shanghai, he served on the editorial staff of the Commercial Press, edited the *Fu-nü tsa-chih* [women's magazine] and the *Chung-hsüeh-sheng* [middle school student], and edited a series of secondary school textbooks on literature and rhetoric.

In 1936 Yeh joined a newly formed anti-Japanese literary group which also included Lu Hsün, Kuo Mo-jo, and Mao Tun. When the Sino-Japanese war began in 1937, Yeh moved to Szechwan, where he was employed as an editor at the K'ai-ming Book Company. In 1941 Yeh became professor of Chinese at Wuhan University, then located in Loshan, Szechwan. There, in an atmosphere charged with political conflict, he maintained a position of detachment, identifying himself with neither the Nationalist nor the Communist cause. A soft-spoken man with a heavy Soochow accent, Yeh seems to have been respected by both sides for his scholarship, his abilities, and his modest and unassuming manner. A volume of miscellaneous writings *Hsi-ch'uan-chi* [western Szechwan], published in 1945, commemorated his wartime experiences. Much of the book was devoted to essays, in which Yeh discussed a variety of topics, including education, literary criticism, and the war situation, but the book also contained several patriotic short stories. Both the essays and stories, however, were laced with sharp criticisms of the National Government.

At war's end, Yeh returned to Shanghai, where he continued to work for the K'ai-ming Book Company. When the North China People's Government was formally established in August 1948, Yeh was named director of the education committee bureau for examining and editing textbooks. After the People's Republic of China was established, he received a number of similar appointments, including membership on the executive committee of the Union of Chinese Writers in 1953, and appointment in 1954 and 1959 as a delegate from Kiangsu to the National People's Congress. In October 1954 he became vice minister of education in the Central People's Government. He was a delegate to the Asian Writers' Congress in 1956 and joined a Scientific Planning Committee group studying classical texts. After 1949 Yeh wrote little fiction. With Communist accession to power, his role became one of confirming and supporting the cultural policies of the new regime. Collections of Yeh's works continued to appear after 1949. In 1951 he published *Yeh Sheng-t'ao hsüan-chi* [an anthology of Yeh Sheng-t'ao], and in 1958 there appeared *Yeh Sheng-t'ao wen-chi* [collected essays of Yeh Sheng-t'ao].

Yeh Sheng-t'ao married Hu Mo-lin in 1916. They had three children.

Yeh Te-hui　　　　　　葉 德 輝
T. Huan-pin　　　　　　奐 份
H. Chih-shan　　　　　　直 山

Yeh Te-hui (1864–11 April 1927), prominent Hunanese classical scholar and political conservative. He was executed by the Chinese Communists in 1927.

The eldest son of Yeh Chün-lan, who achieved the rank of expectant magistrate in Chihli (Hopei), Yeh Te-hui received a classical education. After obtaining his sheng-yuan degree, however, he deserted scholarship for several years to follow a business career. He then returned to his books, passing the examinations for the chü-jen degree in 1885 and obtaining the chin-shih degree in 1892. Hsü Jen-chu (ECCP, II, 703), later director of education in Hunan, was one of Yeh's examiners in 1892, and as such, was considered as one of Yeh's teachers. As a new chin-shih, Yeh entered immediately on an official career, but he did not find it to his taste. In 1892 he served briefly as an assistant secretary in the appointment and transfer department in the Board of Civil Office, where he enjoyed the rank and privileges of a second-class board secretary. After a few months, he resigned to return to Hunan and scholarship.

In Hunan, Yeh Te-hui took a leading role in gentry affairs and became identified with the strongly conservative faction centering around such men as Wang Hsien-ch'ien (q.v.). Yeh and Wang exchanged and compared rare books and also joined forces to take a strong line against the then governor of Hunan, Ch'en Pao-chen, and his director of education, Hsü Jen-chu, both well known for their reformist sympathies. Hsü had written a book entitled *Yu-hsüan chin-yü* expounding the teachings of the Kung-yang school of classical interpretation (*see* Liao P'ing). Yeh wrote a barbed critique of this work entitled *Yu-hsüan chin-yü p'ing*. That Yeh, whose relationship to Hsü was that of pupil to master, could have written such a work caused a major scandal. Not content with this blow, Yeh wrote a conservative political manifesto entitled "Cheng-chieh-lun" [on reforming the world], which, together with a number of other articles critical of K'ang Yu-wei and the other reformers, he contributed to the *I-chiao ts'ung-pien* [materials for the defense of Confucianism] of Su Yü (d. 1914). On the eve of the Hundred Days Reform in 1898, Yeh Te-hui and Wang Hsien-ch'ien addressed a joint petition to Ch'en Pao-chen demanding that Liang Ch'i-ch'ao (q.v.) and his associates be dismissed at once from the Changsha Shih-wu hsüeh-t'ang [academy of current affairs]. This plan nearly backfired when Liang, a few weeks later, arrived in Peking and sought orders for the arrest of Yeh and Wang. The speedy collapse of the reform party, however, effectively prevented any action from being taken.

From 1896 on, Yeh spent most of his time on scholarship and in dabbling in local politics. He taught at the Ts'un-ku Academy and cultivated his cordial association with Wang Hsien-ch'ien and other conservative scholars. During the Boxer Uprising of 1900, Yeh was accused of complicity in the arrest and execu-

tion of T'ang Ts'ai-ch'ang (*see* ECCP, I, 30) and was himself imprisoned at the orders of T'ang's son, T'ang Mang. Yeh's involvement in the affair appears nebulous, and, at the request of Chang Ping-lin (q.v.), he was released. In 1910, as a result of one of their periodic attacks on the local authorities, both Yeh Te-hui and Wang Hsien-ch'ien were cashiered from the civil service, Yeh's alleged crime being his refusal to sell more than 100 piculs of rice from his private granary during a famine. With the coming of the 1911 revolution and the republic, Yeh became even more iconoclastic. For example, when street signs in Changsha were changed to honor Huang Hsing (q.v.), Yeh ordered them torn down and the old names restored. But for all this, Yeh remained an important civic leader in Changsha, serving for a time as chairman of the council on educational affairs and subsequently as chairman of the Changsha Chamber of Commerce.

Because of his outspoken conservatism, Yeh was frequently marked for attack, but he managed to survive the unruly early years of the republic by a combination of sarcasm, toughness, and sagacity. In 1926–27 new foes crossed Yeh's path: Communists enrolled in the Kuomintang. These, at last, brought Yeh's downfall. When the cadres arrived in Changsha, Yeh, in a typical outburst of contemptuous derision, composed a couplet for the farmer's association in which he referred to the Communists as tsa-chung [half-breeds] and ch'u-sheng [beasts], two of the most derogatory expressions in the Hunan dialect. The Communists were not hasty in responding, but when on 1 April 1927 a special court for the trial of "local bullies and vicious gentry" was established, Yeh was in the dock. Ten days later Yeh, together with scores of others, was executed.

Yeh Te-hui was a prolific writer on scholarly and bibliographic topics, and it was as a bibliographer and editor that he earned national fame. Yeh was also an ardent coin collector, and in 1902 he published a booklet on the subject, *Ku-ch'ien tsa-yung*. He was the first Chinese to publish openly a collection of traditional medical works on sex, which he did in 1907 under the title *Shuang-mei ching-an ts'ung-shu* and for which he received much criticism. In 1908 he published one of the two best editions extant of the *Yüan-ch'ao pi-shih* [secret history of the Mongols]. In 1910 he completed his

Shu-lin ch'ing-hua, a charming and complete introduction to Chinese book collecting. *Kuan-ku-t'ang ts'ang-shu-mu,* a catalogue of the more than 350,000 *chüan* of fine editions contained in his personal library, appeared in 1915. Like other Chinese scholars of his time, Yeh wrote much occasional prose and poetry. These works, together with his more substantial writings, were collected in 1902 and published under the title *Kuan-ku-t'ang so-chu-shu;* in 1911 further collections were published. In 1935 Yeh's son Yeh Ch'i-cho published the definitive edition of his father's writings, *Hsi-yüan hsien-sheng ch'uan-shu.*

Yeh T'ing 葉挺
Orig. Yeh Hsi-p'ing 葉西平
T. Hsi-i 希弟

Yeh T'ing (1897–8 April 1946), Communist military commander who led the Independent Regiment attached to the Fourth Army on the Northern Expedition in 1926 and, with Ho Lung (q.v.), directed the Nanchang uprising of 1 August 1927. He commanded the New Fourth Army from 1938 until January 1941, when his forces clashed with Nationalist troops. Yeh was charged with insubordination and detained by the Nationalists for the duration of the Sino-Japanese war.

The Waichow (Huichou) district of Kwangtung, a mountainous area adjacent to Hong Kong, was the birthplace of Yeh T'ing. Born into a peasant family, he received his early education at the local school at Huiyang. In 1911 he enrolled at the Waichow Agricultural School, but he soon left that institution to prepare for a military career. He gained admission to the Whampoa Military Primary School near Canton, where the students were affected by the strong nationalist tradition established by its dean, Teng K'eng (q.v.). After graduation from the Whampoa school in 1916, Yeh went to Wuchang, where he studied for two years at the Second Military Preparatory School.

Yeh T'ing then returned to the south, where he began active military service as a company commander in the Kwangtung Army led by Ch'en Chiung-ming (q.v.). He took part in the campaign against Lu Jung-t'ing (q.v.) which led to the reoccupation of Canton by the republican forces in October 1920, and he became a battalion commander and a member of the Kuomintang. At this early stage in his career, Yeh was associated with an energetic group of young Cantonese officers, many of whom became prominent in later years. This group included Chang Fa-k'uei, Hsueh Yueh, Teng Yen-ta, and Yü Han-mou (qq.v.), a number of whom had been members of the sixth class, graduated in 1919, at the Paoting Military Academy. In 1921, a Nationalist garrison regiment was organized to guard Sun Yat-sen's presidential headquarters; its three battalions were commanded by Chang Fa-k'uei, Hsueh Yueh, and Yeh T'ing. In June 1922, when supporters of Ch'en Chiung-ming besieged that headquarters, Yeh helped to provide the resistance that permitted Sun to escape to a gunboat in the Pearl River.

After the republican forces established a new government at Canton in 1923, Sun Yat-sen moved forward with plans for reorganization of the Kuomintang, construction of an alliance with the Communists, and expansion of a Nationalist party-army. The following year, Liao Chung-k'ai (q.v.), the senior Kuomintang representative at the new Whampoa Military Academy, selected Yeh T'ing to go to Moscow for advanced training. In the Soviet Union, Yeh spent ten months at the Communist University for Toilers of the East and the Red Army Academy, where he was a contemporary of Nieh Jung-chen (q.v.). In 1925 Yeh joined the Moscow branch of the Chinese Communist party. From the Soviet Union he went to western Europe. Teng Yen-ta, also a native of the Waichow district of Kwangtung, had then resigned his post at Whampoa and was in Germany; and he and Yeh T'ing became acquainted with Chu Teh (q.v.), Kao Yü-han, and other members of the Chinese Marxist group at Berlin.

After his return to south China, Yeh T'ing became a regimental commander in the military forces commanded by Li Chi-shen (q.v.). In October-November 1925, the combined efforts of Li Chi-shen and Chiang Kai-shek succeeded in defeating Ch'en Chiung-ming and establishing Kuomintang control over eastern Kwangtung. In preparation for the Northern Expedition, forces under the new National Government at Canton were reorganized and given standard designations as elements of the new National Revolutionary Army. A part of the Kwangtung Army was reconstituted, under Li Chi-shen, as the Nationalist Fourth Army, composed of four divisions. Yeh T'ing was ordered to command and train an independent regiment attached to the Fourth Army, and he actively recruited young Communists from Whampoa to join that unit. Ch'en Yi (1901–; q.v.) was assigned as a political officer, and Lin Piao (q.v.) and other infantry graduates of Whampoa became platoon leaders.

When the Northern Expedition was launched in July 1926, the Nationalist war plan called for a drive through Hunan to support T'ang Sheng-chih (q.v.) against the armies of Wu P'ei-fu (q.v.) to the north. Yeh T'ing's Independent Regiment was assigned to this campaign, along with two divisions, those commanded by Chang Fa-k'uei and Ch'en Ming-shu (q.v.), of the Fourth Army. His regiment played an important part in Chang Fa-k'uei's capture in August 1926 of the two strategic points of Ting-ssu-ch'iao and Ho-sheng-ch'iao south of Wuhan and contributed directly to earning for Chang Fa-k'uei's 12th Division the name "Ironsides." By the time of the Nationalist victory at Wuhan in October, Yeh T'ing had established a reputation as an aggressive and resourceful combat commander, and the Independent Regiment had sustained heavy casualties. Kuo Mo-jo, who headed the propaganda section of the National Revolutionary Army's general political department under Teng Yen-ta, wrote of Yeh's exploits in his book *Pei-fa* [northern expedition], in which he gave him the nickname Chao Tzu-lung, a well-known military hero from the *Romance of the Three Kingdoms*.

After occupation of the Wuhan area, the units of the Fourth Army were reorganized and expanded under the command of Chang Fa-k'uei. Because of his excellent performance during the first stage of the Northern Expedition, Yeh T'ing was promoted to command the 24th Division of the Eleventh Army; and in the spring of 1927 he was assigned concurrently as garrison commander at Wuhan. During 1927 the growing split within the Kuomintang led to the establishment of two rival political centers at Nanking and Wuhan headed, respectively, by Chiang Kai-shek and Wang Ching-wei. Chang Fa-k'uei moved on Kaifeng in

April and won control of most of Honan province. In an effort to take advantage of the reduced military forces in the Wuhan area, a Nanking-backed Hupeh force under Hsia Tou-yin declared itself anti-Communist and attacked Wuhan in early May. Yeh T'ing, as garrison commander, mobilized available troops at Wuchang and quickly repulsed Hsia's move. Yün Tai-ying (q.v.), Communist chief political instructor at the Wuhan branch of the Central Military Academy, played a key role in organizing its cadets to support Yeh T'ing during the crisis.

As tensions heightened, it appeared that the differences between the rival Kuomintang factions at Wuhan and Nanking might have to be settled on the battlefield. Yeh was ordered to lead his troops eastward as part of the advance by Chang Fa-k'uei's Second Front Army. In July, however, when the Kuomintang authorities at Wuhan began a purge of the Communists, Yeh moved southward toward Nanchang in Kiangsi. In the early morning hours of 1 August 1927, Yeh, commander of the 24th Division, and Ho Lung (q.v.), commander of the Twentieth Army, staged a coup to seize Nanchang. Chu Teh, who was then head of the Kiangsi public security bureau, supported the insurrection. Yeh T'ing's coup was successful in gaining control of the city, but within a few days units under Chang Fa-k'uei moved in to reestablish Nationalist control. Despite its failure, the Nanchang uprising became famous in the annals of the Chinese Communist movement, and 1 August 1927 came to be marked as the official birth date of the Red Army in China. After the Nanchang defeat, Yeh T'ing, Ho Lung, Chu Teh, and other military and political figures who had been associated with that action retreated southward to establish a territorial base in Kwangtung, where the peasant movement (*see* P'eng P'ai) had organizational roots. In September 1927 these Communist forces seized Swatow, but again they were driven out within a few days. Yeh T'ing and Ho Lung fled to Hong Kong, while remnants of their forces were reorganized by Chu Teh, who later joined Mao Tse-tung in Kiangsi in the spring of 1928.

From Hong Kong, Yeh T'ing went secretly to Canton, where the Communists planned a new urban insurrection. There he reportedly had disagreements with Chang T'ai-lei (q.v.)

and others who represented the central organization of the Chinese Communist party. When the Canton Commune was established on 11 December 1927, Yeh T'ing was listed as commander of the Workers and Peasants Red Army, but his deputy Yeh Chien-ying (q.v.) actually led the troops that attempted to provide military support for the final, abortive Communist uprising of the year 1927. After the collapse of the Canton Commune, Yeh T'ing again went to the Soviet Union. Later, however, he severed connections with the Chinese Communist party and went to western Europe, where he spent time in Berlin and Vienna at the same time that his erstwhile schoolmate Teng Yen-ta was surveying European conditions. Yeh T'ing's activities during the early 1930's are obscure; he apparently avoided politics and lived in retirement in Hong Kong.

After the outbreak of war with Japan in the summer of 1937, a new Nationalist-Communist united front emerged, and the main Chinese Communist military forces in Shensi were reorganized as the Eighth Route Army. The Communists proposed that efforts be made to mobilize and regroup scattered units of the Red Army, left behind in 1934 at the start of the Long March, which remained operational in central China. The Kuomintang refused this proposal on the ground that it would be inadvisable to have these units continue under Communist command. Yeh T'ing then sent a message to Chiang Kai-shek proposing that he be assigned to command the Communist units in the Yangtze valley in action against the invading Japanese. Perhaps because Yeh T'ing had had no formal connection with the Chinese Communists for a decade, perhaps because of the personal support of Hsueh Yueh and other Nationalist officers regarded as politically reliable, Chiang approved the proposal. In late September 1937, the Military Affairs Commission of the National Government ordered the establishment of the so-called New Fourth Army; the designation was used in allusion to the earlier Fourth Army of the Northern Expedition period. Yeh T'ing at once proceeded to Shensi for conferences with Chu Teh and Mao Tse-tung.

The New Fourth Army was formally created in January 1938, with its headquarters at Nanchang. Yeh T'ing was named commander, with the Communist Hsiang Ying

(q.v.) as deputy commander and political commissar, and Ch'en Yi as commander of its first column. The army was assigned a 150-mile-long sector along the Yangtze. During the spring of 1938 the New Fourth Army established a field command post in southern Anhwei and began to extend its area of operations. Raids were mounted against the Nanking-Shanghai and Nanking-Wuhu rail lines and along the road linking Nanking and Hangchow. After the Japanese captured Hsüchow in northern Kiangsu in May 1938, Yeh deployed elements of his army north of the Yangtze to operate behind Japanese lines.

During 1939–40, as Yeh T'ing's forces extended operations in the Kiangsu-Anhwei area, Ku Chu-t'ung (q.v.), the Nationalist commander of the Third War Area which included these provinces, came to view these Communist units as a greater competitive threat than the Japanese. Frictions increased. In December 1940, Ku ordered some 9,000 men of the New Fourth Army in southern Anhwei to move to bases north of the Yangtze. While these troops were on the march in January 1941, they came into conflict with Nationalist units under the command of Ku Chu-t'ung. The ensuing battle (6–14 January 1941) near Maolin in southern Anhwei ended in virtually complete rout of the greatly outnumbered Communist forces. In that action—known in Chinese Communist history as the New Fourth Army, or Southern Anhwei, incident—Hsiang Ying was killed, and Yeh T'ing was captured. Ku Chu-t'ung's move diminished, but by no means eradicated, Communist military strength in the lower Yangtze valley. The top command at Yenan moved quickly to reorganize these forces. Ch'en Yi was assigned as acting commander of the New Fourth Army, with Liu Shao-ch'i (q.v.) as political commissar and Su Yü (q.v.) as deputy commander.

The Nationalists charged Yeh T'ing with insubordination to military orders and imprisoned him for the remainder of the war. He was held for a time at Shangjao, Kiangsi, but later moved to Enshih in southwestern Hupeh and then to Kweilin in Kwangsi. After the Japanese surrender in 1945, he was sent to Chungking. In the Nationalist-Communist negotiations in the early autumn of 1945, the Communists repeatedly requested that Yeh T'ing be set free He was finally released on 4 March 1946 after over five years of confinement. The next day he requested reinstatement of his membership in the Chinese Communist party, and on 7 March Yenan confirmed that the request had been granted. A month later, Yeh left by plane for Shensi. On the flight to Yenan, the plane crashed in Shansi on 8 April 1946. In addition to Yeh T'ing, a number of other Communist leaders, including Ch'in Pang-hsien, Teng Fa, and Wang Jo-fei (qq.v.), died in the crash. Nationalist sabotage was widely rumored but never proved.

In 1925, while training the Independent Regiment in south China, Yeh T'ing married Li Hsiu-wen. She was the daughter of a prosperous gentry family of Nanhai (Namhoi), Kwangtung, and had graduated from a women's normal college in Canton. She, together with two of the Yeh children, died in the April 1946 plane crash. Six other children, who were at the time living in either Kwangtung or Shensi, survived their parents. Yeh Chun, the wife of Lin Piao who gained political prominence at Peking in 1969, was reportedly a daughter of Yeh T'ing.

Yen Chia-kan   嚴家淦
West. C. K. Yen

Yen Chia-kan (23 October 1905–), known as C. K. Yen, government official who initiated the tax collection system of "land levies in kind." Beginning in 1946 he held a variety of financial posts in Taiwan and stabilized the economy of that island. He served as minister of finance of the National Government in Taiwan in 1950–54 and 1958–63 and as governor of Taiwan in 1955–57. Yen became premier in 1963 and vice president in 1966.

Born into a gentry family in Soochow, Kiangsu, C. K. Yen studied the Chinese classics at home with his grandfather and father, both of whom were scholars. He also attended modern schools in Soochow. Upon graduation from the Tao-wu Middle School, a missionary institution in Soochow, he enrolled at St. John's University in Shanghai. Like many other young Chinese of his day, he believed that science was the key to strengthening China's position in the family of nations.

Accordingly, he chose theoretical chemistry as his major. Upon graduation in 1926, he became director of supplies for the Nanking-Shanghai railroad bureau in Shanghai. Yen held a variety of jobs in 1926–37, but little is known about his activities during that period.

After the Sino-Japanese war began, C. K. Yen became commissioner of reconstruction in the Fukien provincial government in the winter of 1938. In August 1939 the governor, Ch'en Yi (q.v.), appointed him commissioner of finance. Yen restored Fukien to self-sufficiency by setting up a complete budget system and by reforming the system for collecting land taxes. The reform, known as "land levies in kind," dated back to pre-Ming China, when a certain percentage of rice or wheat crops was collected from farmers by local governments and sent to the emperor. Thereafter, taxes were paid in silver until November 1935, when the National Government abandoned the silver standard in favor of a managed paper currency. Because of inflation during the Sino-Japanese war, the value of tax revenues dropped precipitously. Land levies were the principal source of National Government income, but with inflation the tax revenues did not cover the expense of collecting them in the various provinces. For this reason, C. K. Yen decided to initiate a system of tax payment in grain in 1941. The new system was so successful in Fukien that in 1942 Yen was summoned to Chungking to report on land levies in kind to the Executive Yuan of the National Government. As a result, the system was extended to other provinces. Rice and wheat collections strengthened the financial situation of the National Government as well as the provinces, and soldiers at the front began to receive food supplies regularly and without delay. C. K. Yen's contribution to wartime China won him considerable renown.

C. K. Yen was appointed director of procurement of the war production board established in Chungking at the end of 1944. He assumed office in February 1945 and took charge of all procurement under the United States Lend-Lease and the British and Canadian loan programs. At war's end, he was sent to Nanking as a member of the army general headquarters planning committee for taking over party and political offices and as a standing committee member of the ministry of economic affairs committee for reorganizing industrial and mining enterprises in Japanese-occupied areas. Chinese Nationalist forces took control of Taiwan in the early autumn of 1945, and Yen went there in December 1945 as communications commissioner, again serving under Ch'en Yi, and as ministry of economic affairs representative for taking over railroad, telecommunication, and navigation facilities from the Japanese. In April 1946 he became Taiwan finance commissioner and board chairman of the Bank of Taiwan. He issued banknotes for exclusive use in Taiwan, thereby sparing Taiwan the inflation then plaguing mainland China. After Wei Tao-ming (q.v.) became the first regular governor of Taiwan in May 1947, Yen served in his administration as commissioner of finance. He retained that post after Ch'en Ch'eng (q.v.) succeeded Wei as governor in January 1949.

The influx of more than 2,000,000 Nationalist refugees in 1949 created serious financial problems in Taiwan. With many more mouths to feed and troops to support, inflation became inevitable. Accordingly, C. K. Yen undertook a currency reform in June 1949. The exchange rate of the New Taiwan Dollar (NT $) was fixed at NT$5 to US$1. The official price of gold was set at NT$300 per tael, and the old Taiwan currency was exchanged for the new at a ratio of 40,000 to 1. This reform soon brought stability to the economy of Taiwan.

In December 1949 C. K. Yen was appointed chief of the second section in the office of the tsung-ts'ai [party leader] of the Kuomintang and chairman of the board of directors of the China Petroleum Corporation. The following month, he became minister of economic affairs and vice chairman of the Council for United States Aid. When Ch'en Ch'eng became president of the Executive Yuan in March 1950, Yen was made minister of finance. He held that post until 1955, when he became governor of Taiwan. In September 1957 he was appointed minister without portfolio and chairman of the Council for United States Aid, and in 1958 he again became minister of finance. His success in financial administration was such that he was named to succeed Ch'en Ch'eng as premier in December 1963 even though he was not a veteran Kuomintang leader. Indeed, he had not become a Central Executive Committee member until 1963. The soundness of Yen's

financial and economic policies was confirmed by the fact that Taiwan did not suffer a crisis when United States economic aid was terminated in July 1965. The economic growth rate and the volume of foreign trade in Taiwan continued to rise, and the index of wholesale prices was kept under firm control.

In March 1966 C. K. Yen was elected vice president of the Government of the Republic of China in Taiwan. He assumed office on 20 May, at which time President Chiang Kai-shek reappointed him president of the Executive Yuan, observing that "C. K. Yen's merits will complement my weaknesses, while my merits will complement his weaknesses." After 1966 C. K. Yen often traveled abroad representing Nationalist China. In May 1967 he visited the United States at the invitation of President Lyndon B. Johnson for an exchange of views. After two days of conferences in Washington and a trip to Cape Kennedy, he visited New York, Chicago, San Francisco, Los Angeles, and Honolulu before returning to Taipei at the end of May. Yen's cogent presentation of the Chinese Nationalist case, together with his detailed knowledge of economic and financial matters, made a favorable impression on many influential groups in the United States.

C. K. Yen was married to Liu Chi-shun, a native of Shanghai. They had five sons and four daughters.

Yen Fu   嚴 復
Orig. T'i-ch'ien   體 乾
T. Yu-ling   又 陵
Alt. Tsung-kuang 宗 光

Yen Fu (8 January 1854–27 October 1921), naval officer who became the foremost translator-commentator of his day. Through his translations, the works of such Western thinkers as Charles Darwin, Herbert Spencer, John Stuart Mill, and Adam Smith were introduced to China.

The only son of a practitioner of Chinese medicine, Yen Fu was born in Houkuan hsien, Foochow fu, Fukien. He began his formal education at the age of five and at nine studied with a private tutor, Huang Shao-yen, who was well versed in both Han Learning and Neo-Confucian doctrines. Following his father's death, financial difficulties forced Yen to discontinue his classical education. He sat for the entrance examination to the newly established Ma-chiang Naval Academy attached to the Foochow Shipyard, a scholarship which provided maintenance for both students and their families. After gaining admittance with top marks, he was allowed to choose between the School of Naval Architecture, where the French language and French instruction prevailed, and the School of Navigation, where the language of instruction was English. His choice of the School of Navigation was to determine the course of his intellectual development. The English language was to be his medium of access to Western ideas, Great Britain was to become his model state, and English ideas were to dominate his intellectual outlook. During a five-year course at the school, he studied English, mathematics, physics, chemistry, astronomy, and naval science under English and French instructors. He supplemented this curriculum by studying the *Hsiao-ching* [book of filial piety] and the *Sheng-yü kuang-hsün* [the imperial instructions and profound teachings]. He also practiced the composition of examination essays.

After being graduated *summa cum laude* in 1871, Yen Fu was assigned for practical training on the warship Chien-wei. The following year he visited Japan after being transferred to another warship, the Yang-wu. In 1874 he assisted the minister of naval affairs, Shen Pao-chen (ECCP, II, 642–44), his fellow provincial and patron, in drafting reports for the Chinese government following an investigation of the murder by Formosan aborigines of certain Ryukyu islanders under the legal protection of Japan shipwrecked on the Formosan coast.

Yen Fu was one of the earliest Chinese students sent by the Ch'ing government to study in Europe. Upon arrival in 1877, Yen entered a school at Portsmouth, England. He then transferred to the Greenwich Naval College, where he studied mathematics, chemistry, physics, and naval science. Apart from one trip to France, Yen devoted the whole of his two years' stay in the West to study in England. His performance in class was more than satisfactory, but he completely neglected practical training at sea so that he could devote time to examining the British political system and the theories which lay behind it. He seems to have been obsessed by the question of the

bases or secret of Western wealth and power, a question which preoccupied the best minds of his generation and which was to underlie most of his own subsequent study. The answer, he determined to his satisfaction, lay in the manner in which the British judicial and political system operated. He was much impressed by the British jury system, which, in his opinion, guaranteed impartial justice for the people. He believed that the important differences between China and the West had to do with despotism and constitutionalism. Under a despotic ruler there was no national accord because the people were forbidden to participate in politics. Under the representational system of election, the strength of local government served to unite public benefit with self-interest of the people. Because of these political observations, Yen came to regard the Chinese as "coolies" and Westerners as "patriots." It was probably Yen Fu's eager search for understanding which attracted the attention of China's first minister to England (later concurrently minister to France), Kuo Sung-t'ao (ECCP, I, 438–39), who was responsible for the Chinese students of naval science in Europe. Despite differences in age and rank, the two often held long discussions on the differences between Chinese and Western political systems. Kuo was so favorably impressed by the young Yen that he wrote to an official in Peking describing Yen as better qualified than himself to hold the post of minister to Great Britain— praise which was regarded as extravagant and absurd by officials in Peking.

After graduation from the naval college at Greenwich in 1879, Yen Fu returned to China, where he began to experience a series of frustrations which was to lend an edge of personal resentment to his general dissatisfaction with the plight of China. He taught for a year at the Foochow Naval Academy. In 1881 Li Hung-chang (ECCP, I, 464–67), the governor general of Chihli (Hopei), who had become chief manager of China's naval affairs after Shen Pao-chen's death in 1879, appointed Yen dean of the newly founded Peiyang Naval Academy in Tientsin. Yen, however, was not taken into Li's confidence, and his critical comments on China's weakness as reflected in her loss of the Ryukyu Islands to Japan won him the distrust and displeasure of the official class. Because his Western training did not qualify him for an important position in the government bureaucracy, Yen decided to seek advancement through the conventional channels provided by the traditional civil service examination system. In 1885 he purchased the chien-sheng degree and then sat for the chü-jen examination in Fukien, but failed it. He made two more attempts to pass the examination in 1888 and 1889, but without success. At this point, Li Hung-chang made some conciliatory gestures to the disappointed Yen, promoting him to the position of vice chancellor of the Peiyang Naval Academy in 1889 and to the post of chancellor in 1890. Yen was granted the title of expectant tao-t'ai in Chihli in 1892 on the recommendation of the ministry of naval affairs. Aware, however, that he had no real power or prestige, he made a fourth and final attempt to pass the chü-jen examination in 1893, but again he was unsuccessful.

Thwarted by his repeated failures with the examinations, chafing under the limitations of his position in the academy, and disturbed by Japan's defeat of China in 1895, Yen Fu turned his energies to writing. Some of his ideas had taken shape long before they found expression. In England he had become familiar with Darwinism and with works of Herbert Spencer. Early in 1881 he had read Spencer's *Study of Sociology*, a sort of prolegomenon to the study of sociology, and in this book he had found similarities between Western and Chinese thought. In his opinion, *Study of Sociology* contained the essence of the Confucian scriptures *Ta-hsüeh* [the great learning] and *Chung-yung* [doctrine of the mean] in the idea that good government depends on the principles of investigation of things, sincerity, and moderation. Spencer's work surpassed its Chinese counterparts only in precision and accuracy resulting from scientific discipline.

In 1895 Yen Fu published four important essays which first appeared in a Tientsin newspaper and which later were reprinted in the *Shih-wu-pao*, the reform magazine edited by Liang Ch'i-ch'ao (q.v.) in Shanghai. Yen first attacked the conservatives' insistence on preserving the old world. He considered that history developed according to definite laws which were beyond human control. The isolationist policy adopted by the conservatives was impracticable and nothing short of fantasy. As aggression by the West on backward China

was irrevocable, the Chinese could only accept this fact and strive to strengthen their own country on the pattern of their opponents. The strength of the West lay not in weapons and technology, but in the realm of thought and knowledge. He attributed the great advances in Western knowledge to the contributions of Charles Darwin and Herbert Spencer. The importance of these two men to Western thinking was, in Yen's estimation, comparable to that of Isaac Newton in physics. Darwin's contribution was his conception of the struggle for existence and natural selection, while Spencer's lay in the application of Darwin's theories to the social sciences. Using Spencer's standards for judging the strength of a nation and its people by their physical, intellectual, and moral qualities, Yen proposed a threefold reform program. To improve his people's physical stamina he advocated prohibition of opium smoking and foot binding. To enlighten the people's minds, he suggested replacing the writing of eight-legged essays with Western learning. And to regenerate the nation's virtue, he recommended establishing a parliamentary system as the most effective way of arousing patriotism in the Chinese when confronted by their foreign enemies. Yen Fu's commitment to democratic principles of government, however, was not immediate but ultimate, for, with the viewpoint of a social evolutionist, he conceived the emergence of any polity as a gradual process. The condition of the Chinese people could not be changed overnight, and they were not yet ready for self-government. What was needed in the immediate future was an enlightened elite who could educate the people and render them capable of moving toward self-government over a long span of time.

Thus, the years 1895–98 saw Yen Fu setting to work as an educator and intellectual publicist. In 1896 he participated in the establishment of a Russian-language school in Peking and the T'ung-i School in the same city. He also helped Liang Ch'i-ch'ao establish the *Shih-wu pao* in Shanghai. In 1897, together with Hsia Tseng-yu and others, he founded two newspapers in Tientsin, the *Kuo-wen pao*, a daily, and the *Kuo-wen hui-pien*, issued every ten days to provide news summaries of the *Kuo-wen pao*. These two papers had the declared aims of reflecting and transmitting opinions between officialdom and the people, and providing information about foreign countries. In comparison with other embryo Chinese newspapers at the time, the scale of operations of these two newspapers was quite impressive, for they had correspondents stationed in almost every province in China as well as major cities in the West. They were closed down after the 1898 *coup d'etat*.

Because he believed that education was the first step on China's way to strength, Yen Fu set out to improve the content of education. He found translation, interlaced with commentaries, a most effective medium, and it was on his role as a translator-commentator that his subsequent national fame and contribution were to rest. Yen's first translation had appeared in 1892—a rendering of Alexander Michie's *Missionaries in China*, an attack by a Westerner on the methods of missionaries in China. In 1895 he embarked on the translation of the first two chapters of Thomas Huxley's *Evolution and Ethics and Other Essays* under the title *T'ien-yen lun*, and in 1897 he published the results in the *Kuo-wen pao*. The publication of these translations as a book in 1898 was a resounding success and instantly won Yen recognition as a serious writer on national affairs. The work also illustrated Yen's method, it being more than a translation of Huxley's lectures as published in 1893. An appreciative preface by Yen's literary mentor Wu Ju-lun (ECCP, II, 870–72) testified to Yen's high stylistic achievement. Yen's footnotes and commentaries were often as long as the direct translation of the original text, and the work as a whole was both an exposition of Spencer's essential views as opposed to those of Huxley and an adaptation of social Darwinism to China's needs. While approving of Spencer's ethic of self-assertion and enlightened self-interest, Yen rejected Huxley's idea of protecting human ethical values against the efforts to create an evolutionary ethic. Turning to China's needs, Yen contended that she could overcome her weakness by asserting herself in the universal struggle for existence. A master of classical Chinese, he skillfully coined such elegant phrases as *t'ien-yen* [evolution], *wu-ching* [the struggle for existence], and *t'ien-tse* [natural selection], which immediately were adopted by young reformers.

Despite his personal association with reformers, Yen Fu was, by and large, an outsider to the constitutional movement of 1898. Although he agreed with the reform program in principle, he disagreed with K'ang Yu-wei (q.v.) and his associates about the timing of constitutional government in China. He believed that the intellectual and moral level of the Chinese people was not yet high enough for representative government. In September 1898, as the reform movement was approaching its climax, Yen had an audience with the Kuang-hsü emperor, who ordered him to submit a copy of his open "Ten Thousand Word Memorial" published in the *Kuo-wen pao* earlier in the year. This memorial, in which Yen suggested that the emperor make inspection tours within and beyond China's boundaries in order to win the confidence of the people and to establish friendly relations with other nations, probably never received imperial perusal, however; for shortly after the audience, Yen learned of the conservatives' plan to crush the reformers in Peking and returned in haste to Tientsin.

In his search for the sources of national strength, Yen Fu had long been aware of the importance of economics. His reading of Adam Smith's works dated back at least to 1895. He began translating Smith's *An Inquiry into the Nature and Causes of the Wealth of Nations* in 1897 and completed the task in 1900. As in the case of *T'ien-yen lun*, the translation from Smith, entitled *Chi-hsüeh* (later changed to *Yüan-fu*), was favored with a preface by Wu Ju-lun. In this translation Yen reiterated the idea that the wealth and power of the state can only be achieved by a release of energies and capacities of the individual. He attributed England's wealth to Smith's principle of economic individualism, which had encouraged the release of the economic energies of the people.

Between 1898 and 1900 Yen Fu was also engaged in the translation of John Stuart Mill's *On Liberty*, a tract aimed at defending the liberty of individuals against society and upholding the value of freedom as an end in itself. Yen again adapted ideas in the original text to his own concerns. Liberty was interpreted by Yen as the right to a free struggle for existence. It contributed to the improvement of men's moral, physical, and intellectual powers, a prerequisite, in his eyes, to the advance of the wealth and strength of the state.

Yen Fu served as chancellor of the Peiyang Naval Academy until 1900, when the Boxer Uprising broke out in Chihli. He then terminated his naval career by leaving Tientsin for Shanghai. He took part in the formation of a "Society for the Study of Logic" and held various offices for short periods of time. In 1901 he became one of the two Chinese members on the board of directors of the Kaiping mining company. When Wu Ju-lun became chancellor of Imperial University at Peking in 1902, Yen was appointed director of the university's newly established translation bureau. He held the post without much enthusiasm and finally resigned in 1904. That winter he went to London in an official capacity to settle litigation regarding the Kaiping mines. He also visited France, Switzerland, and Italy. Upon his return to China, he helped Ma Liang (q.v.) establish the Fu-tan Academy, and in 1906 he served briefly as its principal. He then was invited by En-ming to supervise the Anhwei Normal School, where he stayed one year. In 1908 he was appointed chief editor of the Bureau of Terminology, a post he held until 1911. He was awarded the chin-shih degree by the Ch'ing government in 1909 and was appointed a member of the advisory council for political affairs in 1910.

In the meantime, Yen Fu continued to expend most of his energies on translation. In 1903 he published a translation of Herbert Spencer's *Study of Sociology* under the title of *Ch'ün-hsüeh i-yen*. His main purpose in translating this work was to discredit then-current revolutionary propaganda. As a follower of Spencer's theory that the law of natural evolution determines the development of human societies, Yen believed that the drastic political reorganization advocated by the Chinese revolutionaries and reformers at that time would only bring harm to the country. In 1904 he published translations of Edward Jenks' *A History of Politics* under the title of *She-hui t'ung-ch'üan* and of Charles Louis Montesquieu's *Esprit des Lois* under the title of *Fa-i*. He also made Chinese versions of two important books on logic: *A System of Logic* by John Stuart Mill appeared in 1905 as *Mu-le ming-hsüeh*, and *Primer of Logic* by William S. Jevons was published in 1909 as *Ming-hsüeh ch'ien-shuo*. In Yen's view, logic was the disciplinary foundation of Western knowledge.

Yen Fu was unsympathetic to the revolutionary movement at the turn of the century. During a 1905 conversation with Sun Yat-sen, Yen insisted that because the Chinese people were backward in both moral and intellectual outlook, the evils banished in one area might simply reappear in another. The immediate task was to transform the national character through education. In Yen's opinion, revolution was a destructive force and would delay the evolution of Chinese society. It would be harmful to the people because it would deepen the conflicts among the various nationalities in China.

It is not surprising that Yen Fu was unhappy when the Chinese republic was established. The political and social chaos which followed the revolution reinforced his conviction that the majority of the Chinese people were incapable of using their political rights properly. In addition to deploring the actions of the revolutionaries and the militarists, he charged K'ang Yu-wei and Liang Ch'i-ch'ao with responsibility for the chaotic conditions then prevailing. He saw the need for a strong government to remedy the turbulent situation. The only form of government suitable for China was one strong enough to maintain order within her own territory, which had to be defended against foreign aggression. Any means used to achieve the goal of national security could be justified in view of the deplorable situation.

Yen Fu's extreme views on government to some extent explain his connection with Yuan Shih-k'ai during the first years of the republican period. Yen and Yuan seem to have known each other at least as early as 1902, when Yuan figured prominently in national politics as the governor general of Chihli and concurrently commissioner for north China trade. Because of his respect for Yen, Yuan intended to enlist him as an adviser. Yen declined several offers because he disapproved of Yuan's personal character as a politician. Nevertheless, when appointed chancellor of Peking University by Yuan in 1912, Yen accepted the post. In 1913 he became an adviser on legal and foreign affairs to the president's office. When Yuan's campaign to become monarch was in full swing during 1915, Yen was a member of the Cheng-chih hui-i [political conference] and the Constitutional Conference. Eventually, his name was listed as one of the "six gentlemen" of the Ch'ou-an-hui [society to plan for stability]. Although Yen later claimed that Yang Tu (q.v.), the leading spirit of the Ch'ou-an-hui, used his name without approval, Yen never publicly repudiated the monarchical plan as a whole. Because of his evaluation of Yuan Shih-k'ai as a political leader, however, he was reluctant to give his wholehearted support to the movement, and he refused Yuan's bribe to write an essay refuting Liang Ch'i-ch'ao's article "How Strange the so-called Question of the Form of State," which vehemently repudiated the monarchical plan. After Yuan's death, Yen Fu went into complete retirement and grew increasingly pessimistic about the contemporary situation.

After 1916, Yen Fu developed a tendency to reject Chinese imitation of Western culture and to seek the restoration of the culture of Chinese antiquity. This change of thinking emerged gradually, becoming increasingly apparent as he advanced in age. His interest in Chinese antiquity gradually led him to advocate revival of the Chinese traditions of the pre-Ch'in period. In order to perpetuate the cultural heritage of China, he maintained, it was mandatory for students of all grades to study the Confucian classics, which in his view would enable the younger generation to cultivate proper moral sentiments and to learn to esteem the sages of the past. When the Confucian Society petitioned Parliament in 1913 to adopt Confucianism as the state religion, Yen Fu supported this course of action. The outbreak of the First World War dealt another blow to his already shaken confidence in the West and contributed to his final reappraisal of its culture as a whole. In 1918 he wrote: "In my old age I have seen the Republic during the seven years of its existence and an unprecedented bloody war of four years in Europe. I feel that the evolution of their [Western] races in the last three hundred years has only made them kill one another for self-interest, without a sense of shame. Today, when I reconsider the way of Confucius and Mencius, I feel it is broad enough to cover the whole cosmos and to benefit the entire world."

These views ran contrary to the ideas then prevalent among intellectuals in China. Yen Fu opposed the May Fourth Movement, whose main aims, science and democracy, he had championed more than a quarter of a century

earlier. He considered the students' attempt to voice their opinions in national politics as useless and the vernacular style as vulgarization of the Chinese language. Suffering from asthma and declining in health, he wrote little except a number of letters to one of his former students, in which he expressed his growing apprehension over the course of contemporary affairs. He found his only consolation in the *Chuang-tzu*. In 1920 he returned to his home town, Foochow, from Peking and died there on 27 October 1921. Among his deathbed instructions to his children was the injunction: "Though the old traditions may be modified, they must never be overthrown."

As a translator-commentator, Yen Fu made an indelible imprint on modern Chinese intellectual history, his only rival being a fellow provincial, Lin Shu (q.v.), who performed a role similar to Yen's in the field of literature. Yen's standard for translation was expressed in the three-word motto "hsin, ta, ya," meaning fidelity to the original, intelligibility of expression, and elegance of style. Such prominent men as Liang Ch'i-ch'ao, Lu Hsün, Hu Shih, and Mao Tse-tung all acknowledged Yen's influence on their thought. Although his use of the classical language made his works difficult to read for the generation which came after the May Fourth Movement, many of the concepts of social Darwinism which he first introduced to China continued to captivate Chinese minds. In this sense, Yen did much to spur intellectual transformation of the Chinese people. Paradoxically, the effects of the ideological changes resulting in social and political reforms were not what he had anticipated.

In addition to his translations, Yen excelled in writing poetry in the traditional style. Two collections of his poems were published: the *Yen Chi-tao shih-wen ch'ao* of 1922 and the *Yü-yeh-t'ang shih-chi* of 1926. Yen was also the author of a commentary on the annotations made by Wang Pi (226–249) to the *Tao-te ching;* this work was published in Japan in 1905 as *Yen-shih p'ing-tien Lao-tzu.* A similar treatise devoted to the *Chuang-tzu* appeared under the title *Chuang-tzu p'ing-tien.* Five of Yen's most important translations were collected and published under the title Yen-i ming-chu ts'ung-k'an. In 1959 a selection of his prose and poetry was published in Peking under the title *Yen Fu shih-wen hsüan*, and in 1965 a number of his translations were reprinted in Taipei. An excellent study by Benjamin Schwartz, *In Search of Wealth and Power: Yen Fu and the West*, was published in 1964.

Yen Fu was survived by his second wife, a concubine, five sons, and four daughters. Yen's first wife, whom he had married at the age of 12, died in 1892. A granddaughter, Isabella Yiyun Yen, became a professor of Chinese and linguistics at the University of Washington at Seattle, where she completed an important work on Chinese syntax, *A Grammatical Analysis of Syau Jing*, published in 1960.

Yen Hsi-shan
T. Pai-ch'uan

閣 錫 山
百 川

Yen Hsi-shan (1883–24 May 1960), Shansi warlord and one of the outstanding political strategists of the republican period. In 1930 he joined with Feng Yü-hsiang (q.v.) in an unsuccessful northern coalition against Chiang Kai-shek. During the Sino-Japanese war, he served as commander in chief of the Second War Area. After being forced out of Shansi early in 1949, he became president of the Executive Yuan and minister of national defense in the National Government. He held those posts until the National Government was reorganized in Taiwan in March 1950.

The village of Hopien in Wut'ai hsien, Shansi, was the birthplace of Yen Hsi-shan. His father, Yen Tzu-ming, managed a small bank. As a boy, Yen Hsi-shan studied the Chinese classics at the village school and served as an apprentice in the bank. After his father lost everything in the depression that overtook Shansi banking at the beginning of the twentieth century, Yen arranged settlements with his father's creditors. In 1901 he left home and enrolled at the government-supported provincial military college in Taiyuan. Three years later, he received a government scholarship for advanced study in Japan. He spent the next two years studying Japanese, science, and military technology at the Shimbu Gakkō [military preparatory academy]. During this period, he joined the T'ung-meng-hui and enlisted as a member of the Dare-to-Die Corps. After a trip to north China in 1907 with his fellow revolutionary and

former teacher Chao Tai-wen, he went back to Japan in 1908 and enrolled at the Shikan Gakkō [military academy]. Upon graduation in 1909, he returned to Shansi to become an instructor at the Shansi Military Primary School. He passed the chü-jen degree examinations later that year and then became a training officer in the 2nd Regiment of the New Shansi Army. In 1910 he received command of that regiment, with the rank of colonel.

When news of the Wuchang revolt reached Shansi, Yen Hsi-shan and the 1st and 2nd regiments of the New Shansi Army seized Taiyuan on 28 October 1911 and declared Shansi's independence the following day. Late in November, a large Ch'ing force headed by Ts'ao K'un (q.v.) began to move toward Shansi. Yen advanced into Chihli (Hopei) to meet this force, but he soon was forced back into Shansi. Only the abdication of the emperor and the subsequent termination of hostilities saved his army from destruction. When Yuan Shih-k'ai succeeded Sun Yat-sen as provisional president of the republican government, he appointed Yen military governor of Shansi. However, he virtually excluded Yen from the civil government of Shansi. Yen remained aloof from both Yuan's monarchical plot and the opposition to it. In July 1917, a year after Yuan's death, Yen drove from power the civil governor and other officials appointed by Yuan. Thereafter, Yen Hsi-shan was the sole ruler of Shansi. With the aid of Chao Tai-wen, he undertook a social reform program that eventually won Shansi the designation of "model province."

During the disorderly decade that followed Yuan Shih-k'ai's death, Yen Hsi-shan shifted from one armed coalition to another, invariably emerging on the winning side. Although weaker than other warlords, he frequently held the balance of power between factions. For this reason, even those whom he betrayed hesitated to attack him lest they need his help in the future. Despite his political adroitness and ability to inspire loyalty in military subordinates, however, Yen might well have fallen from power had he not been a friend and supporter of one of the most powerful of the northern militarists, Tuan Ch'i-jui (q.v.). In 1917 Yen helped Tuan thwart the restoration attempt of Chang Hsün (q.v.). Tuan returned the favor by allowing Yen to oust the Shansi civil officials appointed by Yuan Shih-k'ai and by securing Yen's appointment as civil governor of Shansi. When the Peiyang militarists split into factions, Yen allied himself with the Anfu Club (*see* Hsü Shu-cheng) of Tuan Ch'i-jui. In 1919, in connection with Tuan's program for the unification of China by military force, Yen sent an army into Honan to bring a defiant militarist to terms.

In April 1920 Ts'ao K'un and other militarists formed an alliance directed against Tuan Ch'i-jui and Hsü Shu-cheng. Yen Hsi-shan immediately sensed where the balance of power lay and refrained from participation in the military action launched by Tuan and Hsü in July. He sided with the Chihli faction led by Ts'ao and Wu P'ei-fu (q.v.), for he feared the army of Wu's powerful subordinate Feng Yü-hsiang (q.v.). For this reason, he supported the Chihli faction in its 1922 and 1924 wars with the Manchurian warlord Chang Tso-lin (q.v.). To his dismay, in October 1924 Feng effected a coup at Peking, ousted Ts'ao and Wu from power, and entered into an alliance with Chang Tso-lin and Tuan Ch'i-jui. To assure Feng of his support, Yen occupied the important rail junction of Shihchiachuang, thereby preventing Wu P'ei-fu from bringing up reinforcements from the south. Nevertheless, Feng brought parts of northern Shansi under his dominance, and Yen dared not object.

When war broke out between Feng Yü-hsiang and the coalition of Chang Tso-lin and Wu P'ei-fu early in 1926, Yen Hsi-shan played a double role in the hostilities, forming an alliance with Chang and Wu but dealing also with the Kuominchün. After Feng resigned his posts and went to Moscow, the Kuominchün retreated to Suiyuan by way of northern Shansi. Yen sent forces led by Shang Chen (q.v.) into Suiyuan, providing a shield for the Kuominchün and occupying most of Suiyuan, which Chang Tso-lin coveted. Yen then appointed Shang military governor of the Suiyuan special district.

After the National Revolutionary Army launched the Northern Expedition in mid-1926, Yen Hsi-shan attempted to avoid committing himself by offering to mediate between the Chang Tso-lin faction and the Nationalists. After much vacillation, on 5 June 1927 he announced his allegiance to the Nationalists and accepted an appointment as commander in chief of the revolutionary armies in the north. Once again, Yen found himself allied with Feng Yü-hsiang, who had returned from Moscow and had joined the Kuomintang in September 1926. Yen Hsi-shan's forces, reorganized as the Third Army Group, went into action in September 1927. Shang Chen captured the Fengtien general Yü Chen at Tatung and drove through Kalgan into Chihli (Hopei). Fu Tso-yi (q.v.) captured Chochow. These forces soon met with difficulties, however, because the Nationalist advance fell behind schedule. Shang was forced to withdraw, and Fu was forced to surrender at Chochow after withstanding a siege of three months' duration.

After Chiang Kai-shek returned to power at the beginning of 1928, the final stage of the Northern Expedition was launched. Yen Hsi-shan's forces played a decisive role in this offensive, for they led the drive on Peking. On 4 June, the day of Chang Tso-lin's death, Chiang Kai-shek appointed Yen garrison commander of the Peking-Tientsin area. Yen formally occupied Peking on 8 June. He was richly rewarded for his role in the final drive on Peking with appointments as governor of Shansi, head of the Taiyuan branch of the Political Council, vice chairman of the Military Affairs Commission, and member of the Kuomintang Central Executive Committee and the Central Political Council.

The question of troop disbandment soon strained relations between Feng Yü-hsiang and Chiang Kai-shek to the breaking point. In May 1929 Feng in effect declared his independence of the National Government. Soon afterwards, thousands of Kuominchün troops led by Han Fu-chü, Ma Hung-k'uei (qq.v.), and Shih Yü-san defected to the National Government side, greatly weakening Feng's position in Honan. At this juncture, Chiang Kai-shek wired Feng, urging him to go abroad. Yen Hsi-shan then offered to go abroad with Feng, thereby serving notice that if the National Government tried to break up the Kuominchün, it would have to fight him as well. A settlement was reached by the contending parties. In October, however, Kuominchün officers denounced the policies of the National Government and called on Yen and Feng to rectify the situation. Fighting began in western Honan in mid-October, but Yen remained aloof from the conflict despite his alliance with Feng and despite his appointment by Chiang as deputy commander in chief of the national land, sea, and air forces. The conflict ended when the Kuominchün withdrew from Honan in late November.

In February 1930 Yen Hsi-shan announced his support of Feng Yü-hsiang, thereby forming what came to be known as the northern coalition or the Yen-Feng movement. On 10 February, Yen proposed that Chiang Kai-shek retire. The Kwangsi clique (see Li Tsung-jen), Chang Fa-k'uei (q.v.), and the Reorganizationist faction of Wang Ching-wei (q.v.) joined in the opposition to Chiang. At the beginning of April, Yen took office as commander in chief of the anti-Chiang forces, with Feng as his deputy. The National Government removed Yen from his posts and issued an order for his arrest. The fighting began in May in Honan and Shantung. While Chiang and the Kuominchün fought savagely in Honan, Yen's forces advanced almost without opposition into Shantung and took Tsinan. The Kwangsi forces were eliminated from the campaign in mid-June after a defeat near Hengyang (see Huang Shao-hung). In July, representatives of various dissident groups met in the so-called enlarged conference to organize an opposition government at Peiping. The deliberations of the conference were interrupted by news of a decisive military setback in August. Chiang Kai-shek suddenly mounted an offensive in Shantung and virtually destroyed the forces of Fu Tso-yi. It now became apparent that only the intervention of Chang Hsueh-liang (q.v.) could save the northern coalition. Thus, when Yen Hsi-shan assumed office as chairman of the state council at Peiping on 9 September, he appointed Chang to the council. Chang, however, refused to support the northerners, and on 18 September he called for peace and sent his forces into north China. Yen Hsi-shan withdrew from the new government at Peiping, severed relations with the Kuominchün, and ordered what remained of his army to return to Shansi. He then announced his decision to retire from public life and went to live in Dairen.

After the Japanese attacked Mukden on 18 September 1931, Yen Hsi-shan returned to Shansi. By this time, his former subordinates Hsü Yung-ch'ang (q.v.) and Fu Tso-yi were governing Shansi and Suiyuan, respectively.

Through these men, Yen reasserted his authority over his native region. In 1932 the National Government appointed him pacification commissioner of Shansi and Suiyuan, a post he retained until 1937. In the hope of amassing sufficient strength to withstand both Japanese and the Chinese Communist threats to Shansi, in 1934 Yen initiated a ten-year plan of economic development. He constructed roads and a railway, developed light industry, increased Shansi's agricultural and mining production, and redistributed land holdings. To finance and control these projects, he endeavored to establish a government monopoly of commerce, industry, and agriculture. He curtailed the power of the village gentry, developed a public school system, increased women's rights, and curbed drug addiction. To strengthen Yen's ties to the National Government, Chiang Kai-shek invited him to the Fifth National Congress of the Kuomintang in 1935 and appointed him vice chairman of the Military Affairs Commission in 1936.

When the Sino-Japanese war began in July 1937, Yen Hsi-shan was appointed commander in chief of the Second War Area. Before long, only a small part of Shansi was left unoccupied by either the Japanese or the Chinese Communists. This situation finally led to a clash between Yen's troops and Communist forces in 1939. Because of continuing Communist pressure, Yen apparently established cordial relations with the Japanese, prompting allegations of collaboration. After the Japanese surrender in 1945, he used Japanese troops to defend the provincial capital and otherwise resist the advancing Communists. During this period, he served as Taiyuan defense commissioner and commander in chief for "bandit-suppression" in north China. He endeavored to combat the Communists' popular appeal by going ahead with his plans for social and economic reforms. The result was a peculiar combination of traditionalism and radicalism which apparently failed to satisfy the basic demands of the Shansi population. By April 1949, he had been forced out of the province. That June, he became president of the Executive Yuan and minister of national defense in the National Government. He stayed on the mainland until 8 December 1949, when he flew to Taipei. There he continued to serve as premier until March 1950, when Ch'en Ch'eng (q.v.) succeeded him in that post and Chiang Kai-shek resumed the presidency of the National Government in Taiwan. Thereafter Yen served as a presidential adviser and member of the Central Advisory Committee of the Kuomintang until his death on 24 May 1960.

Yen Hsi-shan's unusual feat of retaining control of all or part of his native province of Shansi from 1912 to 1949 gained him a reputation as one of the outstanding political strategists of north China during the Nationalist period. A comprehensive biography treating both political and military aspects of Yen's active career, *Warlord: Yen Hsi-shan in Shansi Province, 1911–1949*, by Donald G. Gillin, appeared in 1967.

Yen Hui-ch'ing　　　　顔惠慶
T. Chün-jen　　　　　　　駿人
West. W. W. Yen

Yen Hui-ch'ing (2 April 1877–23 May 1950), known as W. W. Yen, American-trained scholar, government official, and diplomat. He served as ambassador to the Soviet Union from 1933 to 1936.

Shanghai was the birthplace of W. W. Yen. Both of his parents were Christians. His father, the Reverend Yen Young-kiung (Yen Yung-ching), became proctor and professor of mathematics and natural philosophy at St. John's College upon its founding in 1879; and he was pastor of the (Episcopal) Church of Our Savior in Hongkew from 1887 until his death in 1898. The elder Yen had received his higher education in the United States, and all of his children, five sons and a daughter, studied either in the United States or in England. W. W. Yen studied at St. John's College, Anglo-Chinese College, and the T'ung-wen-kuan in Shanghai before going to the United States in 1895 to enter an Episcopal-sponsored secondary school in Virginia. In 1897 he enrolled at the University of Virginia, where he won a number of academic prizes, served as secretary of the Blackford Literary Society in 1897–98, and became a member of Phi Beta Kappa in 1899.

Upon graduation from the University of Virginia in 1900, W. W. Yen returned to China to accept an appointment as professor of English at St. John's College, which became a university

in 1905. Yen remained at St. John's until 1906. During this period, he translated various English-language works into Chinese and participated in the intellectual and civic life of the community, becoming a member of the Chinese Educational Association, the Anti-Footbinding Society, and other social welfare organizations. He also was a founder of the Chinese World Students Association. In 1906 he accepted a position at the Commercial Press as editor in chief of the *English and Chinese Standard Dictionary*, which was published in 1908.

In 1907 Yen went to The Hague to serve as interpreter in the Chinese legation, then headed by Lu Cheng-hsiang (q.v.). The following year, he was transferred to Washington as second secretary, under Wu T'ing-fang (q.v.) as minister. He was promoted to the post of first councillor after Chang Yin-t'ang succeeded Wu T'ing-fang in 1909. Yen returned to China in 1910 to organize a press bureau for the Ch'ing government, and in August 1911 he became junior councillor in the Board of Foreign Affairs.

With the establishment of the republican government at Peking in March 1912 and the organization of the cabinet under T'ang Shao-yi (q.v.), W. W. Yen became vice minister of foreign affairs. He held that post until 1913, when he was appointed minister to Germany, Denmark, and Sweden. At the time of the so-called second revolution (*see* Li Lieh-chün), Yen, then residing in Germany, joined several other Chinese ministers abroad in urging domestic peace. He remained loyal to the Peking government throughout the tumultuous 1913–19 period. When China entered the First World War on the side of the Allies in August 1917 (*see* Tuan Ch'i-jui), he left Germany and took up residence in Denmark.

In May 1920 W. W. Yen returned to China and established residence in the seaside resort town of Peitaiho, Chihli (Hopei). On 11 August, Chin Yün-p'eng (q.v.), then the premier at Peking, appointed Yen minister of foreign affairs. About this time, the Far Eastern Republic, organized in eastern Siberia in April 1920, sent a mission to Peking which was headed by Ignatius Yurin. In September, Yen informed the Tsarist envoy to Peking, Prince N. A. Kaudacheff, that his voluntary retirement would help simplify a complicated situation. Kaudacheff rejected the suggestion, and on 23

September the Peking government issued a mandate terminating relations with the Tsarist minister. The next step toward the regularization of Sino-Russian relations came with the reception at Peking of Alexander K. Paikes, representing both the Chita and the Moscow governments, in December 1921. Paikes presented his credentials to Yen on 16 December, and soon afterwards the ministries of foreign affairs and communications were authorized to undertake negotiations with him. These negotiations collapsed when it was discovered that Soviet Russia had signed a treaty with Outer Mongolia on 5 November 1921. In the meantime, Yen had concluded a treaty with Germany in May 1921 which had reestablished peaceful Sino-German relations.

After serving under Li Yuan-hung (q.v.) as officiating premier as well as foreign minister from June to August 1922, W. W. Yen was dropped from the cabinet. He then served as chairman of the Western-Returned Students Club and president of the Chinese Social and Political Science Association until August 1923, when he was appointed chairman of the newly formed commission for the readjustment of finance. It was the function of this commission to determine the total amount of the Peking government's domestic and foreign debts and the methods of adjustment and redemption to be used. The creation of this commission aroused hopes among foreign creditors that China was about to begin funding its debts, but Yen's preliminary report, issued in April 1924, disclosed that the Peking government was virtually bankrupt. Yen, who initially thought that the commission's work could be completed in six months, served as chairman for four years.

In January 1924 W. W. Yen assumed additional responsibility as minister of agriculture and commerce in the cabinet of his father-in-law, Sun Pao-ch'i (q.v.). When Sun resigned in July, V. K. Wellington Koo (Ku Wei-chün, q.v.) became acting premier. Ts'ao K'un (q.v.), then the president at Peking, nominated Yen to succeed Sun, but the Parliament did not approve Yen's appointment until September. Yen formed a new cabinet on 15 September, but he resigned when Feng Yü-hsiang (q.v.) effected a coup at Peking in October. After a few months of political inactivity, Yen was appointed to the commission charged with investigating the May Thirtieth Incident at

Shanghai. In October 1925 he was named minister to the Court of St. James's, but that appointment was superseded later in October by his designation as a delegate to the customs tariff conference at Peking. In May 1926 Yen again became premier, but Chang Tso-lin (q.v.) opposed his appointment and forced him to resign in June. Yen appointed Tu Hsi-kuei acting premier on 22 June and retired to Tientsin.

W. W. Yen then devoted his attention to civic and business affairs. In Tientsin he operated an import-export firm, served as a member of the Chinese Ratepayers Association in the British concession, and became associated with Nankai University. He also served as a director of such Peking institutions as Yenching University and the Peking Union Medical College. In June 1931 he accepted an appointment as chairman of the China International Famine Relief Commission.

In September 1931 W. W. Yen fully emerged from political retirement to succeed C. C. Wu (Wu Ch'ao-shu, q.v.) as Chinese minister to the United States. In 1932 he also represented China in the Assembly and the Council of the League of Nations. While in Geneva, he negotiated with the Soviet foreign minister, Maxim Litvinov, for the restoration of Sino-Soviet relations, which had been interrupted in 1927. Agreement was reached in mid-December, and Yen was appointed Chinese ambassador to the Soviet Union on 27 December. He presented his credentials at Moscow early in 1933. That year he also served as a delegate to the League Assembly, and he attended the World Monetary and Economic Conference at London in May. In January 1934 Soviet military intervention in Sinkiang in support of Sheng Shih-ts'ai (q.v.) focused the National Government's attention on that province. Yen was called to Nanking in February for consultations regarding the matter. After his return to Moscow, he was directed to forward an inquiry to the Soviet authorities about the nature of Soviet dealings in Sinkiang. Sino-Soviet relations worsened as support of Sheng Shih-ts'ai and Soviet commercial penetration of Sinkiang continued. In an effort to improve relations, the National Government appointed T. F. Tsiang (Chiang T'ing-fu, q.v.) to succeed W. W. Yen as ambassador to the Soviet Union in October 1936.

W. W. Yen's return to China late in 1936 marked the end of his career as a diplomat of importance. During the Sino-Japanese War his only post was that of member of the People's Political Council. At war's end, he received another largely honorary appointment as chairman of the Far Eastern Regional Committee of the United Nations Relief and Rehabilitation Administration. In 1947 he became a member of the State Council at Nanking. He undertook his last mission for the National Government in February 1949, when he headed an unofficial delegation that went to north China for an exchange of views with Mao Tse-tung and Chou En-lai at Shihchiachuang. Yen then went to Shanghai. After the People's Republic of China was established in October 1949, he became chairman of the Shanghai branch of the Sino-Soviet Friendship Association. Yen died in Shanghai on 23 May 1950, at the age of 73. He was survived by three sons—Ti-sheng, Chih-sheng, and Pao-sheng—and by three daughters—Ying-sheng, Nan-sheng, and Pin-sheng.

Yen Yang-ch'u   晏 陽 初
T.   Tung-sheng   東 昇
West. Y. C. James Yen

Yen Yang-ch'u (26 October 1893–), known as James Yen, leader of the mass education and rural reconstruction movements in republican China. In the 1950's, as president of the International Committee of the Mass Education Movement, he helped form the Philippine Rural Reconstruction Movement, and in 1960 he became president of the International Institute of Rural Reconstruction.

Little is known about James Yen's family background or early life except that he was born in Pachung, Szechwan, and that he was brought up as a Christian. After attending Hong Kong University, he won the King Edward Scholarship in 1913, refused it, and spent a short period in Europe before going to the United States to enroll at Yale University. Upon graduation from Yale in 1918, he accepted an invitation from the War Work Council of the American YMCA to undertake social work in the Chinese labor battalions recruited by the British in Shantung to help the Allies behind the lines in France. While writing letters home for these illiterate workers, he conceived the idea of teaching them several hundred basic Chinese characters. He later enlarged the number of characters to 1,000 and founded the *Chinese Workers' Weekly*, which used only those characters. This paper soon expanded its operations, and it was distributed to all Chinese workers in France after Yen was transferred to Paris as director of an educational program for the entire Chinese labor corps.

At war's end, James Yen went to the United States, where in 1920 he received an M.A. in history from Princeton University. Upon his return to China in 1921, he became public education secretary of the national committee of the YMCA and immediately embarked on the development of the *People's Thousand Character Reader*, which was published in February 1922 by the Association Press of the YMCA in Shanghai. With this book in hand, he launched a large-scale literacy campaign at Changsha in March–June 1922. Elaborate publicity preceeded the campaign, and about 1,300 people enrolled in the course. A group of volunteer teachers was trained to aid in teaching others. Almost 1,200 successful students were awarded "literate citizen" certificates at the graduation ceremonies. The success of this pilot program in Changsha led the YMCA to sponsor programs in other cities. As the mass education movement gathered momentum, Yen began work on the problem of providing reading material for the newly literate, who had a limited vocabulary and different interests from the traditionally literate segment of the population. Thus began the "People's Library" of 1,000 booklets in basic Chinese ranging from the classics, folk tales, and songs to modern farming, rural hygiene, and cooperatives. In August 1923, after the YMCA-sponsored literacy program had demonstrated the practicability of its approach to the illiteracy problem, a group of educators established at Peking the National Association of the Mass Education Movement, with Yen as executive secretary. This association, committed to carrying out the literacy movement and related programs for the masses on a continuing basis, remained active under Yen's leadership until 1950, when it was dissolved by the Chinese Communist leadership.

In 1925 James Yen attended the first meeting of the Institute of Pacific Relations at Honolulu. There he had occasion to speak to overseas

Chinese about mass education in China, and he began collecting contributions for that cause. In 1928 he made a fund-raising tour in America and obtained about US $500,000, which subsequently benefitted some 400,000 people in Tinghsien, Hopei, through a project Yen had founded in 1926. A model village was created at Tungt'ing hsiang ch'u, and adults were taught to read, to be more sanitary in their living habits, and to improve their economic conditions. Yen soon succeeded in enlisting the aid of other American-trained Chinese in fields ranging from medicine to agricultural economics. In 1929 Yen and his associates moved with their families to Tinghsien in the belief that in order to teach the country people they themselves had to experience rural living. With this added impetus, the Tinghsien program blossomed, winning international recognition and drawing a number of sociologists from Peking to conduct social investigations and community studies. The best known studies about Tinghsien were those by Sidney Gamble and Li Ching-han. An integrated four-fold program of rural reconstruction was developed: livelihood, health, literacy, and self-government to combat poverty, disease, illiteracy, and misgovernment—the four basic problems of the peasants of China.

James Yen's contribution to mass education was recognized both in China and abroad. In 1928 he was invited to lecture in the United States by the American National Association of Education and was awarded an honorary M.A. degree by Yale University; the following year, St. John's University in Shanghai awarded him an honorary doctorate. Although the National Government had given him little assistance in his venture, in 1933 it recognized his achievement by publishing "Plans for Establishing Experimental Stations in the Several Provinces." In 1931–33 Yen was a member of the National Economic Council; in 1935 he became chairman of the North China Council for Rural Reconstruction; and in 1935–37 he was president of the Hopei Provincial Institute of Social and Political Reconstruction, also known as the Hopei Provincial College of County Administration.

By 1937 Japanese aggression in north China had made the continuation of the Tinghsien program impossible, and Yen therefore carried his program to other parts of China. He was vice president of the Szechwan provincial

planning commission in 1936–39 and executive director of the Hunan Provincial School of Public Administration in 1938–39. In 1938, when there was imminent danger of a Japanese invasion of the strategic rice-bowl province of Hunan, the provincial government invited the Association of the Mass Education Movement to help mobilize some 30 million people for resisting the Japanese. With the active participation of hundreds of intellectuals and professionals who had retreated to Hunan from the coastal provinces, 75 hsien governments were reorganized and some 5,000 civil servants and 30,000 village heads were retrained. The reorganization brought confidence to the people and stability to the province. After the fall of Changsha to the Japanese, Yen went back to Szechwan, where he joined with T'ao Hsing-chih (q.v.) in founding the College of Rural Reconstruction and worked to train hsien administrative personnel at the Institute for Administrative Cadres. He also served as a member of the Supreme National Defense Council and the People's Political Council.

James Yen was in the United States in 1944–45, probably for fund-raising purposes. During this sojourn, he was awarded honorary degrees by Syracuse University (LL.D., 1944), the University of Maine (L.H.D., 1944), Temple University (LL.D., 1945), and the University of Louisville (LL.D., 1945). In 1947 Yen again went to the United States. At the suggestion of Secretary of State George C. Marshall, he prepared a memorandum in which he recommended that a joint Sino-American commission be established to administer a program of rural reconstruction in China and that ten percent of United States economic aid to China be earmarked for this program. With a shrewd eye on his American audience, Yen argued that the expenditure of US $6 on a Chinese should effectively prevent him from being influenced by Communist ideology. The China Aid Act of 1948 subsequently allocated US $27 million solely to rural reconstruction, including a mass education program in Szechwan. In October 1948 the Joint Commission on Rural Reconstruction (JCRR) became operational, with Chiang Monlin (Chiang Meng-lin, q.v.) as its chairman and James Yen and Shen Tsung-han (q.v.) as its other Chinese members.

Although the JCRR had only a little over one year in which to operate on the mainland

and although it spent only US$4 million of the total funds allotted, its programs in the fields of agriculture, land tenure reform, cooperative organization, public health, and literacy affected millions of Chinese peasants. Paul G. Hoffman, the first administrator of the Economic Cooperation Administration, commented in 1951 that "it was in the very provinces that the JCRR program had got underway—in Szechwan, Kwangsi, and Fukien—the Communist invaders found some of the most stubborn resistance to their drive. What a different story might have been told in China if this alternative to Communist strategy had been started a few years earlier." In November 1949 Yen left mainland China for Hong Kong. He remained optimistic about his mass education and rural reconstruction programs in west China even after the Communists took control of Szechwan. However, on 1 December 1950 the Chungking Military Control Commission dissolved the National Association of the Mass Education Movement, the College of Rural Reconstruction, and other affiliated organs.

James Yen and his friends continued to believe that the basic problems of the masses throughout the Far East were the same, namely, a full rice bowl and human dignity, and that the mass education movement idea could be adapted to other Asian countries. In 1951, therefore, they formed the International Committee of the Mass Education Movement in New York to promote rural reconstruction in countries that requested it. As president of this committee, Yen made a survey trip early in 1952 to the Philippines, Thailand, Indonesia, India, and Pakistan. With the enthusiastic backing of President Ramon Magsaysay of the Philippines, Yen helped form the Philippine Rural Reconstruction Movement, which began operations in July 1952 with Neuva Ecija in central Luzon as its pilot area. The Philippine Rural Reconstruction Movement aimed to give new purpose to educated young people who had been easy prey for Communist propaganda. As village missionaries, these young people began to find new outlets for their energies, patriotism, and idealism in helping rural people to achieve a better living. The techniques that Yen had perfected in 30 years of mass education in China proved successful in the Philippines. His contribution was recognized when he received the 1960 Ramon Magsaysay Award

for International Understanding and an honorary LL.D. degree from the Philippine Women's University at Manila. Also in 1960 the members of the International Committee of the Mass Education Movement decided to extend their activities to other countries in Asia, Latin America, and Africa through the establishment of the International Institute of Rural Reconstruction in the Philippines, with Yen as president.

James Yen was married to Alice Huie, a sister of the wife of Y. Y. Tsu (q.v.). The Yens had three sons and two daughters.

Yen, W. W.: *see* YEN HUI-CH'ING.

Yi P'ei-chi   易 培 基
T. Yen-ts'un   寅 村
H. Lu-shan   鹿 山

Yi P'ei-chi (28 February 1880–September 1937), Hunanese scholar and Kuomintang member who became president of Labor University at Shanghai, minister of agriculture and mines at Nanking, and curator of the Palace Museum at Peiping. His administration of the Palace Museum caused a major scandal, and Yi was accused of criminal acts, including massive theft.

Little is known about Yi P'ei-chi's background or early life except that he was a native of Changsha, Hunan, and that he visited Japan after being graduated from the Wuchang Language School. In 1913 he joined the staff of the Hunan Higher Normal School as a teacher of Chinese. The following year, he transferred to the First Provincial Normal School, where his students included Mao Tse-tung and Ts'ai Ho-sen (qq.v.). In 1918 Yi and other teachers, with the support of the Hunan provincial headquarters of the Kuomintang, formed an organization to resist the oppressive administration of the Peiyang general Chang Ching-yao, then the military governor of Hunan. This organization aided T'an Yen-k'ai (q.v.) in his successful campaign against Chang in the spring of 1920. That autumn, in an attempt to restore the Hunan educational system, which had suffered seriously under Chang Ching-yao's rule, T'an appointed Yi

P'ei-chi head of the provincial education committee and principal of the First Provincial Normal School at Changsha. Yi carried out a thorough-going reform of the school's faculty, bringing in a number of graduates of Peking universities whose attitudes had been shaped by the May Fourth Movement of 1919. He also invited Mao Tse-tung to teach Chinese literature and to head the primary school attached to the Normal School. In 1921 Yi himself became secretary general in the governor's office and director of the provincial library at Changsha.

In 1922 Yi P'ei-chi went south to Canton, where he became an adviser to Sun Yat-sen. When Kwangtung University was founded in 1924, he joined its faculty. Tsou Lu (q.v.), the president of Kwangtung University, sent Yi to Peking as the university's resident representative to recruit professors and to procure textbooks and other teaching materials. In addition, Yi was to promote the cause of the Kuomintang among the students in Peking, especially the Hunanese students who had supported him in the movement against Chang Ching-yao. In the northern capital, Yi became a close associate of Li Shih-tseng (q.v.).

After Feng Yü-hsiang (q.v.) took control of Peking in October 1924, a new cabinet was formed by Huang Fu (q.v.) on 3 November of that year. On 10 November, Yi P'ei-chi was named acting minister of education, but he held that post for only two weeks, resigning with the rest of the cabinet on 24 November. By that time, Yi had been named to the committee in charge of the inventory and custody of the palace treasures. This committee, chaired by Li Shih-tseng, had been formed after the eviction of P'u-yi (q.v.), the last Manchu emperor, from the Forbidden City on 5 November. In 1925 the Peking Palace Museum was founded, with Li as chairman of the board and Yi as curator. Also in 1925 Yi helped Feng Tzu-yu (q.v.) found the so-called Kuomintang Comrades Club in Peking. When Chang Shih-chao (q.v.), then minister of education, announced the reorganization of the Women's Higher Normal School in Peking to counter a student strike at that institution, Yi and Li, who supported the student movement, worked to turn public opinion against Chang. In December, after Chang had been forced to resign, Yi became chancellor of the institution

and minister of education. He held the latter post until March 1926.

After the 8 March 1926 incident at the Taku harbor and the 18 March demonstration at Peking which resulted in more than 40 fatalities (*see* Feng Yü-hsiang), Tuan Ch'i-jui (q.v.), then the chief executive at Peking, ordered the arrest of Hsü Ch'ien, Li Ta-chao, Ku Meng-yü (qq.v.), Li Shih-tseng, and Yi P'ei-chi on charges of instigating the demonstration and disseminating Communist propaganda. Yi escaped to the Legation Quarter, and he fled south in April 1927. That summer, he helped to found and became president of Labor University at Shanghai, which trained personnel for the labor movement of the Kuomintang. After the Ta-hsueh-yuan [board of universities] was established to replace the ministry of education (*see* Ts'ai Yuan-p'ei), he served on its universities committee.

After the successful completion of the Northern Expedition, the National Government promulgated regulations for the Palace Museum at Peiping and appointed a 27-man board of directors, with Li Shih-tseng as chairman and Yi P'ei-chi as a member. The board confirmed Li as chairman and elected Yi curator of the museum, and these designations were approved by the National Government in February 1929. On 5 March, Yi announced that Li Tsung-tung (his son-in-law and Li Shih-tseng's nephew) would serve as secretary general of the museum and that he himself would serve as head of its antiques division, with Ma Heng as his deputy.

On 19 October 1928 Yi P'ei-chi was appointed minister of agriculture and mines in the National Government. Because he also was serving as president of Labor University and curator of the Palace Museum, he had to divide his time among Shanghai, Peiping, and Nanking. Yi reorganized the ministry, created a new forestry division, and formulated new regulations to encourage mining investments. His burdens were lightened somewhat when, on 24 September 1930, Chiang Monlin (Chiang Menglin, q.v.), the minister of education, relieved him of the presidency of Labor University. At the end of 1930 the ministry of agriculture and mines was merged with the ministry of industry and commerce, under H. H. K'ung (q.v.). Yi then proceeded north to take charge of the Palace Museum. From 4 December 1930 to

7 February 1931 he also served as president of Peking Normal University.

In Peiping, Yi P'ei-chi supervised the inventorying and registration of the objects in the Palace Museum and embarked on a program to evaluate the objects in terms of quality and age. Photographic reproductions of paintings, manuscripts, and examples of calligraphy were made available to the public. The museum was divided into three sections, which were opened to the public in rotation. The museum published weekly and monthly bulletins to announce current exhibits and the discovery of new treasures, and it issued catalogues of its holdings. To finance these projects, Yi held sales of gold dust, silver ingots, tea, silk, and clothing from the palaces. The slipshod manner in which these sales were conducted caused considerable dissatisfaction in Peiping, and Yi P'ei-chi and Li Tsung-tung were accused of criminal acts. Investigations disclosed that Yi had not received National Government approval for the sale of gold bars and some other objects.

Because of the Japanese threat to north China, Yi P'ei-chi had drawn up a plan for the removal of cultural objects to the south, and the plan had been approved by the Executive Yuan. In the autumn of 1932 the packing of objects began. As preparations for shipment got underway, Peiping citizens and newspapers began to complain that more attention was being paid to objects than to people. The Japanese attacked at the Great Wall in January 1933. Disregarding all objections to his plans, Yi shipped some 13,000 boxes of ancient objects to the south between February and May 1933. In the meantime, the Supreme Court sent procurator Chu Shu-sheng from Nanking to Peiping to investigate the charges against Yi and others. Despite the efforts of Li Shih-tseng and others, a formal indictment was made against Yi and Li Tsung-tung on 13 October 1933. Yi fled to the Japanese concession at Tientsin. He published a book entitled *The Truth About the Palace Case* and inserted announcements in newspapers attacking Cheng Lieh, the attorney general of the Supreme Court. After collecting additional evidence against Yi, Cheng issued an order for Yi's arrest on 30 December 1933. At the same time, Sun Wei of the Kiangning district court, who was in charge of the case, undertook investigations at Peiping and at the custodial office of the antiques in Shang-

hai. On 13 October 1934 new indictments were brought against Yi and Li on charges of massive theft from the Palace Museum. Yi also was charged with using his authority as minister of agriculture and mines to foster personal interests. Although every effort was made to apprehend Yi and Li, negotiations for their extradition failed. They assumed disguises and moved about in the foreign concessions of Tientsin and Shanghai and in Hong Kong and Dairen. In the meantime, the investigations went forward, and a new indictment was issued in September 1937 together with a document of certification in two huge volumes. By that time, the Japanese had begun the invasion of Shanghai, where Yi was living under an assumed name. According to a report later made by his family, the objects he had hidden in Kiangwan were destroyed by fire, and the shock of their loss caused Yi P'ei-chi's death.

Ying Hua   英 華
T.   Lien-chih   歛 之
H.   Wan-sung yeh-jen   萬 松 野 人
West. Vincent Ying

Ying Hua (28 October 1866–10 January 1926), known as Ying Lien-chih, an eminent Catholic scholar who was the founder of the *Ta Kung Pao* and the lay founder of Fu-jen (Catholic) University.

Born into a Manchu family in Wanp'ing, Chihli (Hopei), Ying Lien-chih showed his natural taste for literary and intellectual pursuits at an early age. Although he had no formal schooling, he apparently had the benefit of private instruction in the Chinese classics. Ying was a serious lad who found his studies congenial, but he had a normal enthusiasm for play as well as for work. He became a skilled swordsman and archer, and he kept himself in trim by lifting weights.

Even as a youth, Ying enjoyed reflective speculation on philosophical questions. He read widely in the literature of Confucianism, Buddhism, Taoism, and Islam. While pursuing these interests, Ying encountered the Roman Catholic faith for the first time through the Sisters of Charity, who were nursing his fiancée back to health in a Peking hospital. His favorable impression of the attitudes and skills of the Sisters led him to inquiries about the Roman Catholic Church and to wider contacts with Catholic priests. At the same time, he began an intensive study of Christian doctrine and of the Chinese works of the eminent Catholic missionary Matteo Ricci (1552–1610). In 1895, at the age of 29, he became a Catholic. Two years later, Ying and his fiancée were married despite strong objections from her father to Ying's religious affiliation. After the marriage, Ying's wife also became a Catholic.

As a member of the Plain Red Banner, Ying Lien-chih served for two years as an imperial guardsman assigned to the household of Prince Su. He then spent about two years (1898–1900) as a minor government official in Annam. The effects of the tropical climate on his health forced him to return to China in 1900. On his return to north China, he decided to establish a newspaper "to help China become a modern and democratic nation." Thus in June 1902, with the assistance of Ts'ai Fu-ning and Wang Tsu-san, he founded the *Ta Kung Pao* in Tien-tsin. During the next decade he served both as director and editor in chief, and his literary and managerial abilities did much to make the newspaper a success. Founded as an instrument of reform in the critical years when the imperial throne was under pressure to introduce wide-spread changes in many areas, the *Ta Kung Pao* soon acquired the reputation of being a fearless critic of both domestic and international policies. Ying Lien-chih openly attacked the empress dowager, recommending that she retire from the throne. After the republican revolution of 1911, the *Ta Kung Pao* continued its criticism of measures which it considered inim-ical to democratic reform and the public interest.

Ying Lien-chih was also one of the pioneers in the use of pai-hua [the vernacular] in order to reach wider audiences and to spread his appeals for modernization and reform. As early as 1902 he began writing in pai-hua, and during the next few years he published books in pai-hua in which he denounced foot-binding and other customs of the period. He also advocated more governmental initiative in encouraging industry in China. Yet his zeal for reform and his vision of a modernized nation were consistently tempered by his desire to conserve essential elements of Chinese culture, particularly its literature and calligraphy.

In 1912 Ying Lien-chih turned from editing the *Ta Kung Pao* to problems of education which he had come to feel were critical in any program for the modernization of China. He joined with Ma Liang (q.v.) in addressing an eloquent plea to Pope Pius X in July 1912 urging the establishment of a Catholic univer-sity in Peking to advance the cause of Catholicism among the Chinese intelligentsia.

Although poor health forced Ying Lien-chih to retire in 1912 to a quiet retreat in the Western Hills near Peking, he continued his active interest in educational and social problems. His friend Ma Liang prevailed upon him to establish and manage for a brief period a vocational school for girls. In 1913, in another effort to promote learning and to revive Chinese culture, he and Ma established the Fu-jen School as a "means of developing a group of Chinese Catholics who would be as cultured and well-educated as any other class or circle in China and whose conversation would redound to the glory of the Holy Mother Church and to the good of their native country." He personally supported this school until 1918, when a lack of funds and related difficulties forced it to close.

Throughout this period, Ying Lien-chih and his associates were increasingly concerned over the slow progress which the Catholic Church was making in the realm of higher education in China. Prior to the republican period, there were several Protestant-sponsored universities but only one Catholic university—Aurora in Shanghai, founded in 1903. Ying and his friends were troubled by opposition within the Catholic Church to proposals that the Church itself stimulate and sponsor work in the field of secular education. To combat this lethargy and hostility, Ying and a small group of educated Catholic scholars and missionaries, including Ma Liang and Father Vincent Lebbe (Lei Ming-yuan, q.v.), initiated a religio-intellectual movement in north China which resulted in a number of prominent families being brought into the Catholic Church in 1914–15. In June 1917 Ying published an "Exhortation to Study." This sharply worded document attacked the obscurantism of some of the Catholic missionaries and urged the native clergy and laity to seek greater proficiency in their own language and literature. He also submitted a Latin translation of his exhortation together with a sequel, "An Answer to a Friend Who Objects," to Pope Benedict XV, who acknowledged them with sympathetic encouragement.

The first steps toward improving Catholic higher education in China were taken in 1920, when Dr. George B. O'Toole, a seminary professor and a Benedictine Oblate of St. Vincent's Arch-abbey in Pennsylvania, visited China to discuss with Ying Lien-chih his proposal for a Catholic university. Dr. O'Toole left China in January 1921 and reported his findings in Rome on his way back to the United States. As a result, Pope Benedict XV directed the head of the Benedictine Order to consult American representatives of the order regarding the possibility of establishing such a university. The American Benedictines accepted this new responsibility in 1923, and the first monks of that order arrived in Peking in 1924, followed the next year by Abbot Stehle and Dr. O'Toole, whom the Holy See had appointed chancellor and rector, respectively, of the new university.

In 1925 Fu-jen (Catholic) university was established on its new campus at Peking together with the MacManus Academy of Chinese Studies. Throughout the arduous preparations for opening the new university, Ying Lien-chih bore a major share of such practical responsibilities as supervising the renovation of the new premises, managing finances, and establishing admission procedures for the first classes. Because he was participating in the fulfillment of a lifelong dream, he refused to accept compensation for his many labors. In the summer of 1925, despite poor health, he accepted the deanship of the MacManus Academy of Chinese Studies. Though his strength failed rapidly during the remaining months of that year, he continued to work on a book about Benedictine monasticism and completed a syllabus of courses for the academy.

Ying Lien-chih died of cancer on 10 January 1926 in Peking. Two months later, on 2 March 1926, Pope Pius XI honored him with the Knighthood of St. Gregory the Great for his exemplary life and for his services to Fu-jen University. Ying's life was characterized not only by his religious devotion but also by his broad interest in learning and education. At a time when the Catholic Church was making few converts among the Chinese intelligentsia, Ying worked to extend the influence of the Church and its philosophy among Chinese intellectuals and, through them, into the life of modern China. He also worked for the reorientation of the Catholic Church's educational policy and for the rise of the Chinese clergy. As a Chinese patriot, Ying was a firm believer in "reform through evolution rather than revolution" and thought that the Church, as an agent of modern education, was potentially an important aid in the rehabilitation of traditional China. Ying Lien-chih was also widely known as a humanitarian. As a calligrapher of some repute, he turned his considerable income from calligraphy to charitable purposes in north China, working particularly for the assistance of orphans and for the relief of famine victims.

Yolbars

Yolbars (1888–), Uighur leader who opposed the oppressive administrations of Chin Shu-jen and Sheng Shih-ts'ai (qq.v.) in Sinkiang. After holding office in the National Government at Nanking and Chungking, he returned to Sinkiang to lead guerrilla forces against the Chinese Communists. The National Government appointed him governor of Sinkiang in April 1950. He retained that title after he moved to Taiwan in 1951.

Yanghissar in the Kashgar district of western Sinkiang was the birthplace of Yolbars, who was a Uighur. His parents died when he was young, and he was reared by an elder sister at Hami, where he received his early education. At the age of 15, Yolbars entered the service of the Muslim prince of Hami. Hami (or Komul), the key point of ingress to Central Asia across the desert road from China's northwestern province of Kansu, had long been a semi-independent Uighur (Turki) principality, with local affairs handled by its own ruling house. Yolbars was gradually promoted in the administrative hierarchy at Hami, and in 1911 he became a member of the local assembly there.

During the early years of the republican period, Yolbars remained at Hami. In 1922 he gained promotion to a rank which entitled him to the honorific title of khan; and in 1927 he became commissioner of communications. Between 1912 and 1928 the political situation in Sinkiang remained reasonably stable under the firm hand of Yang Tseng-hsin (q.v.). But the assassination of Yang in July 1928 introduced a period of turmoil when the province came under the corrupt and inefficient rule of his successor, Chin Shu-jen (q.v.).

When Maksud Shah, the reigning Muslim prince of Hami, died in November 1930, Chin laid the groundwork for disequilibrium by attempting to impose his direct rule, on the pretext that hereditary principalities should not be permitted to exist within the territory of the Chinese republic. He ordered Nasir, the young successor prince, to reside at the provincial capital of Urumchi (Tihwa), and plans were made to divide the khanate of Hami into three administrative districts on the Chinese pattern. At the same time, Chin encouraged Chinese famine refugees from his native Kansu to move into Turki farmlands. Local unrest grew, and in March 1931 the abduction of a Muslim woman by a Chinese tax collector sparked an anti-Chinese rebellion in the Hami area.

The outbreak assumed significant proportions when Yolbars and his colleague Khoja Niaz, both advisers of the prince of Hami, sought the aid of Muslim co-religionists in Kansu, a move which enlisted the military support of Ma Chung-ying (q.v.) and led to a bloody period of civil conflict within Sinkiang. After being wounded on his first sortie into eastern Sinkiang in the autumn of 1931, Ma Chung-ying temporarily withdrew to Kansu to regroup his forces. Muslim unrest spread in Sinkiang during 1932. In April 1933 a political coup at Urumchi brought the downfall of Chin Shu-jen, who fled the province, and the accession to power of Sheng Shih-ts'ai (q.v.). In May, Yolbars sent a new message to Ma Chung-ying stating that the time was ripe for a full-scale anti-Chinese drive. Ma and his forces at once took the field to attack Urumchi, with Yolbars in command of a reserve column. A large figure of a man, bearded and burly, Yolbars Khan was described by the Swedish explorer Sven Hedin, who was then in Sinkiang, as the Tiger Prince.

Shortly thereafter, Khoja Niaz disassociated himself from Ma Chung-ying's cause and in November 1933 established a so-called East Turkestan Republic in southern Sinkiang. Yolbars remained with Ma Chung-ying, and by the end of the year the rebel forces were threatening the provincial capital. In January 1934, however, the Muslim outbreak confronted a new obstacle when the Soviet Union, for strategic reasons related to Japanese pressure, intervened in Sinkiang to support Sheng Shih-ts'ai. Ma Chung-ying fled southward and destroyed the weakened political organization of the East Turkestan Republic, then located near Kashgar. By July the rebellion had been quelled. Ma Chung-ying transferred command of his remaining troops to his brother-in-law Ma Hu-shan and disappeared into the Soviet Union. Khoja Niaz by then had decided to work with Sheng Shih-ts'ai, and perhaps on his recommendation, Yolbars was named district magistrate of Hami, with the concurrent post of garrison commander there.

Sheng Shih-ts'ai then proceeded to consolidate political control of Sinkiang. In 1937 he carried out one of the many purges that characterized his rule in that province. The move was nominally directed against an "imperialist Japanese plot," but the actual objective was to extend his authority through southern Sinkiang. Again with Soviet military support, Sheng was able to oust Ma Hu-shan from his base at Khotan. A Soviet regiment was then moved to Hami; and Yolbars, under suspicion of being opposed to the autocratic rule of Sheng Shih-ts'ai, fled from the province.

Yolbars then went to Nanking, where he was given the rank of lieutenant general and appointed counselor to the Military Affairs Commission. When the Japanese drive up the Yangtze valley in 1937–38 forced the National Government to evacuate, Yolbars accompanied it to Chungking. There he spent the remaining war years, holding a sinecure position as counselor of the Szechwan-Sikang pacification office. He also became a member of the board of directors of the Islamic National Salvation Society (later China Islamic Association), headed by Pai Ch'ung-hsi (q.v.), an organization designed to mobilize the Muslims of China to support the war effort against Japan. In 1945, when the Sixth National Congress of the Kuomintang met at Chungking, Yolbars was elected to membership in its Central Supervisory Committee.

The year 1944 brought the downfall of Sheng Shih-ts'ai in Sinkiang, and the Kuomintang moved to extend Nationalist authority into

China's largest frontier province. That effort was complicated by the eruption in November 1944 of a new anti-Chinese rebellion in the Ili district, which excluded Chinese authority from the northwestern districts of the province. In 1946 Yolbars attended the meetings of the National Assembly at Nanking. He then returned to Sinkiang to serve as adviser to the provincial government at Urumchi. A temporary truce agreement with the Ili rebels had been arranged in January 1946, and in July of that year a coalition government under Chang Chih-chung (q.v.) was organized at Urumchi. At that time Yolbars was named special executive commissioner for the ninth district in eastern Sinkiang.

Civil war between the Nationalists and Communists in China flared up again in the summer of 1946, and that conflict complicated the efforts of Chang Chih-chung to consolidate stability in Sinkiang. In 1947 Yolbars was named executive supervisory commissioner and peace preservation commander at Hami. In 1948 he was given the additional title of strategy adviser to Chiang Kai-shek. In the following year he was made deputy commander of peace preservation forces in Sinkiang.

When elements of the Communist First Field Army moved from Kansu into Sinkiang in the autumn of 1949, scattered local forces attempted to mobilize resistance. These resistance forces in Sinkiang were composed chiefly of Kazakhs, Mongols, and Uighurs, but they fought under the Chinese Nationalist flag and under the command of Yolbars. Although Burhan (q.v.) had remained as governor of Sinkiang at the time of the "peaceful surrender" of that province to the Communists, the Chinese National Government in April 1950 named Yolbars governor of Sinkiang and commander in chief of pacification for the province. The vast extent of Sinkiang made it impossible for the Chinese Communists to consolidate control quickly, and Yolbars was able to carry on guerrilla warfare operations for several months. By July 1950, however, the resistance forces confronted shortages of grain, fodder, and ammunition; and they were forced to seek refuge, first in the mountains of Sinkiang, later in the Tunhuang area of Kansu.

Pursued by Chinese Communist units, Yolbars and his troops were forced to retreat deep into Tsinghai province in northeastern Tibet. There they were joined by anti-Communist forces led by Osman (q.v.). Yolbars argued that further resistance against Chinese Communist power was fruitless and counseled retreat into Tibet proper. Osman, however, had some 4,000 Kazakh refugees in his charge, and he refused to abandon his people. In September 1950 the two leaders parted. Osman remained in northern Tsinghai, where he was captured in February 1951. Yolbars led his party, then numbering some 90-odd persons, southward into the K'unlun mountain range and on to the lofty Tibetan plateau. After a two-month trek over difficult terrain in deepening winter weather, they reached the border of Tibet proper, which had still not been occupied by the Chinese Communists. After a three-week wait to permit communication with the Tibetan authorities, Yolbars and the remnants of his band reached Lhasa in January 1951.

In Lhasa the government of the fourteenth Dalai Lama was already negotiating with Peking regarding the future status of Tibet in the People's Republic of China. When the Yolbars group requested permission to leave Tibet, the government of India granted entry permits for only six persons. Yolbars was forced to leave remaining personal troops, as well as several White Russian refugees from Sinkiang, behind in Tibet. With a handful of survivors, he proceeded overland to Calcutta. He then flew to Taiwan, arriving on that island on 1 May 1951.

In Taiwan, Yolbars, in his titular capacity as governor-in-exile of Sinkiang, established a provincial government office for his native province. He also continued to serve as a strategy adviser in the office of President Chiang Kai-shek. In view of his advancing years, the duties assigned were not onerous.

In Taiwan, at the age of 65, Yolbars married a girl of 19 to take the place of his former wife, who had died on the arduous march through Tibet. He had two sons by his first wife, Niaz Beg and Yakub Beg. The latter derived his name from the prominent Muslim adventurer from Khokand who had seized power in Sinkiang during the anti-Chinese rebellion in northwest China in the nineteenth century. From 1865 to 1877 Yakub Beg, in defiance of Ch'ing authority, ruled much of the Tarim basin as an independent Muslim state.

Yü Han-mou   余 漢 謀
T. Wo-ch'i   握 奇

Yü Han-mou (1891–), Kwangtung Army commander and subordinate of Ch'en Chi-t'ang (q.v.) whose defection to the National Government in 1936 contributed to the avoidance of civil war between Canton and Nanking. In 1948 he served briefly as commander in chief of the Chinese land forces.

Little is known about Yü Han-mou's family background or early life except that he was born in Kaoyao hsien, Kwangtung. He enrolled in the Paoting Military Academy about 1913, and he was graduated in 1919 with the sixth class, a class which produced such well-known Cantonese military men of the period as Teng Yen-ta, Hsueh Yueh (qq.v.), and Li Han-hun. Li Yang-ching, another Cantonese member of the same class, became a close colleague of Yü Han-mou, and they served together under Ch'en Chi-t'ang (q.v.).

Yü Han-mou began his active military career in 1923 as a battalion commander in the 1st Division of the Kwangtung Army under Teng K'eng (q.v.). By the time Ch'en Chi-t'ang assumed control of Kwangtung province in 1930, Yü had become commander of the 1st Division. After the short-lived secessionist movement at Canton in 1931, the province of Kwangtung maintained itself in a state of semi-autonomy with respect to the National Government and the central authorities of the Kuomintang based at Nanking. As Ch'en Chi-t'ang began to consolidate power in south China, he expanded his military forces. Yü Han-mou then was made commander of the First Army under Ch'en Chi-t'ang and pacification commissioner of the northwestern portion of Kwangtung. He came to be regarded as Ch'en's most trusted military assistant.

As the aggressive military intentions of the Japanese became increasingly obvious during the 1930's, the anomalous semi-autonomy of the southern provinces of Kwangtung and Kwangsi became increasingly intolerable to the National Government at Nanking. In the spring of 1936 Ch'en Chi-t'ang, with the support of Li Tsung-jen (q.v.) in adjacent Kwangsi province, moved to settle their differ-

ences with Chiang Kai-shek through open military action. Ch'en then organized an expeditionary force to march northward, ostensibly to go to Manchuria to fight the Japanese but actually to bring about the downfall of Chiang Kai-shek at Nanking. Yü Han-mou's army served as the vanguard force, moving toward Kanchow in Kiangsi province.

Ch'en Chi-t'ang's move won no real support, and a series of defections soon began. The Canton air force, which Ch'en had built up, was the first to act; on 4 July 1936 a group of pilots flew their aircraft to Nanchang, where they surrendered to the National Government authorities. On 8 July, Yü Han-mou flew to Nanking, where he discussed problems of mutual interest with Chiang Kai-shek. Yü then issued an appeal which called for a halt to hostilities, requested his colleagues in the Kwangtung military forces to join him in forcing Ch'en Chi-t'ang to retire, and stated that he was moving his army back toward Canton. Details of the practical arrangements which stimulated this action were not disclosed.

Yü Han-mou's defection was generally considered the greatest single factor in the avoidance of civil war between Canton and Nanking in 1936. Seeing that the situation was lost, Ch'en Chi-t'ang quietly left Canton for Hong Kong and retired from the political and military scene. For his contribution to national unification, Yü Han-mou was rewarded with an assignment as the top military commander of Kwangtung, with the title of pacification commissioner at Canton. The National Government simultaneously made a careful choice in the appointment of Huang Mu-sung (q.v.) as civil governor of Kwangtung. Huang had previously been dean of the Paoting Military Academy and Yü Han-mou's teacher there, and the move was clearly designed by Nanking to avert possible friction between the civil and military authorities in that important southern province.

After the outbreak of war between China and Japan in 1937 and the fall of Canton to the Japanese forces, Yü Han-mou moved his army to northern Kwangtung, where it was reorganized as the Twelfth Group Army. As its commander in chief, Yü was also named deputy commanding general of the Fourth War Area, later redesignated the Seventh War Area. Later, after a further administrative demarcation,

Yü Han-mou [62]

Yü received command of the South China War Area. After the Japanese surrender in 1945, he was assigned for a period as pacification commander based at Chuchow in Kiangsi province. In May 1948 the National Government appointed him commander in chief of the land forces of the Chinese Army. By then, however, the military situation was rapidly deteriorating for the Nationalists as Chinese Communist forces moved southward over the mainland. At the beginning of 1949, when plans were made to make a final stand against the Communists in south China, Hsueh Yueh (q.v.) was assigned to replace T. V. Soong (q.v.) as governor of Kwangtung province, and Yü Han-mou was transferred back to Canton as pacification commissioner. In the spring of that year, the National Government also reorganized Hainan Island as a special district and placed Ch'en Chi-t'ang in charge with the intention of securing that island as a last base. When Canton fell to the Chinese Communist forces in October 1949, Yü Han-mou moved to Hainan to assist his former chief. But the effort on Hainan was made too late, and the Nationalist commanders also had to evacuate that island in April 1950.

Yü Han-mou then went to Taiwan, where he was given a sinecure post as a member of the military advisory council. Following the deaths in Taiwan during the 1950's of such veteran Cantonese personalities as Wu T'ieh-ch'eng, Ch'en Chi-t'ang, and Wang Ch'ung-hui, Yü Han-mou came to be regarded by his fellow provincials as one of the most senior Kwangtung leaders on the island.

Yü Hsueh-chung 于 學 忠
T. Hsiao-hou 孝 侯

Yü Hsueh-chung (1889–22 September 1964), governor of Hopei in 1932–35 and of Kansu in 1936. He took part in the Sian Incident of December 1936. During the Sino-Japanese war, he served as commander of the Third and Fifth Group armies and as vice chairman of the Military Advisory Council. After 1949 he held minor government posts in the People's Republic of China.

Little is known about Yü Hsueh-chung's family background or early life except that he

was born in P'englai hsien, Shantung, and that he was graduated from a battalion school at Tungchow, Chihli (Hopei), in 1911. In 1914 Yü became aide de camp to the defense commissioner of Linsi, Jehol. After the death of Yuan Shih-k'ai in 1916 and the breakup of the Peiyang party, Yü was associated with the Chihli clique, serving in the forces of Ts'ao K'un and Wu P'ei-fu (qq.v.). He rose steadily in rank, becoming commander of the 18th Mixed Brigade in 1923 and commander of the 26th Division and of the Chingchow-Hsiang-yang defense area in Hupeh in 1926. When Wu P'ei-fu's troops were defeated by the Northern Expedition forces in 1926, Yü left his service and remained in western Hupeh. In the spring of 1927 he received command of the Fifteenth Army of the Chihli-Shantung Joint Army. In the final battles of 1928 between the northern warlords led by Chang Tso-lin (q.v.) and the Northern Expedition forces, Yü commanded the Twentieth Fengtien Army of the Ankuochün [national pacification army]. With the defeat of the Ankuochün and the death of Chang Tso-lin, Yü retreated with the Manchurian forces to Shanhaikuan.

Yü Hsueh-chung then became military affairs counselor in the Northeastern frontier defense headquarters of Chang Hsueh-liang (q.v.). In addition, he served as Luanchow defense commander. When the Northeastern forces intervened in north China in 1930 at the climax of the struggle between the National Government and the northern coalition of Feng Yü-hsiang and Yen Hsi-shan (qq.v.), Yü occupied Tientsin as commander of the First Northeastern Army and became Peiping-Tientsin garrison commander. In 1931 he was appointed to the Northeast Political Council.

In September 1932 Yü Hsueh-chung reached the peak of his power in north China when he was made governor of Hopei, with concurrent command of the Fifty-first Army. He held that post until June 1935 when, in accordance with Sino-Japanese agreements (see Ho Ying-ch'in), he and his army were transferred to northwest China. Yü was designated commander of the Szechwan-Shensi-Kansu border area and governor of Kansu. Later in 1935 he was elected to the Central Executive Committee of the Kuomintang.

In 1935–36 Yü Hsueh-chung participated in

campaigns against the Chinese Communists in northern Shensi. At the time of the Sian Incident in December 1936 (*see* Chang Hsueh-liang; Chiang Kai-shek), Yü was at Sian, and when Chang Hsueh-liang accompanied Chiang Kai-shek to Nanking on 25 December, Yü and Yang Hu-ch'eng (q.v.) were left in charge of military affairs at Sian. They promptly demanded implementation of the agreement to end the civil war with the Communists and to establish a united front against the Japanese. They also demanded the release of Chang Hsueh-liang, who was being held at Nanking. Early in January 1937 the National Government removed Yü and Yang from their posts, appointing Wang Shu-ch'ang to succeed Yü as governor of Kansu. Although Yü and Yang disagreed about strategy, they acted together in challenging the National Government and then agreeing at the end of January to the reorganization and redeployment of their troops. In March, the Fifty-first Army of Yü Hsueh-chung was ordered to the Huaiyin-Huaian-Pengpu sector of Kiangsu. At about the same time, Yü and Yang called on Chiang Kai-shek at Hangchow "to receive instructions." Yang was sent abroad, but Yü was appointed to a new post—military affairs commissioner for Kiangsu.

After the Sino-Japanese war began in 1937, Yü Hsueh-chung was given responsibility for military operations in the Tsingtao sector, where Japanese naval forces had landed in mid-August. The Japanese then advanced in the direction of Tsinan. In mid-December, Yü's force entered Tsingtao to destroy Japanese-owned enterprises. He was forced to withdraw after the Shantung governor, Han Fu-chü (q.v.), abandoned Tsinan to the Japanese on 25 December. The Japanese occupied Tsingtao without resistance on 10 January 1938. With the arrest of Han Fu-chü on 11 January on charges of dereliction of duty, the Shantung troops were transferred to Yü Hsueh-chung's command, together with one division each of Kwangtung and Szechwan troops. Yü's combined forces became the Third Group Army, and it participated in the stubborn defense of Hsuchow and Pengpu. The campaign in that sector ended with the battle of Taierhchuang, and Yü then was transferred to command of the Fifth Group Army. In 1939 he was appointed commander in chief of the Kiangsu-

Shantung War Area, which, however, was both Communist-controlled and behind the Japanese lines. In 1941 Yü was named chairman of the Nationalist provincial government of Shantung. He was removed from field command in 1944 and was made vice chairman of the Military Advisory Council in Chungking. After the Japanese surrender, he served as a member of the Military Strategy Advisory Commission at Nanking.

Yü Hsueh-chüng remained in China after the People's Republic of China was established in October 1949. In December 1952 he was named a member of the Hopei provincial government; and he was a delegate from that province to the National People's Congress in 1954. In September 1954 he received membership in the National Defense Council at Peking, and in 1956 he was elected to the central committee of the Kuomintang Revolutionary Committee. Yü Hsueh-chung died at Peking, of illness, on 22 September 1964, at the age of 73 sui.

Yü Hung-chün   俞鴻鈞
West. O. K. Yui

Yü Hung-chün (1897–1 June 1960), known as O. K. Yui. After holding office as mayor of Shanghai in 1937, he served as vice minister of finance in 1941–44 and as minister of finance in 1945–48. In Taiwan, he was governor in 1953 and president of the Executive Yuan in 1954–57.

Although O. K. Yui was born at Shanghai, his ancestral home was in Hsinhui (Sunwui) hsien, Kwangtung. His family was part of the well-to-do Cantonese business community at Shanghai. Yui received a modern education and was graduated from St. John's University in Shanghai in 1919. He then went to the United States, where he took graduate work in economics at the University of Michigan, studying under Professor C. F. Remer and others. After his return to China, he worked for a time as a reporter on the staff of the Shanghai English-language newspaper, *China Press.* He later entered the government service and worked in the ministry of foreign affairs.

O. K. Yui's first significant period of public service began in 1930, when he joined the staff of the Shanghai municipal government as a secretary handling foreign affairs. His task grew more difficult as Japanese military pressure on China increased, but Yui discharged his duties so well that he soon became secretary general of the Shanghai municipal government. He held that position until 1937. Early in 1937 he was appointed to succeed Wu T'ieh-ch'eng (q.v.) as acting mayor of Shanghai. In April 1937, as the international situation became increasingly critical, Yui was confirmed as mayor.

War between China and Japan broke out in July 1937. Only a month later, in August, the hostilities spread to Shanghai. The civic center district, in which the offices of the municipal government were located, was the first area to be affected by fighting. That area soon became untenable, and the government had to be moved to the old native city area of Shanghai. During the emergency, O. K. Yui's administrative abilities were heavily taxed, for he had to confront several complex tasks simultaneously: maintenance of order, relief of war refugees, removal of supplies, and, above all, the evacuation of the municipal government and its personnel. His performance in the 1937 crisis demonstrated his fine administrative capacities. After the evacuation to Chungking, Yui continued to hold the title of mayor of Shanghai. In that capacity he made broadcasts from the wartime capital to the people of Shanghai to bolster their morale and to call for their patience under the Japanese occupation pending the return of his government to Shanghai.

During his service in Shanghai, O. K. Yui had become known to the influential Soong family (q.v.). Due partly to his personal connections with two of its members, Soong Ai-ling, the wife of H. H. K'ung (q.v.), and Soong Mei-ling (q.v.), the wife of Chiang Kai-shek, Yui gained new prominence in the field of public finance during the Sino-Japanese war. From 1938 to 1941 he was managing director of the Central Trust of China, a government bank. During the decade after 1938, Yui also wrestled with the perplexing fiscal and economic problems of the National Government. For more than three years, from June 1941 until November 1944, he served as vice minister of finance under H. H. K'ung. He succeeded K'ung as minister of finance of the National Government at the end of 1944 and held that

position until May 1948. In 1945 Yui was concurrently appointed governor of the Central Bank of China, succeeding H. H. K'ung. In 1948, when official corruption, inflation, and the black market clogged the Chinese economic system, Yui also served as chairman of the supervisory committee for enforcement of economic controls in the Shanghai area.

After the Communist victory on the mainland in 1949 and the transfer of the National Government to Taiwan, O. K. Yui also moved to that island. There he was appointed governor of the Bank of Taiwan, chairman of the central financial affairs committee, and a member of the economic stabilization board. In April 1953 he was named to succeed K. C. Wu (Wu Kuo-chen, q.v.) as governor of Taiwan. O. K. Yui reached the peak of his public career in June 1954, when he was appointed president of the Executive Yuan at Taipei. His four-year tenure in that post coincided with several international crises in the Far East and with continued tensions within the Kuomintang. Although O. K. Yui was known as a loyal Kuomintang member, he was confronted in the winter of 1957 with impeachment proceedings brought by members of the Control Yuan in Taiwan. Several charges were leveled, including abuse of power and failure to permit the Control Yuan to inspect the books of the Central Bank of China, of which Yui, as premier, was governor. The dispute in early 1958, which reflected intraparty jealousies and frictions within the Kuomintang, led to an official reprimand for the premier. O. K. Yui then submitted his resignation as president of the Executive Yuan to Chiang Kai-shek. It was accepted at the end of June 1958, and Yui retired to private life. He died of asthma at Taipei two years later, on 1 June 1960.

Yü Jih-chang　　　　余 日 章
　Alt.　Yui Zek-tsang
　West. David Z. T. Yui

Yü Jih-chang (25 November 1882–22 January 1936), known as David Yui, general secretary of the YMCA in China from 1916 to 1932.

The son of a Christian minister in Hupeh, David Yui received his early education in the Chinese classics at Wuchang and his higher education at two mission institutions, Boone University at Wuchang and St. John's University at Shanghai. He received a B.A. degree from St. John's in 1905. In 1908 he went to the United States for graduate study in education at Harvard University, where he received his M.S. with honors in 1910, together with the Bowdoin prize for his essay "Schools in Old China."

In the autumn of 1910 David Yui was appointed associate general secretary of the Chinese Student Christian Association in the United States, but illness in his family required him to return to China in November. His first appointment on his return to Wuchang was that of headmaster at the Boone School. He also served briefly as commissioner for foreign affairs in Hupeh province. In 1912 he was associate editor of the *Peking Daily News*, the semi-official organ of the republican government in Peking. He also became private secretary to Li Yuan-hung (q.v.), the first vice president of the new government at Peking and a fellow provincial from Hupeh. In 1913 Yui was appointed secretary of the lecture division of the national committee of the Young Men's Christian Association. He devoted the next two years to lecturing in major cities throughout China to promote interest in YMCA programs designed to extend modern education. At the same time he cooperated with Huang Yen-p'ei (q.v.) in establishing the influential Kiangsu provincial education association. When John R. Mott, founder and foremost leader of the international student Christian movement, visited China in 1913, Yui accompanied him on his speaking tour, sharing interpreting duties with Ch'eng Ching-yi (q.v.). In 1915, at the invitation of Chang Chien (q.v.), then minister of agriculture and commerce in the Peking government, Yui served as adviser and honorary secretary to a Chinese trade commission touring the United States. For almost two months (May–June) the commission visited principal centers throughout the country under the auspices of the Associated Chambers of Commerce of the Pacific Coast.

During the first five years of his career in China, David Yui demonstrated abilities which led to his appointment in 1916 to the highest administrative post in the Chinese YMCA. After four years as secretary of the lecture division and as acting head of the education division, he became, at the age of 34, acting general secretary of the national committee of the YMCA. He soon advanced to the post of general secretary, succeeding C. T. Wang (Wang Cheng-t'ing, q.v.). He held that post for the remaining 16 years of his active career. In the 1920's and the early 1930's the YMCA developed rapidly as it responded to abrupt and radical changes in Chinese life.

At the time of the Washington Conference of 1921, the Shanghai Chamber of Commerce and the National Federation of Educational Associations organized a league of foreign relations to send two observers to the meeting. The league commissioned David Yui and Chiang Monlin (Chiang Meng-lin, q.v.), who left Shanghai on 15 October 1921 as "citizens' representatives" to ensure that Chinese interests were adequately interpreted and considered. Yui and Chiang were particularly involved in the protracted negotiations over the disposition of the Kiaochow-Tsinan railway in Shantung. Despite the active opposition of the Chinese premier at Peking, Liang Shih-i (q.v.), the presence of David Yui and Chiang Monlin encouraged the official Chinese delegation, headed by Sao-ke Alfred Sze (Shih Chao-chi, q.v.), to accept the Japanese proposal that China redeem the railway with funds to be raised in China. David Yui, aware of the divided counsel at Peking and of the Chinese government's disinclination to enter into such a commitment, was confident that private groups within China, given adequate leadership, could guarantee the necessary funds. Thus the task of raising the equivalent of ¥40 million fell largely to him. He organized a society for the redemption of the Shantung railway and personally administered its fund-raising drive. The full amount, in Chinese government treasury notes, was remitted to Japan in 1922.

When the National Christian Council of China was organized in 1922, David Yui was elected chairman. He continued to hold this position, in addition to his YMCA duties, for the next ten years. At the same time, he served as an officer of the World Student Christian Federation. In June 1923, when he was just over 40, Yui's health deteriorated to such an extent that he was obliged to restrict the pace of his work drastically. Nevertheless, he continued to bear heavy responsibilities, and his influence bore directly upon many activities of international significance. As a founder and chairman of the Institute of Pacific Relations in China, he led the Chinese delegation to the second international conference of the IPR at Honolulu in 1927, where, according to the *North China Herald*, "the Chinese delegation dominated all others. Dr. David Yui was the outstanding personality of the Conference. He developed such a keen interest in Chinese affairs that many of the delegates took a new view of the Far Eastern situation." In 1928 he was a prominent figure at the Jerusalem conference of the International Missionary Council.

After the Japanese invasion of Manchuria in 1931, David Yui undertook a special mission to the United States in 1932 in an attempt to arouse American support for China. While in Washington for conferences with Secretary of State Henry L. Stimson, he suffered a cerebral hemorrhage on 4 January 1933. After resting for a few months in the United States, Yui returned to Shanghai in August 1933, where he remained, largely incapacitated, until his death in January 1936.

Two major principles underlay David Yui's philosophy of life and work. He believed that individual character was the key to the solution of national problems. He thought that adequate and widespread programs aimed at individual character development among Chinese youth a generation earlier would have greatly aided the Chinese nation as he knew it in the republican period. "National salvation through the development of individual integrity" (jen-ko chiu-kuo), a phrase attributed to David Yui, gained wide acceptance in China during the 1920's and 1930's. Yui's second basic principle was that the YMCA was an instrument for the development and strengthening of China, not an end in itself. Throughout his career in the YMCA, he promoted training in citizenship for all age groups. In the early 1920's, when there was general skepticism of the possibility of extending literacy on a mass basis, David Yui invited James Yen (Yen Yang-ch'u, q.v.) to join his staff and provided both personal encouragement and congenial working conditions while Yen planned a long-range program to attack the problem of illiteracy in China.

David Yui's deliberate commitment to the ideal of the YMCA as a service organization devoted to the national good of modern China led him to decline many offers of important posts in government, education, business, and

banking. Significantly, his active career was spent in directing an organization whose program included an explicit definition of moral principles and in which his contribution to the welfare of individuals and of China depended solely upon the force of personal influence and persuasion.

Yü Pin 于 斌
West. Paul Yu-pin
T.   Yeh-sheng 野 聲
H.   Kuan-wu 冠 五

Yü Pin (1901–), Archbishop of Nanking and rector of Fu-jen University in Taiwan. In 1969 he became the second Chinese to be designated a cardinal of the Roman Catholic Church.

Although his ancestral home was at Ch'angi, Shantung, Yü Pin was born at Wu-chia-o-p'eng, Lanhsi, in Heilungkiang province. He was the son of Yü Shui-yuan. Both of Yü Pin's parents and his sister died before he was seven years old, and he went to Hai-pei-chen in the Hailun district to live with his grandparents. His grandfather, Yü Kang, was a practitioner of native medicine. From 1910 to 1912 Yü Pin attended the Hsing family school, and in 1912 he entered the Hailun county grammar school. Both of his grandparents were converts to Roman Catholicism, and under their guidance he became a regular churchgoer. In 1913 he was baptized and was given the Christian name Paul. He entered the Heilungkiang Provincial Normal School in 1915. During the May Fourth Movement of 1919 he was chosen to represent his school at a student mass protest meeting at Tsitsihar. Because he was an earnest student, Yü scheduled his school's demonstrations on holidays only.

In the autumn of 1919 Yü Pin entered the Sheng-lo hsueh-yuan, or Latin Academy, in Kirin province, a preparatory school for young men who wished to enter the priesthood. There he began to study French, English, Italian, and Spanish. His progress in all areas was such that the Bishop of Kirin sent him to study at Aurora University (*see* Ma Liang) in Shanghai, where he specialized in French. Yü finished his course of study within a year and returned to Kirin. In December 1924 he enrolled at the Collegium Urbanum in Rome. While in Rome, Yü served successively as vice president and president of the Chinese Students Association, which then had a membership of six. He passed his examinations with honors in 1925 and received a Ph.D. degree from the St. Thomas Academy in 1926. On 22 December 1928 he was ordained a priest. The following year, he received a Th.D. from the Collegium Urbanum, where he also taught. At the same time, he studied ecclesiastical law at the College of Apollonaris. His diplomatic abilities were recognized in 1929, when Pope Pius XI appointed him to a five-man delegation to Ethiopia.

After the Japanese attacked Mukden in September 1931 Father Yü helped form and served as vice president of the Sino-Italian Amity Society, which worked to win support for China. In 1933 he received a doctorate in political economy from the University of Perugia. That December, he returned to China as the head of the newly formed Chung-kuo kung-chiao chin-hsing-hui, or Chinese Catholic Action Committee. In China, he also served as secretary to the office of the Papal Nuncio and as professor of ethics at Fu-jen (Catholic) University. In 1934 he received a concurrent appointment as chief inspector of Catholic schools in China.

On 7 July 1936 Yü Pin was appointed Bishop of Nanking. After the Sino-Japanese war began in July 1937, Bishop Yü also served as head of the Chung-hua t'ien-chu-chiao chiu-hu tsung-hui, or General Catholic Relief and Welfare Association of China, which gave aid to wounded soldiers and war refugees. He accompanied the National Government to Chungking, where he became a member of the People's Political Council in 1938. Throughout the war, Bishop Yü made frequent trips to Europe and the United States as an envoy of the National Government.

At the time of the Japanese surrender in 1945, Bishop Yü was in Rome discussing the establishment of a regular hierarchy in China. This was done on 11 April 1946, and Yü Pin was appointed Archbishop of Nanking with jurisdiction over the entire province of Kiangsu. Upon his return to China, Archbishop Yü worked to build up a national circulation for the *I-shih pao* (see Lei Ming-yuan), and made that newspaper the organ of the Chinese Catholic Cultural Association. Archbishop Yü continued to travel extensively. In 1946 and 1947 he visited Manchuria, and in 1947 he also went to Taiwan to inspect Catholic churches there. He participated in the National Assembly at Nanking in March 1948 and served on its presidium. That winter, he went to the United States and thence to Rome. In 1949 he visited the United States again and went on to Rome by way of London, Paris, and Geneva. He also visited Portugal before his return to Canton that summer.

When the Chinese Communists emerged victorious in the contest for control of the mainland, neither Archbishop Yü Pin nor Cardinal T'ien (T'ien Keng-hsin, q.v.) was in China. Archbishop Yü traveled to the United States by way of Taiwan. He then organized the Chinese Catholic Cultural Mission to South America to enlist support for the Nationalists. He returned to the United States in 1950 to lead a Chinese Eucharistic mission to the Vatican that July and in 1952 to establish the Sino-American Amity Fund in New York. Also in 1952 he traveled to Spain for the International Eucharist Congress at Barcelona and to arrange for the resumption of diplomatic relations between Spain and Nationalist China. At his behest, an academy was established for Chinese students in Spain.

During the 1960's, Archbishop Yü, though he had no diocesan authority in Taiwan, continued as an energetic leader of Catholic activities there while he also served as a member of the National Assembly and of the ruling political party, the Kuomintang. Commissioned by Pope John XXIII to reestablish Fu-jen (Catholic) University of Peking (see Ying Lien-chih) in Taiwan, he worked actively to raise funds for the new institution and became its first rector when it was opened in 1963 on a campus near Taipei. In March 1969 Pope Paul VI named Yü Pin, in his capacity as exiled Archbishop of Nanking, to the college of cardinals as the successor to Thomas Cardinal T'ien, the first Chinese cardinal, who died in Taiwan in 1967.

Yü P'ing-po　　　　　　　俞　平　伯
　Orig. Ming-heng　　　　　銘　衡
　T.　Chih-min　　　　　　　直　民
　H.　Ch'ü-chai　　　　　　　屈　齋

Yü P'ing-po (1899–), essayist, poet, critic, scholar, and professor. He was best known for his writings on the *Hung-lou-meng* and for the nation-wide campaign against them and him in 1954.

A native of Tech'ing, Chekiang, Yü P'ing-po was born into a family which had a long tradition of scholarship and literary endeavor. He was the great-grandson of the famous classical scholar Yü Yueh (ECCP, II, 944–45) and the son of Yü Pi-yün (1868–1950; T. Chieh-ch'ing), a chin-shih degree holder and Hanlin compiler who in 1902 became assistant examiner in the provincial examinations in Szechwan. After the republican revolution, he lived in retirement in Peking. His publications included an itinerary of the journey to Szechwan entitled *Ju Shu i-ch'eng chi*, a collection of poems in the tz'u form entitled *Lo ching tz'u*, and an introduction to the "regulated verse" of the T'ang dynasty entitled *Shih ching ch'ien shuo*.

Although his parents resided in Peking after 1912, Yü P'ing-po seems to have spent the first 16 years of his life at the family home in Soochow. In the absence of his parents, his elder half-sisters supervised him. Yü P'ei-hsün, the second of his elder sisters, who died when Yü P'ing-po was about 30, wrote poems which were collected after her death and published as *Han yen T'ang ch'in shih i shih, Ju ying lou tz'u*. In 1916 Yü P'ing-po enrolled at Peking University. The following year, he married Hsü Ying-huan. Her brothers Hsü Pao-k'uei and Hsü Pao-lu became close friends of Yü and collaborated with him on a translation of Edgar Allen Poe's "The Oblong Box," which was published in the *Hsin-yueh yueh-k'an* [crescent moon monthly]. While at Peking University, Yü came under the influence of Lu Hsün (Chou Shu-jen) and Chou Tso-jen (qq.v.), and he began writing in pai-hua [the vernacular]. Yü was also associated with the student group at Peking University which in 1919 began publication of the magazine *Hsin-ch'ao* [renaissance]; the group also included Chu Tzu-ch'ing, Feng Yu-lan, Fu Ssu-nien, and Yeh Sheng-t'ao (qq.v.).

After being graduated from Peking University in 1919, Yü P'ing-po spent a few months at Hangchow before sailing for Europe with Fu Ssu-nien in January 1920. It is unlikely that Yü derived much pleasure or profit from this trip, for he was a lifelong xenophobe. He quickly succumbed to homesickness after arrival in England. Although Fu Ssu-nien followed him to Paris and Marseilles in a vain effort to dissuade him, Yü returned to Peking in 1921. At that time Ku Chieh-kang (q.v.), who had been reading the first draft of the *Hung-lou-meng k'ao cheng* by Hu Shih (q.v.), was collecting materials bearing on the origins of the great eighteenth-century novel, the *Hung-lou-meng* (*The Dream of the Red Chamber*). His enthusiasm infected Yü P'ing-po who, when Ku Chieh-kang went to Soochow to care for his ailing grandmother, corresponded with him on the subject in April–July 1921. This correspondence became the nucleus of Yü's *Hung-lou-meng pien*, completed in 1921 and published, with a preface by Ku, by the Oriental Book Company in 1923.

In 1922 Yü P'ing-po went to the United States. While in New York, he wrote "Ch'ang-shih ti wen-i t'an" [common-sense talk about literature], which appeared in *Chien Ch'iao*, a collection of essays and short stories by Yü and Yeh Sheng-t'ao which was published in 1924. *Hsi huan* [return from the West], a collection of poems published after his return from America, also must have been written abroad, for Yü wrote elsewhere that the postscript to *Hsi huan* was composed "in 1922 on a ship in the Pacific."

Yü spent most of the period from the autumn of 1922 to the autumn of 1924 in central China, teaching for a time at Shanghai University and then living in his great-grandfather's house on West Lake in Hangchow. Yü's account of a 1923 excursion on the Ch'in-huai river with his life-long friend Chu Tzu-ch'ing, "Chiang-sheng teng-ying li ti Ch'in-huai ho," was a classic of its kind. After witnessing the collapse in September 1925 of the tenth-century Thunder Peak Pagoda, he wrote two scholarly studies about it—one on the history of the pagoda and another on the miniature sutras sealed inside it. On the basis of lectures he had delivered at Shanghai University, in October 1923 he wrote what was to become the main part of the *Tu shih cha chi* [notes on the Book of Songs]. Yü's comical preface to this book describes the difficulties and delays he encountered before it was finally published in 1934. Parts of it appeared in 1924 in the *Yenching Journal* and in 1931 in the third volume of the *Ku-shih pien*, edited by Ku Chieh-kang.

In the late autumn of 1924 Yü P'ing-po went to Peking to join the faculty of Yenching

University. He later taught at Tsinghua and Peking universities. Apart from some early experiments in "new poetry" collected in *Tung yeh*, *Hsi huan*, and *I*, his creative writing in the pre-war period consisted almost entirely of short prose pieces, many of which were introductions, prefaces, and appreciations written for or about books by his friends. Some were in wen-yen, others in pai-hua, and still others in that strange mixture of the two which is peculiarly characteristic of his style. Very few of his essays dealt with political matters. He wrote a few articles deploring foreign encroachments on China's rights, one of which showed that he was familiar with Marxist terminology and turns of phrase. On such topics as education or the position of women in society, he expressed conservative views. Collections of these shorter writings include *Tsa pan erh*, of 1928; *Tsa pan erh II*, of 1933; *Yen chiao chi*, of 1936, and *Ku huai meng yü*, of 1936. His scholarly publications included an introduction to the tz'u form entitled *Tu tz'u ou te*, which was published in 1934.

Yü P'ing-po remained in Peiping after the Sino-Japanese war began in July 1937, and he taught at Peking University throughout the Japanese occupation. At war's end, he was allowed to resume his duties as a professor of literature after the professors and students who had been in west China returned to Peiping and reestablished Peking University. His research during and after the Second World War centered on tz'u poetry and on the poets Chou Pang-yen and Tu Fu. He published a revised edition of *Tu tz'u ou te* in 1947 and a commentary on selected poems of Chou Pang-yen, *Ch'ing-chen tz'u shih*, in 1948. He also produced a revised version of the *Hung-lou-meng pien* entitled *Hung-lou-meng yen-chiu*, which was published in Shanghai in 1952.

Although Yü P'ing-po remained in Peking after the People's Republic of China was established, he made no attempt to incorporate Marxist ideas into his published writings. His lack of enthusiasm for political indoctrination, his slightly haughty manner, and his sometimes unintelligible Chekiang accent made him a far from popular lecturer. In 1952 he resigned to become a member of the Peking University Literary Research Institute, where he devoted his time to the task of collating all available manuscripts of the so-called Chih-yen-chai commentary on the *Hung-lou-meng*.

In the autumn of 1953, a year after the publication of Yü's *Hung-lou-meng yen-chiu*, a congress of the Writers' Union took as its theme the rehabilitation of China's literary heritage, a matter which had been discussed by Wen Huai-sha in his postscript to Yü's work. The Tso-chia ch'u-pan-she [author's publishing company] and a related institute of literary studies were established to publish new editions of Chinese classical literature. The first publication of this new organization, a three-volume edition of the *Hung-lou-meng*, appeared in December 1953. As an authority on the *Hung-lou-meng*, Yü P'ing-po was now under constant pressure to produce articles and reviews for popular consumption. Because he realized that anything he wrote of this nature probably would be politically unacceptable, he was unwilling to comply with most of these requests. It appears that several articles published under his name at this time were partly or wholly the work of his research assistant, Wang P'ei-chang. He offended an important Chinese Communist party propagandist, Hu Ch'iao-mu, by failing to incorporate suggested alterations in an article entitled "Hung-lou-meng chien lun," which was published in the magazine *Hsin chien-she*. He also published a savagely critical review of the Tso-chia ch'u-pan-she edition of the *Hung-lou-meng* in the 1 March 1954 issue of the *Kuang-ming jih-pao*.

Late in 1954 Chou Yang (q.v.) and others launched a campaign against Yü P'ing-po and Hu Shih which began with the publication of articles attacking them for failing to interpret the *Hung-lou-meng* as a novel of class struggle and an indictment of the extended Chinese family system of traditional times. On 24 October 1954, at a plenary session of the Writers' Union, Yü was directed to study Marxism and to mend his ways. Thereafter, he was denounced in the press, in periodicals, and at meetings (which he was forced to attend) throughout China for the better part of three months. Feng Hsueh-feng lost the editorship of the *Wen-i pao* because he defended Yü. Under the circumstances, it is surprising that Yü managed to publish an important contribution to *Hung-lou-meng* studies in

December 1954, the *Chih-yen-chai Hung-lou-meng chi-p'ing* [collected commentaries on the *Hung-lou-meng*]. Although Wang Erh was listed as the chief compiler of this work, his sole contribution to it was a three-paragraph foreword stating that the book had been examined carefully because of the serious charges against Yü and that it had been judged fit to print.

When the campaign against him ended, Yü P'ing-po, who had shown signs of breaking down in the course of it, demonstrated a remarkable resilience in returning to his *Hung-lou-meng* studies. In 1958, assisted by Wang Hsi-shih, he published the four-volume *Hung-lou-meng pa-shih-hui chiao pen*, a definitive edition of the *Hung-lou-meng* with extensive notes. In the preface to this work Yü admitted that he formerly had been misled by Hu Shih and conceded that the general sense of the *Hung-lou-meng* is "anti-feudal," but he carefully pointed out that in no sense are its characters "politically conscious."

Yü Ta-fu   郁 達 夫
T. Wen   文

Yü Ta-fu (1896–September 1945), a founding member of the Creation Society and one of the most important Chinese writers of the 1920's.

The youngest of three boys born into a poor but scholarly family in Fuyang, Chekiang, Yü Ta-fu received his early education in a variety of schools, including the Hangchow First Middle School. He read widely as a boy, devouring the Chinese classics, vernacular fiction, and translations by Lin Shu (q.v.) of Western fiction. After the republican revolution of 1911, he was sent to Japan, where he enrolled at the Tokyo First Middle School in 1912. Upon graduation in 1916, he entered Tokyo Imperial University, where he studied economics until 1922. During this period, most of Yü's time was spent in reading fiction and in the enjoyment of the pleasures which the Japanese capital afforded. He later estimated that in his four years at the Tokyo First Middle School alone he read close to 1,000 Western novels and short stories and that "if I was not reading novels, I was most often seen in cafes, seeking girl companions to drink wine with me. No one was studying hard . . . ."

During his sojourn in Japan, Yü Ta-fu came to know Kuo Mo-jo, Chang Tzu-p'ing, T'ien Han (qq.v.), and other Chinese students who were interested in literature. When Yü first met them he wrote only in classical Chinese, and he was accounted a good poet in the traditional forms. Under the influence of discussions with his new friends, Yü began to write in the vernacular style being advocated by Hu Shih and Ch'en Tu-hsiu (qq.v.). In the summer of 1921 Yü Ta-fu and his friends organized the Ch'uang-tsao she (Creation Society) to promote interest in modern literature. Also in 1921, Yü published his first collection of stories, *Ch'en-lun* [sinking]. The title story was a thinly disguised autobiographical account of the loneliness and sexual temptation experienced by a young Chinese student in Japan. The neurotic hero, after several voyeuristic experiences, is humiliated in a Japanese brothel because of his Chinese nationality. He spends the night drinking and kills himself the next day by walking into the sea. "Ch'en-lun" ends with a supplication that China and her people make themselves sufficiently strong to avoid all humiliations and sufferings. In this story, Yü dealt squarely with the themes of sexual discovery and national shame and in a way which appealed to young Chinese readers. His work was bitterly attacked as pornographic and worse by conservative critics, but it was defended by Chou Tso-jen (q.v.) and others. In little more than a few weeks 20,000 copies of *Ch'en-lun* were sold; and when Yü returned to China in 1922, he found himself a literary hero.

Yü Ta-fu spent the next six years adding to his literary reputation, taking a leading role in the affairs of the Creation Society, and teaching in various colleges. As a member of the editorial staff or as a contributor, Yü participated in the *Ch'uang-tsao chi-k'an* [creation quarterly], begun in 1922; the *Ch'uang-tsao chou-k'an* [creation weekly], begun in 1923; the *Ch'uang-tsao jih-pao* [creation daily] and the *Hung-shui* [the flood], both begun in 1925; the *Ch'uang-tsao yüeh-k'an* [creation monthly], begun in 1926; and in the Creation Society series of modern fiction, in which his own *Ch'en-lun* appeared as the first selection. Yü's stories, mostly in his original decadent vein, remained popular with the public, especially his "Wei-ping" [stomach trouble], "Huai-hsiang ping-che" [victim of nostalgia], and "Feng-ling" [bell in the wind], all written in Japan, and his "Mang-mang yeh" [boundless night] and "Ch'iu-liu" [autumn willow], written in 1922 in China. Like "Ch'en-lun," the stories are autobiographical and neurotic in tone, with themes ranging from poverty, harassed domestic life, and the cruelty of the world to fetishism, homosexuality, masochism, and kleptomania. Skilled as he was at portraying anguish and vacillation, Yü was at his best in leading the reader into the depths of a character by revelation of the character's darkest secrets and innermost feelings. Yü's early stories are, as he described them, decadent, and they focus on one subject, sex. It is probably here that Yü had his greatest influence and appeal, for in dealing with sex and modern love he shattered old taboos and won the interest and admiration of thousands of Chinese young people. Yü's pellucid style, derived in part from his devotion to classical poetry, also contributed to his popularity, and as the years went by, his psychological insight, at first limited to the thwarted and abnormal, expanded to embrace a wide variety of Chinese types.

Like other writers of the period, Yü was obliged to supplement his income from writing with teaching jobs in various places. In the early months of 1923, he taught briefly at the Anking School of Law and Political Science in Anhwei. That September, Yü accepted appointment as an instructor in literature at Peking University, a post which he held on and off for nearly two years. In 1925, while teaching at Wuchang University, he fell ill of tuberculosis and was obliged to suspend all activity for six months. This period of enforced leisure, endured though it was in anxiety and straitened circumstances, gave Yü ample time to ponder his career and to meditate upon his future; and when he finally recovered, he was much changed from the writer with whom the public had grown familiar.

In 1923 Yü Ta-fu had begun to study the life and thought of Alexander Herzen. Under the influence of this Russian champion of revolutionary democracy, as well as that of his fellow provincial Lu Hsün (Chou Shu-jen, q.v.), whom Yü had come to know in 1924 and whose close friend he later became, Yü slowly began to evolve a new attitude toward writing.

As before, the inner life of the individual remained at the center of his interest, but he now turned to exploration of this life against the background of society as a whole. From preoccupation with self-portrayal and the infirmities of love, Yü moved on to explore the themes of poverty and the vitality of the masses. Beginning with "Ch'un-feng ch'en-tsui-ti wan-shang" [one intoxicating spring evening], of 1923, Yü abandoned decadence for a somberly moral point of view. In that story, the hero, an out-of-work writer living in a slum, is looked after by an orphaned factory girl who suspects that he is a thief because of his habit of sleeping all day and taking long walks at night. At the climax of the story, when an unexpected check makes it possible for the writer to repay the girl and the two are enjoying a late evening snack, she solemnly asks him to give up smoking and to end his association with thieves. The girl's sincerity and innocence are a profound revelation to the writer, and the story concludes with his suppressing his amatory desires and promising to reform. The milieu and the neurotic hero are familiar from Yü's earlier work, but a new, and healthy, note is struck in the exploration of the effects of poverty on two young people and the emphasis on the powers of innocence.

Restored to health and armed with his new outlook, Yü joined the staff of Sun Yat-sen University at Canton in March 1926 together with such Creation Society members as Kuo Mo-jo, Wang Ta-ch'ing, Ch'eng Fang-wu, and Mu Mu-t'ien. Yü's tenure at Canton was short and coincided with the failure of the Communist revolution there. Yü then returned to Shanghai, where he resumed a leading role in direction of the Creation Society, took over the editorship of *Hung-shui*, and began to collect his writings for the *Ta-fu ch'üan-chi* [collected works of Yü Ta-fu], which was subsequently published over four years, 1928–31.

About this time, Yü fell in love with Wang Ying-hsia, a young left-wing writer. Through her and through Ch'ien Hsing-ts'un (A-ying), a proletarian critic, Yü became acquainted with what then passed for revolutionary literature in China. The romance and the new associations also contributed to Yü's new point of view. His account of the affair, *Jih-chi chiu-chung* [nine diaries], was published in 1927 and became an immediate best seller, breaking all previous records for Chinese books. "Kuo-ch'ü" [the past], which some critics consider Yü's best work, was also published in 1927. In its exploration of love disappointed and disclosed too late, it achieved depths of psychological insight which were acknowledged by critics and public alike.

Yü's return to Shanghai in 1926 coincided with Kuo Mo-jo's absence on the Northern Expedition, and it appears that Yü, who could now be described as a humanistic socialist, soon fell out with the Communist-inspired elements of the Creation Society because of their emphasis on discipline and propaganda at the expense of art. Accordingly, Yü reorganized the society, expelled three of the most radical members, and seemed on the point of joining forces with the Yü-ssu [threads of talk] group, centered around Chou Tso-jen and his brother, Lu Hsün. The more numerous pro-Kuo Mo-jo members of the society disapproved of this course of action and, after many acrimonious discussions, forced Yü to quit. Yü announced his withdrawal from the Creation Society on 15 August 1927, thus terminating an association of nearly a decade with what was the most influential literary and cultural group of its time.

Yü's association with Lu Hsün, Chiang Kuang-tz'u, a Russian-trained proletarian writer, and others of Lu Hsün's circle became closer after his departure from the Creation Society. Yü admired Lu Hsün and rated his writing as the most mature and profound among his contemporaries. Lu Hsün reciprocated this feeling, and the friendship between the two culminated in Yü's editing the monthly Pen-liu [the torrent] jointly with Lu Hsün in 1928. At this time Yü also became interested in Rousseau and Nietzsche, both of whose works he translated, and for a time he meditated a novel on the life of the German philosopher. Some of this material subsequently appeared in his collection Chi-ling [trivia], notable for its overtly Marxist cast of thought.

In 1928 Yü also published his first novel, Mi-yang [lost sheep], which was not so well received as his short stories had been. Mi-yang was a typical Yü autobiographical short story expanded to novel length, and it was praised principally for its style. After 1928, Yü's association with Lu Hsün and his followers became sporadic. In 1929 he gave in to left-wing pressures and took over the editorship of Ta-chung wen-i [mass literature], but later he joined Soong Ch'ing-ling, Ts'ai Yüan-p'ei, Yang Ch'uan (qq.v.), Lu Hsün, and others in sponsoring the China League for Civil Rights. In 1930 Yü became a member of the League of Left-wing Writers, but he soon found the group too demanding of time and "agitprop" output. He left the league to become an associate of Lin Yü-t'ang (q.v.) and Chou Tso-jen, who at that time stood for a nonpolitical humanistic literature. Typical of Yü's writing during this period was Han-hui [cold ashes], a miscellany devoted mostly to literary essays but containing some short stories. The piece in it which won most immediate attention was his open letter to a young student, in which Yü bitterly castigated the warlords, decried the worthlessness of the degree the young man was soon to take, and advised him that stealing is the only way to success.

In 1932 Yü withdrew formally from the field of proletarian literature with the publication of his second and last novel, T'a shih i-ko jo nü-tzu [she is a weak woman]. A year later he retired with Wang Ying-hsia to the scenic West Lake at Hangchow, where he spent most of his time sightseeing and writing about the city and its environs. He also visited most of the historic and scenic places of interest in Chekiang, and he eventually produced more than 30 travel diaries of varying lengths detailing his visits to them. Between travel writing and extensive reading in the Chinese classics, another of Yü's diversions at Hangchow, he had very little time for fiction. He completed only one important work, Ch'u-pen [flight], a novel which appeared in 1935 and which was destined to be the last important piece of fiction by Yü to be published during his lifetime.

In February 1936, possibly on account of his Japanese educational background, Yü was appointed a counselor to the Fukien provincial government, headed by Ch'en Yi (q.v.). In this capacity he took a short trip to Japan, but the nature of his business is unknown. While in Tokyo, he called on Kuo Mo-jo and renewed their friendship. Also in 1936, Yü published a collection of amorous correspondence under the title Hsien-tai ming-jen ch'ing-shu [love letters of famous men of modern times], which included billets doux penned by such personages as Kuo Mo-jo, Lu Hsün, Hsü Chih-mo (q.v.), and Chang Tzu-p'ing.

When the Sino-Japanese war began in July 1937, Yü Ta-fu resigned his post in Fukien. At Kuo Mo-jo's invitation, he joined the literary propaganda section of the Military Affairs Commission's political department at Hangchow. He wrote anti-Japanese propaganda and visited troops on several fronts.

In the winter of 1938 Yü accepted an invitation from a friend in Singapore to assume the editorship of the *Hsing-chou jih-pao* [Singapore daily] and the *Hua-ch'iao jih-pao* [overseas Chinese daily]. He also joined various anti-Japanese organizations in Singapore and soon became a leading figure in the work of rallying overseas Chinese support against Japan. When Singapore fell to Japanese troops early in 1942, Yü fled to Sumatra in the company of the writer Wang Jen-shu (Pa Jen) and others. There he changed his name to Chao Lien and opened a wine shop. One day Yü inadvertently spoke some Japanese and was immediately conscripted as an interpreter by the Japanese military police. Wang Jen-shu and others later reported that Yü used his position with the Japanese to protect patriotic Chinese and to attack traitors. In the course of his language duties, Yü probably also learned of a number of Japanese atrocities. The week after the Japanese surrender and a few days before the Allied Command took over Sumatra on 17 September 1945, Yü left his home in answer to a midnight summons. He was never seen again. It was assumed at the time that he had been executed on orders of the Japanese military police.

Yü's works continued to be popular with the postwar reading public. New editions of the *Ta-fu ch'üan-chi* appeared in 1947 and 1966. In addition, a number of anthologies of his writings appeared: *Yü Ta-fu yu-chi* [the travel accounts of Yü Ta-fu], published in 1948 and reprinted in 1956; *Ta-fu shih-tz'u chi* [poems in various styles by Yü Ta-fu], of 1954; *Yü Ta-fu nan-yu chi* [Yü Ta-fu's accounts of travels in the south], of 1956; *Yü Ta-fu jih-chi* [Yü Ta-fu's diaries], of 1961; and *Yü Ta-fu shih-tz'u ch'ao* [selection of Yü Ta-fu's poetry in various styles], of 1962.

Yü Ta-wei   俞 大 維

Yü Ta-wei (1899–), Western-educated scholar who served during the Sino-Japanese war as army ordnance director and vice minister of war. From 1946 to 1948 he was minister of communications. After serving in the Chinese embassy at Washington during the Korean war (1950–53), he was minister of national defense in Taiwan in 1954–64.

Born into a scholar-official family in Shaohsing, Chekiang, Yü Ta-wei was the son of the Hanlin scholar Yü Ming-chen. Because the elder Yü was a man of liberal ideas, most of his children studied for a time in the United States or Europe. Yü Ta-wei, after completing his secondary school and college education at missionary institutions in Shanghai, went to the United States for graduate work in philosophy at Harvard University. His dissertation was entitled "Theories of Abstract Implication: A Constructive Study," and he received the Ph.D. in 1922, one of the youngest Chinese ever to gain that degree at Harvard.

During the years just following the May Fourth Movement of 1919, many young Chinese came to believe that the study of science was essential to strengthen the Chinese nation and to improve China's international position. For this reason Yü Ta-wei left the United States in 1922 to study mathematics and ballistics in Germany. He remained an admirer of the encyclopedic knowledge of Voltaire, Dr. Johnson, and other great men of the Enlightenment, however, and he studied music and classical Greek literature in addition to scientific and military subjects. He also became acquainted with other young Chinese scholars then in Berlin, notably Ch'en Yin-k'o and Fu Ssu-nien (qq.v.). The three became close friends, and Fu Ssu-nien later married Yü Ta-ts'ai, the younger sister of Yü Ta-wei.

Yü returned to China in 1926. Through the influence of his mother, a sister of T'an Yen-k'ai (q.v.), he joined the National Government at Canton as an official of the Shih-lung Arsenal. After Nationalist military power had been extended to the Yangtze late in 1926, he served for several years in government arsenals at Nanking and Shanghai. After the Japanese invasion of Manchuria beginning in September 1931, the National Government began to replace Japanese personnel with German military advisers. Because of his experience in Germany and his knowledge of the language, Yü Ta-wei was sent to Berlin to serve as liaison commissioner. In 1933, when Colonel-General

Hans von Seeckt became Chiang Kai-shek's principal German military adviser, Yü was assigned as deputy director of the ordnance department of the Chinese army. With German advice, he supervised development of the Chinese munitions industry to equip new German-trained units for the campaigns against the Chinese Communists in Kiangsi. In July 1937, when the Sino-Japanese war began, he was named director of the ordnance department. He retained that post until December 1944, when he became vice minister of war. He resigned from that ministry at war's end in 1945.

In May 1946 Yü Ta-wei was named minister of communications in the National Government. This post was both demanding and frustrating, for most of China's principal rail lines had been disrupted or destroyed during the war years. Under Yü's supervision, many of the railways were rebuilt and restored to operation in 1946–47, but they were again destroyed in the ensuing Nationalist-Communist civil war. During his tenure in the ministry of communications, Yü also directed reorganization of the Chinese postal system, long noted for its efficiency even amidst wartime circumstances. Late in 1948, he resigned from his government post and went to the United States.

After the reestablishment of the National Government in Taiwan in 1950, Yü returned to its service. When the changed strategic situation in the Far East resulting from the outbreak of war in Korea in 1950 led to a resumption of American military and economic assistance to Taiwan, Yü Ta-wei in July 1951 was appointed vice director of the Executive Yuan's council for the utilization of United States aid. During the Korean war, he also served as special assistant to Wellington Koo (Ku Wei-chün, q.v.), Chinese ambassador at Washington, with responsibility for coordinating the United States aid program.

After the conclusion of hostilities in Korea, Yü Ta-wei was named minister of national defense in the National Government at Taipei in June 1954. During the following decade he did much to direct the reorganization and regeneration of the Chinese Nationalist military establishment which, with the aid of a substantial United States aid program, developed into one of the most efficient military forces in non-Communist Asia. In March 1964, however, Chiang Ching-kuo (q.v.) was named deputy minister of national defense. Chiang then succeeded Yü Ta-wei as minister of national defense in January 1965, at which time Yü resigned. He then virtually retired from public life, though he continued to serve as minister without portfolio in the cabinet.

Yü Ta-wei was married to Ch'en Hsin-wu, younger sister of Ch'en Yin-k'o. They had three sons, one of whom married Amy Chiang, the daughter of Chiang Ching-kuo.

Yü Yu-jen 于右任

Yü Yu-jen (11 April 1879–10 November 1964), scholar, T'ung-meng-hui revolutionary, poet, journalist, army commander, government official, and calligrapher. He first gained prominence as the editor of such anti-Manchu newspapers as the *Min-li pao*. From 1930 until his death in 1964 he was president of the Control Yuan.

Sanyuan, Shensi, was the birthplace of Yü Yu-jen. The Yü family had tilled the land in Sanyuan and in the neighboring hsien of Chingyang for generations, but a series of natural calamities in the nineteenth century had made farming increasingly difficult. Yü's father, Yü Pao-wen (T. Hsin-san), had been obliged to leave home for Szechwan province to seek a better living. He returned to Shensi in 1878 to marry, and Yü Yu-jen was born in the following year. After the birth of his first son, Yü Pao-wen went back to Szechwan. In 1881, when Yü Yu-jen was only three sui, his mother died. Thereafter he was raised by an aunt in a nearby village, where he received his early education in a school established by an elderly scholar. In 1889, at 11 sui, Yü Yu-jen was taken back to Sanyuan, where he studied the Chinese classical curriculum under a local teacher and received initial instruction in calligraphy. That year his father returned home to Shensi and remarried, but the young Yü continued to live with his aunt. His father was belatedly acquiring an education, and father and son often studied together in the evenings. To help the family, the boy worked part time in a local firecracker shop.

In 1895, at 17 sui, Yü Yu-jen placed first in the examinations for the sheng-yuan degree.

Three years later he was appointed a salaried licentiate. The Shensi provincial commissioner of education, Yeh Erh-kai, was so impressed with Yü's intellectual promise that he presented him with a copy of the diaries of the scholar-diplomat Hsueh Fu-ch'eng (ECCP, I, 331–32). This work, which recorded Hsueh's impressions of Europe in 1890–94, stimulated Yü's interest in world affairs. Also in 1898 Yü married Kao Chung-lin. In 1903, at the age of 25 sui, he passed the chü-jen examinations. By this time, however, Yü had become alarmed at the ineffectiveness of Manchu rule and attracted to the cause of republican revolution. Heretical thoughts found expression in his writings, notably in a collection of poems published at this time. In 1904, while Yü Yu-jen was preparing for the metropolitan examinations, his criticisms were reported to the Ch'ing court. The Peking authorities issued an order for his arrest and rescinded his chü-jen degree. Yü then fled to Shanghai, a political refugee at the age of 26 sui.

Upon arrival at Shanghai, Yü was fortunate enough to secure the attention of the educator Ma Liang (q.v.), who enrolled him at the Aurora Academy under the pseudonym Liu Hsueh-yu. In 1905 Ma Liang resigned as principal of that academy because of frictions with European Jesuit priests. He and Yen Fu (q.v.) then established the Futan Academy, with Yü serving on the committee which prepared its inauguration. Yü also took part in the organization of the Chung-kuo kung-hsueh, established to accommodate Chinese students who were returning from Japan in protest against restrictions on political activity imposed by the Japanese government. Yü taught Chinese at both institutions, while he studied French at the Futan Academy.

After the banning of the newspaper Su Pao (see Chang Ping-lin) in 1903, the republican revolutionaries were left without a medium for distribution of their views in Shanghai. Yü Yu-jen determined to continue the work that had been begun by the editors of the Su Pao, and he started a career in political journalism which, though only a few years in duration, ensured him a place of honor in the annals of the T'ung-meng-hui. In the summer of 1906 he went to Japan to study the Japanese press and to meet with T'ung-meng-hui leaders. In Japan, Yü also had his first contact with Sun

Yat-sen and joined the T'ung-meng-hui. For the remainder of his life he remained a faithful supporter of Sun's republican ideals.

Yü returned to Shanghai early in 1907, and in April he launched his first newspaper, the Shen-chou jih-pao. The paper's revolutionary stand was asserted in its first issue, which omitted the year of the reigning Ch'ing emperor from its dating system. Early in 1908 its premises were destroyed by a fire started from an adjoining building. Because of disagreements among the shareholders about establishing new offices, Yü decided to go his separate way and establish a new paper. Late in 1908 he received word of the illness of his father and made a secret trip to Shensi to see him. His father died while Yü was on his way back to Shanghai.

Yü Yu-jen's career as revolutionary journalist continued unabated. In May 1909 he launched the Min-hu pao, which took an even more radically anti-Manchu stance than its predecessor. In August the Ch'ing government had Yü jailed for a month by the authorities of the International Settlement, and the Min-hu pao was shut down. After his release in September, Yü organized a third newspaper, the Min-yu pao, which began publication at the beginning of October. In November he was arrested again when the Japanese consular authorities protested over an editorial which attacked the Japanese demand for rights to build a railroad from Chinchow to Tsitsihar in Manchuria. He was released only when he agreed to suspend publication of the Min-yu pao. Yü then made another brief trip to Japan.

He returned to Shanghai early in 1910 to plan the establishment of a fourth newspaper to support the cause of republican revolution. After some delay, the Min-li pao [people's strength] began publication on 11 October 1910. It was the most successful of Yü's journalistic ventures. For a time it was virtually the official organ of the revolutionary movement led by Sun Yat-sen, and ranking T'ung-meng-hui members, notably Ch'en Ch'i-mei, Sung Chiao-jen (qq.v.), and Ma Chün-wu, were associated with its editorial staff. After the failure of the Huang-hua-kang uprising at Canton in April 1911, a central China bureau of the T'ung-meng-hui was established in July; and the Min-li pao offices in the International Settlement of Shanghai served as an important communications and planning center. After the Wuchang revolt of October 1911, the *Min-li pao* continued to play a major role in presenting the republican case. In November, Sun Yat-sen, then on his way back to China, sent the paper a cable from Paris in which he outlined his proposals for structuring the new government. In this message Sun suggested that either Li Yuan-hung or Yuan Shih-k'ai (qq.v.) might be considered for the presidency of the republic. In publishing the cable in the *Min-li pao*, Yü Yu-jen commented that it revealed Sun's noble character in not striving to win the presidency for himself. He then confirmed the paper's support for Sun as the man best suited for the post.

Sun Yat-sen assumed office as provisional president on 1 January 1912. In organizing his new government at Nanking, Sun named Yü Yu-jen to be vice minister of communications. When Sun resigned from the presidency early in 1912, Yü returned to Shanghai. During his absence, Chang Shih-chao (q.v.) had assumed editorial charge of the *Min-li pao* and had advocated the need for reorganization of the revolutionary party. Yü Yu-jen appeared to side with Chang in this reappraisal of party politics in China; and their proposals evoked vigorous opposition from Wu Chih-hui (q.v.) and other leaders. Meanwhile, another journal, the *Min-ch'üan pao*, edited by Tai Chi-t'ao (q.v.), had been established at Shanghai late in 1911, and it soon began to overshadow the *Min-li pao*.

Early in 1913 Yü Yu-jen's plans to go abroad to study the press in Europe were frustrated by the shooting of his close friend Sung Chiao-jen. Yü attended to Sung during his dying hours and later took charge of the funeral arrangements. After the failure of the so-called second revolution (*see* Li Lieh-chün), the position of Sun Yat-sen and his supporters in China became untenable due to the opposition of Yuan Shih-k'ai. The *Min-li pao* suspended publication on 4 September 1913, and Yü fled to Japan. He returned to Shanghai in 1914 but found that the environment was still too hostile to permit resumption of active journalism. He thus organized the Min-li Book Company to provide cover for continuation of the Kuomintang campaign against Yuan Shih-k'ai. During the next few years, Yü moved chiefly among scholars, book sellers, and collectors. He also undertook some academic research and wrote poetry. But his attention was never deflected from the contemporary political scene, and poems written by Yü during these years reflect his anxiety about the drab prospects of the republican cause.

In August 1918 Yü Yu-jen left Shanghai to return to northwest China. This move was prompted by an invitation from leaders of the republican forces in Shensi, which had been reorganized as the Ching-kuo chün [national pacification army]. Yü became commander in chief of this force. Although he had had no previous military training or experience, he did his best to strengthen the Shensi forces. His task was complicated by internecine rivalries among the republican leaders of the province. For four years the Ching-kuo chün conducted roving campaigns in Shensi designed to undermine the superior power of militarists allied with the Peiyang government at Peking. By 1922, however, Yü's position in Shensi had become untenable, and the Ching-kuo chün had to be disbanded. Yü himself fled to Szechwan and then traveled down the Yangtze to Shanghai. He reached that city in August 1922. There he was reunited with Sun Yat-sen, also a leader in distress, who had just returned to Shanghai following Ch'en Chiung-ming's revolt at Canton.

After the republican forces established a new government at Canton early in 1923, Sun Yat-sen moved forward with plans for reorganization of the Kuomintang, construction of an alliance with the Communists, and development of military forces. In the same year, Yü Yu-jen became president of Shanghai University, a new institution designed to inspire young Chinese to join the Kuomintang and to support its programs. Yü's position there was largely nominal, however, and Shanghai University during the 1924–25 period came to be controlled by the Chinese Communists. Ch'ü Ch'iu-pai, Teng Chung-hsia, Yün Tai-ying (qq.v.), and other prominent Communists served on its faculty, and the institution trained many young cadres who served as political workers during the Northern Expedition. Yü himself attended the First National Congress of the reorganized Kuomintang at Canton in January 1924, and he was elected to the Central Executive Committee. When Sun Yat-sen made his final journey to north China, he named Yü to organize a Peking political committee to supervise Kuomintang affairs in that area.

Early in 1925 Yü traveled to Mukden for discussions with Chang Tso-lin (q.v.) and thus was not present when Sun died at Peking in March.

During this period, the Kuominchün of Feng Yü-hsiang (q.v.), who had shown some inclination to support the Kuomintang and the Nationalist-Communist alliance based at Canton, was threatened by a combination of Chihli and Fengtien forces. Feng himself expressed interest in joining the Kuomintang and went to the Soviet Union for consultation. Yü Yu-jen, who in July 1925 had been elected a member of the State Council of the National Government at Canton, went to Russia in the spring of 1926 to confer with Feng in Moscow. Yü then returned to China by way of Siberia and Outer Mongolia. On the way, he met Feng again, and together they reached Wuyuan in Suiyuan province on 14 September 1926. There Feng's officers had assembled to greet him; and Feng formally accepted membership in the Kuomintang. When Feng resumed command of the Kuominchün, Yü Yu-jen, as a member of the Central Executive Committee of that party, presented the Kuomintang flag, an action which symbolized the formal incorporation of Feng's armies into the Nationalist military forces.

Yü Yu-jen then assumed office as commander of the Kuominchün units in Shensi and governor of that province. But he quickly recognized that there was much friction among the army commanders in that area and that the measure of official deference accorded him far exceeded his practical authority. By the spring of 1927 Feng Yü-hsiang had consolidated control over northern Honan province and held a key strategic position in the intramural conflict between the contending Kuomintang regimes then based at Wuhan and at Nanking. In June 1927 Wang Ching-wei (q.v.) and other Kuomintang leaders from Wuhan went to Chengchow for what proved to be abortive discussions with Feng. Yü Yu-jen then estimated that his personal position was vulnerable at best and dangerous at worst, and he returned to Wuhan with the Wang Ching-wei group. When the feuding Kuomintang factions were able to resolve their differences in early 1928, Yü resumed his official posts as member both of the Central Executive Committee of the party and of the State Council of the National Government.

In July 1928 Yü was named to head the newly created board of audit, then directly subordinate to the National Government at Nanking. In December 1930, at the first plenum of the fourth Central Executive Committee of the Kuomintang, Yü was elected president of the Control Yuan of the National Government. He officially assumed that post in February 1931 and held it until his death more than 30 years later. The former board of audit then was reorganized as the ministry of audit and placed under the jurisdiction of the Control Yuan. That Yuan, part of the five-yuan system of government designed by Sun Yat-sen, to a large extent inherited the functions of the former censorate system under the imperial dynasties. Its primary responsibilities were the impeachment of public functionaries and the auditing of public funds. Yü Yu-jen did much to formulate procedures and regulations to make the control system effective, but he did not succeed in getting the National Government to invest the Control Yuan with unquestioned general authority either to impeach public officials or to punish those found guilty of malpractices. Yü also advocated the appointment of regional offices of the Control Yuan. Practical difficulties prevented this system from being implemented immediately; but, as an alternative, members of the Control Yuan were assigned circuit duty to inspect conditions in various parts of China.

While the National Government functioned at Nanking before the Sino-Japanese war, the Control Yuan gained prominence in several cases involving senior government officials. In January 1933 Yi P'ei-chi (q.v.) was impeached in connection with a scandal involving the theft of so-called national treasures: art objects in the Palace Museum at Peiping. Later in 1933 Ku Meng-yü (q.v.), then minister of railways, was impeached for alleged irregularities connected with the purchase of materials. The Ku Meng-yü affair led to sharp conflict between the Control Yuan and the Executive Yuan, headed by Wang Ching-wei, over procedural measures relating to exercise of the impeachment power. Wang sternly criticized Yü Yu-jen for releasing details of the case before a decision had been reached.

During the Sino-Japanese war, Yü Yu-jen moved with the National Government to Chungking. There he was generally regarded as a party elder, along with Lin Sen, Yeh Ch'u-ts'ang (qq.v.), and other veterans of the T'ung-meng-hui period. Yü continued to hold responsibilities as head of the Control Yuan, and after 1940 inspectors from that yuan were sent to various areas of China under National Government control. In 1941 Yü Yu-jen made a trip to inspect conditions in his native Shensi and adjacent Kansu; in 1946 he made a trip to Sinkiang. In the spring of 1948, Yü, then 70, was defeated in the competition for candidacy to run for the office of vice president of the Republic of China. In June, however, he was reelected to the presidency of the Control Yuan. In 1949, as Communist military offensives gained momentum, Yü moved southward with the government from Nanking to Canton. In November he flew to Taiwan.

Early in 1950, as the National Government moved to reconstitute itself at Taipei, the Control Yuan brought impeachment proceedings against Li Tsung-jen (q.v.) on charges of misconduct for remaining abroad while nominally president of the Republic of China. (Li, who had become acting President in January 1949, had gone to the United States.) Li was removed from his position, and Chiang Kai-shek was reelected President in March 1950. During later years in Taiwan, the Control Yuan again came into conflict with the Executive Yuan. In 1957 the yuan requested O. K. Yui (Yü Hung-chün, q.v.), president of the Executive Yuan, to appear before it to explain certain activities of the government. When Yui refused to accede to the request, the Control Yuan in December 1957 instituted impeachment proceedings against him. Several charges were made, including abuse of power and failure to permit the Control Yuan to inspect the records of the Central Bank of China, of which Yui was *ex officio* governor. The dispute, which reflected intramural jealousies and frictions within the Kuomintang, led to an official reprimand to Yui by the committee for disciplinary action against public functionaries, an organ under the Judicial Yuan.

Yü Yu-jen served as a member of the Central Executive Committee of the Kuomintang from 1924 until 1950, when he was elected to membership in the Central Appraisal Committee, which replaced the former Central Supervisory Committee. During the final years of his life in Taiwan, Yü Yu-jen was one of the genial oldsters of the Kuomintang, widely known for his calligraphy, poetry, and flowing white beard. Throughout his adult life Yü was known for his excellence in the so-called grass (ts'ao-shu) calligraphy, a style which he developed into something approaching a science. He was also popular because of his accessibility to seekers of samples of his flowing calligraphy. Yü also had a life-long interest in Chinese poetry, which he composed in the classical style. In 1941, while in Chungking, he had inaugurated the custom of observing as Poets Day the fifth day of the fifth moon in the lunar calendar, an occasion traditionally celebrated in China as the Dragon Boat Festival to honor the ancient Chou dynasty patriot-poet Ch'ü Yuan. In Taiwan, Yü annually took charge of the observance of Poets Day; and in 1964 he was voted Chinese poet laureate. Yü was hospitalized at Taipei in August 1964 and, after three months of unsuccessful treatment, he died on 10 November, at the age of 85.

Yü Yu-jen was survived by three sons and four daughters. The first two sons were at his bedside when he died. The eldest son, Yü Wang-te (1910–), studied in England, Germany, and France. He later served in the diplomatic service. After the Second World War, Yü Wang-te was Chinese Nationalist minister to a number of nations of Latin America: Colombia, Venezuela, Ecuador, Panama, Honduras, and El Salvador. He later returned to Taiwan to serve as adviser to the ministry of foreign affairs (1957) and adviser to the Executive Yuan (1958). George T. Yu, a grandson of Yü Yu-jen, studied in the United States and later taught political science at the University of Illinois. He was co-author of *The Chinese Anarchist Movement* (1961) and author of *Party Politics in Republican China: the Kuomintang, 1912–1924* (1966).

Yuan Shih-k'ai   袁世凱
H. Jung-an   容庵

Yuan Shih-k'ai (16 September 1859–6 June 1916), Peiyang militarist and high Ch'ing official who succeeded Sun Yat-sen as president of the Chinese republic in 1912. After ridding Peking of Kuomintang influence, he attempted to establish a constitutional monarchy.

The forebears of Yuan Shih-k'ai had risen to prominence as civil officials and military leaders during the middle decades of the nineteenth century. Hsiangch'eng, Honan, the native hsien of the Yuan family, bordered on the home region of the Nien rebels. Yuan's great-uncle, Yuan Chia-san (ECCP, II, 949–53), played an important part in the government campaigns against these rebels in the 1850's and 1860's. Assisting Yuan Chia-san in these military campaigns were such members of the family as his son Yuan Pao-heng (1826–1878; T. Chen-shu, H. Yu-wu), a chin-shih of 1850 who later went with Tso Tsung-t'ang (ECCP, II, 762–67) to northwest China and then served at Peking in 1876–78 as vice president of the Board of Punishments, and his nephew Yuan Pao-ch'ing (1829–1873), a chü-jen of 1858 who later held various posts in Shantung and Kiangsu. While other members of the family were engaged in fighting the Nien rebels, Yuan Shih-k'ai's father, Yuan Pao-chung (d.1875; T. Shou-ch'en), remained at the family seat to organize local defenses against the marauders.

Yuan Shih-k'ai, the fourth of six sons born to Yuan Pao-chung, was adopted by his father's younger brother, Yuan Pao-ch'ing, in 1866. After spending several years in Shantung and then at Nanking, where his adopted father died in 1873 while serving as acting salt tao-t'ai, Yuan Shih-k'ai returned to his native place. He then went to live in Peking under the supervision of Yuan Pao-heng and other uncles until 1878, when he returned to Hsiangch'eng. By that time, he had become a high-spirited youth who spent his leisure hours in horseback riding and other robust pursuits. Although he had been trained since childhood in the Chinese classical tradition of scholarship and had become a licentiate, he had no real liking for the conventional education that would prepare him for the civil service examinations. After failing the examinations for the chü-jen degree in 1876 and 1879, he decided to seek advancement through other channels. In 1880 he purchased the title of expectant secretary in the Grand Secretariat and went to Tengchow, Shantung, the military headquarters of Wu Ch'ang-ch'ing (1834–1884; T. Hsiao-hsuan), who was in command of the maritime defenses of Shantung province. Wu had been a close friend of Yuan Pao-ch'ing, and he gave Yuan Shih-k'ai a position on his staff on the strength of that relationship.

THE KOREAN YEARS

Yuan Shih-k'ai's first call to active military service came in 1882, when trouble flared in Korea. After the signing of the Japanese-Korean treaty of 1876, Japanese influence had begun to challenge Chinese suzerainty over Korea, while in Seoul itself there raged a fierce struggle for power between the king's father, the Tai Wön Kun, and the Min family, led by the queen, who had gained ascendancy over the weak and indecisive king. In July 1882 the Tai Wön Kun seized power in Seoul. During this *coup d'état* rioters, stirred up by the Tai Wön Kun, attacked the queen's supporters at the palace and then destroyed the Japanese legation, forcing the Japanese minister, Hanabusa Yoshimoto, and his staff to flee the city. News of the disturbance quickly reached Peking and, before the Japanese minister could return to Seoul with an escort of Japanese troops, the Chinese government ordered Wu Ch'ang-ch'ing to rush his soldiers to Korea in an attempt to stabilize the political situation. Wu dispatched 3,000 men, including Yuan Shih-k'ai, to the Korean capital.

Under Wu Ch'ang-ch'ing's direction, peace was restored to Seoul, the leaders of the coup were arrested, and the Tai Wön Kun was seized and shipped off to China, where he was held at Paoting until the summer of 1885. Much of the success of the Chinese operation was the result of the efforts of such members of Wu's staff as Ma Chien-chung (1844–1900; T. Mei-shu), Chang Chien (q.v.), and Yuan Shih-k'ai. On Wu's recommendation, Yuan was made an expectant subprefect by the Chinese government. He remained on Wu's staff in Korea as his deputy in charge of foreign affairs, and when Wu was transferred to Manchuria in the spring of 1884, he left Yuan in command of three Chinese divisions in Korea. Meanwhile, at the request of the Korean king, Yuan had begun to train Korean troops, which he organized as the Hsin-chien ch'in chün [newly created royal guard troops] and the Chen-fu chün [pacification troops].

After the outbreak of 1882, the Chinese government had adopted a policy of intervention in Korea in an attempt to reassert China's suzerainty over that country and to counteract the growing encroachments of other powers, especially Japan. Li Hung-chang (ECCP, I, 464–71) directed the implementation of this policy. The presence in Korea of both Chinese and Japanese troops, however, exacerbated the already bitter tensions between pro-Japanese progressives, who wanted an independent Korea, and pro-Chinese conservatives, who wanted to retain Korea's traditional ties to China. Violence erupted on 4 December 1884 when, on the occasion of the opening of the new post office in Seoul, a group of Korean radicals staged a *coup d'état*, attacked the conservative cabinet ministers, formed a new cabinet, and appealed to the Japanese for help in the name of the king. The Japanese minister responded by dispatching a company of Japanese soldiers to guard the king and protect the radicals in the palace. The conservative Min faction, having been ousted from power, turned to Yuan Shih-k'ai and the Chinese garrison for help. Yuan led a force of 2,000 men to the palace, rescued the Korean king, and forced the Japanese minister and his troops to retire from Seoul. The resulting strain on Sino-Japanese relations was relieved for a time when Ito Hirobumi met with Li Hung-chang at Tientsin and negotiated the Tientsin Convention of April 1885, by which both China and Japan agreed to withdraw their garrisons and military instructors from Korea.

Although the Tientsin Convention virtually acknowledged Japan as China's equal in Korea, Li Hung-chang continued his efforts to regain for China the paramount position there. As his chief instrument for carrying out his policy, Li chose the 26-year-old Yuan Shih-k'ai, who had proven himself an energetic and resourceful subordinate. In August 1885, after a leave of several months in China, Yuan returned to Korea. On 30 October he was appointed commissioner of commerce and Chinese resident in Korea. For the next nine years he used his influence as China's ranking representative in Korea to reestablish China's ascendancy over the Korean government and to minimize the influence of Japan, Russia, and other foreign powers. Such was his success that he was able to obstruct the Korean government's attempt to establish diplomatic relations with Great Britain and other European nations and to persuade it to ban the sale of Korean rice to Japanese merchants. However, Yuan's aggressive and somewhat high-handed actions stirred resentment in the Korean government and aroused antagonism among the Japanese.

After the Tientsin Convention of 1885, Japan had followed a policy of relative inaction in Korea. By 1892, however, the Japanese government had begun protesting that China was seeking to monopolize trade and communications in Korea. A more serious threat to Chinese interests, however, was that posed by the rabidly anti-foreign Tonghaks (Tung-hsueh tang), members of an ultra-conservative politico-religious society whose purpose was the expunging from Korea of all traces of alien culture. In July 1894 Tonghak uprisings broke out in the south and moved swiftly northward. Although the Korean government was able to suppress the revolt, it requested military assistance from China. At the urgent request of Yuan Shih-k'ai, Li Hung-chang reluctantly dispatched some 1,500 troops to Korea. This was the first in a series of events that led to the outbreak of the Sino-Japanese war in July 1894. On 19 July, only a few days before hostilities began, Yuan left Seoul secretly and boarded a ship for Tientsin, thus bringing to an end a period of 12 years' service in Korea. During much of this time, Yuan had wielded great influence in Korea; working in this atmosphere of rivalry and intrigue had taught him many valuable lessons in the art of diplomacy and in the manipulation of political and military power.

PEI-YANG TA-CH'EN

On his return to China, Yuan Shih-k'ai was appointed intendent of the Wenchow-Ch'uchow circuit in Chekiang, but he did not take up the duties of this post. At the request of Li Hung-chang, he assisted Chou Fu (*see under* Chou Hsueh-hsi) in supervising the transportation of military supplies to the Chinese forces fighting the Japanese in Korea and Manchuria. By war's end, Yuan had won the confidence of such influential Manchu officials in Peking as Jung-lu (ECCP, I, 405–9) and I-k'uang (Prince Ch'ing). As a result of the defeat by Japan, the Manchu court recognized the urgent need for military reforms. At the suggestion of Jung-lu, Yuan Shih-k'ai began work on a manual of modern Western methods of military training. The resulting (*Ch'ih-chin*) *Hsün-lien tsao-fa hsiang-hsi t'u-shuo*, which favored the use of German training methods, was presented to the throne in 1899.

In December 1895 Jung-lu and other members of the Grand Council recommended that Yuan Shih-k'ai be chosen to organize and train a modern military force. Later that month, Yuan was appointed to succeed Hu Yü-fen (d.1906; T. Yun-mei) as commander of the Pacification Army (Ting-wu-chün), which had been organized during the Sino-Japanese war. Yuan's new command, renamed the Newly Created Army (Hsin-chien lu-chün), was stationed near Tientsin at Hsiaochan, the military encampment formerly used by the famous Anhwei Army (Huai-chün) of Li Hung-chang.

Although derived from the Anhwei Army in several respects, especially personnel, the Newly Created Army differed from the regional armies formed during the Taiping Rebellion in that it was financed by, and hence was dependent upon, the central government at Peking. Nevertheless, like the leaders of the earlier armies, Yuan was able to foster among his men a strong sense of personal loyalty to him. Under his direction, the Newly Created Army was expanded from about 4,000 to about 7,000 men. Most of the new men were recruited from the northern provinces of Shantung, Honan, Anhwei, and Kiangsu. With the assistance of German military officers, he established officer training schools and reorganized his troops along modern Western lines into units of infantry, cavalry, artillery, and engineers. He also instituted a modern military staff system, and he appointed his old friend Hsü Shih-ch'ang (q.v.) chief of staff and T'ang Shao-yi (q.v.) as secretary to staff headquarters.

In the course of building up the Newly Created Army, Yuan Shih-k'ai frequently was subjected to criticism. On one occasion, in the spring of 1896, he was impeached by a censor on charges of extravagance in his management of the establishment at Hsiaochan. However, Jung-lu, who was sent by the imperial court to investigate the charges, was much impressed by the smart appearance of Yuan's troops, and he sent in a report which praised Yuan's achievements. That Yuan enjoyed the favor of the Manchu court was demonstrated further by his appointment as provincial judge of Chihli in July 1897. He also was regarded with favor by reformers because he had declared his support of the Ch'iang-hsueh-hui, a reform

group that had been organized by K'ang Yu-wei (q.v.) and his associates.

In 1898, during the Hundred Days Reform, Yuan Shih-k'ai was promoted to the rank of board vice president by the young Kuang-hsü emperor. Soon afterwards, T'an Ssu-t'ung (ECCP, II, 702–5) tried to enlist his help in staging a coup to oust the empress dowager and the conservatives and to place the emperor and the reform faction in complete control of the government. Yuan is generally believed to have divulged this plot to Jung-lu, the leader of the empress dowager's faction. Jung-lu took counteraction that brought a sudden end to the reform movement, removed the emperor from power, and restored the empress dowager to her former position of undisputed authority. Although Yuan later prepared a wu-hsü jih-chi, or diary, in which he tried to absolve himself of responsibility for the fate of the Kuang-hsü emperor and the reformers, it should be noted that after the conservative action of September 1898 he became a favorite of the empress dowager and that in June 1899 he was made junior vice president of the Board of Works.

Late in 1898 Jung-lu, then in command of all military forces in north China, reorganized military units in that area as a single army, the Guards Army (Wu-wei-chün). This new force consisted of five divisions: the Front Division, formerly the Tenacious Army (Wu-i-chün) of Nieh Shih-ch'eng (*see under* Feng Kuo-chang); the Rear Division, formerly the Kansu troops (Kan-chün) of Tung Fu-hsiang (1839–1908; T. Hsing-wu); the Center Division, a newly organized unit of bannermen under the direct command of Jung-lu; the Left Division, formerly the Resolute Army (I-chün) of Sung Ch'ing (ECCP, II, 686–88); and the Right Division (Wu-wei yu-chün), formerly the Newly Created Army of Yuan Shih-k'ai. Of these five divisions, most of which were made up of old-style troops, Yuan's Right Division, still stationed at Hsiaochan, was by far the best trained and equipped. In May 1899 a detachment of his troops was transferred to Shantung to reinforce local units, then beset by German encroachments from Kiaochow and by increasing unrest, particularly the anti-foreign outbreaks of the Boxers (I-ho-t'uan). The Boxer disturbances in Shantung increased in frequency and violence, and diplomatic pressures by foreign governments resulted in the December

1899 recall of the anti-foreign governor, Yü-hsien (d.1901; T. Tso-ch'en). Yuan Shih-k'ai was ordered to Shantung as acting governor; he took the bulk of his division with him.

During the Boxer Uprising of 1900 Yuan Shih-k'ai sought to follow a course of non-involvement in the pro-Boxer activities of the imperial court. Despite repeated injunctions from Peking to deal mildly with the Boxers, he firmly suppressed their uprisings in Shantung and succeeded in forcing the Boxers to retreat into Chihli. Evading imperial commands to send his troops to bolster anti-foreign forces in Peking, he joined with Chang Chih-tung (ECCP, I, 27–32) and Liu K'un-i (ECCP, I, 523–24) in keeping the central and southern provinces free of Boxers and at peace with foreign powers. Thus, in contrast to other units of Jung-lu's Guards Army, which suffered heavy casualties in fighting both Boxers and foreign troops, Yuan's division not only was preserved intact but also was expanded to include some 26 new battalions in Shantung. In July 1901 these forces were augmented further by the transfer to Yuan's command of the crack Self-Strengthening Army (Tzu-ch'iang-chün), originally organized by Chang Chih-tung.

As commander of the largest military force in north China and as one whose anti-Boxer policies in Shantung had made him acceptable to the foreign powers, Yuan Shih-k'ai was the logical choice to direct the defense organizations of the war-ravaged metropolitan area after the imperial court returned from Sian to Peking. With the death of Li Hung-chang in November 1901, Yuan was appointed to succeed his former mentor as governor general of Chihli and as Pei-yang ta-ch'en, or high commissioner of military and foreign affairs in north China. During the six years he held the powerful post of Pei-yang ta-ch'en, Yuan was responsible for administering many of the post-Boxer reform policies adopted by the Manchu regime. As governor of Shantung, Yuan had begun to introduce reforms in education, industry, and commerce, and he had placed his reform programs under the direction of such protégés as T'ang Shao-yi and Chou Hsueh-hsi (q.v.). Yuan brought his assistants with him to Chihli at the end of 1901 and assigned them to initiate and direct numerous modernization projects in Chihli. A collection of his official papers of the 1901–6 period, the *Pei-yang kung-tu lei-tsuan*, compiled by Kan Hou-tz'u and published in 1907, gives a fairly clear idea of Yuan's activities in Chihli.

Yuan Shih-k'ai's principal concern, however, was military reform. On his recommendation a new standing army was authorized, and in the autumn of 1902 he began to organize its first new divisions. Late in 1903 the impending Russo-Japanese conflict in Manchuria spurred the Manchu court to accelerate its military reform program; in December 1903 it set up a commission for army reorganization (Lien-ping-ch'u) to coordinate the training of provincial armies. This commission was modelled on the provincial staff that Yuan had organized in Chihli, and Yuan himself, as associate director of the new commission (the nominal head was Prince Ch'ing), was its dominating spirit. In September 1904 the court approved the commission's detailed plans for creating a new army patterned after Yuan's divisions. This new force, known as the Peiyang Army (Pei-yang lu-chün), had come to include six full divisions by February 1905. During this period, Yuan also organized a police force to patrol Tientsin and other cities under his jurisdiction and established a police academy (Hsün-ching hsueh-t'ang) in Tientsin staffed with foreign instructors. In the autumn of 1905 the Manchu court accepted Yuan's proposal for the establishment of a Board of Police (Hsün-ching-pu) and his recommendation to place at its head his close associate Hsü Shih-ch'ang. About this time, at his vast military encampment at Paoting, Chihli, Yuan set up a network of training schools including a staff college and a military academy to train his officers in modern military techniques.

As Pei-yang ta-ch'en, Yuan Shih-k'ai had at his disposal both the political authority and the finances needed to expand his military power. Although a severe disciplinarian, he was popular with his troops because he showed a personal interest in their well-being and was careful to see that they were paid regularly. With the expansion of the forces under his command, he was able to grant rapid promotions to his protégés and thus to command their loyalty. A number of his subordinates who had been with him since the formation of the Newly Created Army, such as Tuan Ch'i-jui, Feng Kuo-chang, and Wang Shih-chen (qq.v.), became commanders of the first new Peiyang divisions. These and other senior officers under his command, including Ts'ao K'un, Chang Hsün (qq.v.), Lu Yung-hsiang, and Ni Ssu-ch'ung, owed their subsequent rise to prominence as military or political leaders to the fact that they had been Yuan's protégés. With these subordinates, Yuan was able to create a web of close interpersonal relationships that was to be a major factor in the development of his own military power and of the northern or Peiyang military clique.

Yuan Shih-k'ai inevitably incurred the jealousy of other ambitious officials at the Ch'ing court. Because he was well aware of the dangers involved in his position as the most powerful Chinese official in a Manchu regime, he was careful to retain the favor of his principal supporter, the empress dowager, and to cultivate the friendship of highly placed Manchu princes and nobles. Although he recommended a number of Manchus, such as Prince Ch'ing, Yin-ch'ang (T. Wu-lou), and T'ieh-liang (1863–1938; T. Pao-ch'en), to share in the control of the military establishment, by 1906 there had arisen at the Manchu court an influential group of young noblemen, led by Liang-pi (1872–1912; T. Lai-ch'en) and Yuan's one-time protégé T'ieh-liang, which favored a policy of centralizing the new military forces under Manchu leadership. In 1906 the Manchu court removed four of the six Peiyang divisions from Yuan's command, and in August 1907 Yuan was removed from his posts as governor general of Chihli and Pei-yang ta-ch'en.

Because he retained the personal favor of the empress dowager, Yuan Shih-k'ai, though deprived of direct command of the divisions he had created, continued to exercise considerable influence on military affairs through his powerful friends at court and his high-ranking protégés in the army. He was transferred to Peking as minister of foreign affairs and grand councillor. However, his fortunes underwent a dramatic reversal in November 1908, when both the Kuang-hsü emperor and the empress dowager died. For a decade, Yuan had owed his high position in the government largely to the backing of the empress dowager; now his career and even his life were endangered by his enemies at the imperial court, chief among whom was Prince Ch'un (Tsai-feng), the new prince regent and the father of the infant

Hsuan-t'ung emperor. Although Prince Ch'un as a younger brother of the Kuang-hsü emperor was eager to avenge Yuan's alleged complicity in the *coup d'etat* of 1898, he lacked courage and feared Yuan's still potent influence in the Peiyang Army. Accordingly, he decided to limit his vengeance to the issuance on 2 January 1909 of an edict commanding Yuan to retire from his official duties on the obviously fictitious pretext that he had been incapacitated by a foot injury.

REVOLUTION AND THE PRESIDENCY

For almost three years, Yuan Shih-k'ai lived in retirement in Changte (Anyang), situated in the northern part of Honan on the Peking-Hankow railway. Many of his former associates in Peking, including Hsü Shih-ch'ang and Prince Ch'ing, remained discreetly in touch with him, as did such old Peiyang Army subordinates as Feng Kuo-chang and Tuan Ch'i-jui. Thus, when the revolt of 10 October 1911 broke out at Wuchang, Yuan still wielded considerable hidden influence in both civil and military circles. On the recommendation of Prince Ch'ing and Hsü Shih-ch'ang, Prince Ch'un reluctantly turned to his old enemy in an effort to save the tottering dynasty; on 14 October 1911 he appointed Yuan governor general of Hu-Kwang and instructed him to suppress the revolutionaries. Yuan, however, was in no hurry to come to the aid of the regime that had cashiered him so summarily; he declined the appointment on the grounds that his alleged leg ailment had not been cured.

At the time of Yuan's refusal, the imperial armies that had been sent south to put down the revolutionaries at Wuhan were composed of Peiyang divisions which had been trained under Yuan's command. Though nominally headed by Yin-ch'ang, they were actually led by Feng Kuo-chang and Tuan Ch'i-jui, both of whom regarded Yuan as their patron. With the backing of these and other Peiyang officers, Yuan was in a position to bargain with both the Manchu court and the revolutionaries. In response to continued pressure from the Manchu court to resume office, he submitted a list of conditions under which he would agree to serve the dynasty: the convening of a national assembly within a year, the organizing of a cabinet which would be responsible to the assembly, the lifting of the ban on political parties, the granting of an amnesty to all republican revolutionaries, the granting to himself of complete control over all the military forces, and the providing of adequate military funds. The Manchu regent, hard pressed by spreading revolts, finally acceded to these demands. On 27 October, Yuan was named to replace Yin-ch'ang as imperial high commissioner of all military forces fighting the revolutionaries, and the Peiyang forces, which had remained inactive on the Honan-Hupeh border for several days, mounted an attack on Hankow. Not until the beginning of November, however, did Yuan emerge from retirement and take command of his troops at Hsiaokan, outside of Hankow. By that time, the Manchu court had convened a provisional parliament (tzu-cheng-yuan) and had named Yuan to replace Prince Ch'ing as prime minister and as head of a new cabinet. On 13 November, Yuan moved north to Peking with a sizable bodyguard. Three days later, he announced the composition of his cabinet; the key posts went to his supporters—Wang Shih-chen was named minister of war, with Chao Ping-chün as minister of internal affairs and T'ang Shao-yi as minister of posts and communications. Thereafter, Yuan moved swiftly to remove the Manchus from the remaining positions of influence at Peking and to consolidate his authority. He persuaded the Manchu prince Tsai-t'ao to relinquish command of the imperial guard forces and, on 6 December, compelled his old adversary Prince Ch'un to turn over the regency to the helpless empress Lung-yü, the adoptive mother of the Hsuan-t'ung emperor.

Yuan's ties of loyalty to the Ch'ing dynasty apparently had been dissolved by the death of the empress dowager, his patron, in 1908 and by his dismissal from office in 1909, for he had no noticeable qualms about exploiting the infant emperor and the widowed regent to further his own political ends. Having secured control over the imperial forces in north China, he proceded to play the hapless Manchus against the revolutionaries for his own benefit. As early as 27 October 1911 he had attempted to negotiate secretly with the revolutionaries in Wuchang, but his overtures had been rebuffed. To improve his bargaining position, he had ordered Feng Kuo-chang to press the attack upon Hankow. Feng's men then had

taken both Hankow and Hanyang. By alternately applying and relaxing military pressure on the revolutionaries Yuan, by early December, had succeeded in persuading the Manchus, the revolutionaries, and the foreign powers which had interests in China that he alone held the key to order or chaos in China. Because all parties were anxious to avert widespread civil conflict in China, arrangements were made for an armistice at Wuhan, during which representatives of Yuan Shih-k'ai and of the revolutionary commander Li Yuan-hung (q.v.) met and agreed to hold peace talks. On 9 December 1911 Yuan dispatched a delegation headed by T'ang Shao-yi to Hankow; four days later, T'ang and Wu T'ing-fang (q.v.), the plenipotentiary for the revolutionary army, began formal negotiations in Shanghai.

While the peace negotiations were still underway, the revolutionaries set up a provisional republican government at Nanking and elected Sun Yat-sen provisional president on 29 December 1911. Because he was perturbed by this challenge to his own bid for national supremacy and dissatisfied with the trend of the negotiations in Shanghai, Yuan rejected the agreement reached by T'ang Shao-yi and Wu T'ing-fang. However, he found it necessary to continue negotiations with the revolutionaries because he lacked the funds necessary to finance a full-scale military operation against the provisional government in Nanking. As a result, an understanding was reached early in January 1912 whereby Sun Yat-sen would resign from the provisional presidency in favor of Yuan Shih-k'ai, on the condition that the Manchu emperor abdicated and a republican government was established in Peking. Yuan then was faced with the embarrassing prospect of reversing his earlier stand in support of constitutional monarchy and of persuading the Manchus to agree to abdicate. His old friend Prince Ch'ing agreed to present the possibility of voluntary abdication to the Manchu nobles and did so, but they strongly opposed the idea. Yuan received unexpected assistance from a revolutionary assassin who, by killing Liang-pi, the head of the Imperial Clan party (Tsung-jen-she), removed one of the most dangerous opponents of Yuan's plans and frightened some other members of the Imperial Clan party into hiding. In a final effort to coerce the reluctant Manchus into an abdication agreement, Yuan made use of his ultimate argument, the threat of military force. On 27 January 1912 some 40 Peiyang military commanders, headed by Tuan Ch'i-jui, sent a telegram to the Ch'ing government urging, for the safety of the imperial family and the security of the country, that the emperor abdicate immediately in favor of a republican form of government. On 12 February, an imperial edict announced the abdication of the emperor, stating that "Yuan Shih-k'ai should have full power to organize a provisional republican government to negotiate with the revolutionary government for unification measures."

On 13 February 1912 Sun Yat-sen presented his resignation to the provisional national assembly (ts'an-i-yuan) in Nanking and recommended that Yuan Shih-k'ai succeed him as provisional president. The Nanking assembly unanimously elected Yuan provisional president on 15 February and named Li Yuan-hung vice president on 20 February. However, certain conditions that Sun Yat-sen had attached to his resignation were yet to be met: that Nanking should be the seat of the new government; that he would retire from office only when the new president came to Nanking to be inaugurated; and that the new president should honor the provisional constitution then being drafted by the provisional assembly in Nanking. A few days later, the provisional assembly sent to Peking a group of five envoys, including Ts'ai Yuan-p'ei, Wang Ching-wei, and Sung Chiao-jen (qq.v.), who were to escort Yuan to Nanking for his inauguration. Although Yuan professed to accept Sun's conditions, he did not intend to leave his power base in north China; he claimed that his departure for the south would make it difficult for him to maintain order in the north. As if to substantiate his claims, the well-disciplined troops of the 3rd Division, commanded by Ts'ao K'un (q.v.), mutinied and set fire to many buildings in the center of Peking just four days after the envoys arrived in Peking. Other Peiyang units rioted at Tientsin and Paoting. These military riots, probably ordered by Yuan, convinced the Nanking envoys that Yuan's presence was needed in north China. On their recommendation, the Nanking government telegraphed permission for Yuan to assume office in Peking. He was inaugurated provisional president of the Chinese republic on 12 March 1912.

SUPPRESSION OF THE KUOMINTANG

Although he had sworn in his inaugural address to uphold the republic and to observe the constitution, Yuan Shih-k'ai tended to view his presidential mandate as giving him an authority which differed little from that formerly enjoyed by the Manchu emperors. His idea of republican government was fundamentally different from the idea held by the revolutionary leaders, whose aim was to curb the authority that Yuan sought to expand. Consequently, the first years of the republic saw the development of a struggle for power between Yuan and the revolutionary party. Before resigning as provisional president in Nanking, Sun Yat-sen had tried to diminish Yuan's power by drawing him away from Peking, the center of his political and military influence. Having foiled this attempt, Yuan used a similar strategem to maneuver the Nanking government out of its stronghold in the Yangtze valley and into his sphere of authority; by the end of April 1912 he had managed to persuade the provisional government to move to Peking.

Sun Yat-sen and other revolutionary leaders also had tried to limit Yuan's power by means of the lin-shih yueh-fa, or provisional constitution. This document, drafted in Nanking in February and promulgated at the time of Yuan's inauguration, was designed to make the premier, rather than the president, the chief custodian of power. However, the vague wording of many of the constitution's provisions led to disagreements between the premier and his cabinet on the one hand, and the president on the other, for it permitted Yuan to claim many powers that he was not intended to have. Yuan's ability to subvert the original purposes of the provisional constitution was demonstrated in the workings of the first republican cabinet, headed by T'ang Shao-yi. Although the cabinet included several members of the revolutionary party, the key posts went to such trusted Yuan adherents as Tuan Ch'i-jui (war), Lin Kuan-hsiung (navy), and Chao Ping-chün (internal affairs). Because T'ang Shao-yi was a long-time friend and protégé, Yuan expected to be able to dominate the cabinet with ease. T'ang, however, was a man of character and independence who joined the T'ung-meng-hui at Shanghai in 1912 and who supported its political ideals. As premier, he sought to enforce the constitutional provisions limiting the powers of the president, and when Yuan persisted in acting without his consent, he resigned in June 1912. Under his successors, all of whom were appointed by Yuan, the cabinet gradually degenerated into a powerless adjunct of the president's office.

Having reduced the cabinet system to impotence, Yuan Shih-k'ai turned his attention to the political parties in the National Assembly. These parties, particularly the T'ung-meng-hui, constituted the chief remaining obstacle to the fulfillment of his ambitions. While privately working to undermine the influence of the T'ung-meng-hui, he publicly sought its coopera- tion. In the summer of 1912 he invited Sun Yat-sen and Huang Hsing (q.v.) to Peking to discuss plans for national unification. While they were in Peking late that summer, Yuan impressed them favorably with his courteous attention to their proposals and successfully enlisted their public support of his candidacy for president in the approaching elections. Before leaving Peking, Sun took part in the ceremonies inaugurating the Kuomintang. He then left Sung Chiao-jen (q.v.), the organizer of the new party, in charge of its political affairs in north China. Unlike his colleagues, Sung Chiao-jen was a vigorous proponent of constitu- tional government by a cabinet, which, in turn, would be controlled by the majority party in the National Assembly. He came out strongly against Yuan's administration while electioneer- ing in the provinces. In the elections held early in 1913 the Kuomintang became the majority party in the National Assembly. As *de facto* leader of the party, Sung Chiao-jen constituted a serious threat to Yuan's control of the cabinet and of the government itself. On 20 March 1913, as he was about to board a train for Peking, Sung Chiao-jen was assassinated in Shanghai. The assassin and his accomplice were arrested soon afterwards, and documents found in their homes implicated Chao Ping- chün, the premier, Hung Shu-tsu, the secretary of the cabinet, and even Yuan himself.

The assassination of Sung Chiao-jen led to a rapid deterioration of relations between Yuan Shih-k'ai and the Kuomintang. Another cause of this growing antagonism was the Reorganiza- tion Loan Agreement. In April 1913 Yuan's administration concluded negotiations with a five-power consortium, representing banks of Great Britain, Germany, France, Russia, and

Japan, which resulted in an agreement for a loan of £125 million. The agreement was signed without the formal approval of the National Assembly. Strengthened by this new source of funds and supported in the National Assembly by the Progressive party, Yuan decided that it no longer was necessary to tolerate opposition from the Kuomintang. On 6 May 1913 he issued an order banning that party and began to transfer troops in prepara- tion for an attack on the provinces controlled by Kuomintang governors. In June, he dis- missed three governors: Li Lieh-chün (q.v.) of Kiangsi, Po Wen-wei of Anhwei, and Hu Han- min (q.v.) of Kwangtung. He then ordered Peiyang divisions to advance southward toward Kiukiang and Nanking. Kuomintang resistance (for details, *see* Li Lieh-chün) to the Peiyang onslaught was scattered and ineffectual. By September, the so-called second revolution had been crushed, and the area under Yuan's military control had been extended to include the provinces of Hupeh, Anhwei, Kiangsi, and Kiangsu.

THE MONARCHICAL MOVEMENT

Having destroyed the political and military authority of the Kuomintang, Yuan Shih-k'ai was free to proceed with plans to consolidate his power. In mid-1913 he still was only the provisional president; and to secure formal recognition from foreign powers, he needed confirmation of his status as chief of state by the National Assembly. Yuan succeeded in persuading the National Assembly to pass a new presidential election law and to elect him president. On 10 October 1913, the second anniversary of the revolution, he formally assumed the presidency at the T'ai-ho-tien, where the Manchu emperors had been enthroned. That day, the Chinese republic received formal recognition from Great Britain, Russia, France, Japan, and other powers.

After being installed as president, Yuan Shih-k'ai pressed the National Assembly to amend the provisional constitution of March 1912 so that his authority no longer would be restricted by the assembly or the cabinet. When this proposal encountered opposition from members of the National Assembly, Yuan decided that the continued existence of the National Assembly was unnecessary. On 4 November 1913 he ordered the dissolution of the Kuomintang and the arrest of Kuomintang members still in Peking. This action paralyzed the National Assembly, for it now lacked a quorum. Yuan dissolved it on 10 January 1914 and replaced it with an interim group, the political council (cheng-chih hui-i). This docile body, composed mainly of friends or protégés of Yuan, created the constitutional council (yueh-fa hui-i), which was charged with drafting a new constitution which would meet Yuan's specifications. The new document, known as the constitutional compact (yueh-fa), was promulgated by Yuan himself on 1 May 1914. In addition to bestowing almost unlimited powers upon the president, it called for the establishment of a council of state (ts'an-cheng-yuan) and a legislative council (li-fa-yuan). The council of state was established on 20 June, but the legislative council was never organized. In accordance with the constitutional compact, Yuan also set up an office of government affairs (cheng-shih-t'ang) attached to the presidential office and appointed his old friend Hsü Shih-ch'ang to head it. By creating this office, which served in lieu of a cabinet, and the council of state, Yuan sought to give a democratic air to a regime that was rapidly acquiring the characteristics of a military dictatorship. Such potential sources of opposition as political parties and the press were subjected to restrictions and regulations which were enforced by the military and the secret police. Through revisions made in the constitutional compact, Yuan obtained the presidency for life and the authority to appoint his own successor.

In the autumn of 1914, as Yuan Shih-k'ai was approaching the zenith of his power, his regime encountered unforeseen difficulties in the field of foreign policy, difficulties created by the outbreak of the First World War. Yuan had been aware of the Japanese threat to China for many years, but since his rise to power he had been content to follow the policy of his predecessors, relying upon other foreign powers to check the ambitions of Japan. However, as the European powers became increasingly involved in European affairs after 1914, Japan was left relatively free to extend its influence in China. Japan quickly took over Tsingtao, Kiaochow, and other German concessions in Shantung province. On 18 January 1915, under conditions of extreme secrecy, the Japanese minister in Peking personally presented Yuan

with his government's Twenty-one Demands upon China, which, had they all been granted, would have transformed China into a Japanese protectorate. Because no other foreign power would intervene and because Yuan was unwilling to commit the Peiyang Army to military action against Japan, he had to acquiesce to a Japanese ultimatum. On 9 May he acceded to all but the most sweeping of these demands. His capitulation was a serious blow to his prestige and that of his regime.

Yuan Shih-k'ai's decision to yield to the Japanese was influenced by his plans to found another imperial dynasty in China, a scheme for which he required non-interference, if not cooperation, from Japan. Just when Yuan conceived his monarchical plan cannot be determined. However, an official tendency to revert to the institutions and the terminology of the late Ch'ing period had become evident by mid-1914. Efforts were made, with Yuan's approval, to restore and reinstitute the examination system and the censorate; civil (and later military) officials were ranked into a hierarchy with titles reminiscent of those used under the Ch'ing dynasty. Resumption of the official worship of Confucius was ordered throughout the country. The ceremony of the sacrifices at the Altar of Heaven at the winter solstice, formerly practiced by the emperors, was revived by Yuan, who personally carried out the ceremony in December 1914. Yuan's plans received support from various quarters. From the Japanese premier, Okuma Shigenobu, and from Yuan's Japanese advisers came hints that Japan, itself a monarchy, would not be unsympathetic to the establishment of a new monarchy in China. Yuan's American consultant on constitutional law, Frank J. Goodnow, a professor at Columbia University who later became president of the Johns Hopkins University, submitted a report to Yuan in which he maintained that monarchy was a more suitable form of government for China than was a republican system. Many of Yuan's relatives and advisers also supported the monarchical idea, some because they believed that it would benefit China and others because they saw opportunities for their own advancement.

The monarchical movement began in earnest in August 1915 with the creation of the Ch'ou-an-hui [society for planning stability]. Yuan's personal adviser Yang Tu (q.v.) and his associates used the society to promote the idea of constitutional monarchy. By flooding the political council with petitions to change the system of government, they hoped to create an impression of widespread public support for the establishment of a monarchy. In October, Yuan's supporters hastily formed the kuo-min tai-piao ta-hui [national congress of representatives], allegedly to represent public opinion, and by 20 November this body had cast a unanimous vote in favor of a monarchy. In response to this action, the political council petitioned Yuan on 11 December, asking that he become monarch. On 12 December, a series of orders were issued which prepared the way for the transformation of the state from a republic to a monarchy. Newly created titles of nobility in five ranks were bestowed upon Yuan's most important civil and military subordinates; the designation tsung-t'ung-fu [president's office] was changed to hsin-hua-kung [new China palace]; and in the new official calendar the name Hung-hsien, chosen to designate Yuan's reign period, was scheduled to be used beginning 1 January 1916.

Although Yuan Shih-k'ai carefully gauged the probable reactions of the Chinese people and the foreign powers before establishing the monarchy, events soon proved that he had blundered. The Japanese, who previously had indicated their approval, were the first of several foreign powers to register strong objections; in China, even Yuan's oldest friends and colleagues opposed this venture. Yuan had given too much weight to the casual opinions of foreigners and to his followers' misleading assessments of public opinion. Soon after its inception in the summer of 1915 the monarchical movement had come under increasingly bitter attack from Liang Ch'i-ch'ao (q.v.), the influential leader of the Progressive party. Liang's former student Ts'ai O (q.v.) then had begun in secret to organize military opposition to Yuan's regime.

Yuan's opponents made their first public move on 25 December 1915, when Ts'ai O joined with T'ang Chi-yao (q.v.), Tai K'an, and other military leaders in Yunnan in sending Yuan an open telegram which denounced him as the betrayer of the republic and proclaimed Yunnan's independence from his rule. Soon afterwards, the National Protection Army, led by Ts'ai O, began to advance on Szechwan.

Yuan ordered troops into Szechwan early in January 1916 to crush this opposition, but despite his military efforts, Kweichow declared its independence on 27 January and Kwangsi followed suit on 15 March. These successive blows to Yuan's prestige, together with reports of military reverses in Szechwan and increasing pressure from the foreign powers, persuaded Yuan to postpone further plans for the monarchy. On 22 March 1916, after 83 days as monarch, he issued an order which formally restored the republican government.

THE END OF PEIYANG UNITY

Although the revolt of the southwestern provinces and the opposition of foreign powers contributed substantially to the collapse of the monarchical movement, perhaps the principal reason for Yuan's failure was lack of support from his own military subordinates. In the early days of the Peiyang Army, Yuan had exercised direct control over his troops. After he became chief executive of the Chinese republic, however, the claims made on his attention by matters of state, diplomacy, finance, and politics obliged him to entrust much of his military authority to his top lieutenants. Further delegation of power was necessitated by the rapid expansion of the Peiyang Army during and after the so-called second revolution of 1913 and by the decision to garrison the newly conquered provinces with large Peiyang units, the commanders of which would act as military governors. Once placed in control of large areas located at some distance from the center of authority, these commanders, though outwardly remaining loyal to Yuan, tended to become increasingly independent. Thus, Yuan's military authority diminished in 1913–14 as his political authority increased. Yuan, who was aware of this trend, sought to reestablish direct control over the military by transferring the central direction of military affairs from the ministry of war to a newly organized ta-yuan-shuai t'ung-shuai pan-shih-ch'u [generalissimo's office], which he headed, and by creating a new model army under his personal command to offset the growing power of the older Peiyang commanders. He also tried to reduce the regional power of his commanders by shifting them frequently to new command posts or by transferring them to sinecure posts in Peking. Many of the senior officers, however, had been schooled by Yuan himself in the art of acquiring and keeping power, and they managed to thwart his efforts to dislodge them from their regional bases. By the time the monarchical movement began, Yuan's relations with his two most important subordinates, Tuan Ch'i-jui and Feng Kuo-chang, had become strained; this deterioration seriously weakened Yuan's prestige in the minds of other Peiyang officers.

Yuan Shih-k'ai's failure to retain the support of his top military commanders and to crush the secessionist movement in the southwestern provinces marked a decisive turn in his political fortunes. Faced with the possibility of complete military collapse, he sought to negotiate a compromise with the southwestern military leaders which would allow him to retain the presidency. Ts'ai O and his colleagues responded by demanding that Yuan resign and leave China. The weight of these demands increased with the secession of Kwangtung, Chekiang, Shensi, Szechwan, and Hunan in April and May 1916 and with the formation of a military council (chün-wu-yuan) at Chaoch'ing, Kwangtung, by T'ang Chi-yao and other secessionist leaders, who announced their refusal to recognize Yuan or his administration. Meanwhile, signs of impending defection began to appear among Yuan's subordinates. In mid-May 1916 Feng Kuo-chang convened a conference of political representatives at Nanking which discussed the matter of the presidency and finally adopted a resolution favoring Yuan's retirement from office. In an attempt to keep his hold on the central administration, Yuan tried to regain the support of Tuan Ch'i-jui by appointing him premier of a reorganized government. However, Tuan resumed his attitude of indifference to Yuan's plight when Yuan refused his demands for greater political and military powers.

On 6 June 1916 Yuan Shih-k'ai, exhausted by successive disappointments, humiliations, and desertions and by his own feverish efforts to cling to power, died of uremia at the age of 56. Official funeral ceremonies, conducted by Tuan Ch'i-jui, were held in Peking on 23 June. Six days later, his body was laid to rest at Changte, Honan.

Yuan Shih-k'ai was said to have been the father of some 30 children, 16 of whom were sons. At the age of 17, he married a girl whose surname was Yü, and his household later came to include a number of concubines. Of his sons, the best known were Yuan K'o-ting (1887–; T. Yun-t'ai), who for a time hoped to succeed his father as monarch, and Yuan K'o-wen (1889–1931; T. Han-yun, H. Pao-ts'en), noted for his literary and artistic accomplishments. Another son, Yuan K'o-huan (b.1885; T. Chung-jen, H. Tzu-wu) in 1937 published a collection of his father's public papers from the years 1898–1907, *Yuan-shou-yuan tsou-i chi-yao*, which had been compiled by Shen Tsu-hsien. A collection of Yuan's official papers from the period of his presidency, compiled by Lu Shun and Hsü Yu-p'eng, was published in 1914 as the *Yuan ta-tsung-t'ung shu-tu hui-pien*.

Chinese historians generally have portrayed Yuan Shih-k'ai as the betrayer of the infant republic who bequeathed to China more than a decade of military misrule and political chaos. A traditionalist, Yuan had little sympathy for the political ideals and institutions of the West. His political style was compounded largely of personal ambition and political expediency, and his desire for power may well have blinded his political judgment and led him to undertake the disastrous monarchical movement. Nevertheless, Yuan Shih-k'ai was a seasoned and capable administrator, a skillful organizer, and an astute politician. At one time, his contemporaries, including revolutionaries and foreigners, regarded his leadership as the only possible alternative to a complete breakdown of order in China—a judgment which was partially vindicated by the chaotic period that followed his death.

Yuan T'ung-li   袁 同 禮
T. Shou-ho   守 和

Yuan T'ung-li (1895–6 February 1965), distinguished library administrator and bibliographer who was a pioneer in the modern library movement in China.

The second son of a government official in Hsushui, Chihli (Hopei), Yuan T'ung-li was brought up in a scholarly environment. His elder brother was Yuan Fu-li, who later became a professor of geology at Tsinghua University. Yuan T'ung-li evinced an avid interest in books and scholarship at an early age. In 1913 he enrolled at Peking University. Upon graduation in 1916, he was appointed assistant librarian of Tsinghua College. The following year, he became acting librarian, in which capacity he was largely responsible for the construction of the college's new library building.

In August 1920 Yuan T'ung-li received a Peking University scholarship for advanced study in the United States. Upon arrival in New York, he enrolled at Columbia University, from which he obtained a B.A. degree in 1922. During the Washington Conference in 1921–22 he served as secretary to Huang Fu (q.v.). After the conference, he enrolled at the New York State Library School in Albany, from which he was graduated with a B.L.S. degree in 1923. During this period, he spent three summers at the Library of Congress helping to catalogue its Chinese collections. In 1923 Yuan went to England for a year's study at the University of London's Institute of Historical Research.

Yuan T'ung-li returned to China in 1924 to become librarian of Kwangtung University. He also assisted in the creation of the National Palace Museum at Peking. He moved to Peking in 1925 as librarian and professor of bibliography at Peking University. In 1926 the Peking Metropolitan Library was organized, with the support of the China Foundation for the Promotion of Education and Culture, as the first step toward the establishment of a national library. Liang Ch'i-ch'ao (q.v.) was appointed its director and Yuan T'ung-li, its librarian. In 1929 the Metropolitan Library and the old National Library merged to form the National Library of Peiping, with Ts'ai Yuan-p'ei (q.v.) as director and Yuan T'ung-li as associate director. This new institution soon became the center of library activity in China. Because Ts'ai was also president of the Academia Sinica, the work of the directorship fell to Yuan, who finally succeeded Ts'ai as director in 1942.

In 1930 Yuan T'ung-li instituted a program for the exchange of librarians with Western libraries. To this end, he sought funds from foundations and other sources to send promising Chinese librarians to the United States, England, France, and Germany for advanced study and training. At the same time, he recruited a staff for the National Library of Peiping. After the library's new building was opened to the public on 25 June 1931, he introduced to China such Western practices as interlibrary loan, a photostat service, the exchange of materials with foreign countries, and the compilation of union catalogues and serial lists. In 1934 he sent a member of his staff to the Bibliothèque Nationale in Paris and the British Museum in London to plan and supervise the photographic reproduction of Tun-huang manuscripts.

The *T'u-shu chi-k'an* [quarterly bulletin of Chinese bibliography], a joint publication of the National Library of Peiping and the Chinese Committee on Intellectual Cooperation, was established by Yuan T'ung-li in 1934. Under his managing editorship, it appeared in separate Chinese and English editions and contained much useful information about books and libraries in China. Yuan also encouraged the publication of source materials on China's foreign relations and supervised the compilation of such works as the *Kuo-hsueh lun-wen so-yin* [index to sinological articles], published in four parts (1929, 1931, 1934, 1936); the *Wen-hsueh lun-wen so-yin* [index to articles on literature], published in three parts (1932, 1933, 1936); and the *Ti-hsueh lun-wen so-yin* [index to articles on historical geography], published in two parts (1934, 1936). Yuan also did much to develop bibliography and library science in China through his position as chairman of the executive board of the Library Association of China. In addition to compiling bibliographies and union lists, from 1926 to 1948 the association published *T'u-shu-kuan-hsüeh chi-k'an* [library science quarterly] and the bi-monthly *Chung-hua t'u-shu-kuan hsieh-hui hui-pao* [bulletin of the Library Association of China].

In February 1934 Yuan T'ung-li embarked on a nine-month tour of Europe and North America. He conferred with leading librarians and educators and established exchange relations with many institutions. While in the United States, he was awarded the University Medal for Excellence by Columbia. In July he represented China at the sixteenth plenary session of the League of Nations International Committee on Intellectual Cooperation, and in November he was a delegate to the International Museum Conference in Madrid. After returning to China by way of the Soviet Union, he urged the organization of the Museums Association of China, which came into existence in May 1935. Under his editorship, a bulletin of the association and a directory of Chinese museums were published. To arouse greater interest in museum work, a joint conference of the Museums Association and the Library Association was held at Tsingtao in July 1936.

To promote cooperative cataloguing, Yuan T'ung-li in 1935 initiated a printed card service patterned on that of the Library of Congress. Many libraries in China and abroad subscribed to this highly successful service until it was forced to suspend operations in 1937 by the outbreak of the Sino-Japanese war. Another mid-1930's innovation of Yuan T'ung-li was the establishment of the Engineering Reference Library at Nanking as an administrative division of the National Library of Peiping.

Before the occupation of north China by the Japanese in 1937, Yuan T'ung-li, with commendable foresight, moved some of the National Library of Peiping's irreplaceable books and manuscripts to south China. These materials, some 2,800 items in all, later were sent to the Library of Congress for safekeeping. The National Library carried on its work after the Japanese occupied Peiping, but Yuan and some staff members left the occupied areas. Yuan went to Kunming and busied himself with the task of providing the students and faculty of Southwest Associated University at Kunming with library services. He launched a campaign to appeal for books and periodicals for war-devastated libraries. Many institutions in the West responded to these appeals by sending scientific and technical books and journals to unoccupied China.

In 1942 Yuan T'ung-li moved to the wartime capital of Chungking, where he set up an office of the National Library of Peiping. At this point in the war, transportation problems were making it extremely difficult to import publications from the West. To keep Chinese scholars and scientists abreast of the latest developments in their fields, Yuan decided that extensive use of microfilm was necessary. As executive secretary of the International Cultural Service of China, an organization sponsored by the ministry of education, Yuan coordinated the activities of two organizations which, at the National Government's request, supplied microfilms of scientific and technical journals. One of these was the Sino-British Cooperation Office, headed by Professor Joseph Needham

of Cambridge University; the other was the American Publications Service, headed by Professor John K. Fairbank of Harvard University. Another important task undertaken by the International Cultural Service was the collecting of scholarly and scientific papers by Chinese authors for publication abroad. This work was entrusted to the service by the Cultural Relations Division of the United States Department of State. A committee was set up to examine and select papers for transmission to the United States. By June 1945 about 200 of these papers had been published in American journals.

At the end of 1944 Yuan T'ung-li was sent abroad by the Executive Yuan to strengthen cultural relations with Great Britain and the United States. During this trip, Yuan made special efforts to observe the changes and advances made in the library world as a result of the Second World War. In 1945 he was an adviser to the Chinese delegation to the United Nations Conference on International Organization in San Francisco. That May, he received an honorary LL.D. degree from the University of Pittsburgh.

Yuan T'ung-li returned to China in September 1945 to resume direction of the National Library of Peiping. Early in 1946 the ministry of education sent him on an acquisitions and investigation trip to the United States and Europe. In London he attended the UNESCO conference and served as vice chairman of the Committee on the Restoration of Art Objects. He then went on to Germany to make an investigation of Chinese cultural objects in that country. He returned to Peiping in September 1946 and remained there until the Chinese Communists threatened the city in December 1948.

In 1949 Yuan T'ung-li went to the United States to become consultant in Chinese literature at the Library of Congress. He edited the *Kuo-hui t'u-shu-kuan ts'ang Chung-kuo shan-pen shu-mu* [descriptive catalogue of rare Chinese books in the Library of Congress], which had been compiled by his former student Wang Chung-min. From 1951 to 1953 he served as the chief bibliographer of the Stanford Research Institute in California. He received a research grant from the Rockefeller Foundation in 1953 which enabled him to spend a year in Europe. In 1957 he joined the Library of Congress as a regular member of its staff. He remained in Washington until the summer of 1964, when he was awarded a research grant by the American Council of Learned Societies and the Social Science Research Council for the compilation of a bibliography on Chinese art and archaeology. While doing research in Munich, Germany, that July, he was taken ill and was compelled to return to the United States for treatment. His health continued to deteriorate, and he retired from the Library of Congress staff on 15 January 1965. He died of cancer on 6 February 1965. Yuan was survived by his wife, *née* Hui Hai, and by two sons and a daughter. Friends and scholars alike mourned the loss of an indefatigable and inspiring worker who devoted his entire life to the promotion of scholarship and of better understanding of the cultural heritage of China.

Yuan T'ung-li was the author of numerous articles published in professional journals. As early as 1924 he developed an interest in the *Yung-lo ta-tien*, an encyclopedic dictionary of unparalleled bulk, compiled (1403–9) by order of Yung-lo, the third emperor of the Ming dynasty, who reigned from 1403 to 1424. This work, which consisted of 11,095 hand-written volumes, has never been printed; only two manuscript copies were made, one of which perished at the fall of the Ming dynasty in 1644. The remaining set was stored in the Hanlin Academy in Peking, which was partly destroyed by fire on 23 June 1900 during the Boxer Uprising. A number of volumes were rescued from the conflagration; they were subsequently scattered all over the world. The National Library of Peiping, through the legacy of its institutional predecessor, possessed the largest number of surviving volumes. Yuan made a census of the extant volumes of this monumental compilation, which first appeared in the February 1924 issue of the magazine *Hsüeh-heng* [critical review]. He brought it up to date several times; the last census he made appeared in the September 1939 issue of the Chinese edition of the *T'u-shu chi-k'an*, in which he listed the location of 367 volumes. A number of additional volumes were discovered later, with the result that a total of about 500 volumes were identified.

Among Yuan's many works his *China in Western Literature: A Continuation of Cordier's Bibliotheca Sinica* of 1958 may be singled out for special mention. It is a comprehensive listing of some 18,000 monographic works on China in English, French, and German and works in Portuguese on Macao published from 1921 to 1957. It is the most important bibliography on China since the appearance of the monumental compilation by Henri Cordier (1849–1925) several decades ago. *Russian Works on China, 1918–1960, in American Libraries*, which appeared in 1961, lists materials in Russian not included in *China in Western Literature*.

To record the academic interests and accomplishments of Chinese students who had pursued advanced studies abroad, Yuan compiled a number of lists of doctoral dissertations. The first to appear, in 1961, was *A Guide to Doctoral Dissertations by Chinese Students in America, 1905–1960*, containing nearly 3,000 titles. This was followed by *Doctoral Dissertations by Chinese Students in Great Britain and Northern Ireland, 1916–1961*, which appeared in the March 1961 issue of *Chinese Culture* (Taipei), and *A Guide to Doctoral Dissertations by Chinese Students in Continental Europe, 1907–1962*, which appeared in installments in 1964 in the same journal. All these publications contributed greatly to a better understanding of the background and trends of higher education in modern China.

In his later years Yuan was interested in Sinkiang. He projected a series of ten titles on this outlying territory, including three bibliographies (of works in Chinese, in Japanese, and in Western languages); a collection of treaties and agreements between China and Russia relating to northwestern China; and reproductions of six older works on the area which were long out of print. Nearly all of these titles were published.

Yui, David: *see* YÜ JIH-CHANG.

Yui, O. K.: *see* YÜ HUNG-CHÜN.

Yün Tai-ying   揮 代 英
  T. Tzu-i   子 毅

Yün Tai-ying (1895–April 1931), Marxist intellectual and leader of the Young China Association, the Socialist Youth League, and the Hupeh branch of the Chinese Communist party. A noted propagandist, he edited the *Hsin Shu Pao* [new Szechwan daily], the *Chung-kuo ch'ing-nien* [China youth], and the *Hung-ch'i-pao* [red flag]. Yün was executed at Nanking in 1931.

Although his family's native place was Wuchin, Kiangsu, Yün Tai-ying was born in Wuchang, Hupeh. Several of his forebears had been scholar-officials. While Yün was a student at Chung-hua University in Wuchang, his family's finances became straitened, and he began to earn his living as a writer. He developed an interest in the work-study movement which was prevalent in student circles in China during the years after the First World War, and he organized the Li-ch'ün Society, sometimes translated as the Social Welfare Society, after his graduation from Chung-hua University in 1919. That society sponsored a bookstore as a channel for distributing materials on Marxism to students and established a small textile factory so that members of the society could earn a living while studying. Although the factory soon went bankrupt because of the relative inefficiency of its operations, the Li-ch'ün Bookstore became a center of radical intellectual activity in the central Yangtze valley. As students who had been exposed to Marxist ideas through the bookstore moved on to become teachers in the area, Yün's reputation grew.

Yün himself found a post as instructor and dean at the normal school in the T'ungch'eng district of Anhwei of which Chang Po-chün (q.v.) was principal. As dean, he organized the students into study groups to discuss Marxist ideas. After these activities came to the attention of the Anhwei provincial authorities, who were generally unsympathetic to radical ideas, Yün returned to Wuchang, where he taught at Chung-hua University.

In the early summer of 1921, Yün Tai-ying convened a meeting of young people who had taken part in the Li-ch'ün movement. Also present at this meeting, held at Huangkang, Hupeh, were representatives of the Wen-hua Bookstore at Changsha in Hunan province, which had been established in the autumn of 1920 through the work of Mao Tse-tung and other Hunanese radicals. Under Yün's leadership, the Hupeh meeting voted to organize the Kung-ts'un-she [mutual preservation society]

and drafted a constitution which approved of the dictatorship of the proletariat and of the principles of the new regime in Russia. Yün himself, however, was still not completely committed to the concept of proletarian revolution, for he was also an active leader of the Shao-nien Chung-kuo hsueh-hui (Young China Association), organized by Li Ta-chao and Tseng Ch'i (qq.v.) at Peking in 1918 and dedicated to the rejuvenation of China with "scientific spirit." When the First National Congress of the Chinese Communist party met at Shanghai in July 1921, Yün was at Nanking, chairing the opening session of the first conference of the Young China Association.

After the First National Congress of the Chinese Communist party, Yün dissolved the Kung-ts'un-she and led most of its members to join the Hupeh branch of the Chinese Communist party and the Socialist Youth League. He then went to Szechwan and became dean of the Lu-chou Normal School. In Szechwan, he and Hsiao Ch'u-nü (1894–1927), another young Communist from Hupeh, edited the *Hsin Shu Pao* [new Szechwan daily], which propagated radical ideas. In a retrospective estimate made in 1950 of Yün Tai-ying's influence upon the youth of Szechwan in the early 1920's, Kuo Mo-jo (q.v.), who became a close associate of Yün during the Northern Expedition of 1926–27, stated that nine out of ten young Sechwanese who left their native towns to enroll in the Whampoa Military Academy in Kwangtung had probably been inspired by Yün's revolutionary propaganda. In Szechwan, Yün also became acquainted with Wu Yü-chang (q.v.), then an influential intellectual in the province who was able to assist in obtaining Yün's release from prison in Szechwan after Yün was arrested in 1922.

In August 1923, when Chang T'ai-lei (q.v.), general secretary of the Socialist Youth League, left for the Soviet Union with Chiang Kai-shek, the Chinese Communist party ordered Yün Tai-ying to Shanghai to assist in youth work. He attended the second congress of the Socialist Youth League and was elected to its central committee. After that meeting, he took charge of Youth League propaganda work. Together with Hsiao Ch'u-nü, he edited its official journal, *Chung-kuo ch'ing-nien* [China youth], the first issue of which appeared in October 1923. While in Shanghai, Yün also taught at Shanghai

University, an institution which, during its brief existence, inspired many young Chinese to join the Northern Expedition and trained many cadres for the Chinese Communist party. After the Kuomintang and the Chinese Communist party began their period of collaboration in 1923, Yün joined the Kuomintang and became secretary of the department of workers and peasants at its Shanghai executive headquarters. He was in Shanghai at the time of the May Thirtieth Incident in 1925 and became a prominent leader of anti-British activities after that affair. Threats from Sun Ch'uan-fang (q.v.), who was then in control of Shanghai, subsequently forced Yün to flee. He went to Canton to attend the Second National Congress of the Kuomintang in January 1926, where he was one of the Communists elected to the Central Executive Committee of that party. After Chiang Kai-shek's anti-Communist coup in March 1926, the Chinese Communist party ordered Yün to the Whampoa Military Academy, where he became a political instructor with the mission of attempting to counterbalance the influence of Chiang Kai-shek.

With the rapid military success of the Northern Expedition during the summer of 1926, Yün moved to Wuhan, where he worked with other Communists in the Hupeh provincial government. Yün's most important post, however, was at the Wuhan branch of the Central Military Academy, of which Chiang Kai-shek was *ex officio* commandant and Teng Yen-ta (q.v.) was acting commandant. Because both Chiang and Teng were occupied with other matters, the actual administration of the Wuhan academy fell largely to Chou Fo-hai (q.v.). When Teng Yen-ta named Yün Tai-ying chief political instructor, Yün took over practical control of the institution's political department. In that capacity he played an important role in mobilizing the academy cadets to support Yeh T'ing (q.v.), the garrison commander at Wuchang, in suppressing the rebellion of Hsia Tou-yin.

In the spring of 1927 Yün Tai-ying was elected to the Central Committee of the Chinese Communist party at its Fifth National Congress, held at Hankow. Following the split between the Wuhan faction of the Kuomintang and the Communists in July, Yün was one of the organizers of the Nanchang Uprising (*see* Yeh T'ing) of 1 August 1927.

He then accompanied Yeh T'ing and Ho Lung (q.v.) on their flight southward from Nanchang. After their defeat at Swatow, Yün went to Hong Kong, which he used as a base for attempts to reorganize the battered Communist forces. He was one of the planners of the Canton Commune of December 1927 (*see* Chang T'ai-lei) and was secretary general of the short-lived Canton soviet government. When the Canton Commune was suppressed, he returned to the British colony of Hong Kong, where he edited the *Hung-ch'i-pao* [red flag], an underground Communist publication.

In mid-1928, when the Sixth National Congress of the Chinese Communist party met in Moscow, Yün went to Shanghai to work in the propaganda department of the Central Committee. His well-known polemical essay, "On Shih Ts'un-t'ung's Theory of the Chinese Revolution," soon was published in *Bolshevik*. In this essay, Yün stated that the reason the Chinese Communist party had not encouraged workers and peasants to enter the Kuomintang —the accusation made by Shih—was because the Communists feared that the workers and peasants might be influenced by the bourgeoisie. In the autumn of 1929 a rumor reached Shanghai to the effect that Mao Tse-tung had died in the countryside. The central authorities of the party dispatched Yün to the Kiangsi-Fukien soviet areas to investigate. Mao, of course, had not died, and Yün returned to become secretary of a district party committee in Shanghai. He was arrested in April 1930. Some reports suggest that Li Li-san (q.v.), annoyed both by Yün's criticism and by his popularity within the party, had intended that Yün be arrested when he assigned him to this position, which entailed great risk for a Communist of Yün's prominence. At the trial, Yün posed as a worker by the name of Wang Tso-lin. His identity was not discovered, and he was sentenced to five years in a Nanking prison rather than to death. When Ch'ü Ch'iu-pai and Chou En-lai (qq.v.) returned from Moscow in August 1930, they immediately set to work to arrange Yün's escape. In April 1931, however, after Ku Shun-chang defected to the Kuomintang, Yün's identity became known. He was executed in Nanking in April 1931, only a few days before the intended escape was scheduled to take place. He died at the age of 36 sui.

Yün Tai-ying married twice. His first wife died before 1927. He married his wife's younger sister, Shen Pao-ying, in 1927. They had a son in 1928. Yün Tzu-ch'iang, in later years a prominent scientist in China, was Yün Tai-ying's younger brother.

Yün Tai-ying reportedly led a simple and frugal life. Some individuals in the Communist party called him the "saint of the proletariat" and regarded him as the embodiment of the true Communist spirit. An articulate speaker, Yün showed great skill in arousing his audiences. At the same time, he was a prolific and effective writer. Many of his articles appeared in the *Tung-fang tsa-chih* and the *Hsueh-sheng tsa-chih*. He was also a contributor to *Hsin ch'ing-nien* edited by Ch'en Tu-hsiu (q.v.) and others, which published his essays "On the Reality of Matter" and "On Belief." Yün translated from English many articles on social questions and published them in Chinese journals. Most of his original writings were on contemporary Chinese problems and were published in *Chung-kuo ch'ing-nien* under the pen names Tan I and Tai Ying. It is because of the widespread influence which this journal exercised over the youth of China in the years just before the Northern Expedition that Yün Tai-ying and his close friend, Hsiao Ch'u-nü, gained a place in the history of the Chinese Communist party.

Zen, H. C.: *see* JEN HUNG-CHÜN.

Zen, Sophia H.: *see* CH'EN HENG-CHE.

Zia, H. L.: *see* HSIEH HUNG-LAI.

BIOGRAPHICAL DICTIONARY
OF REPUBLICAN CHINA

BIBLIOGRAPHY

BIBLIOGRAPHER'S NOTE

The bibliographic section of the *Biographical Dictionary of Republican China* follows the order of the text. The bibliography for each article lists the works, if any, of the subject of the article, as well as the sources used in preparing that article.

WORKS

The contributors of biographical articles submitted sketches in several languages and provided bibliographies of works and sources which varied as widely in form and completeness as did the contributors' nationalities and fields of interest. Their bibliographic listings were supplemented through consultation with the holdings of the East Asian Library of Columbia University, the Library of Congress, the Harvard-Yenching Library, the Wason Collection of the Cornell University Libraries, and the Library of the Hoover Institution on War, Revolution, and Peace. For any book about which complete information was unobtainable, we decided to retain the incomplete item, even if only a title, in the hope that such information will be of some use to scholars and that with their aid the gaps in such items can be filled in.

In consultation with the late Dr. William Bridgwater of Columbia University Press, it was decided to arrange works according to dates of publication, in the belief that the chronological system would reflect the developing careers of the authors, most of whom were not literary men. It should be noted, however, that the chronological arrangement is somewhat imperfect because of the chaotic publishing practices prevalent during the republican period and the resultant difficulty in tracing first editions; works for which no date could be determined

are at the end of the listing. In addition to books and articles, we have included English translations and editorships of periodicals and newspapers.

SOURCES

The source listings, in addition to the materials provided by the contributors of biographical articles, include correspondence, personal interviews, and information acquired from individuals and from the files of various institutions in the course of preparing the articles for publication. The source listings are arranged alphabetically. For personal and political reasons, some of the people who were interviewed did not wish their names to be published. In such instances the form "Persons interviewed: not to be identified" is used. The most commonly used sources (*see* KEY TO ABBREVIATIONS on pp. 101–3) have been abbreviated to avoid repetition of the full facts of publication.

ROMANIZATION

The romanization system used for Chinese materials is the Wade-Giles system, with some diacritical marks omitted in keeping with the style of the text. It should also be noted that the Chinese characters are those usually used in the republican period; titles of articles in periodicals published in the People's Republic of China have been rendered in the older style rather than in simplified characters.

ACKNOWLEDGMENTS

The compilation of this bibliography was made possible, first of all, by the scholars from

Bibliographer's Note   [100]

many parts of the world who contributed articles to the *Biographical Dictionary of Republican China*. Thanks are also due to Dr. Te-kong Tong and Mr. Eddie Wang of the East Asian Library of Columbia University, to Dr. Eugene Wu of the Harvard-Yenching Library, and to Mr. Pei-jan Hsia, who verified some of the supplementary material. Finally, I am greatly indebted to Miss Tsui-jean Chen for her diligent and painstaking labors in the Columbia libraries.

JOSEPH K. H. CHENG

KEY TO ABBREVIATIONS

AADC. Reinsch, Paul Samuel. An American Diplomat in China. Garden City, N.Y.; Toronto: Doubleday, Page & Co.,1922.

AWW. The Asia Who's Who, 3rd Edition. Hong Kong: Pan-Asia Newspaper Alliance, 1960.

BKL. Biographies of Kuomintang Leaders. (mimeo.) Cambridge: Committee on International and Regional Studies, Harvard University, 1948. 3 vols.

BPC. Biographies of Prominent Chinese, ed. by A. R. Burt, J. B. Powell, and Carl Crow. Shanghai: Biographical Publishing Co.

CB. Current Background. Hong Kong: American Consulate General, 1950-.

CBJS. Chūgoku bunkakai jimbutsu sōkan, ed. by Hashikawa Tokio. Peking: Chūka horei inshokan, 1940.
中國文化界人物總鑑。橋川時雄。

CCLTC. Yü Hsueh-lun. Ch'i-ch'ing-lou tsachi. Taipei: Taiwan ch'i ming shu-chü, 1953-55. 2 vols.
喩血輪。綺情樓雜記。

CCM-1. Hsueh Chün-tu. The Chinese Communist Movement, 1921-1937: An Annotated Bibliography of Selected Materials in the Chinese Collection of the Hoover Institution on War, Revolution, and Peace. Stanford: The Hoover Institution on War, Revolution, and Peace, Stanford University, 1960.

CCM-2. Hsueh Chün-tu. The Chinese Communist Movement, 1937-1949: An Annotated Bibliography of Selected Materials in the Chinese Collection of the Hoover Institution on War, Revolution, and Peace. Stanford: The Hoover Institution on War, Revolution, and Peace, Stanford University, 1962.

CECP. Wang Sen-jan. Chin-tai erh-shih chia p'ing-chuan. Peiping: Hsing yen shu wu, 1934.
王森然。近代二十家評傳。

CH. China Handbook, 1937-45: A Comprehensive Survey of Major Developments in China in Eight Years of War; Revised and Enlarged with 1946 Supplement, comp. by Chinese Ministry of Information. New York: The Macmillan Co., 1947.

CH-T. China Handbook, ed. by China Handbook Editorial Board. Taipei, 1951-.

CHMI. Tso Shun-sheng. Chung-kuo hsien-tai ming-jen i-shih. Kowloon: Tzu-yu ch'u-pan she, 1951.
左舜生。中國現代名人軼事。

CHWC. Li I-ming. Chung-kuo hsin wen-hsueh shih chiang-hua. Shanghai: Shih-chieh shu-chü, 1947.
李一鳴。中國新文學史講話。

CHWSK. Wang Yao. Chung-kuo hsin wen-hsueh shih kao. Peking: K'ai-ming shu-tien, 1951 (Vol. 1); Shanghai: Hsin wen-i ch'u-pan she, 1954 (Vol. 2).
王瑤。中國新文學史稿。

CHWYS. Wang Che-fu. Chung-kuo hsin wen-hsueh yün-tung shih. Peiping: Chieh ch'eng yin shu chü, 1933.
王哲甫。中國新文學運動史。

CJC. Chin-shih jen-wu chih, ed. by Chin Liang. Taipei: Kuo-min ch'u-pan she, 1955.
近世人物志。金梁。

CKJMT. Chung-kung jen-ming tien, comp. by Chang Ta-chün. Kowloon: Tzu-yu ch'u-pan she, 1956.
中共人名典。張大軍。

CKJWC. Chung-kung jen-wu chih, comp. by Jen-min nien-chien. Hong Kong: Ta-chung shu-tien, 1951?
中共人物誌。人民年鑑。

CKLC. Chung-kuo kung-ch'an-tang lieh-shih chuan, comp. by Hua Ying-shen. Hong Kong: Hsin min-chu ch'u-pan she, 1949.
中國共產黨烈士傳。華應申。

CKMJT. Chung-kuo ming-jen tien, ed. by Li Hsi-keng and Fang Cheng-hsiang. Peking: Li-chih shu-tien, 1949.
中國名人典。李希更，方正祥。

CMJL. Chung-hua Min-kuo jen-shih lu, comp. by Chung-hua Min-kuo jen-shih lu pien-tsuan wei-yuan-hui. Taipei: Hsing T'ai yin-shua ch'ang, 1953.
中華民國人事錄。中華民國人事錄編纂委員會。

CMMC. Chung-hua Min-kuo ming-jen chuan, comp. by Chia I-chün. Peiping: Wen-hua hsueh-she, 1932-33. 2 vols.
中華民國名人傳。賈逸君。

CMTC. Chung-hua Min-kuo ta-shih chi, comp. by Kao Yin-tsu. Taipei: Shih-chieh she, 1957.
中華民國大事記。高蔭祖。

CPR. *Chinese Press Review*. Shanghai: American Consulate General.

CTIW. T'ao Chü-yin. Chin-tai i-wen. Shanghai: Chung-hua shu-chü, 1940.
陶菊隱。近代軼聞。

CTMC. Chung-kuo tang-tai ming-jen chuan, comp. by Fu Jun-hua. Shanghai: Shih-chieh wen-hua fu-wu she, 1948.
中國當代名人傳。傅潤華。

CWR. *China Weekly Review*, June, 1917-July, 1953. Shanghai: Millard Publishing Co.

CWT. Ku Feng-ch'eng. Chung wai wen-hsueh-chia tz'u-tien. Shanghai: Le hua t'u-shu kung-ssu, 1934.
顧鳳城。中外文學家辭典。

CYB. The Chinese Year Book, 1935-45, ed. by the Council of International Affairs. Shanghai, Chungking.

CYB-W. The China Year Book, 1916-20, ed. by H. T. Montague Bell and H. G. W. Woodhead. London: George Routledge & Sons.
The China Year Book, 1921-30, ed. by G. H. W. Woodhead. Tientsin: Tientsin Press.
The China Year Book, 1931-39, ed. by G. H. W. Woodhead. Shanghai: The North-China Daily News & Herald.

DPGOCC. Department of State, Bureau of Intelligence and Research. Biographic Dictionary: Directory of Party and Government Officials of Communist China. Washington: Department of State, 1960. 2 vols.

ECC. Erh-shih chin jen chih, ed by Jen chien shih she. Shanghai: Liang-yu t'u-shu kung-ssu, 1935.
二十今人志。人間世社。

GCCJK. Gendai Chūgoku Chōsen jimmei kan, ed. by Gaimushō Ajia-kyoku. Tokyo, 1953.
現代中國朝鮮人名鑑。外務省アジア局。

GCJ. Gendai Chūgoku jiten, ed. by Chūgoku kenkyū-jo. Tokyo, 1950.
現代中國辭典。中國研究所。

GCJJ. Gendai Chūgoku jimmei jiten, ed. by Kasumigaseki-kai. Tokyo, 1957, 1962.
現代中國人名辭典。霞関会。

GCMMTJK. Gendai Chūka Minkoku Manshū Teikoku jimmei kan, ed. by Gaimushō jōhō-bu. Tokyo, 1937.
現代中華民國滿洲帝國人名鑑。外務省情報部。

GSJJ. Gendai Shina jimmei jiten, ed. by Tairiku bunka kenkyū-jo. Tokyo, 1939.
現代支那人名辭典。大陸文化研究所。

GSJK. Gendai Shina jimmei kan, comp. by Gaimushō jōhōbu. Tokyo, 1928.
現代支那人名鑑。外務省情報部。

GSSJ. Hatano Ken'ichi. Gendai Shina no seiji to jimbutsu. Tokyo, 1937.
波多野乾一。現代支那の政治と人物。

HCJC. Hsin Chung-kuo jen-wu chih, ed. by Chou-mo pao she. Hong Kong: Chou-mo pao she, 1950. 2 vols.
新中國人物誌。週末報社。

HCMW. T'an-tang-tang-chai chu (pseud.). Hsien-tai Chung-kuo ming-jen wai-shih. Peiping: Shih pao she, 1935.
坦蕩蕩齋主。現代中國名人外史。

HKLC. Hunan ko-ming lieh-shih chuan, comp. by Chung-kung Hunan sheng wei hsuan-ch'uan pu. Changsha: Hunan t'ung-su tu-wu ch'u-pan she, 1952.
湖南革命烈士傳。中共湖南省委宣傳部。

HMTT. Hsin ming-tz'u tz'u-tien, ed. by Hu Chi-t'ao. Shanghai: Ch'un ming shu-tien, 1950.
新名詞辭典。胡濟濤。

HSWT. Li Ang. Hung se wu-t'ai (Tang-tai shih-liao). Hong Kong: Sheng-li ch'u-pan she, 1941.
李昂。紅色舞台（當代史料）。

HWP. Fang Ch'ing. Hsien-tai wen-t'an pai-hsiang. Hong Kong: Hsin shih-chi ch'u-pan she, 1953.
方青。現代文壇百象。

JMST. Jen-min shou-ts'e, 1950-1965. Ta kung pao she.
人民手冊。

KHC. Ko-ming hsien-lieh chuan-chi, comp. by Wang Shao-tzu. Shanghai: Ching-wei shu-chü.

革命先烈傳記。王紹子。

KMWH. Ko-ming wen-hsien, ed. by Chung-kuo kuo-min-tang chung-yang wei-yuan-hui tang shih shih-liao pien-tsuan wei-yuan-hui. Taipei, 1953–65. 35 vols.
革命文獻。中國國民黨中央委員會黨史史料編纂委員會。

K-WWMC. Klein, Donald W. Who's Who in China: Biographical Sketches of 542 Chinese Communist Leaders. New York, 1959. 3 vols.

MCNP. Schyns, Jos. *et al.* 1500 Modern Chinese Novels and Plays. Peiping: Catholic University Press, 1948.

MMH. T'ang Tsu-p'ei. Min-kuo ming-jen hsiao-chuan. Hong Kong: Hsin shih-chi ch'u-pan she, 1953.
唐祖培。民國名人小傳。

MMT. Min-kuo ming-jen t'u-chien, ed. by Yang Chia-lo. Tz'u-tien kuan. 1937–. 3 vols.
民國名人圖鑑。楊家駱。

MSICH. Min-kuo shih-wu nien i-ch'ien chih Chiang Kai-shek hsien-sheng, comp. by Mao Ssu-ch'eng. 1935. 20 vols.
民國十五年以前之蔣介石先生。毛思誠。

PCCP. Pei chuan chi pu, comp. by Min Erh-ch'ang. Peiping: Yenching ta-hsueh kuo-hsueh yen-chiu so, 1931. 24 vols.
碑傳集補。閔爾昌。

RCCL. Readings in Contemporary Chinese Literature, ed. by Liu Wu-chi and Li Tien-yi. New Haven: Institute of Far Eastern Languages, Yale University, 1953–. 3 vols.

RD. Wales, Nym (pseud. of Helen Foster Snow). Red Dust: Autobiographies of Chinese Communists. Stanford: Stanford University Press, 1952.

RNRC. Snow, Edgar. Random Notes on Red China (1936–1945). Cambridge: Distributed by Harvard University Press, 1957.

RSOC. Snow, Edgar. Red Star over China. New York: Random House, 1938.

SCMP. Survey of China Mainland Press. Hong Kong: American Consulate General, 1951–.

SHPC. Lu Man-yen. Shih hsien pieh-chi. Chungking: Wen hsin shu-chü, 1943.
陸曼炎。時賢別記。

SJ. Shina jinshiroku, ed. by Sawamura Yukio and Ueda Toshio. Osaka, 1929.
支那人士錄。澤村幸夫,植田捷雄。

SMJ. Shina mondai jiten, comp. by Fujita Chikamasa. Tokyo: Chûô Kôron-sha, 1942.
支那問題辭典。藤田親昌。

SSKR. Saishin Shina kanshin roku, ed. by Shina kenkyū-kai. Tokyo, 1919.
最新支那官紳錄。支那研究會。

SSYD. Saishin Shina yōjin den, comp. by Tōa mondai chōsa-kai. Osaka: Asahi shimbun-. sha, 1941.
最新支那要人傳。東亞問題調查會。

TCJC. Tang-tai Chung-kuo jen-wu chih. ed. by Chung liu shu-chü. Shanghai: Chung liu shu-chü, 1938.
當代中國人物誌。中流書局。

TCMC. Hsiao Hsiao and Hu Tzu-li. Tang-tai Chung-kuo ming-jen chih. Shanghai: Shih-chieh p'ing-lun ch'u-pan she, 1940.
蕭瀟,胡自立。當代中國名人誌。

TCMC-1. Tzu-yu Chung-kuo ming-jen chuan, ed. by Ting Ti-sheng. Taipei, 1952.
自由中國名人傳。丁滌生。

TCMT. Tang-tai Chung-kuo ming-jen tz'u-tien, comp. by Jen Chia-yao. Shanghai: Tung-fang shu-tien, 1947.
當代中國名人辭典。任嘉堯。

TKLH. Tsui-chin kuan-shen lü-li hui lu, ed. by Peking Fu-wen-she. Peking: Fu-wen-she, 1920.
最近官紳履歷彙錄。北京敷文社。

TTJWC. Lu Tan-lin. Tang-tai jen-wu chih. Shanghai: Shih-chieh shu-chü, 1947.
陸丹林。當代人物誌。

USRWC. The China White Paper, August 1949. (Originally issued as United States Relations with China, with Special Reference to the Period 1944–1949.) Stanford: Stanford University Press, 1967. 2 vols.

WWARS. Who's Who of American Returned Students, ed. by Tsing Hua College. Peking, 1917.

WWC. Who's Who in China, ed. by the China Weekly Review. Shanghai, 1915–50.

WWCC. Who's Who in Communist China. Hong Kong: Union Research Institute, 1966.

WWMC. Who's Who in Modern China, ed. by Max Perleberg. Hong Kong: Ye Olde Printerie, 1954.

BIBLIOGRAPHY

Ai Ssu-ch'i　艾思奇

Works

1935–37. ed. of *Tu-shu sheng-huo*.
讀書生活。

1936. Che-hsueh chiang-hua. Shanghai: Tu-shu
sheng-huo she.
哲學講話。

1936. Ju-ho yen-chiu che-hsueh. Shanghai: Tu-
shu sheng-huo ch'u-pan she.
如何研究哲學。

1936. Ssu-hsiang fang-fa lun. Shanghai: Sheng-
huo shu-tien.
思想方法論。

1937. Che-hsueh yü sheng-huo.
哲學與生活。

1938. Ai Ssu-ch'i *et al*. Sun Chung-shan te ssu-
hsiang yü hsueh-shuo.
艾思奇等。孫中山的思想與學說。

1939. Che-hsueh hsuan-chi. Shanghai: Ch'en
kuang shu-tien.
哲學選輯。

1939. Che-hsueh yen-chiu kang-yao. T'o-huang
ch'u-pan she.
哲學研究綱要。

1939. Ju-ho yen-chiu che-hsueh. Shanghai: Tu-
shu sheng-huo ch'u-pan she.
如何研究哲學。

1947. K'o-hsueh li-shih kuan chiao-ch'eng. with
Wu Li-p'ing. Shanghai: Tu-shu ch'u-pan she.
科學歷史觀教程。吳黎平。

1947. Ai Ssu-ch'i *et al*. Yang ko lun-wen hsuan-
chi (comp. by Tung-pei wen-i kung-tso t'uan).
Dairen: Chung Su yu-hao hsieh-hui.
艾思奇等。秧歌論文選集。東北文藝工作團。

1948. She-hui fa-chan chien-shih.
社會發展簡史。

1949. Lun tu-shu. Hong Kong: Hsin min-chu
ch'u-pan she.
論讀書。

1949. Ssu-hsiang fang-fa shang te ko-ming. with
Wu Li-p'ing *et al*. Hong Kong: Hung mien
ch'u-pan she.
思想方法上的革命。吳黎平等。

1950. Li-shih wei-wu-lun—she-hui fa-chan shih
chiang-shou t'i-kang. Canton: Hsin hua shu-
tien.
歷史唯物論—社會發展史講授提綱。

1950. Ta chung che-hsueh. Foochow: Hsin hua
shu-tien Fukien fen-tien.
大象哲學。

1950. Ts'ung-t'ou hsueh ch'i. Peking: Sheng-
huo, tu-shu, hsin chih san lien shu-tien.
從頭學起。

1950–51. Li-shih wei-wu-lun—she-hui fa-chan
shih. Peking: Sheng-huo, tu-shu, hsin chih
san lien shu-tien. 2 vols.
歷史唯物論—社會發展史。

1951. Li-shih wei-wu-lun—she-hui fa-chan shih
chiang-i. Peking: Kung-jen ch'u-pan she.
歷史唯物論—社會發展史講義。

1952. Hsueh-hsi te mu-ti yü chi-pen fang-fa.
with Teng Ch'u-min, Shu Wen. Shanghai:
Chan-wang chou-k'an she.
學習的目的與基本方法。鄧初民舒文。

1952, March. "Jen ch'ing tzu-ch'an chieh-chi
ssu-hsiang te fan-tung hsing." *Hsueh-hsi*, 48:
3–7.
認清資產階級思想的反動性。學習。

1952. Lun ssu-hsiang kai-tsao wen-t'i. Peking:
Hsueh-hsi tsa-chih she.
論思想改造問題。

1955. Hu Shih shih-yung chu-yi p'i-p'an.
胡適實用主義批判。

1955. P'i-p'an Hu Shih te fan-tung che-hsueh
szu-hsiang. Peking: Chung-kuo ch'ing-nien
ch'u-pan she.
批判胡適的反動哲學思想。

1955. Shen-mo shih wo-men te yuan-ta ch'ien-t'u.
Peking: Chung-kuo ch'ing-nien ch'u-pan she.

什麼是我們的遠大前途。

1956. P'i-p'an Liang Shu-ming te che-hsueh szu-hsiang. Peking: Jen-min ch'u-pan she.
批判梁漱溟的哲學思想。

1956. She-hui li-shih shou-hsien shih sheng-ch'an che te li-shih—lao-tung ch'uang-tsao jen-lei te shih-chieh (comp. by Chung-kuo wen-hsueh i-shu chieh lien-ho hui). Peking: Sheng-huo, tu-shu, hsin chih san lien shu-tien.
社會歷史首先是生產者的歷史—勞動創造人類的世界。中國文學藝術界聯合會。

1956. Wei-wu pien-cheng-fa te fan-ch'ou chien-lun. Shanghai: Jen-min ch'u-pan she.
唯物辯證法的范疇簡論。

1957. Pien-cheng wei-wu chu-yi chiang-k'o t'i-kang. Peking: Jen-min ch'u-pan she.
辯證唯物主義講課提綱。

1958. P'o-ch'u mi-hsin ta-chia hsueh che-hsueh. Peking: Chung-kuo ch'ing-nien ch'u-pan she.
破除迷信大家學哲學。

1961. Chin i pu hsueh-hsi chang-wo wu-ch'an chieh-chi shih-chieh-kuan—tu "Mao Tse-tung hsuan-chi" ti-ssu chüan pi-chi. Hong Kong: Sheng-huo, tu-shu, hsin chih san lien shu-tien.
進一步學習掌握無產階級世界觀—讀「毛澤東選集」第四卷筆記。

1964, November 1. "Po Yang Hsien-chen t'ung-chih te 'tsung-ho ching-chi chi-ch'u lun'." *Jen-min jih-pao*. Peking.
駁楊獻珍同志的「綜合經濟基礎論」。人民日報。

SOURCES

Person interviewed: Chang Kuo-t'ao.
GCJJ
WWMC

Burhan　　鮑爾漢

WORKS

1962. Huo-yen shan te nu hou. Shanghai: Shang-hai wen-i ch'u-pan she.
火焰山的怒吼。

SOURCES

Chang Ta-chün. Sinkiang chin ssu-shih nien pien-luan chi-lueh. Taipei: Chung-yang wen-wu kung-ying she, 1954.
張大軍。新疆近四十年變亂紀略。

Hung Ti-ch'en. Sinkiang shih ti ta-kang. Nanking: Cheng-chung shu-chü, 1935.
洪滌塵。新疆史地大綱。

Wu Shao-lin. Sinkiang kai-kuan. Nanking: Jen sheng yin shu chü, 1933.
吳紹璘。新疆概觀。

Buyantai

SOURCES

Persons interviewed: not to be identified.

Cha-ch'i-ssu-ch'in. Meng-ku chih chin hsi. Tai-pei: Chung-hua wen-hua ch'u-pan shih-yeh wei-yuan-hui, 1955. 2 vols.
札奇斯欽。蒙古之今昔。

CMJL
MMT
MSICH
SMJ

Sun Wen. Kuo-fu ch'üan-shu (ed. by Chang Ch'i-yun). Taipei: Kuo-fang yen-chiu-yuan, 1960.
孫文。國父全書。張其昀。

Chan Ta-pei　　詹大悲

SOURCES

CBJS

Feng Tzu-yu. Chung-kuo ko-ming yun-tung erh-shih-liu nien tsu-chih shih. Shanghai: Shang-wu yin shu kuan, 1948.
馮自由。中國革命運動二十六年組織史。

Hsin-hai ko-ming, ed. by Ch'ai Te-keng *et al*. Shanghai: Jen-min ch'u-pan she, 1957. 8 vols.
辛亥革命。柴德賡等。

Li I-tung. "Chan Ta-pei chuan," in Chang Nan-hsien, *Hupeh ko-ming chih chih lu*. Shanghai: Shang-wu yin shu kuan, 1945.
李翊東。詹大悲傳。張難先。湖北革命知之錄。

Yü Hsueh-lun. "Ch'ing mo Min ch'u Hankow pao t'an shih." *Pao hsueh*, I-9 (June, 1956): 28-31.
喻血輪。清末民初漢口報壇史。報學。

Chan T'ien-yu　　詹天佑

SOURCES

Person interviewed: Ling Hung-hsun.

Chan T'ien-yu hsien-sheng nien-p'u, ed. by Ling Hung-hsun. Taipei: Chung-kuo kung-ch'eng-shih hsueh-hui, 1961.
詹天佑先生年譜。凌鴻勛。

Ching Chang t'ieh-lu kung-ch'eng chi-lueh.
京張鐵路工程紀略。
La Fargue, Thomas Edward. China's First Hundred. Pullman: State College of Washington, 1942.
Li Po-yuan and Jen Kung-t'an. Kwangtung chi-ch'i kung-jen fen-tou shih. Taipei: Chung-kuo lao-kung fu-li ch'u-pan she, 1955.
李伯元，任公坦。廣東機器工人奮鬥史。
Ling Hung-hsun. Chung-kuo t'ieh-lu chih. Taipei: Ch'ang liu pan-yueh-k'an she, 1954.
凌鴻勛。中國鐵路誌。
"Ming kung-ch'eng-shih Chan T'ien-yu." *Hua Mei jih-pao.* New York, January 9, 1958.
名工程師詹天佑。華美日報。
MMH
San-shih nien lai chih Chung-kuo kung-ch'eng, ed. by Chung-kuo kung-ch'eng-shih hsueh-hui. Chungking: Chung-yang yin-shua ch'ang, 1946.
三十年來之中國工程。中國工程師學會。
Yung Wing. My Life in China and America. New York: Henry Holt & Co., 1909.

Chang Chi   張繼

WORKS

1905-6, 1908. ed. of *Min pao.*
民報。
1943. P'ing-chün ti-ch'üan yü t'u-ti kai-ko. Chungking: Shang-wu yin shu kuan.
平均地權與土地改革。
1951-52. Chang P'u-ch'üan hsien-sheng ch'üan-chi; cheng-pien, pu-pien (ed. by Chung-yang kai-tsao wei-yuan-hui tang shih shih-liao pien-tsuan wei-yuan-hui). Taipei.
張溥泉先生全集；正編，補編。中央改造委員會黨史史料編纂委員會。

SOURCES

BKL
Chang Chi. Chang P'u-ch'üan hsien-sheng ch'üan-chi; cheng-pien, pu-pien (ed. by Chung-yang kai-tsao wei-yuan-hui tang shih shih-liao pien-tsuan wei-yuan-hui). Taipei, 1951-52.
張繼。張溥泉先生全集；正編，補編。中央改造委員會黨史史料編纂委員會。
Scalapino, Robert A., and George T. Yu. The Chinese Anarchist Movement. Berkeley: Center for Chinese Studies, Institute of International Studies, University of California, 1961.

T'ang Leang-li. The Inner History of the Chinese Revolution. New York: E. P. Dutton & Co., 1930.

Chang Chi-luan   張季鸞

WORKS

1915-16. ed. of *Min hsin jih-pao.* Shanghai.
民信日報。
1944. Chi-luan wen-ts'un. Chungking. 2 vols.
季鸞文存。
ed. of *Chung-hua hsin pao.*
中華新報。
ed. of *Hsia sheng tsa-chih.*
夏聲雜誌。
ed. of *Min li pao.*
民立報。
ed. of *Ta kung-ho jih-pao.*
大共和日報。
ed. of *Ta kung pao.*
大公報。

SOURCES

Chang Chi-luan. Chi-luan wen-ts'un. Chungking, 1944. 2 vols.
張季鸞。季鸞文存。
Ch'en Chi-ying. Po-jen Chang Chi-luan. Taipei: Wen yu ch'u-pan she, 1957.
陳紀瀅。報人張季鸞。
Li Yuan-ting. Chung-hua Min-kuo ku po-jen Yü-lin Chang Chi-luan hsien-sheng pei-ming.
李元鼎。中華民國故報人榆林張季鸞先生碑銘。
SHPC

Chang Ch'i-huang   張其鍠

WORKS

1931. Mo ching t'ung-chieh. Kweilin: Chang shih tu-chih-t'ang. 2 vols.
墨經通解。
1932. Tu-chih-t'ang ts'ung kao.
獨志堂叢稿。

SOURCES

Chang Ch'i-huang. "Hsien-fu-chün hsing shu," in Chang Ch'i-huang, *Tu-chih-t'ang ts'ung-kao.* 1932.
張其鍠。先府君行述。張其鍠，獨志堂叢稿。
CMMC

CTIW

Hsü Liang-chih. Liang-chai tsa-pi. Hong Kong: Tzu-yu ch'u-pan she, 1951.

徐亮之。亮齋雜筆。

MMT

Tao Chü-yin. Wu P'ei-fu chiang-chün chuan. Shanghai: Chung-hua shu-chü, 1946.

陶菊隱。吳佩孚將軍傳。

Tseng Chi-fen. Ch'ung-te lao-jen tzu-ting nien-p'u. 1931.

曾紀芬。崇德老人自訂年譜。

Chang Ch'i-yün 張其昀

WORKS

1928. Chung-kuo min-tsu chih. Shanghai: Shang-wu yin shu kuan.

中國民族誌。

1932. Jen ti hsüeh lun-ts'ung; ti-i chi. Nanking: Chung-shan shu-chü.

人地學論叢；第一集。

1932. Pen kuo ti-li. Nanking: Chung-shan shu-chü. 2 vols.

本國地理。

1942. Chung-hua li-tai ta chiao-yü chia shih-lueh (ed. by Kuo-li Chekiang ta-hsüeh shih ti chiao-yü yen-chiu shih). Kweiyang: Chung-shan shu-chü.

中華歷代大教育家史略。國立浙江大學史地教育研究室。

1942. Tung-pei wen-t'i; ti-i chi. Tsunyi: Chekiang ta-hsüeh shih ti chiao-yü yen-chiu shih.

東北問題；第一輯。

1945. The Natural Resources of China. New York: Sino-International Economic Research Center.

1946. Lü Mei chien-wen lu. Shanghai: Shang-wu yin shu kuan.

旅美見聞錄。

1947. Chung-kuo jen ti kuan-hsi-lun. Shanghai: Ta tung shu-chü.

中國人地關係概論。

1948. Chung-kuo te ch'ien-t'u. Canton: Hsien-tai wen-t'i ts'ung-k'an pien-chi she.

中國的前途。

1948. Tsunyi hsin chih. Hangchow: Kuo-li Chekiang ta-hsüeh shih ti yen-chiu so.

遵義新志。

1949. Fei Han chi hsing. Taipei: Cheng-chung shu-chü.

菲韓紀行。

1950. San min chu-yi kai-lun. Taipei: Chung-yang kai-tsao wei-yuan-hui wen-wu kung-ying-she.

三民主義概論。

1951–52. Tang shih kai-yao. Taipei: Chung-yang kai-tsao wei-yuan-hui wen-wu kung-ying she. 5 vols.

黨史概要。

1952. Hsin sheng-huo yun-tung. Taipei: Chung-yang wen-wu kung-ying she.

新生活運動。

1952. San min chu-i te li-lun. Taipei: Chung-hua wen-hua ch'u-pan shih-yeh wei-yuan-hui. 2 vols.

三民主義的理論。

1953. China of the Fifty Centuries. Taipei: China Culture Publishing Foundation.

1953. Chung-hua Min-kuo ch'uang-li shih. Taipei: Chung-hua wen-hua ch'u-pan shih-yeh wei-yuan-hui.

中華民國創立史。

1953. Climate and Man in China. Taipei: China Culture Publishing Foundation.

1953. Ke-ming che-hsüeh chih chi-ch'u. Taipei: Chung-yang wen-wu kung-ying she.

革命哲學之基礎。

1953. Kuo-min-tang te hsin-sheng. Taipei: Chung-yang wen-wu kung-ying she.

國民黨的新生。

1953. Shih-yeh chi-hua chieh-shuo. Taipei: Chung-yang wen-wu kung-ying she.

實業計劃解說。

1953. Ta-lu lun-hsien te t'ung-shih yü kuang-fu ta-lu te nu-li. Taipei: Chung-yang wen-wu kung-ying she.

大陸淪陷的痛史與光復大陸的努力。

1953–54. (ed.) Kuo shih shang te wei-ta jen-wu. Taipei: Chung-hua wen-hua ch'u-pan shih-yeh wei-yuan-hui.

國史上的偉大人物。

1954. Chang Ch'i-yün et al. Chung-kuo chan shih lun chi. Taipei: Chung-hua wen-hua ch'u-pan shih-yeh wei-yuan-hui. 2 vols.

張其昀 等。中國戰史論集。

1954. Chang Ch'i-yün et al. Chung-kuo wen-hua lun-chi. Taipei: Chung-hua wen-hua ch'u-pan shih-yeh wei-yuan-hui. 3 vols.

張其昀 等。中國文化論集。

1954. "Chung-kuo cheng-chih che-hsüeh te pen-yuan," in Chung-kuo cheng-chih ssu-hsiang yü chih-tu shih lun-chi. Taipei: Chung-hua wen-hua ch'u-pan shih-yeh wei-yuan-hui. 3 vols.

中國政治哲學的本原。中國政治思想與制度史論集。

1954. Education in Free China. Taipei: China Culture Publishing Foundation.

1954. K'ung tzu chuan. Taipei: Chung-yang wen-wu kung-ying she.
孔子傳。

1955. Chung-kuo ti-li-hsueh yen-chiu. Taipei: Chung-hua wen-hua ch'u-pan shih-yeh wei-yuan-hui.
中國地理學研究。

1955. Ko-ming chiao-yü, ti-i chi. Taipei: Chung-kuo hsin-wen ch'u-pan kung-ssu.
革命教育，第一輯。

1955-57. Hsin chiao-yü lun-chi. Taipei: Chung-kuo hsin-wen ch'u-pan kung-ssu. 5 vols.
新教育論集。

1956. (ed.) Chung-kuo chih tzu-jan huan-ching. Taipei: Chung-hua wen-hua ch'u-pan shih-yeh wei-yuan-hui.
中國之自然環境。

1956. Chung-kuo chün-shih shih-lueh. Taipei: Chung-hua wen-hua ch'u-pan shih-yeh wei-yuan-hui.
中國軍事史略。

1956. San min chu-yi mo-fan sheng chih chien-she. Taipei: Chung-hua wen-hua ch'u-pan shih-yeh wei-yuan-hui.
三民主義模範省之建設。

1956. Tsung-chiao chiao-yü. Taipei: Chung-kuo hsin-wen ch'u-pan kung-szu.
宗教教育。

1957. The Essence of Chinese Culture. Taipei: China News Press.

1957. Mei-kuo wen-hua yü Chung Mei kuan-hsi. Taipei: Chung-hua wen-hua ch'u-pan shih-yeh wei-yuan-hui.
美國文化與中美關係。

1958. Chang Ch'i-yün et al. Chung-kuo wen-hsueh shih lun chi. Taipei: Chung-hua wen-hua ch'u-pan shih-yeh wei-yuan-hui. 4 vols.
張其昀等。中國文學史論集。

1958. Chung-kuo ch'ü-yü chih. Taipei: Chung-hua wen-hua ch'u-pan shih-yeh wei-yuan-hui.
中國區域志。

1959-62. (ed.) Chung-hua Min-kuo ti-t'u chi. Taipei: Kuo-fang yen-chiu yuan. 5 vols.
中華民國地圖集。

1960. (ed.) Chung Mei kuan-hsi shih—hua chi. Taipei: Chung-hua wen-hua ch'u-pan shih-yeh she.
中美關係史—畫集。

1960. (ed.) K'ung Meng sheng-chi t'u-shuo. Taipei: Chung-hua wen-hua ch'u-pan shih-yeh she.
孔孟聖蹟圖說。

1962. Chien-kuo fang-lueh yen-chiu. Taipei: Chung-kuo wen-hua yen-chiu so.
建國方略研究。

1962. Ching-fu-men hui-i-lu. Taipei: Chung-kuo hsin-wen ch'u-pan kung-ssu.
景福門回憶錄。

1962. "Chung-kuo hsien-tai ssu-hsiang te chu-liu," in Chung-hua Min-kuo k'ai-kuo wu-shih nien shih lun-chi. Taipei: Kuo-fang yen-chiu-yuan. 2 vols.
中國現代思想的主流。 中華民國開國五十年史論集。

1962. "Chung-kuo tsai shih-chieh te ti-wei," in Chung-hua Min-kuo k'ai-kuo wu-shih nien shih lun-chi. Taipei: Kuo-fang yen-chiu-yuan. 2 vols.
中國在世界的地位。 中華民國開國五十年史論集。

1962. "Kuo-fu yü tsung-t'ung te ko-ming wei-yeh," in Chung-hua Min-kuo k'ai-kuo wu-shih nien shih lun-chi. Taipei: Kuo-fang yen-chiu-yuan. 2 vols.
國父與總統的革命偉業。 中華民國開國五十年史論集。

1962. (ed.) National Atlas of China. Taipei: The National War College, College of Chinese Culture.

1962. (ed.) Wen-wu ching-hua. Taipei: Chung-kuo wen-hua yen-chiu so. 10 vols.
文物精華。

1962-65. (sup. ed.) Chung-wen ta tz'u-tien. Taipei: Chung-kuo wen-hua yen-chiu so.
中文大辭典。

1965. (ed.) Shih-chieh ti-t'u chi. Taipei: Kuo-fang yen-chiu-yuan, Chung-kuo ti-li yen-chiu so.
世界地圖集。

1966. (sup. ed.) Ch'ing tai i t'ung ti-t'u. Taipei: Kuo-fang yen-chiu-yuan, Chung-hua ta tien pien yin hui.
清代一統地圖。

1966. (sup. ed.) Kung fei ch'ieh chü hsia te Chung-kuo ta-lu fen sheng ti-t'u (with Ts'an-k'ao tzu-liao). Taipei: Kuo-fang yen-chiu-yuan ti ch'ing yen-chiu so, Chung-kuo wen-hua hsueh-yuan ta-lu chin-k'uang yen-chiu so.
共匪竊據下的中國分省地圖 (附參考資料)。

SOURCES

Chang Ch'i-yün. Ching-fu-men hui-i-lu. Taipei: Chung-kuo hsin-wen ch'u-pan kung-ssu, 1962.
張其昀。景福門回憶錄。

Chang Ch'i-yün. Hsin chiao-yü lun-chi. Taipei: Chung-kuo hsin-wen ch'u-pan kung-ssu, 1955–57. 5 vols.
張其昀。 新教育論集。

———. Mei-kuo wen-hua yü Chung Mei kuan-hsi. Taipei: Chung-hua wen-hua ch'u-pan shih-yeh wei-yuan-hui, 1957.
張其昀。 美國文化與中美關係。

Chang Chia-ao   張嘉璈

WORKS

1934. Yin-hang hang-yuan te hsin sheng-huo. Nanking: Cheng-chung shu-chü.
銀行行員的新生活。

1943. China's Struggle for Railroad Development. New York: The John Day Co.

1958. The Inflationary Spiral: The Experience in China, 1939–1950. Cambridge: Technology Press of Massachusetts Institute of Technology.

SOURCES

BKL

Chang Chia-ao. China's Struggle for Railroad Development. New York: The John Day Co., 1943.

CTMC

CYB-W, 1928, 1929–30, 1935, 1939.

WWC, 1936.

Chang Chia-sen   張嘉森

WORKS

1911–? ed. of *Chin Ching shih-pao.*
津京時報。

1916. Sheng chih ts'ao-an. Shanghai: T'ai tung shu-chü.
省制草案。

1922. Das Lebensproblem in China und Europa. with Rudolf Eucken. Leipzig.

1924. Kuo-nei chan-cheng liu chiang. Shanghai: Kuo-li cheng-chih ta-hsueh.
國內戰爭六講。

1926. Wuhan chien-wen.
武漢見聞。

1936. Ming-jih chih Chung-kuo wen-hua. Shanghai: Shang-wu yin shu kuan.
明日之中國文化。

1942. Wei-wu shih-kuan p'i-p'an. Chungking.
唯物史觀批判。

1942. Yin-tu fu-kuo yun-tung. Chungking: Shang-wu yin shu kuan.
印度復國運動。

1947. Chung-hua Min-kuo min-chu hsien-fa shih chiang. Shanghai: Shang-wu yin shu kuan.
中華民國民主憲法十講。

1947? Chung-kuo min-chu she-hui tang cheng-kang shih-i; ti-i ts'e. Hong Kong: Tsai-sheng she.
中國民主社會黨政綱釋義；第一冊。

1952. Chung-hua min-tsu ching-shen. Djakarta: T'ien sheng jih-pao she.
中華民族精神。

1952. Chung-hua min-tsu ching-shen—ch'i-chieh. Hong Kong: Tsai-sheng tsa-chih she.
中華民族精神—氣節。

1952. The Third Force in China. New York: Bookman Associates.

1955. Chung-hua Min-kuo tu-li tzu-chu yü Ya-chou wen-t'i. Kowloon: Tzu-yu ch'u-pan she.
中華民國獨立自主與亞洲問題。

1955. I li hsueh shih chiang kang-yao. Taipei: Hua kuo ch'u-pan she.
義理學十講綱要。

1955. Pi-chiao Chung Jih Yang-ming hsueh. Taipei: Chung-hua wen-hua ch'u-pan shih-yeh wei-yuan-hui.
比較中日陽明學。

1956. China and Gandhian India. Calcutta: The Book Co.

1957-62. The Development of Neo-Confucian Thought. New York: Bookman Associates. 2 vols.

1958. Pien-cheng wei-wu chu-yi po lun. Hong Kong: Yu lien ch'u-pan she.
辯證唯物主義駁論。

1959. Chang Chün-mai hsin ta-lu yen-lun chi. Kowloon: Tzu-yu ch'u-pan she.
張君勱新大陸言論集。

1962. Wang Yang-ming: Idealist Philosopher of Sixteenth Century China. Jamaica, New York: St. John's University Press.

SOURCES

Chang, Carsun (Chang Chia-sen). The Third Force in China. New York: Bookman Associates, 1952.

Hsia K'ang-nung. Lun Hu Shih yü Chang Chün-mai. Shanghai: Hsin chih shu-tien, 1948.
夏康農。論胡適與張君勱。

Liang Jen-kung hsien-sheng nien-p'u ch'ang pien ch'u-kao, comp. by Ting Wen-chiang. Taipei: Shih-chieh shu-chü, 1958. 2 vols.
梁任公先生年譜長編初稿。丁文江。

MMT

Shao Chung-i. Chung-kuo ko tang-p'ai ch'üan-mao. Foochow: Wen-hua ch'u-pan she, 1946.
邵重毅。 中國各黨派全貌。

Shih I. "Wo so chih-tao Chang Chün-mai hsien-sheng te sheng-p'ing." *Tsai sheng*, 345–46 (December, 1953–January, 1954).
士一。 我所知道張君勱先生的生平。 再生。

WWC, 1931.

Chang Chien   張謇

WORKS

1925. Se-weng tzu ting nien-p'u. Nan-t'ung: Chang shih.
嗇翁自訂年譜。

1931. Chang Chi-tzu chiu lu (ed. by Chang Hsiao-jo). Shanghai.
張季子九錄。 張孝若。

1964. Chiu lu lu. Taipei: Kuo feng ch'u-pan she.
九錄錄。

Chang Chien tao Huai chi-hua hsuan-kao shu.
張謇導淮計劃宣告書。

SOURCES

AADC

Chang Chien. Chang Chi-tzu chiu lu (ed. by Chang Hsiao-jo). Shanghai, 1931.
張謇。 張季子九錄。 張孝若。

———. Se-weng tzu ting nien-p'u. Nan-t'ung: Chang shih, 1925.
張謇。 嗇翁自訂年譜。

Chang Chien te sheng-p'ing, ed. by Chu Hsi-shang. Taipei: Chung-hua ts'ung-shu pien-shen wei-yuan-hui, 1963.
張謇的生平。 朱希尚。

Chu, Samuel C. Reformer in Modern China: Chang Chien, 1853–1926. New York: Columbia University Press, 1965.

Liu Hou-sheng. Chang Chien chuan-chi. Shanghai: Lung-men lien-ho shu-chü, 1958.
劉厚生。 張謇傳記。

MCNP

Nan-t'ung Chang Chi-chih hsieh-sheng chuan-chi, ed. by Chang Hsiao-jo. Shanghai: Chung-hua shu-chü, 1935.
南通張季直先生傳記。 張孝若。

T'ung-chou hsing-pan shih-yeh chih li-shih, ed. by Han mo lin pien i yin shu chü. T'ung-chou, Kiangsu: Han mo lin pien i yin shu chü, 1910. 2 vols.
通州興辦實業之歷史。 翰墨林編譯印書局。

Chang Chih-chiang   張之江

SOURCES

BKL

Feng Yü-hsiang. Feng Yü-hsiang jih-chi; ti-i pien. Peiping?: Min-kuo shih-liao pien-chi she, 1932.
馮玉祥。 馮玉祥日記； 第一編。

———. Wo te sheng-huo. Shanghai: Chiao-yü shu-tien, 1947. 3 vols.
馮玉祥。 我的生活。

Kuo-min ko-ming chün chan shih, comp. by Kuo-min ko-ming chün chan shih pien-tsuan wei-yuan-hui. Ts'an-mou pen-pu, 1934. 17 vols.
國民革命軍戰史。 國民革命軍戰史編纂委員會。

Chang Chih-chung   張治中

WORKS

1942. Chang shu-chi-chang hsun-tz'u lun-wen hsuan. Chungking: San min chu-i ch'ing-nien t'uan chung-yang t'uan-pu.
張書記長訓詞論文選。

1942. Pen t'uan hsing-chih yü kung-tso chiang-p'ing. Chungking: San min chu-i ch'ing-nien t'uan chung-yang t'uan-pu.
本團性質與工作講評。

1943. Chang pu-chang chung-yao hsun-shih chi. Chungking: Chün-shih wei-yuan-hui cheng-chih pu.
張部長重要訓示集。

1943. Chiang hsien-sheng chih jen-ko yü hsiu-yang. Chungking: San min chu-i ch'ing-nien t'uan chung-yang t'uan-pu.
蔣先生之人格與修養。

1947, December. "Dilemma in Sinkiang." *Pacific Affairs*, 20: 422–29.

SOURCES

AWW
BKL

Chang Chih-chung. "Dilemma in Sinkiang." *Pacific Affairs*, 20: 422–29.

Chassin, Lionel Max. La Conquête de la Chine par Mao Tse-tung. Paris: Payot, 1952.

CMTC
CTMC

Lattimore, Owen. Pivot of Asia: Sinkiang and the Inner Asian Frontiers of China and Russia. Boston: Little, Brown & Co., 1950.

Liang Sheng-chün. Chiang Li tou-cheng nei-mu. Hong Kong: Ya lien ch'u-pan she, 1954.
梁升俊。蔣李鬥爭內幕。
USRWC
Whiting, Allen S., and Sheng Shih-ts'ai. Sinkiang: Pawn or Pivot? East Lansing: Michigan State University Press, 1958.
WWC, 1936, 1950.
WWMC

Chang Chün-hsiang　　張駿祥

WORKS

1945. Shan ch'eng ku-shih. Shanghai: Wen-hua sheng-huo ch'u-pan she.
山城故事。
1946. Fu-kuei fu-yun. Shanghai: Shih-chieh shu-chü.
富貴浮雲。
1946. Mei-kuo tsung-t'ung hao. Shanghai: Wen-hua sheng-huo ch'u-pan she.
美國總統號。
1946. Pien ch'eng ku-shih. Shanghai: Wen-hua sheng-huo ch'u-pan she.
邊城故事。
1946. Wan shih shih piao. Shanghai: Wen-hua sheng-huo ch'u-pan she.
萬世師表。
1947. Hsiao ch'eng ku-shih. Shanghai: Wen-hua sheng-huo ch'u-pan she.
小城故事。
1958. Kuan-yü tien-ying te t'e-shu piao-hsien. Peking: Chung-kuo tien-ying ch'u-pan she.
關於電影的特殊表現。

SOURCES

CHWSK
CKJMT
GCCJK
GCJJ
HWP
MCNP
RCCL
TCMT
WWMC

Chang Ch'ün　　張群

WORKS

1939. K'ang-chan chien-kuo kang-ling chih shih-shih. Chungking.
抗戰建國綱領之實施。

1951. "Shou Chiang tsung-t'ung i shou Chunghua Min-kuo," in *Pen tang yü kung fei po-tou shih-shih*. Taipei: Chung-yang kai-tsao wei-yuan-hui wen-wu kung-ying she.
壽蔣總統以壽中華民國。本黨與共匪博鬥史實。
1952. Chung Jih kuan-hsi yü Mei-kuo. Taipei: Chung-kuo hsin-wen ch'u-pan kung-ssu.
中日關係與美國。
Eng. tr., *Sino-Japanese Relations and America*. Taipei: Office of the Goverment Spokesman, 1952.
1953. Chang Yueh-chün hsien-sheng fang Jih yen-lun chi, ed. by Chung Jih wen-hua ching-chi hsieh-hui. Taipei: Chung-kuo hsin-wen ch'u-pan kung-ssu.
張岳軍先生訪日言論集。中日文化經濟協會。
1954. T'an hsiu-yang. Taipei: Ko-ming shih-chien yen-chiu yuan.
談修養。
1957. Jen-shou chi-ho. Taipei.
人壽幾何。

SOURCES

BKL
CH
Chang Ch'ün. Chung Jih kuan-hsi yü Mei-kuo. Taipei: Chung-kuo hsin-wen ch'u-pan kung-ssu, 1954.
張群。中日關係與美國。
———. "Shou Chiang tsung-t'ung i shou Chunghua Min-kuo," in *Pen tang yü kung fei po-tou shih-shih*. Taipei: Chung-yang kai-ts'ao wei-yuan-hui wen-wu kung-ying she, 1951.
張群。壽蔣總統以壽中華民國。本黨與共匪博鬥史實。
Chang Ch'ün mi-shu-chang fang-wen Jih Han chi-yao, ed. by Chung Jih ho-tso ts'e-chin wei-yuan-hui. Taipei, 1964.
張群秘書長訪問日韓輯要。中日合作策進委員會。
Chang Ch'ün t'e-shih ta fang Jih-pen chi. Taipei: Chung-Jih wen-hua ching-chi hsieh-hui, 1958.
張群特史答訪日本記。
Ch'ien Tuan-sheng. The Government and Politics of China. Cambridge: Harvard University Press, 1950.
CH-T, 1954–55, 1956–57.
CMJL
CMMC
CTMC
CYB-W, 1929–30, 1931, 1934, 1936, 1938, 1939.

"Foreign Minister Chang Chün Appeals to Japan for Peace." CWR, 450 (May, 30, 1936).
Free China Weekly, August 23, 1964; November 28, 1965.
GCJJ
Kuomintang Year Book, 1929.
TCMC-1
TCMT
Tong, Hollington K. Chiang Kai-shek. Taipei: China Publishing Co., 1953.
Wai-chiao ta tz'u-tien, ed. by Wai-chiao hsueh-hui. Kunming: Chung-hua shu-chü, 1937.
外交大辭典。外交協會。
WWC, 1928, 1931.
WWMC

Chang En-p'u   張 恩 溥

WORKS

"Cheng i ching chi." Unpublished manuscript.
正一經籙。
"Fu-lu hsueh." Unpublished manuscript.
符籙學。
"Tao hsueh yuan-liu." Unpublished manuscript.
道學源流。

SOURCES

Liu Ch'eng-yü. Hung-hsien chi-shih shih. Chungking: Ching-hua yin shu kuan.
劉成禺。洪憲紀事詩。
Welch, Holmes H. "Chang T'ien-shih and Taoism in Taiwan." Unpublished manuscript.
Wu Tsung-tz'u. Chang Tao-ling tien-shih shih-chia. 1947.
吳宗慈。張道陵天師世家。

Chang Erh-t'ien   張 爾 田

WORKS

1911. Shih wei; nei p'ien pa chüan. San ch'an shou chai. 4 vols.
史微；內篇八卷。
1917. Yü-ch'i-sheng nien-p'u hui-chien. Nan-lin: Liu shih ch'iu shu chai.
玉谿生年譜會箋。
1932. (ed.) Meng-ku yuan-liu chien-cheng.
蒙古源流箋證。
1933, July. "Huai chü ch'ang ho." *Hsueh heng*, 79: 1-8.
槐居唱和。學衡。

1936. "Ju a-p'i ta-mo chü-she lun chiang-shu hsuan-i," in *Hattori sensei koki shukuga kinen rombun shu*. Tokyo.
人阿毘達磨俱舍論講疏玄義。一服部先生古稀祝賀紀念論文集。
1939. "Ch'an-shou-chai jih-chi." *Shih-hsueh nien-pao*, II-5: 341-69.
屛守齋日記。史學年報。
Hsin hsueh shang tui.
新學商兌。
Man-shu chiao-pu.
蠻書斠補。
Yuan-ch'ao pi-shih chu.
元朝秘史注。

SOURCES

Teng Chih-ch'eng. "Chang chün Meng-ch'ü pieh-chuan." *Yen-ching hsueh-pao*, 30 (June, 1964): 323-25.
鄧之誠。張君孟劬別傳。燕京學報。
T'u-shu chi-k'an, new series, III-3, 4 (December, 1941): 36.
圖書季刊。
Wang Chü-ch'ang. "Chia-hsing Shen Mei-sou hsien-sheng nien-p'u ch'u-kao." *Tung-fang tsa-chih*, XXVI-16 (August, 1929): 63-74.
王蘧常。嘉興沈寐叟先生年譜初稿。東方雜誌。

Chang Fa-k'uei   張 發 奎

SOURCES

CTMC
Devillers. Histoire du Vietnam de 1940 à 1952. Saigon.
Huang Hsü-ch'u. "Kwangsi yü chung-yang pei huan li ho i-shu pu-cheng chih ssu: Kuo chün chan pai pi ju Yueh-nan ching-kuo hsiang-ch'ing." *Ch'un-ch'iu*, 152 (November 1, 1963).
黃旭初。廣西與中央悲歡離合憶述補正之四：國軍戰敗避入越南經過詳情。春秋。
Kwangtung shih jen chih.
廣東時人志。
Ti-ssu chün chi-shih, ed. by Ti-ssu chün chi-shih pien-tsuan wei-yuan-hui. Canton: Huai yuan wen-hua shih-yeh fu-wu she, 1949.
第四軍紀實。第四軍紀實編纂委員會。

Chang Hsueh-liang   張 學 良

WORKS

1934? Chang fu-ssu-ling chiang-yen chi. Wu-

chang: Yü O Wan san sheng chiao fei tsung-
ssu-ling pu chi-yao tzu.
張副司令講演集。

SOURCES

Bertram, James M. First Act in China: The
Story of the Sian Mutiny. New York: The
Viking Press, 1938.

Chang Hsueh-liang te tzu-yu wen-t'i. Hong
Kong: Shih-tai p'i-p'ing she, 1941.
張學良的自由問題。

Cheng T'ien-feng. A History of Sino-Russian
Relations. Washington: Public Affairs Press,
1957.

CTMC

CWR, November 7, 1931.

CYB-W

Hong Kong Tiger Standard, July 22, 1964.

Hsiao Pai-fan. Chung-kuo chin pai nien ko-
ming shih. Kowloon: Ch'iu shih ch'u-pan
she, 1951.
蕭白帆。中國近百年革命史。

Hu Ch'iao-mu. Thirty Years of the Communist
Party of China. Peking: Foreign Languages
Press, 1959.

Hua Mei jih-pao. New York, September 2, 1961.
華美日報。

Koo Hui-lan. Hui-lan Koo: An Autobiography
as Told to Mary Van Rensselaer Thayer. New
York: Dial Press, 1943.

Kung shang jih-pao. Hong Kong, June 3, 1964.
工商日報。

Lei Hsiao-ts'en. San-shih nien tung-luan Chung-
kuo. Hong Kong: Ya-chou ch'u-pan she,
1955.
雷嘯岑。三十年動亂中國。

Lien-ho pao. Taipei, June 2, July 21, August 2,
1964.
聯合報。

Lu Pi *et al*. Lun Chang Hsueh-liang. Hong
Kong: Shih-tai p'i-p'ing she, 1948.
魯泌等。論張學良。

Mao Tse-tung. "Statement on Chiang Kai-
shek's Statement," in Selected Works of Mao
Tse-tung. London: Lawrence & Wishart,
1954-56. 4 vols.

Michael, Franz H., and George E. Taylor. The
Far East in the Modern World. New York:
Holt, Rinehart & Winston, 1956.

Ming Hu. "Chang Hsueh-liang kuo-chen huo
shih ch'i yung?" *Chung Mei chou-pao*, 920
(July 21, 1960): 39.
明胡。張學良果真獲釋起用？中美週報。

RNRC

RSOC

Selle, Earl Albert. Donald of China. New
York: Harper & Bros., 1948.

Sian shih-pien chen-shih; ti-i chi. Hong Kong:
Ch'un-ch'iu tsa-chih she, 1965.
西安事變珍史；第一輯。

Tang, Peter S. H. Russian and Soviet Policy in
Manchuria and Outer Mongolia, 1911-1931.
Durham: Duke University, 1959.

Wang Cho-jan. Chang Hsueh-liang tao-ti shih
ko tsen-yang te jen. Peiping: Tung-fang fu-
wu pu.
王卓然。張學良到底是個怎樣的人。

Woodhead, Henry George Wandesforde. A
Visit to Manchukuo. Shanghai: The Mercury
Press, 1932.

WWC, 1936.

Yu Chün. "Sian shih-pien i-lai ts'ung wei kung-
k'ai kuo te chen shih." *Ch'un-ch'iu*, 52-58
(September 1, 1959-December, 1, 1959).
右軍。西安事變以來從未公開過的珍史。
春秋。

Chang Hsün   張 勳

WORKS

Sung-shou-lao-jen tzu-hsü.
松壽老人自敍。

English tr. by Reginald F. Johnston. "Autobiography of the Old Man of the Pinetree,"
in *Twilight in the Forbidden City*. New York:
Appleton-Century, 1934.

SOURCES

AADC

The Case of the Refuge of Chang Hsün in the
Dutch Legation. China: Ministry of Foreign
Affairs, 1917.

Chang Hsün. Sung-shou-lao-jen tzu-hsü.
張勳。松壽老人自敍。

Ch'en San-li. San-yuan ching-she wen-chi. Taipei: Taiwan chung-hua shu-chü, 1961.
陳三立。散原精舍文集。

Chin Liang. Kua-p'u shu-i. 1923?
金梁。瓜圃述異。

——. Kua-p'u ts'ung-k'an hsü-lu hsü-pien.
1935. 2 vols.
金梁。瓜圃叢刊敍錄續編。

Chin shan shih pao. San Francisco, November 7,
1956.
金山時報。

Chung-kuo chin-tai shih tzu-liao hsü pien, ed. by Tso Shun-sheng. Shanghai: Chung-hua shu-chü, 1933. 2 vols.
中國近代史資料續編。左舜生。
CMMC

Hsin-hai ko-ming, ed. by Ch'ai Te-keng *et al.* Shanghai: Jen-min ch'u-pan she, 1957. 8 vols.
辛亥革命。柴德賡等。

"Hu fa shih-liao," in KMWH.
護法史料。

Johnston, Reginald F. Twilight in the Forbidden City. New York: Appleton-Century, 1934.

Ma Ch'i-ch'ang. Pao-jun-hsuan wen-chi. Peking, 1923.
馬其昶。抱潤軒文集。
MMT
PCCP

Sun Yueh. Chung-hua Min-kuo shih-liao. Shanghai: Wen-ming shu-chü, 1929. 3 vols.
孫曜。中華民國史料。

Wu K'ai-sheng. Pei-chiang hsien-sheng wen-chi. 6 vols.
吳闓生。北江先生文集。

Chang I-lin   張一麐

WORKS

1947. Hsin t'ai-p'ing shih chi (comp. by Ku T'ing-lung). Shanghai. 4 vols.
心太平室集。顧廷龍。

SOURCES

Chang I-lin. Hsin t'ai-p'ing shih chi (comp. by Ku T'ing-lung). Shanghai, 1947. 4 vols.
張一麐。心太平室集。顧廷龍。
CMMC
CYB-W, 1926–27.
Kuo shih kuan kuan k'an, I-4 (November, 1948).
國史館館刊。
Kuo wen chou-pao, III-16 (May 2, 1926).
國聞週報。
MMT
WWC, 1918–19, 1925, 1936.

Chang Jen-chieh   張人傑

SOURCES

BKL
Ch'en Kuo-fu. "Min-kuo shih-wu-liu nien chien i-tuan tang shih," in Ch'en Kuo-fu hsien-sheng i-chu pien yin wei-yuan-hui, *Ch'en Kuo-fu hsien-sheng ch'üan-chi.* Taipei: Cheng chung shu-chü, 1952. 10 vols.
陳果夫。民國十五六年間一段黨史。陳果夫先生遺著編印委員會。陳果夫先生全集。

Ch'en T'ien-hsi. Tai Chi-t'ao hsien-sheng pien-nien chuan-chi.
陳天錫。戴季陶先生編年傳記。

Chiang Yung-ching. Hu Han-min hsien-sheng nien-p'u kao.
蔣永敬。胡漢民先生年譜稿。

Ch'ing tang ts'ung-shu.
清黨叢書。

Kai-tsao, 3.
改造。

Li Shu-hua. Wu Chih-hui hsien-sheng sheng-p'ing lueh shu.
李書華。吳稚暉先生生平畧述。

Ling Hung-hsun. Chung-kuo t'ieh-lu chih. Taipei: Ch'ang liu pan-yueh-k'an she, 1954.
凌鴻勛。中國鐵路志。
MSICH

Shih nien lai te Chung-kuo, ed. by Chung-kuo wen-hua chien-she wei-yuan-hui. Shanghai: Shang-wu yin shu kuan, 1937.
十年來的中國。中國文化建設委員會。

Ti Ying. Chang Ching-chiang hsien-sheng shih lueh.
狄膺。張靜江先生事略。

Wu Chih-hui hsieh-sheng wen-ts'ui.
吳稚暉先生文粹。

Chang Kuo-t'ao   張國燾

WORKS

1942. K'ang Jih min-tsu t'ung-i chan-hsien te fen-hsi yü p'i-p'an. T'ung-i ch'u-pan she.
抗日民族統一戰線的分析與批判。

SOURCES

Person interviewed: Chang Kuo-t'ao.
BKL
HSWT
Schwartz, Benjamin I. Chinese Communism and the Rise of Mao. Cambridge: Harvard University Press, 1951.
Smedley, Agnes. The Great Road: The Life and Times of Chu Teh. New York: Monthly Review Press, 1956.
Wales, Nym (pseud. of Helen Foster Snow). Inside Red China. New York: Doubleday, Doran & Co., 1939.

Chang Lan   張 瀾

WORKS

1943. Chung-kuo hsü-yao chen-cheng min-chu cheng-chih.
中國需要眞正民主政治。

SOURCES

Persons interviewed: not to be identified.

Chang Li-sheng   張 厲 生

WORKS

1939. Chün-tui cheng-chih kung-tso chih chin-chan. Chungking: Chung-yang hsun-lien t'uan tang-cheng hsun-lien pan.
軍隊政治工作之進展。
1939. Tang wu shih-shih shang chih wen-t'i. Chungking.
黨務實施上之問題。
1940. (ed.) Chung-kuo chih min-tsu ssu-hsiang yü min-tsu ch'i-chieh. Chungking: Ch'ing-nien shu-tien.
中國之民族思想與民族氣節。

SOURCES

BKL
Chang Ching-yuan. Chang Li-sheng hsien-sheng te li-shen hsing-shih.
張敬原。張厲生先生的立身行事。
Free China Weekly. NN-LXIII-40: 1. October 1, 1963.
Li Hsü. Cheng-chih hsieh-shang hui-i chih chien-t'ao.
李旭。政治協商會議之檢討。
Nei-cheng pu kung-tso pao-kao.
內政部工作報。
Tang-wu kung-tso pao-kao.
黨務工作報告。

Chang Mo-chün   張 默 君

WORKS

1911. "Chi i t'ung-i" *Ta han pao*, 14.
急宜統一。大漢報。
1911. "Ching-kao kuo-min shu." *Ta han pao*, 12.
敬告國民書。大漢報。
1911. "Ching kao Nanking chu chien-erh." *Ta han pao*, 29.
敬告南京諸健兒。大漢報。
1911. "Ch'ou hsiang wen-t'i." *Ta han pao*, 17.

籌餉問題。大漢報。
1911. "Chung-kuo yü." *Ta han pao*, 25.
忠告語。大漢報。
1911. "Ho-p'ing hsi-wang chih chieh-chueh." *Ta han pao*, 30.
和平希望之解決。大漢報。
1911, November. "Pen pao tsui-hou chih tseng-yen." *Ta han pao*.
本報最後之贈言。大漢報。
1911. ed. of *Ta han pao*.
大漢報。
1911. "Wu-jen tui-yü i-ho chih kuan-ch'a." *Ta han pao*, 28.
吾人對於議和之觀察。大漢報。
1911. "Yuan Shih-k'ai chih chien-mou." *Ta han pao*, 19.
袁世凱之奸謀。大漢報。
1920. ed. of *Shang-hai shih-pao*.
上海時報。
1959. Yü-tieh shan-fang mo-shen. Taipei: Yü-tieh shan-fang.
玉諜山房墨瀋。
1960. Ta-ning-t'ang chi. Taipei: Chung-hua ts'ung-shu pien shen wei-yuan-hui. 4 vols.
大凝堂集。
Chan-hou chih Ou-Mei nü-tzu chiao-yü.
戰後之歐美女子教育。
Cheng-ch'i hu-t'ien chi.
正氣呼天集。
Chiang shu pai yun shan kuan tz'u.
江樹白雲山館詞。
Chung-kuo cheng-chih yü min-sheng che-hsüeh.
中國政治與民生哲學。
Chung-kuo ku-yü yü li-tai wen-hua chih shan-chin. Taipei.
中國古玉與歷代文化之壇晉。
Hangchow shih chiao-yü hsing-cheng liu nien shih-shih kang-yao.
杭州市教育行政六年實施綱要。
Hsien-cheng p'ing-lun.
憲政評論。
Mo-chün shih-ts'ao. 2 vols.
默君詩草。
Ou Mei chiao-yü k'ao-ch'a lu.
歐美教育考察錄。
Pai-hua ts'ao-t'ang shih.
白華草堂詩。
Tsui-chin chiao-yü yen-lun.
最近教育言論。
Wo chih chia-shih chiao-yü kuan.
我之家事教育觀。
Yang ling chi.
楊靈集。

SOURCES

"Chang Mo-chün." *Chung-yang jih-pao*. Taipei, October 3–5, 1962.
張默君。中央日報。

"Chang Mo-chün nü-shih chien-li." *Hsin-shen pao*. Taipei, January 31, 1965.
張默君女士簡歷。新生報。

Ch'en Ku-t'ing. "Chang Mo-lao yü *ta han pao*—ching chu Chang hsien-sheng ch'i-chiu jung-ch'ing." *Chung-yang jih-pao*. Taipei, October 4, 1962.
陳固亭。張默老與大漢報一敬祝張先生七九榮慶。中央日報。

Chia. "Chi chüan-hsien ku-yü te Chang Mo-chün." *Chin-shan shih-pao*. San Francisco, April 11–12, 1957.
家。記捐獻古玉的張默君。金山時報。

CH-T, 1954–55.

CMJL

GCCJK

Huang Shun-hua. "Tao nü chung hao-chieh Chang Mo-lao." *Hsin-sheng pao*. Taipei, January 31, 1965.
黃順華。悼女中豪傑張默老。新生報。

Li Yü-hsi. "Chin shu hai-chün ch'uang-chien ching-kuo i shou tang kuo yuan-lao Chang Mo-chün hsien-sheng." *Chung-yang jih-pao*. Taipei, October 3, 1962.
黎玉璽。謹述海軍創建經過以壽黨國元老張默君先生。中央日報。

MMT

Shen Chien-shih. "Wei i-chieh kao-k'ao t'ung-nien ying-yin Chang Mo-chün hsien-sheng ching-wei shih-kao chin-chu sung-shou hsü." *Chung-yang jih-pao*. Taipei, October 3, 1962.
沈兼士。爲一屆高考同年影印張默君先生京闈詩稿晉祝嵩壽序。中央日報。

TCMC-1

TCMT

WWMC

Yü Yu-jen. "Shao fu-jen Chang Mo-chün hsien-sheng ch'i-shih chin chiu shou hsü." *Chung-yang jih-pao*. Taipei, October 5, 1962.
于右任。邵夫人張默君先生七十晉九壽序。中央日報。

Chang Nai-ch'i 章乃器

WORKS

1936. Chung-kuo huo-pi chin-jung wen-t'i. Shanghai: Sheng-huo shu-tien.
中國貨幣金融問題。

1944. An Inscribed Chinese Ingot of the XII Century A.D. New York: The American Numismatic Society.

1944, September. "Kung-yeh ch'ung-pien yü Sikang chien-she." *Szechwan ching-chi chi-k'an*, I-4.
工業重編與西康建設。四川經濟季刊。

1951. Lun Chung-kuo ching-chi te kai-tsao, hsiao-chung, ch'ü fu, sheng hsin. Peking: Wu-shih nien tai ch'u-pan she.
論中國經濟的改造，消腫，去腐，生新。

Ch'u yü ch'ien hou. Shanghai: Shanghai tsa-chih kung-ssu.
出獄前後。

SOURCES

GCCJK

GCJJ

Hsueh-hsi, July 18, 1957.
學習。

Jen-min jih-pao. Peking, June 18, 1957; April 16, 1960.
人民日報。

K-WWMC

Li Shou-tung. Chiu-kuo wu-tsui ch'i chün-tzu. Shih-tai wen-hsien she, 1936.
李守東。救國無罪七君子。

SCMP, 32 (December 17–18, 1950): 16–18; 284 (February 28, 1952): 6–7, 10–11; 289 (March, 1952): 17–21; 335 (May 14, 1952): 9–10; 687 (November 12–13, 1953): 31–34; 938 (December 1, 1954): 19; 1563 (July, 1957): 7–10; 1570 (July 16, 1957): 4–11, 11–16; 2936 (March 12, 1963); 1.

Smedley, Agnes. Battle Hymn of China. New York: Alfred A. Knopf, 1943.

Tsou T'ao-fen. Huan-nan yü-sheng chi. Shanghai: Sheng-huo shu-tien, 1936.
鄒韜奮。患難餘生記。

Chang Pi-shih 張弼士

SOURCES

Chu Shou-p'eng. T'ung-hua hsü-lu. Shanghai: Chi-ch'eng t'u-shu kung-ssu, 1909. 64 vols.
朱壽朋。東華續錄。

Hua-ch'iao ming-jen chuan, ed. by Chu Hsiu-hsia. Taipei: Chung-hua wen-hua ch'u-pan shih-yeh wei-yuan-hui, 1955.
華僑名人傳。祝秀俠。

Shang-wu kuan-pao. March 9, 1907.
商務官報。

Chang Ping-lin 章炳麟

WORKS

1906-8. ed. of *Min pao*.
民報。

1910. Chang T'an ho ch'ao. with T'an Ssu-t'ung.
Shanghai: Kuo-hsueh fu lun she.
章譚合鈔。譚嗣同。

1917-19. Chang shih ts'ung-shu. 24 vols.
章氏叢書。

1925. Chang T'ai-yen kuo-hsueh yen-chiang lu.
Shanghai: Liang hsi t'u-shu-kuan.
章太炎國學演講錄。

1935-37, 1939. ed. of *Chih yen*.
制言。

1939. Chang shih ts'ung-shu san pien (ed. by Chang shih kuo-hsueh chiang-hsi hui).
章氏叢書三編。章氏國學講習會。

1957. Chang T'ai-yen i lun (Ts'u ping hsin lun).
Peking: Jen-min wei-sheng ch'u-pan she.
章太炎醫論 (猝病新論)。

1957. Po Chung-kuo yung wan kuo hsin yü shuo.
Peking: Wen-tzu kai-ko ch'u-pan she.
駁中國用萬國新語說。

1958. Ch'iu-shu. Shanghai: Ku-tien wen-hsueh ch'u-pan she.
訄書。

1962. Chang T'ai-yen hsien-sheng chia-shu (ed. by Chung-hua shu-chü Shanghai pien-chi so).
Peking: Chung-hua shu-chü.
章太炎先生家書。中華書局上海編輯所。

1965. Kuo-hsueh kai-lun. Kowloon: Hong Kong hsueh lin shu-tien.
國學概論。

1965. T'ai-yen hsien-sheng tzu-ting nien-p'u.
Hong Kong: Lung-men shu-tien.
太炎先生自訂年譜。

Chang shih ts'ung-shu hsü pien. Peiping.
章氏叢書續編。

Ch'i-lueh pieh-lu i-wen cheng.
七略別錄佚文徵。

Ch'i wu lun shih.
齊物論釋。

Chien lun.
檢論。

Chuang-tzu chieh-ku.
莊子解故。

Ch'un-ch'iu tso-chuan hsü-lu.
春秋左傳敍錄。

Hsiao-hsueh ta wen.
小學答問。

Hsin fang-yen.
新方言。

Kao-lan-shih cha-chi.
膏蘭室札記。

Ku-wen shang-shu shih-i.
古文尙書拾遺。

Kuo-ku lun-heng.
國故論衡。

Liu Tzu-cheng tso-shih shuo.
劉子政左氏說。

Po Kang Yu-wei cheng-chien shu.
駁康有爲政見書。

Shou-wen pu-shou chün-yü.
說文部首均語。

T'ai-shih-kung ku-wen shang-shu k'ao.
太史公古文尙書考。

Wen shih.
文始。

Wu-ch'ao fa-lü so-yin.
五朝法律索隱。

SOURCES

Chang Ping-lin, ed. by Hsü Shou-shang. Chungking: Sheng-li ch'u-pan she.
章炳麟。許壽裳。

Chang T'ai-yen te pai-hua-wen, ed. by Wu Ch'i-jen.
章太炎的白話文。吳齊仁。

Feng Tzu-yu. "Chang T'ai-yen chih hu tang chiu-kuo kung-han." *I-ching*, 11 (August, 1936): 38.
馮自由。章太炎之護黨救國公函。逸經。

———. "Chang T'ai-yen shih-lueh." *I-ching*, 6 (May, 1936): 28-30.
馮自由。章太炎事略。逸經。

———. "Chang T'ai-yen yü Chih-na wang-kuo chi-nien hui." *I-ching*, 9 (July, 1936): 14-16.
馮自由。章太炎與支那亡國紀念會。逸經。

Feng Tzu-yu. "Chi Chang T'ai-yen yü yü ting chiao shih-mo." *Ta feng pan-yueh-k'an*, 64 (March, 1940).
馮自由。記章太炎與余訂交始末。大風半月刊。

———. "Chi Shanghai chih-shih yü ko-ming yun-tung." *Ta feng pan-yueh-k'an*, 74 (September, 1940): 2372-73.
馮自由。記上海志士與革命運動。大風半月刊。

———. "Hsing-chung-hui shih-tai chih ko-ming t'ung-chih (Kung Pao-ch'üan)." *Ta feng pan-yueh-k'an*, 66 (April, 1940): 2034.
馮自由。興中會時代之革命同志 (龔寶銓)。大風半月刊。

I-shih. "Chang Ping-ling pei pa Peking i-shih tsa-chi." *I-ching*, 11 (August, 1936): 5-8.

一士。章炳麟被霸北京軼事雜記。逸經。

I-shih. "T'an Chang T'ai-yen." *Kuo wen chou-pao*, XIII-36 (September, 1936): 1-8; XIII-48 (December, 1936): 1-3.

一士。談章太炎。國聞週報。

———. "Tsai chi Chang Ping-lin pa liu Peking i-shih." *I-ching*, 12 (August, 1936): 26-28.

一士。再記章炳麟霸留北京軼事。逸經。

Li Tao-chung. "Tao Chang T'ai-yen hsien-sheng." *Wen lan hsueh-pao*, II-2 (June, 1936): 1-5.

李道中。悼章太炎先生。文瀾學報。

Man Hua. "T'ung-meng-hui shih-tai min-pao shih-mo chi," in Ch'ai Te-keng *et al.*, *Hsin-hai ko-ming*. Shanghai: Jen-min ch'u-pan she, 1957. 8 vols.

曼華。同盟會時代民報始末記。柴德賡等。辛亥革命。

MMH

Tan T'ao. "Chang hsien-sheng pieh-chuan." *Kuo-shih-kuan kuan k'an*, 1 (December, 1947): 98-99.

但燾。章先生別傳。國史館館刊。

———. "Chang T'ai-yen hsien-sheng hsueh an hsiao shih." *Ta-lu tsa-chih*, XII-5 (March, 1956): 1-6.

但燾。章太炎先生學案小識。大陸雜誌。

Wang Sen-jan. "Chang Ping-lin hsien-sheng p'ing-chuan," in CECP.

王森然。章炳麟先生評傳。

Wu Chih-hui. "Hui-i Chiang Chu-chuang hsien-sheng chih hui-i." *Tung-fang tsa-chih*, XXXIII-1.

吳稚暉。回憶蔣竹莊先生之回憶。東方雜誌。

Wu Tsung-tz'u. "Kuei-ping chih-chien Chang T'ai-yen hsien-sheng yen-hsing i-shih." *I-ching*, 13 (September, 1936): 23-27.

吳宗慈。癸丙之間章太炎先生言行軼事。逸經。

Yao Yü-hsiang. "Kuan-yü Chang Ping-lin lueh chuan." *Ta-lu tsa-chih*, XII-8 (April, 1956): 4, 29.

姚漁湘。關於章炳麟略傳。大陸雜誌。

Chang Po-chün   章伯鈞

SOURCES

GCCJK

JMST, 1950, 1957, 1958.

K-WWMC

Liao Shao-i. "Chang Po-chün—p'an-t'u, cheng-k'o, yeh-hsin chia." *Chung-kuo ch'ing-nien*, 14 (July 16, 1957): 34-35.

廖少儀。章伯鈞一叛徒，政客，野心家。中國青年。

SCMP, 24 (December 6, 1950): 1; 118 (June 17-18, 1951): 1; 200 (October 23, 1951): 4; 597 (June, 1953): 19; 644 (September 4, 1953): 34-41; 809 (May 15-17, 1954): 40; 922 (November 5, 1954): 38-41; 958 (December 31, 1954): 36; 1558 (June 26, 1957): 12-13; 1561 (July 2, 1957): 19-22; 1656 (November 21, 1957): 8; 1669 (December 11, 1957): 9-10; 1977 (March 20, 1959): 3.

Stevenson, William. The Yellow Wind. Boston: Houghton Mifflin, 1959.

Chang Po-ling   張伯苓

SOURCES

Persons interviewed: not to be identified.

Barnett, Eugene E., "Chang Po-ling's Fifty Years with the YMCA." Unpublished manuscript, YMCA Historical Library, June 17, 1946.

BKL

Lenz, Frank B., "The Mystery of Personality." *Association Men*, May, 1929.

There is Another China: Essays and Articles for Chang Poling of Nankai. New York: King's Crown Press, 1948.

Chang Shih-chao   章士釗

WORKS

1906. Su pao an chi-shih.

蘇報案紀事。

1912, July 15-19. "Cheng-tang tsu-chih an." *Min li pao*.

政黨組織案。民立報。

1925. Chung-teng kuo-wen tien. Shanghai: Shang-wu yin shu kuan.

中等國文典。

1926. Chia yin tsa-chih ts'un-kao (with Tu-li chou-k'an ts'un-kao). Shanghai: Shang-wu yin shu kuan. 2 vols.

甲寅雜誌存稿（附：獨立週刊存稿）。

1929. Changsha Chang shih ts'ung-kao. Shanghai.

長沙章氏叢稿。

1930. Fu-lo-i-te hsü chuan. Shanghai.

茀蘿乙德序傳。

1943. Lo-chi chih-yao. Chungking.
邏輯指要。

Chang Shih-chao shou han.
章士釗手函。

Shih-pi-po (Editor's Note: Sperber).
師辟伯。

Shuang ch'eng chi.
双枰記。

SOURCES

Chang Shih-chao. "Lun ying-yin ssu-k'u-ch'üan-shu pu ch'eng shih." *Kuo wen chou-pao*, III-33 (August, 1926): 7-8.
章士釗。論影印四庫全書不成事。國聞週報。

Feng Tzu-yu. "Hsing-chung-hui shih-tai chih ko-ming t'ung-chih." *Ta feng pan-yueh-k'an*, 67 (May, 1940): 2095.
馮自由。興中會時代之革命同志。大風半月刊。

———. "Shanghai *min-kuo jih-pao ching chung pao*." *I ching*, 32 (June, 1937): 23.
馮自由。上海民國日報警鐘報。逸經。

Ho Chih. "Chang Hsing-yen ti Kang tso shuo-k'o." *Hua Mai jih-pao*. New York, December 19, 1956.
何知。章行嚴抵港作說客。華美日報。

———. "Chang Shih-chao, Chang Chün-mai, yü Tso Shun-sheng." *Hua Mei jih-pao*. New York, November 21-24, 25-27, 1957.
何知。章士釗，張君勱，與左舜生。華美日報。

Hsin-hai ko-ming hui-i lu, ed. by Chung-kuo jen-min cheng-chih hsieh-shang hui-i ch'üan-kuo wei-yuan-hui wen-shih tzu-liao yen-chiu wei-yuan-hui. Peking: Chung-hua shu-chü, 1961-63.
辛亥革命回憶錄。中國人民政治協商會議全國委員會文史資料研究委員會。

Hu Hsien-su. "P'ing Hu Shih-chih wu-shih nien lai Chung-kuo chih wen-hsueh." *Hsueh heng*, 18 (June, 1923): 1-26.
胡先驌。評胡適之五十年來中國之文學。學衡。

Wang Sen-jan. "Chang Shih-chao hsien-sheng p'ing-chuan," in CECP.
王森然。章士釗先生評傳。

Chang Ta-ch'ien　張大千

WORKS

1947. Chang Ta-ch'ien *et al*. Chang Ta-ch'ien lin fu Tun-huang mo kao k'u chi An-hsi Yü-lin k'u pi-hua. Shanghai: San yuan yin-shua ch'ang.
張大千等。張大千臨撫燉煌漠高窟暨安西榆林窟壁畫。

1961. Chang Ta-ch'ien hua (ed. by Kao Ling-mei). Kowloon: Tung-fang i-shu kung-ssu.
張大千畫。高領梅。

SOURCES

Persons interviewed: not to be identified.
Chiao-yü yü wen-hua shuang-chou-k'an, December 12, 1950; 208 (April 16, 1959): 37-38.
教育與文化雙週刊。

Chang T'ai-lei　張太雷

SOURCES

Chiang K'ang-hu. Hsin O yu-chi. Shanghai: Shang-wu yin shu kuan, 1924.
江亢虎。新俄遊記。

Ch'ü Ch'iu-pai. Ch'ü Ch'iu-pai wen-chi (ed. by Ch'ü Ch'iu-pai wen-chi pien-chi wei-yuan-hui). Peking: Jen-min wen-hsueh ch'u-pan she, 1953-54. 4 vols.
瞿秋白。瞿秋白文集。瞿秋白文集編輯委員會。

Documents on Communism, Nationalism, and Soviet Advisers in China 1918-1927; Papers Seized in the 1927 Peking Raid, ed. by C. Martin Wilbur and Julie Lien-ying How. New York: Columbia University Press, 1956.

Eudin, Xenia Joukoff, and Robert C. North. Soviet Russia and the East, 1920-1927: A Documentary Survey. Stanford: Stanford University Press, 1957.

GCCJK

GCJ

GSSJ

HSWT

Scalapino, Robert A. Democracy and the Party Movement in Prewar Japan: The Failure of the First Attempt. Berkeley: University of California Press, 1953.

Whiting, Allen S. Soviet Policies in China, 1917-1924. New York: Columbia University Press, 1953.

Chang Tao-fan　張道藩

WORKS

1942. Wo-men so hsü-yao te wen-i cheng-ts'e. Chungking.

我們所需要的文藝政策。

1953. Hsing hsien liu nien lai te li-fa-yuan. Taipei.
行憲六年來的立法院。

1962, June. "Suan t'ien k'u la te hui-wei."
Chuan-chi wen-hsueh, I-6: 37–41.
酸甜苦辣的回味。傳記文學。

SOURCES

BKL
Chang Tao-fan. "Suan t'ien k'u la te hui-wei."
Chuan-chi wen-hsueh, I-6: 37–41.
張道藩。酸甜苦辣的回味。傳記文學。

Chang T'ien-yi   張天翼

WORKS

1928. San jih pan chih meng.
三日半之夢。

1931. Ts'ung k'ung-hsü tao ch'ung-shih.
從空虛到充實。

1933. Chi-pei yü nai-tzu. Shanghai: Liang yu t'u-shu yin-shua kung-ssu.
脊背與奶子。

1933. I nien.
一年。

1933. Mi-feng. Shanghai: Hsien-tai shu-chü.
蜜蜂。

1934. I hsing. Shanghai: Liang yu fu-hsing t'u-shu yin-shua kung-ssu.
移行。

1935. Shan-chü. Tientsin.
善舉。

1935. T'uan-yuan. Shanghai: Wen-hua sheng-huo ch'u-pan she.
團圓。

1936. Ch'ing-ming shih-chieh. Wen-hsueh ch'u-pan she.
清明時節。

1936. Ch'un feng. Shanghai: Wen-hua sheng-huo ch'u-pan she.
春風。

1936. Hsiao Pi-te. Shanghai: Fu-hsing shu-chü.
小彼德。

1936. Yang-ching-pin ch'i-hsia. Shanghai: Hsin chung shu-chü.
洋涇濱奇俠。

1937. Ch'i-kuai te ti-fang. Shanghai: Wen-hua sheng-huo ch'u-pan she.
奇怪的地方。

1937. Tsai ch'eng-shih li. Shanghai: Liang yu t'u-shu yin-shua kung-ssu.
在城市裏。

1939. Chui. Shanghai: K'ai-ming shu-tien.
追。

1939. Hao hsiung-ti. Shanghai: Wen-hua sheng-huo ch'u-pan she.
好兄弟。

1939. T'ung-hsiang men. Shanghai: Wen-hua sheng-huo ch'u-pan she.
同鄉們。

1940. Chang T'ien-yi *et al*. Hsin-sheng (ed. by Shih Jo-lin). Kunming: Hsin liu shu-tien.
張天翼等。新生。施若霖。

1943. Hua Wei hsien-sheng.
華威先生。

1945. Chang T'ien-yi *et al*. K'ang-chan hsiao-shuo hsuan. Shanghai: Shanghai wen-i shu-chü.
張天翼等。抗戰小說選。

1946. Su-hsieh san-p'ien. Shanghai: Wen-hua sheng-huo ch'u-pan she.
速寫三篇。

1947. T'an jen-wu miao-hsieh.
談人物描寫。

1949. Chang T'ien-yi *et al*. Lun A Q. Shanghai: Keng-yun ch'u-pan she.
張天翼等。論阿 Q。

1949. Ch'i jen chi. Shanghai: Chien-kuang ch'u-pan kung-ssu.
畸人集。

1951. Chang T'ien-yi hsuan-chi (ed. by Mao Tun). Peking: K'ai-ming shu-tien.
張天翼選集。茅盾。

1952. Lo Wen-ying te ku-shih. Peking: Ch'ing-nien ch'u-pan she.
羅文應的故事。

1954. Stories of Chinese Young Pioneers. Peking: Foreign Languages Press.

1956. Ta Lin ho hsiao Lin. Peking: Chung-kuo shao-nien erh-t'ung ch'u-pan she.
大林和小林。

1959. Kei hai-tzu men. Peking: Jen-min wen-hsueh ch'u-pan she.
給孩子們。

1959. Pao hu-lu te pi-mi. Peking: Jen-min wen-hsueh ch'u-pan she.
寶葫蘆的秘密。

1961. Pao-fu. Hong Kong: Shanghai shu-chü.
報復。

1962. Lü-t'u chung. Hong Kong: Chien wen shu-chü.
旅途中。

Ch'ih-lun.
齒輪。

Chin ya ti-kuo.

金鴨帝國。

Ch'ou-hen.

仇恨。

Ho-shang ta-tui-chang.

和尙大隊長。

Kuei t'u jih-chi.

鬼土日記。

P'i-tai.

皮帶。

Shan nü-jen.

善女人。

T'a-men ho wo-men.

他們和我們。

T'an Chiu hsien-sheng te kung-tso

譚九先生的工作。

T'u t'u ta-wang.

禿禿大王。

Wan jen yueh.

萬仭約。

SOURCES

Chao Ching-shen. Wen-jen chien-ying. Shanghai: Pei hsin shu-chü, 1936.

趙景深。 文人剪影。

CHWC

CHWSK

CHWYS

CKJMT

Contemporary Chinese Stories, tr. by Wang Chichen. New York: Columbia University Press, 1944.

CWT

GCCJK

Hightower, James Robert. Topics in Chinese Literature: Outlines and Bibliographies. Cambridge: Harvard University Press, 1962.

HMTT

HWP

Living China, ed. by Edgar Snow. New York: John Day & Reynal & Hitchcock, 1936.

MCNP

RCCL

WWMC

Chang Tso-lin 張 作 霖

SOURCES

Bertram, James M. First Act in China: The Story of the Sian Mutiny. New York: The Viking Press, 1938.

BPC

Chin Tao. "Chung Tso-lin ko-chü Tung-sansheng ch'ien-hou." Ch'un ch'iu, 121 (July 16, 1962): 20–21.

金刀。 張作霖割據東三省前後。

"Early Life of Chang Tso-lin." Manchuria, September 15, 1936.

The Encyclopedia Britannica, 14th ed.

Gibert, Lucien. Dictionnaire Historique et Geographique de la Mandchourie. Hong Kong: Imprimerie de la Société des Missions-étrangères, 1934.

Gould, Randall. China in the Sun. Garden City, New York: Doubleday & Co., 1946.

Hsiao Pai-fan. Chung-kuo chin pai nien koming shih. Kowloon: Ch'iu shih, 1951.

蕭白帆。 中國近百年革命史。

Hudson, Geoffrey Francis. The Far East in World Politics. London: Oxford University Press, 1939.

Komoto Daisaku. "Watakushi ga Chang Tso-lin o koroshita." Bungei shunju, December, 1954.

河本大作。 私が張作霖を殺した。 文藝春秋。

Koo, Hui-lan. Hui-lan Koo: An Autobiography as Told to Mary Van Rensselaer Thayer. New York: Dial Press, 1943.

Koo, V. K. Wellington. Memoranda Presented to the Lytton Commission. New York: Chinese Cultural Society, 1932.

Lattimore, Owen. Manchuria: Cradle of Conflict. New York: The Macmillan Co., 1935.

Li Chien-nung. The Political History of China 1840–1928 (tr. and ed. by Teng Ssu-yu, Jeremy Ingalls). Princeton: D. Van Nostrand Co., 1956.

Mitsuda Iwao. Showa fûun-roku. Tokyo, 1942.

滿田巖。 昭和風雲錄。

Morishima Morito. Imbô, ansatsu, guntô. Tokyo: Iwanami shoten, 1950.

森島守仁。 陰謀，暗殺，軍刀。

Reischauer, Robert Karl. Japan: Goverment-Politics. New York: T. Nelson & Sons, 1939.

RSOC

Seki Kanji. "1917 nen no Harbin kakumei." Kokusai seiji, Summer, 1958.

關寬治。 1917年のハルビン革命。 國際政治。

SMJ

Snow, Edgar. Far Eastern Front. New York: H. Smith & R. Haas, 1933.

Tanaka Giichi denki, ed. by Tanaka Giichi denki kanko kai. Tokyo, 1958-60.

田中義一傳記。 田中義一傳記刊行會。

T'ang Leang-li. The Inner History of the Chinese Revolution. New York: E.P. Dutton & Co., 1930.

Usui Katsumi. "Chang Tso-lin bakushi no shinso." *Chisei*, December, 1956.
白井勝美。張作霖爆死の眞相。知生。

Vinacke, Harold Monk. A History of the Far East in Modern Times. New York: Crofts, 1942.

Waln, Nora. The House of Exile. Boston: Little, Brown, & Co., 1934.

Wei, Henry. China and Soviet Russia. Princeton: Van Nostrand Co., 1956.

WWC, 1925, 1926, 1930.

Young, Arthur Morgan. Imperial Japan, 1926–1938. New York: W. Morrow & Co., 1938.

———. Japan in Recent Times, 1912–1926. New York: W. Morrow & Co., 1929.

Young, C. Walter. The International Relations of Manchuria. Chicago: University of Chicago Press, 1929.

Chang Tsung-ch'ang　張宗昌

SOURCES

Abend, Hallet. My Life in China 1926–41. New York: Harcourt, Brace & Co., 1943.

BPC

Cheng Chi-ch'eng. "Wo sha-ssu kuo tsei Chang Tsung-ch'ang chih ching-kuo hsiang-ch'ing." *I-ching*, 7 (June 5, 1936): 36–41.
鄭繼成。我殺死國賊張宗昌之經過詳情。逸經。

Chien Yu-wen. "Chung hsiao yung hsia te Cheng Chi-ch'eng chiang-chün." *I-ching*, 7 (June 5, 1936): 34–35.
簡又文。忠孝勇俠的鄭繼成將軍。逸經。

CMTC

CYB-W, 1928, 1929–30.

Koo, V. K. Wellington. Memoranda Presented to the Lytton Commission. New York: The Chinese Cultural Society, 1932.

Kung Yao *et al*. "Ho-kuo yang-min t'an-wu ts'an-pao chih Chang Tsung-ch'ang." *I-ching*, 6 (May 20, 1936): 44–48; 7 (June 5, 1936): 29–30.
工爻等。禍國殃民貪污殘暴之張宗昌。逸經。

Lin Yü-t'ang. With Love and Irony. New York: The John Day Co., 1940.

WWC, 1925.

Chang Tsung-hsiang　章宗祥

SOURCES

AADC

Chang Chung-fu. Chung-hua Min-kuo wai-chiao shih. Taipei: Cheng chung shu-chü, 1954–?
張忠紱。中華民國外交史。

CMTC

Hsin-hai ko-ming, Vol. VIII, ed. by Ch'ai Te-keng *et al*. Shanghai: Shanghai jen-ming ch'u-pan she, 1951. 8 vols.
辛亥革命。柴德賡。

Hu Shih. "Chi-nien 'wu-ssu'," in Pao Tsun-peng, Li Ting-i, and Wu Hsiang-hsiang, *Chung-kuo chin-tai shih lun-ts'ung*, I-8. Taipei: Cheng chung shu-chü, 1956–?
胡適。紀念五四。包遵彭，李定一，吳相湘。中國近代史論叢。

Li Chien-nung. The Political History of China 1840–1928 (tr. and ed. by Teng Ssu-yu, Jeremy Ingalls). Princeton: D. Van Nostrand Co., 1956.

Pollard, Robert T. China's Foreign Relations, 1917–1931. New York: The Macmillan Co., 1933.

Shih Chün-min. Chung Jih kuo-chi shih. Peking: Ming pao she, 1919.
史俊民。中日國際史。

T'ao Chü-yin. Pei-yang chün-fa t'ung-chih shih-ch'i shih-hua. Peking: Sheng-huo, tu-shu, hsin chih san lien shu-tien, 1957. 6 vols.
陶菊隱。北洋軍閥統治時期史話。

Treaties and Agreements with and Concerning China, 1894–1919, comp. and ed. by John V. A. MacMurray. New York: Oxford University Press, 1921.

Wai-chiao ta tz'u-tien, ed. by Wai-chiao hsueh-hui. Kunming: Chung-hua shu-chü, 1937.
外交大辭典。外交學會。

WWMC

Chang Tung-sun　張東蓀

WORKS

1924. K'o-hsueh yü che-hsueh. Shanghai: Shang-wu yin shu kuan.
科學與哲學。

1928. Jen-sheng-kuan ABC. Shih-chieh shu-chü.
人生觀ABC。

1929. Ching-shen fen-hsi hsueh ABC. Shih-chieh shu-chü.

精神分析學ABC。

1929. Hsin che-hsueh lun-ts'ung. Shanghai: Shang-wu yin shu kuan.
新哲學論叢。

1930. Tao-te che-hsueh. Chung-hua shu-chü.
道德哲學。

1931. Che-hsueh. Shih-chieh shu-chü.
哲學。

1931. "Ch'üan-kuo tung-yuan yü hsueh che-hsueh te jen-men," in Ch'u An-p'ing *et al.*, *Chung Jih wen-t'i yü ko chia lun chien.* Shanghai: Hsin-yüeh shu-tien.
全國動員與學哲學的人們。儲安平等。中日問題與各家論見。

1933. Chang Tung-sun *et al.* Che-hsueh shang chih t'ao-lun. Shanghai: Shang-wu yin shu kuan.
張東蓀等。哲學上之討論。

1934. Hsien-tai che-hsueh. Shih-chieh shu-chü.
現代哲學。

1934. Hsien-tai lun-li-hsueh. Shih-chieh shu-chü.
現代倫理學。

1934. Jen-shih-lun. Shih-chieh shu-chü.
認識論。

1934. (ed.) Wei-wu pien-cheng-fa lun-chan. Min yu shu-chü.
唯物辨證法論戰。

1937. "To-yuan jen-shih-lun ch'ung-shu," in Hu Shih *et al.*, *Chang Chü-sheng hsien-sheng ch'i-shih sheng-jih chi-nien lun-wen chi.* Shang-wu yin shu kuan.
多元認識論重述。胡適等。張菊生先生七十生日紀念論文集。

1946. Chih-shih yü wen-hua. Shang-wu yin shu kuan.
知識與文化。

1946. Li-hsing yü min-chu. Shang-wu yin shu kuan.
理性與民主。

1946. Ssu-hsiang yü she-hui. Shanghai: Shang-wu yin shu kuan.
思想與社會。

1947. Min-chu chu-i yü she-hui chu-i. Shanghai: Kuan-ch'a she.
民主主義與社會主義。

Chia-chih che-hsueh. Shih-chieh shu-chü.
價值哲學。

Chin-tai hsi-yang che-hsueh shih kang-yao. Chung-hua shu-chü.
近代西洋哲學史綱要。

ed. of *China Times.*

ed. of *Hsueh teng.*
學灯。

ed. of *Shih-shih hsin pao.*
時事新報。

SOURCES

Person interviewed: James T. C. Liu.

Brière, O. Fifty Years of Chinese Philosophy, 1898–1950 (tr. by Laurence G. Thompson). New York: The Macmillan Co., 1956.

CB, 169, 182, 185, 213.

CBJS

Chan Wing-tsit. Religious Trends in Modern China. New York: Columbia University Press, 1953.

Chang Tung-sun te to-yuan jen-shih-lun chi ch'i p'i-p'ing, ed. by Chan Wen-hu. Shanghai: Shih-chieh shu-chü, 1936.
張東蓀的多元認識論及其批評。詹文滸。

Chow Tse-tsung. The May Fourth Movement: Intellectual Revolution in Modern China. Cambridge: Harvard University Press, 1960.

Ch'üan-kuo tsung shu-mu, ed. by P'ing Hsin (Chao I-p'ing). Shanghai: Sheng-huo shu-tien, 1935.
全國總書目。平心 (趙一萍)。

Chung-kuo shih-hsueh lun-wen so-yin, ed. by Chung-kuo ko-hsueh yuan li-shih yen-chiu so ti i, erh so, Peking ta-hsueh li-shih hsi. Peking: K'o-hsueh ch'u-pan she, 1957. 2 vols.
中國史學論文索引。中國科學院歷史研究所第一，二所，北京大學歷史系。

Edwards, Dwight Woodbridge. Yenching University. New York: United Board for Christian Higher Education in Asia, 1959.

Forke, Alfred. Geschichte der Neueren Chinesischen Philosophie. Hamburg: Friederichsen, de Gruyter & Co., 1938.

HCJC

Kuo Chan-po. Chin wu-shih nien Chung-kuo ssu-hsiang shih. Peiping: Jen-wen shu-tien, 1935.
郭湛波。近五十年中國思想史。

"Selected List of Articles of Ideological Reform and Self-Criticism." CB, 169: 145.

Yeh Ch'ing (Jen Cho-hsuan). Chang Tung-sun che-hsueh p'i-p'an. Shanghai: Hsin k'en shu-chü, 1934.
葉青 (任卓宣)。張東蓀哲學批判。

Chang Tzu-p'ing　張資平

WORKS

1926. Ch'ung-chi ch'i hua-shih. Shanghai: Ch'uang-tsao she ch'u-pan pu.

冲積期化石。

1927. T'ai-li. Shanghai: Ch'uang-tsao she.
苔莉。

1928. Ai chih chiao-tien. Shanghai: T'ai tung shu-chü.
愛之焦點。

1928. Tsui-hou te hsing-fu.
最後的幸福。

1928-? ed. of *Hsin yü-chou*.
新宇宙。

1928-? ed. of *Lo-ch'ün yueh-k'an*.
樂群月刊。

1929. Ch'ang-t'u. Shanghai: Nan ch'iang shu-chü.
長途。

1929. Ch'ing-ch'un. Shanghai: Hsien-tai shu-chü.
青春。

1929-? Tzu-p'ing hsiao-shuo chi. Shanghai: Lo-ch'ün shu-tien. 3 vols.?
資平小說集。

1930. Mei-ling chih ch'un. Shanghai: Kuang-hua shu-chü.
梅嶺之春。

1930. Mi-lan. Shanghai: Le-ch'ün shu-tien.
糜爛。

1930. T'iao-yao che te jen-men.
跳躍着的人們。

1930. T'ien sun chih nü. Shanghai: Wen-i shu-chü.
天孫之女。

1931. Ai chih wo-liu. Shanghai: Kuang-ming shu-chü.
愛之渦流。

1931. Ch'ün hsing luan fei. Shanghai: Kuang-hua shu-chü.
群星亂飛。

1931. Hung wu. Shanghai: Yueh hua shu-tien.
紅霧。

1931. Ming-chu yü hei-t'an. Shanghai: Kuang-ming shu-chü.
明珠與黑炭。

1931. Pei-chi-ch'üan li te wang-kuo.
北極圈裡的王國。

1931. Shang-ti te erh-nü men. Shanghai: Kuang-ming shu-chü.
上帝的兒女們。

1931. (ed.) She-hui-hsueh kang-yao. Shanghai: Shang-wu yin shu kuan.
社會學綱要。

1931. Shih-liu hua.
柘榴花。

1931. Su-miao chung-chung. Shanghai: Kuang-ming shu-tien.
素描種種。

1931. T'o le kuei-tao te hsing-ch'iu (Tung yu shih nien). Shanghai: Hsien-tai shu-chü.
脫了軌道的星球 (東遊十年)。

1932. Ai li ch'üan wai. Shanghai: Yueh hua t'u-shu kung-ssu.
愛力圈外。

1933. Hsueh te ch'u-hsi. Shanghai: Shang-wu yin shu kuan.
雪的除夕。

1933. Pu p'ing-heng te ou li. Shanghai: Shang-wu yin shu kuan.
不平衡的偶力。

1933. Shih-tai yü ai te ch'i-lu. Ho chung shu-tien.
時代與愛的岐路。

1934. Tzu-p'ing tzu-chuan (Ts'ung huang-lung tao wu se). Shanghai: Ti-i ch'u-pan she.
資平自傳 (從黃龍到五色)。

1935. (ed.) Wen-chang kou-tsao fa. Shanghai: Shang-wu yin shu kuan.
文章構造法。

1936? Chang Tzu-p'ing hsuan-chi (ed. by Hsü Ch'en-ssu, Yeh Wang-yu). Shanghai: Wan-hsiang shu wu.
張資平選集。徐沉泗，葉忘憂。

1936. Fei-hsü. Shanghai: Fu-hsing shu-chü.
飛絮。

1936. Ti-t'u hsueh chi ti-t'u hui-chih fa. Shanghai: Shang-wu yin shu kuan.
地圖學及地圖繪製法。

1937. Huan-hsi-t'o yü ma-t'ung. Shanghai: Fu-hsing shu-chü.
歡喜陀與馬桶。

1939. Lien-ai ts'o-tsung. Shanghai: Chung-hua shu-chü.
戀愛錯綜。

1951. Ch'ing-ch'un k'uang-hsiang ch'ü. Hong Kong: Ho ming shu-tien.
青春狂想曲。

1952. Ko-ming ch'ing-lü. Hong Kong: Ho ming shu-tien.
革命情侶。

Chang Tzu-p'ing *et al*. Hsien-tai lien-ai hsiao-shuo hsuan. Shanghai: Nan hua shu-chü.
張資平等。現代戀愛小說選。

Ch'en-i. (tr.)
襯衣。

Chih-shu chieh.
植樹節。

Hsing te teng-fen-hsien.
性的等分線。

Hua-shih jen-lei hsueh. Shang-wu yin shu kuan.
化石人類學。

I-pan jung-yuan te sheng-huo.
　一般冗員的生活。

Jen-lei chin-hua lun. Shang-wu yin shu kuan.
　人類進化論。

Jen-wen ti-li hsueh.
　人文地理學。

Kai-chi chuan-lueh. Shang-wu yin shu kuan.
　蓋基傳略。

K'ou la sha.
　扣拉沙。

Kung-chai wei-yuan.
　公債委員。

K'ung-hsü. (tr.)
　空虛。

Liang jen.
　兩人。

Mou nü-jen te fan-tsui. (tr.)
　某女人的犯罪。

Mu-ma.
　木馬。

Ou-chou wen-i shih ta-kang.
　歐洲文藝史大綱。

P'ing-ti feng-po. (tr.)
　平地風波。

P'u-lo wen-i lun.
　普羅文藝論。

P'u-t'ung ti-chih hsueh. Shang-wu yin shu kuan.
　普通地質學。

Shih-tzu-chia shang.
　十字架上。

Shih-yu yü shih-t'an. Shang-wu yin shu kuan.
　石油與石炭。

Ti-chih hsueh che Ta-erh-wen. Shang-wu yin shu kuan.
　地質學者達爾文。

Ti-chih k'uang-wu hsueh. Shang-wu yin shu kuan.
　地質鑛物學。

Ts'ao-ts'ung chung. (tr.)
　草叢中。

Tzu-jan ti-li hsueh. Shang-wu yin shu kuan.
　自然地理學。

Wen-i shih kai-yao.
　文藝史概要。

Ya-p'o. (tr.)
　壓迫。

Yueh-po chih lei.
　約伯之淚。

Sources

Chang Tzu-p'ing. Tzu-p'ing tzu-chuan (Ts'ung huang-lung tao wu se). Shanghai: Ti-i ch'u-pan she, 1934.

張資平。資平自傳（從黃龍到五色）。

Chang Tzu-p'ing p'ing-chuan, ed. by Shih Ping-hui. Shanghai: Kai ming shu-tien, 1936.

張資平評傳。史秉慧。

Ch'u-pan chou-k'an, 131 (June 1, 1935): 22.

出版週刊。

Ch'uang-tsao she lun, ed. by Huang Jen-ying (pseud. of Ku Feng-ch'eng). Shanghai: Kuang-hua shu-chü, 1932.

創造社論。黃人影（顧鳳城）。

CHWC
CHWSK
CHWYS
CMMC
CWT
GCCJK
GCJJ

Ho Yü-po. Hsien-tai Chung-kuo tso-chia lun. Shanghai: Kuang-hua shu-chü, 1932. 2 vols.

賀玉波。現代中國作家論。

MCNP
MMT

Chang Wen-t'ien　　張聞天

Works

1920, March 1. "Nung-ts'un kai-tsao fa-tuan." *Shao-nien shih-chieh*: 32–34.

農村改造發端。少年世界。

1924. Po-ko-sen chih pien-i che-hsueh. (tr.) Shanghai: Min chih shu-chü.

柏格森之變易哲學。

1925. Chang Wen-t'ien *et al*. Tan-ti yü Ko-te. Shanghai: Shang-wu yin shu kuan.

張聞天等。但底與哥德。

1926. Lü-t'u. Shanghai: Shang-wu yin shu kuan.

旅途。

1932. Man-chou shih-pien chung ko-ko fan-tung cheng-chih p'ai-pieh tsen-yang yung-hu kuo-min-tang te t'ung-chih. Juichin: Chung-hua Su-wei-ai chung-yang ch'u-pan chü.

滿洲事變中各個反動政治派別怎樣擁護國民黨的統治。

1934. Hsin te ling-tao fang-shih.

新的領導方式。

1936. Ch'ing-ch'un te meng. Shanghai: Chung-hua shu-chü.

青春的夢。

1938. Chang Wen-t'ien *et al*. Shih nien lai te Chung-kuo kung-ch'an-tang. Hankow: Yang-tzu Chiang ch'u-pan she.

張聞天等。十年來的中國共產黨。

1940. Hsin wen-hua yün-tung lun. Shanghai?
Kuang-ta ch'u-pan she.
新文化運動論。

1947. San min chu-i yü kung-ch'an chu-i. with
Ch'en Po-ta *et al.* Hong Kong: Hsien-shih
ch'u-pan she.
三民主義與共產主義。陳伯達等。

Ch'i-o-k'ang-t'ao. (tr. of Gabriele L. D'An-
nunzio's *Gioconda*). Chung-hua shu-chü.
琪瑤康陶。

Kuo te t'iao-wu. (tr. of Leonid Andreyev's *The
Waltz of the Dogs*). Shang-wu yin shu kuan.
狗的跳舞。

ed. of *Tou-cheng.*
鬥爭。

Yü chung chi. (tr. of Oscar Wilde's *Ballad of
Reading Gaol*). with Wang Fu-ch'üan. Shang-
wu yin shu kuan.
獄中記。汪馥泉。

SOURCES

Person interviewed: Chang Kuo-t'ao.
Chang Wen-t'ien. "Nung-ts'un kai-tsao fa-
tuan." *Shao-nien shih-chieh*, (March 1, 1920):
32–34.
張聞天。農村改造發端。少年世界。
Chung-kuo kung-ch'an-tang te chung-yao jen-
wu, ed. by Min-chien ch'u-pan she. Peking:
Min-chien ch'u-pan she, 1949.
中國共產黨的重要人物。民間出版社。
CPR, 1071 (January 20, 1950).
GCJJ
GSSJ
Hua shang pao shou-ts'e, 1949. Hong Kong: *Hua
shang pao* she.
華商報手冊。
JMST, 1957.
Mao Tse-tung. Selected Works. London:
Lawrence & Wishart, 1954–56. 4 vols.
Mif, Pavel A. Heroic China, Fifteen Years of
the Communist Party of China. New York:
Workers Library, 1937.
RNRC
RSOC
Schwartz, Benjamin I. Chinese Communism
and the Rise of Mao. Cambridge: Harvard
University Press, 1951.
Shao-nien Chung-kuo, III-2 (September 1, 1921):
14–20.
少年中國。
Wales, Nym (pseud. of Helen Foster Snow).
Inside Red China. New York: Doubleday,
Doran & Co., 1939.

Chang Yuan-chi   張元濟

WORKS

1901–? ed. of *Wai-chiao pao.*
外交報。
1904–? ed. of *Tung-fang tsa-chih.*
東方雜誌。
1911. Hai-yen Chang shih she-yuan ts'ung-k'o.
8 vols.
海鹽張氏涉園叢刻。
1916–31. Han-fen-lou pi-chi. with Sun Yü-hsiu.
Shanghai: Shang-wu yin shu shu kuan. 80
vols.
涵芬樓秘笈。孫毓修。
1917. (comp.) Wu-hsü liu chün-tzu i chi. with
Chuang Yü, Chiang Wei-ch'iao, Sun Yü-hsiu.
Shang-wu yin shu kuan. 6 vols.
戊戌六君子遺集。莊兪，蔣維喬，孫毓修。
1925. Wu-t'ai-shan.
五臺山。
1926. K'ung-lin.
孔林。
1931. T'ien-t'ai-shan.
天臺山。
1937. Chung-hua min-tsu te jen-ko. Shanghai:
Shang-wu yin shu kuan.
中華民族的人格。
1938. Chiao shih sui-pi. Changsha: Shang-wu
yin shu kuan.
校史隨筆。
1949. (ed.) (Chieh-pen) K'ang-hsi tzu-tien.
Shanghai: Shang-wu yin shu kuan.
(節本) 康熙字典。
1951. Han-fen-lou chin-yü shu-lu. with Ku
T'ing-lung.
涵分樓燼餘書錄。顧廷龍。
1957. She-yuan hsü-pa chi-lu (ed. by Ku T'ing-
lung). Shanghai: Ku-tien wen-hsueh ch'u-
pan she.
涉園序跋集錄。顧廷龍。
Pai na pen erh-shih ssu shih.
百衲本二十四史。

SOURCES

Chang Ching-lu. Chung-kuo ch'u-pan shih-liao
pu-pien. Peking: Chung-hua shu-chü, 1957.
張靜廬。中國出版史料補編。
———. Chung-kuo hsien-tai ch'u-pan shih-liao.
Shanghai: Chung-hua shu-chü, 1954–? 3 vols?
張靜廬。中國現代出版史料。
Chin shan shih-pao. San Francisco, February 21,
1957.
金山時報。

Chung-kuo chin-tai ch'u-pan shin-liao, ed. by Chang Ching-lu. Shanghai: Shang tsa ch'u-pan she, ch'ün lien ch'u-pan she, 1953-54. 2 vols.
中國近代出版史料。張靜廬。

Ho Ping-sung. "Shang-wu yin shu kuan pei hui chi-lueh." *Tung-fang tsa-chih*, XXIX-4 (October, 1932): 9.
何炳松。商務印書館被燬紀略。東方雜誌。

Ma Hsü-lun. Wo tsai liu-shih sui i-ch'ien. Shanghai: Sheng-huo shu-tien, 1947.
馬敍倫。我在六十歲以前。

SCMP, 2080 (August 20, 1959).

Shang-wu yin shu kuan chih-lueh, ed. by Shang-wu yin shu kuan. Shanghai: Shang-wu yin shu kuan, 1929.
商務印書館志略。商務印書館。

Sun Shih-cheng. "Shuo lin." *Chia-yin chou-k'an*, I-30: 24-25.
孫師鄭。說林。甲寅周刊。

Yang Shou-ch'ing. Chung-kuo ch'u-pan chieh chien shih. Shanghai: Yung hsiang yin shu kuan, 1946.
楊壽清。中國出版界簡史。

Chao Erh-sun   趙爾巽

WORKS

1902. (comp.) Hsing an hsin pien. 30 vols.
刑案新編。

1903. Chao liu-shou kung lueh.
趙留守攻略。

1928. (ed.) Ch'ing shih kao. with K'o Shao-min *et al*. Peking: Ch'ing shih kuan. 132 vols.
清史稿。柯劭忞等。

SOURCES

CBJS

Chao Erh-sun (1844-1927) ai wan lu. Min-kuo chien.
趙爾巽哀輓錄。

Chin Liang. Ssu ch'ao i-wen. Peiping? 1936.
金梁。四朝佚聞。

Chin Yü-fu. "Tu Ch'ing shih cha-chi." *Kuo shih kuan kuan-k'an*, I-3 (August, 1948): 25-54.
金毓黻。讀清史劄記。國史館館刊。

Chu Shih-ch'e. Ch'ing shih shu wen. Peking, 1957.
朱師轍。清史述聞。

CJC

CYB-W, 1936.

Hsin-hai ko-ming, ed. by Ch'ai Te-keng *et al*. Shanghai: Shanghai jen-min ch'u-pan she, 1957. 8 vols.
辛亥革命。柴德賡等。

Hsü I-shih. "Ch'ing shih kao yü Chao Erh-sun." *I ching*, 2 (March 20, 1936): 11-14.
徐一士。清史稿與趙爾巽。逸經。

Kuang-hsü pa nien jen-wu Shun-t'ien hsiang-shih t'ung-nien ch'ih lu.
光緒八年壬午順天鄉試同年齒錄。

MMT

Shih Liang. Yeh-t'ang-hsuan ch'üan-chi. Pei-ping, 1929. 6 vols.
奭良。野棠軒全集。

Wang I-t'ang. "Chin ch'uan shih lou shih hua." *Kuo wen chou-pao*, V-14 (April, 1928).
王揖唐。今傳是樓詩話。國聞週報。

Chao Heng-t'i   趙恒惕

SOURCES

CMJL

GSJK

Hsien-tai p'ing-lun, I-6 (March, 1925): 2-3; I-19 (April, 1925): 2-3; III-74 (May, 1926): 1-2.
現代評論。

Huang Hui-ch'üan and Tiao Ying-hua. Hsin Chung-kuo jen-wu chih (tr. of Sonoda Kazuki's *Shin Chugoku jimbutsushi*). Shanghai: Liang yu, 1932?
黃惠泉，刀英華。新中國人物誌。

Kuo wen chou-pao, III-9 (March, 1926): 2-3.
國聞週報。

Ta Chung-hua tsa-chih, II-8 (August, 1916); II-9 (September, 1916).
大中華雜誌。

TCML

Tung-fang tsa-chih, XVII-13 (June, 1920): 136; XVIII-9 (March, 1921): 131; XIX-3 (February, 1922): 129; XIX-8 (May, 1922): 127; XIX-20 (October, 1922); XX-2 (January, 1923): 135; XX-10 (May, 1923): 142; XX-15 (August, 1923): 7; XX-16 (August, 1923): 149; XX-18 (July, 1923): 143; XX-19 (August, 1923): 133; XXI-21 (November, 1924): 5-6; XXII-10 (March, 1925): 3; XXIII-8 (February, 1926): 132-133; XXIII-12 (April, 1926): 141-143; XXIII-14 (July, 1926): 141; XXIII-15 (August, 1926): 134; XXV-1 (January, 1928): 15-30.

東方雜誌。
WWC, 1931.

Chao Shih-yen　　趙世炎

Works

ed. of *Cheng-chih sheng-huo*.
政治生活。

Sources

GCCJK
GCJ
Ho Ch'ang-kung. Ch'in kung chien hsueh sheng-huo hui-i. Peking: Kung-jen ch'u-pan she, 1958.
何長工。勤工儉學生活回憶。
Hsiao Pai-fan. Chung-kuo chin pai nien ko-ming shih. Kowloon: Ch'iu shih ch'u-pan she, 1951.
蕭白帆。中國近百年革命史。

Chao Shu-li　　趙樹理

Works

1940. ed. of *Hsin ta-chung*.
新大象。
1942. ed. of *Lao-pai-hsing*.
老百姓。
1946. Li Yu-ts'ai pan-hua. Shanghai: Chih-shih ch'u-pan she.
李有才板話。
1947. Hsiao-erh-hei chieh-hun. Hong Kong: Hsin min-chu ch'u-pan she.
小二黑結婚。
1947. Li-chia-chuang te pien-ch'ien. Shanghai: Hsin chih shu-tien.
李家莊的變遷。
Eng. tr. by Gladys Yang, *Changes in Li Village*. Peking: Foreign Languages Press, 1953.
1949. Meng Hsiang-ying fan-shen (ed. by Sun Feng). Shanghai: Chiao-yü ch'u-pan she.
孟祥英翻身。孫風。
1949-59. (ed.) Chien-kuo shih nien wen-hsueh ch'uang-tso hsuan—ch'ü i. with Tao Tun. Peking: Chung-kuo ch'ing-nien ch'u-pan she.
建國十年文學創作選—曲藝。陶鈍。
1950. Chao Shu-li *et al.* Ta-chung wen-i lun-chi. Peking: Kung-jen ch'u-pan she.
趙樹理等。大象文藝論集。

1950. Fu kuei. Shanghai: Jen-min shu-pao kung-ying she.
福貴。
1950-? ed. of *Shuo shuo ch'ang ch'ang*.
說說唱唱。
1951. Chieh-hun teng-chi. Peking: Ta-chung t'u-hua ch'u-pan she.
結婚登記。
1952. Chao Shu-li hsuan-chi (ed. by Mao Tun). Shanghai: K'ai-ming shu-tien.
趙樹理選集。茅盾。
1953. Teng-chi. Peking: Kung-jen ch'u-pan she.
登記。
1954. Lao Yang t'ung-chih. Peking: Jen-min wen-hsueh ch'u-pan she.
老楊同志。
1955. San li wan. Peking: T'ung-su tu-wu ch'u-pan she.
三里灣。
Eng. tr. by Gladys Yang, *Sanliwan Village*. Peking: Foreign Languages Press, 1957.
1957. Piao-ming t'ai-tu. Peking: T'ung-su wen-i ch'u-pan she.
表明態度。
1959? Ling ch'üan tung. Peking: Tso-chia ch'u-pan she.
靈泉洞。
1962. San fu chi. Peking: Tso-shia ch'u-pan she.
三复集。
1963. Hsia-hsiang chi. Peking: Tso-chia ch'u-pan she.
下鄉集。
1963. Kai ch'ü. Peking: Chung-kuo hsi-chü ch'u-pan she.
開渠。
Ch'uan chia pao.
傳家寶。
Hsieh pu ya cheng.
邪不壓正。
P'ang Ju-chu.
龐如珠。
Shih Pu-lan kang che.
石不爛趕車。
Ti-pan.
地板。

Sources

Birch, Cyril. "Chao Shu-li: Creative Writing in a Communist State." *New Mexico Quarterly*, XXV-2, 3 (1955): 185-95.

Chao Shu-li. Chao Shu-li hsuan-chi (ed. by Mao Tun). Shanghai: K'ai-ming shu-tien, 1952.
趙樹理。趙樹理選集。茅盾。

Chi Chen-huai. "Chu Tzu-ch'ing hsien-sheng nien-p'u," in Chu Tzu-ch'ing hsien-sheng ch'üan-chi pien-chi wei-yuan-hui, *Chu Tzu-ch'ing wen-chi*. Peking: Kai-ming shu-tien, 1953.
季鎮淮。朱自清先生年譜。朱自清全集編輯委員會。朱自清文集。

Chou Yang. "Lun Chao Shu-li te ch'uang-tso," in Peking shih-fan ta-hsueh wen-i hsueh-hsi she, *Tso-chia yü tso-p'in lun*. Peking: Wu-shih nien-tai ch'u-pan she, 1952.
周揚。論趙樹理的創作。北京師範大學文藝學習社，作家與作品論。

CHWSK
CKJMT
GCJJ
HMTT
HWP

New Publications from China. Peking: Guozi shudian, Summer, 1958.

RCCL

Ta kung pao. Hong Kong, June 1, 1952.
大公報。

Ting Miao. P'ing Chung-kung wen-i tai-piao tso. Hong Kong: Hsin shih-chi ch'u-pan she. 1953.
丁淼。評中共文藝代表作。

Chao Tzu-ch'en   趙紫宸

WORKS

1926. Yeh-su te jen-sheng che-hsueh. Shanghai: Chung-hua chi-tu-chiao wen she.
耶穌的人生哲學。

1934. Yeh-su chuan. Shanghai: Ch'ing-nien hsieh-hui shu-chü.
耶穌傳。

1948. Sheng Pao-lo chuan. Shanghai: Ch'ing-nien hsieh-hui.
聖保羅傳。

1950. Chi-tu-chiao chin-chieh. Shanghai: Ch'ing-nien hsieh-hui.
基督教進解。

SOURCES

Person interviewed: Frank W. Price.
China Rediscovers Her West, ed. by Wu Yi-fang, Frank W. Price. New York: Friendship Press, 1940.
WWC, 1931.

Chao Yuen-ren   趙元任

WORKS

1930. Kwangsi Yao ko chi yin. Peiping: Ta pei yin shu chü.
廣西猺歌記音。

1931. A-li-ssu man-yu ch'i-ching chi (tr. of Lewis Carroll's *Alice's Adventures in Wonderland*). Shanghai: Shang-wu yin shu kuan.
阿麗思漫游奇境記。

1933. Kuo-yin hsin shih yün. Shanghai: Shang-wu yin shu kuan.
國音新詩韻。

1935. Hsien-tai Wu yü te yen-chiu. Ch'ing-hua ta-hsueh.
現代吳語的研究。

1936. September. "A Critical List of Errata for Bernhard Karlgren's Études sur la Phonologie Chinoise." *Quarterly Bulletin of Chinese Bibliography*, III-3.

1939. Chung-hsiang fang-yen chi. Shanghai: Shang-wu yin shu kuan.
鐘祥方言記。

1947. Autobiography of a Chinese Woman, Buwei Yang Chao, Put into English by Her Husband Yuenren Chao. (tr.) New York: The John Day Co.

1947. Cantonese Primer. Cambridge: Harvard University Press.

1947. Concise Dictionary of Spoken Chinese. with Yang Lien-sheng. Cambridge: Harvard University Press.

1948. Chao Yuen-ren *et al*. Hupeh fang-yen tiao-ch'a pao-kao. Shanghai: Shang-wu yin shu kuan. 2 vols.
趙元任等。湖北方言調查報告。

1948. Mandarin Primer, an Intensive Course in Spoken Chinese. Cambridge: Harvard University Press.

1959. Yü-yen wen-t'i. Taipei: Kuo-li Taiwan ta-hsueh wen-hsueh yuan.
語言問題。

1968. A Grammer of Spoken Chinese. Berkeley: University of California Press.

Hsin Kuo-yü liu-sheng-p'ien k'o-pen. Shanghai: Shang-wu yin shu kuan.
新國語留聲片課本。

SOURCES

Chao, Buwei Yang. Autobiography of a Chinese Woman, Buwei Yang Chao, Put into English by Her Husband Yuenren Chao. New York: The John Day Co., 1947.

Chao, Buwei Yang. How to Cook and Eat in Chinese. New York: The John Day Co., 1963.

Chao Yuen-ren hsien-sheng liu-shih-wu sui chi-nien lun-wen chi. Taipei: Chung-yang yen-chiu yuan li-shih yü-yen yen-chiu so, 1958.
趙元任先生六十五歲紀念論文集。

Liu Mei hsueh-sheng t'ung-hsin, 20 (1959).
留美學生通訊。

Who's Who in America, 1962–63.

Ch'en Ch'eng   陳誠

WORKS

1945. Tsung-ts'ai ko-ming chih li-lun yü shih-chien. Shanghai: Cheng chung shu-chü.
總裁革命之理論與實踐。

1946. Pa nien k'ang-chan ching-kuo kai-yao. Nanking.
八年抗戰經過概要。

1951. An Approach to China's Land Reform. Taipei: Cheng chung Book Co.

1951. Ju-ho shih-hsien keng che yu ch'i t'ien. Taipei: Cheng chung shu-chü.
如何實現耕者有其田。

1951. Ju-ho tsou hsiang an-ch'üan ho-p'ing chih lu. Taipei: Lien-ho kuo Chung-kuo t'ung-chih hui.
如何走向安全和平之路。

1952. Shih-cheng pao-kao. Taipei.
施政報告。

1953. Shih-shih keng che yu ch'i t'ien chung-yao wen-hsien. Taipei.
實施耕者有其田重要文獻。

1954. An Oral Report on Free China by Premier Chen Cheng to the Second Session of the First Nationalist Assembly on March 4, 1954. Taipei: Government Information Bureau.

1955. Ch'en Ch'eng *et al*. Cheng-fu shou-chang ssu-shih-san nien-tu yen-lun chi (ed. by Hsing-cheng yuan hsin-wen chü. Taipei: Hsing-cheng yuan hsin-wen chü.
陳誠等。政府首長四十三年度言論集。

1960. Kai-shan t'ou-tzu huan-ching yü ching-chi fa-chan (ed. by Kung-yeh fa-chan t'ou-tzu yen-chiu hsiao-tsu). Taipei.
改善投資環境與經濟發展。工業發展投資研究小組。

1961. Land Reform in Taiwan. Taiwan: China Publishing Co.

1961. Taiwan t'u-ti kai-ko chi-yao. Taipei: Chung-hua shu-chü.

臺灣土地改革紀要。
Ko-ming te tao-te.
革命的道德。
Ts'ung-cheng hui-i.
從政回憶。

SOURCES

BKL
Ch'en Ch'eng. Pa nien k'ang-chan ching-kuo kai-yao. Nanking, 1946.
陳誠。八年抗戰經過概要。
————. Taiwan t'u-ti kai-ko chi-yao. Taipei: Chung-hua shu-chü, 1961.
陳誠。臺灣土地改革紀要。
————. Tsung-cheng hui-i.
陳誠。從政回憶。
Ch'en Ch'eng p'ing chuan. Taipei: Shanghai shu pao she, 1949.
陳誠評傳。
Ch'en fu tsung-t'ung hua-chuan.
陳副總統畫傳。
"Ch'en fu tsung-t'ung nien-piao." *Hong Kong shih pao*. Hong Kong, March 6, 7, 8, 1965.
陳副總統年表。香港時報。
Chiao fei chün ti-i lu Chin hsi chiao fei tso-chan chi-yao.
剿匪軍第一路晉西剿匪作戰紀要。
Chün-cheng pu ta-shih chi.
軍政部大事記。
Chung-yang jih-pao. Taipei, March 23, 1960.
中央日報。
CTMC
Free China Weekly, NN-LXI-31 (August 1, 1961): 1–2; NN-LXI-32 (August 8, 1961): 1–3; NN-LXI-30 (July 25, 1961): 1–2; NN-LXI-33 (August 15, 1961): 1–2; NN-LXIII-10 (March 5, 1963): 1–2; NN-LXIII-11 (March 12, 1963): 1; NN-LXIII-12 (March 19, 1963): 1; NN-LXIII-13 (March 26, 1963): 1–3; NN-LXIII-35 (September 4, 1963): 1.
Hsin Hupeh chien-she chi-yao.
新湖北建設紀要。
Hsin-sheng pao. Taipei, March 6, 1965.
新生報。
Hua Mei jih-pao. New York, January 18, 1962.
華美日報。
Huang Kuo-shu *et al*. Ch'en Ch'eng yü Chung-kuo. Taipei: Shih-tai wen-hua ch'u-pan she, 1965.
黃國書等。陳誠與中國。
Japan Times. Tokyo, November 8, 1961.
Kuo chün cheng-kung shih-kao.
國軍政工史稿。

Liang Kuang shih-pien chih chün-shih ching-
kuo.
兩廣事變之軍事經過。
Lu-chün cheng-li ch'u cheng-chün ching-kuo
kai-yao.
陸軍整理處整軍經過概要。
The New York Times, May 15, 1961; March 5,
1965.
Sian shih-pien shih-chi.
西安事變實紀。
Ti-chiu chan-ch'ü Wuhan hui-chan chan-tou
hsiang pao.
第九戰區武漢會戰戰鬥詳報。
Ti-i chan-ch'ü ssu-ling chang-kuan pu tzu-liao
chi.
第一戰區司令長官部資料集。
Ti shih-pa chün chien shih.
第十八軍簡史。
Ti-ssu chi-tuan chün tui-yü Hsi-pei shih-pien
chün-shih hsing-tung.
第四集團軍對於西北事變軍事行動。
White, Theodore H., and Annalee Jacoby.
Thunder Out of China. New York: William
Sloane Associates, 1946.
Yuan-cheng chün ssu-ling chang-kuan pu tzu-
liao.
遠征軍司令長官部資料。

Ch'en Chi-t'ang   陳濟棠

SOURCES

BKL
Carlson, Evans Fordyce. The Chinese Army,
Its Organization and Military Efficiency.
New York: International Secretariat, Insti-
tute of Pacific Relations, 1940.
CH
Chang Ch'i-yün. Tang shih kai-yao. Taipei:
Chung-yang kai-tsao wei-yuan-hui wen-wu
kung-ying she, 1951–52. 5 vols.
張其昀。黨史概要。
Ch'en Chi-t'ang hsien-sheng chi-nien chi, ed.
by Ho Shao-ch'iung *et al.* Kowloon: Ta han
shu-chü, 1957.
陳濟棠先生紀念集。何紹瓊等。
Ch'en Chi-t'ang hsien-sheng chui-tao hui t'e-
k'an. Hong Kong: Ch'en Chi-t'ang hsien-
sheng chui-tao ta-hui ch'ou-pei ch'u.
陳濟棠先生追悼會特刊。
Ch'en Po-nan hsien-shing jung-ai lu, ed. by
Ch'en Chi-t'ang hsien-sheng chih-sang wei-
yuan-hui. Taipei, 1954.

陳伯南先生榮哀錄。陳濟棠先生治喪委員
會。
Chung-hua Min-kuo ta-shih chih.
中華民國大事志。
CMJL
Gannes, Harry. When China Unites: An Inter-
pretive History of the Chinese Revolution.
New York: Alfred A. Knopf, 1937.
Hsing tao jih-pao. Hong Kong, November 4, 7,
1954.
星島日報。
Ko-ming shih ts'an-k'ao tzu-liao.
革命史參考資料。
Kuo wen chou-pao, X-13, XIII-33.
國聞週報。
Tong, Hollington K. Chiang Kai-shek. Taipei:
China Publishing Co., 1953.
Ts'ai T'ing-k'ai. Ts'ai T'ing-k'ai tzu-chuan.
Hong Kong: Tzu-yu hsun-k'an she, 1946. 2
vols.
蔡廷鍇。蔡廷鍇自傳。
Yeh Yün-sheng *et al.* Kwangtung shih-jen chih.
Canton: K'ai t'ung ch'u-pan she, 1946.
葉雲笙等。廣東時人志。

Ch'en Ch'i-mei   陳其美

SOURCES

Chung-kuo kuo-min-tang shih-kao i chih ssu
p'ien, comp. by Tsou Lu. Chungking: Shang-
wu yin shu kuan, 1944. 4 vols.
中國國民黨史稿一至四篇。鄒魯。
Chung-yang jih-pao. Taipei, October 10, 1961.
中央日報。
CMMC
MSICH
P'an Kung-chan. Ch'en Ch'i-mei. Taipei:
Sheng-li ch'u-pan kung-ssu, 1954.
潘公展。陳其美。
Shao Yuan-ch'ung. Ch'en Ying-shih hsien-
sheng ko-ming hsiao-shih. Shanghai: Min
chih shu-chü, 1925.
邵元沖。陳英士先生革命小史。

Ch'en Chia-keng   陳嘉庚

WORKS

1941. Hua-ch'iao ling-hsiu Ch'en Chia-keng
chiu-kuo yen-lun chi (ed. by Shen Chung-jen).
Shanghai: Hua-mei t'u-shu kung-ssu.
華僑領袖陳嘉庚救國言論集。沈仲仁。

1946. Chu-wu yü wei-sheng. Singapore: Nan-yang hua-ch'iao ch'ou chen tsu-kuo nan-min tsung-hui.
住屋與衛生。

1946. Wo kuo hsing te wen-t'i. Singapore: Hsin Nan-yang ch'u-pan she.
我國行的問題。

1949. Ch'en Chia-keng yen-lun chi. Singapore: Hsing-chou nan ch'ao yin-shua she.
陳嘉庚言論集。

1950. Hsin Chung-kuo kuan-kan chi. Singapore: Nan-yang hua-ch'iao ch'ou chen tsu-kuo nan-min tsung-hui.
新中國觀感集。

1950. Nan ch'iao hui-i-lu. Nan-t'ai: Foochow chi-mei hsiao-yu hui.
南僑回憶錄。

1956. Wu-wan li lu tsu-kuo hsing (Hua-ts'e) (ed. by Ching-chi tao pao she). Hong Kong.
五萬里路祖國行（畫冊）。經濟導報社。

SOURCES

Ch'en Chia-keng. Ch'en Chia-keng yen-lun chi. Singapore: Hsing-chou nan ch'iao yin-shua she, 1949.
陳家庚。陳家庚言論集。

———. Nan ch'iao hui-i-lu. Nan-t'ai: Foochow chi-mei hsiao-yu hui, 1950.
陳嘉庚。南僑回憶錄。

Ch'en Chia-keng hsien-sheng chi-nien ts'e, ed. by Ch'en Chia-keng hsien-sheng chi-nien ts'e pien-chi wei-yuan-hui. Peking: Chung-hua ch'üan-kuo kuei-kuo hua-ch'iao lien-ho hui, 1961.
陳嘉庚先生紀念冊。陳嘉庚先生紀念冊編輯委員會。

Cheng Liang. Ch'en Chia-keng. Hong Kong: Hsin ch'ao ch'u-pan she, 1952.
鄭良。陳嘉庚。

CMTC

Hua Mei jih-pao. New York, August 14, 1961.
華美日報。

Yeh I-chün *et al.* Ch'en Chia-keng hsien-sheng an-ch'üan ch'ing-chu ta-hui t'e-k'an, 1945.
葉貽俊等。陳嘉庚先生安全慶祝大會特刊。

Ch'en Chin-t'ao   陳錦濤

SOURCES

AADC
The Chinese Year Book, 1935–36. Nanking.
Li Chien-nung. The Political History of China

1840–1928 (tr. and ed. by Teng Ssu-yu, Jeremy Ingalls). Princeton: D. Van Nostrand Co., 1956.

T'ang Leang-li. The Inner History of the Chinese Revolution. New York: E. P. Dutton & Co., 1930.

Wai-chiao ta tz'u-tien, ed. by Wai-chiao hsueh-hui. Kunming: Chung-hua shu-chü, 1937.
外交大辭典。外交學會。

Who's Who in the Orient, 1915. Tokyo.
WWARS
WWMC

Ch'en Ch'ing-yun   陳慶雲

SOURCES

Persons interviewed: not to be identified

Ch'en Chiung-ming   陳烱明

SOURCES

Ch'en Ching-ts'un hsien-sheng nien-p'u, ed. by Ch'üeh Ming. Hong Kong: Hong Kong wen-hua yin-shua so, 193?.
陳競存先生年譜。闕名。

Ch'en Ching-ts'un hsien-sheng shih lueh.
陳競存先生史略。

Ch'en kung Ching-ts'ung jung-ai lu. Hong Kong, 1934.
陳公競存榮哀錄。

Chung-kuo hsien-tai shih ts'ung-k'an, ed. by Wu Hsiang-hsiang. Taipei: Cheng chung shu-chü, 1960. 6 vols (vols. 5–6 published by Wen hsing shu-tien).
中國現代史叢刊。吳相湘。

Chung-kuo kung-ch'an-tang chien shih, ed. by Hsueh-hsi tsa-chih ch'u-chi pan tzu-liao shih. Peking: Jen-min ch'u-pan she, 1955.
中國共產黨簡史。學習雜誌初級版資料室。

Chung-kuo kuo-min-tang shih kao i chih ssu p'ien, comp. by Tsou Lu. Chungking: Shang-wu yin shu kuan, 1944. 4 vols.
中國國民黨史稿一至四篇。鄒魯。

Hsiang-tao chou-pao, I-16.
響導週報。

Hsin-hai ko-ming, ed. by Ch'ai Te-keng *et al.* Shanghai: Shanghai jen-min ch'u-pan she, 1956. 8 vols.
辛亥革命。柴德賡等。

Kuo-fu nien-piao, ed. by Chung-yang tang shih shih-liao pien-tsuan wei-yuan-hui. Taipei:

Chung-yang tang shih shih-liao pien-tsuan wei-yuan-hui, 1952.

國父年表。中央黨史史料編纂委員會。

Li Chien-nung. Tsui-chin san-shih nien Chung-kuo cheng-chih shih. Shanghai: T'ai-p'ing-yang shu-tien, 1930.

李劍農。最近三十年中國政治史。

MSICH

P'eng Pai. Hai-feng nung-min yün-tung. 1926.

彭湃。海豐農民運動。

Ts'ao Ya-po. Wuchang ko-ming chen shih.

曹亞伯。武昌革命眞史。

Tsou Lu. Hui-ku lu. Nanking: Tu-li ch'u-pan she, 1946–47. 2 vols.

鄒魯。回顧錄。

Wu T'ing-fang. Kung-ho kuan-chien lu.

伍庭芳。共和關鍵錄。

Yueh-tung hen sheng chu-jen (pseud.). Ch'en Chiung-ming p'an-kuo shih. Amoy, 1922.

粵東恨生主人。陳炯明叛國史。

Chen, Eugene   陳 友 仁

SOURCES

Chang Ch'i-yün. Tang shih kai-yao. Taipei: Chung-yang kai-tsao wei-yuan-hui wen-wu kung-ying she, 1951–52. 5 vols.

張其昀。黨史概要。

Ch'en Kung-lu. Chung-kuo chin-tai shih. Shanghai: Shang-wu yin shu kuan, 1935.

陳恭祿。中國近代史。

Documents on Communism, Nationalism, and Soviet Advisers in China, 1918–1927: Papers Seized in the 1927 Peking Raid, ed. by C. Martin Wilbur, Julie Lien-yin How. New York: Columbia University Press, 1956.

Je feng, 7 (December 16, 1953).

熱風。

Kuo wen chou-pao, IV-4.

國聞週報。

Levi, Werner. Modern China's Foreign Policy. Minneapolis: Uuiversity of Minnesota Press, 1953.

Liang Yun-li. "Wuhan cheng-fu shih-tai chih Chung-kuo wai-chiao." *Wai-chiao p'ing-lun*, III-7 (1934): 11–25.

梁鋆立。武漢政府時代之中國外交。外交評論。

Sharman, Lyon. Sun Yat-sen, His Life and Its Meaning: A Critical Biography. Hamden, Conn.: Archon Books, 1965.

T'ang Leang-li. The Inner History of the Chinese Revolution. New York: E. P. Dutton & Co., 1930.

Wai-chiao ta tz'u-tien, ed. by Wai-chiao hsueh-hui. Kunming: Chung-hua shu-chü, 1937.

外交大辭典。外交學會。

WWC

Young, Arthur A. "The Story of Eugene Chen." CWR, January 12, 1929: 278–79.

Ch'en Heng-che   陳 衡 哲

WORKS

1926. Hsi-yang shih. Shanghai: Shang-wu yin shu kuan.

西洋史。

1928. Hsiao yü-tien. Shanghai: Hsin yueh shu-tien.

小雨點。

1931. (ed.) Symposium on Chinese Culture. Shanghai: China Institute of Pacific Relations.

1934. Hsin sheng-huo yü fu-nü chieh-fang. Nanking: Cheng chung shu-chü.

新生活與婦女解放。

1938. Heng-che san-wen chi. Shanghai: Kai ming shu-tien. 2 vols.

衡哲散文集。

1947, January. "What Is the Spiritual Resort of a Chinese?" *National Reconstruction Journal*, VII-3.

ed. of *Liu Mei hsueh-sheng chi-pao*.

留美學生季報。

Wen-i fu-hsing hsiao shih. Shanghai: Shang-wu yin shu kuan.

文藝復興小史。

Wen-i fu-hsing shih. Shanghai: Shang-wu yin shu kuan.

文藝復興史。

SOURCES

CH

Ch'en Heng-che. Heng-che san-wen chi. Shanghai: Kai ming shu-tien, 1938. 2 vols.

陳衡哲。衡哲散文集。

———. Hsiao yü-tien. Shanghai: Hsin yueh shu-tien, 1928.

陳衡哲。小雨點。

———. "What Is the Spiritual Resort of a Chinese?" *National Reconstruction Journal*, VII-3.

CHWC

CHWYS

CMMC

Hsien-tai Chung-kuo nü tso-chia, comp. by Huang Ying. Shanghai: Pei hsin shu-tien, 1931.

現代中國女作家。黃英。

Kuo wen chou-pao, IX-1.

國聞週報。

MCNP

TCMT

Tzu-chuan chih i chang, ed. by T'ao K'ang-te. Canton: Yü-chou feng she, 1938.

自傳之一章。陶亢德。

WWMC

Ch'en Hsing-shen　　陳省身

WORKS

ed. of *American Journal of Mathematics*.
ed. of *Annals of Mathematics*.
ed. of *Illinois Journal of Mathematics*.
ed. of *Journal of Mathematics and Mechanics*.

SOURCES

American Men of Science. New York: R. R. Bowker, 1965.

Ch'en Hsing-shen. "Hsueh suan ssu-shih nien." *Chuan-chi wen-hsueh*, V-5 (November, 1964).

陳省身。學算四十年。傳記文學。

———. "Wo so jen-shih te liang-wei shu-hsueh ta-shih." *Chuan-chi wen-hsueh*, VII-5 (November, 1965).

陳省身。我所認識的兩位數學大師。傳記文學。

Chou Hung-ching. "Shu-hsueh chih," in *Chung-hua Min-kuo k'o-hsueh chih*. Taipei: Chung-hua wen-hua ch'u-pan shih-yeh wei-yuan-hui, 1955.

周鴻經。數學誌。中華民國科學誌。

Ch'en Keng　　陳賡

WORKS

1953. Ch'en Keng *et al*. Tao-ch'u shih hung-ch'i; ti-erh tz'u kuo-nei ko-ming chan-cheng shih-ch'i te chi-ko ku-shih (ed. by Chung-kuo ch'ing-nien ch'u-pan she). Peking: Chung-kuo ch'ing-nien ch'u-pan she.

陳賡等。到處是紅旗；第二次國內革命戰爭時期的幾個故事。中國青年出版社。

SOURCES

CPR, 993 (October 18, 1949).

Hsing tao wan-pao. Hong Kong, November 12, 1951.

星島晚報。

The New York Times, March 17, 1961.

SCMP, 2467 (March 30, 1961).

Ch'en Kuang-fu　　陳光甫

SOURCES

Persons interviewed: Chang Chia-ao; others not to be identified.

Ch'en Kung-po　　陳公博

WORKS

1920–? ed. of *Ch'ün pao*.

群報。

1928. Chung-kuo kuo-min-tang so tai-piao te shih shen-mo? Shanghai.

中國國民黨所代表的是什麼？

1928. Chung-kuo li-shih shang te ko-ming. Shanghai: Fu-tan shu-tien.

中國歷史上的革命。

1928. ed. of *Ko-ming p'ing-lun*.

革命評論。

1928. Kuo-ming ko-ming te wei-chi ho wo-men te ts'o-wu.

國民革命的危機和我們的錯誤。

1937. Ssu nien ts'ung-cheng lu. Shanghai: Shang-wu yin shu kuan.

四年從政錄。

1940. Chung-hua Min-kuo kuo-min cheng-fu fu Jih ta-li chuan-shih Ch'en Kung-po hsien-sheng yen-lun chi (ed. by Hsuan-ch'uan pu). Nanking.

中華民國國民政府赴日答禮專使陳公博先生言論集。宣傳部。

1940. San min chu-i yü k'o-hsueh. Canton: Chung-shan yueh-pao she.

三民主義與科學。

1942. Ch'en Kung-po hsien-sheng erh-shiu-chiu nien wen-ts'un (ed. by Hsuan-ch'uan pu). Nanking: Hsuan-ch'uan pu.

陳公博先生二十九年文存。宣傳部。

1944. Han feng chi. Shanghai: Ti-fang hsing-cheng she.

寒風集。

1960. The Communist Movement in China: An Essay Written in 1924 (ed. by C. Martin Wilbur). New York: East Asian Institute of Columbia University.

SOURCES

Person interviewed: Chang Kuo-t'ao.
CBJS
"Chang Kuo-t'ao's Autobiography." Unpublished manuscript, ed. by Robert Burton.
Ch'en Kung-po. The Communist Movement in China: An Essay Written in 1924 (ed. by C. Martin Wilbur). New York: East Asian Institute of Columbia University, 1960.
———. Han feng chi. Shanghai: Ti-fang hsing-cheng she, 1944.
陳公博。 寒風集。
———. Ssu nien ts'ung-cheng lu. Shanghai: Shang-wu yin shu kuan, 1937.
陳公博。 四年從政錄。
Chou Fo-hai. Wang i chi. Hong Kong: Ho chung ch'u-pan she, 1955.
周佛海。 往矣集。
Chu Tzu-chia (pseud. of Chin Hsiung-pai). "Chi Ch'u Min-i Ch'en Kung-po chih ssu." *Chin shan shih-pao*. San Francisco, November 30, December 1, 3, 4, 1956.
朱子家 (金雄白)。 記褚民誼陳公博之死。 金山時報。
———. Wang cheng-ch'üan te k'ai-ch'ang yü shou-ch'ang. Hong Kong: Ch'un-ch'iu tsa-chih she, 1964. 5 vols.
朱子家 (金雄白)。 汪政權的開場與收場。
CMMC
Dai jin mei jiten, ed. by Heibon-sha. Tokyo: Heibon-sha, 1953-55.
大人名事典。 平凡社。
GCMMTJK
GSJK
GSSJ
Japanese-Sponsored Governments in China, 1937-1945: An Annotated Bibliography Compiled from Materials in the Chinese Collection of the Hoover Library. Stanford: Stanford University Press, 1954.
Kuo Mo-jo. Pei fa. Pei yen, 1937.
郭沫若。 北伐。
Kuo wen chou-pao, IX-1 (January 1, 1932).
國聞週報。
RD
SMJ
SSYD
T'ang Leang-li. The Inner History of the Chi-

nese Revolution. New York: E. P. Dutton & Co., 1930.
TCJC
Teng Chung-hsia. Chung-kuo chih-kung yün-tung chien shih (1919-1926). Peking: Jen-min ch'u-pan she, 1953.
鄧中夏。 中國職工運動簡史。
WWC, 1926.

Ch'en Kuo-fu   陳 果 夫

WORKS

1947. The Chinese Cooperative Movement. Nanking: The China Co-operators' Union.
1952. Ch'en Kuo-fu hsien-sheng ch'üan-chi (ed. by Ch'en Kuo-fu hsien-sheng i-chu pien yin wei-yuan-hui). Taipei: Cheng chung shu-chü. 10 vols.
陳果夫先生全集。 陳果夫先生遺著編印委員會。

SOURCES

BKL
Ch'en Kuo-fu. Ch'en Kuo-fu hsien-sheng ch'üan-chi (ed. by Ch'en Kuo-fu hsien-sheng i-chu pien-yin wei-yuan-hui). Taipei: Cheng chung shu-chü, 1952.
陳果夫。 陳果夫先生全集。 陳果夫先生遺著編印委員會。
Ch'en Kuo-fu hsien-shen nien-p'u. Taipei.
陳果夫先生年譜。
Chung-yang lu-chün chün-kuan hsueh-hsaoi shih-kao. Nanking, 1931.
中央陸軍軍官學校史稿。
Ho Chung-hsiao. Ch'en Ying-shih hsien-sheng nien-p'u.
何仲簫。 陳英士先生年譜。
Ho Jui-yao. Feng-yün jen-wu hsiao chih. Canton, 1947.
何瑞瑤。 風雲人物小誌。
Kung-chi Ch'en Kuo-fu hsien-sheng chi-nien-ts'e.
公祭陳果夫先生紀念冊。
MSICH
Smedley, Agnes. Battle Hymn of China. New York: Alfred A. Knopf, 1943.

Ch'en Li-fu   陳 立 夫

WORKS

1928. Wu pi chien tzu fa chih yuan-li hsiao-yung. Shanghai: Chung-hua shu-chü.

五筆檢字法之原理效用。

1934. Hsin sheng-huo yü min sheng shih kuan. Nanking: Cheng-chung shu-chü.
新生活與民生史觀。

1935. The Function of the Commission on Land Research and Planning. Nanking: International Relations Committee.

1940. Kuo-chi hsien-shih. Chekiang sheng ti-fang hsing-cheng kan-pu hsun-lien t'uan.
國際現勢。

1941. Four Years of Chinese Education (1937–1941). Chungking: China Information Committee.

1943. Chinese Eduction during the War (1937–1942). Chungking? The Ministry of Education.

1944. Shih-yeh chi-hua chih tsung-ho yen-chiu tsung-lun (cheng-chih fang-mien te k'ao-ch'a). Chungking: Chung-yang hsun-lien t'uan tang cheng kao-chi hsun-lien pan.
實業計劃之綜合研究總論 (政治方面的考察)。

1945. Sheng chih yuan-li. Shanghai: Cheng-chung shu-chü.
生之原理。
Eng. tr. by Jen Tai, *Philosophy of Life*. New York: Philosophical Library, 1948.

1945. Wei sheng lun. Shanghai: Cheng chung shu-chü.
唯生論。

Ch'en Li-fu yen-chiang chi.
陳立夫演講集。

ed. of *Ching pao*.
京報。

Chung-kuo tien-ying shih-yeh.
中國電影事業。

SOURCES

BKL
CH
Ch'en Li-fu. Philosophy of Life (tr. by Jen Tai). New York: Philosophical Library, 1948.
Ch'en Po-ta. Chung-kuo ssu ta chia-tsu. Hong Kong: Chung-kuo ch'u-pan she, 1947.
陳伯達。中國四大家族。
Ch'eng T'ien-fang. A History of Sino-Russian Relations. Washington: Public Affairs Press, 1957.
Chiang Kai-shek. Soviet Russia in China: A Summing-up at Seventy. New York: Farrar, Straus & Cudahy, 1957.
CH-T
CMJL
CTMC
GCJJ
Lin Yü-tang. The Vigil of a a Nation. New York: The John Day Co., 1945.
Smedley, Agnes. Battle Hymn of China. New York: Alfred A. Knopf, 1943.
Stuart, John Leighton. Fifty Years in China. New York: Rondom House, 1954.
Tong, Hollington K. Chiang Kai-shek. Taipei: China Publishing Co., 1953.
White, Theodore H., and Annalee Jacoby. Thunder Out of China. New York: William Sloane Associates, 1946.
WWC, 1931.

Ch'en Lu   陳籙

WORKS

1917. Chih shih pi-chi. Shanghai: Shang-wu yin shu kuan.
止室筆記。

SOURCES

Persons interviewed: not to be identified.

Ch'en Ming-shu   陳銘樞

WORKS

1933. Ch'en Ming-shu *et al*. Hai-nan-tao chih. Shanghai: Shen-chou kuo kuang she.
陳銘樞等。海南島志。

SOURCES

CH, 1938–43.
Chung-hua Jen-min Kung-ho-kuo k'ai-kuo wen-hsien, ed. by Hsin min-chu ch'u-pan she. Hong Kong: Shang-wu yin shu kuan, 1949.
中華人民共和國開國文獻。新民主出版社。
CMTC
CYB-W, 1929–30.
GCCJK
Jen-min jih-pao. Peking, July 16, 1957.
人民日報。
T'ang Leang-li. The Inner History of the Chinese Revolution. New York: E. P. Dutton & Co., 1930.
Tong, Hollington K. Chiang Kai-shek. Taipei: China Publishing Co., 1953.
Ts'ai T'ing-k'ai. Ts'ai T'ing-k'ai tzu-chuan. Hong Kong: Tzu-yu hsun k'an she, 1946. 2 vols.

蔡廷鍇。 蔡廷鍇自傳。

RSOC

Yeh Yün-sheng *et al*. Kwangtung shih-jen chih.
Canton: K'ai-t'ung ch'u-pan she, 1946.
葉雲笙等。 廣東時人誌。

Ch'en Pai-ch'en   陳白塵

WORKS

1936. Man t'o lo chi. Wen-hua sheng-huo ch'u-
pan she.
曼陀羅集。

1936. Ni t'ui-tzu. Liang-yu.
泥腿子。

1936. Shih Ta-k'ai te mo-lu. Shanghai: Shanghai wen-hsueh ch'u-pan she.
石達開的末路。

1937. Hsiao Wei te chiang-shan. Wen-hua
sheng-huo ch'u-pan she.
小魏的江山。

1937? Pao-wei Lu-kou-ch'iao. with A Ying *et al*.
保衞蘆溝橋。 阿英。

1938. Tsui-chin chiu wang hsi-chü hsuan-chi.
with T'ien Han *et al*. Nu-hou ch'u-pan she.
最近救亡戲劇選集。 田漢等。

1940. Han-chien. Hua-chung t'u-shu kung-ssu.
漢奸。

1940. Luan-shih nan-nü. Shanghai tsa-chih
kung-ssu.
亂世男女。

1941. Hou-fang hsiao hsi-chü. Wen-hsueh ch'u-
pan she.
後方小喜劇。

1944-45. ed. of *Hua-shi wan-pao*. Chengtu?
華西晚報。

1946. (ed.) Sui han t'u kung-yen t'e chi. Chungking: Chung-kuo i-shu chü she.
歲寒圖公演特輯。

1947. Hsuan-yai chih lien. Shanghai: Ch'ün i
ch'u-pan she.
懸崖之戀。

1948. Ch'a-yeh pang-tzu. Shanghai: K'ai-ming
shu-tien.
茶葉棒子。

1948. Sheng-kuan t'u. Shanghai: Ch'ün i ch'u-
pan she.
陞官圖。

1956. Sui han chi. Peking: Jen-min wen-hsueh
ch'u-pan she.
歲寒集。

1957. Hei ch'i ying-hsiung chuan. Hong Kong:
Chung-yuan ch'u-pan she.

黑旗英雄傳。

1957. Sung ching shih li-shih tiao-ch'a chi. Peking: Jen-min ch'u-pan she.
宋景詩歷史調查記。

1958. Ch'en Pai-ch'en *et al*. Mei-kuo ch'i-t'an
(San ko tu-mu feng-tz'u chü). Peking: Chung-
kuo hsi-chü ch'u-pan she.
陳白塵等。 美國奇譚 (三個獨幕諷刺劇)。

1960.   Chieh-hun chin-hsing-ch'ü. Peking:
Chung-kuo hsi-chü ch'u-pan she.
結婚進行曲。

Chieh-t'ou yeh-ching.
街頭夜景。

Ch'iu-shou (Ta-ti huang-chin or Mo shang
ch'iu).
秋收 (大地黃金, 陌上秋)。

Ch'u-hsi.
除夕。

Chung-ch'iu yueh.
中秋月。

Fen-ho wan.
汾河灣。

Feng yü chih yeh. Ta tung.
風雨之夜。

Fu tzu hsiung ti.
父子兄弟。

Kuei-lai.
歸來。

Kung-hsi fa-ts'ai.
恭喜發財。

Mo k'u (Ch'ün mo luan wu or hsin kuan shang-
jen).
魔窟 (群魔亂舞, 新官上任)。

Sheng-li hao.
勝利號。

Sui han t'u.
歲寒圖。

Ta-ti hui ch'un.
大地回春。

T'ai-p'ing T'ien-kuo. Sheng-huo.
太平天國。

Wu Tse-t'ien.
武則天。

Yü chi.
虞姬。

SOURCES

CHWSK
CKJMT
GCCJK
GCJJ
HMTT
HWP

Liu Shou-sung. Chung-kuo hsin wen-hsueh shih ch'u-kao. Peking: Tso-chia ch'u-pan she, 1956. 2 vols.

劉綬松。中國新文學史初稿。

MCNP
RCCL
TCMT
WWMC

Ch'en Pi-chün   陳璧君

SOURCES

Persons interviewed: not to be identified.

Chu Tzu-chia (pseud. of Chin Hsiung-pai). Wang cheng-ch'üan te k'ai-ch'ang yü shou-ch'ang. Hong Kong: Ch'un-ch'iu tsa-chih she, 1964.

朱子家（金雄白）。汪政權的開場與收場。

San min chu-i yueh-k'an, II-6 (December, 1933).

三民主義月刊。

Sun Wen. Chung-shan ch'üan shu. Hsin-min shu-chü? 4 vols.

孫文。中山全書。

Ch'en Po-ta   陳伯達

WORKS

1935? Wei-lan-hsuan tsa ts'un.

味蘭軒雜存。

1939. San min chu-i kai-lun. Hong Kong? Chung-kuo wen-hua she.

三民主義概論。

1942-43. ed. of *Hsin hua jih-pao*. Chungking.

新華日報。

1943. Chieh-shao "Chung-kuo chih ming-yün." Yenan: Chieh-fang she.

介紹「中國之命運」。

1947. Ch'en Po-ta *et al*. Jen-hsing, tang-hsing, ko-hsing. Hong Kong: Wen ch'ao she.

陳伯達等。人性，黨性，個性。

1947. Chung-kuo ssu ta chia-tsu. Hong Kong: Chung-kuo ch'u-pan she.

中國四大家族。

1947. San min chu-i yü kung-ch'an chu-i. with Chang Wen-t'ien *et al*. Hong Kong: Ch'iu shih ch'u-pan she.

三民主義與共產主義。張聞天等。

1947. Yu shih ho ch'ün-chung shang-liang. Chi Lu Yü shu-tien.

有事和群眾商量。

1948. Ch'en Po-ta *et al*. Kuan-yü kung-shang-

yeh te cheng-ts'e. Hong Kong: Chung-kuo ch'u-pan she.

陳伯達。關於工商業的政策。

1949. Ch'ieh kuo ta-tao Yuan Shih-k'ai. Peking: Hsin hua shu-tien.

竊國大盜袁世凱。

1949. Ch'en Po-ta *et al*. Chung-kuo ching-chi te kai-tsao. Hong Kong: Hsin min-chu ch'u-pan she.

陳伯達等。中國經濟的改造。

1949. Chin-tai Chung-kuo ti-tsu kai-shuo. Peking: Jen-min ch'u-pan she.

近代中國地租概說。

1949. Jen-min kung-ti Chiang Chieh-shih. Hong Kong: Cheng pao ch'u-pan she.

人民公敵蔣介石。

1949. Lun nung-min wen-t'i. Mukden: Tung-pei shu-tien.

論農民問題。

1949. P'ing "Chung-kuo chih ming-yün." Peking: Hsin hua shu-tien.

評「中國之命運」。

1951. Lun Mao Tse-tung ssu-hsiang; Ma-k'o-ssu Lieh-ning chu-i yü Chung-kuo ko-ming te chieh-ho; wei chi-nien Chung-kuo kung-ch'an-tang te san-shih chou-nien erh tso. Peking: Jen-min ch'u-pan she.

論毛澤東思想；馬克思列寧主義與中國革命的結合；為紀念中國共產黨的三十週年而作。

1951. Tu "Hunan nung-min yün-tung k'ao-ch'a pao-kao." Peking: Jen-min ch'u-pan she.

讀「湖南農民運動考察報告」。

1952. Ch'en Po-ta tsai Chung-kuo k'o-hsueh yuan yen-chiu jen-yuan hsueh-hsi hui shang te chiang-hua. Peking: Jen-min ch'u-pan she.

陳伯達在中國科學院研究人員學習會上的講話。

Eng. tr., *Speech before the Study Group of Research Members of Academia Sinica*. Peking: Foreign Languages Press, 1953.

1952. Ssu-ta-lin ho Chung-kuo ko-ming. Peking: Jen-min ch'u-pan she.

斯大林和中國革命。

Eng. tr., *Stalin and the Chinese Revolution, in Celebration of Stalin's Seventieth Birthday*. Peking: Foreign Languages Press, 1953.

1953. Mao Tse-tung on the Chinese Revolution. Peking: Foreign Languages Press.

1954. Kuan-yü shih nien nei-chan. Peking: Jen-min ch'u-pan she.

關於十年內戰。

Eng. tr., *Notes on Ten Years of Civil War (1927–*

1936). Peking: Foreign Languages Press, 1954.

1956. Chung-kuo nung-yeh te she-hui chu-i kai-tsao. Peking: Jen-min ch'u-pan she.
中國農業的社會主義改造。

1958. A Study of Land Rent in Pre-Liberation China. Peking: Foreign Languages Press.

1958-? ed. of *Hung ch'i.*
紅旗。

1960-61. Ch'en Po-ta *et al.* Hsueh-hsi Mao Tse-tung ssu-hsiang. Hong Kong: Sheng-huo, tu-shu, hsin chih san lien shu-tien. 2 vols.
陳伯達等。 學習毛澤東思想。

SOURCES

Person interviewed: Chang Kuo-t'ao.
HCJC
Jen-min jih-pao. Peking, December 14, 1964.
人民日報。
WWC
WWMC

Ch'en Pu-lei   陳布雷

WORKS

1911-12. ed. of *T'ien to pao.*
天鐸報。

1928-? ed. of *Shih-shih hsin pao.*
時事新報。

1949. Ch'en Pu-lei hui-i-lu. Shanghai: Erh-shih shih-chi ch'u-pan she.
陳布雷回憶錄。

1954. (ed.) Chronology of President Chiang Kai-shek. with Tang Cheng-chu (tr. by Sampson C. Shen). Taipei: China Cultural Service.

SOURCES

Ch'en Pu-lei. Ch'en Pu-lei hui-i-lu. Shanghai: Erh-shih shih-chi ch'u-pan she, 1949.
陳布雷。 陳布雷回憶錄。

Chiang Chung-cheng. San min chu-i chih t'i-hsi chi ch'i shih-hsing ch'eng-hsü. Mukden: Kuan-tung yin shu kuan, 1946.
蔣中正。 三民主義之体系及其實行程序。
CHMI

Meng Chang-yung. "The Renewed Peace Movement in China." *China Weekly Review,* (December 4, 1948).

Pao-hsueh tsa-chih, I-6 (November 16, 1948).
報學雜誌。

Ch'en San-li   陳 三 立

WORKS

1922. San-yuan-ching-she shih hsü-chi. Shang-wu yin shu kuan. 2 vols.
散原精舍詩續集。

1931. San-yuan-ching-she shih pieh-chi. Shang-wu yin shu kuan.
散原精舍詩別集。

1936. San-yuan-ching-she shih. Shanghai: Shang-wu yin shu kuan. 5 vols.
散原精舍詩。

1961. San-yuan-ching-she shih-chi. Taipei: Tai-wan Chung-hua shu-chü.
散原精舍詩集。

1961. San-yuan-ching-she wen-chi. Taipei: Tai-wan Chung-hua shu-chü.
散原精舍文集。

Tao-te ching Ch'en chu.
道德經陳註。

SOURCES

Chang Chen-yung. Chung-kuo wen-hsueh shih fen-lun. Shanghai: Shang-wu yin shu kuan, 1934. 4 vols.
張振鏞。 中國文學與史論。

Ch'en San-li. San-yuan-chih-she wen-chi. Tai-pei: Taiwan Chung-hua shu-chü, 1961.
陳三立。 散原精舍文集。

Ch'en Yen. Shih-i-shih shih-hua. Shanghai: Shang-wu yin shu kuan, 1935. 4 vols.
陳衍。 石遺石詩話。

Ch'ien Chi-po. Hsien-tai Chung-kuo wen-hsueh shih. Shanghai: Shih-chieh shu-chü, 1933.
錢基博。 現代中國文學史。

Chin Liang. Ch'ing shih kao pu. Peiping, 1942?
金梁。 清史稿補。

Ch'ing shih, ed. by Ch'ing shih pien-tsuan wei-yuan-hui. Taipei: Kuo-fang yen-chiu-yuan, 1961. 8 vols.
清史。 清史編纂委員會。

Kuo Sung-t'ao. Yang chih shu wu wen-chi. 1892. 29 vols.
郭嵩燾。 養知書屋文集。

Kuo shih kuan kuan k'an, II-1 (1949): 78-79.
國史館館刊。

Liang Ch'i-ch'ao. Shih hua.
梁啟超。 詩話。

———. Wu-hsü cheng-pien chi. Peking: Chung-hua shu-chü, 1954.
梁啟超。 戊戌政變記。

———. Yin-ping-shih shih-hua. Taipei: Tai-wan Chung-hua shu-chü, 1957.

梁啟超。飲冰室詩話。

P'eng Ch'un-shih. "Ch'en San-li" Unpublished manuscript.
彭醇士。陳三立。

Sawada Fusakiyo. Chung-kuo yun-wen shih (tr. by Wang Ho-i). Shanghai: Shang-wu yin shu kuan, 1937. 2 vols.
澤田總淸。中國韻文史。王鶴儀。

T'an K'ai-kuang. "Shih hsueh ch'üan-wei Ch'en Yin-ko." *Ta feng pan-yueh-k'an*, 97 (September 5, 1941).
譚凱光。史學權威陳寅恪。大風半月刊。
TTJWC

Wu Tsung-tz'u. "Ch'en San-li chuan-lueh." *Kuo shih kuan kuan k'an*, Ch'uang-k'an hao (December, 1947): 100-2.
吳宗慈。陳三立傳略。國史館館刊。

Yü Ta-kang. "Ch'en San-yuan hsien-shen chuan." Unpublished manuscript.
俞大綱。陳散原先生傳。

Ch'en Shao-k'uan   陳紹寬

SOURCES

Persons interviewed: not to be identified.
BKL

Ch'en Shao-pai   陳少白

WORKS

1899-1905. ed. of *Chung-kuo jih-pao*. Hong Kong.
中國日報。

SOURCES

Corbett, Charles Hodge. Lingnan University, a Short History Based Primarily on the Records of the University's American Trustees. New York: Trustees of Lingnan University, 1963.

Hsin-hai ko-ming, ed. by Ch'ai Te-keng *et al.* Shanghai: Jen-min ch'u-pan she, 1957. 8 vols.
辛亥革命。柴德賡等。
New Horizons, XXXII-2.

Ch'en Shao-yü   陳紹禹

WORKS

1933. (ed.) Su-wei-ai Chung-kuo. Moscow: Su-lien wai-kuo kung-jen ch'u-pan she.
蘇維埃中國。

1934. Revolutionary China Today. with Kang Sin. New Work: Workers Library.

1935. Lun fan ti t'ung-i chan-hsien wen-t'i. Paris: Ya-chou shu-tien.
論反帝統一戰線問題。

1935. The Revolutionary Movement in the Colonial Countries. New York: Workers Library.

1936. "Chi-nien wo-men te hui-tsu t'ung-chih Ma Chün." in Ta Sheng *et al.*, *Lieh-shih chuan.* Moscow.
紀念我們的回族同志馬駿。大生等。烈士傳。

1936. Hsin hsing-shih yü hsin cheng-ts'e. Paris: Ya-chou shu-tien.
新形勢與新政策。

1937. China Can Win! The New Stage in the Aggression of Japanese Imperialism and the New Period in the Struggle of the Chinese People. New York: Workers Library.

1940. Wei Chung-kung keng-chia pu-erh-sai-wei-k'o erh tou-cheng. Chieh-fang she. 3 vols.
爲中共更加布爾塞唯克而鬥爭。

SOURCES

Person interviewed: Chang Kuo-t'ao.

Ch'en Shao-yü. "Chi-nien wo-men te hui-tsu t'ung-chih Ma Chün." in Ta Sheng *et al.*, *Lieh-shih chuan.* Moscow, 1936.
陳紹禹。紀念我們的回族同志馬駿。大生等。烈士傳。

Chung-kuo kung-ch'an-tang te chung-yao jen-wu, ed. by Min-chien ch'u-pan she. Peiping: Min-chien ch'u-pan she, 1949.
中國共產黨的重要人物。民間出版社。
GCCJK
GCJJ
GSSJ
HSWT
JMST, 1950, 1957.

Mif, Pavel A. Heroic China, Fifteen Years of the Communist Party of China. New York: Workers Library, 1937.

Schwartz, Benjamin I. Chinese Communism and the Rise of Mao. Cambridge: Harvard University Press, 1951.

Ch'en Shu-jen   陳樹人

WORKS

1903-4. ed. of *Kwangtung jih-pao*.
廣東日報。

Ch'en Shu-jen

1917. ed. of *Hsin min-kuo pao*.
新民國報。
1947. Chuan ai chi. Shanghai: Chung-hua shu-chü.
專愛集。
1948. Tzu-jan mei ou-ko chi. Shanghai? Shih-chieh shu-chü.
自然美謳歌集。

SOURCES

BKL
CCLTC
CH
Feng Tzu-yu. "Ch'en Shu-jen shih-lueh." *Kuo shih kuan kuan k'an*, I-4 (November, 1948).
馮自由。陳樹人事略。國史館館刊。
WWC, 5th ed.

Ch'en Ta　陳達

WORKS

1921. Japanese Emigration to China. New York? Chinese Patriotic Committee of New York City.
1927. The Labor Movement in China. Peking: Peking Leader Press.
1929. Chung-kuo lao-kung wen-t'i. Shanghai: Shang-wu yin shu kuan.
中國勞工問題。
1931. Study of the Applicability of the Factory Act of the Chinese Government. Shanghai: China Institute of Scientific Management.
1933, June. "Kuan-yü sheng-yü chieh-chih chi-chung k'an-wu te chieh-shao." *Ch'ing-hua hsueh-pao*, VIII-2: 6-16.
關於生育節制幾種刊物的介紹。清華學報。
1934, January. "Jen-k'ou pien-ch'ien te yuan-su." *Ch'ing-hua hsueh-pao*, IX-I: 15-68.
人口變遷的原素。清華學報。
1934. Jen-k'ou wen-t'i. Shanghai: Shang-wu yin shu kuan.
人口問題。
1938. Nan-yang hua-ch'ao yü Min Yueh she-hui. Shanghai: Shang-wu yin shu kuan.
南洋華僑與閩粵社會。
1939. Emigrant Communities in South China: A Study of Overseas Migration and Its Influence on Standards of Living and Social Change (ed. by Bruno Lasker). New York: Secretariat, Institute of Pacific Relations.
1946. Lang chi shih nien. Shanghai: Shang-wu yin shu kuan.

浪跡十年。
1957, May. "Wan-hun chieh-yü yü hsin Chung-kuo jen-k'ou wen-t'i." *Hsin chien-she*, 5: Appendix, 1-16.
晚婚節育與新中國人口問題。新建設。

SOURCES

Persons interviewed: not to be identified.

Ch'en T'an-ch'iu　陳潭秋

WORKS

1936, October. "Reminiscences of the First Congress of the Communist Party of China." *Communist International* (N.Y. edition), XIII: 1361-66.

SOURCES

Person interviewed: Chang Kuo-t'ao.
Chang Ta-chün. Ssu-shih nien tung-luan Sinkiang. Hong Kong: Ya-chou ch'u-pan she, 1956.
張達鈞。四十年動亂新疆。
Chang Wen-ch'iu. "Ch'en T'an-ch'iu t'ung-chih erh san shih." *Hung ch'i p'iao p'iao*, 5 (December 15, 1957): 149-51.
張文秋。陳潭秋同志二三事。紅旗飄飄。
Ch'ang-chiang jih-pao, June 28, 1951.
長江日報。
Chow Tse-tsung. The May Fourth Movement: Intellectual Revolution in Modern China. Cambridge: Harvard University Press, 1960.
Chung-kuo kung-ch'an-tang tsai Chung-nan ti-ch'ü ling-tao ko-ming tou-cheng te li-shih tzu-liao, ti-i chi, comp. by Wuhan shih chi-kuan Ma-k'o-ssu Lieh-ning chu-i yeh-chien hsueh-hsiao. Hankow: Chung-nan jen-min ch'u-pan she, 1951.
中國共產黨在中南地區領導革命鬥爭的歷史資料，第一輯。武漢市機關馬克思列寧主義夜間學校。
Hsiao Pai-fan. Chung-kuo chin pai nien ko-ming shih. Kowloon: Ch'iu shih ch'u-pan she, 1951.
蕭白帆。中國近百年革命史。
RD
SCMP, 787 (April 13, 1954); 2545 (July 26, 1961).
Wai-shih Shih (pseud.). "Mao Tse-min Sinkiang tso yuan kuei." *Ch'un-ch'iu*, 51 (July 16, 1957): 7-8.
外史氏。毛澤民新疆作怨鬼。春秋。
Whiting, Allen S., and Sheng Shih-ts'ai. Sin-

kiang: Pawn or Pivot? East Lansing: Michigan State University Press, 1958.

Ch'en Tu-hsiu　　陳獨秀

WORKS

1914–15? ed. of *Chia-yin tsa-chih*.
甲寅雜誌。
1915. ed. of *Ch'ing-nien tsa-chih*.
青年雜誌。
1915–? ed. of *Hsin ch'ing-nien*.
新青年。
1925. Tzu-i lei-pieh. Shanghai: Ya-tung t'u-shu-kuan.
字義類別。
1926. Ch'en Tu-hsiu hsien-sheng yen-chiang lu (ed. by Hsin ch'ing-nien she). Shanghai: P'ing-min shu she.
陳獨秀先生演講錄。新青年社。
1927. Chung-kuo ko-ming wen-t'i lun-wen chi (hsuan-chih).
中國革命問題論文集　(選集)。
1927. Tu-hsiu wen-ts'un. Shanghai: Ya-tung t'u-shu kuan. 4 vols.
獨秀文存。
1937. K'ang Jih chan-cheng chih i-i. Shanghai: Sheng-huo ch'u-pan she.
抗日戰爭之意義。
1950. Ch'en Tu-hsiu tsui-hou tui-yü min-chu cheng-chih te chien-chieh (lun-wen ho shu-hsin). Hong Kong: Tzu-yu Chung-kuo ch'u-pan she.
陳獨秀最後對於民主政治的見解　(論文和書信)。
1964. Ch'en Tu-hsiu wen-chi (ed. by Lung wen shu-tien). Hong Kong: Lung wen shu-tien.
陳獨秀文集。龍文書店。

SOURCES

CCM-1
CECP
Ch'en Tu-hsiu p'ing-lun, ed. by Ch'en Tung-hsiao. Peiping, 1933.
陳獨秀評論。陳東曉。
Ch'ing Ch'en. "Wo so chih-tao te Ch'en Tu-hsiu." *Ku chin*, 5 (July, 1942): 16–19.
青塵。我所知道的陳獨秀。古今。
Chow Tse-tsung. The May Fourth Movement: Intellectual Revolution in Modern China. Cambridge: Harvard University Press, 1960.
GCCJK
GCJJ

GSSJ
HSWT
Kuo Chan-po. Chin wu-shih nien Chung-kuo ssu-hsiang shih. Hong Kong: Lung men shu-tien, 1965.
郭湛波。近五十年中國思想史。
Kuo wen chou-pao, IV-14 (April 17, 1927).
國聞週報。
Ma Hsü-lun. Wo tsai liu-shih sui i-ch'ien. Shanghai: Sheng-huo shu-tien, 1947.
馬敍倫。我在六十歲以前。
SMJ
Wang Shih-chao. Chung-kuo wen-jen hsin lun. Hong Kong: Hsin shih-chi ch'u-pan she, 1953.
王世昭。中國文人新論。

Ch'en Wen-k'uan　　陳文寬

SOURCES

Persons interviewed: not to be identified.

Ch'en Yen-nien　　陳延年

SOURCES

Persons interviewed: not to be identified.

Ch'en Yi　　陳儀

SOURCES

Ch'en Chia-keng. Nan ch'iao hui-i lu. Nan-t'ai: Foochow chi-mei hsiao-yu hui, 1950.
陳嘉庚。南僑回憶錄。
CYB-W, 1934.
WWC, 1935.

Ch'en Yi　　陳毅

WORKS

1937. Tsen-yang tung-yuan nung-min ta-chung. Shanghai: Shanghai tsa-chih kung-ssu.
怎樣動員農民大衆。

SOURCES

Chinese Press Survey; a Translation Service Covering the More Important Articles Appearing in Chinese Newspapers and Magazines. Shanghai: Millard Publishing Co., November 1, 1948–April 1, 1951.
HCJC

Rigg, Robert B. Red China's Fighting Hordes. Harrisburg, Pa.: Military Service Publishing Co., 1951.

Schwartz, Benjamin I. Chinese Communism and the Rise of Mao. Cambridge: Harvard University Press, 1951.

Smedley, Agnes. The Great Road: The Life and Times of Chu Teh. New York: Monthly Review Press, 1956.

WWC

WWMC

Ch'en Yin-ko　陳寅恪

Works

1940. Ch'in fu yin chiao chien. Kunming.
秦婦吟校箋。

1943. T'ang-tai cheng-chih shih shu-lun kao. Chungking: Shang-wu yin shu kuan.
唐代政治史述論稿。

1945. Sui T'ang chih-tu yuan-yuan lueh lun kao. Chungking: Shang-wu yin shu kuan.
隋唐制度淵源略論稿。

1945. T'ao Yuan-ming chih ssu-hsiang yü ch'ing-t'an chih kuan-hsi. Peiping: Yen-ching ta-hsueh ha-fo yen-ching hsueh-she.
陶淵明之思想與清談之關係。

1950. Yuan Pai shih-chien cheng kao. Canton: Ling-nan ta-hsueh Chung-kuo wen-hua yen-chiu shih.
元白詩箋證稿。

1959. Lun tsai sheng yuan. Kowloon: Yu lien ch'u-pan she.
論再生緣。

Sources

Persons interviewed: not to be identified.

Ch'en Yuan　陳垣

Works

1922. Shansi Ta-t'ung Wu-chou-shan shih-k'u-ssu chi.
山西大同武州山石窟寺記。

1923. Kaifeng i-tz'u-lo-yeh-chiao k'ao. Shang-hai: Shang-wu yin shu kuan.
開封一賜樂業教考。

1923. Yuan Yeh-li-k'o-wen k'ao. Shanghai: Shang-wu yin shu kuan.
元也里可溫考。

1925. Erh-shih shih shuo-jun piao (with Hsi li hui li). Peking: Kuo-li Peking ta-hsueh yen-chiu so.
二十史朔閏表　（附：西曆回曆）。

1926. Chung hsi hui shih jih-li. Peking: Kuo-li Peking ta-hsueh yen-chiu so. 5 vols.
中西回史日曆。

1931. (ed.) Shen k'o Yuan tien-chang chiao-pu. Peking: Kuo-li Peking ta-hsueh yen-chiu so. 5 vols.
沈刻元典章校補。

1931. (ed.) Tun-huang chieh yü lu. Kuo-li chung-yang yen-chiu-yuan li-shih yen-chiu-so. 6 vols.
敦煌刼餘錄。

1933. Shih-hui chü-li. Li yün shu wu. 2 vols.
史諱舉例。

1934. Yuan pi-shih i yin yung tzu k'ao. Peiping: Kuo-li chung-yang yen-chiu-yuan li-shih yen-chiu-so.
元秘史譯音用字考。

1934. Yuan tien-chang chiao-pu shih-li liu chüan. Peiping: Kuo-li chung-yang yen-chiu-yuan li-shih yü-yen yen-chiu-so.
元典章校補釋例六卷。

1937. Chiu Wu-tai shih chi-pen fa-fu (with Hsueh shih chi-pen pi-hui li). Peiping: Fu-jen ta-hsueh.
舊五代史輯本發復　（附：薛史輯本避諱例）。

1937. Wu Yü-shan (Li) hsien-sheng nien-p'u. Peiping: Fu-jen ta-hsueh.
吳漁山(歷)先生年譜。

1938. (ed.) Shih shih yi nien lu. 4 vols.
釋氏疑年錄。

1940. Ming chi Tien Ch'ien fo-chiao k'ao. Peiping: Fu-jen ta-hsueh.
明季滇黔佛教考。

1941. Nan Sung ch'u Ho-pei hsin tao-chiao k'ao. Peiping: Fu-jen ta-hsueh.
南宋初河北新道教考。

1945–46. T'ung-chien Hu chu piao-wei. Peiping: Fu-jen ta-hsueh.
通鑑胡注表微。

1955. Chung-kuo fo-chiao shih-chi kai-lun. Peking: K'o-hsueh ch'u-pan she.
中國佛教史籍概論。

1962. Ch'ing ch'u seng cheng chi. Peking: Chung-hua shu-chü.
清初僧諍記。

Sources

Persons interviewed: not to be identified.
Shirin, IX-4 (October, 1924): 611–19.
史林。

T'u-shu chi-k'an, new series, I–1 (March, 1939); II–4 (December, 1940); III–4 (December, 1936); V–1 (March, 1944).
圖書季刊。

Ch'en Yün   陳雲

WORKS

1950. Kuan-yü ching-chi hsing-shih t'iao-cheng kung shang yeh ho t'iao-cheng shui-shou chu wen-t'i. Peking: Hsin hua shu-tien.
關於經濟形勢調整工商業和調整稅收諸問題。

SOURCES

Person interviewed: Chang Kuo-t'ao.
Brandt, Conrad, Benjamin Schwartz, and John K. Fairbank. A Documentary History of Chinese Communism. Cambridge: Harvard University Press, 1952.
HCJC
Mao's China: Party Reform Documents, 1942–44, ed. and tr. by Boyd Compton. Seattle: University of Washington Press, 1952.
RD
WWC
WWMC

Cheng Chen-to   鄭振鐸

WORKS

1922–27. ed. of *Hsiao-shuo yueh-pao*.
小說月報。
1925. T'ai-ko-erh chuan. Shanghai: Shang-wu yin shu kuan.
太戈爾傳。
1927. Cheng Chen-to *et al*. Hsueh hen. (tr.) Shanghai: K'ai-ming shu-tien.
鄭振鐸等。血痕。
1927. Chung-kuo wen-hsueh yen-chiu. Shanghai: Shang-wu yin shu kuan.
中國文學研究。
1927. (ed.) Wen-hsueh ta-kang. Shanghai: Shang-wu yin shu kuan. 4 vols.
文學大綱。
1927–? ed. of *Erh-t'ung shih-chieh*.
兒童世界。
1928. (ed.) Pai-hsueh i yin tieh. Shanghai: K'ai-ming shu-tien.
白雪遺音迭。

1929. Lien-ai te ku-shih. Shanghai: Shang-wu yin shu kuan.
戀愛的故事。
1931. Chia-t'ing ku-shih. K'ai-ming shu-tien.
家庭故事。
1931. (ed.) Ch'ing jen tsa chü ch'u chi. Ch'ang-lo Cheng shih. 10 vols.
清人雜劇初集。
1932. Ch'a-t'u pen Chung-kuo wen-hsueh shih. Peiping: P'u she ch'u-pan pu.
插圖本中國文學史。
1932. Hai yen. Hsin Chung-kuo shu-chü.
海燕。
1934. (ed.) Ch'ang-lo Cheng shih hui yin ch'uan-ch'i; ti-i chi. 12 vols.
長樂鄭氏彙印傳奇；第一集。
1934. Chin pai nien ku-ch'eng ku-mu fa-chueh shih. Shanghai: Shang-wu yin shu kuan.
近百年古城古墓發掘史。
1934. Chung-kuo wen-hsueh lun-chi. Shanghai: K'ai-ming shu-tien.
中國文學論集。
1934. Ch'ü huo che te tai-p'u. Shanghai: Shang-hai Sheng-huo shu-tien.
取火者的逮捕。
1934. (ed.) Ming chi shih-liao ts'ung-shu. Sheng tse yuan.
明季史料叢書。
1934. O-kuo wen-hsueh shih-lueh.
俄國文學史略。
1935. (ed.) Shih-chieh wen-k'u. Shanghai: Sheng-huo shu-tien.
世界文庫。
1936. Cheng Chen-to wen-hsuan. Wan-hsiang.
鄭振鐸文選。
1936. (ed.) Hsing shih heng yen. Shanghai: Sheng-huo shu-tien.
醒世恒言。
1936. Tuan chien chi. Shanghai: Wen-hua sheng-huo ch'u-pan she.
短劍集。
1938. Chan hao. Shanghai: Sheng-huo shu-tien.
戰號。
1938. Chung-kuo su wen-hsueh shih. Changsha: Shang-wu yin shu kuan. 2 vols.
中國俗文學史。
1940–45? (ed.) Chung-kuo pan hua shih. Shanghai.
中國版畫史。
1941. K'un hsueh chi. Changsha: Shang-wu yin shu kuan.
困學集。

1947–? (ed.) Chung-kuo li-shih ts'an-k'ao t'u p'u (ti 10–14 chi). Shanghai: Shanghai t'u-shu kung-ssu. 5 vols.
中國歷史參考圖譜 (第 10–14 輯)。

1947–48. ed. of *Wen-i fu-hsing*.
文藝復興。

1951. Chih chü san chi. Shanghai: Shanghai ch'u-pan kung-ssu.
蟄居散記。

1952? (ed.) Wei-ta te i-shu ch'uan-t'ung t'u lu. Chung-kuo ku-tien i-shu ch'u-pan she.
偉大的藝術傳統圖錄。

1953. (ed.) Ch'u tz'u t'u. Peking: Jen-min wen-hsueh ch'u-pan she. 2 vols.
楚辭圖。

1956. Chieh chung te shu chi. Shanghai: Shanghai ku-tien wen-hsueh ch'u-pan she.
刦中得書記。

1957. Cheng Chen-to hsuan-chi. Hong Kong: Wen-hsueh ch'u-pan she.
鄭振鐸選集。

1957. Kuei kung t'ang. Hong Kong: Chung liu ch'u-pan she.
桂公塘。

1957. (ed.) Sung jen hua-ts'e. With Chang Heng, Hsü Pang-ta. Peking: Chung-kuo ku-tien i-shu ch'u-pan she.
宋人畫冊。 張珩, 徐邦達。

1957. T'ang tao p'ien. Shanghai: Ku-tien wen-hsueh ch'u-pan she.
湯禱篇。

1958. Hsi-la shen-hua yü ch'uan-shuo chung te lien-ai ku-shih. Peking: Tso-chia ch'u-pan she.
希臘神話與傳說中的戀愛故事。

1958. Hsi-la shen-hua yü ying-hsiung ch'uan-shuo. Peking: Jen-min wen-hsueh ch'u-pan she.
希臘神話與英雄傳說。

1958. (ed.) T'ien-chu ling ch'ien. Shanghai: Ku-tien wen-hsueh ch'u-pan she.
天竺靈籤。

1959–63. Cheng Chen-to wen-chi. Peking: Jen-min wen-hsueh ch'u-pan she. 2 vols.
鄭振鐸文集。

1960. San nien. Hong Kong: Jih hsin shu-tien.
三年。

1966. Tso-chia t'an Lu Hsun. with Hsü Shou-shang *et al.* Hong Kong: Wen-hsueh yen-chiu she.
作家談魯迅。 許壽裳等。

(ed.) Wan Ch'ing wen-hsuan. Shanghai: Sheng-huo shu-tien.
晚清文選。

ed. of *Wen-hsueh chi-k'an*.
文學季刊。

ed. of *Wen-hsueh chou-pao*.
文學週報。

SOURCES

Cheng Chen-to. Chieh chung te shu chi. Shang-hai: Shanghai ku-tien wen-hsueh ch'u-pan she, 1956.
鄭振鐸。 刦中得書記。

———. Chung-kuo wen-hsueh lun-chi. Shang-hai: K'ai-ming shu-tien, 1934.
鄭振鐸。 中國文學論集。

HCJC

Cheng Ho-fu   鄭和甫

SOURCES

Persons interviewed: not to be identified.
China Mission Year Book, 1919. Shanghai: Christian Literature Society, 1920.
The Chinese Recorder, LX–3 (March, 1922): 197; LXIV–4 (April, 1926): 267.
Forth, CIX–7 (July, August, 1944): 14–16; CXXII–10 (November, 1947): 13.
Handbook on the Mission of the Episcopalian Church, No. 1, China. National Council of the Protestant Episcopal Church, 1932.
The Living Church, CVIII–24 (June, 1944): 11; CX–2 (January, 1945): 7; CXVII–26 (December, 1948): 10.
Lund, F.E. "The Lengthened Shadow of a Man." *The Spirit of Missions*, LXXXVIII–7 (July, 1923): 450.
Shanghai Newsletter, XXIX–3 (May, 1948): 7.
The Spirit of Missions, LXXXVII–4 (April, 1922): 215; XCIV–1 (January, 1929): 41; XCV–11 (November, 1930): 767; C–8 (August, 1935): 339.
Wood, G.W. "A Soldier of Christ Gallantly Holds Post." *The Spirit of Missions*, XCII–11 (November, 1927): 656.

Cheng Hsiao-hsü   鄭孝胥

WORKS

1919. K'ung chiao hsin pien. Shanghai: Shang-wu yin shu kuan.
孔敎新編。

1932. Wang-tao chiu-shih chih yao-i.
王道救世之要義。
1934. Wang-tao chiang-i chi. Hsinching (Changchun).
王道講義集。
1937. Hai-ts'ang-luo shih.
海藏樓詩。

SOURCES

Ch'en Pao-shen. Ts'ang-ch'ü-lou shih-chi. Peking, 1938. 4 vols.
陳寶深。滄趣樓詩集。
Ch'en Pin-ho. Man-chou wei kuo. Peiping: Jih-pen yen-chiu she, 1933.
陳彬龢。滿洲偽國。
Ch'en Yen. Shih-i-shih shih-hua. Taipei: Tai-wan shang-wu yin shu kuan, 1961.
陳衍。石遺室詩話。
———. Shih-i-shih ts'ung-shu. 1906–29. 14 vols.
陳衍。石遺室叢書。
Cheng Ch'ui. Jih-chi.
鄭垂。日記。
Ch'ien Chi-po. Hsien-tai Chung-kuo wen-hsueh shih. Shanghai: Shih-chieh shu-chü, 1933.
錢基博。現代中國文學史。
Ch'in Han-ts'ai. Man kung ts'an-chao chi. Shanghai: Chung-kuo k'e-hsueh t'u-shu i-ch'i kung-ssu, 1947.
秦翰才。滿宮殘照記。
"First Manchoukuo Premier Dies." *Manchuria*, April 15, 1938: 220.
GCMMTJK
Johnston, Reginald F. Twilight in the Forbid-den City. New York: Appleton-Century, 1934.
Jones, Francis Clifford. Manchuria Since 1931. New York: Oxford University Press, 1949.
Kawakami Kiyoshi Karl. Manchoukuo, Child of Conflict. New York: The Macmillan Co., 1933.
Kuo T'ing-i. Chin-tai Chung-kuo shih jih-chih (Ch'ing chi). Taipei: Cheng-chung shu-chü, 1963. 2 vols.
郭廷以。近代中國史日誌 (清季)。
Li Nien-tz'u. "Man-chon-kuo" chi-shih. Hong Kong: Tzu-yu ch'u-pan she, 1954.
李念慈。「滿洲國」紀實。
Manchoukuo Foreign Office. Manchoukuo Today. Hsinking (Changchun), 1940.
The Manchuria Year Book, 1932–33.
Wang I-t'ang. Chin ch'uan shih lou shih-hua. Tientsin, 1933.
王揖唐。今傳是樓詩話。
Woodhead, Henry George Wandesforde. A Visit to Manchukuo. Shanghai: The Mercury Press, 1932.

Cheng T'ien-hsi   鄭天錫

WORKS

1923. The Chinese Supreme Court Decisions. (tr.) Peking: Commission on Extraterritor-iality.
1946. China Moulded by Confucius, the Chinese Way in Western Light. London: Stevens & Sons.
1951. East and West: Episodes in a Sixty Years Journey. London.

SOURCES

Persons interviewed: not to be identified.
Cheng T'ien-hsi. East and West: Episodes in a Sixty Years Journey. London, 1951.

Cheng Yü-hsiu   鄭毓秀

WORKS

1926. (ed.) Kuo-chi lien-meng kai-k'uang. Shanghai: Shang-wu yin shu kuan.
國際聯盟概況。
1927. Chung-kuo pi-chiao hsien-fa lun. Shang-hai: Shih-chieh shu-chü.
中國比較憲法論。
1943. My Revolutionary Years, the Autobio-graphy of Madame Wei Tao-ming. New York: Charles Scribner's Sons.

SOURCES

Kuo wen chou-pao, IV-16.
國聞週報。
Wei Cheng Yü-hsiu. My Revolutionary Years, the Autobiography of Madame Wei Tao-ming. New York: Charles Scribner's Sons, 1943.
WWC
WWMC

Ch'eng Ch'ien   程潛

WORKS

1942. Yang-fu-yuan shih-chi. Chungking.
養復園詩集。

1948. Ch'eng Ch'ien tsui-chin yen-lun.
程潛最近言論。

1955. Ch'eng Ch'ien *et al.* Chung-yen chi.
Canton: Lien yu shu-tien.
程潛等。忠言集。

SOURCES

BKL

Chao Ts'eng-ch'ou, Wu Hsiang-hsiang *et al.* K'ang chan chi-shih.
趙曾儔，吳相湘等。抗戰紀實。

Ch'en Ching-ts'un hsien-sheng nien-p'u, ed. by Ch'üeh Ming. Hong Kong: Wen-hua yin-shua so, 193?.
陳競存先生年譜。闕名。

Ch'eng Ch'ien. Yang-fu-yuan shih-chi. Chung-king, 1942.
程潛。養復園詩集。

Chiang Yung-ching. Wuhan ch'ih se cheng-ch'üan.
蔣永敬。武漢赤色政權。

CTMC

HCJC

Ho Ying-ch'in. Ho shang-chiang k'ang chan ch'i-chien chün-shih pao-kao. Taipei: Wen hsing shu-tien, 1962. 2 vols.
何應欽。何上將抗戰期間軍事報告。

Hsiang tsai chi-lueh, ed. by Hunan shan-hou hsieh-hui.
湘災紀略。湖南善後協會。

Hunan tzu-chih yün-tung shih.
湖南自治運動史。

Kuo-fang pu shih cheng chü. Pei fa chan shih. Taipei: Kuo-fang pu shih cheng chü, 1959. 4 vols.
國防部史政局。北伐戰史。

Kuo-fu nien-p'u, ch'u kao, ed. by Kuo shih kuan shih-liao pien-tsuan wei-yuan-hui, Chung-kuo kuo-min-tang tang-shih shih-liao pien-tsuan wei-yuan-hui. Taipei: Kuo shih kuan shih-liao pien-tsuan wei-yuan-hui, Chung-kuo kuo-min-tang tang-shih shih-liao pien-tsuan wei-yuan-hui, 1959. 2 vols.
國父年譜，初稿。國史館史料編纂委員會，中國國民黨黨史史料編纂委員會。

Li Ken-yuan. Hsueh-sheng (Li Ken-yuan) nien-lu. Ch'ü-shih-ching-lu, 1934.
李根源。雪生 (李根源) 年錄。

Li Lieh-chün. Li Lieh-chün tzu-chuan. Chung-king, 1944.
李烈鈞。李烈鈞自傳。

———. Wu Ning wen-tu.
李烈鈞。武寧文牘。

MSICH

Wang Ching-wei hsien-sheng wen-chi.
汪精衛先生文集。

Wen Kung-chih. Tsui-chin san-shih nien Chung-kuo chün-shih shih. Taipei: Wen hsing shu-tien, 1962.
文公直。最近三十年中國軍事史。

WWC, 5th ed.

Ch'eng Ching-yi   誠靜怡

SOURCES

Persons interviewed: not to be identified.

Bitton, Nelson. "Cheng Ching-yi: A Christian Statesman." *International Review of Missions,* October, 1941: 513–20, 579.

China Mission Year Book, 1919. Shanghai: Christian Literature Society, 1920.

National Christian Council of China, Annual Report, 1928–29. Shanghai, 1929.

The Outlook of Missions, XXXII-2 (February, 1940): 35–36.

Sparham, C.G. "A Chinese Christian Leader." *Missionary Review of the World,* LXV-12 (December, 1922): 952–53.

Who's Who of the Madras Meeting of the International Missionary Council. Madras, 1938.

Ch'eng She-wo   成舍我

WORKS

1956. Pao hsueh tsa chu. Taipei: Chung-yang wen-wu kung-ying she.
報學雜著。

SOURCES

Ch'eng She-wo. Pao hsueh tsa chu. Taipei: Chung-yang wen-wu kung-ying she, 1956.
成舍我。報學雜著。

CMJL

CMMC

GCJJ

Lin Yü-t'ang. A History of the Press and Public Opinion in China. Chicago: University of Chicago Press, 1936.

Lo Tun-wei. Wu-shih nien hui-i-lu.
羅敦偉。五十年回憶錄。

TCMT

Ts'ao Chü-jen. Ts'ai-fang wai chi. Hong Kong: Ch'uang k'en ch'u-pan she, 1955.
曹聚仁，採訪外記。

Ch'eng T'ien-fang　程 天 放

WORKS

1919. ed. of *Hsueh-sheng lien-ho hui jih-k'an*.
學生聯合會日刊。

1923-? ed. of *Hsing hua jih-pao*. Toronto.
醒華日報。

1944. Hsien-fa yü chiao-yü. Chungking: Cheng-chung shu-chü.
憲法與敎育。

1951. Ch'eng T'ien-fang *et al*. Lien-ho-kuo ju-ho chih-ts'ai ch'in-lueh. Taipei: Ta-lu tsa-chih she.
程天放等。聯合國如何制裁侵略。

1952. Lien chiao tsu-chih ti liu chieh ta-hui chih-tz'u. Taipei.
聯敎組織第六屆大會致辭。

1954. Ch'eng pu-chang T'ien-fang wu nien lai yen-lun hsuan-chi. (ed. by Chiao-yü pu chiao-yü tzu-liao yen-chiu shih). Taipei: Chiao-yü pu.
程部長天放五年來言論選集。敎育部敎育資料研究室。

1957. A History of Sino-Russian Relations. Washington: Public Affairs Press.

1958. Ou Ya kuei-t'u. Taipei: Cheng-chung shu-chü.
歐亞歸途。

1959. Mei-kuo lun. Taipei: Kuo-li cheng-chih ta-hsueh ch'u-pan wei-yuan-hui.
美國論。

1962. Ch'eng T'ien-fang *et al*. Hu Shih yü Chung-kuo. Taipei: Chung-kuo wen-i she.
程天放等。胡適與中國。

1962, October. "Wo so ch'in li te ssu-erh shih-pien." *Chin-jih ta-lu*, 146.
我所親歷的四二事變。今日大陸。

1964. (ed.) Cheng-chih hsueh. Taipei: Cheng-chung shu-chü.
政治學。

Pai hua chou p'an te hsien-sung.
百花洲畔的絃誦。

Wo te chia-shu sheng-huo.
我的家熟生活。

SOURCES

AWW, 1960.

Chang Ch'i-yün *et al*. Chung-hua Min-kuo ta-hsueh chih. Taipei: Chung-hua wen-hua ch'u-pan shih-yeh wei-yuan-hui, 1954. 2 vols.
張其昀等。中華民國大學誌。

Ch'eng T'ien-fang. A History of Sino-Russian Relations. Washington: Public Affairs Press, 1957.

Ch'eng T'ien-fung. Pai hua chou p'an te hsien-sung.
程天放。百花洲畔的絃誦。

———. "Wo so ch'in li te ssu-erh shih-pien." *Chin-jih ta-lu*, 146 (October, 1962).
程天放。我所親歷的四二事變。今日大陸。

———. Wo te chia-shu sheng-huo.
程天放。我的家熟生活。

CH-T, 1956-57.

CMJL

GCJJ

WWC, 1934.

Ch'eng Yen-ch'iu　程 硯 秋

WORKS

1959. Ch'eng Yen-ch'iu wen-chi (ed. by Chung-kuo hsi ch'ü yen-chiu yuan). Peking: Chung-kuo hsi-chü ch'u-pan she.
程硯秋文集。中國戲曲研究院。

1959. Hsi ch'ü piao-yen te ssu kung wu fa. Peking: Peking pao-wen-t'ang shu-tien.
戲曲表演的四功五法。

1959. T'an ju-ho hsueh i. Peking: Peking pao-wen-t'ang shu-tien.
談如何學藝。

SOURCES

Persons interviewed: not to be identified.

SCMP, 1732 (March 10, 1958): 4.

Chi Ch'ao-ting　冀 朝 鼎

WORKS

1933-36. ed. of *China Today*.

1936. Key Economic Areas in Chinese History, As Revealed in the Development of Public Works for Water-Control. London: George Allen & Unwin.

1937-? ed. of *Amerasia*.

SOURCES

AWW

Doonping, Richard. Militarist Wars and Revolution in China: A Marxist Analysis of the New Reactionary Civil War and Prospects of the Revolution in China. New York: Chinese Vanguard Publishing Co., 1930.

HCJC

James, Maurice, and Richard Doonping. Soviet China. New York: International Pamphlets, 1932.
K-WWC

Ch'i Hsieh-yuan   齊燮元

SOURCES

BPC
Chu Tzu-chia (Chin Hsiung-pai). Wang cheng-ch'üan te k'ai-ch'ang yü shou-ch'ang. Hong Kong: Ch'un-ch'iu tsa-chih she, 1964. 5 vols.
朱子家（金雄白）。汪政權的開場與收場。
Hsü Kao-yang. Kuo-fang nien-chien. 1952.
許高陽。國防年鑑。
Li Ch'ao-ying. Wei tsu-chih cheng-chih ching-chi kai-k'uang. Chungking: Shang-wu yin shu kuan.
李超英。偽組織政治經濟概況。
Li Chien-nung. Chung-kuo chin pai nien cheng-chih shih. Shanghai: Shang-wu yin shu kuan, 1947. 2 vols.
李劍農。中國近百年政治史。
Powell, Ralph L. The Rise of Chinese Military Power, 1892–1912. Princeton: Princeton University Press, 1955.
Shanghai hung wen t'u shu kuan. Chiang Che chan shih. Shanghai: Hung wen t'u-shu kuan, 1924.
上海宏文圖書館。江浙戰史。
SMJ
T'ao Chü-yin. Liu chü-tzu chuan. Shanghai: Chung-hua shu-chü, 1946.
陶菊隱。六君子傳。
———. Wu P'ei-fu chiang-chün chuan. Shang-hai: Chung-hua shu-chü, 1941.
陶菊隱。吳佩孚將軍傳。
Taylor, George E. The Struggle for North China. New York: International Secretariat, Institute of Pacific Relations, 1940.
Ts'ao Chü-jen and Shu Tsung-ch'iao. Chung-kuo k'ang chan hua shih. Shanghai: Lien-ho hua-pao she, 1947.
曹聚仁，舒宗僑。中國抗戰畫史。

Ch'i Ju-shan   齊如山

WORKS

1964. Ch'i Ju-shan ch'üan-chi. Taipei: Ch'i Ju-shan i-chu pien yin wei-yuan-hui, 1964. 8 vols.

齊如山全集。

SOURCES

Ch'i Ju-shan. Ch'i Ju-shan hui-i-lu. Taipei: Chung-yang wen-wu kung-ying she, 1956.
齊如山。齊如山回憶錄。
———. Ch'i Ju-shan sui-pi. Taipei: Chung-yang wen-wu kung-ying she, 1953.
齊如山。齊如山隨筆。

Ch'i Pai-shih   齊白石

WORKS

1932. Ch'i Pai-shih hua-ts'e. Shanghai: Chung-hua shu-chü.
齊白石畫冊。
1936. Ch'i Pai-shih hua-chien, ti-i chi. Peiping: Ch'ing-pi-ko.
齊白石畫箋，第一集。
1945. Pai-shih lao-jen hsiao ts'e.
白石老人小冊。
1952. Ch'i Pai-shih hua-chi. Peking: Yung-pao-chai hsin chi.
齊白石畫集。
1953. Pai-shih lao-jen hua-ts'e. Peking: Yung-pao-chai hsin chi.
白石老人畫冊。
1958. Ch'i Pai-shih hua-hui ts'e. Peking: Yung-pao-chai hsin chi.
齊白石花卉冊。
1958. Pai-shih ts'ao ch'ung ts'e. Peking: Yung-pao-chai hsin chi.
白石草蟲冊。
1959. Ch'i Pai-shih tso-p'in hsuan-chi (ed. by Li Chin-hsi, Ch'i Liang-chi). Peking: Jen-min mei-shu ch'u-pan she.
齊白石作品選集。黎錦熙，齊良己。
1959. K'o-hsi wu sheng.
可惜無聲。
1959. Pai-shih lao-jen i-mo. Peking: Yung-pao-chai.
白石老人遺墨。
1959. Pai-shih mo miao. Peking: Yung-pao-chai.
白石墨妙。
1961. Ch'i Pai-shih shih wen chuan k'o chi (ed. by Ch'en Fan). Hong Kong: Shanghai shu-chü.
齊白石詩文篆刻集。陳凡。
1962. Pai-shih lao-jen tzu-chuan. Peking: Jen-min mei-shu ch'u-pan she.
白石老人自傳。

1963. Ch'i Pai-shih tso-p'in chi (ed. by Ch'i Pai-shih tso-p'in chi pien-chi wei-yuan-hui). Peking: Jen-min mei-shu ch'u-pan she. 3 vols.
齊白石作品集。齊白石作品集編輯委員會。

1963. Pai-shih yin-chi. Peking: Chung-kuo mei-shu hsieh-hui. 4 vols.
白石印集。

SOURCES

Chi Tang. "Chi Pai-shih, a Great Artist." *Chinese Literature*, (January-February, 1958): 142-44.

Ch'i Pai-shih. Pai-shih lao-jen tzu-chuan. Peking: Jen-min mei-shu ch'u-pan she, 1962.
齊白石。白石老人自傳。

Ch'i Pai-shih nien-p'u, ed. by Hu Shih, Li Chin-hsi, Teng Kuang-ming. Shanghai: Shang-wu yin shu kuan, 1949.
齊白年譜。胡適，黎錦熙，鄧廣銘。

Ch'ü Hsuan-yin. "Ch'i Pai-shih weng hua yü lu." *Ku-chin pan-yueh-k'an*, 35 (November 16, 1943): 12-17.
瞿宣穎。齊白石翁畫語錄。古今半月刊。

ECC

GCJJ

Hu P'ei-heng and Hu T'o. Ch'i Pai-shih hua fa yü hsin-shang. Peking: Jen-min mei-shu ch'u-pan she, 1959.
胡佩衡，胡橐。齊白石畫法與欣賞。

Hu Wen-hsiao. Ch'i Pai-shih chuan-lueh. Peking: Jen-min mei-shu ch'u-pan she, 1959.
胡文效。齊白石傳略。

Li K'o-jan. "A Reminiscence of Ch'i Pai-shih." *Chinese Literature*, (October, 1959): 140-47.

"The Living Art of Chi Pai-shih." *China Reconstructs*, VII-4 (April, 1958): 27.

MMT

Wang Chao-wen. "Chi Pai-shih and His Art." *People's China*, 22 (November 16, 1957): 18-20, 25-27.

Wang Chao-wen *et al*. Ch'i Pai-shih yen-chiu. Shanghai: Jen-min mei-shu ch'u-pan she, 1959.
王朝文等。齊白石研究。

Chiang Ch'ang-ch'uan   江長川

SOURCES

China Christian Advocate, XXIII-12 (December, 1936): 19; XXV-2 (February, 1938): 15; XXIX-4 (April, 1941): 8.

CWR, XCVII-5 (July 5, 1941): 159.

Nance, W.B. Soochow University. New York: United Board for Christian Higher Education in Asia, 1956.

The New York Times, August 28, 1958.

Price, Frank W. China—Twilight or Dawn?

Studley, Ellen M. "Z.T. Kaung: Prince for God." *World Outlook*, July, 1948: 337-39.

Who's Who of the Madras Meeting of the International Missionary Council. Madras, 1938.

World Outlook, XXVIII-11 (November, 1938): 461.

Zion's Herald, December 11, 1947.

Chiang Ching-kuo   蔣經國

WORKS

1943. Sheng lu. Kan-hsien, Kiangsi: Chung-hua cheng-ch'i ch'u-pan she.
生路。

1947. Wo-te sheng-huo. Shanghai: Ch'ien feng ch'u-pan she.
我的生活。

1955. Chiang Ching-kuo hsien-sheng chiang-tz'u chi; ti-i chi. Taipei: Kuo-fang pu tsung cheng-chih pu.
蔣經國先生講詞集；第一輯。

1955. T'ung ting ssu t'ung. Taipei.
痛定思痛。

1956. Wo-te fu-ch'in. Taipei.
我的父親。

1959. Ch'ang yen shih lu (comp. by Huang Chi-tz'u). Taipei.
常言實錄。黃寄慈。

1960. Fu chung chih yuan. Taipei: Kuo-fang pu yin chih ch'ang.
負重致遠。

1963. Sheng-li chih lu. Taipei: Yu shih shu-tien.
勝利之路。

1963. Sung po ch'ang ch'ing. Taipei.
松柏常青。

1967. Feng-yü chung te ning-ching. Taipei: Kuo-fang pu cheng-chih tso-chang pu.
風雨中的寧靜。

Wei-chi ts'un wang chih ch'iu.
危急存亡之秋。

SOURCES

AWW

Bullitt, William C. "Shall We Support an Attack on Red China?" *Look*, August 24, 1954.

CH-T, 1956-57.

Chiang Ching-kuo. Ch'ang yen shih lu (comp. by Hung Shou-tz'u). Taipei, 1959.
蔣經國。 常言實錄。 黃守慈。
———. Fu chung chih yuan. Taipei: Kuo-fang pu yin chih ch'ang, 1960.
蔣經國。 負重致遠。
———. Wo-te fu-ch'in. Taipei, 1956.
蔣經國。 我的父親。
———. Wo-te sheng-huo. Shanghai: Ch'ien-feng ch'u-pan she, 1947.
蔣經國。 我的生活。
Chiang Kai-shek. Soviet Russia in China: A Summing-up at Seventy. New York: Farar, Straus & Cudahy, 1957.
Ch'un-ch'iu, June 16, July 1, 1963.
春秋。
CMTC
Current Biography, 1954.
"Guerrilla War Hits Red China." *U.S. News & World Report*, March 4, 1963.
Hahn, Emily. Chiang Kai-shek: An Unauthorized Biography. New York: Doubleday & Co., 1955.
———. "Our Far-flung Correspondents." *New Yorker*, November 7, 1953: 137–52.
"Hero's Welcome." *Time*, February 1, 1954.
Ho Jui-yao. Feng-yun jen-wu hsiao-chih. Canton: Yü-chou feng she, 1947.
何瑞瑤。 風雲人物小誌。
International Who's Who, 1962–63.
Min-kuo shih-wu nien i-ch'ien chih Chiang Chieh-shih hsien-sheng, comp. by Mao Ssu-ch'eng. 1937. 20 vols.
民國十五年以前之蔣介石先生。 毛思誠。
Newsweek, October 7, 1946.
The Reporter, June 13, 1957.
Sun Chia-ch'i. Chiang Ching-kuo ch'ieh kuo nei-mu. Hong Kong: Tzu li ch'u-pan she, 1961.
張家麒。 蔣經國竊國內幕。
Ts'ao Chü-jen. Chiang Ching-kuo lun. Hong Kong: Ch'uang k'en ch'u-pan she, 1954.
曹聚仁。 蔣經國論。
Tsou Tang. America's Failure in China 1941–50. Chicago: University of Chicago Press, 1963.
Tung Hsien-kuang (Hollington K. Tong). Chiang tsung-t'ung chuan. Taipei: Chung-hua wen-hua ch'u-pan shih-yeh wei-yuan-hui, 1952. 3 vols.
董顯光。 蔣總統傳。
U.S. News & World Report, December 2, 1955.
Whiting, Allen S. "Mystery Man of Formosa." *Saturday Evening Post*, March 12, 1955.

Wu, K.C. "The K.C. Wu Story." *The Reporter*, April 27, 1954.
———. "Your Money Has Built a Police State on Formosa." *The Reporter*, June 29, 1954.

Chiang Fang-chen 蔣方震

WORKS

1922. Ts'ai ping chi-hua shu. Shanghai: Shang-wu yin shu kuan.
裁兵計劃書。
1924. Ou-chou wen-i fu-hsing shih. Shanghai: Shang-wu yin shu kuan.
歐洲文藝復興史。
1937. Kuo-fang lun.
國防論。
1938. Jih-pen jen—i ko wai-kuo jen te yen-chiu.
日本人——個外國人的研究。
1939. Chiang Pai-li wen-hsuan (ed. by Huang P'ing-sun). Chin-hua, Chekiang: Hsin chen-ti t'u-shu she.
蔣百里文選。 黃萍蓀。
1947. Chiang Pai-li hsien-sheng wen-hsuan (ed. by Huang P'ing-sun). Kuo-fang hsueh-hui.
蔣百里先生文選。 黃萍蓀。
Chün-shih ch'ang-shih. 2 vols.
軍事常識。
ed. of *Kai-tsao tsa-chih*.
改造雜誌。

SOURCES

T'ao Chü-yin. Chiang Pai-li hsien-sheng chuan. Shanghai: Chang-hua shih-chü, 1948.
陶菊隱。 蔣百里先生傳。

Chiang Hai-ch'eng 蔣海澄

WORKS

1936. Ta-yen-ho.
大堰河。
1942. Pei-fang.
北方。
1945. Hsueh li tsuan. Chungking: Hsin ch'ün ch'u-pan she.
雪裡鑽。
1946. Shih lun. Shanghai: Shanghai hsin hsin ch'u-pan she.
詩論。
1946. Wu Man-yu. Yenan: Chen chih ch'u-pan she.
吳滿有。

1947. Hsien-kei hsiang-ts'un te shih. Pei-men ch'u-pan she.
獻給鄉村的詩。

1947. K'uang-yeh. Shanghai: Sheng-huo shu-tien.
曠野。

1947. Shih hsin min-chu chu-i te wen-hsueh. Hong Kong: Hai-yang shu wu.
釋新民主主義的文學。

1949-52. ed. of *Jen-min wen-hsueh*.
人民文學。

1950. Tsou hsiang sheng-li. Shanghai: Wen-hua kung-tso she.
走向勝利。

1951. Ai Ch'ing hsuan-chi. Peking: K'ai-ming shu-tien.
艾青選集。

1952. Hsin wen-i lun-chi. Shanghai: Shanghai hsin wen-i ch'u-pan she.
新文藝論集。

1953. Pao-shih te hung-hsing. Peking: Jen-min wen-hsueh ch'u-pan she.
寶石的紅星。

1955. Ai Ch'ing shih-hsuan. Peking: Jen-min wen-hsueh ch'u-pan she.
艾青詩選。

1955. Hei man. Peking: Tso-chia ch'u-pan she.
黑鰻。

1956. Ch'un-t'ien. Peking: Jen-min wen-hsueh ch'u-pan she.
春天。

1957. Hai-chia shang. Peking: Tso-chia ch'u-pan she.
海岬上。

Fan fa-hsi-ssu.
反法西斯。

Huo-pa.
火把。

Hsiang t'ai-yang.
向太陽。

Li-ming te t'ung-chih.
黎明的通知。

T'a ssu tsai ti-erh tz'u.
他死在第二次。

SOURCES

CHWSK
Liu Shou-sung. Chung-kuo hsin wen-hsueh shih ch'u kao. Peking: Tso-chia ch'u-pan she, 1956. 2 vols.
劉綏松。中國新文學史初稿。
RCCL
WWMC

Chiang Kai-shek   蔣介石

WORKS

1925. Chiang Chieh-shih hsiao-chang tsai kuo-min cheng-fu chün-shih wei-yuan-hui chiang-yen tz'u. Canton: Kuo-min ko-ming chün ti-i chün cheng-chih pu.
蔣介石校長在國民政府軍事委員會講演詞。

1926. Chiang Chieh-shih hsien-sheng tsui-chin chih yen-lun (ed. by Peking min she). Peking: Min she.
蔣介石先生最近之言論。北京民社。

1928. (comp.) Tseng pu Tseng Hu chih ping yü-lu. Canton: Chung-kuo kuo-min-tang lu-chün chün-kuan hsueh-hsiao.
增補曾胡治兵語錄。

1933? Chiao fei wen-hsien. Nanchang: Kuo-min cheng-fu chün-shih wei-yuan-hui wei-yuan-chang Nanchang hsing-ying.
剿匪文獻。

1935. Chiang wei-yuan-chang yen-lun chi (comp. by Chung-kuo kuo-min-tang chung-yang chih-hsing wei-yuan-hui hsuan-ch'uan wei-yuan-hui). Chung-kuo kuo-min-tang chung-yang chih-hsing wei-yuan-hui hsuan-ch'uan wei-yuan-hui.
蔣委員長言論集。中國國民黨中央執行委員會宣傳委員會。

1936. Chiang Chieh-shih hsien-sheng chia-yen lei ch'ao (comp. by P'eng Kuo-tung). Shanghai: Shang-wu yin shu kuan.
蔣介石先生嘉言類鈔。彭國棟。

1937. Chiang Chieh-shih ch'üan-chi (ed. by Wen-hua pien i kuan). Wen-hua pien i kuan.
蔣介石全集。文化編譯館。

1937. Chiang wei-yuan-chang Chung-cheng ch'üan-chi (comp. by Chin Ch'eng). Min-tsu ch'u-pan she. 2 vols.
蔣委員長中正全集。金成。

1937. Chiang wei-yuan-chang Sian pan-yueh chi (with Chiang fu-jen Sian shih-pien hui-i-lu). Nanking: Cheng-chung shu-chü.
蔣委員長西安半月記 （附：蔣夫人西安事變回憶錄）。
Eng. tr., Sian: *A Coup d'etat, by Mayling Soong Chiang (with A Fortnight in Sian: Extracts from a Diary by Chiang Kai-shek).* Shanghai: China Publishing Co., 1937.

1938. Huang-p'u hsun-lien chi hsuan-chi. Chungking? Kuo-min cheng-fu chün-shih wei-yuan-hui cheng-chih pu.
黃埔訓練集選集。

1938.   Ling-hsiu k'ang-chan yen-lun hsü-chi. Chungking: Tu-li ch'u-pan she.
領袖抗戰言論續集。

1939.   Cheng-chih chien-she yen-lun chi (comp. by Chung-kuo kuo-min-tang chung-yang hsuan-ch'uan pu). Chungking: Cheng-chung shu-chü.
政治建設言論集。中國國民黨中央宣傳部。

1939.   Chiang wei-yuan-chang chiang tsung-li i-chiao. Chungking: Ch'ing-nien shu-tien.
蔣委員長講總理遺教。

1939.   Tsung-ts'ai tui-yü hsun-lien kung-tso chih chih-shih. Chungking: Chung-kuo kuo-min-tang chung-yang chih-hsing wei-yuan-hui hsun-lien wei-yuan-hui. 3 vols.
總裁對於訓練工作之指示。

1940.   Generalissimo Chiang's Statement Following the Publication of Wang Ching-wei's Secret Agreement with Japan. Chungking: The China Information Committee.

1941.   Chiang tsung-t'ung chih yu-jen shu (ed. by Wang Ming-ta). Kweilin: Ch'ing pai she.
蔣總統致友人書。王明達。

1941.   Generalissimo Chiang Kai-shek's Speech on the Communist Question Delivered at the People's Political Council, Chungking, March 6, 1941. Chungking: The China Information Committee.

1942?   Tsung-ts'ai yen-lun hsuan-chi (comp. by Chung-kuo kuo-min-tang chung-yang chih-hsing wei-yuan-hui hsun-lien wei-yuan-hui). Chungking: Chung-kuo kuo-min-tang chung-yang chih-hsing wei-yuan-hui hsuan-ch'uan pu. 4 vols.
總裁言論選集。中國國民黨中央執行委員會訓練委員會。

1943.   Chung-kuo chih ming-yun. Chungking: Cheng-chung shu-chü.
中國之命運。
Eng. tr. by Wang Chung-hui, *China's Destiny*. New York: The Macmillan Co., 1947.

1943.   Resistance and Reconstruction: Messages During China's Six Years of War, 1937–1943. New York: Harper & Bros.

1945.   Before Final Victory: Speeches by Generalissimo Chiang Kai-shek, 1943–44. New York: Chinese News Service.

1945.   Chiang chu-hsi tui ch'ing-nien wen-t'i chih chih-shih (comp. by Tu Ch'eng-hsiang). Chungking: Ch'ing-nien ch'u-pan she.
蔣主席對青年問題之指示。杜呈祥。

1945.   China's Post War Economic Reconstruc- tion. with T.V. Soong. Shanghai: International Publishers.

1945.   President Chiang Kai-shek's Selected Speeches and Messages, 1937–1945. Taipei: China Cultural Service.

1945–46. Statements and Speeches (with Chinese Texts). Shanghai: International Publishers. 2 vols.

1946.   Chiang chu-hsi chan hou chung-yao yen-lun chi; ti-i chi. Pa-ch'eng: Kuo-min shu-chü.
蔣主席戰後重要言論集；第一集。

1946.   Chiang chu-hsi chia-shu. Shanghai: Ch'ang feng shu-tien tai wen shih yen-chiu hui.
蔣主席家書。

1946.   Chiang Feng shu chien. with Feng Yü-hsiang. Shanghai: Chung-kuo wen-hua hsin-t'o fu-wu she.
蔣馮書簡。馮玉祥。

1946.   The Collected Wartime Messages of Generalissimo Chiang Kai-shek, 1937–1945 (comp. by Chinese Ministry of Information). New York: The John Day Co. 2 vols.

1946.   Sheng-li hou i nien chien Chiang Chu-hsi chung-yao hsun-tz'u. Canton: Kwangtung sheng san-shih-wu nien-tu hsing-cheng hui-i pi-shu ch'u.
勝利後一年間蔣主席重要訓詞。

1947.   Chiang Chieh-shih hsien-sheng k'ang chan chien kuo ming-yen ch'ao (ed. by Ch'en Fu-hua). Shanghai: Shang-wu yin shu kuan.
蔣介石先生抗戰建國名言鈔。陳福華。

1947.   Chiang chu-hsi chih ping yü-lu (comp. by Teng Wen-i). Nanking: Hsin Chung-kuo ch'u-pan she.
蔣主席治兵語錄。鄧文儀。

1947.   O-mei hsun-lien chi (ed. by Teng Wen-i). Nanking: Kuo-fang pu hsin-wen chü.
峨眉訓練集。鄧文儀。

1951.   Tsung-ts'ai tang-wu chung-yao yen-lun chi. Taipei: Kuo-fang pu tsung cheng-chih pu.
總裁黨務重要言論集。

1951–58. Tsung-t'ung wen-kao chiang-tz'u hui-chi.   Yang-ming-shan: Yang-ming-shan chuang. 7 vols.
總統文告講詞彙輯。

1952. Selected Speeches and Messages of President Chiang Kai-shek, 1949–52. Taipei: Office of the Government Spokesman.

1952.   Tsung-ts'ai yen-lun hsuan-chi (comp. by Ko-ming shih-chien yen-chiu-yuan). Taipei: Chung-yang kai-tsao wei-yuan-hui. 5 vols.

總裁言論選輯。革命實踐研究院。

1953. Min-sheng chu-i yü lo liang p'ien pu shu. Taipei: Kuo-fang pu tsung cheng-chih pu.

民生主義育樂兩篇補述。

Eng. tr. by Durhan S.F. Chen, *Chapters on National Fecundity, Social Welfare, Education, and Health and Happiness: Written as Supplements to Dr. Sun Yat-sen's Lectures on the Principle of People's Livelihood.* Taipei: China Cultural Service, 1953?

1954. Message on KMT's 60th Anniversary, November 12, 1954 (with Chinese Text). Taipei: China Cultural Service.

1954. President Chiang's Statement to All Members of the Kuomintang, September, 1949 (with Chinese Text). Taipei: China Cultural Service.

1954. Ti-i chieh kuo-min ta-hui ti-erh tz'u hui-i Chiang tsung-t'ung pao-kao ch'üan-wen (Chung-hua Min-kuo ssu-shih-san nien erh-yueh shih-chiu jih). Taipei: Hsing-cheng yuan hsin-wen chü.

第一屆國民大會第二次會議蔣總統報告全文 (中華民國四十三年二月十九日)。

1955. President Chiang Kai-shek's Messages, October 10, 1954-February 14, 1955. Taipei: Fourth Department, Central Committee of the Kuomintang.

1956. Chiang tsung-t'ung yen-lun hui-pien (ed. by Chiang tsung-t'ung yen-lun hui-pien pien-chi wei-yuan-hui). Taipei: Cheng-chung shu-chü. 24 vols.

蔣總統言論彙編。蔣總統言論彙編編輯委員會。

1956-64. Chiang tsung-t'ung yen-lun chi (ed. by Hsing-cheng yuan hsin-wen chü). Taipei: Hsing-cheng yuan hsin-wen chü. 5 vols.

蔣總統言論集。行政院新聞局。

1957. Chiang tsung-t'ung ssu-shih-liu nien tu yen-lun chi. Taipei: Hsing-cheng yuan hsin-wen chü.

蔣總統四十六年度言論集。

1957. Selected Speeches and Messages in 1956.

1957. Selected Speeches and Messages in 1957. Taipei.

1957. Su-o tsai Chung-kuo—Chung-kuo yü O kung san-shih nien ching-li chi-yao. Taipei: Chung-yang wen-wu kung-ying she.

蘇俄在中國—中國與俄共三十年經歷紀要。

Eng. tr., *Soviet Russia in China: A Summing-up at Seventy.* New York: Farrar, Straus & Cudahy, 1957.

1958. Chiang tsung-t'ung Yeh-su shou-nan chieh cheng-tao tz'u. Taipei: Hsing-cheng yuan hsin-wen chü.

蔣總統耶穌受難節證道詞。

1958. Kuo-ts'e, fan-kung yü ch'iao-pao—Chiang tsung-t'ung tsui-chin yen-lun chi. Taipei: Hai-wai ch'u-pan she.

國策，反攻與僑胞—蔣總統最近言論輯。

1959. Selected Speeches and Messages in 1958. Taipei: Government Information Office.

1960. Chiang tsung-t'ung ssu-shih-chiu nien-tu yen-lun chi. Taipei: Hsing-cheng yuan hsin-wen chü.

蔣總統四十九年度言論集。

1960. Chiang tsung-t'ung wen-kao hsuan-chi; Chung-hua Min-kuo ssu-shih-pa nien i-yueh chih san-yueh. Taipei: Hsing-cheng yuan hsin-wen chü.

蔣總統文告選輯；中華民國四十八年一月至三月。

1961. Chiang tsung-t'ung tui ti-i chieh kuo-min ta-hui ti-san tz'u hui-i chih-tz'u. Taipei: Kuo-min ta-hui pi-shu ch'u.

蔣總統對第一屆國民大會第三次會議致詞。

1961. Chiang tsung-t'ung Yeh-su fu-huo chieh cheng-tao tz'u. Taipei: Hsin-cheng yuan hsin-wen chü.

蔣總統耶穌復活節證道詞。

1963. Chiang tsung-t'ung chi (ed. by Chiang tsung-t'ung chi pien-chi wei-yuan-hui). Yang-ming-shan: Kuo-fang yen-chiu-yuan. 2 vols.

蔣總統集。蔣總統集編輯委員會。

1965. Chiang tsung-t'ung chi tseng-ting pen (ed. by Chiang tsung-t'ung chi pien-tsuan wei-yuan-hui). Yang-ming-shan: Kuo-fang yen-chiu-yuan, Chung-hua ta tz'u-tien pien-yin hui.

蔣總統集增訂本。蔣總統集編纂委員會。

1966. Chiang tsung-t'ung tui kuo-fu ssu-hsiang chih shih-chien tu-hsing yü jung-hui kuan-t'ung (comp. by Ch'in Hsiao-i). Kuo-fu pai nien tan-ch'en ch'ou-pei wei-yuan-hui.

蔣總統對國父思想之實踐篤行與融會貫通。秦孝儀。

1967. K'ung Yung-chih hsien-sheng shih-lueh. Taipei.

孔傭之先生事略。

SOURCES

Berkov, Robert. Strong Man of China. Boston: Houghton Mifflin, 1938.

Bertram, James M. First Act in China: The Story of the Sian Mutiny. New York: The Viking Press, 1938.

Chang Hsin-hai.　Chiang Kai-shek: Asia's Man of Destiny.　New York: Doubleday & Co., 1944.

Ch'en Po-ta.　Jen-min kung-ti Chiang Chieh-shih.　Chin Ch'a Chi hsin hua shu-tien, 1948.
人民公敵蔣介石。

Ch'en Pu-lei.　Hui-i lu.　Shanghai: Erh-shih shih-chi ch'u-pan she, 1949.
陳布雷。回憶錄。

Chiang Kai-shek.　The Collected Wartime Messages of Generalissimo Chiang Kai-shek, 1937-1945 (comp. by Chinese Ministry of Information).　New York: The John Day Co., 1946.　2 vols.

Chiang tsung-t'ung hua-chuan, ed. by Chiang tsung-t'ung hua-chuan pien-chi wei-yuan-hui.　Taipei: Cheng-chung shu-chü, 1956.
蔣總統畫傳。蔣總統畫傳編輯委員會。

Chiang tsung-t'ung nien-piao, comp. by Wang Te-sheng.　Taipei: Shih-chieh shu-chü, 1956.
蔣總統年表。王德勝。

Chiang tsung-t'ung yen-lun hui-pien, ed. by Chiang tsung-t'ung yen-lun hui-pien pien-chi wei-yuan-hui.　Taipei: Cheng-chung shu-chü, 1956.　24 vols.
蔣總統言論彙編。蔣總統言論彙編編輯委員會。

Ch'ien Tuan-sheng.　The Government and Politics of China.　Cambridge: Harvard University Press, 1950.

Chronology of President Chiang Kai-shek, ed. by Ch'en Pu-lei, Tang Cheng-chu (tr. by Sampson Shen).　Taipei: China Cultural Service, 1954.

Feng Yü-hsiang.　Wo so jen-shih te Chiang Chieh-shih.　Shanghai: Wen-hua kung-tso she, 1949.
馮玉祥。我所認識的蔣介石。

Hedin, Sven.　Chiang Kai-shek, Marshal of China (tr. by Bernard Norbelie).　New York: The John Day Co., 1940.

Hsiung Shih-i.　The Life of Chiang Kai-shek.　London: P. Davies, 1948.

Linebarger, Paul M.A.　The China of Chiang Kai-shek: A Political Study.　Boston: World Peace Foundation, 1941.

Min-kuo shih-wu nien i-ch'ien chih Chiang Chieh-shih hsien-sheng, comp. by Mao Ssu-ch'eng.　1937.　20 vols.
民國十五年以前蔣之介石先生。毛思誠。

The Stilwell Papers, ed. by Theodore H. White.　New York: William Sloane Associates, 1948.

Teng Wen-i.　Chiang Chu-hsi.　Shanghai: Sheng-li ch'u-pan she, 1945.
鄧文儀。蔣主席。

Tsou Tang.　America's Failure in China 1941-50.　Chicago: University of Chicago Press, 1963.

Tong, Hollington K.　(Tung Hsien-kuang).　Chiang Kai-shek, Soldier and Statesman: Authorized Biography.　Shanghai: China Publishing Co., 1937.　2 vols.

———.　Chiang tsung-t'ung chuan.　Taipei: Chung-hua wen-hua ch'u-pan shih-yeh wei-yuan-hui, 1952.　3 vols.
董顯光。蔣總統傳。

White, Theodore H., and Annalee Jacoby.　Thunder Out of China.　New York: William Sloane Associates, 1946.

Wu I-chou.　Chiang tsung-t'ung hsing-i.　Taipei: Cheng-chung shu-chü.
吳一舟。蔣總統行誼。

Chiang K'ang-hu　　江亢虎

WORKS

1913.　Hung-shui chi.
洪水集。

1922.　(ed.) (Mei-kuo) Kuo-hui t'u-shu-kuan han chi t'u-shu fen-lei fa.　with Feng Ch'ing-kui, Wang Kuo-chün et al.　Washington: Nung-yeh pu.
(美國) 國會圖書館漢籍圖書分類法。　馮慶桂，王國鈞等。

1923.　Chiang K'ang-hu po-shih yen-chiang lu i erh chi (ed. by Nan-fang ta-hsueh ch'u-pan pu).　Shanghai: Nan-fang ta-hsueh.
江亢虎博士演講錄一二集。南方大學出版部。

1924.　Hsin O yu-chi.　Shanghai: Shang-wu yin shu kuan.
新俄遊記。

1927.　Ming ho chi.
鳴鶴記。

1928.　Nan yu hui-hsiang chi.　Shanghai: Chung-hua shu-chü.
南遊廻想記。

1939.　K'ang lu chin yen.　Hong Kong: K'ang lu ch'u-pan she.
亢廬近言。

1941.　Hui hsiang tung-fang.　Nanking: Min-i she.
回向東方。

1942.　Wen-miao chiang ching chi.　Nanking: Min-i ch'u-pan she.

文廟講經記。

Chin shih san ta chu-i yü Chung-kuo. Nan-ta Ching hsiao ch'u-pan pu.
近世三大主義與中國。

Hsin ta-lu t'ung-hsin pien.
新大陸通信編。

Sheng hsien ts'ao-an. Shanghai: Nan-fang ta-hsueh ch'u-pan pu.
省憲草案。

Shu-ku yu-chi. Shanghai: Shanghai shih-pao she.
黍谷游記。

T'ien hsien kuan-k'uei.
天憲筦闚。

SOURCES

CBJS

Chang Kuo-t'ao. "Autobiography." Unpublished manuscript, ed. by Robert Burton.

Chiang K'ang-hu yin-mou fu-pi chi nan-ta ch'ü Chiang yun-tung chi-shih, ed. by Shanghai nan-fang ta-hsueh hsueh-sheng hui. Shanghai: Nan-fang ta-hsueh hsueh-sheng hui, 1925.
江亢虎陰謀復辟及南大驅江運動紀實。上海南方大學學生會。

Chow Tse-tsung. The May Fourth Movement: Intellectual Revolution in Modern China. Cambridge: Harvard University Press, 1960.

Wu Hsiang-hsiang. "Chiang K'ang-hu yü Chung-kuo she-hui-tang," in Wu Hsiang-hsiang, *Chung-kuo hsien-tai shih ts'ung-k'an*, II. Taipei: Cheng-chung shu-chü, 1960.
吳相湘，江亢虎與中國社會黨，吳相湘，中國現代史叢刊。

WWC, 1936.

Chiang Kuang-nai   蔣光鼐

SOURCES

Chung-hua Jen-min Kung-ho-kuo k'ai-kuo wen-hsien, ed. by Hsin min-chu ch'u-pan she. Hong Kong: Hsin min-chu ch'u-pan she, 1949.
中華人民共和國開國文獻。新民主出版社。

CKJMT

CYB-W, 1934.

HCJC

Ts'ai T'ing-k'ai. Ts'ai T'ing-k'ai tzu-chuan. Hong Kong: Tzu-yu hsun-k'an she, 1946. 2 vols.
蔡廷鍇。蔡廷鍇自傳。

Chiang Meng-lin   蔣夢麟

WORKS

1933. Kuo-tu shih-tai chih ssu-hsiang yü chiao-yü. Shanghai: Shang-wu yin shu kuan.
過渡時代之思想與教育。

1947. Tides from the West. New Haven: Yale University Press.
Chinese tr., *Hsi ch'ao*. Taipei: Chung-hua jih-pao she.
西潮。

1951. Nung-fu-hui kung-tso yen-chin yuan-tse chih chien-t'ao (tr. by Li Hsun-ho). Taipei: Chung-kuo nung-ts'un fu-hsing lien-ho wei-yuan-hui.
農復會工作演進原則之檢討。李循和。

1954. Meng-lin wen-ts'un. Taipei: Cheng-chung shu-chü.
孟鄰文存。

1955. T'an hsueh-wen. Taipei: Cheng-chung shu-chü.
談學問。

1962. Shu-fa t'an yuan. Taipei: Shih-chieh shu-chü.
書法探源。

1962. Wen-hua te chiao-liu yü ssu-hsiang te yen-chin. Taipei: Shih-chieh shu-chü.
文化的交流與思想的演進。

SOURCES

BKL

Chiang Meng-lin. Hsi ch'ao. Taipei: Chung-hua jih-pao she, 1960.
蔣夢麟。西潮。

Chung-yang jih-pao. Taipei, June 19, 20, 1964.
中央日報。

Hong Kong Tiger Standard. Hong Kong, June 20, 1964.

The New York Times, June, 19, 1964.

Chiang Ting-wen   蔣鼎文

SOURCES

Chang Ch'i-yün. Tang shih kai-yao. Taipei: Chung-yang kai-tsao wei-yuan-hui wen-wu kung-ying she, 1951-52. 5 vols.
張其昀。黨史概要。

Chü-hsiao ti-i ch'i t'ung-hsueh lu.
軍校第一期同學錄。

CMJL

GCJJ

Kuo-fang pu shih cheng chü. Pei fa chan shih.
Taipei: Kuo-fang pu shih cheng chü, 1959. 4
vols.
國防部史政局。北伐戰史。
Kuo-min ko-ming chün chan shih, ed. by Kuo-
min ko-ming chün chan shih pien-tsuan wei-
yuan-hui. Ts'an-mou pen pu, 1934. 17 vols.
國民革命軍戰史。國民革命軍戰史編纂委
員會。
MSICH
T'ao Chü-yin. Chiang Pai-li hsien-sheng chuan.
Shanghai, 1948.
陶菊隱。蔣百里先生傳。
Tung Hsien-kuang. Chiang tsung-t'ung chuan.
Taipei: Chung-hua wen-hua ch'u-pan shih-
yeh wei-yuan-hui. 3 vols.
董顯光。蔣總統傳。

Chiang T'ing-fu   蔣廷黻

WORKS

1923. "Labor and Empire: A Study of the
Reaction of British Labor, Mainly as Represented in Parliament, to British Imperialism
since 1880." Unpublished Ph. D. dissertation,
Columbia University.
1930. Tsu-kuo chu-i lun-ts'ung (tr. of C.J.H.
Hayes's Essays on Nationalism). Shanghai:
Hsin yueh.
族國主義論叢。
1931–34. (ed.) Chin-tai Chung-kuo wai-chiao
shih tzu-liao chi-yao. Shanghai: Shang-wu
yin shu kuan. 2 vols.
近代中國外交史資料輯要。
1945. Shan-huo chiu-chi tsung shu kan shen-mo?
Tsen-yang kan? (ed. by Hsing-cheng yuan
shan-huo chiu-chi tsung shu). Chungking.
善後救濟總署幹什麼？ 怎樣幹？ 行政院善
後救濟總署。
1954. Chuang-kuo chin-tai shih. Hong Kong:
Li ta ch'u-pan she.
中國近代史。
1956. Cheng-p'i chiao-i yü Lien-ho-kuo hsien-
chang; Lien-ho-kuo ta-hui ti-shih chieh
ch'ang-hui Chung-hua Min-kuo chu Lien-ho-
kuo ch'ang-jen tai-piao chi ch'u-hsi an-ch'üan
li-shih-hui tai-piao Chiang T'ing-fu chiu "hsin
hui-yuan ju-hui an" li-tz'u so tso sheng-ming
hui-pien. Taipei: Chu Lien-ho-kuo Chung-
kuo tai-piao t'uan.
整批交易與聯合國憲章； 聯合國大會第十
屆常會中華民國駐聯合國常任代表暨出席

安全理事會代表蔣廷黻就「新會員入會案」
歷次所作聲明彙編。
1959. Chung-kuo chi-tai shih ta-kang. Taipei:
Ch'i ming shu-chü.
中國近代史大綱。
1965. Chiang T'ing-fu hsuan-chi. Taipei: Wen-
hsing shu-tien.
蔣廷黻選集。

SOURCES

Persons interviewed: not to be identified.
The ABMAC Bulletin, XXVI-7, 8 (September,
October, 1965).
CMJL
The New York Times, July 31, 1957; October 11,
1965.

Chiang Tso-pin   蔣作賓

WORKS

1945. Chiang Yü-yen hsien-sheng tzu-chuan.
Chungking.
蔣雨岩先生自傳。

SOURCES

Chiang Tso-pin. Chiang Yü-yen hsien-sheng
tzu-chuan. Chunking, 1945.
蔣作賓。蔣雨岩先生自傳。

Chiang Wei-kuo   蔣緯國

SOURCES

Persons interviewed: not to be identified.
GCJJ

Chien Chao-nan   簡照南

WORKS

1925. (ed.) Nan-yuan ts'ung-shu, shih-erh
chung. Nan-hai.
南園叢書， 十二種。

SOURCES

Chien chün Chao-nan ai wan lu, ed. by Chu
Hsiao-tsang (Tsu-mou). 6 vols.
簡君照南哀輓錄。 朱孝臧(祖謀)。
HCJC
Hua-ch'iao ming-jen chuan, ed. by Chu Hsiu-
hsia. Taipei: Chung-hua wen-hua ch'u-pan
shih-yeh wei-yuan-hui, 1955.
華僑名人傳。 祝秀俠。

Chien Yu-wen   簡又文

WORKS

1935. Hsi-pei tung-nan feng; hsü-chi. Shang-hai: Liang yu t'u-shu yin-shua kung-ssu.
西北東南風；續集。

1935. T'ai-p'ing T'ien-kuo tsa-chi ti-i chi. Shanghai: Shang-wu yin shu kuan.
太平天國雜記第一輯。

1944. Chin-t'ien chih yu chi ch'i-t'a. Shang-wu yin shu kuan.
金田之遊及其他。

1944. T'ai-p'ing chün Kwangsi shou i shih. Chungking: Shang-wu yin shu kuan.
太平軍廣西首義史。

1958. T'ai-p'ing t'ien-kuo tien-chih t'ung-k'ao. Kowloon: Chien shih meng chin shu-wu. 3 vols.
太平天國典制通考。

1960. Chung-kuo chi-tu-chiao te k'ai-shan shih-yeh. Hong Kong: Chi-tu-chiao fu ch'iao ch'u-pan she.
中國基督教的開山事業。

1960. (ed.) Sung huang t'ai chi-nien chi. Hong Kong: Hong Kong Chao tsu tsung-ch'in tsung-hui.
宋皇臺紀念集。

1962. T'ai-p'ing T'ien-kuo ch'üan shih. Kowloon: Meng chin shu-wu. 3 vols.
太平天國全史。

1964. Wu-shih nien lai T'ai-p'ing T'ien-kuo shih chih yen-chiu. Hong Kong: Hong Kong ta-hsueh.
五十年來太平天國史之研究。

1967. Ch'ing shih Hung Hsiu-ch'üan tsai chi. Hong Kong: Chien shih meng chin shu wu.
清史洪秀全載記。

ed. of *I-ching*.
逸經。

ed. of *T'ai-feng*.
颱風。

SOURCES

Persons interviewed: not to be identified.

Ch'ien Hsuan-t'ung   錢玄同

WORKS

1921. Wen-tzu hsueh yin p'ien. Peking: Kuo-li Peking ta-hsueh ch'u-pan pu.
文字學音篇。

1931. Hsin hsueh wei ching k'ao. with K'ang Yu-wei. Peiping: Peiping wen-hua hsueh-she.
新學僞經考。康有爲。

1958. Shuo-wen pu-shou chin tu. Shanghai: Hsin chih-shih ch'u-pan she.
說文部首今讀。

ed. of *Hsin ch'ing-nien*.
新青年。

Shou-wen tuan chu hsiao-chien.
說文段注小箋。

SOURCES

Persons interviewed: not to be identified.
Yen-ching hsueh-pao, 25 (June, 1939): 240-44.
燕京學報。

Ch'ien Mu   錢穆

WORKS

1926. Lun-yü yao-lueh. Shanghai: Shang-wu yin shu kuan.
論語要略。

1931. Kuo-hsueh kai-lun. Shanghai: Shang-wu yin shu kuan.
國學概論。

1931. Mo-tzu. Shanghai: Shang-wu yin shu kuan.
墨子。

1934. Wang Shou-jen. Shanghai: Shang-wu yin shu kuan.
王守仁。

1935. Hsien Ch'in chu tzu hsi nien k'ao pien. Shanghai: Shang-wu yin shu kuan.
先秦諸子繫年考辨。

1943. Wen-hua yü chiao-yü. Chungking: Kuo-min t'u-shu ch'u-pan she.
文化與教育。

1944. (ed.) Huang Ti. Chungking: Cheng-chung shu-chü.
黃帝。

1944. Kuo shih ta-kang. Chungking: Shang-wu yin shu kuan. 2 vols.
國史大綱。

1945. Cheng hsueh ssu-yen. Chungking: Shang-wu yin shu kuan.
政學私言。

1947. Liu Hsiang Hsin fu-tzu nien-p'u. Shanghai: Chung-kuo wen-hua fu-wu she.
劉向歆父子年譜。

1948. Meng-tzu yen-chiu. Shanghai: K'ai-ming shu-tien.
孟子研究。

1949? Chung-kuo-jen chih tsung-chiao she-hui chi jen-sheng-kuan. Kowloon: Tzu-yu Chung-kuo she.
中國人之宗教社會及人生觀。

1950. Chung-kuo ch'uan-t'ung cheng-chih; kuo shih hsin lun chih erh. Hong Kong: Hong Kong Chung-kuo wen-t'i yen-chiu so.
中國傳統政治；國史新論之二。

1950. Chung-kuo she-hui yen-pien; kuo shih hsin lun chih i. Hong Kong: Chung-kuo wen-t'i yen-chiu so.
中國社會演變；國史新論之一。

1951. Chung-kuo ssu-hsiang shih. Taipei: Chung-hua wen-hua ch'u-pan shih-yeh wei-yuan-hui.
中國思想史。

1951. Chung-kuo wen-hua shih tao lun. Taipei: Cheng-chung shu-chü.
中國文化史導論。

1952. Wen-hua hsueh ta-i. Taipei: Cheng-chung shu-chü.
文化學大義。

1953. Ssu-shu shih-i. Taipei: Chung-hua wen-hua ch'u-pan shih-yeh wei-yuan hui. 2 vols.
四書釋義。

1953. Sung Ming li-hsueh kai-shu. Taipei: Chung-hua wen-hua ch'u-pan shih-yeh wei-yuan-hui. 2 vols.
宋明理學概述。

1954. Chung-kuo li-shih ching-shen. Taipei: Kuo-min ch'u-pan she.
中國歷史精神。

1955. Chung-kuo ssu-hsiang t'ung-su chiang-hua. Kowloon: Ch'iu ching yin-wu kung-ssu.
中國思想通俗講話。

1955. Kuo shih hsin lun. Kowloon: Ch'iu ching yin wu kung-ssu.
國史新論。

1955. Yang-ming hsueh shu-yao. Taipei: Cheng-chung shu-chü.
陽明學述要。

1956. Ch'ien Mu et al. Chung-kuo hsueh-shu shih lun-chi. Taipei: Chung-hua wen-hua ch'u-pan shih-yeh wei-yuan-hui.
錢穆等。中國學術史論集。

1956. Chung-kuo li-tai cheng-chih te-shih. Hong Kong: Hsin hua yin-shua ku-fen kung-ssu.
中國歷代政治得失。

1956. Hsien Ch'in chu tzu hsi nien. Hong Kong: Hong Kong ta-hsueh ch'u-pan she.
先秦諸子繫年。

1957. Ch'in Han shih. Hong Kong: Hsin hua yin-shua ku-fen kung-ssu.
秦漢史。

1957. Chuang Lao t'ung pien. Kowloon: Hsin ya yen-chiu so.
莊老通辨。

1957. Chung-kuo chin san-pai nien hsueh-shu shih. Taipei: Taiwan shang-wu yin shu kuan.
中國近三百年學術史。

1957. Yang-ming hsien-sheng ch'uan-hsi-lu ta hsueh-wen chieh-pen. Kowloon: Jen-sheng ch'u-pan she.
陽明先生傳習錄大學問節本。

1958. Hsueh Yueh. Hong Kong: Nan t'ien shu yeh kung-ssu.
學籥。

1958. Liang Han ching-hsueh chin ku wen p'ing-i. Kowloon: Hsin ya yen-chiu so.
兩漢經學今古文平議。

1960. Hu shang hsien ssu lu. Kowloon: Jen-sheng ch'u-pan she.
湖上閒思錄。

1961. Chung-kuo li-shih yen-chiu fa. Kowloon: Meng shih chiao-yü chi-chin hui.
中國歷史研究法。

1962. Min-tsu yü wen-hua. Hong Kong: Hsin ya shu-yuan.
民族與文化。

1963. Chung-kuo wen-hsueh chiang-yen chi. Kowloon: Jen-sheng ch'u-pan she.
中國文學講演集。

1963. Jen-sheng shih lun. Hong Kong: Jen sheng ch'u-pan she.
人生十論。

1964. Lun-yü hsin chieh. Kowloon: Hsin ya yen-chiu so. 2 vols.
論語新解。

SOURCES

Ch'ien Mu. Ch'in Han shih. Hong Kong: Hsin hua yin-shua ku-fen kung-ssu, 1957.
錢穆。秦漢史。
———. Chuang Lao t'ung pien. Kowloon: Hsin ya yen-chiu so, 1957.
錢穆。莊老通辨。
———. Chung-kuo chin san-pai nien hsueh-shu shih. Taipei: Taiwan shang-wu yin shu kuan, 1957.
錢穆。中國近三百年學術史。
———. Chung-kuo ssu-hsiang shih. Taipei: Chung-hua wen-hua ch'u-pan shih-yeh wei-yuan-hui.
錢穆。中國思想史。
———. Chung-kuo wen-hua shih tao-lun. Taipei: Cheng-chung shu-chü, 1951.
錢穆。中國文化史導論。

Ch'ien Mu. Hsien Ch'in chut zu hsi nien. Hong Kong: Hong Kong ta-hsueh ch'u-pan she, 1956.

錢穆。先秦諸子繫年。

———. Kuo-hsueh kai-lun. Shanghai: Shang-wu yin shu kuan, 1931.

錢穆。國學概論。

———. Kuo shih ta-kang. Chungking: Shang-wu yin shu kuan, 1944. 2 vols.

錢穆。國史大綱。

———. Liang Han ching-hsueh chin ku wen p'ing-i. Kowloon: Hsin ya yen-chiu so, 1958.

錢穆。兩漢經學今古文平議。

———. Sung Ming li-hsueh kai-shu. Taipei: Chung-hua wen-hua ch'u-pan shih-yeh wei-yuan-hui, 1953. 2 vols.

錢穆。宋明理學概述。

———. Ssu-shu shih-i. Taipei: Chung-hua wen-hua ch'u-pan shih-yeh wei-yuan hui, 1953. 2 vols.

錢穆。四書釋義。

———. Yang-ming hsueh shu-yao. Taipei: Cheng-chung shu-chü, 1955.

錢穆。陽明學述要。

Ch'ien San-ch'iang   錢三強

SOURCES

Persons interviewed: not to be identified.

Ch'ien Ta-chün   錢大鈞

WORKS

1963. Ch'ien Mu-yin shang-chiang ch'i-shih tzu-chuan. Taipei.

錢慕尹上將七十自傳。

SOURCES

BKL
Ch'ien Ta-chün. Ch'ien Mu-yin shang-chiang ch'i-shih tzu-chuan. Taipei, 1963.

錢大鈞。錢慕尹上將七十自傳。

CMJL
CTMC
MSICH
Pawtucket Times. Pawtucket-Central Falls, R.I., August 22, 1957.

Ch'ien Tuan-sheng   錢端升

WORKS

1927, February. "Mei-kuo tui Hua te wai-chiao." *Hsien-tai p'ing-lun*, V-133: 5-9.

美國對華的外交。現代評論。

1927. April. "Shou-hui Shanghai tsu-chieh te p'o-ch'ieh." *Hsien-tai p'ing-lun*, V-122: 5.

收回上海租界的迫切。現代評論。

1934. Fa-kuo te cheng-fu. Shanghai: Shang-wu yin shu kuan.

法國的政府。

1934. Te-kuo te cheng-fu. Shanghai: Shang-wu yin shu kuan.

德國的政府。

1939. Ch'ien Tuan-sheng *et al*. (ed.). Min-kuo cheng chih shih. Changsha: Shang-wu yin shu kuan. 2 vols.

錢端升等。民國政制史。

1943, December. "Wartime Local Government in China." *Pacific Affairs*, XVI-4: 441-60.

1947. Chan hou shih-chieh chih kai-tsao. Shanghai: Shang-wu yin shu kuan.

戰後世界之改造。

1948, September. "The Role of the Military in Chinese Government." *Pacific Affairs*, XXI-3: 239-51.

1950. The Government and Politics of China. Cambridge: Harvard University Press.

1952, July-August. "How the People's Government Works." *China Reconstructs*, 4: 8-12.

1952-58. ed. of *China Reconstructs*.

1954, August. "Chinese-British Friendship." *People's China*, 16: 14-21.

1956. Tzu-ch'an chieh-chi hsien-fa te fan-tung pen-chih. with Lou Pang-yen. Wuhan: Hupeh jen-min ch'u-pan she.

資產階級憲法的反動本質。樓邦彥。

1957, August 6. "Wo te tsui-hsing." *Jen-min jih-pao*.

我的罪行。人民日報。

SOURCES

"Ch'ien Tuan-sheng shih cheng fa hsueh-chieh te yu p'ai yin-mou chia." *Jen-min jih-pao*. Peking, July 20, 1957.

錢端升是政法學界的右派陰謀家。人民日報。

GCJJ
Johnson, Chalmers A. "An Intellectual Weed in the Socialist Garden: The Case of Ch'ien Tuan-sheng." *China Quarterly*, 6 (April-June, 1961).

Ch'ien Yung-ming   錢永銘

SOURCES

Person interviewed: Chang Chia-ao.

Chin Shu-jen   金樹仁

SOURCES

Chang Ta-chün. Sinkiang chin ssu-shih nien pien-luan chi-lueh. Taipei: Chung-yang wen-wu kung-ying she, 1954.
張大軍。新疆近四十年變亂紀略。
Hung Ti-ch'en. Sinkiang shih ti ta-kang. Chungking: Cheng-chung shu-chü, 1939.
洪滌塵。新疆史地大綱。
Tseng Wen-wu. Chung-kuo ching-ying hsi-yü shih. Shanghai: Shang-wu yin shu kuan, 1936.
曾問吾。中國經營西域史。
Whiting, Allen S., and Sheng Shih-ts'ai. Sinkiang: Pawn or Pivot? East Lansing: Michigan State University Press, 1958.

CKLC
GCCJK
GCJ
RNRC
RSOC
Schwartz, Benjamin I. Chinese Communism and the Rise of Mao. Cambridge: Harvard University Press, 1951.
"Ssu-pa" pei-nan lieh-shih chi-nien-ts'e, ed. by Chung-kuo kung-ch'an-tang tai-piao t'uan. 1946.
「四八」被難烈士紀念冊。中國共產黨代表團。
Nym Wales (pseud. of Helen Foster Snow). Inside Red China. New York: Doubleday, Doran & Co., 1939.
WWMC

Chin Yün-p'eng   靳雲鵬

SOURCES

BPC
CMMC
CMTC
Li Chien-nung. The Political History of China 1840-1928 (tr. and ed. by Teng Ssu-yu, Jeremy Ingalls). Princeton: D. Van Nostrand Co., 1956.
WWC, 1925, 1931.

Ch'in Pang-hsien   秦邦憲

WORKS

1930. ed. of Kung-jen hsiao-pao.
工人小報。
1930. ed. of Lao-tung pao.
勞動報。
1933. Lien kung tang shih yü Lieh-ning chu-i. Ma-k'o-ssu kung-ch'an chu-i hsueh-hsiao chiao-yü ch'u.
聯共黨史與列寧主義。
1941-? ed. of Chieh-fang jih-pao.
解放日報。

SOURCES

Person interviewed: Chang Kuo-t'ao.
Bertram, James M. First Act in China: The Story of the Sian Mutiny. New York: The Viking Press, 1938.
Chin-pu jih-pao. Tientsin, July 13, 1951.
進步日報。

Ch'in Te-ch'un   秦德純

WORKS

1967. Ch'in Te-ch'un hui-i-lu. Taipei: Chuan-chi wen-hsueh tsa-chih she.
秦德純回憶錄。

SOURCES

CH
Chung-yang jih-pao. Taipei, September 8, 1963.
中央日報。
CMJL
CTMC
GCJJ
TCJC

Chou Ch'ang-ling   周長齡

SOURCES

Persons interviewed: not to be identified.
P. & T. Sunday Times, August 6, 1933.

Chou Chih-jou   周至柔

WORKS

1943. Fei-hsing-yuan shou-ts'e. Chungking: Ch'ing-nien ch'u-pan she.
飛行員手冊。
1945. K'ung-chün shih nien. Chungking.
空軍十年。
1959. Taiwan sheng cheng-fu chan-wang. Taipei: Taiwan sheng hsin-wen ch'u.

台灣省政府展望。
Chih-jou hung-chao. Taipei. 2 vols.
至柔鴻爪。

SOURCES

AWW, 1960.
BKL
CH–T, 1956–57.
CMJL
CTMC
GCJJ

Chou En-lai   周恩來

WORKS

1924. "Hsin-ch'ou t'iao-yueh yü ti-kuo chu-i,"
in Kao Erh-sung and Kao Erh-po, *Ti-kuo chu-i yü Chung-kuo*. Shanghai: Hsin wen-hua shu-she.
辛丑條約與帝國主義。高爾松，高爾柏。
帝國主義與中國。

1926. Wo-men hsien-tsai wei shen-mo tou-cheng. with Ch'en Tu-hsiu. Canton: Jen-min chou-k'an she.
我們現在為甚麼鬥爭。陳獨秀。

1929. Mu-ch'ien Chung-kuo tang te tsu-chih wen-t'i.
目前中國黨的組織問題。

1931. "Shao-shan pao-kao; tsai san ch'üan k'uo-ta hui chung kuan-yü ch'uan-ta kuo-chi chueh-i te pao-kao." (mimeo.)
少山報告；在三全擴大會中關於傳達國際決議的報告。

1938. Lun mu-ch'ien k'ang chan hsing-shih. Hankow: Hsin hua jih-pao kuan.
論目前抗戰形勢。

1938. Ti-erh ch'i k'ang chan chi chiang-lai. Chieh-fang she.
第二期抗戰及將來。

1939. Tsui-chin yen-lun. with Teng Ying-ch'ao. Canton: Li-so ch'u-pan she.
最近言論。鄧穎超。

1941. Lun Su Te chan-cheng chi ch'i-t'a. Ch'ing niao ch'u-pan she.
論蘇德戰爭及其他。

1941? T'uan-chieh ch'i-lai ta ti-jen. Shanghai: Huan-ch'iu.
團結起來打敵人。

1944. Chou En-lai *et al*. Kuan-yü hsien-cheng yü t'uan-chieh wen-t'i. Po-chung she.
周恩來等。關於憲政與團結問題。

1950. China Advances: A Report to a Meeting of the People's Political Consultative Conference Held in Commemoration of the Founding of the People's Republic of China. London: Britain-China Friendship Association.

1950. The First Year of the People's China. Bombay: People's Publishing House.

1950. Wei kung-ku ho fa-chan jen-min te sheng-li erh fen-tou. Canton: Hsin hua shu-tien.
為鞏固和發展人民的勝利而奮鬥。

1952. Fan t'an-wu, fan lang-fei, f'an kuan-liao chu-i. Peking: Jen-min ch'u-pan she.
反貪污，反浪費，反官僚主義。

1953. Tsai Chung-kuo jen-min cheng-chih hsieh-shang hui-i ti-i chieh ch'üan-kuo wei-yuan-hui ti-ssu tz'u hui-i shang te cheng-chih pao-kao. Peking: Jen-min ch'u-pan she.
在中國人民政治協商會議第一屆全國委員會第四次會議上的政治報告。

1954. Cheng-fu kung-tso pao-kao; tsai Chung-hua Jen-min Kung-ho-kuo ti-i chieh ch'üan-kuo jen-min tai-piao ta-hui ti-i tz'u hui-i shang te pao-kao. Peking: Jen-min ch'u-pan she.
政府工作報告；在中華人民共和國第一屆全國人民代表大會第一次會議上的報告。
Eng. tr., *Report on the Work of the Government; Made at the First Session of the First National People's Congress of the People's Republic of China, September 23, 1954*. Peking: Foreign Languages Press, 1954.

1954. Chou En-lai *et al*. Chieh-fang Taiwan shih Chung-kuo jen-min te shen-sheng jen-wu. Hankow: Hupeh jen-min ch'u-pan she.
周恩來等。解放台灣是中國人民的神聖任務。

1954. Report on Foreign Affairs at the 33rd Session of the Central People's Government Council. Peking.

1954. Statement at the Geneva Conference. Peking?

1955. Mu-ch'ien kuo-chi hsing-shih ho wo kuo wai-chiao cheng-ts'e—i-chiu-wu-wu nien ch'i-yueh san-shih jih tsai ti-i chieh ch'üan-kuo jen-min tai-piao ta-hui ti-erh tz'u hui-i shang te fa-yen. Peking: Jen-min ch'u-pan she.
目前國際形勢和我國外交政策——一九五五年七月三十日在第一屆全國人民代表大會第二次會議上的發言。

1956. Cheng-chih pao-kao; 1956 nien 1 yueh 30 jih tsai Chung-kuo jen-min cheng-chih hsieh-shang hui-i ti-erh chieh ch'üan-kuo wei-yuan-hui ti-erh tz'u ch'üan-t'i hui-i shang. Peking: Jen-min ch'u-pan she.

政治報告；1956 年 1 月 30 日在中國人民政治協商會議第二屆全國委員會第二次全體會議上。

Eng. tr., *Political Report; Delivered at the Second Session of the Second National Committee of the Chinese People's Political Consultative Conference on January 30, 1956*. Peking: Foreign Languages Press, 1956.

1956. Kuan-yü mu-ch'ien kuo-chi hsing-shih, wo-kuo wai-chiao cheng-ts'e ho chieh-fang Taiwan wen-t'i; 1956 nien 6 yueh 28 jih tsai ti-i chieh ch'üan-kuo jen-min tai-piao ta-hui ti-san tz'u hui-i shang te fa yen. Peking: Jen-min ch'u-pan she.

關於目前國際形勢，我國外交政策和解放台灣問題；1956 年 6 月 28 日在第一屆全國人民代表大會第三次會議上的發言。

Eng. tr., *On Present International Situation, China's Foreign Policy, and the Liberation of Taiwan; Delivered at the Third Session of the First National People's Congress on June 28, 1956*. Peking: Foreign Languages Press, 1956.

1956. "Report on the Proposals for the second Five Year Plan for Development of the National Economy," in Chung-kuo kung-ch'an-tang, *Proposals of the Eighth National Congress of the Communist Party of China for the Second Five-year Plan for Development of the National Economy, 1958–62*.

1956. Report on the Question of Intellectuals, Delivered on January 14, 1956, at a Meeting Held Under the Auspices of the Central Committee of the Communist Party of China. Peking: Foreign Languages Press.

1957. Cheng-fu kung-tso pao-kao—i-chiu-wu-ch'i nien liu-yueh erh-shih-liu jih tsai ti-i cheih ch'üan-kuo jen-min tai-piao ta-hui ti-ssu tz'u hui-i shang. Peking: Jen-min ch'u-pan she.

政府工作報告一一九五七年六月二十六日在第一屆全國人民代表大會第四次會議上。

1958. Mu-ch'ien kuo-chi hsing-shih ho wo kuo wai-chiao cheng-ts'e. Peking: Shih-chieh chih-shih ch'u-pan she.

目前國際形勢和我國外交政策。

1958. Tang-ch'ien wen-tzu kai-ko te jen-wu; 1958 nien 1 yueh 10 jih tsai cheng hsieh ch'üan-kuo wei-yuan-hui chü-hsing te pao-kao hui shang te pao-kao. Peking: Jen-min ch'u-pan she.

當前文字改革的任務；1958 年 1 月 10 日在政協全國委員會舉行的報告會上的報告。

1959. Cheng-fu kung-tso pao-kao; i-chiu-wu-chiu nien ssu-yueh shih-pa jih tsai ti-erh chieh ch'üan-kuo jen-min tai-piao ta-hui ti-i tz'u hui-i shang. Peking: Jen-min ch'u-pan she.

政府工作報告；一九五九年四月十八日在第二屆全國人民代表大會第一次會議上。

Eng. tr., *Report on the Work of the Government; Delivered at the First Session of the Second National People's Congress on April 18, 1959*. Peking: Foreign Languages Press, 1959.

1959. A Great Decade. Peking: Foreign Languages Press.

1959. Report on Adjusting the Major Targets of the 1959 National Economic Plan and Further Developing the Campaign for Increasing Production and Practising Economy; Delivered at the Fifth Meeting of the Standing Committee of the Second National People's Congress on August 26, 1959. Peking: Foreign Languages Press.

1965, November 5. "Chou En-lai Sends Letter to Bertrand Russell." *Peking Review*, 45: 16.

ed. of *Chiu-kuo jih-pao*.

救國日報。

ed. of *Ch'ih kuang*.

赤光。

SOURCES

Persons interviewed: Chang Kuo-t'ao, Hsü Po-ch'i, Li T'ien-min.

A Ta (pseud.) *et al*. Ch'ang cheng ku-shih. Hong Kong: Hsin min-chu, 1949.

阿大等。長征故事。

Band, Claire and William. Two Years with the Chinese Communists. New Haven: Yale University Press, 1948.

Brandt, Conrad. "The French Returned Elite in the Chinese Communist Party," in E.F. Szczepanik, *Symposium on Economic and Social Problems of the Far East*. Hong Kong: Hong Kong University Press, 1962.

Brandt, Conrad, Benjamin Schwartz, and John K. Fairbank. A Documentary History of Chinese Communism. Cambridge: Harvard University Press, 1952.

Chang, Carsun (Chang Chia-sen). The Third Force in China. New York: Bookman Associates, 1952.

Chang Kuo-t'ao. "Chou En-lai is 'Round' Man." *The New York Time Magazine*, April 25, 1954.

Chao Chün-hui. Hung chün shih nien. Shanghai: Hsin sheng-huo ch'u-pan she, 1938.
趙君輝。 紅軍十年。

Chao Kuan-i and Wei Tan-po. Chung-kung jen-wu su-miao. Hong Kong: Tzu-yu ch'u-pan she, 1951.
趙貫一， 韋丹柏。 中共人物素描。

Cheng-chih hsieh-shang hui tai-piao ch'ün-hsiang. Shanghai: Shanghai t'u-shu kung-ying she, 1946.
政治協商會代表群像。

Chiang Kai-shek. Soviet Russia in China: A Summing-up at Seventy. New York: Farrar, Straus, & Cudahy, 1957.

Chow Tse-tsung. The May Fourth Movement: Intellectual Revolution in Modern China. Cambridge: Harvard University Press, 1960.

Ch'ü Ch'iu-pai. Chung-kuo ko-ming yü kung-ch'an-tang: Kuan-yü i-chiu-erh-wu nien chih i-chiu-erh-ch'i nien Chung-kuo ko-ming te pao-kao. Chung-kuo kung-ch'an-tang, 1928.
瞿秋白。 中國革命與共產黨： 關於一九二五年至一九二七年中國革命的報告。

Chung kung jen-wu. Shanghai: She-hui ch'u-pan she, 1949.
中共人物。

Chung kung nei-mu, ed. by Sheng-li ch'u-pan she wen-hua tzu-liao shih. Shanghai: Sheng-li ch'u-pan she wen-hua tzu-liao shih, 1946.
中共內幕。 勝利出版社文化資料室。

Chung-kuo kung-ch'an-tang chien shih. Peking: Hsueh-hsi tsa-chih she, 1952.
中國共產黨簡史。

Chung-kuo kung-ch'an-tang shih-lueh, comp. by Li Chih-kung. T'ung-i ch'u-pan she, 1942.
中國共產黨史略。 李致工。

Chung pao she. Huo min p'an-kuo chi. Hong Kong: Hai-wai shu-tien, 1947.
忠報社。 禍民叛國記。

CKJMT

"Communist Ace Diplomat Usually Gets What He Wants." U.S. News and World Report, May 6, 1955: 71-73.

Durdin, Tillman, " 'Marxist Mandarin' on Another Sales Trip." The New York Times Magazine, April 24, 1960.

Elegant Robert S. China's Red Masters. New York: Twayne, 1951.

Epstein et al. Mao Tse-tung tsai Chungking. Shanghai: Ho-chung ch'u-pan she, 1946.
毛澤東在重慶。

Erh wan wu ch'ien li ch'ang cheng; ti pa lu chün hung chün shih-tai te shih-shih, comp. by Chiu wang yen-chiu she. Shanghai: Chiu wang yen-chiu she, 1937.
二萬五千里長征； 第八路軍紅軍時代的史實。 救亡研究社。

Feng Chü-p'ei. K'ang chan chung te ti-wu lu chün. Hankow, 1938.
馮菊培。 抗戰中的第五路軍。

Fitzgerald, C.P. Revolution in China. London: Cresset, 1952.

GCCJK

GCJJ

Hai-wai kung tu shih-nien chi-shih, comp. by Sheng Ch'eng. Shanghai: Chung-hua shu-chü, 1932.
海外工讀十年紀實。 盛成。

Hatano Kén-ichi. "Chou En-lai and Yen-an's Attitude." Contemporary Japan, XI-8 (August, 1942): 1145-55.

HCJC

Ho Kan-chih. A History of the Modern Chinese Revolution. Peking: Foreign Languages Press, 1959.

Hsien-chin te Fei-chou, yu-i te hai-yang—Chou En-lai tsung-li fang-wen Fei-chou shih kuo t'ung-hsin chi, ed. by Shih-chieh chih-shih ch'u-pan she. Peking: Shih-chieh chih-shih ch'u-pan she, 1964.
先進的非洲， 友誼的海洋─周恩來總理訪問非洲十國通訊集。 世界知識出版社。

Hsin-k'o-lai (Upton Sinclair) et al. Ti-pa lu chün te kan-pu jen-wu chien-ying. Chan-shih ch'u-pan she.
辛克萊等。 第八路軍的幹部人物剪影。

Hsueh Shao-ming. Ch'ien Tien Ch'uan lü-hsing chi. Hong Kong: Chung-hua shu-chü, 1938.
薛紹銘。 黔滇川旅行記。

HSWT

Hu Ch'iao-mu. Chung-kuo kung-ch'an-tang san-shih nien. Peking: Jen-min ch'u-pan she, 1951.
胡喬木。 中國共產黨三十年。

Hu Hua. Chung-kuo hsin min-chu chu-i ko-ming shih. Peking: Jen-min ch'u-pan she, 1951.
胡華。 中國新民主主義革命史。

Hua Kang. 1925 nien chih 1927 nien te Chung-kuo ta ko-ming shih. Shanghai: Ch'un keng shu-tien, 1932.
華崗。 1925 年至 1927 年的中國大革命史。

Huang Yen-p'ei. Yenan kuei-lai. Chungking: Kuo hsin shu-tien, 1945.
黃炎培。 延安歸來。

Hughes, Richard. "Peking's 'Indispensable Man'." *The New York Times Magazine*, October 4, 1964.

Hung ch'i, 1929–31.
紅旗。

Hung ch'i chou-pao, 1931–34; 1936.
紅旗週報。

Jaffe, Sam. "Chou Talks to the West." *Nation*, May 7, 1955.

Jen-min jih-pao. Peking, January 2, 1963.
人民日報。

Kan Yu-lan. Mao Tse-tung chi ch'i chi-t'uan. Hong Kong: Tzu-yu ch'u-pan she, 1954.
甘友蘭。毛澤東及其集團。

K–WWMC

Li Tien-min. "Chou En-lai—a Profile." *Issues & Studies*, I–9 (June, 1965): 42–49.

Liu Shao-ch'i, Chou En-lai. Chu Te t'ung-chih tsai ch'ün-chung chung. Peking: Jen-min ch'u-pan she.
劉少奇，周恩來。朱德同志在群眾中。

Liu-yueh i-lai kuo kung t'an-p'an chung-yao wen-hsien.
六月以來國共談判重要文獻。

Look, April 16, 1957; January, 1961.

MacFarquhar, Roderik L. "The Whampoa Military Academy." *Papers on China*, IX (August, 1955): 146–72. (Duplicated for private distribution by the East Asia Program of the Committee on Regional Studies, Harvard University.)

McLane, Charles B. Soviet Policy and the Chinese Communists, 1931–1946. New York: Columbia University Press, 1958.

Mao Tse-tung. Selected Works. New York: International Publishers, 1956–62. 5 vols.

Mao Tse-tung, comp. by Kirin shu-tien. Kirin shu-tien, 1948.
毛澤東。吉林書店。

The New York Times. September 17, 1939; March 26, 1940; January 29, 1959; April 2, 1965.

North, Robert C. Moscow and the Chinese Communists. Stanford: Stanford University Press, 1953.

Pai Shui. Chou En-lai yü Teng Ying-ch'ao. Hankow: I hsing shu-tien, 1938.
白水。周恩來與鄧穎超。

RD

"Red China's Big Three." *Senior Scholastic*, October 25, 1956.

RNRC

Rowe, David N. China: An Area Manual, I, ORO. The Johns Hopkins University, 1953.

RSOC

Scalapino, Robert A., and George T. Yu. The Chinese Anarchist Movement. Berkeley: University of California Press, 1961.

Schwartz, Benjamin I. Chinese Communism and the Rise of Mao. Cambridge: Harvard University Press, 1951.

Shu Hsin-ch'eng. Chin-tai Chung-kuo liu-hsueh shih. Shanghai: Chung-hua shu-chü, 1929.
舒新城。近代中國留學史。

Smedley, Agnes. The Great Road: The Life and Times of Chu Teh. New York: Monthly Review Press, 1956.

Snow, Edgar. The Other Side of the River. New York: Random House, 1962.

———. "Red China's Gentleman Hatchet Man." *Saturday Evening Post*, 226 (March 27, 1954).

Ssu-ma Hsien-tao. Pei-fa hou chih ko-p'ai ssu-ch'ao. Peiping: Ying shan she, 1930.
司馬仙島。北伐後之各派思潮。

Stein, Guenther. The Challenge of Red China. New York: McGraw-Hill Book Co., 1945.

Stuart, John Leighton. Fifty Years in China. New York: Random House, 1954.

TCMC

Time, June 18, 1951; May 10, 1954.

Tseng Ch'i. "Lü Ou jih-chi," in Tseng Ch'i, *Tseng Mu-han hsien-sheng i-chu*. Taipei: Chung-kuo ch'ing-nien-tang chung-yang chih-hsing wei-yuan-hui, 1954.
曾琦。旅歐日記。曾琦。曾慕韓先生遺著。

Tso Shun-sheng. Chin san-shih nien chien-wen tsa-chi. Hong Kong: Tzu-yu ch'u-pan she, 1952.
左舜生。近三十年見聞雜記。

———. Chung-kuo hsien-tai ming-jen i-shih. Hong Kong: Tzu-yu ch'u-pan she, 1951.
左舜生。中國現代名人軼事。

Wang P'ei-huai. Ko-ming te po-chien. Kiangsi: Wei huang she, 1936.
王培槐。革命的寶劍。

Who's Who of the Chinese Government Service, IV–1 (February, 1926).

Wu Ming. Kung tang yao-jen su-miao. Shanghai: Min-tsu chieh-fang she, 1937.
吳明。共黨要人素描。

Chou Fo-hai   周佛海

WORKS

1921, January. "Lao nung O-kuo te nung-yeh chih-tu." *Hsin ch'ing-nien*, VIII–5.

勞農俄國的農業制度。新青年。

1921, January. "Shih-hsing she-hui chu-i ho fa-
chan shih-yeh." *Hsin ch'ing-nien*, VIII-5.
實行社會主義和發展實業。新青年。

1921, April. "Chin-tai wen ming ti-hsia te yi
chung kuai hsien-hsiang." *Hsin ch'ing-nien*,
IX-1.
近代文明底下的一種怪現象。新青年。

1921, June. "She-hui chu-i kuo-chia yü lao-tung
tsu-ho." *Hsin ch'ing-nien*, IX-2.
社會主義國家與勞働組合。新青年。

1921, June. "Ts'ung tzu-pen chu-i tsu-chih tao
she-hui chu-i tsu-chih ti liang t'iao lu—chin-
hua yü ko-ming." *Hsin ch'ing-nien*, IX-2.
從資本主義組織到社會主義組織底兩條路
一進化與革命。新青年。

1921, September. "Ko-ming ting yao ta-to-shu
jen lai kan ma?" *Hsin ch'ing-nien*, IX-5.
革命定要大多數人來幹嗎？新青年。

1922, July. "Tzu-yu chih yü ch'iang-chih—
p'ing-teng yü tu-ts'ai." *Hsin ch'ing-nien*, IX-6.
自由制與强制一平等與獨裁。新青年。

1924. Ching-chi hsueh shih kai-lun (tr.). Shanghai: Shang-wu yin shu kuan.
經濟學史概論。

1924. Kuo-chi shang-yeh cheng-ts'e (tr.) Shanghai: Shang-wu yin shu kuan.
國際商業政策。

1925. Chung-shan hsien-sheng ssu-hsiang kai-
kuan. Shanghai: Min chih shu-chü.
中山先生思想概觀。

1927. Kuo-chi t'ou-tzu ch'ien-shuo. Shanghai:
Shang-wu yin shu kuan.
國際投資淺說。

1928. San min chu-i chih li-lun te t'i-hsi.
Shanghai: Hsin sheng-ming yueh-k'an she.
三民主義之理論的體系。

1928. Shang-yeh ching-chi kai-lun. (tr.) Shanghai: Shang-wu yin shu kuan.
商業經濟概論。

1928-? ed. of *Hsin sheng-ming yueh-k'an*.
新生命月刊。

1929, January. "Tsung-li tsai Chung-kuo li-shih
shang te ti-wei." *Hsin sheng-ming*, II-6.
總理在中國歷史上的地位。新生命。

1929. San min chu-i te chi-pen wen-t'i. Shanghai: Hsin sheng-ming shu-chü.
三民主義的基本問題。

1930. Ching-chi li-lun chih chi-ch'u chih-shih.
Shanghai: Hsin sheng-ming shu-chü.
經濟理論之基礎知識。

1930. Ko kuo ching-chi shih. (tr.) Shanghai:
Hsin sheng-ming shu-chü.

各國經濟史。

1933. Wu-chia wen-t'i. Shanghai: Shang-wu
yin shu kuan.
物價問題。

1934. She-hui wen-t'i kai-kuan. (tr.) Shanghai:
Chung-hua shu-chü.
社會問題概觀。

1944. Wang i chi (ed. by Chou Li-an). Shanghai: Ku-chin ch'u-pan she.
往矣集。周黎庵。

1955. Chou Fo-hai jih-chi. Hong Kong:
Ch'uang k'en ch'u-pan she.
周佛海日記。

1956. Sheng shuai yueh chin hua ts'ang-sang.
Hong Kong: Wen-hua shu-chü.
盛衰閱盡話滄桑。

Chin-jung ching-chi kai-lun. Shanghai: Shang-
wu yin shu kuan.
金融經濟概論。

SOURCES

Person interviewed: Chang Kuo-t'ao.

CBJS

Chou Fo-hai. Chou Fo-hai jih-chi. Hong Kong:
Ch'uang k'en ch'u-pan she, 1955.
周佛海。周佛海日記。

———. "Tzu hsü." *Hsin sheng-ming*, January,
1928.
周佛海。自序。新生命。

———. Wang i chi (ed. by Chou Li-an).
Shanghai: Ku-chin ch'u-pan she, 1944.
周佛海。往己集。周黎庵。

Chu Chia. "Yu ta nan pu ssu pi yu hou-fu t'an-
tao T'ang Shou-min yü Chou Fo-hai." *Chin-
shan shih-pao*, San Francisco, November 29,
1956.
朱家。由大難不死必有後福談到唐壽民與
周佛海。金山時報。

Chu Tzu-chia (pseud. of Chin Hsiung-pai).
"Wang chen-ch'üan shih-liao pu-p'ien."
Ch'un-ch'iu, 147, 150, 151.
朱子家（金雄白）。汪政權史料補篇。春秋。

———. Wang cheng-ch'üan te k'ai-ch'ang yü
shou-ch'ang. Hong Kong: Ch'un-ch'iu tsa-
chih she, 1964. 5 vols.
朱子家（金雄白）。汪政權的開場收塲。

GCJ

GCMMTJK

GSSJ

I Chün-tso. Hui-meng san-shih nien. Singapore:
Ch'uang k'en ch'u-pan she, 1954.
易君左。迴夢三十年。

Lei Hsiao-ts'en. San-shih nien tung-luan

Chung-kuo. Hong Kong: Ya-chou ch'u-pan she, 1955.
雷嘯岑。三十年動亂中國。
RSOC
T'ao Hsi-sheng. "Luan liu." *Chuan-chi wen-hsueh*, II-4, 5.
陶希聖。亂流。傳記文學。

Chou Hsueh-hsi   周學熙

SOURCES

AADC
Carlson, Ellsworth C. The Kaiping Mines (1877–1912). Cambridge: Chinese Economic and Political Studies, Harvard University; distributed by Harvard University Press, 1957.
Chia Shih-i. Min-kuo ts'ai-cheng shih. Shanghai: Shang-wu yin shu kuan, 1917. 2 vols.
賈士毅。民國財政史。
Chou Fu. "Tzu chu nien-p'u," in *Chou K'o-shen kung ch'üan-chi*. 1922.
周馥。自著年譜。周慤慎公全集。
Chou Shu-chen. Chou Chih-an hsien-sheng pieh-chuan. Peiping, 1948.
周叔媜。周止庵先生別傳。
CJC
CYB-W, 1926.
Ma Ch'i-ch'ang. Pao-jun-hsuan wen-chi. Peking, 1923. 4 vols.
馬其昶。抱潤軒文集。
Pei-yang kung-tu lei-tsuan, ed. by Kan Hou-tz'u. Peking, 1907. 20 vols.
北洋公牘類纂。甘厚慈。
San-shui Liang Yen-sun hsien-sheng (1869–1933) nien-p'u, ed. by Ch'üeh Ming. 1946. 2 vols.
三水梁燕孫先生 (1869–1933) 年譜。闕名。
Wang I-t'ang. "Chin ch'uan shih lou shih-hua." *Kuo wen chou-pao*, IV-25 (July 3, 1927).
王揖唐。今傳是樓詩話。國聞週報。
Yao Yung-p'u. Shui ssu hsuan chi. 1921.
姚永樸。蛻私軒集。

Chou I-ch'un   周詒春

SOURCES

Person interviewed: Franklin L. Ho.
CH
Chang Ch'i-yün *et al.* Chung-hua Min-kuo ta-hsueh chih. Taipei: Chung-hua wen-hua ch'u-pan shih-yeh wei-yuan-hui, 1954. 2 vols.
張其昀等。中華民國大學誌。

Ch'üan kuo yin-hang nien-chien. Shanghai, 1934.
全國銀行年鑑。
CYB-W, 1924, 1925.
Edwards, Dwight Woodbridge. Yenching University. New York: United Board for Christian Higher Education in Asia, 1959.
Handbook of Cultural Institutions in China, ed. and comp. by Chuang Wen-ya. Shanghai: Chinese National Committee on Intellectual Co-operation, 1936.
Kweichow ching-chi, ed. by Chang Hsiao-mei. Shanghai: Chung-kuo kuo-min ching-chi yen-chiu so, 1939.
貴州經濟。張肖梅。
Stuart, John Leighton. Fifty Years in China. New York: Random House, 1954.

Chou Pao-chung   周保中

SOURCES

CKJMT
Huang Hui-ch'uan and Tiao Ying-hua. Hsin Chung-kuo jen-wu jih. (tr.) Shanghai: Liang-yu, 1930.
黃惠泉，刁英華。新中國人物誌。
JMST
TCMC
Wei Tung-ming. Jen-wu yü chi-nien. Mukden: Tung-pei shu-tien, 1949.
魏東明。人物與紀念。

Chou Shu-jen   周樹人

WORKS

1928–? ed. of *Pen-liu yueh-k'an*.
奔流月刊。
1934. (comp.) Shih-chu-chai chien p'u. Peiping: Jung-pao-chai.
十竹齋箋譜。
1936. ed. of *Hai-yen*.
海燕。
1936. Lu Hsün tzu-hsuan chi. Shanghai: T'ien-ma shu-tien.
魯迅自選集。
1937? Lu Hsün tai-piao tso hsuan. Shanghai: Ch'üan-ch'iu shu-chü.
魯迅代表作選。
1938. Lu Hsün ch'üan-chi (comp. by Lu Hsün hsien-sheng chi-nien wei-yuan-hui). Lu Hsün ch'üan-chi ch'u-pan she. 20 vols.
魯迅全集。魯迅先生紀念委員會。

1941. Ah Q and Others: Selected Stories of Lusin (tr. by Wang Chi-chen). New York: Columbia University Press.

1941. Lu Hsün tzu-chuan chi ch'i tso-p'in. (comp. by Meng Chin-tieh). Shanghai: Ying-wen hsueh-hui.
魯迅自傳及其作品。孟津迭。

1949. Lu Hsün lun yü-wen kai-ko (comp. by Ni Hai-shu). Shanghai: Shih-tai ch'u-pan she.
魯迅論語文改革。倪海曙。

1951. Lu Hsün jih-chi (comp. by Feng Hsueh-feng). Shanghai: Shanghai ch'u-pan kung-ssu. 24 vols.
魯迅日記。馮雪峯。

1952. Lu Hsün tsa-kan hsuan-chi (comp. by Ch'ü Ch'iu-pai). Shanghai: Shanghai ch'u-pan kung-ssu.
魯迅雜感選集。瞿秋白。

1953. Lu Hsün ch'üan-chi pu-i, hsü-pien (comp. by T'ang T'ao). Shanghai: Shanghai ch'u-pan kung-ssu.
魯迅全集補遺，續編。唐弢。

1953. The True Story of Ah Q. Peking: Foreign Languages Press.

1954. Lu Hsün ming-tso hsuan-chi (comp. by Ch'en Lei). Hong Kong: Nan-yang t'u-shu kung-ssu.
魯迅名作選集。陳磊。

1954. Lu Hsün tsa-wen chi. Hong Kong: Nan-yang t'u-shu kung-ssu.
魯迅雜文集。

1954. Selected Stories of Lu Hsün. Peking: Foreign Languages Press.

1955. Lu Hsün hsiao-shou hsuan. Hong Kong: Tsa-chih t'u-shu ch'u-pan kung-ssu.
魯迅小說選。

1955. Lu Hsün t'an ch'uang-tso. Peking: Chung-kuo ch'ing-nien ch'u-pan she.
魯迅談創作。

1956. Lu Hsün hsiao-shuo chi. Hong Kong: Hong Kong sheng-huo, tu-shu, hsin chih san lien shu-tien.
魯迅小說集。

1956. Lu Hsün lun lien-huan-hua (comp. by Chiang Wei-p'u). Peking: Jen-min mei-shu ch'u-pan she.
魯迅論連環畫。姜維樸。

1956. Lu Hsün lun Mei-shu (comp. by Chang Wang). Peking: Jen-min i-shu ch'u-pan she.
魯迅論美術。張望。

1956. Lu Hsün t'an wen-tzu kai-ko. Peking: Jen-min wen-hsueh ch'u-pan she.
魯迅談文字改革。

1956. Lu Hsün tzu-hsuan wen-chi. Hong Kong: Hsien-tai wen-chiao she.
魯迅自選文集。

1956-58. Lu Hsün ch'üan-chi. Peking: Jen-min wen-hsueh ch'u-pan she. 10 vols.
魯迅全集。

1956-59. Lu Hsün hsuan-chi. Peking: Chung-kuo ch'ing-nien ch'u-pan she. 4 vols.
魯迅選集。

1956-? Selected Works of Lu Hsün. Peking: Foreign Languages Press. 4 vols.

1957. Lu Hsün tso-p'in lun-chi. Peking: Chung-kuo ch'ing-nien ch'u-pan she.
魯迅作品論集。

1958. Lu Hsün mo-chi (ed. by Wen-wu ch'u-pan she). Peking: Wen-wu ch'u-pan she.
魯迅墨迹。文物出版社。

1958. (comp.) Peking chien p'u. with Cheng Chen-tuo. Peking: Jung-pao-chai. 6 vols.
北京箋譜。鄭振鐸。

1959. A Brief History of Chinese Fiction. Peking: Foreign Languages Press.

1959. Lu Hsün chiu-shih chien chu. Canton: Kwangtung jen-min ch'u-pan she.
魯迅舊詩箋注。

1959. Lu Hsün hsuan-chi. Peking: Jen-min wen-hsueh ch'u-pan she. 2 vols.
魯迅選集。

1959. Lu Hsün lun wen-hsueh. Peking: Jen-min wen-hsueh ch'u-pan she.
魯迅論文學。

1959. Lu Hsün shih-chi. Peking: Wen-wu ch'u-pan she.
魯迅詩集。

1960. Lu Hsün shou-kao hsuan-chi (comp. by Peking Lu Hsün po-wu-kuan). Peking: Wen-wu ch'u-pan she.
魯迅手稿選集。北京魯迅博物館。

1960. Selected Stories of Lu Hsün (tr. by Yang Hsien-yi, Gladys Yang). Peking: Foreign Languages Press.

1960. (comp.) Ssu t'ang chuan wen tsa chi. Peking: Wen wu ch'u-pan she.
俟堂專文雜集。

1961. Lu Hsün lun erh-t'ung chiao-yü ho erh-t'ung wen-hsueh (comp. by Chiang Feng). Shanghai: Shao-nien erh-t'ung ch'u-pan she.
魯迅論兒童教育和兒童文學。蔣風。

1961. Lu Hsün shih kao (ed. by Shanghai Lu Hsun chi-nien kuan). Shanghai: Shanghai jen-min mei-shu ch'u-pan she.
魯迅詩稿。

1961. Old Tales Retold by Lu Hsün (tr. by

Yang Hsien-yi, Gladys Yang). Peking: Foreign Languages Press.

1962. (comp.) K'uai-chi chün ku shu tsa chi. Hong Kong: Hsin-yueh ch'u-pan she.
會稽郡故書雜集。

1962. Lu Hsün shih-ko chu. Hangchow: Chekiang jen-min ch'u-pan she.
魯迅詩歌注。

1963. Lu Hsün shou-kao hsuan-chi hsü-pien (comp. by Peking Lu Hsün po-wu-kuan). Peking: Wen-wu ch'u-pan she.
魯迅手稿選集續編。 北京魯迅博物館。

1964. Lu Hsün shou-kao (ed. by Lu Hsün shou-kao pien-chi wei-yuan-hui). Peking: Wen-wu ch'u-pan she. 3 vols.
魯迅手稿。 魯迅手稿編輯委員會。

1965. Lu Hsün hsiao-shuo hsuan-chi. Hong Kong: Hui t'ung shu-tien.
魯迅小說選集。

1967. A Lu Hsün Reader (comp. and annot. by William A. Lyell, Jr.). New Haven: Far Eastern Publications, Yale University.

1967. Lu Hsün san-shih nien chi (comp. by Hsü Kuang-p'ing). Hong Kong: Hsin i ch'u-pan she. 11 vols.
魯迅三十年集。 許廣平。

1967. Lu Hsün san-shih nien chi pu-i (comp. by Hsü Kuang-p'ing). Hong Kong: Hsin i ch'u-pan she.
魯迅三十年集補遺。 許廣平。

Lu Hsün shu-chien (comp. by Hsü Kuang-p'ing). Shanghai: Lu Hsün hsien-sheng chi-nien wei-yuan-hui.
魯迅書簡。 許廣平。

ed. of *Meng-ya yueh-k'an*.
萌芽月刊。

ed. of *Yü ssu*.
語絲。

SOURCES

Chang Nai-ying. Hui-i Lu Hsün hsien-sheng. Peiping: Sheng-huo shu-tien, 1946.
張逎瑩。 回憶魯迅先生。

Ch'en Meng-shao. Lu Hsün tsai Hsia-men (Amoy). Peking: Tso-chia ch'u-pan she, 1954.
陳夢韶。 魯迅在廈門。

Chou Hsia-shou (pseud. of Chou Tso-jen). Lu Hsün te ku chia. Shanghai: Shanghai ch'u-pan kung-ssu, 1953.
周遐壽 (周作人)。 魯迅的故家。

CWT

Feng Hsueh-feng. Hui-i Lu Hsün. Peking: Jen-min wen-hsueh ch'u-pan she, 1953.

馮雪峯。 回憶魯迅。

Feng Hsueh-feng. "Lu Hsün: His Life and Thought," in *Selected Stories of Lu Hsün*. Peking: Foreign Languages Press, 1954.

———. "Lu Hsün ho Kuo-ko-li—wei Kuo-ko-li shih-shih pai nien chi-nien erh tso." *Jen-min jih-pao*. Peking, March 4, 1952.
馮雪峯。 魯迅和果戈理一爲果戈理逝世百年紀念而作。 人民日報。

Hsia, T.A. "Aspects of the Power of Darkness in Lu Hsün." *The Journal of Asian Studies*, XXIII-2 (February, 1964).

Hsü Kuang-p'ing. Hsin-wei te chi-nien (comp. by Wang Shih-ch'ing). Peking: Jen-min wen-hsueh ch'u-pan she, 1951.
許廣平。 欣慰的紀念。 王士菁。

———. Kuan-yü Lu Hsün te sheng-huo. Peking: Jen-min wen-hsueh ch'u-pan she, 1954.
許廣平。 關於魯迅的生活。

———. Lu Hsün hui-i-lu. Peking: Tso-chia ch'u-pan she, 1961.
許廣平。 魯迅回憶錄。

Hsü Shou-shang. Wang yu Lu Hsün yin-hsiang chi. Shanghai: O-mei ch'u-pan she, 1947.
許壽裳。 亡友魯迅印象記。

———. Wo so jen-shih te Lu Hsün. Peking: Jen-min wen-hsueh ch'u-pan she, 1952.
許壽裳。 我所認識的魯迅。

Jen-min jih-pao. Peking, October 19, 1951.
人民日報。

Lin Chen. Lu Hsün shih-chi k'ao. Shanghai: K'ai-ming shu-tien, 1948.
林辰。 魯迅事蹟攷。

Lu Hsün (Chou Shu-jen). Lu Hsün ch'üan-chi (comp. by Lu Hsün hsien-sheng chi-nien wei-yuan-hui). Lu Hsün ch'üan-chi ch'u-pan she, 1938. 20 vols.
魯迅 (周樹人)。 魯迅全集。 魯迅先生紀念委員會。

———. Lu Hsün jih-chi (comp. by Jen-min wen-hsueh ch'u-pan she). Peking: Jen-min wen-hsueh ch'u-pan she, 1959. 2 vols.
魯迅 (周樹人)。 魯迅日記。 人民文學出版社。

———. Lu Hsün shu-chien (comp. by Hsü Kuang-p'ing). Shanghai: Lu Hsün hsien-sheng chi-nien wei-yuan-hui.
魯迅 (周樹人)。 魯迅書簡。 許廣平。

Lu Hsün sheng-p'ing shih-chi, 1881-1936, comp. by Peking Lu Hsün po-wu-kuan. Peking: Wen-wu ch'u-pan she, 1960.
魯迅生平事迹, 1881-1936。 北京魯迅博物館。

Lu Hsün shou-ts'e, ed. by Teng K'o-yün. Shanghai: Ch'ün-chuug tsa-chih kung-ssu, 1946.
魯迅手冊。鄧珂雲。

Mao Tse-tung. "Hsin min-chu chu-i lun," in Mao Tse-tung, *Mao Tse-tung hsuan-chi.* Peking: Jen-min ch'u-pan she, 1966. 4 vols.
毛澤東。新民主主義論。毛澤東。毛澤東選集。

SCMP, March 1, 1952.

Sun Shih-k'ai. Lu Hsün tsai Peking chu kuo te ti-fang. Peking: Peking ch'u-pan she, 1957.
孫世愷。魯迅在北京住過的地方。

Ts'ao Chü-jen. Lu Hsün p'ing-chuan. Hong Kong: Hong Kong hsin wen-hua ch'u-pan she, 1961.
曹聚仁。魯迅評傳。

Tseng Min-chih. Lu Hsün tsai Kwang-chou (Canton) te jih-tzu. Canton: Kwangtung jen-min ch'u-pan she, 1956.
曾敏之。魯迅在廣州的日子。

Wang Chi-chen. "Lusin: A Chronological Record, 1881–1936." *China Institute Bulletin,* III–4 (January, 1939): 99–125.

Wang Shih-ch'ing. Lu Hsün chuan. Shanghai: Hsin chih shu-tien, 1948.
王士菁。魯迅傳。

Wang Yeh-ch'iu. Min yuan ch'ien te Lu Hsün hsien-sheng (with Hsü Shou-shang. Lu Hsün hsien-sheng nien-p'u). Shanghai: O-mei ch'u-pan she, 1947.
王冶秋。民元前的魯迅先生 (附: 許壽裳。魯迅先生年譜)。

Chou Tso-jen   周作人

WORKS

1906. Ku-erh chi.
孤兒記。

1920. Yü wai hsiao-shuo chi. (tr.) Shanghai: Chung-hua shu-chü. 2 vols.
域外小說集。

1923. Tzu-chi te yuan-ti. Peking: Ch'en pao kuan.
自己的園地。

1925. Yü t'ien te shu. Hsin ch'ao she.
雨天的書。

1926. Chou Tso-jen *et al.* Hsien-tai hsiao-shou i-ts'ung; ti-i chi. (tr.) Shanghai: Shang-wu yin shu kuan.
周作人等。現代小說譯叢；第一集。

1926. K'uang-yen shih-fan. (tr.) Peking: Pei hsin shu-chü.

1927. Ming t'u lü-hsing. Shanghai: Pei hsin shu-chü.
冥土旅行。

1927. Tse hsieh chi. Shanghai: Pei hsin shu-chü.
澤瀉集。

1928. T'an hu chi. Shanghai: Pei hsin shu-chü. 2 vols.
談虎集。

1929. Kuo-ch'ü te sheng-ming. Shanghai: Pei hsin shu-chü.
過去的生命。

1929. Yung jih chi. Shanghai: Pei hsin shu-chü.
永日集。

1930. Ou-chou wen-hsueh shih. Shanghai: Shang-wu yin shu kuan.
歐洲文學史。

1931. I-shu yü sheng-huo. Peking: Ch'ün i.
藝術與生活。

1932. Erh-t'ung wen-hsueh hsiao lun.
兒童文學小論。

1933. Chih-t'ang wen-chi. Shanghai: T'ien-ma shu-tien.
知堂文集。

1933. Chou Tso-jen san-wen ch'ao. Shanghai: K'ai-ming shu-tien.
周作人散文鈔。

1933. Chou Tso-jen shu-hsin; i-chiu-san-san. Shanghai: Ch'ing kuang shu-chü.
周作人書信；一九三三。

1933. K'an yün chi. Shanghai: K'ai-ming shu-tien.
看雲集。

1933. K'u-ch'a-an hsiao-hua hsuan. Pei hsin shu-chü.
苦茶庵笑話選。

1933. T'an lung chi. Shanghai: K'ai-ming shu-tien.
談龍集。

1934. K'u-yü-chai hsü pa wen. Shanghai: T'ien-ma shu-tien.
苦雨齋序跋文。

1935. K'u ch'a sui-pi. Pei hsin shu-chü.
苦茶隨筆。

1936. Chou Tso-jen hsuan-chi (ed. by Hsü Ch'en-ssu, Yeh Wang-yu). Shanghai: Wan-hsiang shu-chü.
周作人選集。徐沉四，葉忘憂。

1936. Chou Tso-jen wen-hsuan (ed. by Shao Hou). Shanghai: Fang-ku shu-tien.
周作人文選。少候。

1936. Feng yü t'an. Peking: Pei hsin shu-chü.
風雨談。

1936. K'u chu tsa-chi. Shanghai: Liang yu.
苦竹雜記。

1937. Kua tou chi. Shanghai: Yü-chou feng.
瓜豆集。

1938. Chou Tso-jen tai-piao tso hsuan (ed. by Chang Chün). Shanghai: Ch'üan-ch'iu shu-tien.
周作人代表作選。張均。

1940. Ping chu t'an.
秉燭談。

1941. Yao-t'ang yü-lu. Tientsin.
藥堂語錄。

1942. Yao wei chi. Peking: Hsin min.
藥味集。

1943? Yao-t'ang tsa-wen. Shanghai Pei hsin shu-chü.
藥堂襍文。

1944. Feng yü hou t'an. Peking: Hsin min.
風雨後談。

1944. Ping chu hou t'an. Peking: Hsin min.
秉燭後談。

1944. Sang hsia t'an. Shanghai: Kai-ming shu-tien.
桑下談。

1944. Shu-fang i-chiao. Peking: Hsin min.
書房一角。

1955. Chung-kuo chin-tai wen-hsueh shih-hua. Hong Kong: T'ai-p'ing-yang t'u-shu kung-ssu.
中國近代文學史話。

1959. Kuo-ch'ü te kung-tso. Hong Kong: Hsin ti ch'u-pan she.
過去的工作。

1961. Chih-t'ang i-yu wen-pien. Kowloon: San yü t'u-shu wen-chü kung-ssu.
知堂乙酉文編。

1963. Ku-shih chi. (tr.) Peking: Jen-min wen-hsueh ch'u-pan she.
古事記。

Huang ch'iang-wei.
黃薔薇。

K'ung ta-ku.
空大鼓。

T'o-lo.
陀螺。

SOURCES

Chou Tso-jen lun, ed. by Chao Ching-shen. Shanghai: Pei hsin shu-chü, 1934.
周作人論。趙景深。

CWT

Jen-chien shih, 1 (April 5, 1934): 4; 13 (October 5, 1934): 66–68; 40 (November 20, 1935): 7–11.
人間世。

Kuo wen chou pao, XII–18.
國聞週報。

Ta kung pao. Shanghai, June 6, August 11, September 21, 1946.
大公報。

Chou Tso-min   周作民

SOURCES

Persons interviewed: Chang Chia-ao; others not to be identified.

Chou Tzu-ch'i   周自齊

SOURCES

Persons interviewed: not to be identified.
BPC
CYB-W, 1932.

Chou Yang   周楊

WORKS

1946. (ed.) Chieh-fang ch'ü tuan-p'ien ch'uang-tso hsuan; ti-i chi. Tung-pei shu-tien.
解放區短篇創作選；第一輯。

1949. Hsin te jen-min te wen-i. Peking: Hsin hua shu-tien.
新的人民的文藝。

1949. Piao-hsien hsin te ch'ün-chung te shih-tai. Peking? Hsin hua shu-tien
表現新的群眾的時代。

1950. Ma-k'o-ssu chu-i yü wen-i. Peking? Chieh-fang she.
馬克斯主義與文藝。

1952. Chien-chueh kuan-ch'e Mao Tse-tung wen-i lu-hsien. Peking: Jen-min wen-hsueh ch'u-pan she.
堅決貫澈毛澤東文藝路綫。

1954. China's New Literature and Art: Essays and Addresses. Peking: Foreign Languages Press.

1959. (ed.) Hung ch'i ko-yao. with Kuo Mo-jo. Peking: Hung ch'i tsa-chih she.
紅旗歌謠。郭沫若。

1960. Wo kuo she-hui chu-i wen-hsueh i-shu te tao-lu; i-chiu-liu-ling nien ch'i-yueh erh-shih-erh jih tsai Chung-kuo wen-hsueh i-shu kung-tso che ti-san tz'u tai-piao ta-hui shang te pao-kao. Peking: Jen-min wen-hsueh ch'u-pan she.

我國社會主義文學藝術的道路；一九六〇年七月二十二日在中國文學藝術工作者第三次代表大會上的報告。

SOURCES

Chieh-fang ch'ü tuan-p'ien ch'uang-tso hsuan; ti-i chi, ed. by Chou Yang. Tung-pei shu-tien, 1946.

解放區短篇創作選；第一輯。周楊。

Chou Yang. Chien-chueh kuan-ch'e Mao Tse-tung wen-i lu-hsien. Peking: Jen-min wen-hsueh ch'u-pan she, 1952.

周楊。堅決貫澈毛澤東文藝路綫。

———. China's New Literature and Art: Essays and Addresses. Peking: Foreign Languages Press, 1954.

———. Ma-k'o-ssu chu-i yü wen-i. Peking? Chieh-fang she, 1950.

周楊。馬克斯主義與文藝。

———. Piao-hsien hsin te ch'ün-chung te shih-tai. Peking? Hsin hua shu-tien, 1949.

周楊。表現新的群衆的時代。

Li Ho-lin. Chin erh-shih nien Chung-kuo wen-i ssu-ch'ao lun. Shanghai: Sheng-huo shu-tien, 1947.

李何林。近二十年中國文藝思潮論。

The New York Times. January 6, August 24, 1964.

Chu Ch'i-hua   朱其華

WORKS

1929. Chung-kuo tzu-pen chu-i chih fa-chan. Shanghai: Lien-ho shu-tien.

中國資本主義之發展。

1929. Tzu-pen chu-i te fa-chan chi ch'i mo-lo. Shanghai: Hsin sheng-ming shu-chü.

資本主義的發展及其没落。

1930. Chung-kuo ko-ming yü Chung-kuo she-hui ko chieh-chi. Shanghai: Lien-ho shu-tien.

中國革命與中國社會各階級。

1930. Chung-kuo nung-ts'un ching-chi kuan-hsi chi ch'i t'e-chih. Shanghai: Hsin sheng-ming shu-chü.

中國農村經濟關係及其特質。

1931. Chung-kuo she-hui te ching-chi chieh-kuo. Shanghai: Hsin sheng-ming ch'u-pan she.

中國社會的經濟結構。

1932. Chung-kuo ching-chi wei-chi chi ch'i ch'ien-t'u. Shanghai: Hsin sheng-ming sh'u-chü.

中國經濟危機及其前途。

1933. Chung-kuo chin-tai she-hui shih chieh-p'o. Shanghai: Hsin hsin ch'u-pan she.

中國近代社會史解剖。

1933. I-chiu-erh-ch'i nien ti hui-i. Shanghai: Hsin hsin ch'u-pan she.

一九二七年底回憶。

1936. Chung-kuo nung-ts'un ching-chi te t'ou-shih. Shanghai: Chung-kuo yen-chiu shu-tien.

中國農村經濟的透視。

1938. "I-ko wu ch'an chieh-chi ch'an-yeh kung-jen te tzu-shu." *K'ang chan yü wen-hua.*

一個無產階級產業工人的自述。抗戰與文化。

1941. (Tang-tai shih-liao) Hung-se wu-t'ai. Hong Kong: Sheng-li ch'u-pan she Hong Kong fen-she.

(當代史料) 紅色舞台。

Hsi-pei san chi.

西北散記。

I-chiu-erh-wu—erh-ch'i ta ko-ming hui-i-lu.

一九二五一二七大革命回憶錄。

SOURCES

Persons interviewed: Ma Meng, John T. Ma.

Chu Ch'i-hua. Chung-kuo ko-ming yü Chung-kuo she-hui ko chieh-chi. Shanghai: Lien-ho shu-tien.

朱其華。中國革命與中國社會各階級。

———. I-chiu-erh-ch'i nien ti hui-i. Shanghai: Hsin hsin ch'u-pan she.

朱其華。一九二七年底回憶。

———. "I-ko wu ch'an chieh-chi ch'an-yeh kung-jen te tzu-shu." *K'ang chan yü wen-hua,* 1938.

朱其華。一個無產階級產業工人的自述。抗戰與文化。

HSWT

Chu Chia-hua   朱家驊

WORKS

1937. China's Postal and Other Communications Services. London: Kegan Paul, Trench, Trubner & Co.

1942. Chu pu-chang tui-yü pien-chiang wen-t'i yü pien-chiang kung-tso chih chih-shih. Chungking: Chung-yang tsu-chih pu pien-chiang yü-wen pien i wei-yuan-hui.

朱部長對於邊疆問題與邊疆工作之指示。

1943. Kung yün yü kung hsün. Chungking: Chung-kuo kuo-min-tang chung-yang tsu-chih pu.

工運與工訓。

1944. Nung yun yü nung hsun. Chungking? Chung-yang tsu-chih pu.

農運與農訓。

1954. Taiwan and Sinkiang (Formosa and Chinese Turkistan). (ed. by Chinese Association for the United Nations.) Taipei: Chinese Association for the United Nations.

SOURCES

BKL
The China Tribune, April 30, 1962.
CH–T, 1956–57.
Chu Chia-hua hsien-sheng shih-lueh, ed. by Chu Chia-hua hsien-sheng chih-sang wei-yuan-hui. Taipei, 1963.

朱家驊先生事略。朱家驊先生治喪委員會。

Chung-yang jih-pao. Taipei, January 4, January 8, May 15, 1963.

中央日報。

CTMC
Lo Chia-lun. "Chu Liu-hsien hsieh-sheng te shih-chi ho hsing-i." *Chung-yang jih-pao*. Taipei, January 9, 1963.

羅家倫。朱騮先先生的事蹟和行誼。中央日報。

T'ao Hsi-sheng. "Ching tao Chu Liu-hsien (Chia-hua) hsien-sheng." *Chung-yang jih-pao*. Taipei, January 9, 1963.

陶希聖。敬悼朱騮先(家驊)先生。中央日報。

Chu Chih-hsin   朱 執 信

WORKS

1914? ed. of *Min-kuo tsa-chih*.
民國雜誌。
1919. ed. of *Min-kuo jih-pao*.
民國日報。
1919–20. ed. of *Chien-she*.
建設。
1921. Chu Chih-hsin chi. Shanghai: Min chih shu-chü. 2 vols.
朱執信集。
1924. Ping te kai-tsao yü ch'i hsin-li. Shanghai: Min chih shu-chü.
兵的改造與其心理。
1927. Chu Chih-hsin wen-ch'ao (ed. by Shao Yuan-ch'ung). Shanghai: Min chih shu-chü.
朱執信文鈔。邵元冲。

1930. Chu Chih-hsin, Hu Han-min, Lü Ssu-mien, Hu Shih, Chi Jung-wu, Liao Chung-k'ai *et al*. Ching-t'ien chih-tu yu wu chih yen-chiu. Shanghai: Hua t'ung shu-chü.

朱執信，胡漢民，呂思勉，胡適，季融五，廖仲愷等。井田制度有無之研究。

1941. Kuan-yü san min chu-i (ed. by Yeh Ch'ing). T'ai-ho: Kiangsi-sheng san min chu-i wen-hua yün-tung wei-yuan-hui.

關於三民主義。葉青。

1958. Chu Chih-hsin hsuan-chi (ed. by Yeh Ch'ing). Taipei: P'a-mi-erh shu-tien.

朱執信選集。葉青。

Chih-hsin hsien-sheng i-chu.

執信先生遺著。

SOURCES

Chu Chih-hsin. Chu Chih-hsin chi. Shanghai: Min chih shu-chü, 1928. 2 vols.

朱執信。朱執信集。

———. Chu Chih-hsin hsuan-chi (ed. by Yeh Ch'ing). Taipei: P'a-mi-erh shu-tien.

朱執信。朱執信選集。葉青。

———. Chu Chih-hsin wen-ch'ao (ed. by Shao Yuan-ch'ung). Shanghai: Min chih shu-chü, 1927.

朱執信。朱執信文鈔。邵元冲。

Kuo-fu nien-p'u ch'u-kao, ed. by Kuo shih kuan shih-liao pien-tsuan wei-yuan-hui, Chung-kuo kuo-min-tang tang shih shih-liao pien-tsuan wei-yuan-hui. Taipei: Kuo shih kuan shih-liao pien-tsuan wei-yuan-hui, Chung-kuo kuo-min-tang tang-shih shih-liao pien-tsuan wei-yuan-hui, 1959. 2 vols.

國父年譜初稿。國史館史料編纂委員會，中國國民黨黨史史料編纂委員會。

Scalapino, Robert A., and Harold Schiffrin. "Early Socialist Currents in the Chinese Revolutionary Movement: Sun Yat-sen Versus Liang Ch'i-ch'ao." *Journal of Asian Studies*, XVIII–3 (May, 1959).

Tsou Lu. Hui-ku lu. Nanking: Tu-li ch'u-pan she.

鄒魯。回顧錄。

Wang Hsi-wen. "Chiu Chih-hsin hsien-sheng wai-chuan." *Ch'un-ch'iu*, 51.

汪希文。朱執信先生外傳。春秋。

Chu Ching-nung   朱 經 農

WORKS

1912. ed. of *Min-chu pao*.
民主報。

1921, October. "Fei-chih 1915 nien Chung Jih t'iao-yueh chi ch'i fu-shu wen-chien chih yen-chiu." *Tung-fang tsa-chih*, XVIII–18, 19.
廢止1915年中日條約及其附屬文件之研究。東方雜誌。

1921, October. "Ko kuo tsai Hua tsu chieh ti hsing-chih chih yen-chiu chi ch'ing-ch'iu fei yueh chih li-yu." *Tung-fang tsa-chih*, XVIII–18, 19.
各國在華租借地性質之研究及請求廢約之理由。東方雜誌。

1923. Ming-jih chih hsueh-hsiao. (tr. of John Dewey's *School of Tomorrow*). with P'an Tzu-nien. Shanghai: Shang-wu yin shu kuan.
明日之學校。潘梓年。

1923, January. "Ch'u-chi chung-hsueh ying fou ts'ai-yung hsuan k'o chih?" *Chiao-yü tsa-chih*, XV–1.
初級中學應否採用選科制？教育雜誌。

1923, March. "Tui-yü ch'u-chung k'o-ch'eng te t'ao-lun (i)." *Chiao-yü tsa-chih*, XV–3.
對於初中課程的討論 (一)。教育雜誌。

1923, November. "Tui-yü ch'u-chung k'o-ch'eng te t'ao-lun (erh) (kung-min k'o)." *Chiao-yü tsa-chih*, XV–11.
對於初中課程的討論 (二) (公民科)。教育雜誌。

1923, December. "Tui-yü ch'u-chung k'o-ch'eng te t'ao-lun (san) (li-shih k'o)." *Chiao-yü tsa-chih*, XV–12.
對於初中課程的討論 (三) (歷史科)。教育雜誌。

1924, March. "Chih-yeh chih-tao yü ch'u-chung k'o-ch'eng." *Chiao-yü yü jen-sheng*, 20.
職業指導與初中課程。教育與人生。

1924, March. "Fu yü t'an-hsing te shih-fan k'o-ch'eng." *Chiao-yü yü jen-sheng*, 20.
富於彈性的師範課程。教育與人生。

1924, March. "Tui-yü ch'u-chung k'o-ch'eng te t'ao-lun (ssu) (ti-li k'o)." *Chiao-yü tsa-chih*, XVI–3.
對於初中課程的討論 (四) (地理科)。教育雜誌。

1924, April. "Tui-yü ch'u-chung k'o-ch'eng te t'ao-lun (wu) (kuo-yü k'o)." *Chiao-yu tsa-chih*, XVI–4.
對於初中課程的討論 (五) (國語科)。教育雜誌。

1924, May. "Kung-min hsun-lien yü ch'u-chi chung-hsueh." *Chiao-yü yü jen-sheng*, 32.
公民訓練與初級中學。教育與人生。

1924, July. "Tui-yü ch'u-chung k'o-ch'eng te t'ao-lun (liu) (wai-kuo yü k'o)." *Chiao-yü tsa-chih*, XVI–7.

1924, September. "Tui-yü ch'u-chung k'o-ch'eng te t'ao-lun (ch'i) (suan-hsueh k'o)." *Chiao-yü tsa-chih*, XVI–9.
對於初中課程的討論 (七) (算學科)。教育雜誌。

1924, October, November. "P'ing ching-chi shih-kuan ho fou-jen yin kuo lü te li-shih che-hsueh." *Chiao-yü yü jen-sheng*, 52, 57.
評經濟史觀和否認因果律的歷史哲學。教育與人生。

1925, May. "Tui-yü ch'u-chung k'o-ch'eng te t'ao-lun (pa) (tzu-jan k'o)." *Chiao-yü tsa-chih*, XVII–5.
對於初中課程的討論 (八) (自然科)。教育雜誌。

1925, June. "Kuan-yü pien-chih ch'u-chung k'o-ch'eng yuan-tse chih cheng-i." *Chiao-yü tsa-chih*, XVII–6.
關於編制初中課程原則之爭議。教育雜誌。

1926, January. "Chiao-yü te mu-ti." *Chiao-yü yü jen-sheng*, 16.
教育的目的。教育與人生。

1928, February. "Tao Kao Jen-shan hsien-sheng." *Chiao-yü tsa-chih*, XX–2.
悼高仁山先生。教育雜誌。

1928, March. "Chih-yeh chih-tao yü chung-hsueh k'o-ch'eng." *Chiao-yü tsa-chih*, XX–3.
職業指導與中學課程。教育雜誌。

1930. Chu Ching-nung *et al*. (ed.) Chiao-yü ta tz'u shu. Shanghai: Shang-wu yin shu kuan. 2 vols.
朱經農等。教育大辭書。

1932, June. "Chieh-shu hsun cheng te shih-chien wen-t'i." *Tu-li p'ing-lun*, 7.
結束訓政的時間問題。獨立評論。

1936, February. "Tsui-hou i ko yueh te Ting Tsai-chü hsien-sheng." *Tu-li p'ing-lun*, 188.
最後一個月的丁在君先生。獨立評論。

1936, July. "Changsha t'ung-hsin." *Tu-li p'ing-lun*, 209.
長沙通訊。獨立評論。

1937, May. "Ts'an-chia Yuan-tung ch'ü chi-pen chiao-yü yen chiu hui-i hou so fa-sheng te chi-tien kan-hsiang." *Chiao-yü tsa-chih*, XXXII–5.
參加遠東區基本教育研究會議後所發生的幾點感想。教育雜誌。

1938, January. "Chung-kuo chiao-yü hsueh-hui te shih-tai shih-ming." *Chiao-yü tsa-chih*, XXXIII–1.
中國教育學會的時代使命。教育雜誌。

1942. Chiao-yü yü ssu-hsiang. Chungking: Shang-wu yin shu kuan.
教育與思想。

1948, January. "Tsai wo chi-i chung te Hsiung

Ping-san hsien-sheng." *Tung-fang tsa-chih*, XLIV-1: 28-34.

在我記憶中的熊秉三先生。東方雜誌。

1963. Chiao-yü ssu-hsiang. Taipei: Taiwan shang-wu yin shu kuan.

教育思想。

1965. Ai-shan-lu shih-ch'ao. Taipei: Taiwan shang-wu yin-shu kuan.

愛山廬詩鈔。

ed. of *Ya-tung hsin-wen*.

亞東新聞。

SOURCES

Person interviewed: Chu Wen-djang.

BKL

Chu Ching-nung. "Tsai wo chi-i chung te Hsiung Ping-san hsien-sheng." *Tung-fang tsa-chih*, XLIV-1 (January, 1948): 28-34.

朱經農。在我記憶中的熊秉三先生。 東方雜誌。

CTMC

Hu Shih. Hu Shih liu-hsüeh jih-chi. Taipei: Taiwan shang-wu yin shu kuan, 1959. 4 vols.

胡適。胡適留學日記。

———. Ssu-shih tzu-shu. Taipei: Yuan-tung t'u-shu kung-ssu, 1959.

胡適。四十自述。

———. "Ta Chu Ching-nung," in Hu Shih, *Hu Shih wen-ts'un*. Taipei: Yuan-tung t'u-shu kung-ssu, 1953. 4 vols.

胡適。答朱經農。胡適。胡適文存。

Wang Yün-wu. "Wo so jen-shih te ch'üan-mien chiao-yü chia Chu Ching-nung hsien-sheng," in Wang Yün-wu, *T'an chiao-yü*. Taipei: Hua kuo ch'u-pan she, 1951.

王雲五。我所認識的全面教育家朱經農先生。王雲五。談教育。

Yu Yu (pseud. of P'an Kung-chan). "Chi-nien i wei Chung-kuo chiao-yü chia." *Hua Mei jih-pao*. New York, March 9, 1961.

悠悠（潘公展）。紀念一位中國教育家。華美日報。

Yü Hsien-li. "Hsiang sheng chiao-yü te hui-huang shih yeh." *Hua Mei jih-pao*. New York, March 9, 1961.

余先勵。湘省教育的輝煌史頁。華美日報。

Chu Hsi-tsu   朱希祖

WORKS

1944. Chung-kuo shih-hsüeh t'ung-lun. Chungking: Tu-li ch'u-pan she.

中國史學通論。

1944. Wei ch'i lu chiao-pu. Chungking: Tu-li ch'u-pan she.

僞齊錄校補。

1948. Hua Ho ching-ying Taiwan shih-liao. with Yao Nan. Singapore: Nan-yang shu-chü.

華荷經營台灣史料。姚枬。

1955. Wei ch'u lu chi pu. Taipei: Cheng-chung shu-chü.

僞楚錄輯補。

1960. Chi chung shu k'ao. Peking: Chung-hua shu-chü.

汲冢書考。

1961. Ming chi shih-liao t'i-pa. Peking: Chung-hua shu-chü.

明季史料題跋。

Chan-kuo shih nien-piao.

戰國史年表。

Hsin Liang-shu i-wen-chih.

新梁書藝文志。

Li-t'ing ts'ang-shu t'i-chi.

酈亭藏書題記。

Wei Ch'i kuo chih ch'ang pien.

僞齊國志長編。

SOURCES

Ch'u-pan chou-k'an. 131 (June, 1935): 25.

出版週刊。

Wang Yü-kao and Wang Yü-cheng. "Chu Hsi-tsu chuan." *Kuo shih kuan kuan k'an*, I-2 (March, 1942): 99-101.

王宇高，王宇正。朱希祖傳。國史館館刊。

Chu Hsiang   朱湘

WORKS

1925. Hsia-t'ien. Shanghai: Shang-wu yin shu kuan.

夏天。

1927. Ts'ao-mang chi. Shanghai: K'ai-ming shu-tien.

草莽集。

1934. Chung shu chi. Shanghai: Sheng-huo shu-tien.

中書集。

1934. Hai-wai chi Ni chün. Shanghai: Pei hsin shu-chü.

海外寄霓君。

1934. Shih men chi. Shanghai: Shang-wu yin shu kuan.

石門集。

1936. Fan-shih-liu chi. (tr.) Shanghai: Shang-
wu yin shu kuan.
番石榴集。

1936. Yung yen chi. Shih-tai.
永言集。

Chu Hsiang shu-hsin chi.
朱湘書信集。

Lu-man-ni-ya min-ko i-pan. (tr.)
路曼尼亞民歌一班。

Ying-kuo chin-tai tuan-p'ien hsiao-shuo chi. (tr.)
英國近代短篇小說集。

SOURCES

Chu Hsiang. Chung shu chi. Shanghai: Sheng-
huo shu-tien, 1934.
朱湘。中書集。

——. Hai-wai chi Ni chün. Shanghai: Pei
hsin shu-chü, 1934.
朱湘。海外寄霓君。

——. Hsia-t'ien. Shanghai: Shang-wu yin
shu kuan, 1925.
朱湘。夏天。

——. Shih men chi. Shanghai: Shang-wu yin
shu kuan, 1934.
朱湘。石門集。

CHWC
CHWSK
CHWYS
CWT
ECC
GCCJK
Jen chien shih, 15 (November 5, 1934): 30–31; 18
(December 20, 1934): 19–20, 49.
人間世。

MCNP
MMT
Su Mei. "Wo so chien yü Chu Hsiang che," in
Su Mei, *Ch'ing niao chi*. Changsha: Shang-wu
yin shu kuan.
蘇梅。我所見於朱湘者。蘇梅。青鳥集。

Wales, Nym (pseud. of Helen Foster Snow).
"The Modern Chinese Literary Movement,"
in Edgar Snow, *Living China: Modern Chinese
Short Stories*. New York: John Day & Reynal
& Hitchcock, 1936.

WWMC

Chu Hsueh-fan   朱學範

SOURCES

GCCJK
GCJJ

JMST, 1950, 1957.
Shen Yü-kuang. Wo so chien te k'ao-lung jen-
wu. Hong Kong: Ya-chou ch'u-pan she,
1953.
沈育光。我所見的靠攏人物。

Chu K'o-chen   竺可楨

WORKS

1929. Chung-kuo ch'i-hou ch'ü-yü lun. Nanking: Pei-chi-ko ch'i-hsiang yen-chiu so.
中國氣候區域論。

1935. (ed.) Chung-kuo chih yü-liang. Tzu-yuan
wei-yuan-hui.
中國之雨量。

1937. Chu K'o-chen *et al*. K'o-hsueh te min-tsu
fu-hsing. Chung-hua k'o-hsueh she.
竺可楨等。科學的民族復興。

1948. Chu K'o-chen *et al*. Ti-li hsueh chia Hsü
Hsia-k'o (ed. by Kuo-li Chekiang ta-hsueh
shih ti yen-chiu so). Shanghai: Shang-wu yin
shu kuan.
竺可楨等。地理學家徐霞客。國立浙江大
學史地研究所。

SOURCES

Persons interviewed: not to be identified.

Chu P'ei-te   朱培德

WORKS

1934. Chün-kuan te hsin sheng-huo (ed. by Yeh
Ch'u-ts'ang). Nanking: Cheng-chung shu-
chü.
軍官的新生活。葉楚傖。

SOURCES

Ch'en Hsiao-hu. Chu I-chih hsien-sheng shih-
lueh, i-mo.
陳歇湖。朱益之先生事略，遺墨。

Chiang Yung-ching. Wuhan ch'ih se cheng-
ch'üan.
蔣永敬。武漢赤色政權。

Chu Ch'i-hua. I-chiu-erh-ch'i nien. Shanghai,
1930.
朱其華。一九二七年。

CMTC
CWR, February 27, 1937.
CYB-W, 1934.
Li Chien-nung. The Political History of China
1840–1928 (tr. and ed. by Teng Ssu-yu, Jeremy

Ingalls).   Princeton.   D. Van Nostrand Co,.
1956.
Li Lieh-chün. Tzu-chuan. Chungking, 1944.
李烈鈞。 自傳。
———.   Wu Ning wen-tu.
李烈鈞。 武寧文牘。
MMT
Smedley, Agnes.   The Great Road: The Life
and Times of Chu Teh.   New York: Monthly
Review Press, 1956.

Chu Shao-liang   朱紹良

SOURCES

Chang Ta-chün. Sinkiang nei-mu. Hong Kong:
Ya-chou ch'u-pan she, 1956.
張達鈞。 新疆內幕。
Chou K'ai-ch'ing. Hsi-pei chien-ying. Chengtu:
Chung hsi shu-chü, 1943.
周開慶。 西北剪影。
CMJL
CWR, 1929-30, 1937.
CYB-W, 1934.
Kuo-wen chou-pao, XIV-41 (October 25, 1937).
國聞週報。
Lattimore, Owen. Pivot of Asia: Sinkiang and
the Inner Asian Frontiers of China and Russia.
Boston: Little, Brown & Co., 1950.
The New York Times, December 27, 1963.
TCJC
Whiting, Allen S., and Sheng Shih-ts'ai. Sin-
kiang: Pawn or Pivot? East Lansing: Michi-
gan State University Press, 1958.

Chu Teh   朱德

WORKS

1938. Chu Teh et al. Ti-pa lu chün chiang-ling
k'ang chan hui-i-lu. (comp. by Ch'en Cho-
tai). Shanghai? Nu-hou ch'u-pan she.
朱德等。 第八路軍將領抗戰回憶錄。 陳卓呆。
1938. Chu Teh et al. Wo-men tsen-yang ta-t'ui
ti-jen. Hankow: Hsin hua jih-pao.
朱德等。 我們怎樣打退敵人。
1938. Lun k'ang Jih yu-chi chan-cheng (comp.
by K'ang Jih yu-chi chan-cheng yen-chiu
hui). Chieh-fang she.
論抗日游擊戰爭。 抗日游擊戰爭研究會。
1938. Lun yu-chi chan. Shanghai: Chung-hua
ta-hsüeh t'u-shu yu-hsien kung-ssu.
論游擊戰。

1938. Pa lu chün te chan-lueh ho chan-shu. with
Mao Tse-tung et al. Shanghai: Sheng-huo
ch'u-pan she.
八路軍的戰略和戰術。 毛澤東等。
1939. Chu Teh et al. "T'ung-tien" erh-shih-pa
nien shih-erh-yueh san-shih jih.
朱德等。 「通電」二十八年十二月三十日。
1939? How the Eighth Route Army Fights in
North China. New China Information Committee.
1940. Chu Teh et al. Pa lu chün chih chung-
yang tien.
朱德等。 八路軍致中央電。
1941. Chu Teh et al. San nien. Wei-kuang she.
朱德等。 三年。
1945. Lun chieh-fang ch'ü chan ch'ang; 1945
nien 4 yueh 25 jih Chu Teh t'ung-chih tsai
Chung-kuo kung-ch'an-tang ti-ch'i tz'u
ch'üan-kuo tai-piao ta-hui shang te chün-shih
pao-kao. Chieh-fang she.
論解放區戰場; 1945 年 4 月 25 日朱德同志
在中國共產黨第 7 次全國代表大會上的軍
事報告。
  Eng. tr., On the Battlefronts of the Liberated
  Areas. Peking: Foreign Languages Press,
  1952.
1947. I-chiu-ssu-ch'i nien tou-cheng jen-wu yü
ch'ien-t'u. with Mao Tse-tung et al. Cheng
pao she.
一九四七年鬥爭任務與前途。 毛澤東等。
1949. Chu Teh et al. Fu-nü yün-tung wen-hsien.
Hong Kong: Hsin min-chu ch'u-pan she.
朱德等。 婦女運動文獻。
1950. Chu Teh et al. Hsueh-hsi Jen Pi-shih
t'ung-chih (comp. by Chung-kuo hsin min-
chu chu-i ch'ing-nien t'uan Hua-nan kung-tso
wei-yuan-hui). Canton: Ch'ing-nien ch'u-pan
she Hua-nan ying-yeh ch'u.
朱德等。 學習任弼時同志。 中國新民主主
義青年團華南工作委員會。
1963. Chu Teh shih tz'u hsuan. Peking: Jen-
min wen-hsueh ch'u-pan she.
朱德詩詞選。

SOURCES

Person interviewed: Chang Kuo-t'ao.
Chiu, S.M. "Chinese Communist Military
Leadership." Military Review, March, 1960.
Chu Teh. On the Battle Fronts of the Liberated
Areas. Peking: Foreign Languages Press, 1952.
Chu Teh chuan, comp. by Ch'en Chen. Canton:
Chan shih tu-wu pien i she, 1937.
朱德傳。 陳眞。

Chung-kuo ko-ming ming-jen chuan, comp. by Hsi Ch'u-ming *et al*. Shanghai: Shang-yeh shu-chü, 1928.
中國革命名人傳。 奚楚明等。
CPR, 1005 (November 1, 1949).
"Elder Statesman." *U.S. News and World Report*, February 6, 1959.
Elegant, Robert S. China's Red Masters. New York: Twayne, 1951.
Hsiao San. Jen-wu yü chi-nien. Peking: Sheng-huo, tu-shu, hsin chih san-lien shu-tien, 1951.
蕭三。 人物與紀念。
HSWT
The International Who's Who, 1958.
Keng I. "Le General Tsai Ngao et son Couvre au Yunnan." *Revue Indochinoise*, 61 (June, 1913): 637–44.
———. "Hsin-hai ko-ming shih-ch'i te Kwangsi." *Chin-tai shih tzu-liao*, 4 (1958): 89–106.
耿毅。 辛亥革命時期的廣西。 近代史資料。
Li Hsü. Ts'ai Sung-p'o. Nanking, 1946.
李旭。 蔡松坡。
Liang Jen-kung hsien-sheng nien-p'u ch'ang-pien ch'u-kao, comp. by Ting Wen-chiang. Taipei: Shih-chieh shu-chü, 1958. 2 vols.
梁任公先生年譜長編初稿。 丁文江。
Liu Kuang-yen. Ts'ai Sung-p'o. Hong Kong: Ya-chou ch'u-pan she, 1958.
劉光炎。 蔡松坡。
The New York Times. March 12, April 28, September 26, 1959.
"Old Warrior May Lead Red China." *U.S. News and World Report*, December 26, 1958.
Peking Review, October 20, 1961.
RSOC
SCMP, 1139.
Smedley, Agnes. Battle Hymn of China. New York: Alfred A. Knopf, 1943.
———. China's Red Army Marches. New York: The Vanguard Press, 1934.
———. The Great Road: The Life and Times of Chu Teh. New York: Monthly Review Press, 1956.
Ts'ai Sung-p'o hsien-sheng i chi, comp. by Liu Ta-wu. Shaoyang: Ts'ai kung i chi pien-yin wei-yuan-hui, 1943. 13 vols.
蔡松坡先生遺集。 劉達武。
Wales, Nym (pseud. of Helen Foster Snow). Inside Red China. New York: Doubleday, Doran & Co., 1939.
WWC, supplement to 5th ed., 1940; 6th ed., 1950.
WWMC

Yü En-yang. Chung-hua hu kuo san chieh chuan.
庚恩暘。 中華護國三傑傳。
———. Yunnan shou i yung-hu kung-ho shih-mo chi. Kunming? Yunnan t'u-shu kuan, 1917.
庚恩暘。 雲南首義擁護共和始末記。

Chu Tzu-ch'ing   朱自清

WORKS

1923. Hui-mieh (ed. by Ch'i ming shu-chü pien-chi pu). Taipei: Ch'i ming shu-chü.
毀滅。 啓明書局編輯部。
1924. Tsung-chi. Shanghai: Ya-tung t'u-shu-kuan.
踪跡。
1934. Ou yu tsa-chi. K'ai-ming shu-tien.
歐遊雜記。
1934–? ed. of *T'ai-po*.
太白。
1934–? ed. of *Wen-hsueh chi-k'an*.
文學季刊。
1935. (comp.) Hsin wen-hsueh ta-hsi shih-chi.
新文學大系詩集。
1943. Lun-tun tsa-chi. K'ai-ming shu-tien.
倫敦雜記。
1943. Pei-ying. Shanghai: K'ai-ming shu-tien.
背影。
1947. Ching-tien ch'ang-t'an. Shanghai: Shang-hai wen-kuang shu-tien.
經典常談。
1947. Shih yen chih pien. Shanghai: K'ai-ming shu-tien.
詩言志辨。
1948. Lun ya su kung shang. Shanghai: Kuan-ch'a she.
論雅俗共賞。
1948. Piao-chun yü ch'ih-tu. Shanghai: Shang-hai wen-kuang shu-tien.
標準與尺度。
1948. Yü-wen ling-shih. Shanghai: Min shan shu-chü.
語文零拾。
1952. Chu Tzu-ch'ing hsuan-chi. Peking: K'ai-ming shu-tien.
朱自清選集。
1953. Chu Tzu-ch'ing wen-chi; 12 chung. Peking: K'ai-ming shu-tien. 4 vols.
朱自清文集; 12種。
1955. Chu Tzu-ch'ing shih wen hsuan-chi. Peking: Jen-min wen-hsueh ch'u-pan she.

朱自清詩文選集。

1957. Chung-kuo ko-yao. Peking: Tso-chia ch'u-pan she.
中國歌謠。

1959. Chu Tzu-ch'ing shih wen hsuan. Hong Kong: Wan li shu-tien.
朱自清詩文選。

1959. Lueh-tu chih-tao chü-yü. Taipei: Taiwan shang-wu yin shu kuan.
略讀指導舉隅。

1963. Hsin shih tsa-hua. Hong Kong: T'ai-p'ing shu-chü.
新詩雜話。

1963. Kuo-wen chiao-hsueh. Hong Kong: T'ai-p'ing shu-chü.
國文教學。

1963. Ni wo. Hong Kong: T'ai-p'ing shu-chü.
你我。

1963. Tu-shu chih-tao. Hong Kong: T'ai-p'ing shu-chü.
讀書指導。

1963. Yü wen ying. Hong Kong: T'ai-p'ing shu-chü.
語文影。

1964. Chu Tzu-ch'ing ch'üan-chi. Taipei: Wen-hua t'u-shu kung-ssu.
朱自清全集。

1964. Ho t'ang yueh se. Hong Kong: Shanghai shu-tien.
荷塘月色。

1965. Ching-tu chih-tao chü-yü. Taipei: Taiwan shang-wu yin shu kuan.
精讀指導舉隅。

Hai hsing tsa-chi.
海行雜記。

Lü-hsing tsa-chi.
旅行雜記。

SOURCES

Chi Chen-huai. "Chu Tzu-ch'ing hsien-sheng nien-p'u," in Chu Tzu-ch'ing, *Chu Tzu-ch'ing wen-chi*. Peking: K'ai-ming shu-tien, 1953. 4 vols.
季鎮淮。朱自清先生年譜。朱自清。朱自清文集。

Chin shan shih-pao. San Francisco, December 29, 1956.
金山時報。

Ch'u-pan chou-k'an, 175 (April 4, 1936): 24.
出版週刊。

CHWC
CHWSK
CHWYS
HMTT

Hsien-tai Chung-kuo tso-chia pi-ming lu, ed. by Yuan Yung-chin. Peiping: Chung-hua t'u-shu-kuan hsieh-hui, 1936.
現代中國作家筆名錄。袁湧進。

HWP

Jen-min jih-pao. Peking, August 19, 1949.
人民日報。

Li Kuang-t'ien. "Chu Tzu-ch'ing hsien-sheng chuan-lueh," in Chu Tzu-ch'ing, *Chu Tzu-ch'ing hsuan-chi*. Peking: K'ai-ming shu-tien, 1951.
李廣田。朱自清先生傳略。朱自清。朱自清選集。

MCNP
MMT
RCCL
TCMT

Ch'u Min-i   褚民誼

WORKS

1939. Ch'u Min-i hsien-sheng tsui-chin yen-lun chi. Shanghai.
褚民誼先生最近言論集。

SOURCES

CH
CMTC
MMT
SMJ

T'ang Leang-li. The Inner History of the Chinese Revolution. New York: E.P. Dutton & Co., 1930.

WWC, 1931.

Chü Cheng   居正

WORKS

1907. ed. of *Chung-hsing pao*.
中興報。

1908. ed. of *Kuang-hua jih-pao*.
光華日報。

1947. On the Reconstruction of the Chinese System of Law (tr. by Chang Chi-tai). Nanking.

1954. Chü Chueh-sheng hsien-sheng ch'üan-chi. Taipei. 2 vols.
居覺生先生全集。

SOURCES

Chang Chün-mai (Chang Chia-sen). Yü Chü Chueh-sheng hsien-sheng lun min-chu hsien-cheng shu. Chungking, 194?.

張君勱。與居覺生先生論民主憲政書。
Chiang Ching-kuo. Wei-chi ts'un-wang chih
　ch'iu.
蔣經國。危急存亡之秋。
Chü Cheng. Chü Chueh-sheng hsien-sheng
　ch'üan-chi. Taipei, 1954. 2 vols.
居正。居覺生先生全集。
Kuo-fu nien-p'u ch'u-kao, ed. by Kuo shih kuan
　shih-liao pien-tsuan wei-yuan-hui, Chung-kuo
　kuo-min-tang tang shih shih-liao pien-tsuan
　wei-yuan-hui. Taipei: Kuo shih kuan shih-
　liao pien-tsuan wei-yuan-hui, Chung-kuo kuo-
　min-tang tang shih shih-liao pien-tsuan wei-
　yuan-hui, 1959. 2 vols.
國父年譜初稿。國史館史料編纂委員會，
中國國民黨黨史史料編纂委員會。
The New York Times. November 25, 1951.
Sung Chiao-jen chuan.
宋教仁傳。

Ch'ü Ch'iu-pai　　瞿秋白

WORKS

1924. Ch'ih-tu hsin shih. Shanghai: Shang-wu
　yin shu kuan.
赤都心史。
1924–27. ed. of *Ch'ien-feng.*
前鋒。
1924–27. ed. of *Hsiang-tao chou-pao.*
嚮導週報。
1924–27. ed of *Hsin ch'ing-nien.*
新青年。
1925. ed. of *Je-hsueh jih-pao.*
熱血日報。
1927. Chung-kuo te shih chieh-chi.
中國的士階級。
1927. Ti-san kuo-chi huan shih ti-ling kuo-chi.
第三國際還是第零國際。
1928. Chung-kuo ko-ming yü kung-ch'an-tang:
　Kuan-yü i-chiu-erh-wu nien chih i-chiu-erh-
　ch'i nien Chung-kuo ko-ming te pao-kao.
中國革命與共產黨：關於一九二五年至一
九二七年中國革命的報告。
1929. Kung-ch'an kuo-chi tang-kang chi chang-
　ch'eng. (tr.)
共產國際黨綱及章程。
1938. Luan t'an chi ch'i-ta. Shanghai: Hsia she.
亂彈及其他。
1938. Wei-ta te Lu Hsün. Canton: Chan-shih
　ch'u-pan she.
偉大的魯迅。
1940. Chieh-t'ou chi. Shanghai: Hsia she.
街頭集。

1947. Lun Chung-kuo wen-hsueh ko-ming.
　Hong Kong: Hai-yang shu wu.
論中國文學革命。
1949. Ch'ü Ch'iu-pai *et al*. Chung-kuo yü-wen
　te hsin-sheng; la-ting hua Chung-kuo tzu yun-
　tung erh-shih nien lun-wen chi (ed. by Ni
　Hai-shu). Shanghai: Shih-tai shu pao ch'u-
　pan she.
瞿秋白等。中國語文的新生；拉丁化中國
字運動二十年論文集。倪海曙。
1949. Luan t'an; shang hsia p'ien. Hong Kong:
　Chia hua yin-shua kung-ssu.
亂彈；上下篇。
1953–54. Ch'ü Ch'iu-pai wen-chi. Peking: Jen-
　min wen-hsueh ch'u-pan she. 4 vols.
瞿秋白文集。
1959. Ch'ü Ch'iu-pai hsuan-chi. Peking: Jen-
　min wen-hsueh ch'u-pan she.
瞿秋白選集。
1959. Lun wen-hsueh. Peking: Jen-min wen-
　hsueh ch'u-pan she.
論文學。
Chung-kuo kuo-min ko-ming yü Tai Chi-t'ao
　chu-i.
中國國民革命與戴季陶主義。
Fan-tui Ch'en Tu-hsiu yü chi-hui chu-i.
反對陳獨秀與機會主義。
Kung-ch'an kuo-chi yü tang-ch'ien wen-t'i.
共產國際與當前問題。
San min chu-i.
三民主義。
Wu san-shih yün-tung chung chih kuo-min ko-
　ming yü chieh-chi tou-cheng.
五卅運動中之國民革命與階級鬥爭。

SOURCES

Brandt, Conrad. Stalin's Failure in China, 1924–
　1927. Cambridge: Harvard University Press,
　1958.
Ch'ü Ch'iu-pai. Ch'ü Ch'iu-pai wen-chi.
　Peking: Jen-min wen-hsueh ch'u-pan she,
　1953–54. 4 vols.
瞿秋白。瞿秋白文集。
Ch'ü Ch'iu-pai chu i hsi-nien mu-lu, ed. by
　Ting Ching-t'ang, Wen Ts'ao. Shanghai:
　Jen-min ch'u-pan she, 1959.
瞿秋白著譯系年目錄。丁景唐，文操。
Ch'ü Ch'iu-pai t'ung-chih hsi-sheng chou-nien
　chi-nien. Moscow, 1936.
瞿秋白同志犧牲週年紀念。
Hsia Tsi-an. "Ch'ü Ch'iu-po's Autobiographical
　Writings." Unpublished seminar paper.
Hsiao Tso-liang. Power Relations within the
　Chinese Communist Movement 1930-1934.

Seattle: University of Washington Press, 1961.

Lewis, John Wilson. Leadership in Communist China. Ithaca: Cornell University Press, 1963.

Lü Chien. Li Ta-chao ho Ch'ü Ch'iu-pai. Shanghai: Shang-wu yin shu kuan, 1951.
呂健。李大釗和瞿秋白。

Ts'ao Tzu-hsi. Ch'ü Ch'iu-pai te wen-hsueh huo-tung. Shanghai: Hsin wen-i ch'u-pan she, 1958.
曹子西。瞿秋白的文學活動。

Dalai Lama

SOURCES

Bacot, Jacques. Introduction à l'histoire du Tibet. Paris: Société Asiatique, 1962.

Bell, Sir Charles. People of Tibet. Oxford: Clarendon Press, 1928.

———. Portrait of the Dalai Lama. London: Collins, 1946.

———. Tibet, Past and Present. Oxford: Clarendon Press, 1924.

———. "Tibet's Position in Asia Today." Foreign Affairs, October, 1931.

CMTC

Eudin, Xenia Joukoff, and Robert C. North. Soviet Russia and the East, 1920–1927: A Documentary Survey. Stanford: Stanford University Press, 1957.

Lang-Sims, Lois. The Presence of Tibet. London: Cresset Press, 1963.

Li Tieh-tseng. The Historical Status of Tibet. New York: King's Crown Press, 1956.

Shen Tsung-lien and Liu Shen-chi. Tibet and the Tibetans. Stanford: Stanford University Press, 1953.

Demchukdonggrub

SOURCES

The China Annual, 1944. Shanghai: The Asia Statistics Co., 1944.

CMTC

CWR, 1934–37.

Daily Report, Foreign Radio Broadcasts, 70–1963 (April 10, 1963): BBB 1–3.

Jen-min jih-pao. Peking, April 10, 1963.
人民日報。

Nei-meng meng-ch'i tzu-chih yün-tung chi-shih, ed. by Huang Fen-sheng. Shanghai: Chung-hua shu-chü, 1935.

內蒙盟旗自治運動紀實。黃奮生。

The Orient Year Book, 1942. Tokyo: The Asia Statistics Co., 1942.

T'an T'i-wu. Nei-meng chih chin hsi. Shanghai: Shang-wu yin shu kuan, 1935.
譚惕吾。內蒙之今昔。

Fan Ch'ang-chiang   范長江

WORKS

1936. Chung-kuo te hsi-pei chiao. Tientsin: Ta kung pao kuan ch'u-pan pu.
中國的西北角。

1938. (ed.) Hsi hsien feng-yün.
西線風雲。

1938. Fan Hsi-wen (Fan Ch'ang-chiang) et al. Hsi-pei hsien.
范希文等。西北綫。

1938. Hua-pei liu sheng k'ang Jih hsueh chan shih. with Shu Ch'ing-ch'un et al. Nu-hou ch'u-pan she.
華北六省抗日血戰史。舒慶春等。

1938. Lun-wang te P'ing Ch'in. with Hsiao Fang et al. Hankow: Sheng-huo shu-tien.
淪亡的平津。小方等。

1938. (ed.) Sung Hu huo-hsien shang. Hankow: Sheng-huo shu-tien.
淞滬火綫上。

1938. (ed.) Tsung Lu-kuo-ch'iao tao Chang-ho. Sheng-huo shu-tien.
從蘆溝橋到漳河。

1949–? ed. of Jen-min jih-pao.
人民日報。

1952. Ch'uan-ti-ts'un te nung-yeh sheng-ch'an ho-tso-she. Peking: Jen-min ch'u-pan she.
川底村的農業生產合作社。

SOURCES

CPR, 906 (June 7, 1949).

Ts'ao Chü-jen. Ts'ai-fang wai-chi. Hong Kong: Ch'uang k'en ch'u-pan she, 1955.
曹聚仁。採訪外記。

Fan Wen-lan   范文瀾

WORKS

1929. Shui ching chu hsieh ching wen ch'ao. Peiping.
水經注寫景文鈔。

1931. Cheng-shih k'ao-lueh. Peiping: Wen-hua hsueh-she.

正史考略。

1933. (ed.) Ch'ün ching kai-lun. Peiping: Ching-shan shu she.
群經概論。

1946. Han-chien kuei-tzu-shou Tsen Kuo-fan te i-sheng. Tung-pei shu-tien.
漢奸劊子手曾國藩的一生。

1947. Chung-kuo chin-tai shih; shang pien; ti-i fen ts'e. Shanghai: Tu-shu ch'u-pan she.
中國近代史；上編；第一分冊。

1948. T'ai-p'ing T'ien-kuo ko-ming yün-tung. Singapore: Hsin min-chu ch'u-pan she.
太平天國革命運動。

1949. Lun cheng-t'ung. Chih-shih shu-tien.
論正統。

1950. Fan Wen-lan et al. T'ai-p'ing T'ien-kuo ko-ming yün-tung lun-wen chi; Chin-t'ien ch'i-i pai-chou-nien chi-nien. (ed. by Hua-pei ta-hsüeh li-shih yen-chiu shih) Peking: Sheng-huo, tu-shu, hsin-chih san lien shu-tien.
范文瀾等。太平天國革命運動論文集；金田起義百週年紀念。華北大學歷史研究室。

1950. Lun Chung-kuo feng-chien she-hui ch'ang-ch'i yen-hsü te yuan-yin. Peking: Ta-chung shu-tien.
論中國封建社會長期延續的原因。

1953. Nien chün, ed. by Fang Wen-lan et al. Shanghai: Shen-chou kuo kuang she. 8 vols.
捻軍。范文瀾等。

Sources

Briere, O. Fifty Years of Chinese Philosophy, 1898-1948. (tr. by Laurence G. Thompson). New York: The Macmillan Co., 1956.
GCJJ
HCJC
Kuo Chan-po. Chin wu-shih nien Chung-kuo ssu-hsiang shih. Hong Kong: Lung men shu-tien, 1965.
郭湛波。近五十年中國思想史。
Ying Tzu. Chung-kuo hsin hsueh-shu jen-wu chih. Hong Kong: Chih ming shu-chü, 1956.
穎子。中國新學術人物誌。

Fan Yuan-lien   范源濂

Sources

Chiao-yü ta tz'u shu, comp. by T'ang Yueh, Chu Ching-nung, Kao Chueh-fu. Shanghai: Shang-wu yin shu kuan, 1930. 2 vols.
教育大辭書。唐鉞，朱經農，高覺敷。
Liang Jen-kung hsien-sheng nien-p'u ch'ang pien

ch'u-kao, comp. by Ting Wen-chiang. Tai-pei: Shih-chieh shu-chü, 1959. 2 vols.
梁任公先生年譜長編初稿。丁文江。
Liang Jung-jo. "Chi Fan Ching-sheng hsien-sheng." Chuan-chi wen-hsueh, I-6 (1962).
梁容若。記范靜生先生。傳記文學。
Yao Yü-hsiang. "Fan Yuan-lien yü Chung-kuo chiao-yü." Chung-yang jih-pao. Taipei, December 23, 24, 1962.
姚漁湘。范源濂與中國教育。中央日報。

Fang Chih-min   方志敏

Works

1922. "Mou-shih." Hsiao-shuo nien-chien, 3.
謀事。小說年鑑。
1952. K'o-ai te Chung-kuo; Fang Chih-min lieh-shih i-chu. Peking: Jen-min wen-hsueh ch'u-pan she.
可愛的中國；方志敏烈士遺著。
1957. Yü chung chi-shih. Peking: Kung-jen ch'u-pan she.
獄中記實。
Fang Chih-min tzu-chuan. Hsia she.
方志敏自傳。

Sources

Person interviewed: Chang Kuo-t'ao.
Chin Tung-p'ing. Yenan chien-wen lu. Chung-king: Tu-li ch'u-pan she, 1945.
金東平。延安見聞錄。
Ch'üan Ch'i-fu. "I-yang jen-min je-ai Chung-kuo kung-ch'an-tang." Ch'ang-chiang jih-pao, July 4, 1951.
權屹夫。弋陽人民熱愛中國共產黨。長江日報。
CKLC
Fang Chih-ch'un. "T'ung tao Fang Chih-min t'ung-chih." Ch'ang-chiang jih-pao, July 1, 1952.
方志純。痛悼方志敏同志。長江日報。
Fang Chih-min. Fang Chih-min tzu-chuan. Hsia she.
方志敏。方志敏自傳。
———. K'o-ai te Chung-kuo; Fang Chih-min lieh-shih i-chu. Peking: Jen-min wen-hsueh ch'u-pan she, 1952.
方志敏。可愛的中國；方志敏烈士遺著。
———. "Mou-shih." Hsiao-shuo nien-chien, 3, 1922.
方志敏。謀事。小說年鑑。
———. Yü chung chi-shih. Peking: Kung-jen ch'u-pan she, 1957.
方志敏。獄中記實。

方志敏。 獄中記實。

GCCJK

GSSJ

Hsiao Pai-fan. Chung-kuo chin pai-nien ko-ming shih. Kowloon: Ch'iu shih ch'u-pan she, 1951.

蕭白帆。 中國近百年革命史。

Liu Chu. "Fang Chih-min lieh-shih nien-piao ch'u-kao." *Chin-pu jih-pao*, September 5, 1952.

劉竚。 方志敏烈士年表初稿。 進步日報。

Miu Min. Fang Chih-min chan-tou te i-sheng. Peking: Kung-jen ch'u-pan she, 1958.

繆敏。 方志敏戰鬥的一生。

———. "Fang Chih-min t'ung-chih chan-tou te i-sheng." *Ch'ang-chiang jih-pao*, July 4, 1951.

繆敏。 方志敏同志戰鬥的一生。 長江日報。

SCMP, 2277 (June 15, 1960): 1.

Ta Sheng *et al*. Lieh-shih chuan; ti-i chi; chi-nien wo-men wei Chung-kuo jen-min chieh-fang fen-tou erh hsi-sheng te chan-shih. Moscow, 1936.

大生等。 烈士傳; 第一集; 紀念我們爲中國人民解放奮鬥而犧牲的戰士。

T'ang T'ieh-hai. Chung-yang lao ken-chü-ti yin-hsiang chi. Shanghai: Hua-tung jen-min ch'u-pan she, 1954.

唐鐵海。 中央老根據地印象記。

Fei Hsiao-t'ung   費孝通

WORKS

1939. Peasant Life in China: A Field Study of Country Life in the Yangtze Valley. London: Kegan Paul, Trench, Trubner & Co.

1943. Lu ts'un nung-t'ien. Chungking: Shang-wu yin shu kuan.

祿村農田。

1945. Earthbound China: A Study of Rural Economy in Yunnan. with Chang Chih-i. Chicago: University of Chicago Press.

1946. Fei Hsiao-t'ung *et al*. Jen-hsing ho chi-ch'i; Chung-kuo shou-kung-yeh te ch'ien-t'u (ed. by P'an Kuang-tan *et al*.). Shanghai: Sheng-huo shu-tien.

費孝通等。 人性和機器; 中國手工業的前途。 潘光旦等。

1947. Ch'u fang Mei-kuo. Shanghai: Sheng-huo shu-tien.

初訪美國。

1947? Ch'ung fang Ying Lun. Shanghai: Ta kung pao kuan.

重訪英倫。

1947. Mei-kuo jen hsing-ko. Shanghai: Sheng-huo shu-tien.

美國人性格。

1947. Sheng-yü chih-tu. Shanghai: Shang-wu yin shu kuan

生育制度。

1948. Fei Hsiao-t'ung *et al*. Huang ch'üan yü shen ch'üan. Shanghai: Kuan-ch'a she.

費孝通等。 皇權與紳權。

1948. Hsiang-t'u Chung-kuo. Shanghai: Kuan-ch'a she.

鄉土中國。

1948. Hsiang-t'u ch'ung-chien. Shanghai: Kuan-ch'a she.

鄉土重建。

1950. Fei Hsiao-t'ung *et al*. Chiu jen-wu te kai-tsao (ed. by T'ung-su wen-hua ch'u-pan she). Canton: Ch'un-ch'iu shu-tien.

費孝通等。 舊人物的改造。 通俗文化出版社。

1950, March. "Ssu-hsiang chen-hsien te i-chiao." *Hsueh-hsi*, XI-1: 17–19.

思想陣線的一角。 學習。

1950. Ta-hsueh te kai-tsao. Shanghai: Shanghai ch'u-pan kung-ssu.

大學的改造。

1950. Wo che i nien. Peking: Sheng-huo, tu-shu, hsin chih san lien shu-tien.

我這一年。

1951. Hsiung-ti min-tsu tsai Kweichow. Peking: Sheng-huo, tu-shu, hsin chih san lien shu-tien.

兄弟民族在貴州。

1951, June. "K'o-fu mang-ts'ung." *Hsueh-hsi*, IV-5.

克服盲從。 學習。

1953. China's Gentry: Essays in Rural Urban Relations (rev. and ed. by Margret Park Redfield). Chicago: University of Chicago Press.

1956. Fei Hsiao-t'ung *et al*. Shen-mo shih min-tsu ch'ü-yü tzu-chih. Hong Kong: Hsin min-chu ch'u-pan she.

費孝通等。 甚麼是民族區域自治。

1956, June. "Old Friends and New Understanding." *People's China*, (June 1, 1956): 12–17.

1957, March 24. "Chih-shih fen-tzu te tsao ch'un t'ien-ch'i." *Jen-min jih-pao*.

知識份子的早春天氣。 人民日報。

SOURCES

CB, 475 (August 28, 1957).

Chen, Theodore Hsi-en. Thought Reform of the Chinese Intellectuals. Hong Kong: Hong Kong University Press, 1960.

Fei Hsiao-tung and Chang Chih-i. Earthbound China: A Study of Rural Economy in Yunnan. Chicago; University of Chicago Press, 1945.

GCJJ

The Hundred Flowers Campaign and the Chinese Intellectuals, ed. by Roderick MacFarquhar. New York: Frederick A. Praeger, 1960.

Li Ta. "P'i-p'an Fei Hsiao-t'ung te mai-pan she-hui-hsueh." *Che-hsueh yen-chiu* 5 (October 15, 1957).
李達。批判費孝通的買辦社會學。哲學研究。

Feng Ch'eng-chün   馮承鈞

WORKS

1928. Fo-hsueh yen-chiu. (tr.)
佛學研究。

1930. Fa-chu-chi chi so-chi O-lo-han k'ao. (tr.)
法住記及所記阿羅漢考。

1956. Hsi-yü Nan-hai shih ti k'ao-cheng i ts'ung liu p'ien. (tr.) Peking: Chung-hua shu-chü.
西域南海史地考證譯叢六篇。

SOURCES

Chou Huan. "Feng Ch'eng-chün hsien-sheng i chu shu-mu." *Yen-ching hsueh-pao*, 32 (June, 1947): 254–59.
周桓，馮承鈞先生譯著書目。燕京學報。
"Feng Ch'eng-chün fan-i chu-shu mu-lu." *T'u-shu chi-k'an* V-3, 4 (December, 1946).
馮承鈞翻譯著述目錄。圖書季刊。
Meng Tzu-wei. "Tung-nan-ya shih ti chuan-chia Feng Ch'eng-chün." *Ta kung pao*. Hong Kong, May 15–16, 1960.
孟子微。東南亞史地專家馮承鈞。大公報。
Wang Ching-ju. "Feng Ch'eng-chün chiao-shou chuan." *Yen-ching hsueh-pao*, 30 (June, 1946): 325–27.
王靜如。馮承鈞教授傳。燕京學報。

Feng Chih   馮至

WORKS

1925–? ed. of *Ch'en chung*.
晨鐘。
1927. Tso-jih chih ko. Shanghai: Pei hsin shu-chü.
昨日之歌。

1930. (ed.) Chu fan chih chiao chu. Changsha: Shang-wu yin shu kuan.
諸蕃志校注。
1930. Shih-chieh chih fen-luan. (tr. of Gustave LeBon's *La Desquilifre du Monde*.)
世界之紛亂。
1931. (ed.) Ching-chiao pei k'ao. Shanghai: Shang-wu yin shu kuan.
景教碑攷。
1931. Li-tai ch'iu fa fan ching lu. Shanghai: Shang-wu yin shu kuan.
歷代求法翻經錄。
1931. (ed.) Yuan-tai pai-hua pei. Shanghai: Shang-wu yin shu kuan.
元代白話碑。
1933. (tr.) Shih ti ts'ung-k'ao hsü-pien. Shanghai: Shang-wu yin shu kuan.
史地叢攷續編。
1934. Ch'eng-chi-ssu-han chuan. Shanghai: Shang-wu yin shu kuan.
成吉思汗傳。
1934. Hsi T'u-chüeh shih-liao. (tr. of Edouard Chavannes' *Documents sur les Tou-kiue (Turcs) Occidentaus*.) Shanghai: Shang-wu yin shu kuan.
西突厥史料。
1935. (tr.) Shih ti ts'ung-k'ao. Shanghai: Shang-wu yin shu kuan.
史地叢攷。
1937. Chung-kuo Nan-yang chiao-t'ung shih. Shanghai: Shang-wu yin shu kuan.
中國南洋交通史。
1938. Hsing ch'a sheng lan chio chu; erh chi. Changsha: Shang-wu yin shu kuan.
星槎勝覽校注；二集。
1941. Shih-ssu hang shih chi.
十四行詩集。
1945. Hsi li tung chien shih. Peiping: Peking hsin min yin shu kuan.
西力東漸史。
1946, November. "Sha-lung." *Kuan-ch'a*, I-12: 13.
沙龍。觀察。
1946. Wu Tzu-hsü. Shanghai: Wen-hua sheng-huo ch'u-pan she.
伍子胥。
1950. Tung-ou tsa-chi.
東歐雜記。
1952. Tu Fu chuan. Peking: Jen-min wen-hsueh ch'u-pan she.
杜甫傳。
1954. Chang Ming-shan ho fan wei p'an. Peking: Kung-jen ch'u-pan she.

張明山和反圍盤。

1955. Feng Chih shih wen hsuan-chi; erh chi. Peking: Jen-min wen-hsueh ch'u-pan she.
馮至詩文選集；二輯。

1957. (comp.) Hsi-yü ti-ming. Peking: Chung-hua shu-chü.
西域地名。

1959. Shih nien shih ch'ao. Peking: Jen-min wen-hsueh ch'u-pan she.
十年詩鈔。

1959. (ed.) Tu Fu shih-hsuan. Hong Kong: Ta kuang ch'u-pan she.
杜甫詩選。

ed. of *Hsien-tai wen-lu*.
現代文錄。

Pen-kuo fa-chih shih kang-yao.
本國法制史綱要。

SOURCES

CHWSK

Contemporary Chinese Poetry, ed. by Pierre Stephen Robert Payne. London: Routledge, 1947.

Feng Chih. Feng Chih shih wen hsuan-chi-; erh chi. Peking: Jen-min wen-hsueh ch'u-pan she, 1955.
馮至。馮至詩文選集；二輯。

GCJJ

JMST, 1955.

Wu Pen-hsing. Wen-hsueh tso-p'in yen-chiu; ti-i chi. Shanghai: Tung-fang, 1954.
吳奔星。文學作品研究；第一輯。

Feng Kuo-chang 馮國璋

SOURCES

AADC

Chan I-lin. Hsin t'ai-p'ing shih chi (ed. by Ku T'ing-lung). Shanghai, 1947. 4 vols.
張一麐。心太平室集。顧廷龍。

CMMC

CYB-W, 1919-20.

Ho-chien Feng kung jung-ai lu. Ho-chien, 1920.
河間馮公榮哀錄。

Li Chien-nung. Tsui-chin san-shih nien Chung-kuo cheng-chih shih. Shanghai: T'ai-p'ing-yang shu-tien, 1931.
李劍農。最近三十年中國政治史。

MMT

Powell, Ralph L. The Rise of Chinese Military Power, 1895-1912. Princeton: Princeton University Press, 1955.

T'ao Chü-yin. Pei-yang chün-fa t'ung-chih shih-ch'i shih-hua. Peking: Sheng-huo, tu-shu, hsin chih san lien shu-tien, 1957. 6 vols.
陶菊隱。北洋軍閥統治時期史話。

Wen Kung-chih. Tsui-chin san-shih nien Chung-kuo chün-shih shih. Shanghai: T'ai-p'ing-yang shu-tien, 1932. 2 vols.
文公直。最近三十年中國軍事史。

Feng Tzu-k'ai 豐子愷

WORKS

1926. Yin-yueh ju-men. Shanghai: K'ai-ming shu-tien.
音樂入門。

1927. Tzu-k'ai hua chi. Shanghai: K'ai-ming shu-tien.
子愷畫集。

1928. I-shu chiao-yü ABC. Shanghai: Shih-chieh shu-chü.
藝術教育 ABC。

1929. Hsien-tai i-shu shih-erh chiang. (tr.) Shanghai: K'ai-ming shu-tien.
現代藝術十二講。

1929. Tzu-k'ai man-hua chi. Shanghai: K'ai-ming shu-tien.
子愷漫畫集。

1930. Hsü Hu sheng hua chi. Shanghai: Mei shang yung-ning yu-hsien kung-ssu.
續護生畫集。

1931. Ch'u-lien. (tr.) Shanghai: K'ai-ming shu-tien.
初戀。

1931. Kuang-ming hua chi. Soochow: Hung hua she.
光明畫集。

1933. Tzu-k'ai hsiao-p'in chi. Shanghai: K'ai-ming shu-tien.
子愷小品集。

1934. Hui-hua yü wen-hsueh. Shanghai: K'ai-ming shu-tien.
繪畫與文學。

1934. I-shu kai-lun. (tr.) Shanghai: K'ai-ming shu-tien.
藝術概論。

1934. I-shu ts'ung-hua. Shanghai: Liang-yu t'u-shu kung-ssu.
藝術叢話。

1935. Ch'e hsiang she-hui. Shanghai: Liang-yu t'u-shu yin-shua kung-ssu.
車箱社會。

1935, February, March. "T'an tzu-chi te hua—tzu shu shih nien lai te sheng-huo ho hsin-ch'ing." *Jen-chien shih*, 22-23.

談自己的畫—自述十年來的生活和心情。
人間世。

1938. "Pu-huo chih li," in Tao K'ang-te, *Tzu-chuan chih i-chang*. Canton: Yü-chou feng she.
不惑之禮。陶亢德。自傳之一章。

1940. Kan mei te hui-wei. Shanghai: K'ai-hua shu-chü.
甘美的回味。

1946. Shuai-chen chi. Shanghai: Wan yeh shu-tien.
率眞集。

1946. Tzu-k'ai man-hua ch'üan-chi. Shanghai: K'ai-ming shu-tien.
子愷漫畫全集。

1946. Yuan-yuan-t'ang sui-pi. K'ai-ming shu-tien.
緣緣堂隨筆。

1947. Tu-shih hsiang. Shanghai? K'ai-ming shu-tien.
都市相。

1947. "Wo-te k'u-hsueh ching-yen," in Wang Li-hsi, *Wo-men te tu-shu sheng-huo*. Shanghai: Sheng-chou kuo kuang she.
我的苦學經驗。王禮錫。我們的讀書生活。

1947. Yu sheng hua chi. Shanghai: K'ai-ming shu-tien.
又生畫集。

1948. "Wo-te mu-ch'in," in *Wo-te mu-ch'in*. Hong Kong: Chung-kuo wen-hua kuan.
我的母親。我的母親。

1948. Yuan-yuan-t'ang tsai pi. Shanghai: K'ai-ming shu-tien.
緣緣堂再筆。

1950. Man-hua AQ cheng chuan. Peking: K'ai-ming shu-tien.
漫畫阿Q正傳。

1955. Tzu-k'ai man-hua hsuan (comp. by Wang Chao-wen). Peking: Jen-min mei-shu ch'u-pan she.
子愷漫畫選。王朝聞。

1956. From Feng Tse-kai's Drawings of Children (selected by Wang Chao-wen). Peking: Foreign Languages Press.

1956. (ed.) Hsueh-tan te sheng-ya yü i-shu (Chinien Jih-pen hua-chia Hsueh-tan shih-shih 450 chou-nien). Shanghai: Shanghai jen-min mei-shu ch'u-pan she.
雪丹的生涯與藝術（紀念日本畫家雪丹逝世450週年）。

1961. Yang-liu. Hong Kong: Shanghai shu-chü.
楊柳。

1963. Feng Tzu-k'ai hua-chi (ed. by Shanghai jen-min mei-shu ch'u-pan she). Shanghai: Shanghai jen-min mei-shu ch'u-pan she.

豐子愷畫集。上海人民美術出版社。
Feng Tzu-k'ai man-hua. 2 vols.
豐子愷漫畫。

SOURCES

CBJS
Chao Ching-shen. "Feng Tzu-k'ai ho t'a te hsiao-p'in wen." *Jen-chien shih*, 30 (June, 1935).
趙景深。豐子愷和他的小品文。人間世。
Chi Ch'eng-hsing. "Tzu-k'ai hsien-sheng kei wo te yin-hsiang." *I feng*, III-2 (February, 1935).
季誠性。子愷先生給我的印象。藝風。
Chin-tai ming-jen chuan-chi hsuan, comp. by Chu Te-chün. Shanghai: Wen hsin shu-chü, 1948.
近代名人傳記選。朱德君。
Chung wai wen-hsueh chia chuan-lueh tz'u-tien. Hong Kong: Shanghai shu-chü, 1959.
中外文學家傳略辭典。
Feng Tzu-k'ai. "Pu-huo chih li," in T'ao K'ang-te, *Tzu-chuan chih i-chang*. Canton: Yü-chou feng she, 1938.
豐子愷。不惑之禮。陶亢德。自傳之一章。
———. "T'an tzu-chi te hua—tzu shu shih nien lai te sheng-huo ho hsin-ch'ing." *Jen-chien shih*, 22–23 (February, March, 1935).
豐子愷。談自己的畫—自述十年來的生活和心情。人間世。
———. "Wo-te k'u-hsueh ching-yen," in Wang Li-hsi, *Wo-men te tu-shu sheng-huo*. Shanghai: Shen-chou kuo kuang she, 1947.
豐子愷。我的苦學經驗。王禮錫。我們的讀書生活。
———. "Wo-te mu-ch'in," in *Wo-te mu-ch'in*. Hong Kong: Chung-kuo wen-hua kuan, 1948.
豐子愷。我的母親。我的母親。
GCMMTJK
Ying Tzu. Chung-kuo hsin hsueh-shu jen-wu chih. Hong Kong: Chih ming shu-chü, 1956.
穎子。中國新學術人物誌。

Feng Tzu-yu   馮自由

WORKS

1920. She-hui chu-i yü Chung-kuo. Hong Kong: She-hui chu-i yen-chiu so.
社會主義與中國。

1938. Chung-kuo ko-ming yün-tung erh-shih-liu nien tsu-chih shih. Shanghai: Shang-wu yin shu kuan.
中國革命運動二十六年組織史。

1939-47. Ko-ming i-shih. Chungking, Shanghai: Shang-wu yin shu kuan. 5 vols.
革命逸史。

1944. Chung-hua Min-kuo k'ai-kuo ch'ien ko-ming shih. Chungking: Chung-kuo wen-hua fu-wu she. 3 vols.
中華民國開國前革命史。

1945. Hua-ch'iao ko-ming shih-hua; shang-ts'e. Chungking: Hai-wai ch'u-pan she.
華僑革命史話；上冊。

1947. Hua-ch'iao ko-ming k'ai-kuo shih. Shanghai: Shang-wu yin shu kuan.
華僑革命開國史。

1954. Hua-ch'iao ko-ming tsu-chih shih-hua. Taipei: Cheng-chung shu-chü.
華僑革命組織史話。

Cheng-chih hsueh. (tr.)
政治學。

Hsin-hai Kweichow ko-ming-tang lieh-chuan.
辛亥貴州革命黨列傳。

San tz'u ke-ming shih.
三次革命史。

Sources

Chung-yang jih-pao. Taipei, April 7, 1958.
中央日報。

CMJL

Feng Tzu-yu. Hua-ch'iao ko-ming k'ai-kuo shih. Shanghai: Shang-wu yin shu kuan, 1947.
馮自由。華僑革命開國史。

———. She-hui chu-i yü Chung-kuo. Hong Kong: She-hui chu-i yen-chiu so, 1920.
馮自由。社會主義與中國。

Feng Yu-lan 馮友蘭

Works

1924. I chung jen-sheng-kuan. Shanghai: Shang-wu yin shu kuan.
一種人生觀。

1926. Jen-sheng che-hsueh. Shanghai: Shang-wu yin shu kuan.
人生哲學。

1935. Chung-kuo che-hsueh hsiao-shih. Shanghai: Shang-wu yin shu kuan.
中國哲學小史。

1936. Chung-kuo che-hsueh shih pu. Shanghai: Shang-wu yin shu kuan.
中國哲學史補。

1939. Hsin li-hsueh. Changsha: Shang-wu yin shu kuan.
新理學。

1940. Hsin shih hsun. Shanghai: K'ai-ming shu-tien.
新世訓。

1941. Chung-kuo che-hsueh shih. Changsha: Shang-wu yin shu kuan. 2 vols.
中國哲學史。

1942. "The Rise of Neo-Confucianism." *Harvard Journal of Asiatic Studies*, VII-2. (tr. by Derk Bodde).

1943. Hsin yuan jen. Chungking. Shang-wu yin shu kuan.
新原人。

1946. Hsin chih yen. Shanghai: Shang-wu yin shu kuan.
新知言。

1947. Hsin shih lun. Shanghai: Shang-wu yin shu kuan.
新事論。

1947. Hsin yuan tao. Shanghai: Shang-wu yin shu kuan.
新原道。
Eng. tr. by E.R. Hughes, *The Spirits of Chinese Philosophy.* London: Kegan Paul, Trench, Trubner, 1947.

1950, October 8. "Hsin li-hsueh te tzu-wo chien-t'ao." *Kuang-ming jih-pao. Peking.*
新理學的自我檢討。光明日報。

1950. "I Discovered Marxism-Leninism." *People's China,* I-6.

1958. Chung-kuo che-hsueh shih lun-wen chi. Shanghai: Shanghai jen-min ch'u-pan she.
中國哲學史論文集。

1958, June. "Tsai shuang fan yün-tung chung te shou-huo ho t'i-hui." *Cheng ming,* 6.
在雙反運動中的收獲和體會。爭鳴。

1958, June 12-13. "Kuan-yü Lao-tzu che-hsueh te liang ko wen-t'i." *Jen-min jih-pao.* Peking.
關於老子哲學的兩個問題。人民日報。

1959. "Hsin li-hsueh te yuan-hsing." *Che-hsueh yen-chiu,* 1.
新理學的原形。哲學研究。

1962. Chung-kuo che-hsueh shih lun-wen erh chi. Shanghai: Shanghai jen-min ch'u-pan she.
中國哲學史論文二集。

1964-? Chung-kuo che-hsueh shih hsin pien. Peking: Jen-min ch'u-pan she. 2 vols.
中國哲學史新編。

Sources

Brière, O. Fifty Years of Chinese Philosophy, 1895-1948. (tr. by Laurence G. Thompson). New York: The Macmillan Co., 1956.

Chan Wing-tsit. An Outline and an Annotated

Bibliography of Chinese Philosophy. New Haven: Yale University, Far Eastern Publications, 1959.

Chan Wing-tsit. Religious Trends in Modern China. New York: Columbia University Press, 1953.

Ch'en Hsi-en. Thought Reform of the Chinese Intellectuals. Hong Kong: Hong Kong University Press, 1960.

China News Analysis, 336 (August 19, 1960): 1–7; 395 (November 3, 1961): 6–7; 423 (June 1, 1962): 3–5.

Chow Tse-tsung. The May Fourth Movement: Intellectual Revolution in Modern China. Cambridge: Harvard University Press, 1960.

Hsin chien-she, January, March, 1960.
新建設。

Jen-min jih-pao. Peking, March 29–30, 1957.
人民日報。

Kuo Chan-po. Chin wu-shih nien Chung-kuo ssu-hsiang shih. Hong Kong: Lung men shu-tien, 1965.
郭湛波。近五十年中國思想史。

Lee, Robert H. G. "Fung Yu-lan: A Biographical Profile." *The China Quarterly*, 14 (April-June, 1963): 141–52.

SCMP, 215.

Sheehan, J. J. "A Summary of Fung Yu-lan: Hsin yuan jen (An 'Ethical Inquiry into the Nature of Man,' First Published in Chungking 1943), Together with a Translation of Chapter IV." Unpublished Master's essay, Columbia University, 1951.

Teng Ssu-yu, John K. Fairbank, Sun Zen E-tu, Fang Chaoying, *et al.* China's Response to the West: A Documentary Survey, 1839–1923. Cambridge: Harvard University Press, 1954.

Feng Yü-hsiang   馮玉祥

Works

1927. Chiu i ch'i hsin sheng-ming.
九一七新生命。

1932. Fan kuo-lien tiao-ch'a t'uan pao-kao shu. Shanghai: Chün hsueh she.
反國聯調查團報告書。

1932. Feng Yü-hsiang jih-chi. Peiping: Min-kuo shih-liao pien-chi she. 2 vols.
馮玉祥日記。

1933. Feng Yü-hsiang chün-shih yao tien hui-pien. Shanghai: Min-kuo shih liao pien-chi she.

馮玉祥軍事要電彙編。

1934. Feng Yü-hsiang hsun-ling hui-pien. Shanghai: Chün hsueh she.
馮玉祥訓令彙編。

1934. Feng Yü-hsiang tu ch'un-ch'iu tso-chuan cha-chi. Shanghai: Chün hsueh she.
馮玉祥讀春秋左傳札記。

1936. Feng tsai Nanking chiang-yen chi.
馮在南京講演集。

1937. Feng tsai Nanking pao-kao chi. Nanking.
馮在南京報告集。

1937. Feng tsai Nanking ti-i nien.
馮在南京第一年。

1938. Feng tsai Nanking ti-erh nien. Kweilin: San hu t'u-shu she.
馮在南京第二年。

1938. K'ai pu tsou. Hankow: Ta-chung wen-hua ts'ung-shu she.
開步走。

1940. Feng fu wei-yuan-chang k'ang-chan yen-lun chi (comp. by Hua Ai-kuo).
馮副委員長抗戰言論集。華愛國。

1942? Feng Yü-hsiang chiang-chün Ch'ing-o yu-chi (comp. by Hua Ai-kuo).
馮玉祥將軍青峨遊記。華愛國。

1944. Ch'uan-hsi-nan chi yu. Kweilin: San hu t'u-shu she.
川西南記遊。

1944. Jung Kuan chi-hsing. Kweilin: San hu t'u-shu she.
蓉灌紀行。

1946. Chiang Feng shu-chien. Shanghai: Chung-kuo wen-hua hsin-t'uo fu-wu she.
蔣馮書簡。

1947. Wo te sheng-huo. Shanghai: Chiao-yü shu-tien. 3 vols.
我的生活。

1947. Wo te tu-shu sheng-huo. Shanghai: Tso-chia shu-wu.
我的讀書生活。

1947, November 5. "Why I Broke with Chiang." *The Nation*: 522–25.

1948, September. "Farewell to America." *Far East Spotlight*, IV-3.

1949. Wo so jen-shih te Chiang Kai-shek. Shanghai: Wen-hua kung-tso she.
我所認識的蔣介石。

1954. Feng Yü-hsiang shih-ko hsuan-chi. Shanghai: Hsin wen-i ch'u-pan she.
馮玉祥詩歌選集。

Sources

Broomhall, Marshall. Marshal Feng: A Good

Soldier of Christ Jesus. London: China Inland Mission, 1924.

Chahar k'ang Jih shih-lu. Shanghai: Chün hsueh she, 1933?
察哈爾抗日實錄。

Ch'eng, Marcus. Marshal Feng—The Man and His Work. Shanghai: Kelly & Walsh, 1926?

Chien Yu-wen. Wo so jen-shih te Feng Yü-hsiang chi Hsi-pei chün.
簡又文。我所認識的馮玉祥及西北軍。

Davis, George Thompson Brown. China's Christian Army, a Story of Marshal Feng and His Soldiers. New York: Christian Alliance Publishing Co., 1925.

Documents on Communism, Nationalism, and Soviet Advisers in China, 1918–1927: Papers Seized in the 1927 Peking Raid, ed. by C. Martin Wilbur, Julie Lien-ying How. New York: Columbia University Press, 1956.

Feng Yü-hsiang. Feng tsai Nanking ti-erh nien. Kweilin: San hu t'u-shu she, 1938.
馮玉祥。馮在南京第二年。

———. Feng Yü-hsiang chün-shih yao tien hui-pien. Shanghai: Min-kuo shih-liao pien-chi she, 1933.
馮玉祥。馮玉祥軍事要電彙編。

———. Feng Yü-hsiang jih-chi. Peiping: Min-kuo shih-liao pien-chi she, 1932. 2 vols.
馮玉祥。馮玉祥日記。

———. Feng Yü-hsiang tu ch'un-ch'iu tso-chuan cha-chi. Shanghai: Chün hsueh she, 1934.
馮玉祥。馮玉祥讀春秋左傳札記。

———. "What China Needs Today." Living Age, January 16, 1926: 131–35.

———. Wo so jen-shih te Chiang Kai-shek. Shanghai: Wen-hua kung-tso she, 1949.
馮玉祥。我所認識的蔣介石。

———. Wo-te sheng-huo. Shanghai: Chiao-yü shu-tien, 1947. 3 vols.
馮玉祥。我的生活。

———· Wo-te tu-shu sheng-huo. Shanghai: Tso-chia shu-wu, 1947.
馮玉祥。我的讀書生活。

Feng Yü-hsiang chiang-chün chi-nien ts'e, ed. by Chung-kuo kuo-min-tang ko-ming wei-yuan-hui. Hong Kong: Chia hua yin-shua yu-hsien kung-ssu, 1949.
馮玉祥將軍紀念冊。中國國民黨革命委員會。

Feng Yü-hsiang te tsung chien-ch'a, ed. by Peiping t'e-pieh shih tang-wu chih-tao wei-yuan-hui. Peiping, 1929.
馮玉祥的總檢查。北平特別市黨務指導委員會。

Fuse Katsuji. Shina kokumin kakumei to Fu Gyoku-sho. Tokyo: Osakayago Shoten, 1929.
布施勝治。支那國民革命と馮玉祥。

Kuo-min chün ko-ming shih. Shanghai: Chün hsueh she.
國民軍革命史。

Li Chien-nung. Tsui-chin san-shih nien Chung-kuo cheng-chih shih. Shanghai: T'ai-p'ing-yang shu-tien, 1930.
李劍農。最近三十年中國政治史。

Li T'ai-fen. Kuo-min chün shih kao. 1930.
李泰棻。國民軍史稿。

Ma Po-yuan. Wo so chih-tao te kuo-min chün yü kuo-min-tang ho-tso shih. 1931.
馬伯援。我所知道的國民軍與國民黨合作史。

Miner, Louella. "Works of Peace in Marshal Feng's Army." Chinese Recorder, LVII-3 (March, 1926): 183–86.

Powell, John B. My Twenty-Five Years in China. New York: The Macmillan Co., 1945.

Sheean, Vincent. Personal History. Garden City, N. Y.: Doubleday, Doran & Co., 1935.

Sheridan, James E. Chinese Warlord: The Career of Feng Yü-hsiang. Stanford: Stanford Univerity Press, 1966.

Shyu Nae-lih. "Feng Yü-hsiang and the Kuo-minchün, 1924–1928." Unpublished Master's thesis, University of Washington, 1960.

Strong, Anna Louise. "Chang and Feng and Wu." Asia, XXVI-7 (July, 1926): 596–601, 649–51.

T'ao Chü-yin. Pei-yang chün-fa t'ung-chih shih-ch'i shih-hua. Peking: Sheng-huo, tu-shu, hsin chih san lien shu-tien, 1957–58. 6 vols.
陶菊隱。北洋軍閥統治時期史話。

Weisshart, Herbert. "Feng Yü-hsiang: His Rise as a Militarist and His Training Programs." Papers on China, VI. Cambridge: Harvard University, 1952.

Wen Kung-chih. Tsui-chin san-shih nien Chung-kuo chün-shih shih. Shanghai: T'ai-p'ing-yang shu-tien, 1932.
文公直。最近三十年中國軍事史。

Fu Ssu-nien   傅 斯 年

WORKS

1932. Tung-pei shih kang, ch'u-kao, ti-i chüan: Ku-tai chih Tung-pei. Peiping: Kuo-li chung-yang yen-chiu-yuan li-shih yü-yen yen-chiu so.

東北史綱，初稿，第一卷：古代之東北。

1933. Fu Ssu-nien *et al.* Ch'en Tu-hsiu p'ing-lun (comp. by Ch'en Hsiao-tung). Peiping: Tung-ya shu-chü.

傅斯年等。陳獨秀評論。陳曉東。

1934. Fu Ssu-nien *et al.* Ch'eng-tzu-yai (Shan-tung Li-ch'eng hsien Lung-shan chen hei-t'ao wen-hua i-chih). Nanking: Kuo-li chung-yang yen-chiu-yuan li-shih yü-yen yen-chiu so.

傅斯年等。城子崖（山東歷城縣龍山鎮黑陶文化遺址）。

1940. Hsing-ming ku-hsun pien-cheng. Chang-sha: Shang-wu yin shu kuan.

性命古訓辨證。

1952. Fu Meng-chen hsien-sheng chi. Taipei: Kuo-li Taiwan ta-hsueh. 6 vols.

傅孟眞先生集。

1967. Fu Ssu-nien hsuan-chi. Taipei: Wen-hsing shu-tien.

傅斯年選集。

SOURCES

Ch'en P'an. "Huai ku en-shih Fu Meng-chen hsien-sheng yu shu." *Hsin shih-tai*, III-3 (July, 1958): 13–14.

陳槃。懷故恩師傅孟眞先生有述。新時代。

Chow Tse-tsung. The May Forth Movement: Intellectual Revolution in Modern China. Cambridge: Harvard University Press, 1960.

Fu Lo-ch'eng. Fu Meng-chen hsien-sheng nien-p'u. Taipei: Wen-hsing shu-tien, 1964.

傅樂成。傅孟眞先生年譜。

———. "Fu Ssu-nien hsien-sheng te min-tsu ssu-hsiang." *Chuan-chi wen-hsueh*, II-5, 6 (May-June, 1963).

傅樂成。傅斯年先生的民族思想。傳記文學。

Fu Ssu-nien. Fu Meng-chen hsien-sheng chi. Taipei: Kuo-li Taiwan ta-hsueh. 6 vols.

傅斯年。傅孟眞先生集。

———. "Hsin ch'ao fa-k'an chih-ch'ü." *Hsin ch'ao*, I-1 (January 1, 1919): 1–5.

傅斯年。新潮發刊旨趣。新潮。

Fu ku hsiao-chang ai wan lu. Taipei: Taiwan ta-hsueh, 1951.

傅故校長哀輓錄。

Ku Chieh-kang. Tang-tai Chung-kuo shih-hsueh. Nanking: Sheng-li ch'u-pan kung-ssu, 1947.

顧頡剛。當代中國史學。

Kung lun pao. Taipei, December 21, 1950.

公論報。

Lao Kan. "Fu Meng-chen hsien-sheng yü chin erh-shih nien lai Chung-kuo shih-hsueh te fa-chan." *Ta-lu tsa-chih*, II-1 (January 1, 1951): 6–8.

勞榦。傅孟眞先生與近二十年來中國史學的發展。大陸雜誌。

Lo Chia-lun. "Yuan-ch'i lin-li te Fu Meng-chen." *Chung-yang jih-pao*. Taipei, December 31, 1950.

羅家倫。元氣淋漓的傅孟眞。中央日報。

Mao Tzu-shui. "Fu Meng-chen hsien-sheng lueh-chuan." *Tzu-yu chung-kuo*, IV-1 (January 1, 1950): 5–7.

毛子水。傅孟眞先生略傳。自由中國。

Taiwan ta-hsueh Fu ku hsiao-chang chi-nien lun-wen chi. Taipei: Taiwan ta-hsueh, 1952.

台灣大學傅故校長紀念論文集。

Tung Tso-pin. "Li-shih yü-yen yen-chiu so tsai hsueh-shu shang te kung-hsien." *Ta-lu tsa-chih*, II-1.

董作賓。歷史語言研究所在學術上的貢獻。大陸雜誌。

Fu Tseng-hsiang   傅增湘

WORKS

1929. (ed.) Shuang-chien-lou shan-pen shu-mu (with Hsü chi erh-chüan). 4 vols.

雙鑑樓善本書目（附：續記二卷）。

1932. Ch'in yu jih lu (with Teng T'ai-hua chi).

秦游日錄（附：登泰華記）。

1933. Ch'ing-tai tien-shih k'ao-lueh. Tientsin: Ta kung pao she.

清代殿試考略。

1935. Heng-lu jih lu. Tientsin: Ta kung pao she.

衡盧日錄。

1935. Nan-yü yu-chi.

南嶽游記。

1938. Ts'ang-yuan ch'ün-shu t'i-chi hsü-chi. Peiping: Ts'ang-yuan tzu k'an. 3 vols.

藏園群書題記續集。

1943. (ed.) Sung-tai Shu wen chi ts'un. 34 vols.

宋代蜀文輯存。

1943. Ts'ang-yuan ch'ün shu t'i chi ch'u chi. Peiping: Ch'i lin hsuan. 4 vols.

藏園群書題記初集。

SOURCES

Fu Tseng-hsiang. Ts'ang-yuan chü-shih liu-shih tzu-shu. 1931.

傅增湘。藏園居士六十自述。

T'u-shu chi-k'an, new series, I-2 (June, 1939): 239–41, 302.
圖書季刊。

Fu Tso-yi   傅 作 義

SOURCES

AWW
BKL
Chang Chih-chung *et al.* Tsen-yang kai-tsao. Hong Kong: Ho-tso shu-tien, 1950?
張治中等。 怎樣改造。
Chassin, Lionel Max. La Conquête de la Chine par Mao Tse-tung, 1945–1949. Paris: Payot, 1952.
Chung-kuo k'ang-chan shih, comp. by Hai-wai liu-tung hsuan-ch'uan t'uan. 1947?
中國抗戰史。 海外流動宣傳團。
CMTC
CTMC
CWR, May–September, 1930; April 29, 1933.
CYB-W, 1933.
GCJJ
HCJC
Hsia Shou-t'ien. Cho-chou chan chi. 1929. 4 vols.
夏壽田。 涿洲戰記。
Ko-ming wen-hsieh, ed. by Chung-kuo kuo-min-tang chung-yang wei-yuan-hui tang shih shih-liao pien-tsuan wei-yuan-hui. Taipei: Chung-yang wen-wu kung-ying she, 1953–69. 35 vols.
革命文獻。 中國國民黨中央委員會黨史史料編纂委員會。
TCJC
WWC, 1936.
WWMC

Han Fu-chü   韓 復 榘

SOURCES

Chung-kuo k'ang-chan shih, comp. by Hai-wai liu-tung hsuan-ch'uan t'uan. 1947?
中國抗戰史。 海外流動宣傳團。
CMTC
CWR, 1932–38.
Kuo wen chou-pao, V-24 (June 24, 1928).
國聞週報。
TCJC

Ho Ch'eng-chün   何 成 濬

WORKS

1961. Pa-shih hui-i. Taipei.
八十回憶。

SOURCES

BKL
Ho Ch'eng-chün. Pa-shih hui-i. Taipei, 1961.
何成濬。 八十回憶。
Huang Fu. Wang Cheng-t'ing chuan.
黃郛。 王正廷傳。
Kuo-min ko-ming chün chan shih, ed. by Kuo-min ko-ming chün chan shih pien-tsuan wei-yuan-hui. Ts'an-mou pen-pu, 1934. 17 vols.
國民革命軍戰史。 國民革命軍戰史編纂委員會。
MMT
MSICH
Sun Wen. Kuo-fu ch'üan-shu (ed. by Chang Ch'i-yün). Taipei: Kuo-fang yen-chiu yuan, 1960.
孫文。 國父全書。 張其昀。
T'ang Sheng-chih chuan.
唐生智傳。

Ho Ch'i-fang   何 其 芳

WORKS

1936. Hua meng lu. Shanghai: Wen-hua sheng-huo ch'u-pan she.
畫夢錄。
1938. K'o i chi. Shanghai: Wen-hua sheng-huo ch'u-pan she.
刻意集。
1940. Huan-hsiang jih-chi. Shanghai: Liang-yu fu-hsing t'u-shu yin-shua kung-ssu.
還鄉日記。
1945. Yeh ko. Chungking: Shih wen hsueh-she.
夜歌。
1947. Yü-yen. Wen-hua sheng-huo ch'u-pan she.
預言。
1949. Wu Yü-chang t'ung-chih ko-ming ku-shih. Hong Kong: Hsin Chung-kuo shu-chü.
吳玉章同志革命故事。
1952. Hsi-yuan chi. Peking: Jen-min wen-hsueh ch'u-pan she.
西苑集。
1952. Hsing huo chi. Shanghai: Hsin wen-i ch'u-pan she.
星火集。

1953. Kuan-yü hsien-shih chu-i. Shanghai: Hsin
wen-i ch'u-pan she.
關於現實主義。

1956. Kuan-yü hsieh shih ho tu shih. Peking:
Tso-chia ch'u-pan she.
關于寫詩和讀詩。

1957. Huang-hun. with Li Kuang-t'ien. Hong
Kong: Wen-hsueh ch'u-pan she.
黃昏。李廣田。

1957. San-wen hsuan-chi. Peking: Jen-min
wen-hsueh ch'u-pan she.
散文選集。

1958. Mei-yu p'i-p'ing chiu pu-neng ch'ien-chin.
Peking: Jen-min wen-hsueh ch'u-pan she.
沒有批評就不能前進。

1962. Shih-ko hsin-shang. Peking: Tso-chia
ch'u-pan she.
詩歌欣賞。

1964. Wen-hsueh i-shu te ch'un-t'ien. Peking:
Tso-chia ch'u-pan she.
文學藝術的春天。

ed. of Ta-chung wen-i.
大眾文藝。

SOURCES

CB, 197 (July 30, 1952).
CHWSK
CKJMT
GCCJK
GCJJ
HMTT
Ho Ch'i-fang. Hsi-yuan chi. Peking: Jen-min
wen-hsueh ch'u-pan she, 1952.
何其芳。西苑集。
MCNP
RCCL
TCMT
WWMC

Ho Chien   何鍵

SOURCES

BKL
CMJL
CMTC
CWR, 1927, 1947.
Feng Yü-hsiang. Wo te sheng-huo. Yü-chou
feng she, 1938.
馮玉祥。我的生活。
Hsü Ch'ien chuan.
徐謙傳。

Hsueh Yueh chuan.
薛岳傳。

Kuo-min ko-ming chün chan shih, ed. by Kuo-
min ko-ming chün chan shih pien-tsuan wei-
yuan-hui. Ts'an-mou pen-pu, 1934. 17 vols.
國民革命軍戰史。國民革命軍戰史編纂委
員會。

Lei Hsiao-ts'en. San shih nien tung-luan Chung-
kuo. Hong Kong: Ya-chou ch'u-pan she,
1955.
雷嘯岑。三十年動亂中國。

Lu-chün shang-chiang Ho Yün-ch'iao hsien-
sheng chuan.
陸軍上將何芸樵先生傳。

MMT

T'ang Sheng-chih chuan.
唐生智傳。

Ti-ssu chün chi-shih. Canton: Huai-yuan wen-
hua shih-yeh fu-wu she, 1949.
第四軍紀實。

Ho Chung-han   賀衷寒

WORKS

1924–25. ed. of Kuo-min ko-ming chou-k'an.
國民革命週刊。

1942. I te chi. Chungking: Pa t'i shu-tien.
一得集。

1947. Hou-ch'i ko-ming te hao-chiao.
後期革命的號角。

1951. Chung-kuo te ping-ken. Taipei: P'a-mi-
erh shu-tien.
中國的病根。

1953. Chiao-t'ung kuan-li lun-ts'ung. Taipei.
交通管理論叢。

1954. Chiao-t'ung kuan-li yao-i. Taipei: Chung-
kuo chiao-t'ung chien-she hsueh-hui.
交通管理要義。

SOURCES

BKL
CH, 1937–43.
CH-T, 1956–57.
CTMC
GCJJ
Ho Chung-han. Chiao-t'ung kuan-li lun-ts'ung.
Taipei, 1953.
賀衷寒。交通管理論叢。
———. Chung-kuo te ping-ken. Taipei: P'a-
mi-erh shu-tien, 1951.
賀衷寒。中國的病根。

Ho Chung-han. I te chi. Chungking: Pa t'i shu-tien, 1942.
賀衷寒。 一得集。

Kuo-chün cheng-kung shih-kao, comp. by Kuo-chün cheng-kung shih pien-tsuan wei-yuan-hui. Taipei: Kuo-fang pu tsung cheng-chih pu, 1960. 3 vols.
國軍政工史稿。國軍政工史編纂委員會。

Ma Ch'ao-chün. Chung-kuo lao-kung yün-tung shih; shang-ts'e. Chungking: Shang-wu yin shu kuan, 1942.
馬超俊。 中國勞工運動史; 上冊。

Ho Hsiang-ning 何香凝

WORKS

1954. Ho Hsiang-ning hua-chi. Peking: Jen-min mei-shu ch'u-pan she.
何香凝畫集。

1957. Hui-i Sun Chung-shan ho Liao Chung-k'ai. Peking: Chung-kuo ch'ing-nien ch'u-pan she.
回憶孫中山和廖仲愷。

1958. Ho Hsiang-ning *et al.* K'o-ai te chia-hsiang. Kowloon: Hong Kong hsin ti ch'u-pan she.
何香凝等。 可愛的家鄉。

1963. Ho Hsiang-ning shih hua chi (ed. by Jen-min mei-shu ch'u-pan she). Peking: Jen-min mei-shu ch'u-pan she.
何香凝詩畫集。 人民美術出版社。

SOURCES

Fei wei jen-shih tzu-liao hui-pien—jen-wu chih, comp. by Fei wei jen-shih tzu-liao tiao-ch'a yen-chiu hui. Taipei? 1956–57. 9 vols.
匪偽人事資料彙編—人物誌。 匪偽人事資料調查研究會。
GCCJK
HCJC
HMTT

Ho Hsiang-ning. Hui-i Sun Chung-shan ho Liao Chung-k'ai. Peking: Chung-kuo ch'ing-nien ch'u-pan she, 1957.
何香凝。 回憶孫中山和廖仲愷。

I Ch'en. "Wo so jen-shih te Ho Hsiang-ning." *Chin shan shih-pao.* San Francisco, November 22, 1956.
移塵。 我所認識的何香凝。 金山時報。

I-chiu-wu-ling jen-min nien-chien, ed. by Shen Sung-fang. Hong Kong: Ta kung shu-chü, 1950.
一九五〇人民年鑑。 沈頌芳。

RD
SCMP, August 22, 1960.

Ho Lung 賀龍

WORKS

1965. Chung-kuo jen-min chieh-fang chün te min-chu ch'uan-t'ung. Peking: Jen-min ch'u-pan she.
中國人民解放軍的民主傳統。

SOURCES

Person interviewed: Chang Kuo-t'ao.
CB, 775 (October 29, 1965).
CKLC
Hsiao San. Jen-wu yü chi-nien. Peking: Sheng-huo, tu-shu, hsin chih san lien shu-tien, 1951.
蕭三。 人物與紀念。
Jen-min jih-pao. Peking, September 12, 1965.
人民日報。
Liu Hsin-huang. Ch'ih mo ch'ün hsiang.
劉心煌。 赤魔群像。
The New York Times. February 22, 1959; January 16, 1966.
People's China, October 16, 1955.
RSOC
SCMP, 3554 (October 8, 1965); 3560 (October 19, 1965).
Sha Ting (pseud. of Yang T'ung-fang). Chi Ho Lung. Peking: Jen-min wen-hsueh ch'u-pan she, 1960.
沙汀 (楊同芳)。 記賀龍。
———. Sui chün san-chi.
沙汀 (楊同芳)。 隨軍散記。
Smedley, Agnes. Battle Hymn of China. New York: Alfred A. Knopf, 1943.

Ho Meng-hsiung 何夢雄

SOURCES

Ch'en, Jerome. Mao and the Chinese Revolution. London: Oxford University Press, 1965.
Chereponov. Notes of a Soviet Adviser in China.
Chiang Yung-ching. Pao Lo-t'ing yü Wuhan cheng-ch'üan. Taipei: Chung-kuo hsueh-shu chu-tso chiang chu wei-yuan-hui, 1963.
蔣永敬。 鮑羅廷與武漢政權。
HKLC
Hsiao Tso-liang. Power Relations Within the Chinese Communist Movement, 1930–1934:

A Study of Documents. Seattle: University
of Washington Press, 1961–67. 2 vols.
Trotsky, Leon. Problems of the Chinese Revolution. (tr. by Max Shachtman.) New York:
Paragon Book Reprint Corp., 1966.

Ho Shu-heng　何叔衡

SOURCES

Persons interviewed: not to be identified.

Ho-tung　何東

SOURCES

"Ho Tung chueh shih ch'eng-kung shih." *Kung
shang jih-pao.* Hong Kong, March 20, 21, 1950.
何東爵士成功史。工商日報。
Kung shang jih-pao. Hong Kong, April 26, 1959.
工商日報。
The New York Times. April 27, 1956.

Ho Yao-tsu　賀耀祖

WORKS

1936, January. "Les Rapports entre les Civili-
sations Chinoise et Turque." *Orient et Occident,*
2: 213–17.

SOURCES

CH
CTMC
GCMMTJK
Ho Yao-tsu. "Les Rapports entre les Civilisa-
tions Chinoise et Turque." *Orient et Occident,*
2 (January, 1936): 213–17.
WWC, 1950.
WWCC

Ho Ying-ch'in　何應欽

WORKS

1945. Ho shang-chiang k'ang chan ch'i-chien
chün-shih pao-kao. Nanking: Kuo-fang pu.
何上將抗戰期間軍事報告。
1946. Pa nien k'ang chan chih ching-kuo. Nanking: Chung-kuo lu-chün tsung-ssu-ling pu.
八年抗戰之經過。
1959. Ho Ying-ch'in chiang-chün tao-te lun-
ts'ung. Taipei: Shih-chieh tao-te ch'ung cheng
yun-tung Chung-hua Min-kuo lien-i hui.

何應欽將軍道德論叢。
Jih-pen fang-wen chiang-yen hsuan-chi.
日本訪問講演選集。
Tao-te ch'ung cheng yun-tung yen-chiang chi.
道德重整運動演講集。

SOURCES

AWW, 1960.
BKL
CH-T, 1956–57.
Chung-kuo chan-ch'ü Chung-kuo lu-chün tsung-
ssu-ling pu ch'u-li Jih-pen t'ou-hsiang wen-
chien hui-pien.
中國戰區中國陸軍總司令部處理日本投降
文件彙編。
Chung-kuo chan-ch'ü Chung-kuo lu-chün tsung-
ssu-ling pu shou hsiang pao-kao shu.
中國戰區中國陸軍總司令部受降報告書。
CMJL
CPR, 840 (March 1, 1949).
CTMC
GCJJ
Ho Ching-chih hsien-sheng chu chün-cheng pu
shih nien chi-nien ts'e.
何敬之先生主軍政部十年紀念冊。
Ho Ying-ch'in. Ho shang-chiang k'ang chan
ch'i-chien chün-shih pao-kao. Nanking: Kuo-
fang pu, 1954.
何應欽。何上將抗戰期間軍事報告。
———. Jih-pen fang-wen chiang-yen hsuan-
chi.
何應欽。日本訪問講演選集。
———. Pa nien k'ang chan chih ching-kuo.
Nanking: Chung-kuo lu-chün tsung-ssu-ling
pu, 1946.
何應欽。八年抗戰之經過。
———. Tao-te ch'ung cheng yün-tung yen-
chiang chi.
何應欽。道德重整運動演講集。
Hsueh Yueh chuan.
薛岳傳。
The International Who's Who, 1944–45.
Kuo-min ko-ming chün chan shih, ed. by Kuo-
min ko-ming chün chan shih pien-tsuan wei-
yuan-hui. Ts'an-mou pen-pu, 1934. 17 vols.
國民革命軍戰史。國民革命軍戰史編纂委
員會。
K'ung Hsiang-hsi. Sian shih-pien hui-i-lu.
孔祥熙。西安事變回憶錄。
MMT
MSICH
The New York Times, June 10, 1962.
Newsweek, May 27, 1946.

Pei fa chan shih, ed. by Kuo-fang pu shih cheng chü. Taipei: Kuo-fang pu shih cheng chü, 1959.

北伐戰史。國防部史政局。

T'ang Leang-li. The Inner History of the Chinese Revolution. New York: E. P. Dutton & Co., 1930.

Tung-fang tsa-chih, XXV-10.

東方雜誌。

White, Theodore H., and Annalee Jacoby. Thunder Out of China. New York: William Sloane Associates, 1946.

WWC, 1931.

Hou Te-pang 候德榜

SOURCES

Persons interviewed: not to be identified.

Hsiang Ching-yü 向警予

SOURCES

Person interviewed: Chang Kuo-t'ao.
CKLC
HKLC
HMTT
Hsiao San. Mao Tse-tung t'ung-chih te ch'ing shao nien shih-tai. Shanghai: Hsin hua shu-tien, 1949.

蕭三。毛澤東同志的青少年時代。

Hsiang Chung-fa 向忠發

WORKS

1931. Chung-yang cheng-chih chü pao-kao. Shanghai.

中央政治局報告。

SOURCES

Hsiang Chung-fa. Chung-yang cheng-chih chü pao-kao. Shanghai, 1931.

向忠發。中央政治局報告。
HSWT

Hsiang Ying 項英

WORKS

1939. Hsiang Ying chiang-chün yen-lun chi (ed. by Chi na ch'u-pan she). Chin-hua? Chi na ch'u-pan she.

項英將軍言論集。集納出版社。

SOURCES

Person interviewed: Chang Kuo-t'ao.
Chang Kuo-chiang. Chung-kung chün-shih. Taipei: Chung-yang kai-tsao wei-yuan-hui ti-liu tsu, 1951.

張國疆。中共軍事。

Chang Kuo-t'ao. "Autobiography" (ed. by Robert Burton). Unpublished manuscript.

Chung-kuo kung-ch'an-tang te chung-yao jen-wu, ed. by Min-chien ch'u-pan she. Peking: Min-chien ch'u-pan she, 1949.

中國共產黨的重要人物。民間出版社。
GCCJK
GCMMTJK
GSSJ
Hsiang Ying. Hsiang Ying chiang-chün yen-lun chi (ed. by Chi na ch'u-pan she). Chin-hua? Chi na ch'u-pan she.

項英。項英將軍言論集。集納出版社。
HSWT
Kreisberg, Paul L. "The New Fourth Army Incident and the United Front in China." Unpublished Master's essay, Columbia University, 1952.

Kung Ch'u. Wo yü hung chün. Kowloon: Nan feng ch'u-pan she.

龔楚。我與紅軍。
Teng Chung-hsia. Chung-kuo chih-kung yün-tung chien-shih. Chieh-fang she, 1949.

鄧中夏。中國職工運動簡史。
Ts'ao Chü-jen. Chiang Ching-kuo lun. Hong Kong: Ch'uang k'en ch'u-pan she, 1954.

曹聚仁。蔣經國論。
Wales, Nym (pseud. of Helen Foster Snow). Inside Red China. New York: Doubleday, Doran & Co., 1939.

Hsiao Fo-ch'eng 蕭佛成

SOURCES

CYB-W, 1934.
Feng Tzu-yu. Hua-ch'iao ko-ming k'ai-kuo shih. Shanghai: Shang-wu yin shu kuan, 1947.

馮自由。華僑革命開國史。
Skinner, George William. Chinese Society in Thailand: An Analytical History. Ithaca: Cornell University Press, 1957.

Hsiao Hua　　蕭華

SOURCES

Person interviewed: Chang Kuo-t'ao.
Asian Analyst, February, 1966.
CPR, 1017 (November 16, 1949).
The New York Times, January 26, 1966.
Who's Who in Communist China. Hong Kong:
　Union Research Institute, 1966.

Hsiao K'o　　蕭克

SOURCES

Person interviewed: Chang Kuo-t'ao.

Hsiao T'ung-tzu　　蕭同玆

SOURCES

CH, 1937–45.
China Yearbook, 1958–59.
Tong, Hollington K. Dateline: China. New
　York: Rockport Press, 1950.

Hsieh Ch'ih　　謝持

WORKS

1934. T'ien feng hsieh t'ao kuan liu-shih tzu-
　shu.
　天風澥濤館六十自述。

SOURCES

Chang Chi. Chang P'u-ch'üan hsien-sheng
　ch'üan-chi; cheng-pien pu-pien (ed. by
　Chung-yang kai-tsao wei-yuan-hui tang shih
　shih-liao pien-tsuan wei-yuan-hui). Taipei:
　Chung-yang wen-wu kung-ying she, 1951–52.
　張繼。張溥泉先生全集；正編補編。中央
　改造委員會黨史史料編纂委員會。
Chü Cheng. Ch'ing tang shih-lu.
　居正。清黨實錄。
Chung-yang k'uo-ta hui-i shih-lu.
　中央擴大會議實錄。
Hsieh Ch'ih. T'ien feng hsieh t'ao kuan liu-
　shih tzu-shu. 1934.
　謝持。天風澥濤館六十自述。
Hsieh Hui-sheng hsien-sheng hsing-shu.
　謝慧生先生行述。
Hsieh Hui-sheng hsien-sheng kuo-tsang t'e-k'an.
　謝慧生先生國葬特刊。

Huang Chi-lu. P'ing-fan te jen-sheng yü wei-ta
　te shih-yeh—tao Hsieh Hui-sheng hsien-sheng.
　(mimeo.) 1939.
　黃季陸。平凡的人生與偉大的事業一悼謝
　慧生先生。
Ko-ming wen-hsien, ed. by Chung-kuo kuo-min-
　tang chung-yang wei-yuan-hui tang shih shih-
　liao pien-tsuan wei-yuan-hui. Taipei: Chung-
　yang wen-wu kung she, 1953–65. 35 vols.
　革命文獻。中國國民黨中央委員會黨史史
　料編纂委員會。
Li Lieh-chün tzu-chuan.
　李烈鈞自傳。
Teng Tse-ju. Chung-kuo kuo-min-tang erh-shih
　nien shih-chi. Shanghai: Cheng-chung shu-
　chü, 1948.
　鄧澤如。中國國民黨二十年史蹟。
Tsou Lu. Ch'eng-lu wen-hsuan (ed. by Chang
　Ching-ying). Shanghai: Cheng-chung shu-
　chü, 1948.
　鄒魯。澄廬文選。張鏡影。

Hsieh Chueh-tsai　　謝覺哉

WORKS

1926–27. ed. of *Hunan min pao*.
　湖南民報。
1931? ed. of *Kung nung pao*.
　工農報。
1945. San san chih te li-lun yü shih-chi.
　三三制的理論與實際。
1951. Hsieh Chueh-tsai *et al*. Kuan-yü jen-min
　min-chu chien cheng (ed. by Hsin chien-she
　tsa-chih pien-chi pu). Peking: Hsin chien-
　she tsa-chih she.
　關於人民民主建政。新建設雜誌編輯　。
1954. Hsieh Chueh-tsai *et al*. Mao Tse-tung te
　ku-shih ho ch'uan-shuo. Peking: Kung-jen
　ch'u-pan she.
　謝覺哉等。毛澤東的故事和傳說。
1957. Kung-tso yü hsueh-hsi. Peking: Chung-
　kuo ch'ing-nien ch'u-pan she.
　工作與學習。
1962. Pu huo chi. Peking: Tso-chia ch'u-pan she.
　不惑集。
ed. of *T'ung-su jih-pao*. Changsha.
　通俗日報。

SOURCES

Person interviewed: Chang Kuo-t'ao.
GCJJ

The New York Times, January 4, 1965.
RD
SCMP, 159 (August 22, 1951).
WWMC

Hsieh Hung-lai   謝洪賚

WORKS

1926. (ed.) Ying huan ch'üan chih. Shanghai:
Shang-wu yin shu kuan.
瀛寰全志。
(ed.) Hsiu hsueh i chu.
修學一助。

SOURCES

Person interviewed: Grace Zia Chu.
Gregg, Alice Henrietta. China and Educational
Autonomy: The Changing Role of the Protestant Educational Missionary in China, 1807–
1937. Syracuse: Syracuse University Press,
1946.

Hsieh Ping-ying   謝冰瑩

WORKS

1932. Chung-hsueh-sheng hsiao-shuo. Chung-
hsueh-sheng shu-chü.
中學生小說。
1933. Ch'ing-nien shu-hsin. Shanghai: Pei-hsin
shu-chü.
青年書信。
1933. Ch'ing-nien Wang Kuo-ts'ai. K'ai hua.
青年王國材。
1934. Lu shan chi. Shanghai: Kuang-ming
shu-chü.
麓山集。
1935. Ch'ien lu. Shanghai: Kuang-ming shu-
chü.
前路。
1936. Hunan te feng. Shanghai: Pei hsin shu-
chü.
湖南的風。
1936. I ko nü ping te tzu-chuan. Shanghai:
Liang-yu yin-shua t'u-shu kung-ssu.
一個女兵的自傳。
Eng. tr. by Adet and Anor Lin, *Girl Rebel, the
Autobiography of Hsieh Pingying, with Extracts
from Her New War Diaries.* New York: The
John Day Co., 1940.
1937. Chan-shih te shou. Tu-li ch'u-pan she.
戰士的手。

1937. Chün chung sui-pi. Shanghai: K'ang chan
ch'u-pan pu.
軍中隨筆。
1937. Hsieh Ping-ying *et al.* Ch'ien-hsien k'ang
ti chiang-ling fang-wen chi. Shanghai: Ch'ien-
chin ch'u-pan she.
謝冰瑩等。前線抗敵將領訪問記。
1937. Tsai huo-hsien shang. Sheng-huo.
在火線上。
1938. Chung Chin-shih sha kuei. Lan t'ien.
鐘進士殺鬼。
1938. Jih chün te pao-hsing. Fang ku shu-tien.
日軍的暴行。
1938. Ti-wu chan-ch'ü hsun-li. Kwangsi jih-pao
she.
第五戰區巡禮。
1940. Hsieh kei ch'ing-nien tso-chia te hsin. Ta
tung.
寫給青年作家的信。
1940. Mei tzu ku-niang. Hsin Chung-kuo wen-
hua ch'u-pan she.
梅子姑娘。
1940. Ping-ying k'ang chan wen-hsuan chi. Ta
tung.
冰瑩抗戰文選集。
1940–43. ed. of *Huang-ho*.
黃河。
1942. Tsai Jih-pen yü chung. Sian: Hua-pei
hsin-wen she.
在日本獄中。
1943. Chieh-chieh. Lan t'ien shu pao ho-tso-
she.
姊姊。
1944. Hsin ts'ung-chün jih-chi. Kweilin: T'ien
ma shu-tien.
新從軍日記。
1945. Hsieh Ping-ying *et al*. Nü tso-chia tzu-
chuan hsuan-chi. Chungking: Keng-yün ch'u-
pan she.
謝冰瑩等。女作家自傳選集。
1945-? ed. of *Ho-p'ing jih-pao*.
和平日報。
1946. Sheng-jih. Shanghai: Pei-hsin shu-chü.
生日。
1947. Wei-ta te mu-chiao. with Wang Ying.
Canton: Hsin-sheng shu-chü.
偉大的母教。王瑩。
1954. Sheng-chieh te ling-hun. Hong Kong: Ya-
chou ch'u-pan she.
聖潔的靈魂。
1955. T'ai-tzu li hsien chi. Taipei: Cheng-chung
shu-chü.
太子歷險記。

1955. Wo te shao-nien shih-tai. Taipei: Cheng-
chung shu-chü.
我的少年時代。

1955. Wu. Taipei: Li-hsing shu-chü.
霧。

1957. Fei-tao chi yu. Taipei: Li-hsing shu-chü.
菲島記遊。

1958. Ku-hsiang. Taipei: Li-hsing shu-chü.
故鄉。

1958. Lin Chueh-min. Chung wai hua-pao she.
林覺民。

1959. Ai wan t'ing. Taipei: Ch'ang liu pan-
yueh-k'an she.
愛晚亭。

1960. Pi-yao chih lien. Taipei: Li hsing shu-chü.
碧瑤之戀。

1961. Ping-ying yu-chi. Taipei: Hsin lu shu-
chü.
冰瑩遊記。

1961-? Ma-lai-ya yu-chi. Taipei: Hai-ch'ao yin
yueh-k'an she.
馬來亞遊記。

1963. Wo tsen-yang hsieh-tso. Taipei: San wen
yin-shua ch'ang.
我怎樣寫作。

1964. Wen-hsueh hsin-shang. with Tso Sung-
ch'ao. Taipei: San min shu-chü.
文學欣賞。左松超。

Hsueh liu.
血流。

Ping-ying ch'uang-tso hsuan. Fang ku shu-tien.
冰瑩創作選。

Wei-ta te nü-hsing.
偉大的女性。

ed. of Wen-i yü sheng-huo.
文藝與生活。

SOURCES

CHWYS
CWT
GCCJK

Hsieh Ping-ying. I ko nü ping te tzu-chuan.
Shanghai: Liang-yu yin-shua t'u-shu kung-ssu.
謝冰瑩。一個女兵的自傳。
Eng. tr. by Adet and Anor Lin, Girl Rebel, the
Autobiography of Hsieh Ping ying, with Extracts
from Her New War Diaries. New York: The
John Day Co., 1940.

Hsieh Ping-ying et al. Nü tso-chia tzu-chuan
hsuan-chi. Chungking: Keng-yün ch'u-pan
she, 1945.
謝冰瑩等。女作家自傳選集。

HWP

Jen-chien shih, 20 (January 20, 1935): 38–42; 21
(February 5, 1935): 32–35; 22 (February 20,
1935): 29–31; 24 (March 20, 1935): 20–22; 27
(May 5, 1935): 38–40; 28 (May 20, 1935): 12–14.
人間世。

MCNP

MMH

MMT

TCMT

Tzu-chuan chih i chang, ed. by T'ao K'ang-te.
Canton: Yü-chou feng she, 1938.
自傳之一章。陶亢德。

WWMC

Hsieh Wan-ying   謝婉瑩

WORKS

1930. Chi hsiao tu-che. Shanghai: Pei hsin shu-
chü.
寄小讀者。

1943. Ping Hsin san-wen chi (ed. by Li Fei-kan.)
Kweilin: K'ai-ming shu-tien.
冰心散文集。李芾甘。

1947. Ping Hsin hsiao-shuo chi (ed. by Li Fei-
kan). Shanghai: K'ai-ming shu-tien.
冰心小說集。李芾甘。

1948. Tung erh ku-niang. Shanghai: Pei hsin
shu-chü.
冬兒姑娘。

1949. Ping Hsin shih-chi. Shanghai: K'ai-ming
shu-tien.
冰心詩集。

1949. Wang-shih. Shanghai: K'ai-ming shu-tien.
往事。

1952. Ping Hsin hsuan-chi (ed. by Pa Lei). Hong
Kong: Hsin hsiang shu-tien.
冰心選集。巴雷。

1954. Ping Hsin hsiao-shuo san-wen hsuan-chi.
Peking: Jen-min wen-hsueh ch'u-pan she.
冰心小說散文選集。

1965. Ping Hsin hsuan-chi. Wen-hsueh ch'u-pan
she.
冰心選集。

1956. T'ao Ch'i te shu-ch'i jih-chi. Shanghai:
Shao-nien erh-t'ung ch'u-pan she.
陶奇的暑期日記。

1957. Huan-hsiang tsa-chi. Shanghai: Shao-nien
erh-t'ung ch'u-pan she.
還鄉雜記。

1958. Kuei-lai i-hou. Peking: Tso-chia ch'u-pan
she.
歸來以後。

1958. Ping Hsin hsiao-shuo hsuan. Hong Kong:
Hong Kong wan li shu-tien.
冰心小說選。

1958. Ping Hsin san-wen hsuan. Hong Kong:
Hong Kong wan li shu-tien.
冰心散文選。

1960. Wo-men pa ch'un-t'ien ch'ao hsing le.
Tientsin: Pai hua wen-i ch'u-pan she.
我們把春天吵醒了。

1963. (ed.) Erh-t'ung wen-hsueh hsuan, 1959–
1961. Peking: Jen-min wen-hsueh ch'u-pan
she.
兒童文學選， 1959–1961。

1964. Shih sui hsiao cha. Peking: Tso-chia ch'u-
pan she.
拾穗小札。

Chi Jih-pen hsiao tu-che.
寄日本小讀者。

Hsü chi hsiao tu-che.
續寄小讀者。

Ping Hsin ming-tso hsuan-chi (ed. by Ch'en Lei).
Hong Kong: Nan-yang t'u-shu kung-ssu.
冰心名作選集。 陳磊。

SOURCES

CHWC
CHWSK
CHWYS
CMMC
CWT
Fairbank, John K., and Liu Kwang-ching. Mod-
ern China: A Bibliographical Guide to Chinese
Works, 1898–1937. Cambridge: Harvard Uni-
versity Press, 1950.
GCCJK
HMTT
Hsien-tai Chung-kuo nü tso-chia, ed. by Huang
Ying. Shanghai: Pei hsin shu-chü, 1931.
現代中國女作家。 黃英。
Living China: Modern Chinese Short Stories,
ed. and comp. by Edgar Snow. New York:
John Day & Reynal & Hitchcock, 1936.
MCNP
MMT
Ping Hsin (pseud. of Hsieh Wan-ying). Chi hsiao
tu-che. Shanghai: Pei hsin shu-chü, 1930.
謝婉瑩。 寄小讀者。
———. "Tzu hsü," in Ping Hsin hsiao-shuo chi.
Kweilin: K'ai-ming shu-tien, 1943.
謝婉瑩。 自序。 謝婉瑩。 冰心小說集。
Ping Hsin lun, ed. by Li Hsi-t'ung. Shanghai:
Pei hsin shu-chü, 1932.
冰心論。 李希同。

RCCL
SCMP, 679 (October, 1953): 28–31.
Ta kung pao. Hong Kong, October 29, 1953;
February 28, 1954.
大公報。
TCMT
WWMC

Hsien Hsing-hai   冼星海

WORKS

1956. Huang-ho ta-ho-ch'ang (comp. by Chung-
kuo yin-yueh chia hsieh-hui). Peking: Yin-
yueh ch'u-pan she.
黃河大合唱。 中國音樂家協會。

1960. Hsien Hsing-hai ho-ch'ang ch'ü chi (comp.
by Yin-yueh ch'u-pan she pien-chi pu). Peking: Yin-yueh ch'u-pan she.
冼星海合唱曲集。 音樂出版社編輯部。

SOURCES

Jen-min yin-yueh, 10–12 (October-December,
1960).
人民音樂。
Jen-min yin-yueh chia Hsien Hsing-hai. Shanghai: Hsin hua shu-tien, 1949.
人民音樂家冼星海。
Shen Ya-hsuan. Yin-yueh chia Hsien Hsing-hai.
Peking: Peking ch'u-pan she, 1957.
諶亞選。 音樂家冼星海。

Hsiung Fo-hsi   熊佛西

WORKS

1919. Ch'ing-ch'un te pei-ai. Shang-wu yin shu
kuan.
青春的悲哀。

1925. Yang chuang-yuan.
洋狀元。

1930–? ed. of Hsi-chü yü wen-i.
戲劇與文藝。

1931. Fo-hsi lun chü. Shanghai: Hsin-yueh shu-
tien.
佛西論劇。

1933–35. Fo-hsi hsi-chü. Shanghai: Shang-wu
yin shu kuan. 3 vols.
佛西戲劇。

1940. T'u-hu. Shanghai: Chung-hua shu-chü.
屠戶。

1941. Sai chin hua—ssu mu hua-chü. Chungking: Hua-chung t'u-shu kung-ssu.

賽金花一四幕話劇。

1947. Hsi-chü ta-chung hua chih shih-yen.
Shanghai: Cheng-chung shu-chü.
戲劇大衆化之實驗。

Hsieh chü yuan-li.
寫劇原理。

SOURCES

CHWC
CHWSK
CHWYS
CWT
GCCJK
GCJJ
HMTT
Hsiung Fo-hsi. Fo-hsi lun chü. Shanghai: Hsin-
yueh shu-tien, 1931.
熊佛西。佛西論劇。
————. Hsi-chü ta-chung hua chih shih-yen.
Shanghai: Cheng-chung shu-chü, 1947.
熊佛西。戲劇大衆化之實驗。
HWP
MCNP
MMT
RCCL
TCMT
WWMC

Hsiung Hsi-ling   熊 希 齡

WORKS

1914–? Hsiung Hsi-ling et al. Cheng-fu ta cheng
fang-chen hsuan-yen. Peking.
熊希齡等。政府大政方針宣言。
Shun chih ho-tao kai-shan chien-i an.
順直河道改善建議案。
Tung-san-sheng i-min k'ai-k'en i-chien shu.
東三省移民開墾意見書。

SOURCES

AADC
Chih (pseud.) "'Feng-huang tsung-li' Hsiung
Hsi-ling." Chin shan shih-pao. San Francisco,
December 8, 9, 10, 1960.
芝。「鳳凰總理」熊希齡。金山時報。
CMTC
CYB-W, 1934.
Liu Ch'eng-yü. Hung-hsien chi-shih shih.
劉成禺。洪憲紀事詩。
TCJC
WWC, 1931.

Hsiung K'o-wu   熊 克 武

SOURCES

CYB-W, 1934.
Hua Kang. Chung-kuo min-tsu chieh-fang yün-
tung shih. Peking: Sheng-huo, tu-shu, hsin-
chih san lien shu-tien, 1951–?
華崗。中國民族解放運動史。
Kuo-fu nien-p'u ch'u-kao, ed. by Kuo shih kuan
shih-liao pien-tsuan wei-yuan-hui, Chung-kuo
kuo-min-tang tang shih shih-liao pien-tsuan
wei-yuan-hui. Taipei: Kuo shih kuan shih-
liao pien-tsuan wei-yuan-hui, Chung-kuo kuo-
min-tang tang shih shih-liao pien-tsuan wei-
yuan-hui, 1959. 2 vols.
國父年譜初稿。國史館史料編纂委員會,
中國國民黨黨史史料編纂委員會。
Li Keng-yuan. Hsueh Sheng (Li Ken-yuan)
nien-lu. Ch'ü-shih-ching-lu, 1934.
李根源。雪生（李根源）年錄。

Hsiung Shih-hui   熊 式 輝

WORKS

1945. (ed.) Mei-kuo chih chung kung-yeh.
Chungking: Shang-wu yin shu kuan.
美國之重工業。

SOURCES

BKL
Chang Ch'i-yün. Chung-hua Min-kuo shih-
kang. Taipei: Chung-hua wen-hua ch'u-pan
shih-yeh wei-yuan hui, 1954–? 7 vols.
張其昀。中華民國史綱。
CMTC
CTMC
Feis, Herbert. The China Tangle: The American Effort in China from Pearl Harbor to the
Marshall Mission. Princeton: Princeton University Press, 1953.
Hsiung Shih-hui chuan-lueh.
熊式輝傳略。
Kuo-min ko-ming chün chan shih, ed. by Kuo-
min ko-ming chün chan shih pien-tsuan wei-
yuan-hui. Ts'an-mou pen-pu, 1934. 17 vols.
國民革命軍戰史。國民革命軍戰史編纂委
員會。
Kuo wen chou-pao, V-9 (March 21, 1928).
國聞週報。
MSICH
Ts'ai I-tien. Tung-pei te p'an-chü yü chieh-lueh.
蔡以典。東北的盤踞與刼掠。

WWMC

Hsiung Shih-li   熊 十 力

WORKS

1918. Chen hsin shu.
眞心書。

1933. P'o p'o wei shih lun. Peiping: Peking ta-hsueh.
破破唯識論。

1935. Shih-li yü yao. Peiping: Peking ta-hsueh.
十力語要。

1937. Fo-chia ming hsiang t'ung-shih. Peiping: Kuo-li Peking ta-hsueh ch'u-pan tsu. 2 vols.
佛家名相通釋。

1947. Shih-li ts'ung-shu.
十力叢書。

1948. Tu ching shih-yao.
讀經示要。

1949. Shih-li yü yao ch'u hsü. Hong Kong: Tung sheng yin wu chü.
十力語要初續。

1956. Yuan ju. Shanghai: Lung men lien-ho shu-chü. 2 vols.
原儒。

Tu chih-lun ch'ao.
讀智論抄。

Yin-ming ta-shu shan-chu.
因明大疏刪注。

SOURCES

Brière, O. Fifty Years of Chinese Philosophy, 1898–1948 (tr. by Laurence G. Thompson). New York: The Macmillan Co., 1956.

Chan Wing-tsit. Religious Trends in Modern China. New York: Columbia University Press, 1953.

———. A Source Book in Chinese Philosophy. Princeton: Princeton University Press, 1963.

Chou Ku-ch'eng. Chung-kuo shih-hsueh chih chin-hua. Shanghai: Sheng-huo shu-tien.
周谷城。中國史學之進化。

Hsiung Shih-li. Shih-li yü yao. Peiping: Peking ta-hsueh, 1935.
熊十力。十力語要。

Hsü Ch'ien   徐 謙

WORKS

1917. "Kung-ho lien-pang che-chung chih shang-ch'ueh shu," in Tai Chi-t'ao, *Chung-hua Min-kuo yü lien-pang tsu-chih.*

共和聯邦折中制商搉書。 戴季陶。 中華民國與聯邦組織。

1933. Min-fa tsung-lun. Shanghai: Fa-hsueh pien i she.
民法總論。

1943. Hsü Chi-lung hsien-sheng i shih. New York: Shen shih ying-yin.
徐季龍先生遺詩。

ed. of *I shih pao.*
益世報。

Sheng-huo kung-t'ung chih.
生活共同制。

SOURCES

Chung-kuo kuo-min-tang ti-i tz'u chi ti-erh tz'u ch'üan-kuo tai-piao ta-hui hui-i lu.
中國國民黨第一次及第二次全國代表大會會議錄。

Chung-yang t'e-k'an, 3 (December 12, 1927).
中央特刊。

Feng Yü-hsiang. Feng Yü-hsiang jih-chi; ti-i pien. Peiping? Min-kuo shih-liao pien-chi she, 1932.
馮玉祥。 馮玉祥日記，第一編。

———. Wo te sheng-huo. Shanghai: Chiao-yü shu-tien, 1947. 3 vols.
馮玉祥。 我的生活。

Hsü Chi-lung hsien-sheng ai-jung lu.
徐季龍先生哀榮錄。

Hsü Ch'ien. Hsü Chi-lung hsien-sheng i shih. New York: Shen shih ying-yin.
徐謙。 徐季龍先生遺詩。

"Hsü Ch'ien te tsung chien-ch'a." *Chung-yang pan-yueh-k'an,* 5–6.
徐謙的總檢查。 中央半月刊。

Kuo-fu mo-pao.
國父墨寶。

Tai Chi-t'ao. Chung-hua Min-kuo yü lien-pang tsu-chih. 1917.
戴季陶。 中華民國與聯邦組織。

Wuhan shih-ch'i ko-chung hui-i chi-lu.
武漢時期各種會議紀錄。

Hsü Chih-mo   徐 志 摩

WORKS

1925. Chih-mo te shih. Shanghai: Hsin-yueh shu-tien.
志摩的詩。

1925. Hsueh-hua te k'uai-lo.
雪花的快樂。

1927. Lo-yeh. Shanghai: Pei hsin shu-chü.

落葉。

1927. Pa-li te lin-chao. Shanghai: Hsin-yueh
shu-tien.
巴黎的鱗爪。

1928. Fei-leng-ts'ui te i yeh. Shanghai: Hsin-
yueh shu-tien.
翡冷翠的一夜。

1928. Pien-k'un-kang. with Lu Hsiao-man.
Shanghai: Hsin-yueh shu-tien.
卞昆岡。陸小曼。

1928. Tzu-p'o. Shanghai: Hsin-yueh shu-tien.
自剖。

1930. (ed.) Jih-pen hsien-tai ming-chia hsiao-
shuo chi; ti-erh chi. (tr. by Ch'a Shih-yuan).
Shanghai: Chung-hua shu-chü.
日本現代名家小說集，第二輯。查士元。

1931. Meng-hu chi. Shanghai: Hsin-yueh shu-
tien.
猛虎集。

1932. Ch'iu. Shanghai: Liang-yu t'u-shu yin-
shua kung-ssu.
秋。

1932. Yün yu.
雲遊。

1936. Ai mei hsiao cha (with Hsiao-man jih-chi).
Shanghai: Liang-yu fu-hsing t'u-shu yin-shua
kung-ssu.
愛眉小札 （附：小曼日記）。

1936. Lun-p'an. Shanghai: Chung-hua shu-chü.
輪盤。

1947. Chih-mo jih-chi (with Hsiao-man jih-chi)
(ed. by Lu Hsiao-man). Shanghai: Ch'en-
kuang ch'u-pan kung-ssu.
志摩日記 （附：小曼日記）。陸小曼。

1956. Hsü Chih-mo shih-hsuan (erh chi). Taipei:
Ch'i ming shu-chü.
徐志摩詩選 （二集）。

1957. Mei hsueh cheng ch'un. Taipei: Ch'i
ming shu-chü.
梅雪爭春。

1959. I ko hsing-ch'i. (tr.) Taipei: Ch'i ming
shu-chü.
一個星期。

1964. Hsü Chih-mo ch'üan-chi. Taipei: Wen-
hua t'u-shu kung-ssu.
徐志摩全集。

1966. Chih-mo san-wen hsuan-chi. Hong Kong:
Hui t'ung shu-tien.
志摩散文選集。

ed. of Hsin-yueh yueh-k'an.
新月月刊。

"Wo te shih-ko ch'uang-tso chih hui-ku." Hsien-
tai, IV-4.

我的詩歌創作之回顧。現代。

SOURCES

Chu Hsiang. "P'ing Hsü Chih-mo te shih," in
Chu Hsiang, Chung shu chi. Shanghai: Sheng-
huo shu-tien, 1934.
朱湘。評徐志摩的詩。朱湘。中書集。

CHWC

CHWSK

CHWYS

CMMC

CWT

ECC

Fairbank, John K., and Liu Kwang-ching.
Modern China: A Bibliographical Guide to
Chinese Works, 1898–1937. Cambridge: Har-
vard University Press, 1950.

HMTT

Hsü Chih-mo. Chih-mo jih-chi (with Hsiao-man
jih-chi) (ed. by Lu Hsiao-man). Shanghai:
Ch'en-kuang ch'u-pan kung-ssu, 1947.
徐志摩。志摩日記 （附：小曼日記）。陸小
曼。

———. Fei-leng-ts'ui te i yeh. Shanghai: Hsin-
yueh shu-tien, 1928.
徐志摩。翡冷翠的一夜。

———. Lo-yeh. Shanghai: Pei hsin shu-chü,
1927.
徐志摩。落葉。

———. Tzu-p'o. Shanghai: Hsin-yueh shu-
tien, 1928.
徐志摩。自剖。

Hsü Chih-mo nien-p'u, ed. by Ch'en Ts'ung-
chou. Shanghai: Ch'en shih tzu yin, 1949.
徐志摩年譜。陳從周。

HWP

Li Ho-lin. Chin erh-shih nien Chung-kuo wen-
i ssu-ch'ao lun. Shanghai: Sheng-huo shu-tien,
1947.
李何林。近二十年中國文藝思潮論。

Liu Hsin-huang. Hsü Chih-mo yü Lu Hsiao-
man. Taipei: Ch'ang liu pan-yueh-k'an
she.
劉心皇。徐志摩與陸小曼。

Living China: Modern Chinese Short Stories,
ed. and comp. by Edgar Snow. New York:
John Day & Reynal & Hitchcock, 1936.

MCNP

MMT

RCCL

Su Hsueh-lin. Ch'ing niao chi. Changsha:
Shang-wu yin shu kuan, 1938.
蘇雪林。青鳥集。

Wu, John Ching-hsiung. *Beyond East and West.* New York: Sheed & Ward, 1951.
WWMC
Yü Ta-fu. "Chih-mo tsai hui-i li." *Hsin-yueh yueh-k'an*, IV-1.
郁達夫。志摩在回憶裡。新月月刊。

Hsü Ch'ung-chih   許崇智
SOURCES
BKL
Chin shan shih-pao. San Francisco, December 22, 1956.
金山時報。
Kung shang jih-pao. Hong Kong, January 26, 1965.
工商日報。

Hsü Hai-tung   徐海東
SOURCES
Person interviewed: Chang Kuo-t'ao.
Chung-kuo kung-ch'an-tang te chung-yao jen-wu, ed. by Min-chien ch'u-pan she. Peiping: Min-chien ch'u-pan she, 1949.
中國共產黨的重要人物。民間出版社。
GCCJK
GCJJ
RSOC

Hsü Hsiang-ch'ien   徐向前
SOURCES
Person interviewed: Chang Kuo-t'ao.
Chung-kuo kung-ch'an-tang te chung-yao jen-wu, ed. by Min-chien ch'u-pan she. Peiping: Min-chien ch'u-pan she, 1949.
中國共產黨的重要人物。民間出版社。
Feng Shao-lieh. Shih nien hung chün. Shanghai: Chieh-fang ch'u-pan she, 1938.
馮紹烈。十年紅軍。
GCCJK
GCJJ
GSSJ
HCJC
Kung Ch'u. Wo yü hung chün. Kowloon: Nan feng ch'u-pan she, 1955.
龔楚。我與紅軍。
RD
RSOC

Hsü Hsin-liu   徐新六
SOURCES
CBJS
GCMMTJK
TKLH
WWC, 1931.

Hsü Kuang-p'ing   許廣平
WORKS
1937. (ed.) Lu Hsün shu chien. Shanghai: San hsien shu-wu.
魯迅書簡。
1937. Lu Hsün yü k'ang Jih chan-cheng. with Li Fei-kan *et al.* Canton: Chan-shih ch'u-pan she.
魯迅與抗日戰爭。李芾甘等。
1946. "Lu Hsün ho ch'ing-nien men," in Hsiao Hung (pseud. of Chang Nai-ying), *Hui-i Lu Hsün hsien-sheng.* Peiping: Sheng-huo shu-tien.
魯迅和青年們。蕭紅（張迺瑩）。回憶魯迅先生。
1947. Tsao-nan ch'ien-hou. Shanghai: Shanghai ch'u-pan kung-ssu.
遭難前後。
1951. Hsin-wei te chi-nien. Peking: Jen-min wen-hsueh ch'u-pan she.
欣慰的紀念。
1954. Kuan-yü Lu Hsün te sheng-huo. Peking: Jen-min wen-hsueh ch'u-pan she.
關於魯迅的生活。
1961. Lu Hsün hui-i-lu. Peking: Tso-chia ch'u-pan she.
魯迅回憶錄。
ed. of *Min-chu.*
民主。

SOURCES
China News Analysis, 197 (September 20, 1957): 1.
Ching Sung (pseud. of Hsü Kuang-p'ing). "Lu Hsün ho ch'ing-nien men," in Hsiao Hung (pseud. of Chang Nai-ying), *Hui-i Lu Hsün hsien-sheng.* Peiping: Sheng-huo shu-tien, 1946.
景宋（許廣平）。魯迅和青年們。蕭紅（張迺瑩）。回憶魯迅先生。
CKJMT
GCCJK
HCJC
HMTT

I-chiu-wu-ling jen-min nien-chien, ed. by Shen
  Sung-fang. Hong Kong: Ta kung shu-chü,
  1950.
  一九五〇人民年鑑。沈頌芳。
Ho Ch'un-ts'ai. "Lu Hsün tsai Kuang-chou
  (Canton) te sheng-huo." *Ta kung pao*. Hong
  Kong, October 18, 1951.
  何春才。魯迅在廣州的生活。大公報。
Kao Lang. "I ko ch'i-tzu yen chung te chang-
  fu." *Ta kung pao*. Hong Kong, October 14,
  1951.
  高朗。一個妻子眼中的丈夫。大公報。
TCMT
WWMC

Hsü Mo   徐謨

WORKS

ed. of *I shih pao*.
益世報。

SOURCES

CH-T, 1953–54.
The International Who's Who.
The New York Times, June 30, 1956.
WWC, 1931.

Hsü Pei-hung   徐悲鴻

WORKS

1930. Pei-hung hui-chi. Shanghai: Chung-hua
  shu-chü.
  悲鴻繪集。
1931–32. Pei-hung miao chi. Shanghai: Chung-
  hua shu-chü. 4 vols.
  悲鴻描集。
1932–39. Pei-hung hua-chi. Shanghai: Chung-
  hua shu-chü. 4 vols.
  悲鴻畫集。
1939. (ed.) Hsü Pei-hung hua fan (Tung-wu).
  Shanghai: Chung-hua shu-chü.
  徐悲鴻畫範（動物）。
1939. (ed.) Hua fan. Kunming: Chung-hua
  shu-chü.
  畫範。
1939. (ed.) Li T'ang Po I Shu Ch'i ts'ai wei t'u.
  Kunming: Chung-hua shu-chü.
  李唐伯夷叔齊采薇圖。
1939. (ed.) T'ien-ch'i shu-wu ts'ang hua. Chung-
  hua shu-chü.
  田溪書屋藏畫。

1954. Hsü Pei-hung hsien-sheng mo-hua (comp.
  by Jen-min mei-shu ch'u-pan she). Peking:
  Jen-min mei-shu ch'u-pan she.
  徐悲鴻先生墨畫。人民美術出版社。
1954. Pei-hung mo-hua hsuan-chi. Peking: Jen-
  min mei-shu ch'u-pan she.
  悲鴻墨畫選集。
1954. Pei-hung su-miao hsuan. Peking: Jen-min
  mei-shu ch'u-pan she.
  悲鴻素描選。
1955. Pei-hung su-miao hsuan (comp. by Hsü
  Pei-hung hsien-sheng i-tso chan-lan hui ch'ou-
  pei hui). Peking: Jen-min mei-shu ch'u-pan
  she.
  悲鴻素描選。徐悲鴻先生遺作展覽會籌備
  會。
1956. Hsü Pei-hung te ts'ai mo hua (comp. by
  Ch'en Hsiao-nan). Peking: Chao hua mei-shu
  ch'u-pan she.
  徐悲鴻的彩墨畫。陳曉南。
1958. Hsü Pei-hung su-miao. Peking: Jen-min
  mei-shu ch'u-pan she.
  徐悲鴻素描。
1959. Hsü Pei-hung ts'ai mo hua (ed. by Jen-min
  mei-shu ch'u-pan she). Peking, 1959.
  徐悲鴻彩墨畫。人民美術出版社。
1960. Hsü Pei-hung yu-hua. Peking: Jen-min
  mei-shu ch'u-pan she.
  徐悲鴻油畫。

SOURCES

Ai Chung-hsin. "Hsu Pei-hung—an Outstanding
  Painter." *People's China*, 3 (1954): 36–40.
CBJS
Fan Tseng. Hsu Pei-hung. Shanghai: Jen-min
  mei-shu ch'u-pan she, 1962.
  范曾。徐悲鴻。
Krebsová, B. "Sü Pej-chung." *Nový Orient*, 9
  (1954): 10.
Levina, L. "Syui Bei-Khun, 1894–1953." *Iskus-
  stvo*, 1 (1954): 67–70.
MMT
Sch, F. W. "Plants from China (On the Paintings
  of Ju Péon)." *Visvabharati Quarterly*, N. S. 5
  (1939–40): 350–52.

Hsü Shih-ch'ang   徐世昌

WORKS

1911. (comp.) Tung-san-sheng cheng lueh. 40
  vols.
  東三省政略。

1914? T'ui-keng-t'ang cheng shu. 28 vols.
退耕堂政書。

1914. T'ui-keng-t'ang chi. Tientsin: Hsü shih.
2 vols.
退耕堂集。

1915. (ed.) Cheng-shih-t'ang li-chih-kuan li shu.
with others. 8 vols.
政事堂禮制館禮書。

1915. Kuei-yün-lou yen p'u.
歸雲樓硯譜。

1918. Shui-chu-ts'un-jen chi.
水竹邨人集。

1918. Shui-chu-ts'un-jen shih-hsuan. Tientsin:
Hsü shih. 4 vols.
水竹邨人詩選。

1919. Chiang li fa yen.
將吏法言。

1919. Li-tai li-chih chü-yao.
歷代吏治學要。

1920. Ou chan hou chih Chung-kuo—ching-chi
yü chiao-yü. Shanghai: Chung-hua shu-chü.
歐戰後之中國一經濟與教育。

1922. La Chine Après la Guerre. Paris: A.
Pedone.

1924? Kuei-yün-lou t'i hua shih.
歸雲樓題畫詩。

1931. T'ao-chai shu hsueh.
弢齋述學。

1932. Hai hsi ts'ao t'ang chi. Tientsin: Hsü
shih. 6 vols.
海西草堂集。

1935. (ed.) Shu-sui-lou ts'ang shu mu. 4 vols.
書髓樓藏書目。

1939. (ed.) Ch'ing ju hsueh an. 100 vols.
清儒學案。

(comp.) Yen Li shih ch'eng chi (with Hsi-chai
yü yao; Shu-ku yü yao). 5 vols.
顏李師承記（附：習齋語要，恕谷語要）。

SOURCES

CBJS
Chueh I. "Hsü Shih-ch'ang." *Shih pao pan-yueh-k'an*, II-6 (January 1, 1937): 33–36.
覺篨。徐世昌。實報半月刊。
CMMC
CTIW
CYB-W, 1926–27.
Fei Hsing-chien. Hsü Shih-ch'ang. Shanghai,
1919.
費行簡。徐世昌。
Feng Yü-hsiang. Wo te sheng-huo. Shanghai:
Chiao-yü shu-tien, 1947. 3 vols.
馮玉祥。我的生活。

Johnston, Reginald F. Twilight in the Forbidden
City. New York: Appleton-Century, 1934.
Kuang-hsü ping-hsü k'o hui shih t'ung ch'ih lu.
1886.
光緒丙戌科會試同齒錄。
Li Chien-nung. Tsui-chin san-shih nien Chung-kuo cheng-chih shih. Shanghai: T'ai-p'ing-yang shu-tien, 1931.
李劍農。最近三十年中國政治史。
MMT
Powell, Ralph L. The Rise of Chinese Military
Power, 1895–1912. Princeton: Princeton University Press, 1955.
TTJWC
WWC, 1925.

Hsü Shih-ying   許世英

WORKS

1914. Chih Feng ch'i-shih jih cheng chi. Peking.
治奉七十日政記。

1915. Min hai hsün chi.
閩海巡記。

1952. "Huai-nien Tu Yueh-sheng hsien-sheng,"
in Heng she, *Tu Yueh-sheng hsien-sheng chi-nien
chi, ch'u chi*. Taipei: Heng she.
懷念杜月笙先生。恒社。杜月笙先生紀念
集，初集。

1953. Hsueh-lou chi-shih. Taipei.
雪樓紀事。

1961, October 31. "Fu-ying san-shih-ch'i nien
ssu chi." *Chung-yang jih-pao*. Taipei.
服膺三十七年私記。中央日報。

1966. Hsü Shih-ying hui-i-lu. Taipei: Jen-chien
shih yueh-k'an she.
許世英回憶錄。

Chih Min kung-tu. 2 vols.
治閩公牘。

SOURCES

BPC
Chia I-chün. Chung-hua Min-kuo cheng-chih
shih. Peiping, 1931.
賈逸君。中華民國政治史。
CMJL
CMTC
CYB-W, 1934.
GCJJ
Hsin-sheng pao. Taipei, October 14, 1964.
新生報。
Hsü Shih-ying. Chih Feng ch'i-shih jih cheng
chi. Peking, 1914.

許世英。治奉七十日政記。
Hsü Shih-ying. Chih Min kung tu. 2 vols.
許世英。治閩公牘。
———. "Fu-ying san-shih-ch'i nien ssu chi."
Chung-yang jih-pao. Taipei, October 31, 1961.
許世英。服膺三十七年私記。中央日報。
———. Hsü Shih-ying hui-i-lu. Taipei: Jen-
chien shih yueh-k'an she, 1966.
許世英。許世英回憶錄。
———. Hsueh-lou chi-shih. Taipei, 1953.
許世英。雪樓紀事。
———. "Huai-nien Tu Yueh-sheng hsien-
sheng," in Heng she, *Tu Yueh-sheng hsien-sheng
chi-nien chi, ch'u chi.* Taipei: Heng she, 1952.
許世英。懷念杜月笙先生。恆社。杜月笙
先生紀念集，初集。
Hsü Shih-ying hsien-sheng chi-nien chi. Taipei,
1965.
許世英先生紀念集。
Kuo-fu nien-p'u ch'u-kao, ed. by Kuo shih kuan
shih-liao pien-tsuan wei-yuan-hui, Chung-kuo
kuo-min-tang tang shih shih-liao pien-tsuan
wei-yuan-hui. Taipei: Kuo shih kuan shih-
liao pien-tsuan wei-yuan-hui, Chung-kuo kuo-
min-tang tang shih shih-liao pien-tsuan wei-
yuan-hui, 1959. 2 vols.
國父年譜初稿。國史館史料編纂委員會。
中國國民黨黨史史料編纂委員會。
Liu Ch'eng-yü. "Hsien tsung-li chiu te lu."
Kuo shih kuan kuan k'an, ch'uang-k'an hao
(1947).
劉成禺。先總理舊德錄。國史館館刊。
MSICH
The New York Times, June 3, October 25, 1936;
July 22, September 2, 1937; January 18, 20,
1938; February 5, 1938; October 14, 1964.
Pai Chiao. Yuan Shih-k'ai yü Chung-hua Min-
kuo (ed. by Wu Hsiang-hsiang). Taipei: Wen-
hsing shu-tien, 1962.
白蕉。袁世凱與中華民國。吳相湘。
Shan-hou hui-i shih, ed. by Fei Pao-yen. Peking:
Huan-yü yin-shua chü, 1925.
善後會議史。費保彥。
T'ao Chü-yin. Pei-yang chün-fa t'ung-chih
shih-ch'i shih-hua. Peking: Sheng-huo, tu-
shu, hsin chih san lien shu-tien, 1957–58.
6 vols.
陶菊隱。北洋軍閥統治時期史話。
TCMC-1
WWMC
Yang Chia-lo. Chia-wu i-lai Chung Jih chün-
shih wai-chiao ta-shih chi-yao. Chungking:
Shang-wu yin shu kuan, 1941.

楊家駱。甲午以來中日軍事外交大事紀要。

Hsü Shu-cheng   徐樹錚

WORKS

1921. Chien-kuo ch'üan-chen. Peking? Hsü
shih ying-yin.
建國詮真。
1931. Shih-hsi-hsuan i-kao. 2 vols.
視昔軒遺稿。
1962. Hsü Shu-cheng hsien-sheng wen-chi nien-
p'u ho k'an (ed. by Hsü Tao-lin). Taipei:
Shang-wu yin shu kuan.
徐樹錚先生文集年譜合刊。徐道鄰。
1962. Hsü Shu-cheng tien-kao (ed. by Chung-
kuo k'o-hsueh yuan chin-tai shih yen-chiu so
chin-tai shih tzu-liao pien-chi tsu). Peking:
Chung-hua shu-chü.
徐樹錚電稿。中國科學院近代史研究所近
代史資料編輯組。

SOURCES

CCLTC
Chin Liang. Kua-pu shu i. 1936?
金梁。瓜圃述異。
Chung-kuo tsui-chin san-shih nien shih, comp.
by Ch'en Kung-fu. Shanghai: Shang-wu yin
shu kuan, 1933.
中國最近三十年史。陳功甫。
CMMC
CMTC
Hsü I-shih. "T'an Hsü Shu-cheng." *I ching*, 9
(July 5, 1936): 32–35; 10 (July 20, 1936): 8–13.
徐一士。談徐樹錚。逸經。
Hsü Liang-chih. Liang-chai tsa-pi. Hong Kong:
Tzu-yu ch'u-pan she, 1951.
徐亮之。亮齋雜筆。
Hsü Shu-cheng hsien-sheng wen-chi nien-p'u ho
k'an, ed. by Hsü Tao-lin. Taipei: Shang-wu
yin shu kuan, 1962.
徐樹錚先生文集年譜合刊。徐道鄰。
Kuo-fu nien-p'u, ed. by Chung-kuo kuo-min-
tang chung-yang tang shih shih-liao pien-
tsuan wei-yuan-hui. Taipei: Chung-hua
Min-kuo ko-chieh chi-nien kuo-fu pai nien
tan-ch'en ch'ou-pei wei-yuan-hui, 1965. 2 vols.
國父年譜。中國國民黨中央黨史史料編纂
委員會。
Lei Hsiao-ts'en. San-shih nien tung-luan
Chung-kuo. Hong Kong: Ya-chou ch'u-pan
she, 1955.
雷嘯岑。三十年動亂中國。

Li Chien-nung. Tsui-chin san-shih nien Chung-kuo cheng-chih shih. Shanghai: T'ai-p'ing-yang shu-tien, 1931.
李劍農。最近三十年中國政治史。
Ma wu hsien-sheng (pseud. of Lei Hsiao-ts'en). Hsin shih shuo. Taipei: Tzu-yu T'ai-p'ing-yang wen-hua shih-yeh kung-ssu, 1965.
馬五先生 (雷嘯岑)。新世說。
MMT
Pollard, Robert Thomas. China's Foreign Relations, 1917-1931. New York: The Macmillan Co., 1933.
San-shui Liang Yen-sun hsien-sheng (1869-1933) nien-p'u, comp. by Feng-kang chi men ti-tzu. 1946. 2 vols.
三水梁燕孫先生 (1869-1933) 年譜。鳳岡及門弟子。
Tang, Peter S. H. Russian and Soviet Policy in Manchuria and Outer Mongolia, 1911-1931. Durham: Duke University Press, 1959.
Wai-meng chiao-she shih-mo chi, comp. by Pi Kuei-fang. Peking: Pi shih, 1928.
外蒙交涉始末記。畢桂芳。
Wen Kung-chih. Tsui-chin san-shih nien Chung-kuo chün-shih shih. Shanghai: T'ai-p'ing-yang shu-tien, 1932. 2 vols.
文公直。最近三十年中國軍事史。
Wu K'ai-sheng. Pei-chiang hsien-sheng wen-chi (with Shih-chi).
吳闓生。北江先生文集 (附: 詩集)。
WWC, 1919; 1925.

Hsü T'e-li   徐 特 立

Works

1951. Hsü T'e-li et al. Lun ai-kuo chu-i chiao-yü. Peking: Ch'ün-chung shu-tien.
徐特立等。論愛國主義教育。

Sources

Person interviewed: Chang Kuo-t'ao.
Chung-kuo kung-ch'an-tang te chung-yao jen-wu, ed. by Min-chien ch'u-pan she. Peiping: Min-chien ch'u-pan she, 1949.
中國共產黨的重要人物。民間出版社。
GCCJK
GCJJ
HCJC
Hsiao San. Jen-wu yü chi-nien. Peking: Sheng-huo, tu-shu, hsin chih san lien shu-tien, 1951.
蕭三。人物與紀念。
JMST, 1957.

Peking Review, 17 (April 27, 1962): 19.
RD
SCMP, 2489 (May 4, 1961): 11; 2505 (May 29, 1961).
"Ssu-pa" pei-nan lieh-shih chi-nien-ts'e, comp. by Chung-kuo kung-ch'an-tang tai-piao t'uan. Chung-kuo kung-ch'an-tang tai-piao t'uan, 1946.
"四八" 被難烈士紀念冊。中國共產黨代表團。

Hsü Ti-shan   許 地 山

Works

1920. "Taoism," in W. L. Hare, Religions of the Empire.
1924. "The History of the Canon of the Chinese Classics." Journal of the American Oriental Society, 44: 273-84.
1926. "The Solitary Star by the Sea." Chinese Students Monthly, XXII-2: 27-29. (tr. by Yusu Koo.)
1927. Yü-t'i wen-fa ta-kang. Shanghai: Chung-hua shu-chü.
語体文法大綱。
1928. Wu-fa t'ou-ti chih yu-chien. Peiping: Wen-hua hsueh-she.
無法投遞之郵件。
1931. (ed.) Ta chung chi (Ya-p'ien chan-cheng ch'ien Chung Ying chiao-she shih-liao). Shanghai: Shang-wu yin shu kuan.
達衷集 (鴉片戰爭前中英交涉史料)。
1933. Chieh-fang che. Peiping: Hsing-yün-t'ang shu-chü.
解放者。
1933. (comp.) Combined Indices to the Authors and Titles of Books and Chapters in Four Collections of Buddhistic Literature. Cambridge: Harvard-Yenching Institute Sinological Index Series No. 11. 3 vols.
1934. (ed.) Tao-chiao shih; shang-pien. Shanghai: Shang-wu yin shu kuan.
道教史, 上編。
1935. K'ung shan ling yü. Peiping: Wen-hsueh yen-chiu she.
空山靈雨。
1936. Lo-hua-sheng ch'uang-tso hsuan (comp. by Ch'en Hsiao-mei). Shanghat: Ch'i chin shu-chü.
落華生創作選。陳筱梅。
1936. "Tao in Today's China." Asia, 3: 781-84.
1938. "Wuu Shiunn: The Great Beggar and

Promoter of Free Education." *T'ien-hsia Monthly*, 7: 235–55.

1939. (comp.) Nü kuo-shih.

女國士。

1941. Hsü Ti-shan yü-wen lun-wen chi. Hsin wen-tzu hsueh-hui.

許地山語文論文集。

1946. Fu chi mi-hsin ti yen-chiu. Shanghai: Shang-wu yin shu kuan.

扶箕迷信底研究。

1946. Tsa kan chi. Shanghai: Shang-wu yin shu kuan.

雜感集。

1947. Kuo-ts'ui yü kuo-hsueh. Shanghai: Shang-wu yin shu kuan.

國粹與國學。

1947. Wei ch'ao chui chien. Shanghai: Shang-wu yin shu kuan.

危巢墜簡。

1952. Hsü Ti-shan hsuan-chi. Peking: K'ai-ming shu-tien.

許地山選集。

1955. Erh-shih yeh chien. (tr.) Peking: Tso-chia ch'u-pan she.

二十夜間。

1957. Ch'un te lin-yeh. Taipei: Ch'i ming shu-chü.

春的林野。

1961. Kuei-t'u. Hong Kong: Shanghai shu-chü.

歸途。

1963. Ch'un t'ao. Peking: Jen-min wen-hsueh ch'u-pan she.

春桃。

Sources

Bodde, Derk. "Hsü Ti-shan, 1893–1941." *Harvard Journal of Asiatic Studies*, 6 (1941): 403–4.

CBJS

Ching Fu. "Lo Hua Sheng yin-hsiang chi." *Tu-shu ku-wen*, I-3 (October, 1934).

景福。落花生印象記。讀書顧問。

Chung wai wen-hsueh chia chuan-lueh tz'u-tien. Hong Kong: Shanghai shu-chü, 1959.

中外文學家傳略辭典。

GCMMTJK

Jung Ch'ao-tsu. "Hsü Ti-shan hsien-sheng chuan." *Wen shih tsa-chih*, I-12 (1940).

容肇祖。許地山先生傳。文史雜誌。

Li Pin. "Lo Hua Sheng—Hsü Ti-shan." *Tainan wen-hua*, III-2 (September, 1953): 62–64.

林斌。落華生—許地山。台南文化。

Lien Ching-ch'u. "Hsü Nan-ying yü Hsü Ti-shan." *Tainan wen-hua*, II-2 (April, 1952): 62–65.

連景初。許南英與許地山。台南文化。

Lin Kuang-hao. "Chi Lo Hua Sheng—Hsü Ti-shan." *Chuan-chi wen-hsueh*, VIII-6 (June, 1966): 50–52.

林光灝。記落花生—許地山。傳記文學。

Mao Tun (Shen Yen-ping). "Lo Hua Sheng lun." *Wen-hsueh*, III-4 (October, 1934).

矛盾（沈雁冰）。落花生論。文學。

MMT

Shen Ts'ung-wen. "Lun Lo Hua Sheng." *Tu-shu yueh-k'an*, I-1 (June, 1931).

沈從文。論落花生。讀書月刊。

Hsü Yung-ch'ang   徐永昌

Works

"Ssu nien lai ti wo chan-lueh chan-shu te tsung chien-t'ao," in Chun-shih wei-yuan-hui cheng-chih pu, *K'ang chan ssu nien*.

四年來敵我戰略戰術的總檢討。軍事委員會政治部。抗戰四年。

Sources

BKL

Chiang Ching-kuo. Wei-chi ts'un-wang chih ch'iu.

蔣經國。危急存亡之秋。

CH-T, 1956–57.

CMJL

CMMC

CTMC

CWR, 1929.

Feng Yü-hsiang. Wo te sheng-huo. Shanghai: Chiao-yü shu-tien, 1947. 3 vols.

馮玉祥。我的生活。

GCJJ

Hsü Yung-ch'ang. "Ssu nien lai ti wo chan-lueh chan-shu te tsung chien-t'ao," in Chün-shih wei-yuan-hui cheng-chih pu, *K'ang chan ssu nien*.

徐永昌。四年來敵我戰略戰術的總檢討。軍事委員會政治部。抗戰四年。

Hsü Yung-ch'ang hsien-sheng chi-nien chi, comp. by Hsü Yung-ch'ang hsien-sheng chih-sang wei-yuan-hui. Taipei, 1962.

徐永昌先生紀念集。徐永昌先生治喪委員會。

Hsü Yung-ch'ang hsien-sheng shih-lueh.

徐永昌先生事略。

Kuo-min chün ko-ming shih ch'u-k'ao. Chung-king, 1940.

國民軍革命史初稿。

Kuo-min ko-ming chün chan shih, comp. by
Kuo-min ko-ming chün chan shih pien-tsuan
wei-yuan-hui. Ts'an-mou pen-pu. 1934. 17
vols.
國民革命軍戰史。國民革命軍戰史編纂委
員會。

Liu Chih-pu. A Military History of Modern
China, 1924–1949. Princeton: Princeton University Press, 1956.

TCJC

WWC, Supplement to 4th ed., 1931

WWMC

Hsueh Min-lao   薛敏老

SOURCES

Persons interviewed: not to be identified.
Manila Times, August 9, 1955.

Hsueh Yueh   薛岳

WORKS

1937. Chiao fei chi-shih. Kweiyang.
剿匪紀實。

1941. Hsueh Yueh *et al*. Hsiang cheng san nien
(comp. by Hunan sheng-cheng-fu pi-shu ch'u
pien i shih). Changsha: Hunan sheng-cheng-
fu pi-shu ch'u pien i shih.
薛岳等。湘政三年。湖南省政府秘書處編
譯室。

1942. Hunan sheng ti-fang hsing-cheng kan-pu
hsun-lien t'uan kung-tso pao-kao (Min san-
shih-i nien-tu). Hunan sheng ti-fang hsing-
cheng kan-pu hsun-lien t'uan.
湖南省地方行政幹部訓練團工作報告 (民
三十一年度)。

1942? Hunan tang cheng. Changsha.
湖南黨政。

1948. Hsueh Yueh k'ang chan shou-kao (ed. by
Wu Ching-mo).
薛岳抗戰手稿。吳敬模。

SOURCES

Hsueh Yueh. Chiao fei chi-shih. Taipei: Wen
hsing shu-tien, 1961.
薛岳。剿匪紀實。

———. Hsueh Yueh k'ang chan shou-kao (ed.
by Wu Ching-mo). 1948.
薛岳。薛岳抗戰手稿。吳敬模。

Hsuchow sui-ching kai-yao, ed. by Hsieh Sheng-
i.
徐州綏靖概要。謝聲溢。

K'ang chan chi-shih, ed. by Chao Tseng-ch'ou.
Taipei: Taiwan shang-wu yin shu kuan.
4 vols.
抗戰紀實。趙曾儔。

Kuo-min ko-ming chün chan shih, comp. by
Kuo-min ko-ming chün chan shih pien-tsuan
wei-yuan-hui. Ts'an-mou pen-pu, 1934. 17
vols.
國民革命軍戰史。國民革命軍戰史編纂委
員會。

MSICH

The Stilwell Papers, ed. by Theodore H. White.
New York: William Sloane Associates, 1948.

Sui-ching chi-shih, ed. by Wu Ching-mo *et al*.
1947.
綏靖紀實。吳敬模等。

Ti-ssu chün chi-shih. Canton: Huai yuan wen-
hua shih-yeh fu-wu she.
第四軍紀實。

Wu I-chih. Hsueh Po-ling chiang-chün shih-chi
t'ung-shuai fa chih kai-shu. Changsha, 1941.
吳逸志。薛伯陵將軍實際統帥法之概述。

Hu Feng   胡風

WORKS

1937. Wen-i pi-t'an. Shanghai: Wen-hsueh
ch'u-pan she.
文藝筆談。

1937–38. ed. of *Ch'i-yueh.*
七月。

1938. Mi yün ch'i feng hsi hsiao chi. Hankow:
Hai yen ch'u-pan she.
密雲期風習小紀。

1945, January. "Chih-shen tsai wei min-chu te
tou-cheng li-mien." *Hsi-wang*, 1.
置身在為民主的鬥爭裡面。希望。

1945. Tsai hun-luan li-mien; Hu Feng ti-ssu
p'i-p'ing lun-wen chi. Chungking: Tso-chia
shu-wu.
在混亂裡面，胡風第四批評論文集。

1946. Min-tsu chan-cheng yü wen-i hsing-ko.
Shanghai: Hsi-wang she.
民族戰爭與文藝性格。

1947. Ni-liu te jih-tzu. Shanghai: Hsi-wang she.
逆流的日子。

1947. (comp.) Wo shih ch'u lai te—shih-ssu shih-
jen hsuan-chi. Shanghai: Hsi-wang she.
我是初來的一十四詩人選集。

1948. Hu Feng wen-chi. Shanghai: Ch'un ming
shu-tien.
胡風文集。

1948. Lun hsien-shih chu-i te lu. Shanghai:
Ch'ing lin she.
論現實主義的路。

1952. Ho hsin jen-wu tsai i-ch'i. Shanghai:
Hsin wen-i ch'u-pan she.
和新人物在一起。

1952. Ts'ung yuan-t'ou tao hung-liu. Shanghai:
Hsin wen-i ch'u-pan she.
從源頭到洪流。

1953. Wei-le ch'ao-hsien, wei-le jen-lei! Peking:
Jen-min wen-hsueh ch'u-pan she.
為了朝鮮，為了人類！

Mien-hua. Wen-hua sheng-huo she.
棉花。

Shan ling. Wen-hua sheng huo she.
山靈。

Weh-hsueh yü sheng-huo. Shanghai: Sheng-huo
shu-tien.
文學與生活。

Yeh-hua yü chien. Wen-hua sheng-huo she.
野花與箭。

SOURCES

Chan Shau-wing. "Literature in Communist
China." *Problems of Communism*, VII-1 (January-February, 1958).

"Kuan-yü Hu Feng fan ko-ming chi-t'uan te ti-
erh p'i ts'ai-liao." *Wen-i pao*, 11.
關於胡風反革命集團的第二批材料。文藝報。

"Kuan-yü Hu Feng fan ko-ming chi-t'uan te ti-
san p'i ts'ai-liao." *Wen-i pao*, 11.
關於胡風反革命集團的第三批材料。文藝報。

"Kuan-yü Hu Feng fan tang chi-t'uan te i-hsieh
ts'ai-liao." *Wen-i pao*, 9-10.
關於胡風反黨集團的一些材料。文藝報。

Lu Wei-jan. Hu Feng shih-chien te ch'ien-yin
hou-kuo. Hong Kong: Nan feng ch'u-pan
she, 1956.
魯喟然。胡風事件的前因後果。

The New York Times, June 11, July 19, 1957.

SCMP, 1955-56.

Hu Han-min   胡漢民

WORKS

1919, October-November. "Chung-kuo che-
hsueh shih chih wei-wu te yen-chiu." *Chien-
she*, I-3, 4.
中國哲學史之唯物的研究。建設。

1919, December. "Wei-wu shih-kuan p'i-p'ing
chih p'i-p'ing." *Chien-she*, I-5: 954-89.
唯物史觀批評之批評。建設。

1925. Government Headquarters Declarations.
Canton.

1925. Selected Documents and Addresses.
Canton: Ministry of Foreign Affairs.

1925. Wei-wu shih-kuan yü lun-li chih yen-chiu
(ed. by Huang Ch'ang-ku). Shanghai: Min
chih shu-chü.
唯物史觀與倫理之研究。黃昌穀。

1927. Chiang Hu tsui-chin yen-lun chi. with
Chiang Kai-shek. (comp. by Chung-yang
chün-shih cheng-chih hsueh-hsiao t'e-pieh
tang-pu.) Huang-p'u, Kwangtung: Chung-
yang chün-shih cheng-chih hsueh-hsiao.
蔣胡最近言論集。蔣介石。中央軍事政治
學校特別黨部。

1927. (Hu Han-min hsien-sheng) tsai O yen-
chiang lu; ti-i chi. Canton: Min chih shu-chü.
（胡漢民先生）在俄演講錄，第一集。

1927. Hu Han-min hsien-sheng yen-chiang chi.
Shanghai: Min chih shu-chü. 3 vols.
胡漢民先生演講集。

1927. San min chu-i che chih shih-ming. Shanghai: Min chih shu-chü.
三民主義者之使命。

1927. San min yü CP. Shanghai: Ko-hsin shu-
tien.
三民與 CP。

1927. She-hui chu-i shih. (tr.) Shanghai: Min
chih shu-chü. 2 vols.
社會主義史。

1929. Hu Han-min hsien-sheng yen-hsing lu.
Shanghai: Kuang i shu-chü.
胡漢民先生言行錄。

1929, February. "Ko-ming yü fan ko-ming tsui
hsien-chu te i-mu." *Chung-yang pan-yueh-k'an*,
II-10.
革命與反革命最顯著的一幕。中央半月刊。

1929. San min chu-i chih jen-shih. Nanking:
Chung-kuo kuo-min-tang chung-yang chih-
hsing wei-yuan-hui hsuan-ch'uan pu.
三民主義之認識。

1930. Ching-t'ien chih-tu yu-wu chih yen-chiu.
with Chu Chih-hsin, Hu Shih, Liao Chung-
k'ai *et al.* Shanghai: Hua t'ung shu-chü.
井田制度有無之研究。朱執信，胡適，廖
仲愷等。

1932. Ko-ming li-lun yü ko-ming kung-tso. with
Wang Yang-ch'ung. Shanghai: Min chih
shu-chü.
革命理論與革命工作。王養冲。

1934. Hu Han-min hsien-sheng cheng-lun hsuan-pien—erh-shih nien shih-yueh chih erh-shih-san nien san-yueh. Canton: Hsien tao she.
胡漢民先生政論選編一二十年十月至二十三年三月。

1934. Hu Han-min tui shih-chü chung-yao hsuan-yen. Shao-nien Chung-kuo ch'en pao.
胡漢民對時局重要宣言。

1935. Lun so-wei fa-hsi-ssu-ti. Canton: Min chih shu-chü.
論所謂法西斯蒂。

1936. Hsi-nan k'ang Jih chiu-kuo yen-lun erh chi. Canton: P'ei ying yin-wu chü.
西南抗日救國言論二輯。

1936. Hu Han-min hsien-sheng cheng-lun hsuan-pien ti-erh chi; erh-shih-san nien ssu-yueh chih erh-shih-wu nien i-yueh. Canton: Hsien tao she.
胡漢民先生政論選編第二輯，二十三年四月至二十五年一月。

1936. Min-tsu chu-i yü tzu-li keng-sheng. Canton: Hsien tao she.
民族主義與自力更生。

1941. San min chu-i lun ts'ung (comp. by Wu Man-chün). Kiangsi sheng san min chu-i wen-hua yün-tung wei-yuan-hui.
三民主義論叢。吳曼君。

1945. San min chu-i te lien-huan hsing. Shanghai: Wen hua shu-chü.
三民主義的連還性。

1953. "Hu Han-min tzu-chuan," in Chung-kuo kuo-min-tang chung-yang wei-yuan-hui tang shih shih-liao pien-tsuan wei-yuan-hui, Ko-ming wen-hsien, ti-san chi. Taipei: Chung-yang wen-wu kung-ying she.
胡漢民自傳。中國國民黨中央委員會黨史史料編纂委員會。革命文獻，第三輯。

1958. Pu-kuei-shih shih-ch'ao. Taipei: Chung-hua ts'ung-shu wei-yuan-hui.
不匱室詩鈔。

1959. Hu Han-min hsuan-chi. Taipei: P'a-mi-erh shu-tien.
胡漢民選集。

Hu Han-min hsien-sheng i-chiao chi lu.
胡漢民先生遺教輯錄。

ed. of Ling hai pao.
嶺海報。

ed. of Min-kuo tsa-chih.
民國雜誌。

SOURCES

Chiang Yung-ching. "Hu Han-min hsien-sheng nien-p'u kao," in Wu Hsiang-hsiang, Chung-kuo hsien-tai shih ts'ung-k'an, III. Taipei: Cheng-chung shu-chü, 1961.
蔣永敬。胡漢民先生年譜稿。吳相湘。中國現代史叢刊。

Chow Tse-tsung. The May Fourth Movement: Intellectual Revolution in Modern China. Cambridge: Harvard University Press, 1960.

Chu Ho-chung. "Yü Hu Han-min hsien-sheng yu O pa ko yueh chih hui-hsiang," in Wu Hsiang-hsiang, Chung-kuo hsien-tai shih ts'ung-k'an, III. Taipei: Cheng-chung shu-chü, 1961.
朱和中。與胡漢民先生遊俄八個月之回想。吳相湘。中國現代史叢刊。

Ch'un-ch'iu, 165 (May 16, 1964).
春秋。

Chung-kuo kuo-min-tang shih-kao i chih ssu p'ien, comp. by Tsou Lu. Chungking: Shang-wu yin shu kuan, 1944.
中國國民黨史稿一至四篇。鄒魯。

Cochrane, Donna E. "Hu Han-min's Articles in the Min Pao." Unpublished Master's essay, Columbia University, 1960.

Hu Han-min. "Hu Han-min tzu-chuan," in Chung-kuo kuo-min-tang chung-yang wei-yuan-hui tang shih-liao pien-tsuan wei-yuan-hui, Ko-ming wen-hsien, ti-san chi. Taipei: Chung-yang wen-wu kung-ying she, 1953.
胡漢民。胡漢民自傳。中國國民黨中央委員會黨史史料編纂委員會，革命文獻，第三輯。

Hu hsien-sheng chi-nien chuan k'an, comp. by Hu chu-hsi chih-sang wei-yuan hui. Canton: Hu chu-hsi chih sang wei-yuan-hui, 1936.
胡先生紀念專刊。胡主席治喪委員會。

Kennedy, Melville T., Jr. "Hu Han-min: Aspects of His Political Thought," in Papers on China, VIII. Cambridge: Harvard University, 1954. (Duplicated for private distribution by the Committee on International and Regional Studies, Harvard University.)

Kuo-fu nien-p'u, ed. by Chung-kuo kuo-min-tang chung-yang tang shih shih-liao pien-tsuan wei-yuan-hui. Taipei: Chung-hua Min-kuo ko-chieh chi-nien kuo-fu pai nien tan-ch'en ch'ou-pei wei-yuan-hui, 1965. 2 vols.
國父年譜。中國國民黨中央黨史史料編纂委員會。

Shirley, James R. "Control of the Kuomintang After Sun Yat-sen's Death." The Journal of Asian Studies, XXV-1 (November, 1965): 69-82.

Tong, Hollington K. Chiang Kai-shek, Soldier

and Statesman. Shanghai: China Publishing Co., 1937.

Yao Yü-hsiang. Hu Han-min hsien-sheng chuan. Taipei: Chung-yang wen-wu kung-ying she, 1954.
姚漁湘。 胡漢民先生傳。

Hu Lin　　胡霖

WORKS

1916–? ed. of *Ta kung pao*.
大公報。

SOURCES

Person interviewed: Chang Chia-ao.
CH, 1937–45.
Chang Tan-feng. Chin pai nien lai Chung-kuo pao-chih chih fa-chan chi ch'i ch'ü-shih. Kweilin: K'ai-ming shu-tien, 1942.
章丹楓。 近百年來中國報紙之發展及其趨勢。
GCCJK
Lin Yü-t'ang. A History of the Press and Public Opinion in China. Chicago: The University of Chicago Press, 1936.
TCMT
Tong, Hollington K. Dateline: China. New York: Rockport Press, 1950.

Hu Shih　　胡適

WORKS

1908–? ed. of *Ching yeh hsun pao*.
競業旬報。
1914, May. "The Confucianist Movement in China." *The Chinese Students' Monthly*, IX-7.
1914, October. "Japan and Kiao-chau." *The Chinese Students' Monthly*, X-11.
1914, November. "History of the German Leased Territory of Kiao-chau." *The Chinese Students' Monthly*, X-2: 68.
1915, April. "A Plea for Patriotic Sanity." *The Chinese Students' Monthly*, X-7.
1916, April. "A Chinese Philosopher on War." *The Chinese Students' Monthly*, XI-5.
1917, January. "Classical Confucianism." *The Monist*, 27: 157–60.
1919. Chung-kuo che-hsueh shih ta-kang; chüan shang. Shanghai: Shang-wu yin shu kuan.
中國哲學史大綱；卷上。

1920. Ch'ang-shih chi. Peking: Pei-ta ch'u-pan pu.
嘗試集。
1922. The Development of the Logical Method in Ancient China. Shanghai: The Oriental Book Co.
1923? Yen-chiu kuo-hsueh shu-mu. with Liang Ch'i-ch'ao. Shanghai: Ya-chou shu-chü.
研究國學書目。
1925, December. "Present Crisis in Christian Education." *Religious Education Association*, 20: 434–38.
1926, February. "New Crisis in China Missions." *Missionary Review of the World*, 49.
1926, December. "China and the Missionaries." *London Spectator*, 137: 85–87.
1927, May. "Cultural Rebirth in China." *The Trans-Pacific*, May 14, 1927.
1927, June. "China and Christianity." *Forum*, 78: 1–2.
1927. Kuo-yü wen-hsueh shih chiang-i (with Wu-shih nien lai Chung-kuo chih wen-hsueh). Peking: Wen-hua hsueh-she.
國語文學史講義（附：五十年來中國之文學）。
1927. Tai Tung-yuan te che-hsueh. Shanghai: Shang-wu yin shu kuan.
戴東原的哲學。
1928. Hu Shih *et al.* (Hsien-tai ming-chu) Hsin chu-i p'ing-lun (ed. by Ch'en Pen-wen). Shanghai: Hsin chu-i yen-chiu she. 2 vols.
胡適等。(現代名著) 新主義評論。陳本文。
1929. Pai-hua wen-hsueh shih; shang chüan. Shanghai: Hsin-yueh shu-tien.
白話文學史；上卷。
1930. Ching-t'ien chih-tu yu-wu chih yen-chiu. with Chu Chih-hsin *et al*. Shanghat: Hua t'ung shu-chü.
井田制度有無之研究。朱執信等。
1930. Hu Shih *et al*. Jen-ch'üan lun chi. Shanghai: Hsin-yueh shu-tien.
胡適等。人權論集。
1930. (ed.) Shen-hui ho-shang i chi. Shanghai: Ya tung t'u-shu-kuan.
神會和尚遺集。
1931. China's Own Critics. with Lin Yü-t'ang. Peiping.
1931. Huai-nan-wang shu. Shanghai: Hsin-yueh shu-tien.
淮南王書。
1931. Lu-shan yu-chi. Shanghai: Hsin-yueh shu-tien.
廬山遊記。

1931-37. Tuan-p'ien hsiao-shuo. (tr.) Shanghai: Ya tung t'u-shu kuan. 2 vols.
短篇小說。

1932, January. "Development of Zen Buddhism in China." *The Chinese Social and Political Science Review*, 15: 475-505.

1932. Chung-kuo wen-t'i. with P'an Kuang-tan *et al*. Hsin yueh shu-tien.
中國問題。潘光旦等。

1932, October. "World Opinion Will Finally Curb Japan." CWR, 62: 254-55.

1933. Chang Shih-chai hsien-sheng nien-p'u. Shanghai: Shang-wu yin shu kuan.
章實齋先生年譜。

1933. Hsin sheng-huo lun. Shanghai.
新生活論。

1933. Ssu-shih tzu-shu. Shanghai: Ya tung t'u-shu kuan.
四十自述。

1933, August. "They Stand Out from the Crowd." *The Literary Digest*, 116: 11.

1934, January. "Task of Modern Religion." *The Journal of Religion*, 14: 104-8.

1934, January. "Types of Cultural Response." *The Chinese Social and Political Science Review*, 17: 529-52.

1934. The Chinese Renaissance. Chicago: The University of Chicago Press.

1934. Hu Shih jih-chi. Shanghai: Wen-hua yen-chiu she.
胡適日記。

1935, April. "Japanese Consular Conference on the Boycott: Hu Shih's Views on Cooperation." CWR, 72: 208-10.

1936, January. "Dr. Hu Shih's Demand for Open Diplomacy and Some Recent Developments." CWR, 75: 185-86.

1936. Hu Shih lun shuo wen-hsuan (comp. by Cheng Chih-kuang). Shanghai: Hsi-wang ch'u-pan she.
胡適論說文選。鄭之光。

1936, March. "Word to the Japanese People." *Asia*, 36: 166-68.

1936, November. "Reconstruction in China." *Asia*, 36: 737-40.

1937, January. "Can China Survive?" *Forum and Century*, 97: 39-44.

1937. "Confucianism." *Encyclopedia of the Social Sciences*, IV: 198-201.

1937, May. "My People and the Japanese." *The Living Age*, 352: 251.

1938, September. "What Can America Do in the Far East Situation." CWR, 86: 106-7.

1943. Chung-kuo chang hui hsiao-shuo k'ao-cheng. Dairen: Shih-yeh yin shu kuan.
中國章回小說考證。

1947. Liu hsueh jih-chi. Shanghai: Shang-wu yin shu kuan. 4 vols.
留學日記。

1948. Ch'i Pai-shih nien-p'u. with Li Chin-hsi, Teng Kuang-ming. Shanghai: Shang-wu yin shu kuan.
齊白石年譜。黎錦熙，鄧廣銘。

1950. Wo-men pi-hsü hsuan-tse wo-men te fang-hsiang. Hong Kong: Tzu-yu Chung-kuo ch'u-pan she.
我們必須選擇我們的方向。

1951. (ed.) Taiwan chi-lu yü chung. with Lo Erh-kang. Taipei: Taiwan sheng wen-hsien wei-yuan-hui. 2 vols.
台灣紀錄兩種。羅爾綱。

1953. Hu Shih wen-hsuan. Taipei: Liu i ch'u-pan she.
胡適文選。

1953. Hu Shih wen-ts'un; ti-i chi. Taipei: Yuan-tung t'u-shu kung-ssu. 4 vols.
胡適文存；第一集。

1953. Hu Shih wen-ts'un; ti-erh chi. Taipei: Yuan-tung t'u-shu kung-ssu. 2 vols.
胡適文存；第二集。

1953. Hu Shih wen-ts'un; ti-san chi. Taipei: Yuan-tung t'u-shu kung-ssu. 4 vols.
胡適文存；第三集。

1953. Hu Shih wen-ts'un; ti-ssu chi. Taipei: Yuan-tung t'u-shu kung-ssu. 4 vols.
胡適文存；第四集。

1953. Hu Shih yen-lun chi (ed. by Tzu-yu Chung-kuo she). Taipei: Hua kuo ch'u-pan she. 2 vols.
胡適言論集。自由中國社。

1954. Chih-hsueh fang-fa lun. Taipei: Yuan-tung t'u-shu kung ssu.
治學方法論。

1954. "The Gest Oriental Library at Princeton University." *The Princeton University Library Chronicle*, XV-3.

1954. Kuo-yü wen-fa kai-lun. Taipei: Yuan-tung t'u-shu kung-ssu.
國語文法概論。

1954. Nan yu tsa i. Hong Kong: Ling nan ch'u-pan she.
南遊雜憶。

1954. Shen-mo shih wen-hsueh. Taipei: Yuan-tung t'u-shu kung-ssu.
什麼是文學。

1956. Ting Wen-chiang te chuan-chi. Taipei: Kuo-li chung-yang yen-chiu yuan.

丁文江的傳記。

1958. Chung-kuo hsin wen-hsueh yün-tung hsiao-shih. Taipei: Ch'i ming shu-chü.
中國新文學運動小史。

1959. Tz'u hsuan. Taipei: Shang-wu yin shu kuan.
詞選。

1961. Hu Shih *et al*. Chung-kuo wen-i fu-hsing yün-tung. Taipei: Chung-kuo wen-i hsieh-hui.
胡適等。中國文藝復興運動。

1963. Chung-kuo wen-hsueh shih hsuan li. Taipei: Taiwan shang-wu yin shu kuan.
中國文學史選例。

1963. Hu Shih shu-hsin hsuan. Taipei: Taiwan lien-ho shu-chü.
胡適書信選。

1964. Hu Shih-chih hsien-sheng shih-ko shou-chi. Taipei: Taiwan shang-wu yin shu kuan.
胡適之先生詩歌手迹。

1964? Hu Shih lun hsueh chin chu. Hong Kong: San ta ch'u-pan she.
胡適論學近著。

1964. Hu Shih te shih (comp. by Wen Lei). Taipei: T'ien-hsia ch'u-pan she.
胡適的詩。文雷。

1965. P'u-lin-ssu-tun ta-hsueh; Kai-ssu-t'e tung-fang shou-ts'ang (tr. by Ch'en Chi-ying). Taipei: Wen-yu ch'u-pan she.
普林斯頓大學；蓋斯特東方收藏。陳紀瀅。

1966. Hu Shih shou-kao. Nan-kang: Chung-yang yen-chiu yuan Hu Shih chi-nien kuan. 10 vols.
胡適手稿。

1966. Hu Shih te i-ko meng-hsiang. Nan-kang: Hu Shih chi-nien kuan.
胡適的一個夢想。

"Ching-shih ta-hsueh-t'ang k'ai-pan jih-ch'i." *Min-chu ch'ao*, X-1.
京師大學堂開辦日期。民主潮。

Hsien Ch'in Ming-hsueh shih.
先秦名學史。

ed. of *Hsin ch'ing-nien*.
新青年。

Wu-shih nien lai shih chieh chih che-hsueh.
五十年來世界之哲學。

SOURCES

Person interviewed: Li Shu-hua.

Cameron, Meribeth Elliott. The Reform Movement in China, 1898–1912. New York: Octagon Books, 1963.

Chen Ta. "New Teacher of the East." *The Survey*, 48 (May 27, 1922): 328–29.

Ch'en Tuan-chih. Wu-ssu yün-tung chih shih te p'ing-chia. Shanghai: Sheng-huo shu-tien? 1935.
陳端志。五四運動之史的評價。

Ch'eng T'ien-fang *et al*. Hu Shih yü Chung-kuo. Taipei: Chung-kuo wen-i she, 1962.
程天放等。胡適與中國。

Childs, M. W. "Hu Shih: Sage of Modern China." *The Atlantic Monthly*, 166 (October, 1940): 424–29.

China Research Service, XXVII-1 (April 3, 1962).

Chung-kuo hsin wen-hsueh ta-hsi, comp. by Chao Chia-pi. Shanghai: Liang-yu t'u-shu kung-ssu, 1935. 10 vols.
中國新文學大系。趙家璧。

Chung-yang jih-pao. Taipei, February 25, 1962; February 26, 1962.
中央日報。

Creel, Herrlee Glessner. Chinese Thought: From Confucius to Mao Tse-tung. Chicago: University of Chicago Press, 1953.

Current Biography, 1942.

CWT

Grieder, Jerome B. "Hu Shih and Liberalism: A Chapter in the Intellectual Modernization of China, 1917–1980." Unpublished Ph. D. dissertation, Harvard University, 1963.

Harvey, E. D. The Mind of China. New Haven: Yale University Press, 1933.

Hsia K'ang-nung. Lun Hu Shih yü Chang Chün-mai. Shanghai: Hsin chin shu-tien, 1948.
夏康農。論胡適與張君勱。

Hu Shih. Hsin sheng-huo lun. Shanghai, 1933.
胡適。新生活論。

———. Hu Shih lun hsueh chin chu. Hong Kong: San ta ch'u-pan she, 1964?
胡適。胡適論學近著。

———. Hu Shih wen-ts'un; ti i-ssu chi. Taipei: Yuan-tung t'u-shu kung-ssu, 1953. 14 vols.
胡適。胡適文存；第一一四集。

———. Liu-hsueh jih-chi. Shanghai: Shang-wu yin shu kuan. 4 vols.
胡適。留學日記。

———. Pai-hua wen-hsueh shih; shang chüan. Shanghai: Hsin-yueh shu-tien, 1929.
胡適。白話文學史；上卷。

———. Ssu-shih tzu-shu. Shanghai: Ya tung t'u-shu kuan, 1933.
胡適。四十自述。

Hu Shih *et al*. Jen-ch'üan lun-chi. Shanghai: Hsin-yueh shu-tien, 1930.
胡適等。人權論集。

Hu Shih and Lin Yü-t'ang. China's Own Critics. Peiping, 1931.

Hu Shih, P'an Kuang-tan *et al*. Chung-kuo wen-t'i. Hsin-yueh shu-tien.

胡適，潘光旦等。中國問題。

Hu Shih yü kuo-yün lun-chi, ed. by Ch'en K'o-ch'ou, Lo T'ien-pai, Ch'en P'ei-ken. Kowloon: Wen shan ch'u-pan she, 1958.

胡適與國運論集。陳克疇，羅天白，陳培根。

Hu Shih-chih hsien-sheng chi-nien chi, ed. by Feng Ai-ch'ün. Taipei? Hsueh-sheng shu-chü, 1962.

胡適之先生紀念集。馮愛群。

Jen-chien shih, 3 (May 5, 1934): 41–42; 40 (November 20, 1935).

人間世。

Ku Chieh-kang. The Autobiography of a Chinese Historian, Being the Preface to a Symposium on Ancient Chinese History (Ku shih pien) (tr. and annot. by Arthur W. Hummel). Leyden: E. J. Brill, 1931.

Kung shang jih-pao. Hong Kong, February 27, 28, 1962.

工商日報。

Kuo Chan-po. Chin wu-shih nien Chung-kuo ssu-hsiang shih. Hong Kong: Lung men shu-tien, 1965.

郭湛波。近五十年中國思想史。

Kuo, P. W. "China's Revolt against the Old Order." *Current History*, XXVI-3 (June, 1927): 372–78.

Li Ao. Hu Shih p'ing chuan. Taipei: Wen hsing shu-tien, 1964.

李敖。胡適評傳。

———. Hu Shih yen-chiu. Taipei: Wen hsing shu-tien, 1964.

李敖。胡適研究。

Li Shu-hua. "Hu Shih-chih hsien-sheng sheng-p'ing chi ch'i kung-hsien." *Ta-lu tsa-chih*, XXIV-10 (May 31, 1962).

李書華。胡適之先生生平及其貢獻。大陸雜誌。

Li Ta. Hu Shih fan-tung ssu-hsiang p'i-p'an. Hankow: Hupeh jen-min ch'u-pan she, 1955.

李達。胡適反動思想批判。

Li Ta, Ai Ssu-ch'i *et al*. Hu Shih ssu-hsiang p'i-p'an wen-chi. 1955.

李達，艾思奇等。胡適思想批判文集。

Liu Hsi-san. "Wu-ssu i-hou Chung-kuo ko p'ai ssu-hsiang chia tui-yü hsi-yang te t'ai-tu." *She-hui hsueh-chieh*, 7 (June, 1933): 271–317.

劉錫三。五四以後中國各派思想家對於西洋的態度。社會學界。

The New York Times, February 25, March 24, 1962.

Sun Ting-kuo. Hu Shih che-hsueh ssu-hsiang fan-tung shih-chih te p'i-p'an. Peking: Jen-min ch'u-pan she, 1955.

孫定國。胡適哲學思想反動實質的批判。

Teng Ssu-yü, John K. Fairbank, *et al*. China's Response to the West: A Documentary Survey, 1893–1923. Cambridge: Harvard University Press, 1954.

Ts'ai Yuan-p'ei. "Development of Chinese Education." *Asiatic Review*, 20 (1924): 499–509.

Wang Huan-hsun. Hu Shih chiao-yü ssu-hsiang p'i-p'an yin-lun. Wuhan: Hupeh jen-min ch'u-pan she, 1956.

王煥勛。胡適教育思想批判引論。

Yang Ch'eng-pin. Hu Shih che-hsueh ssu-hsiang. Taipei: Taiwan shang-wu yin shu kuan, 1966.

楊承彬。胡適哲學思想。

Yang, T. P. "Hu Shih vs. the Kuomintang." CWR, December 28, 1929: 150.

Zucker, A. E. "China's Literary Revolution." *The China Review*, 4 (June, 1923): 253–54.

Hu Tieh   胡蝶

SOURCES

CBJS

Chu Chia-hsuan. "Hu Tieh t'an wang." *Chung-yang jih-pao*. Taipei, November 1, 1956.

朱稼軒。胡蝶談往。中央日報。

Chung Lei. Wu-shih nien lai te Chung-kuo tien-ying. Taipei: Cheng-chung shu-chü, 1965.

鐘雷。五十年來的中國電影。

GCMMTJK

Kung-sun Lu. Chung-kuo tien-ying shih-hua. Hong Kong: Nan t'ein shu-yeh kung-ssu, 1962?

公孫魯。中國電影史話。

Hu Tsung-nan   胡宗南

WORKS

1963. Tsung-nan wen-ts'un. Taipei: Chung-kuo wen-hua yen-chiu so.

宗南文存。

SOURCES

BKL

Chung-yang jih-pao. Taipei, February 15, 1962.

中央日報。

Hu Tsung-nan chuan, ed. by Kuo-fang pu shih cheng chü. Taipei: Kuo-fang pu shih cheng chü, 1962.
胡宗南傳。國防部史政局。

Hu Tsung-nan hsien-sheng chi-nien chi, ed. by Hu ku shang-chiang Tsung-nan hsien-sheng chi-nien chi pien-chi wei-yuan-hui. Taipei: Lu-chün tsung-ssu-ling pu yin chih ch'ang, 1963.
胡宗南先生紀念集。 胡故上將宗南先生紀念集編輯委員會。

Hua Mei jih-pao. New York, May 2, 1962.
華美日報。

Lo Lieh. "Ching tao Tsung-nan hsien-sheng." *Chung-yang jih-pao.* Taipei, February 17, 1962.
羅列。敬悼宗南先生。中央日報。

The New York Times, February 15, 1962.

Hu Wen-hu   胡文虎

SOURCES

Biography of Prominent Chinese in Singapore. Singapore: Nan Kok Publishing Co., 1956.

Collier's Magazine, March 1949.

Hu Wen-hu hsien-sheng liu-shih chin wu shou-ch'en chuan-k'an. Singapore: Hsing-tao jih-pao, 1947.
胡文虎先生六秩晉五壽辰專刊。

The New York Times, September 6, 1954.

Straits Times. Singapore, May 6, 1956.

WWC, 1931, 1936.

WWMC

Hu Yeh-p'in   胡也頻

WORKS

1927. Sheng t'u. Shanghai: Hsin-yueh shu-tien.
聖徒。

1928. Huo chu-tzu. Shanghai: Kuang-hua.
活珠子。

1928. Shih kao. Shanghai: Hsien-tai.
詩稿。

1936. Yeh-p'in hsiao-shuo chi. Shanghai: Ta kuang shu-chü.
也頻小說集。

1951. Hu Yeh-p'in hsuan-chi (ed. by Ting Ling). Peking: K'ai-ming shu-tien.
胡也頻選集。丁玲。

1954. Hu Yeh-p'in hsiao-shuo hsuan-chi. Peking: Jen-min wen-hsueh ch'u-pan she.
胡也頻小說選集。

1959. Kuang-ming tsai wo-men te ch'ien-mien. Peking: Jen-min wen-hsueh ch'u-pan she.
光明在我們的前面。

SOURCES

Chung-kuo hsin wen-hsueh ta-hsi, comp. by Chao Chia-pi. Shanghai: Liang-yu t'u-shu yin-shua kung-ssu, 1935. 10 vols.
中國新文學大系。趙家璧。

CHWSK

Huo I-hsien. Tsui-chin erh-shih nien Chung-kuo wen-hsueh shih kang. Canton: Pei hsin shu-tien, 1936.
霍衣仙。最近二十年中國文學史綱。

Li Ho-lin. Kuan-yü Chung-kuo hsien-tai wen-hsueh. Shanghai: Hsin wen-i ch'u-pan she, 1956.
李何林。關於中國現代文學。

Shen Ts'ung-wen. Chi Hu Yeh-p'in. Shanghai: Kuang-hua shu-chü, 1932.
沈從文。記胡也頻。

———. Chi Ting Ling; ch'u hsü chi. Liang-yu, 1939. 2 vols.
沈從文。記丁玲；初續集。

"Ting Ling chuan," in Hsü Ch'en-ssu, Yeh Wang-yu, *Ting Ling hsuan-chi.* Shanghai: Wan-hsiang shu-wu, 1936.
丁玲傳。徐沉泗。葉忘憂。丁玲選集。

Hu Yuan-t'an   胡元倓

SOURCES

Ch'en Pi-t'ao. Hu Tzu-ching hsien-sheng chia-chuan.
陳蔧濤。胡子靖先生家傳。

Ch'ien Wu-chiu. Ming-te hsiao shih. Chang-sha, 1948.
錢无咎。明德校史。

Chung-kuo chin ch'i-shih nien lai chiao-yü chi-shih, ed. by Ting Chih-p'ing. Taipei: Kuo-li pien i kuan, 1961.
中國近七十年來教育記事。丁致聘。

Lung Yü-chün. Lin-chao lu. Chungking: Cheng-chung shu-chü, 1945.
龍毓峻。鱗爪錄。

Lung chang hsing chuang.
龍璋行狀。

Su pao. Shanghai, April 21, 1903.
蘇報。

Ta kung pao. Tientsin, April 28, 1934.
大公報。

Hu Yuan-t'an

Tso Shun-sheng. Chin san-shih nien chien-wen tsa-chi. Kowloon: Tzu-yu ch'u-pan she, 1952.
左舜生。 近三十年見聞雜記。

Wang Feng-chieh. Chung-kuo chiao-yü shih. Shanghai: Kuo-li pien i kuan, 1947.
王鳳喈。 中國教育史。

Wang K'ai-yün. Hsiang-ch'i-luo jih-chi. Shanghai: Shang-wu yin shu kuan, 1927. 6 vols.
王闓運。 湘綺樓日記。

Hu Yün   胡筠

SOURCES

Persons interviewed: not to be identified.

Hua Lo-keng   華羅庚

SOURCES

Persons interviewed: not to be identified.

Huang Chieh   黃節

WORKS

1924. (ed.) Pao ts'an-chün shih chu. Peking: Kuo-li Peking ta-hsueh.
鮑參軍詩註。

1925. Shih hsueh. Peking: Kuo-li Peking ta-hsueh ch'u-pan pu.
詩學。

1936. Shih chih tsuan tz'u. Peking: Peking ta-hsueh.
詩旨纂辭。

1957. (ed.) Ts'ao Tzu-chien shih chu. Peking: Jen-min wen-hsueh ch'u-pan she.
曹子建詩註。

1958. (ed.) Hsieh K'ang-lo shih chu. Peking: Jen-min wen-hsueh ch'u-pan she.
謝康樂詩註。

1958. (ed.) Wei Wen Wu Ming ti shih chu. Taipei: I wen yin shu kuan.
魏文武明帝詩註。

1958. (ed.) Wei Wu-ti Wei Wen-ti shih chu. Peking: Jen-min wen-hsueh ch'u-pan she.
魏武帝魏文帝詩註。

1961. Yuan Pu-ping yung huai shih chu (revised by Hua Chen-chih). Shanghai: Shang-wu yin shu kuan.
阮步兵詠懷詩註。 華忱之。

SOURCES

Chang Ping-lin. "Huang Hui-wen mu-chih-ming," in Chang Ping-lin, T'ai-yen wen-lu hsü-

pien. Hankow: Wuhan yin shu kuan, 1938. 4 vols.
章炳麟。 黃晦聞墓誌銘。 章炳麟。 太炎文錄續編。

Mao Ho-t'ing. "Huan Chieh chuan." Kuo shih kuan kuan k'an, ch'uang k'an hao (December, 1947): 83-84.
冒鶴亭。 黃節傳。 國史館館刊。

Huang Fu   黃郛

WORKS

1914, August 9-12. "Ou chan chih chieh-p'o kuan." Kuo-min jih-pao. Singapore.
歐戰之解剖觀。 國民日報。

1921, September 5-7. "Hua-sheng-tun hui-i fa-ch'i chih nei-jung chi chiang-lai chih ch'ü-shih." Hsin-wen pao. Shanghai.
華盛頓會議發起之內容及將來之趨勢。 新聞報。

1924, October 10. "Chung O hua-chieh ch'u-yen." Shen pao. Shanghai.
中俄劃界芻言。 申報。

1928. Huang shih tsung-tz'u chi.
黃氏宗祠記。

1932. ed. of Fu-hsing yueh-k'an.
復興月刊。

1935. Chan hou chih shih-chieh. Shanghai: Hsin Chung-kuo chien-she hsueh-hui.
戰後之世界。

1935. Ou-chan chih chiao-hsun yü Chung-kuo chih chiang-lai. Shanghai: Hsin Chung-kuo chien-she hsueh-hui.
歐戰之教訓與中國之將來。

1936. Huai-pao ssu ch'in t'u chi-lueh.
懷抱思親圖記略。

Jou-tan. (tr.)
肉彈。

SOURCES

BPC

Chang Ch'i-yün. Tang shih kai-yao. Taipei: Chung-yang kai-tsao wei-yuan-hui wen-wu kung-ying she, 1951-52. 5 vols.
張其昀。 黨史概要。

Chin Wen-ssu et al. Huang Ying-pai hsien-sheng ku-chiu kan il lu (ed. by Wu Hsiang-hsiang). Taipei: Wen hsing shu-tien, 1962.
金問泗等。 黃膺白先生故舊感憶錄。 吳相湘。

The China Critic, 1928: 23; 1933: 755; 1934: 343, 749, 801, 872.

CMMC

CWR, August 26, 1933; September 22, 1934; June 8, 1935,

Feng Tzu-yu. Ko-ming i-shih. Shanghai, Chungking: Shang-wu yin shu kuan, 1939–47. 5 vols.
馮自由。革命逸史。

Huang Shen I-yün. Huang Ying-pai hsien-sheng chia-chuan (with Chui-tao chi-nien ts'e, Kuchiu kan i lu). Taipei: Wen hai ch'u-pan she.
黃沈亦雲。黃膺白先生家傳 (附：追悼紀念冊，故舊感憶錄)。

Jen-wen, VIII-2-10 (March-December, 1937).
人文。

Li Chien-nung. The Political History of China 1840–1928 (tr. and ed. by Teng Ssu-yu, Jeremy Ingalls). Princeton, N. J.: D. Van Nostrand Co., 1956.

MSICH

SMJ

Wai-chiao ta tz'u-tien, ed. by Wai-chiao hsueh-hui. Kunming: Chung-hua shu-chü, 1937.
外交大辭典。外交學會。

Washio, S. "Huang Fu's Resignation Causes Anxiety over China Situation." Trans-Pacific, July 20, 1933.

Woodhead, Henry George Wandesforde. "Huang Fu Improves Outlook for Peace." Trans-Pacific, June 1, 1933.

WWC, 1925, 1931, 1933.

WWMC

Yün Nung. "Huang Ying-pai hsien-sheng nien-p'u ch'u-kao." Hsin Chung-kuo p'ing-lun, January, 1960-April, 1961.
耘農。黃膺白先生年譜初稿。新中國評論。

Huang Hsing   黃興

Works

1914. Huang Hsing hsien-sheng yen-shuo tz'u hui-pien. San Francisco: Chin shan ta pu hua-ch'iao t'uan.
黃興先生演說詞彙集。

1947, March. "San-yueh erh-shih-chiu ko-ming chih ch'ien-yin hou-kuo." Ko-ming wen-hsien ts'ung-k'an, I-5: 7–8.
三月廿九革命之前因後果。革命文獻叢刊。

1956. Huang K'o-ch'iang hsien-sheng shu-han mo-chi, ed. by Chung-kuo kuo-min-tang chung-yang wei-yuan-hui tang shih shih-liao pien-tsuan wei-yuan-hui. Taipei: Chung-yang wen-wu kung-ying she?
黃克強先生書翰墨蹟。中國國民黨中央委員會黨史史料編纂委員會。

1962. Huang Liu-shou shu-tu (comp. by Wu Yen-yün). Taipei: Wen hsing shu-tien.
黃留守書牘。吳硯雲。

Sources

Chang Chi. Chang P'u-ch'üan hsien-sheng ch'üan-chi; cheng-pien pu-pien (ed. by Chung-yang kai-tsao wei-yuan-hui tang shih shih-liao pien-tsuan wei-yuan-hui). Taipei: Chung-yang wen-wu kung-ying she. 2 vols.
張繼。張溥泉先生全集；正編補編。中央改造委員會黨史史料編纂委員會。

Chang Ch'i-yün. Chung-hua Min-kuo ch'uang-li shih. Taipei: Chung-hua wen-hua ch'u-pan shih-yeh wei-yuan-hui, 1953.
張其昀。中華民國創立史。

Chang Chien. Chang Chi-tzu chiu lu (ed. by Chang Hsiao-jo). Shanghai, 1931.
張謇。張季子九錄。張孝若。

Chang Chih-tung. Chang wen-hsiang-kung kung-tu kao. 8 vols.
張之洞。張文襄公公牘考。

———. Chang wen-hsiang-kung tien-kao. 22 vols.
張之洞。張文襄公電稿。

———. Chang wen-hsiang-kung tsou-kao. 26 vols.
張之洞。張文襄公奏稿。

Chang Ch'un-t'ing. Chang wen-hsiang-kung chih O chi. Wuchang: Hupeh t'ung-chih kuan, 1947.
張春霆。張文襄公治鄂記。

Chang Hsiao-jo. Nan-t'ung Chang Chi-chih hsien-sheng chuan-chi. Shanghai: Chung-hua shu-chü, 1935.
張孝若。南通張季直先生傳記。

Chang Nan-hsien. Hupeh ko-ming chih chih lu. Chungking: Shang-wu yin shu kuan, 1945.
張難先。湖北革命知之錄。

Chang Ping-lin. Chang shih ts'ung shu. Shanghai: Yu wen she, 1915. 22 vols.
章炳麟。章氏叢書。

Chang Yü-k'un. Wen-hsüeh she Wuchang shou i chi-shih. Peking: Sheng-huo, tu-shu, hsin-chih san lien shu-tien, 1952.
章裕昆。文學社武昌首義記實。

Chang wen-hsiang-kung nien-p'u, comp. by Hsü T'ung-hsin. Chungking: Shang-wu yin shu kuan, 1944.
張文襄公年譜。許同莘。

Ch'en Po-ta. Ch'ieh kuo ta-tao Yuan Shih-k'ai. Peking: Hsin hua shu-tien, 1949.
陳伯達。竊國大盜袁世凱。

Ch'en Shao-pai. Hsing-chung-hui ko-ming shih

lueh. Taipei: Chung-yang wen-wu kung-ying she, 1956.

陳少白。 興中會革命史略。

Ch'en T'ien-hua. Ch'en T'ien-hua chi. Chungking, 1944.

陳天華。 陳天華集。

Ch'ing shih kao, ed. by Chao Erh-sun *et al*. 1927. 132 vols.

清史稿。 趙爾巽等。

Chü Cheng. Mei-ch'uan jih-chi (Hsin-hai cha-chi). Shanghai: Ta tung shu-chü, 1947.

居正。 梅川日記 (辛亥札記)。

———. Mei-ch'uan p'u chieh (with Hsing i yin). Taipei.

居正。 梅川譜偈 (附: 行役吟)。

Chün wu yuan k'ao shih (with Liang Kuang tu ssu-ling-pu k'ao shih), comp. by Liang Kuang tu ssu-ling-pu ts'an-mou t'ing. Shanghai: Shang-wu yin shu kuan, 1916.

軍務院考實 (附: 兩廣都司令部考實)。 兩廣都司令部參謀廳。

Chung-hua Min-kuo shih-liao, comp. by Sun Yao. Shanghai: Wen-ming shu-chü, 1929. 3 vols.

中華民國史料。 孫曜。

Chung-kuo kuo-min-tang shih-kao i chih ssu p'ien, comp. by Tsou Lu. Chungking: Shang-wu yin shu kuan, 1944. 4 vols.

中國國民黨史稿一至四篇。 鄒魯。

Chung-kuo shih-hsueh lun-wen so-yin, ed. by Chung-kuo k'o-hsueh-yuan li-shih yen-chiu so ti-i, erh so, Peking ta-hsueh li-shih hsi. Peking: K'o-hsueh ch'u-pan she, 1957. 2 vols.

中國史學論文索引。 中國科學院歷史研究所第一, 二所, 北京大學歷史系。

Feng Tzu-yu. Chung-hua Min-kuo k'ai-kuo ch'ien ko-ming shih. Chungking: Chung-kuo wen-hua fu-wu she, 1944. 3 vols.

馮自由。 中華民國開國前革命史。

———. Chung-kuo ko-ming yün-tung erh-shih-liu nien tsu-chih shih. Shanghai: Shang-wu yin shu kuan, 1948.

馮自由。 中國革命運動二十六年組織史。

———. Hua-ch'iao ko-ming k'ai-kuo shih. Shanghai: Shang-wu yin shu kuan, 1947.

馮自由。 華僑革命開國史。

———. Ko-ming i-shih. Chungking, Shanghai: Shang-wu yin shu kuan, 1944–47. 5 vols.

馮自由。 革命逸史。

Ho Po-yen. Huang K'o-ch'iang. Nanking, 1946.

何伯言。 黃克強。

Hou I. Hung-hsien chiu-wen (with Hsiang-ch'eng chiu-jen pi wen). 1926.

侯毅。 洪憲舊聞 (附: 項城就任秘聞)。

Hsi Wen. "Huai Huang Hsing hsien-sheng." *Chin shan shih-pao*. San Francisco, January 19, 1957.

希文。 懷黃興先生。 金山時報。

Hsiang shih chi, comp. by Tzu hsü tzu (pseud.). Peking, 1914.

湘事記。 子盧子。

Hsin-hai ko-ming, ed. by Ch'ai Te-keng *et al*. Shanghai: Shanghai jen-min ch'u-pan she, 1957. 8 vols.

辛亥革命。 柴德賡等。

Hsin-hai shou i hui-i lu, ed. by Chung-kuo jen-min cheng-chih hsieh-shang hui-i Hupeh sheng wei-yuan-hui. Wuhan: Hupeh jen-min ch'u-pan she, 1957–?

辛亥首義回憶錄。 中國人民政治協商會議湖北省委員會。

Hsuan-t'ung cheng chi, ed. by Chin Yü-fu. Liao hai shu-she, 1934. 16 vols.

宣統政紀。 金毓黻。

Hsueh Chün-tu. Huan Hsing and the Chinese Revolution. Stanford: Stanford University Press, 1961.

Hsueh shu, comp. by Han hsia. 1911? 3 vols.

血書。 漢俠。

Huang Hsing. Huang K'o-ch'iang hsien-sheng shu-han mo-chi, ed. by Chung-kuo kuo-min-tang chung-yang wei-yuan-hui tang shih shih-liao pien-tsuan wei-yuan-hui. Taipei: Chung-yang wen-wu kung-ying she? 1956.

黃興。 黃克強先生書翰墨蹟。 中國國民黨中央委員會黨史史料編纂委員會。

Huang-hua-kang ko-ming lieh-shih hua shih, ed. by Lo Chia-lun. Taipei: Chung-yang tang shih shih-liao pien-tsuan wei-yuan-hui, 1952.

黃花岡革命烈士畫史。 羅家倫。

Jung Meng-yuan. "O-kuo i-chiu-ling-wu nien ko-ming tui Chung-kuo te ying-hsiang." *Li-shih yen-chiu*, I-2 (1954): 53–69.

榮孟源。 俄國一九〇五年革命對中國的影響。 歷史研究。

Ko Kung-ch'en. Chung-kuo pao hsueh shih. Peking: San lien shu-tien, 1955.

戈公振。 中國報學史。

Ko-ming hsien-lieh wen-i chi; ti-i chi, ed. by Chung-yang hsuan-ch'uan pu. Nanking: Chung-yang hsuan-ch'uan pu, 1930.

革命先烈文藝集; 第一集。 中央宣傳部。

Ko-ming wen-hsien, I-VI, ed. by Chung-kuo kuo-min-tang chung-yang wei-yuan-hui tang shih shih-liao pien-tsuan wei-yuan-hui. Taipei: Chung-yang wen-wu kung-ying she, 1953–54.

革命文獻。中國國民黨中央委員會黨史史料編纂委員會。
Ko-ming wen-hsien ts'ung-k'an, I-7 (September, 1947): 18-20.
革命文獻叢刊。

Ku Chung-hsiu. Chung-hua Min-kuo k'ai-kuo shih. Shanghai: T'ai tung shu-chü, 1926.
谷鐘秀。中華民國開國史。

Kuan tu lu (pseud. of Wu T'ing-fang). Kung-ho kuan-chien lu. Shanghai, 1912.
觀渡盧 (伍廷芳)。共和關鍵錄。

Kuo-fu nien-piao, ed. by Chung-yang tang shih shih-liao pien-tsuan wei-yuan-hui. Taipei: Chung-yang tang shih shih-liao pien-tsuan wei-yuan-hui, 1952.
國父年表。中央黨史史料編纂委員會。

Kuo shih kuan kuan k'an, I-1, 2, 3, 4 December, 1947-November, 1948); II-1 (1949).
國史館館刊。

Li Chien-nung. Chung-kuo chin pai nien cheng-chih shih. Shanghai: Shang-wu yin shu kuan, 1947. 2 vols.
李劍農。中國近百年政治史。

Li Lien-fang. Hsin-hai Wuchang shou i chi. Wuhan: Hupeh t'ung-chih kuan, 1947. 2 vols.
李廉方。辛亥武昌首義記。

Li Nai-han (Li Shu). Hsin-hai ko-ming yü Yuan Shih-k'ai. Peking: Sheng-huo, tu-shu, hsin-chih san lien shu-tien, 1950.
黎乃涵 (黎澍)。辛亥革命與袁世凱。

Li Shu. "I-chiu-ling-wu nien O-kuo ko-ming ho Chung-kuo." *Li-shih yen-chiu*, II-1 (1955): 1-17.
黎澍。一九○五年俄國革命和中國。歷史研究。

Li Yuan-hung. Li fu tsung-t'ung cheng shu. Wuchang: Wuchang kuan yin-shua chü, 1914. 16 vols.
黎元洪。黎副總統政書。

Liu Ch'eng-yü. "Hsien tsung-li chiu te lu." *Kuo shih kuan kuan k'an*, ch'uang k'an hao (December, 1947): 44-56.
劉成禺。先總理舊德錄。國史館館刊。

———. Hung-hsien chi-shih shih pen-shih pu chu. Chungking: Ching hua yin shu kuan.
劉成禺。洪憲紀事詩本事簿註。

Liu K'uei-i. Huang Hsing chuan-chi. Taipei: P'a-mi-erh shu-tien, 1952.
劉揆一。黃興傳記。

Lo Chia-lun. "Ts'ung mo-chi chung t'i-jen tao te Huang K'o-ch'iang hsien-sheng." *Hua Mei jih-pao*. New York, October 31-November 8, 1957.
羅家倫。從墨蹟中体認到的黃克強先生。華美日報。

Lu Tan-lin. Ko-ming shih t'an. Chungking: Tu-li ch'u-pan she, 1945.
陸丹林。革命史譚。

Lung Yü-chün. Lin chao lu. Chungking: Cheng-chung shu-chü, 1945.
龍毓峻。鱗爪錄。

Ma Ta-chung. Ta Chung-hua Min-kuo shih. Peiping: Chung-hua yin shu chü, 1929.
馬大中。大中華民國史。

Man i hua hsia shih-mo chi, ed. by Yang Tun-i. Shanghai: Hsin Chung-hua t'u-shu kuan, 1912. 12 vols.
滿夷猾夏始末記。楊敦頤。

Min kuo tsa-chih, 6 (1914).
民口雜誌。

Min-kuo ching shih wen pien, ed. by Ching shih wen she. Shanghai: Ching shih wen she, 1914. 40 vols.
民國經世文編。經世文社。

Min pao, 1-26 (1905-10). Peking: K'o-hsueh ch'u-pan she, 1957. 4 vols.
民報。

Pai Chiao. Yuan Shih-k'ai yü Chung-hua Min-kuo. Shanghai: Jen-wen yueh-k'an she, 1936.
白蕉。袁世凱與中華民國。

P'an Kung-chan. Ch'en Ch'i-mei. Taipei: Sheng-li ch'u-pan kung-ssu, 1954.
潘公展。陳其美。

A Revelation of the Chinese Revolution; a Retrospect and Forecast, by a Chinese Compatriot, ed. by John James Mullowney. New York: Fleming H. Revell Co., 1914.

Shang Ping-ho. Hsin-jen ch'un-ch'iu. Hsin-jen li-shih pien-chi she, 1924.
尚秉和。辛壬春秋。

Sung Chiao-jen. Wo chih li-shih. T'ao-yuan: San-yü i chung nung hsiao, 1920.
宋教仁。我之歷史。

Sung Yü-fu and Tai T'ien-ch'ou. Wen-chi ho k'an. Shanghai: Kuo kuang t'u-shu-kuan, 1921.
宋漁父，戴天仇。文集合刊。

Sung Yueh-lun. Tsung-li tsai Jih-pen chih ko-ming huo-tung. Taipei: Chung-yang wen-wu kung-ying she, 1953.
宋越倫。總理在日本之革命活動。

Teng Tse-ju. Chung-kuo kuo-min-tang erh-shih nien shih chi. Shanghai: Cheng-chung shu-chü, 1948.
鄧澤如。中國國民黨二十年史蹟。

Ts'ao Ya-po. Wuchang ko-ming chen shih. Shanghai, 1930. 3 vols.
曹亞伯。武昌革命眞史。

Tsou Lu. Ch'eng-lu wen-hsuan (comp. by Chang Ching-ying). Shanghai: Cheng-chun shu-chü, 1948.
鄒魯。 澄廬文選。 張鏡影。
———. Kuang-chou (Canton) san-yueh erh-shih-chiu ko-ming shih (ed. by Ko-ming chi-nien hui). Shanghai: Min chih shu-chü, 1926.
鄒魯。 廣州三月二十九革命史。 革命紀念會。
Tu Ch'eng-hsiang. Tsou Jung chuan. Taipei: P'a-min-erh shu-tien, 1953.
杜呈祥。 鄒容傳。
Wang Chao-ming. Wang Ching-wei wen-ts'un. Canton: Min chih, 1927.
汪兆銘。 汪精衛文存。
Wang Hsing-jui. "Ch'ing chi Fu-jen wen-she yü ko-ming yün-tung te kuan-hsi." *Shih-hsueh tsa-chih*. I-1 (December 5, 1945): 35–45.
王興瑞。 清季輔仁文社與革命運動的關係。 史學雜誌。
Wu Chih-hui. Wu Chih-hui ch'üan-chi (ed. by Fang Tung-liang). Shanghai: Ch'ün-chung t'u-shu kung-ssu, 1927. 5 vols.
吳稚暉。 吳稚暉全集。 方東亮。
Yang Yu-chiung. Chung-kuo cheng-tang shih. Shanghai: Shang-wu yin shu kuan, 1936.
楊幼烱。 中國政黨史。
Yu hsueh i pien, 1–12 (1902–3).
游學譯編。
Yün Tai-ying. Chung-kuo min-tsu ko-ming yün-tung shih. Shanghai, 1926?
惲代英。 中國民族革命運動史。

Huang K'an   黃侃

WORKS

1927. Yu Lu-shan shih.
游廬山詩。
1933. Jih-chih-lu chiao chi.
日知錄校記。
1935, December 1. "Yin lueh." *Chih yen*.
音略。 制言。
1936. Chi yün sheng lei piao. Shanghai: K'ai-ming shu-tien.
集韵聲類表。
1960. Liang-shou-lu tz'u-ch'ao. Taipei: Kuo-min ch'u-pan she.
量守廬詞鈔。
1962. Wen hsin tiao lung cha-chi (ed. by Chung-hua shu-chü Shanghai pien-chi so). Peking: Chung-hua shu-chü.
文心雕龍札記。 中華書局上海編輯所。

1964. Chi yün sheng lei piao shu li. Hong Kong: Hsin ya shu-yuan.
集韻聲類表述例。
1964. Huang K'an lun hsueh tsa chu (ed. by Chung-hua shu-chü Shanghai pien-chi so). Peking: Chung-hua shu-chü.
黃侃論學雜著。 中華書局上海編輯所。
Hsi-ch'iu-hua-shih.
繡秋華室。
Wen hsin tiao lung Huang chu pu-cheng.
文心雕龍黃注補正。

SOURCES

Chang Ping-lin. T'ai-yen wen-lu hsü-pien. Taipei, 1956.
章炳麟。 太炎文錄續編。
Chiang Fu-sen. "Chang T'ai-yen yü Liang Jen-kung." *Ta feng pan-yueh-k'an*, 79 (November, 1940): 2561.
姜馥森。 章太炎與梁任公。 大風半月刊。
Liu Ch'eng-yü. "Hung-hsien chi-shih shih pen-shih chu." *I ching*, 15 (October, 1936): 41.
劉成禺。 洪憲紀事詩本事註。 逸經。
Man Hua. "T'ung-meng-hui shih-tai min pao shih-mo chi," in Ch'ai Te-keng *et al.*, *Hsin-hai ko-ming*. Shanghai: Shanghai jen-min ch'u-pan she, 1957. 8 vols.
曼華。 同盟會時代民報始末記。 柴德賡 等。 辛亥革命。
Wang Pi-chiang. "Tao Huang Chi-kang hsien-sheng." *Chih yen*, 4 (October, 1935): 1–7.
汪辟疆。 悼黃季剛先生。 制言。
Wei Sheng. "Lun Huang Chi-kang hsien-sheng te shih." *Kuo wen chou-pao*, XII-30 (August, 1935): 1–4.
微生。 論黃季剛先生的詩。 國聞週報。

Huang K'o-ch'eng   黃克誠

SOURCES

Person interviewed: Chang Kuo-t'ao.
Ch'ang-chiang jih-pao. Hankow, August, 1950.
長江日報。
K'ang chan pa nien lai te pa lu chün yü hsin ssu chün. Hua-pei hsin-hua shu-tien, 1946.
抗戰八年來的八路軍與新四軍。
Liu Pai-ming. Kuang-ming chao-yao che Shen-yang (Mukden). Hsin hua shu-tien, 1948.
劉白明。 光明照耀着瀋陽。
The New York Times, October 13, 1958.
Wang Chin-mu. Chung-kuo k'ang chan shih yen-i. Peking: Hsin ch'ao shu-tien, 1951.

王金穆。中國抗戰史演義。

Huang Kuang-jui   黃光瑞

SOURCES

Persons interviewed: not to be identified.

Huang Lu-yin   黃廬隱

WORKS

1925. Hai-pin ku-jen.
海濱故人。

1927. Ma-li.
瑪麗。

1930. Kuei yen.
歸雁。

1931. Hsien-tai Chung-kuo nü tso-chia. Shanghai: Pei hsin shu-chü.
現代中國女作家。

1931. Yün ou ch'ing-shu chi.
雲鷗情書集。

1932. Hsiang-ya chieh-chih.
象牙戒指。

1933. Mei-kuei te tz'u.
玫瑰的刺。

1934. Lu-yin tzu-chuan. Shanghai: Ti-i ch'u-
pan she.
廬隱自傳。

1935. Lu-yin tuan-p'ien hsiao-shuo hsuan. Shanghai: Nü-tzu shu-tien.
廬隱短篇小說選。

Chi-lü hsien-sheng.
畸侶先生。

Chi-mo.
寂寞。

Chi t'ien-hsia i ku-hung.
寄天下一孤鴻。

Chi Yen pei ku-jen.
寄燕北故人。

Ch'iao-ts'ui li-hua.
憔悴梨花。

Ch'in chiao-shou te shih-pai.
秦教授的失敗。

Chiu kao.
舊稿。

Ch'iu-feng ch'iu-yü ch'ou sha jen.
秋風秋雨愁煞人。

Fang-tung.
房東。

Fu-ch'in.
父親。

ed. of *Fu-nü chou-k'an*.
婦女週刊。

Ho jen te pei-ai.
或人的悲哀。

Hsueh feng t'a hsia.
雪峯塔下。

Hsueh-p'o chung te ying-hsiung.
血泊中的英雄。

ed. of *Hua yen pan-yueh-k'an*.
華嚴半月刊。

Huo-yen.
火燄。

I feng hsin.
一封信。

I ko chu-tso-chia.
一個著作家。

Li-shih te jih-chi.
麗石的日記。

Liang ko hsiao hsueh-sheng.
兩個小學生。

Ling hai ch'ao hsi.
靈海潮汐。

Ling-hun k'o-i ch'u-mai ma?
靈魂可以出賣嗎?

Lun-lo.
淪落。

Nü-jen te hsin.
女人的心。

P'ang-huang.
徬徨。

Shih-tai te hsi-sheng che.
時代的犧牲者。

Tsui hou.
醉後。

Tung-ching hsiao-p'in.
東京小品。

Wei-chi.
危機。

Yü-ch'ing i-lü fu cheng hung.
慾情一縷付征鴻。

Yü lei.
餘淚。

Yueh-hsia ku-chou.
月下孤舟。

Yueh-hsia te hui-i.
月下的回憶。

SOURCES

CHWC
CHWSK
CHWYS
CWT
ECC

Fairbank, John K., and Liu Kwang-ching. Modern China: A Bibliographical Guide to Chinese Works, 1898–1937. Cambridge: Harvard University Press, 1950.
GCCJK
HMTT
Huang Lu-yin. Lu-yin tzu-chuan. Shanghai: Ti-i ch'u-pan she, 1934.
黃廬隱。廬隱自傳。
Huang Ying (Pseud of Huang Lu-yin). Hsien-tai Chung-kuo nü tso-chia. Shanghai: Pei hsin shu-chü, 1931.
黃英 (黃廬隱)。現代中國女作家。
HWP
Jen-chien shih, 5 (June 5, 1934): 40–41; 12 (September 20, 1934): 17–18.
人間世。
MCNP
Su Hsueh-lin. Ch'ing niao chi. Changsha: Shang-wu yin shu kuan, 1938.
蘇雪林。青鳥集。
Wales, Nym (pseud. of Helen Foster Snow). "The Modern Chinese Literary Movement," in Edgar Snow, Living China: Modern Chinese Short Stories. New York: John Day & Reynal & Hitchcock, 1936.
WWMC

Huang Mu-sung   黃慕松

SOURCES

CWR, 1933, 1937.
Kuo wen chou-pao. X-23 (June 12, 1933).
國聞週報。
Li Tieh-tseng. The Historical Status of Tibet. New York: King's Crown Press, 1956.
MMT
TCJC
Tseng Wen-wu. Chung-kuo ching-ying hsi-yü shih. Shanghai: Shang-wu yin shu kuan, 1936.
曾問吾。中國經營西域史。
Whiting, Allen S., and Sheng Shih-ts'ai. Sinkiang: Pawn or Pivot? East Lansing: Michigan State University Press, 1958.
WWC, 1934.

Huang Shao-hung   黃紹竑

WORKS

1945. Wu-shih hui-i. Hangchow: Feng-yün ch'u-pan she. 2 vols.

五十回憶。

SOURCES

AWW
BKL
CTMC
CWR, April 8, 1933: 229.
Huang Hsü-ch'u. "Kwangsi yü chung-yang erh-shih yü nien lai pei huan li ho i shu." *Ch'un-ch'iu*, 103 (October 16, 1961): 2–5; 104 (November 1, 1961): 4–8.
黃旭初。廣西與中央廿餘年來悲歡離和憶述。春秋。
Huang Shao-hung. Wu-shih hui-i. Hangchow: Feng-yün ch'u-pan she, 1945. 2 vols.
黃紹竑。五十回憶。
Lei Hsiao-ts'en. San-shih nien tung-luan Chung-kuo. Hong Kong: Ya-chou ch'u-pan she, 1955.
雷嘯岑。卅年動亂中國。
WWMC

Huang Shao-ku   黃紹谷

SOURCES

BKL
Chiang Ching-kuo. Wei-chi ts'un wang chih ch'iu.
蔣經國。危急存亡之秋。
———. Wo-te fu-ch'in.
蔣經國。我的父親。
Kuo chün cheng-kung shih-kao.
國軍政工史稿。
Lo Tun-wei. Wu-shih nien hui-i-lu. Taipei: Chung-kuo wen-hua kung-ying she, 1952.
羅敦偉。五十年回憶錄。

Huang Yen-p'ei   黃炎培

WORKS

1915. Hsin ta-lu chih chiao-yü.
新大陸之教育。
1917. (comp.) Chung-kuo shang chan shih-pai shih. with P'ang Sung. Shanghai: Shang-wu yin shu kuan.
中國商戰失敗史。龐淞。
1922. Huang Yen-p'ei k'ao-ch'a chiao-yü jih-chi. Shanghai: Shang-wu yin shu kuan. 2 vols.
黃炎培考察教育日記。
1922. (comp.) Tung nan-yang chih hsin chiao-yü. Shanghai: Shang-wu yin shu kuan. 2 vols.
東南洋之新教育。

1923. (ed.) Tsui-chin chih wu-shih nien 1872–1922. Shanghai: Shen pao kuan.
最近之五十年1872-1922。

1929. Ch'ao-hsien. Shanghai: Shang-wu yin shu kuan.
朝鮮。

1930. Chung-kuo chiao-yü shih yao. Shanghai: Shang-wu yin shu kuan.
中國教育史要。

1936. Shu tao. Shanghai: K'ai-ming shu-tien.
蜀道。

1941. Shu-nan san chung. Chungking: Kuo-hsin shu-tien.
蜀南三種。

1944. Chung-hua fu-hsing shih chiang. Chungking: Kuo hsin shu-tien.
中華復興十講。

1945. Yenan kuei-lai. Chungking: Kuo hsin shu-tien.
延安歸來。

1946. Pao sang chi. Shanghai: K'ai-ming shu-tien.
苞桑集。

1947. Min-chu hua te chi-kuan kuan-li. Shanghai: Shang-wu yin shu kuan.
民主化的機關管理。

1950. Hung sang. Hong Kong: Hsin Chung-kuo hua-pao she.
紅桑。

SOURCES

CMMC
CWR, April 27, 1946: 195.
GCCJK
Huang Yen-p'ei. Huang Yen-p'ei k'ao-ch'a chiao-yü jih-chi. Shanghai: Shang-wu yin shu kuan, 1922. 2 vols.
黃炎培。黃炎培考察教育日記。
———. Yenan kuei-lai. Chungking: Kuo hsin shu-tien, 1945.
黃炎培。延安歸來。
JMST, 1950.
Li Chien-nung. Chung-kuo chin pai nien cheng-chih shih. Shanghai: Shang-wu yin shu kuan, 1947. 2 vols.
李劍農。中國近百年政治史。
The New York Times, December 22, 1965.
SCMP, 103 (May 8–10, 1951): 38; 1557 (June 25, 1957): 19; 675 (October 24, 1963): 14–15.
SSYD
Tsou T'ao-fen. Huan-nan yü-sheng chi. Shanghai: Sheng-huo shu-tien, 1936.
鄒韜奮。患難餘生記。
WWC, 1931.
Yang Ming. Tsou T'ao-fen te liu-wang sheng-huo. Peking: Sheng-huo, tu-shu, hsin-chih san lien shu-tien, 1951.
楊明。鄒韜奮的流亡生活。

Hung Shen   洪 深

WORKS

1931. Hung Shen hsi-ch'ü chi. Hsien-tai shu-chü.
洪深戲曲集。

1934. Hung Shen hsi-chü lun-wen chi. Shanghai: T'ien ma shu-tien.
洪深戲劇論文集。

1935. Tien-ying hsi-chü piao-yen shu. Sheng-huo shu-tien.
電影戲劇表演術。

1935. Tien-ying hsi-chü te pien-chü fang-fa. Cheng-chung shu-chü.
電影戲劇的編劇方法。

1935. Tien-ying shu-yü tz'u-tien. T'ien ma shu-tien.
電影術語辭典。

1935. "Ts'ung Chung-kuo te hsin hsi shuo-tao hua-chü," in Chao Chia-pi, *Chung-kuo hsin wen-hsueh ta-hsi*. Shanghai: Liang-yu t'u-shu yin-shua kung-ssu. 10 vols.
從中國的新戲說到話劇。趙家璧。中國新文學大系。

1936. I-ch'ien i-pai ko chi-pen han-tzu chiao-hsueh shih-yung fa. Sheng-huo shu-tien.
一千一百個基本漢字教學使用法。

1939. Pao Te-hsing. Shanghai: Shanghai tsa-chih kung-ssu.
包得行。

1941. Mi. Chungking: Hua-chung t'u-shu kung-ssu.
米。

1943. Hsi-chü tao-yen te ch'u-pu chih-shih. Chungking: Chung-kuo wen-hua fu-wu she.
戲劇導演的初步知識。

1951. Che chiu shih "Mei-kuo te sheng-huo fang-shih." Peking: Sheng-huo, tu-shu, hsin chih san lien shu-tien.
這就是「美國的生活方式」。

1951. Hung Shen hsuan-chi (comp. by Hsin wen-hsueh hsuan-chi pien-chi wei-yuan-hui). Peking: K'ai-ming shu-tien.
洪深選集。新文學選集編輯委員會。

1954, July. "Wei jen-min te hsien-fa huan-hu." *Jen-min wen-hsueh*.
為人民的憲法歡呼。人民文學。

1957–? Hung Shen wen-chi. Peking: Chung-
kuo hsi-chü ch'u-pan she.
洪深文集。

1962. Hsiang tao-mi. Peking: Jen-min wen-
hsüeh ch'u-pan she.
香稻米。

Chi-ming tsao k'an t'ien.
鷄鳴早看天。

Chieh-hou t'ao-hua.
刼後桃花。

Chiu shih ching hua.
舊時京華。

Fei chiang-chün.
飛將軍。

Feng ta shao-yeh.
馮大少爺。

Hai-t'ang-hung.
海棠紅。

Ho ting hung.
鶴頂紅。

Hsi-chü te nien-tz'u yü lang-sung.
戲劇的唸辭與朗誦。

Huang pai tan ch'ing.
黃白丹青。

Ko-nü hung mou-tan.
歌女紅牡丹。

Kou yen.
狗眼。

ed. of *Kuang-ming*.
光明。

Nü-ch'üan.
女權。

Nü-jen nü-jen.
女人女人。

Nü shu-chi.
女書記。

Pa-pa ai ma-ma.
爸爸愛媽媽。

Ssu-yueh li ch'iang-wei ch'u-ch'u k'ai.
四月裡薔薇處處開。

Ta chia-t'ing.
大家庭。

Ti-i liu; hsü-pien. with Ho Chia-huai *et al* (ed.
by Mei I). Ti-ch'iu ch'u-pan she,
第一流，續編。何家槐等。梅衣。

Tao-yen te chi-pen chi-shu.
導演的基本技術。

Tsou-ssu.
走私。

Wu-k'uei-ch'iao. Shanghai: T'ieh liu shu-tien.
五奎橋。

Wu-shih nien-tai.
五十年代。

Wu shih t'ung-t'ang.
五世同堂。

SOURCES

Chao Ching-shen. Wen-jen chien-ying. Shanghai: Pei hsin shu-chü, 1936.
趙景深。文人剪影。

CHWC
CHWSK
CHWYS
CKJMT
CWT
HCJC
HMTT

Hung Shen. Hung Shen hsuan-chi (comp. by
Hsin wen-hsueh hsuan-chi pien-chi wei-yuan-
hui). Peking: K'ai-ming shu-tien, 1951.
洪深。洪深選集。新文學選集編輯委員會。

Liu Shou-sung. Chung-kuo hsin wen-hsueh shih
ch'u-kao. Peking: Tso-chia ch'u-pan she,
1956. 2 vols.
劉綬松。中國新文學史初稿。

MCNP
MMT
RCCL
SCMP, 1120 (August 39–31, 1955).
TCMT
WWMC

Jao Shu-shih   饒漱石

WORKS

1945. Jao Shu-shih *et al*. Shang-jao chi-chung
ying (comp. by Hsin hua she hua-chung fen-
she). Su Chung ch'u-pan she.
饒漱石等。上饒集中營。新華社華中分社。

1950. Jao Shu-shih *et al*. Hua-tung, Chung-nan,
Hsi-pei, Hsi-nan ssu ta hsing-cheng ch'ü kung-
tso ch'ing-k'uang chi kung-tso jen-wu (comp.
by Hsin hua shih-shih ts'ung-k'an she). Shanghai: Hsin hua shu-tien.
饒漱石等。華東，中南，西北，西南四大
行政區工作情況及工作任務。新華時事叢
刊社。

SOURCES

Person interviewed: Chang Kuo-t'ao.
CB, 324 (April 4, 1955).
Chang Hsueh-chai. An Interpretation of the
Purge of Kao and Jao in Chinese Communist
Party. Taipei: Asian People's Anti-Commu-
nist League, 1955.

GCJJ
HCJC
Ho Ch'i-fang. Wu Yü-chang t'ung-chih ko-ming
ku-shih. Hong Kong: Hsin Chung-kuo shu-
chü, 1949.
何其芳。吳玉章同志革命故事。
I-chiu-wu-ling jen-min nien-chien, ed. by Shen
Sung-fang. Hong Kong: Ta kung shu-chü,
1950.
一九五〇人民年鑑。沈頌芳。
Jen-min jih-pao. Peking, February 3, 1950.
人民日報。
K'ang Jih chan-cheng shih-ch'i te Chung-kuo
jen-min chieh-fang chün, ed. by Jen-min ch'u-
pan she. Peking, 1954.
抗日戰爭時期的中國人民解放軍。人民出
版社。
Tang, Peter S.H. Communist China Today. New
York: Frederick A. Praeger, 1957-58. 2 vols.
T'ien Ch'i *et al*. Chung-kung Kao Jao shih-chien
mien-mien kuan (comp. by Shih Chia-lin).
Kowloon: Tzu-yu ch'u-pan she, 1955.
田豈等。中共高饒事件面面觀。史家麟。
WWMC

Jen Cho-hsuan   任卓宣

Works

1934.   Chang Tung-sun che-hsueh p'i-p'an.
Shanghai: Hsin k'en shu-tien. 2 vols.
張東蓀哲學批判。
1934.   Che-hsueh tao ho-ch'u ch'ü. Shanghai:
Hsin k'en shu-tien.
哲學到何處去。
1934.   Hu Shih p'i-p'an.
胡適批判。
1935.   (comp.) Che-hsueh lun chan. Shanghai:
Hsin k'en shu-tien.
哲學論戰。
1936.   Che-hsueh wen-t'i.
哲學問題。
1936?   Min-tsu cheng-chih ti fa-chan (comp. by
Hang-k'ung wei-yuan-hui cheng-chih pu).
Hang-k'ung wei-yuan-hui cheng-chih pu.
民族政治底發展。航空委員會政治部。
1937.   K'ang chan te ken-pen wen-t'i. Chungking: Kuo-min cheng-fu chün-shih wei-yuan-
hui pieh tung tsung-tui pu.
抗戰的根本問題。
1937.   Wei fa-chan hsin che-hsueh erh chan; ti-i
chi. Shanghai: Chen-li ch'u-pan she.
為發展新哲學而戰；第一集。

1938.   Chung-kuo ti hsien chieh-tuan chi ch'i
chiang-lai. Wuchang: K'ang chan ch'u-pan
she.
中國底現階段及其將來。
1941.   San min chu-i chih wan-mei. Chungking:
Chung-kuo wen-hua fu-wu she.
三民主義之完美。
1941.   San min chu-i yü tzu-yu. T'ai-ho, Kiangsi:
Shih-tai ssu-ch'ao she.
三民主義與自由。
1944.   Chung-kuo cheng-chih wen-t'i. Chungking: Kuo-min t'u-shu ch'u-pan she.
中國政治問題。
1945.   Min-chu cheng-chih hsin-lun. Chungking: Tu-li ch'u-pan she.
民主政治新論。
1946?   Kung-ch'an-tang shih-pai chih pi-jan.
Nanking: K'ung-chün tsung-ssu-ling pu
cheng-chih pu.
共產黨失敗之必然。
1946.   San min chu-i yü min-chu cheng-chih.
Chungking: Ch'ing-nien ch'u-pan she.
三民主義與民主政治。
1949.   Fan kung wen-t'i. Taipei: Hsin Chung-
kuo wen-hua kung-ssu.
反共問題。
1949.   Kung-ch'an-tang wen-t'i. Nanking: Hsin
Chung-kuo ch'u-pan she.
共產黨問題。
1949.   Wei shui erh chan. Hsin Chung-kuo wen-
hua kung-ssu.
為誰而戰。
1950.   Chung-kuo mu-ch'ien te pien-hua chi ch'i
ch'u-lu. Taipei: Chung-kuo cheng-chih shu-
k'an sheng-ch'an ho-tso she.
中國目前的變化及其出路。
1950.   Kuo-fu che-hsueh yen-lun chi chieh.
Taipei: P'a-mi-erh shu-tien.
國父哲學言論輯解。
1950.   Shih-chieh wang ho-ch'u ch'ü. Taipei:
Tzu-yu Chung-kuo she ch'u-pan pu.
世界往何處去。
1951.   Ko-ming che-hsueh yao-i. Taipei: P'a-mi-
erh shu-tien.
革命哲學要義。
1951.   Min-chu chu-i. Taipei: Cheng-chung
shu-chü.
民主主義。
1951.   San min chu-i ti chi-pen jen-shih. Taipei:
P'a-mi-erh shu-tien.
三民主義底基本認識。
1951.   Tsen-yang yen-chiu san min chu-i. Taipei:
P'a-mi-erh shu-tien.

怎樣研究三民主義。

1951. Tsu-chih yuan-li. Taipei: P'a-mi-erh shu-tien.
組織原理。

1951. Wu ch'üan hsien-fa yü min-chu cheng-chih. Taipei: P'a-mi-erh shu-tien.
五權憲法與民主政治。

1952. Chung-kuo wang ho-ch'u ch'ü. Taipei: P'a-mi-erh shu-tien.
中國往何處去。

1952. Hsin min-chu chu-i p'i-p'an. Taipei: Chung-yang wen-wu kung-ying she.
新民主主義批判。

1952. Kung-ch'an chu-i p'i-p'an. Taipei: P'a-mi-erh shu-tien.
共產主義批判。

1952. Kuo-fu chü-jen ching-shen chiao-yü yen-chiu. Taipei: P'a-mi-erh shu-tien.
國父軍人精神教育研究。

1952. Min-sheng chu-i chen chieh. Taipei: P'a-mi-erh shu-tien.
民主主義眞解。

1952. San min chu-i yü tzu-yu. Taipei: P'a-mi-erh shu-tien.
三民主義與自由。

1952. Wei shen-mo fan kung. Taipei: P'a-mi-erh shu-tien.
爲甚麼反共。

1954. Chung-kuo hsien-fa wen-t'i. Taipei: P'a-mi-erh shu-tien.
中國憲法問題。

1954. Fei tang li-lun p'i-p'an. Taipei: Kuo-fang pu tsung cheng-chih pu.
匪黨理論批判。

1955. (comp.) Hei-ko-erh sheng-p'ing chi ch'i che-hsueh. Taipei: Chung-hua wen-hua ch'u-pan shih-yeh wei-yuan-hui.
黑格爾生平及其哲學。

1955. Ma-k'o-ssu cheng-chih ssu-hsiang p'i-p'an. Taipei: P'a-mi-erh shu-tien.
馬克思政治思想批判。

1957. Kung tang li-lun p'i-p'an ta-kang (with Kung tang ts'e-lueh p'i-p'an). Taipei: P'a-mi-erh shu-tien.
共黨理論批判大綱 (附: 共黨策略批判)。

1957. Wu ch'üan hsien-fa yü Chung-kuo hsien-fa. Taipei: P'a-mi-erh shu-tien.
五權憲法與中國憲法。

1961. Mao Tse-tung p'i-p'an. Taipei: P'a-mi-erh shu-tien.
毛澤東批判。

1961. Ssu-hsiang fang-fa lun (comp. by San min chu-i yen-chiu so). Taipei: P'a-mi-erh shu-tien.
思想方法論。三民主義研究所。

1962. Jen Cho-hsuan *et al*. Min-tsu yü li-shih (ed. by Cheng-chih p'ing-lun she). Taipei: P'a-mi-erh shu-tien.
任卓宣等。民族與歷史。政治評論社。

1964. San-min chu-i hsin chieh (ed. by San min chu-i yen-chiu so). Taipei: P'a-mi-erh shu-tien.
三民主義新解。三民主義研究所。

ed. of *Erh-shih shih-chi*.
二十世紀。

Hsin che-hsueh lun chan chi.
新哲學論戰集。

ed. of *Ko-hsin chou-k'an*.
革新週刊。

ed. of *K'o-hsueh ssu-hsiang*.
科學思想。

Kuo-fu i-chiao ta-kang.
國父遺敎大綱。

Kuo-fu yü ssu-hsiang chan.
國父與思想戰。

Ssu-wei k'o-hsueh.
思維科學。

ed. of *Yen-chiu yü p'i-p'an*.
研究與批判。

SOURCES

Brière, O. Fifty Years of Chinese Philosophy, 1898–1948 (tr. by Laurence G. Thompson). New York: The Macmillan Co., 1956.

CMJL

GCCJK

GCJJ

Jen Cho-hsuan. Che-hsueh tao ho-ch'u ch'ü. Shanghai: Hsin k'en shu-tien, 1934.
任卓宣。哲學到何處去。

———. Hei-ko-erh sheng-p'ing chi ch'i che-hsueh. Taipei: Chung-hua wen-hua ch'u-pan shih-yeh wei-yuan-hui, 1955.
任卓宣。黑格爾生平及其哲學。

———. K'ang chan te ken-pen wen-t'i. Chungking: Kuo-min cheng-fu chün-shih wei-yuan-hui pieh tung tsung-tui pu, 1937.
任卓宣。抗戰的根本問題。

———. Kung-ch'an chu-i p'i-p'an. Taipei: P'a-mi-erh shu-tien, 1952.
任卓宣。共產主義批判。

———. Mao Tse-tung p'i-p'an. Ta kung ch'u-pan she, 1941.
任卓宣。毛澤東批判。

———. Tang-p'ai wen-t'i. Hong Kong: Chung-yang ch'u-pan she, 1940.
任卓宣。黨派問題。

Jen Cho-hsueh. Wei shen-mo fan kung. Taipei:
P'a-mi-erh shu-tien.

任卓宣。爲什麼反共。

Jen Cho-hsuan p'ing chuan, comp. by P'a-mi-
erh shu-tien pien-chi pu. Taipei: P'a-mi-erh
shu-tien, 1965.

任卓宣評傳。帕米爾書店編輯部。

Siao Yu. When Mao Tse-tung and I Were Beggars. Syracuse: Syracuse University Press,
1959.

Wei Hsi-wen *et al*. Jen Cho-hsuan hsueh-shu
ssu-hsiang lun (comp. by Jen Cho-hsuan hsueh-
shu ssu-hsiang lun pien-chi wei-yuan-hui).
Taipei: P'a-min-erh shu-tien, 1965.

魏希文等。任卓宣學術思想論。任卓宣學
術思想論編輯委員會。

Jen Hung-chün   任鴻雋

WORKS

1912. ed. of *Min-i pao*.

民意報。

1922. Wu te fen-hsi. (tr.) Shanghai: Shang-wu
yin shu kuan.

物的分析。

1923. Chiao-yü lun. (tr. of Herbert Spencer's
On Education). Shanghai: Shang-wu yin shu
kuan.

教育論。

1926. K'o-hsueh kai-lun. Shanghai: Shang-wu
yin shu kuan.

科學概論。

1953. Tsui-chin pai nien hua-hsueh te chin-
chan. (tr.)

最近百年化學的進展。

1956. Ai-yin-ssu-t'an yü hsiang-tui lun.

愛因斯坦與相對論。

SOURCES

CH

Chang Ch'i-yün *et al*. Chung-hua Min-kuo ta-
hsueh chih. Taipei: Chung-hua wen-hua
ch'u-pan shih-yeh wei-yuan-hui, 1954. 2 vols.

張其昀等。中華民國大學誌。

Chung-kuo k'o-hsueh erh-shih nien, comp. by
Liu Hsien. Shanghai: Chung-kuo k'o-hsueh
she, 1937.

中國科學二十年。劉咸。

JMST, 1950, 1955.

Tu-li p'ing-lun, 1932-37.

獨立評論。

WWMC

Jen Pi-shih   任弼時

WORKS

1948? T'u-ti kai-ko chung te chi-ko wen-t'i.
Yün feng pao she.

土地改革中的幾個問題。

1949. Jen Pi-shih *et al*. Chung-kuo hsin min-chu
chu-i ch'ing-nien t'uan te jen-wu yü kung-tso.
Hong Kong: Hsin min-chu ch'u-pan she.

任弼時等。中國新民主主義青年團的任務
與工作。

SOURCES

Person interviewed: Chang Kuo-t'ao.

CB, 26 (November 12, 1950).

Ch'en, Jerome. Mao and the Chinese Revolution.
New York: Oxford University Press, 1965.

Chiang Nan-hsiang. "Ching tao Chung-kuo
ch'ing-nien yün-tung te tao-shih—Jen Pi-shih
t'ung-chih." *Chung-kuo ch'ing-nien*, November
4, 1950.

蔣南翔。敬悼中國青年運動的導師一任弼
時同志。中國青年。

CKLC

Chu Teh *et al*. Ti-pa lu chün chiang-ling k'ang
chan hui-i-lu (ed. by Ch'en Cho-tai). 1938.

朱德等。第八路軍將領抗戰回憶錄。陳卓呆。

"A Great Fighter, a Great Statesman." *People's
China*, II-10 (November 16, 1950): 10-11.

HKLC

Hsueh-hsi Jen Pi-shih t'ung-chih, comp. by
Chung-kuo hsin min-chu chu-i ch'ing-nien
t'uan Hua-nan kung-tso wei-yuan-hui. Canton: Ch'ing-nien ch'u-pan she, 1950.

學習任弼時同志。中國新民主主義青年團
華南工作委員會。

Jen-min jih-pao. Peking, July 4, 1945.

人民日報。

Jen Pi-shih. "Tsai Chung-kuo hsin min-chu
chu-i ch'ing-nien t'uan ti-i tz'u ch'üan-kuo
tai-piao ta-hui shang te cheng-chih pao-kao,"
in *Chung-kuo hsin min-chu chu-i ch'ing-nien t'uan
te jen-wu yü kung-tso*. Hong Kong: Hsin min-
chu ch'u-pan she, 1949.

任弼時。在中國新民主主義青年團第一次
全國代表大會上的政治報告。中國新民主
主義青年團的任務與工作。

"Jen Pi-shih t'ung-chih chien-li," *Chung-kuo
ch'ing-nien*, November 4, 1950.

任弼時同志簡歷。中國青年。

Li Jui. Mao Tse-tung t'ung-chih te ch'u-ch'i ko-
ming huo-tung. Peking: Chung-kuo ch'ing-
nien ch'u-pan she, 1957.

李銳。毛澤東同志的初期革命活動。
Ta kung pao. Hong Kong, January 18, 19, 1952.
大公報。
Wang Shou-tao. "In Memory of Comrade Jen Pi-shih." SCMP, 216 (November 15, 1951): 20–22.
WWC, 1950.

Kan Nai-kuang   甘乃光

WORKS

1925. Sun Wen chu-i fa-fan. Kuo-min shu-chü.
孫文主義發凡。
1926. Chung-kuo kuo-min-tang chi ko ken-pen wen-t'i. Wuchang: Hupeh sheng tang-pu chin-hsing wei-yuan-hui hsuan-ch'uan pu.
中國國民黨幾個根本問題。
1926. Sun Wen chu-i chih li-lun yü shih-chi.
孫文主義之理論與實際。
1926. Sun Wen chu-i ta-kang. Canton: Kuo-min ko-ming chün chung-yang chün-shih cheng-chih hsueh-hsiao cheng-chih pu.
孫文主義大綱。
1927. Sun Chung-shan yü Lieh-ning. Shanghai: San min shu-tien.
孫中山與列寧。
1928. Chung-kuo kuo-min-tang te tang shih. Nanking: Chung-yang chih-tao wei-yuan-hui.
中國國民黨的黨史。
1930. Hsien Ch'in ching-chi ssu-hsiang shih. Shanghai: Shang-wu yin shu kuan.
先秦經濟思想史。
1931. (comp.) Chung-shan ch'üan-shu fen-lei so-yin. Shanghai: Liang-yu t'u-shu yin-shua kung-ssu.
中山全書分類索引。
1947. Chung-kuo hsing-cheng hsin lun. Shanghai: Shang-wu yin shu kuan.
中國行政新論。

SOURCES

BKL
CH
Chin shan shih-pao. San Francisco, January 12, 1957.
金山時報。
Documents on Communism, Nationalism, and Soviet Advisers in China 1918–1927: Papers Seized in the 1927 Peking Raid, ed. by C. Martin Wilbur, Julie Lien-ying How. New York: Columbia University Press, 1956.

Linebarger, Paul. The China of Chiang Kai-shek. Boston: World Peace Foundation, 1941.

K'ang Ch'eng   康成

SOURCES

Burton, Margaret E. Notable Women of Modern China. New York: Fleming H. Revell, 1912.
China Christian Advocate, XIX-1 (January, 1932): 7–8.

K'ang Sheng   康生

SOURCES

Person interviewed: Chang Kuo-t'ao.
CB, 308 (December 16, 1954).
CPR, 889 (May 11, 1949).
North, Robert C. Kuomintang and Chinese Communist Elites. Stanford: Stanford University Press, 1952.
WWC, 1950.
WWMC

K'ang Yu-wei   康有爲

WORKS

1891. Ch'ang hsing hsueh chi. Canton: Wan-mu-t'ang.
長興學記。
1897. K'ung-tzu kai-chih k'ao. Shanghai: Wan-mu-ts'ao-t'ang.
孔子改制考。
1901. Chung-yung chu. Shanghai: Chung-kuo t'u-shu kung-ssu ho chi.
中庸注。
1902. Lun-yü chu. Shanghai: Wan-mu-ts'ao-t'ang. 6 vols.
論語注。
1908. Wu-chih chiu-kuo lun. Shanghai: Kuang chih shu-chü.
物質救國論。
1911. Wu-hsü tsou kao (comp. by Mai Chung-hua).
戊戌奏稿。麥仲華。
1914. K'ang Liang shih ch'ao. with Liang Ch'i-ch'ao. Shanghai: Chung-hua t'u-shu-kuan. 4 vols.
康梁詩鈔。梁啓超。
1915. K'ang Nan-hai wen-chi. Shanghai. 8 vols.
康南海文集。

1916. Ni Chung-hua Min-kuo hsien-fa ts'ao-an. Shanghai: Kuang chih shu-chü.
擬中華民國憲法草案。

1916. Shu ching. Shanghai: Kuang chih shu-chü.
書鏡。

1917. Ch'un-ch'iu pi hsiao ta-i wei-yen k'ao. Peiping. 10 vols.
春秋筆削大義微言考。

1917. K'ang Nan-hai hsien-sheng shu k'ai sui hu liu-shih shih. Peking: Ya-tung chih pan yin-shua chü.
康南海先生書開歲忽六十詩。

1918. Kung-ho p'ing i. Shanghai: Ch'ang hsing shu-chü.
共和平議。

1918. (comp.) Wan-mu-ts'ao-t'ang ts'ang hua mu. Shanghai: Ch'ang hsing shu-chü.
萬木草堂藏畫目。

1918. Wei ching k'ao. 6 vols.
偽經考。

1921. Nan-hai hsien-sheng wu-hsü chueh-pi shu pa.
南海先生戊戌絕筆書跋。

1930. K'ang Nan-hai chu t'ien chiang (with Yueh-ch'iu t'u). 2 vols.
康南海諸天講 (附：月球圖)。

1931. Hsin hsueh wei ching k'ao. Peiping: Peiping wen-hua hsueh-she.
新學偽經考。

1932. Ta-t'ung shu. Shanghai: Chung-hua shu-chü.
大同書。
Eng. tr. by Laurence G. Thompson, *Ta T'ung Shu; the One-World Philosophy of K'ang Yu-wei*. London: Allen & Unwin, 1958.

1958. K'ang Yu-wei shih wen hsuan (ed. by Jen-min wen-hsueh ch'u-pan she pien-chi pu). Peking: Jen-min wen-hsueh ch'u-pan she.
康有為詩文選。人民文學出版社編輯部。

1960. Wan-mu-ts'ao-t'ang i-kao (comp. by Lo K'ang T'ung-pi). Peking, 1960. 4 vols.
萬木草堂遺稿。羅康同璧。

Ch'un-ch'iu Tung shih hsueh (with Shih chi ju-lin lieh-chuan).
春秋董氏學 (附：史記儒林列傳)。

Lao t'ai-fu-jen chi K'ang Kuang-jen lieh-shih ai lieh lu. Canton: Yü min yin-shua kung-ssu.
勞太夫人及康廣仁烈士哀烈錄。

Li-ts'ai chiu-kuo lun.
理財救國論。

Nan-hai hsien-sheng ssu shang shu chi. Shanghai: Shih-wu pao kuan.
南海先生四上書記。

Pu-hsin erh yen chung pu t'ing tse kuo wang. Ch'ang hsing shu-chü.
不幸而言中不聽則國亡。

SOURCES

AADC

Chang Po-chen. Nan-hai K'ang hsien-sheng chuan. Peiping: Wen-k'ai-chai, 1932?
張伯楨。南海康先生傳。

Chao Feng-t'ien. "K'ang Ch'ang-su hsien-sheng nien-p'u." *Shih-hsueh nien-pao*, II-1 (September, 1934): 173–240.
趙豐田。康長素先生年譜。史學年報。

Chin shan shih-pao. San Francisco, June 9, 10, 1960.
金山時報。

Hsiao Kung-ch'üan. "K'ang Yu-wei and Confucianism." *Monumenta Serica*, 18 (1959): 96–212.

K'ang Yu-wei. Ta-t'ung shu. Shanghai: Chung-hua shu-chü, 1932.
康有為。大同書。
Eng. tr. by Laurence G. Thompson, *Ta T'ung Shu; the One-World Philosophy of K'ang Yu-wei*. London: Allen & Unwin, 1958.

Li Tse-hou. K'ang Yu-wei T'an Ssu-t'ung ssu-hsiang yen-chiu. Shanghai: Shanghai jen-min ch'u-pan she, 1958.
李澤厚。康有為譚嗣同思想研究。

Liang Ch'i-ch'ao. K'ang Nan-hai chuan (with Kung Ch'iang-li, K'ang Nan-hai hsien-sheng hsing-chuang). New York: Wei-hsin pao, 1928.
梁起超。康南海傳 (附：龔强立，康南海先生行狀)。

———. "Nan-hai K'ang hsien-sheng chuan," in Liang Ch'i-ch'ao, *Yin-ping-shih ho chi*. Shanghai: Chung-hua shu-chü, 1936. 40 vols.
梁起超。南海康先生傳。梁起超。飲冰室合集。

Lu Nai-hsiang and Lu Tun-k'uei. K'ang Nan-hai hsien-sheng chuan. Shanghai: Wan-mu-ts'ao-t'ang, 1919.
陸乃翔，陸敦騤。康南海先生傳。

Sung Yün-pin. K'ang Yu-wei. Shanghai: Shang-wu yin shu kuan, 1951.
宋雲彬。康有為。

Wu Hsien-tzu. Chung-kuo min-chu hsien-cheng tang tang shih. San Francisco: Shih-chieh jih-pao, 1952.
伍憲子。中國民主憲政黨黨史。

Wu Tse. K'ang Yu-wei yü Liang Ch'i-ch'ao. Shanghai: Hua-hsia shu-tien, 1948.
吳澤。康有為與梁啟超。

Kao Kang

Kao Kang　高崗

WORKS

1943. Pien ch'ü tang te li-shih wen-t'i chien-t'ao. Chung-kuo kung-ch'an-tang Hsi-pei chü.
邊區黨的歷史問題檢討。

1945. Shih-shih k'o-k'o wei lao-pai-hsing hsing li ch'u pi—ling-tao fang-fa yü tso-feng. Chi Lu Yü shu-tien.
時時刻刻爲老百姓興利除弊—領導方法與作風。

1950. Chan-tsai Tung-pei ching-chi chien-she te tsui ch'ien-mien. Canton: Hsin hua shu-tien.
站在東北經濟建設的最前面。

1950. Mi-ch'ieh tang yü jen-min ch'ün-chung te lien-hsi—i-chiu-wu-ling nien ch'i-yueh i jih Kao Kang t'ung-chih tsai Tung-pei chü ch'ing-chu Chung-kuo kung-ch'an-tang tan-sheng erh-shih-chiu chou-nien te kan-pu ta-hui shang te chiang-hua. Hankow? Hsin hua shu-tien chung-nan fen-tien.
密切黨與人民群衆的聯繫——一九五〇年七月一日高崗同志在東北局慶祝中國共產黨誕生二十九週年的幹部大會上的講話。

SOURCES

Person interviewed: Chang Kuo-t'ao.
CB, 290 (September 5, 1954).
Chao Kuan-i and Wei Tan-po. Chung-kung jen-wu su-miao. Kowloon: Tzu-yu ch'u-pan she, 1951.
趙貫一，韋丹柏。中共人物素描。
Chao Kuo-chun. "The Government and Economy of Manchuria." *Far Eastern Survey*, XXII-13 (December, 1953): 169-75.
Chung-kung Kao Jao shih-chien mien-mien kuan, comp. by Shih Chia-lin. Kowloon: Tzu-yu ch'u-pan she, 1955.
中共高饒事件面面觀。史家麟。
Chung-kuo hsin min-chu chu-i ko-ming shih ts'an-k'ao tzu-liao, ed. by Tai I, Yen Ch'i. Shanghai: Shang-wu yin shu kuan, 1951.
中國新民主主義革命史參考資料。戴逸，彥奇。
CKLC
CPR, 1005 (November 1, 1949): 11-12.
GCCJK
HCJC
Hsing-tao wan-pao. Hong Kong, November 13, 1951.
星島晚報。
I-chiu-wu-ling jen-min nien-chien, ed. by Shen

Sung-fang. Hong Kong: Ta kung shu-chü, 1950.
一九五〇人民年鑑。沈頌芳。
Jen-min jih-pao. Peking, July 4, 1951.
人民日報。
Mao Tse-tung. Mao Tse-tung hsuan-chi. Peking: Jen-min ch'u-pan she, 1951-60. 4 vols.
毛澤東。毛澤東選集。

Kao Lun　高侖

WORKS

1935. Chien-fu hua-chi. Shanghai: Shang-wu yin shu kuan.
劍父畫集。
1955. Wo-te hsien-tai kuo-hua kuan. Kowloon: Yuan ch'üan ch'u-pan she.
我的現代國畫觀。
Chien-fu sui chin.
劍父碎金。
Ch'un shui i t'an.
春睡藝談。
Chung-kuo hsien-tai te hui-hua.
中國現代的繪畫。
Fo-chiao ko-ming lun.
佛教革命論。
Fo kuo chi.
佛國記。
Hsi-ma-la-ya-shan te yen-chiu.
喜馬拉亞山的研究。
Hui-hua fa wei.
繪畫發微。
Kuo-hua hsin lu hsiang.
國畫新路向。
Wa sheng chi.
蛙聲集。
Yin-tu i-shu.
印度藝術。

SOURCES

"Art Chronicle." *T'ien-hsia Monthly*, III-2 (September, 1936): 163-65; IX-1 (August, 1939): 82-85.
Chu Hsiu-hsia. "I Kao Chien-fu hsien-sheng." *Tzu-yu Chung-kuo*, V-3.
祝秀俠。憶高劍父先生。自由中國。
Hua Ch'ing. "I Ling-nan liang hua-chia." *Ta hua*, June 7, 1959.
花清。憶嶺南兩畫家。大華。
"Kao Chien-fu hsien-sheng chuan-lueh," in Kao Chien-fu, *Wo-te hsien-tai kuo-hua kuan*. Kowloon: Yuan ch'üan ch'u-pan she, 1955.

高劍父先生傳略。高劍父。我的現代國畫觀。
Li Chien-erh. Kwangtung hsien-tai hua-jen
chuan. Hong Kong, 1941.
李健兒。廣東現代畫人傳。
MMT
Sullivan, Michael. Chinese Art in the Twentieh
Century. Berkeley: University of California
Press, 1959.

Kao Weng   高嶺

WORKS

1935. Kao Ch'i-feng hsien-sheng i hua chi; ti-i
chi. Shanghai: Hua-ch'iao t'u-shu yin-shua
kung-ssu.
高奇峰先生遺畫集；第一輯。
1935. Kao Ch'i-feng hsien-sheng jung-ai-lu.
Nanking.
高奇峰先生榮哀錄。
Ch'i-feng hua-chi.
奇峰畫集。
Ch'i-feng hua fan.
奇峰畫範。
Hsin hua hsueh.
新畫學。
Mei-shu shih.
美術史。

SOURCES

An Exhibition of Paintings by Kao Weng and
Chang K'un-i. New York: The Metropolitan
Museum of Art, 1944.
Hua Ch'ing. "I Ling-nan liang hua-chia." *Ta
hua*, June 7, 1959.
花濟。憶嶺南兩畫家。大華。
Kao Weng. Kao Ch'i-feng hsien-sheng jung-ai-
lu. Nanking, 1935.
高嶺。高奇峰先生榮哀錄。
Li Chien-erh. Kwangtung hsien-tai hua jen
chuan. Hong Kong, 1941.
李健兒。廣東現代畫人傳。
MMT
Sullivan, Michael. Chinese Art in the Twentieth
Century. Berkeley: University of California
Press, 1959.

Ko Kung-chen   戈公振

WORKS

1913–27. ed. of *Shih pao*.
時報。

1925. Hsin-wen-hsueh ts'o-yao.
新聞學撮要。
1927. Chung-kuo pao-hsueh shih. Shanghai:
Shang-wu yin shu kuan.
中國報學史。
1935. Ts'ung Tung-pei tao Su-lien. Shanghai:
Sheng-huo shu-tien.
從東北到庶聯。
1940. Hsin-wen-hsueh. Shang-wu yin shu kuan.
新聞學。
ed. of *Shen pao*.
申報。

SOURCES

CBJS
Chao Chün-hao. Chung-kuo chin-tai chih pao
yeh. Changsha: Shang-wu yin shu kuan,
1940.
趙君豪。中國近代之報業。
CMMC
GCJJ
Handbook on People's China. Peking: Foreign
Languages Press, 1957.
JMST, 1950–51.
Ko Kung-chen. Chung-kuo pao-hsueh shih. Pe-
king: Sheng-huo, tu-shu, hsin-chih san lien
shu-tien, 1955.
戈公振。中國報學史。
Kuo wen chou-pao, III-10 (March, 1926).
國聞週報。
WWMC

K'o Ch'ing-shih   柯慶施

WORKS

1959, February. "Lun 'ch'üan-kuo i p'an ch'i'."
Hung ch'i, 4: 9–12.
論「全國一盤棋」。紅旗。

SOURCES

GCJJ
Hsi-wu Lao-jen (pseud. of Tung Pi-wu).
"Chung-kuo kung-ch'an-tang ch'eng-li ch'ien-
hou chien-wen." *Hsin kuan-ch'a*, 13 (July 1,
1957): 16–18.
栖梧老人（董必武）。中國共產黨成立前後
見聞。新觀察。
K'o Ch'ing-shih. "Lun 'ch'üan-kuo i p'an ch'i'."
Hung ch'i, 4 (February, 1959): 9–12.
柯慶施。論「全國一盤棋」。紅旗。
K-WWMC
Snow, Edgar. The Other Side of the River: Red

China Today. New York: Random House, 1962.

王桐齡。介紹柯鳳孫先生新元史。學衡。

K'o Shao-min　　柯劭忞

WORKS

1917. Ch'un-ch'iu ku-liang chuan chu. 4 vols.
春秋穀梁傳注。

1922. Hsin Yuan shih. Tientsin: T'ui-keng-t'ang. 60 vols.
新元史。

1924. Liao-yuan shih-ch'ao.
蓼園詩鈔。

1928. (ed.) Ch'ing shih kao. with Chao Erh-sun et al. Peking: Ch'ing shih kuan. 132 vols.
清史稿。趙爾巽等。

1935. Hsin Yuan shih k'ao-cheng. Peiping: Peking ta-hsueh yen-chiu yuan wen shih pu.
新元史考證。

Hsin Yuan shih shih huo chih.
新元史食貨志。

(comp.) Kung Kuang-lu kung nien-p'u.
龔光祿公年譜。

SOURCES

Chang Erh-t'ien. "Ch'ing ku hsueh pu tso ch'eng K'o chün mu-chih-ming." Shih-hsueh nien-pao, III-1 (1939): 115-16.
張爾田。清故學部左丞柯君墓誌銘。史學年報。

I-shih. "Kuan-yü K'o Shao-min." I ching, 25 (March, 1937): 66-69.
一士。關於柯劭忞。逸經。

———. "Tsai shu K'o Shao-min i-shih." I ching, 28 (April, 1937): 18-19.
一士。再述柯劭忞軼事。逸經。

Liu I-cheng. "K'o Shao-min." Kuo shih kuan kuan k'an, I-2 (March, 1948): 89-92.
柳詒徵。柯劭忞。國史館館刊。

Mou Jun-sun. "K'o Feng-sun hsien-sheng i-shu san-chung." T'u-shu chi-k'an, II-4 (December, 1935): 237-38.
牟潤孫。柯鳳蓀先生遺書三種。圖書季刊。

Wang Po-hsiang. "Hsin-hai ko-ming te hui-ku." Tung-fang tsa-chih, XXVIII-19 (October, 1931): 84.
王伯祥。辛亥革命的回顧。東方雜誌。

Wang Sen-jan. "K'o Shao-min hsien-sheng p'ing-chuan," in CECP.
王森然。柯劭忞先生評傳。

Wang T'ung-ling. "Chieh-shao K'o Feng-sun hsien-sheng hsin Yuan shih." Hsueh heng, 30 (June, 1924): 1-4.

Ku Cheng-lun　　谷正倫

SOURCES

BKL
CH
CMJL
CTMC
GCJJ
GCMMTJK
Ku Chi-ch'ang hsien-sheng ai ssu lu, comp. by Ku Cheng-lun hsien-sheng chih-sang wei-yuan-hui. Taipei, 1954.
谷紀常先生哀思錄。谷正倫先生治喪委員會。
WWC, 1950.

Ku Cheng-ting　　谷正鼎

SOURCES

Persons interviewed: not to be identified.

Ku Chieh-kang　　顧頡剛

WORKS

1924. Chung-kuo hsueh-shu nien-piao te shuo-ming. Peking: Peking ta hsueh yen-chiu so.
中國學術年表的說明。

1925-27. Pen-kuo shih. Shanghai: Shang-wu yin shu kuan. 3 vols.
本國史。

1926-41. Ku Chieh-kang et al. Ku shih pien. Peiping: P'u she. 7 vols.
顧頡剛等。古史辨。

1928-33. Ku Chieh-kang et al. (comp.) Pien wei ts'ung-k'an. Peiping: P'u she. 8 vols.
顧頡剛等。辨偽叢刊。

1933. Shang-shu yen-chiu chiang-i. 3 vols.
尚書研究講義。

1933. Shu hsü pien. Peiping: Ching-shan shu she.
書序辨。

1936. San huang k'ao. with Yang Hsiang-k'uei. Peiping: Ha-fo Yen-ching hsueh-she.
三皇考。楊向奎。

1936. (ed.) Shang-shu t'ung chien. Peiping: Ha-fo Yen-ching hsueh-she.
尚書通檢。

1938. Chung-kuo chiang-yü yen-ko shih. with Shih Nien-hai. Shanghai: Shang-wu yin shu kuan.

中國疆域沿革史。 史念海。

1938. Han-tai hsueh-shu shih-lueh. Shanghai: Ya-hsi-ya shu-chü.
漢代學術史略。

1944. Ch'in Shih huang-ti. Chungking: Sheng-li ch'u-pan she.
秦始皇帝。

1947. Ku Chien-kang t'ung-su lun-chu chi. Shanghai: Ya-tung t'u-shu-kuan.
顧頡剛通俗論著集。

1947. Tang-tai Chung-kuo shih-hsueh. Nanking: Sheng-li ch'u-pan kung-ssu.
當代中國史學。

1955-? (ed.) Ku-chi k'ao-pien ts'ung-k'an. Peking: Chung-hua shu-chü.
古籍考辨叢刊。

1963-? Shih lin tsa shih. Peking: Chung-hua shu-chü.
史林雜識。

ed. of *Shih-hsueh tsa-chih*.
史學雜誌。

ed. of *T'ung-su tu-wu*.
通俗讀物。

ed. of *Yü-kung*.
禹貢。

SOURCES

Persons interviewed: not to be identified.
The Autobiography of a Chinese Historian, Being the Preface to a Symposium on Ancient Chinese History (Ku shih pien), tr. and annot. by Arthur W. Hummel. Leyden: E. J. Brill, 1931.

Ku Chu-t'ung   顧祝同

SOURCES

AWW
BKL
CH
CTMC
GCJJ
MMT
WWC, supplement to 4th ed., 1933.
WWMC

Ku Hung-ming   辜鴻銘

WORKS

1910. Chang Wen-hsiang mu-fu chi-wen. 2 vols.
張文襄幕府紀聞。

1922? Tu i ts'ao t'ang wen-chi.
讀易草堂文集。

SOURCES

Persons interviewed: not to be identified.
Arkush, R. David, "Ku Hung-ming," *Papers on China,* 19 (1965), pp. 194-238.
Tung Nan-ya. "Ku Hung-ming yü Nan-yang." *Ta kung pao.* Hong Kong, August 6, 1962.
董南亞。 辜鴻銘與南洋。 大公報。

Ku Meng-yü   顧孟餘

WORKS

1965. Ku Meng-yü *et al*. Chung-kuo li-tai jen-k'ou wen-t'i lun chi (comp. by Hong Kong Ya-tung hsueh-she). Hong Kong: Lung men shu-tien.
顧孟餘等。 中國歷代人口問題論集。 香港亞東學社。

SOURCES

CH
Documents on Communism, Nationalism, and Soviet Advisers in China, 1918-1927: Papers Seized in the 1927 Peking Raid, ed. by C. Martin Wilbur, Julie Lien-ying How. New York: Columbia University Press, 1956.
Lei Hsiao-ts'en. San-shih nien tung-luan Chung-kuo. Hong Kong: Ya-chou ch'u-pan she, 1955.
雷嘯岑。 三十年動亂中國。
Tong, Hollington K. Chiang Kai-shek. Taipei: China Publishing Co., 1953.

Ku Wei-chün   顧維鈞

WORKS

1912, March. "A Short History of the Chinese Students' Alliance in the United States." *The Chinese Students' Monthly*: 420-31.

1912. The Status of Aliens in China. New York: Columbia University Press.

1915, December. "History of the Chinese Education Mission." *The Chinese Students' Monthly*: 91-93.

1916, April. "American Commercial Opportunities in China." *The Chinese Students' Monthly*.

1918, November. "Dedication of Chinese Flag to the Cause of the War." *The Chinese Students' Monthly*.

1919. China and the League of Nations. with C. T. Wang. London: Unwin.

1931. Ku Wei-chün wai-chiao wen-tu tieh ts'un (V. K. Wellington Koo's Foreign Policy) (comp. by Chin Wen-ssu). Shanghai: Kelly and Walsh Co.
顧維鈞外交文牘迭存。金問泗。

1931, December 31. "Dr. Wellington Koo's Appeal to America." CWR.

1932. Memoranda Presented to the Lytton Commission. New York: The Chinese Cultural Society. 3 vols.

1933. Views of the Chinese Government on the Lytton Report: Statement. Nanking: Intelligence and Publicity Department.

1935, December. "The Future of Sino-American Trade." *Chinese Economic Journal*.

1939. The Open Door Policy and World Peace. London: Oxford University Press.

1941, October. "China and the War Against Aggression." *Asiatic Review*: 836–41.

1941, November. "Reconstruction in Wartime China." *The Scottish Geographical Magazine*: 97–103.

1942, January. "China and the Problem of World Order." *New Commonwealth Quarterly*: 183–90.

1943. "Introduction," in George W. Keeton, *China, the Far East and the Future*. London: Jonathan Cape.

1943, November 13–27. "Trends of Future Development in China." *Great Britain and the East*.

ed. of *Chinese Students' Annual*.

ed. of *Chinese Students' Monthly*.

ed. of *Columbia Daily Spectator*.

ed. of *Dragon*.

SOURCES

AWW

BKL

BPC

Chang Ch'i-yün. Tang shih kai-yao. Taipei: Chung-yang kai-tsao wei-yuan-hui wen-wu kung-ying she, 1951–52. 5 vols.
張其昀。黨史概要。

Chang Chung-fu. Chung-hua Min-kuo wai-chiao shih. Taipei: Cheng-chung shu-chü, 1954?
張忠紱。中華民國外交史。

Ch'en Kung-lu. Chung-kuo chin-tai shih. Shanghai: Shang-wu yin shu kuan, 1935.
陳恭祿。中國近代史。

The China Critic, July 19, 1934.

The Chinese Students' Monthly, June 10, 1913; December, 1915; March, 1919; December, 1920; March, 1921.

Chung-kuo wai-chiao shih, comp. by Tseng Yu-hao. Shanghai: Shang-wu yin shu kuan, 1926.
中國外交史。曾友豪。

CMJL

CMTC

CTMC

Dictionaire Diplomatique. Geneva, 1953.

GCJJ

Hong Kong Standard, March 9, 1953.

Kao Tien-chün. Chung-kuo wai-chiao shih. Taipei: P'a-mi-erh shu-tien, 1952.
高殿均。中國外交史。

Koo Hui-lan (Madame Wellington Koo). Hui-lan Koo: An Autobiography as Told to Mary Van Rensselaer Thayer. New York: Dial Press, 1943.

Ku Wei-chün. Ku Wei-chün wai-chiao wen-tu tieh ts'un (V. K. Wellington Koo's Foreign Policy) (comp. by Chin Wen-ssu). Shanghai: Kelly and Walsh Co., 1931.
顧維鈞。顧維鈞外交文牘迭存。金問泗。

Kuo wen chou-pao, I-13.
國聞週報。

Levi, Werner. Modern China's Foreign Policy. Minneapolis: University of Minnesota Press, 1953.

Li Chien-nung. The Political History of China, 1840–1928 (tr. and ed. by Teng Ssu-yu, Jeremy Ingalls). Princeton: D. Van Nostrand Co., 1956.

Liu Yen. Ti-kuo chu-i ya-p'o Chung-kuo shih. Shanghai: T'ai-p'ing-yang shu-tien, 1932. 2 vols.
劉彥。帝國主義壓迫中國史。

The New York Times, November 17, 1916; April 20, 1917; October 2, 1918; December 16, 1920; April 24, 1932; February 5, December 14, 1939; August 23, 1940; February 2, 5, 15, 1943; December 2, 1948; December 5, 1948; August 8, 1949; April 30, 1950; July 15, 1952; February 3, 1953; August 21, 1955; January 12, 1957; August 28, 1960; October 6, 1963.

Pollard, Robert Thomas. China's Foreign Relations, 1917–1931. New York: The Macmillan Co., 1933.

Quan Lau-king. China's Relations with the League of Nations, 1919–1936. Hong Kong: The Asiatic Litho. Printing Press, 1939.

Sze, Sao-ke Alfred (Shih Chao-chi). Sao-ke Alfred Sze; Reminiscences of His Early Years, as Told to Anming Fu (tr. by May C. Wu). Washington, 1962.

T'ang Leang-li. The Inner History of the Chinese Revolution. New York: E. P. Dutton & Co., 1930.

Wai-chiao ta tz'u-tien, ed. by Wai-chiao hsueh-hui. Kunming: Chung-hua shu-chü, 1937.
外交大辭典。外交學會。

Who's Who in America, 1954–55.

Who's Who in the Orient, 1915.

Willoughby, Westel Woodbury. China at the Conference. Baltimore: The Johns Hopkins Press, 1922.

WWARS

WWMC

Yueh Ch'ien. Chung Su kuan-hsi shih-hua. Singapore, Hong Kong: Ch'uang k'en ch'u-pan she, 1952.
岳騫。中蘇關係史話。

Ku Ying-fen   古應芬

Works

1926. Sun ta yuan-shuai tung cheng jih-chi. Shanghai: Min chih shu-chü.
孫大元帥東征日記。

Sources

Chia Shih-i. Min-kuo ts'ai-cheng shih. Taipei: Taiwan shang-wu yin shu kuan, 1962. 7 vols.
賈士毅。民國財政史。

Chiang Yung-ching. Hu Han-min hsien-sheng nien-p'u kao. Taipei: Cheng-chung shu-chü, 1960.
蔣永敬。胡漢民先生年譜稿。

CMMC

Hsi-nan chih-hsing pu tang-wu nien-k'an.
西南執行部黨務年刊。

Ku Ying-fen. Sun ta yuan-shuai tung cheng jih-chi. Shanghai: Min chih shu-chü, 1926.
古應芬。孫大元帥東征日記。

Kuo-fu nien-p'u, ed. by Chung-kuo kuo-ming-tang chung-yang tang shih shih-liao pien-tsuan wei-yuan-hui. Taipei: Chung-hua Min-kuo ko-chieh chi-nien kuo-fu pai-nien tan-ch'en ch'ou-pei wei-yuan-hui, 1965. 2 vols.
國父年譜。中國國民黨中央黨史史料編纂委員會。

Kuo wen chou-pao, IV-26 (July 10, 1927).
國聞週報。

MSICH

Kuan Hsiang-ying   關向應

Sources

Chang T'ung-chün. "Shantung kung ch'ing t'uan tsao-ch'i te ling-tao che ho tsu-chih che—Kuan Hsiang-ying t'ung-chih." Shantung sheng chih tzu-liao, 3 (July, 1959): 56.
張同俊。山東共青團早期的領導者和組織者一關向應同志。山東省志資料。

CKLC

GCCJK

K'uang Fu-cho   鄺富灼

Sources

Association Men, December, 1922.

China Christian Advocate, October, 1938.

Ch'ing-nien hsieh-hui wu-shih chou-nien chi-nien ts'e. Shanghai, 1935.
青年協會五十周年紀念冊。

CMMC

Green, Katherine R. "Some Christian Leaders of Present Day China." Unpublished manuscript, Missionary Research Library, New York.

North China Daily News, June 23, 1931.

WWC, 1936.

Year Book of the Young Men's Christian Association of China, 1936. Shanghai: Association Press, 1937.

K'ung, H. H.   孔祥熙

Works

1928? Erh-shih-wu nien lai Chung-kuo chih kung shang.
二十五年來中國之工商。

1935? K'ung pu-chang tui-yü so-te-shui chih chiang-yen tz'u. Nanking: Ts'ai-cheng pu so-te-shui shih-wu so.
孔部長對於所得稅之講演詞。

1939. Wo kuo ts'ai-cheng chin-jung chih kou-ch'ü yü hsien-tsai. Chungking: Chung-yang hsun-lien t'uan tang cheng hsun-lien pan.
我國財政金融之過去與現在。

1941. Ssu nien lai te ts'ai-cheng chin-jung. Chungking: Chung-kuo kuo-min-tang chung-yang chih-hsing wei-yuan-hui hsuan-ch'uan pu.

四年來的財政金融。

1942. K'ang chan i-lai te ts'ai-cheng (ed. by P'an Kung-chan). Chungking: Sheng-li ch'u-pan she.
抗戰以來的財政。潘公展。

1960. K'ung Jung-chih hsien-sheng yen-chiang chi (comp. by Liu Chen-tung). New York: Chung Mei wen-hua hsieh-hui. 2 vols.
孔庸之先生演講集。劉振東。

SOURCES

Chou Shun-hsin. The Chinese Inflation, 1937–1949. New York: Columbia University Press, 1963.

Edwards, Dwight W. Yenching University. New York: United Board for Christian Higher Education in Asia, 1959.

Young, Arthur N. China and the Helping Hand, 1937–1945. Cambridge: Harvard University Press, 1963.

Yü Liang. K'ung Hsiang-hsi. Hong Kong: K'ai-yuan shu-tien, 1955.
瑜亮。孔祥熙。

K'ung Te-ch'eng　孔德成

WORKS

Li-chi shih-i.
禮記釋義。

1938. "Japanese Imperialism in the Light of Confucianism." *People's Tribune*, new series, XXII: 204–7.

SOURCES

CBJS
CH
China Yearbook, 1964–65. Taipei: China Publishing Co., 1966.
CMJL
GCJJ
New Yorker, 24 (May, 1948): 19–20.

Kuo Hua-jo　郭化若

WORKS

1938. Kuo Hua-jo *et al.* Yu-chi chan-cheng te chi-pen chan-shu. Shanghai: Chien-she she.
郭化若等。游擊戰爭的基本戰術。

1939. Kuo Hua-jo *et al.* K'ang Jih yu-chi chan te chan-shu wen-t'i. Chung-kuo wen-hua she.
郭化若等。抗日游擊戰的戰術問題。

1950. Chün-shih pien-cheng fa. Shanghai: Hsin ch'ün ch'u-pan she.
軍事辨證法。

1950. Hsin chiao-yü te chiao-hsueh fa. Shanghai: Hsin ch'ün ch'u-pan she.
新教育的教學法。

1959. (Chin i hsin pien) Sun-tzu ping-fa. Peking: Jen-min wei-sheng ch'u-pan she.
（今譯新編）孫子兵法。

1961. (ed.) Sung pen shih-i chia chu Sun-tzu. Peking: Chung-hua shu-chü. 4 vols.
宋本十一家註孫子。

1962. (tr.) Shih-i chia chu Sun-tzu. Shanghai: Chung-hua shu-chü.
十一家注孫子。

SOURCES

Chung kung jen-ming lu. Taipei: Kuo-chi kuan-hsi yen-chiu so, 1967.
中共人名錄。
GCJJ

Kuo Mo-jo　郭沫若

WORKS

1923–27. ed. of *Hsueh i*.
學藝。

1925–? ed. of *Hsien-tai p'ing-lun*.
現代評論。

1926. Wei-i lun-chi. Shanghai: Kuang-hua shu-chü.
文藝論集。

1928. Kuo Mo-jo *et al.* Ko-ming wen-hsueh lun (ed. by Ting Chia-shu). Shanghai: T'ai tung t'u-shu chü.
郭沫若等。革命文學論。丁嘉樹。

1928. Nü-shen. T'ai tung shu-chü.
女神。

1929. Hsueh-lai shih-hsuan. (tr.) Shanghai: T'ai tung shu-chü.
雪萊詩選。

1929. Wu te yu-nien. Kuang-hua shu-chü.
我的幼年。

1930. Chung-kuo ku-tai she-hui yen-chiu. Shanghai: Lien-ho shu-tien.
中國古代社會研究。

1930. Fou-shih-te. (tr. of Johann Wolfgang von Goethe's *Faust*, Part I). Shanghai: Hsien-tai shu-chü.
浮子德。

1930. Hsing k'ung. T'ai tung shu-chü.
星空。

1930. Mo-jo shih ch'üan-chi. Shanghai: Hsien-tai shu-chü.
沫若詩全集。

1930. T'a. Shanghai: Shang-wu yin shu kuan.
塔。

1931. Chan-cheng yü ho-p'ing; ti-i fen ts'e. (tr. of part of Leo N. Tolstoi's *War and Peace*). Shanghai: Wen-i shu-chü.
戰爭與和平；第一分冊。

1931. Chia-ku wen-tzu yen-chiu. Shanghai: Ta tung shu-chü. 2 vols.
甲骨文字研究。

1931. Chin wen yü shih chih yü. Tokyo: Wen-ch'iu-t'ang shu-tien.
金文餘釋之餘。

1931. Shao-nien Wei-t'e te fan-nao. (tr. of Johann Wolfgang von Goethe's *The Sorrows of Young Werther*). Shanghai: Hsien-tai shu-chü.
少年維特的煩惱。

1931. Yin Chou ch'ing-t'ung ch'i ming wen yen-chiu. Shanghai: Ta tung shu-chü. 2 vols.
殷周青銅器銘文研究。

1932. Chin wen ts'ung k'ao. Tokyo: Wen-ch'iu-t'ang. 4 vols.
金文叢攷。

1932. Mo-jo hsiao-shuo hsi-ch'ü chi. Kuang-hua shu-chü.
沫若小說戲曲集。

1932. Mo-jo shih-chi. Shanghai: Hsien-tai shu-chü.
沫若詩集。

1933. Ch'uang-tsao shih nien. Shanghai: Hsien-tai shu-chü.
創造十年。

1933. Ku-hung. Shanghai: Kuang-hua shu-chü.
孤鴻。

1933. Ku-tai ming-k'o hui-k'ao. Tokyo: Wen-ch'iu-t'ang shu-tien. 3 vols.
古代銘刻彙考。

1933. Lo-yeh. Shanghai: Kuang-hua shu-chü.
落葉。

1934. Hou-hui. Shanghai: Kuan-hua shu-chü.
後悔。

1934. Ku-tai ming-k'o hui-k'ao hsü-pien. Tokyo: Wen-ch'iu-t'ang.
古代銘刻彙考續編。

1934. "Wen-i chih she-hui shih-ming," in Chang Jo-ying, *Chung-kuo hsin wen-hsueh yün-tung tzu-liao*. Shanghai.
文藝之社會使命。張若英。中國新文學運動資料。

1935. Liang Chou chin wen tz'u ta-hsi k'ao-shih. Tokyo: Wen-ch'iu-t'ang shu-tien. 3 vols.
兩周金文辭大系考釋。

1936. Hua lun ssu t'ai. (tr.) Sheng-huo shu-tien.
華倫斯太。

1936. Kuo Mo-jo hsiao-shuo hsuan (ed. by Shao-hou). Shanghai: Fang-ku shu-tien.
郭沫若小說選。少候。

1936. Li Hu chih ch'ien. Shanghai: Chih tai shu-chü.
離滬之前。

1937. Kuo Mo-jo *et al*. Ch'ien-hsien k'ang chan chiang-ling fang-wen chi. Shanghai: Ch'ien-chin ch'u-pan she.
郭沫若等。前綫抗戰將領訪問記。

1937. Hai-t'ao. Shanghai: Hsin wen-i ch'u-pan she.
海濤。

1937. K'ang chan yü chueh-wu. Shanghai: Ta shih-tai ch'u-pan she.
抗戰與覺悟。

1937. Kuei ch'ü lai. Shanghai: Pei hsin shu-chü.
歸去來。

1937. Kuo Mo-jo ch'uang-tso hsiao-shuo hsuan (ed. by Shen Wen-yao). Shanghai: Shih-tai ch'u-pan she.
郭沫若創作小說選。沈文耀。

1937. Kuo Mo-jo shu-hsin chi. Shanghai: T'ai tung shu-chü.
郭沫若書信集。

1937. Mo-jo chin chu. Pei hsin shu-chü.
沫若近著。

1937. Pei fa. Shanghai: Pei yen ch'u-pan she.
北伐。

1937. (ed.) Yin ch'i ts'ui pien. Tokyo: Wen-ch'iu-t'ang. 5 vols.
殷契粹編。

1938. Chan-shih hsuan-ch'uan kung-tso (ed. by Huang-p'u ch'u-pan she). Chungking: Chung-yang lu-chün chün-kuan hsueh-hsiao.
戰時宣傳工作。黃埔出版社。

1938. Ch'ang-tsao shih nien hsü-pien. Shanghai: Pei hsin shu-chü.
創造十年續編。

1938. Chung-kuo wei shen-mo k'ang chan. Shanghai: I hsin shu-tien.
中國爲甚麼抗戰。

1938. Ch'üan-mien k'ang chan te jen-shih. Canton: Pei hsin shu-chü.
全面抗戰的認識。

1938. Kuo Mo-jo *et al*. Ch'ih-chiu k'ang-chan yü tsu-chih min-chung. Chiu wang ch'u-pan she.
郭沫若等。持久抗戰與組織民衆。

1938. Kuo Mo-jo *et al*. Lun hsin cheng hsieh. Hong Kong: Nan feng shu wu.
論新政協。郭沫若等。

1938. Kuo Mo-jo hsien-sheng tsui-chin yen-lun (ed. by Hsiung Ch'i). Li sao she.
郭沫若先生最近言論。熊琦。

1939. Fan-cheng ch'ien-hou. Li she.
反正前後。

1939. Mo-jo tai-piao tso hsuan (ed. by Chang Chün). Shanghai: Ch'üan-ch'iu shu-tien.
沫若代表作選。張均。

1940. Chou-i te kuo-ch'eng shih-tai (ed. by Chung Fa wen-hua ch'u-pan wei-yuan-hui). Changsha: Shang-wu yin shu kuan.
周易的構成時代。中法文化出版委員會。

1944. Chia-shen san-pai nien chi. Chungking: Hsin hua shu-tien.
甲申三百年祭。

1945. Ch'ing-t'ung shih-tai. Chungking: Wen-chih ch'u-pan she.
青銅時代。

1945. Hsien Ch'in hsueh-shuo shu lin. Yung-an: Tung-nan ch'u-pan she.
先秦學說述林。

1945. Nan kuan ts'ao; wu mu pei-chü. Chungking: Ch'ün i ch'u-pan she.
南冠草；五幕悲劇。

1945. Shih p'i-p'an shu. Chungking: Ch'ün i ch'u-pan she.
十批判書。

1946. Ch'ü Yuan yen-chiu. Shanghai: Ch'ün i ch'u-pan she.
屈原研究。

1946. Hu fu. Shanghai: Ch'ün i ch'u-pan she.
虎符。

1946. K'ung-ch'ueh tan. Shanghai: Ch'ün i ch'u-pan she.
孔雀胆。

1946. Nanking yin-hsiang. Shanghai: Ch'ün i ch'u-pan she.
南京印象。

1946. Po. Shanghai: Ch'ün i ch'u-pan she.
波。

1947. Fo keng chi. Shanghai: Ta fu ch'u-pan kung-ssu.
沸羹集。

1947. Kuo Mo-jo *et al*. Hu-han (ed. by Mei-chou hua-ch'iao ch'ing-nien wen-i she). Hong Kong? Hua-ch'iao chih-shih she.
郭沫若等。呼喊。美洲華僑青年文藝社。

1947. Li-shih jen-wu. Shanghai: Hai-yen shu-tien.
歷史人物。

1947. Ti-hsia te hsiao-sheng. Shanghai: Hai-yen shu-tien.
地下的笑聲。

1947. T'ien ti hsuan huang. Shanghai: Ta fu ch'u-pan kung-ssu.
天地玄黃。

1947. Yü shu chi. Shanghai: Ch'ün i ch'u-pan she.
羽書集。

1949. Chung Su wen-hua chih chiao-liu. Peking: Sheng-huo, tu-shu, hsin chih san lien shu-tien.
中蘇文化之交流。

1950. Kuo Mo-jo *et al*. Jen-min yin-yueh chia Hsien Hsing-hai. Shanghai: Hsin hua shu-tien.
郭沫若等。人民音樂家冼星海。

1950. Kuan-yü wen-hua chiao-yü kung-tso te pao-kao (ed. by Hsin hua shih-shih ts'ung-k'an she). Peking: Hsin hua shu-tien.
關於文化教育工作的報告。新華時事叢刊社。

1950. Kuo Mo-jo *et al*. Lu Hsün hsien-sheng hsiao le (ed. by Su Tung). Hong Kong: Ta-chung t'u-shu kung-ssu.
郭沫若等。魯迅先生笑了。蘇東。

1951. Kuo Mo-jo hsuan-chi. Peking: K'ai-ming shu-tien. 2 vols.
郭沫若選集。

1952. Ch'ü Yuan wu mu shih chü. Peking: Jen-min wen-hsueh ch'u-pan she.
屈原五幕史劇。

1952. Nu-li chih shih-tai. Shanghai: Hsin wen-i ch'u-pan she.
奴隸制時代。

1953. Hsin hua sung. Peking: Jen-min wen-hsueh ch'u-pan she.
新華頌。

1953. Kuo Mo-jo *et al*. K'ang Mei yuan Ch'ao shih-hsuan (ed. by Jen-min wen-hsueh ch'u-pan she pien-chi pu). Peking: Jen-min wen-hsueh ch'u-pan she.
郭沫若等。抗美援朝詩選。人民文學出版社編輯部。

1953. Mao Tse-tung te ch'i-chih ying-feng p'iao-yang. Peking: Jen-min wen-hsueh ch'u-pan she.
毛澤東的旗幟迎風飄揚。

1954. Chu. Shanghai: Hsin wen-i ch'u-pan she.
筑。

1954. Kuo Mo-jo *et al*. Chung-kuo wen-tzu p'in-yin hua wen-t'i (ed. by Chung-kuo yü-wen tsa-chih she). Shanghai: Chung-hua shu-chü.

郭沫若等。中國文字拼音化問題。中國語
文雜誌社。

1954. T'ang ti chih hua. Shanghai: Hsin wen-
i ch'u-pan she.
棠棣之花。

1955. Kuo Mo-jo *et al*. Chung-kuo jen-lei hua-
shih te fa-hsien yü yen-chiu; Chung-kuo yuan-
jen ti-i ko t'ou-kai-ku fa-hsien erh-shih-wu
chou-nien chi-nien-hui pao-kao chuan-chi.
(ed. by Chung-kuo k'o-hsueh-yuan ku chi-
ch'ui tung-wu yen-chiu shih). Peking: K'o-
hsueh ch'u-pan she.
郭沫若等。中國人類化石的發現與研究；
中國猿人第一個頭蓋骨發現二十五周年紀
念會報告專集。中國科學院古脊椎動物研
究室。

1955. Pao chien chi. Shanghai.
抱箭集。

1956. (tr.) Mo-jo i shih chi. Peking: Jen-min
wen-hsueh ch'u-pan she.
沫若譯詩集。

1956. Mo-jo tzu-chuan. Shanghai: Hsin wen-i
ch'u-pan she. 2 vols.
沫若自傳。

1956. Tsai she-hui chu-i ko-ming kao-ch'ao chung
chih-shih fen-tzu te shih-ming (1956 nien 1
yueh 31 jih tsai Chung-kuo jen-min cheng-
chih hsieh-shang hui-i ti-erh chieh ch'üan-kuo
wei-yuan-hui ti-erh tz'u ch'üan-t'i hui-i shang
te pao-kao). Peking: Jen-min ch'u-pan she.
在社會主義革命高潮中知識分子的使命
(1956年1月31日在中國人民政治協商會議
第二屆全國委員會第二次全体會議上的報
告)。

1957-63. Mo-jo wen-chi. Hong Kohg: Sheng-
huo, tu-shu, hsin chih san lien shu-tien. 17
vols.
沫若文集。

1959. Ch'ang ch'un chi. Peking: Jen-min jih-
pao ch'u-pan she.
長春集。

1959. (ed.) Hung ch'i ko-yao. with Chou Yang.
Peking: Hung ch'i tsa-chih she.
紅旗歌謠。周揚。

1959. Ts'ai Wen-chi. Peking: Wen-wu ch'u-pan
she.
蔡文姬。

1961. Chung-kuo li-shih chü hsuan. with T'ien
Han. Hong Kong: Shanghai shu-tien.
中國歷史劇選。田漢。

1961. Ts'an ch'un. Hong Kong: Tung-ya shu-
chü.
殘春。

1961. Wen shih lun-chi. Peking: Jen-min ch'u-
pan she.
文史論集。

1962. Kuo Mo-jo *et al*. Ts'ao Ts'ao lun-chi. Peking: Sheng-huo, tu-shu, hsin chih san-lien
shu-tien.
郭沫若等。曹操論集。

1962. Mo-jo tzu hsuan chi. Hong Kong: Hsin-
yueh ch'u-pan she.
沫若自選集。

1962. Tu sui yuan shih-hua cha-chi. Peking:
Tso-chia ch'u-pan she.
讀隨園詩話札記。

1963. Tung feng chi. Peking: Tso-chia ch'u-
pan she.
東風集。

1963. Wu Tse-t'ien. Peking: Chung-kuo hsi-
chü ch'u-pan she.
武則天。

Kuo Mo-jo *et al*. Chung-kuo ho-p'ing chih yin
(ed. by Wen-hua ch'u-pan she). Peking: Wen-
hua ch'u-pan she.
郭沫若等。中國和平之音。文化出版社。

Kuo Mo-jo ming-tso hsuan-chi (ed. by Ch'en
Lei). Hong Kong: Nan-yang t'u-shu ch'u-pan
kung-ssu.
郭沫若名作選集。陳磊。

Tsai hung-cha chung lai ch'ü.
在轟炸中來去。

Kuo Mo-jo *et al*. Yu Jih-pen hui-lai le. Hong
Kong: San kuang t'u-shu kung-ssu.
郭沫若等。由日本回來了。

SOURCES

Ch'ien Hsing-ts'un. Hsien-tai Chung-kuo wen-
hsueh tso-chia; ti-i chüan. Shanghai: T'ai-
tung shu-chü, 1929.
錢杏邨。現代中國文學作家；第一卷。

HMTT
Kuo Mo-jo. Mo-jo tzu-chuan. Shanghai: Hsin
wen-i ch'u-pan she, 1956. 2 vols.
郭沫若。沫若自傳。

———. Wo-te yu-nien. Kuang-hua shu-chü,
1929.
郭沫若。我的幼年。

Kuo Mo-jo p'ing-chuan, ed. by Li Lin. Shanghai: Mei ch'eng shu-chü, 1936.
郭沫若評傳。李霖。

Living China: Modern Chinese Short Stories,
comp. and ed. by Edgar Snow. New York:
John Day & Reynal & Hitchcock, 1936.

MMT
Shih Chien (pseud. of Ma Pin). Kuo Mo-jo p'i-

Kuo Mo-jo

p'an. Hong Kong: Ya-chou ch'u-pan she, 1954.

史劍 (馬彬)。郭沫若批判。

Yin Ch'en (pseud. of Chin Tsu-t'ung). Kuo Mo-jo kuei kuo pi chi.

殷塵 (金祖同)。郭沫若歸國秘記。

Kuo Ping-wen   郭秉文

WORKS

1909-10. ed. of *Wooster Voice.*

1914. The Chinese System of Public Education. New York: Teachers College, Columbia University.

1924. (ed.) Webster's Collegiate Dictionary with Chinese Translation. with S. L. Chang *et al.* Shanghai: Commercial Press.

ed. of *Chinese Students' Monthly.*

(ed.) A Practical English Chinese Dictionary.

SOURCES

Persons interviewed: not to be identified.

Chung-hua Min-kuo ta-hsueh chih, ed. by Chung-kuo hsin-wen ch'u-pan kung-ssu. Taipei: Chung-kuo hsin-wen ch'u-pan kung-ssu, 1953.

中華民國大學誌。中國新聞出版公司。

WWC, 1931.

Kuo T'ai-ch'i   郭泰琪

WORKS

1910, December. "The Patriotism of the Future." *The Chinese Students' Monthly.*

1912, February. "The Chinese Revolution." *The Chinese Students' Monthly.*

1920, January. "China's Fight for Democracy." *The Chinese Students' Monthly.*

1935, January. "Interaction of China and the West." *People's Tribune,* 6: 73.

1935, May. "China's Responsibility in Asia." *People's Tribune,* 6: 537.

1935, July. "China's Progress and China's Needs." *Asiatic Review,* 31: 532-37.

ed. of *Pennsylvanian.*

SOURCES

Barrett, R. T. "Chinese Ambassador on the War, Interview with Quo Tai-chi." *Great Britain and the East,* January 27, 1938.

BKL
CH

Chang Ch'i-yün. Tang shih kai-yao. Taipei: Chung-yang kai-tsao wei-yuan-hui wen-wu kung-ying she, 1951-52. 5 vols.

張其昀。黨史概要。

CTMC

The International Who's Who, 1951.

Kuo wen chou-pao, IV-29, 31, 49.

國聞週報。

Levi, Werner. Modern China's Foreign Policy. Minneapolis: University of Minnesota Press, 1953.

The New York Times, April 10, 13, 1927; December 15, 1927; April 25, 1934; January 29, 1938; April 22, 1939; February 16, 1940; December 11, 1941; August 20, 1942; June 28, 1946; March 1, 1952.

SMJ

TCMT

Wai-chiao ta tz'u-tien, ed. by Wai-chiao hsueh-hui. Hong Kong: Chung-hua shu-chü, 1937.

外交大辭典。外交學會。

WWARS

WWC, 1925, 1931.

WWMC

Lao Nai-hsuan   勞乃宣

WORKS

1886. Ku ch'ou suan k'ao shih. Wan-hsien kuan-she. 4 vols.

古籌祘考釋。

1889. Hsü ku ch'ou-suan k'ao shih.

續古籌算考釋。

1891. Ko kuo yueh chang tsuan yao.

各國約章纂要。

1897. Ch'ou-suan ch'ien-shih. Ch'ing-yuan. 2 vols.

籌算淺釋。

1899. I-ho-ch'üan chiao-men yuan-liu k'ao.

義和拳教門源流考。

1907. Chien tzu wu chung. Nanking. 5 vols.

簡字五種。

1907. Ch'üan an san chung. 2 vols.

拳案三種。

1910? (comp.) Hsin hsing-lü hsiu-cheng-an hui-lu.

新刑律修正案彙錄。

1927. T'ung-hsiang lao hsien-sheng i-kao. 6 vols.

桐鄉勞先生遺稿。

1957. Chien tzu p'u lu. Peking: Wen-tzu kai-ko ch'u-pan she.

簡字譜錄。

Chou-i tsun ch'eng. Tsingtao. 10 vols.
周易遵程。

German tr. by Richard Wilhelm, *I Ging, das Buch der Wandlungen*. Jena: Eugen Diederichs, 1924?.

Ch'üan an san chung.
拳案三種。

Ch'üan chiao hsi i shuo.
拳教析疑說。

Tu-yin chien-tzu t'ung p'u.
讀音簡字通譜。

SOURCES

De Francis, John F. Nationalism and Language Reform in China. Princeton: Princeton University Press, 1950.

K'o Shao-min. "Kao-shou kuang-lu-tai-fu Lao kung mu-chih-ming," in Lao Nai-hsuan, *T'ung-hsiang Lao hsien-sheng i-kao*. 1927. 6 vols.
柯劭忞。誥授光錄大夫勞公墓誌銘。勞乃宣。桐鄉勞先生遺稿。

Lang, Erwin. Hoffnung auf China. Wien: Haybach Verlag, 1922.

Lao Nai-hsuan. "Jen-sou tzu ting nien-p'u," in Lao Nai-hsuan, *T'ung-hsiang Lao hsien-sheng i-kao*. 1927. 6 vols.
勞乃宣。靭叟自訂年譜。勞乃宣。桐鄉勞先生遺稿。

Meijer, Marinus Johan. The Introduction of Modern Criminal Law in China. Batavia: De Unie, 1950.

PCCP

Purcell, Victor. The Boxer Uprising: A Background Study. Cambridge: Cambridge University Press, 1963.

Tan, Chester C. The Boxer Catastrophe. New York: Columbia University Press, 1955.

Wilhelm, Richard. I Ging, das Buch der Wandlungen. Jena: Eugen Diederichs Verlag, 1924?.

———. Die Seele Chinas. Berlin: Reimar Hobbing, 1926.

Wilhelm, Salome. Richard Wilhelm, Geistige Mitteln zwischen China und Europa. Dusseldorf: Eugen Diederichs Verlag, 1956.

Lei Hai-tsung　　雷海宗
WORKS

1927. "The Political Ideas of Turgot." Unpublished Ph. D. dissertation, University of Chicago.

1934. (ed.) Chung-kuo t'ung-shih hsuan-tu. 6 vols.
中國通史選讀。

1940. Chung-kuo wen-hua yü Chung-kuo te ping. Changsha: Shang-wu yin shu kuan.
中國文化與中國的兵。

1946. Wen-hua hsing-t'ai shih-kuan. with Lin T'ung-chi. Shanghai: Ta tung shu-chü.
文化形態史觀。林同濟。

Huang-ti chih-tu chih ch'eng-li. Peking: Tsing-hua ta-hsueh.
皇帝制度之成立。

SOURCES

Persons interviewed: not to be identified.

Lei Ming-yuan　　雷鳴遠
WORKS

1910. She-hui-hsueh chiang-i.
社會學講義。

1912-? ed. of *Kuang i lu*.
廣益錄。

ed. of *Kuang i pao*.
廣義報。

SOURCES

Fang Hao. "Lei ku ssu-to Ming-yuan shih-lueh," in Fang Hao, *Fang Hao wen-lu*. Peiping: Shang chih pien i kuan, 1948.
方豪。雷故司鐸鳴遠事略。方豪。方豪文錄。

Goffart, Sohier A. Lettres du père Lebbe. Tournai, 1960.

De Jaegher, Raymond. Vincent Lebbe. Louvain, 1953.

Leclerq, Jacques. Vie du père Lebbe. Paris, 1953.

Legrand, F. "A Life of Father Lebbe." *Christ to the World*, I-2.

Levaux, Leopold. Le Père Lebbe, Apôtre de la Chine Moderne. Brussels, 1948.

Ma Liang. Ma Hsiang-po hsien-sheng wei-chi (comp. by Fang Hao). Peiping: Shang chih pien i kuan, 1947.
馬良。馬相伯先生文集。方豪。

———. Ma Hsiang-po hsien-sheng wen-chi hsü-pien (comp. by Fang Hao). Peiping: Shang chih pien i kuan, 1948.
馬良。馬相伯先生文集續編。方豪。

T'ang Huai-yuan. "Lei shen-fu ts'an-chia k'ang-chan shih-mo chi." *I shih pao*. Chungking, November 29, 1940.

唐淮源。雷神父參加抗戰始末記。 益世報。

Wei, Louis Tsing-sing. La Politique Missionaire de la France en Chine 1842–1856: L'ouverture des Cinq Ports Chinois au Commercé Étranger et la Liberté Religieuse. Paris: Nouvelles Editions Latines, 1960.

Li Chao-lin 李兆麟

SOURCES

Chung-kuo hsin min-chu chu-i ko-ming shih ts'an-k'ao tzu-liao, ed. by Hu Hua, Tai I, Yen Ch'i. Shanghai: Shang-wu yin shu kuan, 1951.

中國新民主主義革命史參考資料。 胡華, 戴逸, 彥奇。

CKLC

Shih Ch'eng Chih. Lun Chung-kung te chün-shih fa-chan. Kowloon: Yu lien ch'u-pan she, 1952.

史誠之。 論中共的軍事發展。

Li Chi 李濟

WORKS

1925. "Yu lan." Ch'ing-hua hsueh-pao, II-2.
幽蘭。 清華學報。

1927. Hsi-yin-ts'un shih-ch'ien te i ts'un. Peking: Ch'ing-hua hsueh-hsiao.
西陰村史前的遺存。

1928. The Formation of the Chinese People: An Anthropological Inquiry. Cambridge: Harvard University Press.

1929. "Hsiao-t'un ti-mien hsia ch'ing-hsing fen-hsi ch'u-pu pao-kao," in Li Chi et al., An-yang fa-chueh pao-kao, 1. Peiping: Kuo-li chung-yang yen-chiu-yuan li-shih yü-yen yen-chiu so.
小屯地面下情形分析初步報告。 李濟等。 安陽發掘報告。

1929. "Yin Shang t'ao-ch'i ch'u lun," in Li Chi et al., An-yang fa-chueh pao-kao, 1. Peiping: Kuo-li chung-yang yen-chiu-yuan li-shih yü-yen yen-chiu so.
殷商陶器初論。 李濟等。 安陽發掘報告。

1929–33. Li Chi et al. (ed.) Án-yang fa-chueh pao-kao; ti-i ch'i chih ti-ssu ch'i. Peiping, Shanghai: Kuo-li chung-yang yen-chiu-yuan li-shih yü-yen yen-chiu so. 4 vols.
李濟等。 安陽發掘報告; 第一期至第四期。

1930. "Hsiao-t'un yü Yang-shao," in Li Chi et al., An-yang fa-chueh pao-kao, 2. Peiping: Kuo-li chung-yang yen-chiu-yuan li-shih yü-yen yen-chiu so.
小屯與仰韶。 李濟等。 安陽發掘報告。

1930. "Hsien-tai k'ao-ku hsueh yü Yin hsü fa-chueh," in Li Chi et al., An-yang fa-chueh pao-kao, 2. Peiping: Kuo-li chung-yang yen-chiu-yuan li-shih yü-yen yen-chiu so.
現代考古學與殷墟發掘。 李濟等。 安陽發掘報告。

1930. "Min-kuo shih-pa nien ch'iu-chi fa-chueh Yin hsü chih ching-kuo chi ch'i chung-yao fa-hsien," in Li Chi et al., An-yang fa-chueh pao-kao, 2. Peiping: Kuo-li chung-yang yen-chiu-yuan li-shih yü-yen yen-chiu so.
民國十八年秋季發掘殷墟之經過及其重要發現。 李濟等。 安陽發掘報告。

1931. "Fa-chueh Lung-shan Ch'eng-tzu-yai te li-yu chi ch'eng-chi." Shantung sheng-li t'u-shu-kuan chi-k'an, I-1.
發掘龍山城子崖的理由及成績。 山東省立圖書館季刊。

1931. "Fu shen tsang," in Li Chi et al., An-yang fa-chueh pao-kao, 3. Peiping: Chung-yang yen-chiu-yuan li-shih yü-yen yen-chiu-so.
俯身葬。 李濟等。 安陽發掘報告。

1932. (ed., tr.) Manchuria in History; a Summary. Peiping: Peking Union Bookstore.

1933. "An-yang tsui-chin fa-chueh pao-kao chi liu-tz'u kung-tso chih tsung ku-chi," in Li Chi et al., An-yang fa-chueh pao-kao, 4. Shanghai: Kuo-li chung-yang yen-chiu-yuan li-shih yü-yen yen-chiu so.
安陽最近發掘報告及六次工作之總估計。 李濟等。 安陽發掘報告。

1934. "Chung-kuo k'ao-ku hsueh chih kuo-ch'ü yü chiang-lai." Tung-fang tsa-chih, XXXI-7.
中國考古學之過去與將來。 東方雜誌。

1934. "Chung-kuo k'ao-ku pao-kao chi—Ch'eng-tzu-yai pao-kao hsü," in Fu Ssu-nien et al., Ch'eng-tzu-yai; Shantung Li-ch'eng hsien Lung-shan chen hei-t'ao wen-hua i-chih. Nanking: Kuo-li chung-yang yen-chiu-yuan li-shih yü-yen yen-chiu so.
中國考古報告集—城子崖報告序。 傅斯年等。 城子崖; 山東歷城縣龍山鎮黑陶文化遺址。

1941. "Min-tsu hsueh fa-chan chih ch'ien-t'u yü pi-chiao fa ying-yung chih hsien-chih." Kuo-li Yunnan ta-hsueh she-hui k'o-hsueh hsueh-pao, I.
民族學發展之前途與比較法應用之限制。 國立雲南大學社會科學學報。

1944. "Hsiao-t'un ti-mien hsia te hsien Yin wen-hua ts'eng." *Chung-yang yen-chiu-yuan hsueh-shu hui-k'an*, I-2.
小屯地面下的先殷文化層。 中央研究院學術匯刊。

1945–46. Li Chi *et al*. Liu t'ung pieh lu. Li-chuang, Szechwan: Kuo-li chung-yang yen-chiu-yuan li-shih yü-yen yen-chiu-so. 3 vols.
李濟 等。 六同別錄。

1948. "Yen-chiu Chung-kuo ku yü wen-t'i te hsin tzu-liao." *Chung-yang yen-chiu-yuan li-shih yü-yen yen-chiu-so chi-k'an*, 13.
研究中國古玉問題的新資料。 中央研究院歷史語言研究所集刊。

1948–49. "Chi Hsiao-t'un ch'u-t'u te ch'ing-t'ung ch'i." *Chung-kuo k'ao-ku hsueh-pao*, 3–4.
記小屯出土的青銅器。 中國考古學報。

1950. "Chung-hua min-tsu chih shih." *Ta-lu tsa-chih*, I-1.
中華民族之始。 大陸雜誌。

1950. "Chung-kuo ku ch'i-wu hsueh te hsin chi-ch'u." *Kuo-li Taiwan ta-hsueh wen-shih che-hsueh pao*, 1.
中國古器物學的新基礎。 國立台灣大學文史哲學報。

1950. "Jui-yen min-tsu hsueh tiao-ch'a ch'u-pu pao-kao—t'i-chih." *Taiwan sheng wen-hsien wei-yuan-hui wen-hsien chuan-k'an*, 2.
瑞岩民族學調查初步報告一體質。 台灣省文獻委員會文獻專刊。

1950. "Yü-pei ch'u-t'u ch'ing-t'ung kou ping fen-lei t'u-chieh." *Chung-yang yen-chiu-yuan li-shih yü-yen yen-chiu-so chi-k'an*, 22.
豫北出土青銅勾兵分類圖解。 中央研究院歷史語言研究所集刊。

1951. "Chih-te ch'ing-nien hsiao-fa te Fu Meng-chen hsien-sheng." *Tzu-yu Chung-kuo*, IV-1.
值得青年效法的傅孟眞先生。 自由中國。

1951. "Chung-kuo shih ch'ien wen-hua." *Ta-lu tsa-chih*, II-11.
中國史前文化。 大陸雜誌。

1951. "Ts'ung jen-lei hsueh k'an wen-hua." *Ta-lu tsa-chih*, III-11.
從人類學看文化。 大陸雜誌。

1952. "Chi Hsiao-t'un ch'u-t'u chih ch'ing-t'ung ch'i—chung p'ien—feng jen ch'i." *Kuo-li Taiwan ta-hsueh wen-shih che-hsueh pao*, 4.
記小屯出土之青銅器一中篇一鋒刃器。 國立台灣大學文史哲學報。

1952. "Hsiao-t'un t'ao-ch'i chih-liao chih hua-hsueh fen-hsi," in Taiwan ta-hsueh Fu ku hsiao-chang chi-nien lun-wen chi pien-chi wei-yuan-hui, *Fu ku hsiao-chang Ssu-nien hsien-sheng chi-nien lun-wen chi*. Taipei: Kuo-li Taiwan ta-hsueh.
小屯陶器質料之化學分析。 台灣大學傅故校長紀念論文集編輯委員會。 傅故校長斯年先生紀念論文集。

1952. "Kuan-yü T'ai-ta k'ao-ku jen-lei hsueh-hsi chih ch'uang-she." *T'ai-ta wen-tse*, I-4.
關於台大考古人類學系之創設。 台大文摘。

1952. "Peking jen te fa-hsien yü yen-chiu chih ching-kuo." *Ta-lu tsa-chih*, V-7.
北京人的發現與研究之經過。 大陸雜誌。

1952. "Peking jen te t'i-chih yü sheng-huo." *Ta-lu tsa-chih*, V-10.
北京人的体質與生活。 大陸雜誌。

1952. "Yin hsü yu jen shih-ch'i t'u-shuo." *Chung-yang yen-chiu-yuan li-shih yü-yen yen-chiu-so chi-k'an*, 23.
殷墟有刃石器圖說。 中央研究院歷史語言研究所集刊。

1953. "K'ao-ku jen-lei hsueh-k'an fa-k'an-tz'u." *Kuo-li Taiwan ta-hsueh k'ao-ku jen-lei hsueh-k'an*, 1.
考古人類學刊發刊詞。 國立台灣大學考古人類學刊。

1953. "Kuan-yü tsai Chung-kuo ju-ho t'ui-chin k'o-hsueh ssu-hsiang te chi-ko wen-t'i." *Tzu-yu Chung-kuo*, IX-9.
關於在中國如何推進科學思想的幾個問題。 自由中國。

1953. "Kuei tso tun chü yü chi chü." *Chung-yang yen-chiu-yuan li-shih yü-yen yen-chiu-so chi-k'an*, 24.
跪坐蹲踞與箕踞。 中央研究院歷史語言研究所集刊。

1953. "T'ai-p'ing-yang k'o-hsueh hui-i te hsing-chih yü ch'eng-chiu." *Chung-kuo i chou*, 191.
太平洋科學會議的性質與成就。 中國一週。

1954. "Chung-kuo shang-ku shih chih ch'ung-chien kung-tso chi ch'i wen-t'i." *Min-chu p'ing-lun*, V-4.
中國上古史之重建工作及其問題。 民主評論。

1954. "Ju-ho pan k'o-hsueh kuan." *Chung-kuo i chou*, 211.
如何辦科學館。 中國一週。

1954. "Notes on Some Metrical Characters of Calvaria of the Shang Dynasty Excavated from Houchiachuang, Anyang." *Annals of Academia Sinica*, 1.

1954. "Taiwan ta-hsueh hsien-hsing chao-sheng pan-fa chih shang-chueh." *Tzu-yu Chung-kuo*, X-9.
台灣大學現行招生辦法之商榷。 自由中國。

1954. "T'ai-p'ing-yang k'o-hsueh hui-i." *Ta-lu tsa-chih*, VIII-4.

太平洋科學會議。大陸雜誌。

1954, April 23. "Ts'ung Chung-kuo yuan ku shih te chi ko wen-t'i t'an ch'i." *Chung-yang jih-pao*. Taipei.

從中國遠古史的幾各問題談起。中央日報。

1955. "Diverse Backgrounds of the Decorative Arts of Yin Dynasty." *Annals of Academia Sinica*, 2.

1955. "The Importance of Anyang Discoveries in Prefacing Known Chinese History with a New Chapter." *Annals of Academia Sinica*, 2.

1956. Hsiao-t'un t'ao-ch'i. Taipei.

小屯陶器。

1956. "Tui-yü Ting Wen-chiang so t'i-ch'ang te k'o-hsueh yen-chiu chi tuan hui-i." *Chung-yang yen-chiu-yuan yuan-k'an*, 3.

對於丁文江所提倡的科學研究幾段回憶。中央研究院院刊。

1956. Yin hsü ch'i-wu, chia pien: T'ao-ch'i, shang chi. Nan-kang, Taiwan: Chung-yang yen-chiu-yuan li-shih yü-yen yen-chiu-so.

殷墟器物，甲編：陶器，上輯。

1956. "Yin hsü t'ao-ch'i yen-chiu pao-kao hsü." *Kuo-li Taiwan ta-hsueh k'ao-ku jen-lei hsueh-k'an*, 8.

殷墟陶器研究報告序。國立台灣大學考古人類學刊。

1956, August 5. "Chui-ch'iu chen-li ying-kai ts'ung jen-shih tzu-chi shen-t'i tso ch'i." *Chung-yang jih-pao*. Taipei.

論追眞理應該從認識自己身體作起。中央日報。

1956, October 2. "Shih lun Chung-kuo wen-hua te yuan-shih." *Chung-yang jih-pao*. Taipei.

試論中國文化的原始。中央日報。

1956, December 18. "Jen chih ch'u." *Chung-yang jih-pao*. Taipei.

人之初。中央日報。

1957. The Beginnings of Chinese Civilization. Seattle: University of Washington Press.

1957. "Lun Tao-sen shih, hsiao jen an-chien chi yuan-shih tzu-liao chih chien-ting yü ch'u-li." *Hsien-tai hsueh-shu chi-k'an*, I-2.

論道森氏，曉人案件及原始資料之鑒定與處理。現代學術季刊。

1957. "Yin hsü pai-t'ao fa-chan chih ch'eng-hsü." *Chung-yang yen-chiu-yuan li-shih yü-yen yen-chiu-so chi-k'an*, 28.

殷墟白陶發展之程序。中央研究院歷史語言研究所集刊。

1958. "Yu pien hsing yen-pien so k'an-chien te Hsiao-t'un i-chih ho Hou-chia-chuang mu tsang chih shih-tai kuan-hsi." *Chung-yang yen-chiu-yuan li-shih yü-yen yen-chiu-so chi-k'an*, 29.

由笄形演變所看見的小屯遺址和候家莊墓葬之時代關係。中央研究院歷史語言研究所集刊。

1959. "Pien hsing pa lei chi ch'i wen-shih chih yen-pien. *Chung-yang yen-chiu-yuan li-shih yü-yen yen-chiu-so chi-k'an*, 30.

笄形八類及其文飾之演變。中央研究院歷史語言研究所集刊。

1959. "Wen-hua sha-mo." *Tzu-yu Chung-kuo*, XXI-10.

文化沙漠。自由中國。

1959. "Yin hsü chien-chu i ts'un pao-kao hsü." *Tzu-yu Chung-kuo*, XXI-9.

殷墟建築遺存報告序。自由中國。

1960. "Tung-ya hsueh-shu yen-chiu chi-hua wei-yuan-hui kuo-chi hui-i k'ai-hui tz'u." *Kuo-li Taiwan ta-hsueh k'ao-ku jen-lei hsueh-k'an*, 15, 16.

東亞學術研究計劃委員會國際會議開會辭。國立台灣大學考古人類學刊。

1961. "Wo yü Chung-kuo k'ao-ku kung-tso." *Hsin shih-tai*, ch'uang k'an hao.

我與中國考古工作。新時代。

1962. "Chinese People (Chung-kuo min-tsu)." *Kuo-li Taiwan ta-hsueh k'ao-ku jen-lei hsueh-k'an*, 19, 20.

(中國民族)。國立台灣大學考古學人類學刊。

1962. "Tsai t'an Chung-kuo shang-ku shih te ch'ung-chien wen-t'i." *Chung-yang yen-chiu-yuan li-shih yü-yen yen-chiu so chi-k'an*, 33.

再談中國上古史的重建問題。中央研究院歷史語言研究所集刊。

1962. "Wo tsai Mei-kuo te ta-hsueh sheng-huo." *Chuan-chi wen-hsueh*, I-5, 6.

我在美國的大學生活。傳記文學。

1963. "Hei-t'ao wen-hua tsai Chung-kuo shang-ku shih chung so chan te ti-wei." *Kuo-li Taiwan ta-hsueh k'ao-ku jen-lei hsueh-k'an*, 21, 22.

黑陶文化在中國上古史中所佔的地位。國立台灣大學考古人類學刊。

1963. "Yin Shang shih-tai chuang-shih i-shu yen-chiu chih i—pi-chiao ku hsing ch'i te hua-wen so yin ch'i te chi ko wen-t'i." *Chung-yang yen-chiu-yuan li-shih yü-yen yen-chiu so chi k'an*, 34.

殷商時代裝飾藝術研究之一——比較觚形器的花紋所引起的幾個問題。中央研究院歷史語言研究所季刊。

1964. "Nan-yang Tung Tso-pin hsien-sheng yü chin-tai k'ao-ku hsueh." *Chuan-chi wen-hsueh*, IV-3.

南洋董作賓先生與近代考古學。傳記文學。

1964. "Yin Shang shih-tai ch'ing-t'ung chi-shu
te ti-ssu chung feng-ko." *Chung-yang yen-chiu-yuan li-shih yü-yen yen-chiu so chi k'an*, 35.
殷商時代青銅技術的第四種風格。

1965. "Hsiang-hsiang te li-shih yü chen-shih te
li-shih chih pi-chiao." *Hsin shih-tai*, V-9.
想像的歷史與眞實的歷史的比較。新時代。

1965. "'Peking jen' te fa-hsien yü yen-chiu chi
ch'i so yin-ch'i chih wen-t'i." *Kuo-li Taiwan
ta-hsueh wen shih che-hsueh pao*, 14.
「北京人」的發現與研究及其所引起之問題。
國立台灣大學文史哲學報。

1966. "Ju-ho yen-chiu Chung-kuo ch'ing-t'ung
ch'i." *Ku-kung chi-k'an*, I-1.
如何研究中國青銅器。故宮季刊。

1967. Kan chiu lu. Taipei: Chuan-chi wen-
hsueh ch'u-pan she.
感舊錄。

1967. "Wo-te ch'u-hsueh shih-tai." *Chuan-chi
wen-hsueh*, XI-III.
我的初學時代。傳記文學。

ed. of *Chung-yang yen-chiu-yuan yuan-k'an*.
中央研究院院刊。

SOURCES

An-yang fa-chueh pao-kao; ti-i ch'i chih ti-ssu
ch'i, ed. by Li Chi *et al.* Peiping, Shanghai:
Kuo-li chung-yang yen-chiu-yuan li-shih yü-
yen yen-chiu-so, 1929-33. 4 vols.
安陽發掘報告;第一期至第四期。李濟等。

Fu Ssu-nien *et al.* Ch'eng-tzu-yai; Shantung Li-
ch'eng hsien Lung-shan chen hei-t'ao wen-hua
i-chih. Nanking: Kuo-li chung-yang yen-
chiu-yuan li-shih yü-yen yen-chiu-so, 1934.
傅斯年等。城子崖;山東歷城縣龍山鎮黑
陶文化遺址。

Li Chi. The Beginnings of Chinese Civilization.
Seattle: University of Washington Press, 1957.

——. "Chi Hsiao-t'un ch'u-t'u te ch'ing-t'ung
ch'i." *Chung-kuo k'ao-ku hsueh-pao*, 3-4 (1948-
49).
李濟。記小屯出土的青銅器。中國考古學報。

——. "Chung-kuo ku ch'i-wu hsueh te hsin
chi-ch'u." *Kou-li Taiwan ta-hsueh wen shih che
hsueh-pao*, 1 (1950).
李濟。中國古器物學的新基礎。國立台灣
大學文史哲學報。

——. "Chung-kuo shang-ku shih chih ch'ung-
chien kung-tso chi ch'i wen-t'i." *Min-chu
p'ing-lun*, V-4 (1954).
李濟。中國上古史之重建工作及其問題。
民主評論。

Li Chi. The Formation of the Chinese People;
An Anthropological Inquiry. Cambridge:
Harvard University Press, 1928.

——. Hsi-yin-ts'un shih-ch'ien te i ts'un.
Peking: Ch'ing-hua hsueh-hsiao, 1927.
李濟。西陰村史前的遺存。

——. "Hsiao-t'un t'ao-ch'i chih-liao chih
hua-hsueh fen-hsi," in Taiwan ta-hsueh Fu
ku hsiao-chang chi-nien lun-wen chi pien-chi
wei-yuan-hui, *Fu ku hsiao-chang Ssu-nien hsien-
sheng chi-nien lun-wen chi*. Taipei: Kuo-li
Taiwan ta-hsueh, 1952.
李濟。小屯陶器質料之化學分析。台灣大
學傅故校長紀念論文集編輯委員會。傅故
校長斯年先生紀念論文集。

——. "Hsiao-t'un ti-mien hsia te hsien Yin
wen-hua ts'eng." *Chung-yang Yen-chiu-yuan
hsueh-shu hui-k'an*, I-2 (1944).
李濟。小屯地面下的先殷文化層。中央研
究院學術匯刊。

——. "Kuei tso tun chü yü chi chü." *Chung-
yang yen-chiu-yuan li-shih yü-yen yen-chiu-so chi-
k'an*, 24 (1953).
李濟。跪坐蹲踞與箕踞。中央研究院歷史
語言研究所集刊。

——. "Tsai t'an Chung-kuo shang-ku shih te
ch'ung-chien wen-t'i." *Hsin shih-tai*, II-2
(1962).
李濟。再談中國上古史的重建問題。新時
代。

——. "Tui-yü Ting Wen-chiang so t'i-ch'ang
te k'o-hsueh yen-chiu chi tuan hui-i." *Chung-
yang yen-chiu-yuan yuan-k'an*, 3 (1956).
李濟。對於丁文江所提倡的科學研究幾段
回憶。中央研究院院刊。

——. "Yen-chiu Chung-kuo ku yü wen-t'i te
hsin tzu-liao." *Chung-yang yen-chiu-yuan li-shih
yü-yen yen-chiu-so chi-k'an*, 13 (1948).
李濟。研究中國古玉問題的新資料。中央
研究院歷史語言研究所集刊。

——. Yin hsü ch'i-wu, chia pien: T'ao-ch'i,
shang chi. Nan-kang, Taiwan: Chung-yang
yen-chiu-yuan li-shih yü-yen yen-chiu so,
1956.
李濟。殷墟器物,甲編:陶器,上輯。

——. "Yin hsü pai-t'ao fa-chan chih ch'eng-
hsü." *Chung-yang yen-chiu-yuan li-shih yü-yen
yen-chiu-so chi-k'an*, 28 (1957).
李濟。殷墟白陶發展之程序。中央研究院
歷史語言研究所集刊。

——. "Yin hsü yu jen shih-ch'i t'u-shuo."
*Chung-yang yen-chiu-yuan li-shih yü-yen yen-chiu-
so chi-k'an*, 23 (1952).

李濟。殷墟有刃石器圖說。中央研究院歷
史語言研究所集刊。

Li Chi. "Yü-pei ch'u-t'u ch'ing-t'ung kuo ping
fen-lei t'u-chieh." *Chung-yang yen-chiu-yuan
li-shih yü-yen yen-chiu-so chi-k'an*, 22 (1950).

李濟。豫北出土青銅勾兵分類圖解。中央
研究院歷史語言研究所集刊。

Wu Chin-ting. Prehistoric Pottery in China.
London: Kegan Paul, Trench, Trubner, 1938.

Li Chi-shen　李濟深

SOURCES

Persons interviewed: not to be identified.

Liang Sheng-chün. Chiang Li tou-cheng nei-mu.
Hong Kong: Ya lien ch'u-pan she, 1954.
梁升俊。蔣李鬥爭內幕。

New York Herald Tribune. New York, October
10, 1959.

Li Fang-kuei　李方桂

WORKS

1930. Mattole: An Athabaskan Language. Chicago: University of Chicago Press.

1933. "Ancient Chinese -ung, uk, -uong, -wok,
etc. in Archaic Chinese." *Bulletin of the Institute of History and Philology, Academia Sinica*,
3: 375-414.

1935. "Archaic Chinese -iwəng, -iwək and -wəg."
*Bulletin of the Institute of History and Philology,
Academia Sinica*, 5: 65-74.

1943. "The Hypothesis of a Pre-glottalized
Series of Consonants in Primitive Tai." *Bulletin of Institute of History and Philology, Academia Sinica*, 11: 177-88.

1944. "The Influence of the Primitive Tai
Glottal Stop and Pre-glottalized Consonants
on the Tone System of Po-ai." *Bulletin of
Chinese Studies*, 4: 59-68.

1945. "Some Ancient Loan Words in the Tai
Languages." *Harvard Journal of Asiatic Studies*,
8: 333-42.

1947. "Phonology of the Tai Dialect of Wu-
ming." *Bulletin of Institute of History and
Philology, Academia Sinica*, 12: 293-303.

1948. "The Distribution of Initials and Tones
in the Sui Language." *Language*, 24: 160-67.

1949. "Tones in the Riming System of the Sui
Language." *Word*, 5: 262-67.

1954. "Consonant Clusters in Tai." *Language*,
30: 368-79.

1955. "The Tibetan Inscription of the Sino-
Tibetan Treaty of 821-822." *T'oung pao*, 44:
1-99.

1956. "Siamese Wan and Waan." *Language*, 32:
81-82.

1956. "The Type of Noun Formation in Athabaskan and Eyak." *International Journal of
American Linguistics*, 22: 45-48.

1957. "The Jui Dialect of Po-ai and the Northern
Tai." *Bulletin of the Institute of History and
Philology, Academia Sinica*, 29: 315-22.

1957. "The Jui Dialect of Po-ai Phonology."
*Bulletin of the Institute of History and Philology,
Academia Sinica*, 28: 551-66.

1957. "Notes on Tibetan Sog." *Central Asian
Journal*, 3: 139-42.

1959. "Classification by Vocabulary: Tai Dialects." *Anthropological Linguistics*, I-2: 15-21.

1959. "Tibetan Glo-ba-'dring." *Studia Serica
Bernard Karlgren Dedicate.*

1960. "A Tentative Classification of Tai Dialects," in Stanley Diamond, *Culture in History,
Essays in Honor of Paul Radin.* New York:
Published for Brandeis University by Columbia University Press.

1961. A Sino-Tibetan Glossary from Tun-huang.
Leiden: E. J. Brill.

1962. "Initial and Tonal Development in the
Tai Dialects." *Bulletin of the Institute of History
and Philology, Academia Sinica*, 34: 31-36.

1964. "A Chipewyan Ethnological Text." *International Journal of American Linguistics*, 30: 132-
36.

1964. "The Phonemic System of the Tai Lu
Language." *Bulletin of Institute of History and
Philology, Academia Sinica*, 35: 7-14.

1965. "Some Problems in Comparative Athabaskan." *Canadian Journal of Linguistics*, 10:
129-34.

1965. "The Tai and the Kam-Sui Languages."
Lingua, 14.

1966. "Notes on the T'en (Yanghuang) Langu-
age; Part I; Introduction and Phonology."
*Bulletin of the Institute of History and Philology,
Academia Sinica*, 36: 419-26.

1966. "The Relationship Between Tones and
Initials in Tai," in Norman H. Zide, *Studies
in Comparative Austroasiatic Linguistics.*

ed. of the *International Journal of American Linguistics.*

"The Zero Initial and the Zero." *Syallabic*, 42: 300–2.

SOURCES

Persons interviewed: Isabella Yen; others not to be identified.

Li Fei-kan　李芾甘

WORKS

1926. Chih-chia-ko te ts'an-chü. San Francisco: Mei-chou p'ing she.
芝加哥的慘劇。

1928. Mien-pao lueh ch'ü. (tr. of P. Kropotkin's *Conquest of Bread*). Shanghai: Tzu-yu shu-tien.
麵包略取。

1928–29. Jen-sheng che-hsueh: Ch'i ch'i-yuan chi ch'i fa-chan. (tr.) Shanghai: Tzu-yu shu-tien. 2 vols.
人生哲學：其起源及其發展。

1929. Tuan-t'ou-t'ai shang. Shanghai: Tzu-yu.
斷頭台上。

1930. Ts'ung tzu-pen chu-i tao an-na-ch'i chu-i. (tr. of P. Kropotkin's *From Capitalism to Anarchism*). San Francisco: P'ing she.
從資本主義到安那其主義。

1933. Ch'un-t'ien li te ch'iu-t'ien. K'ai-ming shu-tien.
春天裡的秋天。

1934. Ch'en-mo. Shanghai: Sheng-huo shu-tien.
沉默。

1934. Chiang-chün. Shanghai: Sheng-huo shu-tien.
將軍。

1934–? ed. of *Wen-hsueh chi-k'an*.
文學季刊。

1935. Shen kuei jen. Wen-hua sheng-huo ch'u-pan she.
神鬼人。

1936. Ch'en lo. Shang-wu yin-shu kuan.
沉落。

1936. I. Shanghai: Wen-hua sheng-huo ch'u-pan she.
憶。

1936. Ma-sai ti yeh. Shanghai: Wen-hua sheng-huo ch'u-pan she.
馬賽底夜。

1936. Men-chien. (tr.) Shanghai: Wen-hua sheng-huo ch'u-pan she.
門檻。

1936. Pa Chin tuan-p'ien hsiao-shuo chi; ti-i chi. Shanghai: K'ai-ming shu-tien.
巴金短篇小說集；第一集。

1936. Pai niao chih ko. Shanghai: Wen-hua sheng-huo ch'u-pan she.
白鳥之歌。

1937. Ch'ang-sheng t'a. Shanghai: Wen-hua sheng-huo ch'u-pan she.
長生塔。

1937. Li Fei-kan *et al*. Lu Hsün yü K'ang Jih chan-cheng. Canton: Chan-shih ch'u-pan she.
李芾甘等。魯迅與抗日戰爭。

1937. Sha Ting. Shanghai: Wen-hua sheng-huo ch'u-pan she.
砂丁。

1937. Sheng chih ch'an-hui. Shang-wu yin shu kuan.
生之懺悔。

1937. Ya-li An-na. Shanghai: Wen-hua sheng-huo ch'u-pan she.
亞麗安娜。

1937. Yeh wei yang. (tr. of Leopold Kampf's *On the Eve*). Shanghai: Wen-hua sheng-huo ch'u-pan she.
夜未央。

1937. Yueh-yeh. Shanghai: Wen-hua sheng-huo ch'u-pan she.
月夜。

1939. Fa te ku-shih. Shanghai: Wen-hua sheng-huo ch'u-pan she.
髮的故事。

1939. Hai ti meng. K'ai-ming shu-tien.
海底夢。

1939. Hei t'u. Shanghai: Wen-hua sheng-huo ch'u-pan she.
黑土。

1939. (comp.) Hsi-pan-ya te shu-kuang. Shanghai: P'ing ming shu-tien.
西班牙的曙光。

1939. Hsin-sheng. K'ai-ming shu-tien.
新生。

1939. Meng-ya. Shanghai: Hsin sheng ch'u-pan she.
萌芽。

1939. Mieh-wang. Shanghai: K'ai-ming shu-tien.
滅亡。

1939. Ssu-ch'ü te t'ai-yang. Shanghai: K'ai-ming shu-tien.
死去的太陽。

1940. Hsueh. Shanghai: Wen-hua sheng-huo ch'u-pan she.
雪。

1940. Li-na. Shanghai: Wen-hua sheng-huo sheng-ch'u-pan she.
利娜。

1940. Lü-t'u t'ung-hsin. Shanghai: Wen-hua huo ch'u-pan she.
旅途通訊。

1941. Ai ti shih-tzu-chia. Shanghai: Wen-hua sheng-huo ch'u-pan she.
愛底十字架。

1941. Ch'u-lien. Shanghai: Ta-lu shu pao she.
初戀。

1941. Ch'un yü. Shanghai: I liu shu-tien.
春雨。

1941. Li Fei-kan *et al.* Chia te shih chih; chi-t'i ch'uang-tso. Shanghai: Pen-liu shu-tien.
李芾甘等。 家的拾撮； 集体創作。

1941. Li Fei-kan *et al.* Chü hsiang. Hong Kong: Pao-lei shu-tien.
李芾甘等。 巨像。

1941. Lun-li-hsueh te ch'i-yuan ho fa-chan. (tr. of P. Kropotkin's *Ethics, Origin and Development*). Chungking: Wen-hua sheng-huo ch'u-pan she.
倫理學的起原和發展。

1942. Huan hun ts'ao (ed. by Wen chi she). Chungking: Wen-hua sheng-huo ch'u-pan she.
還魂草。 文季社。

1942. Pa Chin tuan-p'ien hsiao-shuo chi; ti-san chi. Kweilin: K'ai-ming shu-tien.
巴金短篇小說集； 第三集。

1943. (comp.) Ping Hsin san-wen chi. Kweilin: K'ai-ming shu-tien.
冰心散文集。

1945. Hui-mieh. Hong Kong? Liang-yu t'u-shu kung-ssu.
毀滅。

1946. Ch'i yuan. Shanghai: Wen-hua sheng-huo ch'u-pan she.
憩園。

1946. Lü-t'u tsa-chi. Shanghai: Wan yeh shu-tien.
旅途雜記。

1947. Han-yeh. Shanghai: Ch'en-kuang ch'u-pan kung-ssu.
寒夜。

1947. Hsiao jen hsiao shih. Shanghai: Wen-hua sheng-huo ch'u-pan she.
小人小事。

1947. Huai-nien. Shanghai: K'ai-ming shu-tien.
懷念。

1947. (ed.) Ping Hsin hsiao-shuo chi. Shanghai: K'ai-ming shu-tien.
冰心小說集。

1947. Ti-ssu ping-shih. Shanghai: Ch'en-kuang ch'u-pan kung-ssu.
第四病室。

1948. Lü-t'u sui-pi. Shanghai: K'ai-ming shu-tien.
旅途隨筆。

1948. Meng yü tsui. Shanghai: K'ai-ming shu-tien.
夢與醉。

1949. Ai-ch'ing san-pu-ch'ü (a trilogy composed of wu, yü, tien). Shanghai: K'ai-ming shu-tien. 3 vols.
愛情三部曲 （霧， 雨， 電）。

1949. Chi-liu (a trilogy composed of chia, ch'un, ch'iu). Shanghai: K'ai-ming shu-tien. 3 vols.
激流 （家， 春， 秋）。

1949. Hai hsing tsa-chi. Shanghai. K'ai-ming shu-tien.
海行雜記。

1949. Tien-ti. Shanghai: K'ai-ming shu-tien.
點滴。

1949–51. Huo; ti-i pu chih ti-san pu. Shanghai, Peking: K'ai-ming shu-tien. 3 vols.
火； 第一部至第三部。

1951. Hua-sha ch'eng te chieh-jih—Po-lan tsa-chi. Peking: Jen-min wen-hsueh ch'u-pan she.
華沙城的節日—波蘭雜記。

1951. Pa Chin hsuan-chi (ed. by Hsin wen-hsueh hsuan-chi pien-chi wei-yuan-hui). Peking: K'ai-ming shu-tien.
巴金選集。 新文學選集編輯委員會。

1953. Sheng-huo te hui-i. Hong Kong: Hui t'ung shu-tien.
生活的回憶。

1953. Sheng-huo tsai ying-hsiung men te chung-chien. Peking: Jen-min wen-hsueh ch'u-pan she.
生活在英雄們的中間。
Eng. tr., *Living Amongst Heroes*. Peking: Foreign Languages Press, 1954.

1953. Sheng yü ssu. Hong Kong: Hsin ti ch'u-pan she.
生與死。

1953. Wo-men hui-chien le P'eng Te-huai ssu-ling-yuan. Peking: Jen-min wen-hsueh ch'u-pan she.
我們會見了彭懷司令員。

1953. Ying-hsiung te ku-shih. Shanghai: P'ing ming ch'u-pan she.
英雄的故事。

1954. Pa Chin *et al.* Fu yü tzu. Hong Kong: Hsin ti ch'u-pan kung-ssu.
巴金等。 父與子。

1954. Mou fu-fu. Hong Kong: Hsin ti ch'u-pan she.
某夫婦。

1954. Pao-wei ho-p'ing te jen-men (ed. by Chieh-fang chün wen-i ts'ung-shu pien-chi pu). Peking: Chung-kuo ch'ing-nien ch'u-pan she.
保衛和平的人們。解放軍文藝叢書編輯部。

1955. Pa Chin san-wen hsuan. Peking: Jen-min wen-hsueh ch'u-pan she.
巴金散文選。

1955. Pa Chin tuan-p'ien hsiao-shuo hsuan-chi. Peking: Jen-min wen-hsueh ch'u-pan she.
巴金短篇小說選集。

1955. T'an Ch'i-k'o-fu. Shanghai: P'ing ming ch'u-pan she.
談契訶夫。

1956. Pa Chin tzu-chuan. Hong Kong: Tzu-li shu-tien.
巴金自傳。

1957. Chien-ch'iang chan-shih—chih-yuan chün ying-hsiung chuan. Peking: Chung-kuo shao-nien erh-t'ung ch'u-pan she.
堅強戰士—志願軍英雄傳。

1957. Ming-chu ho yü chi. Peking: Shao-nien erh-t'ung ch'u-pan she.
明珠和玉姬。

1957. Ta huan-lo te jih-tzu. Peking: Tso-chia ch'u-pan she.
大歡樂的日子。

1958. Pa Chin t'an chia ch'un ch'iu. Hong Kong: Wan li shu-tien.
巴金談家春秋。

1958. The Family (tr. by Sidney Shapiro). Peking: Foreign Languages Press.

1958–62. Pa Chin wen-chi. Peking: Jen-min wen-hsueh ch'u-pan she. 14 vols.
巴金文集。

1959. Hsin sheng chi. Peking: Jen-min wen-hsueh ch'u-pan she.
新聲集。

1959. Lo ch'e shang. Hong Kong: Hsin-yueh ch'u-pan she.
騾車上。

1960. Hsin te ch'an-hui. Hong Kong: Jih hsin shu-tien.
心的懺悔。

1960. Tsan ko chi. Shanghai: Shanghai wen-i ch'u-pan she.
贊歌集。

1961. Li Ta-hai. Peking: Tso-chia ch'u-pan she.
李大海。

1964. Hsien-liang-ch'iao p'an. Peking: Tso-chia ch'u-pan she.

1964. Pa Chin *et al*. Shou—tuan shou tsai chih te ku-shih. Shanghai: Shao-nien erh-t'ung ch'u-pan she.
巴金等。手—斷手再植的故事。

Ch'uang wai. Kowloon: Hong Kong Hua-nan shu-tien.
窗外。

Hua hsueh te jih-tzu. Hong Kong: Tung-ya shu-chü.
化雪的日子。

ed. of *Na-han*.
呐喊。

Pa Chin hsiao-shuo hsuan. Shih-tai ch'u-pan she.
巴金小說選。

Pa Chin ming-tso hsuan-chi (ed. by Ch'en Lei). Hong Kong: Nan-yang t'u-shu kung-ssu.
巴金名作選集。陳磊。

ed. of *Shou-huo*.
收穫。

ed. of *Wen ts'ung*.
文叢。

SOURCES

China News Analysis, 208 (December 6, 1957): 4–5.

Contemporary Chinese Stories, tr. by Wang Chi-chien. New York: Columbia University Press, 1944.

Jen-min wen-hsueh, July, 1957.
人民文學。

Lang, Olga. Pa Chin and His Writings. Cambridge: Harvard University Press, 1967.

Living China: Modern Chinese Short Stories, comp. and ed. by Edgar Snow. New York: John Day & Reynal & Hitchcock, 1936.

Monsterleet, Jean. "Pa Chin et les maitres qui l'ont forme." *Le Revue de la Littérature Comparée*, February, 1954.

Pa Chin (pseud. of Li Fei-kan). Chi-liu (a trilogy composed of Chia, ch'un, ch'iu). Shanghai: K'ai-ming shu-tien, 1949. 3 vols.
巴金 (李芾甘)。激流 (家，春，秋)。

———. I. Shanghai: Wen-hua sheng-huo ch'u-pan she. 1936.
巴金 (李芾甘)。憶。

———. Pa Chin wen-chi. Peking: Jen-min wen-hsueh ch'u-pan she, 1958–62. 14 vols.
巴金 (李芾甘)。巴金文集。

Sun Ling. Wen-t'an chiao-yu lu. Kao-hsiung, Taiwan: Ta yeh shu-tien, 1955.
孫陵。文壇交遊錄。

Yü Ssu-mu. Tso-chia Pa Chin. Hong Kong: Nan kuo ch'u-pan she, 1964.

Li Fei-kan [252]

余思牧。作家巴金。

Li Fu-ch'un　李富春

WORKS

1955. Report on the First Five-year Plan for Development of the People's Republic of China in 1953–1957; Delivered on July 5 and 6, 1955, at the Second Session of the First National People's Congress. Peking: Foreign Languages Press.
1960. Raise High the Red Flag of the General Line and Continue to March Forward. Peking: Foreign Languages Press.

SOURCES

Person interviewed: Chang Kuo-t'ao.
HCJC
Hsing-tao wan-pao. Hong Kong, November 22, 1951.
星島晚報。
RSOC
WWMC

Li Hsien-nien　李先念

SOURCES

GCJJ
I-chiu-wu-ling jen-min nien-chien, ed. by Shen Sung-fang. Hong Kong: Ta kung shu-chü, 1950.
一九五〇人民年鑑。沈頌芳。
Jen-min chiang-ling ch'ün hsiang. Macao: Ch'un-ch'iu shu-tien, 1947.
人民將領群像。
JMST, 1952, 1953.

Li Huang　李璜

WORKS

1920. Fa-kuo wen-hsueh shih. Shanghai: Chung-hua shu-chü.
法國文學史。
1923. Kuo-chia chu-i te chiao-yü. with Yü Chia-chü. Shanghai: Chung-hua shu-chü.
國家主義的教育。余家菊。
1925. Kuo-chia chu-i lun-wen chi. Shanghai: Chung-hua shu-chü.
國家主義論文集。

1932. Li Shih hsueh yü she-hui k'o-hsueh. Shanghai: Ta-lu shu-chü.
歷史學與社會科學。
1933. Ku Chung-kuo te t'iao-wu yü shen-pi ku-shih (with Fa-kuo han-hsueh hsiao-shih). (tr.) Shanghai: Chung-hua shu-chü.
古中國的跳舞與神秘故事　（附：法國漢學小史）。
1955. I-ko min-tsu te fan-hsing. Taipei: Min-chu ch'ao she.
一個民族的反省。
Tu Sung-jen k'ao.
杜松人考。

SOURCES

Person interviewed: Li Huang.
Chow Tse-tsung. The May Fourth Movement: Intellectual Revolution in Modern China. Cambridge: Harvard University Press, 1960.
Free China Weekly, III-12 (May 6, 1965).
Li Huang. Fa-kuo wen-hsueh shih. Shanghai: Chung-hua shu-chü, 1920.
李璜。法國文學史。
———. Li-shih hsueh yü she-hui k'o-hsueh. Shanghai: Ta-lu shu-chü, 1932.
李璜。歷史學與社會科學。
Li Huang and Yü Chia-chü. Kuo-chia chu-i te chiao-yü. Shanghai: Chung-hua shu-chü, 1923.
李璜，余家菊。國家主義的教育。

Li I-chih　李儀祉

WORKS

1956. Li I-chih ch'üan-chi (ed. by Chung-kuo shui-li kung-ch'eng hsueh-hui). Taipei: Chung-hua ts'ung-shu wei-yuan-hui.
李儀祉全集。中國水利工程學會。

SOURCES

Li I-chih. Li I-chih ch'üan-chi (ed. by Chung-kuo shui-li kung-ch'eng hsueh-hui). Taipei: Chung-hua ts'ung-shu wei-yuan-hui, 1956.
李儀祉。李儀祉全集。中國水利工程學會。
WWMC

Li Ken-yuan　李根源

WORKS

1909. (comp.) Tien ts'ui.
滇粹。

1926. Wu-chün Hsi-shan fang ku chi (with Chen yang yu chi). Shanghai: T'ai tung shu-chü.
吳郡西山訪古記 (附: 鎮揚游記)。

1932. Ch'ü shih wen-lu. Soochow: Feng-men ch'ü-shih-lu.
曲石文錄。

1934. Hsueh-sheng nien lu. Ch'ü shih ching lu.
雪生年錄。

SOURCES

Li Ken-yuan. Ch'ü shih wen-lu. Soochow: Feng-men ch'ü-shih-lu.
李根源。曲石文錄。

———. Hsueh-sheng nien lu. Ch'ü shih ching lu, 1934.
李根源。雪生年錄。

"Li Ken-yuan chuan," in East Asian Library, Columbia University, Chuan-chi hsing shu hui-chi. 218 vols.
李根源傳。傳記行述彙輯。

Yunnan Kweichow hsin-hai ko-ming tzu-liao, ed. by Chung-kuo k'o-hsueh-yuan li-shih yen-chiu-so ti-san so. Peking: K'o-hsueh ch'u-pan she, 1959.
雲南貴州辛亥革命資料。中國科學院歷史研究所第三所。

Li K'o-nung   李克農

SOURCES

Person interviewed: Chang Kuo-t'ao.
CPR, 889 (May 11, 1949).
RSOC
Tang, Peter S. H. Communist China Today. New York: Frederick A. Praeger, 1957-58. 2 vols.
WWMC

Li Kuang-ch'ien   李光前

SOURCES

Persons interviewed: not to be identified.

Li Li-san   李立三

WORKS

1929. Fan-tung t'ung-chih te tung-yao yü ko-ming tou-cheng te k'ai-chan.
反動統治的動搖與革命鬥爭的開展。

1949. Kuan-yü fa-chan sheng-ch'an lao tzu liang li cheng-ts'e te chi tien shuo-ming. Tientsin: Tu-che shu-tien.
關於發展生產勞資兩利政策的幾點說明。

1951. Li Li-san et al. Lao-tung pao-hsien kung-tso shou-ts'e; ti-i chi (comp. by Chung-hua ch'üan-kuo tsung kung-hui lao-tung pao-hsien pu). Peking: Kung-jen ch'u-pan she.
李立三等。勞動保險工作手冊; 第一輯。
中華全國總工會勞動保險部。

ed. of Shao-nien.
少年。

SOURCES

Person interviewed: Chang Kuo-t'ao.
Brandt, Conrad, Benjamin Schwartz, and John K. Fairbank. A Documentary History of Chinese Communism. Cambridge: Harvard University Press, 1952.
Chao Kuan-i and Wei Tan-po. Chung-kung jen-wu su-miao. Kowloon: Tzu-yu ch'u-pan she, 1951.
趙貫一, 韋丹柏。中共人物素描。
Chin shih-wu nien lai Shanghai chih pa-kung t'ing-yeh (Strikes and Lockouts in Shanghai Since 1918), comp. by Shanghai shih-cheng-fu she-hui chü. Shanghai: Chung-hua shu-chü, 1933.
近十五年來上海之罷工停業。上海市政府社會局。
Chung-kuo hsin min-chu chu-i ko-ming shih ts'an-k'ao tzu-liao, ed. by Hu Hua, Tai Yi, Yen Ch'i. Shanghai: Shang-wu yin shu kuan, 1951.
中國新民主主義革命史參考資料。胡華, 戴逸, 彦奇。
Chung-kuo lao-kung yün-tung shih, comp. by Chung-kuo lao-kung yün-tung shih pien-chi wei-yuan-hui. Taipei: Chung-kuo lao-kung fu-li she, 1959.
中國勞工運動史。中國勞工運動史編輯委員會。
CPR, 819 (January 28, 1949).
Elegant, Robert S. China's Red Masters. New York: Twayne, 1951.
Feng Shao-lieh. Shih nien hung chün. Shanghai: Chieh-fang ch'u-pan she, 1938.
馮紹烈。十年紅軍。
Harrison, James P. "The Li Li-san Line and the CCP in 1930." The China Quarterly, March-June, July-September, 1963.
Hsiao Tso-liang. Power Relations within the Chinese Communist Movement, 1930-1934; a

Study of Documents. Seattle: University of Washington Press, 1961.

HSWT

Kung Ch'u. Wo yü hung-chün. Kowloon: Nan feng ch'u-pan she, 1955.
龔楚。我與紅軍。

Mao Tse-tung. Mao Tse-tung hsuan-chi. Peking: Jen-min ch'u-pan she, 1951-60. 4 vols.
毛澤東。毛澤東選集。

The New York Times, June 24, 1962.

North, Robert C. Moscow and the Chinese Communists. Stanford: Stanford University Press, 1953.

RD

Schwartz, Benjamin I. Chinese Communism and the Rise of Mao. Cambridge: Harvard University Press, 1951.

Smedley, Agnes. The Great Road: The Life and Times of Chu Teh. New York: Monthly Review Press, 1956.

WWC, 1950.

WWMC

Li Lieh-chün   李烈鈞

WORKS

1935. Li Lieh-chün chih yen-lun.
李烈鈞之言論。

1944. Li Lieh-chün tzu-chuan. Chungking.
李烈鈞自傳。

Wu Ning wen-tu.
武寧文牘。

SOURCES

BKL

CH

Chiu tang t'e-k'an, 8 (December 15, 1927).
救黨特刊。

CMTC

Feng Yü-hsiang. Wo-te sheng-huo. Shanghai: Chiao-yü shu-tien, 1947. 3 vols.
馮玉祥。我的生活。

Kuo-fu nien-p'u ch'u-kao, ed. by Lo Chia-lun. Taipei: Kuo shih kuan shih-liao pien-tsuan wei-yuan-hui, Chung-kuo kuo-min-tang tang shih shih-liao pien-tsuan wei-yuan-hui, 1959. 2 vols.
國父年譜初稿。羅家倫。

Kuo-min chün ko-ming shih. Chungking, 1942.
國民軍革命史。

Kuo-min ko-ming chün chan-shih, comp. by Kuo-min ko-ming chün chan-shih pien-tsuan

wei-yuan-hui. Ts'an-mou pen-pu, 1934. 17 vols.
國民革命軍戰史。國民革命軍戰史編纂委員會。

Lei Hsiao-ts'en. San-shih nien tung-luan Chung-kuo. Hong Kong: Ya-chou ch'u-pan she, 1955.
雷嘯岑。三十年動亂中國。

Li Chien-nung. Chung-kuo chin pai nien cheng-chih shih. Shanghai: Shang-wu yin shu kuan, 1948. 2 vols.
李劍農。中國近百年政治史。

Li Lieh-chün. Li Lieh-chün tzu-chuan. Chung-king, 1944.
李烈鈞。李烈鈞自傳。

————. Wu Ning wen-tu.
李烈鈞。武寧文牘。

Li Lieh-chün chih yen-lun. 1935.
李烈鈞之言論。

Li Lieh-chün ch'u hsün chi.
李烈鈞出巡記。

Mao I-heng. O Meng hui-i-lu. Hong Kong: Ya-chou ch'u-pan she, 1954.
毛以亨。俄蒙回憶錄。

T'ao Chü-yin. Pei-yang chün-fa t'ung-chih shih-ch'i shih-hua. Peking: Tu-shu, sheng-huo, hsin chih san lien shu-tien, 1957. 6 vols.
陶菊隱。北洋軍閥統治時期史話。

Wen Kung-chih. Tsui-chin san-shih nien Chung-kuo chün-shih shih. Shanghai: T'ai-p'ing-yang shu-tien, 1932. 2 vols.
文公直。最近三十年中國軍事史。

WWC, 5th ed.

Li Ming   李銘

SOURCES

Persons interviewed: not to be identified.
The New York Times, September 10, 1961.

Li Shih-tseng   李石曾

WORKS

1928. Li Yü-ying *et al*. Ko-ming yü fan ko-ming (comp. by Lang Hsing-shih). Shanghai: Min chih shu-chü.
李煜瀛等。革命與反革命。郎醒石。

1946. Ssu-k'u-ch'üan-shu hsueh-tien. with Yang Chia-lo. Shanghai: Shih-chieh shu-chü.
四庫全書學典。楊家駱。

1953. (Ying han) Shih-chieh hsueh-tien yü ssu-k'u ch'üan-shu. with Yang Chia-lo. Taipei: Shih-chieh shu-chü.

(英漢) 世界學典與四庫全書。楊家駱。

1960. (ed.) Shih-chieh wen-hsueh ta-hsi. Taipei: Ch'i-ming shu-chü. 12 vols.

世界文學大系。

1961. Shih seng pi-chi. Taipei? Chung-kuo kuo-chi wen-tzu hsueh k'an she.

石僧筆記。

Jou shih lun. Peiping yen-chiu yuan.

肉食論。

Ta-tou. Peiping yen-chiu-yuan.

大豆。

Sources

Person interviewed: Li Shu-hua.

Scalapino, Robert A., and George T. Yu. The Chinese Anarchist Movement. Berkeley: Center for Chinese Studies, Institute of International Studies, University of California, 1961.

Li Shu-hua   李 書 華

Works

1922. "Hsiang-tui-lun chi ch'i ch'an sheng ch'ien-hou chih k'o-hsueh chuang-k'uang." *Tung-fang tsa-chih*, XIX-24.

相對論及其產生前後之科學狀況。東方雜誌。

1923. P'u-t'ung wu-li shih-yen chiang-i, ti-i ts'e. Peking: Peking ta-hsueh ch'u-pan pu.

普通物理實驗講義，第一冊。

1923. Yuan-tzu lun ch'ien-shuo. Shang-wu yin shu kuan.

原子論淺說。

1924, January. "Erh-shih nien lai wu-li hsueh chih chin-pu." *Tung-fang tsa-chih*, Fa-k'an erh-shih chou-nien chi-nien hao.

二十年來物理學之進步。東方雜誌，發刊二十周年紀念號。

1924, February. "T'ai-yang je chih ch'i-yuan." *Hsueh i*, V-9.

太陽熱之起源。學藝。

1926, January. "Ko kuo k'o-hsueh chia tui-yü wu-li te kung-hsien." *Tung-fang tsa-chih*, XXIII-1.

各國科學家對於物理的貢獻。東方雜誌。

1934. ed. of Ta kung pao k'o-hsueh chou-k'an.

大公報科學週刊。

1935. "Huang-shan yu-chi." *Yü kung*, III-10.

黃山遊記。禹貢。

1935. "Yu Hsi-ling chi." *Kuo wen chou-pao*, XII-7.

遊西陵記。國聞週報。

1936. "Fang-shan yu-chi." *Yü kung*, V-2.

房山遊記。禹貢。

1936, October 10. "Peiping yen-chiu-yuan yü k'o-hsueh yen-chiu. *Ta kung pao*. Tientsin.

北平研究院與科學研究。大公報。

1936. "T'ien-t'ai-shan yu-chi." *Yü kung*, VI-1.

天台山遊記。禹貢。

1936. "Yen-tang-shan yu-chi." *Yü kung*, VI-2.

雁蕩山遊記。禹貢。

1937. "Shan yu jih-chi." *Yü kung*, VII-1, 2, 3.

陝遊日記。禹貢。

1941, January 5. "Chung-kuo k'o-hsueh shu-ju yü yen-chin." *Sao-tang pao*. Chungking.

中國科學輸入與演進。掃蕩報。

1943, March. "Chung-kuo k'o-hsueh yen-chiu kuo-ch'ü yü wei-lai." *Tung-fang tsa-chih*, San-shih-chiu chüan fu-k'an hao.

中國科學研究過去與未來。東方雜誌，三十九卷復刊號。

1945, January 1. "Tui-yü k'o-hsueh ying yu te jen-shih." *Sao-tang pao*. Chungking.

對於科學應有的認識。掃蕩報。

1945, May-July. "Origine de la Boussole." *ISIS*, XLV-139, 140.

1947, August. "Lien-chiao tsu-chih chi ch'i ti-i tz'u ta-hui ching-kuo." *Hsien-tai chih-shih*, I-8.

聯教組織及其第一次大會經過。現代知識。

1947, September. "Chieh-shao lien-chiao tsu-chih." *Shih-chieh yueh-k'an*, II-3.

介紹聯教組織。世界月刊。

1948, March 2-7. "Jih-pen i-chou." *Shih-chieh jih-pao*. Peiping.

日本一周。世界日報。

1948. Li Shu-hua *et al*. (ed.) Kuo-li Peiping yen-chiu-yuan ch'u-pan p'in mu-lu.

李書華等。國立北平研究院出版品目錄。

1948. "Lien-chiao tsu-chih ta-hui te ching-kuo chi yu Mo-hsi-ko te kan-hsiang." *Hsien-tai chih-shih*, II-7.

聯教組織大會的經過及遊墨西哥的感想。現代知識。

1951. "Wu Chih-hui hsien-sheng sheng-p'ing lueh-shu," in Taiwan sheng kuo-yü t'ui-hsing wei-yuan-hui, *Wu Chih-hui hsien-sheng te sheng-p'ing*.

吳稚暉先生平略述。台灣省國語推行委員會。吳稚暉先生的生平。

1954, September. "Chih fa-ming i-ch'ien Chung-kuo wen-tzu liu-ch'uan kung-chü" *Ta-lu tsa-chih*, IX-6.

紙發明以前中國文字流傳工具。大陸雜誌。

1954. Chih-nan-chen te ch'i-yuan. Taipei: Ta-lu tsa-chih she.
指南針的起源。

1955, January. "Tsao chih te fa-ming chi ch'i ch'uan-po." *Ta-lu tsa-chih*, X-1, 2.
造紙的發明及其傳播。大陸雜誌。

1957, February. "T'ang tai i-ch'ien yu wu tiao-pan yin-shua." *Ta-lu tsa-chih*, XIV-4.
唐代以前有無雕板印刷。大陸雜誌。

1958, September. "The Early Development of Seals and Rubbings." *Ch'ing-hua hsueh-pao*, Hsin (New Series) I-3.
清華學報。

1958, September. "Yin-shua fa-ming te shih-ch'i wen-t'i." *Ta-lu tsa-chih*, XVII-5, 6.
印刷發明的時期問題。大陸雜誌。

1959. Chih-nan-ch'e yü chih-nan-chen (The South-pointing Carriage and the Mariner's Compass). Taipei: Yi wen yin shu kuan.
指南車與指南針。

1959, May. "Tsai lun yin-shua fa-ming te shih-ch'i wen-t'i." *Ta-lu tsa-chih*, XVIII-10.
再論印刷發明的時期問題。大陸雜誌。

1960. Tsao chih te ch'uan-po chi ku chih te fa-hsien. Taipei: Chung-hua ts'ung-shu pien shen wei-yuan-hui.
造紙的傳播及古紙的發現。

1960, August. "Wu-tai shih-ch'i te yin-shua." *Ta-lu tsa-chih*, XXI-3.
五代時期的印刷。大陸雜誌。

1960, December. "Tun-huang fa-hsien yu nien-tai te yin pen." *Ta-lu tsa-chih*, XXI-11.
敦煌發現有年代的印本。大陸雜誌。

1961, June. "T'ang tai hou-ch'i te yin-shua." *Ch'ing-hua hsueh-pao*, Hsin (New Series) II-2: 18-32.
唐代後期的印刷。清華學報。

1962. Chung-kuo yin-shua shu ch'i-yuan. Kowloon: Hsin ya yen-chiu so.
中國印刷術起源。

Li Shu-hua *et al*. (ed.) Kuo-li Peiping yen-chiu-yuan kai-k'uang (Min-kuo shih-pa nien chiu-yueh chih san-shih-ch'i nien pa-yueh).
李書華等。國立北平研究院概況（民國十八年九月至三十七年八月）。

SOURCES

Person interviewed: Li Shu-hua.
BKL
Ch'en Pu-lei. Ch'en Pu-lei hui-i-lu. Shanghai: Erh-shih shih-chi ch'u-pan she, 1949.
陳布雷。陳布雷回憶錄。

Li Shu-t'ung 李叔同

WORKS

1924. Ssu-fen-lü pi-ch'iu chieh-hsiang piao-chi. Chung-hua shu-chü.
四分律比丘戒相表記。

1929. Li Hsi-weng lin ku fa shu (ed. by Hsia Mien-tsun). Shanghai: K'ai-ming shu-tien.
李息翁臨古法書。夏丏尊。

1929-50. Hu-sheng hua-chi. with Feng Tzu-k'ai. 3 vols.
護生畫集。豐子愷。

1937. (ed.) Fo-hsueh ts'ung-k'an ti-i chi; san-shih chung. Shanghai: Shih-chieh shu-chü. 4 vols.
佛學叢刊第一輯；三十種。

1955. Hung-i ta-shih chiang-yen chi (Wan ch'ing lao-jen chiang-yen lu). Taipei: Taiwan yin ching ch'u.
弘一大師講演集（晚晴老人講演錄）。

1958. Li Shu-t'ung ko-ch'ü chi (comp. by Feng Tzu-k'ai). Peking: Yin-yueh ch'u-pan she.
李叔同歌曲集。豐子愷。

Chieh lü hsi-t'ung k'o piao.
戒律系統科表。

Chieh pen chieh mo sui chiang pieh lu.
戒本羯磨隨講別錄。

Fan wang ching p'u-sa chieh pen ch'ien-shih.
梵網經菩薩戒本淺釋。

Li-lu shih chung.
李廬詩鐘。

Li-lu yin p'u.
李廬印譜。

Ling chih nien-p'u.
靈芝年譜。

Lü hsueh yao lueh.
律學要略。

Nan-shan lü tsai chia pei lan lueh pien.
南山律在家備覽略編。

Nan-shan nien-p'u.
南山年譜。

Nan-shan Tao-hsuan lü-tsu lueh-p'u.
南山道宣律祖略譜。

ed. of *T'ai-p'ing-yang hua-pao*.
太平洋畫報。

Wu chieh hsiang ching chien yao.
五戒相經箋要。

SOURCES

Ch'en Hui-chien. Hung-i ta-shih chuan. Taipei: K'ang-li shu-wu, 1965.
陳慧劍。弘一大師傳。

Ch'en Ting-shan. Ch'un shen chiu-wen. Taipei: Ch'en-kuang yueh-k'an she, 1964.

陳定山。 春申舊聞。

Feng Tzu-k'ai. "Fa wei." *Hsiao-shuo shih-chieh*, XV-10.

豐子愷。 法味。 小說世界。

Jung T'ien-ch'i. "Hung-i fa-shih Li Shu-t'ung." *Chuan-chi wen-hsueh*, VII-5.

容天圻。 弘一法師李叔同。 傳記文學。

Lin Tzu-ch'ing. Hung-i ta-shih nien-p'u. Hong Kong: Hung-hua-yuan, 1959.

林子青。 弘一大師年譜。

Lü Yu-po. "Chi Li Shu-t'ung hsien-sheng." *Hsiao-shuo shih-chieh*, XIV-12.

呂攸伯。 記李叔同先生。 小說世界。

Li Ta   李 達

WORKS

1921–? ed. of *Kung-ch'an-tang yueh-k'an.*

共產黨月刊。

1924? "Ho wei ti kuo chu-i," in Kao Erh-sung, Kao Erh-po, *Ti kuo chu-i yü Chung-kuo.* Shanghai: Chung-kuo ching-chi yen-chiu so.

何謂帝國主義。 高爾松， 高爾伯。 帝國主義與中國。

1927. Chung-kuo kuan-shui chih-tu lun. (tr.) Shanghai: Shang-wu yin shu kuan.

中國關稅制度論。

1929. Hsien-tai she-hui hsueh. Shanghai: K'un-lun shu-tien.

現代社會學。

1930. Chung-kuo ch'an-yeh kai-ko kai-kuan. Shanghai: K'un-lun shu-tien.

中國產業改革概觀。

1930. (tr.) She-hui k'o-hsueh k'ai-lun. with Ch'ien T'ieh-ju. Shanghai: K'un-lun shu-tien.

社會科學概論。 錢鐵如。

1930. She-hui wen-t'i tsung-lan. (tr.) Shanghai: Chung-hua shu-chü. 3 vols.

社會問題總覽。

1948. Hsien tzu-pen chu-i te she-hui ching-chi hsing-t'ai lun. Hong Kong: Sheng-huo shu-tien.

先資本主義的社會經濟形態論。

1949. Huo-pi hsueh kai-lun. Shanghai: Sheng-huo, tu-shu, hsin chih san lien shu-tien.

貨幣學概論。

1951. Hsueh-hsi Mao Tse-tung t'ung-chih te "shih-chien lun" (comp. by Hsueh-hsi tsa-chih pien-chi pu). Shanghai: Hsueh-hsi tsa-chih she.

學習毛澤東同志的「實踐論」。 學習雜誌編輯部。

1951. Li Ta *et al*. Hsueh-hsi "shih-chien lun;" ti-erh chi. Peking: Hsin chien-she tsa-chih she.

李達等。 學習「實踐論」; 第二輯。

1951. "Shih-chien lun" chieh-shuo. Peking: Sheng-huo, tu-shu, hsin chih san lien shu-tien.

「實踐論」解說。

1953. Mao-tun lun chieh-shuo. Peking: Sheng-huo, tu-shu, hsin chih san lien shu-tien.

矛盾論解說。

1955. Hu Shih fan-tung ssu-hsiang p'i-p'an. Hankow: Hupeh jen-min ch'u-pan she.

胡適反動思想批判。

1955. Li Ta *et al*. Hu Shih ssu-hsiang p'i-p'an: Lun-wen hui-pien; ti-erh chi. Peking: Sheng-huo, tu-shu, hsin chih san lien shu-tien.

李達等。 胡適思想批判: 論文彙編; 第二輯。

1955. Li Ta *et al*. Hu Shih ssu-hsiang p'i-p'an wen-chi.

李達等。 胡適思想批判文集。

1956. (ed.) Chung-hua Jen-min Kung-ho-kuo hsien-fa chiang-hua. Peking: Jen-min ch'u-pan she.

中華人民共和國憲法講話。

1958. She-hui chu-i ko-ming yü she-hui chu-i chien-she te kung-t'ung kuei-lü. Wuhan: Hupeh jen-min ch'u-pan she.

社會主義革命與社會主義建設的共同規律。

1961. "Yen che ko-ming te tao-lu ch'ien-chin." *Chung-kuo ch'ing-nien*, 13–14: 14–16.

沿着革命的道路前進。 中國青年。

ed. of *Hsin ch'ing-nien*.

新青年。

SOURCES

Brière, O. Fifty Years of Chinese Philosophy 1898–1950 (tr. by Laurence G. Thompson). New York: The Macmillan Co., 1956.

CB, 182.

China News Analysis, 630 (September 23, 1966).

GCJI

HCJC

Kuo Chan-po. Chin wu-shih nien Chung-kuo ssu-hsiang shih. Hong Kong: Lung men shu-tien, 1965.

郭湛波。 近五十年中國思想史。

Li Ta. "Yen che ko-ming te tao-lu ch'ien-chin." *Chung-kuo ch'ing-nien*, 13–14 (1961): 14–16.

李達。 沿着革命的道路前進。 中國青年。

Li Ta-chao   李 大 釗

WORKS

1916, March 15. "Ch'ing-ch'un." *Hsin ch'ing-nien*.
青春。新青年。
1916-17. ed. of *Ch'en chung jih-pao*.
晨鐘日報。
1916-? ed. of *Hsin ch'ing-nien*.
新青年。
1918, October 15. "Bolshevism te sheng-li." *Hsin ch'ing-nien*.
Bolshevism 的勝利。新青年。
1918, October 15. "Shu-min te sheng-li." *Hsin ch'ing-nien*.
庶民的勝利。新青年。
1926. Shih-hsueh yao-lun. Shanghai: Shang-wu yin shu kuan.
史學要論。
1939. Shou-ch'ang ch'üan-chi. Shanghai: Pei hsin shu-chü.
守常全集。
1950. Shou-ch'ang wen-chi. Shanghai: Pei hsin shu-chü.
守常文集。
1951. Hsü Yin. Shanghai: Wen kung shu-tien.
徐寅。
1962. Li Ta-chao hsuan-chi (ed. by Jen-min ch'u-pan she). Peking: Jen-min ch'u-pan she.
李大釗選集。人民出版社。

SOURCES

Person interviewed: Chang Kuo-t'ao.
CKLC
Documents on Communism, Nationalism, and Soviet Advisers in China, 1918-1927; Papers Seized in the 1927 Peking Raid, ed. by C. Martin Wilbur, Julie Lien-ying How. New York: Columbia University Press, 1956.
GCCJK
Hsiao Pai-fan. Chung-kuo chin pai nien ko-ming shih. Kowloon: Ch'iu shih ch'u-pan she, 1951.
蕭白帆。中國近百年革命史。
Hsin ch'ing-nien, 1916-1921.
新青年。
Huang Sung-k'ang. Li Ta-chao and the Impact of Marxism on Modern Chinese Thinking. The Hague: Mouton, 1965.
Kuo wen chou-pao, IV-15.
國聞週報。
Li Shou-ch'ang (Li Ta-chao). Shih-hsueh yao-lun. Shanghai: Shang-wu yin shu kuan, 1926.
李守常 (李大釗)。史學要論。

Li Shou-ch'ang. Shou-ch'ang wen-chi. Shanghai: Pei hsin shu-chü, 1950.
李大釗。守常文集。
Liu Nung-chao. "Li Ta-chao, a Founder of the Chinese Communist Party." *People's China*, July 1, 1957.
Lü Chien. Li Ta-chao ho Ch'ü Ch'iu-pai. Shanghai: Shang-wu yin shu kuan, 1951.
呂健。李大釗和瞿秋白。
Schwartz, Benjamin I. Chinese Communism and the Rise of Mao. Cambridge: Harvard University Press, 1951.
SCMP, 281 (October 2, 1961).
Shao-nien Chung-kuo, 3 (September 15, 1919).
少年中國。
Ta Sheng. Lieh-shih chuan; ti-i chi; chi-nien wo-men wei Chung-kuo jen-min chieh-fang fen-tou erh hsi-sheng te chan-shih. Moscow, 1936.
大生。烈士傳；第一集；紀念我們為中國人民解放奮鬥而犧牲的戰士。
Yeh Hu-sheng. Hsien-tai Chung-kuo ko-ming shih-hua. Peking: K'ai-ming shu-tien, 1951;
葉蠖生。現代中國革命史話。

Li Ta-ming   李 大 明

WORKS

1937. Pei yu yin-hsiang. Shanghai: Shanghai tu-fang wen-hua ch'u-pan she.
北遊印像。
1938-? ed. of *New China Daily Press*.
1945? Chu Kang Mei tsung-ling-shih pao-kao shu te p'i-p'an. San Francisco: Shih-chieh jih-pao.
駐港美總領事報告書的批判。

SOURCES

Persons interviewed: not to be identified.

Li Te-ch'üan   李 德 全

SOURCES

CWR, February 23, 1924.
Feng Yü-hsiang. Feng Yü-hsiang jih-chi. Peiping: Min-kuo shih-liao pien-chi she, 1932. 2 vols.
馮玉祥。馮玉祥日記。
HCJC
HMTT

(Hsin ting) Hsin ming-tz'u tz'u-tien, ed. by
Ch'un-ming ch'u-pan she pien shen pu hsin
ming-tz'u tz'u-tien tsu. Shanghai: Ch'un-
ming ch'u-pan she, 1952.
（新訂）新名詞辭典。春明出版社編審部新
名詞辭典組。

I-chiu-wu-ling jen-min nien-chien, ed. by Shen
Sung-fang. Hong Kong: Ta kung shu-chü,
1950.
一九五〇人民年鑑。沈頌芳。

Mao I-heng. O Meng hui-i lu. Hong Kong:
Ya-chou ch'u-pan she, 1954.
毛以亨。俄蒙回憶錄。

SCMP, 1962.

梁升俊。蔣李鬥爭內幕。

Martin, R. P. "China's Peace Seeker." *Eastern
World*, III-5 (1949): 8–10.

Peking Review, 40 (October 1, 1965): 22–27.

Ta kung pao. Hong Kong, September 28, 1965.
大公報。

Yin Shih (pseud.). Li Chiang kuan-hsi yü
Chung-kuo. Hong Kong: Tzu-yu ch'u-pan
she, 1954.
隱士。李蔣關係與中國。

Yuan Ch'ing-p'ing. Tang-tai tang kuo ming-jen
chuan. Kwangtung: Ku chin t'u-shu she,
1936.
袁清平。當代黨國名人傳。

Li Tsung-jen　李宗仁

WORKS

1935. Li Tsung-ssu-ling tsui-chin yen-chiang chi
comp. by Kuo-min ko-ming chün ti-ssu chi-
t'uan chün tsung-ssu-ling pu cheng hsun ch'u).
Kwangsi yin-shua ch'ang.
李總司令最近演講集。國民革命軍第四集
團軍總司令部政訓處。

1939. Min-t'uan yü chün-hsun. with Pai Ch'ung-
hsi. Kwangsi: Min-t'uan chou-k'an she.
民團與軍訓。白崇禧。

SOURCES

Person interviewed: T. K. Tong.

GCJJ

HCMW

Huai Hsiang (pseud.). Lun Li Tsung-jen yü
Chung Mei fan-tung pai. Hong Kong. Yü-
chou shu wu, 1948.
懷鄉。論李宗仁與中美反動派。

Li Tsung-jen. Li Tsung-ssu-ling tsui-chin yen-
chiang chi. Kwangsi: Kwangsi yin-shua
ch'ang, 1935.
李宗仁。李總司令最近演講集。

Li Tsung-jen and Pai Ch'ung-hsi. Min-t'uan yü
chün-hsun. Kwangsi: Min-t'uan chou-k'an
she, 1939.
李宗仁，白崇禧。民團與軍訓。

Li Tsung-jen te sheng-yin. Hong Kong: Kuo-
chi wen-tse ch'u-pan she, 1965.
李宗仁的聲音。

Li Tsung-jen yin-hsiang chi. Hong Kong: Chung
nan t'u-shu kung-ssu, 1937.
李宗仁印象記。

Liang Sheng-chün. Chiang Li tou-cheng nei-mu.
Hong Kong: Ya lien ch'u-pan she, 1954.

Li Wei-han　李維漢

WORKS

1938. Li Wei-han *et al.* Shan-pei te ch'ün-chung
tung-yuan (comp. by Yang Shih). Hankow:
Yang-tzu ch'u-pan she.
李維漢等。陝北的群衆動員。楊實。

1946. Lo Mai (pseud. of Li Wei-han) *et al.* Shui
tsai t'o. Hong Kong: Ts'ao-yuan ch'u-pan she.
羅邁（李維漢）等。誰在拖。

1962. Chung-kuo hsin min-chu chu-i ko-ming
shih-ch'i cheng-ch'ü wu-ch'an chieh-chi ling-
tao ch'üan te tou-cheng. Peking: Jen-min
ch'u-pan she.
中國新民主主義革命時期爭取無產階級領
導權的鬥爭。
Eng. tr., *The Struggle for Proletarian Leadership
in the Period of the New-Democratic Revolution
in China.* Peking: Foreign Languages Press,
1962.

1964. Hsueh-hsi Mao chu-hsi chu-tso, chu-pu
kai-tsao shih-chieh kuan. Peking: Jen-min
ch'u-pan she.
學習毛主席著作，逐步改造世界觀。

SOURCES

Person interviewed: Chang Kuo-t'ao.

CPR, 869 (April 12, 1949).

HCJC

WWMC

Li Yuan-hung　黎元洪

WORKS

1912. Li fu tsung-t'ung shu tu.
黎副總統書牘。

1912? Li fu tsung-t'ung Yuan-hung wen tien hui-pien.
黎副總統元洪文電彙編。

1914. Li fu tsung-t'ung cheng-shu. Wuchang: Wuchang kuan yin-shua chü. 16 vols.
黎副總統政書。

1914. Li fu tsung-t'ung shu tu hui-pien (comp. by Wang Yü-sun). Shaghai.
黎副總統書牘彙編。 王鈺孫。

1916. Li ta tsung-t'ung cheng shu. Shanghai.
黎大總統政書。

1934. Li ta tsung-t'ung wen-tu lei pien (ed. by Shanghai hui-wen-t'ang hsin-chi shu-chü). Shanghai: Hui-wen-t'ang hsin-chi shu-chü.
黎大總統文牘類編。 上海會文堂新記書局。

SOURCES

Chang Nan-hsien. Hupeh ko-ming chih chih lu. Chungking: Shang-wu yin shu kuan, 1945.
張難先。 湖北革命知之錄。

Chang Ping-lin. "Ta tsung-t'ung Li kung pei." *Chih yen*, 2 (October 1, 1935).
章炳麟。 大總統黎公碑。 制言。

Chang Tzu-sheng. Jen-hsü cheng-pien chi. Shanghai, 1923.
張梓生。 壬戌政變記。

Chung-hua Min-kuo shih-liao, comp. by Sun Yao. Shanghai: Wen-ming shu-chü, 1929. 3 vols.
中華民國史料。 孫曜。

CMMC

Hsin-hai ko-ming, ed. by Ch'ai Te-keng *et al.* Shanghai. Shanghai jen-min ch'u-pan she, 1957. 8 vols.
辛亥革命。 柴德賡等。

Hsueh shu, comp. by Han Hsia. 3 vols.
血書。 漢俠。

"Jen-wen chih." *Jen-wen*, VIII-2 (March 15, 1937).
人文誌。 人文。

Kuei-hai cheng-pien chi-lueh, comp. by Liu Ch'u-hsiang. Shanghai: T'ai tung t'u-shu, chü, 1924.
癸亥政變紀略。 劉楚湘。

Li Chien-nung. Tsui-chin san-shih nien Chung-kuo cheng-chih shih. Shanghai: T'ai-p'ing-yang shu-tien, 1931.
李劍農。 最近三十年中國政治史。

Li Shih-yueh. Hsin-hai ko-ming shih-ch'i liang Hu ti-ch'ü te ko-ming yün-tung. Peking: San lien shu-tien, 1957.
李時岳。 辛亥革命時期兩湖地區的革命運動。

Li Yuan-hung. Li fu tsung-t'ung cheng-shu. Wuchang: Wuchang kuan yin-shua chü. 16 vols.
黎元洪。 黎副總統政書。

———. Li fu tsung-t'ung shu tu. 1912.
黎元洪。 黎副總統書牘。

———. Li fu tsung-t'ung shu tu hui-pien (comp. by Wang Yü-sun). Shanghai, 1914.
黎元洪。 黎副總統書牘彙編。 王鈺孫。

———. Li ta tsung-t'ung cheng shu. Shanghai, 1916.
黎元洪。 黎大總統政書。

———. Li ta tsung-t'ung wen-tu lei pien (ed. by Shanghai hui-wen-t'ang hsin-chi shu-chü). Shanghai: Hui-wen-t'ang hsin-chi shu-chü, 1934.
黎元洪。 黎大總統文牘類編。 上海會文堂新記書局。

Li Yuan-hung li-shih. Chen hua pien-chi pu.
黎元洪歷史。

MMH

MMT

O luan hui-lu ch'u p'ien, comp. by Chih Yin-sheng. Shanghai, 1911.
鄂亂彙錄初篇。 蟄隱生。

Shen Yün-lung. Li Yuan-hung p'ing-chuan. Taipei: Chung-yang yen-chiu yuan chin-tai shih yen-chiu so, 1963.
沈雲龍。 黎元洪評傳。

T'ao Chü-yin. Pei-yang chün-fa t'ung-chih shih-ch'i shih-hua. Peking: Sheng-huo, tu-shu, hsin chih san lien shu-tien, 1957-58. 6 vols.
陶菊隱。 北洋軍閥統治時期史話。

Wen Kung-chih. Tsui-chin san-shih nien Chung-kuo chün-shih shih. Shanghai: T'ai-p'ing-yang shu-tien, 1931. 2 vols.
文公直。 最近三十年中國軍事史。

Liang Ch'i-ch'ao   梁啓超

WORKS

1896-? ed. of *Shih-wu pao*.
時務報。

1899. Yin-ping-shih tzu-yu shu.
飲冰室自由書。

1902. (ed.) Chung-kuo hun. Shanghai: Kung chih shu-chü. 2 vols.
中國魂。

1902-? ed. of *Hsin-min ts'ung pao*.
新民叢報。

1908-11. Liang Ch'i-ch'ao *et al.* Chung-kuo liu

ta cheng-chih chia. Shanghai: Kuang chih shu-chü. 3 vols.
梁啓超等。中國六大政治家。

1912. Liang Jen-kung hsien-sheng yen-shuo chi; ti-i chi (comp. by Chang Chia-sen, Lan Kung-wu). Peking: Cheng meng yin-shu chü.
梁任公先生演說集；第一輯。張嘉森，藍公武。

1914. K'ang Liang shih ch'ao. with K'ang Yu-wei. Shanghai: Chung-hua t'u-shu-kuan. 4 vols.
康梁詩鈔。康有爲。

1915. Liang Jen-kung wei-chn. Shanghai. 8 vols.
梁任公文集。

1916. Yin-ping-shih ts'ung-chu. Shanghai.
飲冰室叢著。

1919. Chiang t'an ti-i chi. Shanghai: Shih-shih hsin pao kuan.
講壇第一集。

1923. Ju-chia che-hsueh chi ch'i cheng-chih ssu-hsiang. Shanghai: Hsin chin t'u-shu she.
儒家哲學及其政治思想。

1925. (comp.) Yao chi chieh t'i chi ch'i tu-fa. Peking: Ch'ing-hua chou-k'an ts'ung-shu she.
要籍解題及其讀法。

1925? Yin-ping-shih wen-chi (comp. by Liang T'ing-ts'an). Chung-hua shu-chü. 67 vols.
飲冰室文集。梁廷燦。

1925-26. Liang Jen-kung chin chu ti-i chi. Shanghai: Shang-wu yin shu kuan. 3 vols.
梁任公近著第一輯。

1926. Chung-kuo ku-tai hsueh-shu ssu-hsiang pien-ch'ien shih. Shanghai: Ch'ün-chung t'u-shu kung-ssu.
中國古代學術思想變遷史。

1926. Liang Jen-kung hsueh-shu chiang-yen chi; ti i-san chi. Shanghai: Shang-wu yin shu kuan. 3 vols.
梁任公學術講演集；第一一三輯。

1929. Ch'ang-shih wen-fan. Shanghai: Chung-hua shu-chü. 4 vols.
常識文範。

1929. Chung-hsueh i-shang tso-wen chiao-hsueh fa. Shanghai: Chung-hua shu-chü.
中學以上作文教學法。

1929. Chung-kuo chin san-pai nien hsueh-shu shih. Shanghai: Min chih shu-tien.
中國近三百年學術史。

1930. History of Chinese Political Thought, During the Early Tsin Period. New York: Harcourt, Brace & Co.

1932. Liang Jen-kung Hu Shih-chih hsien-sheng shen-ting yen-chiu kuo-hsueh shu-mu. with Hu Shih. Shanghai: Ta chung shu-chü.
梁任公胡適之先生審定研究國學書目。胡適。

1933. Chung-kuo li-shih yen-chiu fa (with Chung-kuo li-shih yen-chiu fa pu-pien). Shanghai: Shang-wu yin shu kuan.
中國歷史研究法（附：中國歷史研究法補編）。

1936. Fo-hsueh yen-chiu shih-pa p'ien. Shanghai: Chung-hua shu-chü. 2 vols.
佛學研究十八篇。

1936. Hsiao-shuo ch'uan-ch'i wu chung. Shanghai: Chung-hua shu chü.
小說傳奇五種。

1936. Kuo shih yen-chiu liu-p'ien. Shanghai: Chung-hua shu-chü.
國史研究六篇。

1936. T'ao hua shan chu. Shanghai: Chung-hua shu-chü.
桃花扇註。

1936. Yin-ping-shih ho chi (comp. by Lin Chih-chün). Shanghai: Chung-hua shu-chü. 40 vols.
飲冰室合集。林志鈞。

1937. Liang Ch'i-ch'ao wen-hsueh (comp. by Ch'en Hsiao-mei). Shanghai: Ch'i chih shu-chü.
梁啓超文學。陳筱梅。

1953. The Great Chinese Philosopher K'ang Yu-wei. San Francisco: Chinese World.

1954. Wu-hsü cheng-pien chi. Peking: Chung-hua shu-chü.
戊戌政變記。

1955. Ku shu yeh wei chi ch'i nien-tai. Peking: Chung-hua shu-chü.
古書頁僞及其年代。

1956. Chung-kuo chih mei wen chi ch'i li-shih. Taipei: Chung-hua shu-chü.
中國之美文及其歷史。

1957. Liang Jen-kung shih kao shou chi. Shanghai: Ku-tien wen-hsueh ch'u-pan she.
梁任公詩稿手蹟。

1957. Yin-ping-shih shih-hua. Taipei: Chung-hua shu-chü.
飲冰室詩話。

1958. Chung-kuo wen-hua shih; she-hui tsu-chih p'ein (with Kuo wen yü yuan chieh; Chung-kuo ku-tai pi ts'ai k'ao). Taipei: Chung-hua shu-chü.
中國文化史；社會組織篇（附：國文語原解；中國古代幣材考）。

1958. Lun Li Hung-chang. Taipei: Chung-hua shu-chü.
論李鴻章。

1958. T'u-shu ta tz'u-tien; pu lu chih pu. Tai-pei: Chung-hua shu-chü.
圖書大辭典；簿錄之部。

1959. Intellectual Trends in the Ch'ing Period (Ch'ing-tai hsueh-shu kai-lun). (tr. by Immanuel C. Y. Hsü.) Cambridge: Harvard University Press.

1960. Kuo-hsueh pi-tu chi-ch'i tu fa. Hong Kong: Chung-nan ch'u-pan she.
國學必讀及其讀法。

1961. Chung-kuo hsien Ch'in ssu-hsiang. Tai-pei: Ch'i ming shu-chü.
中國先秦思想。

1963? Yen-chiu shih-hsueh chi ch'i-t'a. Hong Kong: San ta ch'u-pan kung-ssu.
研究史學及其他。

1965. Kuo-hsueh yao chi chü-mu. Taipei: Kuang wen shu-chü.
國學要籍舉目。

1965. T'ao Yuan-ming. Taipei: Taiwan shang-wu yin shu kuan.
陶淵明。

1966. Chu tzu k'ao shih. Taipei: Taiwan Chung-hua shu-chü.
諸子考釋。

ed. of Chih hsin pao.
知新報。

(Chin ni) Ching-shih ta-hsueh-t'ang chang-ch'eng.
（謹擬）京師大學堂章程。

Chung-kuo fo-chiao yen-chiu shih. Hong Kong: San ta ch'u-pan kung-ssu.
中國佛教研究史。

Liang Jen-kung hsueh-shu ching-hua lu (ed. by Hsü Hsiao-t'ien). Hong Kong: San ta ch'u-pan she.
梁任公學術精華錄。許嘯天。

Wang An-shih p'ing-chuan. Hong Kong: Kuang chih shu-chü.
王安石評傳。

SOURCES

Chang Ch'i-yün. "Liang Jen-kung pieh-lu." *Ssu-hsiang yü shih-tai*, 4.
張其昀。梁任公別錄。思想與時代。

Chang P'eng-yuan. Liang Ch'i-ch'ao yü Ch'ing chi ko-ming. Nan-kang, Taiwan: Chung-yang yen-chiu-yuan chin-tai shih yen-chiu-so, 1964.
張朋園。梁啓超與清季革命。

CWT

d'Elia, Pascal M. "Un Maitre de la Jeune Chine: Liang K'i Tch'ao." *T'oung pao*, XVIII: 249–94.

Hsiao Kung-ch'üan. Chung-kuo cheng-chih ssu-hsiang shih. Shanghai: Kuo-li pien i kuan, 1947. 2 vols.
蕭公權。中國政治思想史。

Levenson, Joseph Richmond. Liang Ch'i-ch'ao and the Mind of Modern China. Cambridge: Harvard University Press, 1959.

Liang Ch'i-ch'ao. "San-shih tzu-shu," in Liang Ch'i-ch'ao, *Yin-ping-shih wen-chi*. Chung-hua shu-chu, 1925? 67 vols.
梁啓超。三十自述。梁啟超。飲冰室文集。

Liang Ch'i-ch'ao, comp. by Wu Ch'i-ch'ang. Chungking: Sheng-li ch'u-pan she, 1944.
梁啓超。吳其昌。

Liang Jen-kung hsien-sheng nien-p'u ch'ang-pien ch'u-kao, comp. by Ting Wen-chiang. Taipei: Shih-chieh shu-chü, 1958. 2 vols.
梁任公先生年譜長編初稿。丁文江。

Liu Hsi-sui. "Liang Jen-kung hsien-sheng chuan." *T'u-shu-kuan hsueh chi-k'an*, IV-1, 2.
劉盻遂。梁任公先生傳。圖書館學季刊。

Sources of Chinese Tradition, ed. by Wm. Theodore de Bary, Wing-tsit Chan, and Burton Watson. New York: Columbia University Press, 1960. 2 vols.

Su Ch'ih (pseud. of Chang Yin-lin). "Chin-tai Chung-kuo hsueh-shu shih shang chih Liang Jen-kung hsien-sheng." *Ta kung pao*. Tientsin, February 11, 1929.
素癡（張蔭麟）。近代中國學術史之上梁任公先生。大公報。

Teng Ssu-yu, John K. Fairbank, *et al*. China's Response to the West; A Documentary Survey, 1839–1923. Cambridge: Harvard University Press, 1954.

Wang Shih-chao. Chung-kuo wen-jen hsin lun. Hong Kong: Hsin shih-chi ch'u-pan she. 1953.
王世昭。中國文人新論。

Wu Tse. K'ang Yu-wei yü Liang Ch'i-ch'ao. Shanghai: Hua-hsia shu-tien, 1948.
吳澤。康有為與梁啓超。

Yang Yin-shen. Chung-kuo wen-hsueh-chia lieh-chuan. Shanghai: Chung-hua shu-chü, 1939.
楊蔭深。中國文學家列傳。

Liang Hung-chih　　梁鴻志

WORKS

1942, July. "Chung-yung tu-pen shu hou." *Ku-chin yueh-k'an*, 5.

中庸讀本書後。古今月刊。

SOURCES

Chu Tzu-chia (pseud. of Chin Hsiung-pai). Wang cheng-ch'üan te k'ai-ch'ang yü shou-ch'ang. Hong Kong: Ch'un-ch'iu tsa-chih she, 1964. 5 vols.
朱子家（金雄白）。汪政權的開塲與收塲。

Jones, Francis Clifford. Japan's New Order in East Asia; Its Rise and Fall, 1937-45. New York: Oxford University Press, 1954.

Li Ch'i-ying. Wei tsu-chih cheng-chih ching-chi kai-k'uang. Chungking, 1943.
李啓英。僞組織政治經濟概況。

Li Chien-nung. Chung-kuo chin pai nien cheng-chih shih. Shanghai: Shang-wu yin shu kuan, 1947. 2 vols.
李劍農。中國近百年政治史。

Liang Hung-chih. "Chung-yung tu-pen shu hou." *Ku-chin yueh-k'an*, 5.
梁鴻志。中庸讀本書後。古今月刊。

MMT
SMJ

Liang Shih-ch'iu   梁實秋

WORKS

1927. Lang-man te yü ku-tien te. Shanghai: Hsin-yueh shu-tien.
浪漫的與古典的。

1928. A-po-la yü Ai-lü-ch'i-ssu te ch'ing-shu. (tr.) Shanghai: Hsin-yueh shu-tien.
阿伯拉與哀綠綺思的情書。

1928. Wen-hsueh te chi-lü. Shanghai: Hsin-yueh shu-tien.
文學的紀律。

1929. P'an Pi-te. (tr.) Shanghai. Hsin-yueh shu-tien.
潘彼得。

1930. Liang Shih-ch'iu *et al*. Jen-ch'üan lun-chi. Shanghai: Hsin-yueh shu-tien.
梁實秋等。人權論集。

1931. Ma-jen te i-shu. Shanghai: Hsin-yueh shu-tien.
罵人的藝術。

1934. P'ien-chien chi. Shanghai: Cheng-chung shu-chü.
偏見集。

1934. Wen-i p'i-p'ing lun. Shanghai: Chung-hua shu-chü.
文藝批評論。

1934. Yueh-han-sun. Shanghai: Shang-wu yin shu kuan.

約翰孫。

1942. The Fine Art of Reviling (tr. by William B. Pettus). New York: The Typophiles.

1949. Ya she hsiao-p'in. Taipei: Cheng-chung shu-chü.
雅舍小品。

1954. Mei-kuo shih tsen-yang te i-kuo kuo-chia. with Chang Fang-chieh. Taipei: Kuo-li pien i kuan.
美國是怎樣的一個國家。張芳杰。

1955. (tr.) China the Beautiful (ed. by Ting Sing-wu). Hong Kong: International Culture Press.

1958. T'an Hsü Chih-mo. Taipei: Yuan-tung t'u-shu kung-ssu.
談徐志摩。

1958. (ed.) Tsui hsin ying han tz'u-tien. Hong Kong: Yuan-tung t'u-shu kung-ssu.
最新英漢辭典。

1959. (ed.) Yuan-tung ying han tzu-tien. Taipei: Yuan-tung t'u-shu kung-ssu.
遠東英漢字典。

1961. Liang Shih-ch'iu hsuan-chi. Taipei: Hsin lu shu-chü.
梁實秋選集。

1962. Ch'ing-hua pa nien. Taipei: Ch'ung kuang wen-i ch'u-pan she.
清華八年。

1964. Ch'iu shih tsa-wen. Taipei: Wen hsing shu-tien.
秋室雜文。

1964. Sha-shih-pi-ya ming chü. (tr.) Taipei: Wen hsing shu-tien. 20 vols.
莎士比亞名劇。

1964. Wen-hsueh yin-yuan. Taipei: Wen hsing shu-tien.
文學因緣。

1965. Hsi-sai-lo wen-lu. (tr.) Taipei: Shang-wu yin shu kuan.
西塞羅文錄。

1967. T'an Wen I-to. Taipei: Chuan-chi wen-hsueh tsa-chih she.
談聞一多。

SOURCES

CBJS

Chung wai wen-hsueh chia chuan-lueh tz'u-tien. Hong Kong: Shanghai shu-chü, 1959.
中外文學家傳略辭典。

Liang Shih-ch'iu. Liang Shih-ch'iu hsuan-chi. Taipei: Hsin lu shu-chü, 1961.
梁實秋。梁實秋選集。

———. Ya she hsiao-p'in. Taipei: Cheng-chung shu-chü, 1957.

梁實秋。雅舍小品。
Wang Chi-ts'ung. "Liang Shih-ch'iu lun."
Hsien-tai yueh-k'an, VI-2 (March, 1935).
王集叢。梁實秋論。現代月刊。

Liang Shih-i 梁士詒

SOURCES

AADC
CMMC
CMTC
Johnston, Reginald F. Twilight in the Forbidden City. New York: Appleton-Century, 1934.
Li Chien-nung. Chung-kuo chin pai nien cheng-chih shih. Shanghai: Shang-wu yin shu kuan, 1948. 2 vols.
李劍農。中國近百年政治史。
———. Tsui-chin san-shih nien Chung-kuo cheng-chih shih. Shanghai: T'ai-p'ing-yang shu-tien, 1931.
李劍農。最近三十年中國政治史。
MMT
San Shui Liang Yen-sun hsien-sheng ai-wan-lu. 1933?
三水梁燕孫先生哀輓錄。
San-shui Liang Yen-sun hsien-sheng (1869–1933) nien-p'u, comp. by Feng-kang chi-men ti-tzu. 1946. 2 vols.
三水梁燕孫先生 (1896–1933) 年譜。鳳岡及門弟子。
T'ao Chü-yin. Pei-yang chün-fa t'ung-chih shih-ch'i shih-hua. Peking: Sheng-huo, tu-shu hsin chih san-lien shu-tien, 1957–58. 6 vols.
陶菊隱。北洋軍閥統治時期史話。
Tso Shun-sheng. Wan Chu-luo sui-pi. Hong Kong: Tzu-yu ch'u-pan she, 1953.
左舜生。萬竹樓隨筆。
WWC, 1925.
Yang Yu-chiung. Chung-kuo cheng-tang shih. Shanghai: Shang-wu yin shu kuan, 1936.
楊幼烱。中國政黨史。
Yen-ching hsueh-pao, XXXIII (December, 1947): 292–302.
燕京學報。

Liang Shu-ming 梁漱溟

WORKS

1919. (ed.) Yin-tu che-hsueh kai-lun. Shanghai: Shang-wu yin shu kuan.

印度哲學概論。
1920. Wei shih shu i. Peking: Wen-hsueh.
唯識述義。
1922. Tung hsi wen-hua chi ch'i che-hsueh. Shanghai: Shang-wu yin shu kuan.
東西文化及其哲學。
1926. Shu-ming san-shih ch'ien wen-lu. Shanghai: Shang-wu yin shu kuan.
漱溟三十前文錄。
1929–30. ed. of *Ts'un chih yueh-k'an*.
村治月刊。
1932. Chung-kuo min-tsu tzu-chiu yün-tung chih tsui-hou chueh-wu. Peiping: Ts'un chih yueh k'an she.
中國民族自救運動之最後覺悟。
1932. Liang Shu-ming *et al*. Ts'un chih chih li-lun yü shih-shih. Peiping: Ts'un chih yueh-k'an she.
梁漱溟等。村治之理論與實施。
1935. Chung-kuo chih ti-fang tzu-chih wen-t'i. Tsou-p'ing, Shantung: Hsiang-ts'un chien-she yen-chiu-yuan ch'u-pan ku.
中國之地方自治問題。
1935. Ts'un hsueh hsiang hsueh hsü chih. Tsi-nan: Shantung Tsou-p'ing hsiang-ts'un chien-she yen-chiu-yuan ch'u-pan ku.
村學鄉學須知。
1937. Hsiang-ts'un chien-she li-lun. Tsou-p'ing, Shantung: Hsiang-ts'un shu-tien.
鄉村建設理論。
1938. Ju-ho k'ang ti. Wuchang: Hsiang-ts'un shu-tien.
如何抗敵。
1945. Chiao-yü lun-wen chi. Chungking: K'ai-ming shu-tien.
教育論文集。
1946. Li Wen pei-hai chen-hsiang. with Chou Hsin-min.
李聞被害眞相。周新民。
1951, November 2. "Liang nien lai wo yu na hsieh chuan-pien." *Kuang-ming jih-pao*. Peking.
兩年來我有那些轉變。光明日報。
1963. Chung-kuo wen-hua yao-i. Kowloon: Chi ch'eng t'u-shu kung-ssu.
中國文化要義。
ed. of *Kuang-ming pao*. Hong Kong.
光明報。

SOURCES

"The Case of Liang Shu-ming." CB, 185 (June 16, 1952).
Chieh-fang jih-pao. Shanghai, December 21, 1955.

解放日報。

Liang Shu-ming. Chiao-yü lun-wen chi. Chung-king: K'ai-ming shu-tien, 1945.

梁漱溟。 教育論文集。

———. Chung-kuo min-tsu tzu-chiu yün-tung chih tsui-hou chüeh-wu. Peiping: Ts'un chih yueh k'an she, 1932.

梁漱溟。 中國民族自救運動之最後覺悟。

———. Chung-kuo wen-hua yao-i. Kowloon: Chi ch'eng t'u-shu kung-ssu, 1963.

梁漱溟。 中國文化要義。

———. "Liang nien lai wo yu na hsieh chuan-pien." Kuang-ming jih-pao. Peking, November 2, 1951.

梁漱溟。 兩年來我有那些轉變。 光明日報。

———. Tung hsi wen-hua chi ch'i che-hsueh. Shanghai: Shang-wu yin shu kuan, 1922.

梁漱溟。 東西文化及其哲學。

Liang Shu-ming ssu-hsiang p'i-p'an (Lun-wen hui-pien). Peking: Sheng-huo, tu-shu, hsin chih san lien shu-tien, 1955. 2 vols.

梁漱溟思想批判 (論文彙編)。

Van Slyke, Lyman P. "Liang Sou-ming and the Problem of Alternatives in Modern Chinese History." Unpublished Master's thesis, University of Calfornia, 1958.

———. "Liang Sou-ming and the Rural Reconstruction Movement." The Journal of Asian Studies, XVIII-4 (August, 1959).

Liang Ssu-ch'eng   梁 思 成

WORKS

1933. Ta-t'ung ku chien-chu tiao-ch'a pao-kao. with Liu Tun-chen (ed. by Chung-kuo ying-tsao hsueh-she). Peiping: Chung-kuo ying-tsao hsueh-she.

大同古建築調查報告。 劉敦楨。 中國營造學社。

1934. Ch'ing shih ying-tsao tse li. Peiping: Chung-kuo ying-tsao hsueh-she.

清式營造則例。

1934. Ying-tsao suan li. Peiping: Ying-tsao hsueh-she.

營造祚例。

1935. Ch'ing Wen-yuan-ko shih ts'e t'u-shuo. with Liu Tun-chen (ed. by Chung-kuo ying-tsao hsueh-she). Peiping: Chung-kuo ying-tsao hsueh-she.

清文淵閣寔測圖說。 劉敦楨。 中國營造學社。

SOURCES

China News Analysis, 87, 377, 433, 471.
Jen-min jih-pao. Peking, November 14, 1957.
人民日報。

Liang Ssu-yung   梁 思 永

WORKS

1930. New Stone Age Pottery from the Prehistoric Site at Hsiyin Tsun, Shansi, China. Menasha, Wis.: The American Anthropological Association.

1932, October, "Ang-ang-ch'i shih-ch'ien i-chih." Chung-yang yen-chiu-yuan li-shih yü-yen yen-chiu so chi k'an, 4: 1-44.

昂昂溪史前遺址。 中央研究院歷史語言研究所集刊。

1933. "Hou-kang fa-chueh hsiao-chi," in Li Chi et al., An-yang fa-chueh pao-kao, 4. Shanghai.

後岡發掘小記。 李濟等。 安陽發掘報告。

1933. "Hsiao-t'un Lung-shan yü Yang-shao," in Ch'ing-chu Ts'ai Yuan-p'ie hsien-sheng liu-shih-wu sui lun-wen chi. 2 vols.

小屯龍山與仰韶。 慶祝蔡元培先生六十五歲論文集。

1936. "Johol Ch'a-pu-kan-miao, Lin-hsi, Shuang-ch'ih-feng teng ti so ts'ai-chi chih hsin shih-ch'i shih-tai i-wu yü t'ao-p'ien," in Li Chi et al., T'ien-yeh k'ao-ku pao-kao, 1.

熱河查不干廟，林西，雙赤峯等地所採集之新石器時代遺物與陶片。 李濟等。 田野考古報告。

1939. "The Lung-shan Culture—a Prehistoric Phase of Chinese Civilization." Proceedings of the Sixth Pacific Science Congress, IV.

1948. (ed.) Hsiao-t'un; ti-erh pen: Yin hsü wen-tzu—chia pien: t'u pan. with Li Chi et al. Shanghai: Kuo-li Chung-yang yen-chiu-yuan li-shih yü-yen yen-chiu-so.

小屯；第二本：殷虛文字—甲編：圖版。 李濟等。

1959. Liang Ssu-yung k'ao-ku lun-wen chi (ed. by Chung-kuo k'o-hsueh yuan k'ao-ku yen-chiu-so). Peking: K'o-hsueh ch'u-pan she.

梁思永考古論文集。 中國科學院考古研究所。

1962-65. Hou-chia-chuang (Honan An-yang Hou-chia-chuang Yin tai mu-ti) (ed. by Kao Ch'ü-hsun). Taipei: Chung-yang yen-chiu-yuan li-shih yü-yen yen-chiu-so.

侯家莊 (河南安陽侯家莊殷代墓地)。 高去尋。

SOURCES

Fu Ssu-nien *et al.* Ch'eng-tzu-yai (Shangtung Li-ch'eng hsien Lung-shan chen hei-t'ao wen-hua i-chih). Nanking: Kuo-li chung-yang yen-chiu-yuan li-shih yü-yen yen-chiu-so, 1934.
傅斯年等。城子崖 (山東歷城縣龍山鎮黑陶文化遺址)。

Liang Jen-kung hsien-sheng nien-p'u ch'ang pien ch'u-kao, comp. by Ting Wen-chiang. Taipei: Shih-chieh shu-chü, 1958. 2 vols.
梁任公先生年譜長編初稿。丁文江。

Liang Ssu-yung. "Ang-ang-ch'i shih-ch'ien i-chih." *Chung-yang yen-chiu-yuan li-shih yü-yen yen-chiu-so chi k'an*, 4 (1932): 1-44.
梁思永。昂昂溪史前遺址。中央研究院歷史語言研究所集刊。

——. "Hou-kang fa-chueh hsiao-chi," in Li Chi *et al.*, *An-yang fa-chueh pao-kao*, 4. Shanghai, 1933.
梁思永。後岡發掘小記。李濟等。安陽發掘報告。

——. "Hsiao-t'un Lung-shan yü Yang-shao," in *Ch'ing-chu Ts'ai Yuan-p'ei hsien-sheng liu-shih-wu sui lun-wen chi*. 1933. 2 vols.
梁思永。小屯龍山與仰韶。慶祝蔡元培先生六十五歲論文集。

——. "Jehol Ch'a-pu-kan-miao, Lin-hsi, Shuang-ch'ih-feng teng ti so ts'ai-chi chih hsin shih-ch'i shih-tai i-wu yü t'ao-p'ien," in Li Chi *et al.*, *T'ien-yeh k'ao-ku pao-kao*, 1. 1936.
梁思永。熱河查不干廟，林西，雙赤峯等地所採集之新石器時代遺物與陶片。李濟等。田野考古報告。

——. Liang Ssu-yung k'ao-ku lun-wen chi (ed. by Chung-kuo k'o-hsueh yuan k'ao-ku yen-chiu-so). Peking: K'o-hsueh ch'u-pan she, 1959.
梁思永。梁思永考古論文集。中國科學院考古研究所。

——. "The Lung-shan Culture—a Prehistoric Phase of Chinese Civilization." *Proceedings of the Sixth Pacific Science Congress*, IV (1939).

Liao Ch'eng-chih   廖承志

SOURCES

Person interviewed: Chang Kuo-t'ao.

Chao Kuo-chün. The Mass Organizations in Communist China. Boston: Center for International Studies, Massachusetts Institute of Technology, 1953.

HCJC

The New York Times, August 10, 1964.
RD
WWC, 1950.
WWMC

Liao Chung-k'ai   廖仲愷

WORKS

1919, August-September. "Chung-kuo jen-min ho ling-t'u tsai hsin kuo-chia chien-she shang chih kuan-hsi." *Chien-she tsa-chih*, I-1, 2.
中國人民和領土在新國家建設上之關係。建設雜誌。

1919, October-November. "Ch'ien-pi ko-ming yü chien-she." *Chien-she tsa-chih*, I-3, 4.
錢幣革命與建設。建設雜誌。

1920, April. "Tsai lun ch'ien-pi ko-ming." *Chien-she tsa-chih*, II-3.
再論錢幣革命。建設雜誌。

1927. Ch'üan-min cheng-chih. (tr. of Delos F. Wilcox's *Government by All the People*). Shanghai: Min chih shu-chü.
全民政治。

1928. Shuang ch'ing tz'u ts'ao. Shanghai: K'ai-ming shu-tien.
雙清詞草。

1930. Liao Chung-k'ai *et al.* Ching-t'ien chih-tu yu wu chih yen-chiu. Shanghai: Hua t'ung shu-chü.
廖仲愷等，井田制度有無之研究。

1963. Liao Chung-k'ai chi (comp. by Chung-kuo k'o-hsueh yuan Kuang-chou che-hsueh she-hui k'o-hsueh yen-chiu-so). Peking: Chung-hua shu-chü.
廖仲愷集。中國科學院廣州哲學社會科學研究所。

SOURCES

Chang Ch'i-yün. Chung-hua Min-kuo shih-kang, I. Taipei: Chung-hua wen-hua ch'u-pan shih-yeh wei-yuan-hui, 1954.
張其昀。中華民國史綱。

Ch'en Kung-po. "Ch'en Kung-po t'ung-chih pao-kao Liao an chien-ch'a ching-kuo," in *Chung-kuo kuo-min-tang ti-erh tz'u ch'üan-kuo tai-piao ta-hui hui-i chi-lu*. 1926.
陳公博。陳公博同志報告廖案檢察經過。中國國民黨第二次全國代表大會會議記錄。

Chun-kuo kuo-min-tang shih-kao i chih ssu p'ien, comp. by Tsou Lu. Chungking: Shang-wu yin shu kuan, 1944. 4 vols.
中國國民黨史稿一至四篇。鄒魯。

Ho Hsiang-ning. Hui-i Sun Chung-shan ho Liao Chung-k'ai. Peking: Chung-kuo ch'ing-nien ch'u-pan she, 1957.
何香凝。回憶孫中山和廖仲愷。

———. "Wo hsueh-hui shao-fan te shih-hou," in T'ao K'ang-te, *Tzu-chuan chih i-chang*. Canton: Yü-chou feng she, 1938.
何香凝。我學會燒飯的時候。陶亢德。自傳之一章。

———. "Wo te hui-i," in Chung-kuo jen-min cheng-chih hsieh-shang hui-i ch'üan-kuo wei-yuan-hui wen shih tzu-liao yen-chiu wei-yuan-hui, *Hsin-hai ko-ming hui-i-lu*. Peking: Chung-hua shu-chü, 1961. 2 vols?
何香凝。我的回憶。中國人民政治協商會議全國委員會文史資料研究委員會。辛亥革命回憶錄。

Hsueh Chün-tu. Huang Hsing and the Chinese Revolution. Stanford: Stanford University Press, 1961.

Hu Han-min. "Hu Han-min tzu-chuan," in Chung-kuo kuo-min-tang chung-yang wei-yuan-hui tang shih shih-liao pien-tsuan wei-yuan-hui, *Ko-ming wen-hsien, ti-san chi*. Taipei: Chung-yang wen-wu kung-ying she, 1953.
胡漢民。胡漢民自傳。中國國民黨中央委員會黨史史料編纂委員會。革命文獻，第三輯。

KHC

Kuo-fu nien-p'u, ed. by Chung-kuo kuo-min-tang chung-yang tang shih shih-liao pien-tsuan wei-yuan-hui. Taipei: Chung-hua Min-kuo ko-chieh chi-nien kuo-fu pai nien tan-ch'en ch'ou-pei wei-yuan-hui, 1965. 2 vols.
國父年譜。中國國民黨中央黨史史料編纂委員會。

Levenson, Joseph R. "Ill Wind in the Well-Field: The Erosion of the Confucian Ground of Controversy," in Arthur F. Wright, Denis Twitchett, *Confucian Personalities*. Stanford: Stanford University Press, 1962.

Liao Chung-k'ai. Liao Chung-k'ai chi (comp. by Chung-kuo k'o-hsueh yuan Kuang-chou che-hsueh she-hui k'o-hsueh yen-chiu so). Peking: Chung-hua shu-chü, 1963.
廖仲愷。廖仲愷集。中國科學院廣州哲學社會科學研究所。

Liao Chung-k'ai hsien-sheng ai ssu lu. 1926.
廖仲愷先生哀思錄。

RD

T'ang Leang-li. The Inner History of the Chinese Revolution. New York: E. P. Dutton & Co., 1930.

Liao P'ing   廖平

Works

1897. Ku hsueh k'ao. Tsun ching shu-chü.
古學考。

1897? Ssu-i-kuan ching hsueh ts'ung-shu. 14 vols.
四益館經學叢書。

1905. T'ien jen hsueh k'ao.
天人學考。

1921. Hsin ting liu i kuan ts'ung-shu. Chengtu: Ts'un ku shu-chü.
新訂六譯館叢書。

1931. Ku-liang ch'un-ch'iu ching chuan ku i shu. Wei-nan: Yen shih. 6 vols.
穀梁春秋經傳古義疏。

Chin ku hsueh k'ao. 2 vols.
今古學考。

Huang-ti chiang-yü t'u piao.
皇帝疆域圖表。

Wang chih chi shuo.
王制集說。

Sources

Chang Ping-lin. "Ch'ing ku Lung-an fu hsueh chiao-shou Liao chün mu chih ming," in Chang Ping-lin, *T'ai-yen wen-lu hsü-pien*. Hankow: Wuhan yin shu kuan, 1938. 4 vols.
章炳麟。清故龍安府學教授廖君墓誌銘。
章炳麟。太炎文錄續編。

Ch'ien Mu. Chung-kuo chin san-pai nien hsueh-shu shih. Shanghai: Shang-wu yin shu kuan, 1937. 2 vols.
錢穆。中國近三百年學術史。

Hsia Ching-kuan. "Liao P'ing chuan." *Kuo shih kuan kuan-k'an*, ch'uang k'an hao (September, 1947): 79-80.
夏敬觀。廖平傳。國史館館刊。

Meng Wen-t'ung. "Ching yen Liao Chi-p'ing shih yü chin-tai chin-wen hsueh." *Hsueh heng*, 80 (July, 1923): 1-13.
蒙文通。井研廖季平師與近代今文學。學衡。

Schwartz, Benjamin I. In Search of Wealth and Power: Yen Fu and the West. Cambridge: Belknap Press of Harvard University Press, 1964.

Lin Ch'ang-min   林長民

Works

1933. "Ts'an-i-yuan i nien shih," in Tso Shun-sheng, *Chung-kuo chin pai nien shih tzu-liao hsü-*

pien. Shanghai: Chung-hua shu-chü. 2 vols.
參議院一年史。 左舜生。 中國近百年史資
料續編。

Ching kao Jih-pen jen shu.
敬告日本人書。

SOURCES

Person interviewed: Liang Ching-tui.

Ch'en Teng-hao. "Lin Ch'ang-min hsien-sheng shih-lueh pu-i." Unpublished manu-script.
陳登皥。 林長民先生事略補遺。

Ch'en Yü-ling. "Lin Pai-shui hsien-sheng chuan." *Tung-fang tsa-chih*, XXXII-13.
陳與齡。 林白水先生傳。 東方雜誌。

Chia Tsung-fu. Chung-kuo chih-hsien chien-shih. Taipei: Hua kuo ch'u-pan she, 1953.
賈宗復。 中國制憲簡史。

Chia-yin tsa-chih, I-33 (February, 1926).
甲寅雜誌。

"Chin-pu-tang ch'eng-li chi." *Shen-chou ts'ung-pao*, I-1 (1913).
進步黨成立記。 神州叢報。

Chung-hua Min-kuo hsien-fa shih, comp. by Wu Tsung-tz'u. Peking: Ta-tung shu-chü, 1923. 2 vols.
中華民國憲法史。 吳宗慈。

CMMC

Hou sun kung yuan tsa lu.
後孫公園雜錄。

Hsin-hai ko-ming, ed. by Ch'ai Te-keng *et al.* Shanghai: Shanghai jen-min ch'u-pan she, 1957. 8 vols.
辛亥革命。 柴德賡等。

Hsü Chih-mo. Chih-mo Jih-chi (with Hsiao-man jih-chi) (comp. by Lu Hsiao-man). Shangnai: Ch'en-kuang ch'u-pan kung-ssu, 1947.
徐志摩。 志摩日記 （附：小曼日記）。 陸小曼。

Hsü Chih-mo nien-p'u, comp. by Ch'en Ts'ung-chou. Shanghai: Ch'en-shih tzu-yin, 1949.
徐志摩年譜。 陳從周。

Hsü I-shih. "T'an Lin Ch'ang-min." *Ku-chin tsa-chih*, XXXVIII-34 (January 1, 1944).
徐一士。 談林長民。 古今雜誌。

Hua Mei hsieh-chin hui Chung-kuo liu-hsueh-sheng t'ung-hsin.
華美協進會中國留學生通訊。

Je feng, July 1, 1956.
熱風。

Jen-wen yueh-k'an, VI-7 (September, 1935).
人文月刊。

Kao I-han. "Erh-shih nien lai chih Chung-kuo cheng-tang." *Tung-fang tsa-chih*, 1924 nien chi-nien hao.
高一涵。 二十年來之中國政黨。 東方雜誌, 1924 年紀念號。

Kuo-fu nien-p'u, ed. by Chung-kuo kuo-min-tang chung-yang tang shih shih-liao pien-tsuan wei-yuan-hui. Taipei: Chung-hua Min-kuo ko-chieh chi-nien kuo-fu pai-nien tan-ch'en ch'ou-pei wei-yuan-hui, 1965. 2 vols.
國父年譜。 中國國民黨中央黨史史料編纂委員會。

Liang Ching-tui. "Chui-nien Lin Ch'ang-min hsien-sheng." *Hua Mei jih-pao*. New York, June 7, 1958.
梁敬錞。 追念林長民先生。 華美日報。

———. "Chui-nien Lin Tsung-meng hsien-sheng." *Hua Mei jih-pao*. New York, April, 1954.
梁敬錞。 追念林宗孟先生。 華美日報。

———. "Lin Ch'ang-min hsien-sheng chuan." *Chuan-chi wen-hsueh*, VII-2 (August, 1965).
梁敬錞。 林長民先生傳。 傳記文學。

"Liang Ching-tui yü Chang Shih-chao lai-wang shu-cha." *Chia-yin chou-k'an*, I-44.
梁敬錞與章士釗來往書札。 甲寅週刊。

Liang Jen-kung hsien-sheng nien-p'u ch'ang pien ch'u-kao, comp. by Ting Wen-chiang. Taipei: Shih-chieh shu-chü, 1958. 2 vols.
梁任公先生年譜長編初稿。 丁文江。

Lin Ch'ang-min. "Ts'an-i-yuan i nien shih," in Tso Shun-sheng, *Chung-kuo chin pai nien shih tzu-liao hsü-pien*. Shanghai: Chung-hua shu-chü. 2 vols.
林長民。 參議院一年史。 左舜生。 中國近百年史資料續編。

Liu I-fen. Min-kuo cheng-shih shih-i; shang-ts'e.
劉以芬。 民國政史拾遺；上冊。

Shen Ssu-ch'i. "Yuan Shih-k'ai yü Lin Ch'ang-min." *Jen-wen yueh-k'an*, VIII-1 (February 15, 1937).
沈思齊。 袁世凱與林長民。 人文月刊。

Tung-fang tsa-chih, XX-6; XXI-6.
東方雜誌。

Wang Chung. "Hsien-tai shih-liao ssu: 'Min-kuo ch'u-ch'i cheng-tang chih yen-pien shih-lueh.'" *Jen-wen yueh-k'an*, VIII-5 (June 15, 1937).
汪中。 現代史料四：「民國初期政黨之演變史略」。人文月刊。

Wu T'ieh-ch'eng. Ssu-shih nien lai chih Chung-kuo yü wo; Wu T'ieh-ch'eng hsien-sheng hui-i-lu. Taipei, 1957.

吳鐵城。四十年來之中國與我；吳鐵城先
生回憶錄。

Lin Hsien-t'ang   林獻堂

WORKS

Huan-ch'iu yu chi.
環球遊記。

SOURCES

Liang Jen-kung hsien-sheng nien-p'u ch'ang
pien ch'u-kao, ed. by Ting Wen-chiang.
Taipei: Shih-chieh shu-chü, 1958. 2 vols.
梁任公先生年譜長編初稿。丁文江。
Lin Hsien-t'ang hsien-sheng chi-nien chi, ed. by
Lo Wan-chü. 1960.
林獻堂先生紀念集。羅萬俥。
Meskill, Johanna M. "The Lins of Wufeng:
The Making of a Taiwanese Gentry Family."
Unpublished manuscript, University Seminar
on Modern East Asia; Columbia University,
November 17, 1965.

Lin K'o-sheng   林可勝

SOURCES

Persons interviewed: not to be identified.
CH
GCJJ

Lin Piao   林彪

WORKS

1959. March Ahead under the Red Flag of the
Party's General Line and Mao Tse-tung's
Military Thinking. Peking: Foreign Languages Press.
1965. Jen-min chan-cheng sheng-li wan-sui; chi-
nien Chung-kuo jen-min k'ang Jih chan-cheng
sheng-li erh-shih chou-nien (I-chiu-liu-wu
nien chiu-yueh san jih). Peking: Jen-min
ch'u-pan she.
人民戰爭勝利萬歲；紀念中國人民抗日戰
爭勝利二十周年（一九六五年九月三日）。
Eng. tr., "Long Live the Victory of People's
War! In Commemoration of the 20th Anniversary of Victory in the Chinese People's
War of Resistance Against Japan." Peking
Review, 36 (September 3, 1965): 9-30.
1966. Lin Piao et al. Tsai Mao Tse-tung ssu-
hsiang te ta-lu shang ch'ien-chin. Peking:
Jen-min ch'u-pan she.

林彪等。在毛澤東思想的大路上前進。
1966. Lin Piao t'ung-chih, Chou En-lai t'ung-
chih tsai chieh-chien ch'üan-kuo ko-ti ko-ming
shih sheng ho ch'ün-chung ta-hui shang te
chiang-hua. with Chou En-lai. Hong Kong:
San lien shu-tien.
林彪同志，周恩來同志在接見全國各地革
命師生和群眾大會上的講話。周恩來。
1966. Lin Piao t'ung-chih kuan-yü wu-ch'an
chieh-chi wen-hua ta ko-ming te liang-p'ien
chiang-hua (1966 nien 8 yueh 18 jih chi 31 jih).
Peking: Jen-min ch'u-pan she.
林彪同志關於無產階級文化大革命的兩篇
講話（1966 年 8 月 18 日及 31 日）。
1966. Lin Piao t'ung-chih lun cheng-ch'üan wen-
t'i. Peking?
林彪同志論政權問題。
1966. Lin Piao t'ung-chih tsai chung-yang kung-
tso hui-i shang te chiang-hua. Peking: Peking
kung nung ping t'i-yü hsueh-yuan Mao Tse-
tung chu-i ping-t'uan.
林彪同志在中央工作會議上的講話。

SOURCES

Person interviewed: Chang Kuo-t'ao.
Chao Kuan-i and Wei Tan-po. Chung-kung
jen-wu su-miao. Kowloon: Tzu-yu ch'u-pan
she, 1951.
趙貫一，韋丹柏。中共人物素描。
"China's Recipe for 'People's War'." Asian Ana-
lyst, October, 1965: 13-17.
Chou Ch'ih-p'ing. "Tung-pei chieh-fang chan-
cheng shih-ch'i te Lin Piao t'ung-chih."
Chung-kuo ch'ing-nien, 8 (April 16, 1960): 20-26.
周赤萍。東北解放戰爭時期的林彪同志。
中國青年。
Chu Wen-lin. "Lin Piao—Mao Tse-tung's Close
Comrade-in-Arms." Issues and Studies, III-4
(January, 1967): 1-11; III-5 (February, 1967):
28-35.
Chung-kuo kung-ch'an-tang te chung-yao jen-
wu. Peiping: Min-chien ch'u-pan she, 1949.
中國共產黨的重要人物。
CKJWC
Gayn, Mark. "To Mao We Are the Prime
Enemy." The New York Times Magazine,
October 24, 1965: 46-47, 172-82.
GCCJK
GCJJ
Halperin, Morton H., and John Wilson Lewis.
"Communist China Army-Party Relations."
Military Review, XLVII-2 (February, 1967):
71-78.

Halperin, Morton H., and John Wilson Lewis. "New Tensions in Army-Party Relations in China." *The China Quarterly*, 26 (April-June, 1966): 58–67.

HCJC

Jen-min chiang-ling ch'ün-hsiang, comp. by Hai Yün. Macao: Ch'un-ch'iu shu-tien, 1947.
人民將領群像。海雲。

Johnson, Chalmers. "Lin Piao's Army and Its Role in Chinese Society." *Current Scene*, IV-13 (July, 1966): 1–10; IV-14 (July, 1966): 1–10.

Kung Ch'u. Wo yü hung chün. Kowloon: Nan feng ch'u-pan she, 1955.
龔楚。我與紅軍。

Li Tien-min. "Rise of Lin Piao in the Chinese Communist Hierarchy." *Issues and Studies*, III-1 (October, 1966): 8–19.

Lin Piao. "Long Live the Victory of People's War! In Commemoration of the 20th Anniversary of Victory in the Chinese People's War of Resistance Against Japan." *Peking Review*, 36 (September 3, 1965): 9–30.

"Lin Piao: Mao's Man." *Communist Affairs*, IV-6 (November-December, 1966): 27–30.

Liu Yuan-shen. "Lin Piao te kuo-ch'ü yü hsien-tsai." *Fei ch'ing yen-chiu*, I-1 (January, 1967): 61–71.
劉原深。林彪的過去與現在。匪情研究。

"Marshals of the People's Republic of China." *People's China*, 20 (October 16, 1955): 36–40.

Mozingo, D. P., and T. W. Robinson. "Lin Piao on 'People's War': China Takes a Second Look at Vietnam." *Memorandum RM-4814-PR* (November, 1965), RAND Corp.

The New York Times, September 18, 1959; March 25, 1965; May 15, August 13, September 5, 1966.

Newsweek, September 5, 1966.

Pen k'an tzu-liao shih. "Chung-kung shou-yao shih-lueh—Lin Piao." *Fei ch'ing-yen-chiu*, I-2 (February, 1967): 114–22.
本刊資料室。中共首要事略—林彪。匪情研究。

"A Plea for People's War; Peking's Manifesto for World Revolution." *Current Scene*, III-28 (October, 1965): 1–10.

RD

RSOC

Snow, Edgar. "The Man Alongside Mao: Deputy Lin Piao's Thoughts and Career." *New Republic*, December 3, 1966: 15–18.

Time, September 9, 1966: 28–32.

Topping, Seymour. "Long Live Chairman Mao! Long Live Lin Piao!" *The New York Times Magazine*, July 17, 1966: 18–19, 38–40.

Ts'ao Chü-jen. Ts'ai-fang wai chi. Hong Kong: Ch'uang k'en ch'u-pan she, 1955.
曹聚仁。採訪外記。

Lin Po-ch'ü 林伯渠

SOURCES

Person interviewed: Chang Kuo-t'ao.

CPR, 993 (October 18, 1949).

Elegant, Robert S. China's Red Masters. New York: Twayne, 1951.

The New York Times, May 30, 1960.

RD

RSOC

SCMP, 2272 (June 7, 1960); 2273 (June 8, 1960); 2274 (June 9, 1960); 2547 (July 28, 1961).

WWMC

Lin Sen 林森

WORKS

1957. Lin chu-hsi i-mo (comp. by Lin Hsi-yueh). Chia-i, Taiwan: Hsing chien wen-hua ch'u-pan she.
林主席遺墨。林希岳。

1966. Ch'ien kuo-min cheng-fu chu-hsi Lin kung Tzu-ch'ao i-chi, ed. by Kuo shih kuan, Chung-kuo kuo-min-tang chung-yang wei-yuan-hui tang shih shih-liao pien-tsuan wei-yuan-hui. Taipei: Ch'ien kuo-min cheng-fu ku chu-hsi Lin Sen hsien-sheng pai nien tan-ch'en chi-nien ch'ou-pei wei-yuan-hui.
前國民政府主席林公子超遺集。國史館，中國國民黨中央委員黨史史料編纂委員會。

SOURCES

Chang Ch'i-yün. "Lin chu-hsi chih feng-fan." *Chuan-chi wen-hsueh*, VIII-2 (February, 1966): 3–9.
張其昀。林主席之風範。傳記文學。

———. Tang shih kai-yao. Taipei: Chung-yang kai-tsao wei-yuan-hui wen-wu kung-ying she, 1951–52. 5 vols.
張其昀。黨史概要。

Ch'ien Tuan-sheng. The Government and Politics of China. Cambridge: Harvard University Press, 1950.

Ch'iu Pin-ts'un. "Lin Tzu-ch'ao hsien-sheng yü Taiwan—ts'ung ssu-shih yü nien ch'ien Lin Sen kei Chang Shao-hsiang te i feng hsin shuo ch'i" *Chuan-chi wen-hsueh*, VIII-2 (February, 1966): 14–15.

丘斌存。林子超先生與台灣一從四十餘年
前林森給張少湘的一封信說起。傳記文學。

Chung-kuo kuo-min-tang shih-kao i chih ssu
p'ien, comp. by Tsou Lu. Chungking: Shang-
wu yin shu kuan, 1944. 4 vols.
中國國民黨史稿一至四篇。鄒魯。

Fang Yü. "Lin Sen erh san shih." *Chin shan
shih-pao*. San Francisco, December 22, 1956.
方聿。林森二三事。金山時報。

Hu Shih *et al*. Lin Sen chi-nien chi. Taipei:
Wen hsing shu-tien, 1966.
胡適等。林森紀念集。

Huang Chi-lu. "I p'ing-tan erh chü yuan-shih
te Lin chu-hsi." *Chuan-chi wen-hsueh*, VIII-2
(February, 1966): 10–13.
黃季陸。憶平淡而具遠識的林主席。傳記
文學。

Jo Ting (pseud.). "Lin ku chu-hsi te feng i."
Hua Mei jih-pao. New York, October 17,
1966.
若定。林故主席的風義。華美日報。

Lin Shu   林紓

WORKS

1904. Chia-yin hsiao chuan. (tr. of H. Rider
Haggard's *Joan Haste*).
迦茵小傳。

1905. Fei-chou yen shui ch'ou ch'eng lu. (tr. of
Haggard's *Allan Quatermain*).
斐洲烟水愁城錄。

1905. Lu-pin-sun p'iao-liu chi. (tr. of Daniel
Defoe's *Robinson Crusoe*).
魯濱遜飄流記。

1905. Sa-k'o-sun chieh hou ying-hsiung lueh.
(tr. of Sir Walter Scott's *Ivanhoe*).
撒克遜劫後英雄略。

1906. Chin feng t'eih yü lu. (tr. of Sir Arthur
Conan Doyle's *Micah Clarke*).
金風鐵雨錄。

1906. Hai-wai hsien ch'ü lu. (tr. of Jonathan
Swift's *Gulliver's Travels*).
海外軒渠錄。

1906. Lü-hsing shu i. (tr. of Washington Irving's
Tales of a Traveller).
旅行述異。

1907? Fu chang lu. (tr. of Washington Irving's
Sketch Book).
拊掌錄。

1907. Hua-chi wai-shih. (tr. of Charles Dickens'
Nicholas Nickleby).
滑稽外史。

1907. Shih-tzu-chün ying-hsiung chi. (tr. of Sir
Walter Scott's *The Talisman*).
十字軍英雄記。

1908. Hsin t'ein fang yeh t'an. (tr. of Robert
Louis Stevenson's *New Arabian Nights*).
新天方夜譚。

1908. Ping hsüeh yin-yuan. (tr. of Charles
Dickens' *Dombey and Son*).
冰雪因緣。

1908. Tsei shih. (tr. of Charles Dickens' *Oliver
Twist*).
賊史。

1910. Wei-lu wen-chi. Shanghai: Shang-wu yin
shu kuan.
畏廬文集。

1914. Chin-ling ch'iu.
金陵秋。

1914. Lin i hsiao-shuo ts'ung-shu. Shanghai:
Shang-wu yin shu kuan. 97 vols.
林譯小說叢書。

1916. Wei-lu hsü-chi. Shanghai: Shang-wu yin
shu kuan.
畏廬續集。

1917. Jen kuei kuan-t'ou. (tr. of Leo Tolstoy's
The Death of Ivan Ilyitch).
人鬼關頭。

1918. Hsien shen shuo fa. (tr. of Leo Tolstoy's
Childhood, Boyhood, and Youth).
現身說法。

1919. Shih wan yuan. (tr.) Shanghai? Chen-t'an
hsiao-shuo she.
十萬元。

1922. Wei-lu man lu. Shanghai: Shang-wu yin
shu kuan. 4 vols.
畏廬漫錄。

1922. Wei-lu so-chi. Shanghai: Shang-wu yin
shu kuan.
畏廬瑣記。

1923. Wei-lu shih ts'un. Shanghai: Shang-wu
yin shu kuan. 2 vols.
畏廬詩存。

1924. Wei-lu san chi. Shanghai: Shang-wu yin
shu kuan.
畏廬三集。

1926. Lin Shu *et al*. Wen-hsueh ch'ang-shih;
cheng-pien chi fu-k'an. (ed. by Liu Chin-
chiang). Shanghai: Yuan chi shu-wu.
林紓等。文學常識；正編及附刊。劉錦江。

1934. Han Liu wen yen-chiu fa. Shanghai:
Shang-wu yin shu kuan.
韓柳文研究法。

1934. Lin Wei-lu i-chi; i chih erh chi. Shanghai:
Shang-wu yin shu kuan. 2 vols.

林畏廬遺蹟；一至二集。

1935. Wei-lu lun-wen. Shanghai: Shang-wu yin shu kuan.
畏廬論文。

1936. Ch'un-chueh-chai lun hua. Peiping: Yen-ching ta-hsueh.
春覺齋論畫。

Ai ch'ui lu. (tr.)
哀吹錄。

Chan ch'ao chi. (tr. of I. R. Wyss' *The Swiss Family Robinson*).
鸛巢記。

Chin-kuo yang ch'iu. Chung-hua pien i she.
中國陽秋。

Hsiao nü nai erh chuan. (tr. of Charles Dickens' *The Old Curiosity Shop*).
孝女耐兒傳。

Huang-t'ang yen. (tr. of tales from Edmund Spenser's *Faerie Queene*).
荒唐言。

Kuei wu. (tr.)
鬼悟。

Mei nieh. (tr. of Henrik Ibsen's *Ghosts*).
梅孽。

Mo hsia chuan. (tr. of Miguel de Cervantes' *Don Quixote*).
魔俠傳。

Shuang hsiung i ssu lu. (tr. of Victor Hugo's *Quatre-vingt-treize*).
雙雄義死錄。

Tung ming chi. (tr.)
洞冥記。

SOURCES

Ch'en Yen. "Lin Shu chuan," in Ch'en Yen, *Min-hou hsien-chih*. 1933. 16 vols.
陳衍。林紓傳。陳衍。閩候縣志。

Cheng Chen-to. "Lin Ch'in-nan hsien-sheng." *Hsiao-shou yueh-pao*, XV-11 (November 10, 1924).
鄭振鐸。林琴南先生。小說月報。

CHMI

Chow Ts'e-tsung. Lin Shu nien-p'u. 1959.
周策縱。林紓年譜。

———. The May Fourth Movement: Intellectual Revolution in Modern China. Cambridge: Harvard University Press, 1960.

Han Kuang. Lin Ch'in-nan. Shanghai: Chung-hua shu-chü, 1935.
寒光。林琴南。

Lin Shu. Lin i hsiao-shuo ts'ung-shu. Shanghai: Shang-wu yin shu kuan, 1914. 97 vols.
林紓。林譯小說叢書。

Lin Shu. Wei-lu hsü-chi. Shanghai: Shang-wu yin shu kuan, 1916.
林紓。畏廬續集。

———. Wei-lu man lu. Shanghai: Shang-wu yin shu kuan, 1922. 4 vols.
林紓。畏廬漫錄。

———. Wei-lu san chi. Shanghai: Shang-wu yin shu kuan, 1924.
林紓。畏廬三集。

———. Wei-lu shih-ts'un. Shanghai: Shang-wu yin shu kuan, 1923. 2 vols.
林紓。畏廬詩存。

———. Wei-lu so-chi. Shanghai: Shang-wu yin shu kuan, 1922.
林紓。畏廬瑣記。

———. Wei-lu wen-chi. Shanghai: Shang-wu yin shu kuan, 1910.
林紓。畏廬文集。

Yang Yin-shen. Chung-kuo wen-hsueh chia lieh chuan. Shanghai: Chung-hua shu-chü, 1939.
楊蔭深。中國文學家列傳。

Lin Wen-ch'ing   林文慶

WORKS

1927. Tragedies of Eastern Life; an Introduction to the Problem of Social Psychology. Shanghai: Commercial Press.

1929. (ed. and tr.) The Li sao, an Elegy on Encountering Sorrows, by Ch'u Yüan, of the State of Ch'u (circa 338–288 B.C.). Shanghai: The Commercial Press.

1930–? ed. of *Chinese Nation*.

SOURCES

Ch'en Chia-keng. Nan ch'iao hui-i lu. Nan-t'ai: Foochow chi mei hsiao-yu hui, 1950. 2 vols.
陳嘉庚。南僑回憶錄。

Feng Tzu-yu. Ko-ming i-shih. Shanghai, Chungking: Shang-wu yin shu kuan, 1939-47. 5 vols.
馮自由。革命逸史。

Wu Lien-teh. Plague Fighter, the Autobiography of a Modern Chinese Physician. Cambridge: W. Heffer, 1959.

Lin Yü-t'ang   林語堂

WORKS

1923. "Altchinesische Lautlehre." Unpublished Ph. D. Dissertation, University of Leipzig.

1929. Nü-tzu yü chih-shih. (tr.) Shanghai: Pei hsin shu-chü.
女子與知識。

1930. Hsin te wen p'ing. (tr.) Shanghai: Pei hsin shu-chü.
新的文評。

1934. Yü-yen hsueh lun-ts'ung. Shanghai: K'ai-ming shu-tien.
語言學論叢。

1936. A History of the Press and Public Opinion in China. Chicago: The University of Chicago Press.

1937. Confucious Saw Nancy, and Essays about Nothing. Shanghai: The Commercial Press.

1937. The Importance of Living. New York: Reynal & Hitchcock.

1937. Yü-t'ang yu-mo wen-hsuan (comp. by Ho Hsü-jen). Shanghai: Wan-hsiang shu-wu.
語堂幽默文選。何須忍。

1938. Chung-kuo yü Chung-kuo jen (tr. by Ting Ching-hsin). Chan shih tu-wu pien i she.
中國與中國人。丁鏡心。

1938. (ed. and tr.) The Wisdom of Confucius. New York: Modern Library.

1939. The Birth of a New China: A Personal Story of the Sino-Japanese War. New York: The John Day Co.

1939. (comp.) Hsien-tai yu-mo wen-hsuan. Shanghai: Wen-hua li-chin she.
現代幽默文選。

1939. Hsin Chung-kuo chih tan-sheng (comp. and tr. by Chung ying ch'u-pan she). Shang-hai: Mei shang sheng tun yin-shua kung-ssu.
新中國之誕生。中英出版社。

1939. Moment in Peking. New York: The John Day Co.

1939. My Country and My People. New York: The John Day Co.
Chinese tr. by Cheng T'o, *Wu kuo yü wu min*. Shanghai: Shih-chieh hsin-wen she, 1939. 2 vols.
鄭陀。吾國與吾民。

1939. Six Chapters of a Floating Life (tr. of Shen Fu's Fu-sheng liu-chi). Shanghai: Hsi feng she.

1940. With Love and Irony. New York: The John Day Co.

1941. Chin hsiu chi (comp. by Liang Nai-chih). Shanghai: Shuo feng shu-tien.
錦秀集。梁迺治。

1941. Chung-kuo sheng-jen (tr. by Shen Ch'en). Shanghai: Shuo feng shu-tien.
中國聖人。沈沉。

1941. Hsing su chi. Hong Kong: Kuang-hua ch'u-pan she.
行素集。

1941. K'ung-tzu chih hsueh (tr. by Lo Ch'ien-shih). Shanghai: I-liu shu-tien.
孔子之學。羅潛士。

1941. A Leaf in the Storm: A Novel of War-Swept China. New York: The John Day Co.

1941. P'ei ching chi. Hong Kong: Kuang-hua ch'u-pan she.
披荊集。

1941. Yü-t'ang sui-pi (tr. by Lin Chün-ch'ien). Shanghai: Jen-chien ch'u-pan she.
語堂隨筆。林俊千。

1941. Yü-t'ang wen-ts'un; ti-i ts'e. Shanghai: Lin shih ch'u-pan she.
語堂文存;第一冊。

1942. (comp.) The Wisdom of China and India. New York: Random House.

1945. Between Tears and Laughter. Garden City, N. Y.: Blue Ribbon Books.

1945. The Vigil of a Nation. New York: The John Day Co.

1947. (ed. and annot.) "Democracy": A Digest of the Bible of Chinese Communism. New York: Chinese News Service.

1947. The Gay Genius: The Life and Times of Su Tungpo. New York: The John Day Co.

1948. Chinatown Family. New York: The John Day Co.

1948. (ed. and tr.) The Wisdom of Laotze. New York: Modern Library.

1950. (comp.) On the Wisdom of America. New York: The John Day Co.

1951. Widow, Nun, and Courtesan. (tr.) New York: The John Day Co.

1953. The Vermilion Gate: A Novel of a Far Land. New York: The John Day Co.

1955. Looking Beyond. New York: Prentice-Hall.

1958. Ni ming (tr. by Chung-yang jih-pao she). Taipei: Chung-yang jih-pao she.
匿名。中央日報社。

1958. The Secret Name. New York: Farrar, Straus & Cudahy.

1959. From Pagan to Christian. Cleveland: World Publishing Co.

1960. The Importance of Understanding: Trans-lations from the Chinese. Cleveland: World Publishing Co.

1961. Imperial Peking: Seven Centuries of China. New York: Crown Publishers.

1961. The Red Peony. Cleveland: World Publishing Co.

1962. The Pleasure of a Non-Conformist. Cleveland: World Publishing Co.

1965. Lady Wu. New York: G. P. Putnam's Sons.

1965. T'ao hsiang tzu-yu ch'eng (tr. by Chang Fu-li).
逃向自由城。張復禮。

1966. (comp.) Chung-kuo ch'uan-ch'i hsiao-shuo. Taipei: T'ien hsiang ch'u-pan she.
中國傳奇小說。

1966. Feng sung chi. Taipei: Chih wen ch'u-pan she.
諷頌集。

1966. Lin Yü-t'ang wen-hsuan. Taichung: I shih shu-chü.
林語堂文選。

1966. Ta huang chi. Taipei: Chih wen ch'u-pan she.
大荒集。

1966. Wo-te hua. Taipei: Chih wen ch'u-pan she.
我的話。

1966. Wu so pu t'ang. Taipei: Wen hsing shu-tien.
無所不談。

1966. Yü-t'ang tsa kan hsuan-chi (tr. by Lin Hsü-huai). Hong Kong: Hui-t'ung shu-tien.
語堂雜感選集。林栩槐。

1966. Yü-t'ang wen-ts'ung—lun-wen, hsiao-p'in, sui-pi, yu-chi. Taipei: Chung hsing shu-chü.
語堂文叢一論文，小品，隨筆，遊記。

1967. The Chinese Theory of Art. New York: G. P. Putnam's Sons.

Jih-pen pi pai lun. Canton: Yü-chou feng she.
日本必敗論。

"Lin Yü-t'ang tzu-chuan." Unpublished manuscript.
林語堂自傳。

ed. of Lun-yü pan yueh-k'an.
論語半月刊。

ed. of The People's Tribune.

ed. of Yü-chou feng.
宇宙風。

SOURCES

East Asian Quarterly of Culture and Synthesis, September 17, 1954.

I ching, 16-34 (1936-37).
逸經。

Kuo wen chou-pao, VII-47.
國聞週報。

Lin, Adet and Anor. Our Family. New York: The John Day Co., 1939.

Lin Yü-t'ang. "Why I Came Back to Christianity." Presbyterian Life, April 15, 1959: 13-15.

Living China: Modern Chinese Short Stories, ed. by Edgar Snow. New York: John Day & Reynal & Hitchcock, 1936.

The New York Times, April 18, 1955.

People's China, 8 (1952).

Ts'ao Chü-jen. Ts'ai-fang wai-chi. Hong Kong: Ch'uang k'en ch'u-pan she, 1955.
曹聚仁。採訪外記。

Liu Chan-en 劉湛恩

WORKS

1922. Non-verbal Intelligence Tests for Use in China. New York: Teachers College, Columbia University.

1926. (ed.) Kung-min yü min-chih. Shanghai: Ch'ing-nien hsieh-hui shu pao pu.
公民與民治。

1926. Liu Chan-en et al. (ed.) Ho-p'ing yün-tung t'ao-lun ta-kang. Shanghai: Ch'ing-nien hsieh-hui shu-chü.
劉湛恩等。和平運動討論大綱。

SOURCES

China Christian Year Book, 1931.

The Chinese Recorder, LXIII-10 (October, 1932): 660; LXIX-4 (April, 1938): 192-194.

GCCJK

I-chiu-wu-ling jen-min nien-chien, ed. by Shen Sung-fang. Hong Kong: Ta kung shu-chü, 1950.
一九五〇人民年鑑。沈頌芳。

Nance, W. B. Soochow University. New York: United Board for Christian Colleges in China, 1956.

North China Herald, April 13, 1938.

WWC, 1936.

Liu Chih 劉峙

WORKS

1947. Huang-p'u chün-hsiao yü kuo-min ko-ming chün. Nanking: Tu-li ch'u-pan she.
黃埔軍校與國民革命軍。

1961. "Tzu-chuan." (mimeo.).
自傳。

Sources

CH
CMMC
CWR, 1929–30; 1936–37.
CYB-W, 1935.
GCJJ
Ho Ying-ch'in. Pa nien k'ang chan chih ching-
kuo. Nanking: Chung-kuo lu-chün tsung-ssu-
ling pu, 1946.
何應欽。八年抗戰之經過。
Kuo-min ko-ming chün chan shih, ed. by Kuo-
min ko-ming chün chan shih pien-tsuan wei-
yuan-hui. Ts'an-mou pen-pu, 1934. 17 vols.
國民革命軍戰史。國民革命軍戰史編纂委
員會。
Liu Chih. "Tzu-chuan." (mimeo.). 1961.
劉峙。自傳。
MSICH
TCJC
Wang Shu-hui. "Liu Ching-fu hsien-sheng shih
kung chi-shih." (mimeo). Chungking, 1944.
王叔惠。劉經扶先生事功紀實。
WWC, 1931.

Liu Chih-tan   劉志丹

Sources

Person interviewed: Chang Kuo-t'ao.
Chung-kung Kao Jao shih-chien mien-mien
kuan, ed. by Shih Chia-lin. Hong Kong:
Kowloon tzu-yu ch'u-pan she, 1955.
中共高饒事件面面觀。史家麟。
Chung-kuo ch'ing-nien, 35 (April 22, 1950).
中國青年。
CKLC
GCCJK
RSOC
Tung Chün-lun. Liu Chih-tan te ku-shih. Pe-
king: Chung-kuo ch'ing-nien ch'u-pan she,
1956.
董均倫。劉志丹的故事。

Liu Fu   劉復

Works

1919. Chung-kuo wen-fa t'ung-lun. Shanghai:
Chung-hua shu-chü.
中國文法通論。
1922. Wa fu chi.
瓦釜集。

1924. Ssu sheng yen lu. Shanghai.
四聲驗錄。
1925. Étude Expérimentale sur les Tons du
Chinois. Paris.
1925. Les Mouvements de la Langue Nationale
en Chine. Paris.
1925. Tun-huang to so. Peking: Kuo-li chung-
yang yen-chiu yuan li-shih yü-yen yen-chiu
so. 2 vols.
燉煌掇瑣。
1926. Ch'a hua nü. (tr. of Alexandre Dumas,
fils, *Dame aux Caméllias*).
茶花女。
1926. (annot.) Ho-tien. Peking: Pei hsin shu-
chu.
何典。
1926. (comp.) T'ai-p'ing t'ien-kuo yu-ch'ü wen-
chien shih-liu chung. Shanghai: Pei hsin shu-
chü.
太平天國有趣文件十六種。
1926. Yang pien chi.
揚鞭集。
1928. Pan-nung t'an ying. Shanghai: K'ai-ming
shu-tien.
半農談影。
1929. Liu-li, han-hsing. Shanghai: Ya-tung t'u-
shu-kuan.
流離，寒星。
1930. (ed.) Sung Yuan i-lai su tzu p'u. with Li
Chia-jui.
宋元以來俗字譜。
1933. Chung-kuo wen-fa chiang-hua. Shanghai:
Pei hsin shu-chü.
中國文法講話。
1933. Ying-yung-wen tso-fa.
應用文作法。
1934. Pan-nung tsa-wen. Peiping: Hsing-yün-
t'ang shu-tien.
半農雜文。
1935. Pan-nung tsa-wen erh chi. Shanghai:
Liang-yu t'u-shu yin-shua kung-ssu.
半農雜文二集。
1935. Shih yün hui-pien. with Lo Ch'ang-p'ei.
Peiping: Kuo-li Peking ta-hsueh yen-chiu
yuan. 3 vols.
十韵彙編。羅常培。
1955. "Tung Jo-yü chuan," in Tung Shuo, *Hsi
yu pu*. Shanghai: Wen-hsueh ku-chi k'an
hsing she.
董若雨傳。董說。西遊補。
1958. Liu Pan-nung shih-hsuan. Peking: Jen-
min wen-hsueh ch'u-pan she.
劉半農詩選。

Liu Fu   [276]

1964. Meng. Hong Kong: Shanghai shu-chü.
夢。

SOURCES

Chou Shu-jen. "I Liu Pan-nung chün," in
Chou Shu-jen, *Lu Hsun ch'üan-chi.* Lu Hsun
hsien-sheng chi-nien wei-yuan-hui, 1938. 20
vols.
周樹人。憶劉半農君。周樹人。魯迅全集。
————. "Wei Pan-nung t'i chi Ho-tien hou tso,"
in Chou Shu-jen, *Hua kai chi (with hsü pien).*
Pei hsih shu-chü, 1935. 2 vols.
周樹人。爲半農題記何典後作。周樹人。
華蓋集（附：續編）。
Hu Shih. "Ting Wen-chiang te chuan-chi."
Chung-yang yen-chiu-yuan yuan k'an, 3.
胡適。丁文江的傳記。中央研究院院刊。
RCCL

Liu Hsiang   劉湘

WORKS

1937. Szechwan sheng k'ang chan shih-ch'i
chung-hsin kung-tso. Chengtu.
四川省抗戰時期中心工作。

SOURCES

CMTC
CWR, 1932–33, 1937–38.
TCJC
WWC
WWMC

Liu Hung-sheng   劉鴻生

SOURCES

China Year Book. Shanghai: The North China
Daily News and Herald, 1934.
Chung-kuo chin-tai kung-yeh shih tzu-liao,
comp. by Ch'en Chen, Yao Lo, Feng Hsien-
chih. Peking: Sheng-huo, tu-shu, hsin chih
san lien shu-tien, 1957-62. 4 vols.
中國近代工業史資料。陳眞，姚洛，逢先
知。
CKJMT
GCCJK
Hsü Ying. Chung-kuo tang-tai shih-yeh jen-wu
chih. Shanghai: Chung-hua shu-chü, 1948.
徐盈。中國當代實業人物誌。
JMST, 1955, 1957.

Liu I-cheng   柳詒徵

WORKS

1929. Po-shan shu ying. Kuo-hsueh t'u-shu-kuan.
盋山書影。
1930. (ed.) T'ao-feng-lou ts'ang ming hsien shou-
chi. Kuo-hsueh t'u-shu-kuan.
陶風樓藏名賢手蹟。
1932. Chung-kuo wen-hua shih. Nanking:
Chung-shan shu-chü.
中國文化史。
1948. Kuo shih yao-i. Shanghai: Chung-hua
shu-chü.
國史要義。

SOURCES

CBJS
GCJJ
Shao Ching-jen. "I shih hsueh chia Liu I-cheng
hsien-sheng." *Chuan-chi wen-hsueh,* I-3 (August
1962).
邵鏡人。憶史學家桺詒徵先生。傳記文學。

Liu Jen-ching   劉仁靜

SOURCES

Persons interviewed: Chang Kuo-t'ao; others
not to be identified.
Ta kung pao. Hong Kong, January 15, 1951.
大公報。

Liu Jui-heng   劉瑞恆

WORKS

1934. Hsin sheng-huo yü chien-k'ang (ed. by
Yeh Ch'u-ts'ang). Nanking: Cheng-chung
shu-chü.
新生活與健康。葉楚傖。
1951. Liu Jui-heng *et al.* Chin-tai i-yao chin-pu
yü wei-sheng shih-yeh chih fa-chan. Taipei:
Ta-lu tsa-chih she.
劉瑞恒等。近代醫藥進步與衞生事業之發
展。

SOURCES

CBJS
GCJJ
New York World-Telegram, August 28, 1961.
TKLH
WWARS
WWC, 1931.

Liu Po-ch'eng　劉伯誠

WORKS

1949. Su-lien kung nung hung chün te pu-ping chan-tou t'iao-ling; ti-i pu. (tr.) with Tso Ch'üan. Hong Kong: Cheng pao ch'u-pan she.
蘇聯工農紅軍的步兵戰鬥條令；第一步。左權。

1952. Liu Po-ch'eng *et al*. Ch'ueh-li wei jen-min fu-wu te jen-sheng-kuan (ed. by Chung-kuo hsin min-chu chu-i ch'ing-nien t'uan Hsi-nan kung-tso wei-yuan-hui). Chungking: Hsi-nan ch'ing-nien ch'u-pan she.
劉伯承等。確立爲人民服務的人生觀。中國新民主主義青年團西南工作委員會。

Ho-t'ung chan-shu.
合同戰術。

SOURCES

Person interviewed: Chang Kuo-t'ao.

Chen Chang-feng. On the Long March with Chairman Mao. Peking: Foreign Languages Press, 1959.

Elegant, Robert S. China's Red Masters. New York: Twayne, 1951.

HCJC

Kan Yu-lan. Mao Tse-tung chi ch'i chi-t'uan. Hong Kong: Kowloon tzu-yu ch'u-pan she, 1954.
甘友蘭。毛澤東及其集團。

Ku Kuan-chiao. San-shih nien lai te Chung kung. Hong Kong: Ya-chou ch'u-pan she, 1955.
古貫郊。三十年來的中共。

Lu Yao-wu. Liu Po-ch'eng chiang-chün hui chün tu Huai-ho. Canton: Hsin hua shu-tien, 1950.
盧耀武。劉伯承將軍揮軍渡淮河。

North, Robert C. Moscow and Chinese Communists. Stanford: Stanford University Press, 1953.

Rigg, Robert B. Red China's Fighting Hordes. Harrisburg, Pa.: Military Service Publishing Co., 1952.

SCMP, 1139.

WWC, 1950.

WWMC

Liu Shao-ch'i　劉少奇

WORKS

1941. Jen te chieh-chi hsing.
人的階級性。

1941. Lun tang nei tou-cheng.
論黨內鬥爭。
Eng. tr., *On Inner-party Struggle: A Lecture Delivered on July 2, 1941, at the Party School for Central China*. Bombay: People's Publishing House, 1951.

1946. Chung kung tsai ti-hou tso le hsieh shen-mo. with P'eng Te-huai *et al*. Chi-lung-p'o: Chung Ma ch'u-pan she.
中共在敵後做了些什麼。彭德懷等。

1947. Kuan-yü hsiu-kai tang-chang te pao-kao. Hong Kong: Chung-kuo ch'u-pan she.
關於修改黨章的報告。

1948. Liu Shao-ch'i *et al*. Chung-kuo kung-ch'an-tang yü kung-ch'an-tang yuan. Hong Kong: Hung mien ch'u-pan she.
劉少奇等。中國共產黨與共產黨員。

1948. Liu Shao-ch'i *et al*. Hsiu-yang chih-nan. Liao-pei: Tung-pei shu-tien.
劉少奇等。修養指南。

1948. Liu Shao-ch'i *et al*. T'u kai cheng tang tien-hsing ching-yen. Hong Kong: Chung-kuo ch'u-pan she.
劉少奇等。土改整黨典型經驗。

1949. Chung Su liang kuo jen-min yung-yuan pu hsiu te yu-i yü ho-tso wan-sui.
中蘇兩國人民永遠不朽的友誼與合作萬歲。

1949. Liu Shao-ch'i *et al*. Chung-kuo ching-chi kai-tsao; ti-erh chi. Hong Kong: Hsin min-ch'u-pan she.
劉少奇等。中國經濟改造；第 2 輯。

1949. Liu Shao-ch'i *et al*. Hsin min-chu chi-i ch'eng-shih cheng-ts'e. Hong Kong: Hsin min-chu chu-i ch'u-pan she.
劉少奇等。新民主主義城市政策。

1949. Liu Shao-ch'i *et al*. Lun ch'ün-chung lu-hsien. Hong Kong: Hsin min-chu ch'u-pan she.
劉少奇等。論群眾路綫。

1949. Lun Kung-ch'an tang-yuan te hsiu-yang; i-chiu-san-chiu nien ch'i-yueh pa jih tsai Yenan Ma Lieh hsueh-yuan te yen-chiang. Shanghai: Hsin hua shu-tien.
論共產黨員的修養；一九三九年七月八日在延安馬列學院的演講。
Eng. tr., *How to be a Good Communist*. Peking: Foreign Languages Press, 1951.

1949. Tsai Chung-kuo jen-min cheng-chih hsieh-shang hui-i ti-i chieh ch'üan-t'i hui-i shang chiang-hua.
在中國人民政治協商會議第一屆全體會議上講話。

1949. Ya-chou Ao-chou kung-hui tai-piao hui-i k'ai-mu-tz'u.

亞洲澳洲工會代表會議開幕詞。

1950. Kuan-yü t'u-ti kai-ko wen-t'i te pao-kao (ed. by Hsin hua shih-shih ts'ung-k'an she). Canton: Hsin hua shu-tien.

關於土地改革問題的報告。 新華時事叢刊社。

1950. Lessons of the Chinese Revolution. with Mao Tse-tung. Bombay: J. Bhatt for People's Publishing House.

1950. Liu Shao-ch'i *et al.* Kung ch'ang kuan-li yü ch'ün chung kung tso. Peking: Kung-jen ch'u-pan she.

劉少奇等。 工廠管理與群眾工作。

1950. Lun tang. Peking: Chieh-fang she.

論黨。

Eng. tr., *On the Party*. Peking: Foreign Languages Press, 1950.

1950. Significance of Agrarian Reforms in China. with Mao Tse-tung. Bombay: J. Bhatt.

1950. Tsai Peking ch'ing-chu wu i lao-tung chieh kan-pu ta-hui shang te yen-shuo (ed. by Hsin hua shih-shih ts'ung-k'an she). Peking: Hsin hua shu-tien.

在北京慶祝五一勞動節幹部大會上的演說。 新華時事叢刊社。

1950, December 9. "Ho kuang-ta te kung nung ping hsiang chieh-ho." *Jen-min jih-pao*. Peking.

和廣大的工農兵相結合。 人民日報。

1951. Hsueh-hsi Chung kung tang shih chung-yao wen-hsien (comp. by Ch'ün-chung jih-pao hsuan-ch'uan pu). Sian: Ch'ün-chung jih-pao t'u-shu ch'u-pan k'o.

學習中共黨史重要文獻。 群眾日報宣傳部。

1951. Lun kuo-chi chu-i yü min tsu chu-i. Peking: Jen-min ch'u-pan she.

論國際主義與民族主義。

Eng. tr., *Internationalism and Nationalism*. Peking: Foreign Languages Press, 1952.

1951. Tsai Chung-kuo kung-ch'an-tang ch'eng-li san-shih chou-nien ch'ing-chu ta-hui shang te chiang-hua.

在中國共產黨成立三十週年慶祝大會上的講話。

1951. (Tsai Peking) Ti-san chieh jen-min tai-piao hui-i shang te chiang-hua. Peking: Jen-min ch'u-pan she.

(在北京) 第三屆人民代表會議上的講話。

1954. Report on the Draft Constitution of the People's Republic of China (with Constitution of the People's Republic of China). Peking: Foreign Languages Press.

1956. Chung-kuo kung-ch'an-tang chung-yang wei-yuan-hui hsiang ti-pa tz'u ch'üan-kuo tai-piao ta-hui te cheng-chih pao-kao (I-chiu-wu-liu nien chiu-yueh shih-wu jih). Peking: Jen-min ch'u-pan she.

中國共產黨中央委員會向第八次全國代表大會的政治報告 (一九五六年九月十五日)。

Eng. tr., *The Political Report of the Central Committee of the Communist Party of China to the Eighth National Congress of the Party, Delivered on September 15, 1956*. Peking: Foreign Languages Press, 1956.

1957. Tsai Peking ko-chieh ch'ing-chu shih-yueh she-hui chu-i ko-ming ssu-shih chou-nien ta-hui shang te chiang-hua (I-chiu-wu-ch'i nien shih-i-yueh liu jih). Peking: Jen-min ch'u-pan she.

在北京各界慶祝十月社會主義革命四十周年大會上的講話 (一九五七年十一月六日)。

1958. Chung-kuo kung-ch'an-tang chung-yang wei-yuan-hui hsiang ti-pa chieh ch'üan-kuo tai-piao ta-hui ti-erh tz'u hui-i te kung-tso pao-kao (I-chiu-wu-pa nien wu-yueh wu jih). Peking: Jen-min ch'u-pan she.

中國共產黨中央委員會向第八屆全國代表大會第二次會議的工作報告 (一九五八年五月五日)。

Eng. tr., "Report on the Work of the Central Committee. Delivered to the Second Section of the 8th National Congress of the Communist Party of China. May 5, 1958." *Current Background*, 507 (June 2, 1958).

1961. Tsai ch'ing-chu Chung-kuo kung-ch'an-tang ch'eng-li ssu-shih chou-nien ta-hui shang te chiang-hua (1960 nien 6 yueh 30 jih). Peking: Jen-min ch'u-pan she.

在慶祝中國共產黨成立四十周年大會上的講話 (1960 年 6 月 30 日)。

Eng. tr., *Address at the Meeting in Celebration of the 40th Anniversary of the Founding of the Communist Party of China*. Peking: Foreign Languages Press, 1961.

1963. Liu Shao-ch'i chu-hsi ho Hu Chih-ming chu-hsi lien-ho sheng-ming. with Hu Chih-ming. Peking: Jen-min ch'u-pan she.

劉少奇主席和胡志明主席聯合聲明。 胡志明。

1966. "Liu Shao-ch'i tzu-wo p'i-p'ing." Facsimile reproduction of manuscript.

劉少奇自我批評。

1967. Liu chu-hsi yü-lu (comp. by Hong Kong tzu lien ch'u-pan she). Hong Kong.
劉主席語錄。香港自聯出版社。

1967. Liu Shao-ch'i hsuan-chi. Tokyo: Chung-hua wen-hua fu-wu she.
劉少奇選集。

SOURCES

Person interviewed: Chang Kuo-t'ao.

Barnett, A. Doak. Communist China and Asia. New York: Harper & Bros. for the Council on Foreign Relations, 1960.

Boorman, Howard L. "How To Be a Good Communist." Asian Survey, III-8 (August, 1963): 372-83.

——. "Liu Shao-ch'i: A Political Profile." The China Quarterly, 10 (April-June, 1962): 1-22.

Brandt, Conrad, Benjamin Schwartz, and John K. Fairbank. A Documentary History of Chinese Communism. Cambridge: Harvard University Press, 1952.

CB, 84; February 20, 1953; 324 (April 5, 1954); 665 (July 12, 1961).

Chang Ai-p'ing. Ts'ung Tsunyi tao Ta-tu-ho. Hong Kong: Sheng-huo, tu-shu, hsin chih san lien shu-tien, 1960.
張愛萍。從遵義到大渡河。

Chao Kuo-chun. "Leadership in the Chinese Communist Party." The Annals of the American Academy of Political and Social Science, 321 (January, 1959): 40-50.

Chen Chang-feng. On the March with Chairman Mao. Peking: Foreign Languages Press, 1959.

Cheng feng wen-hsien, comp. by Chieh-fang she. Peking: Hsin hua shu-tien, 1949.
整風文獻。解放社。

Chesneaux, Jean. Le Mouvement Ouvrier Chinois de 1919 à 1927. Paris: Mouton, 1962.

China News Analysis, 349 (November 18, 1960); 380 (July 14, 1961).

"Chung kung tsai Tung-pei te tsao-ch'i huo-tung." Chin-jih ta-lu, 146 (1961).
中共在東北的早期活動。今日大陸。

Compton, Boyd. Mao's China: Party Reform Documents, 1942-44. Seattle: University of Washington Press, 1952.

Current Biography, October, 1957.

Eckstein, Alexander. "The Strategy of Economic Development in Communist China." The American Economic Review, LI-2 (May, 1961): 508-17.

Eighth National Congress of the Communist Party of China. Peking: Foreign Languages Press, 1956. 3 vols.

Elegant, Robert S. China's Red Masters. New York: Twayne, 1951.

Far Eastern Quarterly, XI-1 (November, 1951): 79-84.

Hinton, Harold C. "China," in George McTurnan Kahin, Major Governments of Asia. Ithaca: Cornell University Press, 1958.

——. "The Eighth Congress of the Chinese Communist Party." Far Eastern Survey, January, 1957.

Ho Kan-chih. A History of the Modern Chinese Revolution. Peking: Foreign Languages Press, 1959.

Houn, Franklin W. "The Eighth Central Committee of the Chinese Communist Party." American Political Science Review, LI (June, 1957): 392-404.

Hsueh-hsi, July 1, 1950.
學習。

Hu Ch'iao-mu. Thirty Years of the Communist Party of China. Hong Kong: American Consulate General, 1950.

Hughes, Richard. "Most Likely to Succeed in Red China." The New York Times Magazine, October 21, 1962.

Hunan li-shih tzu-liao. Changsha: Hunan jen-min ch'u-pan she.
湖南歷史資料。

Hung-se Chung-hua, March 3, 6, April 17, 1933.
紅色中華。

"Kuo kung ho-tso ch'ing tang yün-tung wen-ch'ao." Microfilm, Hoover Institution, Stanford University.
國共合作清黨運動文鈔。

Jen-min jih-pao. Peking, December 9, 1950.
人民日報。

Johnson, Chalmers A. Peasant Nationalism and Communist Power: The Emergence of Revolutionary China, 1937-1945. Stanford: Stanford University Press, 1962.

Lee Ming-hua. "Relations between Mao Tse-tung and Liu Shao-ch'i." Issues and Studies, II-12 (September, 1966): 8-18.

Lewis, John W. Leadership in Communist China. Ithaca: Cornell University Press, 1963.

Lifton, Robert Jay. Thought Reform and the Psychology of Totalism: A Study of "Brainwashing" in China. New York: W. W. Norton, 1961.

Liu Fu-lan. "Liu Shao-ch'i: Mao's Heir Apparent?" *Christian Science Monitor*. Boston, October 13, 1961.

Liu Li-k'ai and Wang Chen. I-chiu-i-chiu chih i-chiu-erh-ch'i nien te Chung-kuo kung-jen yün-tung. Peking: Kung-jen ch'u-pan she 1953.
劉立凱, 王眞。 一九一九至一九二七年的 中國工人運動。

Liu Shao-ch'i. How to Be a Good Communist. Peking: Foreign Languages Press, 1952.

————. On Inner-party Struggle: A Lecture Delivered on July 2, 1941, at the Party School for Central China. Bombay: People's Publishing House, 1951.

————. On the Party. Peking: Foreign Languages Press, 1950.

"Liu Shao-chi'i in Moscow." *China News Analysis*, 349 (November 18, 1960).

Mao Tse-tung. Selected Works. Peking: Foreign Languages Press, 1961. 4 vols.

The New York Times, December 5, 1945; April 27, 28, 1959; December 7, 1960; March 27-29, 1966.

Nivison, David S. "Communist Ethics and Chinese Tradition." *Journal of Asian Studies*, XVI-1 (November, 1956): 51-74.

Pacific Affairs, XXV-4 (December, 1952): 410-11.

The People's Tribune, II-285 (April, 1927); II-289 (April, 1927); II-351 (June, 1927).

SCMP, 751 (February 19, 1954): 1-5; 1911 (December 10, 1958); 2398 (December 15, 1960): 29; 2529 (July 3, 1961).

Snow, Edgar. The Other Side of the River: Red China Today. New York: Random House, 1962.

Teng Chung-hsia. Chung-kuo chih-kung yün-tung chien-shih (1919-1926). Peking: Jen-min ch'u-pan she, 1957.
鄧中夏。 中國職工運動簡史 (1919-1926)。

Time, May 10, 1954; October 12, 1959.

Wang Sze-cheng. The Delicate Relationship between Mao Tse-tung, Liu Shao-chi and Chow En-lai. Taipei: Asian People's Anti-Communist League, 1963.

Wetzel, Hans Heinrich. Liu Shao-ch'i: le Moine Rouge. Paris: Editions Denoël, 1961.

Liu Shih-p'ei   劉師培

WORKS

1904-5. ed. of *Ching chung jih-pao*.
警鐘日報。

1923. Chung-kuo chung-ku wen-hsueh shih chiang-i. Peking: Kuo-li Peking ta-hsueh ch'u-pan pu.
中國中古文學史講義。

1934-38. Liu Shen-shu hsien-sheng i shu (ed. by Cheng Yü-fu). Ning-wu Nan shih. 74 vols.
劉申叔先生遺書。鄭裕孚。

1958. Chung-kuo ku wen-hsueh shih. Hong Kong: Shang-wu yin shu kuan.
中國古文學史。

Mo-tzu shih pu. Taipei: I wen yin shu kuan.
墨子拾補。

SOURCES

CECP

Chow Tse-tsung. The May Fourth Movement: Intellectual Revolution in Modern China. Cambridge: Harverd University Press, 1960.

Feng Tzu-yu. "Chi Liu Kuang-han pien-chieh shih-mo." *Ta feng*, 34 (April 25, 1939): 1127-28.
馮自由。記劉光漢變節始末。大風。

————. Ko-ming i-shih. Shanghai, Chungking: Shang-wu yin shu kuan, 1939-47. 5 vols.
馮自由。革命逸史。

————. "Liu Kuang-han shih-lueh pu-shu." *Ta-feng*, 101 (January 20, 1941).
馮自由。劉光漢事略補述。大風。

————. She-hui chu-i yü Chung-kuo. Hong Kong, 1920.
馮自由。社會主義與中國。

Liu Shih-p'ei. Liu Shen-shu hsien-sheng i shu (ed. by Cheng Yü-fu). Ning-wu Nan shih. 74 vols.
劉師培。劉申叔先生遺書。鄭裕孚。

T'ao Chü-yin. Liu chün-tzu chuan. Shanghai: Chung-hua shu-chü, 1946.
陶菊隱。六君子傳。

Yang Yin-shen. Chung-kuo wen-hsueh chia lieh-chuan. Shanghai: Chung-hua shu-chü, 1939.
楊蔭深。中國文學家列傳。

Liu Ssu-fu   劉思復

WORKS

1914-15. ed. of *Min sheng*.
民聲。

1928. Shih-fu wen-ts'un (ed. by Hsin T'ieh). Canton: Ko-hsin shu-chü.
師復文存。心鐵。

K'ang-hu chi.

亢虎集。
Wu cheng-fu chu-i chi.
無政府主義集。

SOURCES

Feng Tzu-yu. Ko-ming i-shih. Shanghai, Chung-king: Shang-wu yin shu kuan, 1939–47. 5 vols.
馮自由。革命逸史。
Ko-ming te hsien-ch'ü. Shanghai: Tzu-yu shu-tien, 1928.
革命的先驅。
Liu Shih-fu. Shih-fu wen-ts'un (ed. by Hsin T'ieh). Canton: Ko-hsin shu-chü, 1928.
劉師復。師復文存。心鐵。
Min sheng, May 5, 1915.
民聲。

Liu T'ing-fang   劉 廷 芳

WORKS

1920–24. ed. of *Life Journal*.
1922. The Psychology of Learning Chinese Characters.
1922–25. ed. of *Journal of New Education*.
1923. China in American School Textbooks. Peking: Chinese Social and Political Science Association.
1924. Message and Work of the Christian Church in China, a Manual of Worship.
1924. Middle School Intelligence Tests.
1924–26. ed. of *Truth Weekly*.
1928. Mountain Showers.
1928–? ed. of *Truth and Life*.
1929. Feng jen. (tr. of Kahlil Gibran's *Madman*). Shanghai: Pei hsih shu-chü.
瘋人。
1930. Mu-chiang chia (Tu-mu-chü). (tr. of Laurence Housman's *Nazareth*). Shanghai: Pei hsin shu-chü.
木匠家 (獨幕劇)。
1930–? ed. of *The Amethyst*.
1933. Ch'ien-ch'ü che (Yü-yen yü shih-ko). (tr. of Kahlil Gibran's *Forerunner*).
前驅者 (寓言與詩歌)。
1935. Hsin-li hsueh tui-yü tsung-chiao te ying-hsiang (tr. of Eliot's *The Contribution of Modern Psychology to Religion*). Shanghai: Yen-ching ta-hsueh tsung-chiao hsueh-yuan.
心理學對於宗教的影響。
1935. Shan yü. Shanghai: Pei hsin shu-tien.
山雨。
1936. (ed.) Hymns of Universal Praise.

1937. ed. of Book of Common Worship.
ed. of *The Chinese Students' Monthly*.
ed. of *Education for Tommorrow*.
ed. of *Liu Mei ch'ing-nien*.
留美青年。
Problems of the Chinese Church.
The Responsibility of Ministers in the Renaissance Movement.

SOURCES

Person interviewed: Frank W. Price.
"Bibliography of Published Writings of Dr. T.T. Lew, 1921–32." Unpublished manuscript, Missionary Research Library, New York.
China Christian Year Book, 1924, 1925. Shanghai: Christian Literature Society.
The Chinese Recorder, LIII-5 (May, 1922): 290; LIV-12 (December, 1923): 746.
Green, Katherine. "Some Christian Leaders of Present Day China." Unpublished manuscript, Missionary Research Library, New York.
Quarterly Notes. Being the Bulletin of the International Missionary Council, 96 (October, 1947).
Seabury, Ruth I. "Leaders of World Christianity." *Envelope Series*, (XL-1 March, 1939): 22–23.
Who's Who of the Madras Meeting of the International Missionary Council. Madras, 1938.
World Outlook, 3–7 (July, 1917).
WWC, 1936.

Liu Wen-hui   劉 文 輝

WORKS

Chien-she hsin Sikang shih chiang.
建設新西康十講。
Chün-shih che-hsueh kang-yao.
軍事哲學綱要。
Nan hsün chiang-yen chi.
南巡講演集。

SOURCES

AWW, 1960.
CMTC
CTMC
GCJJ
Kuo wen chou-pao, V-36 (September 16, 1928).
國聞週報。
Li I-jen. Sikang tsung-lan. Shanghai: Cheng-chung shu-chü, 1947.
李亦人。西康綜覽。

Li Tieh-tseng. The Historical Status of Tibet. New York: King's Crown Press, Columbia University, 1956.

TCJC

Tsinghai, ed. by Chou Chen-ho. Changsha: Shang-wu yin shu kuan, 1939.
青海。周振鶴。

WWC, 1931.

WWMC

Liu Wen-tao 劉文島

WORKS

1922. Hsin chün lun. (tr. of M. Jaurès' *L'Armée Nouvelle*). Shanghai: Shang-wu yin shu kuan.
新軍論。

1923. Cheng-tang cheng-chih lun. Shanghai: Shang-wu yin shu kuan.
政黨政治論。

1941. Hang-yeh tsu-ho lun. Chungking: Cheng-chung shu-chü.
行業組合論。

1943. Hang-yeh tsu-ho yü chin-tai ssu-ch'ao. Chungking: Shang-wu yin shu kuan.
行業組合與近代思潮。

1944. I-ta-li shih ti. Chungking: Shang-wu yin shu kuan.
意大利史地。

1956. Chung I kuan-hsi te hui-i. Taipei.
中義關係的回憶。

1956. Liu Wen-tao *et al*. Chung I wen-hua lun-chi. Taipei: Chung-hua wen-hua ch'u-pan shih-yeh wei-yuan-hui.
劉文島等。中義文化論集。

SOURCES

BKL

CH-T, 1956–57.

CMJL

CMTC

GCJJ

Kuo chün cheng kung shih kao. Taipei.
國軍政工史稿。

Kuo-min ko-ming chün chan shih, ed. by Kuo-min ko-ming chün chan shih pien-tsuan wei-yuan-hui. Ts'an-mou pen-pu, 1934. 17 vols.
國民革命軍戰史。國民革命軍戰史編纂委員會。

Liu Wen-tao. Chung I kuan-hsi te hui-i. Taipei, 1956.
劉文島。中義關係的回憶。

WWC, 1931.

Liu Ya-tzu 柳亞子

WORKS

1911. ed. of *T'ieh pi pao*.
鐵筆報。

1912. ed. of *Min sheng jih-pao*.
民聲日報。

1912. ed. of *T'ai-p'ing-yang pao*.
太平洋報。

1912. ed. of *T'ien tuo pao*.
天鐸報。

1928. (comp.) Su Man-shu nien-p'u chi ch'i-t'a. with Liu Wu-chi. Shanghai: Pei-hsin shu-chü.
蘇曼殊年譜及其他。柳無忌。

1930–31. (comp.) Su Man-shu ch'üan-chi. Shanghai: Pei hsin shu-chü. 5 vols.
蘇曼殊全集。

1940. Nan she chi lueh. Shanghai: K'ai hua shu-chü.
南社紀略。

1947. Huai chiu chi.
懷舊集。

1959. Liu Ya-tzu shih tz'u hsuan (ed. by Liu Wu-fei, Liu Wu-hou). Peking: Jen-min wen-hsueh ch'u-pan she.
柳亞子詩詞選。柳無非，柳無垢。

Ch'eng fu chi.
乘桴集。

SOURCES

Persons interviewed: Liu Wu-chi; others not to be identified.

Lo Ch'ang-p'ei 羅常培

WORKS

1930. Amoy yin hsi. Peiping: Kuo-li chung-yang yen-chiu yuan li-shih yü-yen yen-chiu so.
廈門音系。

1933. T'ang Wu-tai hsi-pei fang yin. Kuo-li chung-yang yen-chiu yuan li-shih yü-yen yen-chiu so.
唐五代西北方音。

1938. Kuo-yin tzu-mu yen-chin shih. Changsha: Shang-wu yin shu kuan.
國音字母演進史。

1940. Lin-ch'uan yin hsi. Changsha: Shang-wu yin shu kuan.
臨川音系。

1945. Chung-kuo jen yü Chung-kuo wen. Chungking: K'ai-ming shu-tien.
中國人與中國文。

1949. Han-yü yin-yün hsueh tao-lun. Peking:
Peking ta-hsueh.
漢語音韻學導論。

1950. Peking su ch'ü pai chung tse yün. Peking: Lai-hsun-ko shu-tien.
北京俗曲百種摘韻。

1950. Yü-yen yü wen-hua (with Fu-lu ssu chung).
Peking: Kuo-li Peking ta-hsueh.
語言與文化 (附: 附錄四種)。

1952. Lo Ch'ang-p'ei *et al.* I-chiu-wu-ling nien
Chung-kuo yü-wen wen-t'i lun-wen chi-yao
(ed. by Tu Tzu-ching). Peking: Ta-chung
shu-tien.
羅常培等。 一九五〇年中國語文問題論文
輯要。 杜子勁。

1952-58. ed. of *Chung-kuo yü-wen.*
中國語文。

1957. P'u-t'ung yü-yin-hsueh kang-yao. with
Wang Chün. Peking: K'o-hsueh ch'u-pan she.
普通語音學綱要。 王均。

1959. (ed.) Pa ssu pa tzu yü Yuan-tai han-yü
(tzu-liao hui-pien). with Ts'ai Mei-piao. Peking: K'o-hsueh ch'u-pan she.
八思巴字與元代漢語 (資料彙編)。 蔡美彪。

1963. Lo Ch'ang-p'ei yü-yen-hsueh lun-wen
hsuan-chi (ed. by Chung-kuo k'o-hsueh yuan
yü-yen yen-chiu so). Peking: Chung-hua shu-
chü.
羅常培語言學論文選集。 中國科學院語言
研究所。

SOURCES

Persons interviewed: not to be identified.
Chung-kuo yü-wen, October, 1959.
中國語文。
"Lo Ch'ang-p'ei hsien-sheng chu-tso mu-lu (ch'u-
kao)." *Chung-kuo yü-wen*, February, 1959.
羅常培先生著作目錄 (初稿)。 中國語文。
"Tao-nien Lo Ch'ang-p'ei hsien-sheng." *Chung-
kuo yü-wen*, January, 1959: 22-27.
悼念羅常培先生。 中國語文。
Yü-wen hsueh-hsi, 1959.
語文學習。

Lo Chen-yü   羅振玉

WORKS

1913. Ming sha shih shih i shu. Shang-yü Lo
shih ch'en-han-lou. 4 vols.
鳴沙石室佚書。

1914. (ed.) Ch'in Han wa tang wen-tzu. Shang-
yü Lo shih tzu k'o.
秦漢瓦當文字。

1914. Mang lo chung mu i wen. 12 vols.
芒洛冢墓遺文。

1914. Ssu ch'ao ch'ao pi t'u lu (with K'ao shih).
Shang-yü Lo shih.
四朝鈔幣圖錄 (附: 考釋)。

1914-15. (ed.) Hsi ch'ui shih k'o lu. Tzu k'an.
西陲石刻錄。

1915. (ed.) Chi Yin hsü wen-tzu ying t'ieh hui-
pien. Tung-fang hsueh-hui.
集殷虛文字楹帖彙編。

1915. (ed.) Chung-chou chung mu i wen (with
Pu i).
中州冢墓遺文 (附: 補遺)。

1915. (ed.) Han Chin shih-k'o mo ying.
漢晉石刻墨影。

1915? Heng nung chung mu i wen. Yung mu
yuan.
恒農冢墓遺文。

1915? Hsiang-yang chung mu i wen (with Pu
i).
襄陽冢墓遺文 (附: 補遺)。

1915. Sung weng chin kao.
松翁近稿。

1915. (ed.) Tung-tu chung mu i wen.
東都冢墓遺文。

1916? (ed.) Kao-ch'ang pi-hua ching-hua (tr. by
Lo Fu-ch'ang).
高昌壁畫菁華。 羅福萇。

1916? (ed.) Ku ming ch'i t'u lu. Shang-yü Lo
shih.
古明器圖錄。

1916. Shih ku wen k'ao shih.
石鼓文考釋。

1916. (ed.) Sui T'ang i-lai kuan-yin chi-ts'un.
Lo shih.
隋唐以來官印集存。

1916. (ed.) T'ieh yün ts'ang kuei chih yü.
鐵雲藏龜之餘。

1917? (ed.) Heng nung chuan lu.
恒農專錄。

1917. (ed.) Liang Che i chin i shih chi ts'un.
Shang-yü Lo shih.
兩浙佚金佚石集存。

1917? (ed.) Liu ch'ao mu chih ch'ing ying; ch'u,
erh pien. 2 vols.
六朝墓誌青英; 初, 二編。

1917. (ed.) Ming sha shih shih i shu hsü-pien.
Shang-yü Lo shih.
鳴沙石室佚書續編。

1917. (ed.) Ming sha shih shih ku-chi ts'ung ts'an.
Shang-yü Lo shih. 6 vols.
鳴沙石室古籍叢殘。

1917. Yin wen ts'un. Ts'ang sheng ming-chih ta-hsueh.
殷文存。

1918? (ed.) Chuan chih cheng ts'un lu.
專誌徵存錄。

1918? (ed.) Ch'u-chou ch'eng chuan lu.
楚州城甎錄。

1918? (ed.) Erh-shih chia shih nü hua ts'un.
二十家仕女畫存。

1918. Han Chin shu ying (mu-lu). Po-li ch'ang.
漢晉書影（目錄）。

1918. Hsü Ssu-chai hsien-sheng nien-p'u (1622–1694). Shang-yü Lo shih.
徐俟齋先生年譜。

1918? Hsueh-t'ang chiao k'an ch'ün shu hsü lu.
雪堂校刊群書敍錄。

1919. (ed.) Ming chi san hsiao lien chi; wu chung. Shang-yü Lo shih. 10 vols.
明季三孝廉集；五種。

1920. Yung-feng hsiang jen kao; ssu chung. I-an-t'ang. 6 vols.
永豐鄉人稿；四種。

1923. (ed.) Chen-sung-t'ang T'ang Sung i-lai kuan yin chi ts'un. Shang-yü Lo shih.
貞松堂唐宋以來官印集存。

1923. (ed.) Yeh hsia chung mu i wen (with erh pien). 2 vols.
鄴下冢墓遺文（附：二編）。

1924. (ed.) Hsueh-t'ang ts'ang ku ch'i-wu mu-lu. Tung-fang hsueh-hui.
雪堂藏古器物目錄。

1924? (ed.) Hua tu shih t'a ming ts'an pen.
化度寺塔銘殘本。

1924. (ed.) Tun-huang ling-shih; ch'i chung. Shang-yü Lo shih.
敦煌零拾；七種。

1924? (ed.) Tun-huang shih shih i-shu san chung.
敦煌石室遺書三種。

1925. (comp.) Fu chai ts'ang ching. T'an-yin-lu. 2 vols.
簠齋藏鏡。

1925. Hsi-yin hsing-shih cheng. Tung-fang hsueh-hui.
璽印姓氏徵。

1925? (ed.) Kao-yu Wang shih i-shu. Shang-yü Lo shih. 8 vols.
高郵王氏遺書。

1925. (Tseng ting) Li-tai fu p'ai t'u lu. Japan: Tung-fang hsueh-hui.
（增訂）歷代符牌圖錄。

1926? (ed.) Hao li i wen mu-lu. Tung-fang hsueh-hui. 2 vols.
蒿里遺文目錄。

1927. (ed.) Chi-yuan i-lai shuo jun k'ao. Tung-fang hsueh-hui. 3 vols.
紀元以來朔閏考。

1927. (ed.) Hsi-hsia kuan-yin chi ts'un. Shang-yü Lo shih.
西夏官印集存。

1927. Ping-yin kao. Shang-yü Lo shih.
丙寅藁。

1927. Yin hsü shu ch'i k'ao shih. Tung-fang hsueh-hui.
殷虛書契考釋。

1928? (ed.) Shang-shu chen pen ts'an chüan. Peiping: Tung-fang hsueh-hui.
尚書眞本殘卷。

1928. (ed.) Tai shih hsuan ch'uan ku pieh lu.
待石軒傳古別錄。

1928. Yin li tsai ssu t'ang ts'ung-shu. Tung-fang hsueh-hui. 12 vols.
殷禮在斯堂叢書。

1929. (ed.) Han hsi-p'ing shih ching ts'an tzu chi lu. Lo shih tzu yin. 3 vols.
漢熹平石經殘字集錄。

1929. Ting-wu kao.
丁戊稿。

1931. Chen-sung-t'ang chi ku i wen.
貞松堂集古遺文。

1931. Chen-sung-t'ang chi ku i wen pu i. 2 vols.
貞松堂集古遺文補遺。

1933. (ed.) Ch'ing t'ai-tsu kao huang-ti shih-lu kao pen; san chung. Shih-liao cheng-li ch'u. 4 vols.
淸太祖高皇帝實錄稿本；三種。

1933. Liao chü tsa chu i pien. Liao-tung: Shang-yü Lo shih. 4 vols.
遼居雜著乙編。

1934. Chen-sung-t'ang chi ku i wen hsü-pien. Shanghai: T'an-yin-lu. 3 vols.
貞松堂集古遺文續編。

1934. Yung-lu jih-cha.
俑廬日札。

1936. (ed.) Ku ching t'u lu (with Pu i). Shang-yü Lo shih.
古鏡圖錄（附：補遺）。

1936. (ed.) Yin hsü shu ch'i hsü-pien chiao chi liu chüan. Tsinan: Ch'i lu ta-hsueh kuo-hsueh yen-chiu so.
殷虛書契續編校記六卷。

1937. (ed.) Ch'i ching k'an ts'ung-shu k'an; ch'i chung. 10 vols.
七經堪叢書刊；七種。

1943. Wei-shu tsung-shih chuan chu chiao pu.
魏書宗室傳注校補。

(ed.) Ch'u-chou chin shih lu (with Ts'un mu).
Shang-yü Lo shih.
楚州金石錄 （附：存目）。

(ed.) Hsi t'an san shu. Lo shih. 6 vols.
悉曇三書。

K'ao-ku-hsueh ling chien. Shang-wu yin shu
kuan.
考古學零簡。

Ku ch'i-wu hsueh yen-chiu i.
古器物學研究議。

(ed.) Liang Che chung mu i wen (with Pu i).
兩浙冢墓遺文 （附：補遺）。

Liao chü tsa chu ping pien. Shang-yü: Lo shih
ch'i ching k'an yin hang. 2 vols.
遼居襍著丙編。

(ed.) Nung hsueh ts'ung-shu. Shanghai: Shanghai nung hsueh hui. 82 vols.
農學叢書。

Pei peih-tzu. 2 vols.
碑別字。

San-tai chi chin wen-ts'un. 20 vols.
三代吉金文存。

Shan tso chung mu i wen. Shang-yü Lo shih.
山左冢墓遺文。

T'ang che-ch'ung fu k'ao pu.
唐折衝府考補。

(ed.) Ti ch'üan cheng ts'un mu-lu.
地券徵存目錄。

Tun-huang ku hsieh pen Chou i Wang chu chiao-
k'an chi.
敦煌古寫本周易王注校勘記。

Tun-huang ku hsieh pen chu ching chiao k'an chi.
敦煌古寫本諸經校勘記。

(ed.) Tun-huang shih shih i-shu; i erh chung.
Shao-fen-shih.
敦煌石室遺書；一二種。

SOURCES

CBJS

CECP

Ch'ing-hua hsueh-pao, new series, I-1 (June, 1956):
46, 110.
清華學報。

K'o Ch'ang-ssu. "Tiao Shang-yü Lo hsien-
sheng." *Chung-ho*, I-8 (August, 1940): 3–8.
柯昌泗。弔上虞羅先生。中和。

Kuo Mo-jo. Li-shih jen-wu. Shanghai: Hai yen
shu-tien, 1951.
郭沫若。歷史人物。

Li Nien-tz'u. Man-chou-kuo chi-shih. Hong
Kong: Tzu-yu ch'u-pan she, 1954.
李念慈。滿洲國紀實。

Lo Chen-yü. "Chi liao pien," in Lo Chen-yü,

Chen-sung lao-jen i-kao chia chi. Peiping, 1941.
6 vols.
羅振玉。集蓼編。羅振玉。貞松老人遺稿
甲集。

———. "Shang-yü Lo shih chih fen p'u," in Lo
Chen-yü, *Liao chü tsa chu*. 1929. 2 vols.
羅振玉。上虞羅氏支分譜。羅振玉。遼居
雜著。

———. "Sung-weng tzu-hsu." *K'ao-ku*, December, 1935: 175–89.
羅振玉。松翁自敘。考古。

———. "Tun-huang ku hsieh pen Mao shih
chiao chi," in Lo Chen-yü, *Liao chü tsa chu*.
1929. 2 vols.
羅振玉。敦煌古寫本毛詩校記。羅振玉。
遼居雜著。

Man-chou-kuo cheng-fu kung-pao, April, 1932–October, 1933.
滿洲國政府公報。

P'u-yi. Wo te ch'ien pan sheng. Hong Kong:
Wen t'ung shu-tien, 1964. 3 vols.
溥儀。我的前半生。

Selections from China Mainland Magazines, 463
(April 5, 1965): 17.

Wang Kuo-wei. Kuan t'ang chi lin (with Pieh
chi). Peking: Chung-hua shu-chü, 1959. 4 vols.
王國維。觀堂集林 （附：別集）。

Yen-ching hsueh-pao, 28 (December, 1940): 257–66;
31 (December, 1946): 187–90.
燕京學報。

Lo Ch'i-yuan   羅綺園

SOURCES

Persons interviewed: not to be identified.

Lo Chia-lun   羅家倫

WORKS

1927. K'o-hsueh yü hsuan-hsueh. Shanghai:
Shang-wu yin shu kuan.
科學與玄學。

1935. Chung-shan hsien-sheng London meng-nan
shih-liao k'ao-ting. Nanking: Ching hua yin
shu kuan.
中山先生倫敦蒙難史料考訂。

1943. Keng pa chi. Chungking: Shang-wu yin
shu kuan.
耕罷集。

1946. Hei yün pao yü tao ming hsia. Shanghai:
Shang-wu yin shu kuan.

黑雲暴雨到明霞。

1946. Hsin jen-sheng kuan. Shanghai: Shang-wu yin shu kuan.
新人生觀。

1946. Hsin min-tsu kuan; shang-ts'e. Shanghai: Shang-wu yin shu kuan.
新民族觀；上冊。

1951. (ed.) Chung-hua Min-kuo k'ai-kuo ming-jen hsiang; ti-i chi. Taipei: Chung-yang tang shih shih-liao pien-tsuan wei-yuan-hui.
中華民國開國名人像；第一輯。

1952. (ed.) Huang-hua-kang ko-ming lieh-shih hua shih. Taipei: Chung-yang tang shih shih-liao pien-tsuan wei-yuan-hui.
黃花岡革命烈士畫史。

1952. Wen-hua chiao-yü yü ch'ing-nien. Taipei: Hua kuo ch'u-pan she Taiwan fen-she.
文化教育與青年。

1953. Su-o te chi-pen ken kuo-ts'e. Taipei: Chung-yang wen-wu kung-ying she.
蘇俄的基本國策。

1953–65. (ed.) Ko-ming wen-hsien. Taipei: Chung-yang wen-wu kung-ying she. 35 vols.
革命文獻。

1954. (ed.) Kuo-fu hua chuan. Taipei: Chung-kuo kuo-min-tang tang shih shih-liao pien-tsuan wei-yuan-hui.
國父畫傳。

1954. Liu-shih nien lai chih Chung-kuo kuo-min-tang yü Chung-kuo. Taipei: Chung-kuo kuo-min-tang chung-yang wei-yuan-hui ti-ssu tsu tang shih shih-liao pien-tsuan wei-yuan hui.
六十年來之中國國民黨與中國。

1957. Hsin ying yu tsung chi. Taipei. 2 vols.
心影遊蹤集。

1958. (ed.) Kuo-min ko-ming hua shih. Taipei: Chung-kuo kuo-min-tang tang shih shih-liao pien-tsuan wei-yuan-hui.
國民革命畫史。

1959. (ed.) Kuo-fu nien-p'u ch'u-kao. Taipei: Kuo shih kuan shih-liao pien-tsuan wei-yuan-hui, Chung-kuo kuo-min-tang tang shih shih-liao pien-tsuan wei-yuan-hui. 2 vols.
國父年譜初稿。

1961. (ed.) K'ai-kuo ming-jen mo-chi. Taipei: Hsing t'ai yin-shua ch'ang. 2 vols.
開國名人墨蹟。

SOURCES

Chung-kuo chin ch'i-shih nien lai chiao-yü chi-shih, ed. by Ting Chih-p'ing. Taipei: Kuo-li pien i kuan, 1961.
中國近七十年來教育記事。丁致聘。

Lo Chia-lun. Hsin ying yu tsung chi. Taipei, 1957. 2 vols.
羅家倫。心影遊蹤集。

———. Wen-hua chiao-yü yü ch'ing-nien. Taipei: Hua kuo ch'u-pan she Taiwan fen-she, 1952.
羅家倫。文化教育與青年。

Wu-ssu ai-kuo yün-tung ssu-shih chou-nien chi-nien t'e-k'an, ed. by Kuo-li Peking ta-hsueh Taiwan t'ung-hsueh hui. Taipei, 1959.
五四愛國運動四十周年紀念特刊。

Lo I-nung   羅亦農

SOURCES

Person interviewed: Chang Kuo-t'ao.
GCCJK
Hsiao Pai-fan. Chung-kuo chin pai nien ko-ming shih. Hong Kong: Ch'iu shih ch'u-pan she, 1951.
蕭白帆。中國近百年革命史。
RSOC
Ta Sheng *et al*. Lieh-shih chuan, ti-i chi; chi-nien wo-men wei Chung-kuo jen-min chieh-fang fen-tou erh hsi-sheng te chan-shih. Moscow, 1936.
大生等。烈士傳，第一集；紀念我們為中國人民解放奮鬥而犧牲的戰士。

Lo Jui-ch'ing   羅瑞卿

WORKS

1938. Yu-chi-tui chung te cheng-chih kung-tso. with T'ieh-jen. Shanghai: Chien she.
游擊隊中的政治工作。鐵人。

1939. K'ang Jih chün-tui chung te cheng-chih kung-tso. Chung-kuo wen-hua she.
抗日軍隊中的政治工作。

1939. Shen-pei te ch'ing-nien hsueh-sheng sheng-huo. with Ch'eng Fang-wu. Shanghai: Chung-hua ta-hsueh t'u-shu yu-hsien kung-ssu.
陝北的青年學生生活。成仿吾。

1951. Lo Jui-ch'ing *et al*. Chen-ya fan ko-ming pi-hsü ta chang ch'i-ku. Kaifeng: Honan sheng jen-min cheng-fu kung-an t'ing.
羅瑞卿等。鎮壓反革命必須大張旗鼓。

1958. Wo kuo su fan tou-cheng te ch'eng-chiu ho chin hou te jen-wu; 1957 nien 12 yueh 4 jih tsai Chung-kung chung-yang chih-shu chi-kuan chü-le-pu te pao-kao. Peking: Chung-kuo ch'ing-nien ch'u-pan she.

我國肅反鬥爭的成就和今後的任務；　1957
年12月4日在中中共中央直屬機關俱樂部
的報告。

1965. Chi-nien chan sheng Te-kuo fa-hsi-ssu,
pa fan-tui Mei ti-kuo chu-i te tou-cheng
chin-hsing tao-ti. Peking: Jen-min ch'u-pan
she.
紀念戰勝德國法西斯，把反對美帝國主義
的鬥爭進行到底。

SOURCES

Person interviewed: Chang Kuo-t'ao.
Lo Jui-ch'ing. "Chi-nien chan sheng Te-kuo
fa-hsi-ssu, pa fan-tui Mei ti-kuo chu-i te to-
cheng chin-hsing tao-ti." *Hung ch'i*, 5 (May,
1965).
羅瑞卿。紀念戰勝德國法西斯，把反對美
帝國主義的鬥爭進行到底。 紅旗。
The New York Times, May, 11, 13, 1965.
Tang, Peter S. H. Communist China Today.
New York: Frederick A. Praeger, 1957-58.
2 vols.
Time, LXVIII-10 (March 5, 1956).
Union Research Biographical Service, 21 (September
21, 1956).
WWMC

Lo Jung-huan   羅榮桓

WORKS

1932? Ch'üan chün-t'uan i-shang hsuan-ch'uan
hui-i chueh-i an. Chung-kuo kung nung hung
chün ti-ssu chün cheng-chih pu.
全軍團以上宣傳會議決議案。
1932? Tui-yü pai ch'ü kung nung te hsuan-ch'uan
kang-yao. Chung-kuo kung nung chün ti-i
chün-t'uan cheng-chih pu.
對於白區工農的宣傳綱要。
1933? Kuan-yü ch'ing-nien kan-pu hsun-lien.
關於青年幹部訓練。

SOURCES

Person interviewed: Chang Kuo-t'ao.
The New York Times, December 17, 1963.
WWMC

Lo Lung-chi   羅隆基

WORKS

1928. The Conduct of Parliamentary Elections
in England. New York: J. Lewin & Son.

1930. Jen-ch'üan lun chi. with Hu Shih, Liang
Shih-ch'iu. Shanghai: Hsin-yueh shu-tien.
人權論集。 胡適，梁實秋。
1931. Shen-yang (Mukden) shih-chien. Shanghai: Liang yu t'u-shu yin-shua kung-ssu.
瀋陽事件。

SOURCES

GCCJK
JMST, 1950, 1957, 1958.
SCMP, 849 (July 16, 1954): 13-21; 1190 (December 16, 1955): 5-6; 1264 (April 10, 1956); 11-
12; 1571 (July, 1957): 7-11; 1594 (August 20,
1957): 9-10; 1932 (October 16, 1957): 4-12;
1694 (January 20, 1958): 13-17; 1699 (January
27, 1958): 27-34.

Lo Teng-hsien   羅登賢

SOURCES

CKLC
GCCJK
Ta Sheng *et al.* Lieh-shih chuan, ti-i chi; chi-
nien wo-men wei Chung-kuo jen-min chieh-
fang fen-tou erh hsi-sheng te chan-shih. Moscow, 1936.
大生等。烈士傳，第一集；紀念我們為中
國人民解放奮鬥而犧牲的戰士。
WWC, 1936.

Lo Wen-kan   羅文幹

SOURCES

BPC
Chang Ch'i-yün. Tang shih kai-yao. Taipei:
Chung-yang kai-tsao wei-yuan-hui wen-wu
kung-ying she, 1951-52. 5 vols.
張其昀。黨史概要。
Chia I-chün. Chung-hua Min-kuo shih. Shang-
hai: Wen-hua hsueh-she, 1930.
賈逸君。中華民國史。
Kuo wen chou-pao, X-34 (August 28, 1933).
國聞週報。
Li Chien-nung. The Political History of China
1840-1928 (tr. and ed. by Teng Ssu-yu and
Jeremy Ingalls). Princeton: D. Van Nostrand
Co., 1956.
Wai-chiao ta tz'u-tien, ed. by Wai-chiao hsueh-
hui. Kunming: Chung-hua shu-chu, 1937.
外交大辭典。外交學會。
WWMC

Yuan Shih-k'ai ch'ieh kuo chi, ed. by Chung-hua shu-chü pien-chi pu. Taipei: Chung-hua shu-chü, 1954.
袁世凱竊國記。中華書局編輯部。

Lu Cheng-hsiang　陸徵祥

WORKS

1938. (ed.) The Voice of the Church in China, 1931–1932, 1937–1938. London: Longmans, Green & Co.

SOURCES

Ch'eng T'ien-fang. A History of Sino-Russian Relations. Washington: Public Affairs Press, 1957.
Chin shan shih pao. San Francisco, July 20, 1960.
金山時報。
CYB-W, 1924.
Millard's Review, April 27, 1918.
The New York Times, April 18, 28, 1913; January 31, November 7, 1915; October 5, 1916; September 9, 1917; May 13, 19, 21, 22, 24, 25, June 26, July 14, 1918; July 9, 1919; January 28, February 20, 1920.
Powell, John Benjamin. My Twenty-Five Years in China. New York: The Macmillan Co., 1945.
WWC, 5th ed.

Lu Chung-lin　鹿鐘麟

SOURCES

Persons interviewed: not to be identified.

Lu Han　盧漢

SOURCES

AWW
CH, 1937–45.
CMTC
GCJJ
MMT

Lu Jung-t'ing　陸榮廷

SOURCES

BPC
CMTC

Kuo wen chou pao, XIII-12, 14, 16, 18.
國聞週報。
Li Chien-nung. The Political History of China 1840–1928 (tr. and ed. by Teng Ssu-yu and Jeremy Ingalls). Princeton: D. Van Nostrand Co., 1956.

Lu Po-hung　陸伯鴻

WORKS

1914, January. "Conversion and Healing of Sen Men Yuen." Relations de Chine.

SOURCES

Apostolicum, February, 1938.
Bulletin Catholique de Pekin, 1938.
Bulletin de la Commission Synodale, 1938.
Bulletin de la Jeunesse Catholique Chinoise, September, 1925.
Bulletin des Petites Soeurs des Pauvres.
Catholic Review, January, 1938.
China Letter, first semester, 1938.
Glennie, I. T. Lo Pa Hong. Calcutta, 1938.
Gonzaga Annual. Shanghai, 1938.
Jesuites Missionaires, March, 1938; June, 1945.
Journal de Shanghai, December, 31, 1937; January 12, 1938.
Masson, J. Un Millionaire Chinois au Service des Gueux: Joseph Lo Pa Hong. Paris: Custerman-Tournai, 1950.
North China Herald, January 5, 1938.
Nouvelles de la Mission, 604, 1178, 1185.
Osservatore Romano, January 25,1933.
Pierre, M. Lo Pa Hong. Louvain: Xaveriana Collection. 1939.
Poisson, R. P. Lo Pa Hong. Montreal.
Relations de la Chine, October, 1929: 239–242, 247; January, 1926: 315; 1914: 311–318; 1935: 159; January, 1936: 238; April, 1937: 80–81; July, 1937: 173; April, 1938: 359.
Revue Catholique chiang hiao tsa che, February, 1938: 89–95; January, 1938: 53–54.
Thauren, J. Lo Pa Hong.
Todos Missionarios, January–February, 1938: 41–44.

Lu Ti-p'ing　魯滌平

SOURCES

CYB-W, 1934.
SMJ

WWC, 1931.

Lu Ting-yi   陸定一

WORKS

1926–27. ed. of *Chung-kuo ch'ing-nien*.
中國青年。
1949. "Explanations of Severel Basic Questions Concerning the Postwar International Situation," in United States Department of State, *United States Relations with China with Special Reference to the Period 1944–1949*. Washington, D.C.: Government Printing Office, 1949.
1950. Lu Ting-yi *et al*. Tang-ch'ien chiao-yü chien-she te fang-chen (comp. by Chiao-yü tzu-liao ts'ung-k'an she). Shanghai: Hsin hua shu-tien.
陸定一等。當前教育建設的方針。 教育資料叢刊社。
1957. Let Flowers of Many Kinds Blossom, Diverse Schools of Thought Contend: A Speech on the Policy of the Communist Party of China on Art, Literature and Science, Delivered on May 26, 1956. Peking: Foreign Languages Press.
1958. Education Must Be Combined with Productive Labour. Peking: Foreign Languages Press.
1959, November 10. "Great Developments in China's Cultural Revolution." *Peking Review*: 13–16.
1960, May 10. "Reform in Educational Work." *Peking Review*.
1960. Speech at the National Conference of Outstanding Groups and Workers. Peking: Foreign Languages Press.
1965, December 4. "Cultural Revolution of China's National Minorities." *Peking Review*: 22–24.
1965, December 17. "Part-Work, Part Study System Shows Its Advantages." *Peking Review*.
ed. of *Hung-se Chung-hua*.
紅色中華。

SOURCES

Person interviewed: Chang Kuo-t'ao.
Jen-min jih-pao. Peking, June 13, 1956.
人民日報。
Wales, Nym (pseud. of Helen Foster Snow). Inside Red China. New York: Doubleday, Doran & Co., 1939.
The New York Times, June 3, 1966.

Union Research Biographical Service, 31 (October 16, 1956).
WWC, 1950
WWMC

Lu Tso-fu   盧作孚

WORKS

1934. Chung-kuo te chien-she wen-t'i yü jen te hsun-lien. Shanghai: Sheng-huo shu-tien.
中國的建設問題與人的訓練。
1944. Kung shang huan-li. Chunking: Chung-yang hsun-lien t'uan.
工商管理。

SOURCES

Persons interviewed: not to be identified.
Hsü Ying. Tang-tai Chung-kuo shih-yeh jen-wu chih. Shanghai: Chung-hua shu-chü, 1948.
徐盈。當代中國實業人物誌。

Lung Chi-kuang   龍濟光

SOURCES

Li Po-yuan *et al*. Kwangtung chi-ch'i kung-jen fen-tou shih. Taipei: Chung-kuo lao-kung fu-li she, 1955.
李伯元等。 廣東機器工人奮鬥史。
Teng Tse-ju. Chung-kuo kuo-min-tang erh-shih nien shih-chi. Shanghai: Cheng-chung shu-chü, 1948.
鄧澤如。 中國國民黨二十年史蹟。
Wu Hsien-tzu hsien-sheng chuan-chi, ed. by Hu Ying-han. Hong Kong: Ssu ch'iang yin-shua kung-ssu, 1953.
伍憲子先生傳記。胡應漢。

Lung Yün   龍雲

SOURCES

BKL
CKJMT
CMTC
CYB, 1937–45.
Jen-min jih-pao. Peking, July 14, 1957.
人民日報。
Kuang-ming jih-pao. Peking, July 21, 1957.
光明日報。
The New York Times, June 24, 1957; June 29, 1962.

Ma Chan-shan   馬占山

SOURCES

BKL
Ch'en Pin-ho. Man-chou wei kuo. Peiping: Jih-pen yen-chiu she, 1933.
陳彬龢。滿洲僞國。
CMTC
CTMC
CWR, 1931–32.
Lei Ting. Tung-pei i yung chün yün-tung shih-hua. Shanghai: T'ien ma shu-tien, 1932.
雷丁。東北義勇軍運動史話。
Smith, Sara Rector, The Manchurian Crisis, 1931-1932: A Tragedy in International Relations. New York: Columbia University Press, 1948.
WWC, 1936.
WWMC

Ma Ch'ao-chün   馬超俊

WORKS

1927. Chung-kuo lao-kung wen-t'i. Shanghai: Min chih shu-chü.
中國勞工問題。
1942. Chung-kuo lao-kung yün-tung shih; shang ts'e. Chungking: Shang-wu yin shu kuan.
中國勞工運動史；上冊。
1946. Pi-chiao lao-tung cheng-ts'e. with Yü Ch'ang-ho. Shanghai: Shang-wu yin shu kuan. 2 vols.
比較勞動政策。余長河。

SOURCES

Persons interviewed: not to be identified.
Li Po-yuan et al. Kwantung chi-ch'i kung-jen fen-tou shih. Taipei: Chung-kuo lao-kung fu-li she, 1955.
李伯元等。廣東機器工人奮鬥史。
Ta hua chou-k'an, 752 (January 14, 1961).
大華週刊。

Ma Chung-ying   馬仲英

SOURCES

CMTC
CWR, March 17, 1934.
Chang Ta-chün. Sinkiang chin ssu-shih nien pien-luan chi-lueh. Taipei: Chung-yang wen-wu kung-ying she, 1954.
張大軍。新疆近四十年變亂紀略。
———. Ssu-shih nien tung-luan Sinkiang. Hong Kong: Ya-chou ch'u-pan she, 1956.
張達鈞。四十年動亂新疆。
Hedin, Sven. The Flight of "Big Horse": The Trail of War in Central Asia (tr. by F. H. Lyon). New York: E. P. Dutton and Co., 1936.
———. Silk Road. New York: E. P. Dutton & Co., 1938.
Hsi-pei tsui-chin shih nien lai shih-liao, comp. by Sung Ping-shan.
西北最近十年來史料。宋冰珊。
Hung Ti-ch'en. Sinkiang shih ti ta-kang. Nanking: Cheng-chung shu-chü, 1935.
洪滌塵。新疆史地大綱。
Kuo wen chou-pao, X-46 (November 20, 1933).
國聞週報。
Lattimore, Owen. Pivot of Asia: Sinkiang and the Inner Asian Frontiers of China and Russia. Boston: Little, Brown & Co., 1950.
Teichman, Eric. "Chinese Turkestan." Journal of Royal Central Asian Society, October, 1936.
Whiting, Allen S., and Sheng Shih-ts'ai. Sinkiang: Pawn or Pivot? East Lansing: Michigan State University Press, 1958.
Wu, Aitchen K. Turkistan Tumult. London: Methuen & Co., 1940.

Ma Fu-hsiang   馬福祥

WORKS

1931. (ed.) Meng Tsang chuang-k'uang. Nanking.
蒙藏狀況。

SOURCES

Chang Wei. "Ku kuo-min cheng-fu wei-yuan Meng Tsang wei-yuan-hui wei-yuan-chang Ma kung Yün-t'ing chi-nien pei." Kuo shih kuan kuan k'an, I-4 (November, 1948): 110-12.
張維。故國民政府委員蒙藏委員會委員長馬公雲亭紀念碑。國史館館刊。
CMTC
CWR,1929, 1930, 1932.
Lin Ching. Hsi-pei ts'ung pien. Shanghai: Shen-chou kuo kuang she, 1933.
林競。西北叢編。
WWC, 1925, 1931.

Ma Hsü-lun　馬敍倫

WORKS

1918. T'ang hsieh pen ching-tien shih-wen ts'an chüan chiao yü pu-cheng.
唐寫本經典釋文殘卷校語補正。

1928. Shuo-wen chieh-tzu yen-chiu fa. Shanghai: Shang-wu yin shu kuan.
說文解字研究法。

1930. Chuang-tzu i cheng. Shanghai: Shang-wu yin shu kuan. 6 vols.
莊子義證。

1931. Liu-shu chieh li. Shanghai: Shang-wu yin shu kuan.
六書解例。

1931. Tu Lü shih ch'un-ch'iu çhi. Shanghai: Shang-wu yin shu kuan.
讀呂氏春秋記。

1933. Tu-shu hsiao chi (with Hsü chi wu chüan). Shanghai: Shang-wu yin shu kuan. 3 vols.
讀書小記 (附: 續記五卷)。

1935. Shih-ku-wen su-chi. Shanghai: Shang-wu yin shu kuan.
石鼓文疏記。

1939. Tu-shu hsü chi; chüan ti-liu, ti-ch'i. Shanghai: Shang-wu yin shu kuan.
讀書續記; 卷第六, 第七。

1946-47. ed. of *Min-chu*.
民主。

1947. Wo tsai liu-shih sui i-ch'ien. Shanghai: Sheng-huo shu-tien.
我在六十歲以前。

1949. Shih wu hsü shen. Shanghai: Chien wen shu-tien.
石屋續瀋。

1958. Ma Hsü-lun hsüeh-shu lun-wen chi. Peking: K'o-hsüeh ch'u-pan she.
馬敍倫學術論文集。

1962. Tu chin ch'i k'o tz'u. Peking: Chung-hua shu-chü.
讀金器刻詞。

ed. of *Hsin shih-chieh hsüeh-pao*.
新世界學報。

ed. of *Hsuan pao*.
選報。

ed. of *Ta kung-ho jih-pao*.
大共和日報。

SOURCES

Persons interviewed: not to be identified.
Chow Tse-tsung. The May Fourth Movement: Intellectual Revolution in Modern China. Cambridge: Harvard University Press, 1960.

Ma Hsü-lun. Wo tsai liu-shih sui i-ch'ien. Shanghai: Sheng-huo shu-tien, 1947.
馬敍倫。 我在六十歲以前。
Ying Tzu. Chung-kuo hsin hsüeh-shu jen-wu chih. Hong Kong: Chih ming shu-chü, 1956.
穎子。 中國新學術人物誌。

Ma Hung-k'uei　馬鴻逵

SOURCES

BKL
Chou K'ai-ch'ing. Hsi-pei chien-ying. Chengtu: Chung hsi shu-chü, 1943.
周開慶。 西北剪影。
CMTC
CTMC
CYB-W, 1929-30.
Huang Fen-sheng. Pien-chiang jen-wu chih. Chunking, 1945.
黃奮生。 邊疆人物誌。
Fu Tso-lin. Ninghsia-sheng k'ao-ch'a chi. Nanking: Cheng-chung shu-chü, 1935.
傅作霖。 寧夏省考察記。
WWC, 1950.
WWMC

Ma Hung-pin　馬鴻賓

SOURCES

BKL
CMTC
CWR, September 19, 1931.
Hsi-pei tsui-chin shih nien lai shih-liao, ed. by Sung Ping-shan.
西北最近十年來史料。 宋冰珊。
Huang Fen-sheng. Pien-chiang jen-wu chih. Chungking, 1945.
黃奮生。 邊疆人物誌。
TCJC

Ma Liang　馬良

WORKS

1916. Hsien-fa hsiang chieh.
憲法向界。
1916. Hsin shih ho pien chih chiang. (tr.)
新史合編直講。

1926. Chih chih ch'ien-shuo; chüan chih i: Yuan yen. Shanghai: Shang-wu yin shu kuan.
致知淺說；卷之一：原言。

1933. Ma Hsiang-po hsien-sheng kuo-nan yen-lun chi (ed. by Hsü Ching-hsien). Shanghai: Wen hua mei-shu t'u-shu kung-ssu.
馬相伯先生國難言論集。徐景賢。

1947. Ma Hsiang-po hsien-sheng wen-chi (ed. by Fang Hao). Peiping: Shang chih pien i kuan.
馬相伯先生文集。方豪。

1948. Ma Hsiang-po hsien-sheng wen-chi hsü-pien (ed. by Fang Hao). Peiping: Shang chih pien i kuan.
馬相伯先生文集續編。方豪。

SOURCES

Chang Jo-ku. Ma Hsiang-po hsien-sheng nien-p'u. Shanghai: Shang-wu yin shu kuan, 1939.
張若谷。馬相伯先生年譜。
Fang Hao. "Ma Hsiang-po hsien-sheng." *Ssu-hsiang yü shih-tai*, 6 (January, 1942).
方豪。馬相伯先生。思想與時代。
———. "Ma Hsiang-po hsien-sheng ch'ou-she han hsia k'ao wen yuan shih-mo." *Ta-lu tsa-chih*, XXI-1, 2 (July 15, 1960).
方豪。馬相伯先生籌設函夏考文苑始末。大陸雜誌。
———. "Ma Hsiang-po hsien-sheng pai sui hsiao-chuan." *I-shih pao*. Kunming, April 8, 1939.
方豪。馬相伯先生百歲小傳。益世報。
———. "Ma Hsiang-po hsien-sheng te sheng-p'ing chi ch'i ssu-hsiang." *Min-chu p'ing-lun*, VI-8-15 (April 20-August 5, 1955).
方豪。馬相伯先生的生平及其思想。民主評論。
Liang Jen-kung hsien-sheng nien-p'u ch'ang pien ch'u-kao, ed. by Ting Wen-chiang. Taipei: Shih-chieh shu-chü, 1958. 2 vols.
梁任公先生年譜長編初稿。丁文江。
Ma Hsiang-po. Ma Hsiang-po hsien-sheng wen-chi (ed. by Fang Hao). Peiping: Shang chih pien i kuan, 1947.
馬相伯。馬相伯先生文集。方豪。
———. Ma Hsiang-po hsien-sheng kuo-nan yen-lun chi (ed. by Hsü Ching-hsien). Shanghai: Wen hua mei-shu t'u-shu kung-ssu, 1933.
馬相伯。馬相伯先生國難言論集。徐景賢。
Ma Hsiang-po. Ma Hsiang-po hsien-sheng wen-chi hsü pien (ed. by Fang Hao). Peiping: Shang chih pien i kuan, 1948.
馬相伯。馬相伯先生文集續編。方豪。
Shang chih pien i kuan kuan k'an, II-4 (June, 1947); II-5 (October, 1947); III-6 (June, 1948).
上智編譯館館刊。

Ma Pu-ch'ing   馬步青

SOURCES

Chang Ta-chün. Ssu-shih nien tung-luan Sin-kiang. Hong Kong: Ya-chou ch'u-pan she, 1956.
張達鈞。四十年動亂新疆。
Chou K'ai-ch'ing. Hsi-pei chien-ying. Chengtu: Chung hsi shu-chü, 1943.
周開慶。西北剪影。
CMJL
CWR, February 13, 1937.
Huang Fen-sheng. Pien-chiang jen-wu chih. Chungking, 1945.
黃奮生。邊疆人物誌。
Kuo wen chou-pao. XIV-4 (April 12, 1937): 83.
國聞週報。
WWMC

Ma Pu-fang   馬步芳

SOURCES

BKL
CH
Chang Ta-chün. Ssu-shih nien tung-luan Sin-kiang. Hong Kong: Ya-chou ch'u-pan she, 1956.
張達鈞。四十年動亂新疆。
Chou K'ai-ch'ing. Hsi-pei chien-ying. Chengtu: Chung hsi shu-chü, 1943.
周開慶。西北剪影。
CTMC
Hsi-pei tsui-chin shih nien lai shih-liao, ed. by Sung Ping-shan.
西北最近十年來史料。宋冰珊。
Hu Ming. "Yin-hui ta-shih chen-tung ch'ao-yeh." *Chung Mei chou-pao*, May 25, 1961.
胡明。淫穢大使震動朝野。中美週報。
Hua Mei jih-pao. New York, May 10, 1961.
華美日報。

Huang Fen-sheng. Pien-chiang jen-wu chih. Chungking, 1945.

黃奮生。邊疆人物誌。

Pai I. "Ma Pu-fang che-ko mi yang te jen-wu." *Ch'un-ch'iu*, 94 (June 1, 1961): 2-4.

白衣。馬步芳這個謎樣的人物。春秋。

Tsinghai, ed. by Chou Chen-ho. Changsha: Shang-wu yin shu kuan, 1939.

青海。周振鶴。

Wu Ching-fu. "Ma Pu-fang ta-shih pei k'ung luan-lun tu-chih." *Chung Mei chou-pao*, May 25, 1961.

吳敬敷。馬步芳大使被控亂倫瀆職。中美週報,

Ma Yin-ch'u   馬寅初

WORKS

1923. Ma Yin-ch'u yen-chiang chi; ti-i chi. Shanghai: Shang-wu yin shu kuan.

馬寅初演講集;第一集。

1925. Chung-kuo wai hui tui. Shanghai: Shang-wu yin shu kuan.

中國外匯兌。

1925. Ma Yin-ch'u yen-chiang chi; ti-erh chi. Shanghai: Shang-wu yin shu kuan.

馬寅初演講集;第二集。

1926. Chung-kuo kuan-shui wen-t'i. Shanghai: Shang-wu yin shu kuan.

中國關稅問題。

1926. Ma Yin-ch'u yen-chiang chi; ti-san chi. Peking: Ch'en pao she.

馬寅初演講集;第三集。

1928. Ma Yin-ch'u yen-chiang chi; ti-ssu chi. Shanghai: Shang-wu yin shu kuan.

馬寅初演講集;第四集。

1929. Chung-hua yin-hang lun. Shanghai: Shang-wu yin shu kuan.

中華銀行論。

1932. Ma Yin-ch'u ching-chi lun wen chi; ti-i chi. Shanghai: Shang-wu yin shu kuan.

馬寅初經濟論文集;第一集。

1935. Chung-kuo ching-chi kai-tsao. Shanghai: Shang-wu yin shu kuan.

中國經濟改造。

1936. Chung-kuo chih hsin chin-jung cheng-ts'e. Shanghai: Shang-wu yin shu kuan. 2 vols.

中國之新金融政策。

1945. Chan-shih ching-chi lun-wen chi. Chungking: Tso-chia shu wu.

戰時經濟論文集。

1948. Ts'ai-cheng hsueh yü Chung-kuo ts'ai-cheng: Li-lun yu hsien-shih. Shanghai: Shang-wu yin shu kuan. 2 vols.

財政學與中國財政:理論與現實。

1948. T'ung-huo hsin lun. Shanghai: Shang-wu yin shu kuan.

通貨新論。

1949. Ching-chi hsueh kai-lun. Shanghai: Shang-wu yin shu kuan.

經濟學概論。

1956, December 28, 29. "Lien-hsi Chung-kuo shih-chi lai t'an-t'an tsung-ho p'ing-heng li-lun ho an pi-li fa-chan kuei-lü." *Jen-min jih-pao*. Peking.

聯系中國實際來談談綜合平衡理論和按比例發展規律。人民日報。

1957, May 11, 12. "Lien-hsi Chung-kuo shih-chi lai tsai t'an-t'an tsung-ho p'ing-heng li-lun ho an pi-li fa-chan kuei-lü." *Jen-min jih-pao*. Peking.

聯系中國實際來再談談綜合平衡理論和按比例發展規律。人民日報。

1957, July 5. "Hsin jen-k'ou lun." *Jen-min jih-pao*. Peking.

新人口論。人民日報。

1957. "Wo kuo tzu-pen chu-i kung-yeh te she-hui chu-i kai-tsao." *Peking ta-hsueh hsueh-pao*, 13.

我國資本主義工業的社會主義改造。北京大學學報。

1958, May 9. "Tsai t'an wo-te p'ing-heng lun chung te t'uan-t'uan-chuan li-lun." *Kuang-ming jih-pao*. Peking.

再談我的平衡論中的團團轉理論。光明日報。

1959. "Hsiao-hsing t'uan-t'uan-chuan te tsung-ho hsing p'ing-heng lun." *Peking ta-hsueh hsueh-pao*, 1.

小型團團轉的綜合性平衡論。北京大學學報。

1959. "Wo-te che-hsueh ssu-hsiang ho ching-chi li-lun." *Hsin chien-she*, 11.

我的哲學思想和經濟理論。新建設。

1958. Wo-te ching-chi li-lun che-hsueh ssu-hsiang ho cheng-chih li-ch'ang. Peking: Ts'ai-cheng ch'u-pan she.

我的經濟理論哲學思想和政治立場。

SOURCES

CB, 469 (July 25, 1957): 1-18.

China News Analysis, 313 (February 26, 1960): 1-7; 248 (October 10, 1958): 1-7.

Extracts from China Mainland Magazines, 195 (January 11, 1960).

Hsin chien-she, December, 1959; January, 1960.
新建設。

Jen-min jih-pao. Peking, July 5, 1957.
人民日報。

Ma Yin-ch'u. Chung-kuo ching-chi kai-tsao.
Shanghai: Shang-wu yin shu kuan, 1935.
馬寅初。中國經濟改造。

———. Chung-kuo kuan-shui wen-t'i. Shanghai: Shang-wu yin shu kuan, 1926.
馬寅初。中國關稅問題。

———. "Hsin jen-k'ou lun." *Jen-min jih-pao*.
Peking, July 5, 1957.
馬寅初。新人口論。人民日報。

———. "Lien-hsi Chung-kuo shih-chi lai t'an-
t'an tsung-ho p'ing-heng li-lun ho an pi-li fa-
chan kuei-lü." *Jen-min jih-pao*. Peking, December 28, 29, 1956.
馬寅初。聯系中國實際來談談綜合平衡理
論和按比例發展規律。人民日報。

———. "Lien-hsi Chung-kuo shih-chi lai tsai
t'an-t'an tsung-ho p'ing-heng li-lun ho an pi-
li fa-chan kuei-lü." *Jen-min jih-pao*. Peking,
May 11, 12, 1957.
馬寅初。聯系中國實際來再談談綜合平衡
理論和按比例發展規律。人民日報。

———. Ma Yin-ch'u yen-chiang chi; ti-i chi.
Shanghai: Shang-wu yin shu kuan, 1923.
馬寅初。馬寅初演講集。第一集。

———. Ma Yin-ch'u yen-chiang chi; ti-erh chi.
Shanghai: Shang-wu yin shu kuan, 1925.
馬寅初。馬寅初演講集；第二集。

———. Ma Yin-ch'u yen-chiang chi; ti-san chi.
Peking: Ch'en pao she, 1926.
馬寅初。馬寅初演講集；第三集。

———. Ma Yin-ch'u yen-chiang chi; ti-ssu chi.
Shanghai: Shang-wu yin shu kuan, 1928.
馬寅初。馬寅初演講集；第四集。

———. "Wo-kuo tzu-pen chu-i kung-yeh te
she-hui chu-i kai-tsao." *Peking ta-hsueh hsueh-
pao*, 3 (1957).
馬寅初。我國資本主義工業的社會主義改
造。北京大學學報。

———. "Wo-te che-hsueh ssu-hsiang ho ching-
chi li-lun." *Hsin chien-she*, 11 (November 7,
1959).
馬寅初。我的哲學思想和經濟理論。新建
設。

———. Wo-te ching-chi li-lun che-hsueh ssu-
hsiang ho cheng-chih li-ch'ang. Peking: Ts'ai-
cheng ch'u-pan she, 1958.
馬寅初。我的經濟理論哲學思想和政治立
場。

Peking ta-hsueh hsueh-pao, December, 1959.

北京大學學報。

Politics in Command: Chinese Intellectual and
the Communist Party. Bankok: The South-
East Asia Treaty Organization.

Ying Tzu. Chung-kuo hsin hsueh-shu jen-wu
chih. Hong Kong: Chih ming shu-chü, 1956.
穎子。中國新學術人物誌。

Mao Tse-min   毛澤民

SOURCES

Chang Ta-chün. Ssu-shih nien tung-lun Sinkiang. Hong Kong: Ya-chou ch'u-pan she,
1954.
張達鈞。四十年動亂新疆。

SCMP, 787 (April 13, 1954).

SMJ

Tang, Peter S. H. Communist China Today.
Washington: Research Institute on the Sino-
Soviet Bloc, 1961. 2 vols.

Wai-shih shih (pseud.). "Mao Tse-min Sinkiang
tso yuan kuei." *Ch'un-ch'iu*, 51 (July 16, 1957):
7–8, 28.
外史氏。毛澤民新疆作怨鬼。春秋。

Whiting, Allen S., and Sheng Shih-ts'ai. Sin-
kinag: Pawn or Pivot? East Lansing: Michigan State University Press, 1958.

Mao Tse-tung   毛澤東

WORKS

1934. Chih-yu Su-wei-ai neng-kou chiu Chung-
kuo. Moscow: Su-lien wai-kuo kung-jen ch'u-
pan she.
只有蘇維埃能夠救中國。

1934? Red China: President Mao Tse-tung Reports on the Progress of the Chinese Soviet
Republic. New York: International Publishers.

1937. China: The March toward Unity. with
Wang Ming, Georgi Dimitroff *et al*. New
York: Workers Library.

1937. Tsai Su ch'ü tang tai-piao ta-hui shang te
cheng-chih pao-kao chi chieh-lun; i-chiu-san-
ch'i nien wu-yueh san jih chi ch'i jih. Yenan:
Chieh-fang she.
在蘇區黨代表大會上的政治報告及結論；
一九三七年五月三日及七日。

1938. Lun hsin chieh-tuan. Chungking: Hsin
hua jih-pao kuan.
論新階段。

Eng. tr., *The New Stage: Report to the Sixth Enlarged Plenum of the Central Committee of the Communist Party of China*. Chungking: New China Information Committee, 1938?

1938. Mao Tse-tung *et al*. K'ang Jih chiu-kuo chih-nan; ti-i chi. Shanghai: K'an Jih chan-shu yen-chiu she.
毛澤東等。抗日救國指南；第 1 輯。

1938. Mao Tse-tung *et al*. Min-tsu ko-ming chih lu. Hsing hsing ch'u-pan she.
毛澤東等。民族革命之路。

1938. Mao Tse-tung *et al*. T'ung-i chan-hsien hsia tang-p'ai wen-t'i. Shih-shih hsin-wen pien-i she.
毛澤東等。統一戰綫下黨派問題。

1938. (comp.) Pa lu chün te chan-lueh ho chan-shu. with Chu Teh *et al*. Shanghai: Sheng-huo ch'u-pan she.
八路軍的戰略和戰術。朱德等。

1939. China and the Second Imperialist World War. Chungking: New China Information Committee.

1939. Mao Tse-tung chiu-kuo yen-lun hsuan-chi. Chungking: Hsin hua jih-pao kuan.
毛澤東救國言論選集。

1943. Wen-i wen-t'i. Yenan: Chieh-fang she.
文藝問題。

1945. The Fight for a New China. New York: New Century Publishers.

1945. Our Task in 1945.

1946. Sheng-ch'an tsu-chih yü nung-ts'un tiao-ch'a. Hong Kong: Hsin min-chu ch'u-pan she.
生產組織與農村調查。

1947. Chung-kuo ko-ming chan-cheng te chan-lueh wen-t'i. Hong Kong: Cheng pao she.
中國革命戰爭的戰略問題。

1947. I-chiu-ssu-ch'i nien tou-cheng jen-wu yü ch'ien-t'u. with Chu Teh *et al*. Cheng pao she.
一九四七年鬥爭任務與前途。朱德等。

1947. Lun ch'a t'ien yün-tung. Chin Ch'a Chi hsin hua shu-tien.
論查田運動。

1947. Mao Tse-tung *et al*. K'ai-chan ta kuei-mo te ch'ün-chung wen-chiao yün-tung. Hong Kong: Chung-kuo ch'u-pan she.
毛澤東等。開展大規模的群衆文教運動。

1948. Aspects of China's Anti-Japanese Struggle. Bombay: People's Publishing House.

1948. Mao Tse-tung *et al*. Kuan-yü chih-shih fen-tzu te kai-tsao (comp. by Cheng pao ch'u-pan she). Hong Kong: Hsin min-chu ch'u-pan she.
毛澤東等。關於知識份子的改造。正報出版社。

1949. Ching-chi wen-t'i yü ts'ai-cheng wen-t'i. Hong Kong: Hsin min-chu ch'u-pan she.
經濟問題與財政問題。

1949. Chung-kuo kung-ch'an-tang hung chün ti-ssu chün ti-chiu tz'u tai-piao ta-hui i-chueh-an. Hong Kong: Hsin min-chu ch'u-pan she.
中國共產黨紅軍第四軍第九次代表大會議決案。

1949. Mao Tse-tung *et al*. Chih-shih fen-tzu yü chiao-yü wen-t'i. Shanghai: Hsin hua shu-tien.
毛澤東等。知識份子與教育問題。

1949. Mao Tse-tung *et al*. Hsin min-chu chu-i kung shang cheng-ts'e. Hong Kong: Hsin min-chu ch'u-pan she.
毛澤東等。新民主主義工商政策。

1949. Mao Tse-tung *et al*. Lun ssu-hsiang. Pei-ping: Ch'ün-chung shu-tien.
毛澤東等。論思想。

1949. Mao Tse-tung *et al*. T'u-ti kung shang tsen-yang tsai kai-ko (comp. by Ch'un feng she). Shanghai: Ch'un feng she.
毛澤東等。土地工商怎樣在改革。春風社。

1949. Nung-min yün-tung yü nung-ts'un tiao-ch'a. Hong Kong: Hsin min-chu ch'u-pan she.
農民運動與農村調查。

1950. Lessons of the Chinese Revolution. with Liu Shao-ch'i. Bombay: J. Bhatt for People's Publishing House.

1950. Mao Tse-tung *et al*. Lun hsin chieh-fang ch'ü t'u-ti cheng-ts'e. Canton: Hsin hua shu-tien.
毛澤東等。論新解放區土地政策。

1950. Significance of Agrarian Reforms in China. with Liu Shao-ch'i. Bombay: J. Bhatt.

1950. Three Important Writings. Bombay: People's Publishing House.

1951. Chung-kuo kung-ch'an-tang tsai k'ang Jih shih-ch'i te jen-wu. Sian: Ch'ün-chuug jih-pao t'u-shu ch'u-pan k'o.
中國共產黨在抗日時期的任務。

1951-60. Mao Tse-tung hsuan-chi. Peking: Jen-min ch'u-pan she. 4 vols.
毛澤東選集。
Eng. tr., *Selected Works*. Peking: Foreign Languages Press, 1961-65. 4 vols.

1952. Lun p'i-p'ing yü tzu-wo p'i-p'ing. Peking: Jen-min ch'u-pan she.
論批評與自我批評。

1953. Mao Tse-tung *et al*. San nien lai hsin Chung-kuo ching-chi te ch'eng-chiu (comp. by Chung-kuo kuo-chi mao-i ts'u-chin wei-yuan-hui). Peking: Jen-min ch'u-pan she.
毛澤東等。三年來新中國經濟的成就。中國國際貿易促進委員會。

1953. Tsui wei-ta te yu-i. Peking: Jen-min wen-hsueh ch'u-pan she.
最偉大的友誼。

1955. Kuan-yü nung-yeh ho-tso hua wen-t'i. Peking: Jen-min ch'u-pan she.
關於農業合作化問題。
Eng. tr., *The Question of Agricultural Co-operation*. Peking: Foreign Languages Press, 1956.

1956. Chung-kuo kung-ch'an-tang ti-pa tz'u ch'üan-kuo tai-piao ta-hui k'ai-mu tz'u (I-chiu-wu-liu nien chiu-yueh shih-wu jih). Peking: Jen-min ch'u-pan she.
中國共產黨第八次全國代表大會開幕詞 (一九五六年九月十五日)。

1957. Mao chu-hsi tsai Su-lien te yen-lun. Peking: Jen-min jih-pao ch'u-pan she.
毛主席在蘇聯的言論。

1958. Comrade Mao Tse-tung on "Imperialism and All Reactionaries Are Paper Tigers." Peking: Foreign Languages Press.

1958. Kuan-yü cheng-ch'ueh ch'u-li jen-min nei-pu mao-tun te wen-t'i. Peking: Wen-tzu kai-ko ch'u-pan she.
關於正確處理人民內部矛盾的問題。
Eng. tr., *On the Correct Handling of Contradictions among the People*. Peking: Foreign Languages Press, 1957.

1958. Mao Tse-tung lun ts'ai-cheng (comp. by Chung-kuo k'o-hsueh-yuan ching-chi yen-chiu so ts'ai-cheng mao-i tsu). Peking: Ts'ai-cheng ch'u-pan she.
毛澤東論財政。中國科學院經濟研究所財政貿易組。

1958. Mao Tse-tung t'ung-chih lun chiao-yü kung-tso. Peking: Jen-min chiao-yü ch'u-pan she.
毛澤東同志論教育工作。

1959. Poems. Peking: Foreign Languages Press.

195?. Statement on American Military Aid to China.

1960. Chairman Mao Tse-tung's Important Talks with Guests from Asia, Africa and Latin America. Peking: Foreign Languages Press.

1960. Chiang ko-ming chin-hsing tao-ti. Peking: Jen-min wen-hsueh ch'u-pan she.
將革命進行到底。

1960. Kuan-yü mu-ch'ien tang te cheng-ts'e chung te chi-ko chung-yao wen-t'i. Peking: Jen-min wen-hsueh ch'u-pan she.
關於目前黨的政策中的幾個重要問題。

1960. Lun wen-hsuen yü i-shu. Peking: Jen-min wen-hsueh ch'u-pan she.
論文學與藝術。
Eng. tr., *On Art and Literature*. Peking: Foreign Languages Press, 1960.

1960. Mao Tse-tung t'ung-chih lun ch'ing-nien ho ch'ing-nien kung-tso. Peking: Chung-kuo ch'ing-nien ch'u-pan she.
毛澤東同志論青年和青年工作。

1960. New-Democratic Constitutionalism. Peking: Foreign Languages Press.

1960. Struggle to Mobilize All Forces in Winning Victory in the Armed Resistance. Peking: Foreign Languages Press.

1960. Tsai Chung-kuo kung-ch'an-tang ti-ch'i chieh chung-yang wei-yuan-hui ti-erh tz'u ch'üan-t'i hui-i shang te pao-kao. Peking: Jen-min ch'u-pan she.
在中國共產黨第七屆中央委員會第二次全體會議上的報告。

1961. Mao chu-hsi shih tz'u ch'ien-shih. Shanghai: Shanghai wen-i ch'u-pan she.
毛主席詩詞淺釋。

1961. Mao Tse-tung lun tiao-ch'a yen-chiu (comp. by Chung-kuo jen-min ta-hsueh chi-hua t'ung-chi hsi t'ung-chi tzu-liao shih). Hong Kong: Sheng-huo, tu-shu, hsin chih san lien shu-tien.
毛澤東論調查研究。中國人民大學計劃統計系統計資料室。

1961. On Guerrilla Warfare (tr. by Samuel B. Griffith). New York: Praeger.

1961. On the U.S. White Paper. Peking: Foreign Languages Press.

1962. Mao chu-hsi shih-tz'u erh-shih-i shou: Chu-ho Chung-kuo kung-ch'an-tang ssu-shih chou-nien (comp. by Chung-kuo min-chu t'ung-meng chung-yang wei-yuan-hui). Peking: Jen-min mei-shu ch'u-pan she.
毛主席詩詞二十一首：祝賀中國共產黨四十周年。中國民主同盟中央委員會。

1963. Mao chu-hsi shih tz'u. Peking: Jen-min wen-hsueh ch'u-pan she.
毛主席詩詞。

1963. Selected Military Writings. Peking: Foreign Languages Press.

1964. Chieh-shao i-ko ho-tso-she. Peking: Jen-min ch'u-pan she.
介紹一個合作社。

1964. Ch'üan shih-chieh jen-min t'uan-chieh ch'i-lai ta pai Mei-kuo ch'in-lueh che chi ch'i i-ch'ieh tsou-kou; kuan-yü chih-ch'ih Mei-kuo hei-jen, Yueh-nan nan-fang jen-min, Pa-na-ma jen-min, Jih-pen jen-min ho Kang-kuo (Li) jen-min fan-tui Mei ti-kuo chu-i te cheng-i tou-cheng te sheng-ming ho t'an-hua. Peking: Jen-min ch'u-pan she.

全世界人民團結起來打敗美國侵略者及其一切走狗；關于支持美國黑人，越南南方人民，巴拿馬人民，日本人民和剛果（利）人民反對美帝國主義的正義鬥爭的聲明和談話。

1964. Jen-te cheng-ch'ueh ssu-hsiang shih ts'ung na-li lai te. Peking: Jen-min ch'u-pan she.

人的正確思想是從那裡來的。

1964. Mao chu-hsi shih-tz'u san-shih-ch'i shou. Wen-wu ch'u-pan she.

毛主席詩詞三十七首。

1964. Mao chu-hsi te ssu p'ien che-hsueh lun-wen. Peking: Jen-min ch'u-pan she.

毛主席的四篇哲學論文。

1964. Mao Tse-tung chu-tso hsuan-tu. Peking: Jen-min ch'u-pan she. 2 vols.

毛澤東著作選讀。

1965. Mao chu-hsi shih-tz'u—ch'i-lü ch'ang-cheng. Peking: wen-wu ch'u-pan she.

毛主席詩詞一七律長征。

1965. Mao Tse-tung shih tz'u fan-i (with Chu-chieh) (tr. by Chin Fang). Kowloon: Han min shu-chü.

毛澤東詩詞翻譯（附：註解）。金芳。

1966. Mao chu-hsi yü-lu (comp. by Chung-kuo jen-min chieh-fang chün tsung cheng-chih pu) Shanghai: Chung-kuo jen-min chieh-fang chün tsung cheng-chih pu.

毛主席語錄。中國人民解放軍總政治部。

Eng. tr., *Quotations from Chairman Mao Tse-tung*. Peking: Foreign Languages Press, 1966.

1966. On War. Dehra Dun, India: The English Book Depot.

1966. Tsai Chung-kuo kung-ch'an-tang ch'üan-kuo hsuan-ch'uan kung-tso hui-i shang te chiang-hua. Peking: Jen-min ch'u-pan she.

在中國共產黨全國宣傳工作會議上的講話。

1967. Mao chu-hsi kuan-yü wen-hsueh i-shu te wu-ko wen-chien. Hong Kong: Hong Kong san lien shu-tien.

毛主席關於文學藝術的五個文件。

1968. Mao chu-hsi kuan-yü hsueh-sheng yün-tung te yü-lu. Hong Kong: Hong Kong san lien shu-tien.

毛主席關於學生運動的語錄。

Mao Tse-tung *et al*. Chung-kuo kung-ch'an-tang yü t'u-ti ko-ming. Hong Kong: Cheng pao she.

毛澤東等。中國共產黨與土地革命。

Mao Tse-tung *et al*. Hsiang-ch'ih chieh-tuan te hsing-shih yü jen-wu. 2 vols.

毛澤東等。相持階段的形勢與任務。

SOURCES

Ch'en Chang-feng. On the Long March with Chairman Mao. Peking: Foreign Languages Press, 1959.

———. The Long March: Eyewitness Account. Peking: Foreign Languages Press, 1963.

Ch'en, Jerome. Mao and the Chinese Revolution. New York: Oxford University Press, 1965.

Ch'en Kung-po. The Communist Movement in China: An Essay Written in 1924 (ed. by C. Martin Wilbur). New York: East Asian Institute, Columbia University, 1960.

The China White Paper, August 1949. Stanford: Stanford University Press, 1967. 2 vols.

Chow Tse-tsung. The May Fourth Movement: Intellectual Revolution in Modern China. Cambridge: Harvard University Press, 1960.

George, Alexander L. The Chinese Communist Army in Action: The Korean War and Its Aftermath. New York: Columbia University Press, 1967.

Hinton, Harold C. Communist China in World Politics. Boston: Houghton Mifflin Co., 1966.

Hsiao San. Mao Tse-tung t'ung-chih te ch'ing shao nien shih-tai. Shanghai: Hsin hua shu-tien, 1949.

蕭三。毛澤東同志的青少年時代。

Hsiao Tso-liang. Power Relations within the Chinese Communist Movement, 1930–1934. Seatle: University of Washington Press, 1961.

Hsiao Yü. Mao Tse-tung and I were Beggars. Syracuse: Syracuse University Press, 1959.

Hu Chiao-mu. Thirty Years of the Communist Party of China. London: Lawrence & Wishart, 1951.

Hunan chin pai nien ta-shih chi-shu (Hunan sheng chih ti-i chüan), comp. by Hunan sheng chih pien-tsuan wei-yuan-hui. Changsha: Hunan jen-min ch'u-pan she, 1959.

湖南近百年大事記述（湖南省誌第一卷）。湖南省志編纂委員會。

Ko-ming wen-hsien, ti-pa chi, ed. by Chung-kuo kuo-min-tang chung-yang wei-yuan-hui tang shih shih-liao pien-tsuan wei-yuan-hui. Tai-

pei: Chung-yang wen-wu kung-ying she, 1955.
革命文獻，第八輯。中國國民黨中央委員
會黨史史料編纂委員會。

Kung Ch'u. Wo yü hung chün. Hong Kong:
Nan feng ch'u-pan she, 1955.
龔楚。我與紅軍。

Li Jui. Mao Tse-tung t'ung-chih te ch'u-ch'i
ko-ming huo-tung. Peking: Chung-kuo
ch'ing-nien ch'u-pan she, 1957.
李銳。毛澤東同志的初期革命活動。

Mao Tse-tung. Mao chu-hsi shih tz'u ch'ien-
shih. Shanghai: Shanghai wen-i ch'u-pan she.
毛澤東。毛主席詩詞淺釋。

———. Selected Works. Peking: Foreign Languages Press, 1961-65. 4 vols.

Michael, Franz H., and George E. Taylor. The
Far East in the Modern World. New York:
Holt, Rinehart & Winston, 1956.

North, Robert C. Chinese Communism. New
York: McGraw-Hill Book Co., 1966.

Payne, Pierre Stephen Robert. Portrait of a
Revolutionary: Mao Tse-tung. New York:
Abelard-Schuman, 1961.

RSOC

SCMP, 2575 (September 11, 1961).

Schram, Stuart. Mao Tse-tung. Middlesex,
England: Penguin Books, 1966.

———. The Political Thought of Mao Tse-tung.
London: Pall Mall Press, 1964.

Schwartz, Benjamin I. Chinese Communism
and the Rise of Mao. Cambridge: Harvard
University Press, 1951.

Smedley, Agnes. The Great Road: The Life
and Times of Chu Teh. New York: Monthly
Review Press, 1956.

Snow, Edgar. The Other Side of the River: Red
China Today. New York: Random House,
1962.

Masud Sabri

SOURCES

An Ning. Sinkiang nei-mu. Singapore: Ch'uang
k'en ch'u-pan she, 1952.
安寧。新疆內幕。

BKL

CH, 1937-45.

CH-T, 1956-57.

Chang Ta-chün. Ssu-shih nien tung-luan Sinkiang. Hong Kong: Ya-chou ch'u-pan she,
1956.
張達鈞。四十年動亂新疆。

Hsin hua yueh-pao, 2 (December, 1945).
新華月報。

Kuo wen chou-pao, XIII-14 (April, 1936).
國聞週報。

Lattimore, Owen. Pivot of Asia: Sinkiang and
the Inner Asian Frontiers of China and Russia.
Boston: Little, Brown & Co., 1950.

WWMC

Mei Kuang-ti   梅光迪

WORKS

1956. Mei Kuang-ti wen-lu. Taipei: Chung-
hua ts'ung-shu wei-yuan-hui.
梅光迪文錄。

SOURCES

CBJS

GCMMTJK

Kuo Pin-ho. "Mei Ti-sheng hsien-sheng Kuang-
ti." *Chiao-yü t'ung-hsin,* VI-2 (Sepember, 1948):
45.
郭斌龢。梅迪生先生光迪。教育通訊。

Mei Kuang-ti. Mei Kuang-ti wen-lu. Taipei:
Chung-hua ts'ung-shu wei-yuan-hui, 1956.
梅光迪。梅光迪文錄。

"Mei Kuang-ti." *Harvard Journal of Asiatic Studies,* 9 (June, 1946): 189.

Mei Lan-fang   梅蘭芳

WORKS

1957. Tung yu chi. Peking: Chung-kuo hsi-chü
ch'u-pan she.
東遊記。

1959. Mei Lan-fang hsi-chü san lun. Peking:
Chung-kuo hsi-chü ch'u-pan she.
梅蘭芳戲劇散論。

1962. Mei Lan-fang wen-chi (ed. by Chung-kuo
hsi-chü chia hsieh-hui). Peking: Chung-kuo
hsi-chü ch'u-pan she.
梅蘭芳文集。中國戲劇家協會。

1962. Wo te tien-ying sheng-huo. Peking:
Chung-kuo tien-ying ch'u-pan she.
我的電影生活。

SOURCES

Ch'i Ju-shan. Mei Lan-fang i-shu i-pan. Peiping: Peiping kuo chü hsueh-hui, 1935.
齊如山。梅蘭芳藝術一斑。

Jen-min jih-pao. Peking, August 4, 19, 1962.

人民日報。

Leung, George Kin. Mei Lan-fang, Foremost Actor of China. Shanghai: Commercial Press, 1929.

Mei Lan-fang ko-ch'ü p'u, ed. by Liu T'ien-hua. 1930. 2 vols.
梅蘭芳歌曲譜。劉天華。

"Mei Lan-fang tsai Su-lien." *Kuo wen chou-pao*, XII-22.
梅蘭芳在蘇聯。國聞週報。

Mei Lan-fang yen-ch'u chü-pen hsuan-chi; shih pen, ed. by Chung-kuo hsi-chü chia hsieh-hui. Peking: Peking i-shu ch'u-pan she, 1954.
梅蘭芳演出劇本選集；十本。中國戲劇家協會。

Mei Lan-fang yu Mei chi, ed. by Ch'i Ju-shan. Peiping: Shang-wu yin shu kuan, 1933.
梅蘭芳遊美記。齊如山。

The New York Times, August 9, 1961.

The San Francisco Chronicle, August 9, 1961.

Ta-chung tien-ying, September, 1962.
大眾電影。

Wen hui pao. Hong Kong, August 7, 8, 13, 17, 18, 1962.
文匯報。

Wen-i pao, August, 1961: 3–5.
文藝報。

Mei Yi-ch'i   梅貽琦
SOURCES

Person interviewed: Liu Ch'ung-hung.
BKL
Chiao-yü yü wen-hua, 25 (March 2, 1961): 71.
教育與文化。

Chung-hua Min-kuo ta-hsueh chih, ed. by Chung-kuo hsin-wen ch'u-pan kung-ssu. Taipei: Chung-kuo hsin-wen ch'u-pan kung-ssu, 1953.
中華民國大學誌。中國新聞出版公司。

"Mei hsiao-chang Yueh-han po-shih ch'i chih nien-p'u chi-yao chi ch'i yü ch'ing-hua yu kuan shih-chi." *Ch'ing-hua hsueh-pao*, t'e-k'an, 1 (December, 1959).
梅校長月涵博士七秩年譜紀要及其與清華有關事蹟。清華學報。
Eng. tr., "A Seventy-Year Chronology of Dr. Y. C. Mei's Life and Work with Special Reference to His Association with Tsing Hua." *Tsing Hua Journal of Chinese Studies*, special number 1 (December, 1959).

The New York Times, May 20, 1962.

Mei Yi-pao   梅貽寶
WORKS

1959. "Yenching University in Chengtu," in Dwight W. Edwards, *Yenching University*. New York: United Borad for Christian Higher Education in Asia.

SOURCES

CH
Chinese Christian Student, November, 1945.

Edwards, Dwight W. Yenching University. New York: United Board for Christian Higher Education in Asia, 1959.

Oberlin College 125th Annual Alumni Catalogue.

Princeton-Yenching News, December, 1954.

Robbins, Martin. "Bringing East and West Together." *On Iowa*, November–December, 1959.

Meng Sen   孟森
WORKS

1905. Kwangsi pien shih p'ang chi. Shanghai: Shang-wu yin shu kuan.
廣西邊事旁記。

1908–9. ed. of *Tung-fang tsa-chih*.
東方雜誌。

1910. (ed.) Ch'eng chen hsiang ti-fang tzu-chih shih-i hsiang-chieh. Shanghai: Shang-wu yin shu kuan.
城鎮鄉地方自治事宜詳解。

1913. Jih-pen min fa yao-i tsung-tse pien. (tr.) Shanghai: Shang-wu yin shu kuan.
日本民法要義總則編。

1913. Min-fa yao-i; chai-ch'üan pien. (tr.) Shanghai: Shang-wu yin shu kuan.
民法要義；債權編。

1916. T'ung-chi t'ung-lun. (tr.) Shanghai: Shang-wu yin shu kuan.
統計通論。

1930. Ch'ing ch'ao ch'ien chi. Shanghai: Shang-wu yin shu kuan.
清朝前紀。

1934–37. Ming Yuan Ch'ing hsi t'ung chi. Peking: Peking ta-hsueh. 16 vols.
明元清系通紀。

1935. Ch'ing ch'u san ta i-an k'ao shih. Peking: Peking ta-hsueh.
清初三大疑案考實。

1935. Hsin shih ts'ung k'an. Shanghai: Ta tung shu-chü. 3 vols.

心史叢刊。

1936, September. "Hsuan-t'ung san-nien tiao-ch'a chih O Meng chieh-hsien t'u k'ao-cheng." *T'u-shu chi-k'an*, III-3: 117–28.
宣統三年調查之俄蒙界線圖考證。 圖書季刊。

1936. Pa ch'i chih-tu k'ao shih.
八旗制度考實。

1947. Ch'ing shih chiang-i. Shanghai: Chung-kuo wen-fu-wu she.
清史講義。

1957. Ming tai shih. Taipei: Chung-hua ts'ung-shu wei-yuan-hui.
明代史。

1959. Ming Ch'ing shih lun chu chi k'an. Peking: Chung-hua shu-chü. 2 vols.
明清史論著集刊。

1960. Chung-hsueh pen-kuo shih wen-ta. Hong Kong: T'ai-p'ing-yang t'u-shu kung-ssu.
中學本國史問答。

SOURCES

Persons interviewed: not to be identified.

Miao Ch'üan-sun   繆荃孫

WORKS

1896. (ed.) Liao wen ts'un (with I wen chih chin shih mu). Lai-ch'ing-ko. 2 vols.
遼文存 （附：藝文志金石目）。

1901. I-feng-t'ang wen-chi. 8 vols.
藝風堂文集。

1901. I-feng ts'ang shu chi. 6 vols.
藝風藏書記。

1901. (ed.) Wu shih shih-lien-an k'o-pen tso jen tz'u. Chin-ling. 10 vols.
吳氏石蓮庵刻本左人詞。

1901–7. I-feng-t'ang wen man ts'un. 5 vols.
藝風堂文漫存。

1903. Jih yu hui-pien. 4 vols.
日遊彙編。

1905. (ed.) Tui-yü-lou ts'ung-shu. 10 vols.
對雨樓叢書。

1906. I-feng-t'ang chin shih wen-tzu mu. 6 vols.
藝風堂金石文字目。

1910. (ed.) Hsü pei-chuan chi. Chiang ch'u pien i chü. 24 vols.
續碑傳集。

1910. (ed.) Ou hsiang ling-shih. Chiang-yin Miao shih. 32 vols.
藕香零拾。

1918. Ching-shih fang chiang chih. with Chu I-hsin. Pao-chen-t'ang.
京師坊巷志。朱一新。

1920. (ed.) Yen hua tung t'ang hsiao-p'in. Miao shih. 2 vols.
煙畫東堂小品。

1936. (ed.) I feng lao-jen nien-p'u. Peiping.
藝風老人年譜。

1939. I-feng-t'ang shih ts'un (with Pi hsiang tz'u i chüan). Peiping: Yen-ching ta-hsueh t'u-shu kuan.
藝風堂詩存 （附： 碧香詞一卷）。

1940. I-feng-t'ang ts'ang shu tsai hsü chi. Peiping: Yen-ching ta-hsueh t'u-shu kuan.
藝風堂藏書再續記。

1965. (ed.) Ch'ing tai ts'ang shu t'i-pa hui-lu. Hong Kong: Lung wen shu-tien. 2 vols.
清代藏書題跋彙錄。

(ed.) Ch'ing hsueh pu t'u-shu kuan fang-chih mu.
清學部圖書館方志目。

(ed.) Ch'ing hsueh pu t'u-shu kuan shan-pen shu-mu.
清學部圖書館善本書目。

K'ung Pei-hai (Jung) nien-p'u. Yen hua tung t'ang.
孔北海(融)年譜。

Kuo shih ju lin chuan.
國史儒林傳。

Liu-li ch'ang shu-ssu hou chi.
琉璃廠書肆後記。

Shu shih ching chiao chi.
蜀石經校記。

(ed.) Te-yueh-lou shu-mu.
得月樓書目。

Yun tzu tsai k'an pi-chi.
雲自在龕筆記。

(ed.) Yun tzu tsai k'an ts'ung-shu. 26 vols.
雲自在龕叢書。

SOURCES

Hsia Sun-t'ung. "Miao I-feng hsien-sheng hsing-chuang," in PCCP.
夏孫桐。 繆藝風先生行狀。

I feng lao-jen-nien-p'u, ed. by Miao Ch'uan-sun. Peiping.
藝風老人年譜。 繆全孫。

Miao Pin   繆斌

SOURCES

Persons interviewed: not to be identified.
GCCMMTJK

Mo Te-hui   莫德惠

SOURCES

AWW

Ch'eng T'ien-fang. A History of Sino-Russian Relations. Washington: Public Affairs Press, 1957.

CMJL

CTMC

CWR, 1929-30.

GCJJ

Tang, Peter S. H. Russian and Soviet Policy in Manchuria and Outer Mongolia, 1911-1931. Durham: Duke University Press, 1959.

Wei, Henry. China and Soviet Russia. Princeton: D. Van Nostrand Co., 1956.

WWC, 1931.

WWMC

Mu Hsiang-yueh   穆湘玥

WORKS

1926. Ou-ch'u wu-shih tzu-shu (with Ou-ch'u wen lu). Shanghai: Shang-wu yin shu kuan.
藕初五十自述 (附：藕初文錄)。

SOURCES

Persons interviewed: not to be identified.

CYB-W, 1934.

Mu Hsiang-yueh. Ou-ch'u wu-shih tzu-shu (with Ou-ch'u wen lu). Shanghai: Shang-wu yin shu kuan, 1926.
穆湘玥。 藕初五十自述 (附：藕初文錄)。

Nieh Erh   聶耳

WORKS

1959. Chung-hua Jen-min Kung-ho-kuo kuo-ko —kuan-hsien-yueh tsung p'u. Peking: Yin-yueh ch'u-pan she.
中華人民共和國國歌一管弦樂總譜。

1960. Nieh Erh ko-ch'ü hsuan-chi (with Kang-ch'in pan-tsou) (ed. by Yin-yueh ch'u-pan she pien-chi pu). Peking: Yin-yueh ch'u-pan she.
聶耳歌曲選集 (附：鋼琴伴奏)。 音樂出版社編輯部。

SOURCES

Chinese Literature Monthly, November, 1959.

Jen-min yin-yueh, 10-12 (October-December, 1960).

人民音樂。

Nieh Erh hua-chuan, comp. by Lien K'ang. Peking: Yin-yueh ch'u-pan she, 1958.
聶耳畫傳。 聯抗。

Nieh Erh—ts'ung chü-pen tao ying-p'ien, ed. by Chung-kuo tien-ying ch'u-pan she. Peking: Chung-kuo tien-ying ch'u-pan she, 1963.
聶耳一從劇本到影片。 中國電影出版社。

Scott, Adolphe Clarence. Literature and the Arts in Twentieth Century China. Garden City, N.Y.: Doubleday, 1963.

Yü Ling, Meng Po, and Cheng Chün-li. Tien-ying wen-hsueh chü-pen—Nieh Erh. Shanghai: Shanghai wen-hua ch'u-pan she, 1964.
于伶， 孟波， 鄭君里。 電影文學劇本一聶耳。

Nieh Jung-chen   聶榮臻

SOURCES

Person interviewed: Chang Kuo-t'ao.

Chung-kuo kung-ch'an-tang te chung-yao jen-wu, ed. by Min-chien ch'u-pan she. Peiping: Min-chien ch'u-pan she, 1949.
中國共產黨的重要人物。 民間出版社。

GCCJK

Jen-min chiang-ling ch'ün-hsiang, comp. by Hai-yün. Macao: Ch'un-ch'iu shu-tien, 1947.
人民將領群像。 海雲。

Rigg, Robert B. Red China's Fighting Hordes. Harrisburg: Military Service Publishing Co., 1952.

RNRC

RSOC

SCMP, 1139.

Smedley, Agnes. The Great Road: The Life and Times of Chu Teh. New York: Monthly Review Press, 1956.

Taylor, George E. The Struggle for North China. New York: International Secretariat, Institute of Pacific Relations, 1940.

Wales, Nym (pseud. of Helen Foster Snow). Inside Red China. New York: Doubleday, Doran & Co., 1939.

WWC, 1950.

WWMC

Niu Hui-sheng   牛惠生

SOURCES

Person interviewed: Y. T. Zee New.

Niu Yung-chien 紐永鍵

SOURCES

Persons interviewed: not to be identified.
BKL
The New York Times, December 26, 1965.

Osman

SOURCES

Chang Ta-chün. Ssu-shih nien tung-luan Sinkiang. Hong Kong: Ya-chou ch'u-pan she,
1956.
張達鈞。 四十年動亂新疆。
Davidson, Basil. Turkestan Alive: New Travels
in Chinese Central Asia. London: Jonathan
Cape, 1957.
Lattimore, Owen. Pivot of Asia: Sinkiang and
the Inner Asian Frontiers of China and Russia.
Boston: Little, Brown & Co., 1950.
Whiting, Allen S., and Sheng Shih-ts'ai. Sinkiang: Pawn or Pivot? East Lansing: Michigan State University Press, 1958.

Ou-yang Ching-wu 歐陽竟無

WORKS

1963. Ching-wu hsiao-p'in. Taipei: Kuang wen
shu-chü.
竟無小品。
Ching-wu nei-wai-hsueh.
竟無內外學。
Wei shih chueh tse t'an.
唯識抉擇談。

SOURCES

Brière, O. Fifty Years of Chinese Philosophy,
1898-1950 (tr. by Laurence G. Thompson).
New York: The Macmillan Co., 1956.
Chan Wing-tsit. Religious Trends in Modern
China. New York: Columbia University
Press, 1953.
Hamilton, Clarence Herbert. "Buddhism," in
Harley Farnsworth MacNair, China. Berke-
ley: University of California Press, 1946.
Li I-cho. "Ou-yang Ching-wu hsien-sheng
Chien." *Chiao-yü t'ung-hsun*, VI-3, 4 (October,
1948).
李翊灼。 歐陽竟無先生漸。 教育通訓。
Ou-yang Chien. Ching-wu hsiao-p'in. Taipei:
Kuang wen shu-chü, 1963.
歐陽漸。 竟無小品。

Ou-yang Chien. "Fu Hsiung Tzu-chen han."
Unpub-lished manuscript, 1935.
歐陽漸。 復熊子眞函。
————. "Kiukiang Kuei Po-hua hsing-shu."
Unpublished manuscript, 1935.
歐陽漸。 九江桂伯華行述。
Ou-yang Ching-wu. Wei shih chueh tse t'an.
歐陽竟無。 唯識抉擇談。
P'i Ming-chü. "P'i Lu-ming hsien-sheng chuan-
lueh." *Kuo-hsueh chi-k'an*, V-2 (1935).
皮名舉。 皮鹿名先生傳略。 國學季刊。
Pratt, James Bissett. The Pilgrimage of Bud-
dhism and a Buddhist Pilgrimage. New York:
The Macmillan Co., 1928.
T'ai Hsü. Fa-hsiang wei shih hsueh. Changsha:
Shang-wu yin shu kuan, 1938.
太虛。 法相唯識學。
Wu Tsung-tz'u. "Ou-yang chien chuan." *Kuo
shih kuan kuan k'an*, I-3 (August, 1948): 99-102.
吳宗慈。 歐陽漸傳。 國史館館刊。

Ou-yang Yü-ch'ien 歐陽予倩

WORKS

1918, October. "Yü chih hsi-chü kai-liang
kuan." *Hsin ch'ing-nien*, V-4.
予之戲劇改良觀。 新青年。
1928. Hui chia i-hou.
回家以後。
1928. P'o-fu. Shang-wu yin shu kuan.
潑婦。
1929-? ed. of *Hsi-chü tsa-chih*.
戲劇雜誌。
1933. Tzu wo yen-hsi i-lai (1907-1928). Peking:
Chung-kuo hsi-chü ch'u-pan she.
自我演戲以來 (1907-1928)。
1939. (ed.) Yü mo (wu mu chü). Hsien-tai hsi-
chü ch'u-pan she.
慾魔 (五幕劇)。
1948. (ed.) T'an Ssu-t'ung shu chien. Shanghai:
Wen-hua kung-ying she.
譚嗣同書簡。
1956. (ed.) Chung-kuo hsi-ch'ü yen-chiu tzu-liao
ch'u chi. Peking: I-shu ch'u-pan she.
中國戲曲研究資料初輯。
1956. Ou-yang Yü-ch'ien chü tso hsuan. Peking:
Jen-min wen-hsueh ch'u-pan she.
歐陽予倩劇作選。
1959. Hua-chü, hsin ko-chü yü Chung-kuo hsi-
chü i-shu ch'uan-t'ung. Shanghai: Shanghai
wen-i ch'u-pan she.
話劇，新歌劇與中國戲劇藝術傳統。

1959. I te yü ch'ao (1951–1959 nien i-shu lun-wen hsuan). Peking: Tso-chia ch'u-pan she.
一得餘抄 (1951–1959年藝術論文選)。

1959. Ou-yang Yü-ch'ien hsuan-chi. Peking: Jen-min wen-hsueh ch'u-pan she.
歐陽予倩選集。

1962. Hei nu hen (Chiu ch'ang hua-chü). Peking: Chung-kuo hsi-chü ch'u-pan she.
黑奴恨 (九場話劇)。

1962. Tien-ying pan-lu ch'u-chia chi. Peking: Chung-kuo tien-ying ch'u-pan she.
電影半路出家記。

Chan-ti yuan-yang.
戰地鴛鴦。

Ch'ang hen ko.
長恨歌。

Ching K'o.
荊軻。

Ch'ing sha chang.
青紗帳。

Hsiao Ying ku-niang.
小英姑娘。

Kuo-ts'ui.
國粹。

Liang Hung-yü.
梁紅玉。

Liu San-mei.
劉三妹。

Pai ku-niang.
白姑娘。

Mu Lan ts'ung-chün.
木蘭從軍。

T'ung-ming yuan-yang.
同命鴛鴦。

Yang Kui-fei.
楊貴妃。

Yü-ch'ien lun chü. T'ai tung.
予倩論劇。

Yü-fu hen.
漁夫恨。

SOURCES

CHWC
CHWSK
CHWYS
CKJMT
GCCJK
HCJC
HMTT
HWP
I-chiu-wu-ling jen-min nien-chien, ed. by Shen Sung-fang. Hong Kong: Ta kung shu-chü, 1950.

一九五〇人民年鑑。沈頌芳。

Liu Shou-sung. Chung-kuo hsin wen-hsueh shih ch'u-kao. Peking: Tso-chia ch'u-pan she, 1956.
劉綬松。中國新文學史初稿。

MCNP
RCCL
TCMT
WWMC

Pai Ch'ung-hsi   白崇禧

WORKS

1935. Pai fu tsung-ssu-ling tsui-chin yen-chiang chi.
白副總司令最近演講集。

1945. Hsien-tai lu-chün chün-shih chiao-yü chih ch'ü-shih.
現代陸軍軍事教育之趨勢。

SOURCES

Kuo-min ko-ming chün chan shih, ed. by Kuo-min ko-ming chün chan shih pien-tsuan wei-yuan-hui. Nanking: Ts'an-mou pen-pu, 1934. 17 vols.
國民革命軍戰史。國民革命軍戰史編纂委員會。

Liang Sheng-chün. Chiang Li tou-cheng nei-mu. Hong Kong: Ya lien ch'u-pan she, 1954.
梁升俊。蔣李鬥爭內幕。

Pai Ch'ung-hsi. Pai fu tsung-ssu-ling tsui-chin yen-chiang chi. 1935.
白崇禧。白副總司令最近演講集。

Yin Shih (pseud. of Ch'en Kuang-yuan). Li Chiang kuan-hsi yü Chung-kuo. Kowloon: Tzu-yu ch'u-pan she, 1954.
隱士 (陳光遠)。李蔣關係與中國。

Pai Yang   白楊

WORKS

1962. Tien-ying piao-yen chi-i man-pi. Shanghai: Shanghai wen-i ch'u-pan she.
電影表演技藝漫筆。

SOURCES

Ch'eng Chi-hua, Li Shao-pai, and Hsing Tsu-wen. Chung-kuo tien-ying fa-chan shih. Peking: Chung-kuo tien-ying ch'u-pan she, 1963.
程季華, 李少白, 邢祖文。中國電影發展史。
GCJJ

Pai Yang [304]

Kung-sun Lu. Chung-kuo tien-ying shih-hua.
Hong Kong: Nan t'ien shu yeh kung-ssu. 2
vols.
公孫魯。中國電影史話。

Pai Yang. Tien-ying piao-yen chi-i man-pi.
Shanghai: Shanghai wen-i ch'u-pan she, 1962.
白楊。電影表演技藝漫筆。

Panchen Lama

SOURCES

AWW

Bell, Charles A. Portrait of the Dalai Lama.
London: Collins, 1946.
———. The Religion of Tibet. Oxford: Clar-
endon Press, 1931.
———. Tibet: Past and Present. Oxford: Clar-
endon Press, 1924.

CMTC

CYB-W, 1933.

GCJJ

Fisher, Margaret W., and Leo E. Rose. England,
India, Nepal, Tibet, China: 1765-1958. Berkeley: University of California, 1959.

Huang Fen-sheng. Pien-chiang jen-wu chih.
Chungking, 1945.
黃奮生。邊疆人物誌。

Li Tieh-tseng. The Historical Status of Tibet.
New York: King's Crown Press, Columbia
University, 1956.

Ma Ho-t'ien. Kan Ch'ing Tsang pien-ch'ü k'ao-
ch'a chi. Shanghai: Shang-wu yin shu kuan,
1947. 3 vols.
馬鶴天。甘青藏邊區考察記。

Richardson, Hugh Edward. A Short History of
Tibet. New York: E. P. Dutton & Co., 1962.

Shen Tsung-lien and Liu Sheng-chi. Tibet and
the Tibetans. Stanford: Stanford University
Press, 1953.

SMJ

WWC, 1931.

P'an Kuang-tan　潘 光 旦

WORKS

1927. Hsiao-ch'ing chih fen-hsi. Shanghai: Hsin-
yueh shu-tien.
小青之分析。

1928. Chung-kuo chih chia-t'ing wen-t'i. Shanghai: Hsin-yueh shu-tien.
中國之家庭問題。

1928. Jen-wen sheng-wu hsueh lun-ts'ung.
Shanghai: Hsin-yueh shu-tien.
人文生物學論叢。

1929, January. "Chung-kuo chia-p'u hsueh lueh
shih." Tung-fang tsa-chih, 26: 107-20.
中國家譜學略史。東方雜誌。

1929. Tzu-jan t'ao-t'ai yü Chung-hua min-tsu
hsing. (tr.) Shanghai: Hsin-yueh shu-tien.
自然淘汰與中華民族性。

1930. Jih-pen Te-i-chih min-tsu-hsing chih pi-
chiao te yen-chiu. Shanghai: Hsin-yueh shu-
tien.
日本德意志民族性之比較的研究。

1930. Tu-shu wen-t'i. Shanghai: Hsin-yueh
shu-tien.
讀書問題。

1934. Hsing te chiao-yü. (tr. of Havelock Ellis's
Sex Education). Shanghai: Ch'ing-nien hsieh-
hui shu-chü.
性的教育。

1934. Hsing te tao-te. (tr.) Shanghai: Ch'ing-
nien hsieh-hui shu-chü.
性的道德。

1937. Jen-wen shih-kuan. Shanghai: Shang-wu
yin shu kuan.
人文史觀。

1941. Chung-kuo ling-jen hsueh-yuan chih yen-
chiu. Changsha: Shang-wu yin shu kuan.
中國伶人血緣之研究。

1946. P'an Kuang-tan et al. (comp.) Jen-hsing
ho chi-ch'i; Chung-kuo shou-kung-yeh te
ch'ien-t'u. Shanghai: Sheng-huo shu-tien.
潘光旦等。人性和機器；中國手工業的前途。

1946. Tzu-yu chih lu. Shanghai: Shang-wu yin
shu kuan.
自由之路。

1946. Yu-sheng kai-lun. Chungking: Shang-wu
yin shu kuan.
優生概論。

1947. "K'o-chü yü she-hui liu-tung." She-hui
k'o-hsueh, 4: 1-21. (with Fei Hsiao-t'ung.)
科舉與社會流動。社會科學。費孝通。

1947. Ming Ch'ing liang tai Chia-hsing te wang-
tsu. Shanghai: Shang-wu yin shu kuan.
明清兩代嘉興的望族。

1947. "P'ai yü hui," in Fei Hsiao-t'ung, Sheng-
yü chih-tu. Shanghai: Shang-wu yin shu kuan.
派與匯。費孝通。生育制度。

1947. Yu-sheng yü k'ang chan. Shanghai:
Shang-wu yin shu kuan.
優生與抗戰。

1948. Cheng hsueh tsui yen. Shanghai: Kuan-
ch'a she.

政學罪言。

1951. P'an Kuang-tan *et al.* Wo-men ts'an-kuan
t'u-ti kai-ko i-hou (ed. by Tientsin shih t'u-ti
kai-ko ts'an-kuan t'uan). Peking: Wu-shih
nien-tai ch'u-pan she.
潘光旦等。我們參觀土地改革以後。天津
市土地改革參觀團。

1952. Su-nan t'u-ti kai-ko fang-wen chi. with
Ch'üan Wei-t'ien. Peking: Sheng-huo, tu-shu,
hsin-chih san lien shu-tien.
蘇南土地改革訪問記。全慰天。

Hsuan-ch'uan pu-shih ko-ming.
宣傳不是革命。

ed. of *Hsueh teng.*
學燈。

SOURCES

GCJJ
JMST, 1958.
MCNP
Ts'ao Chü-jen. Shu lin hsin yü. Hong Kong:
Ta-tung-t'u-shu Kung ssu, 1954.
曹聚仁。書林新語。
Ying Tzu. Chung-kuo hsin hsueh-shu jen-wu
chih. Hong Kong: Chih min shu-chü, 1956.
穎子。中國新學術人物誌。

P'an Kung-chan   潘公展

SOURCES

1930. Ch'ing-nien hsun-lien. Changsha: Shang-
wu yin shu kuan.
青年訓練。

1935. Hsueh-sheng te hsin shen-huo (ed. by Yeh
Ch'u-ts'ang). Nanking: Cheng-chung shu-chü.
學生的新生活。葉楚傖。

1938. Wo-men te k'ang chan ling-hsiu. Changsha: Shang-wu yin shu kuan.
我們的抗戰領袖。

1945. (ed.) Wu-shih nien lai te Chung-kuo.
Chungking: Sheng-li ch'u-pan she.
五十年來的中國。

1945. (ed.) Wu-shih nien lai te shih-chieh.
Chungking: Sheng-li ch'u-pan she.
五十年來的世界。

1954. Ch'en Ch'i-mei. Taipei: Sheng-li ch'u-
pan kung-ssu.
陳其美。

SOURCES

CBJS
Chung-kuo hsin-wen shih, ed. by Tseng Hsü-

pai. Taipei: Kuo-li cheng-chih ta-hsueh,
1966.
中國新聞史。曾虛白。
CTMC
GCJJ
WWC, 1933.
Yuan Ch'ang-ch'ao. Chung-kuo pao yeh hsiao
shih. Hong Kong: Hsin-wen t'ien-ti she, 1957.
袁昶超。中國報業小史。

Pei Tsu-yi   貝祖詒

SOURCES

Person interviewed: Chang Chia-ao.
The New York Times Magazine, March 14, 1965.

P'ei Wen-chung   斐文中

WORKS

1931. Mammalian Remains from Locality 5 at
Choukoutien. Peiping: Geological Survey of
China.

1934. On the Carnivora from Locality 1 of
Choukoutien. Peiping: The Geological Survey of China.

1935. Chiu-shih-ch'i shih-tai chih i-shu. Shanghai: Shang-wu yin shu kuan.
舊石器時代之藝術。

1936. On the Mammalian Remains from Locality 3 at Choukoutien. Peiping.

1937. "Palaeolithic Industries in China," in
G. G. MacCurdy, *Early Man.* Philadelphia.

1939. The Upper Cave Industry of Choukoutien.
Peiping: Geological Survey of China.

1940. The Upper Cave Fauna of Choukoutien.
Chungking: Geological Survey of China.

1947. "Chung-kuo ku-tai t'ao-li chi t'ao-ting te
yen-chiu." *Hsien-tai hsueh-pao,* I-2, 3, 4, 5.
中國古代陶鬲及陶鼎的研究。現代學報。

1947. Kansu shih-ch'ien k'ao-ku pao-kao.
(mimeo.).
甘肅史前考古報告。

1948. Chung-kuo shih-ch'ien shih-ch'i chih yen-
chiu. Shanghai: Shang-wu yin shu kuan.
中國史前時期之研究。

1948. Shih-ch'ien shih-ch'i chih Hsi-pei. Lanchow.
史前時期之西北。

1950. Tzu-jan fa-chan chien-shih. Shanghai:
Keng-yün ch'u-pan she.
自然發展簡史。

1951. P'ei Wen-chung *et al*. Yen pei wen-wu k'an-ch'a t'uan pao-kao. Peking.
斐文中等。雁北文物勘察團報告。

1952. P'ei Wen-chung *et al*. Wo-te ssu-hsiang shih tsen-yang chuan-pien kuo-lai te. Peking: Wu-shih nien-tai ch'u-pan she.
斐文中等。我的思想是怎樣轉變過來的。

1954. Chung-kuo shih-ch'i shih-tai te wen hua. Peking: Chung-kuo ch'ing-nien ch'u-pan she.
中國石器時代的文化。

1954, July-August. "New Light on Peking Man." *China Reconstructs*: 33-36.

1954. Ti-erh tz'u ta-chan ch'ien-hou shih-chieh ko-ti tui-yü jen-lei hua-shih te hsin yen-chiu (ed. by Chung-kuo k'o-hsueh yuan ku chi-chui tung-wu yen-chiu shih). Peking: Chung-kuo k'o-hsueh yuan.
第二次大戰前後世界各地對於人類化石的新研究。中國科學院古脊椎動物研究室。

1955. Kuan-yü k'ao-ku ho ti-ssu chi ti-chih kung-tso shang i-hsieh hsin fang-fa. Peking: K'o-hsueh ch'u-pan she.
關于考古和第四紀地質工作上一些新方法。

1957. "Discovery of Gigantopithecus Mandibles and Other Material in Liu-ch'eng District of Central Kwangsi in South China." *Vertebrata Palasiatica*, I-2: 65-71.

1957. "Giant Ape's Jaw Bone Discovered in China." *American Anthropologist*, LIX: 834-38.

1957. Tzu-yang jen. with Wu Ju-k'ang (ed. by Chung-kuo k'o-hsueh yuan ku chi-chui tung-wu yen-chiu so). Peking: K'o-hsueh ch'u-pan she.
資陽人。吳汝康。中國科學院古脊椎動物研究所。

1958. "Discovery of a Third Mandible of Gi-gantopithecus in Liu-ch'eng, Kwangsi, South China." *Vertebrata Palasiatica*, II: 193-200. (with Li Yu-heng.)

1958. P'ei Wen-chung *et al*. Shansi Hsiang-fen hsien Ting-ts'un chiu-shih-ch'i shih-tai i-chih fa-chueh pao-kao. Peking: K'o-hsueh ch'u-pan she.
斐文中等。山西襄汾縣丁村舊石器時代遺址發掘報告。

1960. "Kuan-yü Chung-kuo yuan-jen ku-ch'i wen-t'i te shuo-ming yü i-chien." *K'ao-ku hsueh-pao*, 2: 1-9.
關於中國猿人骨器問題的說明與意見。考古學報。

1963. Chung-kuo shih-ch'i shih-tai. Peking: Chung-kuo ch'ing-nien ch'u-pan she.
中國石器時代。

1965. Liu-ch'eng chü yuan tung fa-chueh ho Kwangsi ch'i-t'a shan-tung te t'an-ch'a. Peking: K'o-hsueh ch'u-pan she.
柳城巨猿洞發掘和廣西其他山洞的探查。

"The Living Environment of the Chinese Primi-tive Man (Resume)." *Vertebrata Palasiatica*, IV-1: 40-44.

"The Zoogeographical Divisions of Quaternary Mammalian Faunas in China." *Vertebrata Palasiatica*, I-1: 9-24.

SOURCES

Persons interviewed: not to be identified.

Chang Kuang-chih. "New Evidence on Fossil Man in China." *Science*, June, 1962.

P'ei Wen-chung *et al*. Wo-te ssu-hsiang shih tsen-yang chuan-pien kuo-lai te. Peking: Wu-shih nien-tai ch'u-pan she, 1952.
斐文中等。我的思想是怎樣轉變過來的。

Tseng Ma-ch'i. "P'ing P'ei Wen-chung hsien-sheng tsai 'k'ao-ku chi-ch'u' chung te 'shih-ch'i shih-tai k'ao-ku tsung-lun'." *K'ao-ku*, 1 (1959): 10-13.
曾馬其。評斐文中先生在「考古基礎」中的「石器時代考古總論」。考古。

Yuan Wei-chou. "Ti-chih hsueh," in Li Hsi-mou, *Chung-hua Min-kuo k'o-hsueh chih*. Taipei, 1955.
阮維周。地質學。李熙謀。中華民國科學誌。

P'eng Chen 彭眞

WORKS

1942. Chung-kung Chin Ch'a Chi pien-ch'ü ko-chung cheng-ts'e. T'ung-i ch'u-pan she.
中共晉察冀邊區各種政策。

1948. Wei ch'un-chieh tang te tsu-chih erh tou-cheng. Hong Kong: Cheng pao t'u-shu pu.
爲純潔黨的組織而鬥爭。

1950. P'eng Chen *et al*. Pa Peking wen-i kung-tso t'ui-chin i-pu (comp. by Peking wen-i she). Peking: Hsin hua shu-tien.
彭眞等。把北京文藝工作推進一步。北京文藝社。

1951. Kuan-yü cheng fa kung-tso te ch'ing-k'uang ho mu-ch'ien jen-wu (ed. by Jen-min ch'u-pan she pien-chi pu). Peking: Jen-min ch'u-pan she.
關於政法工作的情況和目前任務。人民出版社編輯部。

1951. Kuan-yü k'ang Mei yuan Ch'ao pao chia

wei kuo yün-tung te pao-kao. Peking: Jen-min ch'u-pan she.
關於抗美援朝保家衛國運動的報告。
1965. Tsai Yin-tu-ni-hsi-ya A-li-ha-mu she-hui k'o-hsueh hsueh-yuan te chiang-hua. Peking: Jen-min ch'u-pan she.
在印度尼西亞阿里哈姆社會科學學院的講話。

SOURCES

Person interviewed: Chang Kuo-t'ao.
CB, 763; 3443.
I-chiu-wu-ling jen-min nien-chien, ed. by Shen Sung-fang. Hong Kong: Ta kung shu-chü, 1950.
一九五〇人民年鑑。沈頌芳。
The New York Times, June 5, 15, 1964.
Rigg, Robert B. Red China's Fighting Hordes. Harrisburg: Military Service Publishing Co., 1952.
SCMP, 3299 (September 16, 1964).
Union Research Biographic Service, 7 (July 24, 1956).
Wen-hui pao. Hong Kong, March 4, 1951.
文滙報。
WWC, 1950.
WWMC

P'eng Pai   澎湃
SOURCES

Person interviewed: Chang Kuo-t'ao.
Chung I-mou. Hai-lu-feng nung-min yün-tung. Canton: Kwangtung jen-min ch'u-pan she, 1957.
鐘貽謀。海陸豐農民運動。
CKLC
Eto Shinkichi. "Chūgoku saisho no kyōsan sei-ken, Kai-riku-hō so-i-ai shi." *Kindai Chugoku kenkyu*, 2 (December, 1958): 1–97.
衞藤瀋吉。中國最初の共產黨～海陸豐蘇維埃史。近代中國研究。
———. "Hai-lu-feng—the First Chinese Soviet Government" *The China Quarterly*, 8 (October–December, 1961): 161–83; 9 (January–March, 1962): 149–81.
GCCJK
Hou Feng. P'eng Pai lieh-shih chuan-lueh. Canton: Kwangtung jen-min ch'u-pan she, 1959.
候楓。澎湃烈士傳略。
HSWT
Nan-fang jih-pao. July 1, 1951.
南方日報。

RD
"Red Hai-feng." *International Literature*, 2, 3 (1932): 88–103.
WWMC

P'eng Shu-chih   彭述之
WORKS

1968. "Jang li-shih te wen-chien tso-cheng." *Ming pao yueh-k'an*, III-6 (June, 1968): 13–22.
讓歷史的文件作證。明報月刊。

SOURCES

Dowson, Ross. "Chinese Revolution in Exile." *International Socialist Review*, Summer, 1963.
Ming pao yueh-k'an, III-6 (June, 1968).
明報月刊。
World Outlook, August 12, 1966; February 10, 1967.

P'eng Te-huai   彭德懷
WORKS

1937. Cheng-ch'ü ch'ih-chiu k'ang-chan sheng-li te hsien-chueh wen-t'i. Chiao-t'u ch'u-pan she.
爭取持久抗戰勝利的先決問題。
1940. P'eng Te-huai t'ung-chih tsai pei-fang tang te kao-chi kan-pu hui-i shang pao-kao t'i-kang.
彭德懷同志在北方黨的高級幹部會議上報告提綱。
1940. San nien lai te k'ang-chan. Chieh-fang she.
三年來的抗戰。

SOURCES

Person interviewed: Chang Kuo-t'ao.
CB, 137, 192.
Chao Te-hua. Chu Teh yü P'eng Te-huai fang-wen chi. Shanghai: K'ang chan ch'u-pan she, 1937.
趙德華。朱德與彭德懷訪問記。
Charles, David A. "The Dismissal of Marshal P'eng Teh-huai." *The China Quarterly*, 8 (October–December, 1961): 63–76.
CYB-W, 1934.
Elegant, Robert S. China's Red Masters. New York: Twayne, 1951.
HCJC
The New York Times, October 6, 1958.
New York World-Telegram and Sun. New York, September 17, 1959.
North, Robert C. Kuomintang and Chinese

Communist Elites (with the collaboration of Ithiel de Sola Pool). Stanford: Stanford University Press, 1952.

Rigg, Robert B. Red China's Fighting Hordes. Harrisburg: Military Service Publishing Co., 1952.

RSOC

Schwartz, Benjamin I. Chinese Communism and the Rise of Mao. Cambridge: Harvard University Press, 1951.

SCMP, 1139.

Smedley, Agnes. Battle Hymn of China. New York: Alfred A. Knopf, 1943.

Wales, Nym (pseud. of Helen Foster Snow). Inside Red China. New York: Doubleday, Doran & Co., 1939.

WWC, 1950.

WWMC

Po I-po 薄一波

WORKS

1947. Chih-hsing chung yang wu-ssu chih-shih te chi-pen tsung-chieh chi chin hou jen-wu; Po I-po t'ung-chih liu-yueh erh jih tsai ch'üan ch'ü t'u-ti hui-i shang te chieh-lun. Chung-kung Chi Lu Yü ch'ü tang wei hsuan-ch'uan pu.
執行中央五四指示的基本總結及今後任務；薄一波同志六月二日在全區土地會議上的結論。

1952. Po I-po et al. Chung-hua Jen-min Kung-ho-kuo san nien lai te wei-ta ch'eng-chiu (ed. by Jen-min ch'u-pan she). Peking: Jen-min ch'u-pan she.
薄一波等。中華人民共和國三年來的偉大成就。人民出版社。

1952. Wei shen-ju ti p'u-p'ien ti k'ai-chan fan t'an-wu, fan lang-fei, fan kuan-liao chu-i yün-tung erh tou-cheng. Peking: Jen-min ch'u-pan she.
為深入地普遍地開展反貪污，反浪費，反官僚主義運動而鬥爭。

1953. Kuan-yü i-chiu-wu-san nien kuo-chia yü-suan te pao-kao. Peking: Jen-min ch'u-pan she.
關於一九五三年國家預算的報告。

SOURCES

Person interviewed: Chang Kuo-t'ao.

Belden, Jack. China Shakes the World. New York: Harper & Bros., 1949.

Carlson, Evans Fordyce. Twin Stars of China. New York: Dodd, Mead & Co., 1940.

HCJC

The New York Times, September 20, 21, 1953.

WWC, 1950.

WWMC

P'u-ju 溥儒

WORKS

1961. Shih san ching shih-ch'eng lueh chieh. Taipei.
十三經師承略解。

1963. Hua lin yün yeh. Taipei: Kuang wen shu-chü. 2 vols.
華林雲葉。

1964. Han-yü-t'ang shih tz'u lien wen-chi. Taipei: Chung-hua shu-chü.
寒玉堂詩詞聯文集。

1966. P'u Hsin-yü hsien-sheng mo-pao. Taipei: Chen shan mei ch'u-pan she.
溥心畬先生墨寶。

Han-yü-t'ang lun-chi.
寒玉堂論集。

SOURCES

Ch'in Han-ts'ai. Man kung ts'an chao chi. Shanghai: Chung-kuo k'o-hsueh t'u-shu i-ch'i kung-ssu, 1947.
秦翰才。滿宮殘照記。

China Yearbook, 1960–61. Taipei: China Publishing Co., 1961.

Ching, Nora C. "P'u Ju—Scholarly Chinese Artist." *The Asian Student*, October 24, 1964.

Chung-yang jih-pao. Taipei, November 19, 1963.
中央日報。

CMJL

Hui Shan. "I P'u Hsin-yü." *Hua-ch'iao jih-pao*. Hong Kong, May 13, 25, 1964; June 8, 1964.
慧山。憶溥心畬。華僑日報。

Li Hsiu-wen. "Chi P'u Hsin-yü ta shih tsai chou-shan te jih-tzu." *Chuan-chi wen-hsueh*, III-6 (December, 1963).
李秀文。記溥心畬大師在舟山的日子。傳記文學。

Li Tsung-t'ung. "Ching tao P'u Hsin-yü ta-shih chien shu Ch'ing mo ch'ung-wang tui kung-wang cheng-cheng te nei-mu." *Chuan-chi wen-hsueh*, IV-2 (February, 1964).
李宗侗。敬悼溥心畬大師兼述清末醇王對恭王政爭的內幕。傳記文學。

Sullivan, Michael. Chinese Art in the Twentieth Century. Berkeley: University of California Press, 1959.

———. An Introduction to Chinese Art. Berkeley: University of California Press, 1961.

Wan Ta-hung. "Hsi-shan i-shih te chi tuan i-shih." *Chuan-chi wen-hsueh*, V-5 (November, 1964): 48–54.

萬大鉉。西山逸士的幾段逸事。傳記文學。

P'u-yi   溥儀

WORKS

1964. Wo-te ch'ien pan sheng—sun Ch'ing hsuan-t'ung huang-ti tzu-chuan. Hong Kong: Hong Kong wen t'ung shu-tien. 3 vols.
我的前半生—遜清宣統皇帝自傳。

1964–65. From Emperor to Citizen: The Autobiography of Aisin-Gioro Pu Yi. Peking: Foreign Languages Press. 2 vols.

SOURCES

Backhouse, E., and J. O. P. Bland. Annals and Memoirs of the Court of Peking. Boston: Houghton Mifflin Co., 1914.

Blakeney, Ben Bruce. "P'u Yi." *Life*, July 16, 1945.

China's Outcast Emperor." *Literary Digest*, October 12, 1929.

CYB, 1925.

"Daily Life of the Boy Emperor of China." *Current Literature*, December, 1911.

Gilbert, Lucien. Dictionnaire Historique et Géographique de la Manchourie. Hong Kong: Imprimerie de la Société des Missions-étrangères, 1934.

Hoh Chih-hsiang. "Pu Yi, the Betrayer of China and Puppet of Japan." CWR, June 11, 1932.

Hsiao Pai-fan. Chung-kuo chin pai nien ko-ming shih. Hong Kong: Ch'iu shih ch'u-pan she, 1951.
蕭白帆。中國近百年革命史。

Jen-min jih-pao. Peking, July–August, 1956 (Especially July 21, 1956).
人民日報。

Johnston, Reginald F. Twilight in the Forbidden City. New York: Appleton-Century, 1934.

Kawakami, K. K. Manchoukuo: Child of Conflict. New York: The Macmillan Co., 1933.

Kenjiro Hayashide. Epochal Journey to Nippon. Hsinking: Intelligence Bureau, the General Affairs Office of the State Council, 1937.

Koo, V. K. Wellington (Ku Wei-chün). Memoranda Presented to the Lytton Commission by V. K. Wellington Koo. New York: The Chinese Cultural Society, 1932–33. 3 vols.

McAleavy, Henry. A Dream of Tartary: The Origins and Misfortunes of Henry P'u Yi. London: G. Allen & Unwin, 1963.

The Manchoukuo Yearbook, 1942. Hsinking, 1942.

Moule, Arthur Christopher. The Rulers of China, 221 B.C.–A.D. 1949; Chronological Tables. New York: Frederick A. Praeger, 1957.

The New York Times, July–August, 1956 (especially August 10, 1956).

"The Plot to Restore the Imperial Dynasty in China." *Current Opinion*, July, 1914.

Reid, John Gilbert. The Manchu Abdication and the Powers, 1908–1912. Berkeley; University of California Press, 1935.

———. "The Young Manchu Emperor." *The Open Court*, July, 1935.

SCMP, 2472 (April 10, 1961): 13–15.

Ta kung pao. Hong Kong, February 19, 1961.
大公報。

WWC, Supplement to 4th ed., 1933.

Sa Chen-ping   薩鎮冰

SOURCES

Chung-hua Jen-min Kung-ho-kuo k'ai-kuo wen-hsien, comp. by Hsin min-chu ch'u-pan she. Hong Kong: Hsin min-chu ch'u-pan she, 1949.
中華人民共和國開國文獻。新民主出版社。

CYB-W, 1923.

JMST, 1952.

Kuo-fu nien-p'u ch'u-kao, ed. by Kuo shih kuan shih-liao pien-tsuan wei-yuan-hui, Chung-kuo kuo-min-tang tang shih shih-liao pien-tsuan wei-yuan-hui. Taipei: Kuo shih kuan shih-liao pien-tsuan wei-yuan-hui, Chung-kuo kuo-min-tang tang shih shih-liao pien-tsuan wei-yuan-hui, 1959.
國父年譜初稿。國史館史料編纂委員會，中國國民黨黨史史料編纂委員會。

Li Chien-nung. Chung-kuo chin pai nien cheng-chih shih. Shanghai: Shang-wu yin shu kuan, 1947. 2 vols.
李劍農。中國近百年政治史。

San-shui Liang Yen-sun hsien-sheng nien-p'u, ed. by Feng kang chi men ti-tzu.
三水梁燕孫先生年譜。鳳岡及門弟子。

Teng Tse-ju. Chung-kuo kuo-min-tang erh-shih nien shih-chi. Shanghai: Cheng-chung shu-chü, 1948.
鄧澤如。中國國民黨二十年史蹟。

Ts'ai T'ing-k'ai. Ts'ai T'ing-k'ai tzu-chuan.

Sa Chen-ping [310]

Hong Kong: Tzu-yu hsun k'an she, 1946. 2
vols.
蔡廷鍇。蔡廷鍇自傳。

Saifudin

WORKS

1948–? ed. of *Ch'ien-chin pao*. (Editor's Note: A
conflicting datum gives the name as *Hsin meng
jih-pao*.)
前進報。新盟日報。

SOURCES

Chang Ta-chün. Ssu-shih nien tung-luan Sinkiang. Hong Kong: Ya-chou ch'u-pan she,
1956.
張達鈞。四十年動亂新疆。
CPR, 1083 (February 3, 1950).
Davidson, Basil. Turkestan Alive: New Travels
in Chinese Central Asia. London: Jonathan
Cape, 1957.
The New York Times, February 28, 1965.
Wang Hung. "Saifudin t'an Sinkiang." *Chin-pu
jih-pao*. Tientsin, October 1, 1949.
王鴻。賽福鼎談新疆。進步日報。
WWMC

Shang Chen　商震

SOURCES

BKL
CH, 1937–45.
CH-T, 1956–57.
CMTC
CWR, March 30, 1929.
CYB-W, 1928, 1931–32, 1934.
GCJJ
Kuo wen chou-pao, IV-25 (July 3, 1927).
國聞週報。
TCJC
WWMC

Shao Li-tzu　邵力子

WORKS

1944. Su-lien kuei-lai (ed. by Chung Su wen-hua
hsieh-hui pien-i wei-yuan-hui). Chungking:
Chung-kuo wen-hua fu-wu she.
蘇聯歸來。中蘇文化協會編譯委員會。

SOURCES

BKL
Chow Tse-tsung. The May Fourth Movement:
Intellectual Revolution in Modern China.
Cambridge: Harvard University Press, 1960.
CMMC
CMTC
CTMC
GCJJ
Hahn, Emily. The Soong Sisters. New York:
Doubleday, Doran & Co., 1941.
HCJC
Hsiao Yeh-na and Wang Erh-te. Chung Kung
te min-chu tang-p'ai. Kowloon: Tzu-yu
ch'u-pan she, 1951.
蕭也納，王爾得。中共的民主黨派。
K-WWMC
RD
RSOC
SCMP, 9 (November 13–14, 1950); 920 (Novem-
ber 2, 1954): 3–5; 976 (January 28, 1955): 26–
31; 1458 (January, 1957): 6–7.
TCJC
Wu, Aitchen. China and the Soviet Union: A
Study of Sino-Soviet Relations. New York:
The John Day Co., 1950.
WWC, 1934, 1936.

Shao P'iao-p'ing　邵飄萍

WORKS

1923. Shih-chi ying-yung hsin-wen hsueh. Peking: Ching pao kuan.
實際應用新聞學。
1924. Hsin-wen hsueh tsung-lun. Peking: Ching
pao kuan.
新聞學總論。
1924, March. "Wo kuo hsin-wen hsueh chin-pu
chih ch'ü-shih." *Tung-fang tsa-chih*, XXI-6:
24–26.
我國新聞學進步之趨勢。東方雜誌。

SOURCES

CBJS
Ch'en Pu-lei. Ch'en Pu-lei hui-i-lu. Shanghai:
Erh-shih shih-chi ch'u-pan she, 1949.
陳布雷。陳布雷回憶錄。
Chu Hsü-pai. "Chung-kuo ming pao jen i-shih."
Pao hsueh, III-3 (June, 1964): 84–85.
朱虛白。中國名報人軼事。報學。
Hsieh Hsing-lang. "Chui-tao Shao P'iao-p'ing

hsien-sheng." *Ch'ing-hua chou-k'an*, XXV-14 (May, 1926).
謝星朗。追悼邵飄萍先生。清華周刊。
Kuan I-hsien. Hsin-wen hsueh chi-ch'eng. Peking: Chung-hua hsin-wen hsueh-yuan, 1943.
管翼賢。新聞學集成。
Shen shih tien-hsin she chi-nien k'an "shih nien". Shanghai, 1934.
申時電訊社紀念刊「十年」。
Wang Hsin-ming. Hsin-wen ch'üan li ssu-shih nien. Taipei: Chung-yang jih-pao she.
王新命。新聞圈裡四十年。

Shao Yuan-ch'ung　邵元沖

WORKS

1924. Mei-kuo lao-kung chuang-k'uang. Shanghai: Min chih shu-chü.
美國勞工狀況。
1925. Ch'en Ying-shih hsien-sheng ko-ming hsiao-shih. Shanghai: Min chih shu-chü.
陳英士先生革命小史。
1925. Hsun cheng shih-ch'i ti-fang hsing-cheng chi-hua. Shanghai: Min chih shu-chü.
訓政時期地方行政計劃。
1925. Ko kuo ko-ming shih-lueh. Ming ch'iang shu-she.
各國革命史略。
1925. Kung-hui t'iao-li shih-i. Canton: Min chih shu-chü.
工會條例釋義。
1926. Lao-tung wen-t'i chih fa-sheng ching-kuo chi hsien-tai lao-kung shih-yeh chih fa-chan. Shanghai: Min chih shu-chü.
勞動問題之發生經過及現代勞工事業之發展。
1927. (ed.) Chu Chih-hsin wen-ch'ao. Shanghai: Min chih shu-chü.
朱執信文鈔。
1927. Chung-kuo chih ko-ming yün-tung chi ch'i pei-ching. Shanghai: Min chih shu-chü.
中國之革命運動及其背景。
1944. Hsuan pu i-shu t'e-chi. I she.
玄圃遺書特輯。
1954. Hsuan pu i-shu. Taipei: Cheng-chung shu-chü. 2 vols.
玄圃遺書。
Hsun cheng shih-ch'i ch'ing-ch'a jen-k'ou te i-chien.
訓政時期清查人口的意見。
Sun Wen chu-i tsung-lun.

孫文主義總論。
Ti-fang hsing-cheng chi-hua. Shanghai: San min shu-tien.
地方行政計劃。

SOURCES

Chiang Chung-cheng. Sian pan-yueh chi. Chungking: San min t'u-shu kung-ssu, 1945.
蔣中正。西安半月記。
Chung-yang jih-pao. Taipei, December 1956.
中央日報。
CMJL
CMMC

Shen Chia-pen　沈家本

WORKS

1929. Shen Chi-i hsien-sheng i-shu. 40 vols.
沈寄簃先生遺書。
1963. Chu shih so-yen. Peking: Chung-hua shu-chü. 4 vols.
諸史瑣言。
1963. Ku shu-mu san chung. Peking: Chung-hua shu-chü. 2 vols.
古書目三種。
Chi-i wen-ts'un. Hsiu ting fa-lü kuan. 3 vols.
寄簃文存。

SOURCES

Chao Erh-sun *et al*. Ch'ing shih kao. Peking: Ch'ing shih kuan, 1927. 132 vols.
趙爾巽等。清史稿。
Chu Fang. Chung-kuo fa-chih shih. Shanghai: Fa cheng hsueh-she, 1931.
朱方。中國法制史。
Chu Shou-p'eng. Tung hua hsü lu. Shanghai: Chi ch'eng t'u-shu kung-ssu, 1909.
朱壽朋。東華續錄。
Escarra, Jean. Le Droit Chinois; Conception et Évolution, Institutions Legislatives et Judiciaires, Science et Enseignement. Peking: Henri Vetch, 1936.
Liu Chin-tsao. Huang-ch'ao hsü wen-hsien t'ung-k'ao. 32 vols.
劉錦藻。皇朝續文獻通考。
Meijer, Marinus J. Introduction of Modern Criminal Law into China. Batavia: Sinica Indonesiana, 1950.
PCCP
Peake, Cyrus H. "Recent Studies on Chinese Law." *Political Science Quarterly*, LII-1 (March, 1937): 117-38.

Shen Chia-pen. Shen Chi-i hsien-sheng i-shu. 1929. 40 vols.

沈家本。沈寄簃先生遺書。

Ta Ch'ing fa-kuei ta-ch'üan. Cheng hsueh she.

大清法規大全。

Ta Ch'ing Kuang-hsü hsin fa-ling, comp. by Shang-wu yin shu kuan pien i so. Shanghai: Shang-wu yin shu kuan, 1909. 20 vols.

大清光緒新法令。商務印書館編譯所。

Ta Ch'ing li-ch'ao shih-lu. 1937. 30 vols.

大清歷朝實錄。

Yang Hung-lieh. Chung-kuo fa-lü fa-ta shih. Shanghai: Shang-wu yin shu kuan, 1930. 2 vols.

楊鴻烈。中國法律發達史。

Shen Chün-ju　沈鈞儒

WORKS

1922. Hsien-fa yao-lan. with Ho Chi-hung. Peking: Shang-wu yin shu kuan.

憲法要覽。何基鴻。

1948. Ch'i-ssu lao-jen chien-k'ang fang-wen chi (Hsueh wu pi-chi). Hong Kong: Sheng-huo shu-tien.

七四老人健康訪問記（學武筆記）。

SOURCES

CBJS

CPR, 842 (March 3, 1949).

GCCJK

GSJK

Hahn, Emily. The Soong Sisters. New York: Doubleday, Doran & Co., 1941.

JMST, 1950, 1957.

Li Chien-nung. Chung-kuo chin pai nien cheng-chih shih. Sanghai: Shang-wu yin shu kuan, 1948. 2 vols.

李劍農。中國近百年政治史。

Li Shou-tung. Chiu-kuo wu-tsui ch'i chün-tzu. Shih-tai wen-hsien she, 1937.

李守東。救國無罪七君子。

The New York Times, June 12, 1963.

SCMP, 95 (April 17-18, 1951): 8; 110 (June 1-5, 1951): 19; 459 (November 25, 1952): 6; 773 (March 20, 1954): 1; 874 (August 21-23, 1954): 50; 986 (February 11, 1955): 15; 1558 (June 26, 1957): 23-24; 1907 (December 4, 1958): 7-8.

Shen Chün-ju. Ch'i-ssu lao-jen chien-k'ang fang-wen chi (Hsueh wu pi-chi). Hong Kong: Sheng-huo shu-tien, 1948.

沈鈞儒。七四老人健康訪問記（學武筆記）。

Shen Chun-ju and Ho Chi-hung. Hsien-fa yao-lan. Peking: Shang-wu yin shu kuan, 1922.

沈鈞儒，何基鴻。憲法要覽。

SSYD

Tsou T'ao-fen. Huan-nan yü-sheng chi. Shanghai: Sheng-huo shu-tien, 1936.

鄒韜奮。患難餘生記。

WWC, 1936.

Shen Hung-lieh　沈鴻烈

WORKS

1918-19. Ou chan yü hai ch'üan.

歐戰與海權。

1925. Tung-pei hang-ch'üan shih-mo chi.

東北航權始末記。

1930? Wu-shih nien chien ta meng chi.

五十年間大夢記。

1953. Tung-pei pien-fang yü hang-ch'üan.

東北邊防與航權。

Pen sheng shih-cheng fang-chen. Shantung sheng ti-i ch'ü chiu wang kung-tso t'ao-lun hui.

本省施政方針。

SOURCES

Person interviewed: Sheng Hung-lieh.

Lei Fa-chang. Shen Ch'eng-chang hsien-sheng hsiao chuan.

雷法章。沈成章先生小傳。

Shen Hung-lieh. Tung-pei pien-fang yü hang-ch'üan. 1953.

沈鴻烈。東北邊防與航權。

Tung-pei yueh-k'an, 1929-31.

東北月刊。

Shen Tse-min　沈澤民

WORKS

1927. Erh-t'ung te chiao-yü. (tr. of Ellen Karolina Sofia Key's *Education of Children*). Shanghai: Shang-wu yin shu kuan.

兒童的教育。

ed. of *Hsiao-shuo yueh-pao*.

小說月報。

ed. of *Min-kuo jih-pao*.

民國日報。

SOURCES

Person interviewed: Chang Kuo-t'ao.

GCMMTJK

GSSJ

Liu Hsia. Shih-pa nien lai chih Chung-kuo ch'ing-nien-tang. Chengtu: Kuo hun shu-tien, 1941.
柳下。十八年來之中國青年黨。
Shao-nien Chung-kuo, III-2 (September 1, 1921).
少年中國。

Shen Tsung-han   沈宗瀚

WORKS

1926. "Some Suggestions about Cotton Breeding in China." *Proceedings of the Third Pan-Pacific Science Congress*: 1191–96.

1928. "Hao chung-tzu ts'ai te hao chuang-chia." *Chin-ling ta-hsueh nung-lin ch'ien-shuo*, 24.
好種子才得好莊稼。金陵大學農林淺說。

1928. "Kai-liang chung-tzu te chung-yao chi fang-fa," in *Kiangsu sheng nung cheng hui-i hui-pien*.
改良種子的重要及方法。江蘇省農政會議彙編。

1928. "Kuo-li nung shih shih-yen ch'ang chih she-chi chi ch'i yü sheng-li hsien-li nung shih shih-yen ch'ang chih fen-kung ho-tso an." *Nung k'uang kung-pao*, 5.
國立農事試驗場之設計及其與省立縣立農事試驗場之分工合作案。農礦公報。

1928. "Ping nung chih pien yü liang-shih wen-t'i." *Chung-hua nung hsueh hui pao*, 64, 65.
兵農殖邊與糧食問題。中華農學會報。

1928. "Wo kuo nung-tso-wu chung-tzu kai-liang chi t'ui-kuang fang-fa tsou-i." *Chin-ling ta-hsueh nung-lin ts'ung-k'an*, 45.
我國農作物種子改良及推廣方法芻議。金陵大學農林叢刊。

1929. "Kai-liang chung-tzu i tseng-chia wo kuo liang-shih chih chi-hua." *Chien-kuo yueh-k'an*, II-2.
改良種子以增加我國糧食之計劃。建國月刊。

1929. "Shih-ti kai-liang mai chung te fang-fa." *Nung-min*, 11.
實地改良麥種的方法。農民。

1929. "Wo kuo kai-liang chung-tzu te chung-yao yü nung-chia hsuan-chung te fang-fa." *Nung-min*, 6.
我國改良種子的重要與農家選種的方法。農民。

1930, March. "The Field Technic for Determining Comparative Yields in Wheat under Different Environmental Conditions in China." *Journal of the American Society of Agronomy*, XXII-3.

1930. "Nung-yeh chih-wu sheng-ch'an hsueh i nien lai chih chin-pu." *K'o-hsueh*, XIV-6.
農業植物生產學一年來之進步。科學。

1930. "Shui-tao shih-ti yü-chung fa." *Nung min*, 20.
水稻實地育種法。農民。

1931. "Chung-kuo mien tso yü-chung fa chih shang-chueh," in *Chung-kuo mien ch'an kai-chin t'ung-chi hui-i chuan k'an*.
中國棉作育種法之商榷。中國棉產改進統計會議專刊。

1931. "Hua-pei nung-yeh shih-ch'a pao-kao." *Chin-ling ta-hsueh nung-lin hsin pao*, VIII-1, 2.
華北農業視察報告。金陵大學農林新報。

1931, September. "I nien lai chih tso-wu yü-chung." *Chekiang sheng-li nung-yeh kai-liang ch'ang nung-yeh ts'ung-k'an*, 1.
一年來之作物育種。浙江省立農業改良場農業叢刊。

1931. "Kai-liang p'in-chung i tseng-chin Chung-kuo chih liang-shih." *K'o-hsueh*, XV-11.
改良品種以增進中國之糧食。科學。

1932, January. "Contribution of Crop Breeding to China's Food Problem." *The China Critic*, V-4.

1932, July 24. "Chieh yung Mei mien yü t'ui-kuang kai-liang mien chung." *Ta kung pao*. Tientsin.
借用美棉與推廣改良棉種。大公報。

1932, August. "Chai hou chung mai wu ch'i chih pu-chiu." *Chin-ling ta-hsueh nung-lin hsin pao*, IX-26.
災後種麥誤期之補救。金陵大學農林新報。

1932. "Tsai hou chung mai fang-fa t'ao-lun." *Chin-ling ta-hsueh nung-lin hsin pao*, IX-1.
災後種麥方法討論。金陵大學農林新報。

1933, January. "Chekiang mien tao chih kai-chin." *Hsin Chekiang*.
浙江棉稻之改進。新浙江。

1933. "Application of Science to Agriculture in China." *Proceedings of the Fifth Pacific Congress*.

1933, May. "A Comparison between 537 Foreign Wheat Varieties and Certain Chinese Strains." *Nanking Journal*, III-1.

1933. "Inheritance of Quantitative and Qualitative Characters in Wheat Crosses." *Proceedings of the Fifth Pacific Science Congress*.

1933. "Kao-liang yü-chung fa." *Chung-hua nung hsueh hui pao*, 114.
高粱育種法。中華農學會報。

1933. "Studies on the Method of Kaoliang Breeding in China; Part I, Effect of Selfing, Part II, the Method of Kaoliang Threshing and Relation of the Total Weight of Kaoliang Head with the Weight of Grain." *Proceedings of the Fifth Pacific Science Congress.*

1933, December. "Kai-chin Hsi-pei nung-yeh ying ch'ü chih ch'eng-hsü." *Tu-li p'ing-lun,* 79.
改進西北農業應取之程序。獨立評論。

1934. "Chung-kuo yü-chung shih-yeh chih kuo-ch'ü hsien-tsai chi chiang-lai." *Chung-yang nung-yeh shih-yen so nung pao.*
中國育種事業之過去現在及將來。中央農業實驗所農報。

1934. "Improved Varieties Developed through the Cooperative Project of the University of Nanking," in *Special Report, No. 2, College of Agriculture and Forestry, University of Nanking.* Nanking.

1934, May. "A Preliminary Report on the Inheritance of Nematode Resistance and Length of Beak in a Certain Wheat Cross." *Bulletin No. 19 (New Series), College of Agriculture and Forestry, University of Nanking.*

1934, June. "Breeding Rice in China for Resistance to the Stem Borer." *Bulletin No. 20 (New Series), College of Agriculture and Forestry, University of Nanking.*

1934, June. "Direct-planting and Transplanting in Relation to the Breeding Test of Rise in China." *The Journal of the American Society of Agronomy,* XXVI-6.

1934, June. "The Inheritance of Resistance to Flag Smut in Ten Wheat Crosses." *Bulletin No. 17 (New Series), College of Agriculture and Forestry, University of Nanking.*

1936, February. "Mai liang tzu-kei te t'u-ching." *Chung-yang nung-yeh shih-yen so nung pao,* III-5.
麥糧自給的途徑。中央農業實驗所農報。

1936, July. "Kai-chin Szuchwan nung-ch'an chih i-chien." *Chung-yang nung-yeh shih-yen so nung pao,* III-21.
改進四川農產之意見。中央農業實驗所農報。

1936, October. "Chung hsueh-sheng yen-chiu nung-yeh te fang-fa." *Chung-yang nung-yeh shih-yen so nung pao,* III-30.
中學生研究農業的方法。中央農業實驗所農報。

1936, December. "A Coordinated Program of Wheat Breeding in China." *Miscellaneous Publication No. 6, the National Agricultural Research Bureau, Nanking.*

1937. "The Regional Adaptation of Wheat in China." *The National Agricultural Research Bureau Special Publication,* 18.

1937, May. "Nung-yeh chih-yeh hsueh-hsiao chih hsiao-mai yü-chung kung-tso." *Chung-yang nung-yeh shih-yen so nung pao,* IV-13.
農業職業學校之小麥育種工作。中央農業實驗所農報。

1937, August. "I-chao Hai-ssu po-shih chien-i pan-li hsiao-mai kai-chin chih ch'ing-hsing." *Chung-yang nung-yeh shih-yen so nung pao,* IV-22.
依照海斯博士建議辦理小麥改進之情形。中央農業實驗所農報。

1938. "Adaptability of Wheat Varieties in Relation to the Regions and Breeding in China." *Proceedings of the International Congress of Genetics.*

1938, December. "K'ang chan ch'i-chien te mien-yeh wen-t'i." *Hsin ching-chi,* I-2.
抗戰期間的棉業問題。新經濟。

1939, March. "Tseng-chia Hsi-nan nung-ch'an hsü fa-chan kung-shang-yeh." *Hsin ching-chi,* I-8.
增加西南農產須發展工商業。新經濟。

1940, January. "Kai-chin Hsi-nan ma-tai yuan-liao te sheng-ch'an." *Hsin ching-chi,* II-4.
改進西南麻袋原料的生產。新經濟。

1940, January 21. "Ch'ang-ch'i k'ang chan chung nung-ch'an kung-kei." *Sao-tang pao.* Chungking.
長期抗戰中農產供給。掃蕩報。

1940, April. "Nung-ch'an ju-ho shih-ying kung-yeh-hua." *Hsi-nan shih-yeh t'ung-hsin,* I-4.
農產如何適應工業化。西南實業通訊。

1940, November 17. "Szuchwan liang-shih chih kung-kei yü mi-chia." *Ta kung pao.* Chungking.
四川糧食之供給與米價。大公報。

1941, March. "Chung-yang hsieh-chu Hsi-nan ko sheng nung-yeh kung-to chih chien-t'ao." *Nung pao,* VI-4, 5, 6.
中央協助西南各省農業公作之檢討。農報。

1941, May 20. "Szuchwan chin-jih chih liang chia yü liang ch'an." *Ta kung pao.* Chungking.
四川今日之糧價與糧產。大公報。

1941, July 7. "Chien mien Szuchwan liang huang hsü sheng-ch'an chi-shu yü tien-tsu chih-tu pin wei kai-chin." *Ta kung pao.* Chungking.
減免四川糧荒須生產技術與佃租制度並為改進。大公報。

1942. "T'ai-p'ing-yang chan-cheng yü wo kuo chan hou nung-ch'an kai-chin chih fang-chen." *Ta kung pao.* Chungking.

太平洋戰爭與我國戰後農產改進之方針。
大公報。

1942, November. "Yen-chiu nung-yeh sheng-
ch'an chih fang-fa." *Nung-yeh t'ui-kuang t'ung-
hsin*, IV-2.
研究農業生產之方法。農業推廣通訊。

1944, November 26. "Chung-kuo nung kung
p'ei-ho chih shang-chueh." *Ta kung pao.*
Chungking.
中國農工配合之商榷。大公報。

1945, January 21. "Chung-kuo nung-yeh chi-
chieh hua chih k'o-neng." *Ta kung pao.*
Chungking.
中國農業機械化之可能。大公報。

1951. Agricultural Resources of China. Ithaca:
Cornell University Press.

1951, August. "Fu-chih tzu keng nung cheng-
ts'e chih hui-ku yü ch'ien-chan." *Chung-kuo i
chou*, 119.
扶植自耕農政策之回顧與前瞻。中國一周。

1952, April 20. "Taiwan nung-ts'un ching-chi
chan-wang." *Hsin sheng pao.* Taipei.
台灣農村經濟展望。新生報。

1952, May. "Food Production and Administration in Taiwan." *Scientific Monthly*, LXXIV-5.

1952, May. "Rural Economic Conditions in
Taiwan." *Free China Review Monthly*, II-3.

1952-53. Chung-kuo nung-yeh tzu-yuan. Taipei:
Chung-hua wen-hua ch'u-pan shih-yeh wei-
yuan-hui. 3 vols.
中國農業資源。

1953, January 4. "Free China is at Work on
Land Reform." *Iowa Farm & Home Register.*
Des Moines, Iowa.

1953, January 7. "Ts'ung nung-yeh li-ch'ang
k'an keng-che yu ch'i t'ien." *Hsin-sheng pao.*
Taipei.
從農業立場看耕者有其田。新生報。

1953, February 18. "Taiwan nung-yeh ssu nien
chi-hua." *Chung-kuo i chou*, 192.
台灣農業四年計劃。中國一周。

1953. "Taiwan sheng ching-chi chien-she ssu
nien chi-hua" nung-yeh pu-fen kang-yao.
「台灣省經濟建設四年計劃」農業部份綱要。

1953, December. "Farmers' Association in
Taiwan." *Free China Review*, III-12.

1954. Agricultural and Land Programs in Free
China. Taipei: Government Information
Bureau.

1954. Ching-chi chien-she ssu nien chi-hua nung-
yeh pu-fen ssu-shih-san nien kung-tso t'ui-chin
chien-t'ao pao-kao. Taipei: Hsing-cheng
yuan ching an hui.
經濟建設四年計劃農業部分四十三年工作
推進檢討報告。

1954. K'o-nan k'u-hsueh chi. Taipei: Cheng-
chung shu-chü.
克難苦學記。

1954. "Land to the Tiller in Free China." *Annals
of Academia Sinica*, II.

1954. "Rice Production and Improvement in
Taiwan." *Annals of Academia Sinica*, II.

1954. Taiwan chih tao-mi sheng-ch'an yü kai-
chin. with Kung Pi. Taipei: Chung-yang
wen-wu kung-ying she.
台灣之稻米生產與改進。龔弼。

1954. "Taiwan te liang-shih," in *Chung-hua Min-
kuo ssu-shih-erh nien Chung-hua nien pao.* Taipei:
Chung-kuo hsin-wen ch'u-pan kung-ssu.
台灣的糧食。中華民國四十二年中華年報。

1954, April. "The Agricultural Four-Year Plan
at Work in Taiwan." *Free China Review*, IV-4.

1954, April. "Ta-hsueh nung-yeh chiao-yü tsou-
i." *San min chu-i pan-yueh-k'an*, 23.
大學農業教育芻議。三民主義半月刊。

1954, November. "Shih-men shui-k'u chih chan-
wang." *San min chu-i pan-yueh-k'an*, 38.
石門水庫之瞻望。三民主義半月刊。

1954, December 27. "Pen nien nung-yeh ssu
nien chi-hua te chien-t'ao." *Hsin sheng pao.*
Taipei.
本年農業四年計劃的檢討。新生報。

1955. Economic Significance of Agricultural
Development in Taiwan. Taipei: Committee
D., Economic Stabilization Board, Executive
Yuan.

1955. "Nung hui tui nung-yeh ssu nien chi-hua
ying yu chih nu-li." *Min yün tao pao*, 7.
農會對農業四年計劃應有之努力。民運導
報。

1955. Taiwan nung-yeh ssu-nien chi-hua chih
ching-chi i-i. Taipei: Hsing-cheng yuan
ching-chi an-ting wei-yuan-hui.
台灣農業四年計劃之經濟意義。

1955. "Taiwan te liang-shih," in *Chung-hua Min-
kuo ssu-shih-san nien Chung-hua nien pao.* Taipei:
Chung-kuo hsin-wen ch'u-pan kung-ssu.
台灣的糧食。中華民國四十三年中華年報。

1955, May. "Taiwan nung-ts'un yü ch'eng-shih
wen-t'i" *Chu-i yü kuo-ts'e*, 50.
台灣農村與城市問題。主義與國策。

1955, December 11. "Taiwan nung-yeh chin-pu
chung chih hsin wen-t'i." *Chung-yang jih-pao.*
Taipei.
台灣農業進步中之新問題。中央日報。

1956, January. "Nung hui tui nung-yeh ssu nien

chi-hua ying yu chih nu-li." *Nung yu*, VII-1.
農會對農業四年計劃應有之努力。農友。

1956, February. "The Role of Agriculture in Taiwan's Economy." *Free China Review Monthly*, VI-2.

1956, May. "Ssu-chien-hui yü nung-yeh ssu nien chi-hua." *Chiao-yü yü wen-hua*, XI-10.
四健會與農業四年計劃。教育與文化。

1956, June. "Taiwan hsien chieh-tuan nung-yeh kai-chin yü chien-she wen-t'i chiang-tso— Taiwan nung-yeh yü ching-chi fa-chan." *Taiwan ta-hsueh nung hsueh-yuan tsa k'an*, 1.
台灣現階段農業改進與建設問題講座一台灣農業與經濟發展。台灣大學農學院雜刊。

1956, June. "Ts'u-chin Tung-nan-ya nung-yeh ho-tso." *Chung-kuo i chou*, 322.
促進東南亞農業合作。中國一周。

1956, July 10. "Chung-hua nung hsueh hui huan-yen Yuan-tung tso-wu kai-liang hui-i ko-kuo tai-piao chih-tz'u." *Chung-yang jih-pao*. Taipei.
中華農學會歡宴遠東作物改良會議各國代表致詞。中央日報。

1956, September. "Jih-pen nung-yeh kuan-kan." *Chung-hua nung hsueh hui pao*, new series, 15.
日本農業觀感。中華農學會報。

1956, October. "Taiwan liang-shih sheng-ch'an chin-pu chung te hsin wen-t'i." *Chung-kuo liang-shih chi-k'an*, I-1.
台灣糧食生產進步中的新問題。中國糧食季刊。

1956, December 14. "Chin hou Taiwan nung-yeh chih hsin fa-chan." *Hsin-sheng pao*. Taipei.
今後台灣農業之新發展。新生報。

1956. "Wei-ho ch'iu-hsueh yü ju-ho ch'iu-hsueh." *Ying-ts'ui*, III-2.
為何求學與如何求學。英萃。

1957. Chung-nien tzu-shu. Taipei: Cheng-chung shu-chü.
中年自述。

1957, July 1. "Nung-yeh fa-chan chih yu i t'u-ching." *Hsin-sheng pao*. Taipei.
農業發展之又一途徑。新生報。

1957, October. "Ch'u-hsi ti-chiu chieh T'ai-p'ing-yang k'c-hsueh hui-i tso-wu kai-liang tsu pao-kao." *Chiao-yü yü wen-hua* 167.
出席第九屆太平洋科學會議作物改良組報告。教育與文化。

1958, January. "I nien lai te nung-yen fa-chan yü mao-i." *Kuo-chi mao-i yueh-k'an*, I-1.
一年來的農業發展與貿易。國際貿易月刊。

1958, April 17. "Ho mo wei-ho kai-pien nung-yeh cheng-ts'e." *Hsin-sheng pao*. Taipei.
赫魔為何改變農業政策。新生報。

1958, June. "Taiwan ch'un hsiao-mai sheng-ch'an chih yen-chiu." *Chung-hua nung hsueh hui pao*, new series, 22.
台灣春小麥生產之研究。中華農學會報。

1958. Nung-yeh chi-hua yü sheng-ch'an. Taipei: Hsing-cheng yuan ching-chi an-ting wei-yuan-hui.
農業計畫與生產。

1959. Ch'üan-kuo nung-yeh tzu-yuan li-yung chih fen-hsi. Taipei: Kuo-fang yen-chiu yuan.
全國農業資源利用之分析。

1959. Taiwan nung-yeh chien-she chih chien-t'ao. Taipei: Kuo-fang yen-chiu yuan.
台灣農業建設之檢討。

1959, August 27. "Tsai ch'ü nung ch'ing." *Hsin-sheng pao*. Taipei.
災區農情。新生報。

1959, October 8. "Tsai ch'ü fu keng." *Hsin sheng pao*. Taipei.
災區復耕。新生報。

1959, December 28. "Taiwan nung-yeh te chin-chan." *Hsin-sheng pao*. Taipei.
台灣農業的進展。新生報。

1960, January. "Wo-men te nung-yeh cheng-ts'e chi fa-chan t'u-ching." *Kuo-chi ching-chi tzu-liao yueh-k'an*, IV-1.
我們的農業政策及發展途徑。國際經濟資料月刊。

1960, January 25. "T'ai-tung feng-li shih-yeh (shan-p'o ti tzu-yuan k'ai-fa i li)." *Hsin-sheng pao*. Taipei.
台東鳳梨事業（山坡地資源開發一例）。新生報。

1960. Wo kuo nung-yeh chien-she. Taipei: Kuo-fang yen-chiu yuan.
我國農業建設。

1960, May. "Nung shih yen-chiu pan chih ch'eng-hsiao." *Nung yu*, XI-5.
農事研究班之成效。農友。

1961, March 3. "Taiwan nung-yeh chih chan-wang." *Chung-yang jih-pao*. Taipei.
台灣農業之展望。中央日報。

1961, May. "Hsiao ping chia chü so chi." *Tzu-yu t'an*, XII-5.
小病家居瑣記。自由談。

1961, July. "Ts'ung Taiwan nung-ch'ang chih-tu p'ing-lun kung fei nung-yeh te shih-pai." *T'ai t'ang t'ung-hsin*, XVIII-18.
從台灣農場制度評論共匪農業的失敗。台糖通訊。

1961, August. "Taiwan chia-t'ing nung-ch'ang

yü ta-lu chi-t'i nung-ch'ang chi jen-min kung-she chien-jui te tui-chao." *Hsin shih-tai*, I-8.
台灣家庭農場與大陸集體農場及人民公社尖銳的對照。新時代。

1962, March 3. "I Hu Tsung-nan chiang-chün." *Hsin-sheng pao*. Taipei.
憶胡宗南將軍。新生報。

1962, March 18. "Nung-yeh fa-chan te hsin t'u-ching." *Chung-yang jih-pao*. Taipei.
農業發展的新途徑。中央日報。

1962, May. "Taiwan nung-yeh fa-chan t'u-ching chih t'an-t'ao." *Kuo-chi ching-chi tzu-liao yueh-k'an*, VIII-5.
台灣農業發展途徑之探討。國際經濟資料月刊。

1962, May. "Tao nien Shih-chih hsien-sheng." *Tzu-yu t'an*, XIII-5.
悼念適之先生。自由談。

1962, August. "Chi-nien Mei hsiao-chang." *Ch'ing-hua hsiao-yu t'ung-hsin*, 2.
紀念梅校長。清華校友通訊。

1962, September. "Taiwan nung-yeh chih fa-chan." *Hsin shih-tai*, II-9.
台灣農業之發展。新時代。

1962, November. "Agricultural Problems of Taiwan Today and JCRR Program of Assistance." *China Today*, V-11.

1962, November. "JCRR Means Better Farms." *Free China Review*.

1962, November. "Sheng-li hou chieh-shou Hua-pei nung-ch'ang te hui-i." *Chuan-chi wen-hsueh*, I-6.
勝利後接收華北農場的回憶。傳記文學。

1963. Taiwan nung-yeh chih fa-chan. Taipei: Taiwan shang-wu yin shu kuan.
台灣農業之發展。

1963, July. "Ch'u-hsi Lien-ho-kuo k'o-hsueh chi chi-shu ying-yung hui-i pao-kao." *Kuo-chi ching-chi tzu-liao yueh-k'an*, XI-1.
出席聯合國科學及技術應用會議報告。國際經濟資料月刊。

1963, December. "Ts'an-chia Chung Mei nung-yeh chi-shu ho-tso t'uan te ching-kuo." *Chuan-chi wen-hsueh*, III-6.
參加中美農業技術合作團的經過。傳記文學。

1963, December 28. "Tao-nien Cheng Chung-fu po-shih." *Chung-yang jih-pao*.
悼念鄭仲孚博士。中央日報。

1964, March. "Agriculture Development on Taiwan in 1963." *Industry of Free China*, XXI-3.

1964, July. "Tao-nien Chiang Meng-lin hsien-sheng." *Chuan-chi wen-hsueh*, V-1.

悼念蔣孟隣先生。傳記文學。

1964, September. "Chiang Monlin: A Tribute." *Free China Review*, XIV-9.

1964, November. "Nung-fu-hui chin hou chih kung-tso." *Tzu-yu Chung-kuo chih kung-yeh*, XXII-5.
農復會今後之工作。自由中國之工業。

1964, December. "Ju-ho t'i-kao Taiwan t'u-ti sheng-ch'an-li." *Chin-jung chi-k'an*, I-2.
如何提高台灣土地生產力。金融季刊。

1965, January 1. "Chin hou Taiwan nung-yeh fa-chan chih kuan-chien." *Lien-ho pao*. Taipei.
今後台灣農業發展之關鍵。聯合報。

1965, February. "Shan wei chi-hua chin nien hsin kung-tso, wei nung-yeh ch'ang-ch'i fa-chan nu-li." *Taiwan jih-pao*.
善為計劃今年新工作，為農業長期發展努力。台灣日報。

1965, February. "Ssu chien ch'ing-nien yü nung-ts'un chien-she." *Ssu chien hui hsieh-hui t'ung-hsin*, 33.
四健青年與農村建設。四健會協會通訊。

1965. "Agricultural Development in Free China." *Cornell International Agricultural Development Mimeograph*, 10.

1965, October. "Picture Story: African Progress the Taiwan Way and Green Fields for Africa." *Free China Review*.

1965, October 25. "Erh-shih nien lai te Taiwan nung-yeh chien-she." *Chung-yang jih-pao*. Taipei.
二十年來的台灣農業建設。中央日報。

1965, November. "Taiwan te nung-yeh (wei ch'ing-chu kuo-fu tan-sheng pai nien chi-nien erh tso)." *Ssu-hsiang yü shih-tai*, 135-36.
台灣的農業（為慶祝國父誕生百年紀念而作）。思想與時代。

1966, January. "Agriculture and National Policy (Celebration on 100th Birth Anniversary of Dr. Sun Yat-sen)." *Free China Review*.

1966, February. "Chung-hua Min-kuo wu-shih-wu nien ssu chien hui nien hui k'ai-mu tz'u." *Feng-nien*, XVI-5.
中華民國五十五年四健會年會開幕詞。豐年。

1966, April 10. "Taiwan nung-ch'ang ching-ying chih hsin t'u-ching." *Chung-yang jih-pao*. Taipei.
台灣農場經營之新途徑。中央日報。

1966, May. "Ch'u-hsi li-fa yuan ching-chi wei-yuan-hui yeh-wu pao-kao." *Chien-she*, XIV-12.
出席立法院經濟委員會業務報告。建設。

1966, July. "Ch'ung chien chung-nung-so yü ch'uang-pan nung-fu-hui te hui-i." *Chuan-chi wen-hsueh*, IX-1.
重建中農所與創辦農復會的回憶。傳記文學。

1966, July. "Taiwan chia-cheng t'ui-kuang kung-tso te nu-li fang-hsiang." *Feng-nien*, XVI-13.
台灣家政推廣工作的努力方向。豐年。

1966, November. "Agricultural Development in Taiwan Province, Republic of China." *Industry of Free China*, XXVI-5.

1966, November 25. "Tao T'ang ku hsiao-chang Hui-sun." *Chung-yang jih-pao*. Taipei.
悼湯故校長惠蓀。中央日報。

1967, April 9. "Ta-lu kuang-fu hou nung-yeh ch'ung-chien chih shang-chueh." *Hsin-sheng pao*. Taipei.
大陸光復後農業重建之商榷。新生報。

1967, May. "Taiwan nung hui shih-yeh te hui-ku yü ch'ien-chan." *Nung yu*, XVIII-5.
台灣農會事業的回顧與前瞻。農友。

SOURCES

Shen Tsung-han. Chung-nien tzu-shu. Taipei: Cheng-chung shu-chü, 1957.
沈宗瀚。中年自述。

———. K'o nan k'u-hsueh chi. Taipei: Cheng-chung shu-chü, 1962.
沈宗瀚。克難苦學記。

Shen Ts'ung-wen 沈從文

WORKS

1926. Ya-tzu. Shanghai: Pei hsin shu-tien.
鴨子。

1927. Mi kan. Shanghai: Hsin-yueh shu-tien.
蜜柑。

1928. A-li-ssu yu Chung-kuo chi. Shanghai: Hsin-yueh shu-tien. 2 vols.
阿麗思遊中國記。

1928. Hao kuan hsien-shih te jen. Hsin-yueh shu-tien.
好管閒事的人。

1928. Ju-wu hou. Shanghai: Pei hsin shu-tien.
入伍後。

1928. Lao-shih jen.
老實人。

1929. Nan-tzu hsü-chih. Shanghai: Hung hei ch'u-pan ch'u.
男子須知。

1929. Shih-ssu yeh chien.
十四夜間。

1930. Chiu meng. Shang-wu yin shu kuan.
舊夢。

1930. Shen Ts'ung-wen chia chi. Shanghai: Shen-chou kuo-kuang she.
沈從文甲集。

1931. Shen Ts'ung-wen tzu chi. Shanghai: Hsin-yueh shu-tien.
沈從文子集。

1932. Chi Hu Yeh-p'ing. Shanghai: Kuang-hua shu-chü.
記胡也頻。

1932. Hu ch'u.
虎雛。

1932. I-ko nü chü yuan te sheng-huo.
一個女劇員的生活。

1932. Ni t'u.
泥塗。

1932. Shih-tzu ch'uan. Shanghai: Chung-hua shu-chü.
石子船。

1932. Tu-shih i fu-jen.
都市一婦人。

1933. I ko mu-ch'in. Shanghai: Ho ch'eng shu-chü.
一個母親。

1933. Shen-shih te t'ai-t'ai. San t'ung shu-chü.
紳士的太太。

1934. Chi Ting Ling. Shanghai: Liang yu t'u-shu kung-ssu.
記丁玲。

1934. Ju jui chi. Shanghai: Sheng-huo shu-tien.
如蕤集。

1934. Mo mo chi.
沫沫集。

1934. Yu mu chi.
遊目集。

1935. Fu shih chi.
浮世輯。

1935. Pa chün t'u. Shanghai: Wen-hua sheng-huo ch'u-pan she.
八駿圖。

1936. Hsin yü chiu. Shanghai: Liang-yu t'u-shu kung-ssu.
新與舊。

1936. Shen Ts'ung-wen hsuan-chi (comp. by Hsü Ch'en-ssu, Yeh Wang-yu). Shanghai: Wan-hsiang shu-wu.
沈從文選集。徐沉泗，葉忘憂。

1936. Ts'ung-wen hsiao-shuo chi. Shanghai: Ta kuang shu-chü.
從文小說集。

1936. Ts'ung-wen hsiao-shuo hsi tso hsuan.
從文小說習作選。

1937. Fei yu ts'un kao. with Hsiao Ch'ien. Shanghai: Wen-hua sheng-huo ch'u-pan she.
廢郵存稿。蕭乾。

1939. Hsiang hsi. Changsha: Shang-wu yin shu kuan.
湘西。

1939. Kunming tung ching. Shanghai: Wen-hua sheng-huo ch'u-pan she.
昆明冬景。

1940. Chi Ting Ling hsü chi. Shanghai: Liang yu fu-hsing t'u-shu yin shua kung-ssu.
記丁玲續集。

1940. Lü-tien chi ch'i-t'a. Shanghai: Chung-hua shu-chü.
旅店及其它。

1941. Chu hsü. Shanghai: Wen-hua sheng-huo ch'u-pan she.
燭虛。

1942. Yueh hsia hsiao ching. K'ai-ming shu-tien.
月下小景。

1943. Ch'un teng chi. Shanghai: K'ai-ming shu-tien.
春燈集。

1943. Hei feng chi. Kweilin: K'ai-ming shu-tien.
黑鳳集。

1943. Hsiang hsing san chi. K'ai-ming shu-tien.
湘行散記。

1943. Yunnan k'an yün chi. Chungking: Kuo-min t'u-shu ch'u-pan she.
雲南看雲集。

1946. Ts'ung-wen tzu-chuan. Shanghai: K'ai-ming shu-tien.
從文自傳。

1947. Shen Ts'ung-wen chieh-tso hsuan. Shanghai: Hsin hsiang shu-tien.
沈從文傑作選。

1948. Ch'ang ho. Shanghai: K'ai-ming shu-tien.
長河。

1949. A chin. Shanghai: K'ai-ming shu-tien.
阿金。

1949. Ch'un. Shanghai: K'ai-ming shu-tien.
春。

1949. Pien ch'eng. Shanghai: K'ai-ming shu-tien.
邊城。

1949. Shen wu chih ai. Shanghai: K'ai-ming shu-tien.
神巫之愛。

1957. Chung-kuo ssu-ch'ou t'u-an. with Wang Chia-shu. Peking: Chung-kuo ku-tien i-shu ch'u-pan she.
中國絲綢圖案。王家樹。

1957. Shen Ts'ung-wen hsiao-shuo hsuan-chi. Peking: Jen-min wen-hsueh ch'u-pan she.
沈從文小說選集。

1957. Shen Ts'ung-wen hsiao-shuo san-wen hsuan. Hong Kong: Hsin hsueh shu-tien.
沈從文小說散文選。

1959. Chu-fu chi. Hong Kong: Chien-wen shu-chü.
主婦集。

Feng tzu.
鳳子。

SOURCES

A Ying. "Shih-liao so-yin," in Chao Chia-pi, *Chung-kuo hsin wen-hsueh ta-hsi*. Shanghai: Liang-yu t'u-shu yin-shua kung-ssu, 1935. 10 vols.
阿英。史料索引。趙家璧。中國新文學大系。

CHWSK
Contemporary Chinese Stories, tr. by Wang Chi-chen. New York: Columbia University Press, 1944.

GCJJ
Huo I-hsien. Tsui-chin erh-shih nien Chung-kuo wen-hsueh shih kang. Canton: Pei hsin shu-chü, 1936.
霍衣仙。最近二十年中國文學史綱。

Living China: Modern Chinese Short Stories, ed. by Edgar Snow. New York: John Day & Reynal & Hitchcock, 1936.

MMT
Shen Ts'ung-wen. Chi Ting Ling. Shanghai: Liang-yu t'u-shu kung-ssu, 1934.
沈從文。記丁玲。

———. Chi Ting Ling hsü chi. Shanghai: Liang-yu fu-hsing t'u-shu yin-shua kung-ssu, 1940.
沈從文。記丁玲續集。

———. Shen Ts'ung-wen chia chi. Shanghai: Shen-chou kuo-kuang she, 1930.
沈從文。沈從文甲集。

———. Shen Ts'ung-wen hsuan-chi (comp. by Hsü Ch'en-ssu, Yeh Wang-yu). Shanghai: Wan-hsiang shu wu, 1935.
沈從文。沈從文選集。徐沉泗，葉忘憂。

———. Ts'ung-wen tzu-chuan. Shanghai: K'ai-ming shu-tien, 1946.
沈從文。從文自傳。

Ting Ling. "Chi i ko chen-shih jen te i-sheng." *Jen-min wen-hsueh*, III-2.
丁玲。記一個眞實人的一生。人民文學。

Ts'ao Chü-jen. Pei hsing hsiao yü. Hong Kong: San yü t'u-shu kung-ssu, 1957.
曹聚仁。 北行小語。

Shen Tuan-hsien   沈 端 先

WORKS

1929. Ch'u ch'un te feng. (tr.)
初春的風。

1929. Hsi-sheng. (tr.) Pei hsin.
犧牲。

1929. Lien-ai chih lu (tr. of A. Kollontay's *Wege Zu Liebe*). Shanghai: K'ai-ming shu-tien.
戀愛之路。

1929. Ou-chou chin-tai wen-i ssu-hsiang lun. (tr.) K'ai-ming shu-tien.
歐洲近代文藝思想論。

1930. Pai-pei. (tr.) Shen-chou kuo-kuang she.
敗北。

1933. P'ing lin t'ai tzu chi. (tr.) Hsien-tai.
平林泰子集。

1935. Yu tao wu lang chi. (tr.) Chung-hua shu-chü.
有島武郎集。

1937. Sai chin hua. Sheng-huo shu-tien.
賽金花。

1937-41. ed. of *Chiu wang jih-pao*.
救亡日報。

1938. Ch'ou ch'eng chi. K'ai-ming shu-tien.
愁城記。

1938. Ti-ping chen chung jih-chi. (tr.) with T'ien Han. Canton: Li-sao ch'u-pan she.
敵兵陣中日記。 田漢。

1938. "Wo-men tsai kun-nan chung chin-hsing," in Wen Tsai-tao *et al.*, *Pien ku chi*. Shanghai: Wen hui pao.
我們在困難中進行。 文載道等。 邊鼓集。

1940. Shen Tuan-hsien *et al.* Pao shen kung (ed. by Shih Jo-lin). Kunming: Hsin liu shu-tien.
沈端先等。 包身工。 施若霖。

1940. Tu-hui te i-chiao. Shanghai: T'ien-hsia shu-tien.
都會的一角。

1942. Shui hsiang yin (Ssu mu). Chungking: Ch'ün i ch'u-pan she.
水鄉吟 （四幕）。

1945. Fang-ts'ao t'ien-yai. Chungking: Mei-hsueh ch'u-pan she.
芳草天涯。

1945. Li li ts'ao—ssu mu chü. Kunming: Chin-hsiu ch'u-pan chiao-yü she.

1946. Hsi-chü ch'un-ch'iu. with Sung Chih-ti, Yü Ling. Chungking: Mei-hsueh ch'u-pan she.
戲劇春秋。 宋之的，于伶。

1946. Ts'ao mu chieh ping. with Sung Chih-ti, Yü Ling. Chungking: Mei-hsueh ch'u-pan she.
草木皆兵。 宋之的，于伶。

1948. Chieh-yü sui-pi. Hong Kong: Hai-yang shu wu.
劫餘隨筆。

1949. Kuo-lou sui-pi. Hong Kong: Jen-chien shu wu.
蝸樓隨筆。

1953. Hsia Yen chü tso hsuan. Peking: Jen-min wen-hsueh ch'u-pan she.
夏衍劇作選。

1955. K'ao-yen (Wu mu chü). Peking: Jen-min wen-hsueh ch'u-pan she.
考驗 （五幕劇）。
Eng. tr., *The Test: A Play in Five Acts*. Peking: Foreign Languages Press, 1956,

1959. Fa-hsi-ssu te hsi-chün. Peking: Jen-min wen-hsueh ch'u-pan she.
法西斯的細菌。

1959. Hsieh tien-ying chü-pen te chi ko wen-t'i. Peking: Chung-kuo tien-ying ch'u-pan she.
寫電影劇本的幾個問題。

1963. Shanghai wu-yen hsia. Peking: Chung-kuo hsi-chü ch'u-pan she.
上海屋簷下。

1963. Tien-ying lun-wen chi. Peking: Chung-kuo tien-ying ch'u-pan she.
電影論文集。

Chien-hsi. (tr.) Pei hsin.
奸細。

Fu-jen yü she-hui. (tr.)
婦人與社會。

Hsiao shih-min.
小市民。

Hsin-hsing wen-hsueh lun. (tr.)
新興文學論。

ed. of *I-shu yueh-k'an*.
藝術月刊。

ed. of *Keng-yün*.
耕耘。

Lien-ai yü hsin tao-te. (tr.) with Wang Fu-ch'üan.
戀愛與新道德。 汪馥泉。

Mu-ch'in. (tr. of M. Gorky's *Mother*). Ta chiang.
母親。

Ti-yü. (tr.)
地獄。

Wei-ta te shih nien chien wen-hsueh. (tr.)
偉大的十年間文學。

SOURCES

CB, 776 (July 15, 1965).

Chieh-fang jih-pao. Shanghai, July 18, 1952.
解放日報。

CHWC

CHWSK

CKJMT

CWT

GCCJK

GCJJ

HCJC

HMTT

HWP

I-chiu-wu-ling jen-min nien-chien, ed. by Shen Sung-fang. Hong Kong: Ta kung shu-chü, 1950.
一九五〇人民年鑑。沈頌芳。

Liu Shou-sung. Chung-kuo hsin wen-hsueh shih ch'u-kao. Peking: Tso-chia ch'u-pan she, 1956.
劉綬松。中國新文學史初稿。

MCNP

MMT

TCMT

WWMC

Shen Yen-ping   沈雁冰

WORKS

1920-21. ed. of *Hsiao-shuo yueh-pao*.
小說月報。

1934. Hua-hsia-tzu. Liang yu t'u-shu kung-ssu.
話匣子。

1934. Mao Tun tuan-p'ien hsiao-shuo chi. Shanghai: K'ai-ming.
茅盾短篇小說集。

1935. Ch'un ts'an. Shanghai: K'ai-ming.
春蠶。
Eng. tr. by Sidney Shapiro, *Spring Silkworms, and Other Stories*. Peking: Foreign Languages Press, 1956.

1935. San jen hsing. Shanghai: K'ai-ming shu-tien.
三人行。

1935. She mang. K'ai-ming.
宿莽。

1935. Su-hsieh sui-pi. Shanghai: K'ai-ming.
速寫隨筆。

1935. Yeh ch'iang-wei. K'ai-ming yin-shua kung-ssu.
野薔薇。

1936. (ed.) Chung-kuo te i-jih. Shanghai: Sheng-huo shu-tien.
中國的一日。

1936. Lu. Wen-hua sheng-huo ch'u-pan she.
路。

1936. Mao Tun ch'uang-tso hsuan (ed. by Ch'en Hsiao-mei). Shanghai: Fang-ku shu-tien.
茅盾創作選。陳筱梅。

1936. P'ao-mo. Shanghai: Wen-hsueh ch'u-pan she.
泡沫。

1936. To-chiao kuan-hsi. Shanghai: Sheng-kuo shu-tien.
多角關係。

1936. Yin-hsiang, kan-hsiang, hui-i. Shanghai: Wen-hua sheng-huo ch'u-pan she.
印象，感想，回憶。

1937. Chung-ch'iu chih yeh. Shanghai: Wen-hua sheng-huo ch'u-pan she.
中秋之夜。

1937. Hsiao ch'eng ch'un-ch'iu. Shanghai: Wen-hua sheng-huo ch'u-pan she.
小城春秋。

1937. Ku-ling chih ch'iu. Shanghai: Weh-hua sheng-huo ch'u-pan she.
牯嶺之秋。

1937. Yen-yün chi. Liang yu.
煙雲集。

1937-38. ed. of *Wen-i chen-ti*.
文藝陣地。

1938. Shen Yen-ping *et al*. Kei chan-shih shao-nien. Hankow: Shao-nien hsien-feng she.
沈雁冰等。給戰時少年。

1939. P'ao-huo te hsi-li. Chungking: Feng-huo she.
炮火的洗禮。

1939. Ti-i chieh-tuan te ku-shih. Shanghai: K'ai-ming shu-tien.
第一階段的故事。

1940. Hung. Shanghai: K'ai-ming shu-tien.
虹。

1940. T'an. Ta feng ch'u-pan she.
曇。

1941. Ni-ning. Hsin lien ch'u-pan she.
泥濘。

1941. Shen Yen-ping *et al*. Tzu-sha. Hsin lien ch'u-pan she.

茅盾等。 自殺。

1941. Shen Yen-ping *et al*. Wo-te chung-hsueh shih-tai (ed. by Yü Ti). Wen-hua t'u-shu kung-ssu.

沈雁冰等。 我的中學時代。 兪荻。

1943. Chien-wen tsa-chi. Kweilin: Wen kuang shu-tien.

見聞雜記。

1943. Shen Yen-ping *et al*. Hsi-pei hsing (ed. by P'an T'ai-feng). Kweilin: Chung-kuo lü-hsing she.

沈雁冰。 西北行。 潘泰封。

1945. Ch'ing-ming ch'ien-hou. Shanghai: K'ai-ming shu-tien.

清明前後。

1945. Shen te mieh-wang. Liang-yu t'u-shu kung-ssu.

神的滅亡。

1945. Yeh-su chih ssu. Shanghai: Tso-chia shu wu.

耶蘇之死。

1946. Chieh hou shih-i. Shanghai: Hsueh i ch'u-pan she.

劫後拾遺。

1946. Shih-chien te chi-lu. Shanghai: T'ien ti shu wu.

時間的記錄。

1947. Sheng-huo chih i-yeh. Shanghai: Shang-hai hsin ch'ün ch'u-pan she.

生活之一頁。

1947. Shuang yeh hung shih erh-yueh hua. Shanghai: Hua hua shu-tien.

霜葉紅似二月花。

1948. Shih-chieh wen-hsueh ming-chu chiang-hua. Shanghai: K'ai-ming shu-tien.

世界文學名著講話。

1948. Wei po. Shanghai: Wen-hua sheng-huo ch'u-pan she.

微波。

1949. Fu-shih. Mukden: Tung-pei shu-tien.

腐蝕。

1949. Pai Yang li-tsan. Shanghai: Wen-hua sheng-huo ch'u-pan she.

白楊禮讚。

1949. Shao-nü te hsin. Shanghai: Wen-hua shen-huo ch'u-pan she.

少女的心。

1949. Shih. Shanghai: K'ai-ming shu-tien. 3 vols.

蝕。

1949. Su-lien chien-wen lu. Shanghai: K'ai-ming shu-tien.

蘇聯見聞錄。

1949. T'ieh-shu hua. Shanghai: Wen-hua sheng-huo ch'u-pan she.

鉄樹花。

1950. Kuan-yü wen-hsueh hsiu-yang (ed. by Chung-kuo ch'ing-nien she). Peking: Ch'ing-nien ch'u-pan she.

關於文學修養。 中國青年社。

1950. Tsa-t'an Su-lien. Shanghai: Sheng-huo, tu-shu, hsin-chih san lien shu-tien.

雜談蘇聯。

1951. Ch'uang-tso te chun-pei. Peking: San lien shu-tien.

創作的準備。

1951. Tzu-yeh. Peking: K'ai-ming shu-tien.

子夜。

Eng. tr., *Midnight*. Peking: Foreign Languages Press, 1957.

1952. Mao Tun hsuan-chi. Peking: K'ai-ming shu-tien.

茅盾選集。

1954. Mao Tun tzu hsuan san-wen chi. Hong Kong: Hsien-tai wen-chiao she.

茅盾自選散文集。

1955. Mao Tun tuan-p'ien hsiao-shuo hsuan-chi. Peking: Jen-min wen-hsueh ch'u-pan she.

茅盾短篇小說選集。

1956. Ch'iu-shou. Peking: T'ung-su tu-wu ch'u-pan she.

秋收。

1956. Mao Tun san-wen chi. Hong Kong? Hsien-tai wen-chiao she.

茅盾散文集。

1958. Lin chia p'u-tzu (Chu-yin pen). Peking: Wen-tzu kai-ko ch'u-pan she.

林家舖子 (注音本)。

1958. Mao Tun *et al*. Hsin-fu te lan-t'u. Hong Kong: Hsin ti ch'u-pan she.

茅盾等。 幸福的籃圖。

1958. Mao Tun *et al*. (ed.) We Are with You, Arab Brothers. Peking: Foreign Languages Press.

1958. Yeh tu ou chi. Tientsin: Pai hua wen-i ch'u-pan she.

夜讀偶記。

1958-61. Mao Tun wen-chi. Peking: Jen-min wen-hsueh ch'u-pan she. 9 vols.

茅盾文集。

1959. Ts'an tung. Hong Kong: Hsin-yueh ch'u-pan she.

殘冬。

195?. Hung-yeh. Kowloon: Nan hua shu-tien.

紅葉。

195?. Mao Tun ming-tso hsuan-chi (ed. by Ch'en

Lei). Hong Kong: Nan-yang t'u-shu ch'u-pan kung-ssu.

茅盾名作選集。陳磊。

195?. Wei-ch'ü. Hong Kong: Hsin ti ch'u-pan she.

委屈。

1960. Fan-ying she-hui chu-i yao chin te shih-tai, t'ui-tung she-hui chu-i shih-tai te yao chi; i-chiu-liu-ling nien ch'i-yueh erh-shih-ssu jih tsai Chung-kuo wen-hsueh i-shu kung-tso che ti-san tz'u tai-piao ta-hui shang te pao-kao. Peking: Jen-min wen-hsueh ch'u-pan she.

反映社會主義躍進的時代，推動社會主義時代的躍進；一九六〇年七月二十四日在中國文學藝術工作者第三次代表大會上的報告。

1961. T'ao yuan. (tr.) Hong Kong: Ta wen shu-chü.

桃園。

1962. Ku-ch'ui hsü-chi. Peking: Tso-chia ch'u-pan she.

鼓吹續集。

1962. Kuan-yü li-shih ho li-shih chü. Peking: Tso-chia ch'u-pan she.

關於歷史和歷史劇。

196?. Frustration. Hong Kong: English Language Publishing Co.

Hui-i, shu-chien, tsa-chi. (tr.)

回憶，書簡，襍記。

ed. of *Jen-min wen-hsueh*.

人民文學。

Ju-shih wo chien wo wen.

如是我見我聞。

Mao Tun sui-pi.

茅盾隨筆。

SOURCES

Hsia, C. T. A History of Modern Chinese Fiction 1917–1957. New Haven, Yale University Press, 1961.

Mao Tun p'ing chuan, comp. by Yu Chih-ying. K'ai-ming, 1936.

茅盾評傳。優志英。

MCNP
MMT

Shao Po-chou. Mao Tun to wen-hsueh tao-lu. Wuhan: Ch'ang-chiang wen-i ch'u-pan she, 1959.

邵伯周。茅盾的文學道路。

Yeh Tzu-ming. Lun Mao Tun ssu-shih nien te wen-hsueh tao-lu, Shanghai: Shanghai wen-i ch'u-pan she, 1959.

葉子銘。論茅盾四十年的文學道路。

Shen Yi   沈怡

WORKS

1924. She-hui chin-hua shih. (tr.) with T'ao Meng-ho, Liang Lun-ts'ai. Shanghai: Shang-wu yin shu kuan.

社會進化史。陶孟和，梁綸才。

SOURCES

Persons interviewed: not to be identified.

CH-T, 1956–57.

Hong Kong shih-pao. Hong Kong, January 28, 1953.

香港時報。

Shen Yin-mo   沈尹默

WORKS

1919–? ed. of *Hsin ch'ing-nien*.

新青年。

1962. Mao Chu-hsi shih tz'u erh-shih-i shou—hsiao-k'ai hsi tzu t'ieh. Shanghai: Shanghai chiao-yü ch'u-pan she.

毛主席詩詞二十一首—小楷習字帖。

1963. Li tai ming chia hsueh shu ching-yen t'an chi-yao shih-i. Shanghai: Shanghai chiao-yü ch'u-pan she.

歷代名家學書經驗談輯要釋義。

Ch'iu ming chi.

秋明集。

SOURCES

Chow Tse-tsung. The May Fourth Movement: Intellectual Revolution in Modern China. Cambridge: Harvard University Press, 1960.

MMT

Ying Tzu. Chung-kuo hsin hsueh-shu jen-wu chih. Hong Kong: Chih ming shu-chü, 1956.

穎子。中國新學術人物誌。

Sheng Hsuan-huai   盛宣懷

WORKS

1895–97. (ed.) Ch'ang-chou hsien-che i-shu. Wu-chin: Sheng shih. 64 vols.

常州先哲遺書。

1939. Yü-chai ts'un kao. Ssu-pu-lou. 50 vols.

愚齋存稿。

1960. Sheng Hsuan-huai wei k'an hsin kao(comp. by Peking ta-hsueh li-shih hsi chin-tai shih chiao yen shih). Peking: Chung-hua shu-chü.

盛宣懷未刊信稿。北京大學歷史系近代史
教研室。
Yü-chai tung yu jih-chi. Ssu-pu-lou.
愚齋東遊日記。

SOURCES

Fairbank, John K., and Liu Kwang-ching.
Modern China: A Bibliographical Guide to
Chinese Works, 1898–1937. Cambridge: Har-
vard University Press, 1950.
Feuerwerker, Albert. China's Early Industriali-
zation: Sheng Hsuan-huai (1844–1916) and
Mandarin Enterprise. Cambridge: Harvard
University Press, 1958.
Fo-shan jen (pseud.). "Ch'ing mo hsien-huan
Sheng Huan-huai i-shih." *Hua Mei jih-pao*.
New York, January 26, 28, 29, 1957.
佛山人。清末顯宦盛宣懷軼事。華美日報。
Sheng Hsuan-huai. Yü-chai ts'un kao. Ssu-pu-
lou, 1939. 50 vols.
盛宣懷。愚齋存稿。

Sheng Shih-ts'ai   盛世才

WORKS

1941. Cheng-fu mu-ch'ien chu-yao jen-wu. I-
ning: Sinkiang min-chung fan ti lien-ho hui.
3 vols.
政府目前主要任務。
1942. Liu ta cheng-ts'e chiao-ch'eng. I-ning:
Sinkiang min-chung fan ti lien-ho hui. 2 vols.
六大政策教程。
1954. Kuan-yü kuo-min ta-hui ti-i tz'u ta-hui ti-
erh tz'u hui-i tai-piao Ai Pai Tu La hsien-sheng
ti ssu san erh hao t'i-an chih shen-pien. Taipei.
關於國民大會第一次大會第二次會議代表
艾拜都拉先生第四三二號提案之申辯。
1958. Sinkiang: Pawn or Pivot? with Allen S.
Whiting. East Lansing: Michigan State University Press.

SOURCES

Lattimore, Owen. Pivot of Asia: Sinkiang and
the Inner Asian Frontiers of China and Russia.
Boston: Little, Brown & Co., 1950.
Norins, Martin Richard. Gateway to Asia:
Sinkiang, Frontier of the Chinese Far West.
New York: The John Day Co., 1944.
Sheng Shih-ts'ai. Cheng-fu mu-ch'ien chu-yao
jen-wu. I-ning: Sinkiang min-chung fan ti
lien-ho hui, 1941. 3 vols.
盛世才。政府目前主要任務。
Sheng Shih-ts'ai. Liu tac heng-ts'e chiao-ch'eng.
I-ning: Sinkiang min-chung fan ti lien-ho hui,
1942. 2 vols.
盛世才。六大政策教程。
Tu Chung-yuan. Sheng Shih-ts'ai yü Sinkiang.
Hankow: Sheng-huo shu-tien, 1938.
杜重遠。盛世才與新疆。
Wei Chung-t'ien. Sheng Shih-ts'ai ju-ho t'ung-
chih Sinkiang. Hong Kong: Hai-wai t'ung-
hsin she, 1947.
魏中天。盛世才如何統治新疆。
Whiting, Allen S., and Sheng Shih-ts'ai. Sinkiang: Pawn or Pivot? East Lansing: Michigan
State University Press, 1958.

Shih Chao-chi   施肇基

WORKS

1921–22. "Disarmament and China's Development." *The Chinese Students' Monthly*.
1922, February 11. "Future of Chinese Democracy." CWR.
1923, December. "The Human Spirit in International Relations." *The Chinese Students'
Monthly*.
1924, March. "What China Needs." *The Chinese
Students' Monthly*.
1924, December. "A Tribute to S. Wells Wil-
liams." *The Chinese Students' Monthly*.
1925, January. "China at the Opium Conference." *The Chinese Students' Monthly*.
1925, April. "The Geneva Opium Conferences."
The Chinese Students' Monthly.
1925, June. "Why the Geneva Opium Conferences Failed." *The Chinese Students' Monthly*.
1926. Addresses. Baltimore: The Johns Hopkins
University Press.
1926. (comp.) Geneva Opium Conferences:
Statements of the Chinese Delegation. Baltimore: The Johns Hopkins University Press.
1926, May. "China's Unequal Treaties." *The
Chinese Students' Monthly*.
1926, November. "The Future Relations of
China with the Powers." *The Chinese Students'
Monthly*.
1927, January. "China and World Peace."
Advocate of Peace.
1927, February. "What China Asks of the
Powers." *The Chinese Students' Monthly*.
1927, February 15. "Why China's Unequal
Treaties Must Be Ended." *National Popular
Government League Bulletin*, 108.

1927, April. "The International Aspect of the Chinese Situation." *The Chinese Students' Monthly*.

1927, April 2. "Realities Must Be Faced in China." CWR.

1927, May. "China and the Western Powers." *The Chinese Students' Monthly*.

1928, June 14. "China and Western Civilization." CWR.

1928, December. "The Present Day China." *The Chinese Students' Monthly*.

1928, December 29. "China's Nationalism: An Aid to World Peace." CWR.

1929, May 18. "British and Chinese Expression on Extraterritoriality." CWR.

1933, January. "A Chinese View of the Manchurian Situation." *The Annals*.

1934, July 21. "China's Case Versus Japan." CWR.

1935, January. "Reconstruction in China." *The Annals*.

1937. "Boycotting Japanese Goods." *The China Quarterly*, special Fall issue.

1959. Shih Chih-chih hsien-sheng tsao-nien hui-i-lu.

施植之先生早年回憶錄。

Eng. tr. by Amy C. Wu, *Sao-Ke Afred Sze, Reminiscences of His Early Years As Told to Anming Fu*. Washington, D. C., 1962.

ed. of *The Cornellian*.

ed. of *St. John's Echo*.

SOURCES

"Biographical Sketch of Dr. Sao-ke Alfred Sze." Unpublished mimeographed material prepared by the Chinese Embassy, Washington, D. C., January 6, 1958.

BPC

CH

Chang Ch'i-yün. Tang shih kai-yao. Taipei: Chung-yang kai-tsao wei-yuan-hui wen-wu kung-ying she, 1951–52. 5 vols.

張其昀。黨史概要。

Chang Chung-fu. Chung-hua Min-kuo wai-chiao shih; shang chüan. Chungking: Cheng-chung shu-chü, 1943.

張忠紱。中華民國外交史；上卷。

Chin shan shih-pao. San Francisco, January 7, 1958.

金山時報。

"China's New Representative at Washington." *The Chinese Students' Monthly*, February, 1921.

CH-T, 1950, 1954–55, 1956–57.

CMTC

GCJJ

Kao Tien-chün. Chung-kuo wai-chiao shih. Taipei: P'a-mi-erh shu-tien, 1952.

高殿均。中國外交史。

Kuo wen chou-pao, I-17.

國聞週報。

Levi, Werner. Modern China's Foreign Policy. Minneapolis: University of Minnesota Press, 1953.

Li Chien-nung. Chung-kuo chin pai nien cheng-chih shih. Shanghai: Shang-wu yin shu kuan, 1947. 2 vols.

李劍農。中國近百年政治史。

The New York Times, August 3, 1922; November 30, 1925; February 22, 1926; April 11, 1926; November 12, 1926; February 13, 1927; March 7, 1927; December 6, 1931; July 21, 1935; January 5, 1958.

"Dr. Sao-ke Afred Sze Continues as Minister at Washington." CWR, July 14, 1928.

Shih Chao-chi. Sao-ke Alfred Sze, Reminiscences of His Early Years as Told to Anming Fu (tr. by Amy C. Wu). Washington, 1962.

T'ang Leang-li. The Inner History of the Chinese Revolution. New York: E. P. Dutton & Co., 1930.

Tseng Yu-hao. Chung-kuo wai-chiao shih. Shanghai: Shang-wu yin shu kuan, 1926.

曾友豪。中國外交史。

Wai-chiao ta tz'u-tien, ed. by Wai-chiao hsueh-hui. Kunming: Chung-hua shu-chü, 1937.

外交大辭典。外交學會。

Who's Who in the Orient, 1915.

Willoughby, W. W. China at the Conference—a Report. Baltimore: The Johns Hopkins University Press, 1922.

WWARS

WWMC

Shih Liang-ts'ai   史 量 才

SOURCES

Chang T'ai-yen. "Shih Liang-ts'ai mu-chih-ming." *Chih yen*, 3 (October, 1935).

章太炎。史量才墓志銘。制言。

Chung-kuo hsin-wen shih, ed. by Tseng Hsü-pai. Taipei: Kuo-li cheng-chih ta-hsueh hsin-wen yen-chiu so, 1966. 2 vols.

中國新聞史。曾虛白。

GCCJK

Hu Tao-ching. Hsin-wen shih shang te hsin shih-tai. Shanghai, 1946.
胡道靜。新聞史上的新時代。

———. Shen pao liu-shih-liu nien shih. Shanghai, 1931.
胡道靜。申報六十六年史。

Jen-wen, December 15, 1934.
人文。

(Min-kuo erh-shih-liu nien) Shanghai shih nien-chien, comp. by Shanghai shih t'ung chih kuan nien-chien wei-yuan-hui. Shanghai: Chung-hua shu-chü, 1937. 2 vols.
(民國二十六年) 上海市年鑑。上海市通志館年鑑委員會。

Shen pao liu-t'ung t'u-shu-kuan ti-erh nien kung-tso pao-kao—chi-nien Shih Liang-ts'ai hsien-sheng. Shanghai: Shen pao liu-t'ung t'u-shu-kuan, 1935.
申報流通圖書館第二年工作報告一紀念史量才先生。

Tsui-chin chih wu-shih nien; shen pao kuan wu-shih chou-nien chi-nien, comp. by Shen pao kuan.
最近之五十年；申報館五十週年紀念。申報館。

Yuan Ch'ang-ch'ao. Chung-kuo pao-yeh hsiao-shih. Hong Kong: Hsin-wen t'ien-ti she, 1957.
袁昶超。中國報業小史。

Shih Mei-yü　石美玉

SOURCES

Burton, Margaret E. Notable Women of Modern China. New York: Fleming H. Revell Co., 1912.
CWR, August 23, 1924.
Missionary Tidings, June, 1916.
The New York Times, December 31, 1954.
Newsletter of Bethel Mission of China, Inc., (January-March, 1955): 4–5.
World Outlook, II-4 (April, 1916): 11.
Zion's Herald, May 28, 1919.

Shih Ying　石瑛

SOURCES

Chang Ch'i-yün *et al*. Chung-hua Min-kuo ta-hsueh chih. Taipei: Chung-hua wen-hua ch'u-pan shih-yeh wei-yuan-hui, 1954. 2 vols.
張其昀等。中華民國大學誌。

Chü Cheng. "Chi Shih Heng-ch'ing liu ti wen."
居正。祭石蘅青六弟文。

Ho Fu-nien. "Shih Heng-ch'ing hsien-sheng hsing-chuang."
賀甫年。石蘅青先生行狀。

Lai Lien. "Tao Shih Heng-ch'ing hsien-sheng."
賴璉。悼石蘅青先生。

Meng Hsien-chang. "Tao Shih Heng-ch'ing hsien-sheng."
孟憲章。悼石蘅青先生。

Tung Ping-ju. "Wo so jen-shih te Shih Heng-ch'ing hsien-sheng."
董冰如。我所認識的石蘅青先生。

Wu Ching-heng. "Ai Shih Heng-ch'ing hsien-sheng."
吳敬恒。哀石蘅青先生。

Shu Ch'ing-ch'un　舒慶春

WORKS

1928. Lao Chang te che hsueh. Shanghai: Shang-wu yin shu kuan.
老張的哲學。

1929. Chao Tzu-yueh. Shanghai: Shang-wu yin shu kuan.
趙子曰。

1932. T'ang Love Stories; an Address by S. Y. Shu before the Convocation of the North China Union Language School, February 1932. Peiping: North China Union Language School.

1933. Mao ch'eng chi. Shanghai: Hsien-tai shu-chü.
貓城記。
Eng. tr. by James E. Dew, *City of Cats*. Occasional Papers, 3, Center for Chinese Studies, The University of Michigan, 1964.

1934. Hsiao P'o te sheng-jih. Shanghai: Sheng-huo shu-tien.
小坡的生日。

1934. Kan-chi. Shanghai: Liang-yu t'u-shu yin-shua kung-ssu.
趕集。

1934. "Liu chia ta-yuan," in Lao She, *Kan-chi*. Shanghai: Liang-yu t'u-shu yin-shua kung-ssu.
柳家大院。老舍。趕集。
Eng. tr. by Wang Chi-chen, "Liu's Court," in Wang Chi-chen, *Contemporary Chinese Stories*. New York: Columbia University Press, 1944.

1934. "Pao sun," in Lao She, *Kan-chi*. Shanghai: Liang-yu t'u-shu yin-shua kung-ssu.
抱孫。老舍。趕集。
Eng. tr. by Wang Chi-chen, "Grandma Takes Charge," in Wang Chi-chen, *Contemporary Chinese Stories*. New York: Columbia University Press, 1944.

1934. "Yen-ching," in Lao She, *Kan-chi*. Shanghai: Liang-yu t'u-shu yin-shua kung-ssu.
眼鏡。老舍。趕集。
Eng. tr. by Wang Chi-chen, "The Glasses," in Wang Chi-chen, *Contemporary Chinese Stories*. New York: Columbia University Press, 1944.

1936. Ko tsao chi. Shanghai: K'ai-ming shu-tien.
蛤藻集。

1936. Lao She hsuan-chi (comp. by Hsü Ch'en-ssu, Yeh Wang-yu). Shanghai: Wan-hsiang shu-wu.
老舍選集。徐沉泗，葉忘憂。

1937. Niu T'ien-tz'u chuan. Shanghai: Jen-chien shu-wu.
牛天賜傳。

1937. "Shan-jen," in Lao She, *Ying hai chi*. Shanghai: Chung-kuo k'o-hsueh kung-ssu.
善人。老舍。櫻海集。
Eng. tr. by Wang Chi-chen, "The Philanthropist," in Wang Chi-chen, *Contemporary Chinese Stories*. New York: Columbia University Press, 1944.

1937. Ying hai chi. Shanghai: Chung-kuo k'o-hsueh kung-ssu.
櫻海集。

1938. Lao niu p'o ch'e. Canton: Jen-chien shu-wu.
老牛破車。

1938. Lao She tai-piao tso hsuan. Shanghai: Ch'üan-ch'iu shu-tien.
老舍代表作選。

1938, November. "They Gather Heart Again." *Tien-hsia Monthly*, VII-4: 406–17. (tr. by Richard L. Jew.)

1941. Huo-ch'e chi. Shanghai: Shanghai tsa-chih kung-ssu.
火車集。

1941, August-September. "Portrait of a Traitor." *T'ien-hsia Monthly*, XII-1: 75–93.

1941. Ts'an wu. Changsha: Shang-wu yin shu kuan.
殘霧。

1941. Wai mao erh. Shanghai: I liu shu-tien.
歪毛兒。

1941. Wen po-shih. Chen kuang p'ai yin chü.
文博士。

1942. Lao She yu-mo chi. Dairen: Man ta shu-chü.
老舍幽默集。

1943. Hei pai Li. Dairen: Man ta shu-chü.
黑白李。
Eng. tr. by Wang Chi-chen, "Black Li and White Li," in Wang Chi-chen, *Contemporary Chinese Stories*. New York: Columbia University Press, 1944.

1943. Kuei-ch'ü lai hsi. Tso-chia shu-wu.
歸去來兮。

1944. T'ao-li ch'un-feng. with Chao Ch'ing-ko. Chengtu: Chung hsi shu-chü.
桃李春風。趙清閣。
Eng. tr. by George Kao, "Fruit in the Spring." *China Magazine*, March, 1947: 37–53.

1945. Kuo-chia chih shang. with Sung Chih-t'ung. Shanghai: Hsin feng ch'u-pan kung-ssu.
國家至上。宋之同。

1945. Lao tzu-hao. Mukden: Sheng-ching shu-tien.
老字號。

1946. Huo-tsang. Shanghai: Hsin feng ch'u-pan kung-ssu.
火葬。

1946. Lao She yu-mo chieh-tso chi. Shanghai: I-li shu-chü.
老舍幽默傑作集。

1946. Tung-hai Pa-shan chi. Shanghai: Hsin feng ch'u-pan kung-ssu.
東海巴山集。

1947. Lo-t'o Hsiang-tzu. Shanghai: Wen-hua sheng-huo ch'u-pan she.
駱駝祥子。
Eng. tr. by Evan King, *Rickshaw Boy*. New York: Reynal & Hitchcock, 1945.

1947. Mien-tzu wen-t'i. Shanghai: Cheng-chung shu-chü.
面子問題。

1947. Ssu-shih t'ung-t'ang. Shanghai: Ch'en-kuang ch'u-pan kung-ssu. 2 vols.
四世同堂。
Eng. tr. by Ida Pruitt, *The Yellow Storm*. New York: Harcourt, Brace, 1951.

1947. Wei shen chi. Shanghai: Ch'en kuang ch'u-pan kung-ssu.
微神集。

1947. Wo che i-pei-tzu. Hui ch'ün ch'u-pan she.
我這一輩子。

1949. Erh Ma. Shanghai: Ch'en kuang ch'u-pan kung-ssu.
二馬。

1949. K'ai-shih ta-chi. Shanghai: Wen-hua sheng-huo ch'u-pan she.
開市大吉。

1949. Li-hun. Shanghai: Ch'en kuang ch'u-pan kung-ssu.
離婚。
Eng. tr. by Helena Kuo, *The Quest for Love of Lao Lee*. New York: Reynal & Hitchcock, 1948.

1950. Jao-k'ou-ling. Peking: Lai-hsun-ko shu-tien.
繞口令。

1951. Fang chen-chu. Shanghai: Ch'en-kuang ch'u-pan kung-ssu.
方珍珠。

1951. Heavensent. London: J. M. Dent.

1951. Lao She *et al*. Pieh mi-hsin. Shanghai: Hsin hua shu-tien.
老舍等。別迷信。

1951. Lao She hsi-chü chi. Shanghai: Ch'en kuang ch'u-pan kung-ssu.
老舍戲劇集。

1951. Lao She hsuan-chi (comp. by Hsin wen-hsueh hsuan-chi pien-chi wei-yuan-hui). Peking: K'ai-ming shu-tien.
老舍選集。新文學選集編輯委員會。

1952. The Drum Singers (tr. by Helena Kuo). New York: Harcourt, Brace.

1952. Hsi-sheng. Hong Kong: Wen-hsueh ch'u-pan she.
犧牲。

1952. Lao She hsuan-chi (comp. by Pa Lei). Hong Kong: Lü yang shu-wu.
老舍選集。巴雷。

1953. Hui fa.
灰髮。

1953. Lung hsü kou (rev. by Chiao Chü-yin. ed. by Kuan Kuei-k'ai). Peking: Jen-min mei-shu ch'u-pan she.
龍須溝。焦菊隱。關貴楷。
Eng. tr. by Liao Hung-ying, *Dragon Beard Ditch: A Play in Three Acts*. Peking: Foreign Languages Press, 1956.

1954. Ho kung-jen t'ung-chih men t'an hsieh-tso. Peking: Kung-jen ch'u-pan she.
和工人同志們談寫作。

1955. Wu ming kao-ti yu le ming. Peking: Jen-min wen-hsueh ch'u-pan she.
無名高地有了名。

1956. Lao She hsuan-chi. Hong Kong: Wen-hsueh ch'u-pan she.
老舍選集。

1956. Lao She tuan-p'ien hsiao-shuo hsuan. Peking: Jen-min wen-hsueh ch'u-pan she.
老舍短篇小說選。

1956. (rev.) Shih-wu kuan. Peking: Peking ch'u-pan she.
十五貫。

1958. Ch'a-kuan. Peking: Chung-kuo hsi-chü ch'u-pan she.
茶館。

1958. Fu hsing chi. Peking: Peking ch'u-pan she.
福星集。

1958. Lao She hsiao-shuo hsuan. Hong Kong: Wan-li shu-tien.
老舍小說選。

1959. Ch'üan-chia fu. Peking: Tso-chia ch'u-pan she.
全家福。

1959. Hung ta yuan. Peking: Tso-chia ch'u-pan she.
紅大院。

1959. Lao She chü tso hsuan. Peking: Jen-min wen-hsueh ch'u-pan she.
老舍劇作選。

1959, March. "The Little Story." *Chinese Literature Monthly*, 3: 3–5.

1959. Yueh-ya-erh. Peking: Wen-hsueh ch'u-pan she.
月牙兒。
Eng. tr., "Crescent Moon" in Sidney Shapiro, *Chinese Literature*. Peking: Foreign Languages Press, 1957.

1961. T'ing lai te ku-shih. Hong Kong: Nan kuo ch'u-pan she.
聽來的故事。

1962. Ho chu p'ei. Peking: Chung-kuo hsi-chü ch'u-pan she.
荷珠配。

1962. Pu ch'eng wen-t'i te wen-t'i. Hong Kong: Shanghai shu-chü.
不成問題的問題。

1963. Ma hsien-sheng yü Ma Wei. Hong Kong: Ts'ui wen shu-tien.
馬先生與馬威。

1963. Pao ch'uan. Tokyo.
寶船。

1963. Shen ch'üan. Peking: Chung-kuo hsi-chü ch'u-pan she.
神拳。

1964. Ch'u-k'ou ch'eng-chang—lun wen-hsueh yü-yen chi ch'i-t'a. Peking: Tso-chia ch'u-pan she.
出口成章—論文學語言及其他。

1966. Lao She san-wen chi. Hong Kong: Ta
　　fang ch'u-pan she.
　　老舍散文集。

Chang Tzu-chung.
　　張自忠。

Chien pei p'ien.
　　劍北篇。

ed. of *K'ang chan wen-i.*
　　抗戰文藝。

Lao She ming tso hsuan-chi. Hong Kong: Nan-
　　yang t'u-shu kung-ssu.
　　老舍名作選集。

Shei hsien tao le Chungking.
　　誰先到了重慶。

Ta-ti lung she.
　　大地龍蛇。

SOURCES

Chan Shau-wing. "Literature in Communist
　　China." *Problems of Communism*, VII-1 (Janu-
　　ary-February, 1958).

Chu Fu-sung. "Wartime Chinese Literature,"
　　in Hollington K. Tong, *China after Seven Years
　　of War.* Chungking: Chinese Ministry of
　　Information, 1944.

CHWSK

Contemporary Chinese Stories, tr. by Wang Chi-
　　chen. New York: Columbia University Press,
　　1944.

ECC

Kikuchi Saburo. Chūgoku gendai bungaku shi.
　　Tokyo, 1953.
　　菊地三郎。中國現代文學史。

Kuang-ming jih-pao. Peking, April 16, 1954.
　　光明日報。

Lao She (Shu Ch'ing-ch'un). "Hsiao-hsing te fu-
　　huo," in T'ao K'ang-te, *Tzu-chuan te i-chang.*
　　Shanghai: Yü-chou feng she, 1938.
　　老舍。小型的復活。陶亢德。自傳的一章。

———. Lao niu p'o ch'e. Canton: Jen-chien
　　shu-wu, 1938.
　　老舍。老牛破車。

———. "Life, Study and Work." *People's China*,
　　17 (September, 1954): 33-36.

———. "Living in Peking." *China Reconstructs*,
　　IV (1952): 25-29.

———. "The Modern Chinese Novel." *National
　　Reconstruction Journal*, VII-1 (July, 1946): 3-14.

———. "A Writer Speaks of Writing." *China
　　Reconstructs*, VI-11 (November, 1957).

Lo Ch'ang-p'ei. Chung-kuo jen yü Chung-kuo
　　wen. Chungkung: K'ai-ming shu-tien, 1945.
　　羅常培。中國人與中國文。

MCNP

Monsterleet, Jean. Sommets de la Litterature
　　Chinoise Contemporaine. Paris, 1953.

Ying yin, VII-1 (February, 1948).
　　影音。

Shu Hsin-ch'eng　　舒新城

WORKS

1922. (comp.) Hsin-li yuan-li; shih-yung chiao-
　　yü hsueh. Shanghai: Shang-wu yin shu kuan.
　　心理原理；實用教育學。

1924. Tao-erh-tun chih yen-chiu chi. Chung-
　　hua shu-chü.
　　道爾頓制研究集。

1925. Chiao-yü ts'ung-kao. Shanghai: Chung-
　　hua shu-chü.
　　教育叢稿。

1927. Shou-hui chiao-yü ch'üan yün-tung.
　　Chung-hua shu-chü.
　　收回教育權運動。

1928. Chiao-yü t'ung-lun. Shanghai: Chung-
　　hua shu-chü.
　　教育通論。

1928. (comp.) Chin-tai Chung-kuo chiao-yü shih-
　　liao. Shanghai: Chung-hua shu-chü. 4 vols.
　　近代中國教育史料。

1928. (comp.) Chin-tai Chung-kuo chiao-yü ssu-
　　hsiang shih. Shanghai: Chung-hua shu-chü.
　　近代中國教育思想史。

1928. Chung-kuo chiao-yü tz'u-tien. with Yü
　　Chia-chü, Ku Mei. Shanghai: Chung-hua
　　shu-chü.
　　中國教育辭典。余家菊，古梅。

1928. Chung-kuo hsin chiao-yü kai-k'uang.
　　Shanghai: Chung-hua shu-chü.
　　中國新教育概況。

1929. Chin-tai Chung-kuo liu-hsueh shih. Shang-
　　hai: Chung-hua shu-chü.
　　近代中國留學史。

1930. (comp.) Hsien-tai chiao-yü fang-fa. Shang-
　　hai: Shang-wu yin shu kuan.
　　現代教育方法。

1930. Shu Hsin-ch'eng *et al.* (comp.) Chung-hua
　　pai-k'o tz'u-tien. Shanghai: Chung-hua shu-
　　chü.
　　舒新城等。中華百科辭典。

1931? Chih ch'ing-nien shu—t'ao-lun chi chien
　　kuan-yü tu-shu te shih. Shanghai: Chung-
　　hua shu-chü.
　　致青年書—討論幾件關於讀書的事。

1931. Chung-kuo chiao-yü chien-she fang-chen.
　　Shanghai: Chung-hua shu-chü.
　　中國教育建設方針。

1936. Ku-hsiang. Shanghai: Chung-hua shu-chü.

故鄉。

1936. K'uang-ku-lu. Shanghai: Chung-hua shu-chü.

狂顧錄。

1936. Shu yu hsin-ying. Shanghai: Chung-hua shu-chü.

蜀游心影。

1937. Shu Hsin-ch'eng et al. (comp.) Tz'u-hai. Shanghai: Chung-hua shu-chü. 2 vols.

舒新城等。辭海。

1945. Man-yu jih-chi. Shanghai: Chung-hua shu-chü.

漫遊日記。

1945. Shih nien shu. with Liu Chi-ch'ün. Shanghai: Chung-hua shu-chü.

十年書。劉濟群。

1945. Wo ho chiao-yü; san-shih-wu nien chiao-yü sheng-huo shih. Shanghai: Chung-hua shu-chü.

我和教育；三十五年教育生活史。

1961. (comp.) Chung-kuo chin-tai chiao-yü shih tzu-liao. Peking: Jen-min chiao-yü ch'u-pan she. 3 vols.

中國近代教育史資料。

SOURCES

China News Analysis, 345 (October 21, 1961): 4–6.

Shu Hsin-ch'eng. Wo ho chiao-yü; san-shih-wu nien chiao-yü sheng-huo shih. Shanghai: Chung-hua shu-chü, 1945.

舒新城。我和教育；三十五年教育生活史。

Shu Hsin-ch'eng and Liu Chi-ch'ün. Shih nien shu. Shanghai: Chung-hua shu-chü, 1945.

舒新城，劉濟群。十年書。

Wang I-t'ung. "Tz'u-hai k'an-wu." Ch'ing-hua hsueh-pao, II-1 (May, 1960): 130–42.

王伊同。辭海勘誤。清華學報。

Soong, Charles Jones　宋嘉樹

SOURCES

Barnett, Fred T. "The Romance of Charlie Soong." The Duke Divinity School Bulletin, January, 1942.

Fu Ping-hsiang. "The Soong Dynasty." People's Tribune, I (1931): 133–36.

Hahn, Emily. The Soong Sisters. Garden City. Doubleday, Doran & Co., 1941.

Kuo-fu nien-p'u, ed. by Chung-kuo kuo-min-tang chung-yang tang shih shih-liao pien-tsuan wei-yuan-hui. Taipei: Chung-hua Min-kuo ko-chieh chi-nien kuo-fu pai nien tan-ch'en ch'ou-pei wei-yuan-hui, 1965. 2 vols.

國父年譜。中國國民黨中央黨史史料編纂委員會。

Mortensen, Niels, and Alex Haley. "The Cabin Boy Who Sired a Dynasty." Coronet, XLVIII (May, 1960).

Tourtellot, A. "C. J. Soong and the U. S. Coast Guard." U. S. Naval Institute Proceedings, LXXV (February, 1949): 201–3.

Soong Ch'ing-ling　宋慶齡

WORKS

1937. Sung Ch'ing-ling k'ang chan yen-lun chi. K'ang chan hsin-wen she.

宋慶齡抗戰言論集。

1938. Chung-kuo pu wang lun. Shanghai: Sheng-huo shu-tien.

中國不忘論。

1938. Sung Ch'ing-ling tzu-chuan chi ch'i yen-lun. Hong Kong: Kuang-hua ch'u-pan she.

宋慶齡自傳及其言論。

1951. Hsin Chung-kuo hsiang ch'ien mai-chin—Tung-pei lü-hsing yin-hsiang chi. Peking: Jen-min ch'u-pan she.

新中國向前邁進—東北旅行印像記。

1952. The Struggle for New China. Peking: Foreign Languages Press.

1952. Wei hsin Chung-kuo fen-tou. Peking: Jen-min ch'u-pan she.

為新中國奮鬥。

1956. Good Neighbors Meet: Speeches in India, Burma and Pakistan, 1955–56. Peking: Foreign Languages Press.

SOURCES

BKL

China Journal, XXXI-1 (July, 1939): 60–61.

Chiu-kuo wu-tsui, comp. by Shih-tai wen-hsien she. Tung-fang t'u-shu tsa-chih kung-ssu, 1937.

救國無罪。時代文獻社。

CBJS

CMMC

CPR, 1002 (October 28, 1949); 1005 (November 1, 1949).

GCCJK

Gould, Randall. "Madame Sun Keeps Faith." Nation, January 22, 1930.

GSJK

Hahn, Emily. The Soong Sisters. Garden City, N. Y.: Doubleday, Doran & Co., 1941.
HMTT
I-chiu-wu-ling jen-min nien-chien, ed. by Shen Sung-fang. Hong Kong: Ta kung shu-chü, 1950.
一九五〇人民年鑑。沈頌芳。
Isaacs, Harold R. The Tragedy of the Chinese Revolution. Stanford: Stanford University Press, 1951.
JMST
Kuo wen chou-pao, X-47,
國聞週報。
Martin, Bernard. Strange Vigour: A Biography of Sun Yat-sen. London: William Heinemann, 1944.
The New York Times, February 27, 1964.
SCMP, 39 (December 29-31, 1950); 93 (April 10-12, 1951); 96 (April 19-20, 1951), 177 (September 19, 1951); 178 (September 20, 1951), 472 (December 13-15, 1952); 480 (December 25-27, 1952); 481 (December 28-29, 1952); 492 (January 15, 1953); 552 (April, 1953); 955 (December 24-28, 1954); 1407 (November 8, 1956).
Sheean, Vincent. Personal History. Garden City, N. Y.: Doubleday, Doran & Co., 1936.
SSYD
T'ang Leang-li. The Inner History of the Chinese Revolution. New York: E. P. Dutton & Co., 1930.
WWC, 1950.

Soong Mei-ling 宋美齡

WORKS

1937. China at the Crossroads: An Account of the Fortnight in Sian When the Fate of China Hung in the Balance. with Chiang Kai-shek. London: Faber & Faber.

1937. Sian: A Coup d'État. Shanghai: The China Publishing Co.

1938. Christianity in China's National Crisis: An Address Delivered at the Wuhan Monthly Missionary Prayer Meeting on April 6, 1968. Hankow: Chinese League of Nations Union.

1938. War Messages and Other Selections. Hankow: China Information Committee.

1938. Women and the Way: Christ and the World's Womanhood, a Symposium by Madame Chiang Kai-shek, Mrs. Z. K. Matthews, Tseng Pao-swen, and Others. New York: Friendship Press.

1940. A Letter from Madame Chiang Kai-shek to Boys and Girls Across the Ocean. Chungking: China Information Publishing Co.

1940. China in Peace and War. London: Hurst & Blackett.

1940. This Is Our China. New York: Harper.

1941. China Shall Rise Again. New York: Harper.

1942. Little Sister Su: A Chinese Folk Tale. New York: The John Day Co.

1942. The New Life Movement in China. Calcutta: Calcutta Office, Chinese Ministry of Information.

1943. Addresses Delivered before the House of Representatives and the Senate of the United States, February 18, 1943. Stamford: The Overbrook Press.

1943. Addresses Delivered before the Senate of the United States and the House of Representatives on February 18, 1943, Together with Other Addresses Delivered during Her Visit to the United States. Washington, D. C.

1943. I Confess my Faith. New York: Board of Missions and Church Extension, the Methodist Church.

1943. We Chinese Women: Speeches and Writings during the first United Nations Year, February 12, 1942-November 16, 1942. New York: The John Day Co.

1944. China, as Told by Madame Chiang Kaishek in a Series of Addresses, in New York, San Francisco, Chicago, and in Ottawa, Canada, in Behalf of the Chinese Relief and of the Chinese Government. York, Pa.: The Maple Press Co.

1955. The Sure Victory. Westwood, N. J.: Revell.

1956. Chiang fu-jen yen-lun hui-pien (ed. by Chiang fu-jen yen-lun hui-pien pien-chi wei-yuan-hui). Taipei: Cheng-chung shu-chü. 4 vols.
蔣夫人言論彙編。蔣夫人言論彙編編輯委員會。

1957. Selected Speeches. Taipei: Government Information Office.

SOURCES

Bartlett, Robert M. They Did Something About It. New York: Association Press, 1939.
CTMC
Current Biography, 1940.
Gunther, John. Inside Asia. New York: Harper & Bros., 1939.

Hahn, Emily. The Soong Sisters. Garden City, N. Y.: Doubleday, Doran & Co., 1941.

HMTT

Hua shang pao shou-ts'e, 1949. Hong Kong: Hua shang pao she, 1949.

華商報手冊，1949。

Kazangien, Helene. "Madame Chiang Kai-shek—Mayling Soong," in Chung-yang chu-pan Mei-chou kuo-min jih-pao, *Chiang fu-jen yu Mei chi-nien ts'e*. 1943.

中央主辦美洲國民日報。蔣夫人遊美紀念冊。

Mathews, Basel Joseph. Wings over China: Generalissimo and Madame Chiang Kai-shek. New York: Friendship Press, 1940.

Meet the Press, IX-38 (October 31, 1965).

Miller, Basil W. Generalissimo and Madame Chiang Kai-shek: Christian Liberators of China. Grand Rapids, Mich: Zondervan Publishing House, 1943.

The New York Times, August 30, September 4, 6, 8, 1965; April 17, 1966.

Romanus, Charles F., and Riley Sunderland. Stilwell's Command Problems. Washington: Office of the Chief of Military History, Department of the Army, 1956.

———. Stilwell's Mission to China. Washington: Office of the Chief of Military History, Department of the Army, 1953.

Roosevelt, Eleanor. This I Remember. New York: Harper & Bros., 1949.

Sheean, Vincent. Personal History. Garden City, N. Y.: Doubleday, Doran & Co., 1936.

Steinbery, Alfred. Mrs. R, the Life of Eleanor Roosevelt. New York: G. P. Putnam, 1958.

The Stilwell Papers, ed. by Theodore H. White. New York: William Sloane Associates, 1948.

Tong, Hollington K. Dateline: China. New York: Rockport Press, 1950.

WWC, 1950.

WWMC

Soong, T. V. 宋子文

WORKS

1914-15. "The European War and China's Foreign Relations." *The Chinese Students' Monthly*, X: 150-51.

1932. "Japanese Diplomacy at Work." *People's Tribune*, N. S. II: 32-38. (with Quo Tai-chi).

1932. "Japan's Challenge to the Civilized World." *People's Tribune*, N. S. II: 10-14. (with Quo Tai-chi, Wellington Koo).

1932. "Japan's Proposed Recognition of 'Manchukuo' and the Manchurian Customs." *People's Tribune*, N. S. II: 316-23. (with Wang Ching-wei).

1932-33. "The Manchurian Customs." *People's Tribune*, N. S. III: 141-42.

1945. China's Post War Economic Reconstruction. with Chiang Kai-shek. Shanghai: International Publishers.

SOURCES

Ai Meng. "Liang ch'ao kuo-chiu" Sung Tzu-wen pi-shih. Hong Kong: Huan-ch'iu nei-mu pi-wen she.

艾萌。「兩朝國舅」宋子文秘史。

BKL

Ch'en Po-ta. Chung-kuo ssu ta chia-tsu. Hong Kong: Chung-kuo ch'u-pan she, 1947.

陳伯達。中國四大家族。

The China Critic, August 31, 1933; September 7, 1933; October 19, 1933.

CH-T, 1954-55; 1956-57.

Chung-kuo chin-tai kung-yeh shih tzu-liao, comp. by Ch'en Chen, Yao Lo, Feng Hsien-chih. Peking: Sheng-huo, tu-shu, hsin chih san-lien shu-tien, 1957-61. 4 vols.

中國近代工業史資料。陳眞，姚洛，逢先知。

CMTC

CPR, 896 (May 20, 1949).

CTMC

CWR, August 1, 1931: 334; February 15, 1941: 390-93.

Green, O. M. "Mr. T. V. Soong's Visit to England." *Asiatic Review*, XXIX (1933): 506-12.

Gunther, John. Inside Asia. New York: Harper & Bros., 1939.

Holcombe, Arthur N. The Spirit of the Chinese Revolution. New York: Alfred A. Knopf, 1930.

"Isolation and Constructive Pacifism." *The China Quarterly*, special Fall number: 702-4.

Kwangtung shih-jen chih, ed. by Yeh Yün-sheng, Yeh Po-heng. Canton: K'ai-t'ung ch'u-pan she, 1947.

廣東時人志。葉雲笙，葉伯恒。

The New York Times, February 8, 1927; January 9, 1928; December 22, 1932; December 12,

1937; March 19, 1938; January 13, 1943; June 20, 1946; September 21, October 3, 1947; December 9, 26, 1948; April 17, 1949; April 30, May 11, June 10, 13, 16, 1950.

Sheean, Vincent. Personal History. Garden City, N. Y.: Doubleday, Doran & Co., 1935.

Smedley, Agnes. Battle Hymn of China. New York: Alfred A. Knopf, 1944.

Sokolsky, George E. "Modernization of the Chinese Government—a Study of Ideas and Methods Based upon the Annual Report of Mr. T. V. Soong, Minister, of Finance." *The Far Eastern Review*, April, 1930: 145-48, 158.

Sung Tzu-wen hao-men tzu-pen nei-mu, comp. by Ching-chi tzu-liao shih. Hong Kong: Kuang-hua shu-tien, 1948.
宋子文豪門資本內幕。經濟資料室。

"T. V. Soong." *The China Journal*, XXX-6 (June, 1939): 387-88.

Tamagna, Frank M. Banking and Finance in China. New York: International Secretariat, Institute of Pacific Relations, 1942.

Tong, Hollington K. Chiang Kai-shek, Soldier and Statesman: Authorized Biography. Shanghai: China Publishing Co., 1937.

WWMC

Su Chao-cheng   蘇兆徵

SOURCES

Person interviewed: Chang Kuo-t'ao.
CKLC
GCCJK
GCJ

Isaacs, Harold R. The Tragedy of the Chinese Revolution. Stanford: Stanford University Press, 1951.

Nan-fang jih-pao. July 1, 1951.
南方日報。

North, Robert C. Moscow and the Chinese Communists. Stanford: Stanford University Press, 1963.

Ta Sheng *et al.* Lieh-shih chuan, ti-i chi; chi-nien wo-men wei Chung-kuo jen-min chieh-fang fen-tou erh hsi-sheng te chan-shih. Moscow, 1936.
大生等。烈士傳，第一集；紀念我們爲中國人民解放奮鬥而犧牲的戰士。

Teng Chung-hsia. Chung-kuo chih-kung yün-tung chien-shih (1919-1926). Peking: Jen-min ch'u-pan she, 1953.

鄧中夏。中國職工運動簡史。

Su Hsueh-lin   蘇雪林

WORKS

1929. Chi hsin. Shanghai: Pei hsin shu-chü.
棘心。

1938. Ch'ing niao chi. Changsha: Shang-wu yin shu kuan.
青鳥集。

1938. Tu-yü chi. Changsha: Shang-wu yin shu kuan.
鱷魚集。

1941. Nan Ming chung-lieh chuan. Chungking.
南明忠烈傳。

1941. T'u lung chi. Chungking: Shang-wu yin shu kuan.
屠龍集。

1945. Shan shui chi. Chungking: Shang-wu yin shu kuan.
蟬蛻集。

1946. Chiu-na-lo te yen-ching. Shang-wu.
鳩那羅的眼睛。

1950. Chung-kuo ch'uan-t'ung yü t'ien-chu ku chiao.
中國傳統與天主古敎。

1954. Hsueh-lin tzu hsuan chi. Taipei: Sheng-li ch'u-pan kung-ssu.
雪林自選集。

1955. Kuei hung chi.
歸鴻集。

1956. K'un-lun chih mi. Taipei: Chung-yang wen-wu kung-ying she.
崑崙之謎。

1957. Lü t'ien. T'ai-chung: Kuang-ch'i ch'u-pan she.
綠天。

1957. San ta sheng-ti te hsün-li. T'ai-chung: Kuang-ch'i ch'u-pan she.
三大聖地的巡禮。

1957. T'ien-ma chi. Taipei: San min shu-tien.
天馬集。

1958. T'ang shih kai-lun. Shanghai: Shang-wu yin shu kuan.
唐詩概論。

1958. Yü ch'i shih mi (Yuan ming: Li I-shan lien-ai shih-chi k'ao). Taipei: Taiwan shang-wu yin shu kuan.
玉溪詩謎 （原名：李義山戀愛事跡考）。

1961. Su Hsueh-lin hsuan-chi. Taipei: Hsin lu shu-chü.
蘇雪林選集。

1964. Liao Chin Yuan wen-hsueh. Hong Kong: Shang-wu yin shu kuan.
遼金元文學。

SOURCES

Chao Ching-shen. Wen-jen chien-ying. Shanghai: Pei hsin shu-chü, 1936.
趙景深。文人剪影。
CHWC
CHWYS
CMJL
CMMC
CWT
GCCJK
Hsien-tai Chung-kuo nü tso-chia, ed. by Huang Ying. Shanghai: Pei hsin shu-chü, 1931.
現代中國女作家。黃英。
"Jung huo wen-i chiang-chin te Su Hsueh-lin chiao-shou." *Min-hang kung-ssu yueh-k'an*, IX-2 (February, 1956): 7.
榮獲文藝獎金的蘇雪林教授。民航公司月刊。
MCNP
Su Hsueh-lin. Chi hsin. Shanghai: Pei hsin shu-chü, 1929.
蘇雪林。棘心。
————. Ch'ing niao chi. Changsha: Shang-wu yin shu kuan.
蘇雪林。青鳥集。
WWMC

Su Man-shu 蘇曼殊

WORKS

1930-31. Su Man-shu ch'üan-chi (ed. by Liu Ya-tzu). Shanghai: Pei hsin shu-chü. 5 vols.
蘇曼殊全集。柳亞子。
1961. Su Man-shu ch'üan chi. Taipei: Ta Chung-kuo t'u-shu kung-ssu.
蘇曼殊全集。

SOURCES

Huang Ming-ch'i. Su Man-shu p'ing chuan. Shanghai: Pei hsin shu-tien, 1949.
黃鳴岐。蘇曼殊評傳。
McAleavy, Henry. Su Man-shu (1884-1918) a Sino-Japanese Genius. London: China Society, 1960.
Su Man-shu nien-p'u chi ch'i-t'a, ed by Liu Wu-chi. Shanghai: Pei hsin shu-chü, 1928.
蘇曼殊年譜及其他。柳無忌。

Su Yü 粟裕

SOURCES

Persons interviewed: Chang Kuo-t'ao; others not to be identified.

Sun Ch'uan-fang 孫傳芳

SOURCES

Persons interviewed: not to be identified.
MMT
WWC, 1931.

Sun Fo 孫科

WORKS

1919-? ed. of *Canton Times*.
1930. Chung-kuo ko-ming hou te hsin chien-she. Shanghai: Hsin yü-chou shu-tien.
中國革命後的新建設。
1942. Chung-kuo te ch'ien-t'u.
中國的前途。
Eng. tr., *China Looks Forward*. New York: The John Day, Co., 1944.
1948. Sun fu chu-hsi tsui-chin yen-lun chi. Nanking.
孫副主席最近言論集。

SOURCES

BKL
CB, 1944.
Chang Chia-ao. China's Struggle for Railroad Development. New York: The John Day Co., 1943.
Ch'eng T'ien-fang. A History of Sino-Soviet Relations. Washington: Public Affairs Press, 1957.
CH-T, 1956-57.
CYB-W, 1934.
Free China Weekly, November 3, December 12, 1965; August 27, 1967.
Kuo-fu nien-p'u, ed. by Chung-kuo kuo-min-tang chung-yang tang shih shih-liao pien-tsuan wei-yuan-hui. Taipei: Chung-hua Min-kuo ko-chieh chi-nien kuo-fu pai nien tan-ch'en ch'ou-pei wei-yuan-hui, 1965. 2 vols.
國父年譜。中國國民黨中央黨史史料編纂委員會。
Kwangtung shih jen chih.
廣東時人誌。
Lei Hsiao-ts'en. San-shih nien tung-luan Chung-

kuo. Hong Kong: Ya-chou ch'u-pan she, 1955.
雷嘯岑。三十年動亂中國。

Li Yün-han. Ts'ung jung kung tao ch'ing tang. Taipei: Chung-kuo hsueh-shu chu-tso chiang chu wei-yuan-hui, 1966. 2 vols.
李雲漢。從容共到清黨。

Sharman, Lyon. Sun Yat-sen, His Life and Its Meaning: A Critical Biography. New York: The John Day Co., 1934.

Sun Fo. China Looks Forward. New York: The John Day Co., 1944.

T'ang Leang-li. The Inner History of the Chinese Revolution. New York: E. P. Dutton & Co., 1930.

Tong, Hollington K. Chiang Kai-shek, Soldier and Statesman: Authorized Biography. Shanghai: China Publishing Co., 1937.

Wu, Aitchen. China and the Soviet Union: A Study of Sino-soviet Relations. London: Methuen, 1950.

Sun Lan-feng   孫蘭峯

SOURCES

Persons interviewed: not to be identified.
CTMC
GCJJ

Sun Li-jen   孫立人

WORKS

1952. "General Sun Li-jen, '27, Heads Nationalist Army on Formosa." *Virginia Military Alumni Review*.

1952. "Report from Formosa." *Virginia Military Institute Review*.

SOURCES

AWW
CH-T, 1953–54.
Clubb, O. Edmund. "Manchuria in the Balance, 1945–1946." *Pacific Historical Review*, November, 1957: 377–89.
———. "Military Debacle in Manchuria." *Army Quarterly*, January, 1958: 221–32.
CMJL
Fang Ning. Sun Li-jen chiang-chün yü Mien chan. Hong Kong: T'ai hsuan ch'u-an she, 1963.
方寧。孫立人將軍與緬戰。
Ko Shan-k'o. Sun Li-jen shih-chien chen-hsiang.

Hong Kong: Ta ch'ien yin shua kung-ssu, 1955.
高山客。孫立人事件眞相。

The New York Times, August 20, 21, 24, 28, 1955.

Romanus, Charles F., and Riley Sunderland. United States Army in World War II—China-Burma-India Theater. Washington: Department of the Army, 1953–58. 3 vols.

TCMC-1

"Tiger Under Sun." *Newsweek*, July 28, 1947: 37.

Sun Lien-chung   孫連仲

WORKS

1962. Sun Lien-chung hui-i-lu (ed. by Wu Yen-huan). Taipei: Sun Fang-lu hsien-sheng ku-hsi hua-tan ch'ou-pei wei-yuan-hui.
孫連仲回憶錄。吳延環。

SOURCES

BKL
Chung-kuo k'ang chan shih, ed. by Hai-wai liu-tung hsuan-ch'uan t'uan. Canton: Hai-wai liu-tung hsuan-ch'uan t'uan chu Yueh tsung pan-shih-ch'u, 1947.
中國抗戰史。海外流動宣傳團。
CMJL
CTMC
CWR, 1931.
Huang Shao-hung. Wu-shih hui-i. Hangchow: Yün feng ch'u-pan she, 1945. 2 vols.
黃紹竑。五十回憶。
Liu, F. F. A Military History of Modern China, 1924–1949. Princeton: Princeton University Press, 1956.
Sun Lien-chung. Sun Lien-chung hui-i-lu (ed. by Wu Yen-huan). Taipei: Sun Fang-lu hsien-sheng ku-hsi hua-tan ch'ou-pei wei-yuan-hui, 1962.
孫連仲。孫連仲回憶錄。吳延環。
TCJC
TCMC-1
WWMC

Sun Pao-ch'i   孫寶琦

SOURCES

Chia I-chün. Chung-hua Min-kuo shih. Shanghai: Wen-hua hsueh-she, 1930.
賈逸君。中華民國史。

Christian Mission China Book, 1912, 1915.

Kuang-hsü yin sheng t'ung kuan ch'ih lu. Peking: Wen-te-chai. 5 vols.
光緒廳生同官齒錄。

Kuo wen chou-pao, II-6.
國聞週報。

T'ang Leang-li. The Inner History of the Chinese Revolution. New York: E. P. Dutton & Co., 1930.

Wai-chiao ta tz'u-tien, ed. by Wai-chiao hsueh-hui. Kunming: Chung-hua shu-chü, 1937.
外交大辭典。外交學會。

Who's Who in the Orient, 1915.

WWMC

Yuan Shih-k'ai ch'ieh kuo chi, comp. by Taiwan Chung-hua shu-chü. Taipei: Taiwan Chung-hua shu-chü, 1954.
袁世凱竊國記。台灣中華書局。

Sun Yat-sen　　孫文

Works

1905? The True Solution of the Chinese Question.

1927. Memoirs of a Chinese Revolutionary, a Programme of National Reconstruction for China. London: Hutchinson & Co.

1928. San min chu-i, the Three Principles of the People (tr. by Frank W. Price; ed. by L. T. Chen). Shanghai: China Committee, Institute of Pacific Relations.

1930. Tsung-li ch'üan-chi (ed. by Hu Han-min). 5 vols.
總理全集。胡漢民。

1936. Chung-shan ch'üan shu. Shanghai: Ming li shu-chü. 4 vols.
中山全書。

1942. Ten Letters of Sun Yat-sen, 1914-1916. Stanford: Stanford University Libraries.

1952. Tsung-li ch'üan shu, ed. by Chung-yang kai-tsao wei-yuan-hui tang shih shih-liao pien-tsuan wei-yuan-hui. Taipei: Chung-yang kai-tsao wei-yuan-hui. 11 vols.
總理全書。中央改造委員會黨史史料編纂委員會。

1953. Fundamentals of National Reconstruction. Taipei: China Cultural Service.

1953. The International Development of China. Taipei: China Cultural Service.

1956. Sun Chung-shan hsuan-chi. Peking: Jen-min ch'u-pan she. 2 vols.
孫中山選集。

1965. Kuo-fu ch'üan-chi, ed. by Chung-kuo kuo-min-tang chung-yang tang shih shih-liao pien-tsuan wei-yuan-hui. Taipei: Chung-hua Min-kuo ko-chieh chi-nien kuo-fu pai-nien tan-ch'en ch'ou-pei wei-yuan-hui. 3 vols.
國父全集。中國國民黨中央黨史史料編纂委員會。

1965. Kuo-fu fa-lü ssu-hsiang lun-chi (ed. by Hsieh Kuan-sheng, Ch'a Liang-chien). Taipei: Chung-kuo wen-hua hsueh-yuan fa-lü yen-chiu-so.
國父法律思想論集。謝冠生，查良鑑。

Sources

Amann, Gustav. The Legacy of Sun Yatsen: A History of the Chinese Revolution. New York: L. Carrier & Co., 1929.

Chen, Stephen, *et al*. Sun Yat-sen: A Portrait. New York: The John Day Co., 1946.

Chiang Kai-shek. Sun ta tsung-t'ung Kuang-chou (Canton) meng-nan chi. Shanghai: Min chih shu-chü, 1927.
蔣介石。孫大總統廣州蒙難記。

Chien Yu-wen. "Sun tsung-li shao-nien shih-ch'i i-shih." *I ching*, 17 (November 5, 1936): 6-9.
簡又文。孫總理少年時期逸事。逸經。

Chin shan shih-pao. San Francisco, November 10, 1956.
金山時報。

Chu Chi-hsien. A Study of the Development of Sun Yat-sen's Philosophical Ideas. 1950.

Chung-kuo kuo-min-tang shih-kao i chih ssu p'ien, comp. by Tsou Lu. Chungking: Shang-wu yin shu kuan, 1944. 4 vols.
中國國民黨史稿一至四篇。鄒魯。

Documents on Communism, Nationalism, and Soviet Advisors in China, 1918-1927: Papers Seized in the 1927 Peking Raid, ed. by C. Martin Wilbur, Julie Lien-ying How. New York: Columbia University Press, 1956.

Feng Tzu-yu. Chung-hua Min-kuo k'ai kuo ch'ien ko-ming shih. Chungking: Chung-kuo wen-hua fu-wu she, 1944. 3 vols.
馮自由。中華民國開國前革命史。

———. Ko-ming i-shih. Chungking, Shanghai: Shang-wu yin shu kuan, 1944-47. 5 vols.
馮自由。革命逸史。

Hou Wai-lu. "Sun Chung-shan te che-hsueh ssu-hsiang chi ch'i t'ung cheng-chih ssu-hsiang te lien-hsi." *Li-shih yen-chiu*, 2 (1957): 1-21.
候外廬。孫中山的哲學思想及其同政治思想的聯繫。歷史研究。

Hsin-hai ko-ming, ed. by Ch'ai Te-keng *et al.* Shanghai: Jen-min ch'u-pan she, 1957. 8 vols. 辛亥革命。柴德賡等。

Hsü Sung-ling. "I-chiu-erh-ssu nien Sun Chung-shan te pei fa yü Kuang-chou (Canton) shang t'uan shih-pien." *Li-shih yen-chiu*, 3 (1956): 59-69. 徐嵩齡。一九二四年孫中山的北伐與廣州商團事變。歷史研究。

Hsueh Chün-tu. Huang Hsing and the Chinese Revolution. Stanford: Stanford University Press, 1961.

Huang Hui-lung. Chung-shan hsien-sheng ch'in cheng lu (ed. by Ch'en T'ieh-sheng). Shanghai: Shang-wu yin shu kuan, 1930. 黃惠龍。中山先生親征錄。陳鐵生。

Isaacs, Harold R. The Tragedy of the Chinese Revolution. Stanford: Stanford University Press, 1961.

Jansen, Marius B. The Japanese and Sun Yat-sen. Cambridge: Harvard University Press, 1954.

Ko-ming wen-hsien, I-X, ed. by Chung-kuo kuo-min-tang chung-yang wei-yuan-hui tang shih shih-liao pien-tsuan wei-yuan-hui. Taipei: Chung-yang wen-wu kung-ying she, 1953. 革命文獻。中國國民黨中央委員會黨史史料編纂委員會。

Ku Ying-fen. Min-kuo erh-shih nien Sun ta-yuan-shuai tung cheng jih-chi. Shanghai: Min chih shu-chü, 1926. 古應芬。民國十二年孫大元帥東征日記。

Kuo-fu hua chuan, ed. by Lo Chia-lun. Taipei: Chung-kuo kuo-min-tang tang shih shih-liao pien-tsuan wei-yuan-hui, 1954. 國父畫傳。羅家倫。
Eng. tr., *The Pictorial Biography of Dr. Sun Yat-sen.* Taipei: Historical Archives Commission of the Kuomintang, 1955.

Kuo-fu nien-piao, ed. by Chung-yang tang shih shih-liao pien-tsuan wei-yuan-hui. Taipei: Chung-yang tang shih shih-liao pien-tsuan wei-yuan-hui, 1952. 國父年表。中央黨史史料編纂委員會。

Kuo-fu nien-p'u, ed. by Chung-kuo kuo-min-tang chung-yang tang shih shih-liao pien-tsuan wei-yuan-hui. Taipei: Chung-hua Min-kuo ko-chieh chi-nien kuo-fu pai nien tan-ch'en ch'ou-pei wei-yuan-hui, 1965. 2 vols. 國父年譜。中國國民黨中央黨史史料編纂委員會。

Kuo-fu Sun hsien-sheng nien-p'u, ed. by Chung-kuo kuo-min-tang chung-yang chih-hsing wei-yuan-hui Yueh Min ch'ü hsuan-ch'uan chuan-yuan pan-shih-ch'u. Canton? Chung-kuo kuo-min-tang chung-yang chih-hsing wei-yuan-hui Yueh Min ch'ü hsuan-ch'uan chuan-yuan pan-shih-ch'u. 國父孫先生年譜。中國國民黨中央執行委員會粵閩區宣傳專員辦事處。

Leng Shao-chuan and Norman D. Palmer. Sun Yat-sen and Communism. New York: Frederick A. Praeger, 1961.

Li Chien-nung. The Political History of China, 1840-1928 (tr. and ed. by Teng Ssu-yu, Jeremy Ingalls). Princeton: D. Van Nostrand Co., 1956.

Li Tse-hou. "Lun Sun Chung-shan te 'min sheng chu-i' ssu-hsiang." *Li-shih yen-chiu*, 11 (1956): 27-50. 李澤厚。論孫中山的「民生主義」思想。歷史研究。

Linebarger, Paul M. The Political Doctrines of Sun Yat-sen. Baltimore: The Johns Hopkins Press, 1937.

——. Sun Yat-sen and the Chinese Republic. New York: The Century Co., 1925.

Liu Ch'eng-yü. "Hsien tsung-li chiu te lu." *Kuo shih kuan kuan k'an*, I-1 (December, 1947): 44-56. 劉成禺。先總理舊德錄。國史館館刊。

Lo Hsiang-lin. Kuo-fu chia-shih yuan-liu k'ao. Chungking: Shang-wu yin shu kuan, 1942. 羅香林。國父家世源流考。

——. Kuo-fu chih ta-hsueh shih-tai. Chungking: Tu-li ch'u-pan she, 1945. 羅香林。國父之大學時代。

——. Kuo-fu yü Ou Mei chih yu-hao. Taipei: Chung-yang wen-wu kung-ying she, 1951. 羅香林。國父與歐美之友好。

Martin, Bernard. Strange Vigour: A Biography of Sun Yat-sen. London: W. Heinemann, 1952.

Peffer, Nathaniel. The Far East: A Modern History. Ann Arbor: The University of Michigan Press, 1958.

Selle, Earl Albert. Donald of China. New York: Harper, 1948.

Shao Yuan-ch'ung. "Tsung-li hu fa shih-lu," in Shao Yuan-ch'ung, *Hsuan p'u i shu.* Taipei: Cheng-chung shu-chü, 1954. 2 vols. 邵元沖。總理護法實錄。邵元沖。玄圃遺書。

Sharman, Lyon. Sun Yat-sen, His Life and Its Meaning: A Critical Biography. New York: The John Day Co., 1934.

Sun Chung-shan hsien-sheng chuan-chi, comp.
by Lu Yu-pai. Shanghai.
孫中山先生傳記。陸友白。

Sun Chung-shan hsien-sheng nien-p'u, comp. by
Chung-kuo kuo-min-tang chung-yang chih-
hsing wei-yuan-hui hsuan-ch'uan pu. Nanking: Chung-kuo kuo-min-tang chung-yang
chih-hsing wei-yuan-hui hsuan-ch'uan pu.
孫中山先生年譜。中國國民黨中央執行委
員會宣傳部。

Sun Yat-sen. San min chu i, the Three Principles of the People (tr. by Frank W. Price; ed.
by L. T. Chen). Shanghai: China Committee,
Institute of Pacific Relations, 1928.

Sun Yat-sen, His Political and Social Ideals,
comp., tr., and annot. by Leonard Shihlien
Hsu. Los Angeles: University of Southern
California Press, 1933.

Sung Yueh-lun. Tsung-li tsai Jih-pen chih ko-
ming huo-tung. Taipei. Chung-yang wen-
wu kung-ying she, 1953.
宋越倫。總理在日本之革命活動。

Tai Ch'uan-hsien (Tai Chi-t'ao). Sun Wen chu-
i chih che-hsueh chi-ch'u. Shanghai: Min
chih shu-chü, 1925.
戴傳賢 (戴季陶)。孫文主義之哲學基礎。

The Triple Demism of Sun Yat-sen, tr. by Pas-
chal M. d'Elia. Wuchang: The Franciscan
Press, 1931.

Tsung-li nien-p'u ch'ang-pien ch'u-kao, comp.
by Chung-yang tang shih shih-liao pien-tsuan
wei-yuan hui, 1932.
總理年譜長編初稿。中央黨史史料編纂委
員會。

Sung Che-yuan   宋哲元

SOURCES

Ch'ang Jen. "Feng Yü-hsiang te chuan-pien."
Hsien-tai shih-liao, III. Shanghai: Hai t'ien
ch'u-pan she, 1934.
昌人。馮玉祥的轉變。現代史料。

Ch'in Te-ch'un. Ch'in Te-ch'un hui-i-lu. Taipei:
Chuan-chi wen-hsueh ch'u-pan she, 1967.
秦德純。秦德純回憶錄。

CMTC

CWR, 1933–37.

CYB-W, 1926; 1927; 1929–30; 1931–32; 1939.

Feng Yü-hsiang. Feng Yü-hsiang jih-chi. Peiping? Min-kuo shih-liao pien-chi she, 1932.
馮玉祥。馮玉祥日記。

Feng Yü-hsiang. Wo-te sheng-huo. Shanghai:
Chiao-yü shu-tien, 1947. 3 vols.
馮玉祥。我的生活。

Hai-wai liu-tung hsuan-ch'uan t'uan. Chung-
kuo k'ang-chan shih.
海外流動宣傳團。中國抗戰史。

Hsü Shu-hsi. The North China Problem. Shanghai: Kelly & Walsh, 1937.

Liu Ju-ming. Liu Ju-ming hui-i-lu. Taipei:
Chuan-chi wen-hsueh tsa-chih she, 1966.
劉汝明。劉汝明回憶錄。

Mao Ho-t'ing. "Sung Che-yuan chuan." Kuo
shih kuan kuan k'an, I-4 (November, 1948): 74–
76.
冒鶴亭。宋哲元傳。國史館館刊。

Sung Che-yuan hsueh-chan sha ti chi, comp. by
I Lu-p'an. Shanghai: Nan kuo yin-shua so,
1933.
宋哲元血戰殺敵記。逸廬潘。

TCJC

Ting Wei-fen. Chui tseng i chi shang-chiang
Sung kung Ming-hsuan shen-tao pei.
丁惟汾。追贈一級上將宋公明軒神道碑。

WWMC

Sung Chiao-jen   宋教仁

WORKS

1920. Wo chih li-shih. T'ao-yuan, Hunan: San
yü i chung nung-hsiao.
我之歷史。

1921. Wen-chi ho k'o. with Tai T'ien-ch'ou.
Shanghai: Shanghai kuo kuang t'u-shu kuan.
文集合刻。戴天仇。

SOURCES

Hsueh Chün-tu. Huang Hsing and the Chinese
Revolution. Stanford: Stanford University
Press, 1961.

Sung Chiao-jen. Wo chih li-shih. T'ao-yuan,
Hunan: San yü i chung nung-hsiao, 1920.
宋教仁。我之歷史。

Sung Yü-fu; ti-i chi, ed. by Hsü Hsueh-erh et al.
Shanghai: Min li pao kuan, 1913.
宋漁父; 第一集。徐血兒等。

Sung Han-chang   宋漢章

SOURCES

Persons interviewed: Chang Chia-ao; others not
to be identified.

Sung Hsi-lien   宋希濂

SOURCES

BKL

Chang Ta-chün. Ssu-shih nien tung-luan Sin-kiang. Hong Kong: Ya-chou ch'u-pan she, 1956.
張達鈞。 四十年動亂新疆。

CMTC

CTMC

CWR

Liang Sheng-chün. Chiang Li tou-cheng nei-mu. Hong Kong: Ya lien ch'u-pan she, 1954.
梁升俊。 蔣李鬥爭內幕。

Romanus, Charles F., and Riley Sunderland. Stilwell's Mission to China. Washington: Office of the Chief of Military History, Department of the Army, 1953.

WWMC

Tai Ai-lien   戴愛蓮

WORKS

1955, November 28. "Jen-min te wu-tao i-shu tsai ch'eng-chang." *Jen-min jih-pao*. Peking.
人民的舞蹈藝術在成長。 人民日報。

1957, April 5. "Yin-tu te p'o-lo-to-wu." *Jen-min jih-pao*. Peking.
印度的婆羅多舞。 人民日報。

SOURCES

Chung-kung jen-ming lu. Taipei: Kuo-chi kuan-hsi yen-chiu-so, 1967.
中共人名錄。

GCJJ

HCJC

Ying Tzu. Chung-kuo hsin hsueh-shu jen-wu chih. Hong Kong: Chih ming shu-chü, 1956.
穎子。 中國新學術人物誌。

Tai Chi-t'ao   戴季陶

WORKS

1921. Tai T'ien-ch'ou wen-chi ho k'an. Shanghai.
戴天仇文集合刊。

1921. Wen-chi ho k'o. with Sung Yü-fu. Shanghai: Shanghai kuo kuang t'u-shu kuan.
文集合刻。 宋漁父。

1925. Chung-kuo tu-li yün-tung te chi-tien. Canton: Min chih shu-chü.
中國獨立運動的基點。

1925. Sun Wen chu-i chih che-hsueh te chi-ch'u. Shanghai: Min chih shu-chü.
孫文主義之哲學的基礎。

1926. Hsieh-tso she te hsiao-yung (with Ch'an-yeh hsieh-tso she fa ts'ao-an chi ch'i li-yu shu). Shanghai: Min chih shu-chü.
協作社的效用 (附: 產業協作社法草案及其理由書)。

1927. Tai Chi-t'ao *et al*. Chien-she sui chin; ti-i pien (ed. by Min chih shu-chü). Shanghai: Min chih shu-chü.
戴季陶等。 建設碎金; 第一編。 民智書局。

1928. Ch'ing-nien chih lu. Shanghai: Min chih shu-chü.
青年之路。

1928. Jih-pen lun. Shanghai: Min chih shu-chü.
日本論。

1929. Kuo-min ko-ming yü Chung-kuo kuo-min-tang. Shanghai: Ta tung shu-chü.
國民革命與中國國民黨。

1929. Tai Chi-t'ao tsui-chin yen-lun chi. Shanghai.
戴季陶最近言論集。

1932. Tai Chi-t'ao *et al*. Hsi-pei.
戴季陶等。 西北。

1941. Kao pi-yeh chi ju-hsueh t'ung-chih shu. Chung-yang cheng-chih hsueh-hsiao.
告畢業及入學同志書。

1948. Hsueh li lu. Shanghai: Cheng-chung shu-chü.
學禮錄。

1959. Tai Chi-t'ao hsieh-sheng wen-ts'un (ed. by Ch'en T'ien-hsi). Taipei: Chung-kuo kuo-ming-tang chung-yang wei-yuan-hui, 1959. 4 vols.
戴季陶先生文存。 陳天錫。

1962. Tai T'ien-ch'ou wen-chi (ed. by Wu Hsiang-hsiang). Taipei: Wen hsing shu-tien.
戴天仇文集。 吳相湘。

1966. Tai Ch'uan-hsien hsien-sheng mo-pao (Tu li cha chi). Taipei: Cheng-chung shu-chü.
戴傳賢先生墨寶 (讀禮札記)。

Ch'ien-pi kai-ko yao-i.
錢幣改革要義。

Min-kuo cheng-chih kang-ling.
民國政治綱領。

SOURCES

Person interviewed: Chang Kuo-t'ao.

BKL

CH

Chang Ch'i-yün *et al.* Chung-hua Min-kuo ta-hsueh chih. Taipei: Chung-hua wen-hua ch'u-pan shih-yeh wei-yuan-hui, 1954. 2 vols. 張其昀等。中華民國大學誌。

Ch'en T'ien-hsi. Tai Chi-t'ao hsien-sheng pien-nien chuan-chi. Taipei: Chung-hua ts'ung-shu wei-yuan-hui, 1958.
陳天錫。戴季陶先生編年傳記。

Chiang Chung-cheng. Huang-p'u chien chün san-shih nien kai-shu. Taipei: Chung-yang wen-wu kung-ying she, 1954.
蔣中正。黃埔建軍三十年概述。

CMTC

CTMC

CYB-W, 1931–32.

Documents on Communism, Nationalism, and Soviet Advisers in China, 1918–1927; Papers Seized in the 1927 Peking Raid, ed. by C. Martin Wilbur, Julie Lien-ying How. New York: Columbia University Press, 1956.

Ko-ming wen-hsien, ed. by Chung-kuo kuo-min-tang chung-yang wei-yuan-hui tang shih shih-liao pien-tsuan wei-yuan-hui. Taipei: Chung-yang wen-wu kung-ying she, 1953–65. 35 vols.
革命文獻。中國國民黨中央委員會黨史史料編纂委員會。

MSICH

Tai Chi-t'ao. Ch'ing-nien chih lu. Shanghai: Min chih shu-chü, 1928.
戴季陶。青年之路。

———. Jih-pen lun. Shanghai: Min chih shu-chü.
戴季陶。日本論。

———. Tai Chi-t'ao hsien-sheng wen-ts'un (ed. by Ch'en T'ien-hsi). Taipei: Chung-kuo kuo-min-tang chung-yang wei-yuan-hui, 1959. 4 vols.
戴季陶。戴季陶先生文存。陳天錫。

———. Tai Chi-t'ao tsui-chin yen-lun chi. Shanghai, 1929.
戴季陶。戴季陶最近言論集。

———. Tai T'ien-ch'ou wen-chi ho k'an. Shanghai, 1921.
戴季陶。戴天仇文集合刊。

Tai Chi-t'ao hsien-sheng shih-shih shih chou nien chi-nien t'e-k'an. Taipei, 1959.
戴季陶先生逝世十週年紀念特刊。

Wu T'ieh-ch'eng. Ssu-shih nien lai chih Chung-kuo yü wo; Wu T'ieh-ch'eng hsieh-sheng hui-i-lu. Taipei, 1957.
吳鐵城。四十年來之中國與我；吳鐵城先生回憶錄。

WWC, 1936.

Tai Li   戴笠

SOURCES

Persons interviewed: not to be identified.

Chiang Kai-shek. China's Destiny and Chinese Economic Theory. New York: Roy Publishers, 1947.

T'ai-hsü   太虛

WORKS

1924? Yen-shuo chi.
演說集。

1926. Fo hsueh kai-lun.
佛學概論。

1926. Lu shan hsueh. Shanghai: T'ai tung shu-chü.
廬山學。

1927. T'ai Hsü fa-shih wen-ch'ao ch'u chi san pien (comp. by Ch'en Hui-ping *et al.*). Shanghai: Chung-hua shu-chü. 3 vols.
太虛法師文鈔初集三編。陳慧秉等。

1928. "Buddhismus in Geschichte und Gregenwart." *Sinica*, III: 189–96.

1929. "Über das Nichtvorhandensein eines Objektiven Geistes." *Sinica*, IV: 206–15.

1930. Fo-chiao ko tsung-p'ai yuan-liu. Hankow: Hsin chi yin shu kuan.
佛教各宗派源流。

1930. T'ai Hsü ta-shih huan-yu chi. Shanghai.
太虛大師寰遊記。

1931. Fo-chiao tui-yü Chung-kuo wen-hua chih ying-hsiang; chiu hsin ssu-ch'ao chih pien-ch'ien yü fo hsueh chih kuan-hsi. Sian? Chung-kuo fo hsueh hui.
佛教對於中國文化之影響；舊新思潮之變遷與佛學之關係。

1932. Che-hsueh. Shanghai: Fo hsueh shu-tien.
哲學。

1933? Fo shuo shih shan yeh tao ching chiang yao. Hankow: Chung hsi yin-shua kung-ssu.
佛說十善業道經講要。

1934. Hsien-shih chu-i. Shanghai: Shang-wu yin shu kuan.
現實主義。

1935. Fo chiao jen ch'eng cheng fa lun. Hankow: Hankow fo-chiao cheng hsin hui.
佛教人乘正法論。

1938. Fa hsiang wei shih hsueh. Changsha: Shang-wu yin shu kuan.
法相唯識學。

1938. "Wo te fo-chiao ko-ming shih-pai shih,"

in T'ao K'ang-te, *Tzu-chuan te i chang*. Shang-hai: Yü-chou feng she.

我的佛教革命失敗史。 陶亢德。 自傳的一章。

1939. Shih hou lung hsiao. Chengtu: Shih-chieh fo hsueh yuan han tsang chiao-li yuan.

獅吼龍嘯。

1945? Fo-chiao yü t'iao-cheng.

佛教與調整。

ed. of *Chueh she chi-k'an*.

覺社季刊。

ed. of *Hai ch'ao yin*.

海潮音。

SOURCES

Callahan, Paul E. "T'ai Hsu and the New Buddhist Movement." *Papers on China*, VI (March, 1952): 149–88. (Duplicated for private distribution by the East Asia Program of the Committee on Regional Studies, Harvard University.)
CBJS
Wilhelm, R. "Der Grossabt Schi Tai Hsu." *Sinica*, IV (1929): 16.

T'an Chen   覃 振

WORKS

Wuhan ch'i-i hui-i-lu.

武漢起義回憶錄。

SOURCES

BKL
Ch'ing tang shih lu. 1928.

清黨實錄。

Chung-kuo kuo-min-tang shih kao i chih ssu p'ien, comp. by Tsou Lu. Chungking: Shang-wu yin shu kuan, 1944. 4 vols.

中國國民黨史稿一至四篇。 鄒魯。

Hsin-hai ko-ming, ed. by Ch'ai Te-keng *et al.* Shanghai: Jen-min ch'u-pan she, 1957. 8 vols.

辛亥革命。 柴德賡等。

T'an Chen. Wuhan ch'i-i hui-i-lu.

覃振。 武漢起義回憶錄。

"T'an Chen shih-lueh," in Chung-kuo kuo-min-tang chung-yang tang shih shih-liao pien-tsuan wei-yuan-hui, *Ko-ming hsien-lieh hsien-chin chuan*. Taipei: Chung-hua Min-kuo ko-chieh chi-nien kuo-fu pai nien tan-ch'en ch'ou-pei wei-yuan-hui, 1965.

覃振事略。 中國國民黨中央黨史史料編纂委員會。 革命先烈先進傳。

T'an Li-ming hsien-sheng shih-lueh.

覃理鳴先生事略。

Tsou Lu. Ch'eng-lu wen-hsuan. Shanghai: Cheng-chung shu-chü, 1948.

鄒魯。 澄廬文選。

Wu Hsiang-hsiang. "Hsi-shan hui-i erh chien-chiang: Hsieh Ch'ih yü T'an Chen." *Chuan-chi wen-hsueh*, VIII-4: 23–26.

吳相湘。 西山會議二健將： 謝持與覃振。 傳記文學。

T'an Chen-lin   譚 震 林

SOURCES

Person interviewed: Chang Kuo-t'ao.
CPR, 842 (March 3, 1949).
Kung-jen jih-pao. Peking, August 31, 1960.

工人日報。

K-WWMC
SCMP, 2362 (October 21, 1960).
WWC, 1950.
WWMC

T'an Cheng   譚 政

SOURCES

Person interviewed: Chang Kuo-t'ao.
CKJMT
WWC, 1950.

T'an Hsin-p'ei   譚 鑫 培

SOURCES

Chou I-pai. Chung-kuo hsi-chü shih. Shanghai: Chung-hua shu-chü, 1953. 3 vols.

周貽白。 中國戲劇史。

Huang Yün-sheng. "Hsiao-chiao-t'ien hsiao chuan." *Ta kung pao*. Tientsin, February 7–9, 1935.

黃運生。 小叫天小傳。 大公報。

Liu Shou-ho. "T'an Hsin-p'ei chuan chi." *Chü hsueh yueh-k'an*, I-11, 12 (November, December, 1932).

劉守鶴。 譚鑫培專記。 劇學月刊。

Mei Lan-fang. Wu-t'ai sheng-huo ssu-shih nien. Shanghai: P'ing ming ch'u-pan she, 1952–54. 2 vols.

梅蘭芳。 舞台生活四十年。

Meng Yao. Chung-kuo hsi ch'ü shih. Taipei: Wen hsing shu-tien, 1965. 4 vols.

孟瑤。 中國戲曲史。

Pi ko mo wu chai chu (pseud.). "Ching-chün sheng tan liang ko-ming chia." *Chü hsueh yueh-k'an*, III-7 (July, 1934).
筆歌墨舞齋主。京劇生旦兩革命家。劇學月刊。

T'an Hsin-p'ei ch'ang ch'iang chi, comp. by Chung-kuo hsi ch'ü yen chiu yuan. Peking: Yin-yueh ch'u-pan she, 1959.
譚鑫培唱腔集。中國戲曲研究院。

T'an P'ing-shan   譚平山

WORKS

1919-? ed. of *Hsin ch'ao*.
新潮。
1927. Entwicklungswege der Chinesischen Revolution. Hamburg: Carl Hoym Nachfolger.

SOURCES

Person interviewed: Chang Kuo-t'ao.
CBJS
Ch'en Kung-po. Han feng chi. Shanghai: Ti-fang hsing-cheng she, 1944.
陳公博。寒風集。
Chiang Kai-shek. Soviet Russia in China; A Summing-up at Seventy. New York: Farrar, Straus & Cudahy, 1957.
GCCJK
GCJ
GCJJ
GCMMTJK
GSJK
GSSJ
HCJC
Hsin cheng-hsieh jen-wu chih, comp. by Chou-mo pao pien-chi wei-yuan-hui. Hong Kong: Min sheng yin wu chü, 1949. 2 vols.
新政協人物誌。週末報編輯委員會。
HSWT
Isaacs, Harold R. The Tragedy of the Chinese Revolution. Stanford: Stanford University Press, 1961.
Jen-min jih-pao. Peking, April 3, 5, 1956.
人民日報。
JMST, 1955.
RSOC
Schwartz, Benjamin I. Chinese Communism and the Rise of Mao. Cambridge: Harvard University Press, 1951.
Tung-fang tsa-chih, XXIV-8 (February 16, 1927): 107.
東方雜誌。

T'an Yen-k'ai   譚延闓

WORKS

1930. T'an Yen-k'ai ta-k'ai k'u-shu fu. Shanghai: Chung-hua shu-chü.
譚延闓大楷枯樹賦。
(ed.) Sun Chung-shan hsien-sheng shou-cha mo-chi.
孫中山先生手札墨跡。
BPC
CMTC
Feng Tzu-yu. Ko-ming i-shih. Chungking, Shanghai: Shang-wu yin shu kuan, 1944-47. 5 vols.
馮自由。革命逸史。
Hsiao Pai-fan. Chung-kuo chin pai nien ko-ming shih. Hong Kong: Ch'iu shih ch'u-pan she, 1951.
蕭白帆。中國近百年革命史。
Hsin-hai ko-ming, ed. by Ch'ai Te-keng *et al*. Shanghai: Shanghai jen-min ch'u-pan she, 1957. 8 vols.
辛亥革命。柴德賡等。
Li Chien-nung. The Political History of China, 1840-1928 (tr. and ed. by Teng Ssu-yu, Jeremy Ingalls). Princeton: D. Van Nostrand Co., 1956.
T'an Tsu-an hsien-sheng nien-p'u ch'u-pien, comp. by Hsü Chien-shih *et al*. Taipei. Chung-kuo chiao-t'ung chien-she hsueh-hui, 1964.
譚祖安先生年譜初編。徐健實等。
T'ang Leang-li. The Inner History of the Chinese Revolution. New York: E.P. Dutton & Co., 1930.
WWC, 1931.

T'ang Chi-yao   唐繼堯

SOURCES

BPC
Chün wu yuan k'ao shih, comp. by Liang Kuang tu ssu-ling-pu ts'an-mou t'ing. Shanghai: Shang-wu yin shu kuan, 1916.
軍務院考實。兩廣都司令部參謀廳。
CMTC
Li Chien-nung. Chung-kuo chin pai nien cheng-chih shih. Shanghai: Shang-wu yin shu kuan, 1947.
李劍農。中國近百年政治史。
T'ang Chi-yao, comp. by Tung nan pien i she. Taipei: Wen hai ch'u-pan she, 1967.
唐繼堯。東南編譯社。

Yü En-yang. Chung-hua hu kuo san chieh chuan. Yunnan t'u-shu kuan, 1917.
庾恩暘。 中華護國三傑傳。

———. Yunnan shou i yung-hu kung-ho shih mo chi. Yunnan t'u-shu-kuan, 1917.
庾恩暘。 雲南首義擁護共和始末記。

T'ang En-po　　湯恩伯

WORKS

Pu-ping chung-tui (lien) chiao-lien chih yen-chiu.
步兵中隊 (連) 教練之研究。

SOURCES

Chung-kuo k'ang chan hua shih, ed, by Ts'ao Chü-jen, Shu Tsung-ch'iao. Shanghai: Shanghai lien-ho hua-pao she, 1947.
中國抗戰畫史。 曹聚仁, 舒宗僑。

Ho Ying-ch'in. Pa nien k'ang chan chih ching-kuo. Nanking: Chung-kuo lu-chün tsung-ssu-king pu, 1946.
何應欽。 八年抗戰之經過。

Kou Chi-t'ang. Chung-kuo lu-chün ti-san fang-mien chün k'ang chan chi-shih (ed. by Wu Hsiang-hsiang). Taipei: Wen hsing shu-tien, 1962.
茍吉堂。 中國陸軍第三方面軍抗戰紀實。 吳相湘。

Kuo-min ko-ming chün chan shih, ed. by Kuo-min ko-ming chün chan shih pien-tsuan wei-yuan-hui. Ts'an-mou pen-pu, 1934. 17 vols.
國民革命軍戰史。 國民革命軍戰史編纂委員會。

Nan-k'ou hsueh-chan chi. Hankow, 1938.
南口血戰記。

T'ang Erh-ho　　湯爾和

SOURCES

Chow Tse-tsung. The May Fourth Movement: Intellectual Revolution in Modern China. Cambridge: Harvard University Press, 1960.

Chung-kuo k'ang chan hua shih, ed. by Ts'ao Chü-jen, Shu Tsung-ch'iao. Shanghai: Shanghai lien-ho hua-pao she 1947.
中國抗戰畫史。 曹聚仁, 舒宗僑。

Hua-pei kuan-liao ch'ün-hsiang. I pao t'u-shu pu.
華北官僚群像。

Kuo-fu nien-p'u; ch'u-kao, ed. by Kuo shih kuan shih-liao pien-tsuan wei-yuan-hui, Chung-kuo kuo-min-tang tang shih shih-liao pien-tsuan wei-yuan-hui. Taipei: Kuo shih kuan shih-liao pien-tsuan wei-yuan-hui, Chung-kuo kuo-min-tang tang shih shih-liao pien-tsuan wei-yuan-hui, 1959. 2 vols.
國父年譜; 初稿。 國史館史料編纂委員會, 中國國民黨黨史史料編纂委員會。

Li Ch'ao-ying. Wei tsu-chih cheng-chih ching-chi kai-k'uang. Chungking: Shang-wu yin shu kuan, 1943.
李超英。 僞組織政治經濟概況。

Ling Hung-hsun. Chung-kuo t'ieh-lu chih. Taipei: Ch'ang liu pan-yueh-k'an she, 1954.
凌鴻勛。 中國鐵路志。

Ma Hsü-lun. Wo tsai liu-shih sui i-ch'ien. Shanghai: Sheng-huo shu-tien, 1947.
馬敍倫。 我在六十歲以前。

Taylor, George E. The Struggle for North China. New York: International Secretariat, Institute of Pacific Relations, 1940.

T'ang Hua-lung　　湯化龍

SOURCES

Chang Nan-hsien. Hupeh ko-ming chih chih lu. Chungking, 1945.
張難先。 湖北革命知之錄。

Ch'en Kung-lu. Chung-kuo chin-tai shih. Shanghai: Shang-wu yin shu kuan.
陳恭祿。 中國近代史。

Ch'i-shui T'ang hsien-sheng i nien lu. T'ang Hua-lung chih-ts'an ch'u, 1919.
蘄水湯先生遺念錄。

Chü Cheng. Mei-ch'uan jih-chi. Shanghai: Ta tung shu-chü, 1947.
居正。 梅川日記。

Hsin-hai ko-ming, ed. by Ch'ai Te-keng *et al*. Shanghai: Jen-min ch'u-pan she, 1957. 8 vols.
辛亥革命。 柴德賡等。

Liang Jen-kung hsien-sheng nien-p'u ch'ang pien ch'u-kao, comp. by Ting Wen-chiang. Taipei: Shih-chieh shu-chü, 1959. 2 vols.
梁任公先生年譜長編初稿。 丁文江。

T'ao Chü-yin. Liu chün-tzu chuan. Shanghai: Chung-hua shu-chü, 1946.
陶菊隱。 六君子傳。

———. Pei-yang chün-fa t'ung-chih shih-ch'i shih-hua. Peking: Sheng-huo, tu-shu, hsin chih san lien shu-tien, 1957–58. 6 vols.
陶菊隱。 北洋軍閥統治時期史話。

Wu T'ieh-ch'eng. Ssu-shih nien lai chih Chung-kuo yü wo; Wu T'ieh-ch'eng hsien-sheng hui-i-lu. Taipei, 1957.
吳鐵城。四十年來之中國與我；吳鐵城先生回憶錄。
Yang Yu-chiung. Chin-tai Chung-kuo li-fa shih. Shanghai: Shang-wu yin shu kuan, 1936.
楊幼烱。近代中國立法史。

T'ang Shao-yi   唐紹儀

WORKS

1917. "Introduction," in Taraknath Das, *Is Japan a Menace to China?* Shanghai.
1925, October 31. "Unity First." CWR.

SOURCES

"Alleged Tang Shao-yi Would Form Rightist Government." CWR, January 22, 1938.
Bland, J. O. P. Li Hung-chang. New York: Holt, 1917.
Chang Ch'i-yün. Tang shih kai-yao. Taipei: Chung-yang wen-wu kung-ying she, 1951–52. 5 vols.
張其昀。黨史概要。
Chia I-chün. Chung-hua Min-kuo shih. Shanghai: Wen-hua hsueh-she, 1930.
賈逸君。中華民國史。
Ch'ien Tuan-sheng. The Government and Politics of China. Cambridge: Harvard University Press, 1950.
China Mission Year Book, 1911, 1912, 1919.
CYB, 1935–36.
CYB-W, 1913, 1924, 1925, 1929–30, 1931–32, 1933, 1936, 1939.
Hsia Ching-kuan. "T'ang Shao-i chuan." *Kuo shih kuan kuan k'an*, I-2 (March, 1948): 79–80.
夏敬觀。唐紹儀傳。國史館館刊。
Kuo wen chou-pao, I-2; II-41; XIII-40, 42, 44.
國聞周報。
Levi, Werner. Modern China's Foreign Policy. Minneapolis: University of Minnesota Press, 1953.
Li Chien-nung. The Political History of China 1840–1928 (tr. and ed. by Teng Ssu-yu, Jeremy Ingalls). Princeton: D. Van Nostrand Co., 1956.
North China Daily News, November 4, December 23, 1911.
T'ang Leang-li. The Inner History of the Chinese Revolution. New York: E. P. Dutton & Co., 1930.

"Tang Shao-yi's Name Again Linked with Puppet Nanking Regime." CWR, March 5, 1938.
T'ao Chü-yin. Liu chün-tzu chuan. Shanghai: Chung-hua shu-chü, 1946.
陶菊隱。六君子傳。
Vevier, Charles. The United States and China, 1906–1913. New Brunswick: Rutgers University Press, 1955.
Wai-chiao ta tz'u-tien, comp. by Wai-chiao hsueh-hui. Kunming: Chung-hua shu-chü, 1937.
外交大辭典。外交學會。
Who's Who in the Orient. Tokyo, 1915.
WWARS
WWMC

T'ang Sheng-chih   唐生智

SOURCES

Ho Chien chuan.
何鍵傳。
Huang Shao-hung. Wu-shih hui-i. Hangchow: Feng-yün ch'u-pan she, 1945. 2 vols.
黃紹竑。五十回憶。
Liang Jen-kung hsien-sheng nien-p'u ch'ang pien ch'u-kao, ed. by Ting Wen-chiang. Taipei: Shih-chieh shu-chü, 1958. 2 vols.
梁任公先生年譜長編初稿。丁文江。
T'ao Chü-yin. Chiang Pai-li chuan.
陶菊隱。蔣百里傳。
———. Pei-yang chün-fa t'ung-chih shih-ch'i shih-hua. Peking: Sheng-huo, tu-shu, hsin-chih san lien shu-tien, 1957–58. 6 vols.
陶菊隱。北洋軍閥統治時期史話。
———. Wu P'ei-fu chiang-chün chuan. Shanghai: Chung-hua shu-chü, 1941.
陶菊隱。吳佩孚將軍傳。

T'ang Yung-t'ung   湯用彤

WORKS

1922, December. "P'ing chin-jen chih wen-hua yen-chiu." *Hsueh heng*, 12: 1–4.
評近人之文化研究。學衡。
1923, May-July. "Ya-li-shih-to-te che-hsueh ta-kang." *Hsueh heng*, 17: 1–26; 19: 1–15. (tr.)
亞里士多德哲學大綱。學衡。
1924, February. "Fo-chiao shang-tso-pu chiu-hsin-lun lueh-shih." *Hsueh heng*, 20: 1–13:
佛教上座部九心輪略釋。學衡。

1930, September. "Tu hui-chiao kao-seng chuan cha-chi." *Shih-hsueh tsa-chih*, II-3, 4.
讀慧皎高僧傳札記。史學雜誌。

1931. "T'ang T'ai-tsung yü fo-chiao." *Hsueh heng*, 75.
唐太宗與佛教。學衡。

1932, March. "Chu Tao-sheng yü nieh-p'an hsueh." *Kuo-hsueh chi-k'an*, III-1: 1-66.
竺道生與涅槃學。國學季刊。

1933. "Wei Chin ssu-hsiang te liu-pien," in *Kuo-li Peking ta-hsueh yen-chiu yuan wen-k'o yen-chiu so chiang-yen chi, ti-i chi*. (mimeo.).
魏晉思想的流變。國立北京大學研究院文科研究所講演集, 第一集。

1935. "Shih fa yao." *Kuo-hsueh chi-k'an*, V-4: 109-18.
釋法瑤。國學季刊。

1936. "Han Wei fo-hsueh te liang ta hsi-t'ung." *Che-hsueh p'ing-lun*, VII-1.
漢魏佛學的兩大系統。哲學評論。

1936. "She-shan chih san-lun-tsung shih-lueh-k'ao." *Shih-hsueh tsa-chih*.
攝山之三論宗釋略考。史學雜誌。

1937. Chung-kuo fo-chiao shih ling p'ien. Pei-ping: Yen-ching ha-fo hsueh-she.
中國佛教史零篇。

1939. "Yen i chih pien." (mimeo.).
言義之辨。

1943. "Wang Pi chih chou-i lun-yü hsin i." *T'u-shu chi-k'an*, new series, IV-1, 2.
王弼之周易論語新義。圖書季刊。

1945. Yin-tu che-hsueh shih lun. Chungking? Tu-li ch'u-pan she.
印度哲學史論。

1951. "On 'Ko-yi', the Earliest Method by Which Indian Buddhism and Chinese Buddhism Were Synthesised." *Radhakrishnan*: 276-86 (tr. by M. C. Rogers.)

1953, June. "Various Traditions Concerning the Entry of Buddhism into China." *Phi Theta Annual Papers of the Oriental Language Honor Society of the University of California*, IV: 31-93. (tr. by A. E. Link.)

1955. Han Wei liang Chin Nan-pei-ch'ao fo-chiao shih. Peking: Chung-hua shu-chü. 2 vols.
漢魏兩晉南北朝佛教史。

1956. T'ang Yung-t'ung *et al*. Liang Shu-ming ssu-hsiang p'i-p'an; ti-erh chi. Peking: Sheng-huo, tu-shu, hsin chih san lien shu-tien.
湯用彤等。梁漱溟思想批判; 第二輯。

1957. Wei Chin hsuan-hsueh lun kao. Peking: Jen-min ch'u-pan she.
魏晉玄學論稿。

1961, October. "K'ou Ch'ien-chih te chu-tso yü ssu-hsiang." with T'ang I-chieh. *Li-shih yen-chiu*, 5: 64-77.
寇謙之的著作與思想。湯一介。歷史研究。

1962. Wang jih tsa kao. Peking: Chung-hua shu-chü.
往日雜稿。

"Ch'uan nien an-pan ching." *Nei hsueh*.
傅念安般經。內學。

"Nan-k'ang nien an-pan-ching." *Nei hsueh*.
南康念安般經。內學。

"Wei Chin ssu-hsiang te fa-chan." *Hsueh yuan*, I-3.
魏晉思想的發展。學原。

SOURCES

Persons interviewed: not to be identified.

T'ao Hsi-sheng 陶希聖

WORKS

1926. Chung-kuo ssu-fa chih-tu. Shanghai: Shang-wu yin shu kuan.
中國司法制度。

1926. Tui Hua men-hu k'ai-fang chu-i. Shanghai: Shang-wu yin shu kuan.
對華門戶開放主義。

1929. Kuo-chia lun. (tr. of Franz Oppenheimer's *The State, Its History and Development Viewed Sociologically*). Shanghai: Hsin sheng-ming shu-chü.
國家論。

1930. Chung-kuo wen-t'i chih hui-ku yü chan-wang. Shanghai: Hsin sheng-ming shu-chü.
中國問題之回顧與展望。

1931. Chung-kuo she-hui chih shih te fen-hsi. Shanghai: Hsin sheng-ming shu-chü.
中國社會之史的分析。

1931. Chung-kuo she-hui yü Chung-kuo ko-ming. Shanghai: Hsin sheng-ming shu-chü.
中國社會與中國革命。

1931. Hsi-han ching-chi shih. Shanghai: Shang-wu yin shu kuan.
西漢經濟史。

1932. Chung-kuo she-hui hsien-hsiang shih-ling. Shanghai: Hsin sheng-ming shu-chü.
中國社會現象拾零。

1932-33. Chung-kuo cheng-chih ssu-hsiang shih. Shanghai: Hsin sheng-ming shu-chü. 3 vols.
中國政治思想史。

1933. Pien-shih yü yu-hsia. Shanghai: Shang-wu yin shu kuan.

1934. Hun-yin yü chia-tsu. Shanghai: Shang-wu yin shu kuan.
婚姻與家族。

1936. Ch'in Han cheng-chih chih-tu. Shanghai: Shang-wu yin shu kuan.
秦漢政治制度。

1936. Min-fa ch'in-shu. Shanghai: Shang-wu yin shu kuan.
民法親屬。

1937. Nan-pei-ch'ao ching-chi shih. with Wu Hsien-ch'ing. Shanghai: Shang-wu yin shu kuan.
南北朝經濟史。武仙卿。

1940, February 4. "Hsin chung-yang cheng-ch'üan shih shen-mo." Ta kung pao. Hong Kong.
新中央政權是什麼。大公報。

1943. Lun tao chi. Chungking: Nan-fang yin shu kuan. 2 vols.
論道集。

1944. Chung-kuo she-hui shih. Chungking: wen-feng shu-chü.
中國社會史。

1955. Ching-chueh chi. Taipei: Ch'üan-min ch'u-pan she.
警覺集。

1955. Chung-kuo min-tsu chan shih. with Shen Jen-yuan. Taipei: Chung-yang wen-wu kung-ying she.
中國民族戰史。沈任遠。

1955. Hui lei chi. Taipei: Ch'üan min ch'u-pan she.
揮淚集。

1955. Liang tao chi. Taipei: Ch'üan-min ch'u-pan she.
兩刀集。

1955. Shih chü chuan-pien chung chih tzu-yu Chung-kuo. Taipei: Ch'üan min ch'u-pan she.
世局轉變中之自由中國。

1956. Cheng-i chi—min-kuo ssu-shih-ssu nien shih-shih lun-ts'ung. Taipei: Ch'üan-min ch'u-pan she.
正義集一民國四十四年時事論叢。

1958. Fei O yin-mou ts'e-lueh chih p'o-hsi. Taipei: Yang-ming-shan chuang.
匪俄陰謀策略之剖析。

1961-62. "Hsia ch'ung yü ping lu." Fa-ling yueh k'an.
夏蟲語冰錄。法令月刊。

1962, June. "Pei-ta fa-lü hsi te hsueh-sheng." Chuan-chi wen-hsueh, I-1: 9–11.
北大法律系的學生。傳記文學。

1962, July. "Chiang feng t'a ying." Chuan-chi wen-hsueh, I-2: 8–11.
江風塔影。傳記文學。

1964. Ch'ao-liu yü tien-ti. Taipei: Chuan-chi wen-hsueh tsa-chih she.
潮流與點滴。

"Chieh-fa Jih Wang mi yueh te mu-hou." Tzu-yu t'an, XIII-1.
揭發日汪密約的幕後。自由談。

"Huai-nien Shih-chih hsien-sheng." Tzu-yu t'an, XIII-4,
懷念適之先生。自由談。

"Kuan-yü Chung-kuo chih ming-yün." Tzu-yu t'an, XIII-6.
關於中國之命運。自由談。

"San tai yu-i." Tzu-yu t'an, XIII-7.
三代友誼。自由談。

ed. of Shih huo.
食貨。

"Ts'ung wu-ssu tao liu-san." Tzu-yu t'an, XIII-5.
從五四到六三。自由談。

ed. of Tu-li p'ing-lun.
獨立評論。

SOURCES

Ch'en Pu-lei. Ch'en Pu-lei hui-i lu. Shanghai: Erh-shih shih-chi ch'u-pan she, 1949.
陳布雷。陳布雷回憶錄。

Chou Fo-hai. Chou Fo-hai jih-chi. Hong Kong: Ch'uang k'en ch'u-pan she, 1955.
周佛海。周佛海日記。

Chu Tzu-chia (pseud. of Chin Hsiung-pai). Wang cheng-ch'üan te k'ai-ch'ang yü shou-ch'ang. Hong Kong: Ch'un-ch'iu tsa-chih she, 1964.
朱子家（金雄白）。汪政權的開場與收場。

Free China Weekly, NN-LXIII-20 (May 14, 1963); NN-LXIII-28 (July 9, 1963).

The New York Times, April 19, 1966.

Ta kung pao. Hong Kong, January 22, 23, 24, 1940.
大公報。

T'ao Ch'in-hsun. "Wo chia t'o-hsien te ch'ien-hou." Kuo-min jih-pao. Hong Kong, January 1, 1940.
陶琴薰。我家脫險的前後。國民日報。

T'ao Hsi-sheng. Ch'ao-liu yü tien-ti. Taipei: Chuan-chi wen-hsueh tsa-chih she, 1964.
陶希聖。潮流與點滴。

———. "Chiang feng t'a ying." Chuan-chi wen-hsueh, I-2 (July, 1962): 8–11.
陶希聖。江風塔影。傳記文學。

———. "Chieh-fa Jih Wang mi yueh te mu-hou." Tzu-yu t'an, XIII-1.
陶希聖。揭發日汪密約的幕後。自由談。

T'ao Hsi-sheng. Chung-kuo cheng-chih ssu-hsiang shih. Shanghai: Hsin sheng-ming shu-chü, 1932–33. 3 vols.
陶希聖。中國政治思想史。

———. Chung-kuo she-hui yü Chung-kuo ko-ming. Shanghai: Hsin sheng-ming shu-chü, 1931.
陶希聖。中國社會與中國革命。

———. Chung-kuo wen-t'i chih hui-ku yü chan-wang. Shanghai: Hsin sheng-ming shu-chü, 1930.
陶希聖。中國問題之回顧與展望。

———. Hsi-han ching-chi shih. Shanghai: Shang-wu yin shu kuan, 1931.
陶希聖。西漢經濟史。

———. "Hsia ch'ung yü ping lu." Fa-ling yueh-k'an, 1961–62.
陶希聖。夏蟲語冰錄。法令月刊。

———. "Huai-nien Shih-chih hsien-sheng." Tzu-yu t'an, XIII-4.
陶希聖。懷念適之先生。自由談。

———. "Kuan-yü Chung-kuo chih ming-yun." Tzu-yu t'an, XIII-6.
陶希聖。關於中國之命運。自由談。

———. "Pei-ta fa-lü hsi te hsueh-sheng." Chuan-chi wen-hsueh, I-1 (June, 1962): 9–11.
陶希聖。北大法律系的學生。傳記文學。

———. Pien-shih yü yu-hsia. Shanghai: Shang-wu yin shu kuan, 1933.
陶希聖。辯士與游俠。

———. "San tai yu-i." Tzu-yu t'an, XIII-7.
陶希聖。三代友誼。自由談。

———. "Ts'ung wu-ssu tao liu-san." Tzu-yu t'an, XIII-5.
陶希聖。從五四到六三。自由談。

Wang Ching-wei et al. Ho-p'ing fan-kung chien-kuo wen-hsien.
汪精衞等。和平反共建國文献。

T'ao Hsing-chih　陶行知

WORKS

1922. (ed.) Meng-lu te Chung-kuo chiao-yü t'ao-lun. Shanghai: Chung-hua shu-chü.
孟祿的中國教育討論。

1928. Chung-kuo chiao-yü kai-tsao. Ya tung.
中國教育改造。

1929. Chih-hsing shu-hsin. Shanghai: Ya tung.
知行書信。

1944. Yü-ts'ai hsueh-hsiao shou-ts'e. Chung-king: Shih-tai yin-shua ch'u-pan she.
育才學校手冊。

1947. Hsing-chih shih-ko chi. Shanghai: Ta fu ch'u-pan kung-ssu.
行知詩歌集。

1947. T'ao Hsing-chih chiao-yü lun-wen hsuan-chi (ed. by Fang Yü-yen). Chungking: Min lien shu-chü.
陶行知教育論文選集。方與嚴。

1950. Hsing-chih ko-ch'ü chi. Peking: Sheng-kuo, tu-shu, hsin-chih san lien shu-tien.
行知歌曲集。

1950. Wei chih-shih chieh-chi. Peking: Hsin Peking ch'u-pan she.
僞知識階級。

Chai-fu tzu-yu t'an.
齋夫自由談。

ed. of Hsin chiao-yü.
新教育。

Ku miao ku chung lu.
古廟鼓鐘錄。

SOURCES

Fairbank, John K. The United States and China. Cambridge: Harvard University Press, 1955.

Fang Yü-yen. Ta-chung chiao-yü chia yü ta-chung shih-jen. Shanghai, 1949.
方與嚴。大衆教育家與大衆詩人。

Ho Kung-ch'ao. Lu Hsun ho T'ao Hsing-chih te i-shih. Shanghai: Shanghai kuang-mang ch'u-pan she, 1950.
何公超。魯迅和陶行知的軼事。

Hsin hua jih-pao, July 25, 1946.
新華日報。

Mai Ch'ing. T'ao Hsing-chih. Hong Kong: Hong Kong hsin Chung-kuo shu-chü, 1949.
麥青。陶行知。

P'an K'ai-p'ei. T'ao Hsing-chih chiao-yü ssu-hsiang te p'i-p'an. Peking: Peking ta-chung shu-tien, 1952.
潘開沛。陶行知教育思想的批判。

Pai T'ao. T'ao Hsing-chih te sheng-p'ing chi ch'i hsueh-shuo. Peking: San lien shu-tien, 1950.
白韜。陶行知的生平及其學說。

T'ao Hsing-chih. Hsing-chih shih-ko chi. Shanghai: Ta fu ch'u-pan kung-ssu, 1947.
陶行知。行知詩歌集。

T'ao Hsing-chih hsien-sheng chi-nien chi, ed. by T'ao Hsing-chih hsien-sheng chi-nien wei-yuan-hui. Shanghai: T'ao Hsing-chih hsien-sheng chi-nien wei-yuan hui, 1947.
陶行知先生紀念集。陶行知先生紀念委員會。

T'ao Hsing-chih hsien-sheng ssu chou-nien chi. Peking, 1950.
陶行知先生四週年祭。

Teng Chung-hsia   鄧中夏

WORKS

1953. Chung-kuo chih-kung yün-tung chien-shih (1919–1926). Peking: Jen-min ch'u-pan she.
中國職工運動簡史。

SOURCES

CKLC
HKLC
HSWT
Nan-fang jih-pao. July 1, 1951.
南方日報。
Teng Chung-hsia. Chung-kuo chih-kung yün-tung chien-shih (1919–1926). Peking: Jen-min ch'u-pan she, 1953.
鄧中夏。中國職工運動簡史 (1919–1926)。
Tso Shun-sheng. Chin san-shih nien chien-wen tsa-chi. Kowloon: Tzu-yu ch'u-pan she, 1952.
左舜生。近三十年見聞雜記。

Teng Fa   鄧發

WORKS

1931. Chia-ch'iang yü ti-jen chen-t'an tou-cheng.
加强與敵人偵探鬥爭。

SOURCES

Person interviewed: Chang Kuo-t'ao.
CKLC
GCCJK
Nan-fang jih-pao. July 1, 1951.
南方日報。
RSOC
"Ssu-pa" pei-nan lieh-shih chi-nien ts'e, ed. by Chung-kuo kung-ch'an-tang tai-piao t'uan. Chung-kuo kung-ch'an-tang tai-piao t'uan, 1946.
「四八」被難烈士紀念冊。中國共產黨代表團。

Teng Hsi-hou   鄧錫候

SOURCES

BKL
BPC

Chung-kuo k'ang chan shih, comp. by Hai-wai liu-tung hsuan-ch'uan t'uan. Canton: Hai-wai liu-tung hsuan-ch'uan t'uan chu Yueh tsung pan-shih ch'u, 1947.
中國抗戰史。海外流動宣傳團。
CMTC
CTMC
GCJJ
Huang Shao-hung. Wu-shih hui-i. Hankow: Feng-yün ch'u-pan she, 1945.
黃紹竑。五十回憶。
Jen-min jih-pao. Peking, April 1, 1964.
人民日報。
TCJC
WWC, 1931.
WWMC

Teng Hsiao-p'ing   鄧小平

WORKS

1947. Teng cheng wei chieh-ta shih-chü yü jen-wu chung chi-ko wen-t'i te pao-kao. Chin Chi Yü chün-ch'ü cheng-chih pu.
鄧政委解答時局與任務中幾個問題的報告。
1948. Teng cheng wei tsai san ti wei hui shang te pao-kao. Chung-kung Hsin-hsien hsien wei hui.
鄧政委在三地委會上的報告。
1951, July. "To Maintain Close Ties with the Masses Is Our Party's Glorious Tradition." *People's China,* IV-1: 32–35.
1956. Chung-kuo kung-ch'an-tang chang-ch'eng—kuan-yü hsiu-kai tang te chang-ch'eng te pao-kao. Peking: Jen-min ch'u-pan she.
中國共產黨章程一關於修改黨的章程的報告。
1956. Chung-kuo kung-ch'an-tang ti-pa tz'u ch'üan-kuo tai-piao ta-hui t'ung-kuo Chung-kuo kung-ch'an-tang chang-ch'eng (with Kuan-yü hsiu-kai tang te chang-ch'eng te pao-kao). Peking: Jen-min ch'u-pan she.
中國共產黨第八次全國代表大會通過中國共產黨章程（附：關於修改黨的章程的報告）。
1959. Chung-kuo jen-min ta t'uan-chieh ho shih-chieh jen-min ta t'uan-chieh—ch'ing-chu Chung-hua Jen-min Kung-ho-kuo ch'eng-li shih chou-nien. Peking: Jen-min ch'u-pan she.
中國人民大團結和世界人民大團結一慶祝中華人民共和國成立十週年。
ed. of *Hung hsing.*
紅星。

SOURCES

Carlson, Evans Fordyce. Twin Stars of China. New York: Dodd, Mead & Co., 1940.

CB, 170 (April 8, 1952).

Croft, Michael. Red Carpet to China. New York: St. Martin's Press, 1959.

Hung ch'i p'iao-p'iao. Shanghai: Wen-hua, 1958. 紅旗飄飄。

Jen-min hua-pao, 1 (1961). 人民畫報。

Kan Yu-lan. Mao Tse-tung chi ch'i chi-t'uan. Hong Kong: Tzu-yu ch'u-pan she, 1954. 甘友蘭。毛澤東及其集團。

Kung Ch'u. Wo yü hung chün. Hong Kong: Nan feng ch'u-pan she, 1955. 龔楚。我與紅軍。

Lewis, John Wilson. Chinese Communist Party Leadership and the Succession to Mao Tse-tung: An Appraisal of Tensions. Washington, Bureau of Intelligence and Research, U. S. Department of State, 1964.

The New York Times, July 21, 1965.

People's China, April 1, 1953.

RNRC

Selections from China Mainland Magazines, 285 (October 30, 1961).

Teng Hsiao-p'ing. Report on the Rectification Campaign; Delivered at the Third Plenary Session (Enlarged) of the Eighth Central Committee of the Communist Party of China, on September 23, 1957. Peking: Foreign Languages Press, 1957.

"Thrust into the Tapieh Mountains," in *The Great Turning Point*. Peking: Foreign Languages Press, 1962.

Zagoria, Donald S. The Sino-Soviet Conflict, 1956–1961. Princeton: Princeton University Press, 1962.

Teng K'eng   鄧鏗

SOURCES

Persons interviewed: not to be identified.

Kuo shih kuan kuan k'an, II-1 (January, 1948). 國史館館刊。

Teng Tse-ju   鄧澤如

WORKS

1948. Chung-kuo kuo-min-tang erh-shih nien shih-chi. Shanghai: Cheng-chung shu-chü.

中國國民黨二十年史蹟。

SOURCES

Kuo-fu nien-p'u, ed. by Chung-kuo kuo-min-tang chung-yang tang shih shih-liao pien-tsuan wei-yuan-hui. Taipei: Chung-hua Min-kuo ko-chieh chi-nien kuo-fu pai nien tan-ch'en ch'ou-pei wei-yuan-hui, 1965. 2 vols. 國父年譜。中國國民黨中央黨史史料編纂委員會。

Min pao; ho-ting-pen, comp. by Chung-kuo k'o-hsueh-yuan li-shih yen-chiu so ti-san so. Peking: K'o-hsueh ch'u-pan she, 1957. 4 vols. 民報；合訂本。中國科學院歷史研究所第三所。

Teng Tse-ju. Chung-kuo kuo-min-tang erh-shih nien shih-chi. Shanghai: Cheng-chung shu-chü, 1948. 鄧澤如。中國國民黨二十年史蹟。

Yin Kung. "Sun Chung-shan hsien-sheng chuan," in Hsin lü wen-hsueh she, *Ming-chia chuan-chi*. 因公。孫中山先生傳。新綠文學社。名家傳記。

Teng Tzu-hui   鄧子恢

WORKS

1939, June. "Kuan-yü X ti-ch'ü ju-ho yü ti-jen chin-hsing cheng-chih ching-chi tou-cheng." *K'ang ti*, I-4. 關於X地區如何與敵人進行政治經濟鬥爭。抗敵。

1949, September 12. "Lun shui-shou." *Kuang-ming jih-pao*. Peking. 論稅收。光明日報。

1949, December 4. "Hua chung nan te kung-tso ch'ing-k'uang." *Jen-min jih-pao*. Peking. 華中南的工作情況。人民日報。

1950, March. "Chung-yuan lin-shih jen-min cheng-fu chin i nien lai te shih-cheng kung-tso." *Hsin hua yueh pao*, I-5: 1125–31. 中原臨時人民政府近一年來的施政工作。新華月報。

1950. Kuan-yü kung-hui kung-tso chung te san ko chi-pen wen-t'i. Peking: Kung-jen ch'u-pan she. 關於工會工作中的三個基本問題。

1950, September. "Tsai Chung-nan tsung kung-hui ch'ou wei k'uo-ta hui shang te pao-kao." *Hsin hua yueh-pao*, II-5: 1033–36. 在中南總工會籌委擴大會上的報告。新華月報。

1950, October. "Chung-nan i nien hui-ku."
Hsin hua yueh-pao, II-6: 1225-31.
中南一年回顧。新華月報。

1951. Teng Tzu-hui *et al.* Chi-nien Chung-kuo
kung-ch'an-tang te san-shih chou-nien (comp.
by Chung-nan jen-min ch'u-pan she pien-chi
pu). Hankow: Chung-nan jen-min ch'u-pan
she.
鄧子恢等。紀念中國共產黨的三十週年。
中南人民出版社編輯部。

1951. Teng Tzu-hui t'ung-chih tsai Chung-nan
tang cheng chi-kuan kan-pu hui shang kuan-
yü chen-ya fan ko-ming hsueh-hsi tsung chieh
pao-kao. Hankow: Chung-nan jen-min ch'u-
pan she.
鄧子恢同志在中南黨政機關幹部會上關於
鎮壓反革命學習總結報告。

1952. Teng Tzu-hui *et al.* Jen-chen t'ui-kuang
su-ch'eng shih-tzu fa (comp. by Chung-nan
jen-min ch'u-pan she). Hankow: Chung-nan
jen-min ch'u-pan she.
鄧子恢等。認眞推廣速成識子法。中南人
民出版社。

1952. Teng Tzu-hui fu chu-hsi kuan-yü Chung-
nan chün-cheng wei-yuan-hui pan-nien lai
kung-tso ho chin hou kung-tso jen-wu te pao-
kao. Canton: Jen-min ch'u-pan she.
鄧子恢副主席關於中南軍政委員會半年來
工作和今後工作任務的報告。

1954. The Outstanding Success of the Agrarian
Reform Movement in China. Peking: Foreign
Languages Press.

1956. Pan-nien lai nung-yeh ho-tso hua yün-tung
fa-chan te ch'ing-k'uang ho chin hou te kung-
tso jen-wu—tsai ch'uan-kuo hsien-chin sheng-
ch'an che tai-piao hui-i shang te fa-yen.
Peking: T'ung-su tu-wu ch'u-pan she.
半年來農業合作化運動發展的情況和今後
的工作任務—在全國先進生產者代表會議
上的發言。

"Chung-nan kung-ying kung k'uang yeh chin
hou san ta jen-wu yü ch'i-yeh kuan-li min-chu
hua," in *Kan-pu hsueh-hsi tzu-liao.*
中南公營工礦業今後三大任務與企業管理
民主化。幹部學習資料。

SOURCES

Persons interviewed: Chang Kuo-t'ao; Michel
Oksenberg.
AWW, 1957.
Ch'ang-chiang jih-pao. Hankow, May 30, 1950;
August, 1950.
長江日報。

GCCJK
Hu Yü-kao. Kung fei hsi ts'uan chi. Kweiyang:
Yü-kao shu-chü, 1946.
胡羽高。共匪西竄記。

K'ang chan pa nien lai te pa lu chün yü hsin ssu
chün, comp. by Kuo-min ko-ming chün ti
shih-pa chi-t'uan chün tsung cheng-chih pu
hsuan-ch'uan pu. 1945.
抗戰八年來的八路軍與新四軍。國民革命
軍第十八集團軍總政治部宣傳部。

RSOC
SCMP, 272 (February, 1952): 14; 277 (February
17-18, 1952): 24; 288 (March 5, 1952): 12-15.
Ta kung pao. Hankow, December, 1949. Hong
Kong, August, 1950; January 8, 1951.
大公報。

Ting Ming. Ta-pieh shan hsia. 1948.
丁明。大別山下。

Ts'ung "wu ssu" tao Chung-hua Jen-min Kung-
ho-kuo te tan-sheng, comp. by Wu Min,
Hsiao Ch'üan. Peking: Hsin ch'ao shu-tien,
1951.
從「五四」到中華人民共和國的誕生。吳
民,蕭權。

WWMC
Yeh-ts'ao. San nien yu-chi chan. Cheng pao
she.
野草。三年遊擊戰。

Teng Yen-ta 鄧演達

WORKS

1949? Teng Yen-ta hsien-sheng i-chu. Hong
Kong: Yang I-t'ang.
鄧演達先生遺著。

1951. Tuan chin ling-shih. with Ch'iu Che.
Canton: Ch'iu Che tzu yin.
斷金零拾。丘哲。

SOURCES

CWR, August 20, 1927.
Isaacs, Harold R. The Tragedy of the Chinese
Revolution. Stanford: Stanford University
Press, 1951.
Kuo Mo-jo. Ko-ming ch'un-ch'iu. Shanghai:
Shanghai hai-yen shu-tien, 1947.
郭沫若。革命春秋。

Smedley, Agnes. The Great Road: The Life
and Times of Chu Teh. New York: Monthly
Review Press, 1956.
Teng Yen-ta hsien-sheng chi-nien chi.
鄧演達先生紀念集。

Teng Yen-ta te tao-lu, ed. by Teng Yen-ta hsien-sheng hsun-nan shih-wu chou-nien chi-nien hui. Shanghai? Teng Yen-ta hsien-sheng hsun-nan shih-wu chou-nien chi-nien hui, 1946.
鄧演達的道路。鄧演達先生殉難十五週年紀念會。

Ti-san tang cheng-kang.
第三黨政綱。

Ti-ssu chün chi-shih. Canton: Canton huai-yuan wen-hua shih-yeh fu-wu she, 1949.
第四軍紀實。

Tong, Hollington K. Chiang Kai-shek. Taipei: China Publishing Co., 1953.

Teng Ying-ch'ao　鄧穎超

WORKS

1949. Teng Ying-ch'ao et al. Chung-kuo chieh-fang ch'ü te Nan-ting-ko-erh men (ed. by Ch'üan kuo min-chu fu-nü lien-ho hui ch'ou-pei wei-yuan-hui). Hong Kong: Hsin min-chu ch'u-pan she.
鄧穎超等。中國解放區的南丁格爾們。全國民主婦女聯合會籌備委員會。

SOURCES

Chung-kuo kung-ch'an-tang te chung-yao jen-wu, ed. by Min-chien ch'u-pan she. Peiping: Min-chien ch'u-pan she, 1949.
中國共產黨的重要人物。民間出版社。
HCJC
HMTT
I-chiu-wu-ling jen-min nien-chien, ed. by Shen Sung-fang. Hong Kong: Ta kung shu-chü, 1950.
一九五〇人民年鑑。沈頌芳。
JMST, 1949.
The New York Times, October 23, 1960.
SCMP, 2353 (October 7, 1960): 16.
WWC, 1950.
WWMC

T'ien Han　田漢

WORKS

1921. Wu-fan chih ch'ien.
午飯之前。
1925. Kung Cheng-hung chih ssu.
顧正紅之死。
1925. San yeh chi. with Tsung Pai-hua, Kuo Mo-jo. Shanghai: Ya-tung t'u-shu kuan.

三葉集。宗白華，郭沫若。
1927. Wen-hsueh kai-lun. Chung-hua shu-chü.
文學概論。
1928. Ch'iang-wei chih lu. Shanghai: T'ai tung t'u-shu kung-ssu.
薔薇之路。
1930. Ha-meng-lei-t'e. (tr. of Shakespeare's Hamlet). Chung-hua shu-chü.
哈夢雷特。
1930. K'a-men.
卡門。
1930. Lo-mi-ou yü Chu-li-yeh. (tr. of Shakespeare's Romeo and Juliet).
羅密歐與朱麗葉。
1932. Pao-feng-yü chung te ch'i-ko nü-hsing.
暴風雨中的七個女性。
1933. Hsi-chü kai-lun. (tr. of K. Kishida's On Drama). Chung-hua shu-chü.
戲劇概論。
1936. T'ien Han hsuan-chi (ed. by Yeh Wang-yu, Hsü Ch'en-ssu). Shanghai: Wan-hsiang shu wu.
田漢選集。葉忘憂，徐沉泗。
1936. T'ien Han San-wen chi.
田漢散文集。
1937. T'ien Han et al. Chan-ti kuei-lai. Shanghai: Chan-shih ch'u-pan she.
田漢等。戰地歸來。
1937. T'ien Han et al. Ch'ien-hsien k'ang-chan chiang-ling fang-wen chi. Shanghai: Shanghai ch'ien-chin ch'u-pan she.
田漢等。前綫抗戰將領訪問記。
1937. Li-ming chih ch'ien.
黎明之前。
1937. Wan-hui.
晚會。
1937-38. ed. of K'ang chan hsi-chü.
抗戰戲劇。
1938. Chan-ti hsun li. Chan-shih ch'u-pan she.
戰地巡歷。
1938. T'ien Han et al. Tsui-chin chiu wang hsi-chü hsuan-chi. Nu-hou ch'u-pan she.
田漢等。最近救亡戲劇選集。
1938. Tsui-hou te sheng-li. Shanghai: Shanghai tsa-chih kung-ssu.
最後的勝利。
1940. Chiang-han yü ko (Hsin ko-chü) (ed. by Cheng Po-ch'i). Shanghai: Shanghai tsa-chih kung-ssu.
江漢漁歌（新歌劇）。鄭伯奇。
1955. Pai she chuan (Ching-chü). Peking: Tso-chia ch'u-pan she.
白蛇傳（京劇）。

1955. T'ien Han chü tso hsuan. Peking: Jen-
min wen-hsueh ch'u-pan she.
田漢劇作選。

1958. Kuang Han-ch'ing (Hua-chü). Peking:
Chung-kuo hsi-chü ch'u-pan she.
關漢卿 (話劇)。

1959. Li jen hsing (Erh-shih-i ch'ang hua-chü).
Peking: Chung-kuo hsi-chü ch'u-pan she.
麗人行 (21場話劇)。

1959. Yueh kuang ch'ü. Peking: Jen-min wen-
hsueh ch'u-pan she.
月光曲。

1960. T'ien Han *et al*. T'an ch'i p'ai i-shu.
Peking: Chung-kuo hsi-chü ch'u-pan she.
田漢等。談麒派藝術。

1961. (ed.) 1949-1959 chien-kuo shih nien wen-
hsueh ch'uang-tso hsuan: Hsi-chü. Peking:
Chung-kuo ch'ing-nien ch'u-pan she.
1949-1959建國十年文學創作選：戲劇。

1961. Wen-ch'eng kung-chu shih-i ch'ang hua-
chü. Peking: Chung-kuo hsi-chü ch'u-pan
she.
文成公主十一場話劇。

An chuan.
暗轉。

Chan-li.
顫慄。

Ch'ing t'an.
情探。

Ch'iu sheng fu.
秋聲賦。

Fu kuei. (tr.)
父歸。

Han tsai.
旱災。

Hsueh chung hsing shang.
雪中行商。

Huang-hua-kang.
黃花岡。

Huo chih t'iao-wu.
火之跳舞。

Hsiang-ch'ou.
鄉愁。

Hsin erh-nü ying-hsiung chuan.
新兒女英雄傳。

Hsin t'ao hua shan.
新桃花扇。

I-chih.
一致。

Ku t'an li te sheng-yin.
古潭裡的聲音。

La-chi t'ung.
垃圾桶。

Lo hua shih-chieh.
落花時節。

Mu-hsing chih kuang.
母性之光。

Nien yeh fan.
年夜飯。

Piano chih kuei.
Piano 之鬼。

Sha-lo-mei. (tr. of Oscar Wilde's *Salome*.)
沙樂美。

She sao.
射掃。

Sheng chih i-chih.
生之意志。

Shui-yin teng hsia.
水銀燈下。

Sun Chung-shan chih ssu.
孫中山之死。

T'an-t'ai-ch'i-erh chih ssu (tr. of M. Maeter-
linck's *La Mort de Tintagile*.) Hsien-tai.
檀泰棋兒之死。

Tao min-chien ch'ü.
到民間去。

Ti-wu hao ping-shih.
第五號病室。

T'ien Han *et al*. Chan-shih ko-chü hsuan. Chan-
shih ch'u-pan she.
田漢等。戰時歌劇選。

T'ien Han *et al*. Pa-pai ku chün. Chan-shih
ch'u-pan she.
田漢等。八百孤軍。

Wei che kuan te jen-men. (tr.)
圍着棺的人們。

Wu Sung yü P'an Chin-lien.
武松與潘金蓮。

Wu Tse-t'ien.
武則天。

Yin se te meng. Liang-yu.
銀色的夢。

SOURCES

Chao Ching-shen. Wen-jen chien-ying. Shanghai: Pei hsin shu-chü, 1936.
趙景深。文人剪影。

CHWC
CHWSK
CHWYS
CKJMT
CWT
GCCJK
GCJJ
HCJC
HMTT

HWP

Liu Shou-sung. Chung-kuo hsin wen-hsueh shih ch'u-kao. Peking: Tso-chia ch'u-pan she, 1956. 2 vols.

劉綬松。中國新文學史初稿。

MCNP

RCCL

Sun Ling. Wen-t'an chiao-yu lu. Kao-hsiung: Ta yeh shu-tien, 1955.

孫陵。文壇交遊錄。

TCMT

T'ien Han. T'ien Han hsuan-chi (ed. by Yeh Wang-yu, Hsü Ch'en-ssu). Shanghai: Chung-hsing shu-tien, 1947.

田漢。田漢選集。葉忘憂，徐沉泗。

WWMC

T'ien Keng-hsin　　田 耕 莘

SOURCES

Persons interviewed: not to be identified.

Chao Pin-shih. "Yuan-tung ti-i wei shu-chi Peiping tsung chu-chiao T'ien Keng-hsin." *Heng-i yueh-k'an*, VII–3 (October, 1957).

趙賓實。遠東第一位樞機北平總主教田耕莘。恒毅月刊。

Chung-yang jih-pao. Taipei, April 19, 1962; July 9, 1963.

中央日報。

Maloof, Louis J. The Story of China's First Cardinal.

The New York Times, July 25, 1967.

Ting Fu-pao　　丁 福 保

WORKS

1900. Suan-hsueh shu-mu t'i-yao.
算學書目提要。

1902. Tung wen tien wen-ta.
東文典問答。

1916. (comp.) Tu-shu lu lu. Shanghai: I-hsueh shu-chü.
讀書錄錄。

1921. (comp.) Hsueh fo chieh-ching. Shanghai: I-hsueh shu-chü.
學佛捷徑。

1924. (comp.) Shuo wen mu lu.
說文目錄。

1925. Fo-hsueh ta tz'u-tien (with Ch'ou yin chü-shih tzu ting nien-p'u). Shanghai: I-hsueh shu-chü. 16 vols.
佛學大辭典 (附：疇隱居士自訂年譜)。

1928. Shuo wen chieh tzu ku lin t'i-yao. Shanghai: I-hsueh shu-chü.
說文解字詁林提要。

1928. Ting Fu-pao *et al*. Hsien-tai i-hsueh (comp. by I-hsueh shu-chü). Shanghai: I-hsueh shu-chü.
丁福保等。現代醫學。醫學書局。

1929. Chung hsi i fang hui t'ung. Shanghai: Shang-wu yin shu kuan.
中西醫方會通。

1933. (comp.) Shuo wen yao (with Hsü chi). Shanghai: I-hsueh shu-chü. 2 vols.
說文鑰 (附：續集)。

1938. (ed.) Ku-ch'ien ta tz'u-tien. 12 vols.
古錢大辭典。

1939. Ku-ch'ien ta tzu-tien shih-i.
古錢大辭典拾遺。

1948. Ch'ou yin chü-shih tzu-chuan. Shanghai: Ku lin ching she.
疇隱居士自傳。

1949. Ch'ou yin chü-shih hsueh-shu shih. Shanghai: Ku lin ching she.
疇隱居士學術史。

1955. (comp.) Ssu pu tsung lu i-yao pien. with Chuo Yün-ch'ing. Shanghai: Shang-wu yin shu kuan. 3 vols.
四部總錄醫藥編。周雲青。

1956. (comp.) Ssu pu tsung lu t'ien-wen pien. with Chou Yün-ch'ing. Shanghai: Shang-wu yin shu kuan.
四部總錄天文編。周雲青。

1957. (comp.) Ssu pu tsung lu i-shu pien. with Chou Yün-ch'ing. Shanghai: Shang-wu yin shu kuan. 2 vols.
四部總錄藝術編。周雲青。

1957. (comp.) Ssu pu tsung lu suan fa pien. with Chou Yün-ch'ing. Shanghai: Shang-wu yin shu kuan.
四部總錄算法編。周雲青。

1959. (comp.) Ch'üan Han San-kuo Chin Nan-pei-ch'ao shih. Peking: Chung-hua shu-chü. 2 vols.
全漢三國晉南北朝詩。

1959. (comp.) Shuo wen chieh tzu ku lin. Tai-pei: Taiwan shang-wu yin shuk uan. 12 vols.
說文解字詁林。

1963. (comp.) Ch'ing shih-hua. Peking: Chung-hua shu-chü. 2 vols.
清詩話。

1965. Chung-yao ch'ien shuo. Taipei: Taiwan shang-wu yin shu kuan.
中藥淺說。

(comp.) Li-tai shih-hua hsü-pien. Wu-hsi: Ting
shih. 12 vols.
歷代詩話續編。
Wei-sheng hsueh wen-ta.
衞生學問答。

SOURCES

Ting Fu-pao. Ch'ou yin chü-shih hsueh-shu
shih. Shanghai: Ku lin ching she, 1949.
丁福保。疇隱居士學術史。
———. Ch'ou yin chü-shih tzu-chuan. Shanghai: Ku lin ching she, 1948.
丁福保。疇隱居士自傳。
———. "Ch'ou yin chü-shih tzu ting nien-p'u,"
in Ting Fu-pao, *Fo hsueh ta tz'u tien*. Shanghai:
I-hsueh shu-chü, 1925. 16 vols.
丁福保。疇隱居士自訂年譜。丁福保。佛
學大辭典。

Ting Hsi-lin   丁西林

WORKS

1947. Hsi-lin tu-mu-chü chi.
西林獨幕劇集。
1947. Miao feng shan; ssu mu hsi-chü. Shanghai: Wen-hua sheng-huo ch'u-pan she.
妙峯山；四幕喜劇。
1954. Ting Hsi-lin *et al.* (ed.) Han-tzu te
cheng-li ho chien-hua. Peking: Chung-hua
shu-chü.
丁西林等。漢字的整理和簡化。
1955. Ting Hsi-lin chü tso hsuan. Peking: Jen-
min wen-hsueh ch'u-pan she.
丁西林劇作選。
1963. Ya-p'o. Peking: Jen-min wen-hsueh
ch'u-pan she.
壓迫。

SOURCES

CHWSK
CHWYS
CKJMT
CWT
GCCJK
GCJJ
HMTT
MCNP
MMT
RCCL
TCMT
WWMC

Ting Ling   丁玲

WORKS

1906. I-wai chi.
意外集。
1928. Tsai hei-an chung.
在黑暗中。
1930. Wei-hu. Shanghai: Ta chiang shu p'u.
韋護。
1933. Mu-ch'in. Shanghai: Liang-yu t'u-shu
yin-shua kung-ssu.
母親。
1936. Ting Ling wen-hsuan (comp. by Shao-
hou). Shanghai: Fang ku shu-tien.
丁玲文選。少候。
1937. Ting Ling chieh-tso hsuan. Shanghai: Pai
kuang shu-tien.
丁玲傑作選。
1937. Tzu-sha jih-chi. Shanghai: Ta kuang
shu-chü.
自殺日記。
1938. Hsi-pei chan-ti fu-wu t'uan hsi-chü chi.
with Hsi Ju.
西北戰地服務團戲劇集。奚如。
1938. Su ch'ü wen-i.
蘇區文藝。
1938. Tung-ts'un shih-chien. Shanghai: Lü yeh
shu-wu.
東村事件。
1939. Ting Ling *et al.* Huo wang li; chi-t'i pao-
kao wen-hsueh. Shanghai: Hu-chiang ch'u-
pan she.
丁玲等。火網裡；集體報告文學。
1939. I nien. Sheng-huo shu-tien.
一年。
1939. I t'ien. Shanghai: Ch'ing-nien wen-hua
she.
一天。
1940. I ko nü-jen. Shanghai: Chung-hua shu-
chü.
一個女人。
1940. Ting Ling tai-piao tso hsuan (ed. by Chang
Chün). Shanghai: Ch'üan-ch'iu shu-tien.
丁玲代表作選。張均。
1941. Ch'ien san.
遣散。
1941. Chü. Shanghai: I liu shu-tien.
聚。
1941. Hsiao-hsi. Hsin lien ch'u-pan she.
消息。
1946. I k'o wei ch'u-t'ang te ch'iang-tan.
Shanghai: Chih-shih ch'u-pan she.
一顆未出膛的槍彈。

1946. Wo tsai Hsia ts'un te shih-hou. Peiping:
Yuan fang shu-tien.
我在霞村的時候。

1946. Ying-hsiung chuan.
英雄傳。

1949. Ting Ling wen-chi. Shanghai: Ch'un
ming shu-tien.
丁玲文集。

1949. Yao kung. with Ch'en Ming, Lu Fei.
Peking: Ta-chung shu-tien.
窰工。陳明，逯斐。

1950. Fang Su yin-hsiang.
訪蘇印象。

1950. I-erh-chiu shih yü Chin Chi Lu Yü pien-
ch'ü; ti-hou k'ang Jih ken-chü-ti chieh-shao.
Peking: Hsin hua shu-tien.
一二九師與晉冀魯豫邊區；敵後抗日根據
地介紹。

1950. Ting Ling *et al*. Tsai ch'ien-chin te tao-lu
shang. Peking: Ch'ing-nien ch'u-pan she.
丁玲等。在前進的道路上。

1951. (comp.) Hu Yeh-p'in hsuan-chi. Peking:
K'ai-ming shu-tien.
胡也頻選集。

1951. K'ua-tao hsin te shih-tai lai (ed. by Wen-i
chien-she ts'ung-shu pien-chi wei-yuan-hui).
Peking: Jen-min wen-hsueh ch'u-pan she.
跨到新的時代來。文藝建設叢書編輯委員
會。

1951. Shan pei feng-kuang. Peking: Jen-min
ch'u-pan she.
陝北風光。

1951. Ting Ling hsuan-chi (ed. by Hsin wen-
hsueh hsuan-chi pien-chi wei-yuan-hui).
Peking: K'ai-ming shu-tien.
丁玲選集。新文學選集編輯委員會。

1952. Ting Ling *et al*. Ch'ing-nien te lien-ai yü
hun-yin wen-t'i. Peking: Ch'ing-nien ch'u-
pan she.
丁玲等。青年的戀愛與婚姻問題。

1952. Ou hsing san chi (ed. by Wen-i chien-she
ts'ung-shu pien-chi wei-yuan-hui). Peking:
Jen-min wen-hsueh ch'u-pan she.
歐行散記。文藝建設叢書編輯委員會。

1953. T'ai-yang chao tsai sang-ch'ien-ho shang.
Peking: Jen-min wen-hsueh ch'u-pan she.
太陽照在桑乾河上。

1954. Shui. Hong Kong: Hsin ti ch'u-pan she.
水。

1954. Tao ch'ün-chung chung ch'ü lo-hu.
Peking: Tso-chia ch'u-pan she.
到群眾中去落戶。

1954. Ting Ling tuan-p'ien hsiao-shuo hsuan-
chi. Peking: Jen-min wen-hsueh ch'u-pan
she.
丁玲短篇小說選集。

1954. Yenan chi. Peking: Wen-hsueh ch'u-pan
she.
延安集。

1956. I ko hsiao hung chün te ku-shih. Shanghai: Shao-nien erh-t'ung ch'u-pan she.
一個小紅軍的故事。

1956. Ting Ling *et al*. Wu nien chi-hua sung.
丁玲等。五年計劃頌。

1965. Ting Ling ming-chu hsuan (comp. by
K'an-ju). Hong Kong: Hui-t'ung shu-tien.
丁玲名著選。侃如。

A-mao ku-nian.
阿毛姑娘。

Mou yeh.
某夜。

ed. of *Pei-tou*.
北斗。

Sha-fei nü-shih te jih-chi.
莎菲女士的日記。

ed. of *Shih-tzu chieh-t'ou*.
十字街頭。

ed. of *Wen-i hsin-wen*.
文藝新聞。

SOURCES

Anderson, Colena Michael. "Ping Hsin and
Ting Ling." Unpublished Ph. D. dissertation, Claremont College, 1954.

Elegant, Robert S. China's Red Masters. New
York: Twayne, 1951.

Fairbank, John K., and Liu Kwang-ching.
Modern China: A Bibliographical Guide to
Chinese Works, 1898-1937. Cambridge:
Harvard University Press, 1950.

GCJJ

Hsia, C.T. A History of Modern Chinese Fiction 1917-1957. New Haven: Yale University
Press, 1961.

Hsin ming-tz'u tz'u-tien, comp. by Hu Chi-t'ao,
T'ao P'ing-t'ien. Shanghai: Ch'un-ming shu-
tien, 1949.
新名詞辭典。胡濟濤，陶萍天。

I-chiu-ssu-chiu nien shou-ts'e, comp. by Hua
shang pao tzu-liao shih. Hong Kong: Hua
shang pao she, 1949.
一九四九年手冊。華商報資料室。

I-chiu-wu-ling jen-min nien-chien, ed. by Shen
Sung-fang. Hong Kong: Ta kung shu-chü,
1950.
一九五〇人民年鑑。沈頌芳。

JMST

Mao Tun (pseud. of Shen Yen-ping). "Nü tso-chia Ting Ling," in Chiang Ping-chih, *Ting Ling hsuan-chi*. Peking: K'ai-ming shu-tien. 茅盾（沈雁冰）。女作家丁玲，蔣冰之，丁玲選集。

MCNP

The New York Times, August 8, 1957.

Shen T'ung-wen. Chi Ting Ling. Shanghai: Liang-yu t'u-shu yin-shua kung-ssu, 1934. 沈從文。記丁玲。

Smedley, Agnes. Battle Hymn of China. New York: Alfred A. Knopf, 1943.

Ting Ling. Mu-ch'in. Shanghai: Liang-yu t'u-shu yin-shua kung-ssu, 1933. 丁玲。母親。

———. T'ai-yang chao-tsai Sang-ch'ien-ho shang. Peking: Jen-min wen-hsueh ch'u-pan she, 1953. 丁玲。太陽照在桑乾河上。

———. Ting Ling hsuan-chi (ed. by Hsin wen-hsueh hsuan-chi pien-chi wei-yuan-hui). Peking: K'ai-ming shu-tien, 1951. 丁玲。丁玲選集。新文學選集編輯委員會。

———. Wei-hu. Shanghai: Ta chiang shu p'u, 1930. 丁玲。韋護。

———. "Wo-men yung-yuan tsai i-ch'i," in Chung-kuo kung-ch'an-tang tai-piao-t'uan, *Ssu pa pei-nan lieh-shih chi-nien-ts'e*. Chung-kuo kung-ch'an-tang tai-piao-t'uan, 1946. 丁玲。我們永遠在一起。中國共產黨代表團。四八被難烈士紀念冊。

Ting Ling tsai Hsi-pei, tr. by Ch'ing-hua. Canton: Hsin-wen yen-chiu so, 1938. 丁玲在西北。清華。

Ts'ao Chü-jen. Wen-t'an wu-shih nien. Hong Kong: Hsin wen-hua ch'u-pan she, 1955. 2 vols. 曹聚仁。文壇五十年。

WWMC

Yao Peng-tzu. "Wo-men te p'eng-yu Ting Ling," in Chiang Ping-chih, *Ting Ling hsuan-chi*. Peking: K'ai-ming shu-tien. 姚蓬子。我們的朋友丁玲。蔣冰之，丁玲選集。

詁雅堂叢著六種。

SOURCES

Chang Ch'i-yün. Tang shih kai-yao. Taipei: Chung-yang wen-wu kung-ying she, 1951-52. 5 vols. 張其昀。黨史概要。

Ch'ü Wan-li. "Ting Ting-ch'eng hsien-sheng tui-yü hsueh-shu chih kung-hsien," Chung-kuo kuo-min-tang chung-yang tang shih shih-liao pien-tsuan wei-yuan-hui, *Ko-ming hsien-lieh hsien-chin chuan*. Taipei: Chung-hua Min-kuo ko-chieh chi-nien kuo-fu pai nien tan-ch'en ch'ou-pei wei-yuan-hui, 1965. 屈萬里。丁鼎丞先生對於學術之貢獻。中國國民黨中央黨史史料編纂委員會。革命先烈先進傳。

Kuo-fu nien-p'u ch'u-kao, ed. by Chung-kuo kuo-min-tang tang shih shih-liao pien-tsuan wei-yuan-hui, kuo shih kuan shih-liao pien-tsuan wei-yuan-hui. Taipei: Kuo kuang yin chih ch'ang, 1959. 2 vols. 國父年譜初稿。中國國民黨黨史史料編纂委員會，國史館史料編纂委員會。

Ma Hsing-yeh. "Chui-i Ting chiao-yü chang," in Chung-kuo kuo-min-tang chung-yang tang shih shih-liao pien-tsuan wei-yuan-hui, *Ko-ming hsien-lieh hsien-chin chuan*. Taipei: Chung-hua Min-kuo ko-chieh chi-nien kuo-fu pai nien tan-ch'en ch'ou-pei wei-yuan-hui, 1965. 馬星野。追憶丁教育長。中國國民黨中央黨史史料編纂委員會。革命先烈先進傳。

Ting Ting-ch'eng hsien-sheng chi-nien chi. 丁鼎丞先生紀念集。

',Ting Wei-fen shih-lueh," in Chung-kuo kuo-min-tang chung-yang tang shih shih-liao pien-tsuan wei-yuan-hui, *Ko-ming hsien-lieh hsien-chin chuan*. Taipei: Chung-hua Min-kuo ko-chieh chi-nien kuo-fu pai nien tan-ch'en ch'ou-pei wei-yuan-hui, 1965. 丁惟汾事略。中國國民黨中央黨史史料編纂委員會。革命先烈先進傳。

Tsou Lu. Chung-kuo kuo-min-tang shih lueh. Shanghai: Shang-wu yin shu kuan, 1945. 鄒魯。中國國民黨史略。

Ting Wei-fen 丁淮汾

WORKS

1966. Ku-ya-t'ang ts'ung chu liu chung. Taipei: Chung-hua ts'ung-shu pien shen wei-yuan-hui. 3 vols.

Ting Wen-chiang 丁文江

WORKS

1926. Min-kuo chün-shih chin chi; shang pien. Shang-wu yin shu kuan. 民國軍事近記；上編。

1926, October 16. "The Greater Shanghai Municipality." *North China Herald*.

1928? Chung-kuo kuan pan k'uang-yeh shih lueh.
中國官辦礦業史略。

1928–29. (ed.) Hsu Hsia-k'e yu-chi. Shanghai: Shang-wu yin shu kuan. 3 vols.
徐霞客遊記。

1933. (comp.) Chung-kuo fen-sheng hsin t'u. with Wong Wen-hao, Tseng Shih-ying. Shanghai: Shen pao kuan.
中國分省新圖。翁文灝，曾世英。

1934. (comp.) Chung-hua Min-kuo hsin ti-t'u. with Wong Wen-hao, Tseng Shih-ying. Shanghai: Shen pao kuan.
中華民國新地圖。翁文灝，曾世英。

1936. (comp.) Ts'uan wen ts'ung k'e; chia pien. Shanghai: Shang-wu yin shu kuan.
爨文叢刻；甲編。

1956. "Ch'ung yin t'ien kung k'ai wu chüan pa." *Chung-yang yen-chiu-yuan yuan k'an, ti-san chi*; *Ting ku tsung-kan-shih Wen-chiang shih-shih erh-shih chou-nien chi-nien k'an*: 525–28.
重印天工開物卷跋。中央研究院院刊，第三輯；丁故總幹事文江逝世二十週年紀念刊。

1956. "Feng-hsin Sung Ch'ang-keng hsien-sheng chuan." *Chung-yang yen-chiu-yuan yuan k'an, ti-san chi*; *Ting ku tsung-kan-shih Wen-chiang shih-shih erh-shih chou-nien chi-nien k'an*: 523–24.
奉新宋長庚先生傳。中央研究院院刊，第三輯；丁故總幹事文江逝世二十週年紀念刊。

1956. "Man-yu san chi." *Chung-yang yen-chiu-yuan yuan k'an, ti-san chi*; *Ting ku tsung-kan-shih Wen-chiang shih-shih erh-shih chou-nien chi-nien k'an*: 341–437.
漫遊散記。中央研究院院刊，第三輯；丁故總幹事文江逝世二十週年紀念刊。

1956. "Su-o lü-hsing chi." *Chung-yang yen-chiu-yuan yuan k'an, ti-san chi*; *Ting ku tsung-kan-shih Wen-chiang shih-shih erh-shih chou-nien chi-nien k'an*: 439–512.
蘇俄旅行記。中央研究院院刊，第三輯；丁故總幹事文江逝世二十週年紀念刊。

1958. (ed.) Liang Jen-kung hsien-sheng nien-p'u ch'ang pien ch'u-kao. Taipei: Shih-chieh shu-chü. 2 vols.
梁任公先生年譜長編初稿。

ed. of *Chung-kuo ku sheng-wu chih*.
中國古生物誌。

ed. of *Chung-kuo ti-chih hsueh-hui chih*.
中國地質學會誌。

SOURCES

Chung-yang yen-chiu-yuan yuan k'an, ti-san chi; *Ting ku tsung-kan-shih Wen-chiang shih-shih chou-nien chi-nien k'an* (December, 1956).
中央研究院院刊，第三輯；丁故總幹事文江逝世二十週年紀念刊。

CYB-W, 1926–27.

Hu Shih. Ting Wen-chiang te chuan-chi. Taipei: Kuo-li chung-yang yen-chiu-yuan, 1956.
胡適。丁文江的傳記。

Hu Shih *et al*. Ting Wen-chiang che ko jen (comp. by Chuan-chi wen-hsueh tsa-chih she). Taipei: Chuan-chi wen-hsueh ch'u-pan she, 1967.
胡適等。丁文江這個人。傳記文學雜誌社。

The Journal of Asian Studies, XVII-4 (1958): 623–25.

Ts'ai Ch'ang   蔡暢

WORKS

1949. Ts'ai Ch'ang *et al*. Chung-kuo chieh-fang ch'ü fu-nü yün-tung wen-hsien (ed. by Ch'üan-kuo min-chu fu-nü lien-ho hui ch'ou-pei wei-yuan-hui). Shanghai: Hsin hua shu-tien.
蔡暢等。中國解放區婦女運動文獻。全國民主婦女聯合會籌備委員會。

1949. Ts'ai Ch'ang *et al*. Chung-kuo fu-nü ti-i tz'u ch'üan-kuo tai-piao ta-hui chung-yao wen-hsien (ed. by Chung-hua ch'üan-kuo min-chu fu-nü lien-ho hui hsuan-ch'uan chiao-yü pu). Shanghai: Chung-hua ch'üan-kuo min-chu fu-nü lien-ho hui.
蔡暢等。中國婦女第一次全國代表大會重要文献。中華全國民主婦女聯合宣傳教育部。

SOURCES

Person interviewed: Chang Kuo-t'ao.
Chung-kuo kung-ch'an-tang te chung-yao jen-wu, ed. by Min-chien ch'u-pan she. Peiping: Min-chien ch'u-pan she, 1949.
中國共產黨的重要人物。民間出版社。
CKLC
GCJ
HCJC
HMTT
I-chiu-wu-ling jen-min nien-chien, ed. by Shen

Sung-fang. Hong Kong: Ta kung shu-chü, 1950.
一九五〇人民年鑑。沈頌芳。
RD
Wales, Nym (pseud. of Helen Foster Snow). Inside Red China. New York: Doubleday, Doran & Co., 1939.

Ts'ai Ho-sen   蔡和森

Works

1922–25. ed. of *Hsiang-tao chou-pao*.
響導週報。

Sources

Person interviewed: Chang Kuo-t'ao.
Chow Tse-tsung. The May Fourth Movement: Intellectual Revolution in Modern China. Cambridge: Harvard University Press, 1960.
Brandt, Conrad. Stalin's Failure in China, 1924–1927. Cambridge: Harvard University Press, 1958.
Ch'en, Jerome. Mao and the Chinese Revolution. New York: Oxford University Press, 1965.
CKLC
HKLC
Hsiao Tso-liang. Power Relations Within the Chinese Communist Movement, 1930–1934; a Study of Documents. Seattle: University of Washington Press, 1961–67. 2 vols.
Hsin ch'ing-nien, IX–4 (August 1, 1921).
新青年。
HSWT
Hunan li-shih tzu-liao, 9 (1959).
湖南歷史資料。
Li Jui. Mao Tse-tung t'ung-chih te ch'u-ch'i ko-ming huo-tung. Peking: Chung-kuo ch'ing-nien ch'u-pan she, 1957.
李銳。毛澤東同志的初期革命活動。
Lieh-shih Hsiang Ching-yü, ed. by Chung-kuo fu-nü tsa-chih she. Peking, 1958.
烈士向警予。中國婦女雜誌社。
Schwartz, Benjamin I. Chinese Commuism and the Rise of Mao. Cambridge: Harvard University Press, 1951.
Siao, Emi. Mao Tse-tung, His Childhood and Youth. Bombay: People's Publishing House, 1953.
Siao Yü. Mao Tse-tung and I Were Beggars. Syracuse, N.Y.: Syracuse University Press, 1959.

Tung, William. The Political Institutions of Modern China. The Hague: Martinus Nijhoff, 1964.

Ts'ai O   蔡鍔

Works

1917. (ed.) Tseng Hu chih-ping yü-lu. Shanghai: Shang-wu yin shu kuan.
曾胡治兵語錄。
1943. Ts'ai Sung-p'o hsien-sheng i chi, comp. by Liu Ta-wu. Shao-yang: Ts'ai kung i chi pien yin wei-yuan-hui. 12 vols.
蔡松坡先生遺集。劉達武。
1966. Sung-p'o chün chung i-mo. Taipei: Wen-hai ch'u-pan she.
松坡軍中遺墨。
Yueh-nan (Vietnam) yao-sai t'u-shuo.
越南要塞圖說。

Sources

CHMI
Chün wu yuan k'ao shih (with Liang Kuang tu ssu-ling-pu k'ao shih), ed. by Liang Kuang tu ssu-ling-pu ts'an-mou t'ing. Shanghai: Shang-wu yin shu kuan, 1916.
軍務院考實 (附：兩廣都司令部考實)。兩廣都司令部參謀廳。
"Le General Tsai Ngao et Son Oeuvre au Yunnan." *Revue Indochinoise*, 6 (June, 1913): 637–44.
Ho Hui-ch'ing. "Hu kuo chih i Yunnan ch'i-i pi-shih." *I ching*, 21 (January, 1937): 36–41.
何慧青。護國之役雲南起義秘史。逸經。
Hsiao Yuan. "Ts'ai O, Yunnan ch'i-i chih t'ui-tung che." *Kuo wen chou-pao*, XIII–10 (March, 1936): 45–46.
篠圓。蔡鍔，雲南起義之推動者。國聞周報。
I chiao ts'ung pien, ed. by Yeh Te-hui. 1898.
翼教叢編。葉德輝。
Keng I. "Hsin-hai ko-ming shih-ch'i te Kwangsi." *Chin-tai shih tzu-liao*, 4 (1958): 89–106.
耿毅。辛亥革命時期的廣西。近代史資料。
Li Hsü. Ts'ai Sung-p'o. Nanking: Ch'ing-nien ch'u-pan she, 1946.
李旭。蔡松坡。
Liang Ch'i-ch'ao. "Hu kuo chih i hui-ku t'an." *Shih ti hsueh-pao*, II–3 (March, 1923).
梁啟超。護國之役回顧談。史地學報。

Liang Ch'i-ch'ao. Hu ko chih i tien-wen chi
    lun-wen. Taipei: Wen hai ch'u-pan she, 1966.
    梁啟超。護國之役電文及論文。
Liang Jen-kung hsien-sheng nien-p'u ch'ang
    pien ch'u-kao, ed. by Ting Wen-chiang.
    Taipei: Shih-chieh shu-chü, 1958. 2 vols.
    梁任公先生年譜長編初稿。丁文江。
Liu Kuang-yen. Ts'ai Sung-p'o. Hong Kong:
    Ya-chou ch'u-pan she, 1958.
    劉光炎。蔡松坡。
Teng Chih-ch'eng. "Hu kuo chün chi-shih."
    Shih hsueh nien-pao, II-2 (September, 1935).
    鄧之誠。護國軍紀實。史學年報。
Ts'ai O. Ts'ai Sung-p'o hsien-sheng i chi (comp.
    by Liu Ta-wu). Shao-yang: Ts'ai kung i chi
    pien yin wei-yuan-hui, 1943. 12 vols.
    蔡鍔。蔡松坡先生遺集。劉達武。
Wu Hsiang-hsiang. "Hu kuo chün shen Ts'ai
    Sung-p'o." Chuan-chi wen-hsueh, IV-5 (May,
    1964): 29-31.
    吳相湘。護國軍神蔡松坡。傳記文學。
Yü En-yang. Chung-hua hu kuo san chieh
    chuan. Yunnan t'u-shu kuan, 1917.
    庾恩暘。中華護國三傑傳。
Yü Feng-yü. Yunnan shou i yung-hu kung-ho
    shih-mo chi. Yunnan t'u-shu kuan, 1917.
    庾楓漁。雲南首義擁護共和始末記。

Ts'ai T'ing-k'ai   蔡廷鍇

WORKS

1935. Hai-wai yin-hsiang chi. Hong Kong:
    Tung ya yin wu yu-hsien kung-ssu.
    海外印象記。
1946. Ts'ai T'ing-k'ai tzu-chuan. Hong Kong:
    Tzu-yu hsun-k'an she. 2 vols.
    蔡廷鍇自傳。

SOURCES

JMST, 1956-66.
Ts'ai T'ing-k'ai. Ts'ai T'ing-k'ai tzu-chuan.
    Hong Kong: Tzu-yu hsun-k'an she, 1946, 2
    vols.
    蔡廷鍇。蔡廷鍇自傳。

Ts'ai T'ing-kan   蔡廷幹

WORKS

1922. Lao chih lao.
    老解老。

1932. Chinese Poems in English Rhyme.
    Chicago: The University of Chicago Press.

SOURCES

AADC
BPC
Ch'en Po-wen. Chung Jih wai-chiao shih.
    Shanghai: Shang-wu yin shu kuan, 1929.
    陳博文。中日外交史。
CMTC
CYB-W, 1913, 1919, 1928, 1934.
Hsin-hai ko-ming, ed. by Ch'ai Te-keng et al.
    Shanghai: Shanghai jen-min ch'u-pan she,
    1957. 8 vols.
    辛亥革命。柴德賡等。
La Fargue, Thomas E. China's First Hundred.
    Pullman: State College of Washington, 1942.
Liu Yen. Ti-kuo chu-i ya-p'o Chung-kuo shih.
    Shanghai: T'ai-p'ing-yang shu-tien, 1932. 2
    vols.
    劉彥。帝國主義壓迫中國史。
North China Herald, August 16, September 20,
    1913; May 17, 1919; July 7, 10, August 28,
    November 6, 1926.
Pollard, Robert. China's Foreign Relations,
    1917-1931. New York: The Macmillan Co.,
    1933.
Shih Chao-chi. Shih Chih-chih hsien-sheng tsao-
    nien hui-i-lu. 1954?
    施肇基。施植之先生早年回憶錄。
Willoughby, W.W. China at the Conference:
    A Report. Baltimore: The Johns Hopkins
    University Press, 1922.
Yang Chia-lo. Chia-wu i-lai Chung Jih chün-
    shih wai-chiao ta-shih chi-yao. Chungking:
    Shang-wu yin shu kuan, 1941.
    楊家駱。甲午以來中日軍事外交大事紀要。

Ts'ai Yuan-p'ei   蔡元培

WORKS

1917. Yao-kuai hsueh chiang-i lu tsung-lun. (tr.)
    Shanghai: Shang-wu yin shu kuan.
    妖怪學講義錄總論。
1919. Shih-t'ou chi so-yin. Shanghai: Shang-wu
    yin shu kuan.
    石頭記索隱。
1920. Ts'ai Chieh-min hsien-sheng yen-hsing lu
    (ed. by Hsin ch'ao she). Peking: Peking ta-
    hsueh ch'u-pan pu.
    蔡孑民先生言行錄。新潮社。

1927. Chung-kuo lun-li hsueh shih. Shanghai: Shang-wu yin shu kuan.
中國倫理學史。

1931. Che-hsueh ta-kang. Shanghai: Shang-wu yin shu kuan.
哲學大綱。

1937. (ed.) Chang Chü-sheng hsien-sheng ch'i-shih sheng-jih chi-nien lun-wen chi. with Hu Shih, Wang Yün-wu. Shanghai: Shang-wu yin shu kuan.
張菊生先生七十生日紀念論文集。 胡適, 王雲五。

1959. Ts'ai Yuan-p'ei hsuan-chi (ed. by Chung-hua shu-chü). Peking: Chung-hua shu-chü.
蔡元培選集。 中華書局。

1961. Ts'ai Yuan-p'ei hsien-sheng i wen lei ch'ao (comp. by Sun Te-chung). Taipei: Fu-hsing shu-chü.
蔡元培先生遺文類鈔。 孫德中。

1962. Ts'ai Yuan-p'ei min-tsu hsueh lun chu (comp. by Chung-kuo min-tsu hsueh-hui). Taipei: Taiwan chung-hua shu-chü.
蔡元培民族學論著。 中國民族學會。

1963. Ts'ai Yuan-p'ei hsien-sheng chu te-yü chiang-i (ed. by Sun Te-chung). Taipei: Taiwan shu-tien.
蔡元培先生著德育講義。 孫德中。

1967. Ts'ai Yuan-p'ei hsuan-chi. Taipei: Wen-hsing shu-tien.
蔡元培選集。

1967. Ts'ai Yuan-p'ei tzu-shu (comp. by Chuan-chi wen-hsueh tsa-chih she). Taipei: Chuan-chi wen-hsueh ch'u-pan she.
蔡元培自述。 傳記文學雜誌社。

SOURCES

Chin shan shih pao. San Francisco, February 18, 19,1956.
金山時報。

Chung-kuo kuo-min-tang shih-kao, comp. by Tsou Lu. Chungking: Shang-wu yin shu kuan, 1944. 4 vols.
中國國民黨史稿。 鄒魯。

Feng Tzu-yu. Chung-hua Min-kuo k'ai-kuo ch'ien ko-ming shih. Chungking: Chung-kuo wen-hua fu-wu she, 1944. 3 vols.
馮自由。 中華民國開國前革命史。

Li Chien-nung. Tsui-chin san-shih nien Chung-kuo cheng-chih shih. Shanghai: T'ai-p'ing-yang shu-tien, 1931.
李劍農。 最近三十年中國政治史。

Lo Chia-lun. "Kuo-li Peking ta-hsueh," in Chung-kuo hsin-wen ch'u-pan kung-ssu,

Chung-hua Min-kuo ta-hsueh chih. Taipei: Chung-kuo hsin-wen ch'u-pan kung-ssu, 1953.
羅家倫。 國立北京大學。 中國新聞出版公司。 中華民國大學誌。

Teng Ssu-yu and John K. Fairbank. China's Response to the West. Cambridge: Harvard University Press, 1954.

Ts'ai Shang-ssu. Ts'ai Yuan-p'ei hsueh-shu ssu-hsiang chuan-chi. Shanghai, 1950.
蔡尙思。 蔡元培學術思想傳記。

Ts'ai Yuan-p'ei. Che-hsueh ta-kang. Shanghai: Shang-wu yin shu kuan, 1931.
蔡元培。 哲學大綱。

————. Chung-kuo lun-li hsueh shih. Shanghai: Shang-wu yin shu kuan, 1927.
蔡元培。 中國倫理學史。

————. Shih-t'ou chi so-yin. Shanghai: Shang-wu yin shu kuan, 1919.
蔡元培。 石頭記索隱。

————. Ts'ai Chieh-min hsien-sheng yen-hsing lu (ed. by Hsin ch'ao she). Peking: Peking ta-hsueh ch'u-pan pu, 1920.
蔡元培。 蔡子民先生言行錄。 新潮社。

————. Ts'ai Yuan-p'ei hsien-sheng i wen lei ch'ao (comp. by Sun Te-chung). Taipei: Fu-hsing shu-chü, 1961.
蔡元培。 蔡元培先生遺文類鈔。 孫德中。

Tzu-chuan chih i chang, ed. by T'ao K'ang-te. Canton: Yü-chou feng she, 1938.
自傳之一章。 陶亢德。

Ts'ao Ju-lin   曹汝霖

WORKS

1966. I-sheng chih hui-i. Hong Kong: Ch'un-ch'iu tsa-chih she.
一生之回憶。

SOURCES

AADC

BPC

Chang Chung-fu. Chung-hua Min-kuo wai-chiao shih. Chungking: Cheng-chung shu-chü, 1943.
張忠紱。 中華民國外交史。

Ch'en Kung-lu. Chung-kuo chin-tai shih. Shanghai: Shang-wu yin shu kuan, 1935.
陳恭祿。 中國近代史。

Ch'en T'i-ch'ang. Chung-kuo wai-chiao hsing-cheng. Chungking: Shang-wu yin shu kuan, 1945.
陳體強。 中國外交行政。

Chow Tse-tsung. The May Fourth Movement: Intellectual Revolution in Modern China. Cambridge: Harvard University Press, 1960.

CMTC

Hsin-hai ko-ming, ed. by Ch'ai Te-keng *et al.* Shanghai: Jen-min ch'u-pan she, 1957. 8 vols. 辛亥革命。柴德賡等。

Li Chien-nung. Chung-kuo chin pai nien cheng-chih shih. Shanghai: Shang-wu yin shu kuan: 1947. 2 vols. 李劍農。中國近百年政治史。

Pollard, Robert Thomas. China's Foreign Relations, 1917-1931. New York: The Macmillan Co., 1933.

Shih Chao-chi. Sao-Ke Alfred Sze; Reminiscences of His Early Years as Told to Anming Fu (tr. by Amy C. Wu). Washington, D.C., 1962.

T'ang Chung. "Yuan Shih-k'ai chih-cheng shih-tai chih tui Jih wai-chiao." *Wai-chiao p'ing-lun*, III-7: 5. 湯中。袁世凱執政時代之對日外交。外交評論。

T'ao Chü-yin. Pei-yang chün-fa t'ung-chih shih-ch'i shih-hua. Peking: Sheng-huo, tu-shu, hsin chih san lien shu-tien, 1957-58. 6 vols. 陶菊隱。北洋軍閥統治時期史話。

Ts'ao Ju-lin. I-sheng chih hui-i. Hong Kong: Ch'un-ch'iu tsa-chih she, 1966. 曹汝霖。一生之回憶。

Wai-chiao ta tz'u-tien, ed. by Wai-chiao hsueh-hui. Kunming: Chung-hua shu-chü, 1937. 外交大辭典。外交學會。

Ying Ch'ien-li. "T'ieh-ch'uang hui-i." *Chuan-chi wen-hsueh*, II-4 (April, 1963): 13-16. 英千里。鐵窗回憶。傳記文學。

Yuan Shih-k'ai ch'ieh kuo chi, comp. by Tai-wan Chung-hua shu-chü pien-chi pu. Taipei: Taiwan Chung-hua shu-chü, 1954. 袁世凱竊國記。台灣中華書局編輯部。

Ts'ao K'un   曹錕

SOURCES

CMMC
CMTC
CWR, June 4, 25, 1938.
CYB-W, 1923, 1925.
Houn, Franklin W. Central Government of China 1912-1928: An Institutional Study. Madison: University of Wisconsin Press, 1957.
Li Chien-nung. The Political History of China

1840-1928 (tr. and ed. by Teng Ssu-yu, Jeremy Ingalls). Princeton: D. Van Nostrand Co., 1956.

SJ

SMJ

Sonoda Ikki. Hsin Chung-kuo fen sheng jen-wu chih (tr. by Huang Hui-ch'üan, Tiao Ying-hua). Shanghai: Liang-yu, 1930? 園田一龜。新中國分省人物誌。黃惠泉，刁英華。

SSKR

T'ao Chü-yin. Pei-yang chün-fa t'ung-chih shih-ch'i shih-hua. Peking: Sheng-huo, tu-shu, hsin-chih san lien shu-tien, 1957-58. 6 vols. 陶菊隱。北洋軍閥統治時期史話。

T'ao Chü-yin. Wu P'ei-fu chiang-chün chuan. Shanghai: Chung-hua shu-chü, 1941. 陶菊隱。吳佩孚將軍傳。

TKLH

Ts'ao K'un, Wu P'ei-fu ho chuan, ed. by Ti-i t'u-shu-kuan. Ti-i t'u-shu-kuan, 1924. 曹錕，吳佩孚合傳。第一圖書館。

WWC, 1925, 1931.

Yu Yen Chü-shih (pseud.). Chung-hua Min-kuo wu ta tsung-t'ung ta-shih chi. Peking, 1925. 幽燕居士。中華民國五大總統大事記。

Ts'en Ch'un-hsuan   岑春煊

WORKS

1962. Le-chai man-pi (ed. by Wu Hsiang-hsiang). Taipei: Wen hsing shu-tien. 樂齋漫筆。吳相湘。

SOURCES

Chan Chi. Chang P'u-ch'üan hsien-sheng ch'üan-chi; cheng pien, pu pien. Taipei: Chung-yang wen-wu kung-ying she, 1951-52. 張繼。張溥泉先生全集；正編，補編。

Chang Ping-lin. T'ai-yen hsien-sheng tzu-ting nien-p'u (1868-1922). Hong Kong: Lung men shu-tien, 1965. 章炳麟。太炎先生自訂年譜 (1968-1922)。

Chün wu yuan k'ao shih (with Liang Kuang tu ssu-ling pu k'ao shih), ed. by Liang Kuang tu ssu-ling pu ts'an-mou t'ing. Shanghai: Shang-wu yin shu kuan, 1916. 軍務院考實 (附：兩廣都司令部考實)。兩廣都司令部參謀廳。

Chung-kuo chin-shih ming-jen hsiao-shih. 中國近世名人小史。

CMTC

Hsin-hai ko-ming, ed. by Ch'ai Te-keng *et al.* Shanghai: Shanghai jen-min ch'u-pan she, 1957.
辛亥革命。柴德賡等。

I-ho-t'uan tang-an shih-liao, ed. by Kuo-chia tang-an chü Ming Ch'ing tang-an kuan. Peking: Chuang-hua shu-chü, 1959. 2 vols.
義和團檔案史料。國家檔案局明清檔案館。

K'ai-kuo ming-jen mo-chi.
開國名人墨蹟。

Li Ken-yuan. Hsueh sheng (Li Ken-yuan) nien lu. Ch'ü shih ching lu, 1934.
李根源。雪生 (李根源) 年錄。

Li P'ei-sheng. Kuei hsi chü Yueh chih yu-lai chi ch'i ching-kuo. Canton, 1921?
李培生。桂系據粵之由來及其經過。

Liu Ch'eng-yü. Hung-hsien chi-shih shih pen-shih pu chu. Taipei: Wen hai ch'u-pan she, 1966. 2 vols.
劉成禺。洪憲紀事詩本事簿注。

Sun Wen. Kuo-fu ch'üan-chi (ed. by Chung-kuo kuo-min-tang tang shih shih-liao pien-tsuan wei-yuan-hui). Taipei: Chung-hua Min-kuo ko-chieh chi-nien kuo-fu tan-ch'en ch'ou-pei wei-yuan-hui, 1965.
孫文。國父全集。中國國民黨黨史史料編纂委員會。

T'ao Chü-yin. Pei-yang chün-fa t'ung-chih shih-ch'i shih-hua. Peking: Sheng-huo, tu-shu, hsin-chih san lien shu-tien, 1957-58. 6 vols.
陶菊隱。北洋軍閥統治時期史話。

———. Tu-chün t'uan chuan. Shanghai: Chung-hua shu-chü, 1948.
陶菊隱。督軍團傳。

Ts'en Ch'un-hsuan. Le-chai man-pi (ed. by Wu Hsiang-hsiang). Taipei: Wen hsing shu-tien, 1962.
岑春煊。樂齋漫筆。吳相湘。

Ts'en Hsiang-ch'in kung nien-p'u, ed. by Chao Fan.
岑襄勤公年譜。趙藩。

Tseng I. Hu kuo chün chi-shih.
曾毅。護國軍記事。

Wu-hsü pien-fa tang-an shih-liao, ed. by Kuo-chia tang-an chü Ming Ch'ing tang-an kuan. Peking: Chung-hua shu-chü, 1959. 2 vols.
戊戌變法檔案史料。國家檔案局明清檔案館。

Tseng Ch'i   曾琦

WORKS

1941. Shih-pa nien lai chih Chung-kuo ch'ing-nien-tang. Chengtu: Kuo hun shu-tien.
十八年來之中國青年黨。

1954. Tseng Mu-han hsien-sheng i-chu (ed. by Tseng Mu-han hsien-sheng i-chu pien-chi wei-yuan-hui). Taipei: Chung-kuo ch'ing-nien-tang chung-yang chih-hsing wei-yuan-hui.
曾慕韓先生遺著。曾慕韓先生遺著編輯委員會。

ed. of *Hsing shih chou-k'an.*
醒獅週刊。

Kuo-t'i yü ch'ing-nien.
國体與青年。

SOURCES

Chang, Carsun (Chang Chia-sen). The Third Force in China. New York: Bookman Associates, 1952.

Ch'ien Tuan-sheng. The Government and Politics of China. Cambridge: Harvard University Press, 1950.

Chow Tse-tsung. The May Fourth Movement: Intellectual Revolution in Modern China. Cambridge: Harvard University Press, 1960.

CHMI

CH-T, 1952.

Houn, Franklin W. Central Government of China 1912-1928: An Institutional Study. Madison: University of Wisconsin Press, 1957.

Li Chien-nung. The Political History of China 1840-1928 (tr. and ed. by Teng Ssu-yu, Jeremy Ingalls). Princeton: D. Van Nostrand Co., 1956.

Linebarger, Paul M. The China of Chiang Kai-shek. Boston: World Peace Foundation, 1941.

———. Government in Republican China. New York: McGraw-Hill Book Co., 1938.

Tseng Ch'i. Tseng Mu-han hsien-sheng i-chu (ed. by Tseng Mu-han hsien-sheng i-chu pien-chi wei-yuan-hui). Taipei: Chung-kuo ch'ing-nien-tang chung-yang chih-hsing wei-yuan-hui, 1954.
曾琦。曾慕韓先生遺著。曾慕韓先生遺著編輯委員會。

WWC, 1950.

WWMC

Tseng Chung-ming   曾仲鳴

WORKS

1925. Une Goutte d'eau. Paris: E. Leroux.

1930. La Chine et le Kuomintang. Shanghai: Librairie Franco-Chinoise.

1934. Lu cheng lun-ts'ung. Shenghai: K'ai-ming shu-tien.
路政論叢。

SOURCES

Chu Tzu-chia (pseud of Chin Hsiung-pai). Wang cheng-ch'uan te k'ai-ch'ang yü shou-ch'ang. Hong Kong: Ch'un-ch'iu tsa-chih she, 1964. 5 vols.
朱子家（金雄白）。汪政權的開場與收場。
WWC, 1931.

Tsien, H.S.   錢學森

WORKS

1938. "Supersonic Flow over an Inclined Body of Revolution." *Journal of Aeronautical Sciences*, 5: 480–83.

1939. "Two-dimensional Subsonic Flow of Compressible Fluids." *Journal of Aeronautical Sciences*, 6: 399–407.

1940. "Influence of Curvature on Buckling Characteristics of Structures." *Journal of the Aeronautical Sciences*, 7: 276–89. (with T. von Karman, L.G. Dunn).

1941. "Buckling of Thin Cylindrical Shells Under Axial Compression." *Journal of the Aeronautical Sciences*, 8: 303–12. (with T. von Karman.

1942. "Buckling of Column with Non-linear Lateral Supports." *Journal of the Aeronautical Sciences*, 9: 119–32.

1942. "Theory for the Buckling of Thin Shells." *Journal of the Aeronautical Sciences*, 9: 119–32.

1943. "On the Design of the Contraction Cone for a Wind Tunnel." *Journal of the Aeronautical Sciences*, 10: 68–70.

1943, April 8. "Report on High Speed Pressure Distribution over XSB2D-1 Cowl." California Institute of Technology, JPL–27.

1943. "Symmetrical Joukowsky Airfoils in Shear Flow." *Quarterly of Applied Mathematics*, 1: 130–48.

1945. "The Glauert-Prandtl Approximation for Subsonic Flows of a Compressible Fluid." *Journal of the Aeronautical Sciences*, 12: 173–87, 202 (with Lester Lees).

1946. "Atomic Energy." *Journal of the Aeronautical Sciences*, 13: 171–80.

1946. "Propagation of Plane Sound Waves in Rarefied Gases." *Journal of the Accoustical Society of America*, 18: 335–41 (with R. Schomberg).

1946. "Similarity Laws of Hypersonic Flows.' *Journal of Mathematics and Physics*, 25: 247–52.

1946. "Superaerodynamics, Mechanics of Rarefied Gases." *Journal of the Aeronautical Sciences*, 13: 653–64.

1947. "Corrections on the Paper 'One-Dimensional Flows of a Gas Characterized by van der Waal's Equation of State.' " *Journal of Mathematics and Physics*, 26: 76–77.

1947. "One-Dimensional Flows of a Gas Characterized by van der Waal's Equation of State." *Journal of Mathematics and Physics*, 25: 301–24.

1948. "On Two-Dimensional Non-steady Motion of Slender Body in Compressible Fluid." *Journal of Mathematics and Physics*, 27: 220–31 (with C.C. Lin, E. Reissner).

1949. "Airfoils in Slightly Supersonic Flow." *Journal of the Aeronautical Sciences*, 16: 55–61 (with J. R. Baron).

1949. "Interaction Between Parallel Streams of Subsonic and Supersonic Velocities." *Journal of the Aeronautical Sciences*, 16, 515–28 (with M. Finston).

1950. "A Generalization of Alfrey's Theorem for Visco-Elastic Media." *Quarterly of Applied Mathematics*, 8: 104–6.

1950, June. "Instruction and Research at Daniel and Florence Guggenheim Jet Propulsion Center." *American Rocket Society Journal*. 81: 51–64.

1950. "Research in Rocket and Jet Propulsion." *Aero Digest*, 60: 120–22, 124–25.

1951. "Optimum Thrust Programming for Sounding Rocket." *American Rocket Society Journal*, 19: 99–107 (with R.C. Evans).

1951. "Influence of Flame Front on the Flow Field." *Journal of Applied Mechanics*, 18: 188–94.

1952. "Automatic Navigation of Long Range Rocket Vehicle." *American Rocket Society Journal*, 22: 192–99 (with T.C. Adamson, E.L. Knuth).

1952. "Method for Comparing Performance of Power Plants for Vertical Flight." *American Rocket Society Journal*, 22: 200–3, 212.

1952. "Similarity Law for Stressing Rapidly Heated Thin-Walled Cylinders." *American Rocket Society Journal*, 22: 144–49, 167 (with C.M. Cheng).

1952. "Transfer Functions of Rocket Nozzles." *American Rocket Society Journal*, 22: 139–43, 162.

1953. "Physical Mechanics, New Field in Engineering Science." *American Rocket Society Journal*, 23: 14–16, 35.
1954. Engineering Cybernetics. New York: McGraw-Hill Book Co.
1956. "The Poincare-Lighthill-Kuo Method." *Advances in Applied Mechanics*, IV: 281–349.

SOURCES

"Chinese Puzzle." *Technology Week*, IXX–50 (November 7, 1966).
"Jet Scientist Deported to China." *Aviation Weekly*, LXIII–17 (September 19, 1955).
von Karman, Theodore. The Wind and Beyond (with Lee Edson). Boston: Little Brown & Co., 1967.
Keats, E. "Blackboard Jumble." *Saturday Review of Literature*. LI–6 (January 27, 1968).
Kuang-ming jih-pao. Peking, November 2, 1955. 光明日報。
The New York Times, November 7, December 14, 1948; December 2, 1949; September 8, 21, November 16, 17, 1950; January 30, 31, 1951; December 3, 15, 1952; March 6, 1953; September 13, 1955; August 12, 1956; August 27, 1957; January 11, 1960; October 28, 1966.
Ryan, William L., and Sam Summerlin. "How China Got the Bomb." *Look*, July 25, 1967: 19–25.
Time, LIV–46 (December 12, 1949).
Viorst, Milton. "The Bitter Tea of Dr. Tsien." *Esquire*, September, 1967: 125–29, 168–70.

Tso Ch'üan   左權

WORKS

1949. Su-lien kung nung hung chün te pu-ping chan-tou t'iao ling, ti-i pu. (tr.) with Liu Po-ch'eng. Hong Kong: Hong Kong cheng pao ch'u-pan she.
蘇聯工農紅軍的步兵戰鬥條令，第 1 部。
劉伯承。
Chien-chueh chih-hsing ching ping chien cheng.
堅決執行精兵簡政。
Sao-tang yü fan sao-tang.
掃蕩與反掃蕩。

SOURCES

Person interviewed: Chang Kuo-t'ao.
CKLC
GCCJK
HKLC

Tsou Lu   鄒魯

WORKS

1914–? ed. of *Min-kuo tsa-chih*.
民國雜誌。
1927? Hung-hua-kang ssu lieh-shih chuan-chi (comp. by Ko-ming chi-nien hui). Shanghai.
紅花岡四烈士傳記。革命紀念會。
1930. Tsou Lu wen-ts'un (ed. by Mei O). Peiping: Pei hua shu-chü.
鄒魯文存。梅喦。
1939? Ch'eng-lu shih chi.
澄廬詩集。
1939. Kuang-chou (Canton) hsin-hai san-yüeh erh-shih-chiu jih ko-ming chi. Shanghai: Shang-wu yin shu kuan.
廣州辛亥三月二十九日革命記。
1944. (comp.) Chung-kuo kuo-min-tang shih kao. Chungking: Shang-wu yin shu kuan. 4 vols.
中國國民黨史稿。
1944. K'ang chien ho-p'ing chih wo chien. Chungking: Shang-wu yin shu kuan.
抗建和平之我見。
1945. Chung-kuo kuo-min-tang shih lueh. Shanghai: Shang-wu yin shu kuan.
中國國民黨史略。
1946. Chung-kuo kuo-min-tang kai shih. Shanghai: Cheng-chung shu-chü.
中國國民黨概史。
1946–47. Hui-ku lu. Nanking: Tu-li ch'u-pan she. 2 vols.
回顧錄。
1948. Ch'eng-lu wen-hsuan (ed. by Chang Ching-ying). Shanghai: Cheng-chung shu-chü.
澄廬文選。張鏡影。
1951. Erh-shih-chiu kuo yu-chi. Taipei: Taiwan shang-wu yin shu kuan.
二十九國遊記。
1952. Chung-kuo ko-ming shih. Taipei: P'a-mi-erh shu-tien.
中國革命史。

SOURCES

BKL
CH
Chung-yang jih-pao. Taipei, January 31, February 1, 1956.
中央日報。
CMJL
CTMC
Hsien-tai shih-liao, I, ed. by Hai t'ien ch'u-pan

she. Shanghai: Hai t'ien ch'u-pan she, 1933.
現代史料。海天出版社。

Hsing-tao jih-pao. Hong Kong, February 14, 1954.
星島日報。

The New York Times, February 14, 1954.

Tsou Lu. Chung-kuo kuo-min-tang shih luch. Shanghai: Shang-wu yin shu kuan, 1945.
鄒魯。中國國民黨史略。

———. Hui-ku lu. Nanking: Tu-li ch'u-pan she, 1946–47. 2 vols.
鄒魯。回顧錄。

———. Tsou Lu wen-ts'un (ed. by Mei O). Peiping: Pei hua shu-chü, 1930.
鄒魯。鄒魯文存。梅萼。

Tsou T'ao-fen   鄒韜奮

WORKS

1928. Min pen chu-i yü chiao-yü. (tr. of John Dewey's *Democracy and Education*). Shanghai: Shang-wu yin shu kuan.
民本主義與教育。

1932–34. Hsiao yen-lun. Shanghai: Sheng-huo chou-k'an she. 3 vols.
小言論。

1935–? ed. of *Ta-chung sheng-huo*.
大眾生活。

1936. Ta-chung chi.
大眾集。

1936. T'an-pai chi.
坦白集。

1938. Chi-pien. Kwangtung.
激變。

1938. Tsai li chi. Hankow: Sheng-huo shu-tien.
再厲集。

1939. (ed.) Hsien-cheng yün-tung ts'an-k'ao ts'ai-liao. Chungking: Sheng-huo shu-tien.
憲政運動參考材料。

1940. Tsou T'ao-fen *et al*. Hsien-cheng yün-tung lun-wen hsuan-chi. Chungking: Sheng-huo shu-tien.
鄒韜奮等。憲政運動論文選集。

1940. P'ing tsung chi yü. Sheng-huo shu-tien. 2 vols.
萍踪寄語。

1941. K'ang chan i-lai. Hong Kong: Hong Kong hua shang pao-kuan.
抗戰以來。

1941. (ed.) Lun Te Su chan-cheng. Hong Kong: Ta-chung ch'u-pan she.
論德蘇戰爭。

1946. Tsou En-jun *et al*. Hsien-fa ts'ao-an yen-chiu. Shanghai: Sheng-huo shu-tien.
鄒恩潤等。憲法草案研究。

1947. Ching-li. Shanghai: T'ao-fen ch'u-pan she.
經歷。

1947. Huan-nan yü-sheng chi. Shanghai: T'ao-fen ch'u-pan she.
患難餘生記。

1948. P'ing tsung i yü. Shanghai: T'ao-fen ch'u-pan she.
萍踪憶語。

1949. T'ao-fen wen lu (ed. by Hu Yü-chih *et al*.). Shanghai: San lien shu-tien.
韜奮文錄。胡愈之等。

1950. Shih-yeh kuan-li yü chih-yeh hsiu-yang. Peking: San lien shu-tien.
事業管理與職業修養。

1959. T'ao-fen wen-chi. Hong Kong: San lien shu-tien. 3 vols.
韜奮文集。

ed. of *Ch'üan min k'ang chan*.
全民抗戰。

K'ang chan.
抗戰。

ed. of *Sheng-huo chou-k'an*.
生活週刊。

ed. of *Ti-k'ang (San-jih-k'an)*.
抵抗 (三日刊)。

Tsou En-jun *et al*. K'ang chan tsung tung-yuan. Chan-shih ch'u-pan she.
鄒恩潤等。抗戰總動員。

Tu-shu ou i. (tr.)
讀書偶譯。

T'uan-chieh yü-wu te chi-ko chi-pen t'iao-chien yü tsui-ti yao-ch'iu. with Shen Chün-ju, Chang Nai-ch'i, Tao Hsing-chih.
團結禦侮的幾個基本條件與最低要求。沈鈞儒, 章乃器, 陶行知。

SOURCES

Huang I-chih. Tsou T'ao-fen. Shanghai: Shang-wu yin shu kuan, 1950.
黃逸之。鄒韜奮。

Jen-min jih-pao. Peking, July 25, 1964.
人民日報。

Mu Hsin. Tsou T'ao-fen. Hong Kong: Sheng-huo, tu-shu, hsin-chih san lien shu-tien, 1959.
穆欣。鄒韜奮。

T'ao-fen te tao-lu, ed. by Shanghai T'ao-fen chi-nien kuan. Peking: Sheng-huo, tu-shu, hsin-chih san lien shu-tien, 1958.
韜奮的道路。上海韜奮紀念館。

Tsou En-jun. Ching-li. Shanghai: T'ao-fen ch'u-pan she, 1947.
鄒恩潤。 經歷。

———. Huan-nan yü-sheng chi. Shanghai: T'ao-fen ch'u-pan she, 1947.
鄒恩潤。 患難餘生記。

Yang Ming. T'ao-fen hsien-sheng te liu-wang sheng-huo. Shanghai: Min-chu she, 1945.
楊明。 韜奮先生的流亡生活。

Yung tsai chui-nien chung te T'ao-fen hsien-sheng, ed. by T'ao-fen ch'u-pan she. Shanghai: Sheng-huo shu-tien, 1947.
永在追念中的韜奮先生。 韜奮出版社。

Tsu, Y.Y.

WORKS

Friend of Fishermen. Ambler, Pa.: Trinity Press.

SOURCES

Documents of the Three-Self Movement: Source Materials for the Study of the Protestant Church in Communist China, comp. by Far Eastern Office, Division of Foreign Missions, National Council of the Churches of Christ in the U.S.A. New York: Far Eastern Office, Division of Foreign Missions, National Council of the Churches of Christ in the U.S.A., 1963.

Tsu, Andrew Yu-yue. Friend of Fishermen. Ambler, Pa.: Trinity Press.

Tu Chung-yuan   杜重遠

SOURCES

Persons interviewed: not to be identified

Tu Yü-ming   杜聿明

SOURCES

BKL

Clubb, O. Edmund. "Chiang Kai-shek's Waterloo: The Battle of the Hwai-hai." Pacific Historical Review (November, 1956): 389-99.

———. "Manchuria in the Balance, 1945–1946." Pacific Historical Review, (November, 1957): 377-89.

———. "Military Debacle in Manchuria." Army Quarterly and Defense Journal, (January, 1958): 221-32.

CTMC

Liu Chih-pu. A Military History of Modern China, 1924–1949. Princeton: Princeton University Press, 1956.

Romanus, Charles F., and Riley Sunderland. United States Army in World War II—China-Burma-India Theater, Vol. I, Stilwell's Mission to China. Washington: Department of the Army, 1953.

Tu Yueh-sheng   杜月笙

SOURCES

Chang Chün-ku. Tu Yueh-sheng chuan. Taipei: Chuan-chi wen-hsueh ch'u-pan she, 1967-68. 3 vols.
章君穀。 杜月笙傳。

Chin shan shih-pao. San Francisco, November 24, 1956.
金山時報。

Gunther, John. Inside Asia. New York: Harper & Bros., 1939.

Hsing tao chou-pao, 240-42 (January, 1956).
星島週報。

Kuo wen chou-pao, X-9 (March 6, 1933).
國聞週報。

Review of the Hong Kong Chinese Press, 163 (August 17, 1951).

Shih I (pseud.). Tu Yueh-sheng wai-chuan. Hong Kong: Ch'un-ch'iu tsa-chih she, 1962.
拾遺。 杜月笙外傳。

TCML

Tu Yueh-sheng hsien-sheng chi-nien chi. Taipei: Heng she, 1952-54. 2 vols.
杜月笙先生紀念集。

Tui-chih chi-che (pseud.). Ai Chiang-nan. Kowloon: Chen hua ch'u-pan she, 1962-64. 8 vols.
退職記者。 哀江南。

Wang, Y.C. "Tu Yueh-sheng (1888–1951): A Tentative Political Biography." The Journal of Asian Studies, XXVI-3 (May, 1967): 433-55.

Tuan Ch'i-jui   段祺瑞

WORKS

1966. Hsun-lien ts'ao-fa hsiang hsi t'u shuo. with Yuan Shih-k'ai et al. Taipei: Wen hai ch'u-pan she, 1966. 2 vols.

Chung-hua Min-kuo shih-liao, ed. by Sun Yueh.
Shanghai: Shanghai wen-ming shu-chü, 1929.
3 vols.
中華民國史料。孫曜。
CMMC
Fei Hsing-chien. Tuan Ch'i-jui. Shanghai,
1920.
費行簡。段祺瑞。
Godshall, Wilson Leon. Tsingtao under Three
Flags. Shanghai: The Commercial Press, 1929.
Hsin-hai ko-ming, ed. by Ch'ai Te-keng *et al.*
Shanghai: Shanghai jen-min ch'u-pan she,
1957. 8 vols.
辛亥革命。柴德賡等。
Hsü I-shih. I-shih lei kao. Shanghai: Ku-chin
ch'u-pan she, 1944.
徐一士。一士類稿。
"Jen-wen chih." *Jen-wen yueh-k'an*, VIII-2
(March 15, 1937).
人文志。人文月刊。
Kuo wen chou-pao, I-4 (August 28, 1924).
國聞週報。
Li Chien-nung. Tsui-chin san-shih nien Chung-
kuo cheng-chih shih. Shanghai: T'ai-p'ing-
yang shu-tien, 1931.
李劍農。最近三十年中國政治史。
Ma Ta-chung. Ta Chung-hua Min-kuo shih.
Peiping: Chung-hua shu-chü, 1929.
馬大中。大中華民國史。
Nan-hai Yin-tsu (pseud.). An fu t'ung shih.
1926.
南海胤子。安福痛史。
Powell, Ralph L. The Rise of Chinese Military
Power 1895-1912. Princeton: Princeton University Press, 1955.
Pu I-p'eng *et al.* Ts'an-chan shih-lu. Peiping,
1927. 6 vols.
步翼鵬等。參戰實錄。
Shang Ping-ho. Hsin-jen ch'un-ch'iu. Hsin-jen
li-shih pien-chi she, 1924. 16 vols.
訓練操法詳晰圖說。袁世凱等。

SOURCES

AADC
Chang Hsiung. Chung-hua Min-kuo te nei-ko.
Peiping, 1928.
章熊。中華民國的內閣。
Chia I-chün. Chung-hua Min-kuo cheng-chih
shih. Peiping, 1929. 2 vols.
賈逸君。中華民國政治史。
Ch'ien Tuan-sheng. The Government and
Politics of China. Cambridge: Harvard
University Press, 1950.

尚秉和。辛壬春秋。
Shih pao pan-yueh-k'an, 3 (November 16, 1936).
實報半月刊。
T'ao Chü-yin. Pei-yang chün-fa t'ung-chih
shih-chi shih-hua. Peking: Sheng-huo, tu-
shu, hsin-chih san lien shu-tien, 1957-58. 6
vols.
陶菊隱。北洋軍閥統治時期史話。
TKLH
Tuan Ch'i-jui, Chang Tso-lin ho chuan, ed. by
Tun Ken. Hsiao-shuo t'u-shu she, 1925.
段祺瑞，張作霖合傳。鈍根。
Wen Kung-chih. Tsui-chin san-shih nien
Chung-kuo chün-shih shih. Shanghai: T'ai-
p'ing-yang shu-tien, 1932. 2 vols.
文公直。最近三十年中國軍事史。
Wen Shih-lin. Tuan shih huo kuo chi.
溫世霖。段氏禍國記。
WWC, 1918-19.
Wu T'ieh-ch'eng. Ssu-shih nien lai chih Chung-
kuo yu wo (Wu T'ieh-ch'eng hsien-sheng hui-
i lu). Taipei, 1957.
吳鐵城。四十年來之中國與我 （吳鐵城先
生回憶錄）。
Yuan shih tao kuo chi, ed. by Huang I. Taipei:
Wen hsing shu-tien, 1962.
袁氏盜國記。

Tuan Hsi-p'eng　段錫朋

SOURCES

BKL
CH
Chow Tse-tsung. The May Fourth Movement:
Intellectual Revolution in Modern China.
Cambridge: Harvard University Press, 1960.
Liu Chao-pin. "Chi Tuan Hsi-p'eng hsien-
sheng." *Chuan-chi wen-hsueh*, III-4 (October,
1963): 24-25.
劉兆璸。記段錫朋先生。傳記文學。
Tuan Yung-lan. "Wo te fu-ch'in." *Chuan-chi
wen-hsueh*, III-4 (October, 1963): 26-27.
段永蘭。我的父親。傳記文學。

Tung Ch'i-wu　董其武

SOURCES

CTMC
DPGOCC
GCJJ

Tung Hsien-kuang　　董顯光

WORKS

1912-? ed. of *New York Independent*.

1914-16. ed. of *Peking Daily News*.

1918-? ed. of *Millard Review*.

1925-31. ed. of *Yung pao*.
庸報。

1929. Facts about the Chinese Eastern Railway Situation.

1929-35. ed. of *China Press*.

1933. Problems and Personalities in the Far East. Shanghai.

1933-34. Men and Events in the Far East. Shanghai? 3 vols.

1937. Chiang Kai-shek, Soldier and Statesman: Authorized Biography. Shanghai: China Publishing Co., 2 vols.

1937-45. (sup. ed.) *China Handbook*.

1944. (ed.) China After Seven Years of War. Chungking: Chinese Ministry of Information.

1947. (sup. ed.) CH.

1950. Dateline: China; the Beginning of China's Press Relations with the World. New York: Rockport Press.

1953. Chiang Kai-shek. Taipei: China Publishing Co.

1954. Abridged Biography of President Chiang Kai-shek. Taipei: China Cultural Service.

1955. Jih-pen te yu-mo.
日本的幽默。
Eng. tr., *Japanese Sense of Humour*. Tokyo, 1956?

1955. Tung Hsien-kuang *et al*. Hsin-wen hsueh lun-chi. Taipei: Chung-hua wen-hua ch'u-pan shih-yeh wei-yuan-hui.
董顯光等。新聞學論集。

1957. Collection of Speeches, June 1956-February 1957. Washington: Chinese Embassy.

1957. Gems of Chinese Humor. Washington.

1958. Free China's Role in the Asian Crisis: Collection of Speeches, March-November, 1957. Washington.

1961. Christianity in Taiwan: A History. Taipei: China Post.

1962. Chi-tu-chiao tsai Taiwan te fa-chan Taipei.
基督教在台灣的發展。
ed. of *China Republican*.

SOURCES

Baker, Richard T. A History of the Graduate School of Journalism, Columbia University.

New York: Columbia University Press, 1954.
CH
CH-T, 1956-57.
CMJL
Current Biography, 1956.
GCJJ
WWC, 1925, 1931, 1936.

Tung K'ang　　董康

WORKS

1939. Min-fa ch'in-shu chi-ch'eng liang pien hsiu-cheng an (with Ts'an-k'iao t'ao-wen). 2 vols.
民法親屬繼承兩編修正案（附：參考條文）。

1939. Shu po yung t'an. Sung-fen-shih. 5 vols.
書舶庸譚。

(ed.) Ch'ien-ch'iu chueh yen t'u. Wu-chin: Tung shih. 2 vols.
千秋絶艷圖。

(ed.) Sung-fen-shih ts'ung-k'an, ch'u pien, erh pien. 100 vols.
誦芬室叢刊，初編，二編。

SOURCES

Chung-kuo chin-tai hsi-ch'ü shih, tr. and ed. by Wang Ku-lu. Peking: Tso-chia ch'u-pan she, 1958. 2 vols.
中國近代戲曲史。王古魯。

Tung K'ang. Shu po yung t'an. Sung-fen-shih, 1939. 5 vols.
董康。書舶庸談。

Tung Pi-wu　　董必武

WORKS

1945. Memorandum on China's Liberated Areas. San Francisco.

1946. Chung-kuo chieh-fang ch'ü shih-lu. San Francisco: Ho-tso ch'u-pan she.
中國解放區實錄。

1951, October. "Two Years of the People's Republic of China." *People's China*, IV-7: 10-12.

1952, April. "Strengthen the Work of the People's Representative Conference." *People's China*, 8: 4-7, 27-31.

1953. Lun chia-ch'iang jen-min tai-piao hui-i te kung-tso—tsai Hua-pei ti-i tz'u hsien-chang hui-i shang te chiang-hua (i-chiu-wu-i nien chiu-yueh erh-shih-san jih). Peking: Jen-min ch'u-pan she.

論加強人民代表會議的工作─在華北第一
次縣長會議上的講話（一九五一年九月二
十三日）。

1955, April. "The Thirtieth Anniversary of the
Death of Dr. Sun Yat-sen." *People's China*,
7: 3-6.

1956, November. "Sun Chung-shan hsien-sheng
te ko-ming ching-shen." *Hsin kuan-ch'a*, 22:
7-8.
孫中山先生的革命精神。新觀察。

1957, January. "Hui-i Ch'en Yen-nien lieh-
shih." *Hsin kuan-ch'a*, 2: 30-31.
回憶陳延年烈士。新觀察。

1957, February-March. "'Erh ch'i' pa-kung hui-
i." *Hsin kuan-ch'a*, 3-5.
二七罷工回憶。新觀察。

1957, July. "Chung-kuo kung-ch'an-tang
ch'eng-li ch'ien-hou te chien-wen." *Hsin
kuan-ch'a*, 13: 6-8.
中國共產黨成立前後的見聞。新觀察。

1958. Kuan-yü tsui-kao jen-min fa-yuan te kung-
tso pao-kao; i-chiu-wu-ch'i nien ch'i-yüeh erh
jih tsai ti-i chieh ch'üan-kuo jen-min tai-piao
ta-hui ti-ssu tz'u hui-i shang. Peking: Fa-lü
ch'u-pan she.
關於最高人民法院的工作報告；一九五七
年七月二日在第一屆全國人民代表大會第
四次會議上。

SOURCES

Person interviewed: Chang Kuo-t'ao.

Boorman, Howard L. "Tung Pi-wu: A Political
Profile." *The China Quarterly*, July-September, 1964: 66-83.

Chung-kuo kung-ch'an-tang te chung-yao jen-
wu. Peiping: Min-chien, 1949.
中國共產黨的重要人物。

Elegant, Robert S. China's Red Masters. New
York: Twayne, 1951.

K-WWMC

The New York Times, April 22, 1945.

Ray, J. Franklin. UNRRA in China: A Case
Study of the Interplay of Interests in a Program of International Aid to an Underdeveloped Country. New York: Institute of
Pacific Relations, 1947.

RD

Shen Te-ch'un and T'ien Hai-yen. "Chung-kuo
kung-ck'an-tang 'i ta' te chu-yao wen-t'i—
fang-wen ti-i tz'u tai-piao ta-hui tai-piao Tung
Pi-wu t'ung-chih." *Jen-min jih-pao*. Peking,
June 30, 1961.
沈德純，田海燕。中國共產黨「一大」的

主要問題─訪問第一次代表大會代表董必
武同志。人民日報。
WWC, 1950.
WWMC

Tung Tso-pin　　董作賓

WORKS

1919-? ed. of *Hsin Yü jih-pao.*
新豫日報。

1929. "Hsin huo pu-tz'u hsieh pen," in Li Chi
et al.; *An-yang fa-chueh pao-kao*, I. Kuo-li
chung-yang yen-chiu yuan li-shih yü-yen yen-
chiu so.
新獲卜辭寫本。李濟等。安陽發掘報告。

1929. "Shang-tai kuei-pu te t'ui-ts'e," in Li Chi
et al., *An-yang fa-chueh pao-kao*, I. Kuo-li
chung-yang yen-chiu yuan li-shih yü-yen yen-
chiu so.
商代龜卜的推測。李濟等。安陽發掘報告。

1929. "Shih-ch'i nien shih-yüeh shih chueh An-
yang Hsiao-t'un pao-kao shu," in Li Chi *et
al.*, *An-yang fa-chueh pao-kao*, I. Kuo-li chung-
yang yen-chiu yuan li-shih yü-yen yen-chiu
so.
十七年十月試掘安陽小屯報告書。李濟等。
安陽發掘報告。

1930. "Chia-ku-wen yen-chiu te k'uo-ta," in Li
Chi *et al.*, *An-yang fa-chueh pao-kao*, II. Kuo-li
chung-yang yen-chiu yuan li-shih yü-yen yen-
chiu so.
甲骨文研究的擴大。李濟等。安陽發掘報告。

1930. "Yin hsü yen-ko." *Chung-yang yen-chiu
yuan li-shih yü-yen yen-chiu so chi k'an*, 2.
殷墟沿革。中央研究院歷史語言研究所集
刊。

1931. "Pu-tz'u chung so chien chih Yin li," in
Li Chi *et al.*, *An-yang fa-chueh pao-kao*, III.
Kuo-li chung-yang yen-chiu yuan li-shih yü-
yen yen-chiu so.
卜辭中所見之殷曆。李濟等。安陽發掘報告。

1931. "Ta kuei ssu pan k'ao shih," in Li Chi *et
al.*, *An-yang fa-chueh pao-kao*, III. Kuo-li
chung-yang yen-chiu yuan li-shih yü-yen yen-
chiu so.
大龜四版考釋。李濟等。安陽發掘報告。

1932. Chia-ku-wen tuan-tai yen-chiu li.
甲骨文斷代研究例。

1933. "T'an t'an." *Chung-yang yen-chiu yuan li-
shih yü-yen yen-chiu so chi k'an*, 4.
談譚。中央研究院歷史語言研究所集刊。

1934. "Ch'eng-tzu-yai yü Lung-shan-chen," in

Fu Ssu-nien *et al.*, *Ch'eng-tzu-yai (Shantung Li-ch'eng hsien Lung-shan-chen hei t'ao wen-hua i-chih)*. Nanking: Kuo-li chung-yang yen-chiu yuan li-shih yü-yen yen-chiu so.
城子崖與龍山鎮。傅斯年等。城子崖（山東歷城縣龍山鎮黑陶文化遺址）。

1934. P'ing-lu ching p'u.
平廬景譜。

1934. "Yin li chung chi ko chung-yao wen-t'i." *Chung-yang yen-chiu yuan li-shih yü-yen yen-chiu so chi k'an*, 4.
殷曆中幾個重要問題。中央研究院歷史語言研究所集刊。

1936. "Wu teng chueh tsai Yin Shang." *Chung-yang yen-chiu yuan li-shih yü-yen yen-chiu so chi k'an*, 6.
五等爵在殷商。中央研究院歷史語言研究所集刊。

1939. (comp.) Chou-kung ts'e-ching-t'ai tiao-ch'a pao-kao. with Liu Tun-chen, Kao p'ing-tzu. Changsha: Shang-wu yin shu kuan.
周公測景台調查報告。劉敦楨，高平子。

1945. Yin li p'u. Li-chuang, Szechwan: Chung-yang yen-chiu yuan li-shih yü-yen yen-chiu so. 4 vols.
殷曆譜。

1950. "Yin tai yueh-shih k'ao." Chung-yang yen-chiu yuan li-shih yü-yen yen-chiu so chi k'an, 22.
殷代月食考。中央研究院歷史語言研究所集刊。

1951. "Chung-kuo ku-tai wen-hua te jen-shih." *Ta-lu tsa-chih*, III-12.
中國古代文化的認識。大陸雜誌。

1951. Shih-chieh kai li wen-t'i. with Kao P'ing-tzu *et al*. Taipei: Ta-lu tsa-chih she.
世界改曆問題。高平子等。

1951. Tung Tso-pin *et al*. Shih-chieh wen-hua te ch'ien-t'u (chiu): Chung-kuo ku-tai wen-hua te jen-shih. Taipei: Ta-lu tsa-chih she.
董作賓等。世界文化的前途（九）：中國古代文化的認識。

1951. Wu-wang fa Chou nien yueh jih chin k'ao. Taipei: Kuo-li Taiwan ta-hsueh.
武王伐紂年月日今考。

1952. Chung-kuo ku-tai wen-hua te jen-shih. Taipei: Ta-lu tsa-chih she.
中國古代文化的認識。

1952, April. "Chia-ku wen tuan-tai yen-chiu shih ko piao-chun." *Ta-lu tsa-chih*, IV-8.
甲骨文斷代研究十個標準。大陸雜誌。

1952. "Hsi-chou nien li p'u." *Chung-yang yen-chiu yuan li-shih yü-yen yen-chiu so chi k'an*, 23.
西周年曆譜。中央研究院歷史語言研究所集刊。

1952. An Interpretation of the Ancient Chinese Civilization (ed. by Chinese Association for the United Nations). Taipei: Chinese Association for the United Nations.

1952, November. "Chung-kuo wen-hsueh te ch'i-yuan." *Ta-lu tsa-chih*, V-10.
中國文學的起源。大陸雜誌。

1953. (comp.) Chung-kuo li-shih ts'an-k'ao t'u-p'u. Taipei: I wen yin shu kuan.
中國歷史參考圖譜。

1953. "Pu-tz'u chung te po yü shang." *Ta-lu tsa-chih*, VI-1.
卜辭中的亳與商。大陸雜誌。

1955. Chia-ku-hsueh wu-shih nien. Taipei: I wen yin shu kuan.
甲骨學五十年。

1955. Tung Tso-pin *et al*. Chung Han wen-hua lun-chi. Taipei: Chung-hua wen-hua ch'u-pan shih-yeh wei-yuan-hui. 2 vols.
董作賓等。中韓文化論集。

1958. Chia-ku shih-wu chih cheng-li. Taipei: Chung-yang yen-chiu yuan li-shih yü-yen yen-chiu so.
甲骨實物之整理。

1958. "Chung-kuo shang-ku shih nien-tai." *Kuo-li Taiwan ta-hsueh k'ao-ku jen-lei hsueh-k'an*, 11.
中國上古史年代。國立台灣大學考古人類學刊。

1960. Chung-kuo nien-li tsung-p'u. Hong Kong: Hong Kong ta-hsueh ch'u-pan she. 2 vols.
中國年曆總譜。

1962. Tung Tso-pin hsueh-shu lun-chu (ed. by Yang Chia-lo). Taipei: Shih-chieh shu-chü. 2 vols.
董作賓學術論著。楊家駱。

1963. P'ing-lu wen-ts'un. Taipei: I wen yin shu kuan. 2 vols.
平廬文存。

1964. Fifty Years of Studies in Oracle Inscriptions. Tokyo: Center for East Asian Cultural Studies.

1964? P'ing-lu yin ts'un. Hong Kong?
平廬印存。

1965. Chia-ku hsueh liu-shih nien. Taipei: I wen yin shu kuan.
甲骨學六十年。

SOURCES

Shih Chang-ju. K'ao-ku nien-pao. 1952.
石璋如。考古年表。

Tung Tso-pin. "Ch'eng-tzu-yai yü Lung-shan-chen," in Fu Ssu-nien *et al.*, *Ch'eng-tzu-yai* (*Shantung Li-ch'eng hsien Lung-shan-chen hei t'ao wen-hua i-chih*). Nanking: Kuo-li chung-yang yen-chiu yuan li-shih yü-yen yen-chiu so, 1934.

董作賓。城子崖與龍山鎮。傅斯年等。城子崖（山東歷城縣龍山鎮黑陶文化遺址）。

———. Chia-ku hsueh wu-shih nien. Taipei: I wen yin shu kuan, 1955.

董作賓。甲骨學五十年。

———. Chia-ku-wen tuan-tai yen-chiu li. 1932.

董作賓。甲骨文斷代研究例。

———. "Chia-ku wen tuan-tai yen-chiu shih ko piao-chun." *Ta-lu tsa-chih*, IV-8 (April, 1952).

董作賓。甲骨文斷代研究十個標準。大陸雜誌。

———. "Chia-ku-wen yen-chiu te k'uo-ta," in Li Chi *et al.*, *An-yang fa-chueh pao-kao*, II. Kuo-li chung-yang yen-chiu yuan li-shih yü-yen yen-chiu so, 1930.

董作賓。甲骨文研究的擴大。李濟等。安陽發掘報告。

———. "Chung-kuo ku-tai wen-hua te jen-shih." *Ta-lu tsa-chih*, III-12 (1951).

董作賓。中國古代文化的認識。大陸雜誌。

———. Chung-kuo nien-li tsung-p'u. Hong Kong: Hong Kong ta-hsueh ch'u-pan she, 1960. 2 vols.

董作賓。中國年曆總譜。

———. Chung-kuo shang-ku shih nien-tai." *Kuo-li Taiwan ta-hsueh k'ao-ku jen-lei hsueh-k'an*, 11 (1958).

董作賓。中國上古史年代。國立台灣大學考古人類學刊。

———. "Hsi-chou nien li p'u." *Chung-yang yen-chiu yuan li-shih yü-yen yen-chiu so chi k'an*, 23 (1952).

董作賓。西周年曆譜。中央研究院歷史語言研究所集刊。

———. "Hsin huo pu-tz'u hsieh pen," in Li Chi *et al.*, *An-yang fa-chueh pao-kao*, I. Kuo-li chung-yang yen-chiu yuan li-shih yü-yen yen-chiu so, 1929.

董作賓。新獲卜辭寫本。李濟等。安陽發掘報告。

———. P'ing-lu ching p'u. 1934.

董作賓。平廬景譜。

———. "Pu-tzu chung so chien chih Yin li," in Li Chi *et al.*, *An-yang fa-chueh pao-kao*, III. Kuo-li chung-yang yen-chiu yuan li-shih yü-yen yen-chiu so, 1931.

董作賓。卜辭中所見之殷曆。李濟等。安陽發掘報告。

Tung Tso-pin. "P'u-tz'u chung te po yü shang." *Ta-lu tsa-chih*, VI-1 (1953).

董作賓。卜辭中的亳與商。大陸雜誌。

———. "Shang-tai kuei-pu te t'ui-ts'e," in Li Chi *et al.*, *An-yang fa-chueh pao-kao*, I. Kuo-li chung-yang yen-chiu yuan li-shih yü-yen yen-chiu so, 1929.

董作賓。商代龜卜的推測。李濟等。安陽發掘報告。

———. "Shih-ch'i nien shih-yueh shih chueh An-yang Hsiao-t'un pao-kao shu," in Li Chi *et al.*, *An-yang fa-chueh pao-kao*, I. Kuo-li chung-yang yen-chiu yuan li-shih yü-yen yen-chiu so, 1929.

董作賓。十七年十月試掘安陽小屯報告書。李濟等。安陽發掘報告。

———. "Ta kuei ssu pan k'ao shih, in Li Chi *et al.*, *An-yang fa-chueh pao-kao*, III. Kuo-li chung-yang yen-chiu yuan li-shih yü-yen yen-chiu so, 1931.

董作賓。大龜四版考釋。李濟等。安陽發掘報告。

———. "T'an t'an." *Chung-yang yen-chiu yuan li-shih yü-yen yen-chiu so chi k'an*, 4 (1933).

董作賓。談譚。中央研究院歷史語言研究所集刊。

———. Tung Tso-pin hsueh-shu lun-chu (ed. by Yang Chia-lo). Taipei: Shih-chieh shu-chü, 1962. 2 vols.

董作賓。董作賓學術論著。楊家駱。

———. "Wu teng chueh tsai Yin Shang." *Chung-yang yen-chiu yuan li-shih yü-yen yen-chiu so chi k'an*, 6 (1936).

董作賓。五等爵在殷商。中央研究院歷史語言研究所集刊。

———. Wu-wang fa Chou nien yueh jih chin k'ao. Taipei: Kuo-li Taiwan ta-hsueh, 1951.

董作賓。武王伐紂年月日今考。

———. "Yin hsü yen-ko." *Chung-yang yen-chiu yuan li-shih yü-yen yen-chiu so chi k'an*, 2 (1930).

董作賓。殷墟沿革。中央研究院歷史語言研究所集刊。

———. "Yin li chung chi ko chung-yao wen-t'i." *Chung-yang yen-chiu yuan li-shih yü-yen yen-chiu so chi k'an*, 4 (1934).

董作賓。殷曆中幾個重要問題。中央研究院歷史語言研究所集刊。

———. Yin li p'u. Li-chuang, Szechwan: Chung-yang yen-chiu yuan li-shih yü-yen yen-chiu so, 1945. 4 vols.

董作賓。殷曆譜。

———. "Yin tai yueh-shih k'ao." *Chung-yang*

yen-chiu yuan li-shih yü-yen yen-chiu so chi k'an, 22 (1950).

董作賓。殷代月食考。中央研究院歷史語言研究所集刊。

Tung Yuan-feng   董遠峯

SOURCES

Persons interviewed: not to be identified.

Ulanfu

SOURCES

Clubb, O. Edmund. "The Inner Mongolian Autonomous Region." *Eastern World* (April, 1955): 15-17.

HCJC

Lo, J.P. "Political Dynamics in Inner Mongolia." Unpublished manuscript.

Rupen, Robert A. "Mongolian Nationalism." *Royal Central Asian Journal*, XLV (April, July-October, 1958).

WWMC

Unenbayin

SOURCES

Persons interviewed: not to be identified.

Unenbayin. "Meng-ku chin-tai li-shih." Unpublished manuscript.

蒙古近代歷史。

———. "Meng-ku tai-piao-t'uan." Unpublished manuscript.

蒙古代表團。

Wan Chia-pao   萬家寶

WORKS

1936. Jih-ch'u. Shanghai: Wen-hua sheng-huo ch'u-pan she.

日出。

Eng. tr. by A. C. Barnes, *Sunrise, a Play in Four Acts by Tsao Yu*. Peking: Foreign Languages Press, 1960.

1936. Lei-yü. Shanghai: Wen-hua sheng-huo ch'u-pan she.

雷雨。

Eng. tr. by Wang Tso-liang and A.C. Barnes, *Thunderstorm*. Peking: Foreign Languages Press, 1958.

1937. Yuan-yeh. Shanghai: Wen-hua sheng-huo ch'u-pan she.

原野。

1941. Shui-pien. Hong Kong: Shang-wu yin shu kuan.

蛻變。

1946, July. "The Modern Chinese Theater." *National Reconstruction*, VII-1: 33-48.

1947. Chia. Shanghai: Wen-hua sheng-huo ch'u-pan she.

家。

1947. Hei tzu erh-shih-pa. with Sung Chih-ti. Shanghai: Cheng-chung shu-chü.

黑字二十八。宋之的。

1947. Peking jen. Shanghai: Wen-hua sheng-huo ch'u-pan she.

北京人。

1948. Yen yang t'ien (Tien-ying chü-pen). Shanghai: Wen-hua sheng-huo ch'u-pan she.

艷陽天 (電影劇本)。

1952. Ts'ao Yü hsuan-chi. Peking: K'ai-ming shu-tien.

曹禺選集。

1954. Ts'ao Yü chü-pen hsuan. Peking: Jen-min wen-hsueh ch'u-pan she.

曹禺劇本選。

1956. Ming-lang te t'ien. Peking: Jen-min wen-hsueh ch'u-pan she.

明朗的天。

Eng. tr. by Chang Pei-chi, *Bright Skies*. Peking: Foreign Languages Press, 1960.

1958. Ying ch'un chi. Peking: Peking ch'u-pan she.

迎春集。

1962. Tan chien p'ien (wu mu hua-chü). Peking: Chung-kuo hsi-chü ch'u-pan she.

胆劍篇 (五幕話劇)。

SOURCES

Chao Chung. The Communist Program for Literature and Art in China. Hong Kong: Union Research Institute, 1955.

HWP

MCNP

T'ien Ch'in. Chung-kuo hsi-chü yün-tung. Chungking, 1944.

田禽。中國戲劇運動。

Ts'ao Chü-jen. Wen-t'an wu-shih nien; cheng hsü chi. Hong Kong: Hsin wen-hua ch'u-pan she, 1955. 2 vols.

曹聚仁。文壇五十年；正續集。
Wan Chia-pao. "The Modern Chinese Theater." *National Reconstruction*, VII-1 (July, 1946): 33-48.
Ying Tzu. Chung-kuo hsin hsueh-shu jen-wu chih. Hong Kong: Chih ming shu-chü, 1956.
穎子。中國新學術人物誌。

Wan Fu-lin   萬福麟

SOURCES

BKL
CH
CMTC
CWR, 1930, 1931, 1932, 1933, 1937.
Kuo wen chou-pao. VIII-23 (July 15, 1931).
國聞週報。
Li Nien-tz'u. "Man-chou-kuo" chi-shih. Hong Kong: Tzu-yu ch'u-pan she, 1954.
李念慈。「滿洲國」紀實。
WWMC
Yu Chün. "Sian shih-pien i-lai ts'ung wei kung-k'ai kuo te chen shih." *Ch'un-ch'iu*, 52-58 (September 1, 1959–December 1, 1959).
右軍。西安事變以來從來公開過的珍史。春秋。

Wang Chen   王震

SOURCES

Person interviewed: Chang Kuo-t'ao.
HCJC
RD
WWC, 6th ed., 1950.
WWMC

Wang Cheng-t'ing   王正廷

WORKS

1928. Chung-kuo chin-tai wai-chiao shih kai-yao. Nanking? Wai-chiao yen-chiu she.
中國近代外交史概要。
1933. Wang Cheng-t'ing chin yen lu (comp. by Wu T'ien-fang). Shanghai: Chün i, li kuo lien-ho yin-shua kung-ssu.
王正廷近言錄。吳天放。
1937. Democratic China: An Address Delivered before the Philadelphia Board of Trade, October 21, 1937. Philadelphia?
1937. Japan's Aggressions upon China: Address

at the Armistice Eve Banquet of the International Good-will Congress, November 10, 1937, Boston, Massachusetts.
1938. Selected Statements and Addresses Concerning the Sino-Japanese Conflict.
1948. "An p'in jo su te mu-ch'in," in Chung-kuo wen-hua kuan Hong Kong fen kuan, *Wo te mu-ch'in*. Hong Kong: Chung-kuo yin-shua kung-ssu. 2 vols.
安貧若素的母親。中國文化館香港分館。我的母親。

SOURCES

BKL
Chin shan shih-pao. San Francisco, January 3, 1961.
金山時報。
The New York Times, May 22, 1961.
TCJC
Wai-chiao ta tz'u-tien, comp. by Wai-chiao hsueh-hui. Kunming: Chung-hua shu-chü, 1937.
外交大辭典。外交學會。
Wang Cheng-t'ing. "An p'in jo su te mu-ch'in," in Chung-kuo wen-hua kuan Hong Kong fen kuan, *Wo te mu-ch'in*. Hong Kong: Chung-kuo yin-shua kung-ssu, 1948. 2 vols.
王正廷。安貧若素的母親。中國文化館香港分館。我的母親。
——. Wang Cheng-t'ing chin yen lu (comp. by Wu T'ien-fang). Shanghai: Chün i, li kuo lien-ho yin-shua kung-ssu, 1933.
王正廷。王正廷近言錄。吳天放。

Wang Chia-hsiang   王稼祥

WORKS

1941. Chung-kuo kung-ch'an-tang yü ko-ming chan-cheng. Yenan: Chieh-fang she.
中國共產黨與革命戰爭。

SOURCES

Person interviewed: Chang Kuo-t'ao.
CPR, 685 (October 6-7, 1949); 1011 (November 8, 1949).
GCCJK
HCJC
I-chiu-wu-ling jen-min nien-chien, ed. by Shen Sung-fang. Hong Kong: Ta kung shu-chü, 1950.
一九五〇人民年鑑。沈頌芳。
JMST, 1950, 1957, 1958, 1959.

Ssu-ma Lu. Tou-cheng shih-pa nien. Hong
Kong: Ya-chou ch'u-pan she, 1953.
司馬璐。 鬥爭十八年。

Wang Ching-ch'un 王景春

SOURCES

Persons interviewed: not to be identified.

Wang Ching-wei 汪精衞

WORKS

1910. Wang Chao-ming kung-tz'u.
汪兆銘供詞。
1912. Wang Ching-wei hsien-sheng wen-ch'ao.
Shanghai: Hsieh she. 4 vols.
汪精衞先生文鈔。
1919. Wang Ching-wei hsien-sheng tsui-chin
yen-shuo. Tour, France: Chung-hua yin tzu
chü.
汪精衞先生最近演說。
1925. Chung-kuo kuo-min-tang shih kai-lun;
shang p'ien. Canton: Chung-kuo kuo-min-
tang lu-chün chün-kuan hsueh-hsiao cheng-
chih pu.
中國國民黨史概論; 上篇。
1925. Ti-kuo chu-i ch'in-lueh Chung-kuo te
ch'ü-shih ho pien-ch'ien kai-lun. Hangchow:
Chung-kuo kuo-min-tang Chekiang sheng
tang wu chih-tao wei-yuan-hui hsuan-ch'uan
pu.
帝國主義侵略中國的趨勢和變遷概論。
1926. Wang Ching-wei hsien-sheng chiang-yen
chi (comp. by Ai chih she). Shanghai:
Kuang-ming shu-chü.
汪精衞先生講演集。 愛知社。
1926. Wang Ching-wei hsien-sheng chiang-yen
chi (with Liao Chung-k'ai hsien-sheng chuan-
lueh). (ed. by Chung-kuo kuo-min-tang
chung-yang chih-hsing wei-yuan-hui Peking
chih-hsing pu.) Peking: Chung-kuo kuo-min-
tang chung-yang chih-hsing wei-yuan-hui
Peking chih-hsing pu.
汪精衞先生講演集 (附: 廖仲愷先生傳略)。
中國國民黨中央執行委員會北京執行部。
1926. Wang Ching-wei hsien-sheng tsui-chin
chiang-yen chi; ti-i chi. Shanghai: Min chih
shu-chü.
汪精衞先生最近講演集; 第一集。
1926. Wang Ching-wei yen-chiang lu. Chung-
kuo yin shu kuan.

汪精衞演講錄。
1926. Wang Ching-wei yen-shuo chi. Chung-
kuo yin shu kuan.
汪精衞演說集。
1927. China and the Nations (ed. by Teng I-sen,
John N. Smith). New York: Frederick A.
Stodes.
1927. (ed.) Pa-li (Paris) ho hui hou chih shih-
chieh yü Chung-kuo. Shanghai: Min chih
shu-chü.
巴黎和會後之世界與中國。
1927. Wang Ching-wei wen-ts'un. Canton:
Min chih shu-chü.
汪精衞文存。
1928? Wang Ching-wei hsien-sheng tsui-chin
yen-shuo chi.
汪精衞先生最近演說集。
1928. Wang Ching-wei yü Wu Chih-hui te lun-
wen chi (ed. by Yen Hsü-tsai). Shanghai:
Hsin shih-tai shu-tien.
汪精衞與吳稚輝的論文集。 嚴勗哉。
1929. Wang Ching-wei chi (ed. by Hsun Ju).
Shanghai: Kuang-ming shu-chü. 4 vols.
汪精衞集。 恂如。
1929? Wang Ching-wei hsien-sheng te wen-chi.
Shanghai: Chung-shan shu-tien.
汪精衞先生的文集。
1930. Wang Ching-wei *et al*. Tsui-chin yueh-fa
lun-tsung. Hong Kong: Nan hua jih-pao.
汪精衞等。 最近約法論叢。
1930. Wang Ching-wei hsien-sheng tsui-chin te
cheng-lun. Canton: Kwangtung sheng tang-
pu.
汪精衞先生最近的政論。
1930. Wang Ching-wei hsien-sheng tsui-chin
yen-lun chi. Hong Kong: Nan hua jih-pao.
汪精衞先生最近言論集。
1930. Wang Ching-wei shih ts'un. Shanghai:
Kuang-ming shu-chü.
汪精衞詩存。
1931. Wang Ching-wei *et al*. The Chinese National Revolution: Essays and Documents.
Peiping: China United Press.
1932. Poèmes et "tseu" choisis de Wang Ching-
wei (tr. and annot. by Hsü Sung-nien).
Peking: Impr. de la "politique de Pekin."
1933. Wang Ching-wei yen-hsing lu (ed. by Shih
Hsi-sheng). Shanghai: Kuang i shu-chü. 2
vols.
汪精衞言行錄。 時希聖。
1934, January. "Tzu shu." *Tung-fang tsa-chih*,
XXXI-1.
自述。 東方雜誌。

1934. Wang Chao-ming keng-hsü pei tai kung-tz'u.

汪兆銘庚戌被逮供詞。

1936. Hsin sheng-huo yü min-tsu fu-hsing. Nanking: Cheng-chung shu-chü.

新生活與民族復興。

1936. Wang Ching-wei hsien-sheng chih ko tang-pu t'ung-chih shu. Hong Kong: Nan hua jih-pao.

汪精衛先生致各黨部同志書。

1936. Wang Ching-wei hsien-sheng chung-yao chien-i (ed. by Nan hua jih-pao she pien-chi pu). Hong Kong: Nan hua jih-pao ying-yeh pu.

汪精衛先生重要建議。 南華日報社編輯部。

1937. Wang Ching-wei hsien-sheng tsui-chin chih yen-lun (comp. by Lin Po-sheng). Shang-hai: Chung-hua jih-pao kuan.

汪精衛先生最近之言論。 林柏生。

1937. Wang Ching-wei hsien-sheng tsui-chin yen-lun chi (comp. by Lin Po-sheng). Shang-hai: Chung-hua jih-pao kuan. 2 vols.

汪精衛先生最近言論集。 林柏生。

1937. Wang Ching-wei wen-hsuan (comp. by Shao Hou). Shanghai: Ch'i chih shu-chü.

汪精衛文選。 少候。

1938. "Chu Chih-hsin," in Chang Yueh-jui, *Chin-tai chuan-chi wen-hsuan*. Changsha: Shang-wu yin shu kuan.

朱執信。 張越瑞。 近代傳記文選。

1938. K'ang chan yü chien-kuo (comp. by Lin Po-sheng). Hong Kong: Nan hua jih-pao she.

抗戰與建國。 林柏生。

1938. Poems of Wang Ching-wei (tr. by Shu Seyuan). London: G. Allen & Unwin.

1938. Wang Ching-wei hsian-sheng tsui-chin yen-lun chi; hsü pien (comp. by Lin Po-sheng). Hong Kong: Nan hua jih-pao she.

汪精衛先生最近言論集; 續編。 林柏生。

1939. A la Mémoire de M. Tsen Tson-ming. Hanoi: Impr. d'Extrème-Orient.

1939. Tseng Chung-ming hsien-sheng hsing-chuang. Hong Kong: Nan hua jih-pao ying-yeh pu.

曾仲鳴先生行狀。

1939. Wang Ching-wei hsien-sheng chung-yao sheng-ming. Shanghai: Chung-hua jih-pao.

汪精衛先生重要聲明。

1939. Wang Ching-wei hsien-sheng kuan-yü ho-p'ing yün-tung chih chung-yao yen-lun.

汪精衛先生關於和平運動之重要言論。

1939? Wo tui-yü Chung Jih kuan-hsi chih ken-pen kuan-nien chi ch'ien-chin mu-piao (with Ching-kao hai-wai ch'iao-pao). Shanghai: Chung-hua jih-pao.

我對於中日關係之根本觀念及前進目標 (附: 敬告海外僑胞)。

1940. Tsu fu huan tu yen-lun chi. Canton: Chung-kuo kuo-min-tang Kwangtung sheng chih-hsing wei-yuan-hui.

組府還都言論集。

1940. Wang Chu-hsi ho-p'ing chien-kuo yen-lun chi (ed. by Hsuan-ch'uan pu). Nanking: Hsuan-ch'uan pu.

汪主席和平建國言論集。 宣傳部。

1941. Chu-hsi fang Jih yen-lun chi. Nanking: Hsuan-ch'uan pu.

主席訪日言論集。

1942. Wang Chu-hsi ho-p'ing chien-kuo yen-lun chi; hsü-chi (ed. by Hsuan-ch'uan pu). Nanking: Hsuan-ch'uan pu.

汪主席和平建國言論集; 續集。

1943? Lu hai k'ung chün chün-jen hsun t'iao ch'ien-shih. Nanking?

陸海空軍軍人訓條淺釋。

1943. Shuang-chao-lou shih tz'u kao. Hong Kong: Yung t'ai yin-wu kung-ssu.

雙照樓詩詞稿。

ed. of *Min pao*.

民報。

"Pei shang ju Ching chih ching-kuo," in Lu Yu-pai, *Sun Chung-shan hsien-sheng chuan-chi*. Shanghai: Ch'ing yün t'u-shu kung-ssu.

北上入京之經過。陸友白。孫中山先生傳記。

Tsui-chin Wang Ching-wei hsien-sheng chiang-yen chi.

最近汪精衛先生講演集。

SOURCES

Agreements between Wang Ching-wei and Japan. Chungking: Chinese Ministry of Information, 1943.

Bate, Don. Wang Ching-wei: Puppet or Patriot? Chicago: R. F. Seymour, 1941.

Boorman, Howard L. "Wang Ching-wei: China's Romantic Radical." *Political Science Quarterly*, LXXIX-4 (December, 1964).

Butow, Robert J. C. Tojo and the Coming of the War. Princeton: Princeton University Press, 1961.

Chang Ch'i-yün. Chung-hua Min-kuo shih kang. Taipei: Chung-hua wen-hua ch'u-pan shih-yeh wei-yuan-hui, 1954. 7 vols.

張其昀。 中華民國史綱。

Ch'en, Jerome. "The Left Wing Kuomintang—a Definition." *Bulletin of the School of Oriental and African Studies, University of London*, XXV (1962).

Ch'en Kung-po. Ch'en Kung-po tzu-pai shu chi ta-pien shu. 1946.

陳公博。 陳公博自白書及答辯書。

China and Japan: Natural Friends—Unatural Enemies; a Guide for China's Foreign Policy. Shanghai: China United Press, 1941.

Chou Fo-hai. Chou Fo-hai jih-chi. Hong Kong: Ch'uang k'en ch'u-pan she, 1955.

周佛海。 周佛海日記。

———. Wang i chi. Hong Kong: Ho chung ch'u-pan she, 1955.

周佛海。 往矣集。

Chu P'u. "Kuan-yü Wang Ching-wei hsien-sheng." *Ta feng*, 4 (April 5, 1938)

朱樸。 關於汪精衞先生。 大風。

Chu Tzu-chia (pseud. of Chin Hsiung-pai). Wang cheng-ch'üan te k'ai-ch'ang yü shou-ch'ang. Hong Kong: Ch'un-ch'iu tsa-chih she, 1959-61. 5 vols.

朱子家 (金雄白)。 汪政權的開場與收場。

Ch'un-ch'iu, 159 (February, 1964); 160 (March, 1964); 172-74 (September-October, 1965).

春秋。

Chung-kuo kuo-min-tang shih-kao i chih ssu p'ien, comp. by Tsou Lu. Chungking: Shang-wu yin shu kuan, 1944. 4 vols.

中國國民黨史稿一至四篇。 鄒魯。

CMTC

Conroy, Hilary. "Government versus 'Patriot': The Background of Japan's Asiatic Expansion." *Pacific Historical Review*, XX (1951): 31-42.

———. "Japan's War in China: An Ideological Somersault." *Pacific Historical Review*, XXI (1952): 367-79.

CYB-W, 1928.

Feng Tzu-yu. Chung-hua Min-kuo k'ai-kuo ch'ien ko-ming shih. Chungking: Chung-kuo wen-hua fu-wu she, 1944.

馮自由。 中華民國開國前革命史。

Fundamentals of National Salvation: A Symposium by Wang Ching-wei and Others, ed. by T'ang Leang-li. Shanghai: China United Press, 1942.

Gunther, John. Inside Asia. New York: Harper & Bros., 1939.

Harding, Gardner L. "China's Part in the War." *Asia*, 17 (October, 1917).

Hsiao Nan Ch'iang (pseud.). "Ch'en Pi-chün je lien shih." *Chin shan shih-pao*. San Francisco, October 17-19, 1956.

小南强。 陳璧君熱戀史。 金山時報。

Hsü Chih-mo nien-p'u, comp. by Ch'en Ts'ung-chou. Shanghai: Ch'en shih, 1949.

徐志摩年譜。 陳從周。

Jansen, Marius B. The Japanese and Sun Yat-sen. Cambridge: Harvard University Press, 1954.

Johnson, Chalmers A. Peasant Nationalism and Communist Power: The Emergence of Revolutionary China, 1937-1945. Stanford: Stanford University Press, 1962.

Jones, F.C. Japan's New Order in East Asia: Its Rise and Fall, 1937-45. London: Oxford University Press, 1954.

Journal of Asian Studies, XXIII-1 (November, 1963): 126-28.

Kung Te-po. Wang Chao-ming hsiang ti mai-kuo mi-shih. Taipei: Chu che, 1965.

龔德柏。 汪兆銘降敵賣國密史。

Kuo wen chou-pao, IV-16 (May 1, 1927).

國聞週報。

Li Chien-nung. Chung-kuo chin pai nien cheng-chih shih. Shanghai: Shang-wu yin shu kuan, 1947. 2 vols.

李劍農。 中國近百年政治史。

Linebarger, Paul M. The China of Chiang Kai-shek. Boston: World Peace Foundation, 1941.

Lu, David J. From the Marco Polo Bridge to Pearl Harbor: Japan's Entry into World War II. Washington: Public Affairs Press, 1961.

Mao Tse-tung. Selected Works. New York: International Publishers, 1956-62. 5 vols.

Min pao. Peking: K'o-hsüeh ch'u pan she, 1957. 4 vols.

民報。

Mote, Frederick W. Japanese-Sponsored Governments in China, 1937-1945. Stanford: Stanford University Press, 1954.

Ngok, Lee. "The Later Career of Wang Ching-wei, with Special Reference to His National Government's Cooperation with Japan, 1938-1945." Unpublished Master's essay, University of Hong Kong, 1966.

North, Robert C. "M.N. Roy and the Fifth Congress of Chinese Communist Party." *China Quarterly*, 8 (September-December, 1961): 184-95.

North, Robert C., and Xenia J. Eudin. M.N. Roy's Mission to China: The Communist-Kuomintang Split of 1927. Berkeley: University of California Press, 1963.

Shirley, James R. "Political Conflict in the

Kuomintang: The Career of Wang Ching-wei to 1932." Unpublished Ph.D. dissertation, University of California, 1962.

Simon, Paul. Deux Personalities de la Chine Contemporaire: Wu Pei-fu et Wang Ching-wei. Verviers: Leens, 1939.

T'ang Leang-li. The Inner History of the Chinese Revolution. New York: E. P. Dutton & Co., 1930.

———. Wang Ching-wei, a Political Biography. Peiping: China United Press, 1931.

T'ao Chü-yin *et al.* Wang cheng-ch'üan tsa-lu. Macao: Ta-ti ch'u-pan she, 1963.
陶菊隱等。 汪政權雜錄。

Tong, Hollinton K. Chiang Kai-shek, Soldier and Statesman: Authorized Biography. Shanghai: China Publishing Co., 1937.

Wai-chiao ta tz'u tien, ed. by Wai-chiao hsueh-hui. Kunming: Chung-hua shu-chü, 1937.
外交大辭典。 外交學會。

Wang Ching-wei: China's Problems and Their Solution. Shanghai, 1934.

———. "Tzu shu." *Tung-fang tsa-chih*, XXXI-1 (January, 1934).
汪精衞。 自述。 東方雜誌。

———. Wang Ching-wei chi (ed. by Hsun Ju). Shanghai: Kuang-ming shu-chü, 1929. 4 vols.
汪精衞。 汪精衞集。 恂如。

———. Wang Ching-wei hsien-sheng chiang-yen chi (comp. by Ai chih she). Shanghai: Kuang-ming shu-chü, 1926.
汪精衞。 汪精衞先生講演集。 愛知社。

———. Wang Ching-wei hsien-heng chih ko tang-pu t'ung-chih shu. Hong Kong: Nan hua jih-pao, 1936.
汪精衞。 汪精衞先生致各黨部同志書。

———. Wang Ching-wei hsien-sheng tsui-chin chih yen-lun (comp. by Lin Po-sheng). Shanghai: Chung-hua jih-pao kuan, 1937.
汪精衞。 汪精衞先生最近之言論。 林柏生。

———. Wang Ching-wei hsien-sheng tsui-chin yen-lun (comp. by Lin Po-sheng). Shanghai: Chung-hua jih-pao kuan, 1937. 2 vols.
汪精衞。 汪精衞先生最近言論集。 林柏生。

———. Wang Ching-wei hsien-sheng tsui-chih yen-lun chi; hsü pien (comp. by Lin Po-sheng). Hong Kong: Nan hua jih-pao she, 1938.
汪精衞。 汪精衞先生最近言論集; 續集。 林柏生。

———. Wang Ching-wei hsien-sheng wen-ch'ao. Shanghai: Hsieh she, 1912. 4 vols.
汪精衞。 汪精衞先生文鈔。

Wang Ching-wei. Wang Ching-wei shih ts'un. Shanghai. Kuang-ming shu-chü, 1930.
汪精衞。 汪精衞詩存。

———. Wang Chu-hsi ho-p'ing chien-kuo yen-lun chi (ed. by Hsuan-ch'uan pu). Nanking: Hsuan-ch'uan pu, 1940.
汪精衞。 汪主席和平建國言論集。 宣傳部。

———. Wang Chu-hsi ho-p'ing chien-kuo yen-lun chi; hsü-chi (ed. by Hsuan-ch'uan pu). Nanking: Hsuan-ch'uan pu, 1942.
汪精衞。 汪主席和平建國言論集; 續集。 宣傳部。

Wen hui nien-k'an, comp. by Wen hui nien-k'an pien-chi wei-yuan-hui. Shanghai: Wen-hui yu-hsien kung-ssu, 1939.
文滙年刊。 文滙年刊編輯委員會。

Wu Yu-chang. The Revolution of 1911: A Great Democratic Revolution of China. Peking: Foreign Languages Press, 1962.

WWC, 1940.

Yü Mu-jen. Tang kuo ming-jen chuan. Shanghai: Shih-chieh shu-chü, 1928.
余牧人。 黨國名人傳。

Wang Ch'ung-hui   王寵惠

Works

1907. The German Civil Code. (tr.) London: Stevens & Sons.

1919. Law Reform in China. London.

1925, October 3. "Chinese Official Views Regarding Extraterritoriality." CWR.

1928, October 20. "New Five-power Government Explained." CWR.

1930. "Lun kai shu-ju kuan-shui wei chin tan-wei chih pi-yao," in Li Ta-nien, *Chin chang yin lo wen-t'i chi ch'i chiu-chi*. Shanghai: Ch'i chih.
論改輸入關稅為金單位之必要。 李大年。 金漲銀落問題及其救濟。

1937, March 13. "International Cooperation Stressed by Wang Chung-hui." CWR.

1937, June 26. "China's Territorial Integrity Stressed by Wang Chung-hui." CWR.

1937. "Wang hsü," in Wai-chio hsueh-hui, *Wai-chiao ta tz'u-tien*. Kunming: Chung-hua shu-chü.
王序。 外交學會。 外交大辭典。

1940. Wu ch'üan hsien-fa. Chungking: Chün-shih wei-yuan-hui cheng-chih pu.
五權憲法。

1945. "Wu-shih nien lai te wai-chiao ch'ing-hsing," in P'an Kung-chan, *Wu-shih nien lai te Chung-kuo.* Chungking: Sheng-li ch'u-pan she.

五十年來的外交情形。潘公展。五十年來的中國。

1947. China's Destiny. (tr. of Chiang Kai-shek's Chung-kuo chih ming-yun). New York: The Macmillan Co.

1957. K'un-hsueh-chai wen-ts'un (comp. by Hsieh Ying-chou). Taipei: Chung-hua ts'ung-shu wei-yuan-hui.

困學齋文存。謝瀛洲。

ed. of *Journal of the American Bar Association.*

SOURCES

BKL

CH, 1937–45, 1954–55.

Chang Ch'i-yün. Tang shih kai-yao. Taipei: Chung-yang kai-tsao wei-yuan-hui wen-wu kung-ying she, 1951–52. 5 vols.

張其昀。黨史概要。

Chia I-chün. Chung-hua Min-kuo shih. Shanghai: Wen-hua hsueh-she, 1930.

賈逸君。中華民國史。

Christian Mission China Year Book, 1923, 1934–35, 1936–37.

CH-T, 1956–57.

Chung-kuo wai-chiao nien-chien; ti-erh ts'e. Shih-chieh shu-chü, 1935.

中國外交年鑑；第二冊。

Chung-yang jih-pao. Taipei, March 16, 1958.

中央日報。

CMJL

CMTC

CTMC

CYB, 1935–36.

"Dr. Wang Chung-hui's Appointment and the Future Outlook." CWR, March 13, 1937.

Feng Tzu-yu. Ko-ming i-shih. Chungking, Shanghai: Shang-wu yin shu kuan, 1944–47. 5 vols.

馮自由。革命逸史。

GCJJ

Hsiao Pai-fan. Chung-kuo chin pai nien ko-ming shih. Kowloon: Ch'iu shih, 1951.

蕭白帆。中國近百年革命史。

Hsieh Kuan-sheng. "Chui-huai Wang Liang-ch'ou hsien-sheng." *Cheng-lun chou-k'an*, 167 (March, 1958): 1.

謝冠生。追懷王亮疇先生。政論週刊。

———. "Essays by Dr. Wang Chung-hui—Selected and Edited by Dr. Hsieh Ying-chow." *Chinese Culture*, I-1 (July, 1957): 166–69.

Hsieh Kuan-sheng. "Wang Ch'ung-hui hsien-sheng chuan-lueh." *Cheng-lun chou-k'an*, 167 (March, 1958): 2–3.

謝瀛洲。王寵惠先生傳略。政論週刊。

Hsien Shao. "Wang Chung-hui." *Cheng feng*, IV-3 (March, 1937): 269–70.

羨韶。王寵惠。正風。

International Who's Who, 1954.

Kuo wen chou pao, II-9.

國聞週報。

Li Chien-nung. Chung-kuo chin pai nien cheng-chih shih. Shanghai: Shang-wu yin shu kuan. 2 vols.

李劍農。中國近百年政治史。

Ma Shou-hua. "Chui ssu Liang lao lueh shu ch'i erh san shih." *Cheng-lun chou-k'an*, 167 (March, 1958): 4.

馬壽華。追思亮老略述其二三事。政論週刊。

Meng, C.Y.W. "Open Letter to Dr. Wang Chung-hui on National Unification of China." CWR, March 21, 1936.

"New Honor for Dr. Wang Chung-hui." *The China Critic*, 1928.

The New York Times, March 16, 1958.

North China Daily News, January 13, 1912.

Nu-li chou-pao, May 14, 1922.

努力週報。

Pollard, Robert Thomas. China's Foreign Relations 1917–1931. New York: The Macmillan Co., 1933.

T'ang Leang-li. The Inner History of the Chinese Revolution. New York: E.P. Dutton & Co., 1930.

"Tao Wang Liang-ch'ou hsien-sheng." *Cheng-lun chou-k'an*, 167 (March, 1958).

悼王亮疇先生。政論週刊。

Wai-chiao ta tz'u-tien, ed. by Wai-chiao hsueh-hui. Kunming: Chung-hua shu-chü, 1937.

外交大辭典。外交學會。

"Wang Chung-hui Invited by the League of Nations." *The Chinese Students' Monthly*, June, 1921.

Whang, P.K. "Dr. Wang Chung-hui's Mission to Japan." CWR, March 9, 1935.

Who's Who in the Orient, 1915.

WWARS

WWC, 1936.

WWMC

Yuan Shih-k'ai ch'ieh kuo chi, comp. by Taiwan Chung-hua shu-chü pien-chi pu. Taipei: Taiwan Chung-hua shu-chü, 1954.

袁世凱竊國記。台灣中華書局編輯部。

Yueh Ch'ien. Chung Su kuan-hsi shih-hua.
Singapore, Hong Kong: Ch'uang k'en ch'u-
pan she, 1952.
岳騫。中蘇關係史話。

Wang Hsien-ch'ien　　王 先 謙

WORKS

1883. (comp.) Wang I-chi k'an shu. Changsha:
Wang shih. 10 vols.
王益吉刊書。

1884–90. (comp.) (Shih ch'ao) Tung hua lu.
Changsha: Wang shih. 218 vols.
（十朝）東華錄。

1899. Tung hua hsü lu; T'ung-chih ch'ao 100
chüan. Shanghai: Kung chi shu-chuang. 24
vols.
東華續錄；同治朝 100 卷。

1901. (ed.) Jih-pen yuan-liu k'ao. 10 vols.
日本源流考。

1902. (ed.) P'ien-wen lei tsuan. Ssu hsien shu-
chü. 32 vols.
駢文類纂。

1904. Shang-shu k'ung chuan ts'an cheng.
Hsü-shou-t'ang. 6 vols.
尚書孔傳參正。

1921. Hsü-shou-t'ang wen-chi. 8 vols.
虛受堂文集。

1965. Chuang-tzu chi-chieh. Taipei: Taiwan
shang-wu yin shu kuan. 2 vols.
莊子集解。

Hsü-shou-t'ang shih-ts'un.
虛受堂詩存。

(ed.) Nan-ching shu-yuan ts'ung-shu. Nan-ching
shu-yuan. 32 vols.
南菁書院叢書。

(comp.) Wei-shu chiao k'an chi.
魏書校勘記。

SOURCES

Feng Chih-chün. Wu-hsü pien-fa jen-wu chuan
kao. Peking: Chung-hua shu-chü, 1961. 2
vols.
馮志鈞。戊戌變法人物傳稿。

Wang Hsien-ch'ien. Wang Hsien-ch'en tsu ting
nien-p'u. 1908.
王先謙。王先謙自訂年譜。

———. Wang I-wu so k'o shu. Changsha, 1883.
王先謙。王益吾所刻書。

Wu Ch'ing-ch'ih. "Wang K'uei-yuan hsien-
sheng mu-chih-ming," in PCCP.
吳慶坻。王葵園先生墓誌銘。

Wang I-t'ang　　王 揖 唐

WORKS

1912? Chin pien chien chih kai-lueh.
近邊建置概略。

1920. (comp.) Kuang te shou ch'ung kuang chi.
廣德壽重光集。

1923. Hsin O-lo-ssu. (tr.) Shanghai.
新俄羅斯。

1924. Shanghai tsu-chieh wen-t'i. Shanghai.
上海租界問題。

1933. Chin ch'uan shih lou shih hua. Tientsin.
今傳是樓詩話。

1934? Tung yu chi-lueh. Tientsin.
東游紀略。

1941. I-t'ang shih ts'un. Peking?
逸塘詩存。

Shih-chieh tsui hsin chih hsien-fa. (tr.)
世界最新之憲法。

Te huang Wei-lien ti-erh tzu-chuan. (tr.)
Shanghai.
德皇維廉第二自傳。

SOURCES

Ch'en Kung-lu. Chung-kuo chin-tai shih.
Shanghai: Shan-wu yin shu kuan, 1935.
陳恭祿。中國近代史。

BPC

CBJS

GCMMTJK

HCMW

Hsin-hai ko-ming, ed. by Ch'ai Te-keng *et al*.
Shanghai: Jen-min ch'u-pan she, 1957. 8 vols.
辛亥革命。柴德賡等。

I ching, 5 (May 5, 1936): 40–41.
逸經。

Kuo wen chou-pao, V–47 (December 2, 1928); V–50
(December 23, 1928); IX–15 (April 18, 1932).
國聞週報。

Li Chien-nung. Chung-kuo chin pai nien cheng-
chih shih. Shanghai: Shang-wu yin-shu
kuan, 1947. 2 vols.
李劍農。中國近百年政治史。

MMT

Shen Chao-t'i. Chi-lin chi-shih shih. Chin-ling:
Yang ming lin chü chen shu-chü, 1911. 2 vols.
沈兆禔。吉林紀事詩。

SMJ

Ta feng, 3 (March 25, 1938): 90–91.
大風。

Ts'ao Chü-jen and Shu Tsung-ch'iao. Chung-
kuo k'ang chan hua shih. Shanghai: Lien-ho
hua-she, 1947.

曹聚仁，舒宗僑。中國抗戰畫史。
Wang I-t'ang. I-t'ang shih ts'un. Peking? 1941.
王揖唐。逸塘詩存。
Wuhan jih-pao nien-chien, 1947.
武漢日報年鑑。
Yang Yu-chiung. Chin-tai Chung-kuo li-fa shih.
Shanghai: Shang-wu yin shu kuan, 1936.
楊幼烱。近代中國立法史。

Wang Jo-fei 王若飛

SOURCES

Person interviewed: Chang Kuo-t'ao.
Chung-kuo ch'ing-nien, 5-6 (March 16, 1961).
中國青年。
CKLC
Selections from China Mainland Magazines, 266
(June 19, 1961); 267 (June 26, 1961); 269 (July
10, 1961).
"Ssu pa" pei-nan lieh-shih chi-nien-ts'e, comp.
by Chung-kuo kung-ch'an-tang tai-piao t'uan.
Chung-kuo kung-ch'an-tang tai-piao t'uan,
1946.
「四八」被難烈士紀念冊。中國共產黨代表
團。
Yang Chih-lin and Ch'iao Ming-fu. Wang Jo-
fei tsai yü chung. Hong Kong: Sheng-huo,
tu-shu, hsin chih san lien shu-tien, 1965.
楊植霖，喬明甫。王若飛在獄中。

Wang K'ai-yün 王闓運

WORKS

1881. Hsiang chün chih. 4 vols.
湘軍志。
1896. Li ching chien. Tung-chou: Chiang she.
6 vols.
禮經箋。
1906. Hsiang-ch'i-lou ch'üan shu. 80 vols.
湘綺樓全書。
1909. Hsiang-ch'i-lou chien ch'i. Shanghai:
Shang yu shan fang.
湘綺樓箋啟。
1923. Wang Hsiang-ch'i hsien-sheng ch'üan-chi.
94 vols.
王湘綺先生全集。
1927. Hsiang-ch'i-lou jih-chi. Shanghai: Shang-
wu yin shu kuan. 32 vols.
湘綺樓日記。
1956. Hsiang-ch'i-lou wen-chi. Taipei: Hsin-
hsing shu-tien.

湘綺樓文集。
1966. Wang chih erh chüan (ed. by Ch'en Chao-
k'uei). Kowloon: Kuang hua shu-tien.
王志二卷。陳兆奎。
Hsiang-ch'i-lou shih chi.
湘綺樓詩集。

SOURCES

I Shih. "Wang K'ai-yün yü Hsiang Chün chih."
I ching, 14 (September 20, 1936); 15 (October
5, 1936); 16 (October 20, 1936).
一士。王闓運與湘軍志。逸經。
Wang K'ai-yün. Hsiang-ch'i-lou jih-chi. Shanghai: Shang-wu yin shu kuan, 1927. 32 vols.
王闓運。湘綺樓日記。
Wang Tai-kung. Hsiang-ch'i fu-chün nien-p'u.
王代功。湘綺府君年譜。

Wang Kan-ch'ang 王淦昌

SOURCES

China Topics, June 19, 1968.
Far Eastern Economic Review, November 10, 1966.
Fei ch'ing yen-chiu, August 31, 1964.
匪情研究。
I-chiu-liu-ch'i fei ch'ing nien pao.
一九六七匪情年報。
International Who's Who, 1966-1967.
Johnson, Chalmers A. "China's Manhattan
Project." *The New York Times Magazine*,
October 25, 1964.
Frank, Lewis. "Nuclear Weapons Development
in China." *Bulletin of the Atomic Scientists*,
January, 1966.
Who's Who in Atoms. London: Harrap Re-
search Publications, 1965.
WWMC

Wang K'o-min 王克敏

SOURCES

Ch'ing-suan Jih-pen. Chungking: Ta kung pao,
1939.
清算日本。
Chu Tzu-chia (pseud. of Chin Hsiung-pai).
Wang cheng-ch'üan te k'ai-ch'ang yü shou-
ch'ang. Hong Kong: Ch'un-ch'iu tsa-chih
she, 1964. 5 vols.
朱子家（金雄白）。汪政權的開場與收場。
Ch'üan-kuo yin-hang nien-chien. Shanghai,
1934.

全國銀行年鑑。

Hua-pei kuan-liao ch'ün-hsiang. Hong Kong, 1938.
華北官僚群像。

Jones, Francis Clifford. Japan's New Order in East Asia: Its Rise and Fall, 1937–45. New York: Oxford University Press, 1954.

Li Ch'ao-ying. Wei tsu-chih cheng-chih ching-chi kai-kuang. Chungking: Shang-wu yin shu kuan, 1943.
李超英。偽組織政治經濟概況。

Li Chien-nung. Chung-kuo chin pai nien cheng-chih shih. Shanghai: Shang-wu yin shu kuan, 1947. 2 vols.
李劍農。中國近百年政治史。

Taylor, George E. The Struggle for North China. New York: International Secretariat, Institute of Pacific Relations, 1940.

Wai-chiao ta tz'u-tien, ed. by Wai-chiao hsueh-hui. Hong Kong: Chung-hua shu-chü, 1937.
外交大辭典。外交學會。

Wang Kuo-wei 王國維

WORKS

1930? Kuan-t'ang i-mo. Shanghai. 2 vols.
觀堂遺墨。

1933. San-tai Ch'in Han chin-wen chu lu piao (with Pu-i). Dairen: Mo-yuan-t'ang. 4 vols.
三代秦漢金文著錄表（附：補遺）。

1935. Ku shih hsin cheng. Peiping: Lai-hsun-ko.
古史新証。

1940. Wang Ching-an hsien-sheng i-shu (ed. by Chao Wan-li). Shang-wu yin shu kuan. 48 vols.
王靜安先生遺書。趙萬里。

1954. Wang Kuo-wei hsien-sheng san chung. Taipei: Kuo-min ch'u-pan she.
王國維先生三種。

1957. Wang Kuo-wei hsi-ch'ü lun-wen chi. Peking: Chung-kuo hsi-chü ch'u-pan she.
王國維戲曲論文集。

1962. Meng-ku shih-liao ssu chung. Taipei: Cheng-chung shu-chü.
蒙古史料四種。

"Ch'in Han chün k'ao," in Lo Chen-yü, *Hsueh-t'ang ts'ung-k'o*. 20 vols.
秦漢郡考。羅振玉。雪堂叢刻。

"Jen-kuei chi," in Lo Chen-yü, *Hsueh-t'ang ts'ung-k'o*. 20 vols.
壬癸集。羅振玉。雪堂叢刻。

"Ku Hu fu k'ao," in Lo Chen-yü, *Hsueh-t'ang ts'ung-k'o*. 20 vols.
古胡服考。羅振玉。雪堂叢刻。

"Ku li ch'i lueh-shuo," in Lo Chen-yü, *Hsueh-t'ang ts'ung-k'o*. 20 vols.
古禮器略說。羅振玉。雪堂叢刻。

"Kuei-fang K'un-i Yen-yün k'ao," in Lo Chen-yü, *Hsueh-t'ang ts'ung-k'o*. 20 vols.
鬼方昆夷玁狁考。羅振玉。雪堂叢刻。

"Lo kao chien," in Lo Chen-yü, *Hsueh-t'ang ts'ung-k'o*. 20 vols.
洛誥箋。羅振玉。雪堂叢刻。

"Ming t'ang miao ch'in t'ung-k'ao," in Lo Chen-yü, *Hsueh-t'ang ts'ung-k'o*. 20 vols.
明堂廟寢通考。羅振玉。雪堂叢刻。

"Pu ch'i tun kai ming k'ao shih," in Lo Chen-yü, *Hsueh-t'ang ts'ung-k'o*. 20 vols.
不期敦蓋銘考釋。羅振玉。雪堂叢刻。

"San-tai ti-li hsiao-chi," in Lo Chen-yü, *Hsueh-t'ang ts'ung-k'o*. 20 vols.
三代地理小記。羅振玉。雪堂叢刻。

"Sheng pa ssu pa k'ao," in Lo Chen-yü, *Hsueh-t'ang ts'ung-k'o*. 20 vols.
生霸死霸考。羅振玉。雪堂叢刻。

Wang Chung-ch'üeh kung i-shu. 42 vols.
王忠愨公遺書。

SOURCES

Persons interviewed: not to be identified.

Wang Te-i. Wang Kuo-wei nien-p'u. Taipei: Chung-kuo hsueh-shu chu-tso chiang chu wei-yuan-hui, 1967.
王德毅。王國維年譜。

Wang P'eng-sheng 王芃生

WORKS

1941, September 26. "Cheng-lueh chan-lueh t'o-chieh te Jih-pen mang-tung." *Ta kung pao*. Chungking.
政略戰略脫節的日本盲動。大公報。

1944. I-ko p'ing-fan tang-yuan te hui-i yü tzu-wo chien-t'ao. Chungking.
一個平凡黨員的回憶與自我檢討。

1944. San min chu-i kuo-chi wen-t'i yen-chiu fa, piao-chieh, t'u-chieh, li chieh. Chungking: Chün-shih wei-yuan-hui kuo-chi wen-t'i yen-chiu-so ch'ü tang pu.
三民主義國際問題研究法，表解，圖解，例解。

1945. Shih-chü lun-ts'ung. Chungking.
時局論叢。

Hsiao mei ch'i t'ang shih-ts'un.
小梅溪堂詩存。
Jih-pen ku-shih chih wei-tsao.
日本古史之僞造。
Jih-pen ku-shih pien-cheng.
日本古史辨証。
Ku-chün she-chan san-tao chi-yao.
孤軍舌戰三島紀要。
Mo ai ko ts'ao tz'u chi.
莫哀歌草詞集。
Wai-meng chien-wen chi.
外蒙見聞記。

SOURCES

Chin Wen-ssu *et al.* Huang Ying-pai hsien-sheng ku-chiu kan i lu (ed. by Wu Hsiang-hsiang). Taipei: Wen hsing shu-tien, 1962.
金問泗等。黃膺白先生故舊感憶錄。吳相湘。
Ho Yao-tsu. Wang P'eng-sheng hsien-sheng hsing-chuang. Nanking, 1946.
賀耀祖。王芃生先生行狀。
Hsü Shih-ying. Hsü Shih-ying hui-i-lu. Taipei: Jen chien shih yueh-k'an she, 1966.
許世英。許世英回憶錄。
Kung Te-po. Hui-i lu. Hong Kong: Hsin-wen t'ien-ti, 1962.
龔德柏。回憶錄。
Liu Yen. Chung-kuo wai-chiao shih. Taipei: San min shu-chü, 1962.
劉彥。中國外交史。
Wai-chiao yueh-pao, 1932.
外交月報。
Wang P'eng-sheng. I-ko p'ing-fan tang-yuan te hui-i yü tzu-wo chien-t'ao. Chungking, 1944.
王芃生。一個平凡黨員的回憶與自我檢討。
———. Shih-chü lun-ts'ung. Chungking, 1945.
王芃生。時局論叢。
Yuan Jung-sou. Chiao ao chih (ed. by Chao Ch'i). Tsingtao: Chiao ao shang-wu chü, 1928. 10 vols.
袁榮叟。膠澳志。趙琪。

Wang Shih-chen   王士珍

SOURCES

CMMC
Kuo shih kuan kuan k'an, I-2 (March, 1948): 106-9.
國史館館刊。
Kuo wen chou-pao, II-30 (Ausust, 9, 1925); III-27 (July 14, 1930).
國聞週報。

MMT
PCCP
Powell, Ralph L. The Rise of Chinese Military Power, 1895-1912. Princeton: Princeton University Press, 1955.
T'ao Chü-yin. Pei-yang chün-fa t'ung-chih shih, ch'i shih-hua. Peking: Sheng-huo, tu-shu-hsin-chih san-lien shu-tien, 1957-58. 6 vols.
陶菊隱。北洋軍閥統治時期史話。
Wang Shu-nan. T'ao-lu ts'ung-k'o; ch'u-chi erh-shih chung. Hsing-ch'eng: Wang shih, 1883-1917. 46 vols.
王樹枏。陶廬叢刻;初集二十種。
Wen Kung-chih. Tsui-chin san-shih nien Chung-kuo chün-shih shih. Shanghai: T'ai-p'ing-yang shu-tien, 1932. 2 vols.
文公直。最近三十年中國軍事史。
WWC, 1925.

Wang Shih-chieh   王世杰

WORKS

1920? La Repartition des Competences dans les Constitutions Federales.
1934. "Minister Wang on Education Progress." *The China Critic*: 968.
1935. Education in China. Shanghai: China United Press.
1937. "Education in China." *Yearbook of Education*: 555-601.
1938-39, Winter. "Consolidation of Democracy: The People's Political Council." *The China Quarterly*: 17-23.
1946. Pi-chiao hsien-fa. with Ch'ien Tuan-sheng. Shanghai: Shang-wu yin shu kuan.
比較憲法。錢端升。
The Legal Aspect of Slavery in the History of China.

SOURCES

AWW
BKL
CH
Chang Ch'i-yün. Tang shih kai-yao. Taipei: Chung-yang wen-wu kung-ying she, 1951-52. 5 vols.
張其昀。黨史概要。
China Yearbook, 1963-64. Taipei: China Publishing Co., 1964.
Chung-kuo wai-chiao nien-chien; ti-erh ts'e, comp. by Chang Chin. Shanghai: Shih-chieh shu-chü, 1935.

中國外交年鑑；第二冊。章進。
CMJL
CMTC
CTMC
CWR, March 3, 1946.
GCJJ
International Who's Who, 1955.
Levi, Werner. Modern China's Foreign Policy.
  Minneapolis: University of Minnesota Press,
  1953.
MMT
The New York Times, July 15, 1958.
SMJ
Tong, Hollington K. Abridged Biography of
  President Chiang. Taipei: China Cultural
  Service, 1954.
WWC, 1950.
WWMC
Yueh Ch'ien. Chung Su kuan-hsi shih-hua.
  Singapore, Hong Kong: Ch'uang k'en ch'u-
  pan she, 1952.
  岳騫。中蘇關係史話。

Wang Tsao-shih   王造時

WORKS

1932. Kuo-chi lien-meng yü Chung Jih wen-t'i.
  Shanghai: Hsin-yüeh shu-tien.
  國際聯盟與中日問題。
1935. Chung-kuo wen-t'i te fen-hsi. Shanghai:
  Shang-wu yin shu kuan.
  中國問題的分析。
1936. Chin-tai Ou-chou wai-chiao shih, 1815-
  1914. (tr.) Shanghai: Shang-wu yin shu
  kuan.
  近代歐洲外交史，1815-1914。
1936. Li-shih che-hsueh. (tr.) with Hsieh I-
  cheng. Shanghai: Shang-wu yin shu kuan.
  歷史哲學。謝詒徵。
1938-42. ed. of Ch'ien-hsien jih-pao.
  前綫日報。
ed. of Chu-chang yü p'i-p'ing.
  主張與批評。
Huang-miao chi.
  荒謬集。
ed. of Tzu-yu yen-lun.
  自由言論。

SOURCES

GCCJK
GCJJ

Hsing-tao wan-pao. Hong Kong, August 12-13,
  1951.
  星島晚報。
JMST, 1958.
Li Shou-tung. Chiu kuo wu tsui ch'i chün-tzu.
  Shih-tai wen-hsien she, 1937.
  李守東。救國無罪七君子。
SCMP, 157 (August 19-20, 1951).
SSYD
Tsou T'ao-fen. Huan-nan yü-sheng chi. Shang-
  hai: Sheng-huo shu-tien, 1936.
  鄒韜奮。患難餘生記。

Wang Yao-ch'ing   王瑤卿

WORKS

1933, April. "Wo-te chung-nien shih-tai." *Chü-
  hsueh yueh-k'an*, II-4.
  我的中年時代。劇學月刊。

SOURCES

CBJS
Chang Hsiang-ch'ien. "Li-yuan shih-chia,
  Wang shih ssu ch'ing." *Chuan-chi wen-hsueh*,
  III-5 (November, 1963).
  張象乾。梨園世家，王氏四卿。傳記文學。
Huang K'o-pao. Wang Yao-ch'ing yü ching-chü
  "liu yin chi" (ed. by Chung-kuo hsi-ch'ü yen-
  chiu-yuan). Shanghai: Shanghai wen-hua
  ch'u-pan she, 1957.
  黃克保。王瑤卿與京劇「柳蔭記」。中國戲
  曲研究院。
Li-yuan ying shih, comp. by Hsü Mu-yün.
  Shanghai: Hua-tung yin-shua so, 1933.
  梨園影事。徐慕雲。
Mei Lan-fang. "Chi-ch'eng che Yao-ch'ing
  hsien-sheng te ching-shen ch'ien-chin."
  Kuang-ming jih-pao. Peking, June 25, 1954.
  梅蘭芳。繼承著瑤卿先生的精神前進。光
  明日報。
———. Wu-t'ai sheng-huo ssu-shih nien. Shanghai: P'ing ming ch'u-pan she, 1952.
  梅蘭芳。舞台生活四十年。
Pi Ko Mo Wu Chai Chu (pseud.). "Ching-chü
  sheng tan liang ko-ming chia." *Chü-hsueh
  yueh-k'an*, III-7 (July, 1934).
  筆歌墨舞齋主。京劇生旦兩革命家。劇學
  月刊。
Wang Yao-ch'ing. "Wo te chung-nien shih-tai."
  Chü-hsueh yueh-k'an, II-4 (April, 1933).
  王瑤卿。我的中年時代。劇學月刊。

Wang Yin-t'ai　王蔭泰

SOURCES

The China Annual. Shanghai: The Asia Statistics Co., 1944.
Kuo wen chou-pao, IV-29 (July 31, 1927).
國聞週報。
MMT
The Orient Year Book. Tokyo: The Asia Statistics Co., 1942.
SMJ
Who's Who in Japan, with Manchukuo and China, 1940-41. Tokyo.
WWC, 1928, 1931.

Wang Yün-wu　王雲五

WORKS

1926. Wang's System of Chinese Lexicography: The Four-Corner Numeral System in Arranging Chinese Characters. Shanghai: The Commercial Press.
1930. (ed.) Wang Yün-wu ta tz'u-tien. Shanghai: Shang-wu yin shu kuan.
王雲五大辭典。
1933. (ed.) Chih-min-ti tu-li yün-tung. with Li Sheng-wu. Shanghai: Shang-wu yin shu kuan.
殖民地獨立運動。李聖五。
1933. (ed.) Fei chan kung-yueh. with Li Sheng-wu. Shanghai: Shang-wu yin shu kuan.
非戰公約。李聖五。
1933. (ed.) Hsi feng. with Li Sheng-wu. Shanghai: Shang-wu yin shu kuan.
西風。李聖五。
1933. (ed.) Hsien-tai ching-chi ssu-hsiang. with Li Sheng-wu. Shanghai: Shang-wu yin shu kuan.
現代經濟思想。李聖五。
1933. (ed.) K'o-hsueh shang chih hsin kung-hsien. with Li Sheng-wu. Shanghai: Shang-wu yin shu kuan.
科學上之新貢獻。李聖五。
1933. (ed.) Kung-yeh ching-chi. with Li Sheng-wu. Shanghai: Shang-wu yin shu kuan.
工業經濟。李聖五。
1933. (ed.) Kuo-hua mien-mien-kuan. with Li Sheng-wu. Shanghai: Shang-wu yin shu kuan.
國畫面面觀。李聖五。
1933. (ed.) Ou-chou lien-pang wen-t'i. with Li Sheng-wu. Shanghai: Shang-wu yin shu kuan.
歐洲聯邦問題。李聖五。
1933. (ed.) Sheng-ch'an te lao-tso chiao-yü. with

Li Sheng-wu. Shanghai: Shang-wu yin shu kuan.
生產的勞作教育。李聖五。
1933. (ed.) T'ai-p'ing-yang kuo-chi kuan-hsi te fen-hsi. with Li Sheng-wu. Shanghai: Shang-wu yin shu kuan.
太平洋國際關係的分析。李聖五。
1934. (ed.) (Fu-hsing kao-chi chung-hsueh chiao-k'o-shu) Kung-min. with Li Chen-tung *et al*. Shanghai: Shang-wu yin shu kuan. 6 vols.
(復興高級中學教科書) 公民。李震東等。
1937. Pien-tsuan Chung-kuo wen-hua shih chih yen-chiu. Shanghai: Shang-wu yin shu kuan.
編纂中國文化史之研究。
1939. Chung wai t'u-shu t'ung-i fen-lei fa. Changsha: Shang-wu yin shu kuan.
中外圖書統一分類法。
1943. Kung shang kuan-li i-p'ieh. Chungking: Shang-wu yin shu kuan.
工商管理一瞥。
1943. (ed.) Wang Yün-wu hsin tz'u-tien. Chungking: Shang-wu yin shu kuan.
王雲五新詞典。
1945. Fang Ying jih-chi. Chungking: Shang-wu yin shu kuan.
訪英日記。
1946. Hsin mu-lu hsueh te i chiao-lo. Shanghai: Shang-wu yin shu kuan.
新目錄學的一角落。
1946. Lü Yü hsin-sheng. Shanghai: Shang-wu yin shu kuan.
旅渝心聲。
1952. I-chiu-wu-erh nien te shih chü. Taipei: Hua kuo ch'u-pan she.
一九五二年的世局。
1952. T'an shih-chieh. Taipei: Hua kuo ch'u-pan she.
談世界。
1952. Wo-te sheng-huo p'ien-tuan. Hong Kong: Hua kuo ch'u-pan she.
我的生活片段。
1954. T'an cheng-chih. Taipei: Hua kuo ch'u-pan she.
談政治。
1954. T'an kuo-chi chü-shih. Taipei: Hua kuo ch'u-pan she.
談國際局勢。
1954. Tui ch'ing-nien chiang-hua. Taipei: Hua kuo ch'u-pan she.
對青年講話。
1955. Hsien-tai kung-wu kuan-li. Taipei: Chung-hua wen-hua ch'u-pan shih-yeh wei-yuan-hui.

現代公務管理。

1960. (ed.) Wang Yün-wu tsung-ho tz'u-tien. Taipei: Hua kuo ch'u-pan she.

王雲五綜合辭。

1964. Chi chiu yu. Taipei: Tzu-yu t'an tsa-chih she.

紀舊遊。

1964. Hsiu-lu lun cheng. Taipei: Fa-ling yueh-k'an she.

岫廬論政。

1964. T'an wang-shih (ed. by Chuan-chi wen-hsueh tsa-chih she). Taipei: Chuan-chi wen-hsueh ch'u-pan she.

談往事。傳記文學雜誌社。

1965. Hsiu-lu lun chiao-yü. Taipei: Taiwan shang-wu yin shu kuan.

岫廬論教育。

1965. Hsiu-lu lun hsueh. Taipei: Ta hua wan-pao she.

岫廬論學。

1965. Hsiu-lu lun kuan-li. Taipei: Hua kuo ch'u-pan she.

岫廬論管理。

1965. Hsiu-lu lun shih chü. Taipei: Ch'ing-nien chan-shih pao she.

岫廬論世局。

1965. Ssu chiao hao-ma chien tzu fa (with chien tzu piao). Taipei: Taiwan shang-wu yin shu kuan.

四角號碼檢字法 (附檢字表)。

1965. Wang Yün-wu et al. Wo Tsen-yang jen-shih kuo-fu Sun hsien-sheng. Taipei: Chuan-chi wen-hsueh she.

王雲等。我怎樣認識國父孫先生。

SOURCES

P'ang-t'ing che (pseud.). "Wang Yün-wu t'an ch'ang-shou pi-chueh." *Hua Mei jih-pao*, New York, August 31, 1961.

旁聽者。王雲五談長壽秘訣。華美日報。

Wang Yün-wu. T'an wang-shih (ed. by Chuan-chi wen-hsueh tsa-chih she). Taipei: Chuan-chi wen-hsueh ch'u-pan she, 1964.

王雲五。談往事。傳記文學雜誌社。

———. Wo-te sheng-huo p'ien-tuan. Hong Kong: Hua kuo ch'u-pan she, 1952.

王雲五。我的生活片段。

Wei Cho-ming   韋卓明

SOURCES

Persons interviewed: not to be identified.

Wei Li-huang   衞立煌

SOURCES

BKL

CH

CTMC

GCJJ

SMJ

South China Morning Post. Hong Kong, January 18, 1960.

Tai Liao-p'an. "Wei Li-huang chia san jen 'wang'." *Hsin-wen t'ien-ti*, 371 (March 26, 1955).

戴了攀。衞立煌家散人「亡」。新聞天地。

Union Research Biographic Service, 420 (January 1, 1960).

Wei Tao-ching. "Hsieh kei wo-te pa-pa Wei Li-huang." *Hsin-wen t'ien-ti*, 371 (March 26, 1955).

衞道京。寫給我的爸爸衞立煌。新聞天地。

WWMC

Wei Tao-ming   魏道明

WORKS

1940, Autumn. "Important Administrative Measures in the Last Three Years." *China Quarterly*: 559-64.

1944, August 7. "The Future of Chinese-American Economic Relations." *Contemporary China*: 1-4.

1946, April 15. "China's Democratic Ideals." *Contemporary China*: 1-2.

SOURCES

Person interviewed: Chang Chia-ao.

BKL

CH

CH-T, 1954-55, 1956-57.

Chung-yang jih-pao. Taipei, February 10, 1963.

中央日報。

CMTC

Contemporary China, April 15, 1946.

CTMC

Current Biography, 1942.

CWR, April 6, 1929; July 5, 1947.

Free China Weekly, June 12, 1966.

GCJJ

International Who's Who, 1954.

The New York Times, September 2, 1942; August 15, November 28, 1945; May 18, 1947.

T'ang Leang-li. The Inner History of the

Chinese Revolution. New York: E.P. Dutton & Co., 1930.

Wei Tao-ming. "Important Administrative Measures in the Last Three Years." *The China Quarterly*, Autumn, 1940: 559-64.

Wei Yü-hsiu. May Revolutionary Years: The Autobiography of Madame Wei Tao-ming. New York: Charles Scribner's Sons, 1943.

WWMC

Wen I-to 聞一多

WORKS

1915-16. ed. of *Ch'ing-hua chou-k'an*.
清華週刊。

1919-20. ed. of *Ch'ing-hua hsueh-pao*.
清華學報。

1948. Wen I-to ch'üan-chi (ed. by Chu Tzu-ch'ing, Kuo Mo-jo, Wu Han, Yeh Sheng-t'ao). Shanghai: K'ai-ming shu-tien. 4 vols.
聞一多全集。朱自清，郭沫若，吳晗，葉聖陶。

1955. Wen I-to shih wen hsuan-chi (ed. by Jen-min wen-hsueh ch'u-pan she). Peking: Jen-min wen-hsueh ch'u-pan she.
聞一多詩文選集。人民文學出版社。

ed. of *Min-chu chou-k'an*.
民主週刊。

SOURCES

Mien-chih (pseud.). Wen I-to. Peiping: Hsin Chung-kuo shu-chü, 1949.
勉之。聞一多。

Modern Chinese Poetry, tr. by Harold Acton, Ch'en Shih-hsiang. London: Duckworth, 1936.

Shih Ching. Wen I-to te tao-lu. Shanghai: Sheng-huo shu-tien, 1947.
史靖。聞一多的道路。

Shih chien, April 1926.
詩鐫。

Shih k'an, January 20, 1931.
詩刊。

Tsang K'o-chia. "Wen I-to hsien-sheng chuan-lueh," in Jen-min wen-hsueh ch'u-pan she, *Wen I-to shih wen hsuan-chi*. Peking: Jen-min wen-hsueh ch'u-pan she, 1955.
臧克家。聞一多先生傳略。人民文學出版社。聞一多詩文選集。

Wen Chan-min, Wu Han, Chang Po-chün *et al.* Jen-min ying-lieh. 1946.
聞展民，吳晗，章伯鈞等。人民英烈。

Wen I-to. Wen I-to ch'üan-chi (ed. by Chu Tzu-ch'ing, Kuo Mo-jo, Wu Han, Yeh Sheng-t'ao). Shanghai: K'ai-ming shu-tien. 4 vols.
聞一多。聞一多全集。朱自清，郭沫若，吳晗，葉聖陶。

Wong Wen-hao 翁文灝

WORKS

1933. Chung-kuo fen sheng hsin t'u. with Ting Wen-chiang, Tseng Shih-ying. Shanghai: Shen pao kuan.
中國分省新圖。丁文江，曾世英。

1933. The Distribution of Population and Land Utilization in China. Shanghai: China Institute of Pacific Relations.

1934. Chung-hua Min-kuo hsin ti-t'u. with Ting Wen-chiang, Tseng Shih-ying. Shanghai: Shen pao kuan.
中華民國新地圖。丁文江，曾世英。

1938. China's Economic Development. Hankow: Chinese League of Nations Union.

1946. Chung-kuo ching-chi chien-she yü nung-ts'en kung-yeh-hua wen-t'i. with Ku I-ch'ün. Shanghai: Shan-wu yin shu kuan.
中國經濟建設與農村工業化問題。顧翊群。

1946. Report on Economic Affairs. Nanking: International Department, Ministry of Information.

SOURCES

China Reconstructs, January, 1957.

CTMC

CYB-W, 1934.

Hsin-wen t'ien-ti, May 19, 1951.
新聞天地。

Hsü Ying. Tang-tai Chung-kuo shih-yeh jen-wu chih. Shanghai: Chung-hua shu-chü, 1948.
徐盈。當代中國實業人物志。

Wu Ch'ao-shu 伍朝樞

WORKS

1929. "Chinese-American Relations." *Annals of the American Academy of Political and Social Science*, 144: 135-36.

1929. The National Program for China. New Haven: Yale University Press.

An Appeal for Recognition.

China's Position in Tibet.

SOURCES

BPC

CWR, January 6, 1934.

Kuang-hsü yin sheng ·t'ung kuan ch'ih lu. Peking: Wen te chai, 1875–1940. 5 vols.
光緒廩生同官齒錄。

Liang Yuen-li. "In Memory of Dr. C.C. Wu." *The China Critic*, VII-15 (April, 1934): 345-49.

T'ao Lü-ch'ien. "Wu Ch'ao-shu hsing-chuang," in Chung-kuo kuo-min-tang chung-yang tang shih shih-liao pien-tsuan wei-yuan-hui, *Ko-ming hsien-lieh hsien-chin chuan*. Taipei: Chung-hua Min-kuo ko-chieh chi-nien kuo-fu pai nien tan-ch'en ch'ou-pei wei-yuan-hui, 1965.
陶履謙。伍朝樞行狀。中國國民黨中央黨史史料編纂委員會。革命先烈先進傳。

Wu Ch'ao-shu. The Nationalist Program for China. New Haven: Yale University Press, 1929.

WWC, 1925.

Wu Chien-hsiung   吳健雄

SOURCES

Persons interviewed: not to be identified.
The New Yorker, May 12, 1962.

Wu Chien-hsiung po-shih yü Chia-hsin t'e-shu kung-hsien chiang, comp. by Chia-hsin shui-ni kung-ssu wen-hua chi-chin hui. Taipei: Chia-hsin shui-ni kung-ssu wen-hua chi-chin hui, 1965.
吳健雄博士與嘉新特殊貢獻獎。嘉新水泥公司文化基金會。

Wu Chih-hui   吳稚暉

WORKS

1924. Erh-pai chao p'ing-min ta wen-t'i. Shang-wu yin shu kuan.
二百兆平民大問題。

1925. Wu Chih-hui hsien-sheng wen-ts'un (ed. by Chou Yün-ch'ing). Shanghai: I-hsueh shu-chü. 2 vols.
吳稚暉先生文存。周雲青。

1926. Wu Chih-hui chin-chu (ed. by Li Hsiao-feng). Shanghai: Pei hsin shu-chü.
吳稚暉近著。李曉峯。

1926. Wu Chih-hui chin chu hsü-pien (ed. by Chung Tan). Pei hsin shu-chü.
吳稚暉近著續編。仲丹。

1926. Wu Chih-hui hsueh-shu lun-chu (comp. by Liang Ping-huan). Shanghai: Shanghai ch'u-pan ho-tso she.
吳稚暉學術論著。梁冰弦。

1927. I ko hsin-yang te yü-chou kuan chi jen-sheng kuan. Nanking: Chung-yang chün-shih cheng-chih hsueh-hsiao cheng-chih pu.
一個信仰的宇宙觀及人生觀。

1927. Wu Chih-hui hsien-sheng ch'üan-chi (ed. by Fang Tung-liang). Shanghai: Ch'ün-chung t'u-shu kung-ssu. 5 vols.
吳稚暉先生全集。方東亮。

1927. Wu Chih-hui hsueh-shu lun chu hsü-pien (ed. by Liang Ping-hsuan). Shanghai: Shanghai ch'u-pan ho-tso she.
吳稚暉學術論著續編。梁冰弦。

1927. Wu Chih-hui yü Wang Ching-wei. Shanghai: Ko-ming shu-tien.
吳稚暉與汪精衞。

1928. Wu Chih-hui hsien-sheng wen-ts'ui (ed. by T'ao Lo-ch'in). Shanghai: Ch'üan min shu-chü. 4 vols.
吳稚暉先生文粹。陶樂勤。

1928. Wu Chih-hui pai-hua-wen ch'ao. Shanghai: Wen-ming shu-chü.
吳稚暉白話文鈔。

1929. Wu Chih-hui yen-hsing lu (ed. by Shih Hsi-sheng). Shanghai: Kuang i shu-chü.
吳稚暉言行錄。時希聖。

1936. Wu Chih-hui shu-hsin chi (comp. by Shao-hou). Shanghai: Fang ku shu-tien.
吳稚暉書信集。少候。

1939? Tui Wang Ching-wei "chü i ko li" te chin i chieh. Hong Kong.
對汪精衞「舉一個例」的進一解。

1939. Wu Chih-hui hsien-sheng tsui-chin yen-lun chi (ed. by Sao-tang pao). Chungking: Ch'ing-nien shu-tien.
吳稚暉先生最近言論集。掃蕩報。

1944. Chu-yin fu-hao tso-yung chih pien-cheng.
注音符號作用之辨正。

1949. Tsung-li hsing-i. Taipei: Chiao-yü t'ing.
總理行誼。

1952. Kuo-fu nien-hsi chi hsing-i (ed. by Yang Ch'eng-po). Taipei: P'a-mi-erh shu-tien.
國父年系及行誼。楊成柏。

1960. Shang hsia ku-chin t'an. Taipei: Hsin lu shu-chü.
上下古今談。

1964. Chih-hui hsien-sheng i p'ien chung-yao hui-i (ed. by Wu Tse-chung). Taipei: Shih-chieh shu-chü.
稚暉先生一篇重要回憶。吳則中。

1964. Wu Chih-hui hsien-sheng hsuan-chi (comp. by Chung-kuo kuo-min-tang chung-yang wei-yuan-hui tang shih shih-liao pien-tsuan wei-yuan-hui). Taipei. 2 vols.
吳稚暉先生選集。中國國民黨中央委員會黨史史料編纂委員會。

ed. of *Chung-hua jih-pao.*
中華日報。

ed. of *Hsin shih-chi.*
新世紀。

Huang ku yuan jen shih. Wen-ming shu-chü.
荒古原人史。

Wu Chih-hui ch'ih-tu. Shanghai: San min kung-ssu.
吳稚暉尺牘。

SOURCES

BKL

Chang Ch'i-yün. Tang shih kai-yao. Taipei: Chung-yang kai-tsao wei-yuan-hui wen-wu kung-ying she, 1951–52. 5 vols.
張其昀。黨史概要。

———. "Wu Chih-hui hsien-sheng chih ching-shen. *Chung-kuo i chou*, 189 (December 7, 1953).
張其昀。吳稚暉先生之精神。中國一周。

Chang Wen-po. Chih lao hsien-hua. Taipei: Chung-yang wen-wu kung-ying she, 1952.
張文伯。稚老閒話。

———. Wu Chih-hui hsien-sheng chuan-chi. Taipei: Wen hsing shu-tien, 1965.
張文伯。吳稚暉先生傳記。

Ch'i T'ieh-hen *et al.* Wu Chih-hui hsien-sheng te sheng-p'ing (comp. by Taiwan sheng kuo-yü t'ui-hsing wei-yuan-hui). Taipei: Taiwan sheng kuo-yü t'ui-hsing wei-yuan-hui, 1951.
齊鐵恨等。吳稚暉先生的生平。台灣省國語推行委員會。

Chung-kuo i-chou, 185 (November 9, 1953).
中國一周。

CTMC

Hu Shih. "Chui-nien Wu Chih-hui hsien-sheng," in Chung-huo kuo-min-tang chung-yang tang shih shih-liao pien tsuan wei-yuan-hui, *Ko-ming hsien-lieh hsien-chi chuan.* Taipei: Chung-yang wen-wu kung-ying she, 1965.
胡適。追念吳稚暉先生。中國國民黨中央黨史史料編纂委員會。革命先烈先進傳。

Kwok, D.W.Y. "The Ta-t'ung Thought of Wu Chih-hui." Unpublished paper, International Conference on Asian History, University of Hong Kong, August 30–September 5, 1964.

———. "Wu Chih-hui and Scientism." *Tsing-hua Journal of Chinese Studies*, New Series III-1: 160–85.

Lei Hsiao-ts'en. San-shih nien tung-luan Chung-kuo. Hong Kong: Ya-chou ch'u-pan she, 1955.
雷嘯岑。三十年動亂中國。

Li Shu-hua. "Wu Chih-hui hsien-sheng te t'e-tien." *Chung-kuo i chou*, 237 (November 8, 1954).
李書華。吳稚暉先生的特點。中國一周。

Scalapino, Robert A., and George T. Yu. The Chinese Anarchist Movement. Berkeley: Center for Chinese Studies, Institute of International Studies, University of California, 1961.

T'ang Leang-li. The Inner History of the Chinese Revolution. New York: E.P. Dutton & Co., 1930.

Teng Yen-pin. "Wu Chih-hui, Great Man of the Century." *Free China Review*, XIV-5 (May, 1964): 9–17.

Ti Ying. "Chih lao hai-tsang chi ai." *Chung-kuo i chou*, 190 (December 14, 1953).
狄膺。稚老海葬記哀。中國一周。

Wu Chih-hui hsien-sheng chi-nien chi, ed. by Yang K'ai-ling. Taipei: Chung-yang wen-wu kung-ying she, 1954.
吳稚暉先生紀念集。楊愷齡。

Wu Chih-hui hsien-sheng chi-nien chi hsü chi; Wu Chih-hui hsien-sheng shih-shih shih chou-nien chi-nien t'e chi, ed. by Yang K'ai-ling. Taipei: Chung-yang wen-wu kung-ying she, 1963.
吳稚暉先生紀念集續集；吳稚暉先生逝世十週年紀念特輯。楊愷齡。

Wu Ching-hsiung 吳經熊

WORKS

1928. Juridical Essays and Studies. Shanghai: Commercial Press.

1930. Legal Systems of Old and New China, a Comparison. Chicago.

1933. Fa-lü che-hsueh yen-chiu. Shanghai: Shanghai fa-hsueh pien-chi she.
法律哲學研究。

1933. First Draft of the Permanent Constitution of China (tr. by Yui Ming). Shanghai: China Press.

1936. The Art of Law and Other Essays, Juridical and Literary. Shanghai: Commercial Press.

1937. Chung-kuo chih hsien shih. with Huang Kung-chueh. Shanghai: Shang-wu yin shu kuan.
中國制憲史。黃公覺。

1937. (ed.) Fa-hsueh wen-hsuan. with Hua Mou-sheng. Shanghai: Hui-wen-t'ang hsin-chi shu-chü. 2 vols.
法學文選。華懋生。

1938. (comp.) Essays in Jurisprudence and Legal Philosophy. with M.C. Liang. Shanghai: Soochow University Law School.

1939–40. (tr. and annot.) Lao-tzu's the Tao and Its Virtue. Shanghai.

1945. China's Constitutions: Permanent and Provisional. Chungking: Chinese Ministry of Information.

1945. The Organic Law of the Republic of China and the Final Draft Constitution of the Republic of China. New York: Chinese News Service.

1946. Sheng yung i i ch'u-kao. (tr.) Shanghai: Shang-wu yin shu kuan.
聖詠譯義初稿。

1947. The Constitution of the Republic of China. New York: Chinese News Service.

1951. Beyond East and West. New York: Sheed & Ward.

1953. The Interior Carmel: The Threefold Way of Life. New York: Sheed & Ward.

1954. "Victory of Grace," in John Anthony O'Brien, *Roads to Rome*. New York: The Macmillan Co.

1955. Fountain of Justice: A Study in the Natural Law. New York: Sheed & Ward.

1957? Justice Holmes: A New Estimate. Philadelphia: Brandeis Lawyers Society.

1958. Cases and Materials on Jurisprudence. St. Paul, Minn.: West Publishing Co.

1963. Huai lan chi. Taichung: Kuang-ch'i ch'u-pan she.
懷蘭集。

1965. Chinese Humanism and Christian Spirituality: Essays of John C.H. Wu (ed. by Paul K.T. Sih). Jamaica, N.Y.: St. John's University Press.

Hsin-ching ch'üan-chi. (tr. of New Testament).
新經全集。

SOURCES

Catholic Authors, ed. by Mathew Hoehn. St. Mary's Abbey, 1948.
CBJS
GCJJ

K'o I (pseud.). "Chi lü Mei te Wu Ching-hsiung chiao-shou." *Chin shan shih-pao*, San Francisco, August 30, 31, 1960.
可義。記旅美的吳經熊教授。金山時報。

Wu, John C.H. (Wu Ching-hsiung). Beyond East and West. New York: Sheed & Ward, 1951.

———. "Victory of Grace," in John Anthony O'Brien, *Roads to Rome*. New York: The Macmillan Co., 1954.

WWC, 1931.

Wu Chung-hsin   吳忠信

WORKS

1953. Hsi-tsang (Tibet) chi-yao. Taipei.
西藏紀要。

SOURCES

BKL
Chang Ta-chün. Ssu-shih nien tung-luan Sinkiang. Hong Kong: Ya-chou ch'u-pan she, 1956.
張達鈞。四十年動亂新疆。
Chiang Ching-kuo. Wei-chi ts'un-wang chih ch'iu.
蔣經國。危急存亡之秋。
Chou K'un-t'ien. Wu Li-ch'ing hsien-sheng hsing-shu.
周昆田。吳禮卿先生行述。
CH–T, 1956–57.
Feng Tzu-yu. Chung-hua Min-kuo k'ai-kuo ch'ien ko-ming shih. Chungking: Chung-kuo wen-hua fu-wu she, 1944. 3 vols.
馮自由。中華民國開國前革命史。
Sun Fu-k'un. Su-lien lueh-to Sinkiang chi-shih. Kowloon: Tzu-yu ch'u-pan she, 1952. 2 vols.
孫福坤。蘇聯掠奪新疆紀實。
Sun Wen. Kuo-fu ch'üan-shu (ed. by Chang Ch'i-yün). Taipei: Kuo-fang yen-chiu yuan.
孫文。國父全書。張其昀。
Wu Chung-hsin. Hsi-tsang (Tibet) chi-yao. Taipei, 1953.
吳忠信。西藏紀要。
Wu Li-ch'ing hsien-sheng chi-nien chi.
吳禮卿先生紀念集。

Wu Han   吳晗

WORKS

1937, June. "Hu Wei-yung tang-an k'ao." *Yenching hsueh-pao*.

胡惟庸黨案考。燕京學報。

1944. (comp.) Ming-t'ai-tsu. Chungking: Sheng-li ch'u-pan she.
明太祖。

1946. Li-shih te ching-tzu. Shanghai: Sheng-huo shu-tien.
歷史的鏡子。

1948. Huang ch'üan yü shen ch'üan. with Fei Hsiao-t'ung et al. Shanghai: Kuan-ch'a she.
皇權與紳權。費孝通等。

1949. Chu Yuan-chang chuan. Shanghai: Sheng-huo, tu-shu, hsin chih san lien shu-tien.
朱元璋傳。

1950. "Wo k'o-fu le 'ch'ao chieh-chi' kuan-tien," in Chang Chih-chung et al., Tsen-yang kai-tsao. Hong Kong: Ho-tso shu-tien.
我克服了「超階級」觀點。張治中等。怎樣改造。

1951. Wu Han et al. (comp.) Mei-kuo ch'in Hua shih-liao. Peking: Jen-min ch'u-pan she.
吳晗等。美國侵華史料。

1957. Tu shih cha chi. Peking: Tu-shu, sheng-huo, hsin chih san lien shu-tien.
讀史劄記。

1960. Hai-jui te ku-shih. Peking: Chung-hua shu-chü.
海瑞的故事。

1961. Ch'un-t'ien li. Peking: Tso-chia ch'u-pan she.
春天裡。

1961. Hai-jui pa kuan. Peking ch'u-pan she.
海瑞罷官。

1961. Teng hsia chi. Peking: Sheng-huo, tu-shu hsin chih san lien shu-tien.
燈下集。

1964. (ed.) Chung-kuo li-shih ch'ang-shih. Peking: Chung-kuo ch'ing-nien ch'u-pan she.
中國歷史常識。

1967-? Wu Han wen-chi. Hong Kong: Ts'un-chen yin shu kuan. vols. 1-?
吳晗文集。

SOURCES

CB, 783.
Chang Chih-chung et al. Tsen-yang kai-tsao. Hong Kong: Ho-tso shu-tien, 1950.
張治中等。怎樣改造。
GCJJ
MacFarquhar, Roderick. "Mao's Last Revolu-tion." Foreign Affairs, XLV-1 (October, 1966).
SCMP, 3669, 3698, 3699, 3701, 3707-9, 3718.

Selections from China Mainland Magazines, 514, 526.

Wu Hsien　　吳憲

SOURCES

Persons interviewed: not to be identified.
American Men of Science, 9th ed.
International Who's Who in World Medicine.

Wu Hsien-tzu　　伍憲子

WORKS

1929. Wu Hsien-tzu chih hai-wai kuo-min-tang jen shu. San Francisco: Ch'ü kuai pan-yueh-k'an she.
伍憲子致海外國民黨人書。

1930. Meng tieh ts'ung-k'an, ti-i ts'e. San Francisco: Shih-chieh jih-pao she.
夢蝶叢刊; 第一冊。

1952. Chung-kuo min-chu hsien-cheng tang tang shih. San Francisco: Shih-chieh jih-pao she.
中國民主憲政黨黨史。

1956. K'ung-tzu. Kowloon: Tzu-yu ch'u-pan she.
孔子。

1957. Chung-kuo min-chu chu-i. Kowloon: Tzu-yu ch'u-pan she.
中國民主主義。

ed. of Jen-tao.
人道。

SOURCES

Hu Ying-han. Wu Hsien-tzu hsien-sheng chuan-chi. Hong Kong: Ssu ch'iang yin-shua kung-ssu, 1953.
胡應漢。伍憲子先生傳記。
Wu Hsien-tzu. Chung-kuo min-chu hsien-cheng tang tang shih. San Francisco: Shih-chieh jih-pao she, 1952.
伍憲子。中國民主憲政黨黨史。

Wu Hsiu-ch'üan　　伍修權

WORKS

1950. People's China Stands for Peace: Speech at the United Nations Security Council No-vember 28, 1950. New York: Committee for a Democratic Far Eastern Policy.
1951. Wo-kuo tai-piao Wu Hsiu-ch'üan chih-

ch'ih Su-lien tai-piao tsai Lien-ho-kuo cheng-wei-hui k'ung-su Mei-kuo ch'in-lueh wo-kuo te fa-yen.

我國代表伍修權支持蘇聯代表在聯合國政委會控訴美國侵略我國的發言。

SOURCES

Person interviewed: Chang Kuo-t'ao.

Hinton, Harold C. Leaders of Communist China. California: The RAND Corporation, 1956.

WWMC

Wu Kuo-chen   吳 國 楨

WORKS

1928. Ancient Chinese Political Theories. Shanghai: Commercial Press.

1952. Taiwan sheng liu nien lai te shih-cheng ch'eng-kuo; Wu chu-hsi tsai Taiwan sheng lin-shih i-hui ti-i chieh ta-hui chih shih-cheng tsung pao-kao. Taipei: Taiwan sheng hsin-wen ch'u.

台灣省六年來的施政成果；吳主席在台灣省臨時議會第一屆大會之施政總報告。

1954, March 10. "Wu Kuo-chen chih kuo-min ta-hui ch'üan han." *Hsing-tao jih-pao*. Hong Kong.

吳國楨致國民大會全函。星島日報。

1954, June 29. "Your Money Has Built a Police State on Formosa." *Look*.

1962. The Lane of Eternal Stability. New York: Crown.

SOURCES

BKL

Christian Century. Chicago, March 31, 1954.

CH–T, 1953–54.

CMJL

CTMC

Current Biography, 1953.

CWR, 1930.

GCJJ

Hu Shih. "How Free Is Formosa?" *New Leader*, (August 16, 1954): 16–20.

Huang Shao-hung. Wu-shih hui-i. Shanghai: Shih-chieh shu-chü, 1945.

黃紹竑。五十回憶。

"The K. C. Wu Story." *Reporter*, April 27, 1954.

Newsweek, July 26, 1954.

Time, July 31, August 7, 1950; March 8, 22, 1954.

U.S.News & World Report, January 11, 1952.

Wu Kuo-chen. "Wu Kuo-chen chih kuo-min ta hui ch'üan han." *Hsing-tao jih-pao*. Hong Kong, March 10, 1954.

吳國楨。吳國楨致國民大會全函。星島日報。

———. "Your Money Has Built a Police State on Formosa." *Look*, June 29, 1954.

WWMC

Wu Lien-teh   伍 連 德

WORKS

1914–22. (ed.) North Manchurian Plague Prevention Service. Tientsin: Tientsin Press. 3 vols.

1921. Plague in the Orient with Special Reference to the Manchurian Outbreaks. Tientsin: Tientsin Press.

1922. "Progress of Modern Medicine in China." *The Chinese Students' Monthly*, 17: 581–86.

1926. A Treatise on Pneumonic Plague. Nancy, Paris, Strasburg: Berger-Leurault.

1931. "Early Days of Western Medicine in China." *Journal of North China Branch of Royal Asiatic Society*, 62: 1–31.

1932. History of Chinese Medicine: Being a Chronicle of Medical Happenings in China from Ancient Times to the Present Period. with K. Chimin Wong. Tientsin: The Tientsin Press.

1933. "Early Chinese Travellers and Their Successors." *Journal of the North China Branch of the Royal Asiatic Society*, 64: 1–23.

1933. A New Survey of Plague in Wild Rodents and Pneumonic Plague. Shanghai: National Quarantine Service.

1933. "A Short History of the Manchurian Plague Prevention Service." *People's Tribune*, new series, 4: 485–88.

1934. Cholera: A Manual for the Medical Profession in China. with J. W. H. Chun, R. Pollitzer, C. Y. Wu. Shanghai: National Quarantine Service.

1934. (ed.) Manchurian Plague Prevention Service Memorial Volume, 1912–1932. Shanghai: National Quarantine Service.

1936. "Chinese Achievements Overseas." *People's Tribune*, new series, 13: 175–84.

1936. Plague, a Manual for Medical and Public Health Workers. with J. W. H. Chun, R. Pollitzer, C. Y. Wu. Shanghai: National Quarantine Service.

1936. "Public Hospitals in China." *China Quarterly*, I-4: 1-11.
1936. "The Traditional Philosophy of Disease." *People's Tribune*, new series, 15: 221-28.
1936-37. "Hainan, the Paradise of China." *China Quarterly*, II: 225-58.
1937. "Hainan, China's Island Paradise." *China Journal of Science and Art*, 26: 184-88.
1959. Plague Fighter: The Autobiography of a Modern Chinese Physician. Cambridge, England: W. Heffer.

SOURCES

BPC
CBJS
Morrison, George E. Reminiscences of George E. Morrison. Canberra: Institute of Anatomy, 1936.
Wu Lien-teh. Plague Fighter: The Autobiography of a Modern Chinese Physician. Cambridge, England: W. Heffer, 1959.

Wu Mi 吳宓

WORKS

1935. Wu Mi shih-chi. Shanghai: Chung-hua shu-chü.
吳宓詩集。
ed. of *Hsueh heng*.
學衡。

SOURCES

Cho Hao-jan. "Chi Wu Yü-seng hsien-sheng." *Chung-yang jih-pao*, Taipei, May 14, 1963.
卓浩然。 記吳雨僧先生。 中央日報。
Hsin hua jih-pao, Chungking, July 8, 1952.
新華日報。
MMT

Wu P'ei-fu 吳佩孚

WORKS

1930. Hsun fen hsin shu. Ta-hsien, Szechwan.
循分新書。
1932. P'eng-lai Wu kung chiang-hua lu. Peiping: T'ien hua kuan.
蓬來吳公講話錄。
1936. Cheng i tao ch'üan.
正一道詮。
1960. Wu P'ei-fu hsien-sheng chi (comp. by Wu P'ei-fu hsien-sheng chi pien-chi wei-yuan-hui).

Taipei: Wu P'ei-fu hsien-sheng chi pien-chi wei-yuan-hui.
吳佩孚先生集。 吳佩孚先生集編輯委員會。
Ch'un-ch'iu tso-chuan ch'ien chieh.
春秋左傳淺解。

SOURCES

Far Eastern Review, XVII (June, 1922): 367.
Kuo Wei-lien. "Wu P'ei-fu fa-chi shih." *Chin shan shih-pao*. San Francisco, February 4-6, 1957.
郭威廉。 吳佩孚發跡史。 金山時報。
Li Chien-nung. The Political History of China 1840-1928 (tr. and ed. by Teng Ssu-yu, Jeremy Ingalls). Princeton: D. Van Nostrand Co., 1956.
Lu Tan-lin. "Wu P'ei-fu yü Yang Ch'i," in TTJWC.
陸丹林。 吳佩孚與楊圻。
MMT
New China Herald, December 20, 1934.
North China Herald, December 20, 1939.
Okano Masujirō. Go Hai-fu. Banseikaku, 1939.
岡野增次郎。 吳佩孚。
Powell, John B. My Twenty-Five Years in China. New York: The Macmillan Co., 1945.
SHPC
Soter, Richard. "Wu P'ei-fu: Case Study of a Chinese Warlord." Unpublished Ph. D. dissertation, Harvard University, 1958.
Ta feng hsun k'an, 25 (January 5, 1940): 793-94; 46 (August 25, 1939): 1482; 70 (July 5, 1940): 2204-7; 95 (August 5, 1941): 3189-92.
大風旬刊。
T'ao Chü-yin. Pei-yang chün-fa t'ung-chih shih-ch'i shih-hua. Peking: Sheng-huo, tu-shu, hsin chih san lien shu-tien, 1957-58. 6 vols.
陶菊隱。 北洋軍閥統治時期史話。
———. "Ts'ao Wu chih sheng shuai," in CTIW.
陶菊隱。 曹吳之盛衰。
———. Wu P'ei-fu chiang-chün chuan. Shanghai: Chung-hua shu-chü, 1941.
陶菊隱。 吳佩孚將軍傳。
Ts'ao K'un Wu P'ei-fu ho chuan, ed. by Ti-i yin shu kuan. 1924.
曹錕吳佩孚合傳。 第一印書館。
Wen Kung-chih. Tsui-chin san-shih nien Chung-kuo chün-shih shih. Shanghai: T'ai-p'ing-yang shu-tien, 1930.
文公直。 最近三十年中國軍事史。
Wu P'ei-fu. P'eng-lai Wu kung chiang-hua lu. Peiping: T'ien hua kuan, 1932.
吳佩孚。 蓬來吳公講話錄。

Wu P'ei-fu. Wu P'ei-fu hsien-sheng chi (ed. by Wu P'ei-fu hsien-sheng chi pien-chi wei-yuan-hui). Taipei: Wu P'ei-fu hsien-sheng chi pien-chi wei-yuan-hui, 1960.
吳佩孚。 吳佩孚先生集。 吳佩孚先生集編輯委員會。

Wu P'ei-fu, comp. by Wu te pao she. Peking, 1940.
吳佩孚。 武德報社。

Wu P'ei-fu ch'üan chuan, ed. by Chung wai hsin-wen she. Shanghai: Shih-chieh shu-chü, 1922.
吳佩孚全傳。 中外新聞社。

Wu Ying-wei. Wu P'ei-fu chiang-chün sheng-p'ing chuan. Shanghai: Chih-shih shu-tien, 1941.
吳英威。 吳佩孚將軍生平傳。

Wu T'ieh-ch'eng   吳鐵城

WORKS

1927? Wu wei-yuan T'ieh-ch'eng chih cheng-chih pao-kao (ti-erh tz'u). Canton: Chung-kuo kuo-min-tang Kwangtung sheng tang pu hsuan-ch'uan pu.
吳委員鐵城之政治報告 (第二次)。

1957. Ssu-shih nien lai chih Chung-kuo yü wo; Wu T'ieh-ch'eng hsien-sheng hui-i-lu. Taipei.
四十年來之中國與我; 吳鐵城先生回憶錄。
Chiang-yen lu.
講演錄。
Tang cheng chih-tu chi ch'i kuan-hsi.
黨政制度及其關係。

SOURCES

BKL
Chang Ch'ün *et al.* Wu T'ieh-ch'eng hsien-sheng chi-nien chi. 1953.
張群等。 吳鐵城先生紀念集。
Ko-ming hsien-lieh hsien-chin chuan, ed. by Chung-kuo kuo-min-tang chung-yang tang shih shih-liao pien-tsuan wei-yuan-hui. Taipei: Chung-yang wen-wu kung-ying she, 1965.
革命先烈先進傳。 中國國民黨中央黨史史料編纂委員會。
T'ieh-ch'eng t'ung-chih shih-shih shih chou-nien chi-nien, comp. by Wu T'ieh-ch'eng hsien-sheng shih-shih shih chou-nien chi-nien hui. Taipei, 1964.
鐵城同志逝世十週年紀念。 吳鐵城先生逝世十週年紀念會。

Wu Tieh-ch'eng. Ssu-shih nien lai chih Chung-kuo yü wo; Wu T'ieh-ch'eng hsien-sheng hui-i-lu. Taipei, 1957.
吳鐵城。 四十年來之中國與我; 吳鐵城先生回憶錄。
Wu T'ieh-ch'eng hsien-sheng chou chia jung shou t'e-k'an, comp. by Wu Yen-ch'ang. Shanghai: I wen shu-chü, 1947.
吳鐵城先生周甲榮壽特刊。 伍燕昌。

Wu Ting-ch'ang   吳鼎昌

WORKS

1926. Chung-kuo hsin ching-chi cheng-ts'e.
中國新經濟政策。
1960? Hua-ch'i hsien pi. Taipei.
花谿間筆。
(ed.) Chih shih wen lu (with Hsü pien).
誌石文錄 (附: 續編)。

SOURCES

BKL
CTMC
GCMMTJK
TKLH
WWC, 1933.

Wu T'ing-fang   伍廷芳

WORKS

1914. Yen shou hsin fa.
廷壽新法。
1915. Chung-hua Min-kuo t'u chih tsuo-i. Shanghai: Shang-wu yin shu kuan.
中華民國圖治芻議。

SOURCES

BPC
Ch'en Tz'u-sheng. Wu T'ing-fang i-shih. Shanghai: Hung wen t'u-shu kuan, 1925.
陳此生。 伍廷芳軼事。
Chung-hua Min-kuo k'ai-kuo ming-jen hsiang ti-i chi, comp. by Chung-kuo kuo-min-tang chung-yang tang shih shih-liao pien-tsuan wei-yuan-hui. Taipei: Chung-kuo kuo-min-tang chung-yang tang shih shih-liao pien-tsuan wei-yuan-hui, 1951.
中華民國開國名人像第一輯。 中國國民黨中央黨史史料編纂委員會。
Sun Wen. "Wu Chih-yung po-shih mu piao," in Tsou Lu, *Chung-kuo kuo-min-tang shih kao i*

chih ssu p'ien. Chungking: Shang-wu yin shu kuan, 1944. 4 vols.
孫文。伍秩庸博士墓表。鄒魯。中國國民黨史稿一至四篇。
Wu T'ing-fang hsien-sheng ai-ssu lu. 1922.
伍廷芳先生哀思錄。

Wu T'ing-hsieh   吳庭燮

WORKS

1909? Tung-san-sheng yen-ko piao. Tientsin: Hsü shih t'ui-keng-t'ang. 6 vols.
東三省沿革表。
1917. Hsuan-te pieh lu. 2 vols.
宣德別錄。
1928. (ed.) Ch'ing shih kao. with Chao Erh-sun, K'o Shao-min *et al.* Peking: Ch'ing shih kuan. 132 vols.
清史稿。趙爾巽，柯劭忞等。
1937. Li-tai fang-chen nien-piao (Sung, Liao, Chin, Yuan). 8 vols.
歷代方鎮年表（宋，遼，金，元）。
1938. (ed.) Hofei chih-cheng nien-p'u ch'u-kao.
合肥執政年譜初稿。
1948, November. "Ching-mu tzu ting nien-p'u." *Kuo shih kuan kuan k'an,* I-4: 48-56.
景牧自訂年譜。國史館館刊。
1948, November-1949, January. "T'ieh-lu ta-shih chi." *Kuo shih kuan kuan k'an,* I-4: 48-56; II-1. 32-41.
鐵路大事記。國史館館刊。
1962. Hofei chih-cheng nien-p'u (ed. by Wu Hsiang-hsiang). Taipei: Wen hsing shu-tien.
合肥執政年譜。吳相湘。
Ch'ing ts'ai-cheng k'ao-lueh.
清財政考略。

SOURCES

Chin Yü-fu. "Wu hsien-sheng chuan." *Kuo shih kuan kuan k'an,* I-2 (March, 1948): 112-13.
金毓黻。吳先生傳。國史館館刊。
Chu Shih-ch'e. Ch'ing shih shu wen. Peking, 1957.
朱師轍。清史述聞。
MMT
Wu T'ing-hsieh. "Ching-mu tzu ting nien-p'u." *Kuo shih kuan kuan k'an,* I-4 (November, 1948): 48-56.
吳廷燮。景牧自訂年譜。國史館館刊。

Wu Yao-tsung   吳耀宗

WORKS

1927. "William James's Doctrine of Religious Belief." Unpublished Master's essay, Columbia University.
1930. Wu Yao-tsung *et. al.* The Jesus I Know. Shanghai: Published privately by T. Z. Kao.
1933. Kan-ti tzu-chuan. (tr. of Mohandas Karamchand Gandhi's *Mahatma Gandhi: His Own Story*). Shanghai: Ch'ing-nien hsieh-hui shu-chü.
甘地自傳。
1934. K'o-hsueh te tsung-chiao kuan (tr. of John Dewey's *A Common Faith*). Shanghai: Ch'ing-nien hsieh-hui shu-chü.
科學的宗教觀。
1934. She-hui fu-yin. Shanghai: Ch'ing-nien hsieh-hui shu-chü.
社會福音。
1935. Chung-kuo ch'ing-nien ch'u-lu wen-t'i. Shanghai: Ch'ing-nien hsieh-hui shu-chü.
中國青年出路問題。

SOURCES

Barnett, Eugene E. "The Far East in the Summer of 1940." (mimeo.)
Chieh-fang jih-pao. Shanghai, October 2, 1949.
解放日報。
China Bulletin of the Far Eastern Joint Office, III-3 (February 9, 1953): 4; III-4 (February 23, 1953): 2. (New York: Division of Foreign Missions, National Council of Churches.)
China Christian Year Book, 1931.
Chinese Recorder, LV-8 (August, 1923).
Occasional Bulletin, VII-3 (March 15, 1956): 20. (New York: Missionary Research Library.)
Price, Frank W. China: Twilight or Dawn?
SCMP, 236 (December 14-15, 1951).
Seabury, Ruth I. "Leaders of World Christianity." *Envelope Series,* XLII-1 (March, 1939): 20-21. (Boston: American Board of Commission for Foreign Missions.)
Who's Who of the Madras Meeting of the International Missionary Council. Madras, India, 1938.
World Service News, XVI-8 (October, 1930).
Wu Yao-tsung *et al.* The Jesus I Know. Shanghai: Privately published by T. Z. Kao, 1930.
WWC, 1936.
Year Book of the YMCA in China, 1937. Shanghai, 1938.

Ying Tzu. Chung-kuo hsin hsueh-shu jen-wu chih. Hong Kong: Chih ming shu-chü, 1956.
穎子。中國新學術人物誌。

Wu Yi-fang   吳貽芳

WORKS

1940. (ed.) China Rediscovers Her West. with Frank W. Price. New York: Friendship Press.
ed. of *China Reconstructs*,
"A Contribution to the Biology of Simulium." Unpublished Ph. D. dissertation, University of Michigan, 1928.

SOURCES

Asia Calling, October, 1947.
CH, 1937-45.
Chin shan shih-pao. San Francisco, March 24, 1959.
金山時報。
China Rediscovers Her West, ed. by Wu Yi-fang and Frank W. Price. New York: Friendship Press, 1940.
CKJMT
Crouch, Archie R. Rising Through the Dust.
Endicott, Mary Austin. Five Stars over China. Toronto, 1953.
GCCJK
Ginling Association in America Newsletter, 10 (Winter, 1956): 8-14.
Ginling College Primer. 1942.
HMTT
I-chiu-wu-ling jen-min nien-chien, ed. by Shen Sung-fang. Hong Kong: Ta kung shu-chü, 1950.
一九五〇人民年鑑。沈頌芳。
MMT
The New York Times, April 24, 1959.
TCMT
Tien-ying yü po-yin, IV-4 (May, 1945).
電影與播音。
World Outlook, July, 1945.
WWC, 1936.
WWMC
Ying Tzu. Chung-kuo hsin hsueh-shu jen-wu chih. Hong Kong: Chih ming shu-chü, 1956.
穎子。中國新學術人物誌。
Zion's Herald, March 7, 1945.

Wu Yü   吳虞

WORKS

1913. Ch'iu shui chi. Chengtu: Wu shih ai-chih-lu.
秋水集。
1936-37. Wu Yü wen-lu (with Hsü lu). Chengtu: Wu shih ai-chih-lu. 3 vols.
吳虞文錄 (附：續錄)。

SOURCES

Persons interviewed: Not to be identified.

Wu Yü-chang   吳玉章

WORKS

1907-8. ed. of *Szechwan*.
四川。
1938. Wu Yü-chang k'ang Jih yen-lun chi. Chung-kuo ch'u-pan she.
吳玉章抗日言論集。
1949. Chung-kuo li-shih chiao-ch'eng hsü-lun. Peiping: Hsin hua shu-tien.
中國歷史教程緒論。
1949. Wu Yü-chang *et al*. Fan "pai-p'i-shu" hsueh-hsi ts'ai-liao (comp. by Chung kung Tientsin shih wei tsung hsueh wei hui). Tientsin: Chung kung Tientsin shih wei tsung hsueh wei hui.
吳玉章等。反「白皮書」學習材料。中共天津市委總學委會。
1951. Wu Yü-chang *et al*. Chung-kuo chiao-yü kung-hui kung-tso che shou-ts'e. (comp. by Chung-kuo chiao-yü kung-hui ch'üan-kuo wei-yuan-hui). Peking: Kung-jen ch'u-pan she.
吳玉章等。中國教育工會工作者手冊。中國教育工會全國委員會。
1956. Wu Yü-chang *et al*. Chien-tan Han tzu wen-t'i (comp. by Chung-kuo yü-wen tsa-chih she). Peking: Chung-hua shu-chü.
吳玉章等。簡單漢字問題。中國語文雜誌社。
1961. Hsin-hai ko-ming. Peking: Jen-min ch'u-pan she.
辛亥革命。
Eng. tr., *The Revolution of 1911; a Great Democratic Revolution of China*. Peking: Foreign Languages Press, 1962.
ed. of *Chiu-kuo shih pao*. Paris.
救國事報。

Chung-kuo La-ting hua hsin wen-tzu te yuan-tse ho kuei-tse.
中國拉丁化新文字的原則和規則。
Chung-kuo wen-tzu te yuan-liu chi ch'i kai-ko te fang-an.
中國文字的源流及其改革的方案。
Yen-chiu li-shih te i-i.
研究歷史的意義。

SOURCES

Person interviewed: Chang Kuo-t'ao.
GCCJK
HCJC
Ho Ch'i-fang. Wu Yü-chang t'ung-chih ko-ming ku-shih. Hong Kong: Hsin Chung-kuo shu-chü, 1949.
何其芳。吳玉章同志革命故事。
The New York Times, December 16, 1966.
Ta kung pao. Hong Kong, October 10, 1951.
大公報。
Wu Yü-chang. The Revolution of 1911: A Great Democratic Revolution of China. Peking: Foreign Languages Press, 1962.
WWC, 1950.
WWMC

Yang Ch'ang-chi   楊昌濟

WORKS

1916, December-1917, January. "Chih sheng p'ien." *Hsin ch'ing-nien*, II-4, 5.
治生篇。新青年。
1923. Hsi-yang lun-li chu-i shu-p'ing. Shanghai: Shang-wu yin shu kuan.
西洋論理主義述評。
"Chieh-hun lun." *Hsin ch'ing-nien*, V-3.
結婚論。新青年。
"Tsung-chiao lun." *Chia-yin tsa-chih*, I-6.
宗教論。甲寅雜誌。

SOURCES

Hsiao San. Mao Tse-tung t'ung-chih te ch'ing-shao-nien shih-tai. Shanghai: Hsin hua shu-tien, 1950.
蕭三。毛澤東同志的青少年時代。
Hsiao Yü. Mao Tse-tung and I Were Beggars. Syracuse, N. Y.: Syracuse University Press, 1959.
Li Jui. Mao Tse-tung t'ung-chih te ch'u-ch'i ko-ming huo-tung. Peking: Chung-kuo ch'ing-nien ch'u-pan she, 1957.

李銳。毛澤東同志的初期革命活動。
Payne, Pierre Stephen Robert. Portrait of a Revolutionary: Mao Tse-tung. London, New York: Ablelard-Schuman, 1961.
RSOC

Yang Chieh   楊杰

WORKS

1943. Kuo-fang hsin lun. Chung-hua shu-chü.
國防新論。
1945. Chün-shih yü kuo-fang. Shanghai: Shang-wu yin shu kuan.
軍事與國防。
1945. Sun-wu-tzu. Chungking: Sheng-li ch'u-pan she.
孫武子。
1946. Kuo-fang lun. Shanghai: Chung-hua shu-chü.
國防論。
Chan-cheng chueh-yao.
戰爭抉要。
Pao-liu ch'eng-yuan i-chien shu.
保留城垣意見書。
Sun-tzu ch'ien shih.
孫子淺釋。
Tsung ssu-ling hsueh.
總司令學。

SOURCES

BKL
CWR, July 12, 1930; June 10, 1933.
Ho Jui-yao. Feng-yün jen-wu hsiao chih. Canton: Yü-chou feng she, 1947.
何瑞瑤。風雲人物小誌。
Kuo-min ko-ming chün chan shih, ed. by Kuo-min ko-ming chün chan shih pien-tsuan wei-yuan-hui. Ts'an-mou pen-pu yin-shua so, 1934. 17 vols.
國民革命軍戰史。國民革命軍戰史編纂委員會。
Review of the Hong Kong Chinese Press, 82/51 (April 18, 1951).
SMJ
Tong, Hollington K. Chiang Kai-shek, Soldier and Statesman: Authorized Biography. Shanghai: China Publishing Co., 1937.
Wu, Aitchen. China and the Soviet Union, a Study of Sino-Soviet Relations. London: Methuen, 1950.
WWC, 1931.

Yang Ch'üan   楊詮

WORKS

1927. Yang Hsing-fo chiang-yen chi. Shanghai:
Shang-wu yin shu kuan.
楊杏佛講演集。

1929. Yang Hsing-fo wen-ts'un. Shanghai:
P'ing-fan shu-chü.
楊杏佛文存。

SOURCES

Chung-yang yen-chiu-yuan kai-k'uang (Min-kuo
shih-ch'i nien chih ssu-shih-liu nien), comp. by
Chung-yang yen-chiu-yuan. Taipei: Chung-
yang yen-chiu-yuan, 1957.
中央研究院概況 (民國十七年至四十六年)。
中央研究院。

CWR, LXV-4 (June 24, 1933).

Lin Yü-t'ang. A History of the Press and Public
Opinion in China. Chicago: University of
Chicago Press, 1936.

T'ang Yueh. "Yang Ch'üan chuan-lueh," in
Chiao-yü pu chiao-yü nien-chien pien-tsuan
wei-yuan-hui, Ti-i tz'u Chung-kuo chiao-yü nien-
chien. Shanghai: K'ai-ming shu-chü, 1934.
唐鉞。楊詮傳略。教育部教育年鑑編纂委
員會。第一次中國教育年鑑。

Yang Ch'üan. Yang Hsing-fo chiang-yen chi.
Shanghai: Shang-wu yin shu kuan, 1927.
楊詮。楊杏佛講演集。

———. Yang Hsing-fo wen-ts'un. Shanghai:
P'ing-fan shu-chü, 1929.
楊詮。楊杏佛文存。

Yang Hu-ch'eng   楊虎城

SOURCES

CMTC
CWR, 1937.
CYB-W, 1934.
GCJJ
Hsi-pei chin shih nien lai shih-liao, comp. by
Sung Ping-san.
西北近十年來史料。宋冰珊。
Kuo wen chou-pao, VIII-2 (January 5, 1931).
國聞週報。
SCMP, 1110 (August 16, 1955).
TCJC
WWC, 1931.
WWMC
Yu Chün. "Sian shih-pien i-lai ts'ung wei kung-

k'ai kuo te chen-shih." Ch'un-ch'iu, 52–58
(September 1–December 1, 1959).
右軍。西安事變以來從未公開過的珍史。
春秋。

Yang Sen   楊森

WORKS

1966, April. "Wu Tzu-yü hsien-sheng yu Ch'uan
hui-i-lu." Chuan-chi wen-hsueh, VIII-4: 7–10.
吳子玉先生游川回憶錄。傳記文學。

SOURCES

BKL
1966, December. "Yeh t'an Chou Hsi-ch'eng."
Chuan-chi wen-hsueh, IX-6: 35–38.
也談周西成。傳記文學。
Chao Tseng-ch'ou, Wu Hsiang-hsiang et al.
K'ang chan chi-shih. Shanghai: Shang-wu
yin shu kuan, 1961.
趙曾儔，吳相湘等。抗戰紀實。
Ch'en Hsun-cheng. Kuo-min ko-ming chün
chan shih ch'u-kao.
陳訓正。國民革命軍戰史初稿。
Chin-tai shih tzu-liao, 4 (1962).
近代史資料。
Chou K'ai-ch'ing. Min-kuo Szechwan jen-wu
chuan-chi. Taipei: Taiwan shang-wu yin shu
kuan, 1966.
周開慶。民國四川人物傳記。
CMJL
CMTC
CTMC
CWR, 1924, 1926–27.
Free China Weekly, October 11, 1964.
GCJJ
Hsiao Pai-fan. Chung-kuo chin pai nien ko-ming
shih. Hong Kong: Ch'iu shih chu-pan she,
1951.
蕭白帆。中國近百年革命史。
Hsueh Yueh. Chiao fei chi-shih. Taipei: Wen
hsing shu-tien, 1962.
薛岳。剿匪紀實。
Ko-ming wen-hsien, comp. by Chung-kuo kuo-
min-tang chung-yang wei-yuan-hui tang shih
shih-liao pien-tsuan wei-yuan-hui. Taipei:
Chung-yang wen-wu kung-ying she, 1953–65.
35 vols.
革命文獻。中國國民黨中央委員會黨史史
料編纂委員會。
Kuo-fu p'i tu mo-chi, comp. by Chung-kuo kuo-

min-tang chung-yang tang shih shih-liao
pien-tsuan wei-yuan-hui. Taipei: Chung-kuo
kuo-min-tang chung-yang tang shih shih-liao
pien-tsuan wei-yuan-hui, 1955.
國父批牘墨跡。中國國民黨中央黨史史料
編纂委員會。
MSICH
T'ang Leang-li. The Inner History of the Chinese Revolution. New York: E. P. Dutton &
Co., 1930.
TCMC-1
Ts'ai Sung-p'o hsien-sheng i chi, comp. by Liu
Ta-wu. Taipei: Wen hsing shu-tien, 1962.
蔡松坡先生遺集。劉達武。
Wu P'ei-fu hsien-sheng chi, comp. by Wu P'ei-
fu hsien-sheng chi pien-chi wei-yuan-hui.
Taipei: Wu P'ei-fu hsien-sheng chi pien-chi
wei-yuan-hui, 1960.
吳佩孚先生集。吳佩孚先生集編輯委員會。
WWC, 1931.
Yang Chao-jung. "Hsin-hai hou chih Szechwan
chan chi." *Chin-tai shih tzu-liao*, 6 (1958).
楊兆蓉。辛亥後之四川戰記。近代史資料。

Yang Shou-ching   楊守敬

WORKS

1870-77, 1909. (ed.) Wang t'ang chin shih wen-
tzu. 14 vols.
望堂金石文字。
1897. Jih-pen fang shu chih. Su-yuan. 8 vols.
日本訪書志。
1901. Liu chen p'u ch'u pien. I-tu: Yang shih.
12 vols.
留真譜初編。
1901-7. Hui-ming-hsuan kao. Lin-su-yuan. 2
vols.
晦明軒稿。
1902, 1917. Liu chen p'u.
留真譜。
1905. Shui-ching chu t'u.
水經注圖。
1908. (ed.) Huan-yü chen shih t'u. 6 vols.
寰宇貞石圖。
1915. Lin-su lao-jen nien-p'u.
鄰蘇老人年譜。
Tseng-ting ts'ung-shu chü-yao.
增訂叢書舉要。

SOURCES

Ch'en San-li. San yuan ching she wen-chi. Taipei: Taiwan Chung-hua shu-chü, 1961.

陳三立。散原精舍文集。
Ch'en Yuan. Chung-kuo fo-chiao shih-chi kai-
lun. Peking: K'o-hsueh ch'u-pan she, 1957.
陳垣。中國佛教史藉概論。
Liang Ch'i-ch'ao. Yin-ping-shih ho-chi; wen-
chi, vol. 16. Chung-hua shu-chü, 1914.
梁啟超。飲冰室合集；文集。
MMT
PCCP
Wang P'i-chiang. "Yang Shou-ching Hsiung
Hui-chen chuan." *Kuo shih kuan kuan k'an*,
ch'uang-k'an hao: 80-83.
王辟疆。楊守敬熊會貞傳。國史館館刊。
Yang Shou-ching. Lin-su lao-jen nien-p'u. 1915.
楊守敬。鄰蘇老人年譜。
Yeh Ch'ang-chih. Yuan-tu-lu jih-chi ch'ao.
Shanghai: Yin-yin-lu, 1933. 16 vols.
葉昌熾。緣督廬日記鈔。

Yang Tseng-hsin   楊增新

WORKS

1921. Pu-kuo-chai jih-chi. Peking: 20 vols.
補過齋日記。
1921. Pu-kuo-chai wen-tu. 32 vols.
補過齋文牘。

SOURCES

Bailey, Frederick Marshman. Mission to Tash-
kent. London: Jonathan Cape, 1946.
Bosshard, W. "Politics and Trade in Central
Asia." *Journal of the Central Asian Society*,
XVI (1929): 433-54.
Ch'eng T'ien-fang. A History of Sino-Russian
Relations. Washington: Public Affairs Press,
1957.
Conolly, Violet. Soviet Economic Policy in the
East. London: Oxford University, 1933.
Dettmann, Hans Eduard. Unter Chinesen,
Türken und Bolschewiken. Berlin: F. Sch-
neider, 1942.
Etherton, Percy Thomas. In the Heart of Asia.
London: Constable and Company, 1925.
"H. E. Yang Tseng Hsin." *Journal of the Central
Asian Society*, XVI (1929): 87-89, 407.
Ho, David. L'Oeuvre Colonisatrice de la Chine
dans le Turkestan Chinois. Paris: Reçueil
Sirey, 1941.
Hung Ti-ch'en. Sinkiang shih ti ta-kang.
Chungking: Cheng-chung shu-chü, 1939.
洪滌塵。新疆史地大綱。
Lattimore, Owen. "The Chinese as Dominant

Race." *The Journal of the Central Asian Society*. XVI (1928): 278-300.

Lattimor, Owen. High Tartary. Boston: Little, Brown & Co., 1930.

———. Inner Asian Frontiers of China. New York: American Geographical Society, 1940.

———. Pivot of Asia: Sinkiang and the Inner Asian Frontiers of China and Russia. Boston: Little, Brown & Co., 1950.

———. "Political Conditions in Mongolia and Chinese Turkistan." *Annals of the American Academy of Political Science*, 152 (1930): 318-27.

Li Huan. Sinkiang yen-chiu. Chungking: An-ch'ing yin shu chü, 1944.
李寰。新疆研究。

Norins, Martin Richard. Gateway to Asia: Sinkiang, Frontier of the Chinese Far West. New York: The John Day Co., 1944.

Pasvolsky, Leo. Russia in the Far East. New York: The Macmillan Co., 1922.

"The Peoples of Sinkiang." *Journal of the Central Asian Society*, XVII (1930): 232-36.

Pollard, Robert Thomas. China's Foreign Relations, 1917-1931. New York: The Macmillan Co., 1933.

Roerich, George Nicholas. Sur les Pistes de l'Asie Centrale. Paris: Geuthner, 1933.

Shina-sho betsu zenshi: Shinkyo-sho, comp. by Toa dobun kai. Tokyo, 1937.
支那省別全誌：新疆省。東亞同文會。

Sinkiang ching-ying lun, comp. by Chiang Chün-chang. Chungking: Cheng-chung shu-chü, 1939.
新疆經營論。蔣君章。

Skrine, Clarmont Percival. Chinese Central Asia. Boston: Houghton Mifflin, 1926.

Sykes, Ella and Percy. Through Deserts and Oases of Central Asia. London: Macmillan & Co., 1920.

Teichman, Eric. Journey to Turkestan. London: Hodder & Stoughton, 1937.

Three Decades of Nationalist Control in Sinkiang: Report No. 4826 (November, 1947), Division of Research for the Far East, U. S. Department of State.

Tseng Wen-wu. Chung-kuo ching-ying hsi-yü shih. Shang-wu yin shu kuan, 1936.
曾問吾。中國經營西域史。

Wei, Henry. China and Soviet Russia. Princeton: D. Van Nostrand Co., 1956.

Whiting, Allen S. Soviet Policies in China, 1917-24. New York: Columbia University Press, 1954.

Wu, Aitchen. China and the Soviet Union: A Study of Sino-Soviet Relations. London: Methuen, 1950.

———. Turkistan Tumult. London: Methuen, 1940.

Wu Shao-lin. Sinkiang kai-kuan. Nanking: Jen sheng shu-chü, 1933.
吳紹璘。新疆概觀。

Yang Tu   楊度

WORKS

1915. Chün hsien chiu-kuo lun.
君憲救國論。

ed. of *Chung-kuo hsin pao*.
中國新報。

Lun fo tsa-wen.
論佛雜文。

(ed.) *Yu hsueh i pien*.
遊學譯編。

SOURCES

Chang I-lin. Hsin t'ai-p'ing shih chi (comp. by Ku T'ing-lung). Shanghai, 1947. 4 vols.
張一麐。心太平室集。顧廷龍。

Chang Ping-lin. Chang shih ts'ung-shu. Che-kiang t'u-shu-kuan, 1919. 24 vols.
章炳麟。章氏叢書。

CHMI

Huang I. Yuan shih tao kuo chi (comp. by Wu Hsiang-hsiang). Taipei: Wen hsing shu-tien, 1962.
黃毅。袁氏盜國記。吳相湘。

Liang Jen-kung hsien-sheng nien-p'u ch'ang pien ch'u-kao, comp. by Ting Wen-chiang. Taipei: Shih-chieh shu-chü, 1959. 2 vols.
梁任公先生年譜長編初稿。丁文江。

Liu Ch'eng-yü. "Hsien tsung-li chiu te lu." *Kuo shih kuan kuan k'an*, ch'uang k'an hao (December, 1947).
劉成禺。先總理舊德錄。國史館館刊。

Reeves, William, Jr. "Sino-American Cooperation in Medicine: The Origin of Hsiang-ya." *Papers on China*, 14. (Duplicated for private distribution by the East Asia Program of the Committee on International and Regional Studies, Harvard University.)

Sun Wen. Kuo-fu ch'üan-shu (ed. by Chang Ch'i-yün). Taipei: Kuo-fang yen-chiu-yuan, 1960.
孫文。國父全書。張其昀。

Sung Chiao-jen. Wo chih li-shih (ed. by Wu Hsiang-hsiang). Taipei: Wen hsing shu-tien, 1962.
宋教仁。我之歷史。吳相湘。
Ta chiang tsa-chih, 1907.
大江雜誌。
T'ao Chü-yin. Liu chün-tzu chuan. Shanghai: Chung-hua shu-chü, 1946.
陶菊隱。六君子傳。
Tsui-chin kuo-t'i feng-yün lu.
最近國體風雲錄。
Wang K'ai-yün. Hsiang-ch'i-lou jih-chi. Shanghai: Shang-wu yin shu kuan, 1927. 6 vols.
王闓運。湘綺樓日記。
Wang Tai-kung. Hsiang Ch'i-lou fu-chün nien-p'u.
王代功。湘綺樓府君年譜。
Yang Tu. Chün hsien chiu-kuo lun. 1915.
楊度。君憲救國論。

Yang Yung-ch'ing   楊永清

Works

1935. China's Modern Aspiration and Achievements. Honolulu: University of Hawaii.
1943. China's Religious Heritage. New York, Nashville: Abingdon-Cokesbury Press.
ed. of *The Chinese Students' Monthly*.

Sources

CBJS
GCMMTJK
The New York Times, March 28, 1956.
"Social Commission—Vice-Chairman." *United Nations Weekly Bulletin*, 3 (September, 1947): 340.

Yang Yung-t'ai   楊永泰

Works

1915. Wai-chiao cheng-ts'e. (tr.) Shanghai: T'ai tung t'u-shu chü.
外交政策。
1963. Yang Yung-t'ai hsien-sheng yen-lun chi. Jesselton, Sabah, Malaysia: Shen shan kung-ssu.
楊永泰先生言論集。
Chin-tai min-chu cheng-chih.
近代民主政治。
ed. of *Chung-hua hsin pao*.
中華新報。

Sources

Chu Shou-min. "Political Forces in China." *Asia*, XXXVI-12 (December, 1936): 762-63.
Chung-kuo.wen-t'i te ko p'ai ssu-ch'ao, comp. by Chung-kuo chi-tu-chiao hsueh-sheng yün-tung she-hui kai-tsao wen-t'i yen-chiu wei-yuan-hui. Shanghai: Chung-kuo chi-tu-chiao hsueh-sheng yün-tung lin-shih ch'üan-kuo tsung-hui, 1934.
中國問題的各派思潮。中國基督教學生運動社會改造問題研究委員會。
CWR, LXXVIII-8 (October 24, 1936).
Hsin-hai ko-ming, ed. by Ch'ai Te-keng *et al.* Shanghai: Jen-min ch'u-pan she, 1957. 8 vols.
辛亥革命。柴德賡等。
Kuo-fu nien-p'u ch'u-kao, ed. by Chung-kuo kuo-min-tang tang shih shih-liao pien-tsuan wei-yuan-hui, Kuo shih kuan shih-liao pien-tsuan wei-yuan-hui. Taipei: Chung-yang wen-wu kung-ying she, 1958. 2 vols.
國父年譜初稿。中國國民黨黨史史料編纂委員會，國史館史料編纂委員會。
Liu Sheng-min. "'Cheng-hsueh-hsi' t'an yuan." *Hai-wai lun-t'an*, II-7, 8, 9, 10, 11, 12 (July-December, 1961).
劉生旻。「政學系」探原。海外論壇。
The New York Times, October 25, 26, 1936.
Pai Ch'en. "Hsien-hua cheng-hsueh hsi." *Ch'un-ch'iu*, 74 (1957).
白辰。閒話政學系。春秋。
Tong, Hollington K. Chiang Kai-shek, Soldier and Statesman: Authorized Biography. Shanghai: China Publishing Co., 1937.
Yang Yu-chiung. Chin-tai Chung-kuo li-fa shih. Shanghai: Shang-wu yin shu kuan, 1936.
楊幼烱。近代中國立法史。
Yang Yung-t'ai. Yang Yung-t'ai hsien-sheng yen-lun chi. Jesselton, Sabah, Malaysia: Shen shan kung-ssu, 1963.
楊永泰。楊永泰先生言論集。

Yang Yü-t'ing   楊宇霆

Sources

CMTC
CWR, 1929.
CYB-W, 1928.
Hsiao Yuan. "Chi Yang Yü-t'ing." *Kuo wen chou-pao*, XIV-22.
篠園。記楊宇霆。國聞週報。
MMT

Ransome, Arthur. "Yang Yü-t'ing—Brains of
the North." CWR (February 23, 1929): 526.

Yao Yung-p'u   姚永樸

WORKS

1901. Shang-shu i lueh.
尚書誼略。
1906. (ed.) T'ung-ch'eng Yao shih pei chuan lu.
2 vols.
桐城姚氏碑傳錄。
1911. Su yuan ts'ung kao. 2 vols.
素園叢稿。
1921. T'ui ssu hsuan chi.
蛻私軒集。
1926. Wen-hsueh yen-chiu fa. Shanghai: Shang-
wu yin shu kuan. 4 vols.
文學研究法。
1932. T'ui ssu hsuan hsü chi.
蛻私軒續集。
1939. Shih-hsueh yen-chiu fa. Changsha: Shang-
wu yin shu kuan.
史學研究法。
Ch'ün ju k'ao lueh.
群儒考略。
Hsiao hsueh kuang.
小學廣。

SOURCES

Ch'ien Chi-po. Hsien-tai Chung-kuo wen-hsueh
shih. Shanghai: Shih-chieh shu-chü, 1933.
錢基博。現代中國文學史。
Chu Shih-ch'e. Ch'ing shih shu wen. Peking:
Sheng-huo, tu-shu, hsin chih san lien shu-tien,
1957.
朱師轍。清史述聞。
Kuo shih kuan kuan k'an, I-3 (August, 1948): 128–30.
國史館館刊。
Liu Sheng-mu. "T'ung-ch'eng wen-hsueh yuan-
yuan k'ao," in *Chih-chieh-t'ang ts'ung k'o*.
劉聲木。桐城文學淵源考。直介堂叢刻。
Ma Ch'i-ch'ang. Pao-jun-hsuan wen-chi. Pe-
king, 1923. 4 vols.
馬其昶。抱潤軒文集。
MMT
Wang I-t'ang. "Chin ch'uan shih lou shih hua."
Kuo wen chou-pao, IV-40 (October 16, 1927);
V-38 (September 30, 1928).
王揖唐。今傳是樓詩話。國聞週報。
Wang Shu-nan. "T'ao-lu wen-chi," in Wang
Shu-nan, *T'ao-lu ts'ung k'o*. Hsin-ch'eng:
Wang shih, 1883-1917. 46 vols.

王樹枏。陶廬文集。王樹枏。陶廬叢刻。

Yeh Ch'ang-chih   葉昌熾

WORKS

1909. Yü shih. Soochow: Wen-hsueh shan-fang.
4 vols.
語石。
1921. Ch'i-ku-ch'ing wen-chi. 4 vols.
奇觚廎文集。
1921. Han-shan-ssu chih. Wu-hsien: P'an shih.
2 vols.
寒山寺志。
1933. Yuan-tu-lu jih-chi ch'ao (ed. by Wang
Chi-lieh). Shanghai: Yin-yin-lu. 16 vols.
緣督廬日記鈔。王季烈。
1958. Ts'ang-shu chi-shih shih. Shanghai: Ku-
tien wen-hsueh ch'u-pan she.
藏書紀事詩。
Pin-chou shih-shih lu.
邠州石室錄。

SOURCES

Chao Erh-sun, K'o Shao-min *et al*. Ch'ing shih
kao. Peking: Ch'ing shih kuan, 1928. 132
vols.
趙爾巽。柯劭忞等。清史稿。
Ch'ing ju hsueh an, ed. by Hsü Shih-ch'ang.
1939. 100 vols.
清儒學案。徐世昌。
Ts'ang-shu chi-shih shih yin-te, ed. by Ts'ai
Chin-chung. Peking: Ha-fo Yen-ching hsueh-
she, 1937.
藏書紀事詩引得。蔡金重。
Ts'ao Yuan-pi. "Yeh shih chiang mu-chih-
ming." PCCP.
曹元弼。葉侍講墓誌銘。
Yeh Ch'ang-chih. Yuan-tu-lu jih-chi ch'ao (ed.
by Wang Chi-lieh). Shanghai: Yin-yin-lu,
1933. 16 vols.
葉昌熾。緣督廬日記鈔。王季烈。

Yeh Chien-ying   葉劍英

WORKS

1949. Yeh Chien-ying *et al*. Shou-tu ti i erh
chieh ko-chieh jen-min tai-piao hui-i (ed. by
Hsin hua shih-shih ts'ung-k'an she). Peking:
Hsin hua shu-tien.
葉劍英等。首都第一二屆各界人民代表會
議。新華時事叢刊社。

1951. Kuan-yü mu-ch'ien hsing-shih. Canton: Hua-nan jen-min ch'u-pan she.
關於目前形勢。

1951. Yeh Chien-ying et al. T'ui tsu t'ui ya ch'ing fei fan pa yün-tung ch'u-pu tsung-chieh yü chin-hou jen-wu (ed. by Kwangtung sheng t'u-ti kai-ko wei-yuan-hui). Canton: Hua-nan jen-min ch'u-pan she.
葉劍英等。退租退押清匪反霸運動初步總結與今後任務。廣東省土地改革委員會。

SOURCES

Person interviewed: Chang Kuo-t'ao.
Chou-mo pao, September 17, 1949.
週末報。
HCJC
Jen-min chiang-ling ch'ün-hsiang, ed. by Hai Yün. Macao: Ch'un-ch'iu shu-tien, 1947.
人民將領群像。海雲。
RNRC
SCMP, 1139.
Ta kung pao. Hong Kong, September 20, 1950; May 6, 1951.
大公報。
Wales, Nym (pseud. of Helen Foster Snow). Inside Red China. New York: Doubleday, Doran & Co., 1939.
WWC, 1950.
WWMC

Yeh Ch'ien-yü   葉淺予

WORKS

1944. China Today. Calcutta: The Book Emporium.
1950. "Tzu wo p'i-p'an (Yuan t'i: Ts'ung kuo-hua tao man-hua)," in *Wo te ssu-hsiang shih tsen-yang chuan-pien kuo-lai te.* Peking: Wu-shih nien tai ch'u-pan she.
自我批判 (原題: 從國畫到漫畫)。我的思想是怎樣轉變過來的。
1953. Wu-t'ai jen-wu. Peking: Jen-min mei-shu ch'u-pan she.
舞台人物。
1955. Tsen-yang hua su-hsieh. Peking: Jen-min mei-shu ch'u-pan she.
怎樣畫速寫。
1958. Yeh Ch'ien-yü te hua. Shanghai: Jen-min mei-shu ch'u-pan she.
葉淺予的畫。
1963. Ch'ien-yü su-hsieh, 1958–1959. Shanghai: Jen-min mei-shu ch'u-pan she.

淺予速寫, 1958–1959。
1963. Tsai Nei-meng yü Kwangsi. Peking: Jen-min mei-shu ch'u-pan she.
在內蒙與廣西。
1963. Wu-t'ai jen-mu; Ch'ien-yü su-hsieh chi. Peking: Jen-min mei-shu ch'u-pan she.
舞台人物; 淺予速寫集。
1963. Yeh Ch'ien-yü tso-p'in hsuan-chi (ed. by Chung-kuo mei-shu chia hsieh-hui, jen-min mei-shu ch'u-pan she). Peking: Jen-min mei-shu ch'u-pan she.
葉淺予作品選集。中國美術家協會, 人民美術出版社。

SOURCES

GCJJ
Yeh Ch'ien-yü. "Tzu wo p'i-p'an (Yuan t'i: Ts'ung kuo-hua tao man-hua)," in *Wo te ssu-hsiang shih tsen-yang chuan-pien kuo-lai te.* Peking: Wu-shih nien-tai ch'u-pan she, 1950.
葉淺予。自我批判 (原題: 從國畫到漫畫)。我的思想是怎樣轉變過來的。

Yeh Ch'u-ts'ang   葉楚傖

WORKS

1929. Ch'ien-pei hsien-sheng. Shanghai: Kuang-hua shu-chü.
前輩先生。
1929. Ju-tz'u ching-hua. Shanghai: Chung-hua shu-chü.
如此京華。
1935. Hsin sheng-huo yü ch'ing-ts'ao. Nanking: Cheng-chung shu-chü.
新生活與情操。
1936. (ed.) Nan ming hsien-lieh ku-shih chi. with Ch'en Li-fu. Nanking: Cheng-chung shu-chü.
南命先烈故事集。陳立夫。
1939. Tang wu shih-shih shang chih wen-t'i; chung-yang hsun-lien t'uan tang cheng hsun-lien pan chiang-yen lu. Chungking, 1939.
黨務實施上之問題; 中央訓練團黨政訓練班講演錄。
1942. (ed.) Yueh-fu shih-hsuan. Chunking: Cheng-chung shu-chü.
樂府詩選。
1943. The Confucian Concept of Jen. London: The China Society.
1943. (ed.) Yuan Ming Ch'ing ch'ü-hsuan. with Ch'ien Nan-yang. Chungking: Cheng-chung shu-chü.

元明清曲選。錢南揚。

1944. Ch'u-ts'ang wen-ts'un. Shanghai: Cheng-chung shu-chü.
楚傖文存。

1945–46. "Builders of a New China." *Geographical Magazine*, XVIII: 179–89.

1946. "The Industrialization of China." *Journal of the Royal Central Asian Society*, XXXIII: 9–24.

1948. Introducing China. with C. P. Fitzgerald. London: I. Pitman.

1965. "Yeh Ch'u-ts'ang hsuan-chi," in Chung-kuo kuo-min-tang chung-yang tang shih shih-liao pien-tsuan wie-yuan-hui, *Ko-ming hsien-lieh hsien-chin shih wen hsuan-chi*. Taipei: Chung-hua Min-kuo ko-chieh chi-nien kuo-fu tan-ch'en ch'ou-pei wei-yuan-hui. 6 vols.
葉楚傖選集。中國國民黨中央黨史史料編纂委員會。革命先烈先進詩文選集。

1966. "Ch'u-ts'ang wen ch'i shou," in Hu P'u-an, *Nan-she ts'ung hsuan*. Taipei: Wen hai ch'u-pan she.
楚傖文七首。胡樸安。南社叢選。

ed. of *Chung-hua hsin pao*.
中華新報。

ed. of *Min-kuo jih-pao*.
民國日報。

ed. of *Min li pao*.
民立報。

ed. of *T'ai-p'ing-yang pao*.
太平洋報。

SOURCES

BKL
CMJS
CMJL
Chin shan shih-pao. San Francisco, December 25, 1956.
金山時報。
China Yearbook, 1966–67. Taipei: China Publishing Co., 1967.
Chung-kuo hsin-wen shih, ed. by Tseng Hsü-pai. Taipei: Kuo-li cheng-chih ta-hsueh, 1966.
中國新聞史。曾虛白。
GCMMTJK
HCMW
Hua Mei jih-pao. New York, November 20, 25, 1961.
華美日報。
Tzu-yu t'an, XI-11 (September, 1960): 16–19.
自由談。
WWC, 1933.
"Yeh Ch'u-ts'ang chuan," in Chung-kuo kuo-min-tang chung-yang tang shih shih-liao pien-tsuan wei-yuan-hui, *Ko-ming hsien-lieh hsien-chin chuan*. Taipei: Chung-hua Min-kuo ko-chieh chi-nien kuo-fu pai nien tan-ch'en ch'ou-pei wei-yuan-hui, 1965.
葉楚傖傳。中國國民黨中央黨史史料編纂委員會。革命先烈先進傳。
Yuan Ch'ang-ch'ao. Chung-kuo pao yeh hsiao shih. Hong Kong: Hsin-wen t'ien-ti she, 1957.
袁昶超。中國報業小史。
Yuan Ch'ing-p'ing. Tang-tai tang kuo ming-jen chuan. Canton: Ku-chin t'u-shu she, 1936.
袁清平。當代黨國名人傳。
Yü Yu-jen. "Yeh Ch'u-ts'ang hsien-sheng mu-pei," in Chung-kuo kuo-min-tang chung-yang tang shih shih-liao pien-tsuan wei-yuan-hui, *Ko-ming hsien-lieh hsien-chin chuan*. Taipei: Chung-hua Min-kuo ko chieh chi-nien kuo-fu pai nien tan-ch'en ch'ou-pei wei-yuan-hui, 1965.
于右任。葉楚傖先生墓碑。中國國民黨中央黨史史料編纂委員會。革命先烈先進傳。

Yeh Kung-ch'ao　　葉公超

SOURCES

Persons interviewed: not to be identified.

Yeh Kung-cho　　葉恭綽

WORKS

1921. An Industrial Tour Around Manchuria. Peking: Office of the High Industrial Commissioner.

1924. Chiao-t'ung chiu-kuo lun. Shanghai: Shang-wu yin shu kuan.
交通救國論。

1930. Hsia an hui kao, ti-i chi san pien. 4 vols.
遐庵彙稿, 第一輯三編。

1960? Hsia-an shih i pien (with Hsia weng tz'u chui pu). Hong Kong.
遐菴詩乙編（附：遐翁詞贅補）。

1962? Hsia-an t'an i lu.
遐庵談藝錄。

1964. Hsia-an ch'ing pi lu. Hong Kong: Shang-wu yin shu kuan. 2 vols.
遐庵清秘錄。

SOURCES

BPC
Chang Kia-ngau (Chang Chia-ao).　China's

Struggle for Railroad Revelopment. New York: The John Day Co., 1943.

Chu Tzu-chia. Wang cheng-ch'üan te k'ai-ch'ang yü shou-ch'ang. Hong Kong: Ch'un-ch'iu tsa-chih she, 1964. 5 vols.
朱子家。汪政權的開場收場。

CMTC
Kuo shih kuan kuan k'an, II-1 (January, 1949).
國史館刊。

San-shui Liang Yen-sun hsien-sheng nien-p'u, comp. by Feng kang chi men ti-tzu. 2 vols.
三水梁燕孫先生年譜。鳳岡及門弟子。

Yeh Sheng-t'ao   葉聖陶

WORKS

1926. Ch'eng chung. K'ai-ming shu-tien.
城中。

1926. Tso-wen lun. Shanghai: Shang-wu yin shu kuan.
作文論。

1930. Hsien hsia. Shang-wu yin shu kuan.
線下。

1934. (ed.) Shih-san-ching so-yin. K'ai-ming shu-tien.
十三經索引。

1936. Sheng-t'ao tuan-p'ien hsiao-shou chi. Shanghai: Shang-wu yin shu kuan.
聖陶短篇小說集。

1936. Ssu san chi. Shanghai: Liang-yu t'u-shu kung-ssu.
四三集。

1938. Ku-tai ying-hsiung te shih-hsiang. Shanghai: K'ai-ming shu-tien.
古代英雄的石像。

1938. Tao-ts'ao jen. Shanghai: K'ai-ming shu-tien.
稻草人。
Eng. tr., *The Scarecrow.* Peking: Foreign Languages Press, 1961.

1938. Yeh Shao-chün et. al. Kei chan-shih shao-nien. Hankow: Shao-nien hsien-feng she.
葉紹鈞等。給戰時少年。

1941. Yeh Shao-chün et al. I fu tzu (comp. by Hu Hsi-chih). Shanghai: Ti-ch'iu ch'u-pan she.
葉紹鈞等。遺腹子。胡錫之。

1943. Lueh tu chih-tao chü-yü. with Chu Tzu-ch'ing. Chungking: Shang-wu yin shu kuan.
略讀指導舉隅。朱自清。

1945. Hsi-ch'uan chi. Chungking: Wen kuang shu-tien.
西川集。

1947. (ed.) K'ai-ming shu-tien erh-shih chou-nien chi-nien wen-chi. Shanghai: K'ai-ming shu-tien.
開明書店二十週年紀念文集。

1947. Li t'ai-t'ai te t'ou-fa. Shaghai: Po wen shu-tien.
李太太的頭髮。

1947. Wei yen chü hsi tso. Shanghai: K'ai-ming shu-tien.
未厭居習作。

1949. Wen-chang li hua. Shanghai: K'ai-ming shu-tien.
文章例話。

1949. Yeh Shao-chün *et al*. Fang-yen wen-hsueh, ti-i chi (ed. by Chung-hua ch'üan-kuo wen-i hsieh-hui Hong Kong fen-hui fang-yen wen-hsueh yen-chiu hui). Hong Kong: Hsin min-chu ch'u-pan she.
葉紹鈞等。方言文學，第一輯。中華全國文藝協會香港分會方言文學研究會。

1951. Yeh Shao-chün *et al*. Hsieh-tso tsa-t'an. Hong Kong: Hsueh wen shu-tien.
葉紹鈞等。寫作雜談。

1951. Yeh Sheng-t'ao hsuan-chi. Peking: K'ai-ming shu-tien.
葉聖陶選集。

1953. Ni Huan-chih. Peking: Jen-min wen-hsueh ch'u-pan she.
倪煥之。
Eng. tr. by A. C. Barnes, *Schoolmaster Ni Huan-chih*. Peking: Foreign Languages Press, 1958.

1954. Yeh Shao-chün *et al*. Tsen-yang hsueh-hsi kuo-yü (ed. by Yeh K'e). Mukden: Tung-pei jen-min ch'u-pan she.
葉紹鈞等。怎樣學習國語。葉克。

1954. Yeh Sheng-t'ao tuan-p'ien hsiao-shuo hsuan-chi. Peking: Jen-min wen-hsueh ch'u-pan she.
葉聖陶短篇小說選集。

1955. I-ko lien-hsi sheng. Peking: T'ung-su tu-wu ch'u-pan she.
一個練習生。

1958. Hsiao chi shih-p'ien. Peking: Pai hua wen-i ch'u-pan she.
小記十篇。

1958. Yeh Sheng-t'ao wen-chi. Peking: Jen-min wen-hsueh ch'u-pan she. 3 vols.
葉聖陶文集。

1959. Wei po. Hong Kong: Jih hsin shu-tien.
微波。

1961. P'an hsien-sheng tsai nan chung. Hong Kong: Shanghai shu-chü.

潘先生在難中。
ed. of *Chung-hsueh-sheng.*
中學生。
ed. of *Fu-nü tsa-chih.*
婦女雜誌。
Yeh Shao-chün *et al.* I-erh.
葉紹鈞等。義兒。

SOURCES

CHWC
Ho Yü-po. "Yeh Shao-chün fang-wen chi."
Tu-shu yueh-k'an, January 10, 1931.
賀玉波。葉紹鈞訪問記。讀書月刊。
Lu Chien. "A Visit to Yeh Sheng-t'ao." *Chinese Literature*, May, 1963.
"Lueh hsü wen-hsueh yen-chiu hui." *Wen-hsueh p'ing-lun*, January-December, 1959.
略敍文學研究會。文學評論。
Yeh Shao-chün (Yeh Sheng-t'ao). Schoolmaster Ni Huan-chih (tr. by A. C. Barnes). Peking: Foreign Languages Press, 1958.
————. The Scarecrow. Peking: Foreign Languages Press, 1961.
————. Yeh Sheng-t'ao hsuan-chi. Peking: K'ai-ming shu-tien.
葉聖陶。葉聖陶選集。
Ying Tzu. Chung-kuo hsin hsueh-shu jen-wu chih. Hong Kong: Chih ming shu-chü, 1956.
穎子。中國新學術人物誌。

Yeh Te-hui   葉德輝

WORKS

1898. "Ch'ang hsing hsueh chi po i," in Su Yü, *I chiao ts'ung pien*. Wuchang. 3 vols.
長興學記駁義。蘇輿。翼教叢編。
1898. "Cheng chieh lun," in Su Yü, *I chiao ts'ung pien*. Wuchang. 3 vols.
正界論。蘇輿。翼教叢編。
1898. "Fei yu hsueh t'ung i," in Su Yü, *I chiao ts'ung pien*. Wuchang. 3 vols.
非幼學通義。蘇輿。翼教叢編。
1898. "Tu hsi hsueh shu fa shu hou," in Su Yü, *I chiao ts'ung pien*. Wuchang. 3 vols.
讀西學書法書後。蘇輿。翼教叢編。
1898. "Yu hsuan chin yü p'ing," in Su Yü, *I chiao ts'ung pien*. Wuchang. 3 vols.
輶軒今語評。蘇輿。翼教叢編。
1903. Sung Pi-shu sheng hsü pien tao ssu k'u ch'ueh shu-mu. Changsha: Kuan-ku-t'ang.
宋秘書省續編到四庫闕書目。

1907. (ed.) Shuang mei ching an ts'ung-shu. 5 vols.
雙梅景闇叢書。
1908. Yuan-ch'ao pi-shih.
元朝秘史。
1911. Hsi yuan shan-chü wen-lu.
郋園山居文錄。
1911. (ed.) T'ang k'ai-yuan hsiao-shuo liu chung. Changsha: Yeh shih kuan-ku-t'ang. 2 vols.
唐開元小說六種。
1915. Kuan-ku-t'ang ts'ang shu mu.
觀古堂藏書目。
1919. (ed.) Kuan-ku-t'ang hui k'o shu. Changsha: Yeh shih.
觀古堂彙刻書。
1919. (ed.) Li lü ts'ung-shu. Changsha: Yeh shih. 8 vols.
麗廔叢書。
1921. Hsi-yuan pei yu wen-ts'un.
郋園北遊文存。
1928. Hsi-yuan tu-shu chih. Changsha: Yeh shih.
郋園讀書志。
1928. Shu lin yü hua. Shanghai: Tan yuan. 2 vols.
書林餘話。
1931. Hsi-yuan hsiao-hsueh ssu chung. Nanyang: Yeh shih kuan-ku-t'ang.
郋園小學四種。
1935. Hsi-yuan hsien-sheng ch'üan-shu (ed. by Yeh Ch'i-cho). Changsha: Chung-kuo ku-shu k'an yin she.
郋園先生全書。葉啟倬。
1936, December. "Ku T'ing-lin hsien-sheng nien-p'u hsü." *Chih yen*, 301: 1-2.
顧亭林先生年譜序。制言。
1957. Shu lin ch'ing hua (with Shu lin yü hua). Peking: Ku-chin ch'u-pan she.
書林清話（附：書林餘話）。
Ku ch'üan tsa yung.
古泉雜咏。
Kuan-ku-t'ang shih-chi.
觀古堂詩集。

SOURCES

Ch'en Tzu-chan. "Yeh Te-hui yü K'ang Yu-wei." *Jen chien shih*, 7 (July, 1934): 26-27.
陳子展。葉德輝與康有為。人間世。
CHMI
Hsü Ch'ung-hsi. "Hsi-yuan hsien-sheng mu-chih-ming," in PCCP.
許崇熙。郋園先生墓誌銘。

Ku chin Chung wai jen-ming ta tz'u-tien. Tai-pei: Chung hsing shu-chü, 1967.
古今中外人名大辭典。
Yang Yin-shen. Chung-kuo hsueh-shu chia lieh-chuan. Shanghai: Kuang-ming shu-chü, 1939.
楊蔭深。中國學術家列傳。

Yeh T'ing   葉挺

SOURCES

Person interviewed: Chang Kuo-t'ao.
CKLC
GCCJK
HSWT
Kuo Mo-jo. Pei fa. Pei yen, 1937.
郭沫若。北伐。
Nan-fang jih-pao. Canton, July 1, 1951.
南方日報。
"Ssu-pa" pei-nan lieh-shih chi-nien-ts'e, ed. by Chung-kuo kung-ch'an-tang tai-piao t'uan. Chung-kuo kung-ch'an-tang tai-piao t'uan, 1946.
"四八"被難烈士紀念冊。中國共產黨代表團。
Yen Fu. Chung-kuo kung-ch'an-tang te pi-mi. Taipei: Tung-nan ch'u-pan she, 1950.
燕夫。中國共產黨的秘密。

Yen Chia-kan   嚴家淦

WORKS

1955. Taiwan sheng cheng kai-yao. Taipei: Taiwan sheng hsin-wen ch'u.
台灣省政概要。
1956. Taiwan sheng cheng chin-k'uang. Taipei: Taiwan sheng hsin-wen ch'u.
台灣省政近況。
1959. Ching-chi chen-she yü ts'ai-cheng. Taipei: Yang-ming shan chuang.
經濟建設與財政。
1964. Yen Yuan-chang shih-cheng pao-kao; Chung-hua Min-kuo wu-shih-san nien erh-yueh erh-shih-i jih tsai li-fa yuan pao-kao. Taipei: Hsing-cheng yuan hsin-wen chü.
嚴院長施政報告；中華民國五十三年二月二十一日在立法院報告。

SOURCES

Persons interviewed: not to be identified.
China Yearbook, 1964-1965. Taipei: China Publishing Co., 1966.

CMJL
GCJJ

Yen Fu   嚴復

WORKS

1900. Mu-le ming-hsueh. (tr. of John Stuart Mill's *A System of Logic, Ratiocinative and Inductive*). Shanghai: Shang-wu yin shu kuan. 3 vols.
穆勒名學。
1901. Hou kuan Yen shih ts'ung k'o. Nanchang: Tu yu-yung shu chih chai. 4 vols.
候官嚴氏叢刻。
1902. Yuan fu. (tr. of Adam Smith's *Wealth of Nations*). Shanghai: Nan-yang kung hsueh i shu yuan. 7 vols.
原富。
1905. Ch'ün chi ch'üan chieh lun. (tr. of John Stuart Mill's *On Liberty*). Shanghai: Shang-wu yin shu kuan.
羣己權界論。
1922. Yen Chi-tao shih wen ch'ao (ed. by Chiang Chen-chin). Shanghai: Kuo hua shu-chü. 6 vols.
嚴幾道詩文鈔。蔣貞金。
1922, June-1923, August. "Yen Chi-tao yü Hsiung Ch'un-ju shu cha chieh ch'ao." *Hsueh heng*, 6-12.
嚴幾道與熊純如書札節鈔。學衡。
1923. T'ien yen lun. (tr. of Thomas Henry Huxley's *Evolution and Ethics*). Shanghai: Shang-wu yin shu kuan.
天演論。
1930. Cheng-chih chiang-i. Shanghai: Chin ma shu-wu.
政治講義。
1931. Yen i ming-chu ts'ung-k'an. Shanghai: Shang-wu yin shu kuan.
嚴譯名著叢刊。
1953? Chuang-tzu p'ing tien. Hong Kong: Hua ch'iang yin wu kung-ssu.
莊子評點。
1959. Yen Chi-tao hsien-sheng i-chu (ed. by Nan-yang hsueh-hui yen-chiu tsu). Singapore: Nan-yang hsueh-hui.
嚴幾道先生遺著。南洋學會研究組。
1965. Meng-te-ssu-chiu fa i. (tr. of Montesquieu's *de l'Esprit des Loix*). Taipei: Taiwan shang-wu yin shu kuan. 6 vols.
孟德斯鳩法意。

1965. She-hui t'ung-ch'üan. (tr. of Edward Jenks's *History of Politics*). Taipei: Taiwan shang-wu yin shu kuan.
社會通詮。

Sources

Ch'en Pao-shen. "Ch'ing ku tzu-cheng tai-fu hai-chün hsieh tu-t'ung Yen chün mu-chih-ming."
陳寶琛。清故資政大夫海軍協都統嚴君墓誌銘。

Chou Chen-fu. Yen Fu ssu-hsiang shu p'ing. Shanghai: Chung-hua shu-chü, 1940.
周振甫。嚴復思想述評。

Creel, Herrlee G. Chinese Thought, from Confucius to Mao Tse-tung. Chicago: University of Chicago Press, 1953.

Ho Lin. "Yen Fu te fan-i." *Tung-fang tsa-chih*, XXIII-21 (November 25, 1925): 75–87.
賀麟。嚴復的翻譯。東方雜誌。

Lin Yao-hua. "Yen Fu she-hui ssu-hsiang." *She-hui hsueh-chieh*, VII (June, 1933): 1–82.
林耀華。嚴復社會思想。社會學界。

Schwartz, Benjamin I. In Search of Wealth and Power: Yen Fu and the West. Cambridge: Belknap Press of Harvard University Press, 1964.

Wang Ch'ü-ch'ang. Yen Chi-tao nien-p'u. Shanghai: Shang-wu yin shu kuan, 1936.
王蘧常。嚴幾道年譜。

Wang Ju-feng. "Yen Fu ssu-hsiang shih-t'an," in Chung-kuo jen-min ta-hsueh Chung-kuo li-shih chiao yen shih, *Chung-kuo chin-tai ssu-hsiang-chia yen-chiu lun-wen hsuan*. Peking: Sheng-huo, tu-shu, hsin chih san lien shu-tien.
王汝丰。嚴復思想試探。中國人民大學中國歷史教研室。中國近代思想家研究論文選。

Yen Ch'ü. Hou kuan Yen hsien-sheng nien-p'u. Shanghai: Chin ma shu-wu, 1930.
嚴璩。候官嚴先生年譜。

Yen Hsi-shan   閻錫山

Works

1925. Ts'un cheng fa-kuei ling-wen chi-yao. Taiyuan.
村政法規令文輯要。

1928? Chih Chin cheng-wu ch'üan-shu ch'u-kao. 12 vols.
治晉政務全書初稿。

1933. (comp.) Shansi sheng cheng shih nien chien-she chi-hua an.
山西省政十年建設計劃案。

1935. Fang kung yü chieh-chueh t'u-ti wen-t'i. Taiyuan.
防共與解決土地問題。

1935? Wu-ch'an cheng-ch'üan yü an-lao fen-p'ei. Taiyuan: Wu-ch'an cheng-ch'üan yen-chiu hui.
物產證券與按勞分配。

1936. Po-ch'uan hsien-sheng lu mu chih-hsueh lu (comp. by Yen Tzu-ming hsien-sheng feng tsang shih-lu pien-chi hui). 2 vols.
伯川先生廬墓治學錄。閻子明先生奉葬實錄編輯會。

1939. Yen Pai-ch'uan hsien-sheng yen-lun lei-pien. Shanghai. 9 vols.
閻百川先生言論類編。

1939. Yen Po-ch'uan hsien-sheng chiu-kuo yen-lun hsuan-chi (ed. by Fang Han-sung). Min ko ch'u-pan she.
閻伯川先生救國言論選集。方寒松。

1945. Shansi kuang-fu chih ching-kuo. Taiyuan.
山西光復之經過。

1948? Hsien she-hui ping-t'ai chi ch'i chih-fa. Taipei.
現社會病態及其治法。

1949. Mei-kuo pai-p'i-shu chih kuan-kan; Yen yuan-chang min-kuo san-shih-pa nien pa-yueh shih jih tsai fan ch'in-lueh ta t'ung-meng ch'ang wei hui chih chiang-tz'u. Taipei: Hsing-cheng yuan pi-shu ch'u.
美國白皮書之觀感；閻院長民國三十八年八月十日在反侵略大同盟常委會之講詞。

1949? Taiwan chi Hai-nan-tao po-wei an. Canton.
台灣及海南島保衛案。

1950. Tsen-yang su wei (with Tse lu Shansi su wei shih-li i-pai ko). Taipei: Yang-ming shan chuang.
怎樣肅偽（附：擇錄山西肅偽事例一百個）。

1951. Fan kung te shen-mo? P'ing shen-mo fan kung. Taipei: Cheng-chung shu-chü.
反共的什麼？憑什麼反共。

1951. Taiyuan po-wei chan kai shu. Taipei.
太原保衛戰概述。

1952. Taichung chiang-yen chi. Taipei.
台中講演集。

1952. Yen Po-ch'uan hsien-sheng an ho shih-chieh yen-lun hsuan-chi. Taipei.
閻伯川先生安和世界言論選集。

1952. Yen Po-ch'uan hsien-sheng i nien lai yü

Jih-pen (Japan) yu-jen t'an shu chi-yao. Tai-pei.

閻百川先生一年來與日本友人談述紀要。

1952. Yen Po-ch'uan hsien-sheng tsui-chin yen-lun chi (comp. by Chang Ching-an). Taipei: Fu-hsing ch'u-pan she. 2 vols.

閻伯川先生最近言論集。張靖安。

1953? Fan kung fu-kuo te ch'ien-t'u. Taipei.

反共復國的前途。

1954. Ta-t'ung kuo-chi hsuan-yen ts'ao-an. Tai-pei.

大同國際宣言草案。

1956. K'ung-tzu shih ko shen-mo chia. Taipei: Ta kung ch'u-pan she.

孔子是個什麼家。

1956. Yen Pai-ch'uan hsien-sheng yü Tz'u-hang Fa-shih lun tao shu. with Tz'u-hang Fa-shih. Taipei.

閻百川先生與慈航法師論道書。慈航法師。

1960? Chih Chin cheng-wu ch'üan shu ch'u pien. Taipei: Yen Chai.

治晉政務全書初編。

1960. San-pai nien te Chung-kuo. 2 vols.

三百年的中國。

1960. Shih-chieh ta-t'ung. Taipei.

世界大同。

1960. Yen Pai-ch'uan hsien-sheng t'i-tzu chi. Taipei.

閻百川先生題字集。

Chün kuo chu-i t'an.

軍國主義譚。

Jen-min hsü chih.

人民須知。

Yen Hsi-shan *et al.* T'u-ti ts'un kung-yu wen-t'i yen-lun chi; ti-i chi (comp. by T'u-ti ts'un kung-yu shih-shih pan-fa t'ao-lun hui). Tai-yuan? T'u-ti ts'un kung-yu shih-shih pan-fa t'ao-lun hui.

閻錫山等。土地村公有問題言論集；第一輯。土地村公有實施辦法討論會。

SOURCES

Ch'en Po-ta. T'u huang-ti Yen Hsi-shan.

陳伯達。土皇帝閻錫山。

———. Yen Hsi-shan p'i-p'an. Kalgan, 1945.

陳伯達。閻錫山批判。

Chung-kuo kuo-min-tang shih kao i chih ssu p'ien, comp. by Tsou Lu. Chungking: Shang-wu yin shu kuan, 1944. 4 vols.

中國國民黨史稿一至四篇。鄒魯。

CYB-W, 1921-39.

Gillin, Donald G. Warlord: Yen Hsi-shan in Shansi Province, 1911-1949. Princeton: Princeton University Press, 1967.

Hsin Chung-kuo, November 15, 1919.

新中國。

Lü Chu. "Shansi shu cheng t'an." *Hsien-tai p'ing-lun*, August 21-October 9, 1926.

呂著。山西庶政談。現代評論。

North China Herald. Shanghai, 1911-30.

Wen Kung-chih. Tsui-chin san-shih nien Chung-kuo chün-shih shih. Shanghai: T'ai-p'ing-yang shu-tien, 1932. 2 vols.

文公直。最近三十年中國軍事史。

WWC, 1926, 1936.

Yen Hsi-shan. Shansi kuang-fu chih ching-kuo. Taiyuan, 1945.

閻錫山。山西光復之經過。

———. Ts'un cheng fa-kuei ling-wen chi-yao. Taiyuan, 1925.

閻錫山。村政法規令文輯要。

———. Yen Pai-ch'uan hsien-sheng yen-lun lei-pien. Shanghai, 1939. 9 vols.

閻錫山。閻百川先生言論類編。

Yen Hui-ch'ing　　顏惠慶

WORKS

1908. (ed.) English and Chinese Standard Dictionary. Shanghai: The Commercial Press, 2 vols.

1932, February. "On the Manchurian Crisis." *The China Review*, I-1.

1932. "Dr. W. W. Yen's Letter to M. Paul Boncour." *The China Critic*: 262.

1937. Communication from the Chinese Delegation: Telegraphic Message to the Assembly from Dr. W. W. Yen, President of the Chinese Institute of International Relations. Geneva.

1937. "The Sino-Japanese Conflict and American Neutrality." *The China Quarterly*, III, special Fall number: 694-96.

1937, October-December. "The Shanghai International Red Cross." *The China Critic*.

1938, Spring. "Sanctity of Treaty." *The China Quarterly*, IV: 113-24.

1938, Summer. "Reminiscences of Soviet Russia." *The China Quarterly*, IV: 227-36.

1939-40, Winter. "Some Observations on the Institute of Pacific Relations Conference." *The China Quarterly*, V.

1940, Summer. "China's Prospects of Winning the War." *The China Quarterly*, V.

1940, August. "Some Aspects of China's Relations with the Soviet Union." *Asiatic Review*, XXXVI: 338-45.

SOURCES

Person interviewed: Yen Pao-sheng.
BPC
CH
Chang Ch'i-yün. Tang shih kai-yao. Taipei: Chung-yang wen-wu kung-ying she, 1951-52. 5 vols.
張其昀。黨史概要。
Chia I-chün. Chung-hua Min-kuo shih. Shanghai: Wen-hua hsueh-she, 1930.
賈逸君。中華民國史。
Chung-kuo hsueh-sheng, 28 (May, 1926); 31 (June, 1926).
中國學生。
Chung-kuo wai-chiao nien-chien, comp. by Chang Chin. Shanghai: Shih-chieh shu-chü, 1935.
中國外交年鑑。章進。
CMTC
CTMC
CWR, April 2, 1924.
CYB, 1936.
"Dr. W. W. Yen." CWR, December, 1909.
Kuo wen chou-pao, I-9.
國聞週報。
Li Chien-nung. Chung-kuo chin pai nien cheng-chih shih. Shanghai: Shang-wu yin shu kuan, 1947. 2 vols.
李劍農。中國近百年政治史。
"The New Minister of Foreign Affairs (Yen)." *The Chinese Students' Monthly*, December, 1920.
T'ang Leang-li. The Inner History of the Chinese Revolution. New York: E. P. Dutton & Co., 1930.
T'ao Chü-yin. Liu chün-tzu chuan. Shanghai: Chung-hua shu-chü, 1946.
陶菊隱。六君子傳。
TCMT
Tseng Yu-hao. Chung-kuo wai-chiao shih. Shanghai: Shang-wu yin shu kuan, 1926.
曾友豪。中國外交史。
Wai-chiao p'ing-lun, III-9.
外交評論。
Wai-chiao ta tz'u-tien, ed. by Wai-chiao hsueh-hui. Kunming: Chung-hua shu-chü, 1937.
外交大辭典。外交學會。
Whang, P. K. "Will W. W. Yen and Wellington Koo Return to Their Posts?" CWR, July 28, 1934.
WWARS
WWC, 1950.
WWMC
Yueh Ch'ien. Chung Su kuan-hsi shih-hua. Singapore, Hong Kong: Ch'uang k'en ch'u-pan she, 1952.
岳騫。中蘇關係史話。

Yen Yang-ch'u 晏陽初

WORKS

1925. Educating China's Millions for Democracy. Shanghai: The Commercial Press.
1925. The Mass Education Movement in China. Shanghai: The Commercial Press.
1928, June. "Mass Education in China." *Pacific Affairs*: 23-24.
1928-29. "New Citizens for China." *Yale Review*, XVIII: 262-76.
1929. "China's New Scholar-Farmer." *Asia*, 9: 126-33, 158-60.
1938. "Mass Education to Increase China's Fighting Power." *China Review*, V-13: 12-14.
1938. "Mass Education Movement in China's Crisis." *China Forum*, I: 492-501.
1943-44. 1000 Chinese Foundation Characters. with Daniel C. Fu. Toronto: University of Toronto Press, 4 vols.

SOURCES

Buck, Pearl S. Tell the People, Talks with James Yen About the Mass Education Movement. New York: The John Day Co., 1945.
Current Biography, 1946.
Davidson, C. "Jimmy Yen's Proven Aid for Developing Countries." *Reader's Digest*, October, 1961.
GCJJ
Gould, K. M. "Citizen of the World." *Senior Scholastic*, 66 (April 20, 1955).
HCMW
Spencer, Cornelia. China's Leaders in Ideas and Action. Macrai, 1966.

Yi P'ei-chi 易培基

WORKS

"Ch'ing shih li mu cheng wu." *Chia-yin tsa-chih*, I-6.

清史例目證誤。甲寅雜誌。
(ed.) Ku-kung sung-an hsieh-chen.
故宮訟案寫眞。

SOURCES

Chung-kuo chin ch'i-shih nien lai chiao-yü chi-shih, ed. by Ting Chih-p'ing. Taipei: Kuo-li pien i kuan, 1961.
中國近七十年來教育記事。丁致聰。
Lao-ta lun-ts'ung.
勞大論叢。
Ssu-fa hsing-cheng pu. Ku-kung po-wu-yuan wu-pi an shih-lu. Nanking, 1935.
司法行政部。故宮博物院舞弊案實錄。
Tsou Lu. Hui-ku lu. Nanking: Tu-li ch'u-pan she, 1946-47. 2 vols.
鄒魯。回顧錄。
Wu Ying. Ku-kung po-wu-yuan ch'ien-hou wu nien ching-kuo chi. Peiping, 1932.
吳瀛。故宮博物院前後五年經過記。
Yeh O. Yi P'ei-chi teng ch'in-chan ku-kung ku-wu an ch'i-su shu chi chien-ting shu. Nanking, 1937.
葉峨。易培基等侵占故宮古物案起訴書及鑑定書。
Yi Pai-sha. Ti-wang ch'un-ch'iu.
易白沙。帝王春秋。

Ying Hua   英華

WORKS

1902-13. ed. of *Ta kung pao*.
大公報。

SOURCES

CBJS
Fang Hao. "Mr. Ying Lien-chih—Founder of Fu Jen." *China Critic*, December 17, 1956.
Paragon, Donald. "Ying Lien-chih (1866-1926) and the Rise of Fu Jen—the Catholic University of Peking." Unpublished Master's essay, Columbia University, 1957.
Ta kung pao. Tientsin, May 22, 1931.
大公報。

Yolbars

SOURCES

Chang Ta-chün. Ssu-shih nien tung-luan Sinkiang. Hong Kong: Ya-chou ch'u-pan she, 1957.

張達鈞。四十年動亂新疆。
CMJL
GCJJ
Hahn, Emily. "Our Far-flung Correspondents." *New Yorker*, November 7, 1953.
Hedin, Sven. The Flight of Big Horse. New York, 1936.
———. The Silk Road. New York, 1938.
Wu, Aitchen. Turkestan Tumult. London: Methuen, 1940.

Yü Han-mou   余漢謀

SOURCES

BKL
CH
CTMC

Yü Hsueh-chung   于學忠

SOURCES

BKL
Chung-kuo k'ang chan shih, comp. by Hai-wai liu-tung hsuan-ch'uan t'uan. Canton: Hai-wai liu-tung hsuan-ch'uan t'uan chu Yueh tsung pan-shih-ch'u, 1947.
中國抗戰史。海外流動宣傳團。
CMTC
CWR, 1938.
GCJJ
Jen-min jih-pao. Peking, September 25, 1964.
人民日報。
Lei Hsiao-ts'en. San-shih nien tung-luan Chung-kuo. Hong Kong: Ya-chou ch'u-pan she, 1955.
雷嘯岑。三十年動亂中國。
TCJC
WWC, 1931.
WWMC
Yu Chün. "Sian shih-pien i-lai ts'ung wei kung-k'ai kuo te chen-shih." *Ch'un-ch'iu*, 52-58 (September 1-December 1, 1959).
右軍。西安事變以來從未公開過的珍史。春秋。

Yü Hung-chün   兪鴻鈞

WORKS

1955, April. "Hui-i wo te chi-che sheng-yai." *Pao hsueh*, I-7 (April, 1955): 50-52.

回憶我的記者生涯。報學。
1956. Shih-cheng pao-kao yü chiang-yen—Yü
yuan-chang yen-lun chi-yao. Taipei: Hsing-
cheng yuan hsin-wen chü.
施政報告與講演一兪院長言論輯要。
1957. Report on Action Taken by the Government Regarding the Incident on May 24, 1957,
in Taipei. Taipei: Government Information
Office.

SOURCES

BKL
CH
"Chien-lü tu-shih chih Yü Hung-chün hsien-
sheng." *Chung-kuo i-chou*, 529 (June, 1960): 5-
6.
踐履篤實之兪鴻鈞先生。中國一周。
CMJL
Current Biography, 1961.
GCJJ
Ho Shan-yuan. "Wo so chih-tao te Yü hsien-
sheng Hung-chün." *Chung-kuo i-chou*, 541
(September, 1960): 6-8.
何善垣。我所知道的兪先生鴻鈞。中國一
周。
The New York Times, January 10, 1958; June 2,
1960.
WWC, supplement to the 4th ed., 1933.
Yü Hung-chün. "Hui-i wo te chi-che sheng-yai."
Pao hsueh, I-7 (April, 1955): 50-52.
兪鴻鈞。回憶我的記者生涯。報學。
———. Shih-cheng pao-kao yü chiang-yen—Yü
yuan-chang yen-lun chi-yao. Taipei: Hsing-
cheng yuan hsin-wen chü, 1956.
兪鴻鈞。施政報告與講演一兪院長言論輯
要。
Yü Hung-chün hsien-sheng chi-nien chi, comp.
by Yü Hung-chün hsien-sheng chih-sang wei-
yuan-hui. Taipei, 1960.
兪鴻鈞先生紀念集。兪鴻鈞先生治喪委員
會。

Yü Jih-chang   余日章

WORKS

1927. Yü Jih-chang *et al.* Tsui-chin T'ai-p'ing-
yang wen-t'i (ed. by Ch'en Li-t'ing, Ying
Yuan-tao). Shanghai: T'ai-p'ing-yang kuo
chiao t'ao-lun hui.
余日章等。最近太平洋問題。陳立廷，應
元道。

ed. of *Peking Daily News*.

SOURCES

Barnett, Eugene E. "Contemporary Chinese
Christian Leaders: David Z. T. Yui." *The
Chinese Recorder and Missionary Journal*, Janu-
ary, 1927.
Li Chien-nung. Chung-kuo chin pai nien cheng-
chih shih. Shanghai: Shang-wu yin shu kuan,
1947. 2 vols.
李劍農。中國近百年政治史。
The New York Times, January 23, 1936.
Yuan Fang-lai. Yü Jih-chang chuan. Shanghai:
Ch'ing-nien hui shu-chü, 1948.
袁訪賚。余日章傳。

Yü Pin   于斌

WORKS

1937. La Guerre en Extreme-Orient. Brussels:
Édition de la Cité Chrétienne.
1938. The War in the Far East. Oxford: Catholic Social Guild.
1939. Yü Pin chu-chiao k'ang-chan yen-lun chi.
Hong Kong: Chen-li hsueh-hui.
于斌主教抗戰言論集。
1945. Eyes East, Selected Pronouncements of
the Most Reverend Paul Yü Pin. Paterson,
N. J.: St. Anthony Guild Press.
1953. Yü Pin tsung chu-chiao tui liu Mei t'ung-
hsueh yen-chiang chi. Hong Kong: Yu lien
ch'u-pan she.
于斌總主教對留美同學演講集。
1954. Yü Pin tsui-chin yen-shou chi (ed. by I
shih t'ung-hsin she). Taipei: Chung-yang
wen-wu kung-ying she.
于斌最近演說集。益世通訊社。
1960. Yü Pin tsung chu-chiao yen-lun chi (ed.
by Jen-sheng che-hsueh yen-chiu hui; comp.
by Chang Li-hsing). Taipei: Hsin tung-li
tsa-chih she.
于斌總主教言論集。人生哲學研究會。張
力行。
1963. Yü Pin tsung chu-chiao tsung-chiao yen-
lun chi (comp. by Jen-sheng che-hsueh yen-
chiu hui tsung-hui). Taipei: Hsin tung-li
tsa-chih she.
于斌總主教宗教言論集。人生哲學研究會
總會。
1964. Yü Pin tsung chu-chiao yen-lun hsuan-chi
(comp. by Tuan Hung-chün). Taipei: Tzu-yu
T'ai-p'ing-yang wen-hua shih-yeh kung-ssu.

于斌總主教言論選集。段宏俊。

SOURCES

CBJS
Eyes East, Selected Pronoucements of the Most Reverend Paul Yü Pin. Paterson, N. J.: St. Anthony Guild Press, 1945.

GCJJ
Lei Chen-yuan. "Fa-ch'i tzu-yu T'ai-p'ing-yang yün-tung te Yü Pin tsung chu-chiao." *Chung-kuo i-chou*, 527 (May, 1960): 10–12.
雷震遠。發起自由太平洋運動的于斌總主教。中國一周。

Tsiang, Paul Hong-li. "Son Ec. Monseigneur Paul Yü Pin, Vicaire Apostolique de Nankin." *Bulletin de l'Université l'Aurore*, XXXV (1935–36): 83–85.

Yü Pin. Yü Pin chu-chiao k'ang-chan yen-lun chi. Hong Kong: Chen-li hsueh-hui, 1939.
于斌。于斌主教抗戰言論集。

——. Yü Pin tsui-chin yen-shuo chi. Taipei: Chung-yang wen-wu kung-ying she, 1954.
于斌。于斌最近演說集。

——. Yü Pin tsung chu-chiao tui-yü liu Mei t'ung-hsüeh yen-chiang chi. Hong Kong: Yu-lien ch'u-pan she, 1953.
于斌。于斌總主教對留美同學演講集。

Yü Pin tsung chu-chiao yen-lun hsuan-chi, comp. by Tuan Hung-chün. Taipei: Tzu-yu T'ai-p'ing-yang wen-chiao shih-yeh kung-ssu, 1964.
于斌總主教言論選集。段宏俊。

Yü P'ing-po 兪平伯

WORKS

1923. Hung lou meng pien. Shanghai: Ya-tung t'u-shu-kuan.
紅樓夢辨。

1924. Hsi huan. Shanghai: Ya-tung t'u-shu-kuan.
西還。

1925. I. Chih ch'eng shu-chü.
憶。

1927. Tung yeh. Shanghai: Ya-tung t'u-shu-kuan.
冬夜。

1928. Tsa pan erh. Shanghai: K'ai-ming shu-tien.
雜拌儿。

1928. Yen chih ts'ao. K'ai-ming shu-tien.
燕知草。

1933. Tsa pan erh chih erh.
雜拌儿之二。

1934. Tu tz'u ou te. Shanghai: K'ai-ming shu-tien.
讀詞偶得。

1936. Ku huai meng yü. Shih-chieh shu-chü.
古槐夢遇。

1936. Yen chiao chi. Shanghai: Liang-yu t'u-shu yin-shua kung-ssu.
燕效集。

1953. Hung lou meng yen-chiu. Shanghai: T'ang ti ch'u-pan she.
紅樓夢研究。

1955. (ed.) Chih-yen-chai hung-lou-meng chi p'ing. Shanghai: Shanghai wen-i lien-ho ch'u-pan she.
脂硯齋紅樓夢輯評。

1960. Yü P'ing-po et al. Chung-kuo hsien-tai ming-jen yu-chi. Hong Kong: Tung-ya shu-chü.
兪平伯等。中國現代名人遊記。

1962. Yü P'ing-po *et al.* Li Pai shih lun-ts'ung. Hong Kong: Hong Kong wen yuan shu-wu.
兪平伯等。李白詩論叢。

SOURCES

Chan Shau-wing. "Literature in Communist China." *Problems of Communism*, VII-1 (January-February, 1958).

CKJMT
Hightower, James Robert. Topics in Chinese Literature: Outlines and Bibliographies. Cambridge: Harvard University Press, 1962.

Jen chien shih. 11 (September 5, 1934).
人間世。

Jen-min jih-pao. Peking, October 23, 1954; November 29, 1954.
人民日報。

Kuang-ming jih-pao. Peking, October 10, 1954.
光明日報。

MCNP
RCCL
WWMC

Yü Ta-fu 郁達夫

WORKS

1923. Niao meng chi. T'ai tung shu-chü.
蔦夢集。

1928. Lien-ai chih hua. Shanghai: K'ai-ming shu-tien.
戀愛之花。

1929. Mi-yang. Shanghai: Pei hsin shu-chü.
迷羊。

1929. Ta-fu tai-piao tso. Shanghai: Hsien-tai shu-chü.
達夫代表作。

1929-32. Ta-fu ch'üan-chi. Shanghai: Pei hsin shu-chü. 6 vols.
達夫全集。

1929-? ed. of Ta-chung wen-i.
大衆文藝。

1930. Hsiao-shuo lun. Shanghai: Kuang-hua shu-chü.
小說論。

1932? Jao le t'a. Shanghai.
饒了她。

1932. T'a shih i ko jo nü-tzu. Shanghai: Hung feng shu-chü.
她是一個弱女子。

1933. Jih-chi chiu-chung. Shanghai: Pei hsin shu-chü.
日記九種。

1933. Ta-fu tzu hsuan chi. Shanghai: T'ien ma shu-tien.
達夫自選集。

1934. Chi hen ch'u ch'u. Shanghai: Hsien-tai shu-chü.
屐痕處處。

1934. Yü Ta-fu et al. Pan-jih yu-ch'eng. Shanghai: Liang-yu t'u-shu yin-shua kung-ssu.
郁達夫等。半日遊程。

1935. Yü Ta-fu et al. Ch'ih-mu. Shanghai: Sheng-huo shu-tien.
郁達夫等。遲暮。

1936. Hsien shu. Shanghai: Liang-yu t'u-shu yin-shua kung-ssu.
閑書。

1936. (comp.) Hsien-tai ming-jen ch'ing-shu. Shanghai: Hsi-wang ch'u-pan she.
現代名人情書。

1936. Yü Ta-fu hsuan-chi (comp. by Hsü Ch'en-ssu, Yeh Wang-yu). Shanghai: Wan-hsiang shu-wu.
郁達夫選集。徐沉泗, 葉忘憂。

1940. Yü Ta-fu et al. Hui-i Lu Hsün chi ch'i-ta (ed. by Chou Li-an). Yü-chou feng she.
郁達夫等。回憶魯迅及其他。周黎庵。

1948. Ta-fu ch'üan-chi; ti-ch'i chüan, tuan ts'an chi. Shanghai: Pei hsin shu-chü.
達夫全集；第七卷，斷殘集。

1948. Yü Ta-fu yu-chi. Shanghai: Shanghai tsa-chih kung-ssu.
郁達夫遊記。

1954. Ta-fu shih tz'u chi (comp. by Cheng Tzu-yü). Hong Kong: Hsien-tai ch'u-pan she.
達夫詩詞集。鄭子瑜。

1954. Yü Ta-fu hsuan-chi (comp. by Yeh Ting-i). Peking: Jen-min wen-hsueh ch'u-pan she.
郁達夫選集。葉丁易。

1956. Yü Ta-fu nan yu chi (comp. by Wen Tzu-ch'uan). Hong Kong: Shih-chieh ch'u-pan she.
郁達夫南遊記。溫梓川。

1957. Kan-shang te hsing lü. Taipei: Ch'i ming shu-chü.
感傷的行旅。

1960. Ch'u-pen. Hong Kong: Shanghai shu-chü.
出奔。

1960. Ch'un-ch'ao. Hong Kong: Jih hsin shu-tien.
春潮。

1962. Yü Ta-fu shih tz'u ch'ao (comp. by Lu Tan-lin). Hong Kong: Shanghai shu-chü.
郁達夫詩詞鈔。陸丹林。

Erh shih-jen.
二詩人。

Hsiao chia chih wu (Ou Mei hsiao-shuo hsuan i). (tr.) Pei hsin shu-chü.
小家之伍 （歐美小說選譯）。

Hsiao-shuo lun. Kuang-hua.
小說論。

ed. of Hsing-chou jih-pao.
星洲日報。

ed. of Hua-ch'iao chou-pao.
華僑週報。

Pai chin i-shu. (tr.) Pei hsin shu-chü.
拜金藝術。

ed. of Pen-liu.
奔流。

Shen-lou. Pei hsin shu-chü.
蜃樓。

Wen-hsueh kai-shuo. Shang-wu yin shu kuan.
文學概說。

SOURCES

Ch'ien Hsing-ts'un. Hsien-tai Chung-kuo wen-hsueh tso-chia. Shanghai: T'ai tung t'u-shu chü, 1929.
錢杏邨。現代中國文學作家。

CHWC

CHWSK

CHWYS

CWT

Hightower, James Robert. Topics in Chinese Literature: Outlines and Bibliographies. Cambridge: Harvard University Press, 1962.

HMTT

Hsü Chih-mo nien-p'u, comp. by Ch'en Ts'ung-chou. Shanghai: Ch'en shih tzu yin, 1949.
徐志摩年譜。陳從周。

Hu Yü-chih. Yü Ta-fu te liu-wang ho shih-tsung. Hong Kong: Chih yuan shu-wu, 1946.
胡愈之。郁達夫的流亡和失踪。

Huang Ying-jen (pseud. of Ku Feng-ch'eng). Ch'uang-tso-she lun. Shanghai: Kuang-hua shu-chü, 1932.
黃影人 (顧鳳城)。創造社論。

HWP

Jen chien shih, 16 (November 20, 1934); 17 (December 5, 1934): 11–14; 18 (December 20, 1934): 17–19; 19 (January 5, 1935): 29–31; 20 (January 20, 1935): 35–38; 21 (February 5, 1935): 29–31; 23 (March 5, 1935): 33–36; 26 (April 20, 1935): 25–28; 28 (May 20, 1935): 6–8; 31 (July 5, 1935): 6–8.
人間世。

Kuo Mo-jo. Li-shih jen-wu. Shanghai: Hai-yen shu-tien, 1947.
郭沫若。歷史人物。

MCNP

Sun Pai-kang. Yü Ta-fu yü Wang Ying-hsia. Hong Kong: Hong Kong hung yeh shu-chü, 1962.
孫百剛。郁達夫與王映霞。

Ting I. Chung-kuo hsien-tai wen-hsüeh shih-lüeh. Peking: Tso-chia ch'u-pan she, 1957.
丁易。中國現代文學史略。

Tseng Hua-p'eng and Fan Po-ch'ün. "Yü Ta-fu lun." *Jen-min wen-hsüeh*, 91 (May 20, 1957): 184–204.
曾華鵬，范伯群。郁達夫論。人民文學。

Yü Ta-fu. Yü Ta-fu ch'üan-chi. Shanghai: Pei hsin shu-chü, 1929–32. 6 vols.
郁達夫。郁達夫全集。

———. Yü Ta-fu hsüan-chi (comp. by Yeh Ting-i). Peking: Jen-min wen-hsueh ch'u-pan she, 1954.
郁達夫。郁達夫選集。葉丁易。

Yü Ta-fu lun, ed. by Tsou Hsiao (pseud. of Chao Ching-shen). Shanghai: Pei hsin shu-chü, 1933.
郁達夫論。鄒嘯 (趙景深)。

Yü Ta-fu lun, comp. by Ho Yü-po. Shanghai: Ta kuang shu-chü, 1936.
郁達夫論。賀玉波。

Yü Ta-fu t'ao-wang chi, comp. by I mei t'u-shu kung-ssu. Hong Kong, 1960.
郁達夫逃亡記。

Yü Ta-wei   俞大維

Sources

AWW

CH

CH-T, 1956–57.

China Yearbook, 1957–58, 1960–61. Taipei: China Publishing Co.

GCJJ

Liu, F. F. A Military History of Modern China, 1924–1949. Princeton: Princeton University Press, 1956.

Romanus, Charles F., and Riley Sunderland. Stilwell's Command Problems. Washington; Office of the Chief of Military History, Department of the Army, 1956.

———. Stilwell's Mission to China. Washington: Office of the Chief of Military History, Department of the Army, 1953.

SMJ

Yü Yu-jen   于右任

Works

1927. Chung-shan li-shih. Min-chüan shu-chü.
中山歷史。

1930. Yu-jen shih-ts'un. Shanghai: Shih-chieh shu-chü.
右任詩存。

1944. Ts'ao-shu cheng-ch'i-ko chen-chi. Cheng-tu: Yuan-tung t'u-shu kung-ssu.
草書正氣歌眞蹟。

1945. Piao-chun ts'ao-shu. Chungking: Shuo-wen she ch'u-pan pu.
標準草書。

1948. Yü Yu-jen hsien-sheng shih wen hsuan-ts'ui. Shanghai?
于右任先生詩文選粹。

1953. Wo te ch'ing-nien shih-ch'i. Taipei: Cheng-chung shu-chü.
我的青年時期。

1955. Yü Yu-jen et al. Kuo-fu chiu-shih tan-ch'en chi-nien lun-wen chi. Taipei: Chung-hua wen-hua ch'u-pan shih-yeh wei-yuan-hui. 2 vols.
于右任等。國父九十誕辰紀念論文集。

1956. Yu-jen shih-ts'un (ed. by Liu Yen-t'ao) Taipei: Chung-hua ts'ung-shu wei-yuan-hui. 2 vols.
右任詩存。劉延濤。

1956? Yü Yu-jen hsien-sheng ko hsuan. Taipei: Chung-kuo hsin-wen ch'u-pan kung-ssu.

于右任先生歌選。

1957. Yu-jen wen-ts'un (ed. by Liu Yen-t'ao).
Taipei: Chung-hua ts'ung-shu wei-yuan-hui.
右任文存。劉延濤。

1963. Yu-jen shih wen chi. Taipei: Cheng-
chung shu-chü. 3 vols.
右任詩文集。

1963. Yü Yu-jen hsien-sheng shih wen hsuan-
chi (ed. by T'ien sheng ch'u-pan she pien-chi
pu). Taipei: T'ien sheng ch'u-pan she.
于右任先生詩文選集。天聲出版社編輯部。

1965. Yü Yu-jen chi-nien chao-p'ien, mo-pao,
shih wen, chuan-chi, tao-wen lien-ho chuan-
chi (comp. by Chang Yün-chia). Taipei:
Chung-kuo ch'ang hung ch'u-pan she.
于右任紀念照片，墨寶，詩文，傳記，悼
文聯合專集。張雲家。

SOURCES

Chang Chia-yun. Yü Yu-jen chuan. Taipei:
Chung wai t'ung-hsin she, 1958.
張家雲。于右任傳。

The China News. Taipei, November 10, 1964.

Chung-yang jih-pao. Taipei, November 11, 1964.
中央日報。

Feng Yü-hsiang. Wo te sheng-huo. Shanghai:
Chiao-yü shu-tien, 1947. 3 vols.
馮玉祥。我的生活。

Hong Kong shih-pao. Hong Kong, November 1,
1964.
香港時報。

Hsü Tuan-fu. Yü Yu-jen hsien-sheng nien-p'u
ch'u-kuo.
胥端甫。于右任先生年譜初稿。

The New York Times, November 11, 1964.

Wu Hsiang-hsiang. "Ts'ung mu-yang-erh tao
chien-ch'a yuan chang—Yü Yu-jen hsien-
sheng chuan-lueh." *Chuan-chi wen-hsueh,* V-6
(December, 1964): 4–12.
吳相湘。從牧羊兒到監察院長—于右任先
生傳略。傳記文學。

Yü Yu-jen. Wo te ch'ing-nien shih-ch'i. Taipei: Cheng-chung shu-chü, 1953.
于右任。我的青年時期。

———. Yu-jen shih-ts'un. Shanghai: Shih-chieh
shu-chü, 1930.
于右任。右任詩存。

———. Yu-jen wen-ts'un (ed. by Liu Yen-t'ao).
Taipei: Chung-hua ts'ung-shu wei-yuan-hui,
1957.
于右任。右任文存。劉延濤。

Yü Yu-jen hsien-sheng liu-shih sui nien-p'u.
于右任先生六十歲年譜。

Yü Yu-jen hsien-sheng nien-p'u, ed. by Liu
Yen-t'ao. Taipei: Chung-kuo i-chou she.
于右任先生年譜。劉延濤。

Yuan Shih-k'ai   袁世凱

WORKS

1899. Hsün-lien ts'ao-fa hsiang-hsi t'u-shuo.
Tientsin. 22 vols.
訓練操法詳晰圖說。

1926. Yuan Shih-k'ai chia-shu. Shanghai:
Chung-yang shu-tien.
袁世凱家書。

1937. Yang-shou-yuan tsou-i chi-yao (ed. by Shen
Tsu-hsien). Hsiang-ch'eng, Honan: Yuan
shih tsung tz'u. 6 vols.
養壽園奏議輯要。沈祖憲。

1938. "Wu-hsü jih-chi," in Tso Shun-sheng,
Chung-kuo chin pai nien shih tzu-liao. Shanghai:
Chung-hua shu-chü. 2 vols.
戊戌日記。左舜生。中國近百年史資料。

1962. Yuan ta tsung-t'ung shu tu hui-pien (ed.
by Hsü Yu-p'eng). Taipei: Wen hsing shu-
tien.
袁大總統書牘彙編。徐有朋。

1966. (ed.) Hsin chien lu-chün ping-lueh lu ts'un.
Taipei: Wen hai ch'u-pan she.
新建陸軍兵略錄存。

1966. Yang-shou-yuan tien kao (ed. by Shen
Tsu-hsien). Taipei: Wen hai ch'u-pan she.
養壽園電稿。沈祖憲。

SOURCES

AADC

Chang I-lin. Hsin-t'ai-p'ing-shih chi (with Pu-i
fu-lu). (ed. bp Ku T'ing-lung.) Shanghai,
1947. 4 vols.
張一麐。心太平室集（附：補遺附錄）。顧
廷龍。

Ch'en, Jerome. Yuan Shih-k'ai, 1859–1916.
Stanford: Stanford University Press, 1961.

Ch'en K'uei-lung. Meng-chiao-t'ing tsa-chi.
1925.
陳夔龍。夢蕉亭雜記。

Ch'en Po-ta. Ch'ieh kuo ta-tao Yuan Shih-k'ai.
Peking: Hsin hua shu-tien, 1949.
陳伯達。竊國大盜袁世凱。

Ch'ien Tuan-sheng, Sa Shih-chiung *et al.* Min-
kuo cheng chih shih. Shanghai: Shang-wu
yin shu kuan, 1946. 2 vols.
錢端升，薩師炯等。民國政制史。

Chin shan shih-pao. San Francisco, October 31, November, 1, 1956.
金山時報。

Chin-shih wai huo shih, comp. by A Ying (pseud. of Ch'ien Hsing-ts'un). Shanghai: Ch'ao feng ch'u-pan she, 1951. 3 vols.
近世外禍史。阿英 (錢杏邨)。

Chin Yün-chih. Yün yang chi. 1913?
金允植。雲養集。

Chün hsien wen-t'i wen tien hui-pien, comp. by Ch'ou an hui. Peking: Cheng meng shu-chü, 1915. 2 vols.
君憲問題文電彙編。籌安會。

Chung-hua Min-kuo shih-liao, comp. by Sun Yao. Shanghai: Wen-ming shu-tien, 1929. 3 vols.
中華民國史料。孫曜。

Chung-kuo kuo-min-tang shih-kao i chih ssu p'ien, comp. by Tsou Lu. Chungking: Shang-wu yin shu kuan, 1944. 4 vols.
中國國民黨史稿一至四篇。鄒魯。

Hou I. Hung-hsien chiu-wen (with Hsiang-ch'eng chiu-jen pi-wen). 1926.
候毅。洪憲舊聞 (附: 項城就任秘聞)。

Houn, Franklin W. Central Government of China 1912-1928. Madison: University of Wisconsin Press, 1957,

Hsin-hai ko-ming, ed. by Ch'ai Te-keng *et al.* Shanghai: Jen-min ch'u-pan she, 1957. 8 vols.
辛亥革命。柴德賡等。

Jen-wen, VIII-3 (April 15, 1937).
人文。

Kent, Percy Horace. The Passing of the Manchus. London, 1912.

Kao Lao. Ti-chih yün-tung shih-mo chi. Shanghai: Shang-wu yin shu kuan, 1924.
高勞。帝制運動始末記。

Li Chien-nung. Tsui-chin san-shih nien Chung-kuo cheng-chih shih. Shanghai: T'ai-p'ing-yang shu-tien, 1931.
李劍農。最近三十年中國政治史。

Li Shu. Hsin-hai ko-ming ch'ien-hou te Chung-kuo cheng-chih. Peking: Jen min ch'u-pan she, 1954.
黎澍。辛亥革命前後的中國政治。

Liu Ch'eng-yü. Hung-hsien chi-shih shih pen-shih pu chu. Chungking: Ching hua yin shu kuan.
劉成禺。洪憲紀事詩本事簿注。

Ma Ta-chung. Ta Chung-hua Min-kuo shih. Peiping: Chung-hua yin shu chü, 1929.
馬大中。大中華民國史。

MMT

Morse, Hosea Ballou. The International Relations of the Chinese Empire. London: Long-mans, Green & Co., 1910-18. 3 vols.

Naito Juntaro. Seiden En Sei-gai. Tokyo, 1913.
內藤順太郎。正傳袁世凱。

Pai Chiao. Yuan Shih-k'ai yü Chung-hua Min-kuo. Shanghai: Jen-wen yueh-k'an she, 1936.
白蕉。袁世凱與中華民國。

Powell, Ralph L. The Rise of Chinese Military Power, 1895-1912. Princeton: Princeton University Press, 1955.

Reid, John Gilbert. The Manchu Abdication and the Powers, 1908-1912; an Episode in Pre-war Diplomacy: A Study of the Role of Foreign Diplomacy during the Reign of Hsuan-t'ung. Berkeley: University of California Press, 1935.

Shang Ping-ho. Hsin-jen ch'un-ch'iu. Hsin-jen li-shih pien-chi she, 1927.
尚秉和。辛壬春秋。

Shen Tsu-hsien *et al.* Jung an ti-tzu chi (ed. by Wu Hsiang-hsiang). Taipei: Wen hsing shu-tien, 1962.
沈祖憲等。容菴弟子記。吳相湘。

T'ao Ch'ü-yin. Liu chün-tzu chuan. Shanghai: Chung-hua shu-chü, 1946.
陶菊隱。六君子傳。

——. Pei-yang chün-fa t'ung-chih shih-ch'i shih-hua. Peking: Sheng-huo, tu-shu, hsin chih san lien shu-tien, 1957-58. 6 vols.
陶菊隱。北洋軍閥統治時期史話。

"T'ao Yuan shih-liao," in Lo Chia-lun, *Ko-ming wen-hsien; ti-liu chi.* Taipei: Chung-kuo kuo-min-tang chung-yang wei-yuan-hui tang shih shih-liao pien-tsuan wei-yuan-hui, 1954.
討袁史料。羅家倫。革命文献; 第六輯。

Wang Yün-sheng. Liu-shih nien lai Chung-kuo yü Jih-pen. Tientsin: Ta kung pao she, 1932-34. 7 vols.
王芸生。六十年來中國與日本。

Wen Kung-chih. Tsui-chin san-shih nien Chung-kuo chün-shih shih. Shanghai: T'ai-p'ing-yang shu-tien, 1932. 2 vols.
文公直。最近三十年中國軍事史。

Wheeler, W. Reginald. China and the World War. New York: The Macmillan Co., 1919.

WWMC

Yeh-shih shih (pseud.). Yuan Shih-k'ai ch'üan chuan (with I-shih chi i-shih hsü-lu). Shanghai: Wen-i pien i she, 1926.
野史氏。袁世凱全傳 (附: 軼事及軼事續錄)。

Yuan Shih-k'ai ch'üan-chi. Taichung: I-shih shu-chü, 1962.
袁世凱全集。

Yuan Shih-k'ai shih-liao hui-k'an, ed. by Shen Yün-lung. Taipei: Wen hai ch'u-pan she, 1966. 24 vols.
袁世凱史料彙刊。沈雲龍。

Yuan shih tao kuo chi, comp. by Huang I. Taipei: Wen hsing shu-tien, 1962.
袁氏盜國記。黃毅。

Yuan Shih-wen. Hung-hsien kung-wei pi-shih. Shanghai: Hua wen shu-chü, 1925.
袁世文。洪憲宮闈秘史。

Yuan T'ung-li   袁同禮

Works

1933. (ed.) Yung-lo ta-tien hsien-ts'un chüan-mu piao. Peiping: Kuo-li Peiping t'u-shu-kuan.
永樂大典現存卷目表。

1956. Chung-kuo yin-yueh shu-p'u mu-lu. Taipei: Chung-hua kuo-yueh hui.
中國音樂書譜目錄。

1956. Economic and Social Development of Modern China: A Bibliographical Guide. New Haven, Conn.: Human Relations Area Files.

1957. (ed.) Kuo-hui t'u-shu-kuan ts'ang Chung-kuo shan-pen shu lu. Washington: Library of Congress, 1957. 2 vols.
國會圖書館藏中國善本書錄。

1958. China in Western Literature: A Continuation of Cordier's Bibliotheca Sinica. New Haven: Far Eastern Publications, Yale University.

1960. Russian Works on Japan, a Selected Bibliography. Tokyo.

1961. A Guide to Doctoral Dissertations by Chinese Students in America, 1905–1960. Washington.

1961. Russian Works on China, 1918–1960, in American Libraries. New Haven: Far Eastern Publications, Yale University.

1962. (comp.) Sinkiang yen-chiu wen-hsien mu-lu. Washington.
新疆研究文献目錄。

1963. (ed.) Chung O hsi-pei t'iao-yueh chi. Washington.
中俄西北條約集。

1963. Doctoral Dissertations by Chinese Students in Great Britain and Northern Ireland, 1916–1961.

1963. Hsien-tai Chung-kuo shu-hsueh yen-chiu mu-lu. Washington.
現代中國數學研究目錄。

1963. (ed.) K'an-ting Sinkiang chi. Taipei: Taiwan shang-wu yin shu kuan.
戡定新疆記。

1964. A Guide to Doctoral Dissertations by Chinese Students in Continental Europe, 1907–1962. Washington.

Bibliography of Chinese Mathematics, 1918–1960. Washington.

Sources

CBJS
Chung-hua t'u-shu-kuan hsieh-hui hui-pao, 1925–40; 1945–47.
中華圖書館協會會報。
Chung-kuo po-wu-kuan hsieh-hui hui-pao, 1935–37.
中國博物館協會會報。
Kuo-li Peiping t'u-shu-kuan kuan-k'an, 1928–37.
國立北平圖書館館刊。
The New York Times, February 7, 1965.
Quarterly Bulletin of Chinese Bibliography, 1934–37, 1939–48.
T'u-shu chi-k'an, 1934–36, 1939–48.
圖書季刊。
T'u-shu-kuan hsueh chi-k'an, 1926–37.
圖書館學季刊。
Wen hua t'u-shu-kuan hsueh chuan-k'o hsueh-hsiao chi-k'an, 1929–37.
文華圖書館學專科學校季刊。
WWC, 1936.

Yün Tai-ying   惲代英

Works

1926? Chung-kuo min-tsu ko-ming yün-tung shih. Shanghai.
中國民族革命運動史。

ed. of *Hsin Shu pao*.
新蜀報。

ed. of *Hung ch'i pao*.
紅旗報。

Sources

Person interviewed: Chung Kuo-t'ao.
Cheng-chih sheng-huo. Chungking: Cheng-chih sheng-huo she.
政治生活。
CKLC
GCCJK
HSWT

Liu Hsia. Shih-pa nien lai chih Chung-kuo ch'ing-nien-tang. Chengtu: Kuo-hun shu-tien, 1941.

柳下。十八年來之中國青年黨。

Schwartz, Benjamin I. Chinese Communism and the Rise of Mao. Cambridge: Harvard University Press, 1951.

RSOC

Ta Sheng *et al*. Lieh-shih chuan, ti-i chi, chi-nien wo-men wei Chung-kuo jen-min chieh-fang fen-tou erh hsi-sheng te chan-shih. Moscow, 1936.

大生等。烈士傳，第一集，紀念我們爲中國人民解放奮鬥而犧牲的戰士。

WWMC